Catalogue of the Coptic manuscripts in the collection of the John Rylands library, Manchester

John Rylands Library, W E. 1865-1944 Crum

CATALOGUE

OF THE

COPTIC MANUSCRIPTS

BERNARD QUARITCH
11 GRAFTON STREET, NEW BOND STREET, LONDON, W

SHERRATT AND HUGHES
PUBLISHERS TO THE VICTORIA UNIVERSITY OF MANCHESTER
34 CROSS STREET, MANCHESTER, AND
SOHO SQUARE, LONDON, W

CATALOGUE

OF THE

COPTIC MANUSCRIPTS

IN THE COLLECTION OF THE

JOHN RYLANDS LIBRARY

MANCHESTER

By W. E. CRUM

MANCHESTER   AT THE UNIVERSITY PRESS
LONDON: BERNARD QUARITCH, AND
SHERRATT AND HUGHES

1909

A491346

OXFORD   HORACE HART
PRINTER TO THE UNIVERSITY

PREFATORY NOTE

THE present Catalogue forms the second issue in the series of descriptive catalogues or guides to the collection of Oriental and Western manuscripts in the John Rylands Library

The entire cost of producing this volume has been defrayed, in part by Mrs Rylands herself, and in part out of the estate of the deceased lady, by direction of the executors of her will.

HENRY GUPPY,
Librarian

MANCHESTER,
March 10, 1909

TABLE OF CONTENTS

INTRODUCTION

THE manuscripts described in this catalogue are among those bought by Mrs Rylands of the Earl of Crawford, in 1901[1] To these only one (no 433) has since been added. The collection consisted of two distinct parts the earlier to be acquired (A) was brought together by the late (the 25th) Earl, then Lord Lindsay, who bought a number of Archdeacon Tattam's Bohairic MSS[2] Of the Sa'idic literary MSS in the *Bibliotheca Lindesiana*, which had been Tattam's, I have been able to identify nos. 2, 8, 11, 12, 14, 67, 69, 70, 87, 91, 92, 94, 96, 97[3]. Some Sa'idic leaves—I know not which—had been given to Lord Crawford by the Rev R Lieder[4], others (so Mr de Ricci has informed me) were once in J Lee's collection (*ob* 1866). The other section (B) had been bought of two well-known Gizah dealers[5] by the present Earl of Crawford, in 1898 To it belong all the papyri, with a much smaller number of parchment and paper fragments. This section contains no Bohairic texts (excepting no 421)

In 1868 the late Lord Crawford employed the Rev. J M Rodwell to arrange and describe his MSS Mr Rodwell assigned to them the numbers whereby they have since been known, and which, as sub-numbers in square brackets, serve to distinguish this older collection (A) in the present catalogue[6], and he moreover drew up descriptions of 59 of them[7]. To these Dr E A W Budge, in 1893, added short descriptions of four more MSS (nos 63, 434, 443, 455) After the purchase of the second collection (B), I was invited to compile a catalogue of the whole, upon a more extensive scale Lord Crawford, with that liberality whereof many scholars have had advantage, agreed to his MSS being transmitted for this purpose to the British Museum Subsequently Mrs Rylands, and eventually her trustees and librarian, by generously allowing the remainder to be sent me, rendered the continuance and completion of my work possible

The older collection (A) consists of MSS in the two main dialects. The Sa'idic parchment MSS came, as usual, from the library of the White Monastery this is demonstrable from the relationship of many of the fragments to others elsewhere, of ascertained *provenance* The few Bohairic parchments (nos 436 ff) are of Nitrian origin, as their frequent connexion with those brought thence by Tischendorf, and now in Leipzig, testifies The paper volumes came either from Nitria or from the Cairene churches

The ultimate *provenance* of the second collection (B) is not easier to fix than in similar cases elsewhere[8] Internal evidence, however, shows that so large a proportion of it relates to the neighbourhood of Ashmunain, that we may be justified in referring

---

[1] *Bulletin of the John Rylands Library*, i 355

[2] Tattam's sale was at Sotheby's, on June 16, 1868, six months after his death

[3] Thanks to the kind loan by Prof Erman of M Schwartze's copies (1848) The sole reference to his Sa'idic MSS. in Miss PLATT's *Journal of a Tour &c*, 1842, is vol. i, 102. In the list, *ZDMG.* vii. 94, 174 vellum leaves are mentioned, in the sale catalogue (no 401) 'over 130'.

[4] Stated in rough notes by the late Lord Crawford, now in the Rylands Library

[5] With, I think, the eight exceptions mentioned below

[6] *V* Table, p 244

[7] Descriptive list now in the Rylands Library

[8] The fact that it was bought of two dealers makes more than one *provenance* probable

to the whole as 'the Ashmunain collection'—at least in a negative sense, when dealing with the 8 numbers clearly independent of the large body of papyri[1] (nos 232, 255, 288, 291, 316, 347, 365, 465)   The presence in collection (B) of five Fayyûmic fragments may be evidence against a single place of origin   one of them (no 412) is part of a MS elsewhere, which is believed to have been obtained in the Fayyûm   Another curious text, in unmistakable, though perhaps artificial, Bohairic (no 460), is difficult to account for here[2]

More important is the group of papyri showing, in varying proportions, the Aḥmimic dialect   We may count 13 of them, some, however, such small fragments that it is hardly fair to decide their linguistic position   The idiom of this group ranges from a practically pure Aḥmimic (no 396), through a hybrid stage (nos 269, 270, 292, 311, 352), down to fragments where an ε- for ⲁ-, -ⲉⲓ for -ⲓ, -ⲏⲟⲩ for -ⲏⲩ, an ⲣ- with Greek verbs, may perhaps be taken as vanishing traces of the old dialect[3] (nos 271, 273, 274, 275, 301, 312, 314)   Yet we have no grounds so far for assigning these texts to a district appreciably south of Ashmunain, albeit the name of that town itself, so frequent elsewhere, does not occur in them   The presence of this ancient dialect, in unimpeachably Saʿidic surroundings, would alone be a testimony to the varieties of age among our documents, did not remarkable differences of script bear independent evidence of this   The pieces tainted with an Aḥmimic colouring are all, it will be seen, written in hands far older than those usually exemplified in such collections of papyri— older, indeed, than any hitherto published Coptic documentary MSS[4]   Certain of the hands I have ventured to ascribe to the 4th–5th centuries (nos 268 ff), one or two, more closely, to the 4th (nos 270, 311)   A number of these early texts (v no 268) are addressed to an ecclesiastical dignitary, named John   Were I right in regarding the recipient of all as one and the same person—and the assumed chronological diversity between the hands is not too wide to permit this—we should thence have evidence that such varieties of dialect—nos 268, 272, 276, are in a pure Saʿidic—were coeval, though not necessarily coeval in a single district; for we do not know from what distances these letters may have been sent

An estimate, based upon the table, p 241, shows that, among the 298 Saʿidic documents (nos 115–409, 462–465),' the number of MSS. assigned to each succeeding century thenceforth increases rapidly, down to the 8th, which claims a third of the total, and together with which may be counted some 70 more, doubtfully placed in the century preceding or following   Thereafter the numbers again diminish, the latest period (11th–12th century) having only three   A type of script, exceeding all others in obscurity, is that whereof Pll 7 and 8 give the first published specimens[5]   It appears to have developed in the 10th century   Among these younger MSS are of course all those

---

[1] Unless my memory deceives me, these were the papyri which I saw on sale in the neighbourhood of the Ezbekîyah, in the winter of 1897–98

[2] *Papyrus* documents with Bohairic tendency have not hitherto been met with S of the Fayyûm (v Br Mus nos 572, 1237).

[3] Notable peculiarities, unsupported by the published Aḥmimic texts, are ⲁⲉϥ=ⲁⲁϥ, ⲁⲗⲗⲉⲉⲩ, ⲙⲉⲉⲩ, ⲡⲉϫⲉⲩ, ⲥⲁⲛⲉ   V Index. The idiom of districts south of Aḥmim shows similar traces   V CRUM, *Ostr* pp xix, xx

[4] Br Mus *Catal*, Pl 11, 711, Pl 12, 1102 and no 1252 are alone comparable. I am ignoring the old magical texts (Br Mus nos 1223, 1244, Pap Lichatschef, ed Turaief, Russian Archaeol Soc, xviii, 1907)

[5] Excepting Br Mus. *Catal*, Pl 15, 1214

written upon paper (18 nos) or parchment (3 nos)[1]   The paper MSS in the literary sections likewise (e g liturgical and magical), belonging as they do to this same 'Ashmunain collection', must be reckoned to the latest group of our texts.   Further evidence, were it needed, of the late use of these two materials could be had from the fact that only upon them are the texts to be found wherein the idiom displays a Bohairic tendency[2]   Another characteristic of at any rate post-Muslim times may be mentioned here   Krall had noticed[3] that documents emanating from Muslims are distinguished, now and then, by an oblique double stroke, in place of the more usual cross, before the beginning of the text (v Pl 6)   Of the 13 instances in this catalogue, 11 are in texts characterized by Muslim names, and it is noticeable that the Muslim witness in no 214 employs these strokes, while the Christian signatures have the cross[4]

In this connexion I would offer some supplementary comments upon the Plates, and the grounds for the selection of the specimens reproduced

Plate 1 shows first three types of uncial, no. 310 a very uncommon one for private documents.   No 175 confirms Krall's axiom[5], that 8th century scribes tend to avoid ligatures   No 279 appears here by an error   At the time the plates were composed, I had intended to read the final date $\overset{v}{\epsilon\tau}$ ι (assuming some local era or year of office). And, even now, I cannot but record that the final letter bears but small resemblance to the ιυδ, or ιδ, usual in documents of the Muslim period, and further, that the metathesis of ε ι[δ], for ιδ ε, is equally abnormal[6]   No 7 is a specimen of that type of uncial often met with in parchment MSS in 'Ashmunain' (as distinct from 'White Monastery') collections, but hitherto seldom facsimiled[7].   It may be compared with the script of the *Uncanonical Gospel* fragment, *Pap Oxyrh* vol v, Pl 1, placed by the editors as early as the 4th century, a date, however, to which I should not venture to assign our no 7

Plate 2 contains one dated text ('Addenda' = no 464), written in the same year as Br Mus no 162[8], 4 liturgical pieces, nos 49 and 55 showing what scraps were deemed sufficient for use as 'choir slips'; while the two lower specimens are from the series of early letters addressed to 'John' (v above)

Plate 3   These (excepting no 413) are among the oldest MSS in the Rylands collection.   The character of no 311 may, as a whole, be compared with that of *Pap Oxyrh* no 299 (Ep. Rom 1), which is regarded as of the early 4th century, or with *Pap. Amherst*, Pl xxi, 'late 4th or early 5th'.   The writer of the former of these, however, attempts a more regular, literary script than ours

Plate 4   No 271 again recalls the above-named *Oxyrhynchus* and *Amherst* papyri, though the comparison must not be made from the same standpoint as for no 311 No 270 resembles 4th century hands, such as that reproduced in Br Mus *Greek*

---

[1] Ordinary literary uncials upon parchment are not here in question

[2] Witness the use of ποϲ (v Index)   Similarly in Br Mus, where only one instance, and that clearly a late text (no 582), is on papyrus   The earliest dated occurrence known to me is in the colophon Paris 132[1], fol 67, A D 928.

[3] *Führer* (1894) p 53, *Mitth Rain* v 45

[4] *Cf* this sign in B Moritz's *Album*, p 113, l 13 from below (after لمال)   The Brit. Mus instances (in nos 581, 639 only a single stroke) show the same state of things, only the group nos 1167, 1168, 1169 might appear ambiguous (cf here no 279) H I Bell has observed the same usage in the Jkôw (Aphroditô) papyri   [5] *Führer*, p 49

[6] It is to be observed that the edge of the papyrus is not broken

[7] Br Mus *Catal*, Pl 8, no 171 is an instance of a similar type on papyrus

[8] *V* Hyvernai's *Album*, ix, 2

Catal 11, Pll 102, 104, 105 or Deissmann's *Licht vom Osten*, p 146   No 396 is the most outspoken of our Aḫmimic texts   Though not free from literary affectation, its hand approaches certain informal 4th century types in its є, c, ϒ

Plate 5   No 352 resembles Br Mus *Greek Catal* 111, Pll 84, 87 (middle of 6th century); but perhaps it is younger than these   No 312 may be classed with no 276 (Pl 3), no 292 with no 271 (Pl 4)   No 313, though with a preponderance of uncial forms, has certain ligatures and irregularities which I take to point to the 4th or 5th century   (For further specimens of these early hands, *v* Pl 10)

Plate 6 represents a substantially later epoch than those preceding   No 407 much resembles Pl viii of the *Rainer Führer* (A D 827)   No 287 may be somewhat earlier   No 390 has, in l 2, a remarkable ligature used also in the above *Rainer* papyrus and in nos 380 and 405 here.   But whether all three belong to one period, it is difficult to say   No 398 goes a decided step farther towards the highly ligatured type shown in the next two plates

Plate 7   Of these three hands, no 362 is presumably the oldest, but several of its forms (к, п), and especially the ligature ʌι, are already those which characterize the later hands—that of no 372, for example, which is of the same type with Br. Mus *Catal*, Pl. 15, no 1214

Plate 8 gives two more specimens of these most difficult hands   Both may be somewhat earlier than no 372 on the foregoing plate

Plate 9   The tall characters above the tachygraphic text in no 410 recall the conventionalized strokes flanking the Greek [1] and Graeco-Arabic protocols, as well as those heading mediaeval (imperial and papal) deeds, *cf* also Pl 10, no 159.   The Arabic lines in no 214 closely resemble the early 8th century hands of the Jkôw papyri [2]

Plate 10, being the first of three additional plates, not contemplated at the outset, returns again to an earlier period   No 273 may be a rough example of the type *Pap Amherst* Pl xxi, yet it might be considerably younger   No 320 has features in common with *Pap Amh* cl (A D 592); but I should incline to place it later than this   The fantastic subscription to no. 159 is not unlike that in Vitelli's 3rd and 11th plates   This scribe's normal hand is of a type constantly met with among 'Ashmunain' papyri

Plate 11   The subject with which no 277 is concerned—the treatment of 'fugitive' peasants—might incline us to place the MS in the early 8th century, beside the Jkôw texts [3]   The script is indeed not far removed from that of Br Mus *Catal.*, Pl 4, Or. 6205   An 8th century date too for no 319 is suggested by the Greek script of line 1, which is similar to that of the Greek parts of the Arabic papyri from Jkôw, also by the Coptic script, itself quite of the Jkôw type   On the other hand, it is to be observed that the protocol does not appear yet to contain any Arabic text [4]

Plate 12   The Coptic hands in nos. 142 and 180 may be estimated by help of the earlier Greek accompanying them, which is ascribable, in both cases, to the 8th century   In no 137 we may see (ll 4, 5 and subscription) both the Greek and Coptic styles of a single scribe

---

[1] *E g* Br Mus *Catal*, no 171
[2] *Cf Papyri Schott Reinhardt*, ed C H Becker, Taff iii–v

[3] *V* Bell in *J Hell Stud* xxviii 110, note
[4] The supposed Arabic letters are, I think, merely stains, not written characters

Few, beyond the small circle of specialists, can be expected to explore a mass of texts such as those here published. For the benefit, therefore, of such as the literary (theological or historical) materials may interest, I shall here draw attention to some of the pieces especially noteworthy in these respects

Among the Biblical texts is one hitherto unique (no 421), parts of which are in the British Museum[1] It is probably the oldest of Bohairic New Testament MSS

The Liturgical texts comprise a group (nos 25–29) of Greek hymns (printed in this catalogue since they were employed in the service of the Coptic church), showing an unknown system of musical notation   The abbreviated directories, too, of lessons and hymns (nos 54 ff) are of interest   No 430 is an unusually full example of the Theotokia, whereof the analysis given may be a guide in classifying this type of text The collection possesses one of the rare MSS of the Antiphonary (no 435), and that for only a part of the year   The work would well repay investigation   In the hymn-book no 433, two names repeatedly occur (v p 240), which should be those of authors It is to be hoped that a key to their identity may eventually be found

Conspicuous among the Homiletic texts is no 62, which purports to be an unknown work of Athanasius   The problem of authorship in no 65 remains unsolved   John of Lycopolis appears to me the most likely claimant[2]   The fragments of Festal Letters, if such they be (nos 81–83), are not without interest   Perhaps they represent the copies (translations?) communicated to the respective monasteries[3]

Fragments of two Apocryphal texts are here (nos 84, 86), the latter awaiting identification, also part of a new Salomonic legend (no 85)   No 94 is an interesting Encomium on the Forty Martyrs   The indications of authorship are tantalizingly insufficient   No 95 makes it probable, as in so many other cases, that the Bohairic Life of Macarius was adapted from an existing Saïdic version, while no 411 shows us a fourth recension—Saïdic, Bohairic and Syriac are already known—of the popular Story of Dioscorus[4].   No 99 is not without its interest for students of Severus   The apologetic dialogue, no 449, may be noted here

The Magical and Medical section includes several interesting texts   the long recipes in no 106, with their numerous Arabic botanical terms transcribed, and the Arabic charms and magical ritual in no 467.

Turning now to the 'Documents', we have illustrations in nos 128 ff of that surety system, so widely developed in Byzantine and Muslim Egypt[5], interesting contracts (nos 139, 144, 153), unusually lengthy and well preserved leases (nos 158, 159) and remnants of a will (no 462), the only one, so far, from Ashmunain   Among the most curious pieces in the collection are the inventories of church property (no 238), and hangings (no 244), and that of clothes, with many remarkable Arabic terms, including one which suggests an etymology for the obscure Latin *quadrapulus* (no 243)

[1] *Catal* no 739 (v Pl II)

[2] Since no 70 was described, I have found a fragm by the same hand, in the Cairo Patriarch's collection, which, in its lower margin (cf no 65), shows the name [ιωρα]ннкε This, calling in question the authorship of Brit Mus no 204 &c., further complicates the problem

[3] Cf Br. Mus. *Cat*, no 464, CRUM, *Ost* , p 7, n. 4.

[4] But the note on p 240 (*ad* p 29) raises the question as to the true title and principal subject of this work   The vol, to which ZOEGA clxv &c belonged, ended at any rate with a Life of John of Lycopolis.

[5] It is observable that deeds of this class are quite rare in Greek, but plentiful in Coptic papyri (so notably among the Jkôw Aphroditô texts)   The guarantors would be the village peasantry, ignorant of Greek

Finally, among the Letters, the series addressed to 'John' (nos 268 ff.) and already described, is conspicuous by reason of its unusual antiquity   Indeed, these, with the remaining letters of that early period, might be reckoned the most valuable element in the entire collection.   Beside the bishop's official letter (no 267), we may place the private letter of another bishop (no 461), in many ways a highly interesting document   Letters which throw light upon the working of the provincial administration are nos 277, 319, 346, while nos. 320, 321 illustrate fiscal procedure

Something should be said as to certain methodical features of this catalogue   Whereas all the MSS composing the older collection (A) are described, the same has not been done with the later, 'Ashmunain' stock   Here I have been allowed to use discretion, and so have described but a selection of the great mass of fragments, abandoning a considerable quantity of impracticable material to a *limbo*   Such texts as are printed have been all collated, most of them several times, and it is not without satisfaction that, on a final revision, I have, in many cases, found in print corrupt or questionable readings to which a *sic* might deservedly have been added   I am well aware that many a passage, in the documentary texts, has not yet been adequately read   as here printed, it is but too often impossible to extract from them a reasonable meaning[1]   But it is earnestly to be hoped that this and the similar papyrus collections will, in time, be attacked afresh by other students, for such texts are destined to yield invaluable contributions both towards Coptic vocabulary and syntax   The commentary upon the texts offered in the foot-notes may often appear unduly meagre, considering the problems raised   But I have preferred to restrict it to what was needful, seeing no reason to repeat arguments here or multiply evidence which those interested can quite conveniently find elsewhere   The chronological Table on p 241, is a concession to criticisms upon my British Museum Catalogue; but it is still with the utmost diffidence that I print it   The reproduction of dated papyri, primarily of those still lying buried at Vienna, would be among the greatest boons conferable on Coptic scholarship

Only two abbreviations occur frequently   Br Mus, followed by a number, *i e* my *Catalogue of the Coptic MSS in the British Museum*, 1905, and KRALL, *i.e. Corpus Papyr Raineri*, vol ii, KRALL *Rechtsurkunden*, 1895

In conclusion, I must express my hearty thanks to the John Rylands Librarian, Mr H Guppy, who, with unwearied amiability, has acceded to my various requests and throughout facilitated my work in the most liberal way; also to Mr Hart and the readers and staff of the Clarendon Press, whose skill has never been overtaxed nor their patience exhausted in the slow and troublesome task of printing a book so complicated as this   And I would thank those friends too—Dr. Kenyon, Sir Herbert Thompson, the Rev G Horner, and Mr H I Bell—who, by kind loans of books or the verification of references, have made it possible to carry out such work at a distance from all libraries

W. E. CRUM

ALDEBURGH, *February*, 1909

[1] One of the most constant obstacles to the correct reading of non-literary hands is the complete similarity between ⲧ and ϥ

SA'IDIC MANUSCRIPTS

BIBLICAL

1.—Parchment, a fragment, 8 × 7 cm 1 col., 23+ lines Script small, square uncials, ⲁ, ⲙ, ⲩ each in a single stroke.

Genesis xxvi 21-25, 26-29 (?), the latter passage, on the *verso*, being all but illegible The following is the restored text on the *recto*[1] —

```
                        ]ⲉ · ⲁϥⲧⲱⲟⲩⲛ ⲇⲉ]
              [ⲉⲃⲟⲗ ⲟⲙⲡ]ⲙⲁ ⲉⲧⲙ[ⲙⲁⲩ ⲛϭⲓ]
              [ⲓⲥⲁⲁⲕ · ⲁϥ]ϣⲓⲕⲉ ⲛⲕⲉϣ[ⲱⲧⲉ ·]
              [ⲁⲩⲕⲣⲓⲛⲉ ⲁ]ⲉ ⲟⲛ ⲟⲓⲧⲛⲉⲩⲉⲓ[· ⲁϥ]
              [ⲙⲟⲩⲧⲉ ⲉ]ⲡⲉⲥⲣⲁⲛ ⲭⲉⲧⲁⲛ[ⲧⲭⲁ]
         22  [ⲭⲉ · ⲁϥ]ⲧⲱⲟⲩⲛ ⲇⲉ ⲉⲃⲟⲗ ⲟⲙ
              [ⲡⲙⲁ ⲉⲧⲙ]ⲙⲁⲩ ⲁϥϣⲓⲕⲉ ⲛⲕⲉ
              [ϣⲱⲧⲉ · ⲁⲩ]ⲱ ⲙⲡⲟⲩⲙⲓϣⲉ ⲉⲧ
              [ⲃⲏⲛⲧⲉ · ⲁϥⲙ]ⲟⲩⲧⲉ ⲉⲡⲉⲥⲣⲁⲛ
              [ⲭⲉⲧⲉⲧⲟⲩⲟϣⲥ ⲉ]ⲃⲟⲗ · ⲉϥⲭⲱ ⲙ
              [ⲙⲟⲥ ⲭⲉⲧⲉⲛⲟⲩ ⲁⲡⲭⲟⲉⲓⲥ ⲟⲩⲱ
              [ϣⲥ ⲛⲁⲛ ⲉⲃⲟⲗ ⲁ]ⲩⲱ ⲁϥⲁⲩⳅⲁⲛⲉ
         23  [ⲙⲙⲟⲛ ⲟⲓⲭⲙ [2]ⲡⲛⲁⲟ · ⲁϥⲉⲓ
              [ⲇⲉ ⲉⲃⲟⲗ ⲟⲙⲡⲙⲁ ⲉⲧ]ⲙⲙⲁⲩ ⲉⲭⲛ
         24  [ⲧϣⲱⲧⲉ ⲙⲡⲁⲛⲁϣ] · ⲁⲡⲭⲟⲉⲓⲥ
              [ⲟⲩⲱⲛⲟ ⲛⲁϥ ⲉⲃⲟⲗ ⲟ]ⲛⲧⲉⲩϣⲛ
              [ⲉⲧⲙⲙⲁⲩ ⲁⲩⲱ ⲡⲉⲭⲁⲓϥ · ⲭⲉⲁⲛⲟⲕ
              [ⲡⲉ ⲡⲛⲟⲩⲧⲉ ⲛⲁⲃⲣⲁⲟⲁ]ⲙ ⲡⲉⲛ
              [ⲉⲓⲱⲧ · ⲙⲡⲣⲣⲟⲟⲧⲉ ϯ]ϣⲟⲟⲡ
              [ⳅⲁⲣ ⲛⲙⲙⲁⲕ ⲁⲩⲱ ϯⲛⲁⲥⲙⲟⲩ
              [ⲉⲣⲟⲕ ⲛⲧⲁⲧⲁϣⲟ ⲙⲡⲉ]ⲕⲥⲡⲉⲣ
              [ⲙⲁ ⲉⲧⲃⲉⲁⲃⲣⲁⲟⲁⲙ ⲡⲉⲕ]ⲉⲓⲱⲧ
         25                              ⳝⲩ
```

2 [2]—Parchment, 3 complete leaves, now 28 × 21 cm. Pp ⲣ̅ⲁ̅-ⲣ̅ⲝ̅, ⲥ̅ⲅ̅, ⲥ̅ⲭ̅ 2 cols of 30 lines each. Script hand of CIASCA xv and Brit Mus Catal. nos. 17 and 937

Foll. 1, 2 1 Samuel xxviii 16—xxx 5 Published by ERMAN, *Bruchstucke &c* (*Gotting. Nachr*, 1880), and thence by CIASCA, i. 182.

---

[1] References to this passage in ZOEGA, p 583   [2] Or ⲟⲣⲁⲓ ⲟⲙ, as there is space for more in the gap.

Fol 3   2 Samuel xvii. 19-29   Published by Erman and Ciasca

Begins ⲡⲉⲝⲉ ⲥⲁⲙⲟⲩⲏⲗ.   Ends ϩⲛⲧⲉⲣⲅⲙⲟⲥ[

3.—Parchment, a fragment, $5\frac{1}{2} \times 7\frac{1}{2}$ cm   2 cols.   Script   small uncials, ⲁ, ⲙ, ⲩ each in a single stroke

Job vii   8-11 (omitting 8 *b*) in Greek, and 2, 3 in Coptic, with the *cola* marked in the margins

	ⲟⲣⲱ[ⲛⲧⲟⲥ ⲙⲉ]	[ⲛⲟⲩϩⲙϩⲁⲗ] ⲉϥⲣϩⲟⲧⲉ ϩⲏⲧϥ	
ⲉ̄	ⲱⲥⲡⲉⲣ ⲛⲉⲫ[ⲟⲥ ⲁⲡⲟⲕⲁⲑⲁⲣⲑⲉⲛ]	[ⲙⲡⲉϥϫⲟⲉⲓⲥ ⲁⲩⲱ] ⲉⲁϥϩⲉ ⲉⲩϩⲁⲓ·	ⲏ̄
	ⲁⲡ ⲟ̄ⲩ̄ⲛ̄ⲟ̄ⲩ̄	[ⲃⲉⲥ]	
ⲍ̄	ⲉⲁⲛ ⲅⲁⲣ ⲁ̄ⲛ̄ⲟ̄ⲥ̄ [ⲕⲁⲧⲁⲃⲏ ⲉⲓⲥ ⲁⲇⲏⲛ]	[ⲏ ⲛⲑⲉ ⲁⲛⲡⲉ ⲛⲟⲩ]ϫⲁⲓⲃⲉⲕ[ⲉ ⲉϥϩⲉ]	ⲑ̄
	ⲟⲩⲕ ⲉⲧⲓ ⲙⲏ ⲁⲛⲁⲃⲏ	[ⲉⲧ ⲉⲡⲉϥⲃⲉ]ⲛⲉ	
ⲍ̄	ⲟⲩⲇ ⲟⲩ ⲙⲏ ⲥⲡⲓ[ⲥⲧⲣⲉⲯⲏ ⲉⲓⲥ]	[ⲧⲁⲓⲧⲉ ⲧⲁϩⲉ ϩⲱⲱⲧ ⲛ]ⲧⲁⲓϩⲩⲡⲟⲙⲓⲛⲉ	ⲓ̄
	ⲧⲟⲛ ⲓⲁⲓⲟⲛ [ⲟⲓⲕⲟⲛ]	[ⲉϩⲉⲛⲉⲃⲁⲧⲉ] ⲉⲩⲱⲟⲩⲉⲓⲧ	
ⲏ̄	ⲟⲩⲇ ⲟⲩ ⲙⲏ ⲉⲡ[ⲓⲥⲕⲱ ⲁⲩⲧⲟⲛ ⲉⲧⲓ]	[ϩⲉⲛⲟⲩⲱⲏ ⲇⲉ ⲛϩ]ⲓⲥⲉ [ⲛⲉⲧⲟ ⲛⲁⲓ]	ⲓ̄ⲁ̄
	[ⲟ] ⲧⲟⲡⲟⲥ [ⲁⲩⲧⲟⲩ]	]	
ⲑ̄	ⲁ[ⲧⲁⲣ ⲟⲩⲛ ⲟⲩⲇⲉ ⲉⲅⲱ ⲫⲉⲓⲥⲟⲙⲁⲓ]		ⲓ̄ⲃ̄

4.—Parchment, a fragment, $7\frac{1}{2} \times 6$ cm   1 col   Script   rough, irregular uncials.

Psalm iv 7, 8.

After ϩⲛⲟⲩϩⲉⲗⲡⲓⲥ, ⲁⲗⲗⲏⲗⲟⲩⲓⲁ

Verso ⲧⲁⲁⲙ ⲉⲙⲏⲛⲁ ⲛⲁⲯⲁⲗⲙ[

5.—Papyrus, a fragment, 21×20 cm   Pp —,]ⲛ̄ⲅ̄   1 col, in στίχοι   Script   *cf* Ciasca vii for a slight resemblance

Psalms (*recto*) xxxvi 27-34, (*verso*) 38—xxxvii. 4, all incomplete

The only legible variant from Budge's text is ver 27, ⲛϥⲛⲁⲕⲱ

6.—Parchment, a fragment; $13\frac{1}{2} \times 9$ cm (a complete page *ca* 17×14 cm)   1 col Script   *cf* the Berlin Psalter, ed Rahlfs (*Göttinger Abhandl*, N F   iv, 1901), which shows a very similar but not identical hand   About 24 lines in a page

Psalm lxxxviii 14-20, 24-32

The following variants from Budge's text are visible —

ver 20, ⲛⲙ for ⲙⲛ, 26, ϩⲛⲉⲓⲉⲣⲱⲟⲩ, 28, ⲁⲛⲟⲕ ⲛⲇⲉ[1], 29 and 32, ⲁⲣⲉϩ, 31, ⲉⲣϣⲁⲛⲉϥ-, 32, ⲛⲥⲉⲥⲱϣϥ.

---

[1] *V* the Index and C Schmidt, *Acta Pauli* (1904), p 19

7.—Parchment, a complete and a damaged fol , the former 6¾ × 6½ cm 1 col , 18 lines Script minute, square uncials, ⲁ, ⲗ, ⲙ, ⲩ each in a single stroke

Proverbs xxiii 34—xxiv 7, 23-27

The following are the variants from Ciasca's text (ii 176) —

xxiii 35, ⲕⲛⲁϫⲟⲟⲥ ϫⲉ ⲛⲉⲩϯⲟⲩⲉ ⲉⲣⲟⲓ ⲁⲩⲱ ⲙⲡⲓⲙⲕⲁϩ—ⲁⲛⲟⲕ ⲇⲉ ⲛⲉⲓⲥⲟⲟⲩⲛ ⲁⲛ ⲡⲉ ⲉⲣⲉ—ϯⲛⲁⲥⲱⲟⲩ ϩ; xxiv 1, ⲉⲧϩⲟⲟⲩ—ⲛⲁⲙⲙⲱⲟⲩ, 2, [ⲁⲩⲱ] ⲉⲣⲉⲛⲉⲩⲥⲡⲟⲧⲟⲩ [ϫⲱ] ⲙⲡϩⲓⲥⲉ, 3, ⲁⲩⲱ ⲉϣⲁⲩⲥⲁϩⲱϥ—ⲁⲩⲱ ⲟⲛ , 5, ⲛⲁⲛⲟⲩ, 6, ⲉⲣⲉⲧⲃⲟⲏⲑⲉⲓⲁ ⲇⲉ ⲙⲛⲡϩⲏⲧ, 7, ⲉⲣⲉⲧⲥⲟⲫⲓⲁ ⲇⲉ , 8, ⲙⲉⲣⲉ[ⲛⲓ ⲟϥⲟⲥ], 23, ⲛⲉϥⲗⲁⲥ ⲟⲩⲥⲛⲏϥ—ϥⲛⲁⲟⲩⲟϣϥ—ⲛⲓϣⲏⲣⲉ ⲛⲓⲣⲱⲙⲉ ⲟⲛ—ⲛϩⲉⲛⲕⲉⲉⲥ

After ver 23 little is legible, [ⲡⲉⲛⲧⲁ]ϥⲥⲉⲩϩ is the last word discernible

8 [31]—Parchment, 4 complete leaves, now 34½ × 26½ cm Pp ⲣⲕⲉ-ⲣⲗⲅ 2 cols , 35-37 lines Script cf Hyvernat viii 3 and Ciasca xiii , titles being in a sloping hand, cf Hyvernat x Initials, floral scrolls, birds and animals in margins in red, yellow and green.

Jeremiah xxxix (xxxii) 42—xliii (xxxvi) 7 Published by Erman, *Bruchstücke &c*, and thence by Ciasca, ii 256

Begins]ⲉϫⲙⲡⲉⲓⲗⲁⲟⲥ Ends ⲙⲡⲙⲓⲟ ⲉⲃⲟⲗ ⲙⲡ[

9 —Parchment; 10 × 8 cm Palimpsest (a) square uncials, only a few letters visible , (b) of Zoega's 9th class. 1 col

(b) Tobit viii 16, 17 'Finished is the Confession (ἐξομολόγησις) of the father-in-law of Tobias' Then, 'The prayer of Tobit which he pronounced on beholding his son, when he had gone out toward him from the house,' ⲛⲧⲁϥⲉⲓ ϩⲏⲧϥ ⲙⲡⲏⲓ, followed by xi 14 These passages are published by Maspero, *Mission franç*, vi 291

10 —Parchment, a fragment, 12 × 9 cm Script of Zoega's 3rd class P ⲣϫⲁ. Ornaments and pen-trials in margins *Verso* blank

Matthew i 13-16 Begins [ⲁϥ]ⲟⲩⲁ ⲁϥⲟⲩⲁ ⲇⲉ. Ends ⲫⲁⲓ ⲙⲙⲁⲣⲓⲁ] ⲧⲁⲓ. In 13, ⲁϫⲱⲣⲁ, in 14, ⲁⲥⲱⲣⲁⲥ.

11 [3]—Parchment, 6 complete leaves, now 37 × 28 cm 2 cols, about 44 lines Pp ⲓⲑ-ⲗ. Script small; cf Ciasca iii, x, xvii Initials, scrolls and animals in red, green and yellow, the letter ⲫ in red and yellow

Mark ix 19—xiv 26 Published by Amélineau in *Recueil de Travaux &c*, v 106

Begins]ⲛⲟϫϥ ⲉⲃⲟⲗ. Ends ⲛⲧⲉⲣⲟⲩⲥⲙⲟⲩ[

The sections are marked ⲕⲍ at ix 33, ⲕⲏ at x 1, ⲕⲑ at 17, ⲗⲁ (sic) at 46, ⲗⲃ at xi 1, ⲗⲅ at 11, ⲗⲇ at 19, ⲗⲉ at 27, ⲗⲋ at xii 1, ⲗⲍ at 13, ⲗⲏ at 18, ⲗⲑ at 28, ⲙ at 35, ⲙⲁ at 41, ⲙⲅ (sic) at xiii 32, ⲙⲇ at xiv 3, ⲙⲉ at 12

12 [5]—Parchment; 7 leaves, now $35\frac{1}{2} \times 27\frac{1}{2}$ cm   2 cols, 35 lines   Pp. ⲣ̅ⲥ̅ⲑ̅-[ⲥ̅ⲓ̅]. Script *v* Palaeographical Society, Oriental Series, Pl. LXXX   Scrolls red and green, titles to chapters (in top margins) red.

Luke iii 8—vi 37   Published by AMÉLINEAU in *Recueil de Travaux &c*, v 118.

Begins]ⲧⲉⲧⲛ̅ⲧⲁⲁⲣⲭⲉⲓ.   Ends ⲝⲉⲛⲛⲉⲩⲕⲣⲓⲛⲉ ⲙⲙⲱⲧⲛ[

The Ammonian canons and sections are marked as in the Greek   The titles of the larger chapters are   ⲅ̅. ⲉⲧⲃⲉⲛⲉⲛⲧⲁⲩⲝⲛⲉⲓⲱϩⲁⲛⲛⲏⲥ, ⲍ̅. ⲉⲧⲃⲉⲛⲡⲉⲓⲣⲁⲥⲙⲟⲥ ⲙⲡⲥⲱⲧⲏⲣ. ⲙⲉ ⲅ̅ ⲙⲣ ⲗ̅, ⲏ̅. ⲉⲧⲃⲉⲡⲉⲧⲉⲣⲉⲡⲉⲛⲡⲛⲁ̅ ⲛⲁⲁⲓⲙⲟⲛⲓⲟⲛ ϩⲓⲱⲱϥ. ⲙⲣ ⲗ̅, ⲑ̅. ⲉⲧⲃⲉⲧϣⲱⲙⲉ ⲙⲡⲉⲧⲣⲟⲥ. ⲙⲉ ⲏ̅ ⲙⲣ ⲃ̅; ⲓ̅ ⲉⲧⲃⲉⲛⲉⲛⲧⲁⲩⲧⲁⲗϭⲟ ϩⲛ̅ⲟⲩⲉⲛϣⲱⲛⲉ ⲉⲩϣⲟⲃⲉ. ⲙⲉ ⲑ̅. ⲙⲣ ⲅ̅, ⲓ̅ⲁ̅. ⲉⲧⲃⲉⲧⲥⲟⲟⲩϩⲥ ⲛⲛ̅ⲧⲃⲧ, ⲓ̅ⲃ̅. ⲉⲧⲃⲉⲡⲉⲧⲥⲟⲃϩ ⲉⲛⲧⲁϥⲗⲟ. ⲙⲉ ⲅ̅ ⲙⲣ ⲗ̅, ⲓ̅ⲅ̅. ⲉⲧⲃⲉⲡⲉⲧⲥⲛⲅ. ⲓⲱ ⲍ̅. ⲙⲉ ⲓ̅ⲅ̅. ⲙⲣ ⲅ̅, ⲓ̅ⲁ̅ ⲉⲧⲃⲉⲗⲉⲅⲉⲓ ⲛⲧⲉⲗⲱⲛⲏⲥ. ⲙⲉ ⲓ̅ⲁ̅ ⲙⲣ ⲅ̅, ⲓ̅ⲉ̅. ⲉⲧⲃⲉⲛⲉⲣⲉⲧⲉϥϭⲓⲝ ϣⲟⲩⲱⲟⲩ ⲙⲉ ⲕ̅ⲁ̅. ⲙⲣ ⲍ̅, ⲓ̅ⲉ̅. ⲉⲧⲃⲉⲡⲥⲱⲧⲡ ⲛⲛⲁⲡⲟⲥⲧⲟⲗⲟⲥ. ⲙⲉ ⲓ̅ⲑ̅ ⲙⲣ ⲏ̅, ⲓ̅ⲍ̅. ⲉⲓⲃⲉⲙⲙⲁⲕⲁⲣⲓⲥⲙⲟⲥ. ⲙⲉ ⲉ̅.

13 [1]—Parchment; 5 leaves; now $29\frac{1}{2} \times 21$ cm   2 cols, 27 lines   Pp ⲣ̅ⲁ̅-ⲣ̅ⲓ̅. Script that of BALFSTRI, Tab 13 (ZOEGA liv)   Initials, floral scrolls &c, brightly coloured   In the margins are birds (ⲣ̅ⲃ̅), human figures (ⲣ̅ⲍ̅, the blind man, Zacchaeus), and trees (ⲣ̅ⲓ̅)

Luke xvii 18—xix 29   Published by AMÉLINEAU in *Recueil de Travaux &c*, v 126

Begins]ⲉⲓⲙⲏⲧⲓ ⲡⲉⲓϣⲙⲙⲟ.   Ends ⲉϥϫⲱ ⲙⲙⲟⲥ[

The numbers of the sections are written in the margins in a later hand   ⲍ̅ⲁ̅ at xviii 1, ⲍ̅ⲃ̅ at 9, ⲍ̅ⲅ̅ at 18, ⲍ̅ⲁ̅ at 35, ⲍ̅ⲉ̅ at xix. 1, ⲍ̅ⲅ̅ at 11, ⲍ̅ⲍ̅ at 12, ⲍ̅ⲏ̅ at 15, while in the original hand titles are sometimes given   at xviii 1 ⲉⲧⲃⲉⲡⲉⲕⲣⲓⲧⲏⲥ ⲛⲧⲁⲁⲓⲕⲓⲁ, at 9 ⲉⲧⲃⲉⲡⲫⲁⲣⲓⲥⲥⲁⲓⲟⲥ ⲙⲛ̅ⲡⲧⲉⲗⲱⲛⲏⲥ, at 15 ⲉⲧⲃⲉⲛϣⲏⲣⲉ ϣⲏⲙ, at 18 ⲉⲧⲃⲉⲡⲣⲙⲙⲁⲟ, at 35 ⲉⲧⲃⲉⲡⲃⲗ̅ⲗⲉ, at xix 1 ⲉⲧⲃⲉⲍⲁⲭⲁⲓⲟⲥ.

14 [4]—Parchment, 8 leaves, now 35×27 cm.   2 cols, 29 lines, ruled   Pp ⲣ̅ⲓ̅ⲑ̅-ⲥ̅ⲁ̅, being quire ⲓ̅ⲅ̅   Script *of* CIASCA xxiii   Floral scrolls in margins in red, green and yellow

Galatians i 14—vi 16   Published by AMÉLINEAU in *Recueil de Travaux &c*, v 131.

Begins]ϩⲙ̅ⲡⲁⲅⲉⲛⲟⲥ   Ends ⲁⲩⲱ ⲉⲝⲙ̅ⲡⲓⲏ̅ⲗ ⲙ[

The sections are marked in a later hand   ⲃ̅ at ii. 1, ⲅ̅ at iii 2, ⲁ̅ at 15, ⲉ̅ at iv. 12, ⲋ̅ at v 16

15 —Papyrus, a fragment, $3\frac{1}{2} \times 7\frac{1}{2}$ cm   Script: rounded uncials, leaning slightly to left

Recto   Titus iii 15 with subscription

Verso   Philemon 6, 7   All incomplete.

16—Parchment, a fragment; $7\frac{1}{2} \times 9$ cm   2 cols   Script   small, square uncials of early type, *cf Cod Sinaiticus.*

Hebrews IV 12, 13, 15, 16, V 1 (*verso*), 3-5, 7-9

Note the forms ⲣⲣⲉϥ- and ⲧⲉⲉⲓϩⲉ.

IV. 12]ⲛϩⲟ ⲥⲛⲁⲩ
ⲓⲉϣⲁ ⲙⲙⲁ
]. ⲛⲧⲉϥⲯⲩⲭⲏ
ⲓⲡⲛ̄ⲁ̄ ⲛϩⲁⲣⲙⲟⲥ
ⲓⲕⲁⲥ ⲉϥⲟ ⲣⲣⲉϥ
]ⲙⲙⲉⲥⲩⲉ
]ⲉⲕ ⲙ
13   ]ⲙⲛⲥⲱⲡⲧ
]ⲉϥⲓ

15 [ⲉϣⲡϩⲓⲥⲉ ⲙⲙⲙⲁⲛ
ϩⲛⲛⲉⲛⲁⲥⲑⲉⲛⲉ[ⲓⲁ]
ⲁⲗⲗⲁ ⲉϥⲭⲟⲡⲧ [ϩⲛ]
ϩⲱⲃ ⲛⲓⲙ ⲛⲧⲛϩⲓⲉ ϣⲁ]
16 ⲧⲛⲛⲟⲃⲉ · ⲙⲁⲣⲛ[ϯ ⲡⲉⲛ]
ⲟⲩⲟⲉⲓϭⲉ ϩⲛⲟ[ⲩⲡⲁⲣ]
ⲣⲏⲥⲓⲁ ⲉⲡⲉⲑⲣ[ⲟⲛⲟⲥ]
ⲛⲧⲉⲭⲁⲣⲓⲥ ⲝⲉⲕ[ⲁⲥ]
ⲉⲛⲉϫⲓ ⲛⲟⲩⲛ[ⲁ ⲁⲩ
ⲱ ⲛⲧⲛϩⲓ̣ⲉ ⲉⲩⲭⲁⲣⲓⲥ]
ⲉⲩⲟⲩⲟⲉ[ⲓϣ
V. 1 ⲃⲟⲏⲑⲉ[ⲓⲁ · ⲁⲣⲭⲓⲉⲣⲉⲩⲥ]
ⲅⲁⲣ [ⲛⲓⲙ

V 3 ⲧⲁⲗⲟ ⲉϩⲣⲁⲓ [ϩⲁⲡⲗⲁ]
ⲟⲥ ⲛϥⲧⲁⲗⲟ ϩⲱⲱ̣ϥ
[ϩⲁ]ⲣⲟϥ̣ ⲛⲧⲉⲉⲓϩⲉ
4 [ϩⲁ]ⲛⲉϥⲛⲟⲃⲉ · ⲛⲉⲣⲉ
[ⲡⲟ]ⲩⲁ ⲅⲁⲣ ⲡⲟⲩⲁ ϫⲓ
[.] ⲁⲛ ⲙⲡⲧⲁⲉⲓⲟ
[. . .]ⲉⲩⲉⲓⲛⲉ ⲙⲙⲟϥ
ⲓⲉⲃ]ⲟⲗ ϩⲓⲧⲙⲛⲟⲩ
[ⲧⲉ] · ⲕⲁⲧⲁ ⲑⲉ ⲛⲁⲁⲣⲱ̅
5   ]ⲉ ⲙⲡⲉⲭ̅ⲥ̅
]ⲉⲟⲟⲩ ⲛⲁϥ
]. ⲣⲉϥ
ⲛⲁⲣⲭⲓⲉⲣⲉⲩⲥ

7 ⲛⲁϣⲕ[ⲁⲕ . . . ϩⲓⲣⲙ]
ⲉⲓⲏ · ⲁⲩⲱ ⲁ[
ⲉⲣⲟϥ ⲉⲃⲟⲗ ϩ[
8 ⲕⲁⲓⲡⲉⲣ ⲉⲡ[ϣⲏⲣⲉ]
ⲡⲉ ⲁϥⲥⲃⲟ[
ⲉⲃⲟ[ⲗ ϩⲓⲧⲛⲛⲉⲛⲧⲁϥ]
9 ϣⲟⲡⲟⲩ
ⲉⲃⲟⲗ [ⲉⲟⲩ]
ⲟⲛ ⲛⲓⲙ[ⲉⲧ

17—Parchment, a fragment, $19\frac{1}{2} \times 25$ cm   2 cols   Pp ⲣⲟ̅ⲃ̅, ⲣ̅ⲅ̅. Script. *cf* HYVERNAT IX 1, CIASCA IV   Initials moderately enlarged   No ornaments or colours

1 John III 11-14, 15-17, 19-21, 23—IV 1

The principal variants from WOIDE, p 219, are: III 11, ⲁⲛ (*sic*); 15, ⲛⲓⲙ ⲙⲛⲧϥϣⲟⲛϩ ⲙⲙⲁⲩ ϣⲁⲉⲛⲉϩ; 21, ⲉⲣⲉⲧⲙⲡⲉⲛϩⲏⲧ.

18—Papyrus; a fragment; $8 \times 8\frac{1}{2}$ cm   From the same MS as Brit Mus Catal ,
Pl 10, no 967

Presumably a New Testament text, but unidentified

Fibres ↑

]ⲁⲙ	ⲧ[		
]ⲁϥⲧⲁ	ⲧⲛ[		
]ⲡⲣⲟ ⲉⲓⲣⲁ	ⲙⲡ[		
]ϩⲏⲧⲟⲩ	ⲧⲉⲧ|		
]ⲕⲧⲟⲙⲉ	ⲡⲉⲓ[		
]ⲉⲝⲙⲡϣⲁ	ⲧⲉⲧ|		
]ⲛⲁⲩ	ϩⲁⲣⲟ[		
]ⲏⲩ ⲛⲛⲉⲛ	ⲟⲩⲙ[		
] ⲧⲉⲛⲟⲩ			

Fibres →

] . ⲉⲓⲱⲧ	ⲛⲟⲩ[		
] ?	. ⲝ[		
]ⲛⲁ ⲉⲧⲟⲩ	ⲡⲉⲭⲥ[		
]ⲁⲩⲱ ⲁϥⲉ	ⲡⲉⲛⲛ[		
]ⲗⲉⲓ ⲛⲧⲉ	ⲛⲟⲥ[		
] . ⲓⲣⲁⲉ	ϩⲱⲱ[		
] . ϥⲥⲩ	ϩⲁⲣⲁ[		
] ?	ϫⲁ ⲛⲁ[		
	ⲝ . ⲉⲛ[		

LITURGICAL

19—Paper, a fragment; 12 × 9 cm   Script of ZOEGA's 9th class
Prayer of Incense   12 lines

[o]ⲩϣⲗⲏⲗ ⲛ̄ϣⲟⲩϩⲏⲛⲓ. Begins ⲧⲛ̄ⲡⲣⲟⲥⲫⲉⲣⲓⲛ ⲙ̄ⲡⲉⲕⲙ̄ⲧⲟ ⲉⲃⲟⲗ ⲡ̄ϭ̄ⲥ̄ ⲛ̄ⲟⲩϣⲟⲩϩⲏⲛⲓ ⲛ̄ⲥ̄ⲧⲟⲓ
ⲛ̄ⲥ̄ⲧⲓⲛⲟⲩⲃⲉ. After it, ⲉⲓⲥ ⲟⲩ ϩⲓⲧⲁ ⲁ (rest illegible)
Verso. remains of earlier Coptic and Arabic texts.

20—Parchment; a fragment, 17 × 10 cm.   Palimpsest   (*a*) in 2 cols   Script. small,
square uncials, (*b*) at right angles to preceding   Script of ZOEGA's 9th class, often
illegible

(*a*) 2 Peter i 7 and ii 1 in Greek are legible
(*b*) Prayer referring to the Departed   The following can be read —

... ⲛⲁⲓ ⲛ̄ⲧⲁⲡⲉⲕⲙⲟⲛⲟⲅⲉⲛⲏⲥ ⲛ̄ϥ̄ⲥ̄ † ⲡⲉϥⲥⲛⲟϥ ⲉⲧⲟⲩⲁⲁⲃ ϩⲁⲣⲟⲟⲩ ϩⲓϫⲙ̄ⲡϣⲉ ⲙ̄ⲡⲉⲥⲣ̄ⲟⲥ ⲁⲁⲩ
ⲉⲡⲉⲙⲡϣⲁ ⲡ̄ϭ̄ⲥ̄ ⲉⲧⲣⲉⲩⲉⲓ ⲉⲧⲟⲧⲕ ⲛ̄ⲡⲉϩⲟⲟⲩ ⲙ̄ⲙ̄ⲡⲁⲣϩⲟⲩⲥⲓⲁ ⲛ̄ⲡⲉⲕⲙⲟⲛⲟⲅⲉⲛⲏⲥ ⲛ̄ϥ̄ⲥ̄ ϩⲉⲛⲉⲩϩⲓⲕⲟⲛ
ⲉⲛⲟⲩⲟⲉⲓⲛ ⲛ̄ⲑⲉ ⲛ̄ⲛⲓⲕⲱⲛ ⲛ̄ⲛⲁⲅⲅⲉⲗⲟⲥ ⲉⲧⲃⲉⲡⲙⲁⲉⲓⲛ ⲉⲡⲉⲥⲧⲁⲩⲣⲟⲥ ⲉϥⲥⲱⲕⲣⲁⲫⲉⲓⲁ ⲉϫⲛ̄ⲛⲉⲩϩⲓⲕⲱⲛ
ⲉⲣⲉⲡⲉⲩⲥⲱⲙⲁ ⲧⲏⲣϥ̄ ⲟⲩⲟⲃⲉϣ ⲛ̄ⲑⲉ ⲛ̄ⲟⲩⲭⲓⲱⲛ ..

.. ⲣⲏⲧⲟⲛ ⲛ̄ⲡⲉⲣⲣⲟ ⲇⲁⲇ ϫⲉⲛⲁⲓⲁⲧϥ̄ ⲡⲉⲛⲧⲁⲕⲥⲟⲧϥ̄ ⲁⲕϣⲟⲡ ⲉⲣⲟⲛ ⲉϥⲛⲁⲟⲩⲱϩ ϩⲓⲛⲉⲕ ⲁⲩⲗⲏ⸱
ⲛ̄ϥⲥⲓ ϩⲛ̄ⲛⲁⲅⲁⲑⲁ ⲛⲉⲡⲉⲕⲏⲓ⸱ ⲁⲓ° ⲡ̄ϭ̄ⲥ̄ ⲇⲓ ⲛⲁⲩ ⲛ̄ⲟⲩⲙⲉⲣⲟⲥ ⲙ̄ⲙ̄ⲛⲉⲕⲡⲉⲧⲟⲩⲁⲁⲃ ...

. ⲡⲓⲱⲧ ⲡ̄ϭ̄ⲥ̄ ⲙ̄ⲛ̄ⲡ̄ⲛ̄ⲁ̄ ⲧⲟⲩⲁⲁⲃ ⲛ̄ⲣⲉϥⲧⲁⲛϩⲟ ⲁⲩⲱ ⲛ̄ϩ̄ⲙⲟⲩⲥⲓⲱⲛ ※

'those for whom Thine Only begotten Son did give His blood upon the wood
of the cross   Make them worthy, O Lord, to come unto Thee in the day of the appearing
(παρουσία) of Thine Only begotten Son, in a form (εἰκών) of light, like to the form of the
angels, through the sign of the cross that is traced (ζωγράφειν) upon their forms, their
whole body being white as snow'   .   .

Psalm lxiv. 4, 5. 'O Lord, grant unto them a portion with Thy saints' ..

21—Paper, complete; 19 × 7½ cm   Script   irregular, of ZOEGA's 9th class   Was
folded some 9 times.

'A Prayer of the Kiss of Peace (ἀσπασμός) of Saint Gregory'

ⲟⲩϣⲗⲗ ⲛ̄ⲧⲉ ⲡⲁⲅⲓⲟⲥ ⲅⲉⲣⲅⲟⲣⲓⲟⲥ ⲛ̄ⲁⲥⲡⲁⲥⲙⲟ̄ —

ⲕⲥⲙⲁⲙⲁⲁⲧ ⲡ̄ϭ̄ⲥ̄ ⲫ̄ϯ ⲛ̄ⲛⲉⲛⲓⲟⲧⲉ ⲡⲉⲧⲣⲉ ⲛⲓⲛⲟϭ ⲛ̄ϣⲡⲏⲣⲉ ⲙⲁⲩⲁⲁϥ̄ · ⲡⲉⲧⲁⲓ ⲛⲟⲩⲡ̄ⲛ̄ⲁ̄ ⲛ̄ⲱϩ
ⲉⲥⲁⲣⲝ ⲛⲓⲙ · ⲡⲉⲧⲙⲟⲩϩ ⲛ̄ⲛⲉⲛϩⲏⲧ ⲉⲣϣⲉ ϩⲓⲉⲩⲫⲣⲟⲥⲏⲛⲏ[1] · ⲡⲉⲛⲧⲁϥⲟⲩⲱⲛϩ ⲛⲁⲛ ⲉⲃⲟⲗ
ⲙ̄ⲡⲓϣⲙ̄ϣⲉ ⲡⲁⲓ ⲉⲧⲱ ⲛ̄ϩ̄ⲙⲙⲉⲥⲧⲏⲣⲓⲟⲛ ⲉⲛⲁⲧⲁⲅⲟϥ̄ · ⲡⲉⲛⲧⲁϥⲭⲁⲣⲓⲍⲉ ⲛⲁⲛ ⲛ̄ϯⲟⲩⲥⲓⲁ ⲧⲁⲓ ⲛ̄ⲗⲟⲅⲓⲕⲏⲩ

[1] Ac xiv 17

ⲁⲩⲱ ⲛⲁⲧⲡⲉⲣⲧ ⲥⲛⲟϥ ⲉⲃⲟⲗ · ⲡⲉⲛⲧⲁϥⲧⲁϩⲟⲛ ⲉⲣⲁⲧⲛ ⲉⲭⲛⲡⲉϥⲑⲩⲥⲓⲁⲥⲧⲏⲣⲓⲟⲛ ⲉⲧϩⲁⲣⲟⲧⲉ ⲁⲩⲱ
ⲉⲧϩⲁⲉⲟⲟⲩ ⲡⲉⲛⲧⲁϥⲧⲣⲉⲧⲏⲅⲩⲛⲟⲛⲉⲓ ⲛⲛⲁⲅⲅⲉⲗⲟⲥ ϣⲱⲡⲉ ϩⲛⲛⲣⲱⲙⲉ · ⲡⲉⲛⲧⲁϥⲉⲓⲣⲉ ⲙⲡⲥⲱⲧⲉ ⲛⲛⲉⲛ-
ⲧⲁⲩⲉⲣⲛⲟⲃⲉ ϩⲣⲁⲓ ⲛϩⲏⲧϥ ⲉⲙⲓⲛ ⲙⲙⲟϥ · (verso) ⲡⲉⲛⲧⲁϥⲡⲱϩ ⲛⲛⲉⲭⲓⲣⲟⲭⲟⲣⲫⲟⲛ ⲛⲛⲉⲛⲛⲟⲃⲉ
ϫⲓⲛⲉϣⲟⲣⲡ ⲉⲁϥⲡⲱϩ ⲛⲧⲁⲡⲏⲗⲩ ⲙⲡⲉⲥϩⲁⲓ ⲉⲧϣⲟⲟⲡ ⲕⲁⲧⲁⲣⲟⲛ · ⲡⲉϥⲣⲉ ϩⲣⲁⲓ ⲛϩⲏⲧϥ ⲙⲡⲉⲣⲡⲙⲉⲉⲩⲉ
ⲛⲃⲏⲣⲣ ⲛⲛⲉⲡⲉⲧⲛⲁⲛⲟⲩϥ ⲉⲧⲁϥⲁⲁⲩ ⲛⲙⲙⲁⲛ · ⲧⲁⲁⲥ ⲛⲁⲛ ⲡϭ̅ⲥ̅ ⲉⲧⲣⲉⲛⲕⲓⲛⲉ ⲉϩⲟⲩⲛ ϣⲁⲣⲟⲛ ⲛⲛⲉⲛ-
ⲧⲱⲃⲁϩ ϩⲛⲟⲩⲟⲡ ⲙⲛⲟⲩⲇⲓⲕⲉⲟⲥⲛⲏⲛ · ⲧⲁϩⲟⲛ ⲉⲣⲁⲧⲛ ⲉⲭⲛⲡⲉⲕⲑⲩⲥⲓⲁⲧⲏⲣⲓⲟⲛ ⲉⲧⲟⲩⲁⲁⲃ ⲉⲛⲟ
ⲛⲁⲧⲧⲱⲗⲙ ϫⲉⲛⲁⲁⲥ ⲉⲛⲉϯ ⲡⲉⲛⲟⲩⲟⲓ ⲉⲣⲟⲛ ϩⲛⲟⲩⲧⲱⲧ ⲛϩⲏⲧ ⲛⲡⲓⲥϯ · ⲉⲣⲉⲛⲉⲛϩⲏⲧ ⲥⲉⲃⲧⲱⲧ ⲉⲃⲟⲗ
ϩⲛⲥⲛⲛⲉⲧⲥⲥⲓⲥ ⲛⲓⲙ ⲛⲡⲟⲛⲩⲣⲟⲥ · ⲁⲩⲱ ⲛⲧⲁⲁⲛ ⲉⲛⲉⲙⲡϣⲁ ⲉⲧⲣⲉⲛⲁⲥⲡⲁⲍⲉ ⲛⲛⲉⲛⲉⲣⲏⲩ ϩⲛⲟⲩⲡⲓ
ⲉⲥⲟⲩⲁⲁⲃ ⲁϫⲛⲗⲁⲁⲩ ⲛϩⲩⲡⲟⲕⲣⲓⲥⲓⲥ.

'Blessed is the Lord, the God of our fathers, Who alone doeth great marvels; Who
giveth to all flesh a living spirit, Who filleth our hearts with joy and gladness, Who did
reveal to us this (divine) service that is an unspeakable mystery, Who hath granted to
us this reasonable and bloodless sacrifice; Who hath set us at His altar, terrible and
glorious, Who hath caused the fellowship (κοινωνία) of the angels to be with men, Who
did perform the redemption of them that had sinned against Himself,' &c, ending 'and
make us worthy to greet one another with a holy kiss, without any hypocrisy.'

Verso   part of an earlier Arabic text

22—Parchment; a fragment, 14 × 4 cm   Palimpsest   (*a*) script of ZOEGA'S 1st or
2nd class, (*b*) of his 9th class   1 col

(*b*) End of a Prayer in Greek, relating to the Communion, followed by a Rubric
in Coptic —

]ⲉⲓⲥ ⲁⲫⲉⲥⲓⲛ ⲁⲙⲁⲣⲧⲓⲱⲛ ⲛⲉⲱⲛⲧⲏⲥ ⲉϩ ⲁⲩⲧⲱⲛ ⲙⲉⲧⲁⲗⲁⲙⲃⲁⲛⲟⲩⲥⲓⲛ ⲁⲙⲏⲛ—Ⓐ[1] ⲁⲙⲏⲛ—
ⲥⲉⲯⲁⲗ̅ · ⲛⲧⲉⲡⲟⲩⲏⲛⲃ ⲉⲧⲁⲛⲁⲫⲃⲉⲣⲓ ϫⲓ ⲛϯ̅ ⲉⲡⲗⲁⲙⲁ[2] ⲛϥⲧⲁⲁⲩ ⲉⲛⲉⲧⲡⲱϣ ⲛⲙⲙⲁϥ ⲉⲡⲟⲩⲁ[3]
ⲛⲥⲉϩⲁⲙⲁⲗⲟϭⲓ ⲉϩⲣⲁⲓ ⲉϫⲱ[ⲟⲩ] ⲛϥϫⲓⲧⲟⲩ ⲛⲧⲟⲧⲟⲩ ⲟⲛ ⲡⲉⲡⲓⲥⲕ̅/ ⲙ[. .] ⲙϭⲟⲙ[4] ⲛⲗⲁⲁⲩ ⲉⲧⲓ ⲛⲁϥ
ⲁⲗⲗⲁ ⲛⲧⲟϥ ⲡ[ⲉ]ⲧⲛⲁⲧⲓⲛ̅ ⲛⲛⲉⲡⲣⲉⲥ[

'They sing (ψάλλειν), and the celebrating (ἀναφέρειν) priest takes 3 portions(?) and
gives them to them that partake with him, one by one, and they make confession
(ὁμολόγειν) over them and he (then) takes them from them again   To the bishop none
may give, but it is he that gives to the priests'   . .

23.—Papyrus, a fragment, $4\frac{1}{2} \times 14\frac{1}{2}$ cm.   Script   uncials of an early type   Fibres on
recto ↑

From a Prayer, perhaps relating to Ordination.

] ⲧⲟⲧⲅⲟⲩⲧⲛ ⲥⲱⲧⲙⲥⲉ ⲉⲣⲟⲛ ⲁⲛⲟⲛ |]ⲅϣⲱⲡⲉ ⲛϯⲁⲧⲟⲭⲟⲥ ⲛⲁⲡⲟⲥⲧⲟⲗⲟⲥ |]ⲧⲛ ⲛϭⲓ ⲡⲉⲕⲙⲉⲣⲓⲧ
ϣⲏⲣⲉ ⲓ̅ⲥ̅ ⲡⲉⲭ̅ⲥ̅ ⲡⲉⲛϫⲟⲉⲓⲥ | ⲧⲛ]ⲛⲟⲟⲩ ⲙⲡⲉⲕⲡⲛⲉⲩⲙⲁ ⲉⲧⲟⲩⲁⲁⲃ |]ⲙⲧⲟ ⲉⲃⲟⲗ ⲉⲧⲣⲉϥⲧⲉⲃⲟⲗ ⲛϥⲙⲁϩϥ
ⲛϭⲟⲙ |]ⲙⲛⲧⲃⲉⲣ[ⲉ] |

<hr/>

[1] 'Ο λαός   [2] ?? κλάσμα   [3] ? ⲉⲡⲟⲩⲁ ⲡⲟⲩⲁ   [4] ? ⲙⲙⲛϣϭⲟⲙ.

24—Paper, $27\frac{1}{2} \times 4\frac{1}{2}$ cm   Script *cf* Brit Mus Catal, Pl 7, no 490, col 1

Prayer from the paschal Office of Foot-washing (*cf* Brit Mus Catal nos 833, 1247), to be said over the basin (λεκάνη), 'without sprinkling the lentils[1]'   After the text, it is said that this prayer is from 'the book of Joseph,' presumably either the owner of the book copied or the author of some liturgical work

ⲡⲁⲓⲡⲉ ⲡⲉϣⲗⲏⲗ ⲉⲧⲗⲉⲕⲁⲛⲏ ⲙⲡⲟⲩⲱϣ ⲉⲡⲁⲣϣⲓⲛ ·   ⲕⲥⲙⲁⲙⲁⲁⲧ ⲡⲟⲥ

ⲡⲛⲟⲩⲧⲉ ⲡⲡⲁⲛⲧⲱⲕⲣⲁⲧⲱⲣ ⲡⲉⲓⲱⲧ ⲥⲡⲉⲛϫⲟⲉⲓⲥ ⲁⲩⲱ ⲡⲉⲛⲛⲟⲩⲧⲉ ⲡⲉⲛⲥⲱⲣ ⲓⲥ ⲭⲥ : ⲡⲉⲛⲧⲁϥϣⲁϫⲉ
ⲛϣⲟⲣⲡ ϩⲛⲧⲁⲡⲣⲟ ⲛⲛⲉϥⲡⲣⲟⲫⲧ/ ⲉⲧⲟⲩⲁⲁⲃ : ⲡⲉⲛⲧⲁϥⲥⲱⲧⲉ ⲙⲡⲕⲉⲛⲟⲥ ⲙⲡⲣⲱⲙⲉ ⲉⲃⲟⲗ ϩⲛⲧⲙⲛⲧ-
ϩⲙϩⲁⲗ ⲉⲧⲥⲁϣⲉ ⲙⲡⲁⲓⲁⲃ ϩⲛⲡⲉⲧⲉⲣⲉⲡⲉⲕⲙⲟⲛⲟⲅⲉⲛⲏⲥ ⲛϣⲏⲣⲉ ⲉⲓ ϩⲛⲧⲥⲁⲣⲝ ⲡⲉⲛϫⲟⲉⲓⲥ ⲓⲥ ⲭⲥ :
ⲡⲉⲛⲧⲁϥϯ ⲑⲉ ⲛⲁⲛ ⲁⲛⲟⲛ ⲉⲧⲣⲉⲛⲧⲱⲟⲩⲛ ϩⲁⲡⲉϥⲥⲫⲟⲥ ⲁⲩⲱ ⲛⲥⲙⲟⲟϣⲉ ⲉϩⲣⲁⲓ ⲉϫⲛϩⲟⲃ ⲙⲛⲟⲩϩⲟⲣⲉ :
ⲡⲉⲛⲧⲁϥⲭⲁⲣⲓⲍⲉ ⲛⲁⲛ ⲙⲡⲕⲱ ⲉⲃⲟⲗ ⲛⲛⲉⲛⲛⲟⲃⲉ ϩⲓⲧⲙⲡϫⲱⲕⲙ ⲙⲡⲉϩⲛⲟ ⲛⲕⲉⲥⲟⲡ ⲁⲩⲱ ⲁϥⲧⲥⲁⲃⲟⲛ
ⲉⲡⲉϥⲙⲛⲥⲧⲏⲣⲓⲟⲛ ⲉⲧⲟⲩⲁⲁⲃ ϩⲓⲧⲙⲡⲉⲛϫⲟⲉⲓⲥ ⲓⲥ ⲡⲉⲭⲥ : ⲡⲉⲛⲧⲁϥⲧⲁⲁⲃ ⲉⲛⲉϥⲙⲁⲑⲏⲧⲏⲥ ϩⲛⲡⲧⲉⲣⲉϥ-
ⲧⲱⲟⲩⲛ ⲅⲁⲣ ϩⲛⲡⲁⲓⲡⲛⲟⲛ ⲁϥⲕⲁ ⲛⲉϥϩⲟⲓⲧⲉ ⲉϩⲣⲁⲓ ⲁϥϫⲓ ⲛⲟⲩⲗⲩⲛϯⲛⲟⲛ (λέντιον) ⲁϥⲙⲟⲣⲉϥ ⲉⲙⲟϥ ·
ⲉⲓⲧⲁ ⲁϥⲛⲉϫ ⲡⲙⲟⲟⲩ ⲉⲧⲗⲩⲕⲁⲛⲏ ⲁϥⲁⲣⲭⲓ ⲛⲓⲱ ⲛⲛⲥⲟⲩⲉⲣⲏⲧⲉ ⲛⲛⲉϥⲙⲁ ⲁⲩⲱ ⲉⲃⲟⲧⲟⲩ ϩⲛⲡⲗⲏⲛ-
(*verso*)-ϯⲛⲟⲛ ⲉⲧⲙⲏⲣ ⲉⲙⲟϥ ⲁⲩⲱ ⲡⲉϫⲁⲁϥ ⲛⲁϥ ϫⲉⲥⲙⲉ ϫⲉⲟⲩ ⲡⲉⲛⲧⲁⲓⲁⲁⲃ ⲛⲏⲧⲛ ⲛⲧⲟⲟⲧⲛⲥⲉ
ⲁⲉⲧⲙⲙⲟⲩⲧⲉ ⲣⲟⲓ ϫⲉⲡⲟⲧ ⲁⲩⲱ ⲡⲥⲁϩ ⲁⲩⲱ ⲕⲁⲗⲱⲥ ⲧⲉⲧⲛϫⲱ ⲙⲙⲟⲥ ⲁⲛⲟⲛ ⲅⲁⲣⲡⲉ ⲉϣϫⲉ ⲁⲛⲟⲕ ⲇⲉ
ⲁⲓⲁⲓ ⲡⲉⲧⲛⲟⲩⲉⲣⲏⲧⲉ ⲡⲟⲧ ⲁⲩⲱ ⲡⲥⲁϩ ⲉϣϣⲉ ⲉⲣⲟⲧⲛ ⲉⲓⲁ ⲡⲟⲩⲉⲣⲏⲧⲉ ⲛⲛⲉⲧⲉⲛⲉⲣⲏⲩ ⲟⲩⲙⲟⲩⲧ ⲅⲁⲣ
ⲡⲉⲛⲧⲁⲓⲁⲁⲃ ⲛⲏⲧⲛ ⲛⲧⲟⲟⲧⲛ ϩⲱⲱⲧⲧⲏⲩⲧⲛ ⲉⲧⲉⲧⲛⲁⲁⲥ ⲉⲧⲃⲉⲡⲁⲓ ⲡⲟⲧ ⲓⲥ ⲡⲉⲭⲥ ⲭⲁⲣⲓⲍⲉ ⲛⲁⲛ ⲙⲡⲉⲥⲙⲟⲧ
ⲉⲧⲕ/ⲛⲟⲛⲉⲓ ϫⲉⲕⲁⲁⲥ ⲉⲛⲉϣⲱⲡⲉ ⲛⲥⲛⲛⲕⲗⲩⲣⲟⲛⲁⲙⲙⲟⲥ ⲙⲙⲛⲉⲕⲡⲥⲧⲟⲩⲁⲁⲃ ⲉⲛⲁⲡⲟⲥⲧ/ ϩⲓⲧⲛⲧⲉⲭⲁⲣⲓⲥ :—
ⲡⲁⲓⲡⲉ ⲡⲉϣⲗⲗ ⲉⲧⲗⲩⲕⲁⲛⲏ ⲡⲁⲡϫⲱⲱⲙⲉ ⲛⲓⲱⲥⲏⲫⲡⲉ.

'Blessed art Thou, Lord, God, Almighty, the Father of our Lord and our God, our Saviour, Jesus Christ, Who spake first by the mouth of His holy prophets, Who did redeem the race of man from the bitter slavery of the devil by the coming of Thy Only begotten Son in the flesh, our Lord Jesus Christ, Who showed us how to bear His cross and to tread upon serpents and scorpions, Who granted us the remission of our sins by the purifying of a second birth,' &c , followed by an abstract of John xiii 4–15

25.—Paper, complete; 32×5 cm   Script of ZOEGA's 9th class, across width of strip

Greek Hymn to the Virgin, preceding the recital of the diptychs   *V* Daniel, *Cod Liturg*, iv 119[2]   This and the following numbers show a remarkable system of musical notation, consisting in from 1 to 6 oblique strokes, with a few other signs, above certain syllables.   I have failed to find examples of it elsewhere   The R. P. L. PÉTIT (Constantinople) is of opinion that this system, otherwise unknown to him, indicates the duration of the notes, but, at the same time, their rhythmic emphasis   He suggests that in the strokes we may seek the origin of the 'grace notes' now in use in the Greek church music   Dom A WILMART (Solesmes) has referred me to THIBAUT's art., *Byz Zeitschr*, viii 122, where signs somewhat resembling ours are discussed

---

[1] For ⲙⲡⲟⲩϣⲉϣ ⲡⲁⲣϣⲓⲛ or ⲙⲡⲟⲩϣⲱϣ ⲙⲡⲁⲣϣⲓⲛ or perhaps ⲙⲡⲟⲩϣ-ϣⲉⲛ ' when unable to procure'   I know not to what this rubric refers, but there is no doubt about the reading   The Greek rite (Goar **743**) throws no light on it, nor do the native descriptions, Abû'l-Barakât (VANSLEB, *Hist*, 153), or Ibn Sabbâ', 161

[2] I owe the identification to Mr C N Faminsky, anagnostes of the Russian church, London

C

ⲉⲡⲓ ⲥⲩ · ⲭⲁⲓⲣⲟⲓⲥ · ⲕⲁⲓⲭⲁⲣⲓⲧⲱⲙⲉⲛⲟⲓ · ⲛⲁⲥⲁ · ⲟⲓ ⲕⲧⲓⲥⲓⲥ · ⲁⲅⲅⲉⲗⲟⲛ · ⲧⲟ ⲥⲩⲥⲧⲏⲙⲁ ⲕⲁⲓ ⲁⲛⲱⲛ ·
ⲧⲟ ⲅⲉⲛⲟⲥ · ⲟⲓⲅⲓⲁⲥⲙⲉⲛⲟⲛ ⲛⲁⲉ ⲕⲁⲓ ⲡⲁⲣⲁⲇⲓⲥⲟⲥ ⲗⲟⲅⲓⲕⲟⲛ · ⲡⲁⲣⲑⲉⲛⲓⲕⲟⲛ · ⲕⲁⲩⲭⲏⲙⲁ · ⲉⲝ ⲓⲥ ⲑⲥ ·
ⲉⲥⲁⲣⲕⲱⲑⲏ · ⲕⲁⲓ ⲡⲁⲗⲓⲟⲛ ⲅⲉⲅⲟⲛⲉⲛ · ⲟ ⲡⲣⲟ ⲁⲓⲱⲛⲟⲛ ⲩⲡⲁⲣⲭⲏⲥ ⲑⲥ · ⲧⲏⲛ ⲅⲁⲣ ⲥⲩⲛ · ⲙⲏⲧⲣⲁⲛ
ⲑⲣⲟⲛⲟⲛ ⲉⲡⲟⲓⲏⲥⲉⲛ · ⲕⲁⲓ ⲧⲏⲛ ⲥⲩ ⲅⲁⲥⲧⲉⲣⲁ ⲡⲗⲁⲧⲓⲧⲉⲣⲁ ⲟⲩⲛⲟⲛ · ⲁⲡⲓⲣⲅⲁⲥⲁⲧⲟ · ⲉⲡⲓ ⲥⲩ · ⲭⲁⲓⲣⲟⲓⲥ ·
ⲕⲁⲓⲭⲁⲣⲓⲧⲱⲙⲉⲛⲟⲓ · ⲛⲁⲥⲁ · ⲏ ⲕⲧⲓⲥⲓⲥ · ⲇⲟⲝⲁ ⲥⲟⲓ : — : — : —

Below, in different ink and hand　ⲫⲱⲥ ⲏⲡⲁⲣⲭⲏⲥ.

Verso blank

26—Paper, 3 pieces pasted together, complete, 21 × 7½ cm. Script of ZOEGA's 9th class
Greek Hymn on Christ's birth (*cf* Luke ii 11-16)　The superlinear notation is more elaborate than in the preceding number

ⲓⲇⲟⲩ ⲉⲧⲉⲭⲑⲏ · ⲏⲙⲓⲛ ⲥⲏⲙⲉⲣⲟⲛ · ⲓⲥ ⲭⲥ ⲟ ⲕⲥ · ⲉⲛ ⲡⲟⲗⲓ ⲇⲁⲇ ⲓⲇⲟⲩ ⲡⲏⲙⲉⲛⲏⲥ ⲥ ⲏ ⲙⲁⲥⲏ ·
ⲥ ⲥⲧⲣⲁⲧⲓⲉ · ⲧⲟⲛ ⲁⲅⲅⲉⲗⲟⲛ · ⲉⲛⲟⲩⲛⲧⲟⲛ ⲗⲉⲅⲟⲛⲧⲉⲥ · ⲇⲟⲝⲁ ⲉⲛ ⲩⲯⲩⲥⲧⲓ ⲑⲱ · ⲥ ⲉⲡⲓ ⲅⲏⲥ ⲓⲣⲏⲛⲏⲥ · ⲉⲛ
ⲁⲛⲑⲣⲱⲡⲓⲥ · ⲛ ⲩⲇⲟⲕⲓⲁ · ⲥ ⲏⲗⲑⲟⲛ ⲉⲡⲉⲩⲥⲁⲛⲧⲉⲥ · ⲧⲟ ⲃⲣⲉⲫⲟⲥ · ⲕⲓⲙⲉⲛⲟⲛ ⲉⲛ ⲫⲁⲧⲛⲏ ⲇⲓⲟ ⲡⲁⲛⲧⲉⲥ
ⲡⲓⲥⲧⲏ · ⲉⲩⲗⲟⲅⲟⲩⲏⲧⲟⲛ ⲥⲉ · ⲡⲣⲟⲥⲕⲩⲛⲏⲥⲟⲙⲉⲛ : —

Verso　remains of Arabic and Coptic texts (earlier)

27—Paper, complete?, 16 × 7½ cm　Script of ZOEGA's 9th class.　1 col, across width of strip
Greek Hymn on the Flight into Egypt　*Cf* the next number　Superlinear notation as before, though more sparing

ⲙⲏⲣⲓⲟⲛ · ⲙⲉⲅⲁ ⲕ/ ⲡⲁⲣⲁⲇⲟⲝⲟⲛ · ⲕ/ⲟⲡⲧⲉ · ⲓⲁⲑⲉⲓ ⲕⲏ · ⲓⲇⲉⲛ ⲛⲩⲕⲧⲟⲥ ⲧⲱ ⲓⲱⲥⲏⲫ · ⲱⲫⲑⲏ ⲟ
ⲁⲅⲅⲉⲗⲟⲥ ⲑⲱ ⲕ/ ⲗⲉⲅⲓ ⲉⲅⲉⲣⲟⲓⲥ ⲗⲁⲃⲓⲛ · ⲧⲟⲛ ⲡⲉⲇⲓⲟⲛ ⲕ/ [ⲙⲁ]ⲣⲓⲁⲙ / ⲟⲡⲟⲥ ⲉⲡⲗⲏⲣⲱⲥⲁⲥ ⲧⲱⲛ
ⲣⲩⲙⲁⲧⲱⲛ ⲡⲣⲟⲫⲏⲧⲱⲛ ⲉ ⲧⲏ ⲉⲕ[ⲏ]ⲣⲩⲅⲁⲥ ⲥ ⲟ ⲙⲉⲅⲁⲥ ⲟ ⲏⲥⲁⲓⲁⲥ · ⲉⲝ ⲉⲅⲩⲡⲧⲱ ⲉⲕⲁⲗⲁⲥ ⲧⲟⲛ
ⲩⲛ ⲙⲟⲩ ⲥⲩⲛ ⲙⲏⲧⲉⲣⲁ / ⲓⲇⲟⲩ ⲉⲣⲭⲉⲧⲉ ⲟ ⲕⲥ · ⲛⲉⲫⲉⲗⲉ ⲕⲟⲩⲫⲏ ⲏⲡⲟⲭⲟⲩⲙⲉⲛⲟⲥ ⲥ ⲕⲁⲧⲉⲗⲁⲃⲃⲁⲛⲓ
ⲧⲱⲛ ⲉⲅⲩⲡⲧⲓⲟⲛ · ⲁⲩⲧⲟⲥ ⲉⲱⲥⲁⲓ ⲧⲟⲛ ⲗⲁⲟⲛ ⲥⲟⲩ · ⲁⲡⲟ ⲧⲱⲛ ⲁⲙⲁⲣⲧⲱⲛ /

Verso　remains of Arabic accounts (earlier)

28—Paper, a fragment, 17½ × 9½ cm　Script of ZOEGA's 9th class　1 col, across width of strip
Greek Hymn on Christ's sojourn in Egypt and return thence (*cf* Matt ii 15, 20), with superlinear notation

ⲓ]ⲱⲥⲏⲫ ⲛⲩⲕⲧⲟⲥ · ⲓⲛⲉⲛ[　]ⲧⲟⲛ / ⲉⲝ ⲉⲅⲩⲡⲧⲱ ⲉⲕⲁⲗ[ⲁⲥⲁ ⲧⲟⲛ] ⲩⲛ ⲙⲟⲩ ⲥⲩⲛ ⲙⲏⲧⲉⲣ-
[ⲁ · ⲉⲧⲉ]ⲣⲟⲓⲥ ⲗⲁⲃⲓⲛ / [. . . . .]ⲏ · ⲡⲁⲛⲧ[. . . .]ⲏ[. .]ⲗⲟⲛ · ⲇⲓⲁ ⲧⲟⲩⲧⲟ[.]ⲛⲟⲧⲏⲛ / ⲉⲛ ⲥⲩ
ⲉⲅⲩⲡⲧⲱ[.]ⲗ[.]ⲧⲱ ⲓⲏⲗ ⲕⲁⲧⲁ ⲧⲟⲛ ⲁⲣⲭⲉⲟⲛ ⲁⲅⲅⲉⲗⲟⲛ · ⲉⲭⲣⲩⲙⲁⲧⲓⲥⲑⲉⲛⲧⲉⲥ ⲥⲁⲫⲱⲥ / ⲥⲩⲙⲉ-
ⲣⲟⲛ ⲏ ⲉⲅⲩⲡⲧⲟⲛ · ⲡⲣⲟⲫⲁⲛⲓⲥⲟⲩⲥⲁⲛ ⲧⲱ ⲕⲩ · ⲧⲟⲛ ⲓⲇⲱⲗⲟⲛ ⲕⲁⲑⲉⲣⲟⲛⲧⲉⲥ · ⲭⲥ ⲟ ⲥⲱⲣ ⲡⲁⲣⲁⲅⲓⲛⲉⲧⲁⲓ ·
ⲉⲣⲭⲉⲧⲟ ⲟ ⲇⲉⲥⲡⲟⲧⲏⲥ · ⲉⲡⲓ ⲛⲉⲫⲉⲗⲉ ⲕⲟⲩⲫⲏ ⲏⲡⲟⲭⲟⲩⲙⲉⲛⲟⲥ / ⲥ ⲧⲏⲛ ⲉⲅⲩⲡⲧⲱ ⲙⲟⲭⲟⲩⲣⲁⲥ ⲉⲕⲕⲁ-
ⲑⲉⲣⲟⲛⲧⲉⲥ · ⲟ ⲫⲓⲗⲱⲛ ⲁⲅⲧⲏⲥ / ⲟⲑⲉⲛ ⲗⲁⲟⲥ ⲉⲅⲩⲡⲧⲱ ⲁⲛⲉⲃⲟⲁ ⲇⲉⲟⲙⲉⲑⲁ ⲓⲏ/ⲧⲉⲅⲉ · ⲥⲱⲑⲏⲛⲉ ⲧⲁⲥ
ⲯⲩⲭⲁⲥ ⲏⲙⲱⲛ : —

Verso　an Arabic account (earlier)

29—Paper; complete, 12 × 7½ cm   Script of Zoega's 9th class
Greek Psalm verses for liturgical use on the 1st of Epiphi   Superlinear notation
ōн : епн̄п̄ · a   тас саряас (&c, Ps lxxviii 2, 3 without notation), after which,
β' о о̄с̄ ил̄оосал̄н еонн · еıс тн̄н вл̄н̄ро̄но̄мı̄ан соу · емµıанан то̄н наон тωн асıон
соу · оѳēпто̄ ̄ıлн̄н̄ · ωс опорофуλакıон (ib. 1)
Verso Arabic.

30—Paper; complete, 8½ × 7½ cm   Script of Zoega's 9th class
Greek Psalm verses as before.
Heading пес .. етанат : р̄п̄
ωс емесаλумфон та ерса соу н̄е (&c, Ps ciii 24, 1).
Verso 1 line of Coptic

31—Paper, complete, 7 × 7 cm.   Script of Zoega's 9th class
Greek Psalm verses as before, for morning service (ὄρθρον) on the 8th Hathor.
ор̄ ч̄н̄ : аоур̄ : н̄ о к̄с̄ еѣасıλеусен (&c, Ps xcviii. 1[1])
Verso Arabic (earlier)

32—Paper; complete, 10 × 6 cm   Script of Zoega's 9th class
Greek Psalm verses as before, for morning (ὄρθρον) and evening (τὸ λυχνικόν) services
ı̄ζ ор̄ : к, епı та γψγλε (&c, Ps. xvii 34, 35)
λγ̇ : п̄н̄ : ç еınас (&c, Ps lxxxviii 20)
Verso blank

33.—Paper; almost complete, 18 × 8½ cm.   Script of Zoega's 9th class
Greek Psalm verses for the 18th of Thoth[2], followed by a Hymn to Christ
оω̄ соу ı̄н̄ етω [...] пноуте нıноу[те нау]ωнаɡ еѣоλ ɡнс[ıωн]:—ωфонсете о [о̄с̄ тωн]
о̄н̄ еıн сıωн (&c, Ps lxxxiii 8, 9), after which, о ѣасıλеус тнс ɔoɔн[с] проерхете · он
та херо[у]ѣıµ премоусıн ç та [с]арафıµ кpасоусıн асıос асıос асıос еı н̄е · он ̄но ı̄ω
енурнзен · ıαе о аµнос [оӯ][3]:—[. . . .]руса кλатоп:—[. . . . .] асıос о ѳеос епı tω
ıорɔаноу.

Verso perhaps related to the above, естıн саp е нµера еıс тн̄н еλеусıн соу
ɔеснота нµωн ı̄ɣ̄ х̄ɣ̄ еıс аıсунтон[4]:—п неофωтıсѳе н перıµıноусıн. Also an earlier
Arabic text.

¹ It is the festival of the Four Beasts   ³ Perhaps nothing here
² Perhaps the Exaltation of the Cross.   ⁴ According to the calendar, 24th Pachons

34—Paper, complete, 16 × 5¼ cm. Script of ZOEGA's 9th class   1 col, across width of strip

The Trisagion 'farced'

ⲁⲅⲓⲟⲥ ⲟ ⲑ̅ⲥ̅ · ⲟ ⲁⲓ ⲛⲙⲁⲥ ⲁ̅ⲡ̅ⲟ̅ⲥ̅ · ⲕ/ ⲏ ⲅⲟⲏ ⲁⲧⲣⲉⲡⲧⲟⲥ · ⲕ/ ⲙⲓⲛⲁⲥ ⲑ̅ⲥ̅ ⧸ ⲁⲅⲓⲟⲥ ⲓⲥⲭⲩⲣⲟⲥ ⲟ ⲉⲛ ⲁⲥⲑⲉⲛⲓⲁⲛ ⲧⲱ ⲩⲡⲉⲣⲉⲭⲟⲛⲧⲟⲥ · ⲓⲥⲭⲩⲣⲟⲥ · ⲉⲡⲓⲧⲉⲍⲁⲙⲉⲛ ⲁⲅⲓⲟⲥ ⲁⲑⲁⲛⲁⲧⲟⲥ · ⲟ ⲥϥⲟⲑⲓⲥ ⲁⲓ ⲛⲙⲁⲥ · ⲟ ⲧⲟⲛ ⲁⲓⲁ ⲥϥⲱ ⲑⲁⲛⲁ ⲕ/ ⲩⲡⲟⲙⲓⲛⲁⲥ ⲥⲁⲣⲕⲓ · ⲕ/ ⲁⲓⲍⲁⲟⲛ · ⲕ/ ⲑⲁⲛⲁⲧⲱ · ⲕ/ ⲩⲅⲟⲡⲟⲥ ⲩⲡⲁⲣⲭⲏⲥ · ⲁⲑⲁⲛⲁⲧⲟⲥ ⲉⲗⲉⲏⲥⲟⲛ ⲛⲙⲁⲥ ⧸ ⲁⲟⲍⲁ · ⲕ/ ⲛⲏⲛ / ⲁⲅⲓⲁ ⲧⲣⲓⲁⲥ ⲉⲗⲉⲏⲥⲟⲛ ⲛⲙⲁⲥ /

Verso blank

35—Paper, a fragment, 22 × 11½ cm   Script of ZOEGA's 9th class

Greek Hymn to the Virgin, divided into 4 (the first 5)-line stanzas   The name of the melody (ἦχος) is ⲏ̇ ⲡⲁⲥⲁ ⲡⲣⲟ⌊ . Then ⲭⲁⲓⲣⲉ ⲡⲁⲛⲁ[. . . . .   ]ⲙⲛⲏ · ⲭⲁⲓⲣⲉ Each phrase begins with ⲭⲁⲓⲣⲉ[1], *e g* ⲭⲁⲓⲣⲉ ⲁⲅⲁⲑⲏ ⲋ ⲁⲭⲣⲁⲛⲧⲉ · ⲭⲉⲣⲉ ⲁⲓⲏⲥ ⲧⲏⲥ ⲱ̅ⲏ̅ⲥ̅ · ⲭⲉⲣⲉ ⲁⲭⲣⲁⲛⲧⲉ ⲙ̅ⲏ̅ⲣ̅ · ⲭⲁⲓⲣⲉ ⲑⲛⲥⲁⲩⲣⲉ ⲧⲏⲥ ⲟⲛⲧⲟⲥ ⲍⲱⲏⲥ.

Verso Arabic

36—Paper, complete, 28 × 8 cm   Script of ZOEGA's 9th class   1 col, across width of strip

Greek Troparia in honour of Claudius, the Antiochene martyr[2], with the name of the melody (ἦχος)

>ⲭ< ⲧⲣ̊ : ⲏ̊ : ⲟ ⲉⲛ ⲕⲣⲁⲛⲓⲟⲩ :—ⲟ ⲁⲑⲗⲟⲫⲟⲣⲉ ⲧⲟⲩ ⲭ̅ⲩ̅ ⲋ ⲛⲓⲕⲏⲫⲟⲣⲉ ⲕⲗⲁⲩⲧⲓⲟⲥ ⲙⲁⲣⲧⲏⲥ ⲧⲓⲙⲓⲉ ⲉⲛⲓⲏⲛⲥⲁⲥ · ⲋ ⲧⲏⲛ ⲡⲗⲁⲛⲏⲛ ⲧⲱⲛ ⲓⲁⲱⲗⲟⲛ/ ⲋ ⲧⲩⲣⲁⲛⲛⲟⲩ ⲙⲁⲛⲓⲁⲛ ⲁⲡⲓⲗⲏⲛ · ⲃⲁⲥⲁⲛⲟⲥ ⲩⲡⲉⲙⲓⲛⲉⲛ · ⲥⲑⲉⲛ ⲧⲣⲓⲥⲥⲧⲉⲫⲁⲛⲉ ⲕⲗⲁⲩⲧⲓⲟⲥ/ ⲭ̅ⲛ̅ ⲧⲟⲛ ⲑ̅ⲛ̅ ⲛⲙⲱⲛ · ⲧⲉⲥ ⲡⲣⲉⲥⲃⲓⲉⲥ ⲥⲟⲩ ⲥⲱⲑⲏⲛⲉ ⲛⲙⲁⲥ/ ⲱⲥⲡⲉⲣ ⲅⲁⲣ ⲟ ⲕ̅ⲥ̅ · ⲩⲡⲉⲣ ⲧⲟⲩ ⲕⲟⲥⲙⲟⲩ ⲧⲟ ⲉⲙⲁ · ⲧⲟ ⲛⲏⲛⲓⲟⲛⲧⲟⲛ ⲉⲅⲉ⌊ⲉ⌋ⲭⲉⲁⲛ · ⲋ ⲉⲛ ⲁⲟⲍⲏⲥ ⲧⲟⲩⲥ ⲙⲁⲣⲧⲏⲣⲉⲥ/ ⲟ ⲩⲡⲉⲣ ⲧⲱⲛ ⲉⲩⲉⲣⲅⲉⲧⲏⲛ · ⲧⲏⲛ ⲯⲩⲭⲏⲛ ⲥⲟⲩ ⲡⲁⲣⲉⲁⲱⲕⲉⲛ · ⲥⲱⲥⲟⲛ ⲧⲁⲥ ⲯⲩⲭⲁⲥ ⲛⲙⲱⲛ ⧸

ⲁⲗⲗⲟⲥ :—ⲙⲛⲏⲙⲏⲛ ⲥⲛⲁⲟⲍⲟⲛ ⲕⲗⲁⲩⲧⲓⲟⲥ · ⲥⲛⲙⲉⲣⲟⲛ ⲁⲛⲥⲁⲓⲍⲁⲥ · ⲏ ⲡⲓⲥⲧⲏ ⲥⲩⲛⲁⲅⲅⲉⲗⲏⲥ ⲭⲟⲣⲉⲅⲟⲩⲥⲓⲛ · ⲁⲉⲓ ⲉⲟⲣⲧⲁⲍⲟⲙⲉⲛ/ ⲧⲟⲛ ⲁⲅⲱⲛⲁ ⲧⲟⲛ ⲕⲁⲗⲱⲛ · ⲟⲓ ⲁⲅⲱⲛⲓⲥⲁⲙⲉⲛⲟⲥ · ⲋ ⲧⲟⲛ ⲁⲣⲟⲙⲟⲛ ⲕⲁⲗⲟⲛ ⲧⲉⲗⲉⲥⲁⲛⲧ, ⲧⲟⲛ ⲓⲁⲱⲗⲟⲛ ⲧⲏⲛ ⲗⲁⲧⲣⲓⲁⲛ ⲙⲁⲛⲓⲁⲛ ⲕⲁⲧⲉⲡⲁⲧⲏⲥⲉⲛ/ ⲋ ⲧⲟⲛ ⲁⲩⲣⲁⲛⲛⲟⲛ ⲁⲡⲓⲗⲏⲛ · ⲟⲩⲕ/ⲡⲧⲟⲏ̇ⲑⲏⲥⲁⲛ ⲟⲓ ⲁⲅⲓⲟⲓ[3] · ⲋ ⲧⲟⲛ ⲛⲟⲥⲟⲩⲛⲧⲟⲛ ⲑⲉⲣⲁⲡⲉⲩⲟⲩⲥⲓⲛ · ⲋ ⲁⲉⲙⲟⲛⲓⲟⲛ ⲉⲗⲁⲃⲉⲧⲁⲓ · ⲁⲓⲟ ⲁⲩⲥⲱⲛⲏⲥⲟⲛ ⲭ̅ⲛ̅ · ⲓⲛⲁ ⲥⲱⲥⲁⲓ ⲧⲱⲛ ⲁⲛⲑⲣⲱⲡⲱⲛ · ⲕ̅ⲉ̅ ⲁⲟⲍⲁ ⲥⲟⲓ :—:—:

Verso earlier text, cut through, probably same hand   It consisted of Psalm verses,

---

[1] Cf the Ἀκάθιστος Ὕμνος and the Bohairic *Theotokia,* pp 64, 92, 102, 136, 329 &c

[2] *V Synaxarium,* 11th Kihak, 11th Baunah, AMÉLINEAU

Contes, II, Brit Mus Copt Catal nos 328, 1222

[3] In the next number this is ⲟⲩⲕⲉⲡⲧⲟⲏⲑⲏⲥⲁⲛ ⲫⲓⲗⲟⲑⲉⲟⲛ

in Greek with Coptic translations lxvii. 3, cvi. 32, 31 and 41–43 (omitting 42 b). Below this is,

ме]ркоүрιοү : ψαπ : ҳ҃ꙗ :

]еап соү : еχει о҃ѡо҃ : к҃

]аꙗнтап ⸗

]— ·· — ·· — ·· —

]р : к҃а

]— ·· — ·· — ·· —

]мет҄р а̊реп҃пс҄к҄/ · еχει ѳ̊ѡ̊ : н҃ :

]ψаѧ̇ р҃ѧа ψаѧ̇ р҃ѧа (sic) оϊ ιεριс соү

]— ·· — ·· — ·· — ·· —

37—Paper, 3 pieces pasted together; 26½ × 7 cm Script of ZOEGA's 9th class

Greek Troparia to Philotheus, the martyr[1]. *Recto* except for the saint's name, the texts are identical with those of no 36

Verso each of the 3 pieces had a text 2 were Greek, one having коп҄[2] антιφѡпнсιс · геппнсеос.—φѡτι соү φѡτι соү еп еιѧнее нѧѳеп гар соү то ф (*sic expl*), the other Pss. xxvi 16, viii 5 The 3rd was Coptic, apparently a letter.

]ос[ ]ꙗп аүтаееоι

]χρια пѳѡк етаеео

]еιс пааϥ аϥхооү п[а]ϥ

]нпе шаϥерпеϥаѳн

]рѳе нтаϥпаү епса

]таееоι хептаϥхоос

]парраⲋеѧ еιѳнк

]ѧ етоүпаⲅ пеϥхѡѡ

а]ιакѡп ѳеоѧѡрє пхо

38.—Parchment; a fragment, 10 × 13 cm Palimpsest (*a*) script of ZOEGA's 4th class, (*b*) 1 script of ZOEGA's 9th class 1 col, 2 *cf* HYVERNAT x. 1 col

(*b*) 1 Hymns The melody of the first is ннаткет, its text, relating to a saint or martyr, наιатк еток херо · акееιше каѧѡе ⲅепакѡп · атекоүсια ѳѡк еⲅраι шап[р]р[о] пот епеѳоее · акⲅареⲅ епексѡееа еϥтв҄внү · апот аак екеро:—

Title of the second, ιѡ҃[3] Begins аѧⲅ̂ еток оүсаιе · ѡ пкоүι ⲅее[..]ѧеⲅ[..]ос екιпе ноүаⲅⲅеѧо[с

---

[1] *V Synaxarium,* 16th Tybi   [2] *кортáкιор.*   [3] *V Aeg Zeitschr,* xxxix. 109

39—Paper, complete, 20 × 5½ cm   Script of ZOEGA's 9th class
Greek Hymn in honour of Dioscorus, patriarch of Alexandria, and the dogmas which he upheld

ϲ[ⲏ]ⲙⲉⲣⲟⲛ ⲟ ⲕⲁ[..]   ⲟ ⲙⲉ[ⲅⲁⲥ] ⲁⲓⲟⲥⲕⲟⲣⲟⲥ · ⲕ,[..] . ⲣⲁⲓⲟⲛ ⲛⲁⲩⲭⲙⲙⲁ
ⲧⲁⲓ[..]ⲧⲱⲛ ⲥⲟⲩ ⲉⲣⲉ [...] ⲛ / ⲙⲁ[.. ⲛⲁ]ⲧⲉⲫⲣⲟⲛⲏⲥⲁⲛ ⲁⲓⲣⲉⲥⲓⲛ · ⲕ, ⲧⲏⲛ ⲧⲣⲓⲁⲇⲁ ⲕⲩⲣⲏⲝ[..]⳹
ⲟⲥⲓⲉ ⲁⲓⲟⲥⲕⲟⲣⲉ/ ⲱⲥ ⲟ ⲏⲗⲓⲟⲥ ⲗⲁ[..] ⲉⲡ[..]ⲥⲉⲍⲟⲩⲛ ⲟ ⲭⲥ · ⲧⲟⲩⲥ ⲗⲟⲅⲟⲩⲥ ⲥⲟⲩ ⲕⲟⲥⲙⲏⲥⲓⲥ
ⲡⲛⲙⲏⲛ [ⲟ]ⲥⲓⲉ ⲁⲓⲟⲥⲕⲟⲣⲉ ⲕ,[..]ⲗⲱ[.]ⲥⲟⲫ[..] ⲁⲓⲇⲁⲥⲕⲁⲗⲉ ⲧⲏⲥ ⲉⲕⲕⲗⲏⲥⲓⲁⲛ ⲥⲟⲩ ⲉⲫⲣⲟⲛϯⲥⲉⲛ ·
ⲡⲣⲉⲥⲃⲉⲩⲟⲛⲧⲁ ⲩⲡⲉⲣ ⲏⲙⲱⲛ ⲥⲱⲑⲏⲛⲉ ⲧⲁⲥ ⲯⲩⲭⲁⲥ ⲩⲙⲱⲛ.

Verso remains of an Arabic text (earlier)

40.—Paper, 2 pieces pasted together; complete; 16 × 11½ cm   Script of ZOEGA's 9th class
Hymn (?), treating of the Communion, with reference to the deacon's bidding, ἀσπάσασθε ἀλλήλους. The punctuation may indicate the mode of recitation[1] *Cf* nos 25 ff

ⲟⲩⲛⲟϭⲡⲉ ⲡⲉⲟⲟⲩ : ⲛⲛⲉⲓⲁⲣⲭⲓⲉⲣⲉⲩⲥ : ⲛⲧⲁⲡⲛⲟⲩⲧⲉ ⲥⲟⲧⲡⲟⲩ ⲉⲩⲅ̄ⲛⲛⲉϥⲉⲛⲕⲗⲏⲥⲓⲁ ≡ ⲟⲩⲛⲟϭ
ⲟⲛⲡⲉ ⲡⲧⲁⲓⲟ :: ⲛⲛⲓⲡⲣⲉⲥⲃⲩⲧⲉⲣⲟⲥ : ⲙⲛⲛⲓⲁⲓⲛ̄ⲟⲥ[2]·: ⲉⲩⲕⲱⲧⲉ ⲉⲡⲙⲁ ⲛⲉⲣϣⲟⲩϣⲟⲩ = ϣⲁⲣⲉⲡⲇⲓ̄ⲕ̄/
ⲱϣ ⲉⲃⲟⲗ ⲉⲡⲗⲁⲟⲥ : ϫⲁⲥⲡⲁⲍ ⲛⲛⲉⲧⲕⲉⲣⲏⲩ : ϩⲛⲟⲩⲡⲓ ⲉⲥⲟⲩⲁⲁⲃ ⳥ ϣⲁⲣⲉⲡⲗⲁⲟⲥ ϩⲱⲱⲃ · ⲛϣⲏⲣⲉ
ⲛⲧⲉ ⲡⲟⲩⲟⲉⲓⲛ : ⲧⲓ ⲡⲉⲩⲟⲩⲟⲓ ⲉϩⲟⲩⲛ :: ⲛⲥⲉⲁⲥⲡⲁⲍ ⲛⲛⲉⲩⲉⲣⲏⲩ ≡ (*verso*) ⲙⲁⲣⲛⲉⲙⲡϣⲁ ⲧⲉⲛⲟⲩ ≡
ⲛⲡⲉⲕⲁⲥⲡⲁⲥⲙⲟⲥ ⲉⲧⲟⲩⲁⲁⲃ ⲛⲧⲉⲛⲥⲙⲟⲩ ⲉⲣⲟⲕ : ⲙⲛⲛⲉⲁⲅⲅⲉⲗⲟⲥ =: : ϫⲉⲕⲁⲁⲥ ϩⲓⲧⲛⲛⲁⲓ : ⲉⲛⲉϭⲓⲛⲉ
ⲉⲛⲟⲩⲛⲁ :. ⲙⲡⲟⲩⲕⲱ ⲉⲃⲟⲗ ⲛⲛⲉⲛⲛⲟⲃⲉ ⲕⲁⲧⲉ ⲡⲉⲛⲛⲟϭ ⲛⲛⲁ :—

41.—Parchment ; a fragment, 12 × 13 cm   Palimpsest   (*a*) illegible (erased ?), (*b*) 1 col   Script small, of ZOEGA's 9th class
(*b*) Hymns, divided by lines   The following, relating to the reception of the law by Moses, can be read

]ⲡⲣⲟⲫⲏⲧⲏⲥ ⲉⲙⲏ ⲡⲉⲛⲧⲁ[ⲓⲧⲁⲙ]ⲟϥ ⲉⲡⲁⲉⲟⲟⲩ ⲁⲙⲟⲩ ⲛⲁⲓ ⲉϩⲣⲁⲓ [ⲉϫⲙ]ⲡⲓⲧⲟⲟⲩ ⲧⲁϯ ⲛⲁⲕ
ⲉⲡⲙⲛⲧ [ⲉϣⲁϫⲉ] ϥⲓⲧⲟⲩ ⲛⲥⲧⲁⲁⲩ ⲉⲡⲁⲗⲁⲟⲥ · ⲉⲩϣⲁⲛϩⲁⲣⲉϩ ⲉⲛⲁⲛⲧⲟⲗⲏ ϣⲁⲓϣⲉ ⲧⲁⲕⲁⲥ
ⲁⲗⲗⲟ[3]:—ⲁⲙⲟⲩ ⲧⲁϯ ⲡⲙⲛⲧ ⲉϣⲁϫⲉ ⲛⲁⲕ ⲙⲱⲩⲥⲏⲥ ⲡⲉⲡⲣⲟⲫⲏⲧⲏⲥ ⲉⲙⲏ ϫⲓ ⲛⲡⲙⲛⲧ ⲉϣⲁϫⲉ
ⲛⲁⲕ ϥⲓⲧⲟⲩ ⲛⲥⲧⲁⲁⲩ ⲉⲡⲁⲗⲁ[ⲟⲥ] ⲉⲩϣⲁⲛϩⲁⲣⲉϩ ⲉⲛⲁⲛⲅⲟⲗⲏ ⲁⲩⲱ ⲛⲥⲉⲥⲱⲧⲙ ⲉⲥⲱⲓ ϣⲁⲓ[ϣⲉ]
(dividing line here)
Verso illegible.

42.—Parchment, a complete leaf, 12 × 10   Palimpsest   (*a*) script of ZOEGA's 4th class, (*b*) clumsy script of ZOEGA's 9th class.   1 col , 12 lines
Hymn to the melody ⲁⲓⲕⲏⲗⲉ (= ⲧⲓⲅⲩⲗⲏ)[4] and referring to Isaiah xxvi 2   Begins
ⲁⲙⲟⲩ ϣⲁⲣⲟⲛ ⲧⲉⲛⲟⲩ ⲱ ⲡⲁⲡⲛⲟϭ ⲉⲛϩⲣⲟⲟⲩ ⲛⲥⲁⲉⲓⲁⲥ[5] ⲡⲉⲡⲣⲟⲫⲏⲧⲏⲥ ⲡⲉⲛⲧⲁϥϫⲉ ⲛⲉϥϣⲁϫⲉ
ϩⲓⲧⲉⲙⲡⲛⲟⲩⲧⲉ.   Ends ⲛⲉ ⲛⲓⲙⲡⲉ ⲡⲓⲗⲁⲟⲥ ⲉⲧⲛⲁⲃⲱⲕ ⲉϩⲟⲩⲛ ⲉⲛϩⲏⲧⲟⲩ.

[1] Brit Mus Catal no 973 has a somewhat similar punctuation
[2] ⲁⲓⲕⲁⲓⲟⲥ, error for ⲁⲓⲁⲕⲟⲛⲟⲥ.
[3] ἄλλος, *i e* another hymn to the same melody *Cf*

Aeg Zeitschr, xxxix 110
[4] *V l c*, 109
[5] 'Loud-voiced Esaias' *Cf* Leyden, *MSS. Coptes*, 125, ⲛⲥⲁⲓⲁⲥ ⲛⲁⲡⲉⲛⲟϭⲝ(? ⲛⲟⲭ) ⲉⲛϩⲣⲟⲟⲩ.

43.—Parchment, a fragment, 7½×9 cm. Palimpsest (*a*) illegible, (*b*) script small, of Zoega's 9th class

(*b*) Hymns One, relating to Zacharias, begins ⲉⲧⲃⲉⲟⲩ ⲙⲡⲉⲍⲁⲭ[ⲁⲣⲓⲁⲥ   ] ⲉⲃⲟⲗ ⲭⲉⲁϥⲛⲁⲩ [   ] ⲁϥⲉⲣⲁⲡⲓⲥⲧⲟⲥ. Above it is ⲥ[×] (στίχοϛ) One on the other side refers to the Redemption, Paradise and the Virgin.

44—Parchment, a complete double leaf; together 12½×18 cm Script uneven, of Zoega's 9th class 1 col

Hymns, relating (1) to John the Baptist and (2) to Shenoute.

(1) narrates Christ's baptism Its first part ends ⲭⲉⲡⲁⲓⲡⲉ ⲡⲁϣⲏⲣⲉ ⲙⲡⲣⲣⲁⲧⲥⲱⲧⲙ ⲛⲥⲱϥ Then ⲗⲟⲅ/ ⲕ/ ⲏⲏ ⲕ//, followed by a second part, ⲟⲩϣⲁⲭⲉ ⲛⲧⲉ ⲫϯ ⲁϥϣⲱⲡⲉ ϣⲁⲓⲱⲁ ⲡϣⲏⲣⲉ ⲛⲍⲁⲭⲁⲣⲓⲁⲥ &c, which ends ⲡⲁⲣⲁⲕⲁⲗⲉⲓ ⲙⲙⲟϥ ϩⲁⲣⲟⲛ ⲱ ⲡⲃⲁⲡⲧⲓⲥⲧⲏⲥ ⲓⲱⲁ ϥϣⲉⲛⲉⲣⲧⲏϥ ϩⲁⲣⲟⲛ ⲧⲉϥⲛⲁ ⲛⲉⲛⲛⲟⲃⲉ ⲉⲃⲟⲗ. This contains the verse 'At the tenth hour (ⲭⲉⲙⲙⲏⲧ) of the night[1] came Jesus to the Jordan, to John.'

(2) headed ⲉⲭ ⲡⲉⲭⲥ : ⲟⲩⲁⲥⲡⲁⲥⲙⲟⲥ ⲉⲭⲙⲡⲛⲓⲱⲧ ⲁⲡⲁ ϣⲉⲛⲟⲩⲧⲉ. Begins ⲛⲧⲕⲟⲩⲙⲁ ⲕⲁⲣⲓⲟⲥ ⲡⲓⲱⲧ ⲁⲡⲁ ϣⲉⲛⲟⲩⲧⲉ ⲡⲉⲡⲛⲁⲧⲟⲫⲟⲣⲟⲥ. Ends ⲁⲕⲣϣⲁ ⲙⲡⲓⲥⲱⲧⲏⲣ ϩⲛⲧⲉϥⲙⲛⲧⲉⲣⲟ ⲥⲡⲥ ⲙⲡⲟⲥ ⲉⲭⲱⲛ ⲡⲉⲛⲉⲓⲱⲧ ⲁⲡⲁ ϣ ϥϣⲉⲛⲉⲣⲧⲏϥ ϩⲁⲣⲟⲛ ϥ̅ⲛ̅ⲁⲕⲉⲛⲛⲟⲃⲉ ⲉⲃⲟⲗ.

45.—Paper, a fragment, 16×5½ cm. Script of Zoega's 9th class.

Hymns referring to Christ's appearances after the Resurrection. The beginning of the first is lost After 3 broken lines ⲡⲉ·ⲃⲉⲉⲅⲉ :—[. . .] ⲕⲁⲓ ⲡⲉⲧⲕⲩⲡⲱⲣⲟⲥ[2] · ⲡⲣⲱⲙⲉ ⲡⲁⲧⲉϣⲓⲛ ⲙⲁⲣⲓⲁ ⲧⲡⲁⲣ̅ ⲉⲥⲁⲃⲏ / ⲁⲛⲟⲕ ⲡⲉⲛⲧⲁⲓⲙⲟⲩ ⲁⲓⲱⲛϩ · ⲁⲓⲧⲱⲟⲩⲛ ϩⲓⲛⲉⲧⲙⲟⲟⲩⲧ · ⲁⲓⲥⲱ[3] :—

ⲡ ⲁ^ⲗ· ⲟⲩⲥⲙⲏ ⲉⲥϩⲟⲗϭ ⲁⲓⲥⲱⲧⲙ ⲉⲣⲟⲥ · ⲉϩⲟⲩⲛ ⲉⲡⲧⲁⲫⲟⲥ ⲉⲡⲉⲣ̅ · ⲭⲉⲙⲁⲣⲓϩⲁⲙ ⲉⲣϣⲓⲛⲉ ⲛⲥⲁⲛⲓⲙ ⲉⲓⲥ ϩⲏⲧⲉ ⲁϥⲧⲱⲟⲩⲛ ϩⲓⲛⲉⲧⲙⲟⲟⲩⲧ / ⲁⲗⲗ^{sic} ⲃⲱⲕ ⲉⲧⲅⲁⲗⲓⲗⲉⲁ · ⲧⲉⲧⲛⲁϭⲛⲧϥ ϩⲓⲡⲙⲁ ⲉⲧⲙⲙⲁⲩ^{sic} · ⲧⲉⲧⲟⲩⲱϣⲧ ⲉⲡⲉϥⲙⲧⲟ ⲉⲃⲟⲗ · ⲛⲧⲁⲣϯ ⲛⲟⲩⲭⲁⲓ ⲉⲛⲓⲗⲁⲟⲥ ⲧ[ⲏⲣⲟⲩ][5] :—

46.—Paper, a fragment, 8½×12 cm Script of Zoega's 9th class

Hymn to the Twenty-four Elders, for the 24th Hathor[6], using the words of Revelation iv. 2, 4

ⲡ ⲁ^ⲓ ϯ ⲁⲥⲡⲁⲥⲙ : ⲁⲉⲩⲣ̅ : ⲕⲁ ⁛

ⲁⲓⲛⲁⲩ ⲁⲛ[ⲟⲕ] ⲓⲱⲁⲛⲛⲏⲥ ⲉϩⲛⲑⲣⲟⲛⲟⲥ ϩⲓⲡⲉⲡⲛⲩⲉ ⲉⲩⲕⲱⲧⲉ ⲡⲉⲑⲣⲟⲛⲟⲥ ⲉⲡⲉ[.] ⲉⲣⲉⲕⲁ ? [. . . . .] ⲉⲣⲉⲕⲁ [. . . . . . .] ϩⲙⲟ[ⲟⲥ

Verso · remains of an Arabic text

---

[1] Cf the homily of Proclus, Rossi, *Papiri* II ii 61

[2] Perhaps the name of a melody, v *Aeg. Zeitschr* xxxix 109, Brit Mus Catal no 975

[3] Name of a melody, v. *Aeg. Zeitschr*, l.c, 108

[4] (ἦχοϛ) πλάγιοϛ δ, v l.c, 109

[5] Perhaps nothing here

[6] V *Synaxarium, sub die*

[7] (ἦχοϛ) πλάγιοϛ α

47.—Parchment, $13\frac{3}{4} \times 4$ cm   Script small, of Zoega's 9th class.   1 col., across width of strip

Four Hymns relating to Theodore Stratelates[1]   The strophes refer to his birth (?), to his heathen mother and Christian father, and to his employment by Diocletian as a general.   Each is preceded by the name of its melody

ⲅ̄   ⲙ̄ⲡⲓⲛⲁⲩ ⲉⲣⲟⲕ ⲉⲛⲉϩ · ⲛ̄ⲧⲁⲕⲓ ⲁⲕⲟⲩⲱϣⲧ ⲉⲡⲁⲛⲟⲩⲧⲉ ⲍ̄ⲛ̄ⲧⲟⲩ ⲡⲉⲛⲧⲁϥϯ ⲛⲁⲛ · ⲉⲡⲓ-
ϣⲏⲣϣⲏⲙ ⲛ̄ⲥⲁⲓⲉ ⲛ̄ϫⲱⲱⲣⲉ · ⲁⲛⲁⲩ ⲛⲁⲕ ⲉⲡⲉϥϩⲟ · ϫⲉⲙ̄ⲡⲉⲧⲛ̄ⲧⲱⲛ ⲉⲣⲟϥ · ⲟⲩⲡⲉⲧϣ̄ϣⲉ ⲣⲟⲕⲡⲉ ·
ⲛⲕⲟⲩⲱϣⲧ ⲛⲁⲛ ⲛⲛ̄ϯ ⲉⲟⲟⲩ ⲛⲁϥ :—

ⲃ̄ ⲇ   ⲧⲁⲙⲟⲓ ⲉⲡⲙⲁ ⲉⲣⲉⲡⲁⲓⲱⲧ ⲛ̄ϩⲏⲧϥ · ⲁⲩⲱ ⲛ̄ⲧⲉⲣⲧⲁⲙⲟⲓ ⲉⲡϥ̄ⲣⲁⲛ · ⲉⲃⲟⲗ ϫⲉⲙ̄ⲡⲓⲛⲁⲩ
ⲉⲣⲟϥ ⲉⲛⲉϩ ⲧⲁⲙⲙⲁⲩ ⲡⲣ̄ⲉⲡ ⲗⲁⲁⲩ ⲉⲣⲟⲓ · ⲉϣⲱⲡ ϥⲟⲛϩ ⲧⲁⲙⲟⲓ ⲉⲧⲙⲉ · ⲧⲁⲃⲱⲕ ϣⲁⲣⲟϥ ⲧⲁϭⲱ
ϩⲁϩⲧⲛ̄ϥ · ⲛϥ̄ⲧⲁⲙⲟⲓ ⲉⲧⲡⲓⲥϯ ⲉⲧⲥⲟⲩⲧⲱⲛ · ⲧⲉⲡⲁⲣⲁϣⲉ :—

ⲡⲁϣⲏⲣ ·   ⲁⲣⲁⲁⲧ ⲉϣⲉⲙⲟ · ⲉⲡⲁⲓⲱⲧ ⲕⲁⲧⲁ ⲥⲁⲣⲝ · ⲉⲧⲃⲉⲟⲩⲉⲓⲇⲱⲗⲟⲛ · ⲉϣⲁϥⲟⲩⲱϣϥ
ⲛϥ̄ⲃⲱⲗ ⲉⲃⲟⲗ ⲝ

(verso) ϣⲁⲓⲡⲱⲣϫ ⲉⲣⲟ ϩⲱⲱⲧⲉ ⲧⲁⲕⲁⲁⲧⲉ ⲛ̄ⲥⲱⲓ ⲱ ⲧⲁⲙⲙⲁⲩ · ⲧⲁⲡⲓⲥⲧⲉⲩⲉ ⲡⲉⲭ̄ⲥ̄ · ⲧⲁⲣϣⲁ
ϩⲓⲧⲥⲙ̄ⲛⲧⲣⲣⲟ :—

ⲡⲉϫⲁⲥ   ⲡⲣⲣⲟ ⲇⲓⲟⲕⲗⲏϯⲁⲛⲟ ⲥⲱⲧⲙ ⲉⲣⲟⲛ ⲧⲛ̄ϣⲁϫⲉ ⲛⲉⲙⲁⲕ · ⲙ̄ⲡⲣⲗⲩⲡⲓ ⲙ̄ⲡⲣⲟⲩⲱⲗⲥ
ⲉϩⲛⲧ · ⲉⲧⲃⲉⲡⲡⲟⲗⲟϭ ϫⲉϥⲛⲁϣⲧ ⲉⲙⲁⲧⲉ · ⲉⲓⲥ ⲑⲉⲟⲇⲱⲣⲟⲥ ⲡϣ̄ⲏⲣⲟⲥ ⲡ̄ϥ̄ⲥⲛⲉϥ ⲥⲉ ⲟⲩϫⲱⲟⲣ ⲙ̄ⲙⲁⲧⲉⲡⲉ
ϩⲓⲧⲥϭⲟⲙ ϫⲟⲟⲩ ⲉⲥⲱϥ ⲧⲁⲣϥ̄ⲙⲓϣⲉ ϫⲱⲕ · ⲧⲉϥϭⲱⲧⲡ ⲉⲡⲉⲕϫⲁϫⲉ ⲧⲏⲣⲟⲩ :—

48—Parchment, $16 \times 2\frac{1}{2}$ cm   Script small, of Zoega's 9th class   Text across width.

Hymns relating to Theodore Stratelates   The war in Arabia (sic) in which he took part and the dragon which he slew at Euchaita are mentioned

]ⲟⲥ [ⲡⲉ]ⲥⲧⲣ[ⲁⲧⲏ]ⲗⲁⲧⲏⲥ ⲡ̄ⲡⲟⲗⲩⲙⲁⲣⲭⲏⲥ ⲉϣⲟⲩⲧⲁⲓⲟϥ ⲝ ⲁⲡⲉⲕⲙⲁⲣⲧⲩⲣⲓⲟⲛ ϣⲱⲡⲉ ⲛⲟⲩⲛⲟϭ
ⲉϣⲏⲛ ⲉⲣⲉⲡⲉϥⲕⲁⲣⲡⲟⲥ ⲉⲩⲫⲣⲁⲛⲉ ⲙ̄ⲡϩⲏⲧ ⲉⲛⲓⲗⲁⲟⲥ · ⲟⲩⲟⲛ ⲛⲓⲙ ⲉⲧⲛⲁⲉⲓ ⲉⲡⲉⲕ[ⲙ]ⲁ ⲛϣ̄ⲱⲡⲉ
ⲛⲁⲩ ⲉⲛⲟⲩϫⲁⲓ · ϩⲓⲙⲁ ⲛⲓⲙ : [. . .]ⲛ ⲉⲧⲁⲓⲛⲁⲩ ⲉⲩⲛⲟϭ ⲉϩⲟⲧⲉ ⲁⲛⲟⲕ ϩⲓⲡⲡⲟⲗⲉⲙⲟⲥ ⲉⲧⲁⲣⲁⲃⲓⲁ ·

(verso) ⲉⲣⲉⲛⲃⲁⲣⲃⲁⲣⲟⲥ ⲥⲟⲟⲩϩ ⲉϩⲟⲩⲛ ⲉⲩⲙⲓϣⲉ ⲙ̄ⲡⲑⲉⲟⲇⲱⲣ ⲝ ⲁⲓⲛⲁⲩ ⲥⲉⲥⲟⲇⲱⲣ ⲉⲣⲉⲡⲉϥ-
ⲕⲟⲛⲧⲁⲣⲓⲟⲛ ϩⲛ̄ⲧⲉϥϭⲓϫ ⲛ̄ⲧⲁϥϩⲱⲗ ⲉⲃⲟⲗ ⲁϥⲃⲱⲕ ⲉⲡϫⲓⲥⲉ · ⲁϥϭⲱⲧⲡ ⲉⲡⲉⲧϯ ⲛⲉⲙⲁϥ :

ϣⲟⲙⲉⲧⲧ ⲉϣⲡⲏⲣ ⲛ̄ⲧⲁⲓⲛⲁⲩ ⲉⲣⲟⲥ · ϩⲙ̄ⲡⲉⲇⲣⲁⲕⲛ̄ ⲉⲩⲭⲏⲧⲟⲥ ⲛ̄ⲧⲁⲑⲉⲟⲇⲱ[

49—Parchment; irregular shape, 12×5 cm   Script small, of Zoega's 9th class
Text across width of strip, divided into paragraphs

Initial words of Hymns referring to various events in the story of Theodore Stratelates

]ⲉⲥ[. .] ⲁⲛϩⲁⲥ[ⲓⲟⲥ] ⲧⲏⲟⲟⲩ

ϯⲉⲓ · ⲣ · ⲛⲣⲟⲙⲡⲉ · ϫⲉⲡⲁⲅ̄ⲥ̄ ⲇⲓⲟⲕⲗⲏ[2].

ⲭⲉ ⲡⲉⲥⲧⲣⲁ · ⲭⲉⲣⲉ ⲡⲙⲁⲣⲧ ⲛⲉϣⲟⲩⲧⲁⲓⲟϥ : ϫⲉϫⲣⲟ ⲙⲟⲛ ⲱ ⲑⲉⲟⲇⲉⲓⲥ ϩⲏⲧⲉ ⲁⲥϥⲱⲛ ⲉϩⲟⲩⲛ
ⲛϭⲓ ⲧⲉⲩ[3]:

ϣⲉⲡⲟⲩϫⲁⲓ[4]   ⲡⲉϫⲁϥ ⲛⲁϥ ϫⲉⲉⲧ · ⲁⲣⲏⲩ ⲕⲛⲁⲥⲱⲧⲙ ⲛ̄ⲥⲱⲓ ⲛ̄ⲥⲉⲣⲃⲟⲗ ·

---

[1] On this martyr v Nilles in *Z f Kath Theol*, 1880,
120   Coptic texts are Zoega, pp 28, 56, Cairo no 8021
Leyden no 55 refers to Theod the Eastern

[2] ⲇⲓⲟⲕⲗⲏⲧⲓⲁⲛⲟⲥ.
[3] ⲧⲉⲩϣⲏ.
[4] Presumably names of melodies

πεϩλοσ   απτημιος τηρϥ αϩε ρατϥ πεχαγ μπρρο χερεπηογτε

[ο]γαπε πηογτε : [. . . .] παιαβολο[c . . . .] πεπταϥογ[. . . . .] χιϣοχπ :

Verso

]ϩε θεο̅ ̅ ητε[. . . . . .]με ηαι αϥμογϩ ε

]   [. . . .]ε χεπαο̅c̅ αητογχρ̅c̅ ηϙοcοπ

καλωc :   πετογααβ ϫε θεο̅ αϥτηοογ αϥειπε επετογααβ εγλοcιο ·

cωτμ ε   χεω ϩια μποογ πιχιηcοηc ηταϥϣωπε ϩιτ̅πολιc :

ϩωκ ηη̅η   χεϣογη ητετηϩωκ επρπε

λ̅

η̅ τ̅ χε θεοϫω πεcρατηλα εμοϥ:χεθεο̅ ϙρμϩα[λ] μπχ̅c̅ χρο ηϭμϭομ ϯριιη μπαο̅c̅

αηαcταcι παμεριτ [. .]τογ[. .]εη[. .]

50.—Parchment; 13½ × 3 cm   Script small, of ZOEGA's 9th class   Text across width of strip

Hymn relating to Theodore Stratelates, who here promises help to some one in distress, perhaps merely any one invoking him.

[. .]ϫιc[. .] χαηοηπε θεοϫω · πεcρατη πιωτ μπιτοπο[2] · ταιει ϣαροκ ταηογϫμ εμ · ταογωηϩ ερο επαϭοογ · μπρρϩοτε παμεριτ ϯϣοοπ ηεμακ εϭ̇ο · τατογχοκ ϩιηκ- ελπιϥιc τηρ · τεπεκραϣ :—

Verso blank

51.—Leather, apparently complete, 6 × 16½ cm.   Script   sloping uncials; *cf* CRUM, *Ostraca*, Pl I, no 71

Pen-trials, consisting of phrases from Hymns.

ϯ μπιογτε εροκ μπαι αηπε πιϙιρι χαιρε | χεχαιρε πογοειη ηρρο ηταϥει μπραϣε | χεμμοη παιπε χεχαιρε πογοειη μμε ηταϥει ηαη αϥρογοειη εροη ϯ

Verso beginning of same text, in upright uncials.

52.—Papyrus; a fragment; 18 × 13   This facsimile represents all that allows of being traced

Text in a peculiar script   Line 1 begins with απαcκαφοc, 2 with παλλ, t e ? ἄλλος (*cf* no 41[3]), perhaps names of melodies   The signs resemble certain musical characters[4], but also some stenographic systems[5].

[1] (ἦχος) πλάγιος γ
[2] 'The father of this τόπος,' here the patron saint, not the abbot (Brit. Mus Catal, pp 58, 84 a, GEORGI, *Colluth* 26, CLÉDAT, *Baouit*, II 96)   Three churches of S Theodore at Ashmunain (?) are in the list, Brit Mus Catal no 1100, to one of which the *Inventum* in the present Catalogue should relate   [3] And ERMAN, *Kopt Volkslit* 43

[4] GAISSER in *Or Christ* iii 423

[5] J HAVET in *Ac. des Inscr*, CR. 1887, 351

53 [20 a].—Parchment, 3 complete leaves; now 29½ × 21½ cm   Pp. ᄀ̄ᄀ̄-ᄀ̄ᄃ̄. 1 col,
28-33 lines   Script . *cf* ZOEGA, class VII, no. 29, or (especially for ⲁ) CIASCA XIV.   All
initials and rubrics in red[1].   From the same MS as Brit. Mus Catal no 147, and most
probably Leyden no 32

Directory of Hymns in Greek[2] and Coptic for certain days in the months Thoth,
Phaophi and Hathor. *Cf* Brit Mus Catal nos 157-159, Leyden nos 32, 37, 38,
Paris 129[20] foll. 115-120, Clarendon Press nos 18, 19, and GEORGI, *Frag Ev S Joh*, 203,
for similar texts

The following are the rubrics and the opening words of the hymns, the former
are underlined

Ⲣ ᄀ̄ᄀ̄   ⲛϭⲓ ⲡⲁⲧⲙⲟⲩ ⲙⲁⲅⲁⲁϥ ⲙⲡⲉⲓⲙⲁⲩ ⲉⲩⲇⲓⲕⲁⲓⲟⲥ ⲉⲁⲡϫⲟⲉⲓⲥ ⲕⲁⲁϥ ⲛⲥⲱϥ[3] ⲡⲉⲛⲧⲁϥ-
ⲧⲱⲟⲩⲛ ⲉⲃⲟⲗ ϧⲛⲛⲉⲧⲙⲟⲟⲩⲧ ϣⲛϧⲧⲏⲣ ⲛⲉⲛⲁ ⲛⲁⲛ

ⲩⲙⲛⲟⲥ ⲉⲝⲙⲡⲉⲩⲁⲅⲅⲉⲗⲓⲟⲛ ⲉⲛ ⲧⲟⲓⲧⲱ ⲙⲉⲛ ⲉⲓⲥ ⲧⲉϥϧⲣⲓⲟⲛ ϧⲛϫⲟⲓⲁϧⲛ ⲩⲙⲛⲟⲥ ⲉⲝⲙⲡⲁⲥⲡⲁⲥⲙⲟⲥ

ⲉⲛⲟⲏⲙⲉⲛⲑⲉⲛⲧⲟⲥ ⲧⲁⲩⲧⲁ ⲓⲱⲥⲏⲫ ⲧⲟⲩ ⲇⲓⲕⲁⲓⲟⲩ[4] &c

ⲩⲙⲛⲟⲥ ⲉⲝⲛϯⲣⲏⲛⲏ ⲧⲁⲩⲟ ⲉⲝⲙⲡⲡⲉⲧⲟⲩⲁⲁⲃ

ⲁⲗⲕⲉ ⲛⲑⲟⲟⲩⲧ ⲛϣⲁ ⲛⲁⲡⲁ ⲓⲱⲥⲏⲫ ⲡⲛⲟⲧⲁⲣⲓⲟⲥ[5]

ⲩⲙⲛⲟⲥ ⲉⲝⲛϯⲣⲏⲛⲏ ⲉⲓⲥ ⲙⲛⲟⲙⲙⲱⲥⲩⲛⲟⲛ ⲟ ⲡⲟⲓⲙⲉⲛⲟⲛ ⲇⲓⲕⲁⲓⲟⲥ ⲱⲥ ⲫⲟⲓⲛⲓⲝ[6] ⲁⲛ

ⲥⲟⲩϣⲙⲟⲩⲛ ⲙⲡⲁⲟⲡⲉ ⲛϣⲁ ⲙⲡⲉⲛⲉⲓⲱⲧ ⲁⲡⲁ ⲡⲁⲡⲛⲟⲩⲧⲉ[7] ⲛⲛⲁⲩ ⲛⲥⲩⲛⲁⲅⲉ ⲧⲣⲓⲥⲁⲅⲓⲟⲥ

ⲝⲉⲙⲱⲩⲥⲏⲥ ⲟⲩⲁⲁⲃ ⲙⲡⲛⲁⲁⲣⲱⲛ ϧⲛⲛⲉϥⲟⲩⲏⲏⲃ ⲁⲅⲓⲟⲥ ⲟ ⲑ̄ⲥ̄ ⲁⲅⲱ ⲥⲁⲙⲟⲩⲏⲗ ϧⲛⲛⲉⲧⲉⲡⲉⲓ-
ⲛⲁⲗⲉⲓ ⲙⲡⲉϥⲣⲁⲛ[8] ⲁⲅⲓⲟⲥ ⲉⲓⲥⲭⲩⲣⲟⲥ &c

ⲩⲙⲛⲟⲥ ⲉⲝⲙⲡⲉⲩⲁⲅⲅⲉⲗⲓⲟⲛ ⲅⲯⲟⲩⲧⲉ ⲧⲟⲛ ᄀ̄ᄀ̄

ⲩⲙⲛⲟⲥ ⲉⲝⲙⲡⲁⲥⲡⲁⲥⲙⲟⲥ ⲙⲉⲗⲭⲓⲥⲉⲇⲉⲕ ⲟ ⲉⲣⲉⲩⲥ ⲉⲓⲥ ⲧⲉϥϧⲡⲁⲇⲟⲩ ϧⲛⲟⲩⲥⲁϣϥ ⲛⲑⲟⲟⲩⲧ

ⲩⲙⲛⲟⲥ ⲉⲝⲛⲧⲥⲟⲟⲩϧⲥ ⲉϩⲉⲗⲉⲝⲁⲧⲟ[9] ⲇⲁⲩⲉⲓⲇ ⲩⲙⲛⲟⲥ ⲉⲝⲛϯⲣⲏⲛⲏ ⲟ ⲉⲓⲣⲟⲓⲥ ⲥⲟⲩ[10] *ⲇⲟⲝⲁ ⲡⲁⲧⲣⲓ*
ⲟⲙⲟⲥⲉⲛ ᄀ̄ⲥ̄[11] *ⲕⲁⲓ ⲛⲏⲛ* ⲟⲥ ⲉⲡⲟⲓⲛⲟⲓⲥⲱⲙⲉⲛ ⲅⲏⲛ

Ⲣ ᄀ̄ᄇ̄   ⲥⲟⲩⲥⲟⲟⲩ ⲛⲁⲑⲱⲣ ⲛϣⲁ ⲛⲛⲉⲛⲉⲓⲟⲧⲉ ⲉⲧⲟⲩⲁⲁⲃ ⲛⲁⲡⲟⲥⲧⲟⲗⲟⲥ[12] ⲛⲛⲁⲩ ⲛⲥⲩⲛⲁⲅⲉ
ⲧⲣⲓⲥⲁⲅⲓⲟⲥ ⲉⲝⲙⲡⲣⲁⲝⲓⲥ

ⲇⲟⲝⲁ ⲥⲟⲓ ⲭ̄ⲥ̄ ⲁⲡⲟⲥⲧⲟⲗⲱⲛ ⲕⲁⲩⲭⲏⲙⲁ ⲙⲁⲣⲧⲩⲣⲱⲛ ⲁⲅⲁⲗⲗⲓⲁ, with τρισάγιον &c
ⲡⲉϥⲃⲱⲗ

ⲡⲉⲟⲟⲩ ⲛⲁⲕ ⲡⲉⲭ̄ⲥ̄ ⲡϣⲟⲩϣⲟⲩ ⲛⲛⲁⲡⲟⲥⲧⲟⲗⲟⲥ ⲡⲧⲉⲗⲏⲗ ⲛⲙⲙⲁⲣⲧⲩⲣⲟⲥ &c

---

[1] The alternations of black and red seem here, as else-where, to be often irregular

[2] On the Greek of such texts *v* HESSELING in *Het Museum*, VI, no 11

[3] Ps xxxvi 25   [4] *Cf* Matt 1 20

[5] *V* Leyden Catal, p 213   Joseph was Shenoute's secretary and δευτεράριος, *v Miss franç*, IV, 65, 424, 459, 465   He is not found in the Bohairic calendar

[6] Ps xci 13

[7] *Cf* Leyden Catal, p 214, though this may be the archimandrite of Tabennese, *cf* Brit Mus Catal no 146, LEIPOLDT, *Schenute*, 90, 160   Several saints of this name are in the Bohairic calendar, *v.* 15th Mechir, 25th Pharm., 11th Pachon, as well as martyrs   In Brit. Mus Catal no 175 is apparently a dignitary of the White Monastery

[8] Ps xcvii 6   [9] Ps lxvii 70

[10] Ps cxxxi 9

* * Words between stars are in smaller, sloping script

[11] Ps cix 4

[12] This festival does not occur in the calendars

ⲩⲙⲛⲟⲥ ⲉⲝⲙⲡⲉⲩⲁⲅⲅⲉⲗⲓⲟⲛ

ⲧⲱⲛ ⲙⲁⲣⲧⲩⲣⲟⲛ ⲟ ⲭⲟⲣⲟⲥ ⲕⲁⲓ ⲧⲏⲛ ⲡⲁⲣⲑⲉⲛⲟⲩ ⲟ ⲡⲗⲏⲑⲱⲥ &c.

ⲩⲙⲛⲟⲥ ⲉⲝⲛⲡⲁⲥⲡⲁⲥⲙⲟⲥ ⲛ̄ⲃⲱⲗ

ⲛⲉⲛⲧⲁⲛⲛⲟⲩⲧⲉ ⲕⲁⲁⲩ ϩⲛⲧⲉⲕⲕⲗⲏⲥⲓⲁ ⲛϣⲟⲣⲡ ⲛⲉⲧⲛϩⲏⲧⲟⲩⲛⲉ ⲛⲁⲡⲟⲥⲧⲟⲗⲟⲥ &c *ⲇⲟⲝⲁ ⲡⲁⲧⲣⲓ*

ⲁϥⲥⲱⲧⲛ ⲙⲡⲙⲛⲧⲥⲛⲟⲟⲩⲥ ⲛⲛⲉⲧⲟⲩⲏϩ ⲛⲥⲱϥ ⲁϥϯⲣⲁⲛ ⲉⲣⲟⲟⲩ ϫⲉⲁⲡⲟⲥⲧⲟⲗⲟⲥ[1] &c *ⲕⲁⲓ ⲛⲩⲛ
ⲕⲁⲓ ⲁⲓⲁⲉⲓⲛ*

ⲁϥⲥⲱⲧⲛ ⲙⲡⲁⲩⲗⲟⲥ ⲛ̄ϩⲁⲉ ⲙⲙⲟⲟⲩ ⲧⲏⲣⲟⲩ &c

Ⲣ ⲡⲍ̄. ⲩⲙⲛⲟⲥ ⲉⲝⲛⲧⲥⲟⲟⲩⲥ ⲛⲟⲓⲕⲕⲟⲛ

ⲇⲟⲝⲁ ⲥⲟⲓ ⲁⲡⲟⲥⲧⲟⲗⲱⲛ ⲕⲁⲩⲭⲏⲙⲁ ⲡⲁⲥⲁ ⲡⲛⲟⲛ ⲉⲛⲉⲥⲁⲧⲟ ⲧⲟⲛ ⲕⲛ̄[2]

ⲩⲙⲛⲟⲥ ⲉⲝⲛϯⲣⲏⲛⲏ

ⲁⲡⲟⲥⲧⲟⲗⲟⲓ ⲕⲁⲓ ⲙⲁⲣⲧⲩⲣⲟⲓ ⲕⲁⲓ ⲡⲁⲛⲧⲉⲥ ⲡⲣⲟⲫⲏⲧⲟⲓⲥ &c

ⲡⲉϥⲃⲱⲗ

ⲛⲁⲡⲟⲥⲧⲟⲗⲟⲥ ⲙⲛⲙⲙⲁⲣⲧⲩⲣⲟⲥ ⲁⲩⲱ ⲛⲉⲡⲣⲟⲫⲏⲧⲏⲥ &c

ⲡⲟⲓⲕⲕⲟⲛ

ⲧⲣⲓⲁⲇⲁ ⲟⲙⲟⲟⲩⲥⲓⲟⲛ ⲛⲙⲉⲓⲥ ⲇⲟⲝⲟⲗⲟⲅⲟⲩⲙⲉⲛ ⲡⲁⲧⲏⲣⲁ ⲕⲁⲓ ⲩⲓⲱ ⲥⲩⲛ ⲁⲅⲓⲱⲛ ⲡⲛⲓ̄ &c

ⲡⲉϥⲃⲱⲗ

ⲧⲉⲧⲣⲓⲁⲥ ⲙⲁⲩⲁⲁⲥ ⲧⲁⲓ ⲉⲧⲛϯⲉⲟⲟⲩ ⲛⲁⲥ ⲡⲉⲓⲱⲧ ⲙⲛⲡϣⲏⲣⲉ ⲙⲛⲡⲉⲡⲛ̄ⲁ̄ ⲉⲧⲟⲩⲁⲁⲃ &c

ⲡⲟⲓⲕⲕⲟⲛ

ⲙⲁⲣⲧⲩⲣⲱⲛ ⲧⲱ ⲕⲁⲩⲭⲏⲙⲁ ⲭ̄ⲥ̄ ⲟ ⲑ̄ⲥ̄ ⲟ ⲉⲣⲉⲓⲥ ⲧⲱⲛ ⲡⲟⲗⲩⲧⲉⲩⲙⲁ ⲧⲟⲛ ⲁⲡⲟⲥⲧⲟⲗⲱⲛ &c.

ⲥⲟⲩϣⲙⲟⲩⲛ ⲡϣⲁ ⲙⲡⲉϥⲧⲟⲟⲩ ⲛ̄ϩⲱⲛ[3] *ⲧⲣⲓⲥⲁⲅⲓⲟⲥ*

ⲁⲅⲓⲟⲥ ⲟ ⲑ̄ⲥ̄ ⲁⲅⲓⲟⲥ ⲉⲓⲥⲭⲩⲣⲟⲥ ⲁⲅⲓⲟⲥ ⲁⲑⲁⲛⲁⲧⲟⲥ ⲟ ⲥⲁⲣⲛⲱⲑⲉⲓⲥ ⲇⲓ ⲛⲙⲁⲥ ⲉⲗⲉⲏⲥⲟⲛ ⲛⲙⲁⲥ
ⲟⲧⲓ ⲫⲓⲗⲁⲛⲑⲣⲱⲡⲱⲥ ⲟⲓ ⲟ ⲉⲡⲓ ⲧⲱⲛ ⲭⲉⲣⲟⲩⲃⲓⲙ ⲕⲁⲑⲏⲙⲉⲛⲟⲥ ⲧⲁ ⲡⲟⲧⲁⲙⲓⲁ ⲩⲇⲁⲧⲁ ⲉⲡⲓ
ⲧⲱⲛ ⲙⲉⲧⲣⲟⲛ ⲁⲩⲧⲟⲩ ⲧⲟⲩⲥ ⲕⲁⲣⲡⲟⲥ ⲧⲏⲥ ⲅⲏⲥ ⲁⲩⲝⲏⲥⲟⲛ ⲕⲁⲓ ⲡⲗⲏⲑⲏⲛⲟⲛ ⲧⲁ ⲥⲉⲛⲙⲓⲁ
ⲧⲏⲥ ⲅⲏⲥ ⲟⲓ ⲁⲅⲅⲉⲗⲟⲓ ⲉⲡⲉⲛⲟⲓⲥⲟⲩⲥⲉⲛ ⲥⲉ ⲕⲁⲓ ⲟ ⲭⲟⲣⲟⲥ ⲧⲱⲛ ⲇⲓⲕⲁⲓⲱⲛ ⲇⲟⲝⲁⲥⲟⲩⲥⲓⲛ ⲥⲉ
ⲧⲁ ⲡⲟⲓⲟⲩⲛⲧⲁ ⲉⲓⲣⲏⲛⲏ

ⲩⲙⲛⲟⲥ ⲉⲝⲙⲡⲉⲩⲁⲅⲅⲉⲗⲓⲟⲛ[4]

ⲡⲟⲓⲙⲉⲛⲟⲛ ⲧⲟⲛ ⲓⲥⲣⲁⲏⲗ ⲡⲣⲟⲥⲭⲉⲥⲟ ⲟⲧⲓⲛⲟ (sic)

Ⲣ. ⲡⲁ̄. ⲩⲙⲛⲟⲥ ⲉⲝⲙⲡⲁⲥⲡⲁⲥⲙⲟⲥ

ⲥⲟⲓ ⲡⲣⲉⲡⲉⲓ ⲇⲟⲝⲁ ⲁⲅⲅⲉⲗⲟⲓ ⲇⲟⲝⲁⲥⲟⲩⲥⲓⲛ ⲛ ⲟⲩⲣⲁⲛⲟⲓ ⲧⲱⲛ ⲟⲩⲣⲁⲛⲱⲛ[5] &c

ⲩⲙⲛⲟⲥ ⲉⲝⲛⲧⲥⲟⲟⲩⲥ ⲛⲧⲉⲩϣⲏ

ⲧⲁ ⲡⲟⲗⲩⲟⲙⲁⲧⲁ ⲭⲉⲣⲟⲩⲃⲉⲓⲛ ⲕⲁⲓ ⲉⲝⲁⲡⲧⲉⲣⲩⲅⲁ ⲥⲉⲣⲁⲫⲓⲛ, with *tersanctus*.

---

[1] Luke vi 13   [2] Ps cl 6.
[3] This corresponds to the Bohairc calendar
[4] After this the following rubric has been erased.

[1] ⲟⲩⲣⲁⲛⲟⲓ ⲧⲱⲛ ⲟⲩⲣⲁⲛⲟⲛ ϣⲁϥⲉⲓ ⲉⲝⲙⲡⲁⲣⲁⲅⲅⲉⲗⲟⲥ
ⲙⲓⲭⲁⲏⲗ ⲟⲛ ⲉϣⲱⲡⲉ ⲧⲕⲩⲣⲓⲁⲕⲏⲧⲉ.
[5] Ps. cxlviii 4

ὑμνος εϩⲛⲧⲥⲟⲟⲩϩⲥ ⲙ̄ⲡⲛⲁⲩ ⲛ̄ⲥⲩⲛⲁⲅⲉ

    μετα των χαιρουβιμ ὑμνον αναπεμπομεν &c

ὑμνος εϩⲛ︦ϯⲣⲏⲛⲏ

    δοξασουσιν σε τον θ̄ν̄ ⲛ̄ⲙⲱⲛ των εγερϲητε τον ψυχον ⲛ̄ⲙⲱⲛ &c

ⲡⲉϥⲃⲱⲗ

    τηϯⲉⲟⲩ ⲛⲁⲕ ⲡⲉⲭⲥ︦ ⲡⲉⲛⲛⲟⲩⲧⲉ ⲡⲉⲓⲣⲉϥⲣ̄ⲡⲉⲧⲛⲁⲛⲟⲩϥ ⲙ̄ⲛ̄ⲙ̄ⲯⲩⲭⲏ &c.

ⲡⲟⲓⲏⲕⲟⲛ

    τα χερουβιν μετα των σεραφιμ ὑμνον απεμπομεν, with *tersanctus*

ⲧⲁⲅⲟ ⲛⲁⲓ ⲉϩⲙ̄ⲡⲛⲁⲩ ⲉⲛϣⲁⲛϩⲁϯⲁⲍⲉ

    τριας αγιας εν ομοουϲιον την εⲕⲕⲗⲏⲥⲓⲁⲛ ⲥⲟⲩ [1] διαφυλαζον και μη εις παντες
    εν πιϲτον φυλαζον ο εν αγιας αναπαυϲομενος

ⲡⲟⲓⲏⲕⲟⲛ   χορος επουρανιε ὑⲙⲛⲟⲙⲉⲛ σε, with *tersanctus*

    ⲣ̄ ⲕ̄ⲉ.

ⲡⲟⲓⲏⲕⲟⲛ (*sic*) δοξαν του θ̄ῡ ⲡⲗⲏϲον τη ϲⲕⲏⲛⲏⲥ οτι παρεⲅθη αυτος ⲙⲱⲩϲⲏⲥ [2] &c.
ⲡⲉϥⲃⲱⲗ   απεοου ⲙ̄ⲡⲛⲟⲩⲧⲉ ⲙⲟⲩϩ ⲛ̄ⲧⲉⲥⲕⲏⲛⲏ ϩⲙ̄ⲡⲣⲉ ⲙⲱⲩϲⲏⲥ ⲃⲱⲕ ⲉϩⲟⲩⲛ ⲉⲣⲟⲥ &c
ⲧⲕⲩⲣⲓⲁⲕⲏ ⲥⲙ̄ⲡⲁⲣⲭⲁⲅⲅⲉⲗⲟⲥ ⲙⲓⲭⲁⲏⲗ ⲡⲛⲁⲩ ⲛ̄ⲥⲩⲛⲁⲅⲉ τριϲαγιος

    δοξα εν ὑψιϲτιϲ θ̄ῡ και επι ϲⲏⲥ ειρⲏⲛⲏ αγιοϲ ο θ̄ϲ̄ [3] &c

ⲡⲉϥⲃⲱⲗ   ⲡⲉⲟⲟⲩ ⲙ̄ⲡⲛⲟⲩⲧⲉ ⲥ︦ϩ̄ⲛⲉⲧϫⲟⲥⲉ ⲧⲉϥⲉⲓⲣⲏⲛⲏ ϩⲓϫⲙ̄ⲡⲕⲁϩ [4] ϥ̄ⲟⲩⲁⲁⲃ ⲛ̄ϭⲓ ⲡⲛⲟⲩⲧⲉ &c
ⲩⲙⲛⲟⲥ ⲥⲙ̄ⲡⲥⲩⲁⲅⲅⲉⲗⲓⲟⲛ ⲡⲟⲓⲏⲕⲟⲛ

    οι ουρανοι των ουρανων ενεϲον ϲου κ̄ⲉ̄ [5] &c, ending αλληλογια

    ⲣ̄. ⲕ̄ⲉ̄. ⲩⲙⲛⲟⲥ ⲉϫⲙ̄ⲡⲁⲥⲡⲁⲥⲙⲟⲥ

    χορος αⲅⲅⲉⲗⲓⲕⲟⲛ, ending αλληλογια

ⲩⲙⲛⲟⲥ ⲉϩⲛ︦ϯⲣⲏⲛⲏ

    χορος αⲅⲅⲉⲗⲓⲕⲟⲛ και ⲡⲡⲁⲧⲁ δⲓⲕⲁⲓⲱⲛ, ending ὑⲙⲛⲉⲓⲧⲉ και ὑⲡⲉⲣ-ὑⲯⲟⲩⲧⲉ &c

ⲡⲟⲓⲏⲕⲟⲛ δοξα πατρι [6]

    ϲⲩⲛⲉⲓ αⲅⲅⲉⲗⲱⲛ ο χορος των ὑⲡⲉⲣⲁⲛⲱⲛ των ουρⲁⲛⲟⲛ &c, ending αλληλογια
ⲡⲟⲓⲏⲕⲟⲛ   οι αⲅⲅⲉⲗⲟⲓ ὑⲙⲛⲟⲩⲥⲓⲛ ϲε ⲉ̄ (*sic*) βαϲιλευϲ των απαντον &c

ⲥⲟⲩⲙⲛⲧⲥⲛⲟⲟⲩⲥ ⲛⲁⲑⲱⲣ ⲡ̄ϣⲁ ⲙ̄ⲡⲁⲣⲭⲁⲅⲅⲉⲗⲟⲥ ⲉⲧⲟⲩⲁⲁⲃ ⲙⲓⲭⲁⲏⲗ ⲩⲙⲛⲟⲥ ⲉϩⲛⲧⲥⲟⲟⲩϩⲥ
    ⲛ̄ⲧⲉⲩϣⲏ

    ⲙⲓⲭⲁⲏⲗ αρχⲁⲅⲅⲉⲗⲟⲩ ⲗⲓⲧⲟⲩⲣⲅⲟⲥ του θ̄ῡ πρεⲥⲃⲉⲩⲥⲟⲛ επερ ⲛ̄ⲙⲱⲛ &c.

ⲡⲉϥⲃⲱⲗ

    ⲙⲓⲭⲁⲏⲗ ⲡⲁⲣⲭⲁⲅⲅⲉⲗⲟⲥ ⲁⲩⲱ ⲡ̄ⲗⲓⲧⲟⲩⲣⲅⲟⲥ ⲙ̄ⲡⲛⲟⲩⲧⲉ ⲉϥⲉⲡⲣⲉⲥⲃⲉⲩⲉ ϩⲁⲣⲟⲛ &c

---

[1] From ⲇⲓⲁ to ⲡⲁⲛⲧⲉⲥ has been altered   [4] Then ϩⲛ̄ⲡⲣⲱⲙⲉ ⲙ̄ⲡⲉϥⲟⲩⲱ̄ⲉ erased
[2] *Cf* Exod xl 28, 29   [5] *Cf* Ps cxlviii 4
[3] Luke ii 14   [6] *Cf* on ⲣ̄ ⲕ̄

ппат псγпаϩε τρισαϭιος

стратіє των аϭϭελων τω πληθωс των оіктеірμων &c , with τρισάγιον

γμποс εχμπεγαϭϭελιон

арχαϭϭελογ μιχαнλ .... των аϭϭελων γμηογсιη сε &c

54.—Parchment; 9 × 7½ cm   1 col   Script of ZOEGA's 9th class
Directory of Lessons[1] for the 4th Mesore, commemoration of Besa, Shenoute's successor

>ϫ< μεсоρ̄ · ⲇ̄ · ⲃⲏсα παρμαнⲁ̄ρⲓ̄ · пр̄[2] : о̄ϩ · αϥсωтп птеφγλ/ · ϯⲙⲟ̈ · ⲃ̄ · нток ⲇⲉ
анотⲁ̄ϩк псатаⲓⲃω · н̄ коⲣ̄ ⲇ̄ · ϩωс соφос нαрχⲓⲡ̄ · петⲣ̄ · ⲇ̄ · εϣϫεатетнⲝⲓϯ [θес ·] ⲇ̄
текклⲏсⲓⲁ сε. пε · етⲣнϯотⲇⲁⲓ · ⲯ/ · о̄ς · арⲓ пⲙετε птенсγнаϭⲱ · н̄ ϩ̄н̄ ϫепкотте
папотⲣⲙ псⲓⲱ̄ · λⲟ̄ϭ · ⲓ̄н̄ · отонсе п̄н̄ етⲏнт ϣароⲓ стсωтⲙ εнаϣϫϫε ϣⲁ/ нтⲏⲗαατ
ϩⲙⲡⲓ̄ⲗ̄ · н̄ к̄ε · ϩⲙⲡⲧρⲉⲓ̄с ⲕⲟⲧϥ :—

Verso blank

55.—Parchment; 22 × 2½ cm   Script small, of ZOEGA's 9th class   Text across width
Directory of Lessons[3] for the 10th Tybi.

тⲩⲃⲓ · ⲓ̄ · пр̄[4] · ⲙⲁ̄ · корⲓ̄н · ⲃ̄ · εγнтⲁн ⲇⲉ ⲙⲙⲁⲧ нпⲓсрⲏт · петⲣ̄ · ⲃ̄ · пⲉⲓϣϫϫε нотωт
па[ⲙ]ерⲁ̄[T] · [пр̄]ⲁ · ⲃ̄ · ϩнтпаϣε ⲇⲉ нтеγϣн паγλос · ⲯⲁ/ · ⲕ̄ⲃ̄ · ⲙⲁ̄ нтереϥⲃωк ⲇⲉ εϩотн
ⲉⲡⲣⲡⲉ · ϣⲁ/ ⲉⲓⲉⲓⲣⲉ ннаⲓ ϩнаϣ неϩотсⲓⲁ :

Verso н̄ паⲓ · ⲙⲁθⲁ̈ⲓ · ϩⲣⲁⲓ ϩⲙⲡⲉϩοοⲧ ⲉⲧⲙⲙⲁⲧ (blank)

56.—Parchment, 13 × 3 cm   Script small, of ZOEGA's 9th class   Text across width
Directory of Lessons[5]

п[.....] нтаϥтⲉϩⲙ · н̄ колⲁ̄ нтωтн ⲙпⲓⲟⲧⲟⲉⲓϣ ετετⲓ · ⲯ/ · ϥ̄ · ⲙⲁⲣⲓⲡⲏⲧⲉ оⲧноϭ
ⲙⲁⲣ̄ ·] аγω пеϫⲁϥ наγ ϩⲙⲡⲉϩοοⲧ ⲉⲧⲙⲙⲁⲧ : пр̄ · п̄н̄ · ⲙпⲙⲏⲧⲉ наотωнϩ εⲃολ · корⲓ̄
ⲇ̄ ϯотωϣ ⲇⲉ ετρετнⲉⲓⲙⲉ паснⲏⲧ [ϫε]ⲙⲉⲛⲉⲓοⲧⲉ

Verso

нте]реотн[оϭ] нотоеⲓ[ϣ] отⲉⲓⲛⲉ а[γ]рϩⲃⲁ ϩⲙⲡⲉсоⲏⲣ ετⲃεϫεатⲕⲉⲛⲓстϯ · ⲯ/ рⲣ̄ⲉ̅[sic]
θⲁλασса ϯноϭ ετοτοϣс · н̄ ⲙ̄ⲅ̄ · ϩнотⲏⲧ ноосⲙ[6] ϥнαотωϣ ⲙⲁ λ̄ · нтеγнот
аϥапасⲕⲁ̄ⲍⲉ [

---

[1] The lessons are Ps lxxvii 68, 2 Tim iii 10 *or* 1 Cor iii 10, 1 Pet ii 3, 1 Thess ii 14, Ps lxxiii 2 *or* lxvii 36, Luke vi 47—vii. 9 *or* vii. 40. B's death, 6th Mesore in Ethiop. calendar.

[2] προκείμενον , *cf* Brit. Mus Catal, pp. 32, 517

[3] The lessons are Ps. xli, 2 Cor vii 1, 2 Pet iii 8 (*or* 7),

Acts xvi 25, Ps xxii, Matt xxi 12–24 *or* iii 1

[4] προκείμενον.

[5] The lessons are ? *or* Col. i 21, Ps xcv 11, ? (Gosp), Ps lxxxviii 6, 1 Cor x 1, Acts xxvii. 9, Ps ciii 26 *or* xlvii 8, Matt xiv 22

[6] Note ⲥⲟⲥⲙ for the usual ⲥⲟⲛⲥ.

SA'IDIC MANUSCRIPTS

22

57—Paper, 2 pieces pasted together; almost complete, 18 × 5 cm. Script of Zoega's 9th class

Psalm Verses and Directory of Lessons[1] for the 2nd Payni

p̄ⲙ̄ⲑ ⲕⲁⲩⲭⲏⲥⲟⲛⲧⲁⲓ ⲟⲥⲓⲁⲓ ⲉⲛ ⲁⲟⲍⲏ (&c, Psalm cxlix. 5)

Verso

ⲡⲁⲅ ⲃ ⲕ̄ⲁ̄ ⲙ̄ⲁ̄ ⲟⲩⲁⲟ̄ ⲉⲩⲟⲏⲡ ⲟⲣ̅[2] ⲙ̄ⲁ̄ ⲁⲥⲱ̄ ⲛ̄ⲧⲉⲣⲉⲧ̄ⲥ̄ ⲟⲩⲱ ⲉⲩⲟⲩⲉⲣⲥⲁⲟⲛⲉ ⲡⲣ̄[3] ⲗ̄ⲅ̄ :
ⲉⲃ̄ⲣ̄ ⲟⲛⲟⲩⲡⲓⲥ†ⲉ ⲓⲁⲕⲱⲃ &c

Across this, an earlier Arabic text

58.—Parchment; irregular shape; 11 × 5½ cm. Script small, of Zoega's 9th class. Text across width

Directory of Psalms, in Coptic and Greek[4], for the — Hathor

ⲁⲑⲱⲣ · ⲥⲉⲡ̄[6] · ⲗ̄ⲅ̄[6] ⲟⲉ · ⲟⲩⲟⲛ ⲛⲓⲙ ⲉⲧⲁⲡⲉⲩⲕⲱⲧⲉ ⲛⲁⲭⲓ ⲁ'ⲱⲣⲟⲛ] ⲛⲁⲩ : ⲡⲁⲛⲧⲉⲥ [ⲏ] ⲕ[ⲅ]-
ⲕⲗⲱ ⲁⲩⲧⲟⲩ · ⲟⲓⲥⲟⲩⲥⲓⲛ ⲁⲱⲣⲁ :—

ⲟⲣ̄[7] ⲡⲇ ⲡⲭⲟⲥ ⲁⲕⲟⲩⲉⲱ ⲡ̄ⲕⲕⲁⲟ : ⲛ̄ⲩⲁⲟⲕⲏⲉⲁⲥ ⲡ̄ⲉ̄ ⲧⲏⲛ ⲅⲏⲛ ⲥⲟⲩ · ⲁⲡⲉⲥⲧⲣⲉⲯⲁⲥ · ⲧⲏⲛ
ⲁⲓⲭⲙⲁⲗⲱⲥⲓⲁⲛ ⲓⲁⲕⲱⲃ :

Verso

ⲧ̄ⲅ̄ · ⲯⲁⲗ/ ⲕⲏ ⲥⲉⲡ̄ · ⲁⲛⲓ[ⲛⲉ] ⲙ̄ⲡⲟ̄ⲧ̄ : ⲗ̄ⲅ̄ · ⲉⲛⲉⲥⲕⲁⲧⲱ ⲧⲱ ⲕ̄ⲱ̄ · ⲅⲓⲟⲓ ⲑ[ⲉⲟⲩ] (blank)

59.—Parchment · 11 × 2½ cm. Script (in 2 inks) small, of Zoega's 9th class. Text across width.

Above, remains of an earlier(?) text. Then

ⲯⲁⲗ̄ⲙ̄ ⲩⲃ ⲁⲛⲁⲥ̄ ⲥ ⲁⲛⲁⲗⲩ̄ⲙ̄[8] ⲟⲩϣⲡⲏⲣⲉⲡⲉ ⲡⲟ̄ⲧ̄ ⲟⲛⲉⲭⲟⲥⲉ ·

ⲩⲅ ⲙⲁⲣⲉⲙⲡⲛⲩ[ⲉ

Verso, in 1 column

ⲑ̄ⲱ̄ ⲓⲑ, ⲡ̄ⲁ̄ · ⲋ, [ⲁ]ⲑ/ ⲣⲕ, ⲭⲓ̄ ⲋ, ⲧ̄ⲅ̄ · ⲅ, ⲙⲉ̄ ⲅ, ⲫⲁ̄ⲙ̄ ?, ⲁⲛⲁⲥ̄ ⲏ, ⲫⲁⲣ̄ // (sic),
ⲡ̄ⲁ̄ ⲇ, ⲡ̄ⲁ̄ⲅ̄ ⲅ, ⲉⲡⲓ̄ · ⲃ (blank)

60—Paper, complete, 18 × 14½ cm. Script of Zoega's 9th class

Directory of Lessons for (1) the Enthronement of a Bishop and (2) for his return
to the city[9]

---

[1] The lessons are Ps xxiv. Matt. xiii. 44; *ib* xi 1,
Ps xxxiii, Heb xi 21

[2] ὄρθρον.   [3] προκείμενον

[4] The Psalms are lxxv. 11, lxxxiv. 2, xxviii. 1.

[5] ? γεννήσεως, cf no 37, *verso*

[6] τὸ λυχνικόν.   [7] ὄρθρον

[8] ἀνάστασις καὶ ἀνάληψις The two Psalms are xcii 4,
xcv 11.

[9] The lessons are (1) John xvii. 4, Matt xvii 1, Ps.
lxxxviii. 15, Heb. v 1, 1 Pet. ii. 9, Acts xiii 14, Ps cix (?),
Luke vii 9 (or x. 22); (2) Pss cxx, lxxxiv, Heb. ?, 1 Pet. ii
16 (?), Acts x. 25, Ps ix. 4, Luke viii 40

ⲡⲉⲑⲣⲟⲛⲓⲥⲙ̄ ⲛⲟⲩ | ⲡⲗⲁ̄ⲝ : ⲓ̄ⲱ ⲁⲛⲟⲕ | ⲁⲓϯⲉⲟⲟⲩ ⲛⲁⲕ ϩⲓ : | ⲟ̊ⲣ̄ ⲙⲁ̄ : ⲙⲛⲛⲥⲁⲥ | ⲁⲉ¹ ⲛϩⲟⲟⲩ |
ⲡⲣ̊ ⲡ̄ⲙ̄ : ⲧⲁⲓⲕ̸ⲟ | ⲥⲩⲛⲛ ⲙⲙⲛⲟⲁⲡ | ⲉϥⲣⲉⲟⲥ : ⲁⲣⲭⲓ | ⲉⲣⲉⲅⲉ̊ ⲅⲁⲣ ⲛⲓⲙ | ⲡⲉⲧⲣ̊ ⲍ̄ ⲛ̄ⲧⲱⲧⲛ̄ | ⲁⲉ
ⲡⲓⲉⲧⲛⲟⲩⲧⲉ | ⲡⲣ̸ ⲁⲩⲱ ⲛ̄ⲧⲉⲣⲟⲩ | ⲃ̄ⲱⲕ ⲉϩⲟⲩⲛ ⲉⲓ̸ⲥⲩ | ⲛⲁⲥⲱⲧⲛ̸ ⲯⲁⲗ | ⲣ̄ⲟ̄ : ⲁⲡⲟ̄ⲥ̄... | [ⲗ]ⲟⲩ
ⲁⲩⲱ ⲁϥⲕⲟⲧϥ | (here dividing line) ⲡⲉϩⲟⲟⲩ ⲛϣⲁⲣⲉⲟⲩ | ⲉⲡ̄ⲥ̄ ⲕⲟⲧϥ ⲉⲧⲡⲟⲗ | ⲡⲣ̄ ⲣ̄ⲕ̄ ⲋ ⲡ̄ⲁ̄ |
ⲉϥⲣⲉ̊ · ⲛⲉⲣⲉⲡⲟⲩⲁ | ⲡⲉⲧⲣ̊ · ⲍ̄ : ⲛϩⲙ | ϩⲁⲗ : ⲡⲣ̸ ⲁⲥ|ϣ̄ⲱ ⲁⲉ ⲛ̄ⲧⲣⲉ | ⲡⲉⲧⲣ̊ ⲃ̄ⲱⲕ ⲉϩⲟⲩ̄ | ⲯⲁⲗ ⲑ :
ⲁⲕϩⲙⲟ|ⲟⲥ ϩⲙⲡⲉⲕⲑⲣⲟ | ⲗⲟⲩ ϩⲙⲡⲧⲣⲉⲓ̄ⲥ̄ ⲕⲟⲧϥ ⲁⲡⲙⲛ|ⲛϣⲉ |

Verso ⲗⲟⲩ̄ ⲕ̄ⲉ̄ : ϩⲙⲡⲧ|ⲣⲉⲓ̄ⲥ̄ ⲕⲟⲧϥ ⲁⲡⲙⲛⲛϣⲉ | ϣⲟⲡϥ ⲉⲣⲟⲟⲩ |

Also remains of an earlier Arabic text.

61.—Parchment; (1) a complete leaf, $24\frac{1}{2} \times 16$ cm, and (2) a fragment. Palimpsest
(1) *a* Script *cf* CIASCA III, 2 cols, *b* at right angles to preceding Script of ZOEGA's
9th class, 1 col. (2) *a* Script *cf* CIASCA II or VII, 2 cols ; *b* as in (1) *b*

(1) *a* On S. Mercurius *V.* below

b Abbreviated Concordance (?) to the Psalter, for liturgical use *Cf* Brit Mus.
Catal no. 977[2] Section 1, filling *recto* and *verso*, headed ⲛ̄ϥⲁⲗ ⲙⲡⲟⲗⲓⲥ, contains
Psalms xxx 22, IX 15, xlv 5, xliv 10, xlvii 2, xliv. 11 &c, referring alternately to 'city'
and 'daughter' Most verses are separated by =, only once by ※

(2) *a* shows Mark XIII 33, 34.

b The Concordance continued by Psalms lxii 2 (with title), lxxiv 7, lxxviii. 7
and 5 or 6 more, each containing the word 'desert' Another section, headed ⲯⲁⲗⲗⲉⲓ
ⲛⲧⲱⲣⲧⲣ, contains verse 2 of Psalms cxix, cxx, cxxi and following, several of the titles
being included. A third section, headed ⲯⲁⲗⲗⲉⲓ ⲉϫⲱⲧⲃⲓ, contains Psalm lvi 7 Here
all verses appear to be separated by ※

The idiom is marked by the forms ⲫ̄ϯ and ⲡ̄ⲟ̄ⲥ̄.

---

[1] The positions of these letters show that the paper was already in holes when the Coptic was written

[2] Also Berlin, Kgl Bibl, Or 409 (RAHLFS, *Sahid Ps*, 6 Anm)

HOMILIES, EPISTLES ETC

62 [25].—Parchment; 6 complete leaves, now $32\frac{1}{2} \times 21\frac{1}{2}$ cm A palimpsest (1) the *earlier* texts, 2 cols, about 30 lines Script of Zoega's 6th–8th classes, (2) the *later*, 1 col, 50–60 lines Script small, sloping, *cf* Hyvernat ix. 2, col 2, or Brit Mus Catal, Pl 6, no 465. From same MS as Brit Mus Catal no 185 &c

I The *later* texts are from several Homilies The leaves, as now bound, are not consecutive, it is however most probable from their contents that foll 2, 5 and 6 should follow each other in that order

Foll 2, 5, 6 A passage from this text is, on p $\overline{\gamma\lambda\lambda}$ of the Curzon fragment of no 63, cited and attributed to Athanasius It does not however appear among his published works, *cf* the biblical quotations, not to be found, in this sequence, in the Benedictine edition The text is moreover identical with that of Brit. Mus Catal no 990 The following is an abstract

Vain swearing is to be avoided, that our life be profitable and worthy Those that 'walk angelically' must shun the desires of the flesh, must live on herbs and water, not on flesh and wine, eat sparingly, keep vigil rather than sleep But let such as cannot attain the heights ('hill tops') at least cast away worldly desires, that they be not led astray from God's service Fleshly desires, gluttony ($-\kappa o\iota\lambda\iota\alpha\kappa\acute{o}\varsigma$[1]), cunning, drunkenness &c beget greed of wealth and divers cares Let us be like Lot, who was content with a small city. Let fornication be far from us, lest we nourish a consuming fire Let us not be unbelieving, rather let faith be displayed Let[2] none see thee behaving unseemly and say, 'This is he that disciplines himself ($\dot{\alpha}\sigma\chi\epsilon\tilde{\iota}\nu$), to attain the gift of heaven, this is the disciple and pupil of the wise teacher, this is the man chosen from the world and reckoned to the angels of heaven' Let Christ be glorified in thee, if worthy of Him, show forth His glory. Thy limbs have been sanctified, let them not be joined unto harlots Abuse not nature marriage is for the begetting of children alone A help ($\beta o\eta\theta\acute{o}\varsigma$) has been given thee, make use thereof in holiness The flesh should not overrule the spirit Converse spiritually, sing psalms, these are the medicines of God's house, healing the soul Follow not fleshly pleasures, such as wine feasts ($\sigma\nu\mu\pi\acute{o}\sigma\iota o\nu$), though wine may be used moderately This I say not to the baptized ('enlightened') alone, but to those also that prepare. The baptized must be worthy of their light Great is Christ's grace, but see thou sin not after knowledge. Who receives a king but first prepares his house? Thus came John, to prepare for Christ Return then not to evil, even though nature draw thee thither The word of God and prayer, these will conquer the passions. For a little pleasure's sake, estrange not thyself from the eternal blessedness We are able to repent, let us pray for one another Woe to unbelievers, estranged at the last from God, none can then bewail but his own sins

---

[1] The Coptic prefix shows that the Greek word was an abstract noun   [2] This is the passage cited, *v.* p 27.

Now is the time to struggle and to help ourselves and to put on the wedding garment. Christ set up for us a cross, which is our salvation, He who with His father created man, Who took flesh in the Virgin Mary, on our behalf, very God of very God, true light of true light, without beginning nor end, unto Whose Godhead the prophets did testify, this deathless Jesus, Who died in the flesh for us, was made man like us, like us died according to human dispensation (οἰκονομία), but on the third day rose again, according to the scriptures and, in unspeakable glory, ascended into heaven and there sat upon His father's right, this same Jesus, God's Son, Who in the Holy Spirit entered Mary's womb, declared to His disciples that the very body which dies shall rise again. They believed on Him and worshipped, let us do likewise and henceforth depart from all sin—list of sins—, for such as do these shall not inherit the kingdom What shame to us to remain in sin, when once we have known God What shame to hear a layman (λαικός) swearing falsely, by God's name, above all a monk or son of the church Better they had not known God, than thus to set His commandments at naught Let us pay heed to Him, and so become united unto Him Through Him the martyrs were strong and would not deny Him, and thus, in the persecution, they, by their good choice (προαίρεσις), became His comrades, and when brought to Alexandria (Rakote) and set before the tyrant's judgement seat, arrayed like thieves in skins, they heard his exhortation 'Obey the laws of our lords the emperors and be ashamed before them For in their benevolence and care for us, they do counsel (συνβουλεύειν) us to worship the gods Obey them, then, and be saved from an evil death, giving joy to us and all that behold you For because of your disobedience are these tortures set here' Hearing this, the martyrs looked toward heaven, remembering Jesus that had died for them, and elected to die rather at men's hands, than to fall into the hands of the living God Their various deaths All ended their martyrdom bravely, trusting that Christ would give their bodies to them again May we also, through His name, attain forgiveness

Quotations John xv. 8, *cf* I Cor xv 31, Gal v 24, 2 Cor. x 3, Gen xix 16, *ib* 22, *ib* xiv 8, Ezek xvi 49, I Sam ii 30, *cf* I Cor iii 17, 2 Cor vi 14, James ii 12, Rom viii 13, Eph v 18, 19, *cf* I Tim v 23, *ib* i 13, 14, Luke iii 8, 7, 2 Pet ii 22, Matt xxii 12, Jer xlviii 10, *ib* xvii 5, Gen i 26, Ps ci 28, Luke xxiv 37–39, John v. 29, Rom x. 12, 11, *ib* xii 5, Matt x 32 *or* Luke xii 8, Matt x 28

Fol 3 *a*. Basil of Caesarea, from *Prooem in Regul fus tractat* (MIGNE, *P G*, 31, 892, 893) Title at top of page ⲟⲙⲁⲓⲟⲥ ⲡⲣⲁⲥⲓⲟⲥ ⲃⲁⲥⲓⲗⲓⲟⲥ ⲡⲉⲡⲓⲥⲕⲟⲡⲟⲥ ⲛⲧⲕⲁⲓⲥⲁⲣⲓⲁ ... ⲉϥⲧⲥⲃⲱ ⲛⲟⲩⲉⲛⲥⲏⲏⲩ ⲙⲙⲁⲓⲛⲟⲩⲧⲉ ⲉϥⲡⲣⲣⲟⲧⲣⲉⲡⲓ ⲙⲙⲟⲟⲩ ⲉⲧⲣⲉⲩⲁⲅⲱⲛⲓⲍⲉ ϩⲛⲛⲉϩⲃⲏⲩⲉ ⲛⲧⲙⲛⲧⲉⲩⲥⲉⲃⲏⲥ ⲕⲁⲓ ⲉⲧⲁⲡⲟ ⲛⲁⲛ ⲙⲡⲱⲛϩ ϣⲁⲉⲛⲉϩ ϩⲛⲟⲩⲉⲓⲣⲏⲛⲏ ⲛⲧⲉ [ⲡⲛⲟⲩⲧⲉ] Begins ϯⲡⲁⲣⲁⲕⲁⲗⲉⲓ ⲙⲙⲱⲧⲛ ⲉⲃⲟⲗ ϩⲓⲧⲛⲧⲁⲅⲁⲡⲏ ⲙⲡⲉⲛϫⲟⲉⲓⲥ ⲓ̅ⲥ̅ ⲡⲉⲭ̅ⲥ̅ ⲡⲁⲓ ⲛⲧⲁϥⲧⲁⲁϥ ⲙⲙⲓⲛ ⲙⲙⲟϥ ϩⲁⲛⲉⲛⲛⲟⲃⲉ ⲙⲁⲣⲉⲛϩⲓⲧⲟⲟⲧⲛ ⲗⲟⲓⲡⲟⲛ ⲉⲡⲣⲟⲟⲩϣ ⲛⲛⲉⲙⲯⲩⲭⲏ ⲙⲁⲣⲉⲛⲙⲕⲁϩ ⲛϩⲏⲧ ⲉⲭⲛⲙⲡⲉⲧϣⲟⲩⲉⲓⲧ ⲙⲡⲉⲛϣⲟⲣⲡ ⲛⲃⲓⲟⲥ ... The text however differs considerably from the Greek, which is longer *Quotations* Matt xxv 46, xxiv 46, xxviii 19, 2 Cor vi 3, Matt v 22, John xiii 8, Rom x. 13, 14, Matt vii 21, vi 5, I Cor xiii 3

Fol 4 *a* Chrysostom, from the 6th Discourse commenting upon the Epistle to the Hebrews Title at top of page ⲟⲙⲁⲓⲟⲥ ⲙⲙⲉϩⲥⲟⲟⲩ ⲛⲗⲟⲅⲟⲥ ⲛⲧⲉ ⲡϩⲩⲡⲟⲙⲛⲏⲙⲁ ⲉⲁϥⲧⲁⲩⲟϥ

L

ⲛϭⲓ ⲡⲙⲁⲕⲁⲣⲓⲟⲥ ⲓⲱⲁⲛⲛⲏⲥ ⲡⲉⲭⲣⲏⲥⲟⲥⲧⲟⲙⲟⲥ .. ⲉϥⲉⲣⲙⲉⲛⲉⲩⲉ ⲛⲧⲉⲡⲓⲥⲧⲟⲗⲏ ⲙⲡⲣⲟⲥ ϩⲉⲃⲣⲁⲓⲟⲥ
ϩⲛⲟⲩⲉⲓⲣⲏⲛⲏ   Begins ⲉⲡⲓⲁⲛϭⲉ ⲁⲛϣⲏⲣⲉϣⲏⲙ ⲕⲟⲓⲛⲱⲛⲉⲓ ⲉⲥⲛⲟϥ ϩⲓⲥⲁⲣⳉ ⲛⲧⲟϥ ϩⲱⲱϥ ⲟⲛ
ⲛ̄ⲧϩⲉ ⲁϥⲙⲉⲧⲉⲭⲉ ⲉⲛⲁⲓ ⲙⲁⲣⲟⲩⳉⲓϣⲓⲛⲉ ⲧⲉⲛⲟⲩ ⲛϭⲓ ⲛϩⲁⲓⲣⲉⲇⲓⲕⲟⲥ ⲛⲁⲓ ⲉⲧⲡⲱⲣϫ ⲙⲡⲗⲟⲅⲟⲥ ⲉⲃⲟⲗ
ⲛⲧⲉϥⲥⲁⲣⳉ ⲁⲩⲱ ⲙⲁⲣⲟⲩⳉⲓϣⲓⲛⲉ ⲟⲛ ⲛϭⲓ ⲛⲫⲁⲛⲧⲁⲥⲓⲁⲥⲧⲏⲥ ⲛⲁⲓ ⲉⲧϫⲱ ⲙⲙⲟⲥ ϫⲉⲙⲡⲉϥⲉⲣⲣⲱⲙⲉ
ϩⲛⲟⲩⲙⲉ ⲙⲛⲟⲩⲙⲛⲧⲁⲧⲡⲱⲛⲥ ⲉⲩⲧⲱϭⲉ ⲉⲣⲟϥ ⲛⲟⲩⲫⲁⲛⲧⲁⲥⲓⲁ ⲙⲛⲟⲩⲙⲛⲧⲉⲣϩⲁⲗ ... The text ends
with the story of Lazarus and Dives *Quotation* Heb ii 14 The only homily on Hebrews
quoting this verse is no 5, with the text of which the Coptic passage does not correspond

Fol 1 *a*   This passage resembles more than one in Chrysostom's Homilies
(*e g* hom 3 on 1 Thess iii), but is not identical with any On rejoicing at afflictions
An athlete expects not luxury but rigour If there are no longer persecutions to face,
yet have we those from within to withstand It is not for Christians to fight with others,
but rather to shed their blood for Christ and to crucify the flesh and the world (Fol *b*)
Now the battle is with all our inward passions *Quotations* John xvi 33, 2 Tim iii 12,
1 Cor x 13, Matt xxvi 41, xvi 24, Eph vi 12–14, Isa xxi 3 (?), Job xxxi 12

II The *earlier* texts From parts of at least two MSS Foll 1, 2, 3, 5 appear to
be by one scribe (*cf* Ciasca ix), foll 4, 6 by another (*cf* Ciasca xiv, Hyvernat xii 2 or
Georgi, *Fragm*, tab iii, p 304)
Fol 1, the last of a quire P ⲧ̄, all but illegible The first words refer to God's
choice of Saul as king P ⲧ̄ⲍ treats of Herod, Pilate and Christ brought before them
The following is the text :—

]ⲑⲓⲗⲙⲁ ⲛⲛⲉⲓϩⲟⲟⲩ ⲛⲧⲉⲣⲉϩⲏⲣⲱⲇⲏⲥ ⲇⲉ ⲛⲁⲩ ⲉⲓ̄ⲥ̄ ⲁϥⲣⲁϣⲉ ⲉⲙⲁⲧⲉ ⲱ ϩⲏⲣⲱⲇⲏⲥ ⲙⲁⲧⲁⲙⲟⲓ
ϫⲉⲁϣⲡⲉ ⲡⲉⲕⲣⲁϣⲉ ⲛⲧⲉⲣⲉⲕⲛⲁⲩ ⲉⲡⲉⲭ̄ⲥ̄ ⲉϣϫⲉⲕⲣⲁϣⲉ ⲉⲧⲃⲉⲟⲩ ⲙⲡⲉⲕⲟⲩⲱϣⲧ ⲛⲁϥ ⲉⲧⲃⲉⲟⲩ ⲙⲡⲉⲕ-
ⲡⲓⲥⲧⲉⲩⲉ ⲉⲡⲉⲛⲧⲁϥϯ ⲛⲁⲕ ⲛⲧⲉⲓⲁⲣⲭⲏ ⲛⲧⲕⲟⲩⲣⲣⲟ ⲁⲙⲡⲉ ϩⲏⲣⲱⲇⲏⲥ ⲛⲧⲕⲟⲩⲧⲉⲧⲣⲁⲁⲣⲭⲏⲥ ⲅⲁⲣ ⲁⲩⲱ
ⲉⲛⲉⲛⲧⲁⲕⲡⲓⲥⲧⲉⲩⲉ ⲉⲣⲟϥ ⲡⲁⲛⲧⲱⲥ ⲉⲛⲉϥⲛⲁϯ ⲛⲁⲕ ⲉⲛⲟⲩⲙⲛⲧⲉⲣⲟ ⲉⲛⲁⲁⲥ ⲉⲧⲁⲓ ⲉⲧⲉⲧⲁⲓⲧⲉ ⲧⲁⲧⲡⲉ ⲁⲗⲗⲁ
ⲛⲧⲁⲕⲥⲟⲟⲩϥ ⲁϩⲏⲣⲱⲇⲏⲥ ⲥⲟⲟⲩϥ ⲉⲛⲓ̄ⲥ̄ ⲁϥⲧⲛⲛⲟⲟⲩϥ ⲙⲡⲓⲗⲁⲧⲟⲥ ⲉⲁϥⲁⲓⲧⲉⲓ ⲉⲛⲟⲩⲉⲓⲣⲏⲛⲏ ⲉⲃⲟⲗ
ϩⲓⲧⲟⲟⲧϥ ⲕⲁⲧⲁ ⲑⲉ ⲛⲧⲁⲡⲉⲩⲁⲅⲅⲉⲗⲓⲥⲧⲏⲥ ϫⲟⲟⲥ ϫⲉⲁϩⲏⲣⲱⲇⲏⲥ ⲥⲟⲟⲩϥ ⲙⲛⲡⲉϥⲥⲧⲣⲁⲧⲉⲩⲙⲁ[1] ▨
ⲁϥϭⲟⲟⲗⲉϥ ⲉⲛ[ⲟⲩ]ϩⲃⲥⲱ ⲛⲟⲩⲱⲃ[ϣ] ⲁϥϫⲟⲟⲩϥ ⲙⲡⲓⲗⲁⲧⲟⲥ ⲁⲩ[ⲣ]ϣⲃⲏⲣ ⲉⲛⲉⲩⲉⲣⲏⲩ ϫⲓⲙⲙⲡⲉ-
ϩⲟ[ⲟⲩ] ⲉⲧⲙⲙⲁⲩ ⲛϭⲓ ϩⲏⲣⲱⲇⲏⲥ ⲙⲛ[ⲡⲓ]ⲗⲁⲧⲟⲥ ⲕⲁⲗⲱⲥ ⲁϥϫⲟⲟⲥ ⲛϭⲓ ⲡⲁⲡⲟⲥⲧⲟⲗⲟⲥ ϫⲉⲧ-
ⲙⲛⲧ]ϣⲃⲏⲣ ⲙⲡⲉⲓⲕⲟⲥⲙⲟⲥ ⲟⲩⲙⲛⲧ[ϫⲁ]ϫⲉⲧⲉ ⲉⲛⲛⲟⲩⲧⲉ[2] ⲉϣϫⲉⲙⲙⲟ[ⲛ▨ⲥⲱ]ⲧⲙ ϫⲉⲁϩⲏⲣⲱⲇⲏⲥ
ⲥⲟⲟ[ϥ] ⲙⲡⲉϥⲥⲧⲣⲁ[ⲧⲉⲩ]ⲙⲁ ⲛⲓⲙ ⲡⲉⲧⲛⲁⲥⲱⲃⲉ ▨ⲛⲓⲙ ⲱ ⲛⲁϩⲏⲧ ⲟⲩⲡⲉ ⲡⲁⲓ ⲛⲧ[ⲁⲕ]ⲁⲁϥ ⲱ
ϩⲏⲣⲱⲇⲏⲥ ⲉⲛϩⲙⲟⲟⲥ ⲉ[ⲣⲉ]ⲛⲛⲟⲩⲧⲉ ⲙⲡ[ⲧⲏ]ⲣϥ ⲁϩⲉⲣⲁⲧϥ ⲉ.

Fol 2 *a*   Apparently from a Homily upon Easter The following is the text, from
col 2, l 3   ⲡⲁⲓⲡⲉ ⲡⲉϩⲟⲟⲩ ⲙⲡⲣⲁϣⲉ ⲡⲁⲓⲡⲉ ⲡⲉϩⲟⲟⲩ ⲛⲧⲉⲩⲫⲣⲟⲥⲩⲛⲏ ⲉⲁⲛⲉⲓ ⲉϩⲣⲁⲓ ⲉϫⲙⲡⲉⲓ-
ϩⲟⲟⲩ ⲛϣⲁ ⲙⲁⲣⲉⲛⲥⲱⲟⲩϩ ⲉϩⲟⲩⲛ ⲙⲡⲉⲛⲉⲣⲏⲩ ⲛⲧⲉⲛⲟⲩⲛⲟϥ ⲙⲙⲟⲛ ϩⲛⲟⲩⲟⲩⲛⲟϥ ⲙⲡⲛⲓⲕⲟⲛ
ⲙⲁⲣⲉⲛⲁⲣⲭⲓⲥⲑⲁⲓ ⲉⲡⲉⲓϩⲟⲟⲩ ⲛⲥⲙⲟⲩ ⲉⲛϫⲱ ⲉⲃⲟⲗ ⲉⲛⲙⲙⲙⲩⲥⲧⲏⲣⲓⲟⲛ ⲉⲧⲟⲩⲁⲁⲃ ϩⲛⲟⲩⲧⲃⲃⲟ
ⲛⲥⲱⲙⲁ ⲙⲁⲣⲉⲛϩⲱⲧⲡ ⲙⲙⲡⲉⲛⲉⲣⲏⲩ ⲉϫⲛⲕⲣⲓⲣⲓⲙ ⲙⲁⲣⲉⲛⲁⲥⲡⲁⲍⲉ ⲛⲛⲉⲛⲉⲣⲏⲩ ϩⲛⲟⲩⲡⲓ ⲉⲥⲟⲩⲁⲁⲃ
ⲁⲡϫⲟⲉⲓⲥ ⲧⲱⲟⲩⲛ ⲙⲁⲣⲉⲛⲧⲱⲟⲩⲛ ⲛⲙⲙⲁϥ ⲛⲧⲉⲛⲥⲱⲧⲙ ⲉⲛⲉⲧⲭⲟⲣⲉⲩⲉ ϩⲓⲱⲛ ⲙⲙⲟϥ. Fol *b* illegible

---

[1] Luke xxiii 11.   [2] James iv 4

Fol 3 *a* illegible; fol *b* blank

The remainder of these earlier texts are described in the next section of the Catalogue

63 [24 c + 66]—Parchment, (1) the larger part of a leaf and (2) a small fragment, the former 22 × 20 cm   Paging lost   2 cols, 27+ ruled lines   Script *cf* Pl 6 in *Not et Extr des MSS*, xxxiv (AMÉLINEAU)   Initials not enlarged but accompanied by small scroll-ornaments in red   From same MS as Curzon 109 (ff 15–76) and ZOEGA no ccIV

Besa[1], Epistle of, (1) addressed to a woman, reproving her for vice or misconduct The authorship is to be presumed from the titles preserved in the other fragments of the MS   The text consists chiefly of *quotations* 'As thou hast turned from me, so will I turn from thee, saith the Lord,' Luke xiv 35, Ps xlviii 20, Rom viii 35 (here cited as from 'our holy fathers').   The following phrase is also legible (fol 1 *b*) —

ⲁⲣϩⲙⲟⲟⲥ ⲛⲁⲩ ϩⲛⲛⲟⲩϩⲓⲟⲟⲩⲉ ⲛⲑⲉ ⲛⲟⲩⲁⲃⲟⲕⲉ ⲉⲥϭⲉⲉⲧ ⲙⲁⲩⲁⲁⲥ ⲁⲩⲱ ⲁⲣⲭⲱϩⲙ ⲙⲡⲕⲁϩ
ϩⲛⲛⲟⲩⲡⲟⲣⲛⲉⲓⲁ ⲙⲛⲛⲟⲩⲕⲁⲕⲓⲁ ⲁⲣⲭⲓ ⲛⲉ ⲛⲟⲩⲙⲉⲉϣⲉ ⲛⲉϣⲱ ⲉⲩⲭⲣⲟⲛ ⲛⲉ ⲟⲩϩⲟ ⲙⲡⲟⲣⲛⲏ ⲁϥϣⲱⲡⲉ
ⲛⲉ ⲁⲣⲭⲓϣⲓⲡⲉ ⲛⲛⲁϩⲣⲛⲟⲩⲟⲛ ⲛⲓⲙ ⲙⲛⲛⲉⲙⲟⲩⲅⲉ ⲉⲣⲟⲓ ϩⲱⲥ ⲣⲙⲛⲏⲓ ⲁⲩⲱ ϩⲱⲥ [

ZOEGA's leaves show parts of at least three epistles, while the Curzon fragment (ⲧⲙ–ⲧⲙⲉ, ⲧϥⲍ–ⲅⲗⲟ, ⲅⲙⲥ–ⲅⲙⲏ, ⲅⲛⲁ–ⲫⲍ, ⲫⲓ–ⲫⲕⲃ, with many inaccuracies of pagination) has ten complete and part of an eleventh.   These are addressed (ⲧϥⲥ) to Maria, mother of John, and Talou[2], mother of Macarius, reproving discontent and insubordination, (ⲧⲟⲥ) to certain disturbers of the congregation, (ⲧⲟⲑ) to Maria, sister of Matai, chiding her for pride, (ⲧϥⲏ) to certain who have stolen the belongings of the sick, (ⲅⲑ) also to thieves, apparently nuns, (ⲅⲓⲥ) to such as break the commandments of 'our fathers', (ⲅⲕⲁ) horatory, to the brethren, quoting (ⲅⲗⲁ) 'the beloved of God, Apa Athanasius[3] Let none see thee behaving unseemly (ἀσχημονεῖν) and say, "This is the man that disciplines himself (ἀσκεῖν) to attain the gift that belongeth unto heaven"' &c, (ⲅⲓⲥ) to Matthew, who had renounced the monastic virtues and gone to Thessalonica[4], (ⲅⲝⲍ) to Antinoe[5], reproved for quarrelsomeness, (ⲅⲟⲍ) to Herai, quoting 'our holy father, Apa Antonius[6] Of a truth, my beloved, our carelessness and our humiliation and our departure (from righteousness) are not hurtful to us alone, but to the angels also they are a pain and to all the saints in Christ Jesus', (ⲅⲛⲑ) to 'those that have renounced their constancy (ὑπομονή) and departed from us.'   'Our holy fathers, from the day when they brought together these monasteries, sent not after men to make them

---

[1] Other works by him   ZOEGA ccxxxvi, Brit Mus Catal no 175, Paris 130[5], fol 128 (an Epistle 'to the people that dwell in the ἐποίκια, at the time when they set to fighting one with another   Begins ⲁ̄ ⲛⲉⲓⲉⲗⲁⲭⲓⲥⲧⲟⲥ ⲡⲉⲧⲥϩⲁⲓ ⲛⲛⲉⲡⲣⲉⲥⲃⲩⲧⲉⲣⲟⲥ ⲙⲛⲛⲇⲓⲁⲕⲟⲛⲟⲥ ⲙⲛⲛⲉⲡⲣⲟⲛⲟⲏⲧⲏⲥ ⲙⲛⲛⲕⲉⲫⲁⲗⲁⲓⲱⲧⲏⲥ), Clarendon Press no 22, ⲧⲙⲉ, ⲧⲛⲍ (so LEIPOLDT, *Schenute* 41)

[2] *Cf* Cairo 8474 ⲧⲉⲗⲟⲩ (Ταλοῦς SPIEGELBERG, *Eigennamen*, no 333)

[3] From the text no 62, *q v*

[4] 'which is foolishness'   *Cf* 2 Tim iv 10

[5] *V* ZOEGA 510

[6] Letter to the Arsinoites, *P G* 40, 986 D   Antony is cited by Shenoute also   Cambridge Univ Libr, Add 1876, 2 (as quoting Prov xxiv 8, not found in his works, *P G* 40)   S also cites A's βίος (referring to Christ's visit to the spirits in hell), ZOEGA 419   But the passage has no relation to any in Athanasius' *Vita*

monks by force, nor compelled they any man on account of his possessions   Neither
have we done this, for man shall not be forced to virtue[1]   ,' (ϥ̄ϥ̄ⲃ̄) to Herai, who had
renounced her constancy.

64 —Parchment, 2 double consecutive leaves, 17 × 13 cm   1 col   Script in 2 sizes,
cf CIASCA XXI.
   Cyril of Alexandria, from the Explanation (ἐπίλυσις) of the Twelve Chapters[2] = MIGNE,
P G. 76, 309, ANATHEMA XI
   Fol 1 a   Above text   ⲧⲟⲩ ⲁⲅⲓⲟⲩ ⲕⲩⲣⲓⲗⲗⲟⲩ.

ⲡⲉⲧⲉⲛⲉϥϩⲟⲙⲟⲗⲟⲅⲉⲓ ⲁⲛ ⲛ̄ⲧⲥⲁⲣⲝ ⲙ̄ⲡ̄ϫⲟⲉⲓⲥ ⲓ̄ⲥ̄ ⲡⲉⲭ̄ⲥ̄ ϫⲉⲧⲥⲁⲣⲝ ⲙ̄ⲡⲗⲟⲅⲟⲥⲧⲉ ⲁⲩⲱ ϫⲉⲟⲩⲣⲉϥ-
ⲧⲁⲛϩⲟⲧⲉ ⲙⲁⲣⲉϥϣⲱⲡⲉ ⲛⲁⲛⲁⲑⲉⲙⲁ

   ⲁⲩⲱ ⲡⲉⲧⲛⲁϫⲟⲟⲥ ϫⲉⲅⲁⲛⲉⲟⲩⲁⲧⲉ ⲉϥϩⲟⲧⲣ ⲛⲙⲙⲁϥ ⲕⲁⲧⲁ ⲟⲩⲁϫⲓⲁ ⲏ ϫⲉϥⲟⲩⲏϩ ⲛϩⲏⲧⲥ ⲙⲙⲁⲧⲉ
ϩⲱⲥ ⲉⲥⲟⲩⲁⲁⲃ ⲛⲉϥⲧⲁⲙϫⲟⲟⲥ ⲙⲁⲗⲗⲟⲛ ϫⲉⲟⲩⲱⲛϩⲧⲉ ⲁⲩⲱ ⲟⲩⲣⲉϥⲧⲁⲛϩⲟⲅⲉ ⲕⲁⲧⲁ ⲑⲉ ⲛ̄ⲧⲁⲓϣⲣⲡϫⲟⲟⲥ
ϫⲉⲧⲥⲁⲣⲝ ⲙ̄ⲡⲗⲟⲅⲟⲥⲧⲉ ⲧⲁⲓ ⲉⲧ(fol b)-ⲧⲁⲛϩⲟ ⲉⲙⲡⲧⲏⲣϥ ⲙⲁ[ⲣ]ⲉϥϣⲱⲡⲉ ⲛⲁⲛⲁⲑⲉⲙⲁ :—

ⲉⲣⲙⲏⲛⲓⲁ

   ⲉⲛⲧⲁⲗⲟ ⲉϩⲣⲁⲓ ⲁⲩⲱ ⲛϫⲱⲕ ⲉⲃⲟⲗ ⲛⲟⲩⲟⲩⲥⲓⲁ ⲉⲥⲧⲁⲛϩⲟ ⲁⲩⲱ ⲉⲥⲟⲩⲁⲁⲃ ⲉⲥⲟ ⲛⲁⲧⲧⲱⲗⲙ
ϩⲛⲧⲉⲕⲕⲗⲏⲥⲓⲁ ⲉⲛⲡⲓⲥⲧⲉⲩⲉ ⲉⲣⲟϥ ϫⲉⲡⲟⲩⲥⲱⲙⲁ ⲛ̄ⲣⲱⲙⲉ ⲁⲛ ⲛⲑⲉ ⲛⲟⲩⲟⲛ ⲛⲓⲙ ⲡⲉⲧⲛϫⲓ ⲙⲙⲟϥ
ϩⲟⲙⲟⲓⲱⲥ ⲇⲉ ⲟⲛ ⲡⲉⲥⲛⲟϥ ⲉⲧⲧⲁⲓⲏⲩ ⲁⲗⲗⲁ ϩⲱⲥ ⲉⲛⲥⲱⲙⲁ ⲙ̄ⲡⲉⲥⲛⲟϥ ϩⲛⲟⲩⲙⲉ ⲙ̄ⲡⲗⲟⲅⲟⲥ
ⲛ̄ⲧⲁϥⲣⲥⲁⲣⲝ ⲡⲉⲧⲛϫⲓ ⲙⲙⲟϥ ⲡⲁⲓ ⲉⲧ⳨ⲱⲛϩ ⲙ̄ⲡⲧⲏⲣϥ ⲟⲩ̇ⲓⲁ(fol 2 a)-ⲣⲝ ⲅⲁⲣ ⲉⲛⲑⲉ ⲛ̄ⲧⲁⲩⲟⲩⲟⲛ
ⲛ̄[ⲓⲙ] ⲙ̄ⲛϭⲟⲙ ⲙⲙⲟⲥ ⲉⲧⲁⲛϩⲟ ⲏ ⲉ⳨ ⲱⲛϩ ⲛ̄ⲧⲟϥ ⲅⲁⲣ ⲡⲉⲥⲱⲧⲏⲣ ⲁϥⲣⲙⲛⲧⲣⲉ ⲙ̄ⲡⲁⲓ ⲉϥϫⲱ ⲙⲙⲟⲥ
ϫⲉⲛⲧⲥⲁⲣⲝ ⳨ ϩⲏⲩ ⲁⲛ ⲛ̄ⲗⲁⲁⲩ ⲡⲉⲡⲛⲁ̄ ⲇⲉ ⲡⲉⲧⲧⲁⲛϩⲟ ⲉⲡⲉⲓⲇⲁⲛ ⲇⲉ ⲧⲥⲁⲣⲝ ⲙ̄ⲡⲗⲟⲅⲟⲥ ⲧⲉⲧⲛϫⲓ
ⲙⲙⲟⲥ ⲧⲏⲛⲟⲓ ⲙⲙⲟⲥ ϫⲉⲟⲩⲣⲉϥⲧⲁⲛϩⲟ ⲇⲉ ⲛⲑⲉ ⲉⲧⲉⲣⲉⲡⲥⲱⲧⲏⲣ ϫⲱ ⲙⲙⲟⲥ ϫⲉⲕⲁⲧⲁ ⲑⲉ ⲛ̄ⲧⲁϥⲧⲁⲟⲩⲟⲓ
ⲛ̄ϭⲓ ⲡⲁⲓⲱⲧ ⲉⲧⲟⲛϩ ⲁⲛⲟⲕ ϩⲱ ⳨ⲟⲛϩ ⲉⲧⲃⲉⲡⲁⲓⲱⲧ ⲁⲩⲱ ⲡⲉⲧⲛⲁⲟⲩⲟⲙⲧ ⲡⲉ ⲙⲙⲁⲩ ϩⲱⲱϥ ⲟⲛ ⲛⲁⲱⲛϩ
ⲉⲧⲃⲏⲏⲧ (fol b) ⲉⲛⲉⲓⲇⲁⲛⲧⲉ ⲛⲉⲥⲧⲱⲣⲓⲟⲥ ⲙ̄ⲛⲉⲧⲉⲓⲛⲉ ⲙⲙⲟϥ ϩⲙⲡⲉⲓϣⲟϫⲛⲉ ⲛⲟⲩⲱⲧ ⲥⲉⲃⲱⲗ ⲉⲃⲟⲗ
ⲛ̄ⲧϭⲟⲙ ⲙ̄ⲡⲉⲓⲛⲟϭ ⲙ̄ⲙⲩⲥⲧⲏⲣⲓⲟⲛ ⲉⲧⲃⲉⲡⲁⲓ ⲁⲛϩⲁⲓ ⲙ̄ⲡⲉⲓⲁⲛⲁⲑⲉⲙⲁⲧⲓⲥⲙⲟⲥ ⲉⲛⲟⲩⲱⲛϩ ⲉⲃⲟⲗ
ⲛ̄ⲧⲉⲩⲙⲛⲧⲁⲥⲉⲃⲏⲥ :—

ⲕⲉⲫⲁⲗⲁⲓⲟⲛ ⲓⲃ

   ⲡⲉⲧⲉⲛϥϩⲟⲙⲟⲗⲟⲅⲉⲓ ⲁⲛ ϫⲉⲁⲡⲗⲟⲅⲟⲥ ⲙ̄ⲡⲛⲟⲩⲧⲉ ϣⲡ(fol 3 a)-ϩⲓⲥⲉ ϩⲛⲧⲥⲁⲣⲝ ⲁⲩⲱ ϫⲉⲁⲩⲥ⳨ⲟⲩ
ⲙⲙⲟϥ ϩⲛⲧⲥⲁⲣⲝ ⲁⲩⲱ ϫⲉⲁϥϫⲓ ⳨ⲡⲉ ⲙ̄ⲡⲙⲟⲩ ϩⲛⲧⲥⲁⲣⲝ ⲉⲁϥϣⲱⲡⲉ ⲛ̄ϣⲣⲡ ⲙⲙⲓⲥⲉ ⲉⲃⲟⲗ ϩⲛⲛⲉⲧ-
ⲙⲟⲟⲩⲧ ⲕⲁⲧⲁ ⲟⲥ ϫⲉⲡϣⲟⲣⲡⲉ ⲁⲩⲱ ⲡⲣϥⲧⲁⲛϩⲟⲡⲉ ϩⲱⲥ ⲛⲟⲩⲧⲉ ⲙⲁⲣϥϣⲱⲡⲉ ⲛⲁⲛⲁⲑⲉⲙⲁ :—

(fol. b)   ⲉⲣⲙⲉⲛⲓⲁ

   ⲟⲩⲁⲧϣⲡϩⲓⲥⲉ ⲙⲙⲡⲉ ⲁⲩⲱ ⲟⲩⲁⲧⲙⲟⲩⲡⲉ ⲡⲗⲟⲅⲟⲥ ⲡⲉⲉⲃⲟⲗ ϩⲓⲧⲛⲡⲛⲟⲩⲧⲉ ⲡⲓⲱⲧ ⲧⲉⲫⲩⲥⲓⲥ
ⲅⲁⲣ ⲙⲡⲛⲟⲩⲧⲉ ⲛⲁⲧϣⲁϫⲉ ⲉⲣⲟⲥ ⲟⲩⲏⲩ ⲉⲃⲟⲗ ⲙ̄ⲡϩⲓⲥⲉ ⲁⲩⲱ ⲛ̄ⲧⲟⲥ ⲧⲉⲧⲧⲁⲛϩⲟ ⲙ̄ⲡⲧⲏⲣϥ ⲁⲩⲱ
ⲉⲣϫⲁⲉⲓⲧ ⲉⲛⲙⲟⲩ ⲁⲗⲗⲁ ⲕⲉ ⲧⲟⲓ ⲉϥϣⲟⲟⲡ ⲉⲃⲟⲗ ϩⲛⲟⲩⲟⲩⲥⲓⲁ ⲛⲟⲩⲱⲧ ⲛ̄ϭⲓ ⲡⲗⲟⲅⲟⲥ ⲡⲉⲉⲃⲟⲗ *(sic)*
ϩⲙⲡⲛⲟⲩⲧⲉ ⲡⲓⲱⲧ ⲁϥⲧⲁⲙⲓⲟ ⲛⲁϥ ⲙⲙⲓⲛ ⲙⲙⲟϥ (fol 4 a) ⲛⲟⲩⲥⲁⲣⲝ ⲉϣⲁⲩⲭⲡⲟⲥ ⲉ[. . .] ϫⲉⲕⲁⲥ
ⲉϥⲛⲁϣⲡ ϩⲓⲥⲉ ⲉⲧⲃⲏⲏⲧⲛ ϩⲙⲡⲉⲧⲛ ⲉϣ⳨ ϩⲓ[ⲥⲉ] ⲁⲩⲱ ⲛϥⲙⲟⲩ ϫⲉⲕⲁⲥ ⲉϥⲉⲛⲁϩⲙⲛ ⲉⲃⲟⲗ ϩⲙⲡⲧⲁⲕⲟ
ⲙⲙⲡⲙⲟⲩ ϩⲟⲙⲁⲓⲟⲥ ⲛ̄ϥⲧ[ⲟⲩ]ⲛⲥ ⲡⲉϥⲥⲱⲙⲁ ⲙⲙⲓⲛ ⲉⲙⲙ[ⲟϥ] ϩⲱⲥ ⲛⲟⲩⲧⲉ ⲛ̄ϥϣⲱⲡⲉ ⲛⲁⲡⲁⲣⲭⲏ
ⲛ̄ⲛⲉⲛⲧⲁⲩⲉⲛⲕⲟⲧⲕ ⲙ̄ⲡⲣⲱⲙⲉ ⲅⲁⲣ ⲉⲛⲧⲉⲡⲉ ϣⲟⲟⲡ ⲛ̄ϣⲣⲡ ⲙⲙ[ⲓ]ⲥⲉ ⲉⲃⲟⲗ ϩⲛⲛⲙⲟⲟⲩⲧ ⲉⲛⲥⲁⲡⲗⲟⲅⲟⲥ
ⲡⲉⲉⲃⲟⲗ ϩⲙⲡⲛⲟⲩⲧⲉ ⲡⲓⲱⲧ ⲡⲁⲓ ⲛ̄ⲧⲁϥϩⲩⲡⲟⲙⲟⲛⲏ ⲉⲡⲥ⳨ⲟⲥ ⲉⲁϥϫⲓ ⳨ⲡⲉ ⲙ̄ⲡⲙⲟⲩ ⲉⲧⲃⲏⲏⲧⲛ] ⲉⲛⲧⲟⲩⲡⲉ
ⲡϫⲟⲉⲓⲥ ⲙⲡⲉⲟⲟⲩ ⲉⲁϥϣⲡ ϩⲓⲥⲉ ϩⲛⲧⲥⲁⲣⲝ ⲕⲁⲧⲁ ⲛⲅⲣⲁⲫⲏ (fol b) [ⲉⲡⲓⲇⲁⲛ ⲇⲉ ⲛⲁⲛⲁⲇⲟⲕⲙⲁ [ⲉ]ⲧⲟⲟⲩⲣⲟⲩ
ⲁⲩⲱ ⲉⲧⲁϩⲙ [ⲥⲉ]ⲟⲩⲱϣ ⲉⲉⲓⲛⲉ ⲉϩⲟⲩⲛ ⲉⲧⲡⲓⲥ[ⲧⲓ]ⲥ ⲉⲧⲥⲟⲩⲧⲱⲛ ⲛⲟⲩⲣⲱⲙⲉ ⲛⲑⲉ ⲛⲣⲱⲙⲉ ⲛⲓⲙ

---

[1] V *Journ Theol Stud* v 131   [2] Paris 131³, fol 42 appears to be from the same work

[e]ϥⲭⲱ ⲙⲙⲟⲥ ⲭⲉⲛⲧⲟϥ ⲡⲛⲧⲁϥⲟⲩⲡⲟⲙⲟⲛⲏ ⲉⲡⲥ[ϯ]ⲟⲥ ϧⲁⲣⲟⲛ [ⲉ]ⲧⲃⲉⲡⲁⲓ ⲁⲛⲉϧⲁⲓ ⲙⲡⲉⲓⲁⲛⲁ-
ⲑⲩⲙⲁⲧⲓⲥⲙⲟⲓ :—ⲥⲛⲟⲩⲱⲛϧ ⲉⲃⲟⲗ ⲛⲛⲉⲩⲙⲛⲧⲁⲥⲉⲃⲏⲥ :—

Below, an ornament and ⲓⲥ ⲭⲥ ⲛⲓⲕⲁ.

65 [32].—Parchment, a complete leaf, now 29 × 22½ cm   Pp ⲥ̄ⲉ̄, ⲥ̄ⲁ̄, being the last
fol of qu ⲓ̄ⲉ̄, so presumably from the second volume of the MS   2 cols, 26 lines
Script *cf* CIASCA XXVI. No colours Characteristic is the variously ornamented monogram ⲓ̄ⲥ̄, ⲓ̄ⲥ̄ ⲡⲉⲭ̄ⲥ̄ &c, in the lower margin of many pages. To the same MS belonged
Curzon no. 110 (pp ⲝ̄ⲉ̄-ⲡ̄, ⲥ̄ⲉ̄-ⲥ̄ⲛ̄ⲃ̄), ZOEGA ccxliii[1] (ⲣ̄ⲙ̄ⲉ̄-ⲣ̄ⲙ̄ⲏ̄), Paris Vol. 131¹, foll 39, 40
(ⲥ̄ⲛ̄ⲉ̄-ⲥ̄ⲛ̄ⲋ̄)

Homily or Epistle. On p ⲥ̄ⲛ̄ⲁ̄ the work ends with the subscription ⲓⲱⲁⲛⲛⲟⲩ ⲉϧⲏ-
ⲛⲥⲕ ² The next page is occupied with a colophon, which, after the recital of a short
creed[3], states that 'this κανών of the blessed Apa John' had been lost, until 'God gave
it us in a small book, written in ancient writing' ⲉϥⲥⲏϧ ⲛⲁⲣⲭⲁⲓⲟⲛ[4]. This was then transcribed ⲁⲛⲙⲟⲟⲛⲉϥ as a memorial and entrusted to 'our fathers that are in the desert,' to
be kept in the church on the hill of the Virgin[5], so that all who wished might get comfort
therefrom and find grace with 'this great and perfect τέλειος archimandrite, Apa John'
That this is not Chrysostom is certain from the biblical quotations and the title archimandrite John of Lycopolis has this title, ZOEGA p. 37, and would be honoured in Shenoute's
monastery; but no work of his is extant[6] The rank of John, bishop of Parallus
(Borlos)[7], likewise excludes him Nor does John 'the monk, of the Thebaid,' as yet
an obscure but prolific homilist, appear to be our author[8]

    The 32 Curzon leaves of this MS are apparently the work of one author, for in
both its fragments frequent reference is made to the 'brethren,' whom the writer
addresses, and who dwell in 'the holy τόποι of Christ,' wearing the habit σχῆμα, and
further, 'our holy father' is cited in both ('the words of scripture and the saints, especially
of our holy father,' 'the commandments given us by God through our holy father,' 'our
holy father, in whom God spake') His 'epistles' are quoted as follows (p ⲟ̄ⲏ̄) 'A
heathen or heretic or a blood-shedding gentile, if he turn to God, it is meet God should
receive him. rather than the brother of this sort, that doeth these abominations in His
holy τόποι, while bearing God's holy name and the (monastic) habit', (p ⲟ̄ⲑ̄) 'All the
sinners that have died, since Cain until now and those that shall die unto the world's

---

[1] ZOEGA's reference to 'classis IV' is a mistake

[2] P ⲟ̄ⲉ̄ has ⲓⲱⲁⲛⲛⲟⲩ in the lower margin

[3] On prefatory creeds *v* VON DER GOLTZ in *Texte u
Unt*, N F, xiv (2), 97

[4] Paris 131³ 49 ⲛⲉⲥϧⲁⲓ ⲛⲁⲣⲭⲁⲓⲱⲛ = *scripti juxta
veterem formam*, P G 43, 357 (EPIPHANIUS, *De Gem*)

[5] More probably 'church of the Virgin on the hill'
Her τόπος in 'the desert of Apa Shenoute,' Paris 131⁷ 35,
her church in the White Monastery, *Synax*, 2 Ter (Tubeh).

[6] Unless he be identical with John ἔγκλειστος, archimandrite of Siût and afterwards bishop of Hermopolis,
contemporary with Theophilus (ZOEGA p 107, Brit Mus
no 184) Another John, of Scete, also a prophet, was con-

temporary with Theodosius II (NAU in *Journ As*, 1903,
i 243, *cf* Brit Mus no 333)

[7] He lived about A D 600 (*v Hist of Patriarchs*
EVETTS, 477, *Synax*, 19th Kihak) Paris 131¹ 15 is heading of a sermon by him 'on St Michael and on the blasphe-
mous books of the heretics read in the churches of the
orthodox')

[8] Mr F W Brooks has kindly sought in the Syriac
MSS of his writings (Brit Mus Add 17,169, 17,170, 14,611
and 17,167) for the long texts here described, but has
failed to find them According to CURETON (*Corp Ignat*
352) he was a contemporary of Evagrius Pont (*ob ca* 401)
The scribe of Add 17,172 held him to be John of Lycopolis

end, are taken down to Hell, even as the Gospel saith', (p c̄κ̄θ) 'Woe, woe unto them that are not in this state and that have not this (*sc* purity) in the congregations of God', (p c̄λ̄ə) 'Woe unto them that are companions one to another in slandering (καταλαλιά), that run one to another in great eagerness, that they may fulfil it together', (p c̄λ̄ι) 'It is said concerning two races (of animals) that they do cast up their ἐπιθυμίαι by their mouths one race is among the birds that are in the waters and the other is among the insects that are upon the earth. Even so are such men as slander and as hearken willingly' The phraseology in some of these strongly recalls Shenoute[1] 'Our holy father Apa Athanasius' is also quoted (p c̄λ̄ə) 'Preserve the honoured image of man, for thou shalt not be called man when thou doest the deeds of bestiality (-αλογον)'

The texts treat (CURZON) of repentance and its especial need for those dwelling in monasteries, of wisdom and its value. The unrepentant are likened to Cain, the men of the Deluge, Pharaoh, those smitten in the desert, Korah, to those that refused the prophets and apostles, to the heathen and the heretics. If the ancient world was not spared, wherefore should we be? (ZOEGA) Of the creation of Adam and his rule over the beasts, of Cain, Abel, Noah, Abraham &c (RYLANDS, CURZON) Of philanthropy and misanthropy, the charitable and the uncharitable. The latter shall stand upon the left, they belong all to the Devil. Of diligence at prayers (σύναξις) Of the blessedness of those 'of our βίος,' and of them that understand good and evil. Of slanderers and their hearers, they are like fornicators and thieves. What man sows shall grow and spread, whether evil or good. Of the Lord's Prayer, which is commented at length. Finally, a long doxology, blessing God

Characteristic of the largest fragment is the expression 'the Almighty (παντοκρ) Jesus'

The occasion of writing is indicated by pp ō̄ε̄ and c̄λ̄ of the Curzon fragment, where reference is made to 'these five days' that are quickly passing. But I do not know to what season this could apply. The fast of Holy Week would last six days[2]

The biblical *quotations* in the various parts of the MS are (CURZON) Matt viii 12, Prov xxvi 3, x 13, Jer vii 23 (*or* xi 4 *or* xxiv 7 ?), Ps lvii 5, 6, Prov xviii 9, xvii 28, xviii 9, 10, Exod iii 5, Josh v 15, Acts viii 23, Ps xxiii 6, John viii 21, Heb xi 7, Gen vi 15, 2 Pet ii 5, *ib*, 2 Cor xi 13, John v 25, (ZOEGA) Isa i 3, Gen i 28, xxvi 23, xiii 10, xxvi 12, xxxi 12, xxxvii 14, (RYLANDS) Prov xvii 5, Exod iv 17, Ps cxxxvi 11, 12, Mark xii 28–32, (CURZON) *ib* 34, Luke x 29 ff, 1 Cor iii 3, Matt xvi 27, 1 John ii 11, 2 Thess ii 3, 1 Cor vi 18, iii 16, 17, Matt xxv 41, Amos vi 12, Isa xlv 22, Jer iii 22, 2 Cor vi 17, 1 Cor vi 2, Matt vii 12, 13, *ib* v 44–48, Luke iii 10, 11, Heb xiii 1, 2, Jer ix 7–9, Matt vi 3, v 16, x 26, 1 Tim v 25, Jer xxvii (l) 22, Prov xxv 28, xix 21, xx 6, Ps xxiii 6, Gal v 10, Ps xxxii 12, lxxxviii 16–19, Eccles i 15, Col i 5, Job ix 25, Ps cxxvi 1, 1 Cor xii 3, John xv 5 ('without us'), Heb xiii 8, 2 Cor ix 7, Isa lv 2 ('Wherefore do ye labour'), Eccles i 9, 2 Tim ii 19, James i 26, Ps c 5, xlix 20-23, Matt xiii 31, James iv 11, Jer ii 26, Matt vi 9 ff, Eph iv 32, Matt xii 47–50, 2 Cor vi 3, Gen iii 19, Isa xl 6, 22, 15

---

[1] Dr LEIPOLDT observes that this is true conspicuously of the first quotation

[2] So in a sermon on Easter, Paris 131° 51 ⲛⲉⲓⲥⲟⲟⲩ ⲛϩⲟⲟⲩ.

Portions of these texts are in Leyden no 81, ZOEGA no ccxliv, Paris Vol 131².
125-133, while Brit Mus Catal no 229, Paris Vol 130² 70, 126, Vol 131⁵ 23 belong at any
rate to the same MS as the two last of these

66 [60].—Paper, a bound volume, 20 foll, 34 × 24 cm 2 cols Script a modern
Egyptian hand Copy made presumably for the Rev H TATTAM, since there are many
annotations in his hand in the margins A note, also by him, states that the transcript
was finished at Malta in 1839

The text is that of the Curzon fragment of the preceding number, which had probably
been lent to TATTAM by the 14th Baron Zouche (Robert Curzon) The original leaves
are copied in the sequence c̅e̅–cn̅b̅, x̅e̅–n̅, i e that in which they are at present, and presumably were then already, bound

67 [24 b]—Parchment, 6 complete leaves, now 31 × 22 cm Pp ⊤q̅e̅–ᵧ̅c̅ 2 cols,
30 ruled lines. Script v the photograph of the last page, HYVERNAT VIII 4 Small, red
ornaments beside each initial From the same MS as Brit Mus Catal no 198, Leyden
no 67, Paris Vol 130 120, Vol 131⁷ 66, 105, 106, 109, Curzon no 109, ff 7-14, and
possibly ZOEGA no cc, though this has no coloured ornaments and a different style of
page numbers

Shenoute, Homilies or Epistles of Pp ⊤q̅e̅–⊤q̅n̅ contain denunciations of various carnal
sins, on pp ⊤q̅θ̅–ᵧ̅c̅ the text takes the form of a prayer or thanksgiving to God; on
p ᵧ̅c̅, a new homily The large initial letter of this last contains the scribe's name,
ⲭⲣⲓⲥⲧⲟⲫⲟⲣⲟⲥ ⲕⲁⲗⲗⲓⲟⲅⲣⲁⲫⲟⲩ (v HYVERNAT, l c) The text embraces that of ZOEGA
no ccxˣ and the passage pp ᵧ̅b̅–ᵧ̅ⲁ̅ recurs in Brit Mus Catal no 194, f 4, while ib no 193
shows passages identical with the Curzon fragment of the present MS The following
are examples of the text —

Ⲣ ⊤q̅e̅ ⲟⲩⲟⲉⲓ ⲛⲉ ⲧⲁⲡⲉ ⲛ̅ϩⲟⲟⲩ ⲛⲁⲓⲁⲓϥ ⲙ̅ⲡⲉⲓⲉⲙ̅ⲡⲉⲧⲙⲁⲧⲟⲩ ⲉ̅ⲛⲧⲁⲣ̅ⲛⲟϫⲉ ⲉϩⲟⲩⲛ ⲉ̅ϩⲣⲁϥ
ⲁⲩⲱ ⲉⲁⲣⲛⲉϥⲧ̅ ⲉⲃⲟⲗ ϩⲓⲣⲱ ⲧⲁϩⲟϥ ⲛ̅ⲟⲉ ⲉⲛⲧⲁⲣ̅ⲣϩⲁϩ ⲛ̅ⲃ̅ⲗⲗⲉ ϩⲙ̅ⲡⲧⲣⲉⲛⲱⲣⲡ ⲛ̅ⲧⲱⲙ ⲛ̅ⲛⲟⲩⲃⲁⲗ
ⲙⲁⲩⲁⲁⲧⲉ ϩⲛⲟⲩⲥⲓⲝ ⲙⲙⲓⲛ ⲙⲙⲟ · ⲡⲣⲱⲙⲉ ⲉⲧⲥⲟⲩⲟⲣⲧ ⲉⲧⲉⲙ̅ⲛ̅ⲥⲉⲥⲁϩⲟⲩ ϫⲉⲛ̅ϥ ϩⲓϫⲱϥ ⲁⲛ ⲉⲃⲟⲗ
ϫⲉⲙ̅ⲛ̅ⲥⲉⲡⲁⲣⲁⲫⲩⲥⲓⲥ ϫⲉⲙ̅ⲡϥ̅ϫⲁⲁⲩ · ⲟⲩⲟⲛ ⲁⲛⲡⲉ ⲛ̅ⲧⲁⲓϫⲟⲟϥ ϫⲉⲛ̅ϣⲁϫⲉ ⲛⲁⲡⲁⲧⲓ ⲛ̅ⲧⲥⲙ̅ⲙⲉ ⲡⲣⲱⲙⲉ
ⲁⲩⲱ ⲛⲉϥⲙ̅ⲗⲟⲧ ⲙ̅ⲡⲟⲛⲏⲣⲟⲛ ⲥⲉϩⲟⲟⲩ ϯⲡⲉⲩⲁⲕⲁⲑⲁⲣⲥⲓⲁ ⲁⲩⲱ ⲡⲉⲩⲁⲕⲁⲑⲁⲣⲥⲓⲁ ϩⲟⲟⲩ ⲉⲡⲉⲧⲏⲛⲩ ⲉⲃⲟⲗ
ϩⲛ̅ⲣⲱⲟⲩ ⲁⲩⲣⲁⲧⲥⲟⲟⲩⲛ ⲉⲡⲧⲁⲓⲟ ⲙ̅ⲡⲱⲙⲁ ⲑⲓⲕⲱⲛ ⲙ̅ⲡⲛⲟⲩⲧⲉ ⲡⲓⲁ ⲛ̅ⲟⲩⲱϩ ⲛ̅ⲛⲁⲅⲅⲉⲗⲟⲥ ⲁϥⲁⲁϥ
ⲙⲙⲁ ⲛ̅ⲥⲟⲉⲓⲗⲉ ⲛ̅ⲛⲁⲓⲙⲟⲛⲓⲟⲛ ⲁⲛⲧⲓ ⲧⲣⲉϥⲙⲟⲩϩ (ⲡ ⊤q̅c̅) ⲙ̅ⲡⲡ̅ⲛ̅ⲁ̅ ⲉϥⲟⲩⲁⲁⲃ ⲁϥⲙⲟⲩϩ ⲙ̅ⲡⲡ̅ⲛ̅ⲁ̅
ⲛ̅ⲁⲕⲁⲑⲁⲣⲧⲟⲛ.

ⲟⲩⲣⲱⲙⲉ ⲙⲉⲛ ⲕⲁⲧⲁ ⲑⲓⲕⲱⲛ ⲙ̅ⲡⲛⲟⲩⲧⲉⲡⲉ ⲡⲣⲱⲙⲉ ⲁⲗⲗⲁ ⲟⲩⲕⲁⲕⲟⲇⲁⲓⲙⲱⲛ ⲁⲗⲏⲑⲱⲥⲡⲉ
ⲡⲣⲱⲙⲉ ⲉⲛⲧⲁϥϣⲱⲡ ⲛ̅ⲧⲉϥⲁⲥⲭⲏⲙⲟⲥⲩⲛⲏ ⲉⲡⲉⲧⲉⲣⲉⲟⲩⲥⲛϥⲉ ⲛ̅ⲧⲟⲟⲧⲩ ⲉⲁϥⲛ̅ⲧⲥ ⲉϩⲣⲁⲓ ϩⲙ̅ⲡⲉⲥⲛⲟϥⲥⲓ
ⲉⲣⲟϥ ⲙⲙⲓⲛ ⲙⲙⲟϥ ⲥⲧⲣⲉϥⲙⲟⲟⲩⲧ ⲛ̅ϩⲏⲧⲥ ⲁⲩⲱ ⲛ̅ϥⲙⲟⲩⲟⲩⲧ ⲛ̅ϩⲉⲛⲕⲟⲟⲩⲉ ⲛⲙⲙⲁϥ ⲛⲁⲓⲛⲉ
ⲡⲣⲱⲙⲉ ⲥⲧⲥⲟⲟϥ ⲉⲛⲧⲁⲛⲉⲓⲟⲧⲉ ⲉⲧⲟⲩⲁⲁⲃ ⲁⲩⲱ ⲉⲧⲛⲟⲉⲓ ϩⲛ̅ϩⲱⲃ ⲛⲓⲙ ⲥϩⲁⲓ ⲉⲧⲃⲏⲏⲧⲟⲩ ϩⲛ̅ⲛⲉⲩⲉⲡⲓⲥⲧⲟⲗⲏ
ϫⲉⲉⲣⲉⲧⲥⲏϥⲉ ⲙ̅ⲡⲉⲩⲧⲁⲕⲟ ϩⲁⲡⲉⲩ ⲅⲟⲡ ⲉⲩϭⲟⲣϭ ϩⲛⲙ̅ⲡⲩⲗⲏ ⲛⲁⲙ̅ⲛⲧⲉ¹.

---

¹ ‘The holy fathers in their epistles "The sword of
their destruction is in their bosoms, while they dwell (?) at
the gates of hell"' Another quotation is added in ZOEGA

p 522, 5 The prophets and apostles are called 'our holy
fathers' by Shenoute, e g Clar Press no 31, 2

Ρ ⲧ̄ⲍ̄ ⲡⲉⲧⲉⲙⲡϥⲥⲟⲩⲱⲛϥ ⲙⲁ̅ⲩⲁⲁϥ ⲛⲁϣ ⲛϩⲉ ⲉϥⲛⲁⲥⲟⲩⲛⲡⲛⲟⲩⲧⲉ ⲏ ⲛⲧⲁϥⲥⲟⲩⲛⲡⲉⲭ̅ⲥ̅
ϩⲙⲟⲩ ⲛ̄ϭⲓ ⲡⲉⲧⲉⲓⲣⲉ ⲛ̄ⲛⲉϥⲙⲉⲗⲟⲥ ⲙ̄ⲙⲉⲗⲟⲥ ⲙ̄ⲙⲁⲗⲁⲕⲟⲥ ϩⲓⲣⲉϥⲛⲕⲟⲧⲕ ⲙ̄ⲛϩⲟⲟⲩⲧ ⲁⲩⲱ ⲥⲱⲱϥ
ϩⲓⲛⲟⲉⲓⲕ ϩⲓⲡⲟⲣⲛⲏ ϩⲓⲍⲓⲛϭⲟⲛⲥ ⲙ̄ⲛⲃⲟⲧⲉ ⲛⲓⲙ

Ρ ⲧ̄ⲕ̄ⲑ̄ ⲛⲧⲟⲕⲡⲉ ⲡⲛⲟⲩⲧⲉ ⲙ̄ⲙⲉ ⲙⲁ̅ⲁⲃ ⲁⲩⲱ ⲡⲟⲩⲟⲉⲓⲛ ⲁⲩⲱ ⲡⲱⲛϩ ⲡⲁⲅⲁⲑⲟⲥ ⲡϫⲟⲉⲓⲥ
ⲡⲣⲣⲟ ⲡⲡⲁⲛⲧⲟⲕⲣⲁⲧⲱⲣ ⲁⲩⲱ ⲉϣϫⲉ ⲟⲩⲛⲣⲱⲙⲉ (ⲡ ⲣ̄) ϩⲓϫⲙ̄ⲡⲕⲁϩ ⲉⲣⲉⲧⲉⲛⲙⲉ ⲛϩⲏⲧⲟⲩ ϩⲟⲩⲙ̄ⲙⲉ
ⲛⲁⲓ ⲡⲉⲧⲙⲡϣⲁ ⲛⲟⲩⲱϣⲧ ⲛⲁⲕ ⲁⲛⲟⲛ ϫⲉ ⲁⲛⲟⲛ ϩⲉⲛⲃⲟⲗ ⲁⲩⲱ ⲁⲛⲟⲛ ϩⲉⲛⲣⲱⲙⲉ ⲁⲛ ⲁⲙⲙⲉⲛⲧⲁⲙ
ⲥⲃⲟⲕ ⲉⲃⲟⲗ ϩⲛⲣⲱⲛ ⲁⲛⲡⲣⲥⲁⲙⲙⲉⲛⲧⲟⲩⲝ ⲧⲏⲣⲛ ⲁⲛⲡⲗⲁⲛⲁ ϩⲓⲟⲩⲥⲟⲡ ⲁⲛϣⲱⲡⲉ ⲁⲗⲏⲑⲱⲥ ⲛⲑⲉ ⲛϭⲉⲡⲁ
ⲕⲁⲑⲁⲣⲧⲟⲥ ⲙ̄ⲡⲉⲕⲙⲧⲟ ⲉⲃⲟⲗ ⲉⲧⲃⲉⲛⲁⲓ ϥϫⲡⲓⲟ ⲛ̄ⲧⲉⲛⲙⲉⲛⲧⲁⲧⲥⲃⲱ ⲛ̄ϭⲓ ⲡⲉⲡⲛ̅ⲁ̅ ⲛⲧⲙⲉ ⲉⲧϣⲁϫⲉ ϩⲛⲛⲉⲕ
ⲡⲣⲟⲫⲏⲧⲏⲥ ⲉⲛⲧⲁⲩⲥⲟⲩⲱⲛϥ ⲉⲃⲟⲗ ϫⲉⲁϥⲟⲩⲱϩ ⲛⲙⲙⲁⲩ.

Ρ ⲧ̄ⲉ̄ ⲛⲥⲙⲁⲙⲁⲁⲧ ⲁⲩⲱ ⲛⲁⲓⲁⲧⲟⲩ ⲛⲛⲉⲧⲕⲛⲁⲧⲃⲃⲟⲟⲩ ⲉⲃⲟⲗ ϩⲙⲡⲥⲁⲧⲁⲛⲁⲥ ⲙ̄ⲛⲛⲉϥⲇⲁⲓⲙⲱⲛ
ⲁⲩⲱ ⲡⲉϥⲙⲛ̄ⲧⲁⲥⲉⲃⲏⲥ ⲛⲥⲙⲁⲙⲁⲁⲧ ⲉⲛⲉⲓⲣⲉ ⲛⲛⲉⲧⲙⲉ ⲙ̄ⲙⲟⲕ ⲛⲁⲡϣⲁ ⲛϭⲉⲡⲙⲁ ⲛϣⲟ(ⲣ ⲧ̄ⲥ̄)-ⲡⲉ
ⲛⲁⲕ ⲁⲩⲱ ⲡⲉⲕⲉⲓⲱⲧ ⲙ̄ⲡⲉⲕⲡⲛ̅ⲁ̅ ⲁⲩⲱ ⲡⲉⲕⲁⲅⲅⲉⲗⲟⲥ ⲙ̄ⲡⲉⲕⲟⲩⲱϣ ⲧⲏⲣⲟⲩ ⲛⲥⲙⲁⲙⲁⲁⲧ ⲁⲩⲱ
ⲛⲁⲓⲁⲧⲟⲩ ⲛⲛⲉⲛⲧⲁⲕⲛⲧⲟⲩ ⲉϩⲣⲁⲓ ϩⲛⲛⲉⲣⲃⲏⲩⲉ ⲙ̄ⲡⲇⲓⲁⲃⲟⲗⲟⲥ ⲛⲑⲉ (read ⲙ̄ⲡϩⲉ) ⲉϩⲣⲁⲓ ϩⲛⲛⲛⲟⲩⲛ
ⲁⲩⲱ ⲉⲕϩⲁⲣⲉϩ ⲟⲛ ⲉⲣⲟⲟⲩ ⲉⲧⲙ̄ⲧⲣⲉ ⲉϩⲣⲁⲓ ⲉⲡϣⲱⲛϩ ⲉⲧⲙ̄ⲙⲁⲩ ϫⲉⲁⲕⲟⲩⲁϣⲟⲩ ⲛϩⲟⲩⲟ ϫⲉ ⲛⲉⲧⲉ
ⲙ̄ⲡⲟⲩⲧⲉⲛ ⲧ̄ⲡⲉ ⲉⲛⲉϩ ⲛ̄ⲛⲉϥϩⲛⲁⲁⲩ ⲉⲧⲥϩⲟⲩⲟⲣⲧ ϫⲉⲩⲛⲁϣⲱⲡⲉ ⲛⲁⲕ ⲙ̄ⲙⲉⲣⲓⲧ ⲛⲟⲩⲏⲣ. (End
of homily)

The beginning of another homily refers to the crowds which had fled to the gate
of the monastery on the occasion of a Nubian inroad[1] —

ⲉⲓⲟⲩⲱϩ ⲟⲛ ⲉⲧⲟⲟⲧ ⳿ⲧⲉⲟⲟⲩ (read ⲉ⳿ⲧ-) ⲙ̄ⲡϫⲟⲉⲓⲥ ⲡⲛⲟⲩⲧⲉ ⲁⲩⲱ ⲉϣⲡϩⲙⲟⲧ ⲛⲧⲟⲟⲧϥ ϩⲛⲛⲉϥ
ⲁⲅⲁⲑⲟⲛ ⲧⲏⲣⲟⲩ ⲉⲛⲧⲁϥⲁⲁⲩ ⲛⲙⲙⲁⲛ ⳿ⲧⲛⲁϫⲟⲟⲥ ϫⲉⲡⲛⲟϭ ⲙ̄ⲙⲛ̄ϣⲉ ⲛⲧⲁⲉⲓⲛⲉ ⲉⲛⲧⲁⲩⲥⲟⲉⲓⲗⲉ
ⲉⲣⲟⲛ ⲏ ⲉⲁⲩⲟⲩⲱϩ ⲙ̄ⲡⲙⲁ ⲙ̄ⲡⲣⲟ ⲛⲡⲉⲥⲩⲛⲁⲅⲱⲛ ⲁⲩⲱ ⲡⲉⲩⲕⲱⲧⲉ ⲧⲏⲣϥ ⲙ̄ⲛⲛⲉⲩⲅⲓⲟⲙⲉ ⲙ̄ⲛⲛⲉⲩ
ϣⲏⲣⲉ ϩⲱⲥⲧⲉ ⲉⲧⲣⲉⲩⲣⲁϫⲟⲩⲱ ⲛⲛϣⲟ ⲛⲣⲱⲙⲉ ⲏ ϩⲟⲩⲟ ⲉⲣⲟⲟⲩ ⲉⲣⲉⲛⲉⲥⲛⲏⲩ ⲧⲏⲣⲟⲩ ϣⲁⲓⲛⲛⲉⲧⲉⲙ̄ⲛ̄ϭⲟⲙ
ⲙ̄ⲙⲟⲟⲩ ⲇⲓⲁⲕⲟⲛⲉⲓ ⲛⲁⲩ ⲛ̄ϣⲟⲙⲧ ⲡ̄ⲉ(sic expl)

68 [23].—Parchment, 6 complete leaves, now 27¼×21 cm   Pp ⲥⲛ̄ⲑ̄-ⲥⲟ̄.   2 cols,
25 lines   Script *cf* CIASCA III, especially for ⲕ and ϩ   Initials enlarged and, on some
pages, coloured red, as are the letters ⲫ and ⲟ, other pages have no colours   From
same MS as ZOEGA no clxxxix

Shenoute, Homily by   ZOEGA's fragment shows that it is directed against an idolater,
possibly the δούξ (*v* p ⲥ̄ϫ̄ⲁ̄), who was seducing the people   The following are examples —

Ρ ⲥ̄ϫ̄ ⲁⲗⲗⲁ ⲛⲛⲁϩⲣⲛⲡⲣⲙⲙⲁⲟ ⲛⲣⲉϥϫⲓⲛϭⲟⲛⲥ ⲉⲧⲙⲙⲁⲩ ⲙ̄ⲛⲧⲟⲩⲗⲁⲁⲩ ⲛϩⲱⲃ ⲉϫⲱ ⲉⲣⲟⲓ
ⲛⲥⲁⲧⲣⲉⲩϫⲟⲟⲥ ϫⲉⲉⲕⲛⲧⲟ ⲛⲡϩⲏⲧ ⲛⲡⲡⲣⲛⲛⲉ ⲉⲃⲟⲗ ⲙ̄ⲙⲟⲛ ⲉⲧⲙⲉⲣⲛ̄ⲃⲁ ϩⲉⲓϭⲱⲙ ϩⲉⲓϩⲱⲃ ⲛⲓⲙ ⲡⲁⲣⲁ
ⲧⲉⲩϭⲟⲙ ⲁⲩⲱ ⲉⲧⲣⲉⲩϫⲟⲟⲥ ϫⲉⲁϥⲉⲓ ⲉϩⲟⲩⲛ ⲉⲡⲉⲡⲏⲓ ⲫⲁⲛⲉⲣⲱⲛ ⲁϥϫⲉⲓ ⲛⲛⲉⲧⲉⲛⲟⲩⲱϣⲧ ⲛⲁⲩ ⲉ⳿ⲧϣⲓⲡⲉ
ⲛⲁⲛ ϫⲉⲙ̄ⲡⲉⲛⲉϣⲡⲙ̄ϭⲟⲙ ⲉⲕⲱⲗⲩ ⲙ̄ⲙⲟϥ.

Ρ ⲥ̄ϫ̄ⲁ̄ ⲛⲑⲉ ⲟⲛ ⲉⲧⲁⲡⲉϥⲟⲩⲉⲓⲧⲉ ⲙ̄ⲡⲗⲁⲥ ⲛⲛⲉⲧϫⲉⲓⲟⲩⲁ ⲉⲣⲟϥ ⲧⲉⲛⲟⲩ ⲁⲩⲱ ⲙ̄ⲡⲉϥⲧⲣⲉⲡⲥⲁⲣⲝ
ⲛⲛⲉⲧϫⲱ ⲙ̄ⲙⲟⲥ ϫⲉⲟⲩⲛⲟⲩⲧⲉ ⲁⲛⲡⲉ ⲡⲟⲧⲡⲉⲧ ⲉⲡⲉⲥⲏⲧ ⲁⲗⲗⲁ ⲥⲉⲛⲁⲡⲟⲧⲡⲉⲧ ⲁⲩⲱ ⲛⲥⲉⲡⲱϩ ⲁⲩⲱ
ⲡⲉⲩⲗⲁⲥ ⲛⲁⲡⲱϩⲥ ⲁⲩⲱ ⲛϥϫⲉⲓⲧⲉ ⲙ̄ⲡⲥⲟⲛ ⲉⲧⲉⲣⲉⲛϫⲟⲉⲓⲥ ⲓ̄ⲥ̄ ⲛⲁⲧⲥⲁⲃⲟⲟⲩ ⲉⲡⲉϩⲟⲟⲩ ⲉⲡⲉⲩⲕⲱⲱⲛⲥ.

Ρ ⲥ̄ϫ̄ⲃ̄ ⲡⲉⲧⲣϩⲟⲧⲉ ϩⲏⲧϥ ⲉⲛⲟⲩⲣⲱⲙⲉ ⲉϣⲁϥⲙⲟⲩ ⲁⲩⲱ ⲉϩⲣⲏⲧϥ ⲉⲛⲟⲩϣⲏⲣⲉ ⲛⲣⲱⲙⲉ ⲛⲁⲓ
ⲉϣⲁⲩϣⲟⲟⲩⲉ ⲛⲑⲉ ⲛⲟⲩⲭⲟⲣⲧⲟⲥ ⲛⲉⲩϣⲟⲃⲉ ⲁⲛ ⲉϩⲉⲛϣⲏⲣⲉ ϣⲏⲙ ⲉⲛⲁⲧⲥⲟⲟⲩⲛ ⲉϣⲁⲩϭⲱϣⲉ ⲁⲩⲱ
ⲛⲥⲉⲧⲣⲣⲉ ϩⲙ̄ⲡⲧⲣⲉⲩⲥⲱⲧⲙ ⲉⲡⲉϩⲣⲟⲟⲩ ⲉⲛϩⲉⲛⲃⲁϣⲟⲟⲣ ⲏ ⲁⲩⲛⲁⲩ ⲉⲣⲟⲟⲩ.

[1] *V* LEIPOLDT's *Schenute* 172 and in *Aeg Zeitschr* xl 130, where this text is printed from Paris MSS   *Cf* also Brit Mus no 351

P ⲥ̅ⲕ̅ⲁ̅ ⲉⲧⲃⲉⲡⲁⲓ ⲙⲡⲁⲣⲟⲟⲩϣ ⲁⲛⲡⲉ ⲛⲁⲓ ⲙⲛⲡⲉⲓⲕⲟⲟⲩⲉ ⲁⲛ ⲙⲡⲉⲟⲩⲗⲟⲩϩ ⲅⲉⲛⲛⲥⲉ ⲛⲟⲩⲗⲟⲩϩ ⲛϩⲉⲗⲗⲏⲛ ⲁⲟⲗⲟⲙⲁ ⲉϫⲟⲟⲥ ϩⲙⲡⲧⲣⲉϥϫⲓ ⲉⲡⲉⲓⲙⲁ ϫⲉⲁⲓⲣⲙⲟⲓϭⲉ ⲣⲱ ϫⲉⲛⲣⲟⲟⲩⲧ.

P ⲥ̅ⲕ̅ⲉ̅. ⲥⲉⲥⲟⲩⲟⲣⲧ ⲛϭⲉⲓ ⲛⲉⲧϫⲱ ⲙⲙⲟⲥ ϫⲉⲛⲉϣⲁⲩⲅⲓϥⲟⲩ ⲡⲛⲟⲩⲧⲉ ⲏ ϫⲉϣⲁⲣⲉⲛⲟⲩⲧⲉ ⲙⲟⲩ ⲥⲉⲥⲟⲩⲟⲣⲧ ⲛϭⲉⲓ ⲛⲉⲧϫⲱ ⲙⲙⲟⲥ ϫⲉⲉⲩϫⲧⲟⲩⲛⲟⲩⲧⲉⲡⲉ ⲡⲛⲟⲩⲧⲉ ⲁϥⲣⲟϥ ⲙⲡⲉϥⲥⲓⲙⲉ ϫⲉⲛⲧⲁⲡⲁⲓⲁⲃⲟⲗⲟⲥ ⲉⲓ ⲧⲱⲛ ⲛⲧⲁⲩϫⲉⲡⲁⲓ ⲉⲃⲟⲗ ϫⲉⲁⲩⲥⲱⲧⲙ ϩⲛⲉⲓⲱⲃ ⲡⲣⲣⲟ ⲡⲛⲟⲩⲧⲉ ⲡⲡⲁⲛⲧⲱⲛⲣⲁⲧⲟⲣ ⲉϥϫⲛⲟⲩ ⲛⲛⲁⲁⲓⲙⲱⲛ ⲉⲧⲙⲙⲁⲩ ϫⲉⲛⲧⲁⲕⲉⲓ ⲧⲱⲛ ⲙⲡⲟⲩⲅⲉⲓⲙⲉ ⲉⲡⲓⲟⲩⲉ ⲛⲛⲉⲩⲥⲱⲧⲙ ⲉⲣⲟⲟⲩ ϫⲉϩⲁⲡ (*read* ϩⲁϩ) ⲛⲥⲟⲡ ⲁⲛⲛⲟⲩⲓⲉ ϣⲁϫⲉ ϩⲛⲛⲉⲧⲅⲣⲁⲫⲏ. This is compared to Elisha's question to Gehazi (2 Kings v 25), and similar lessons are then drawn from God's questions to Adam (Gen iii 9) and to Moses (Exod iv 2), Joseph's to his brethren (Gen xlii 7), Christ's concerning Lazarus (John xi 34), God's to Abraham (Gen xviii 9), the angel's to the women (? John xx 13), Christ's to Mary (ⲙⲁⲣⲓϩⲁⲙ, *ib* 15), or on the road to Emmaus (Luke xxiv 17), or to the disciples (John xxi 5 and Mark vi 38), or the woman (Luke viii 45) Then p ⲥ̅ⲟ̅: ϩⲟⲙⲟⲓⲱⲥ ⲉⲣϣⲁⲛⲧⲛⲁⲕⲓⲁ ⲁⲛⲡⲉⲛⲉⲓⲱⲧ ⲛⲥⲁⲁⲛⲁⲥ ⲡⲱϩ ⲏ ⲛⲥⲥⲡⲱϭⲉ ⲛϭⲏⲧⲛ ⲱ ⲛϩⲉⲗⲗⲏⲛ ⲛⲉⲣⲣⲟⲩⲉⲓⲁϩⲕ ⲙⲙⲛⲧⲁⲧϩⲁⲣⲧⲉ ϯⲛⲁϫⲟⲟⲥ ⲉⲓϩⲟⲙⲟⲗⲟⲅⲉⲓ ⲛⲧⲁⲉ ϫⲉⲟⲩ ⲙⲟⲛⲟⲛ ϥⲥⲟⲟⲩⲛ ϫⲉⲉⲓⲥ ⲡⲉⲥⲛⲟϥ ϩⲁⲣⲟⲥ ⲙⲙⲛⲧⲥⲛⲟⲟⲩⲥ ⲛⲣⲟⲙⲡⲉ ⲁⲗⲗⲁ ϥⲥⲟⲟⲩⲛ ⲙⲙⲟⲥ ϫⲓⲛⲉⲥⲛϩⲧⲉ ⲛⲧⲉⲥⲙⲙⲁⲁⲩ ⲉⲣϣⲁⲛⲟⲩⲑⲉⲣⲁⲙⲉⲩⲥ ⲣⲁⲧⲥⲟⲟⲩⲛ ⲙⲡⲉⲣⲛⲁⲁⲩ ⲛⲧⲁϥⲧⲁⲙⲓⲟϥ ϩⲛⲛⲉϥϭⲓϫ ϩⲙⲡⲉϥϣⲱⲛϩ ⲓ̅ⲥ̅ ⲛⲧⲟϥ ⲥⲟⲟⲩⲛ ⲉⲡⲉⲛⲧⲁϥⲡⲗⲁⲥⲥⲁ ⲙⲙⲟⲩ ϩⲛⲑⲉ ⲛⲉⲧⲥⲟⲟⲩⲛ ϫⲉⲛⲉϥ (*sic expl*)

69 [**34, 28, 23 a**, in this order]—Parchment, 8 complete leaves, now from $28\frac{1}{2} \times 24\frac{1}{2}$ to 32×25 cm   Pp ⲙ̅ⲉ̅-ⲅ̅ (the last of qu ⲍ̅). 2 cols, about 30 lines   Script *cf* CIASCA xi, HYVERNAT xi 4   Its peculiarities are indicated in Brit Mus Catal no 202   From same MS or by same scribe as Brit Mus no 202, Paris Vol 130³ 75-83, Vol 130⁶ 62, Vol 131⁴ 111, Vol 131⁶ 91, 110, Vol 131⁷ 38, Vol 129¹⁴ 130, ZOEGA cxciv, cccviii (2), Leyden no 80, Cairo no 8006   It is clear from some of the pagination and incidental quire-marks that all these are from at least two distinct volumes, *e g* our leaves have the same pages as some of ZOEGA cxciv, while the pages of another part of that fragment are the same as part of Brit Mus no 202; again, Leyden 80, pp ⲥ̅ⲕ̅ϩ̅, ⲥ̅ⲟ̅ with quire-mark ⲓ̅ⲏ̅, would scarcely be from the first volume of the MS

Shenoute, Homily or Epistle by[1]   The text is partly identical with ZOEGA no cci (p ⲛ̅ = Z, pp ⲛ̅ⲟ̅, ⲟ̅, p ⲛ̅ⲟ̅ col 2 = Z, p ⲟ̅ⲁ̅, p ⲅ̅ col 2 = Z, p ⲟ̅ⲉ̅)   The author rebukes vice and exhorts to virtue, addressing himself to nuns as well as to monks   The following are examples of the text not given by ZOEGA —

P ⲛ̅. ⲡⲁⲕⲁⲑⲁⲣⲧⲟⲥ ⲁⲛ ⲙⲙⲁⲧⲉⲡⲉ ⲟⲩⲣⲱⲙⲉ ⲉϥϫⲁϩⲙ ⲉⲩⲡⲱⲣϫ ⲙⲙⲟϥ ⲉⲃⲟⲗ ⲙⲡⲣⲱⲙⲉ ⲉⲧⲟⲩⲁⲁⲃ ⲟⲩⲁⲉ ⲟⲩϩⲛⲟ ⲁⲛ ⲙⲙⲁⲧⲉ ⲉϥⲛⲁⲣϣⲁⲩ ⲁⲛ ⲉⲁⲁϥ ⲛⲟⲩⲥⲓⲁ ⲙⲡϫⲟⲉⲓⲥⲡⲉ ⲡⲉⲧϫⲁϩⲙ ⲉⲩⲡⲱⲣϫ ⲙⲙⲟϥ ⲉⲃⲟⲗ ⲙⲡⲉⲧⲧⲃⲃⲏⲩ ⲕⲁⲧⲁ ⲛⲉⲛⲧⲟⲗⲏ ⲁⲗⲗⲁ ⲡⲟⲛⲏⲣⲟⲛ ⲛⲓⲙ ϫⲓⲛⲛϩⲁⲡ ⲉⲧⲥⲟⲟⲩⲥ ϣⲁϩⲣⲁⲓ ⲉⲟⲩⲡⲟⲕⲣⲓⲥⲓⲥ ϩⲉⲛⲁⲕⲁⲑⲁⲣⲧⲟⲛⲛⲉ ⲁⲩⲱ ⲡⲉⲧⲛⲁϫⲱϩ ⲉⲣⲟⲟⲩ ⲥⲧⲡⲁⲓⲡⲉ ⲛϭⲁⲁⲩ ⲉϥϣⲁⲛⲧⲁϩⲟⲩ ⲉⲃⲟⲗ ⲙⲙⲟⲟⲩ ϥⲛⲁϣⲱⲡⲉ ⲛⲁⲕⲁⲑⲁⲣⲧⲟⲥ ⲛⲛⲁϩⲣⲛⲡⲛⲟⲩⲧⲉ ⲛⲑⲉ ⲉⲧⲉϩⲉⲛⲁⲕⲁⲑⲁⲣⲥⲓⲁⲛⲉ ⲛⲟⲃⲉ ⲛⲓⲙ ⲛⲛⲁϩⲣⲛⲡⲙⲛⲟⲩⲧⲉ ⲕⲁⲙⲉ ⲧⲁⲓⲧⲉ ⲑⲉ ⲉⲧⲟⲩⲕⲱ ⲙⲙⲟⲥ ⲉϩⲉⲛⲁⲓⲕⲁⲥⲧⲏⲥ ⲛⲥⲉⲥⲟⲩⲧⲱⲛ ⲁⲛ ϫⲉⲁⲕⲁⲑⲁⲣⲧⲟⲥ ⲉⲧⲃⲉⲛⲉⲩϩⲃⲏⲩⲉ ⲛⲁⲕⲁⲑⲁⲣⲧⲟⲛ ⲁⲩⲱ ⲛⲉⲧⲥⲟⲩⲧⲱⲛ ϫⲉⲛⲁⲑⲁⲣⲟⲥ ⲉⲧⲃⲉⲛⲉⲩϩⲃⲏⲩⲉ ⲛⲁⲓⲕⲁⲓⲟⲛ ⲁⲩⲱ ⲛⲉⲩⲣⲁⲛ ⲙⲙⲉ.

---

[1] LEIPOLDT, *Schenute* 160, holds the authorship doubtful.

Р п͞с. ⲛⲧⲁⲓⲧⲁⲅⲉⲛⲁⲓ ⲁⲛ (ⲣ ⲡ͞ⲍ) ⲛⲑⲉ ⲛϩⲉⲛⲣⲁⲥⲟⲩ ⲛⲉⲛϩⲃⲏⲩⲉ ⲅⲁⲣ ⲛⲉⲧⲧⲣⲉⲛⲉⲓϣⲁϫⲉ †ϩⲁⲡ ⲉⲣⲟⲛ ⲁⲩⲱ ⲛⲁⲛⲟⲩⲥ ⲉⲩ† ⲁⲣⲁ ⲧⲛⲛⲁⲙⲉⲧⲁⲛⲟⲉⲓ ⲁⲣⲁ ⲧⲛⲛⲁϩⲱ ⲉⲣⲟⲛ ⲉⲛⲥⲱⲟⲩϩ ⲛⲁⲛ ⲉϩⲟⲩⲛ ⲛⲟⲩⲟⲣⲅⲏ ϩⲙⲡⲉϩⲟⲟⲩ ⲛⲧⲟⲣⲅⲏ ⲙⲙⲡϭⲱⲗⲡ ⲉⲃⲟⲗ ⲙⲡⲣⲁⲡ ⲙⲙⲉ ⲙⲡⲛⲟⲩⲧⲉ ⲉϣϫⲉⲛⲉⲓⲡⲟⲛⲏⲣⲟⲛ ⲛⲧⲉⲓϭⲟⲧ ϣⲟⲟⲡ ⲁⲛ ⲉⲓⲥ ⲟⲩⲛⲟⲩⲟⲛ ⲉⲣⲟϥ[1] ⲙⲡⲉⲧϣⲁϫⲉ ϫⲉϥϫⲱ ⲙⲡⲉⲧⲉⲛϥϣⲟⲟⲡ ⲁⲛ ⲉϣϫⲉⲥⲉϣⲟⲟⲡ ϫⲉ ⲁⲩⲱ ⲥⲉⲣϩⲟⲩⲟ ⲉⲓⲉ ⲥⲉⲣⲛⲟⲃⲉ ⲛϭⲓ ⲛⲉⲧϭⲛⲁⲣⲓⲛⲉ ⲉⲡⲉⲧϣⲁϫⲉ.

70 [24 a].—Parchment, 8 complete leaves, now 32·3 × 24 3 cm　Pp $\overline{\text{ⲥⲗⲑ}}$-$\overline{\text{ⲥⲛⲁ}}$. 2 cols, 32 lines.　Script· *v* MINGARELLI, *Aeg Codd Reliq*, p 30, no iv　Initials moderately -enlarged, without ornaments or colours　By same scribe as ZOEGA ccxiii, cclxxvii(i), Brit Mus Catal no 204, Paris Vol 78 41, Vol 131[5] 54, 67, Vol 131[6]. 32[2] and MINGARELLI no iv

Homily, probably by Shenoute, on God's (or Christ's) creation of the universe, His favour and protection to Israel, on Christ's humble birth, human life, sufferings and passion (with very many quotations from or references to the Gospels); on the punishment of the wicked and the blessedness of true believers.　P $\overline{\text{ⲥⲛⲁ}}$ shows the end of the homily　The following are examples —

Р $\overline{\text{ⲥⲗⲑ}}$ ⲡⲉⲛⲧⲁϥⲡⲁⲧⲁⲥⲥⲉ ⲛⲛⲓⲛⲟϭ ⲛⲣⲣⲟ ⲉⲁϥⲙⲟⲩⲟⲩⲧ ⲛϩⲉⲛⲣⲣⲱⲟⲩ (ⲣ $\overline{\text{ⲥⲙ}}$) ⲉⲩⲧⲁϫⲣⲏⲩ ⲉⲁϥϫⲱⲧⲉ ⲉⲃⲟⲗ ⲛϩⲉⲛϩⲉⲑⲛⲟⲥ ⲉⲛⲁϣⲱⲟⲩ ⲛⲁⲓ ⲉⲧⲉⲣⲉⲧⲟⲣⲅⲏ ϩⲓϫⲛⲛⲉⲩⲕⲉϣⲱⲡⲛ ⲡⲉⲛⲧⲁϥⲧⲣⲉⲡⲥⲉⲣⲱⲃ ⲙⲙⲱⲩⲥⲏⲥ ⲛⲧⲟϥ ⲉⲩϩⲟϥ ⲡⲁⲗⲓⲛ ⲟⲛ ⲉⲁϥⲕⲧⲟϥ ⲉⲩϭⲉⲣⲱⲃ ⲁϥϣⲱⲡⲉ ϩⲛⲧⲉϥϭⲓϫ ⲛⲑⲉ ⲉⲧⲉⲛⲉϥⲟ ⲙⲙⲟⲥ

Р $\overline{\text{ⲥⲙⲃ}}$. ⲕⲁⲓ ⲅⲁⲣ ⲁϥϣⲓⲛⲉ ϩⲱⲱϥ ⲉⲧⲃⲉϩⲉⲛϩⲃⲏⲩⲉ ⲛⲑⲉ ⲛⲟⲩⲣⲱⲙⲉ ⲛⲁⲧⲥⲟⲟⲩⲛ ⲛⲑⲉ ⲛⲧⲁϥϫⲛⲉⲡⲉⲓⲱⲧ ⲙⲡϣⲏⲣⲉϣⲏⲙ ⲛⲧⲁϥⲟⲩⲱϣ ⲉⲧⲁⲗϭⲟϥ ϫⲉⲉⲓⲥ ⲁⲟⲩⲏⲣ ⲛⲟⲩⲟⲉⲓϣ ϫⲓⲛⲧⲁⲡⲁⲓ ⲧⲁϩⲟϥ ϩⲱⲥ ⲉϣϫⲉⲛϥⲥⲟⲟⲩⲛ ⲁⲛ ⲛⲑⲉ ⲟⲛ ⲛⲧⲁϥϣⲓⲛⲉ ⲉⲧⲃⲉⲗⲁⲍⲁⲣⲟⲥ ϫⲉⲛⲧⲁⲧⲉⲧⲛⲕⲁⲁϥ ⲧⲱⲛ.

Р $\overline{\text{ⲥⲛⲁ}}$. †ϩⲧⲏⲕ ⲉⲡⲉⲥⲙⲟⲧ ⲙⲡⲣⲱⲙⲉ ⲛⲧⲁⲣⲁϩ ⲛϭⲱⲃ ⲧⲁⲕⲟ ⲛⲧⲟⲟⲧϥ ⲏ ⲡⲉϭⲉⲓⲛⲉ ϫⲉⲉϥⲟ ⲛⲁϣ ⲙⲙⲓⲛⲉ ⲁⲩⲱ ⲕⲛⲁⲉⲓⲙⲉ ϫⲉⲡⲉⲓⲛⲉ ⲛⲧⲁϥϣⲱⲡⲉ ⲙⲡⲣⲱⲙⲉ ϩⲙⲡⲧⲣⲉϥⲣⲛⲟⲃⲉ ⲙⲛⲛⲥⲁⲡⲥⲱϣ ⲛⲧⲁϥϣⲱⲡⲉ ⲙⲙⲟⲛ ⲁⲡϫⲟⲉⲓⲥ ϣⲱⲡⲉ ⲛϩⲏⲧϥ ⲉⲧⲃⲏⲏⲧⲛ ϩⲙⲡⲧⲣⲉϥ ⲣⲣⲱⲙⲉ ϣⲁⲛⲧϥⲙⲡⲣⲱⲙⲉ ⲉⲧⲉϥⲁⲣⲭⲏ ⲏ ⲧⲉϥⲙⲛⲧⲁⲧⲛⲟⲃⲉ ⲙⲛⲧⲙⲛⲧⲥⲁⲉⲓⲉ ⲛⲧⲉϥⲯⲩⲭⲏ ⲛϣⲟⲣⲡ ϩⲁⲑⲏ ⲙⲡⲁⲧϥϣⲱⲡⲉ ⲛⲁⲛⲁⲑⲁⲣⲧⲟⲥ

ⲧⲱ ⲉⲧⲱ ⲧⲉⲛⲟⲩ ⲛⲛⲉⲧⲙⲉ ⲙⲡϫⲟⲉⲓⲥ ⲓ͞ⲥ ⲛⲥⲉⲛⲁⲩ ⲉⲣⲟϥ ⲁⲛ ⲛⲑⲉ ⲉⲧⲛϩ.... ⲧⲱ ⲉⲧⲱ ⲛⲛⲉⲧⲣⲙⲟⲉⲓϩⲉ ⲧⲉⲛⲟⲩ ⲉϫⲛⲛⲉϥϭⲟⲙ ⲙⲛⲛⲉϥϩⲃⲏⲩⲉ ⲧⲏⲣⲟⲩ ⲉⲩⲥⲱⲧⲙ ⲉⲣⲟⲟⲩ ϩⲛ (ⲣ $\overline{\text{ⲥⲛⲃ}}$) ⲛⲉⲩⲙⲁⲁϫⲉ ⲙⲙⲛⲕⲉⲛⲧⲁⲩⲛⲁⲩ ⲉⲛⲙⲁⲉⲓⲛ ⲙⲛⲛⲧⲁⲗϭⲟ ⲧⲏⲣⲟⲩ ⲛⲧⲁϥⲁⲁⲩ ⲙⲡⲉⲩⲙⲧⲟ ⲉⲃⲟⲗ ⲏ ϩⲛⲧⲉⲩⲙⲛⲧⲉ ⲁⲩⲣⲁⲧϩⲁⲣⲧⲉ ⲟⲩⲏⲣ ⲛⲧⲩⲡⲟⲥ ⲙⲡⲟⲛⲏⲣⲟⲛ ⲉⲁⲩϫⲟⲕⲟⲩ ⲉⲃⲟⲗ ϩⲙⲡⲙⲁ ⲙⲡⲉⲕⲣⲁⲛⲓⲟⲛ ϩⲙⲡⲧⲣⲉⲩ ϣⲱⲡⲉ ⲛⲟⲩⲙⲟⲩϫϭ ⲛⲟⲩⲱⲧ ϩⲓⲧⲕⲁⲕⲓⲁ ϩⲓⲧⲛⲧⲉⲥⲃⲱ ⲛⲛⲉⲧⲟⲓϩⲱⲟϥ.

---

[1] The use of ⲟⲩⲟⲛ with ⲟⲩⲛ is sometimes remarkable It means either (1) 'There is (are) who ,' *e g* ZOEGA 352 ⲟⲩⲛⲟⲩⲟⲛ ⲙⲙⲁⲩ ⲧⲉⲛⲟⲩ, 355 ⲟⲩⲛⲟⲩⲟⲛ ⲉϥⲉⲓⲣⲉ, 437 ⲛⲉⲧⲉⲟⲩⲛⲟⲩⲟⲛ ⲛⲧⲟⲟⲧⲟⲩ, Rossi II, i 74 ⲟⲩⲛⲟⲩⲟⲛ ⲉⲁϥⲣϩⲟⲩⲟⲧⲉ, STERN § 265 ⲟⲩⲛⲟⲩⲟⲛ ⲉϥⲟ ⲛⲉⲗⲁⲭⲓⲥⲧⲟⲥ and Boh, *Mus. Guim* xxv 8 ⲟⲩⲛⲟⲩⲟⲛ ⲟⲩⲣⲟ ⲉϫⲛⲛⲓⲕⲁϩⲓ, Luke xxiv 39 ⲟⲩⲛⲟⲩⲟⲛ ⲙⲙⲟⲓ *ἐμὲ ἔχοντα* (Boh ⲉⲟⲩⲟⲛ), or (2) 'There is a debt, responsibility, with him towards ,' *e g*. in the present text, and in no 68, ⲉⲝ, ⲛⲛⲁϩⲣⲛⲣⲱⲙⲉ ⲅⲁⲣ ⲛⲓⲙ ⲉⲧϩⲉⲗⲡⲓⲥ (*sic*) ⲉⲓ͞ⲥ ⲟⲩⲟⲩⲟ (*sic*) ⲛⲟⲩⲟⲛ ⲉⲣⲟⲓ ⲛⲧⲟⲟⲧⲟⲩ ⲁⲩⲱ ⲟⲩⲉⲛⲧⲁⲩ ⲉⲣⲟⲓ ⲙⲙⲁⲧⲉ, *ib* ⲥϫⲁ, ⲉⲣϣⲁⲛ ⲛϥϭⲟⲩⲓ . ⲥϭⲟⲩⲉⲣ ϩⲉⲛⲣⲱⲙⲉ ... ⲟⲩⲉⲛⲟⲩⲟⲛ ⲉⲣⲟⲟⲩ, Brit Mus Catal p 163 ⲡⲉⲧⲉⲟⲩⲛⲟⲩⲟⲛ ⲉⲣⲟⲓ ⲛϩⲏⲧϥ, ZOEGA 480 ⲉⲧⲣⲉⲡⲉⲧⲉⲟⲩⲛⲟⲩⲟⲛ ⲉⲣⲟϥ ⲕⲱ ⲉⲃⲟⲗ. Obscure is here no 70 ⲥⲙⲉ=Mark xiv 63 ⲛⲉⲣⲭⲣⲓⲁϭⲉ ⲧⲉⲛⲟⲩ ⲙⲙⲛⲧⲣⲉ ⲉⲣⲟⲩ ⲛⲟⲩⲟⲛ (WOIDE, Balestri ⲉⲣⲟⲩ ϫⲓⲛⲧⲉⲛⲟⲩ, *cf* Boh)

[2] Correct reference thus to Paris MSS in Brit. Mus Catal.

Ρ ⲥⲙⲑ. ⲉⲁⲩⲉϣⲧⲡⲉⲩⲣⲣⲟ ⲇⲉ ϩⲱⲱϥ ⲁⲩⲱ ⲡⲛⲟⲩⲧⲉ ⲛⲥⲁⲣⲝ ⲛⲓⲙ ⲉⲡϣⲉ ⲁⲩⲟⲩⲱⲙ ⲉⲣⲉⲡⲉⲥⲛⲟϥ ϩⲣⲁⲓ ϩⲓϫⲛⲧⲥⲟⲟⲩϩⲉ ⲛϫⲱⲟⲩ ⲙⲡⲉⲩⲕⲉϣⲏⲣⲉ ⲕⲁⲧⲁ ⲧϭⲟⲧ ⲙⲡⲥⲁⲙⲟⲩⲗ ⲙⲙⲁⲧⲉ ⲁⲛ ⲉⲧⲣⲟⲣϣ
ⲉϩⲣⲁⲓ ⲉϫⲱⲟⲩ ⲛⲧⲁⲩⲟⲩⲙⲛϥ ⲁⲗⲗⲁ ⲕⲁⲧⲁ ⲡϣⲓ ⲛⲧⲟⲣⲅⲏ ⲧⲏⲣⲥ ⲛⲧⲁⲥⲟⲩⲱ ⲉⲥⲉⲓ ⲉϩⲣⲁⲓ ⲉϫⲱⲟⲩ ⲁⲩⲱ
ⲟⲛ ⲉⲥⲛⲁⲉⲓ

Ρ ⲥⲛⲁ. ϩⲉⲛⲟⲩⲏⲏⲃ ⲉⲩϫⲱ ⲉⲃⲟⲗ ⲙⲡⲉⲩϣⲙϣⲉ ⲕⲁⲗⲱⲥ ϩⲁⲡⲏⲓ ⲙⲡⲛⲟⲩⲧⲉ ϩⲉⲛⲙⲟⲛⲁⲭⲟⲥ
ⲉⲩⲡⲟⲗⲓⲧⲉⲩⲉ ϩⲛⲟⲩⲙⲉ ϩⲟⲉⲓⲛⲉ ⲉⲩⲁⲥⲛⲉⲓ ϩⲛⲟⲩⲙⲛⲧⲡⲁⲣⲑⲉⲛⲟⲥ ϩⲉⲛⲕⲟⲟⲩⲉ ⲉⲩϩⲁⲣⲉϩ ⲉⲡⲉⲩⲥⲁⲙⲟⲥ
ϩⲟⲓⲛⲉ ⲉⲁⲩϥⲓ ⲙⲡⲉⲩⲥⲧⲟⲥ ⲁⲩⲟⲩⲁϩⲟⲩ ⲛⲥⲱϥ ϩⲉⲛⲕⲟⲟⲩⲉ ⲉⲩⲥⲁⲁⲛϣ ⲛⲏ̄ϩⲏⲕⲉ ϩⲛⲛⲉⲧϣⲟⲡ ⲛⲁⲩ
ϩⲟⲓⲛⲉ ⲉⲩϣⲙϣⲉ ϩⲛϩⲉⲛϣⲗⲏⲗ ⲙⲛϩⲉⲛⲛⲏⲥⲧⲓⲁ[1].

71 [30].—Parchment, 2 complete leaves, now 31 × 24 cm   Pp [ϥⲁ, ϥⲃ], ϥⲅ, ϥⲇ.
2 cols, 27 or 28 lines. Script *cf* HYVERNAT XI 3, though there the character is smaller
From same MS as Brit. Mus no 213, Leyden no 68 and Cairo no 8009[2]

From a Homily or Epistle by a successor or disciple of Shenoute. On the blessings
of Christ for the righteous and on the punishment of the wicked *Quotations*: 1 Cor vi 9
and v 11; also the following from 'our holy father[3], which he said and wrote as a testimony to all generations unto the world's end,' (p. ϥⲃ) ⲝⲉⲟⲩⲟⲓ ⲛⲁⲓ ⲝⲉⲁⲩⲥⲟⲡⲧ ⲛⲑⲉ ⲛⲟⲩⲣⲉϥ
ⲝⲓⲟⲩⲉ ⲁⲩⲱ ⲁⲩⲥⲟⲛϩⲧ ⲛⲑⲉ ⲛⲟⲩⲣⲉϥϩⲱⲧⲃ ⲁⲩⲛⲧ ϩⲓⲧⲛⲟⲩⲁⲅⲅⲉⲗⲟⲥ ⲕⲁⲧⲛⲁ ⲉϩⲣⲁⲓ ⲉⲡⲧⲟⲡⲟⲥ ⲉϥ
ⲛϩⲏⲧϥ ⲝⲉⲕⲁⲥ ⲉⲧⲉⲧⲛⲁⲉⲓⲙⲉ ⲝⲉⲙⲡⲉⲛϩⲉⲗⲁⲁⲩ ⲛϣⲁⲝⲉ ⲉϥϣⲟⲃⲉ ⲉⲡⲁⲉⲡⲓⲅⲣⲁⲫⲏ; and again, ⲁⲩⲱ
ϥⲣⲙⲛⲧⲣⲉ ⲟⲛ ⲛⲙⲙⲁⲛ ⲛϭⲓ ⲡⲉⲛⲡⲉⲧⲟⲩⲁⲁⲃ ⲛⲉⲓⲱⲧ ϩⲛⲛⲉⲛⲧⲁⲛϫⲟⲟⲩ ⲝⲓⲛⲛ̄ϣⲟⲣⲡ ⲝⲉⲧⲁⲓⲧⲉ ⲑⲉ
ⲉⲧⲛⲁϣⲱⲡⲉ ⲛⲛⲣⲉϥⲣⲛⲟⲃⲉ ⲧⲏⲣⲟⲩ. The first of these (to ⲛϩⲏⲧϥ) recurs in Brit Mus no 214
and LEMM (*Kl Kopt Stud* no xlv 0194) has shown that the words are Shenoute's
Those immediately following (ⲝⲉⲕⲁⲥ), on the other hand, occur in MS. Curzon 110, ⲥⲍ̄
(on which *v* no 65), and, together with the writer's style, suggest that this fragment is
likewise by the 'John' to whom the other is ascribed

Further examples of the text.—

ⲥⲟⲩⲛⲡⲉⲧⲛϣⲓⲛⲉ ⲁⲩⲱ ⲧⲉⲧⲓⲙⲛ ⲙⲡⲉⲧⲛϩⲱⲃ ⲱ ⲡⲉⲧⲣⲟⲥ ⲛⲥⲁ ⲛⲉⲓⲟⲧⲉ ⲁⲩⲱ ⲉⲧⲣϩⲟⲩⲟ̄ⲝⲱⲛ
ⲙⲙⲟⲟⲩ ⲉⲃⲟⲗ ϩⲛⲛⲧⲟⲡⲟⲥ ⲙⲡⲉⲭ̄ⲥ̄ ⲛⲥⲉⲝⲓⲧⲏⲩⲧⲛ ϩⲱⲟⲩ ⲉϩⲟⲩⲛ ϩⲛⲙⲡⲩⲗⲏ ⲉⲛⲧⲁⲩⲟⲩⲱⲛ ⲙⲙⲟⲟⲩ
ⲛⲏⲧⲛ ⲉⲣⲁⲧⲟⲩ ⲛⲛⲁⲅⲅⲉⲗⲟⲥ ⲉⲛⲧⲁⲩⲕⲱ ⲛⲥⲱⲟⲩ ⲛⲧⲉⲩⲁⲣⲭⲏ ⲁⲩⲉⲓ ⲉϩⲣⲁⲓ ⲁⲩⲡⲟⲣⲛⲉⲩⲉ ⲙⲛⲛϣⲉⲉⲣⲉ
ⲛⲛⲣⲱⲙⲉ ⲁⲩⲱ ⲉⲣⲁⲧⲟⲩ ⲛⲛⲥⲓⲧⲁⲥ ⲛⲁⲣⲭⲁⲓⲟⲥ ⲛⲧⲁⲩϣⲧⲟⲣⲧⲣⲡⲛⲁϩ ϩⲛⲡⲉⲩⲱⲛϩ ⲁⲩⲱ ⲉⲣⲁⲧⲟⲩ
ⲛⲛⲣⲙⲥⲟⲇⲟⲙⲁ ⲙⲛⲧⲅⲟⲙⲟⲣⲣⲁ ⲛⲁⲓ ⲛⲧⲁⲟⲩⲕⲱⲧ ϩⲱⲟⲩ ⲉⲃⲟⲗ ϩⲓⲧⲡⲉ ⲙⲛⲟⲩⲕⲱϩⲧ ⲁϥⲣⲟⲕϩⲟⲩ
ⲉⲧⲃⲉⲙⲛⲧⲣⲉϥⲛⲕⲟⲧⲕ ⲙⲛϩⲟⲟⲩⲧ ⲛⲉⲓϣⲉⲉⲣⲉ ⲥⲁⲣⲛⲉ ⲧⲁⲩⲱ ⲛⲡⲉⲧⲛⲥⲛⲏⲩ ⲁⲛⲛⲉ ⲉⲣⲁⲧⲟⲩ ⲛⲛϩⲉⲗ
ⲗⲏⲛ ⲛⲣⲉϥϣⲙϣⲉⲉⲓⲇⲱⲗⲟⲛ ⲉⲣⲁⲧⲟⲩ ⲛⲛϩⲁⲓⲣⲉⲧⲓⲕⲟⲥ ⲙⲛⲟⲩⲟⲛ ⲛⲓⲙ ⲉⲧⲡⲟⲣⲝ ⲉⲃⲟⲗ ⲛⲧⲕⲁⲑⲟⲗⲓⲕⲏ
ⲉⲛⲕⲗⲏⲥⲓⲁ ⲉⲣⲁⲧⲟⲩ ⲛⲛⲓⲟⲩⲇⲁⲓ ⲛⲧⲁⲩⲥⲧⲟⲩ ⲙⲡⲉⲭ̄ⲥ̄ ⲙⲛⲟⲩⲟⲛ ⲛⲓⲙ ⲛⲧⲁⲩⲝⲓϣⲟⲕⲛⲉ ⲉϩⲟⲩⲛ ⲉⲣⲟϥ
ⲝⲓⲛⲛ̄ϣⲟⲣⲡ

ⲉⲡⲁⲓ ⲡⲉⲧⲛⲁⲝⲟⲟϥ ϩⲛⲟⲩⲥⲓϣⲉ ϩⲛⲧⲃⲁⲥⲁⲛⲟⲥ ⲙⲡⲕⲱϩⲧ ⲙⲡⲛϭⲓⲛⲧ ⲉⲧⲣⲱⲕϩ ⲙⲡⲉⲧⲛⲥⲱⲙⲁ
ⲙⲛⲧⲉⲧⲛⲯⲩⲭⲏ ⲙⲙⲁⲗⲁⲥⲟⲥ ⲁⲩⲱ ⲉⲧⲝⲓⲕⲃⲁ ⲛⲧⲉⲧⲛⲯⲩⲭⲏ ⲙⲙⲡⲉⲧⲛⲥⲱⲙⲁ ⲉⲁⲙⲡⲉⲧⲉⲧⲛⲝⲓ ⲉⲃⲟⲗ
ϩⲙⲡⲉϥⲥⲛⲟϥ ⲡⲉⲭ̄ⲥ̄ ⲓ̄ⲥ̄ ⲱ ⲛⲣⲉϥⲛⲕⲟⲧⲕ ⲙⲛϩⲟⲟⲩⲧ ⲁⲧⲥⲧⲓⲣⲟⲩⲁ ⲛⲟⲩⲱⲧ ⲙⲙⲡⲇⲓⲁⲃⲟⲗⲟⲥ ϩⲛϩⲉⲛⲝⲏⲣ
ⲉⲩⲧⲟⲟⲙⲉ ⲉⲣⲱⲧⲛ ⲁⲛ ⲁⲩⲱ ϩⲛϩⲉⲛⲥⲡⲁⲧⲁⲗⲁ ⲛⲛⲟⲩⲧⲛ ⲁⲛⲛⲉ ⲉⲁϥⲙⲉϩⲡⲉⲧⲛϩⲏⲧ ⲁϥⲡⲟⲟⲛⲉϥ ⲁⲩⲱ
ⲁϥⲥⲉⲣⲙⲡⲉⲧⲛⲟⲩⲓ.

---

[1] This passage has a marked resemblance to that from
SHENOUTE's *Didascalia* in CRUM, *Copt Ostraca*, no 13
[2] On the title occurring in the Cairo fragment, *v* Brit
Mus. Catal no. 213
[3] 'My holy father' also in the Leyden fragment
(p. 333)

72 [36].—Parchment, 6 complete leaves, now 32½ × 24½ cm   Pp T̄λ̄Θ T̄Z̄. 2 cols,
36 lines, pricked down middle of leaf   Script *cf* CIASCA xxv, though there the letters
are heavier and closer   Initials moderately enlarged, accompanied by small floral scrolls
in red and green   By the scribe of Brit Mus Catal no 257 and a number of leaves in
Paris (*v op cit*), of which 132¹ 56 at least seems related in contents to ours   *V.* also
FORBES ROBINSON, *Copt Apocr Gosp*, xxii

From a Homily, apparently upon the Virgin or the Birth of Christ   Mary is likened
to Gideon's fleece, to a well-watered land whence the rod of Jesse springs   Joseph
renounced all worldly possessions to obtain Mary ¹   She is a pearl in the midst of other
jewels, in a meadow girt about by the sea, the fish in which live all at peace   When
the pearl's time is fulfilled, it joins that other pearl which lies below the water in its
shell ⲝⲉⲕ, and together they mount up and illuminate the field and trees   The pearl in
the meadow is now named ⲁⲭⲁⲧⲏⲥ, according to the reckoning ⲛⲱⲱⲛ of its time, which
is 1110, that is, 1000 and 100 and 10   Now 100 is 10 times 10 ⲙⲏⲧ ⲙⲙⲏⲧ, and this is
Jesus, for He is ⲙⲏⲧ (truth) ²   On the road to Jerusalem, Mary brings forth her child
in a wayside tomb and lays him in a manger   Joseph calls in Salome, the midwife,
who forthwith proclaims the virgin-birth. The very flesh which Jesus had from Mary
shall sit on the Father's right   For Him who bade the earth be the μήτρα of all men
did the Virgin suffer in childbirth   The magi forsake their magic and bring gifts   Herod
thinks they come to seek John the Baptist, whom, being unable to find, he slays
Zacharias   The latter is secretly buried, none see his blood   The weeping of Rachel
(Matt ii 18) is explained by the story of an Israelite mother's bereavement in Egypt
There was joy in all the world at Christ's birth, he reopened to men the gates of Paradise
and took in the soul of Abel, so that his blood, which still cried out, might be silenced.
The phoenix, burnt upon the altar, rises on the third day as a worm from the ashes, grows,
again puts forth wings and every 500 years returns to the temple and altar (*sic expl*)

FORBES ROBINSON, *l c*, xxiii 196, 235, has translated considerable passages of the
text and noticed its relations to the *Protevangelium* &c

.

73.—Parchment, a fragment, 19½ × 25 cm   2 cols   Script *cf* HYVERNAT xii 2
Initials &c red

Homily (?) relating here to the Virgin's conception (Luke i 39 ff)   The following
occur —

[ⲉⲓ]ϣⲁⲛⲉⲙⲙⲉ ⲝⲉⲁⲧⲁⲥⲣⲏⲕ ⲱⲱ ⲧⲉⲛⲧⲁⲛⲥⲱⲛⲧ ⲛⲛⲉϩⲓⲟⲙⲉ ⲟⲩⲉ ⲙⲙⲟⲥ ⲉⲓⲉ ϯⲛⲁⲡⲓⲥⲧⲉⲩⲉ ⲝⲉⲁⲛⲟⲕ
ϩⲱ ϯⲛⲁⲱⲱ ⲭⲱⲣⲓⲥ ⲥⲩⲛⲟⲩⲥⲓⲁ ϯⲛⲁⲟⲙⲙⲥⲙ ϩⲛⲛⲁⲟⲓⲝ ⲉⲧⲛⲁⲗⲁϩⲏ ⲛⲧⲁⲥⲣⲏⲕ ⲧⲁⲛⲁⲩ ⲝ[ⲉⲁ.]ⲟⲥⲟⲉ ³
ⲛⲛϩⲏ[ⲧ]ϭ ⲃ]ⲱⲣⲉ ⲉⲃⲟⲗ [ⲧⲁ]ⲛⲁⲩ ⲉⲛⲉⲕⲓⲃⲉ ⲛⲧⲁⲩⲱⲥⲕ ⲛⲁⲧⲧⲥⲛⲕⲟ ⲙⲛⲛⲥⲁⲡⲉⲓⲭⲣⲟⲛⲟⲥ ⲉⲁⲩⲙⲟⲩϩ ⲛⲉⲣⲱⲧⲉ
ⲛϯⲛⲁⲕⲁⲧⲟⲟⲧ ⲉ[ⲃⲟⲗ

ⲛⲧⲉⲣⲉⲓⲱϩⲁⲛⲛⲏⲥ ⲛⲁⲩ [ⲉ]ⲧⲙⲁⲁⲩ ⲙⲡⲉϥ[ⲝⲟ]ⲉⲓⲥ ⲁⲥⲉⲓ ⲉⲣⲁⲧ[ⲥ ⲛ]ⲧⲉϥⲙⲁⲁⲩ ⲁϥ[ϣⲧⲟⲣ]ⲧⲣ ⲉⲧⲉⲓ
ⲉϥϩ[ⲛⲟⲏ] ⲁϥⲥⲕⲓⲣⲧ[ⲁ

---

¹ *Cf* Matt xiii 45
² For this obsolete word *cf* ERMAN, *Aeg Zeitschr*,
1883, 96, 1895, 49, also Leyden Catal 459   The play

upon the word here should show that the writer was an
Egyptian
³ ⲡⲗⲟⲅⲟⲥ seems unsuitable

ⲛⲧⲉⲣⲉⲙⲁⲣⲓⲁ ⲗⲟⲓⲡⲟⲛ ⲁⲥⲡⲁⲍⲉ ⲛⲉⲗⲓⲥⲁⲃⲉⲧ ⲁⲥⲙⲟⲩϩ ⲉⲃⲟⲗ ϩⲙⲡⲉⲡⲛⲁ ⲉⲧⲟⲩⲁⲁⲃ ⲡⲉⲡⲛⲁ ⲉⲧⲟⲩ-
ⲛⲟⲃϣⲁ ⲙⲙⲁⲣⲓⲁ ⲛⲧⲟϥ ⲡⲉⲛⲧⲁϥⲙⲟⲩϩ ⲛⲉⲗⲓⲥⲁⲃⲉⲧ |ⲟⲩ|ⲡⲛⲁ ⲉϥⲟⲩⲁⲁⲃ |ⲛ|ⲥϥⲛⲟⲩϥⲉ

ⲧⲥⲁⲣⲝ ⲙⲡⲗⲟⲅⲟⲥ ⲧⲁⲓ ⲉⲧⲟ ⲛⲟⲩⲁ ⲛⲟⲩⲱⲧ ⲙⲛⲧⲙⲛⲧⲛⲟⲩⲧⲉ ⲡⲛⲉϩ ⲛⲧⲁⲩⲥⲟⲧϥ ⲉⲣⲟⲥⲧⲉ ⲧϭⲟⲙ
ⲙⲡⲉⲡⲛⲁ ⲉⲧⲟⲩⲁⲁⲃ.

74.—Papyrus, a fragment; 11 × 15½ cm   Script   *cf* Brit Mus Catal, Pll 9, no 279,
and 10, no 967   2 cols.

Homily (?), relating here to Christ's conception and birth, on the 27th of Epiphi
The following phrases can be read   ]ⲣⲛ ⲉϥⲣⲁϣⲉ ⲁⲩⲱ ⲉϥⲣⲟⲟⲩⲧ ⲡⲉⲝⲁϥ ⲛⲁⲥ ⲝⲉⲭⲁⲓⲣⲉ
ⲧⲉⲛⲧⲁⲥϭⲛϩⲙⲟⲧ ⲡⲝⲟⲉⲓⲥ ⲛⲙⲙⲉ ⲭⲁⲓⲣⲉ ⲧⲣⲣⲱ ⲁⲩⲱ ⲧⲙⲁⲁⲩ [. .] ⲛⲣⲣⲟ[

]ⲁⲩⲱ ⲡⲉϩⲟⲟⲩ ⲛⲧⲁⲥⲝⲡⲟϥ ⲛϩⲏⲧϥⲡⲉ ⲥⲟⲩⲝⲟⲩⲧⲥⲁϣϥⲉ ⲙⲡⲉⲃⲟⲧ ⲉⲡⲏⲡ ⲕⲁⲧⲁ ⲟⲉ ⲝⲉϥⲟ ⲛⲛ[

75.—Parchment, a complete leaf, 13 × 14 cm   Script   *cf* Hyvernat x   1 col.

Homily (?), relating here to Christ's birth and baptism and to our redemption thereby
The baptism by John is narrated, with incidents of attendant angels and of waters in
awe receding   The heavenly voice says 'This is my beloved son, in whom my will
hath been fulfilled   Obey ye him'

Begins]ⲛⲁⲣ̄ ⲉⲧⲟⲩⲁⲁⲃ ⲙⲁⲣⲓⲁ ⲁⲥⲝⲡⲟϥ ⲛⲁⲛ ⲉϩⲣⲁⲓ ⲉⲝⲙⲡⲕⲁϩ.   Ends ⲙⲁⲣⲉⲛϥⲓ ⲉⲃⲟⲗ ϩⲙ[

76.—Papyrus, a fragment, 9½ × 13 cm.   Script· *cf* Ciasca vii for certain features
Homily (?)[1], commenting on the narrative of Christ's Passion.

]ⲥⲛⲟϥ ⲧⲁⲓ ⲟⲩⲛⲧⲉ ⲧⲉϯⲁ ⲛⲧⲁⲡⲉⲭ̄ⲥ̄ ⲝⲟⲟⲥ ⲝⲉϥⲟⲃⲉ ⲉⲧⲃⲏⲛⲧⲉ ϩⲙⲡⲉⲥϥⲟⲥ · ⲛⲧⲉⲣⲉⲛⲓⲟⲩⲇⲁⲓ
ⲉⲧⲙⲡⲕⲱⲧⲉ ⲙⲡⲉⲥϥⲟⲥ ⲥⲱⲧⲙ ⲝⲉϥⲟⲃⲉ ⲁⲩⲱ ⲉⲡⲉⲁⲩⲛⲁⲩ ⲙⲙⲁⲧⲟⲓ [

]ϩⲙⲝ ⲉϩⲟⲩⲛ ⲉⲧⲁⲧⲁⲡⲣⲟ ⲝⲉⲉⲓⲛⲁϭⲛⲁⲡⲟⲗⲟⲅⲓⲁ ⲛϫⲱ ⲙⲡⲉϩⲟⲟⲩ ⲙⲡⲥⲏⲩ ⲉⲓⲛⲏⲩ ϩⲙⲡϩⲁⲉ
ⲛϩⲟⲟⲩ ⲁⲓⲧⲁⲙⲟⲟⲩ ⲅⲁⲣ ⲙⲡⲁⲧⲟⲩⲧⲁⲗⲟⲓ ⲉⲡⲉⲥϥⲟⲥ ⲝⲉϯ[

] blood.   This then is the reason (αἰτία) why Christ said, 'I thirst,' upon the cross
When the Jews that were around the cross heard (the words) 'I thirst,' and had beheld
the soldiers [

] vinegar into my mouth, that I may (?) find cause (ἀπολογία) to give, on that day,
in the time when I come in the last day   For I told them, ere I was raised upon the cross,
that I [

77.—Parchment, a fragment, 23 × 22 cm   Pp ⲅ̄, ⲝ̄.   2 cols   Script   hand of Brit.
Mus Catal no 230[2]

Homily, here quoting the Beatitudes (Matt. v 4 ff) and admonishing to piety, charity
and other virtues

---

[1] The 1st pers sing in the second passage suggests a text like that in Revillout's *Apocr. Coptes, Patr. Or* II 163
[2] *Cf. ib*, p 519·

78.—Papyrus, a fragment, 14½ × 11 cm　　Script *recto*, rounded, upright uncials, *verso*, sloping, ligatureless　Fibres on *recto* →

Recto　Greek text, treating of doctrinal (Christological) questions

т]ω πρῑ ειηαι |] αγτογ τοιϲ ктι |] ⲅⲥ̄ ϵκ τω πρῑ |]ⲩ ⲑϵⲟⲧⲏⲥ ⲉⲇⲏ | ҟⲁ⳿ ⲁⲩⲧⲟⲥ
т |]ⲏⲏⲧϵ[

Verso　Coptic text, on similar subjects

] ⲉⲡⲉϩⲟⲩⲟ ⲙ[|] ⲛⲥⲙⲟⲧ ⲛⲛⲉⲧϫⲓ ⲉϩⲟⲩⲛ ⲉϩ[| ϩⲛⲟⲩⲙⲉ ⲡⲉⲛⲧⲁⲩϫⲡⲟϥ[| ⲉⲣⲉⲡⲁⲓ ⲡⲏϣ ⲁⲛ ⲛⲥⲉⲛ[| ⲛϭⲓ ⲧϭⲓⲛϫⲟⲟⲥ ⲕⲁⲧⲁ [ⲧ]ϥⲫⲱⲛⲏ [|]ⲡϫⲟⲉ]ⲓⲥ ϩⲙⲡⲧⲣⲉϥϣⲱⲡⲉ ⲛⲥⲁⲣ̄ⲝ[|]ⲁϥ ⲁⲛⲟⲛ ⲛⲉⲧⲙⲛⲣ ⲁⲩⲱ[|]ⲛ-
ⲡⲏⲩⲥ (ⲧⲟⲩⲧⲉⲥⲧⲓⲛ erased) ϩⲓⲧ[|]ⲉⲧⲣⲛⲉⲧⲟⲩⲏⲩ ⲉⲃⲟⲗ ⲉ[|]ⲁⲧⲙⲛⲧⲟⲩⲁ ⲡⲉⲧⲟⲩⲑⲉⲱⲣ[ⲉⲓ ⲙⲙⲟϥ

79.—Papyrus, a fragment, 4½ × 18½ cm　　Script sloping uncials, *cf* HYVERNAT x
Homily (?), here relating to Susanna and the elders

Fibres →]ϫⲟⲩⲧⲁϥⲧⲉ ⲛ... ⲛⲣⲱ.... ⲙⲁⲣⲓⲛⲁⲩ ⲟⲛ | ϫⲉⲟⲩ ⲡⲉⲛⲧⲁϥϣⲱⲡⲉ ⲛⲛⲉⲡⲣⲉⲥⲃⲩⲧⲉⲣⲟⲥ
ⲥⲛⲁⲩ | ⲉⲧϩⲛⲧⲃⲁⲃⲩⲗⲱⲛ ϩⲙⲡⲧⲣⲉⲩⲉⲡⲓⲑⲩⲙⲓ ⲥⲥⲟⲩⲥⲁⲛ[ⲛⲁ] | ϩⲁ...[....ⲛ]ⲛⲟⲧⲕ ⲛⲉⲙⲁⲥ ⲁⲡⲛⲟⲩⲧⲉ |

Fibres ↑. ⲛ]ⲧⲟⲕ ⲇⲉ ϩⲱⲱⲕ ⲥⲉⲙⲟⲩϩ ⲛⲙⲟⲕ ⲁⲩⲱ ⲭⲱⲣⲓⲥ ⲡⲁ... | ⲟⲩⲛ ⲟⲩⲛⲟϭ ⲛϫⲁⲥⲙ ⲁϣ
... ⲛⲧⲁⲕⲙⲛ.ⲛ ⲥⲙⲛⲧⲓ | ϫⲉⲕⲁⲁⲥ ⲉϥ..ⲛⲟⲩ..... . ϣⲁⲛϩⲁϩ | ⲛ ⲛϥⲧⲉⲙϭⲙϭⲟⲙ....[|
..]ⲝⲛⲧⲓⲧⲣⲁⲡⲓⲍⲁ ⲥⲧ[

80.—Papyrus, a fragment, 11½ × 11 cm　　Script small, few ligatures　Fibres on *recto* (?) ↑

A collection of Aphorisms, mostly from Solomon or Sirach, but with extra-biblical additions.　One quotes 'a philosopher'

+ ⲉⲓⲟ ⲉⲓⲛⲁⲩ [1] ⲉⲡⲁⲥⲉⲃⲏⲥ ⲉϥϫⲓⲥⲉ[ⲙⲙⲟϥ | ⲛⲑⲉ ⲛⲡⲕⲉⲇⲣⲟⲥ ⲉⲡⲗⲓⲃⲁⲛⲟⲥ ⲁⲓ[ⲥⲁⲧϥ | ⲁⲃⲱϫⲉⲛ
ⲛⲡⲉⲓϭⲛⲧϥ ⲁⲓϣⲓⲛⲉ [....] 　　　 ⲛⲁ[... | + ⲁⲩϫⲓⲛⲟⲩ ⲟⲩⲫⲩⲗⲟⲥⲟⲫⲟⲥ ϫⲉⲟⲩⲡⲉ ⲡ | ⲧⲁϩⲟ
ⲉⲣⲁⲧϥ ⲥⲛⲟⲩⲡⲟⲗⲓⲥ ⲡⲉϫⲁϥ ϫⲉ | ϩⲟⲧⲁⲛ ⲧⲉ ⲉⲣϣⲁⲛⲛⲉⲕⲟⲩⲓ ⲥⲱⲧⲙ | ⲉⲓⲁⲛⲛⲟϭ ⲁⲩⲱ ⲛⲧⲛⲛⲟϭ
ϩⲁⲣⲉϩ ⲉⲧⲣⲟⲧ[ⲉ | ⲛⲡϫⲟⲉⲓⲥ ⲡⲁⲛϫⲱⲥ ⲥⲛⲁϣⲱⲡⲉ ⲉⲥⲧⲁⲭⲣⲏⲩ | + ⲥⲟⲗⲟⲙⲱⲛ ⲁϥⲛⲱⲧ ⲉⲛⲟⲩϩⲓ ⲁⲗⲗⲁ
ⲙⲉⲡⲉⲛ | ⲉⲧϫⲟⲥⲉ ⲟⲩⲱϩ ϩⲛⲧⲁⲙⲓⲟ ⲛϭⲓϫ ⲕⲁⲧⲁ ⲧ|ϩⲉ ⲉⲧⲥⲏϩ [2] ϫⲉⲡⲉⲧⲉ ⲡⲁⲑⲣⲟⲛⲟⲥ ⲁⲩⲱ ⲡⲕⲁϩⲡⲉ |
ⲡⲥ ⲡⲅⲩⲡⲟⲡⲟⲧⲓⲟⲛ ⲉⲛⲁⲩⲉⲣ⳿ⲏⲧ|ⲉ +

Verso (other direction) + ⲡⲁϣⲏⲣⲉ ⲥⲱⲧⲙ ⲉⲥⲁⲧⲁⲥⲃⲱ ⲛⲡⲉⲣⲧⲁⲛ | ϩⲟⲧⲕ [3] ⲙⲛⲥⲁⲣⲉϩ ⲛⲓⲙ
ⲉϫⲱ ⲛⲡⲉⲛⲙⲛⲥⲧⲏⲣ[ⲓ | 　　　 ⲟⲛ ⲉⲣⲟϥ | + ϣⲁⲣⲉⲡⲉⲧⲓ [4] ϩⲉⲛⲟⲩϩⲱⲡ ⲕⲧⲟ ⲉⲃⲟⲗ | ⲉϩⲉⲛⲱⲣⲏⲛ ϣⲁⲣⲉ-
ϩⲉⲛϩⲱⲣⲟⲛ [5] ϣⲱⲃ | ⲛⲉⲃⲁⲗ ⲉⲛⲉⲣⲱⲟⲩ 　　　 | + ⲛⲡⲉⲣⲉⲣϣⲃⲏⲣ ⲉⲛⲧⲓϩⲉ ϫⲛⲛⲉⲧⲉⲧ[.]| 　　　 ⲛⲥⲟⲩ-
ⲥⲱⲃⲉ ⲛⲥⲱ[ⲕ | + ⲟⲩϩⲙⲕⲉ [6] ⲛϫⲁⲥⲓϩⲏⲧ ⲙⲛⲟⲩⲣⲉⲙⲙ[ⲁⲟ | ⲡⲣⲉϥϫⲓⲛϭⲟⲛⲥ ⲡϫⲟⲉⲓⲥ ⲙⲟⲥⲧⲉ ⲛⲙ[ⲟⲟⲩ] |

81.—Papyrus, a fragment, 4½ × 9½ cm　　Script sloping semi uncials　Fibres on *recto* ↑.

Festal Epistle (?)　This is made likely by the phrase 'as the time . .. (we ?)

---

[1] Ps xxxvi 35　　　[2] Isa lxvi 1　　　[4] Prov xxi 14　　　[5] *Cf* ? Eccli viii 2
[3] Eccli xxxiii 21 (xxx 29)　This, with the same addi-　　[6] *Cf* Eccli xxv 2
tion, in Berlin *Aeg Urk*, Kopt no 32, § 50

approach the Feast of the Resurrection,' by the literary script and by the text being
confined to one side of the leaf[1].

]ⲁⲩⲱ ⲛ̄ϥⲛ . . . ϩⲣⲁⲓ [|] ⲁⲩⲱ ϩⲙ̄ⲛⲧⲣⲉⲡⲉⲩⲟⲉⲓϣ ⲓ[| ϩⲱ]ⲛ ⲉϩⲟⲩⲛ ⲉⲡϣⲁ ⲛ̄ⲧⲁⲛⲁⲥⲧⲁ[ⲥⲓⲥ |
]ⲣⲡⲙⲉⲉⲩⲉ ⲙⲡⲉⲟⲟⲩ ⲡⲙ[

Verso blank.

82.—Papyrus, a fragment, 8 × 15 cm   Script *cf* ZOEGA's 9th class for some features.
1 col

Festal Epistle (?, *cf*. no 81) with a quotation from the 2nd λόγος of 'Gregory, the
most saintly bishop[2]'

]ⲅⲉⲛⲛⲭⲉⲓⲣⲓ ⲅⲁⲣ ⲉϥⲓ ⲙⲙⲁⲩ ⲛ[,   ]ⲛⲡⲉⲟⲟⲩ ϩⲓⲧⲛⲛⲉⲡⲉⲟⲟⲩ[,   ]ⲣⲟϥ ⲛⲛⲉϩⲓⲟⲟⲩⲉ
ⲉⲧⲥⲟⲩⲧⲱ[ⲛ,   ]ⲉⲣⲏⲅⲟⲣⲓⲟⲥ ⲡϩⲁⲅⲓⲱⲧⲁⲧⲟⲥ ⲛⲉ[ⲡⲓⲥⲕⲟⲡⲟⲥ,   ]ϩⲙ̄ⲙⲉϩⲥⲛⲁⲩ ⲛ̄ⲗⲟⲅⲟⲥ ⲛ̄ⲧⲁ[,
]ⲛⲁⲕ ⲛⲛⲉⲧⲉⲣⲉⲡⲗⲟⲅⲟⲥ ϣⲡϩⲓⲥⲉ ⲛϩⲏ[ⲧⲟⲩ

Verso blank

83.—Papyrus; a fragment, 11 × 40 cm   Script . slightly sloping uncials, *cf* HYVER-
NAT x   Fibres on *recto* ↑

Festal Epistle (?, *cf* no. 81), treating here of doctrinal questions (the character and
relations of the persons of the Trinity)

]ϩ ⲉϩⲟ[ⲩⲛ |] ⲛⲁⲧⲭⲡⲟϥ [|] ⲁⲭⲛ̄ⲭⲣⲟⲛⲟⲥ ⲁⲩⲱ ϩⲁⲑⲏ[| ⲉ]ⲓⲱⲧ ⲁⲭⲛ̄ⲭⲣⲟⲛⲟⲥ ⲁⲩⲱ ϩⲁⲑⲏ
. . . . . ⲃ ϩⲛⲟⲩϩⲉ ⲛⲁⲧⲧⲁⲩⲟ ⲙⲉⲣⲉⲡⲉⲓⲱⲧ ⲅⲁⲣ ⲡⲱⲱⲛⲉ ⲉⲛ[|]ⲣϣⲏⲣⲉ ⲏ ⲙ̄ⲡⲛ̄ⲁ̄ ⲉ[ⲧⲟ]ⲩⲁⲁⲃ . .
ⲡ[ϣ]ⲏⲣⲉ ⲙⲉϥⲡⲱⲱⲛⲉ ⲉⲧⲟⲓⲡⲣⲉⲓⲱⲧ ⲏ ⲙ̄ⲡⲛ̄ⲁ̄ ⲉϥⲟⲩⲁⲁⲃ [|] ⲡⲉⲡⲛ̄ⲁ̄ ⲉϥⲟⲩⲁⲁⲃ ⲙⲉϥ[ⲡ]ⲱⲱⲛⲉ .
ⲁ[ⲧⲙ]ⲛ̄ⲧϩⲓⲁⲓⲟⲧⲏⲥ ⲙ̄ⲡⲉⲓⲱⲧ ⲏ ⲡϣⲏⲣⲉ ⲁϥϣⲟⲟⲡ ⲅⲁⲣ ⲛⲁⲧ[| ⲡⲱ]ⲱⲛⲉ ⲛϭⲓ ⲛϩⲓⲁⲓⲟⲧⲏⲥ . ⲭⲁⲣ . .
. . . ⲛ̄ⲧⲟⲩⲉⲓ ⲧⲟⲩⲉⲓ ⲛ̄ⲛⲉⲩⲡⲟⲥⲧⲁⲥⲓⲥ ⲁⲩⲱ ⲉⲩⲡⲟⲣϫ ⲁⲛ ⲉⲧⲙⲛ̄ⲧ |]ϭ ⲛ̄ⲧⲟⲩⲥⲓⲁ ⲧⲉⲧⲣⲓⲁ[ⲥ ⲅ]ⲁⲣ
ⲉⲧ[about 16 let] ⲛⲁⲧⲥⲟⲛⲧⲉ ϣⲁⲩϫⲛ̄ⲛⲉ . . ⲧ ⲙⲙⲟⲥ ϩⲛⲛ[

Verso blank.

---

[1] The only Festal Letter extant in the original, GRENFELL-
HUNT, *Gk Pap* II. 163 = *New Palaeogr Soc*, Pt 3, pl 48,
is written thus.

[2] I have not found the words here visible in the 2nd
Oration of Gregory Nazianzene

NARRATIVES, ACTS, MARTYRDOMS

84—Parchment, a fragment, $5 \times 13\frac{1}{2}$ cm 2 cols Script small, square uncials, ⲁ, ⲙ, ⲩ each in a single stroke as in Brit Mus Catal, Pl 8, no 171

Adam and Eve From the apocryphon *ed* TISCHENDORF, *Apocal Apocr*, 1866, 'Apocr Mosis,' §§ 31, 32 (beg ἡ πόσον χρόνον), but with considerable differences[1]

Recto

```
              ]ⲁ
[.  ]ⲉ ⲧⲛⲁⲣⲏⲉ
[ⲟ]ⲩⲏⲣ ⲛⲣⲟⲙⲡⲉ
[ⲉ']ⲟⲛϩ ⲙⲡⲣϩⲉⲡ
[ⲡ]ϩⲱⲃ ⲉⲣⲟⲓ ⲡⲁ
[ⲝ]ⲟⲉⲓⲥ ⲁⲇⲁⲙ
[ⲡ]ⲥⲱⲧⲡ ⲛⲧⲉ
[ⲡ]ⲛⲟⲩⲧⲉ · ⲧⲟ
[ⲧⲉ ⲁ]ⲇⲁⲙ ⲡⲉ
[ⲝⲁϥ] ⲛⲉⲩϩⲁ ⲝⲉ
```

```
[  ]ϥ ⲛϭⲓ ⲁⲇⲁⲙ
ⲡⲉⲝⲁϥ ⲝⲉⲉⲓϣⲁ̄
ⲙⲟⲩ ⲙⲡⲣ[ⲝ]ⲱϩ
ⲉⲣⲟⲓ ⲙⲡⲁⲙⲁ
ⲛⲁⲙⲁ ϣⲁⲛⲧⲉ
ⲡⲝⲟⲉⲓⲥ ⲧⲛⲛⲟ
ⲟⲩ ⲛϥ́ϣⲁⲝⲉ ⲛⲙ
ⲙⲏⲧⲛ ⲉⲧⲃⲏ
ⲛⲧ ⲛϥⲛⲁⲟⲃϣϥ
ⲅⲁⲣ ⲁⲛ ⲉⲣⲟⲓ · ⲁⲗ
ⲗⲁ ϥⲛⲁϣⲓⲛⲉ ⲛ
```

Verso   ]? ?

```
ⲧⲁⲙⲟ[2] ⲉⲣⲟⲓ ⲝⲉⲛ
ⲧⲥⲟⲟⲩⲛ ⲁⲛ ⲛ
ⲑⲉ ⲉⲧⲛⲁⲁⲡⲁⲛ
ⲧⲁ ⲙⲙⲟⲥ ⲉⲡⲁⲉⲥ
ⲡⲟⲧⲏⲥ ⲙⲡⲧⲏ
ⲣϥ ⲝⲉⲛⲉϥⲛⲁ
ⲁⲡⲓⲗⲓ ⲛⲁⲓ ⲛϭⲓ
ⲡⲛⲟⲩⲧⲉ ⲝⲉⲛ
ⲛⲉϥⲛⲁⲛⲁ ϩⲁⲣⲟⲓ
ⲧⲟⲧⲉ ⲁⲥⲧⲱⲟⲩⲛ
```

```
ⲣ . . ⲙ . [
ⲛⲁ ⲙⲛⲧⲙⲛ[ⲧ]
ⲛⲟϭ ⲧ ⲙⲉⲧ[ⲁ]
ⲛⲟⲓⲁ ⲛⲁⲓ ⲝⲥⲁ[ⲓ]
ⲡⲁⲣⲁⲃⲁ ⲙⲡ[ⲉⲕ]
ⲙⲧⲟ ⲉⲃⲟⲗ · ⲧ[ⲧⲱ]
ⲃϩ ⲙⲙⲟⲕ ⲡⲉⲓ̈ⲱⲧ]
ⲛⲣⲉϥϣⲁⲛϩⲧⲏϥ ⲧ]
ⲙⲉⲧⲁⲛⲟⲓⲁ ⲛⲁⲓ]
```

] how many more years I have to live Hide not the thing from me, my lord Adam, elect of God' Then Adam said unto Eve [

] Adam He said, 'When I die, touch me not in my place, until the Lord send and speak with you (*pl*) concerning me For He will not forget me, but will seek [

] gave it (?) me For I know not the manner of my meeting with the ruler (δεσπότης) of all, whether God will threaten (ἀπελεῖν) me or whether He will have mercy on me' Then [Eve] arose [

] mercy (?) and greatness Give me repentance (μετάνοια), for I have transgressed (παραβαίνειν) before Thee I beseech Thee, merciful father (?), give me repentance [

---

[1] The fragment Berlin *Kopt Urk*, no 181, is also from an Adam apocalypse   [2] Perhaps ⲧⲁⲁⲥ?

85 [25].—From the *earlier* texts of the palimpsest no. 62, which see

Fol. 5   From the same MS as foll 1–3   Pp [ᴋ̄ᴀ], ᴋ̄ʙ̄   Of fol *a* much is illegible or uncertain, while the beginnings or ends of many lines are hidden by the present binding   The text relates a legend of the building of Solomon's temple   Thabôr, king of the gentiles (ἔθνος), appears to meditate war with him, but hearing at night the noise of the spirits (δαιμόνιον) whom Solomon was forcing to build for him, he is terrified and realizes that for such an adversary he is no match, he would be trampled down like the potter's clay   At the end of the fragment is a reference to the δεκανοί.

I have failed to find any trace of such a story. The name Thabôr might suggest the well-known Thamur-Shamir-Sachr[1]; but the legends have apparently no common element except the temple building

P [ᴋ̄ᴀ]		
] . . . coλo	. . . . . aγnoxoγ	
[ʍω]n πρρo ʙнᴋ	eʙoλ ϩaϩтʍn . .	
]ꙇ eꙇeтᴋoꙇ	ʍперпe · aγω	
]ꙇ · πρρo	ϩennoϭ nϩʙнoγe	
[ө]aʙωp ϩωωϥ	naɯɯoγ aγ	
]aтoϥ ϩnoγ	ɯωπe ϩꙇтптa	
]нᴋoтᴋ ʍ	ɯн нꙇɯнe нтaγ	
[п]ʙoλ aγω	noxoγ eʙoλ ϩωc	
[aϥ]ʍoᴋʍeᴋ ʍ	xe eтperпᴋaϩ нꙇʍ	
[ʍoϥ] нϭꙇ өaʙωp	eʍaтe · нтe	
[πρρ]o xeᴀꙇϭꙇ	peϥcωтʍ epooγ н	
]пeoγoeꙇɯ	ϭꙇ өaʙωp πρρo	
p]пoλeʍoc ʍn	aϥɯтopтp eʍa	
[coλo]ʍωn πρρo	тe aγω aϥнeϩcc	
]нeϥxopʍ	ʍπρρo coλoʍωn	
[ʍп]нꙇ ʍнꙇxoeꙇc	пexaϥ наϥ xe	
]c xe ϯнaрпo	пacon coλoʍωn	
[λeʍ]oc нʍʍaϥ	oγпe пeꙇϩpooγ ʍn	
]нaтacтpeп	нeꙇϭ[oʍ] нтaγɯω	
]ʍнтepo	пe · aрнϥ epe	
]ꙇ xeeϥxopʍ ϩн	пнaϩ ʍп . . .	
]т xeϥнaр	ϭωʙe ʍпecнaγ	
[пo]λeʍoc ʍнco	aπρρo coλoʍωn	
[λo]ʍωn · eꙇc	ϭωʙe пexaϥ xe	
[нᴅ]aʍoнꙇoн тн	ʍʍoн пacon ʍ	
[poγ] · aγeꙇ eγ · тп	πρρϩoтe eнᴋoтᴋ	
	(sic) наᴋ	

[1] *V* M Grünbaum, *Neue Beiträge* 288 and in *ZDMG* xxxi 204, also Singer in *Z für deutsches Alterium* xxxv 183

Ρ κ̄β̄.

πειϫοογτ ⲛ̄ⲁⲓ	ⲟⲩⲉ ⲛ̄ϭⲓ ⲑⲁⲃ[ⲱⲣ]
ⲙⲟⲛⲓⲟⲛ ⲛⲉⲛⲧⲁⲩ	ⲡⲣⲣⲟ ⲛ̄ⲛϩⲉ[ⲑⲛⲟⲥ]
ⲉⲓ ⲉⲩⲑⲓⲧ ⲛⲱⲛⲉ	ⲁϥⲃⲱⲕ ⲉϩⲣⲁ[ⲓ ⲉⲛ]
ⲁⲩⲛⲟϫⲟⲩ ⲉⲃⲟⲗ ϧⲁϧ	ⲛⲓ ⲁⲩⲱ[
ⲧⲛ̄ⲛ̄ϫⲟⲓ ⲙⲡⲛⲓ	ⲟⲩⲱϩ ⲉⲧⲟⲟ[ⲧϥ ⲉ]
ⲙⲡ̄ϫⲟⲉⲓⲥ ⲉⲧⲟⲩ	ϣⲓⲛⲉ ⲛ ⲉϩⲟ[ⲣϧⲉⲧ]
ⲕⲱⲧ ⲙ̄ⲙⲟϥ ·	ⲏ ⲉϣⲟϫⲛⲉ ⲉϥϫⲱ ⲙ̄]
ⲛ̄ⲧⲉⲣⲉϥⲥⲱⲧⲙ ⲉⲛⲁⲓ	ⲙⲟⲥ ⲙ̄ⲛ̄ⲡⲣ[ⲣⲟ ⲥⲟ]
ⲛ̄ϭⲓ ⲑⲁⲃⲱⲣ ⲡⲣⲣⲟ	ⲗⲟⲙⲱⲛ · [
ⲛ̄ⲛϩⲉⲑⲛⲟⲥ ⲁϥ	ⲑⲟⲧⲉ ⲛ̄ⲛⲉⲛ[
ϣⲧⲟⲣⲧⲣ ⲉⲙⲁⲧⲉ ⲉϥ	ϩⲩⲡⲟⲧⲁⲥⲥⲉ[ⲛⲁϥ]
ϫⲱ ⲙ̄ⲙⲟⲥ ϧⲙ̄ⲡⲉϥϩⲏⲧ	ⲁⲥϣⲱⲡⲉ ⲇⲉ ⲛ̄ⲧⲉ]
ϫⲉⲉϣϫⲉⲁϥⲧⲣⲉⲛ	ⲣⲉⲡⲣⲣⲟ ⲥⲟⲗ[ⲟⲙⲱⲛ]
ⲇⲁⲓⲙⲟⲛⲓⲟⲛ ⲉⲣⲣ	ⲉⲓ ⲉϩⲣⲁⲓ ⲉⲧⲙ[ⲉϩ]
ⲧ̄ⲁⲥⲓⲁ ⲁⲩϣⲉⲧ ⲱ	ⲅⲏ¹ ⲛ̄ⲣⲟⲙⲡ[ⲉ
ⲡⲉ ⲉⲡⲕⲱⲧ ⲙ̄ⲡⲏⲓ	ⲕⲱⲧ ⲉⲡⲏ[ⲓ ⲙ̄]
ⲙ̄ⲡϫⲟⲉⲓⲥ ⲉⲓⲉ ⲁⲛⲕ	ⲡϫⲟⲉⲓⲥ ⲁ[ⲅⲁⲣ]
ⲛⲓⲙ ⲁⲛⲟⲕ ϫⲉⲉⲓⲉⲣ	ϫⲉⲓ ⲛ̄ϭⲓ ⲛ̄ⲇⲁⲓ[ⲙⲟⲛⲓ]
ⲡⲟⲗⲉⲙⲟⲥ ⲛⲙⲙⲁϥ	ⲟⲛ ⲉⲧⲣⲉⲩⲗ[ⲟ ⲉⲩⲣ]
ϥⲛⲁⲕⲉⲗⲉⲩⲉ ⲛ̄ⲥⲉⲣⲓ	ϩⲱⲃ ⲉⲡⲏⲓ [ⲙ̄ⲡⲛⲟⲩ]
ⲕⲉ ⲉⲃⲟⲗ ⲉϫⲱⲓ ⲙ̄ⲛ	ⲧⲉ ⲁϩⲟⲓⲛ[ⲉ
ⲡⲁⲙⲏⲏϣⲉ ⲛ̄ⲥⲉ	ⲡⲱⲧ ⲛ̄ⲧⲟⲟⲧ[
ⲕⲁⲧⲁⲡⲁⲧⲉⲓ ⲙ̄ⲙⲟⲓ	ⲛ̄ⲛⲁⲉⲕⲁⲛⲟ[ⲥ ⲛ̄ⲛⲁϩ]
ⲛⲟⲥ ⲙ̄ⲡⲟⲙⲉ ⲙⲡⲕⲉ	ⲣⲙⲡⲣⲣⲟ ⲥⲟ[ⲗⲟ]
ⲣⲁⲙⲉⲩⲥ ⲛ̄ⲧⲉ	ⲙⲱⲛ ⲁⲩ[
ⲣⲉϥⲅⲱⲟⲩⲛ ⲇⲉ ⲉϩⲧⲟ	ⲉⲧⲉⲣⲛⲙⲟⲥ [ⲁⲩ]
	ϣⲱⲡⲉ ⲙⲛ[ⲁⲩ]

86.—Papyrus , a complete leaf, $28\frac{1}{2} \times 17\frac{1}{2}$ cm   Script *cf* Brit Mus Catal , Pl 8, 171, Pl 10, 967, Rossi, *I Papiri* II iv, Tav II   2 cols, *ca.* 22 lines   Initials not enlarged Ink brown.   Fibres on *recto* ↑

An apocryphal narrative, probably prefatory to an apocalypse[2]   Whether the twelve apostles are addressed by Christ, or the seventy two disciples, is doubtful.

ⲁⲡⲟⲥ]ⲧⲟⲗⲟⲥ ϫⲓⲛⲡⲉϩⲟⲟⲩ ⲛ̄ⲧⲁϥⲥⲟⲧⲡⲟⲩ ⲛⲁϥ ⲙ̄ⲙⲁⲑⲏⲧⲏⲥ ⲉϥϫⲱ ⲙ̄ⲙⲟⲥ ϫⲉⲉⲓⲥ ϩⲏⲏⲧⲉ ⲁⲓⲥⲉⲡ-
ⲑⲏⲩⲧⲛ ⲛⲁⲓ ⲙ̄ⲙⲁⲑⲏⲧⲏⲥ ⲉⲃⲟⲗ ϩⲛ̄ⲧⲉϣϥⲥⲛⲟⲟⲩⲥ ⲛ̄ⲭⲱⲣⲁ ⲁⲓⲙⲟⲩⲧⲉ ⲉⲣⲱⲧⲛ ϫⲉⲛⲁⲥⲛⲏⲩ ⲁⲩⲱ
ⲡⲁⲕⲗⲏⲣⲟⲛⲟⲙⲟⲥ ⲉⲧⲧⲁⲓⲏⲩ ⲧⲉⲛⲟⲩ ⲇⲉ ϩⲱⲃ ⲛⲓⲙ ⲉⲧⲉⲧⲛⲁϣⲓⲛⲉ ⲛ̄ⲥⲱϥ ⲉⲃⲟⲗ ϩⲓⲧⲟⲟⲧ ⲉⲧⲃⲉⲡⲟⲩⲱϣ
ⲛ̄ⲛⲁⲓⲱⲛ ⲧⲏⲣⲟⲩ ⲙ̄ⲡⲧⲁϩⲟ ⲉⲣⲁⲁⲧϥ ⲛ̄ⲛⲉⲕⲕⲗⲏⲥⲓⲁ ⲧⲏⲣⲟⲩ ⲙ̄ⲡⲧⲁϣⲉⲟⲉⲓϣ ⲛ̄ⲧⲁⲛⲁⲥⲧⲁⲥⲓⲥ ⲉⲧⲟⲩⲁⲁⲃ
ⲙ̄ⲡⲧⲁϩⲟ ⲉⲣⲁⲁⲧϥ ⲛ̄ⲧⲟⲓⲕⲟⲩⲙⲉⲛⲏ ⲧⲏⲣⲥ ⲙ̄ⲡⲧⲱϣ ⲙ̄ⲡⲃⲁⲡⲧⲓ[ⲥ]ⲙⲁ ⲙ̄ⲡⲛ̄.ⲅⲝ . . . ϫ ⲉⲧⲃⲉⲡ-
ϩⲉⲑⲛⲟⲥ] ⲧⲏⲣⲟⲩ ⲉⲃⲟ[ⲗ] ϫⲉⲟⲩⲛⲟⲩⲙ[ⲏ]ⲛϣⲉ ϣⲓϣ[ⲉ] ⲛ̄ⲛⲉⲓⲱⲗ[ⲟⲛ] ⲙ̄ⲡⲉⲟⲩⲟⲉⲓϣ ⲉⲧⲙⲙⲁⲩ · ⲧⲉⲛⲟⲩ
ⲇⲉ ϣⲓⲛⲉ ⲛ̄ⲥⲁϩⲱⲃ ⲛⲓⲙ ⲁⲩⲱ (*verso*) ϯⲛⲁⲟⲩⲟⲛϩⲟⲩ ⲉⲣⲱⲧⲛ ϩⲛ[ⲟ]ⲩⲣⲁϣⲉ ⲉⲃⲟⲗ ϫⲉⲛ̄ⲧⲱⲧⲛⲡⲉ

---

¹ Perhaps = ϯ̄ⲉ (*cf* 1 Kings vi 38)   ² *Cf* phrases *e g* in *Mém de l'Inst franç. au Caire* ix. 100 (LACAU)

ⲛⲉⲡⲓⲧⲣⲟⲡⲟⲥ ⲛⲧⲉϣϥⲉⲥⲛⲟⲟⲩ ⲛⲭⲱⲣⲁ ⲉⲣϣⲁⲛⲟⲩⲁ [ϩⲉ] ⲉⲃⲟⲗ ϩⲛⲛⲁⲉⲥⲟⲟⲩ ⲛⲁⲓ ⲁⲛⲟⲕ ⲛⲧⲁⲓϯ
ⲙⲡⲁⲥⲛⲟϥ ϩⲁⲣⲟⲟⲩ ϯⲛⲁϣⲓⲛⲉ ⲛⲥⲱϥ ⲉⲃⲟⲗ ϩⲓⲧⲟⲟⲧⲧⲏⲩⲧⲛ ϣⲓⲛⲉ ϩⲙⲡⲉⲧⲛϩⲏⲧ ⲧⲏⲣϥ ⲁⲩⲱ ϯⲛⲁⲟⲩⲟⲛϩⲟⲩ ⲉⲣⲱⲧⲛ ⲧⲏⲣⲟⲩ · ⲧⲁⲡⲓⲑⲉ ⲙⲡⲉⲧⲛϩⲏⲧ ⲉⲩϩⲏⲩ ⲙⲡⲕⲟⲥⲙⲟⲥ ⲧⲏⲣϥ ⲉⲃⲟⲗ ϫⲉⲛⲧⲱⲧⲛ ⲙⲛ-
ⲙⲓⲭⲁⲏⲗ ⲙⲛⲅⲁⲃⲣⲓⲏⲗ · ⲛⲁⲥⲱⲧⲡ ⲛⲁⲣⲭⲁⲅⲅⲉⲗⲟⲥ ⲛⲧⲱⲧⲛⲉ ⲛϭⲁⲓϣⲓⲛⲉ ⲛⲟⲩⲟⲛ ⲛⲓⲙ ⲛⲧⲁⲩ-
ⲡⲓⲥⲧⲉⲩⲉ ⲉⲣⲟⲓ ⲙⲛⲡⲁⲙⲟⲩ ⲙⲛⲧⲁⲁⲛⲁⲥⲧⲁⲥⲓⲥ ⲉⲧⲟⲩⲁⲁⲃ · ⲛⲁⲡⲟⲥⲧⲟⲗⲟⲥ ⲇⲉ ⲛⲧⲉⲣⲟⲩⲥⲱⲧⲙ ⲉⲛⲁⲓ
ϩⲓⲣⲱϥ ⲙⲡϣⲏⲣⲉ ⲙⲡⲛⲟⲩⲧⲉ ⲁⲩⲣⲁϣⲉ ⲉⲙⲁⲧⲉ ⲁⲩⲱ ⲁⲩⲣϣⲡⲏⲣⲉ ϫⲉ[

] apostles, from the day when He chose them for Himself as disciples (μαθητής),
saying, 'Lo, I have chosen you for myself as disciples from the 72 regions (χώρα) and
I have called you my brethren and my honoured heirs (κληρονόμος) So now everything
that ye shall ask of me, regarding the desire of all the ages (αἰών) and the establishment
of all the churches (ἐκκλησία) and the preaching of the holy resurrection (ἀνάστασις) and
the establishment of all the world (οἰκουμένη) and the ordinance of baptism and the . .
on behalf of all the gentiles (ἔθνος)—for there was a multitude of idolaters at that time—
so now enquire concerning all things and (verso) I will reveal them unto you gladly,
for ye are entrusted with (ἐπίτροπος) the 72 regions (χώρα) If one fall from among my
sheep, those for whom I gave my blood, I will seek him at your hands Enquire with
all your heart and I will reveal them all unto you and will incline (πείθειν) your heart
toward the benefit of the whole world (κόσμος) For ye, with Michael and Gabriel, my
chosen archangels, ye are the messengers to every one that hath believed (πιστεύειν) on
me and my death and my holy resurrection (ἀνάστασις)'

But (δέ) the apostles, when they had heard these (words) at the mouth of the Son of
God, rejoiced greatly and marvelled that [

87 [29].—Parchment, 4 complete leaves, now 32×23 cm. 2 cols, 32 or 33 lines
Pp. ⲡⲉ-ⲍ̄ Script . cf CIASCA v, though there the letters are smaller and more regular
Initials enlarged and, with the letter ⲫ, coloured red From same MS as ZOEGA
no cxxxii, Brit Mus no 287, Leyden no 51, Berlin, Kgl Bibliothek, Or 1607, ff 1, 2
(ⲙⲉ, ⲕ̄, ⲣ̄ⲟ, ⲣ̄ⲓ), Paris 129¹⁷ 85-87 (ⲣⲙⲉ-ⲣⲛⲃ̄, —, —)

Andrew the Apostle, Acts of[1]. Published by Guidi, Acc dei Linc, Rendic III,
2° sem , 368, and translated by him, Soc Asiat Ital, Giorn II 22 The corresponding
Arabic text is in A S LEWIS, Hor Semit III 3, IV 2, the Ethiopic in BUDGE, The
Contendings &c, I 141, II 164.

88—Parchment, a fragment, 5×31 cm Palimpsest, from the upper part of a double
fol (I) 2 cols Script cf CIASCA xvi, (II) at right-angles to preceding. Script of
ZOEGA's 9th class

[1] On the localities of Andrew's preaching, v Brit Mus
Catal no 297 and Paris Vol 129¹⁸ 88, where the text of
his martyrdom begins 'After A had gone to preach
among the Scythians ⲛⲉⲥⲕⲏⲑⲏⲥ and to ⲟⲣⲧⲓⲁⲕⲟⲥ and

ⲥⲁⲕⲕⲟⲥ, those wicked cities ,' with which cf BUDGE,
l c , I 184, LEWIS, l c, p 26, and LIPSIUS, Apokr Apost I
621 &c

(I) Acts, wherein Jesus and John (the apostle ?) play a part. The sequence of *rectos* and *versos* is uncertain There are probably some 25 lines missing from each column

Fol *a*   Recto.   *Verso*

ϩⲟⲟⲩ ⲉⲧ[ⲙⲙⲁⲩ]   ⲡⲛ̅ⲁ̅ ⲉⲧⲟⲩ

ⲁⲩⲱ ⲛⲧⲉ[ⲣⲉⲓⲱ]   [ⲁⲁϥ ⲁϥⲉⲓⲱ]ⲣⲙ ⲉⲝⲱϥ

ϩⲁⲛⲛⲏⲥ [   ] . . ⲣⲱⲙⲉ

Fol *b*   Recto

ⲝⲉⲧϭⲟⲙ ⲙⲡⲛⲟⲩ   ⲟⲩⲱϣ .[1][ⲁⲟⲕⲓ]

ⲧⲉ ⲝⲟⲟⲣ ⲉϩⲱⲃ ⲛⲓⲙ   ⲙⲁⲍⲥ ⲙⲙⲟϥ ⲁϥ

ⲁⲩⲱ ⲛⲧⲉⲩⲛⲟⲩ ⲁϥ   ⲁⲙⲁϩⲧⲉ ⲛⲧⲉϥϭⲓⲝ

ⲛ ⲧⲉϥϭⲓⲝ ⲉⲡⲉⲥⲏⲧ   ⲁϥⲃⲱⲕ ⲉϩⲣⲁⲓ ⲉ

        ⲩ]ⲧⲏⲛ   ⲝⲛⲧⲣⲟϩⲧⲉ ·

Verso

[ⲙⲙⲟ]ⲥ ⲝⲉⲙⲛⲛⲟⲩ   ⲙⲁϩⲧⲉ ⲛⲩⲟⲙⲛⲧ

ⲩⲁⲝⲉ ⲛⲟⲩⲱⲧ   ⲙⲙⲁⲣ ⲛⲥⲟⲣⲉⲧ ⲁϥ

ⲁⲛ ⲡⲉⲛⲧⲁⲓⲝⲟⲟϥ   ⲥⲟⲛⲟⲩ[2] ⲉϩⲣⲁⲓ ϩⲛ

ⲉⲣⲟⲛ ⲓ̅ⲥ̅ ·ⲁⲉ ⲁϥ   ⲧⲣⲟϩⲧⲉ ⲁⲡⲥⲁϩ

ϩ[ⲙ]ⲟⲟⲥ ⲉⲝⲛⲧⲣⲟϩ   ϭⲱⲩⲧ[

[ⲧⲉ

Fol *a*   ] that day   And when John had [

          ] Holy Spirit (?), he looked (?) upon him [   ] man [

Fol *b*, *ro*   ] saying, 'The power of God is mightier than all', and forthwith he brought

               his hand down [   ] garment [

               he] wished to prove him and he seized his hand and went down to the

               caldron   [

       vo   ] saying, 'Not (?) one word did I say unto thee'   But Jesus sat down (?)

               by the caldron [

              ] took three girths of wool and drew them through (?) the caldron; and

              the teacher looked [

For the other text, *v* below

89 [25]—From the *earlier* texts of the palimpsest no 62, which see

Fol 6   From the same MS as fol 4 (*v* no 90)

Probably from an Encomium on St Michael (*cf* no 90). Dionysius the Areopagite is the narrator, and tells of St Paul's visit to Athens, the earthquake and a vision of the archangel   On Dionysius *v* von LEMM in *Bull de l'Ac imp* , vᵉ ser , xii, and AMÉLINEAU, *Contes* I 1, which deals with the same events

---

        [1] Apparently a straight letter, not ⲉ   [2] Altered from ⲥⲟⲛⲕ.

Fol *a*]ογ ηταϥ ηογcμογ μηογεγχαριcτια μπαρχαггελοc μιχαηλ ετвеηсоλ
μηηεϣηιρε ηταγϣωπε ϩμπεϥτοποc ετογααв εαιηαγ ερооγ ϩηηαвλ εαγϣωπε εвоλ
ϩιταμηογτε εαϥεηερμει ηϩαϩ ηϣηιρε жιηϣορπ ϩιτοотϥ μπεϥηоб ηαρχαггελоc
μιχαηλ αcϣωπε ϫε ϩμπεογоειϣ ηταηθεcπιcιоc αγω ηϩιεрoc ηαпоcтолоc пcαϩ παγλоc
ει εϩογη ε[αθηη]ναιc αϥταϣεоειϣ ηϩητε μπκηργημα μπογжαι εвоλ жετπоλιc ετμμαγ
ηεcλовε ϩηταμητρεϥϣμϣε ειδωλоη επεϩογo ηεγηϩεμμαноc ηϩнтε μηϩεηϥεγτопро-
φнтнc εγπλαηα ηηιρωμε ηναвоλ μпεхc̄ αγжωηει ηcαππμακαριоc παγλоc αϥει εвоλ
ϩηαθнннιαιc τпоλιc αϥϩопϥ ηϩεηκоγι ηϩооγ αηок жε ϫιоηнcιоc αικотк ητεγϣн
(fol. *b*)]εвоλ ϩμπα[3½ lines illegible] ηтоογ ηεнταγαγμιоγрγει ηηεноб ηϩвнγε тпе
μηпκαϩ μηнεφωcтнр μηηϣнн μηηϩαλαατε μηнεογрιоη μηηжατϥε μηнтвноογе
θαλαccα μηнειερωоγ μηнιпγcн μμоογ εвоλ жμпεογоειϣ ετμμαγ ηεμπαιεπcooγн
μπηογτε рογоειη ερопε αλλα ηειоμε ϩωпε ϩηταμητρελλнη αλλα [5 lines illegible]
ϩηκооγε εγαϩερατоγ εμεγεϣμoоc εμεγμоγτε ϩητεγϣогωве μηπ̄н̄ᾱ гαρ ϩηρωоγ
ετι жε εμcoκμεκ επαι ϩιжμπαμαηηκотк αγω ειμελετα μμоογ αϥϩαϩερατϥ ϩιжωι ηбι
оγрωμε ηогоειη μπεcμот ηоγcτρατопεταρхнc ηcεηнαιоc εϥcоoλε ϩηoγλιпоπнϩоη [1]
εϥμнр ηоγμохϩ ϥн[

90 [25].—From the *earlier* texts of the palimpsest no 62, which see

Fol. 4 *a*, illegible, fol *b* has part of the story of the conversion of Matthew, the scribe, attributed to Severus of Antioch (*V.* BUDGE, *St Michael* 86, AMÉLINEAU, *Contes* I 103)

пεже пρρo ηαϥ жεπαειωτ μπλααγ ηακωλγ μμок ϩμпογωϣ тнρϥ μπεκϩнт пεпιcкопоc ϫε αϥcωρ εвоλ ηтεηте μптопоc ερεπατпоλιc тнрc рαϣε ημμαϥ αϥжокϥ εвоλ
ϩμπηгαιε ηιμ αγω αϥϯ μπεϥλωвϣ μпϩoγη ηϣμoγη ηεвот ηϩooγ αϥϩαπαже μμоϥ
ϩηcoγμητcηooγc μпεвот αθωр αγω αϥμoγте επтопоc μпραη μμιχαηλ παρχαггελоc
ερεπατпоλιc тнрc cooγϩ εγρϣα μпαρх. μιχαηλ εγϣooп тнрoγ ηбι μμнηϣε ϩηoγ-
oγрот жεαγρμпϣα μπαρхαггελоc μιχαηλ ηϥϣωпε ϩнтεγпоλιc απϣα μπαρх
μιχαηλ ϣωпε εϥo ηαιπλоγη ηϣα μпεϥαϩо ερατϥ ετιαειηγ αγω ηϣα μпραμιαcμоc
μпεϥтопоc ετогααв μηнcαηαι αιωϩαηηнc пεпιcкопоc ϣαже μпηρρo εϥжω μμоc

91 [26].—Parchment, 8 complete leaves; now 31 × 21½ cm Pp μ̄ε̄-ϥ̄, being quire ϫ̄
2 col, *ca* 26 lines Script. *cf* CIASCA XXII Initials moderately enlarged and coloured
red, marginal ornaments red, green and yellow From same MS as Brit Mus no 334,
ZOEGA clii, Paris Vol 129[16] 82, 83 and Cairo no 8023 (= *Rec de Trav* IV 154)

St George, Miracles of Published by BUDGE, *St George of Cappadocia*, 1888,
p 190 ff

---

[1] On this word *v. Proc. Soc Bibl. Arch.* XXVI 61.

92 [27+44].—Parchment[1]; 4 complete leaves, now 30½×22½ cm　Pp π̄ϭ-ϥ̄, the proper order of the leaves being no 27 1, 2, no 44, no 27 3　2 cols, *ca* 30 lines Script *v.* CIASCA XIII, though there the character is rather thicker.　Initials, marginal ornaments &c in red　From same MS as Paris Vol 129[16] 49-54, Vol 131[5] 61

Ptolemy ⲡⲧⲉⲗⲉⲙⲏ, Martyrdom of　Published by ROSSI, *I Papiri .. di Torino* I, v 49, from a copy of Schwartze.

Ptolemy was 18 years old and the son of Nestorius, a citizen (πολιτευόμενος) of Nekintôre (Denderah[2]) in the Thebais　His teachers were Papnoute of Pboou and Dorotheus, who had urged him to martyrdom　The *hegemon*, whom he finds at 'Tôhe of the Horses[3],' attempts to win him by mildness, but Ptolemy repels him and is condemned to various tortures　The 24th Hathor is mentioned as the date of his trial　The last of the above Paris leaves relates to the miracles at his τόπος[4]　Rossi has published (*l c* 45) fragments of the martyrdom, under Diocletian, of a saint of the same name, whose day is the 11th Kihak and who occurs[5] in Abū 'l-Barakāt's calendar (Paris MS. arabe 203). According to AMÉLINEAU, *Les Actes* 198, these two are identical　ⲡⲧⲟⲗⲟⲙⲉ son of the Eparch is in the list of martyrs in HYVERNAT, *Actes* 100　Paul and Ptolemy are martyrs in Berlin, *Aeg Urk*, Kopt 183　To some one of these a church at Ishnîn was dedicated (Abū Sâlih 91 *a*)

93.—For description *v* no 61

(1) *a*. S Mercurius, Miracles of[6]　*E.g.* ϯⲛⲁⲧⲁⲙⲱⲧⲛ ⲱ ⲡⲗⲁⲟⲥ ⲙⲙⲁⲓⲛⲟⲩⲧⲉ ⲉⲕⲉⲛⲟϭ ⲛϣⲡⲏⲣⲉ ⲛⲧⲁⲥϣⲱⲡⲉ ⲉⲃⲟⲗ ϩⲓⲧⲟⲟⲧϥ ⲙⲡⲣⲁⲅⲓⲟⲥ ⲙ ⲡⲥⲧⲣⲁⲧⲏⲗⲁⲧⲏⲥ · ⲛⲉⲩⲛⲟⲩⲛⲣⲉⲥⲃⲏⲧⲉⲣⲟⲥ ⲁⲉ ϩⲙⲡⲧⲟⲡⲟⲥ ⲙⲡⲣⲁⲅⲓⲟⲥ ⲙ. ⲡⲁⲓ ⲁⲉ ⲉⲛⲉⲁϥⲁⲓⲁⲓ ϩⲛⲛⲉϩⲣⲟⲟⲩ ⲁⲩⲱ ⲛⲉⲟⲩⲥⲟⲫⲟⲥⲡⲉ ⲕⲁⲧⲁ ⲡⲓⲕⲟⲥⲙⲟⲥ ⲁⲩⲱ ⲉⲣⲉ[

94 [33+45].—Parchment, 8 complete leaves and one slightly damaged, now 32½×25 cm　Pp —, —, —, — (last of quire ⲍ̄), —, —, ϥ̄ⲑ-ⲣ̄ⲓ̄.　2 cols, 34 ruled lines Script *cf* CIASCA I and XIII　Initials slightly enlarged and accompanied by small scroll ornaments in red and green　From same MS as Brit Mus no 348 and by the scribe of Paris Vol 130[5]. 121 and Clarendon Press no 29

Sebaste, Forty Martyrs of[7]　The proper order of the leaves is no 33, foll 3 *b a*, 1 *a b* (=pp ϥ̄ⲍ̄, ϥ̄ⲍ̄), 2 *a b* (=pp. ϥ̄ⲏ̄, ϥ̄ⲑ̄), no 45 = pp ϥ̄ⲑ̄-ⲣ̄ⲓ̄.

---

[1] On p π̄ⲍ̄ a pencil note says this MS was given by Mr Leider (*v* Brit Mus no 924)

[2] *V* AMÉLINEAU, *Geogr* 140

[3] A ⲧⲱϩⲉ occurs in *Rec de Trav* xi 134, *Rev Eg* ix 168, in a graffito near Denderah, where a martyr Pt is also named, and in one of the present papyri (*v* Index)

[4] *Cf* Paris MS. arabe 150, 6

[5] As الطّلبا, of which the Ethiop ⲁⲧⲢⲘⲎ: is a misreading　This calendar has other Ptolemies on Babeh 13 and Tubeh 19

[6] *V Synaxarium*, 14th and 25th Hathor, Paris MS arabe 263.　Fourteen of his miracles ⲇⲟⲙ are referred to in Leyden *MSS*, p 436

[7] Paris 129[16] 77 relates to these martyrs.

The Encomium of which this is a part is not identical with any published text. The writer mentions (p. p̄ⲅ̄) his 'first encomium' on the subject[1]. A *terminus a quo* for the time of composition is the quotation (p p̄ⲁ̄) from Severus of Antioch (*ob* 538) The following is the text of 33, fol 3 —

ⲣ̄ⲕ] ⲧⲟⲟⲧⲏ ⲉⲣⲟϥ ⲉⲁⲁϥ ⲟⲩⲛⲟⲩⲛ ⲡⲧⲟⲟⲩ ⲛⲉⲧⲁⲣⲭⲉⲓ ⲥⲟⲉⲥⲧⲱⲣⲓⲁ ⲁⲛⲟⲕ ϩⲱ ⲉⲓⲟⲩⲉϩ ⲛⲥⲱⲟⲩ
ⲉⲓⲥⲁ ⲃⲉⲗⲃⲓⲗⲉ ϩⲓⲡⲁϩⲟⲩ ⲙⲙⲟⲟⲩ ⲕⲁⲧⲁ ⲑⲉ ⲟⲛ ⲛⲧⲁⲩⲟⲩⲉⲣⲥⲁϩⲛⲉ ⲛⲁⲓ ϩⲙⲡⲉⲩϣⲟⲣⲡ ⲛⲉⲛⲕⲱ-
ⲙⲓⲟⲛ · ⲉⲁⲛⲉⲓⲙⲉⲥⲉ ⲧⲉⲛⲟⲩ ⲱ ⲛⲁⲙⲉⲣⲁⲧⲉ ϫⲉⲛⲉⲡⲉⲧⲟⲩⲁⲁⲃ ⲛⲉⲧⲛⲁϣⲱⲡⲉ ⲛⲁⲣⲭⲏⲅⲟⲥ ⲁⲩⲱ ⲛⲥⲱⲧⲏⲣ
ⲉⲡⲉⲩⲉⲥⲕⲱⲙⲓⲟⲛ · ⲙⲁⲣⲓⲥⲱⲧⲙ ϩⲛⲟⲩⲡⲓⲥⲧⲓⲥ ⲁϫⲛⲁⲓⲥⲧⲁⲍⲉ ⲉⲛⲥⲱϣⲧ ⲁⲛ ⲉⲡⲉⲛϣⲁϫⲉ ⲛⲉⲗⲁⲭⲓⲥⲧⲟⲛ
ⲟⲩⲗⲁⲭⲓⲥⲧⲟⲛ ⲅⲁⲣⲡⲉ ⲙⲙⲡⲉϥⲛⲉϣⲁϫⲉ · ⲁⲗⲗⲁ ϩⲛⲟⲩⲙⲉ[ⲡⲓⲥⲧⲉⲩⲉ ϫⲉⲛⲉⲡⲉⲧⲟⲩⲁⲁⲃ ⲛⲉⲧⲛⲁϣⲱⲡⲉ
ⲛⲁⲣⲭⲏⲅⲟⲥ ⲁⲩⲱ ⲛⲥⲱⲧⲏⲣ ⲉⲡⲉⲩⲉⲥⲕⲱⲙⲓⲟⲛ ⲙ[ⲁⲣⲓⲥ]ⲱⲧⲙ ϩⲛⲟⲩⲡⲓⲥⲧⲓⲥ ⲁϫⲛⲁⲓⲥ[ⲧⲁⲍⲉ] ϫⲉⲛⲉⲓⲡⲉ
[(col 2)-ⲧⲟⲩⲁⲁⲃ, 8 lines lost]ⲉⲩⲫⲣⲁⲛⲉ · [. .] ϩⲁⲙⲡϣⲟⲩϣⲟⲩ ⲁⲛ · ⲧⲁⲓⲧⲉ ⲑⲉ ⲥⲛⲱⲡ ⲙⲡⲉⲧϣⲁϫⲉ
ϫⲉⲁⲅⲅⲓⲟⲛ ⲁⲩⲱ ⲛⲉⲡⲉⲧⲟⲩⲁⲁⲃ ⲙⲙⲁⲣⲧⲩⲣⲟⲥ ⲡⲉⲧϣⲁϫⲉ ϫⲉⲡⲏⲣⲡ ⲡⲉⲧⲉⲩⲫⲣⲁⲛⲉ ⲙⲡϩⲏⲧ ⲙⲡⲣⲱⲙⲉ[2]
ⲟⲩⲛⲟⲩⲛ ⲛⲉⲧⲛⲁⲁⲣⲭⲉⲓ ⲉⲡⲥⲱⲣ ⲉⲃⲟⲗ ⲙⲡⲉⲓⲗⲟⲅⲟⲥ ⲏ ⲡⲉⲓⲉⲥⲕⲱⲙⲓⲟⲛ ⲙⲁⲣⲓⲙⲉⲉⲩⲉ ⲉⲃⲟⲗ ϫⲉⲟⲩ-
ⲕⲓⲛⲁⲅⲛⲟⲥ ⲛⲁϣ ⲛϭⲟⲧ ⲡⲉⲧⲧⲁϩⲟ ⲙⲙⲟⲛ · ⲉⲛϣⲁⲛⲧⲁⲗⲁ ⲡⲉⲛϩⲏⲧ ⲉϩⲟⲩⲛ ⲉⲓⲥⲱⲧⲙ ϩⲛⲟⲩⲱⲣⲝ ⲛϭⲉ
ⲉⲣⲟⲥ ⲉⲣⲉⲙⲙⲁⲣⲧⲩⲣⲟⲥ ⲙⲉⲛ ϩⲱⲅⲣⲁⲫⲉⲓ ⲛⲁⲛ ⲁⲩⲱ ⲁⲩⲧⲁϩⲟ ⲉⲣⲟⲛ ⲛⲏ[(ϯ 3 a) 8 lines · ⲁⲥϣ]ⲱⲡⲉ
ϩⲙⲡ[ⲛⲁⲓ]ⲣⲟⲥ ⲙⲡⲁⲓⲱⲧⲙⲟⲥ ⲉⲣⲉⲡⲁⲓⲁⲃⲟⲗⲟⲥ ⲧⲟⲩⲛⲟⲩⲥ ⲛⲟⲩⲛⲟϭ ⲛϭⲓⲙⲱⲛ ⲉϫⲛⲧⲉⲕⲕⲗⲏⲥⲓⲁ ⲁⲛⲣ-
ⲣⲱⲟⲩ ⲙⲡⲁⲣⲁⲛⲟⲙⲟⲥ ϩⲙⲡⲕⲁⲓⲣⲟⲥ ⲉⲧⲙⲙⲁⲩ ϫⲟⲟⲩ ⲛϭⲉⲡⲁⲣⲭⲱⲛ ⲡⲟⲩⲁⲓⲣⲏⲛⲧ ⲕⲁⲧⲁ ⲡⲟⲗⲓⲥ
ⲉⲛⲟⲗⲁⲍⲉ ⲛⲟⲩⲟⲛ ⲛⲓⲙ ⲉⲧⲛⲁϩⲟⲙⲟⲗⲟⲅⲉⲓ ⲙⲡⲣⲁⲛ ⲙⲡⲉⲭ̄ⲥ̄ · ⲉⲁⲛⲁⲣⲭⲱⲛ ⲉⲧⲙⲙⲁⲩ ⲥⲃⲧⲉ ⲛⲕⲟⲗⲁⲥ-
ⲧⲏⲣⲓⲟⲛ ⲉⲩϣⲟⲃⲉ ⲉⲛⲉⲩⲉⲣⲏⲩ ϩⲓⲧⲙⲡϣⲟϫⲛⲉ ⲙⲡⲉⲧϩⲓⲡⲟⲃⲁⲗⲉ ⲛⲁⲩ ⲡⲁⲓⲁⲃⲟⲗⲟⲥ ⲉⲩⲡⲉϣⲗϭⲡⲉ ⲛⲁⲩ
ⲉⲣⲟⲟⲩ ⲉⲩⲕⲏ ⲉϩⲣⲏⲓ ϩⲁⲣⲱⲟⲩ ⲙⲙⲓⲛ ⲙⲙⲟⲟⲩ ⲙ[ⲁ]ⲗ[ⲓⲥⲧⲁ] ⲥⲧⲁⲗⲉ letters ⲉϩⲣⲁⲓ ⲉϫⲱⲟⲩ
ⲁⲩⲙⲙⲛ ⲟⲩⲧⲣⲟⲭⲟⲥ ⲙⲡⲉⲛⲓⲛⲉ ⲙⲡⲉⲥⲙⲟⲧ ⲙⲡⲥⲉⲗϭⲓⲗ ⲙⲡⲣⲟⲓ ⲉⲣⲉⲛⲗⲉϩⲗⲱϭⲉ ⲛⲧⲟⲩⲉⲓⲣⲉ ⲁϣⲉ ⲉⲣⲟϥ
ⲁⲩⲱ ⲛⲉϣⲁⲣⲉⲡⲉⲧⲙⲙⲁⲩ ϫⲧⲉ ⲡⲣⲱⲙⲉ ⲉϫⲙⲡⲛⲟⲧ ⲉⲧⲙⲙⲁⲩ ⲉϫⲛⲧⲉϥϫⲓⲥⲉ ⲉⲩⲥⲱⲕ ⲙⲙⲟϥ ⲉⲡⲁϩⲟⲩ
ⲉϫⲙⲡⲕⲟⲧ ϣⲁⲛⲧⲉϥⲁⲡⲉ ϭⲱⲗϫ ⲉⲛⲉϥϯⲃⲥ[3] · ⲗⲟⲓⲡⲟⲛ ⲛⲥⲉⲡⲉⲣϣⲟⲩⲙⲛⲓϣⲉ ⲛϫⲃⲃⲥ ⲛⲕⲱϩⲧ
ϣⲁⲟⲩⲛⲟϭ ⲛⲛⲟⲩⲉ ϩⲓⲙⲡⲛⲁϩ ⲛⲥⲉⲥⲕⲓⲣⲕⲓⲣⲡⲛⲟⲧ ⲛⲧⲣⲟⲭⲟⲥ ⲙⲡⲛⲣⲱⲙⲉ ⲉⲧⲟⲓⲕⲱϩ ϣⲁⲛⲧⲉⲡⲉϥⲥⲁⲣⲝ
ⲙⲙⲛⲉϥⲕⲉⲉⲥ ϭⲟϫⲉ ⲉϥⲟⲗⲕ ⲛⲥⲁⲡⲁϩⲟⲩ ⲡⲣⲟⲥ ⲡⲕⲱϩⲧ ⲙⲡⲉⲧⲣⲟⲭⲟⲥ · ϩⲟⲙⲁⲓⲟⲥ ϩⲉⲛⲕⲉⲟⲣⲅⲁⲛⲟⲛ
ⲛⲃⲁⲥⲁⲛⲓⲥⲧⲏⲥ ⲟⲛ ⲉⲩⲥⲧⲱⲧⲡ[ⲥ] ⲛⲁⲩ ⲉⲣⲟⲟⲩ ⲙⲁ(f. 1 a)-ⲗⲓⲥⲧⲁ ⲉϫⲓϯⲛⲉ ⲙⲙⲟⲟⲩ ⲧⲟⲧⲉ ⲗⲟⲓⲡⲟⲛ
ⲛⲧⲉⲣⲉⲡⲉϩⲙⲉ ⲙⲙⲁⲧⲟⲓ ⲛⲁⲙⲉ &ⲥ

(*continued*) When the forty soldiers learn that the edict against the Christians has been published, they meet together at the standards (σίγνον) and determine to fight for Christ as they would for their earthly king Candidus, one of their number, moved by God, urges them to go at once to the station of the standards ⲕⲩⲛϩⲏ ⲛⲛⲥⲓⲕⲛⲟⲛ[4]. There all pledge themselves by the golden image of Christ ⲟⲩϩⲓⲕⲱⲛ ⲛⲛⲟⲩϥ ϩⲛⲟⲩⲱϣⲩⲧ ϩⲛⲧⲟ ⲛⲛⲉⲓⲃⲧ to confess Him to the death In the praetorium their comrades try to withhold them, reminding them of their past exploits and of the glory their band (ἀριθμός) has

[1] 'Their encomium,' 33, 3 *b*, means apparently the martyrs themselves
[2] Psalm ciii 15
[3] 'An iron wheel, in the fashion of the water-wheel (?) of the field, with   of   hung thereon And they were wont to lay a man thereon, upon his back, stretching him backward upon the wheel, until his head reached his

heels' With ϭⲉⲗϭⲓⲗ cf ϭⲁⲗⲓⲗ (Brit Mus Catal no 266), also ⲟⲩϭⲗⲓϭ (?) ⲛⲣⲁⲙϣⲉ, BUDGE, *St George* 178=ⲟⲩⲅⲁⲥⲧⲏⲣⲓⲟⲛ, *ib* 9
[4] ⲕⲛϩⲉ, ὥμα in LXX To the instances in *Aeg Zeitschr* 1886 91, add Paris 129¹⁴ 127 (? Severus Ant) brawling priests fetch sticks from ⲧⲕⲛϩⲉ ⲙⲡⲟⲩⲥⲓⲁⲥⲧⲏ-ⲣⲓⲟⲛ.

gained through their valour. (fol 2) But the martyrs push them aside, repeating Christ's
words (Matt v 29, 30) and, presenting themselves to the magistrate (δικαστής), they
loudly proclaim their faith   The magistrate attempts with bribes to dissuade them,
reminding them of the difficulties in their course and of the numbers who have yielded
either to (p ϥⲑ) flattery or threats   They reply that they value only Christ and His faith
(Matt xvi 26), that other gods are but stone and wood, that nothing can turn them from
their purpose and that they are ready for any punishment ⲉⲧⲃⲉⲛⲁⲓ ⲧⲁⲙⲙⲱⲣⲓⲁ ⲉⲧⲣⲁⲛⲁⲕ
ⲁⲡⲟⲫⲁⲛⲉ ⲙⲙⲟⲥ ⲉⲍⲱⲛ ⲙⲛⲑⲉ ⲉⲧⲣⲉⲛⲁⲑⲁⲓⲧⲥⲓ ⲛⲛⲁⲛⲥⲙⲙⲉ ⲛⲧⲁⲛⲥⲙⲛⲧⲟⲩ ⲙⲛⲡⲉⲛⲣⲣⲟ ⲡⲉⲭ̄ⲥ.
The rest of their ἀπολογία consists of *quotations*, Matt xvi 26, Ps lxi 11, Prov xi 4,
Isa xl 6, 7, James i 10, 11, *ib* v 1, 2 and one not identified[1]   In the meantime the
saints are put in prison till the magistrate shall decide on their punishment, and there
Christ appears and greets them with the words of Matt x 22   Next day they are
again brought before the magistrate and condemned to be frozen to death in a lake
near the town ⲟⲩⲗⲓⲙⲛⲏ ϩⲁⲧⲛⲧⲡⲟⲗⲓⲥ ⲉⲣⲉⲡⲉⲭ̄ⲓⲱⲛ ⲙⲛⲡⲉⲭⲣⲏⲥⲧⲁⲗⲗⲟⲥ ϣⲟⲩⲟ ⲉⲍⲱⲥ, where
the cold is such that not only water and oil become as lead ⲧⲁϩⲧϩ[2], but even wine in
its bottles there becomes hard (πήσσειν) like stone   Forthwith the saints cast away
their clothes and hasten to the lake   There, in the freezing night and bitter north wind
ⲉⲣⲉⲧⲕⲉⲡⲛⲟⲛ ⲙⲛⲧⲏⲩ ⲛⲙϩⲓⲧ ⲛⲃⲉ ϩⲛⲟⲩⲥⲓϣⲉ, plunged in the water ⲉⲁⲩⲧⲱⲗⲥ ⲛϩⲏⲧⲥ, they
attempt again to proclaim their faith, but the words are interrupted by the shivering
of their bodies ⲁⲗⲗⲁ ⲛⲉⲣⲉⲛⲟⲩϣⲁⲍⲉ ⲛⲏⲩ ⲉⲃⲟⲗ ϩⲛⲣⲱⲟⲩ ϩⲛⲟⲩⲥⲟⲟⲩⲧⲛ ⲁⲩⲱ ⲛⲉϥⲥⲟⲗⲡ ϩⲓⲧⲉⲩ-
ⲧⲁⲡⲣⲟ ⲕⲁⲧⲁ ⲗⲉⲍⲓⲥ ⲉⲧⲃⲉⲡⲉⲥⲧⲣⲧⲣ ⲙⲡⲉⲩⲥⲱⲙⲁ ⲙⲛⲡⲛⲟⲥⲓⲛ ⲛⲛⲉⲩⲙⲉⲗⲟⲥ, the pain of that frost
penetrating to their marrows ϣⲁⲛⲉⲩⲁⲗⲧⲛⲁⲥ[3].   Who can realize their torture ?   None
can adequately praise (ἐγκωμιάζειν) them, as I said in the προοίμιον of this poor discourse
(λόγος)   I rejoice at the mention of them, as did Severus at the names of Basil and
Gregory, saying, ' If ye will believe me, each time that I mention (ὀνομάζειν) their
names, my soul rejoiceth (εὐφραίνειν) '   I must tell of the bath ⲟⲩϩⲟⲩⲟ ⲉⲣⲟⲙⲉ ϣⲁⲍⲉ ⲉⲣⲟⲥ,
placed near by, as a snare for them, for it seduces one, whereat the rest grieve (1 Cor xii 26),
and their guard (κουβικλάριος) sees 40 angels descending with 40 crowns, yet one returns
heavenward with his   Thereupon declaring himself a Christian, he joins the saints in
the lake, thus being likened to the penitent thief and to the labourer summoned at the
eleventh hour, who received the full wage ⲧⲥⲁⲧⲉⲉⲣⲉ ⲉⲧⲟⲩⲟⲍ   Next day their bodies
are ordered to be burned   One of them, being still alive, is left behind in the hope
that he may recant   But his mother herself, in her zeal ϩⲙⲡⲍⲛⲟⲩϥ ⲙⲡⲉⲥϩⲏⲧ ⲉϩⲟⲩⲛ
ⲉⲛⲛⲟⲩⲧⲉ, though old and weak, seizes and carries him to where the rest are burnt   What
can I add of this woman to what we said in the first encomium ?   True love to God can
bring even forgetfulness of nature, as when Abraham was ready to sacrifice Isaac ⲉⲁϥⲁ-
ⲙⲁϩⲧⲉ ⲛⲧⲥⲁⲣⲧⲉ ⲙⲙⲓⲛ ⲙⲙⲟϥ ⲉⲛⲉⲉⲥ(*read* ⲕⲉⲛⲥ) ⲡⲉϥϣⲏⲣⲉ ⲛⲟⲩⲱⲧ, and did indeed in intention
sacrifice him, for he knew not that God would prevent him, as the wise man (σοφός) saith,

---

[1] ⲟⲩⲉⲡⲣⲱ ⲉⲙⲉⲥⲟⲩⲉⲓⲛⲉⲧⲉ ϫⲉⲉⲕⲛⲁϭ̄ⲱ ⲉⲕⲣⲟⲟⲩⲧ ⲱ
ⲡⲉⲭⲟⲣⲧⲟⲥ ⲛⲛⲉⲕⲣⲟⲟⲩ ⲉⲧⲛⲡ ⲛⲧⲟⲟⲧϥ ⲙⲡⲉⲛⲧⲁϥϫⲟⲕ ⲉⲡⲕⲁϩ
ⲛⲁⲟⲩⲉⲓⲛⲉ ϩⲛⲟⲩϭⲉⲡⲏ ⲁⲩⲱ ⲉⲕⲛⲁϩⲟⲡⲕ ⲉⲧⲱⲛ ⲉϥⲙⲙⲉ
ⲙⲡⲣⲏ ⲙⲛⲡⲕⲁⲓⲣⲟⲥ ⲙⲡϣⲱⲙ, 'It is a winter that passeth
not   For thou shalt cease to flourish, O grass, thy days

that belong unto him that did sow thee on the earth, shall
go by quickly   And where wilt thou hide thee from the
sun's heat and the time of summer?'

[2] For this word *v Aeg Zeitschr* 1883 156

[3] Gen xlv 18 (Paris 43, 196), Job xxi 24   Boh ⲁⲧⲕⲁⲥ.

in recounting (ἱστορίζειν) his life (βίος), or as Jephtha, who made his daughter a sacrifice unto God   To this woman her Isaac was not given back ⲙⲡⲟⲩⲉϩⲙ̅ⲭⲁⲣⲓⲍⲉ ⲛⲁⲥ ⲙⲡⲉⲥⲓⲥⲁⲁⲕ, she must return home comfortless, yet greatly comforted and glad   Should any ask if ever I knew a woman reckoned to the band of martyrs or to the priesthood for offering sacrifice to God, and her sacrifice her own entrails (σπλάγχνον), I should name this woman   She stood by the fire and heard the voice of her son's bones and flesh as they crackled ⲉⲩⲣⲁⲥⲣⲉⲥ, like damp wood ⲉⲩⲗⲏⲕ ⲙⲡⲁⲧⲟⲩϣⲟⲟⲩⲉ in the devouring flames, through the humours ϩⲁⲧⲁϭⲃⲉⲥ of the flesh[1].   She has indeed no part with the mother in Solomon's judgment, who could not bear even to hear of the child's death ⲥⲙⲡⲉⲥⲉϣϭⲓ ⲉⲣⲟⲥ ϩⲟⲗⲱⲥ ⲟⲩⲇⲉ ϣⲁⲡⲣⲁ ⲛⲥⲱⲧⲙ̅ ⲉⲡⲙⲟⲩ.   But this woman of adamant ⲧⲉⲓⲥϩⲓⲙⲉ ⲇⲉ ⲛⲧⲟⲥ ⲛⲁⲇⲁⲙⲟⲥ may be likened to Job in his bereavement (sic expl)

95—Parchment, a fragment, 12 × 31 cm   2 cols   Script *cf* BALESTRI 35 and ZOEGA's 5th class   Marginal ornaments, sometimes red

Macarius the Egyptian, Life of[2]   The following examples correspond respectively to pp 98, l 14, 99, l 11, 100, l. 6, and 101, l 1 of the Bohairic version (*Musée Guimet* xxv)

] ϩⲙⲟⲧ ⲛⲧⲉ ⲡⲛⲟⲩⲧⲉ ⲉϥϫⲱ ⲙⲙⲟⲥ ϫⲉϩⲱⲃ ⲛⲓⲙ ⲛⲧⲁⲡϫⲟⲉⲓⲥ ϫⲟⲟⲩ ⲛⲁⲓ ⲁⲩϫⲱⲕ ⲉⲃⲟⲗ ⲁⲓⲛⲁⲩ ⲉⲣⲟⲟⲩ ⲉⲓⲟⲛϩ ϩⲛⲛⲁⲃⲁⲗ   ⲛⲁⲓ ⲅⲁⲣ ⲛⲉⲣⲙⲉⲛⲕⲏⲙⲉ ⲙⲁⲅⲁⲁⲩ ⲁⲛ ⲛⲉⲧⲟⲩⲏϩ ϩⲙⲡⲙⲁ ⲉⲧⲙⲙⲁⲩ ⲁⲗⲗⲁ ⲁⲩⲥⲱⲟⲩϩ [

ⲁⲩⲛⲱⲗϩ ⲉϩⲟⲩⲛ ⲉⲩϫⲱ ⲙⲙⲟⲥ ϫⲁⲣⲓ ⲡⲛⲁ ⲛⲓⲙⲁⲛ ⲛⲧⲉⲣⲉϥⲥⲟⲩⲉⲛⲧⲉⲩⲥⲙⲏ ⲁϥⲉⲣⲟⲥ ϩⲱⲥ ⲉϥϩⲛⲏϥ ⲡⲉϫⲁⲩ ⲛⲛⲉⲩⲉⲣⲏⲩ ϫⲉϥⲉⲛⲛⲟⲧⲛⲡⲉ ϩⲛⲕⲟⲟⲩⲉ ϫⲉⲁ[

ⲁⲩϩⲟϫϩϫ ⲇⲉ ⲛϭⲓ ⲛⲉⲧⲙⲙⲁⲩ ϩⲓⲧⲙⲡⲉϣⲧⲟⲣⲧⲣ ⲉⲧⲛⲧⲱⲧⲉ ⲉⲣⲟⲟⲩ ⲁⲩⲃⲓⲱⲛⲉ ⲁⲩⲛⲟⲗϩ ⲙⲡⲣⲟ ⲁⲩⲱ ⲁⲩⲛⲟⲩϫ ⲉϩⲟⲩⲛ ⲉⲣⲟϥ ⲛϫⲟⲉⲓⲥ ϫⲉ ⲛⲉϥ[

ⲉⲩⲱϣ ⲉⲃⲟⲗ ϫⲉⲁⲛⲕⲣⲟ ⲉⲣⲟⲛ ⲱ ⲡϩⲗⲗⲟ ⲛⲛⲁⲕⲟⲩⲣⲛⲟⲥ ⲛⲧⲟϥ ⲇⲉ ⲁϥⲉⲡⲉⲧⲓⲙⲁ (ἐπιτιμᾶν) ⲛⲁⲩ ϩⲙⲡⲣⲁⲛ ⲙⲡϫⲟⲉⲓⲥ ⲁϥⲛⲟϣⲡⲟⲩ ⲉⲃⲟⲗ ⲛⲑⲉ ⲛⲛⲓϣϫⲉ ⲡⲉⲥⲛⲏⲩ ⲇⲉ ⲛⲁⲩⲡⲁⲣⲁⲕⲁⲗⲉⲓ ⲙⲙⲟϥ ϫⲉⲕⲁⲥ ⲉϥϯ ⲉⲙⲧⲟⲛ[

---

96 [35]—Parchment; 4 complete leaves, now 32 × 24 cm   Pp ⲣⲕⲁ–ⲣⲕⲍ, numbered in a later (?) hand on *rectos* only   2 cols, 30 ruled lines   Script *cf* HYVERNAT VIII 4, but for ⲁ, *ib* 3   Initials enlarged but plain   From same MS as ZOEGA no clxxxv (1), Brit Mus no 350, Paris Vol 132[1] 3

Hilaria, daughter of Zeno, History of   *Published* by AMELINEAU, *Proc Soc Bibl Arch.* x 198   The last 2 pages correspond in part to ROSSI, *I Papiri* I v 52[3]   Paris Vol 78 39 and Leyden no 56 are from other copies of the same story, which is further narrated in the *Synaxarium*, Tubeh 21   A Syriac version is found in several MSS

---

[1] ⲁϭⲃⲉⲥ, ⲁⲧⲃⲉⲥ, ἰκμάς Trees wither, ⲉⲙⲛⲁⲧⲃ̅ ϩⲁⲣⲟⲟⲩ, Paris 131[5] 32, so too Clar Press 32, ⲡⲟⲍ, Curzon 109, ⲧⲓⲧⲁ.

[2] On this work *v* F C BUTLER, *Lausiac Hist* I 220
[3] *V* VON LEMM in *Bull Ac imp*, NS, I (xxiii) 518

(*v* WRIGHT's Catalogue *sub nom* and NILLES, *Kalendarium*² I. 223), and an Arabic in Brit Mus Or 4403 and Bodleian, *Cod Charsh* xc In these the substance of the story is the same, though they differ from the Coptic in detail¹

97 [37]—Parchment, 6 complete leaves, now 28 × 22 cm Pp ℞–ℕ. 2 cols, 26 lines Script *v* HYVERNAT IX. 2, clearly by the same scribe and dated A M 722 (= A D 1006) Initials, stops &c bright red

Gesius and Isidorus, the Story of² These brothers had a variety of adventures and were at length miraculously led to discover the relics of John the Baptist near Emesa ZOEGA nos clvii, clviii are from other copies of the same story, which, with the present leaves (from a copy by Schwartze), are *published* by STEINDORFF, *Aeg Zeitschr* 1883, 137³ The saints were commemorated on the 12th Pharmouthi (*v*. ZOEGA clvii), but this is apparently recorded only by the Ethiopic *Synaxarium*, 12th Miyazya, where in the *Salâm* the appearance of the Baptist to them and the sick man whom they tended are referred to For parallel legends of the Baptist's relics *v Acta SS* June 24th, 612 ff

98.—Papyrus, a fragment, 21 × 14 cm Script heavy, *cf.* ZOEGA's 4th class 2 cols, 20 + lines Note the system of superlineation

From a narrative wherein a king and his horse occur Whether *recto* and *verso* (sequence doubtful) concern the same persons and incident is uncertain

Recto →

]ⲁϥⲁⲣⲭⲉⲥⲟⲉ ⲛ̄ϫⲟⲟⲥ ϫⲉⲟⲩⲡⲉ ⲡⲙⲟⲩ: ⲛ̄ⲧⲉⲣⲉϥⲙⲟⲟϣⲉ ⲇⲉ ⲉⲑⲏ ⲛⲟⲩⲕⲟ[ⲩⲓ ⲁ]ϥⲉⲓ ⲉϫⲛⲟ[ⲩⲣ]ⲱⲙⲉ ⲉϥⲥⲕⲩⲗⲗⲉⲓ ⲟⲩⲧⲉⲡⲙⲏⲏϣⲉ ⲧⲏⲣϥ̄ ⲁϥϣⲓⲛⲉ ϫⲉ[ⲟⲩ]ⲡⲉ ⲡⲁⲓ: [. . .]ⲉⲁⲩⲧⲁ[ⲙⲟϥ] ⲉⲧⲃⲏⲛ̄[ⲧϥ̄ . . . .] ⲙ[. . .]ⲱϥ[. .]ⲉ ϣⲁⲛⲟ[ ] ⲁⲩⲱ ⲟⲩ[ϫ]ⲱⲱⲣⲉⲡⲉ ⲅ̄ϫ ⲉ|

Verso ↑

|ϫⲁⲓⲭⲁⲣⲓϫⲉ ⲛⲁϥ ⲛ̄ⲧⲙⲛ̄ⲧⲉⲗⲉⲩⲑⲉⲣⲟⲥ ⲉⲧⲃⲏⲏⲧ · ⲁⲩⲱ [ⲙ̄ⲡ]ⲣ̄ⲕⲁⲁϥ ⲉ̄ⲃ[ⲱ]ⲕ ⲉⲡⲡⲟⲗⲥⲙⲟⲥ ϫⲉⲁⲓ ϩ ⲛ̄ⲧⲁⲗⲉ ⲉⲣⲟϥ ⲙ̄ⲡⲛ̄ⲥⲱⲓ ϩⲱⲱϥ ⲁ[ϥ.]ⲟⲩⲟⲁ · ⲁϥⲛⲟ[ⲩϫ]ⲉ ⲙ̄ⲡⲉⲕⲗⲟⲙ [ⲉⲧ]ϩⲓϫⲛ̄[ⲧⲉϥⲁⲡⲉ ⲁϥ[. . . ⲉϩ]ⲣⲁⲓ ⲁϥⲏ[ⲁⲁϥ] ⲛⲁϩⲏⲩ ⲛ̄ⲧ[ⲡⲟⲣ]ⲫⲩⲣⲁ ⲛ[. . · ⲁϥϥⲓⲧ[

] he began to say, 'What is death?' But after he had gone forward a little, he came upon a man striving (σκύλλειν) among (?) all the crowd, and he asked, 'What is this?' And (?) they told him concerning [him   ?   ] and he is a mighty man[

]for(?) I have granted (χαρίζειν) him freedom on my(?) account And suffer him not to go to the war, for I have but lately ridden him' But thereafter he [   ] and cast down the crown that was on his head and he [   ] and stripped him of the purple robe (πορφύρα) of [   ] and took[

---

¹ VON LEMM has also identified the epistle, Brit Mus Catal no 1101, as belonging to this story He intends to edit the whole material

² It seems from *Aeg. Zeitschr* 1883, 157 that this work is ascribed either to Alexander of Alexandria or to Athanasius

³ LEIPOLDT has printed a fragment of another MS. (Berlin Urk, Kopt no 188)

99—Parchment, 1 fol, 35 × 30½ cm   Page numbers lost   2 cols, *ca* 34 lines   Script of Zoega's 8th class   Initials, stops, the letter ϥ &c red

Severus of Antioch, from a Life of   It corresponds verbally with the Syriac version of the *Life* by John of Beth Aphthonia [1], ed Kugener (*Patrol Or*), pp 248 [164], l 8–251, l 10, with the omission of the dogmatic passage, pp 249, 4–250, 7

The passage relates to Severus' refutation of the opinions of Sergius the Grammarian [2] and others of his opponents

ⲁⲗⲗⲁ ⲡⲉⲧⲉⲟⲩⲛϭⲟⲙ ⲙⲙⲟϥ ⲙ̈ⲙⲟϥ ϩⲛ̄ⲧⲡⲓⲥⲧⲓⲥ ⲉⲩⲧⲁⲕⲟ ⲙⲙⲟϥ ϩⲛ̄ⲧⲉⲩⲕⲁⲕⲟⲗⲟⲅⲓⲁ ⲟⲩ-
ⲅⲣⲁⲙⲙⲁϯⲕⲟⲥ ⲇⲉ ϩⲛ̄ⲧⲉϥⲧⲉⲭⲛⲏ ⲉϥϩⲟⲟⲩ ⲡⲁⲣⲁ ⲛⲉⲧϩⲓⲧⲟⲩⲱⲟⲩ ⲧⲏⲣⲟⲩ ⲙⲁⲗⲗⲟⲛ ⲇⲉ ⲡⲁⲣⲁ
ⲛ̄ϩⲁⲓⲣⲉⲥⲓⲁⲣⲭⲏⲥ ⲛⲁⲩ ⲧⲏⲣⲟⲩ ⲛ̄ⲧⲁⲩϣⲱⲡⲉ ϩⲓⲑⲏ ⲙ̄ⲙⲟⲛ · ⲁϥⲥϩⲁⲓ ⲛⲟⲩⲛⲟϭ ⲛⲥⲩⲛⲟⲅⲟⲣⲓⲁ
ϩⲁⲧⲥⲩⲛϩⲟⲣⲟⲥ ⲛ̄ⲭⲁⲗⲕⲏⲇⲱⲛ ⲉϥϫⲱ ⲙⲙⲟⲥ ϫⲉⲕⲁⲗⲱⲥ ⲁⲩⲭⲟⲟⲥ ϩⲓⲧⲥⲩⲛϩⲟⲣⲟⲥ ⲉⲧⲙⲙⲁⲩ
ϫⲉⲁⲡⲉⲛϫⲟⲉⲓⲥ ⲁⲩⲱ ⲡⲉⲛⲛⲟⲩⲧⲉ ⲓ̅ⲥ̅ ⲡⲉⲭ̅ⲥ̅ ϣⲱⲡⲉ ϩⲛ̄ⲫⲩⲥⲓⲥ ⲥⲛⲧⲉ ⲉⲩⲟ ⲉⲛⲟⲩⲁ ⲙⲙⲛⲉⲧⲉⲣⲏⲩ
ⲙⲙⲛ̄ⲥⲁⲧⲉ ⲙ̄ⲧⲟⲩⲁ · ⲁⲩⲱ ⲧⲉϥϩⲩⲡⲟⲥⲧⲁⲥⲓⲥ ⲛ̄ⲟⲩⲱⲧ ⲉϥϫⲱ ⲙⲙⲟⲥ ϫⲉⲛⲉⲧⲡⲓⲥⲧⲉⲩⲉ ⲛ̄ⲑⲉ ⲉⲩⲟ
ⲛⲟⲉ ⲛⲛⲉⲧϫⲱ ⲙⲙⲟⲥ ϫⲉⲟⲩⲫⲩⲥⲓⲥ ⲛ̄ⲟⲩⲱⲧⲧⲉ ⲧⲉϥⲫⲩⲥⲓⲥ ⲙ̄ⲡⲗⲟⲅⲟⲥ ⲉⲁϥϫⲓⲥⲁⲣⲝ ϩⲛ̄ⲟⲩⲙⲉ · ⲡⲗⲟⲅⲟⲥ
ⲇⲉ ⲛ̄ⲧⲁϥⲧⲁⲩⲟϥ ⲁϥⲙⲡⲣⲱϣⲉ ⲙⲙⲛ̄ⲧⲁⲙⲧⲣⲉ ⲛⲁⲛ ⲉϩⲟⲩⲛ ϯⲡⲁⲡⲉⲛⲉⲓⲟⲧⲉ(col 2)ⲛⲉ ⲁⲩⲱ ⲛ̈[. . . . .]
ⲁⲩⲱ ⲁϥⲟⲣϫ[. . . . .] ⲡⲣⲟⲥ ⲑⲉ ⲛ̈[. . . . .] ⲉⲁϥⲡⲗⲁⲥⲧ[ⲉⲩⲉ . . . ⲙⲙⲟⲩ ⲁϥⲟⲩⲁ[. . . . .]
ⲙ̄ⲡϭⲟⲙ ⲅⲁⲣ ⲛ̄ⲗⲁⲁⲩ ⲛ̄ⲣⲱⲙⲉ ⲉⲉⲗⲉⲩⲭⲉⲓ .]ⲛⲁⲧⲣⲉϥⲡⲏ . ⲡⲉ]ⲧⲙⲙⲁⲩ ⲥϩⲁⲓⲥⲟⲩ ⲉⲓⲙⲏⲧⲉⲓ
ⲧϭⲟⲙ ⲙ̄ⲡⲛⲟϭ ⲥⲉⲩⲏⲣⲟⲥ ⲙⲁⲩⲁⲁϥ ⲁϥⲥⲧⲩⲗⲓⲧⲉⲩⲉ ⲅⲁⲣ ⲙⲙⲟϥ ⲛ̄ⲧϩⲉ ⲧⲏⲣⲥ ⲉⲁϥⲉⲗⲉⲭⲉⲓ ⲙⲙⲟϥ
ϩⲱⲥⲧⲉ ⲛ̄ⲧⲉⲛⲉⲛⲧⲁⲩⲟⲩⲉϣ ⲟⲩⲛⲟϭⲓ ϩⲙ̄ⲡⲉϥϫⲟⲕⲙⲁ ⲥⲱⲃⲉ ⲛ̄ⲥⲁⲧⲉϥⲙⲛ̄ⲧⲁⲡⲁⲓⲇⲉⲩⲧⲟⲥ · ⲁⲩⲱ ⲧⲏⲉⲥⲩⲛ-
ϩⲟⲣⲟⲥ ⲙ̄ⲡⲉⲛⲧⲁϥⲣ̄ⲥⲩⲛⲏⲅⲟⲣⲟⲥ ⲛⲁϥ ⲉⲧⲉⲧⲁⲭⲁⲗⲕⲏⲇⲱⲛⲧⲉ ⲁϥϫⲓⲏⲧⲉⲩⲉ ⲙⲙⲟⲥ ⲉⲓⲟ ⲛ̄ⲕⲁⲛⲉ ϩⲓⲛ̄-
ⲛⲉⲛⲧⲁϥϩⲟⲣⲓⲍⲉ ⲙⲙⲟⲟⲩ ⲉⲧⲃⲏⲏⲧⲥ [3] · ⲁⲗⲗⲁ ⲉⲡⲉⲓⲇⲁⲛ ⲡⲕⲁⲓⲣⲟⲥ ⲁⲙⲡⲉ ⲧⲉⲛⲟⲩ ⲛⲁⲟⲥⲙⲁⲧⲓⲍⲉ ⲁⲩⲱ
ⲉⲧⲣⲉⲛⲧⲁⲩⲟ ⲑⲉ ⲛ̄ⲧⲁⲃⲉⲗ ⲛⲉϥⲡ̈ⲉ̈ϣ̈ⲁϫⲉ ⲉⲃⲟⲗ ⲧⲏⲣⲟⲩ ⲉϩ[. . . . .]ⲟϣ[. . . . .] (fol *b*) . . . . .]
ⲛϣⲟⲩⲣ[. . . . .]ϥ ⲥⲉⲩⲏⲣⲟⲥ [. . . . . . .]ϥⲧⲁⲩⲉ ϣⲟ[ⲙⲧ . . .]ϩⲁⲥⲓⲁ ⲉⲛ[. . . . . ⲕⲁ]ⲧⲁ ⲡⲉⲓⲅⲣⲁⲙ-
[ⲙⲁⲧⲓⲕⲟⲥ ⲉϯⲙⲙⲁⲩ [. . . . . .]ⲉ ⲛ̄ⲧⲁⲓⲥⲱ[ⲧⲙ . . . ⲉ]ⲛⲉⲧⲉⲣⲉⲛϩⲁⲓⲣⲉⲧⲓⲕⲟⲥ ⲟϣⲟⲩ ⲁⲓϫⲟⲟⲥ ⲉⲣⲟϥ ϫⲉ
ϩⲁⲙⲟⲓ ⲛ̄ⲧⲁⲛϣⲧⲙ̄ⲣⲱⲙ ϩⲛ̄ⲟⲩⲕⲁⲣⲱϥ ⲙ̄ⲡⲉⲛⲧⲁⲩⲉ ⲗⲁⲁⲩ ϩⲱⲗⲟⲥ ⲛ̄ϩⲟⲩⲟ ⲉⲣⲟⲥ ⲉⲁⲛⲟⲩⲱⲛ ⲛ̄ⲣⲱϣ
ⲙ̄ⲡⲉⲛⲛⲟϭ ⲙ̄ⲙⲟⲅⲓ ⲕⲁⲧⲁⲣⲟⲛ ⲁϥⲥⲱⲗⲡ ⲅⲁⲣ ⲛ̄ⲛⲟⲩⲛⲉ ⲙ̄ⲡⲉⲛϫⲟⲥⲙⲁ ⲛⲑⲉ ⲉϣⲁⲩⲡⲱⲣⲕ ⲛ̄ⲟⲩϣⲏⲛ
ⲙ̄ⲡⲉϥⲛⲟⲩⲛⲉ · ⲛ̄ⲧⲉⲣⲉⲟⲩⲛⲟⲩϯ ⲇⲉ ⲛⲟⲩⲟⲉⲓϣ ϣⲱⲡⲉ ⲁⲡⲇⲓⲁⲃⲟⲗⲟⲥ ⲉⲓⲛⲉ ⲛⲕⲉⲙⲁⲥⲧ̈ⲉ̈ϫ ⲉϫⲙ̄ⲡⲓⲥⲧⲟⲥ
ϩⲱⲥⲧⲉ ⲛ̄ⲧⲉⲧⲉⲡⲣⲟⲫⲓⲧⲁ ⲙ̄ⲡⲁⲩⲗⲟⲥ ⲡϣⲟⲣ̄ϣⲏⲣⲉ ⲙⲙⲟϥ ϫⲱⲕ ⲉⲃⲟⲗ ⲉⲁϥϫⲟⲟⲥ [4] ϫⲉⲟⲩⲛ̄ϩⲉⲛⲣⲱⲙⲉ
ⲛⲁⲓⲱⲟⲩⲛ ϩⲓⲱⲧⲛⲏⲩⲧⲛ ⲉⲩⲧⲁⲩⲟ ⲛ̄ϩⲉⲛϣⲁϫⲉ ⲉⲩⲡⲟⲟⲛⲉ ϩⲱⲥⲧⲉ ⲉⲧⲣⲉⲩⲥⲱⲕ ⲛ̄ⲙ̄ⲙⲁⲑⲏⲧⲏⲥ [ϩⲓⲡⲁϩⲟⲩ
ⲙⲙⲟⲟⲩ · |ⲛⲉⲟⲩⲛⲟⲩϯⲛⲏ]ⲥⲕⲟ(col 2)ⲡⲟⲥ ⲉⲁⲡⲉϥϩⲏⲧ ⲁⲗⲁⲥⲥ[ⲉ] ⲁϥⲗⲟ ⲙⲙⲟϥ ⲉϥⲧⲁϩⲉ ⲇⲉ ϩⲁⲑⲏ
ⲙ̄ⲡⲣⲱϣⲉ ⲉⲛⲟⲩⲟⲉⲓϣ ϩⲙ̄ⲡⲧⲓϩⲉ ⲛ̄ⲟⲩⲁⲗⲉⲡⲧⲛⲁⲛⲟⲥ ⲙ̄ⲙⲙⲁⲣⲕⲓⲱⲛ ⲙ̄ⲡⲉⲩⲧⲏⲭⲏⲥ ⲙ̄ⲡⲉⲩϫⲟⲛⲕⲥⲓⲥ
ⲁϥⲕⲁⲃⲟⲗ ⲛ̄ⲧⲁⲓ ⲛ̄ⲧⲉⲣⲉϥⲥⲉⲛⲡⲉⲩⲟⲩⲟⲉⲓϣ ϩⲁϩⲧⲛ̄ⲡⲉϩⲟϩ ⲁⲛ ⲛⲉⲣⲉⲡⲉⲧⲙⲙⲁⲩ ⲅⲁⲣ ϫⲱ ⲙⲙⲟⲥ ϫⲉⲛⲥⲱⲙⲁ
ⲙ̄ⲡⲉⲛⲛⲟⲩⲧⲉ ⲡⲉⲭ̅ⲥ̅ ⲡⲉⲛⲧⲁϥϫⲁⲁϥ ⲛⲟⲩⲁ ⲛⲟⲩⲱⲧ ⲛⲙⲙⲁϥ ϩⲓⲧⲛ̄ⲧⲡⲁⲣⲑⲉⲛⲁ ⲙⲁⲣⲓⲁ · ⲁϥϩⲟⲩϩⲩⲡⲟⲥⲧⲁⲥⲓⲥ
ⲛⲟⲩⲱⲧ ⲛⲙⲙⲁϥ ⲉⲅⲟⲩⲛ̄ⲯⲩⲭⲏ ⲙⲙⲟϥ ⲛⲛⲟⲉⲣⲁ ϫⲉⲁϥϫⲁⲁϥ ⲛⲁⲧϣⲡⲣⲓⲥⲉ ⲁⲩⲱ ⲛⲁⲧⲙⲟⲩ ϫⲓⲛⲑⲉ
ⲛ̄ⲧⲁϥⲣⲟⲩⲁ ⲛⲟⲩⲱⲧ ⲙ̄ⲡⲗⲟⲅⲟⲥ ⲁⲩⲱ ϫⲉⲉϥϩⲩⲡⲟⲥⲓⲕⲉⲁⲓ ⲁⲛ ⲛ̄ⲛⲉⲛⲡⲁⲑⲟⲥ ⲛⲟⲩⲛ ⲙ̄ⲫⲓⲥⲓⲕⲟⲛ ⲁⲩⲱ
ⲉⲙⲛⲇⲓⲁⲃⲟⲗⲏ ⲛ̄ϩⲏⲧⲟⲩ · ϩⲟⲙⲁⲓⲟⲥ ⲟⲛ ⲡⲉϫⲕⲟ ⲙ̄ⲡⲉⲓⲃⲉ ⲙ̄ⲡ̄ϩⲓⲥⲉ ⲛ̄ⲧⲉϩⲓⲛ ⲙ̄ⲙⲟⲟϣⲉ ⲙ̄ⲡⲙⲟⲩ
ⲁⲗⲗⲁ ϫⲛ̄ⲧⲁϥϣⲡⲛⲁⲓ ϩⲛ̄ⲟⲩⲫⲁⲛⲧⲁⲥⲓⲁ ⲁⲩⲱ ϩⲛ̄ⲟⲩⲙⲉ ⲁⲛ [

---

[1] Cf Kruger in *Byz Zeitschr*. 1905, 633   [3] Here the Syriac is much fuller
[2] Cf Zachar. Rhetor, ed Ahrens-Kruger, 349   [4] Acts xx 30

H 2

MAGIC, MEDICINE

100.—Papyrus, almost complete, $5\frac{1}{2} \times 7\frac{1}{2}$ cm   Script   clumsy uncials

Recto ↑

Prayer to 'the God of Saint Leontius[1]'   'If I remain in the house where I am and stay within, with my mother, my mind shall be at rest and I shall bear (?) a living child' The rest obscure.

Above the text, three crosses

+ ⲡⲛⲟⲩⲧⲉ ⲛⲫⲁⲥⲓⲟ[ⲥ] | ⲗⲉⲟⲛⲧⲓ̅ⲛ̅ ⲉⲓϣⲁⲛϭⲱ | ϩⲓⲡⲏⲓ ⲉⲓϩⲓⲱⲱϥ | ⲧⲁϭⲱ ⲛϩⲟⲩⲛ ⲙⲛⲧ[ⲁ] | ⲙⲁⲁⲩ ⲡⲁϩⲏⲧ ⲛⲁ | ⲙⲧⲟⲛ ⲧⲁⲕⲁ ϣⲏⲣⲉ ⲛ | ⲱⲛϩ ⲛⲁⲛⲉ ⲛϥⲣ ⲟⲩⲛ[| ⲛⲁϩⲉ ⲥ.ⲕ |

Verso   remains of a letter (earlier)

101.—Papyrus, a fragment, $6 \times 8\frac{1}{2}$ cm   Script   rounded uncials

Presumably a Charm, since it preserves (1) the beginning of at any rate one Gospel (Mark 1 2) and (2) part of the list of the Forty Martyrs of Sebaste[2]   Above the latter is a dividing line of dots

Recto   ]ⲕⲁⲧⲁ ⲑⲉ ⲉⲧⲥⲏϩ ϩⲛⲏⲥ | ⲁⲓⲁⲥ ⲡⲉ]ⲡⲣⲟⲫⲏⲧⲏⲥ ⲍⲉⲓⲥ ϩⲛ | ⲛⲧⲉ ϯ̅ⲛⲁⲭⲟⲟⲩ ⲛⲁⲁⲅⲅⲉⲗⲟⲥ | ϩⲁⲧⲉ]ⲕⲣϩ ⲛϥⲥⲟⲃⲧⲉ ⲛⲧⲉⲕ | (margin)

Verso   ⲇⲟⲙⲛⲧⲓⲁⲛⲟⲥ ⲟⲩⲁ[ⲗⲏⲥ | ⲏ]ⲥⲩⲭⲓⲟⲥ ⲥⲙⲁⲣⲁⲕⲧⲟ[ⲥ ⲥⲓⲥⲓ | ⲛ]ⲡⲓⲟⲥ · ⲟⲁⲗⲉⲗⲓⲟⲩ ⲕⲩ[ⲣⲓⲗ- ⲗ | ⲟⲥ] ⲭⲟⲩⲁⲓⲟⲛ ⲕ[ⲁⲓⲟⲥ | (margin)

102—Paper, a fragment, 25×10 cm   Script of ZOEGA's 9th class.

Charms, the first against ophthalmia, the second 'a safeguard in everything'   The former invokes the lance wherewith Christ was pierced and refers presumably to the legend of Longinus' blindness[3]

Above   are   magical   letters[4]   Then one line, [.]ⲧⲁϣϣⲉⲕⲓⲕⲁ , followed   by similar signs   Then   ⲟⲩϯⲕⲁⲥ ⲛ̄ⲃⲁⲗ, followed by 4 signs and this text   ⲡⲉⲛⲓⲡⲉ ⲛϩⲱⲟⲩⲧ ⲡⲉⲛⲓⲡⲉ ⲛⲥⲓⲙⲉ ⲡⲉⲛⲓⲡⲉ ⲛϩ̄ⲥ ⲛⲛⲁ̄ϣⲟⲙ ⲡⲉⲛⲧⲁⲅⲱⲛⲱⲙⲁⲍⲉ ⲙⲙⲟϥ ϩⲓⲭⲙⲡⲧⲟⲟⲩ ⲛⲓⲉⲍⲉⲕⲓⲏⲗ ⲡⲉⲛⲧⲁⲅⲥⲟⲕϥ ⲁⲩⲥⲉⲕⲥⲟⲕϥ ⲁⲅⲁⲁϥ ⲛⲗⲟⲡⲭ[ⲏ] ⲁⲩⲧⲁⲁϥ ⲥⲡⲉⲥⲡⲏⲣ ⲛⲛⲥⲟⲩⲥ ϩⲓⲭⲙⲡϣⲉ ⲙⲡⲉⲥϯⲥ

---

[1] Of Tripolis   For his healing powers *v* NAU in *An Boll* xix 10, RAABE, *Petrus der Iberer* 103, the Ethiop *Synax*, 1st Sanê (Brit Mus Or 659, 101 *a*), Brit Mus Catal p 409

[2] These elements are thus combined in the Leyden charm book (*MSS*, 475), the former also in M A MURRAY, *The Osireion*, p 39 and no 104 here, the latter in Berlin

Urk, Kopt nos 19, 20, *Rec de Trav* xx 174, HALL, *Copt and Gk Texts*, p 39

[3] *V Acta SS*, Mart iii 373 B, GRETSER, *De S Cruce*, Lib I, xxxiv, TILLEMONT, *Mém* I, note xxxix, F DE MÉLY, *Exuviae sacr cpolitan* 55   Christ pierced by the lance is invoked in VASILIEV, *Anecd Gr Byz* 334 γ

[4] *V* Brit. Mus no 369, *PSBA* xxviii 97, pl 1

ⲛ̣ϫⲉⲱⲛ ⲗⲉⲡⲟⲟⲩ ⳨ⲧⲁⲣⲕⲱ ⲗⲗⲟⲕ ⲱ ⲡⲉⲛⲓⲡⲉ ⲗⲡⲉ ⲡ[.]ⲏ̣[ ]ⲏ̣ⲧⲁⲩⲟϥ ⲧⲉⲩ . . ⲏ̣ⲡⲉⲱⲗⲁ ⲙ̅ⲡⲉ ⲡ⳩ⲥ̅
ϫⲉ[. . .] ⲉⲕⲏⲏⲩ ⲉϩⲟⲩⲛ . . . ⲣⲥⲟϥ ⲉⲕⲏⲏⲩ ⲉ[ⲃ]ⲟⲗ ϩⲓⲧⲛ̅ⲧⲥⲟⲗ ⲛ̅ⳤⲡⲣⲟⲥⲉⲩⲭ̅[ⲏ ⲛ̅ⲧⲁⲗ]ⲁⲣⲓⲁ
ⲧⲡⲁⲣⲑ̅ ⲧⲁⲩⲟⲩⲥ ⲥⲁⲃ̣[ⲟⲗ] ⲗⲡⲧⲁⲫⲟⲥ ⲁ̅ⲓ̅ⲟ̅ ⲁ̅ⲓ̅ⲟ̅ ⲧⲁ̅ⲭ̅ⲏ̅. Below this, a line of Arabic letters[1], almost
illegible كلبلبدلبحلاوللادلر

'Male iron, female iron[2], iron of wood of . ⁣ ³, that was named (ὀνομάζειν) upon
Ezekiel's mount⁴, that was pulled and plucked and made a lance (λόγχη) and set in Jesus'
side, upon the tree of the cross of Sion (?), this day ! I adjure thee, O heavenly iron,
which was   the body of Jesus Christ; for   thou goest in   . thou
comest forth by the might of this prayer which Mary the Virgin spake without (?) the
tomb   Yea, yea, quickly !'

Verso Above end of a text   Then a pentagonal frame, wherein a head, with the
letters ⲩ̅ⲁ̅[ ]ϥⲏⲗ̅ above it   Below this, in the hand of *recto* ⲟⲩⲣⲱⲉⲓⲥ ϩⲛϩⲱⲃ ⲕⲁⲁ ⳨ⲁ̅ⲣ̅·
ⲉ̅ⲣ̅ ⲱ̅ⲣ̅ ϥ̅ⲣ̅ ⲣ̅ⲉ̅ ⲣ̅ⲟ̅ ⲣ̅ⲥ̅·ⲑ̅ⲓ̅·ⲟ̅ⲥ̅·ⲟ̅ⲩ̅·ⲟ̅ⲥ̅·ϫⲉ ⲟ̅ⲩ̅ ⲉ̅ⲧ̅·ⲧ̅ⲓ̅·ⲁ̅ϥ̅·ⲧ̅ⲟ̅·ⲟ̅ⲧ̅ ⲁ̅ⲩ̅ ϩ̅ⲣ̅·ⲅ̅ⲣ̅·ⲟ̅ϥ̅·ⲅ̅ⲱ̅·ⲓ̅ⲛ̅
ⲁ̅ⲧ̅·ⲧ̅· ⲕ̅ ⲁ̅ⲧ̅ ⲧ̅ⲓ̅ ⲛ̅ ⲕ̅ⲁ̅ ⲧ̅ⲁ̅ ⲥ̅ⲓ̅·ⲣⲁⲱ ⲱ̅ϥ̅ ⲉⲣ̅·ⲛⲁ̅·ⲥ̅ⲁ̅ ϥⲉⲣ̅·ⲗⲁ̅·ⲕ̅ⲁ̅·, and six more lines of
syllables, ending ⲁϥϫⲱⲕ ⲉⲃⲟⲗ   Below this, one line, ending]ⲉⲩ̣ⲩⲟⲩⲓ .

103—Paper, a fragment, 15×8 cm   Script   small, sometimes ligatured   ⲛ has
the form *ν*.

Charm, most of which is illegible   The following can be read   ⲧⲁⲗⲁⲁⲩⲧⲉ ⲗⲁⲣⲓⲁ
ⲧⲉⲕⲓⲃⲉ . . . . . , ⲧⲉⲕⲓⲃⲉ ⲛ̅ⲧⲁⲡⲉⲛϫⲟⲉⲓⲥ ⲓ̅ⲥ̅ ⲡⲉⲭ̅ⲥ̅ ⲥⲱ ⲉⲃⲟⲗ ⲛϩⲏⲧⲥ ϩⲗⲡⲣⲁⲛ ⲉⲧⲉⲥⲫⲣⲁⲅⲓⲥ
ⲉⲥϣⲟⲗⲉϩ ϩⲓϫⲗⲡϩⲏⲧ ⲉⲗⲁⲣⲓⲁ ⲧⲡⲁⲣⲑⲉⲛⲟⲥ ϩⲗⲡⲣⲁⲛ ⲉⲡⲥⲁϣϥ ⲉⲭ . . . ⲏ ⲉⲧⲟⲩⲁⲁⲃ ⲉⲩϫⲉⲕϫⲱⲕ
ⲉⲧ[ϩⲓϫⲛⲧⲗⲁ]ⲉⲥⲧⲛϩⲏⲧ ⲉⲡⲓⲱⲧ ⲡⲁⲛⲧⲱⲕⲣⲁⲧⲟⲣ ⲁ̅ⲉ̅ⲛ̅ⲓⲟⲩ̅ⲱ̅ ϩⲗⲡⲣⲁⲛ ⲉⲡⲉⲛⲧⲁϥϫⲟⲟⲥ ϫⲉⲁⲛⲟⲕ ⲗⲉⲡⲁⲓⲱⲧ
ⲁⲛⲟⲕ ⲟⲩⲁ ⲉⲧⲉⲡⲁⲓⲡⲉ ⲓ̅ⲥ̅ ⲡⲉⲭ̅ⲥ̅ ϩⲗⲡⲣⲁⲛ ⲉⲁⲃⲃⲁ ⲁⲃⲃⲁ ⲁⲃⲃⲁ · ⲁⲃⲗⲁⲛⲁⲑⲁ · ⲛⲁⲥⲗⲁ · ⲁⲕⲣⲁⲗⲁ
ⲭⲁⲗⲁⲣⲓ · ⲛⲗⲩ · ⲧ̅ⲗⲁⲭ̅ ⲁⲭⲱⲱⲭⲁ · ⳨ⲱⲣⲕ ⲉⲣⲟⲕ ⲉⲧⲉⲟⲩⲥⲓⲁ ⲗⲡⲉⲕⲗⲟⲛⲟⲅⲉⲛⲏⲥ ⲛϣⲏⲣⲉ ⲓ̅ⲥ̅
ⲡⲉⲭ̅ⲥ̅ ϩⲣⲁⲃⲟⲩⲛⲓ · ⲛ̅ⲑⲉ ⲛ̅ⲧⲁⲕⲉⲥⲫⲣⲁⲅⲓ̅ⲍ̅ⲉ ⲗⲡⲟⲧⲏⲣⲓⲟⲛ ⲛϩⲏⲧⲥ.

'   my mother is Mary   The breast   . , the breast whence our Lord Jesus Christ
drank   In the name of the seal (σφραγίς) that is imprinted on Mary the Virgin's heart
In the name of the seven holy, burnished   . that are upon the breast of the Father,
Almighty (*the 7 vowels*)   In the name of Him that said, "I and my Father are one," that
is Jesus Christ   In the name of (*magical names*)   I adjure thee by the sacrifice of Thine
Only begotten Son, Jesus Christ, Rabboni ⁵, in like manner as Thou didst sign the cup '

Verso mostly illegible

104.—Paper, almost complete, 19×14 cm   Script   irregular, of ZOEGA's 9th class
Much faded   The sheet was several times folded.
   Charms and Recipes

---

[1] Dots below indicate doubtful letters

[2] 'Male,' 'female , cf the charms in *Aeg Zeitschr* 1895,
48, 132, also GRIFFITH & THOMPSON, *Demot Magical Pap*,
p 173, note

³ ϩⲁⲩⲟⲩ, 'true,' cannot be read   No Arabic word
seems, in the context, suitable   Is it a Coptic compound ?

⁴ V ? Ezek xvii 22

⁵ Apparently one letter after ϩⲣⲁⲃⲟⲩⲛⲓ

The text is divided into sections   The first is filled chiefly with magical signs or letters (*cf* no 102)

Sect 2   Legible are   ]ⲁⲧ ϩⲓⲱⲱⲥ ⲧⲁϥⲟ ⲛⲁⲓ ϩⲓϫⲛⲟⲩⲛⲏϩⲓ,   ]ϫⲉⲙ: ⲫⲁⲥⲉ ⲙ̄ⲭⲱⲣⲁ. ⲟⲕⲗⲁⲧⲱⲕ: ⲭⲱⲃⲟⲗ ⲙⲁⲣⲉϥⲙⲁⲩ ϩⲉⲛⲁⲛⲁⲕⲉ.

Sect 3   ⲛϩⲁϫ ϭⲟⲡ ⲡⲧⲁⲡⲉⲛ ⲑⲁⲛⲟϥ ϩⲧⲁϣⲟⲩϣ ⲉϥⲗⲏⲕ ⲧⲥⲟϥ ϩⲓⲛⲣ ⲉϭⲟⲙ ⲉϣⲟⲙⲛⲧ ⲉϩⲟⲟⲩ ϣⲁϥⲗⲟ.

Sect 4   ⲟⲩϣⲗⲏⲗ ⲧⲉⲕⲧⲁⲩⲟϥ ⲛⲉⲗⲁⲁⲩ ⲉⲝ̄ⲭⲁⲧⲃⲉ ⲉϣⲗⲟⲕⲥ ⲁⲓ ⲓ̄ⲥ̄ ⲉⲓϩⲛⲙⲁⲣⲓⲁ : ⲁⲓⲉⲓ ⲓⲱⲁⲛⲛⲏⲥ ⲉⲓϩⲛⲗⲓⲥⲁⲃⲉⲧ ⲡⲉϫⲉ ⲡ̄ϫⲟⲉⲓⲥ ⲓ̄ⲥ̄ ϫⲉⲙⲡⲉⲣⲧⲣⲉⲗⲁⲁⲩ ⲛ . ⲟ . . . . ⲉ . . ⲟⲩ ϩⲟⲗⲟⲥ ⲛ .   ⲝ . . . . ϫⲏⲣ . . . . . . ⲗⲁⲁⲩ . . [ⲁ]ⲛⲟⲕ ⲛⲓⲙ ϩⲁⲙⲡϩⲟⲟⲩ ⲡⲁⲓ ⲙⲛⲧⲟⲩϣⲏ ⲧⲁⲓ ⲧⲁⲡⲣⲟ ⲙ̄ⲡⲟ̄ⲥ̄ ⲥⲁⲃⲁⲱⲑ ⲧⲉⲛⲧⲁⲥϫⲉ ⲡⲁⲓ : ϫⲉⲙⲡⲉⲣⲧⲣⲉⲗⲁⲁⲩ ⲛ̄ϫⲁⲧⲃⲉ ⲗⲟⲕⲥ ⲁⲛⲟⲕ ⲁⲗⲗⲁ ⲙⲁⲣⲉⲛϫⲁⲧⲃⲉ ⲧⲏⲣⲟⲩ ⲙ̄ⲡⲕⲁϩ ϣⲱⲡⲉ ⲛⲱⲛⲉ ⲛⲡⲁⲙⲧⲟ ⲉⲃⲟⲗ ⲛ̄ⲧⲉⲛⲉⲧϩⲓϫⲙⲡⲕⲁϩ ⲧⲏⲣⲟⲩ ϣⲱⲡⲉ ⲛⲑⲉ ⲛⲟⲩⲱⲛⲉ ⲙⲛⲟⲩⲡⲉⲛⲓⲡⲉ ⲙⲡⲁⲙⲧⲟⲩ ⲉⲃⲟⲗ ϫⲉⲧⲁⲡⲣⲟ ⲡⲟ̄ⲥ̄ ⲥⲁⲃⲁⲱⲑ ⲧⲉⲛⲧⲁⲥϫⲉ ⲡⲁⲓ ⲁⲩⲱ ⲛϣⲁϫⲉ ⲙⲡ̄ϫⲟⲉⲓⲥ ϩⲛⲙⲉⲛⲉ ⲁϥϫⲱⲕ.

Sect 5   ⲉⲓⲧⲃⲉ ⲧⲉⲣⲙⲟⲛⲧ ⲙⲛⲡⲁⲥⲓⲕ ⲙⲛⲭⲟⲧϣⲟⲙⲧⲉ. Here follow magical letters, the vowels (7 times each) and ⲗⲁⲙⲁⲟ, ⲁⲁⲱⲛⲁⲓ, ⲟⲏⲛⲁⲱⲣⲁ . . , ⲥⲁⲃⲁⲱ[ⲑ], ⲁⲃⲃⲁⲧ . . (*verso*) . . ⲛⲉ ⲛⲛⲁⲓ ⲟⲩⲁ   . ⲧⲏⲥ ϯⲟⲩ ⲛⲁⲡⲛⲉⲛⲥⲟⲟⲉϩⲟⲛⲉⲧ . ⲛ ⲛⲟⲩⲱⲧ ⲧⲁⲁϥ ⲉⲡⲉϥⲙⲟⲧⲉ ⲟ̄ⲓ̄ ⲙⲁⲥϯⲭ̄ⲉ ⲛⲟⲩⲉⲣⲙⲟⲧ.

Sect 6   ⲟⲩϣⲗⲏⲗ ⲧⲉⲕⲧⲁⲩⲟϥ ⲧⲉϥⲛⲟⲩϭⲙ ⲛⲗⲁⲩ ⲛⲓⲙ : ⲡϫⲓⲥⲉ ⲙⲛⲡⲓⲱⲧ ⲡⲟⲛϥ ⲉⲡϣⲏⲣⲉ ⲙⲛⲡⲉⲡⲛⲁ ⲉⲧⲟⲩⲁⲁⲃ ⲧⲁⲣⲭⲏ ⲙⲡⲉϥⲁⲛⲅⲅⲉⲗⲓⲟⲛ ⲉⲧⲟⲩⲁⲁⲃ · ⲕⲁⲧⲁ ⲙⲁⲑⲉⲟⲥ ⲕⲁⲧⲁ ⲙⲁⲣⲕⲟⲥ ⲕⲁⲧⲁ ⲗⲟⲩⲕⲁⲥ ⲕⲁⲧⲁ ⲓⲱⲁⲛⲛⲏⲥ ⲡⲱⲛϩ ⲟⲛ ⲛ̄ⲧⲉⲡⲉⲛϫⲟⲉⲓⲥ ⲉⲓ ⲉϥⲉⲧⲁⲁϥ ⲉⲡⲉϥⲙⲁⲑⲩⲧⲏⲥ ⲉϩⲣⲁⲓ ⲉϫⲛⲡⲟⲩⲉⲥ.[1] (9 lines more, mostly illegible)   Ends ⲛⲉϩⲟⲟⲩ ⲧⲏⲣⲟⲩ ⲙⲡ[ⲁⲱⲛ]ⲁϩ ⲁⲛⲟⲕ ⲛⲓⲙ ⲡϣⲥ ⲝ̄ⲝ̄ ϣⲁⲓⲉⲛⲉϩ ⲛⲉⲛⲉϩ ϩⲁⲙⲏⲛ

Sect 7   ⲟⲩⲙⲁⲁⲩ ⲉϣⲁⲥⲁϩⲉⲣⲁⲧⲉ ϩⲓⲟⲩϭⲣⲙⲉ : ⲁⲓⲉⲓ ⲉⲓ̄ⲥ̄ ⲉⲓ ⲉϥⲙⲟⲩ[ⲧⲉ ⲉⲛ]ϥⲙⲁⲑⲩⲧⲏⲥ ⲁⲩϩⲉ ⲟⲩⲣⲱ ⲛⲕⲛ[2] (9 lines more, illegible)

Sect 2 contains a recipe, in which oil and words apparently magic play a part   Perhaps for the use of 'a mother in childbirth'

Sect 3 'The fever   Take the cummin, pound it with moistened rue[3], soak it with   for three days   He will cease (to be ill)'

Sect 4 'A prayer, which when thou speakest, there shall no insect be able to bite (thee) —O Jesus, I am in Mary!   O John, I am in Elizabeth!   The Lord Jesus said, "Let not any   . at all   me, NN, on this day and this night" The mouth of the Lord Sabaoth it is did say this   "Let not any insect bite me   But let all the insects of the earth become stone in my presence and let all that are upon the earth become even as stone and iron in my presence"   For the mouth of the Lord Sabaoth it was did say this and the words of the Lord are true   It is finished[4].'

Sect. 5 'Concerning the   and the 23 days' fever[5]'   The rest obscure

[1] Not ⲥ̄ϥⲟⲥ   [2] Not ⲣⲱⲙⲉ
[3] *Cf* ⲃⲁϣⲟⲩϣ
[4] Thus, without ⲉⲃⲟⲗ, at the end of several recipes, STERN, *Aeg Zeitschr* 1885, *Tractat* §§ vii, xii, xviii

[5] Also in no 105 below and a charm against ⲛⲉϩⲙⲟⲙ ⲙⲛⲡⲁⲥⲓⲕ, in S DE RICCI's hands   LABÎB, *Dict*, *s v*, gives ⲥⲓⲕ Boh, حمّى الغِبّ 'tertiary fever'   It seems to be Saʿid in Br Mus. Catal no 260

Sect 6 'A prayer which when thou speakest, will protect from everything —The height of the Father, the . . . of the Son and the Holy Ghost, the beginning of the holy Gospel according to Matthew, to Mark, to Luke, to John, the life (?) which our Lord came to give to His disciples upon the   .', 'all the days of my life, NN, the son of NN (ὁ δεῖνα), for ever and ever Amen'

Sect 7 'When a mother stands by (?)[1] a woman —I have come (?)[2] and Jesus is come and calleth His disciples They have found a   .

105—Parchment, 6½ × 6 cm   Script sloping uncials   Was folded 5 times in width and thrice in height

A Charm against various maladies, opening with the palindrome *sator arepo tenet otera rotas*, abbreviated

ϲⲁⲓⲱⲣ ⲉⲣⲓ[3] ⲉⲧⲃⲉⲡⲟⲣⲛⲓ[4] ⲙⲙⲡⲁϲⲓⲕ[4] ⲙⲙⲡⲁⲣⲟϣ ⲙⲙⲡⲉϩⲙⲟ[5] ⲙⲙⲡⲧⲓⲡⲛⲁϲ[6] ⲧⲓⲱⲣⲕ ⲉⲣⲟⲕ
ⲛ̄ⲧⲟⲕ sic ⲡⲉ ⲉⲓⲁⲓⲱ ⲭⲡⲥⲓ .

106.—Paper, 2 fragments joined, complete, 25 × 17 cm   Script *recto*, uneven, of ZOEGA's 9th class, *verso, cf* Brit Mus Catal, Pl 7, no 489

Medical Recipes. Lacunae and uncertainties in reading, apparent irregularities of grammar, besides many unfamiliar words, make the sense often obscure   Help may be had from the other Coptic alchimistic and medical texts STERN's *Tractat* in *Aeg Zeitschr* 1885, 102 (*cf* Brit Mus Catal no 374), BOURIANT's in Ac des Inscr, *CR* 1887, 374, ZOEGA p 626 (*cf* DULAURIER in *Journ As* 1843, 433), Berlin *Urkunden*, Kopt nos 21, 22, 25, 26, the Bodleian papyri *a* 1, *a* 2, *a* 3, and, for the Arabic words, Ibn al-Baithar (LECLERC) in *Not et Extr* XXIII, XXV, XXVI and the articles of STEINSCHNEIDER in *WZKM* XI, XII, XIII and of P GUIGUES in *Journ As* 1905, nos 1 and 3

ϩⲙⲡⲣⲁⲛ ⲉⲛⲛⲟⲧⲉ sic · ⲛⲉⲡⲁⲓϩⲣⲉ ϩⲉⲡⲕⲱⲗⲁϩ
ϫⲓ ⲛⲁⲕ ⲟⲩⲣⲁϥⲧⲟⲟⲩ ⲛⲗⲓⲗⲟⲟϩⲥ ϥϣⲟⲟⲩⲉ
ⲕⲁⲁϥ ⲉⲡⲗⲱⲕ[7] ϣⲁⲛⲧⲉϥⲗⲱⲕ ⲉⲥⲁⲓⲉ⸗ ⲗⲉϩ ϥ
ⲧϥ · ϭⲟⲡ ⲛϥϥⲉⲓ ⲉⲡⲉⲥⲏⲧ (ⲁⲗⲟϥ[8] ⲉⲡⲕⲱϩⲧ ϫ[. . . .])
5 ⲉⲙⲙⲟϥ ϯ ⲥⲟϥⲧϥ ϩⲓⲛⲥⲟⲗⲉϥ ⲥⲁⲧ ⲛⲉϥⲕⲟⲩⲏ[9]
ⲉⲃⲟⲗ · ⲧⲁⲗⲟ ⲡⲉϣⲁϥⲉⲓ ⲉⲡⲉⲥⲏⲧ ϩⲓⲛⲥⲟⲗϥ ⲁⲗⲟϥ
ⲉⲡⲕⲱϩⲧ ϯ ⲡⲁⲥⲱϫⲁⲣ ⲛⲁⲓⲁⲧⲁⲡⲣϥⲓ ⲙⲉⲡⲁⲗ
ⲭⲓⲟⲓⲣⲉ ⲙⲉⲙⲛⲕⲛⲙⲉ ⲛϣⲟⲛⲧⲉ · ⲙⲣⲱⲡⲉⲥ

---

[1] Either subject or verb must have some special meaning   Cf ? Brit Mus p 253, note 9 اﻟﺴﺎﺑﻞ ام
[2] Or the first word the interjection = ⲁⲉⲓⲟ *vai.*
[3] Presumably ⲁⲡⲉ[ⲛⲟ]
[4] *V* no 104   [5] ϩⲙⲟⲙ
[6] ⲧⲕⲁⲧ cannot be read

[7] ⲗⲟⲕ κοτίλη, 'cup'   *V* GRIFFITH & THOMSON, *Demot Magical Pap*, p 76
[8] Scarcely ⲁⲗⲉ for ⲧⲁⲗⲟ, but a-ⲗⲟ 'remove' seems, here and below, to give no sense   The words in brackets are erased
[9] Rind'?

соүс¹∴ мєⲱⲣⲱⲕєⲥⲟⲩⲥ ✝ єⳡⲓ тєⲣϩⲁⲙ

10 ⲕⲁⲧⲁⲅⲟⲅⲁ ⲑⲉⲛⲟⲟⲩ ⳡⲉⲗⳡⲱⲗⲉ ⲧⲁⲁⲩ

ⲉⲧϭⲁⲗⲁϩⲧ · ⲙⲛⲡⲛⲉϥ ⲉⲥⲓⲙ ∴ ⲛⲁⲕ ⲛⲉϩ

ⲛⲁⲓⲣⲉ ∴ ⲁⲓⲛⲧ ⲉⲙⲟⲟⲩ ϩⲓϫⲱⲡⲥⲁⲣⲧⲉ · ⲧⲁⲁⲩ

ⲥⲩⲁⲗⲡⲁⲣⲛⲓⲉ²· ⲟⲩⲱⲙ ⲛⲁⲕ ⲙⲡⲁⲧⲉⲕⲟⲩⲱⲙ

ⲟⲩⲗⲁⲁⲩ ⲡⲣⲟⲩϩⲉ ⲉⲕⲁⲗⲱ ⲉⲛⲟⲩⲱⲙ :—

15 ✝ ⲡⲕⲱⲗⲁϩ ⲟⲛ

ϫⲓ ⲛⲁⲕ ⲛⲛⲏ[. . . . ⲛ]ⲁⲗⲁⲩ · ✝ⲟⲩ ⲉⳡⲓ ⲧⲣϩⲁⲙ ⲉⲩⳡⲗⲱⲗ³

ⲉⲩⳡⲏⲩⲉ ⲧⲁⲁⲥ . . . ⲡⲛⲥⲧⲉ ⲛⲁⲕ ⳡⲁⲛⲧⲉⲛⲥⲟⲟⲩ ∴ ϫⲓ ⲛⲁⲕ

ⲛⲛⲟⲩⲁⲣⲁⲡⲱ⁴ ⲉⲛⲉⲣⲱⲧ ⲛⲛⲁⲗϫⲁⲗⲉⲥ ∴ ϭⲟⲡ ⲧⲉⲥⲡⲁⳡⲉ

ⲁⲗⲟⲓ ⲉ[ⲡⲥ]ⲁϩⲧⲉ ⳡⲁⲛⲧⲉⲥϩⲙⲟⲙ ⲟⲩⲁϩϭⲥ⁵ ⲉⲃⲟⲗ ⲉⲣⲡⲓ

20 ⲉ[. . . . . . .]ⲣ̄ ⲛⲧⲟ · ✝ ⲟⲩⲉⲓ ϩⲓⲛⲓⲧⲟ ⲉⲡⲉⲛⲧ

ⲥⲧⲡⲁⳡ ⲛⲥⲣⲱⲧⲉ ⲉⲥϩⲛⲙ ⲙⲁⲣⲉϥⲥⲟⲟϥ ϩⲓⲧⲃⲛ

ⲧⲉ ⲧⲉϥⲥⲟ ⲡϫⲉ[. .] ⲥⲣⲱⲧⲉ ⲉⲛⲁⲧⲥⲁⲣⲧⲉ ϩⲓϫⲱⲥ

ⲗⲉⲙⲗⲱⲙ ⲉ⳧ⲅⲁ . ⲁ . ⲛ . ⲕⲟⲧⲉⲛⲛ ⳡⲁ . ϩⲓⲡⲕⲁϩ

ⲣⲁⲓ ⲙ ⳧ⲣⲟⲕ ⲕⲥⲁⲧ⁶ ⲟⲩⲗⲁⲁⲩ ⲉϩⲣⲁⲓ ϩⲓ ⲡⲉⲛϩⲏⲧ

25 ⲛⲑⲉ ⲛⲟⲩⲥⲟⲟⲩϩⲥ · ϫⲓ ⲛⲁⲕ ⲉⲩⲧ . ⲓϩⲉ ⲛⲁ ⲡⲉ∴ ⳡⲁ

ⲧϥ ⲙⲉⲛⲉⲕⲥⲡⲟⲧⲟⲩ ⲉⲡⲓⳡⲟⲙⲉⲧ ⲉϩⲟⲟⲩ ⲉⲕⲱ

ⲛⲥⲙⲙⲟϥ ⲉⲕⲥⲓⲧⲉ ⲉϩⲣⲁⲓ ⲁⲩⲱ ⲧⲉⲕϫⲓ ⲧⲉⲩϩⲓⲕⲏ

ⲛⲥⲁⲛⲓⲥ ⲙⲡⲓⳡⲟⲙⲛⲧ ⲥϩⲟⲟⲩ ⲙⲟⲛ⁷ ⳡⲁⲕⲥⲓ

ⲅⲉ ⲉϩⲣⲁⲓ ⲥⲡⲓⳡⲟⲙⲛⲧ ⲉⲛϩⲟⲟⲩ

Verso   30 ⲟⲩⲡⲁϩⲣⲉ ⲛⲥⲁⲓⲉ ⲕⲁⲗⲱⲥ ·

ⲟⲩⲡⲁϩⲣ ⲛⳡⲏⲛ ⲛⲛⲟϭ ⲥⲥⲁⲓⲥ ⲕⲁⲗⲱⲥ ⲥⲩϫⲱⲛⲧ ⲉⲧ

ⲟⲟⲧⲉ⁸ ⲧⲉⲛⲟⲩⲟⲙⲥ ϩⲁⳡⲱⲣⲡ ⲙⲡⲁⲧⲉⲕ[ⲟⲩ]ⲱⲙ ⲗ

ⲁⲩ : ⲉⲕⲟⲩⲱⲙ ⲛⲙⲟⲥⲩ ⲛⲡⳡⲓⲱ ⲉⲕⲉⲟⲩⲟⲙⲥⲩ ⲙⲡⲉⲣⲓ . . ⲛⲥ

ⲡⲉⲓⲁⲛ ⲙⲡⲉⲣⲟⲩⲉⲙⲧⲛⲃⲧ ⲟⲩⲇⲉ ϫⲉⲛⲉ ⳡⲁ[ⲕ]ⲟⲧⲗ ϩ ⲡ

35 ⲉⲕϩⲏⲧ S⁹ ⳡⲁⲕⲟⲩⲱⲙ ϩⲁⲣⲟϥ · ⲁⲩⲱ ⳡⲁϥⲧ[. .]ⲛⲁ

ⲃⲁⲗ ⲛⲥϥⲱⳡⲛ ⲛⲛⲁⲡⲟⲩⲥⲓⲣ¹⁰ ⲛϥⲛⲁⲗⲟⲗ[. . . .] ⲛϩⲙ

ⲟⲩ ⲥⲓⲥ ⲕⲁⲛⲧ . . ⲃⲁⲗ ⲟⲩⲁ ⲡⲟⲩ . . ϩⲛϩⲱⲃ [ⲛⲓⲙ] ⲉⲧⲥⲁϩⲟⲩⲛ [ⲉ]ⲡⲣⲱⲙⲉ

ϫⲓ ⲛⲁⲕ ⲛⲟⲩⲁⲣⲣⲁ[ⲙⲁⲛ] ⲡ ⲉϥⲕⲏⲕ ⲧⲁ

ⲁⲩ ⲉⳡⲙⲟⲩ . . ⲉⲱ . . . ⳧ ⲉϥⲕⲏϥ ⲛⲥ ⲛϩⲟⲟⲩ

40 ⲥⲛⲓⲱ ⲛⲙⲟⲟⲩ . ϩ . . . . ⲉⲙⲟⲟⲩ ⲙⲙⲏⲛⲉ ⲙⲡⲛⲥⲱⲥ

---

¹ This and next word obscure, though reading certain

² الربية

³ ? For ⳡⲗⳡⲱⲗ

⁴ Recurs (v Index) as a measure of flax, written with double p so possibly الرُّبْع , الرُّبْع , 'a quart,' a milk- or corn-measure in Spain, z Dozy i 503, Ducange, *Gloss La¹*, *arroba* Engelmann-Dozy 203

⁵ ? For ⲟⲩⲁϩⲥ   *Cf* Stern, *l c* § xvi

⁶ ⲥⲓⲧⲉ ⲉϩⲣⲁⲓ, here and below, is difficult In Num v 17 (Br Mus 1221) it varies with ⲛⲟⲩϫⲉ ⲉϩⲣⲁⲓ In Wisd xvii 19 (Peyron) it=συνέχεσθαι (though Br Mus Or 5984 has ⲥⲓⲛⲉ ⲉϩⲣⲁⲓ) Elsewhere συνέχεσθαι=ⲱⲧⲛ

ⲉϩⲟⲩⲛ Prov xi 26, Luke xix 43, ⳡⲱⲧⲙ Ezek xxxiii 22, Isa lii 15, besides the usual ⲁⲙⲁϩⲧⲉ Job xxxi 23, Psalm lxviii 18 &c Here the first meaning might be applicable 'evacuate, purge,' if the action of the drug is intended

⁷ 'Certainly' V Crum, *Ostraca* no 83

⁸ ϫⲱⲛⲧ 'try', 'test', but ⲟⲟⲧⲉ 'womb' seems impossible as 2nd sing masc is used throughout ⲟⲟⲧⲉ might perhaps be read

⁹ The signs for 'and' and 'half' in this MS are identical

¹⁰ Scarcely 'hemorrhoid', الثور السور (*cf* Turaief, *Materiale po Archeol Christ Egipta*, no 9, ⲁⲗⲙⲉⲥⲟⲩⲣ)

ϣⲁⲧⲟⲩ ϭⲉⲗ . . . ϩⲓⲝⲛⲟⲩⲥⲟⲗⲓⲃ · ⲧⲁⲁⲩ ⲉⲩϩⲙ

ⲝ ⲉ[ϥ]ⲝⲛ[ϥ ⲛⲃ̄] ⲛϩⲟⲟⲩ ⲙⲛⲃ̄ ⲛⲟⲩϣⲏ · ⲛⲓⲧⲟⲩ ⲉϩⲣ

ⲁⲓ . . . . . . [ⲟ]ⲩⲟⲛ ϩⲓⲝⲛⲟⲩⲥⲟⲗⲓⲃ ⲛⲃ̄ ⲛϩⲟⲟⲩ

ϣⲁⲛⲧⲟⲩ . . ⲉ ϩⲓⲡⲉⲕⲃⲟ ϫⲓ ⲛⲁⲕ ⲛⲟⲩⲁⲥⲥⲓⲡⲛ ⲛⲥⲁⲓ

45   ⲉ ⲛⲛ ⲡⲉϥ[ⲕⲁ]ⲉ ⲉⲃⲟⲗ ϭⲟⲡ ⲃ̄ ⲛⲗⲁ̈ⲓ ⲛⲉϥⲓⲱ ⲙⲙⲉ ⲧⲁⲗⲟⲟⲩ

ⲥⲡⲕⲱϩⲅ ϩⲱⲡ ⲡⲉϥⲥⲃⲁⲓⲉϥ ϯ ⲟⲩϥ ⲗ̄ⲓ ⲛⲉϥⲓⲱ ⲛⲕ . . ⲉ

ⲉϫⲱⲟⲩ · ⲥⲁϭⲧ[ⲉ ϩⲁ]ⲣⲟⲟⲩ . ⲉ ⲡⲉⲩⲥⲃⲁⲓⲉϥ ⲟⲓ ⲡⲉⲱϫ

ⲛ ⲟⲩⲁⲁϥ · ⲟⲓ ⲡⲁⲥ[ⲥⲓ]ⲡⲛ ⲟⲩⲁⲁϥ ⲧⲁⲁⲩ ⲉⲡⲉϥⲓⲱ ⲉϥϩⲓ

ϫⲱⲡⲥⲁⲧⲉ ⲧⲱϩ ⲉⲥⲱⲟⲩ ϣⲁⲛⲧⲟⲩⲃⲱⲗ ⲉⲃⲟⲗ ·

50   ⲟⲓ ⲛⲓⲕⲟⲟⲩⲉ[ ] ⲉⲧⲉⲛⲁⲓⲛⲉ ✻

ⲁⲥⲓⲛϭⲏⲏⲗ · ⲟⲩϣⲓ · ⲧⲁⲣⲥⲓⲛⲉⲓ ϟ ϣⲓ · ⲁⲗⲃⲟⲩⲗⲃⲟⲩⲗ ϟ ϣⲓ

ⲁⲗⲛⲁⲣⲁⲛⲃⲟⲩⲗ ϟ ϣⲓ · ⲃⲣⲁ ϭⲁⲛⲉⲝⲛϥ · ⲁⲗϩⲱⲣ ⲃ̄

. . ⲟⲩⲏⲣⲧ ⲉϥϣⲟⲟⲩ ϟ · ⲙⲁ̄ϥ ϟ ⲁⲥⲛⲙⲛⲟⲩⲗ ϟ ⲁⲥⲥⲁⲑⲁⲣ ⲃ̄

ⲁⲗⲟⲩⲁⲣⲉ ⲉϥϣⲟⲟⲩⲉ ϟ ϭⲗⲟϭ ⲛⲉⲙ ⲃ̄ ⲃⲣⲁ ⲉⲙϫⲱⲗ ϟ

55   ⲥⲓⲛⲁⲡⲛ ϟ ϫⲛⲗⲛⲩϫⲛ ϟ ⲁⲛⲁⲣⲕⲁⲣϩⲁⲣ ⲁ̄ [. .]ⲁⲛⲱⲛ ⲃ̄

ⲟⲓ ⲟⲩⲁ ⲟⲩⲁ ϣⲉⲗϣⲱⲗⲟⲩ ϭⲟⲡ ⲛⲓϣ ϩⲓⲱⲟⲩ ⲧⲁϩⲟⲩⲉ ·

ⲛⲛⲉⲩⲉⲣⲏⲩ ⲉⲧⲉⲡⲉϣϫⲏⲛ ⲙⲙⲡⲉⲥⲥⲓⲡⲛ ϩⲱⲡ ⲡⲉϥ

ⲣⲱ ϩⲓϫⲱⲡⲥⲁⲧⲉ ⲛⲁⲁⲩ ⲧⲟⲩⲕⲃⲟ ⲧⲁϩⲟϥ ⲕⲁⲗⲱⲥ ⲧⲁ

ⲁⲩ ⲉⲩⲁⲗⲛⲁⲣⲱⲣⲉ · ⲉⲕⲉⲟⲩⲱⲙ ⲛⲟⲩ̄ⲥ ⲁⲗⲙⲁⲗⲛⲁⲗ ϩⲓⲱⲟⲩ

60   ⲁⲩ ⲛⲧⲁⲕⲟⲩⲱⲙ ⲟⲩⲉⲙⲥⲓⲟⲛ ⲧⲉⲕϩⲓϣ ⲁⲛ · ⲉⲛⲉⲓϣ ⲁⲛ · ⲛ

ⲱⲫⲉⲗⲓⲉ ϩⲁⲣⲟϥ · ϣⲁϥⲕⲁⲑⲁⲣⲓϫⲉ ⲙⲡⲣⲟ ⲙⲡⲉⲛϩ[ⲏ]ⲧ

ϣⲁϥⲫⲩⲗⲉ ⲛⲧⲁⲡⲉ ⲁⲩⲱ ⲡⲉϩⲟⲟⲩ ⲛϣⲁⲕⲟⲩⲱⲙ ⲛ[ϩⲏ]

ⲧϥ ⲙⲡⲉⲣⲃⲱⲕ ϩⲁⲧⲛⲥϩⲓⲙⲉ ⲙⲡⲉⲣⲟⲩⲉⲙⲧⲛⲃⲧ ⲟⲩⲧⲉ

ϫⲛⲏⲛ ⲟⲩⲉ ⲉⲣⲱⲧⲉ ⲧⲏⲡⲛ ⲛⲛⲉⲡⲁϩⲣⲉⲡⲉ · ⲓ̄ⲱ —

65   ⲟⲩⲡⲁϩⲣ ⲉⲥⲱ ϩⲁⲧⲁⲗϩⲱⲙⲙⲉ · ⲟⲩⲥⲁⲓⲡⲉ ⲙⲡϣⲱⲙ ϩ ⲧⲉⲡⲣⲱ

ϣⲗⲁⲉⲓⲛ · ⲁⲥⲥⲁⲑⲁⲣ ⲗⲁⲕ ⲛϣⲕⲛⲕⲛⲗⲛⲉⲓⲛ ⲁ̄ ⲉⲡⲟⲩⲁ [ⲟⲩⲁ] ·

ⲟⲓ ϣⲉⲗϣⲱⲗⲟⲩ ⲟⲩⲟϣⲙⲟⲩ ϩⲓⲙⲟⲟⲩ ⲛⲛϭⲛⲁⲁⲩ ⲛⲡⲉⲗ[. .]

ⲟⲗⲉ ⲧⲁϩⲉ ⲉⲟⲩⲛⲕⲛⲛ ⲉⲛⲉⲣⲱⲧⲉ ⲛⲁϩⲛ · ⲛⲁⲁⲩ . . .

ⲡⲉⲕⲃⲟ ⲧⲟⲩϣⲟⲟⲩⲉ ⲛϣⲓ ⲛⲱⲗⲕ ⲉⲃⲟϥ

70   ⲡⲉ ⲃ̄ ⲛⲁⲗⲙⲁⲧⲕⲁⲗ · ⲥⲟ ⲡⲉϥϥ́ ϩⲁⲣⲟⲩϩⲉ

ⲁⲩⲱ ⲡⲉϥϥ́ ϩⲁϣⲱⲣⲡ ⲁⲩⲱ ⲛⲛⲉⲕⲉⲣϩⲟⲩⲟ ⲉⲣⲟϥ.

The first recipe is for an unidentified malady[1] It consists of a quart (4th part) of dried *bdellium*[2], to be subjected to the fire and sieve, 5 drams[3] of sugar[4] of . . , gum of *astragalus*[5], and gum arabic[6] respectively being added After grinding and shaking,

[1] A prescription for this malady in Berlin *Urk*, Kopt no 25 The only known meaning is 'strike,' 'knock' In STERN § viii ⲕⲟⲗϩ is different but equally obscure

[2] Also ⲗⲉⲗⲱϩⲉ and ? ⲗⲗⲟϩⲉ (Rossi I, v 48), where it may well be the *doum* palm جمّيز (so LABÎB, *Dict*)

[3] درهم, as often in STERN, thus with ϣⲓ, in no 110 and STERN § xiv

السُّكَّر *Cf* STERN § xiv ϣⲟⲩⲕⲉⲣ, here no 109 ⲥⲟⲩϫϫⲁⲣ

[5] الكثيراء

[6] In Bodl Copt a 2 (P), 28 ⲙⲟⲩ ⲛⲕⲙⲙⲉ (? κόμμι) ⲛϣⲁⲛⲧⲉ.

this is to be mixed with oil of sesame or of nuts and set on[1] the fire. The mixture to be bottled and eaten fasting, in the evening

The second recipe (l 15) is for the same malady. 5 drams[2] of white ., shaken and measured, are to be placed in a   Half a quart (?) of pure[3] milk having been heated, the first ingredient is to be divided (?) into   parts and one of them added to the milk. This is to be drunk and, thereafter apparently, the remaining cold milk   The rest of this recipe (ll 23-29) is obscure

It is difficult to say to what the third (*verso*), 'a very fine medicine,' relates   Its primary ingredients are garlic and dried raisins. It is to be taken fasting in the morning, and after (?) it, neither fish nor certain herbs are to be eaten   From l 38 it may be translated 'Take thee a peeled pomegranate (?)[4]. Place them (*sic*) in cold water of   for 3 days, washing them in (fresh ?) water daily   Afterward cut them up (?) and roll   on a sieve   Put them in strong (*lit* acid) vinegar for 2 days and 2 nights   Take them out, . .. one (?) on a sieve, for 2 days, until (*or* so that) they   in the cool   Take fine dried raisins[5], take out their seeds   Take 2 liters of pure[6] honey and put them on the fire, their froth[7]   Add half a liter of black (?)[8] honey thereto   Set fire beneath them, their froth   Throw in[9] the garlic by itself, throw in the raisins by themselves and add them to the honey that is on the fire   Stir them together[10], till they dissolve   Throw in the remaining (medicaments), namely   ginger[11], 1 measure; .   [12], $\frac{1}{2}$ a measure, pepper[13], $\frac{1}{2}$ a measure, gilliflower[14], $\frac{1}{2}$ a measure, seed of   , 2, dried   of roses[15], $\frac{1}{2}$, mastich, $\frac{1}{2}$; spikenard[16], $\frac{1}{2}$; .. ..[17], 2, dried saffron[18], $\frac{1}{2}$,   of sesame[19], 2; seed of onion, $\frac{1}{2}$, mustard[20], $\frac{1}{2}$;   [21], $\frac{1}{2}$, feverfew[22], 1,   . , 2   Throw them in, one by one   Shake them   Take the   [23] from them   Mix them together, namely the garlic and the raisins   Cover (*lit* hide) its (*sc* the vessel's) mouth (when) on the fire   Allow them to cool   Mix them thoroughly   Put them in a bottle[24]   Thou shalt eat a *mithkal*-weight thereof, and when thou hast eaten a jar[25] (thereof) and hast   , thou shalt have benefit therefrom   it will cleanse (καθαρίζειν) the mouth of thy belly and will benefit (?)[26] the head   And the day thou eatest thereof, go not in unto a woman, neither eat fish nor herbs[27] nor milk   The number of the medicaments is 19

(l 65)   A medicine to drink against fever[28], good in summer and winter —*Nasturtium*,   ,   [29], 1 (measure) of each   Throw (them) in   Shake them   Knead

---

[1] ⲁⲕⲏⲧ in Stern § xii, Bodl Copt *a* 1 (P), fol 2, and here indicates action by fire on a dissolved substance ⲁ- might be imperative

[2] ϯⲟⲩ and ϯ above are assumed identical

[3] الخالص　So in Stern p 118

[4] ⲉⲣⲙⲁⲛ الرمان[5] الرنب

[6] *Lit* 'genuine' Cf ⲱⲛⲉ ⲙⲙⲉ, ⲛⲉϩ ⲙⲙⲉ, ⲭⲏϭⲉ ⲙⲙⲉ (*Journ As* 1905, 3 413) In Brit Mus no 920, f 242 a, ⲛⲉϩ ⲙⲙⲉ رب طيب It is frequent in the Demotic Papyrus (*v* above), pp 44, 50, 76 &c

[7] ? ⲥϩⲛⲛⲧⲉ, but the meaning seems unsuitable

[8] Scarcely ⲕⲁⲙⲉ or ⲕⲁⲕⲉ   Third letter ⲓ, p or ⲩ

[9] ⲟⲓ twice in Turaief, *l c*

[10] ⲧⲱϩ ⲛⲥⲁ-, as in Bodl Copt *a* 2 (P), 16, 19 &c

[11] الزنجبيل

[12] Not arsenic (ⲁⲣⲥⲉⲛⲓⲕⲱⲛ Zoega 630), as for internal use

[13] الفلفل   [14] القرنفل

[15] ⲁⲗⲟⲩⲉⲣⲧ might be read, but *cf* ورد   [16] السنبل

[17] Arabic unidentified, recurs below   [18] الورس

[19] Perhaps both words merely mean 'cabbage,' since ϭⲓⲙ is (sometimes) a general term

[20] σίναπι   [21] Greek ?   [22] العاقرقرحا

[23] ⲓⲏⲓ 'urine' in Isa xxxvi 12, Mid. Eg   So in Bodl Copt *a* 2 (P), 44 ⲟⲩⲏⲓ ⲛⲓⲏϣ ⲉϥⲛⲟⲥⲉ. But here unlikely

[24] القارورة   So in Stern   [25] ἀγγεῖον   [26] ? ὠφελεῖν

[27] ⲭⲛⲉ. In Ac des Inscr, *CR* 1887, 376 ⲭⲏⲛⲉ. Species unidentified

[28] الحمّى

[29] ? شقائق, but here apparently a plural form

them with water   .   .   Mix it with a jar[1] of cow's milk   Place it (?) to cool and dry. The amount of it to be swallowed (?)[2] is 2 *mithkals*   Drink two-thirds thereof in the evening and its (other) third in the morning and thou shalt not go beyond that '

107.—Parchment; a fragment, 9 × 4½ cm   Palimpsest   (*a*) illegible, (*b*) script irregular, of Zoega's 9th class

(*b*) A Medical Recipe   ⲛⲉϣⲱⲛⲉ ⲧⲏⲣⲟⲩ ⲛ̇ⲧⲁⲡⲉ ⲙ̇ⲡⲛⲥⲙⲁⲩ   ⲟⲩⲁⲡⲕⲉⲫⲟⲗⲟⲥ ⲉϥ̇ⲧ̇ⲕⲁⲥ ϫⲓ ⲛⲁⲕ ⲛⲟⲩⲥⲟⲟⲩϩⲉ ⲙ̇ⲡⲁⲡⲟⲓ ⲟⲩⲟ̇ⲡⲥⲡⲉ ϯ ⲟ̇ⲛⲉϩ ⲙ̇ⲛⲟⲩⲕⲟⲩ[ⲓ] ⲛ̇ϩⲙⲝ ⲉϫⲱⲥ ⲧⲁϩⲟⲩ ⲙ̇ⲡⲛ[ⲉ]ⲩ[ⲥⲣⲏ]ⲩ ⲕⲁⲁ[ⲩ] . . . . ⲁ]ⲡⲉ ⲕⲁⲁ[. .]ⲟⲩ ⲛⲥⲟⲣ̇ⲓ ⲛⲁ[ⲗ]ⲁⲩ ⲉϫⲱ[ϥ [.]ϯⲥ.ⲥⲡⲁ[

'All the maladies of the head and eyelids   (For) a   [3] that is painful   Take a hen's (?)[4] egg, break it, add thereto oil and a little vinegar   Mix them together and place them   head   Place   [5] of white wool thereon   '

Verso (different hand)   ⲁⲓⲡⲟⲟⲛⲉ ⲉⲧⲁⲓ ⲙ̇ⲛ̇ⲉϯⲛⲉ ⲙ̇ⲙⲟⲥ.

108.—Parchment, 6½ × 8½ cm   Palimpsest   Script (*a*) and (*b*) Zoega's 9th class

(*a*) An Ophthalmic Recipe   Very faded and illegible

ϩⲁⲃⲁⲗ ⲉⲁⲣⲭⲏ ⲛ̇ⲡⲣⲙⲟⲩ ⲛ̇ϩⲙⲟⲩ ⸫ ⲥⲛⲟϥ ⲉⲛⲱⲕⲱⲡⲁⲧ ⲉϥϩⲙⲙ ⸫ ⲟⲩⲥⲛⲧⲏⲛϭ ϫⲉⲕⲁⲣⲧⲁⲙⲱⲛ ⲙⲙⲛⲧⲣⲙⲛⲕⲏⲙⲉ ϫⲉⲡϣⲓϫⲉ ⲉⲟⲩϣⲏⲛ ⲉϥⲣⲏⲧ ϩⲛⲡⲁⲛⲧⲟⲟⲩ ⲛ[ⲑ]ⲉ ⲛⲟⲩⲃⲱ ⲛ̇ϩⲉⲣⲙⲁⲛ ⲉⲣⲉⲛⲉϥϭⲱⲃⲉ ⸫ ϣⲟⲓ ⲛⲟⲩⲕⲟⲩⲓ ⲛⲑⲉ ⲛϩⲓⲥⲁϥ ⲉⲕⲁϭⲱ ⲡⲉϣϣⲉ ⲉϥⲉⲛⲉ ⲙ̇ⲡⲁⲡϩⲉⲣⲙⲁⲛ

'Eyes that begin to exude salt water—Hoopoe's blood[6], heated, a herb named *cardamum*, in the Egyptian tongue *shife*[7], which is a tree that grows in mountain regions[8], like a pomegranate tree, its leaves being somewhat long[9], like   .   Its wood is like that of the pomegranate '

(*b*) A List (*v* below)

109.—Papyrus, a fragment, 5 × 10 cm   Script   irregular uncials   *Recto* ↑

From a Medical Recipe   Ashes (?)[10] of vine wood are to be placed on the fire, and the face is to be anointed with oil and other things

]ⲕⲁⲣⲃⲱⲛⲉ ⲉⲛ̇ϣⲉⲛⲉⲗⲟⲗⲉ ⲧⲁⲁⲃ ⲉⲡⲕⲱϩⲧ ⲟⲩ ⲙⲁⲥⲙⲟⲩ ϣⲁⲗⲁ[11] ⲛ̇ⲟⲩϣ ⲁⲣⲁ ⲙⲉⲛⲏϩ ⲧⲁϩⲥ ⲡⲉⲕϩⲟ   . ⲉⲙⲙ[

---

[1] ? ἀγγεῖον
[2] But ⲱⲁⲕ ⲉⲙⲟϥ cannot be read
[3] Paris 44, f 68*b* ⲡⲕⲉⲫⲁⲗⲟⲥ μῆνιγξ غِشا, Kircher 74 ⲡⲓⲕⲉⲫⲁⲗⲱⲥ مخ *medulla*   But ⲁⲛ- is obscure
[4] *V* Brit Mus Catal p 263, note, and Index here
[5] ? A bandage
[6] Prescribed in the Demotic Paparus (*v* above), pp 42, 158, 194, its heart in Parthey, *Zwei Zauberpap*, no. 2, 18   *V* Ibn al-Baithar no 2251

[7] Unknown. Or 'in Egyptian (it is) the blight (? ϣⲛⲃⲉ, rust) of a tree &c '
[8] Not known in Sa'idic, except once as ϩⲁⲛ-, Amélineau, *Géogr* 127 (=Paris 129[14] 95)
[9] For ϣⲟⲓ *v* Isa v 18
[10] *Cf* Kircher 199 ⲭⲁⲣⲃⲟⲛⲓⲛ (*leg* ⲭⲁⲣⲃ., *cf* κάρβων, κάρβουνον) جمر (*leg* جمر)
[11] ⲥ or ϥ might be read for ϣ

110.—Paper, complete, 17 × 5½ cm   Script irregular, of Zoega's 9th class

A Recipe for preparing a certain dish, though the final words would apply rather to a medicine   Much is obscure and translation difficult

Ⲧϭⲓⲛⲟⲩⲱⲙ ⲟⲩϣⲏⲙ ⲉⲛⲉⲙϫⲱⲗ ⲉϥϭⲉϣϭⲱϣ ϣⲏⲩ[1] ⲉⲡⲣⲱϣⲉ ⲧⲁ[ⲗ]ⲟ ⲙⲙⲟⲟⲩ ⲉⲡⲕⲱϩⲧ
[ⲧ]ⲁⲁⲩ ⲉϩⲣⲁⲓ ⲉⲣⲟⲁⲃ ⲙⲉⲩⲙⲉϩ ⲉⲥⲙⲙ: ⲧⲁⲗⲓ ⲁϣϣⲉⲣⲓϭ[2]: ⲃⲏⲣⲃⲉⲣ ⲉⲙⲙⲟⲟⲩ ⲉⲅⲁⲃⲏⲃⲉⲣ: ϭⲟⲡ
ⲟⲩⲟⲉⲓⲕ ⲉⲡⲣⲱⲥⲫⲟⲣⲁ ⲗⲟⲕ ⲧⲁⲁⲃ ⲉϩⲣⲁⲓ: ⲉⲧⲗⲟⲃ, ⲁⲗⲗⲟⲩⲭ̄ⲭⲁⲣ[3]· ⲛⲁⲧ̄ ⲉϣⲕ̄: ⲧⲁⲡⲡⲉⲛ: β̄ ϣⲓ.
ⲙⲁⲓ ϯ ⲟⲩϩ ϣⲓ: ⲡⲓⲡⲣⲉ[4] ⲟⲩⲡⲁϣ ϩ ⲧⲁϭ ⲟⲩϣⲓ ⲧⲉⲣϩⲁⲙ[5] ⲁ̄ ⲉϣϫⲏⲛ ⲧⲁⲁⲩ ⲉϩⲣⲁⲓ ⲉⲣⲟⲥ: ⲥⲩⲁⲃⲏⲣⲃⲉⲣ
ⲟⲩⲁϩ ⲉⲃⲟⲗ ⲧⲉⲥⲙⲃⲟ[6]: ⲟⲩⲱⲙ ⲛⲁⲕ ⲃⲱⲕ ⲉⲡⲉⲕϩⲱⲃ ⲡⲉⲣⲟⲩⲱⲙ ⲁⲛ ⲉϫⲱⲥ ⲟⲩⲁ ⲙⲡⲉⲣⲥⲉⲙⲟⲟⲩ ⲁⲛ
ⲉϫⲱⲥ ⲉⲁϥϫⲱⲕ ⲉⲃⲟⲗ ⲕⲁⲗⲱⲥ.

'A food   A few moistened onions, a sufficient measure[7].   Set water upon the fire and put them therein, but (so that) they fill it not   Put (with them) oil of sesame   Boil them and let them boil   Take a light (?) sacramental loaf, add it .   , (also) sugar of   , 5 measures, cummin, 2 measures; mastich (?), 5½ measures, pepper, ½ a measure   ; one dram of garlic   Add them thereto and let them boil; set them aside to cool   Eat (thereof and) go to thy work   Eat not (else) besides it nor drink besides it   It is quite complete '

Verso   remains of an earlier text

111—Parchment, apparently complete, 2 × 9 cm   Script rounded uncials

Possibly used as an Amulet by the writer, 'Matthew the little, of Pȯrb[8] '

✝ ⲙⲁⲑⲑⲉⲟⲥ ⲕⲟⲩⲓ ⲡⲣⲙⲡⲱⲣⲃ: ⲡⲛ̄ⲕ̄ⲁ̄ · ϩⲁⲙⲏⲛ.

---

[1] As in ⲗⲟⲕ, below, the prefix appears to be omitted   [6] As in Stern, *op cit* § xvi

[2] الشيح   [3] *V* no 106   [7] *Cf* τὸ ἀρκοῦν, Parthey, *Zwei Zauberpap*, no 2, 19

[4] πεπερι   [5] *V* no 106, l 9   [8] Recurs only in no 120

MISCELLANEOUS

112.—Parchment, a fragment, $13\frac{1}{2} \times 8$ cm.   Palimpsest   (*a*) 2 cols , rounded uncials, (*b*) 2 cols , small hand, *cf* CIASCA xv   Initials and ornaments red

(*a*) New Testament text, as shown by the number $\overline{\text{ɯϭ}}$, visible in one margin

(*b*) *Recto* and col 1 of *verso* unidentifiable   *Verso*, col 2, part of a colophon, in sloping script, referring to the donation of the MS to a church [1]

```
ϯ  cγⲡ̄ ·  ⲡⲛⲟ[ⲩⲧⲉ ⲡⲉⲛⲧⲁϥϣⲱⲡ]
             ⲉⲣⲟϥ ⲛⲛ[ⲁⲱⲣⲟⲛ ⲛⲁⲃⲉⲗ]
             ⲡⲁⲓⲕⲁⲓ[ⲟⲥ ⲁⲩⲱ ⲧⲉⲑⲩⲥⲓⲁ]
             ⲙⲡⲉⲛⲉⲓⲱ[ⲧ ⲁⲃⲣⲁⲁⲙ ⲁⲩⲱ]
             ⲡⲗⲉⲡⲧⲟⲛ [ⲥⲛⲁⲩ ⲛⲧⲉ ⲧⲉⲭⲏⲣⲁ]
             ⲁⲩⲱ ⲡϣⲟ[ⲩϩⲙⲛⲉ ⲛ
             ⲉϥⲉϣⲱ[ⲡ ⲉⲣⲟϥ ⲙⲡ
             ⲛⲧⲁⲡⲉⲛ[              ⲙⲙⲁⲓ]
             ⲁⲅⲁⲡⲏ [
             ϥⲓ ⲛⲉϥⲣ[ⲟⲟⲩϣ ϩⲙⲡⲉϥⲡⲣⲟⲥ]
             ϩⲟⲁⲟⲥ ⲛ[ⲙⲓⲛ ⲙⲙⲟϥ ⲁϥ]
             ⲥⲙⲛⲧϥ [ ⲁϥⲧⲁⲁϥ ⲉϩⲟⲩⲛ ⲉ]
             ⲧⲉⲕⲕⲗⲏⲥ[ⲓⲁ ⲛ ⲙⲁⲡⲉ          ]
             ⲭ̄ⲥ̄ ⲉⲧ[
```

113.—Parchment, irregular shape, 21×4 in   Script   small, of ZOEGA's 9th class   Text across width, divided into paragraphs

Greek-Coptic Vocabulary   Several of the words are not biblical

```
ⲍⲉ[2].. ⲁⲍⲓⲕⲓⲧⲉ · ⲥⲉⲭⲓ ⲙⲙⲟϥ ⲛϭⲟⲛⲥ ·
ⲍⲱⲏⲥ ϩ ⲍⲱⲟⲛ: ⲡⲱⲛϩ ⳝ
ⲍⲉⲩⲅⲟⲥ  ⲡⲥⲟⲉⲓϣ ⲡϩⲱⲧⲣ ⲡϣⲱⲛⲃ ⳝ
ⲍⲏⲗⲟⲧⲩⲡⲟⲥ · ⲡⲉⲧⲣⲟⲉⲓⲥ ⲉⲧⲉⲥϩⲓⲙⲉ ⳝ
ⲍⲩⲗⲁⲙⲟ̄ · ⲡⲙⲟⲩ ⲛⲥⲏⲃⲉ [3] ·
```

---

[1] Lacunae tentatively filled from a prayer in the Anaphora of Mark (Cyril), *v* the Cairo *Euchologion*, p $\overline{\text{ⲭ̄ⲓ̄ⲁ̄}}$, BRIGHTMAN, p. 129

[2] Possibly belongs to a preceding word, as this is not line 1

[3] Ζιλάπιον 'julap' seems unlikely   The Coptic may be 'water of cedar' or 'of tar'

ϫⲁⲗⲏ : ⲡⲓⲧⲟⲣⲧⲉⲣ :

ϫⲁⲕⲟⲧⲟⲛ : ⲡⲣⲉϥϭⲱⲛⲧ ⲉⲙⲁϣⲟ ¹ :

ϫⲱⲟⲥⲙⲉⲛⲟⲥ : ⲉϥϯ ⲙⲡⲱⲛϧ :

ϫⲱⲁⲣⲕⲉⲥ : ⲛⲉⲧϫⲓ ⲉϧⲟⲩⲛ ⲉⲡⲱⲛϧ :

ϫⲱⲛⲉ ⲁⲣⲭⲏⲅⲟⲥ : ⲡⲁⲣⲭⲏⲅⲟⲥ ⲙⲡⲱⲛϧ :

ϫⲱϯⲕⲟⲥ : ⲡⲉϯ ⲧⲟⲩϫⲏⲩ

ϫⲏⲙⲓⲁ : ⲡⲟⲥⲉ :

ϫⲟⲙⲓⲛ : ⲡⲥⲱⲡⲥ ⲡⲉϥⲁⲉⲓⲛ ² :

(broken off here)

114 [51]—Paper, 12 complete leaves, being foll 35-38, 44, 45, 50, 51, 53-56 of the volume as now bound, 17×13 cm 1 col with Arabic opposite 15 lines Pp n̄-n̄ⲃ, n̄ⲑ, ⲟ̄, ⲟ̄ⲁ, ⲡⲅ, ⲡⲏ, ϥⲁ-ϥⲍ Script regular, sloping, of ZOEGA's 9th class Stops and a few initials red, ornaments red and yellow

Saʿidic-Arabic *Scala* preserved in Paris MSS coptes 43, 44³ These leaves are from the Saʿidic version of the biblical and ecclesiastical سلم of John, bishop of Samannûd⁴ They show words from St Mark, the Pauline and Catholic Epistles, the Odes and the liturgical books The Vocabulary was here followed by the same author's Grammar, also in Saʿidic (v Paris 44, fol 23 b) Preserved (foll 53-56) is a passage corresponding to the Bohairic text in KIRCHER, pp 2a-5a

The text differs not materially from that of Paris 44 a word more is occasionally added, another omitted, the Arabic equivalents are sometimes not identical It may be noted that this scribe does not write ⲉⲧⲅⲩⲣⲓϫ, ⲉⲧⲥⲁⲙⲃⲓⲕⲏ, as in Paris 44

¹ Note this archaic (or Bohairic) word
² *ζώμιον?, since the first Coptic word perhaps means 'drink' The second is obscure Cf ϫⲟⲩⲙⲏⲛ ڟمر, Paris 44, 85 b

³ Cf Brit Mus Catal no 491
⁴ For this work v MALLON in *Mélanges de la Fac Or de l'Univ de St Joseph* (Beyrouth), i 117

LEGAL AND FINANCIAL TEXTS

TAXATION

115.—Papyrus, a fragment; 35 × 30 cm   *Recto* ↑, except first *selis*   Script small, ligatured.

Above the text a 'protocol' in large brown characters, alternately Greek and Arabic, beginning ἐν ὀνόματι   Of the Arabic الله الا الا الا [is legible

The villagers (κοινότης[1]) of Senepo[2] to the treasury (δημόσιος λόγος[3]), represented by the Amir of Shmoun, with a request for a tax remittance (?)

At end legible ζωοποιογ και οι[οογcιογ τριαλος

In middle]πρωτης ιια[

+ αιιοιι τκοιιιωτης επτι[ιι]ε cειιεπο ϩιτοοτιι αιιοιι ϩερογοϫ πεϫελ͞χ ιιπϩ͞ε αγω
πλιοικ,[4] πϣιιιιλκ, [

πιιλκ, ϣειιογτε ιιιιιερειιιας πϣιιιιλκ, κολλογθος ιιιιαθαιιαςς πϣιιιιλκ, φιλ[

5 πιιλκ, πϫιιϭε ιιιιϩηλιας πϣιιιιλκ, παγλος cιϲϩϫι επαϩιιιιοςιος λο͞γ ͞η[τοι] πειι[δ,6
ιιιιαιιιρα ιιτιπολιc ται ϣιιιογιι ιιιιπϲιιτοϣ ϫεεπιιϫη ιιγιιει αιιιιαρακ[αλει π]τιι[ε].[
ιιιιαϣε ιιιιπε . ος ιιτιρουιπε ται ϫεccαρεcκαιϫεκ, ι͞δ, ταρετιιτι εγκλη ε͞6 . . .
προωιι[πειι]τιιε . . ϭω . ιιτcωϣε ιιϩωϫε ιιϩερϩω[ϥ] εϥοιϫαιιιιωιι πϣ . [

In middle]ιιϩοιιιολογι[α

Traces of 3 more lines

Verso ı line]λοϥ [. αι]ϫα κιρ[οϊ [space] α . . ͞χ͞ω cειιοιιϧο +

116.—Papyrus, a fragment; 22 × 15 cm   Script· ll ı, 2 ligatured, the rest ligatureless
Recto ↑

Part of an earlier Arabic account (unpointed), perhaps relating to the text on the other side   It begins[7] الوا اں دوحر عںهم الى العصر [.   This was followed by columns of names

---

[1] Cf Krall cxlv, Brit. Mus no 391 (Jême), Crum, *Ostr* no 407

[2] Cf Σενομβῶ, Mitteis, *Griech Urk* no 99, and the same form on *verso* here

[3] So expressly in a fragment Brit Mus Or 6201 A &c , ιιϫιιιι λ ιιτοι πειιϫοεις ραϣιϫ πεγκλεεςτατος ιιαιιιρα ιιτιπολιc ται ϣ[ιιογιι] ιιιιπϲιιτοϣ Cf no 160   In the Jkôw (Aphroditô) papyri constantly, 'the

δημ λόγ , namely (ἤτοι) Kurra ibn Sharîk'

[4] The διοικητής as village magistrate at Shmoun, Brit Mus nos 1159, 1180, and often in the Jême documents , or as agent or steward of a landowner, BGU 323, 368

[5] Or πειι[ϫοεις

[6] Not ἔγκλημα

[7] الوالى seems impossible. The next may be دوحر, نوحر or دوحر.

with two sums of money opposite each   The names appear to be, دولي بما ساس,
علعه ابرهيم٠ [عــ]سي مودو٠, ٤كريا (؟) [ﺝ|ﺍﻡﺍ]٬ ﻣﻌﺎﺭﻩ ﻓﺮﺩﻋﻮﺱ, ﻓﻠﻮﺻﻠﺴﻦ ﻣﻘﺎﺭﻩ, ﺍﺻﻄﻔﻦ ﺩﻋﺎﻡ٠

Verso a statement of taxes paid by certain villages (?) to the treasury (δημόσιος λόγος),
represented by the Amîr of Shmoun

+βουσιρεως δ, μουσαι υἳ ραζιδ ·ζγ ·δ [| πολεως² δ, κυῶ απα κυρ̅ ε αρ̅ κη [|

+ ϩⲙ̅ⲡⲣⲁⲛ ⲙ̅ⲡⲛⲟⲩ[ⲧⲉ] ⲁⲛⲟⲕ ⲕⲟⲥⲙⲁ ⲇⲓⲟ[ⲓⲕⲏⲧⲏⲥ | ⲡⲣⲱⲙⲡⲙⲟⲛⲁⲥⲧⲏⲣⲓⲟⲛ ⲉⲧⲟⲩⲁⲁⲃ ⲛ̅[|
ⲉⲛⲥϩⲁⲓ ⲛⲡⲁⲏⲙⲟⲥⲓⲟⲥ ⲗⲟⲅⲟⲥ ⲛ ⲡⲉⲛϫⲟⲉⲓⲥ.[| ⲡⲉⲩⲕⲗⲉⲉⲥⲧⲁⲧⲟⲥ ⲛⲁⲙⲓⲣⲁ ⲛ̅ⲧⲓⲡⲟⲗⲓⲥ ⲧⲁⲓ ϣⲙⲟ[ⲩⲛ |
ⲙ̅ⲡⲟⲟⲩ ⲉⲧⲉⲥⲟⲩϣⲟⲙⲧⲉ ⲛ̅ⲭⲟⲓⲁ[ϩ | (the rest blank)

117.—Papyrus; complete, 9½ × 13½ cm   Script small, ligatured, *cf* Brit. Mus Catal.,
Pl 15, no. 1167, and Rossi, *Papiri* I i, Tav iv   *Recto* ↑

Note from Yezîd, son of ʿAbd er-Rahman [3], to Severus, son of Bane [4] of Shmoun,
informing him of the amount due by him for the tax in 'this the 10th Indiction, (for) the
canon, the 9th Indiction'   *Cf* no 118

⳽ ⲥⲩⲛ̅ ⲓⲉϫⲓⲁ ⲩ̊ ⲁⲃⲇⲉⲣ[ⲁ]ⲙ[ⲁⲛ] ⲡϥⲥϩⲁⲓ ⲥⲉⲩⲏⲣⲟⲥ | ⲡϣⲛⲃⲁⲛⲉ ⲡⲣⲱⲙ̅ⲡⲟⲗⲓⲥ ϣⲙⲟⲩⲛ ϫⲉⲛⲁⲓⲛⲉ |
ⲛ̅ⲧⲁⲥⲧⲁϩⲟⲕ ⲙ̅ⲙⲟⲟⲩ ⲛ̅ⲧⲁⲁⲩ ⲉⲡⲗⲟϭ ⲛ̅ⲛⲟⲩⲃ | ⲉ. ⲥⲙ̅ⲛⲉ ⲙ[ⲟⲟ]ⲩ ⲡⲛⲁϩ⁵ ⲛⲁⲙⲓⲣ̅ ⲧⲉⲓⲣⲟⲙⲡⲉ
ⲧⲁⲓ | ϫⲉⲕ, ⲓᵟ, ⲡⲕⲁⲛ̅ ⲑ ⲓᵟ, ⲉⲧⲉⲛⲁⲓⲛⲉ ⲧⲓⲟⲩ ⲟⲩⲥⲟⲥ | ϩⲟⲗⲟⲕ, γν, ·ⲉⲥ πεντα ημισ μ̅, μ̅ αθ̅, η ιᵟ, ι +

The blank papyrus below this is folded and fastened with a clay seal and ribbon
(*cf* no 119), the former having traces of a two lined Cufic inscription

Verso blank

118.—Papyrus; complete, 15 × 18 cm   Script ligatured   *Recto* ↑

Note from Yezîd, son of Seeîd [6], similar to the preceding, addressed to Severus, son
of Mark, the goldsmith   The tax is to be paid to the ὑποδέκτης, what he had already paid
being deducted

ⲥⲩⲛ̅ ⲓⲉϫⲓⲁ ⲩ̊ⲟ ⲥⲉⲉⲓⲁ ⲡϥⲥϩⲁⲓ ⲛⲥⲉⲩⲏⲣⲟⲥ ⲡϣ⳽ ⲛⲙⲁⲣⲕⲟⲥ ⲫⲁⲅⲛⲟⲩϥ | ⲡⲣⲱⲙⲉ ϣⲙⲟⲩⲛ
ϫⲉⲛⲁⲓⲛⲉ ⲉⲛⲧ[ⲁⲥⲧⲁ]ϩⲟⲕ ⲉⲙⲟⲟⲩ ⲛ̅ⲧⲁⲁⲩ ⲉⲧⲣⲩⲡⲟⲇⲟⲭⲏ | ⲛ̅ⲕⲟⲥⲙⲁ ⲡϭⲩⲡⲟⲇⲉⲕ, ϩⲓⲡⲉⲁⲏⲙⲟ
ⲉⲧⲕⲁⲧⲁⲃⲁⲗ, ⲥⲧⲥⲁⲕⲕ̄⁷ ⲛⲁ ⲓᵟ, ⲉⲧⲉⲛⲁⲓⲛⲉ | ⲟⲩϩⲟⲗⲟⲕ, ⲙⲛ̅ⲟⲩⲧⲣⲓⲙⲏⲥⲓⲛ ⲉⲣⲉⲡⲉⲛⲧⲁⲛⲧⲁⲁϥ ϣⲁⲡⲟⲟⲩ
ⲛⲡ ⲉⲣⲟⲕ | γν, αρ̅ ν̅ αγ′ ⲥγρ̅ μ̅ μεϩ̅ η ιᵟ, ϛ | ⳗ ⲓⲇⲓⲕ ουν̅′⁸ [space] αρ̅ ν̅ αγ′ | γν, ν̅ αγ′

---

¹ In ﺍﺑﺮﻫﻢ and ﻋﺒﻬﻢ above, *f* and *n* are not formed
" This should be Shmoun itself
³ Quite uncertain   *Cf* no 119
⁴ Also the addressee in Brit Mus nos 1167–1169 and
in no 118 here   V also no 214
⁵ For ? ⲛⲉⲛⲇⲟϩ(ⲟⲧⲁⲧⲟⲥ), though it cannot be so read

⁶ No 117 apparently in the same hand, but the father's
name is there different.
⁷ Unintelligible to me
⁸ *I* ε ὑπὲρ ἰδικοῦ (?) ονομότων, or simply ἰδικῶν   Ἰδικόν
recurs in no 151 here, Brit Mus no 1088 and *Aeg.
Zeitschr* xxix. 22, where it seems to mean ' own property.'

119.—Papyrus, a fragment; $13\frac{1}{2} \times 16$ cm   Script   moderately ligatured   *Recto* ↑
Note similar to the preceding, addressed to Victor, son of Claudius, of Thône[1].

ⲁⲃⲁⲗⲉⲣⲁⲙⲁⲛ[2] ⲡ̄ⲥ̄ϩ̄ⲁⲓ ⲛⲃⲓⲕⲧⲱⲣ ⲕⲗⲁⲩⲧⲓ ⲡⲣⲱⲙⲉ ⲑⲱⲛⲉ ⲛ |]ⲓ ⲙⲟϥ ⲛⲟⲩⲣⲱⲙⲉ ⲉϥϫⲟⲥⲉ
ⲉϥⲗⲏⲕ ⲛⲉϣⲁ ⲛⲥⲟⲩⲟ |ϫⲉⲛⲁⲓⲛⲉ ⲛϣⲁⲥⲧⲁϫⲟⲕ ⲉⲙⲟⲟⲩ ⲛⲥⲧⲁⲁⲩ ϩⲁⲡⲥⲕⲁⲛ⁴³[.] |]ⲉ ⲓ⁹, ⲉⲧⲉⲛⲁⲓⲛⲉ
ⲥⲛⲁⲩ ⲟⲩϩⲟⲥ ⲛϩⲟⲗⲟⲕ[ᵀ]/ ⲁⲩⲱ ϩⲁⲧⲧⲁⲡⲁⲛⲏ |ⲛⲧⲣⲓⲙⲏⲥⲓ, ⲙⲛⲟⲩⲡⲁϣⲕⲉⲣⲁⲧⲛ ⲁⲩⲱ ⲉⲩϣⲁⲛⲁⲙⲁϩⲉ |
]ⲁⲧⲉⲛⲛⲧⲧⲁⲩⲛ . ⲅⲟⲛ . . ⲉⲥⲃ . . . |]ⲧ β ⲓⲛ⁹, θ ||]   ̊ⲛ β ϛ|]   ̊ⲛ βγ́
μή |] μ́ μ́ ιβ ⲛ̄ γ́ ⲧⲟⲓⲥ ⲕⲟⲓⲛⲱ̄ ⲛ̄ γ́ μή |]   γι ⲛ̄ γ ϛ́ μή |

The ribbon, with its seal, tying the folded end of the leaf, is still attached   The
position of certain worm-holes show that ribbon and seal were folded inwards   Cf no 121.

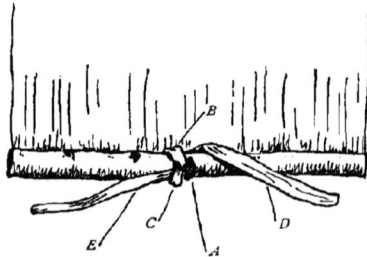

A fragment of clay seal   *B C* passes through the back of the papyrus
                     D continues *C*   *E* continues *B*

120.—Papyrus, a fragment; $11 \times 18\frac{1}{2}$ cm   Script almost ligatureless   This text is on
the *verso*, fibres →   *Recto* is no 160

Receipt ($\dot{\alpha}\pi\dot{o}\delta\epsilon\iota\xi\iota\varsigma$) by Apa Kyros, a husbandman, for money contributions towards
the $\dot{\alpha}\nu\delta\rho\iota\sigma\mu\dot{o}\varsigma$[4], the $\kappa\alpha\nu\dot{\omega}\nu$ of the 6th Indiction[5] and $\delta\alpha\pi\dot{\alpha}\nu\eta$ of the 7th   One apparently of
the contributors is from 'the eastern Pôrf[6].'

ⲁ|ⲡⲁ ⲕⲩⲣⲓ ⲡⲟⲩⲟⲟⲓⲉ ⲡϣⲉ ⲛⲡⲙⲁⲕ/ ⲓⲱⲥⲏϥ ⲡⲣⲱⲙⲉ ϣⲙⲟⲩⲛ | ⲓⲱϩⲁⲛⲛⲏⲥ ⲡϣⲉ ⲛⲡⲙⲁⲕ/
ⲉⲩⲥⲉⲃⲉ ⲡⲁⲡⲱⲣϥ ⲛⲉⲓⲛⲃ̄ⲧ |] ⲛⲙⲉⲣⲟⲥ ϫⲉⲁⲓϫⲓ ⲁⲩⲱ ⲁⲡⲗⲏⲣⲟⲩ ⲛⲧⲟⲟⲧⲛ ⲡⲉⲕⲁⲛⲁⲣⲓⲙ̄ⲟⲥ᷐ᵗⁱᶜ |]ⲛⲕⲁⲛⲱⲛ
ⲛⲉⲕⲧⲏⲥ ⲓⲛ⁹, ⲙⲛⲁⲡⲁⲛⲏ ⲛⲉⲃⲇⲟⲙⲏⲥ ⲓⲛ⁹, ⲉⲧⲉⲛ[ⲁⲓⲛⲉ |]ⲥ ⲛⲕⲟⲩⲃ̄ γⲓ/ αρ ᷎θ ⁰ν̄ α ⲉⲛ μ/ ⲉⲩⲱⲣϫ ⲛⲁⲕ

ⲁⲓⲙⲛ ⲧⲉⲓⲁⲡⲟⲇⲉⲓϫⲓⲥ | ⲥⲧⲟ|ϣⁱ ⲉⲣⲟⲥ +γⲉ̄ν μⲉⲥⲟⲣ [] ⲓⲛ⁹, $\frac{\sigma\eta\mu/}{\alpha\pi\alpha \ \kappa'}$ + ⲟⲓ |ⲧⲓ]ⲁⲡⲟⲇⲉⲓϫⲓⲥ ⲛⲟⲉ ⲉⲥⲥⲏϩ [

121.—Papyrus, a fragment, $11\frac{1}{2} \times 18$ cm.   Script   uneven, ligatured   *Recto* ↑
   1 Receipt by Bane of . . . . ., on the north of Shmoun, to Apa Severus, for the

---

[1] *V* Brit Mus no 1042   Presumably the Θῦνıς of
the Greek documents.
[2] عـ الرحمن   *Cf* no 117.
[3] 'Ανδρισμός, *v* no 120.
[4] Δημόσιον, ἀνδρ, δαπανη paid together in an 8th cent

Jkôw papyrus (Brit Mus Or 6208)   'Ανδρ also in Cairo
no 8076   *V* no. 222 below
[5] *Cf* Brit Mus no 1050 and here no 117
[6] Or Ôrf   *V* no 111

δημόσιον (half a *solidus*) of the 7th Indiction, the deed being dated in the 9th   Whether Severus is himself the contributor is uncertain   Reference is made to sea-service in Africa[1]

+ ⲁⲛⲟⲕ ⲃⲁⲛⲉ ⲡϣⲉ ⲛⲡⲙⲁⲕ/ ⲓⲁⲕⲱⲃ ⲡⲣⲱⲙⲉ[| ⲡⲉⲙϩⲓⲧ ⲛⲏⲩⲙⲟⲩⲏ ⲧⲡⲟⲗⲓⲥ ⲉⲓⲥϩⲁⲓ ⲛⲡⲁ‐
ⲥⲉⲩⲏⲣⲟⲥ [| ϣⲙⲟⲩⲏ ⲍⲉⲉ ⲟⲩⲡⲁϣⲉ ⲛϩⲟⲗⲟⲕᵀ, ⲁⲥⲉⲓ ⲧⲟⲟⲧ ϩ . [| .ⲣⲏⲗⲁ..ⲟⲥ ⲡⲣⲱⲙⲉ ⲛⲡⲥⲓⲧⲙⲉ
ⲛⲛⲟⲩⲱ[ᵗⲉⲉϥ ⲛⲧⲁⲫⲣⲏⲕⲏ ϩⲁⲧⲉⲙⲟⲥⲓⲟⲛ ⳽ ⲓⲛᵟ, ⲟⲓ, ⲏ[| ⲥⲓⲛ ⲃⲁⲛⲉ ⲥⲧⲟⲓ̅ + ⲫⲁⲟⲫⲏ ⲕ ⲑ ⲓⲛᵟ/
ⲃⲁⲛⲉ ⲥⲧⲟⲓⲭ[

2 In the other direction and a different hand, the opening formula of a deed, mentioning Babylon

[+ⲉⲛ ⲟⲛⲟⲙⲁⲧⲓ ⲧⲏⲥ] ⲁⲅⲓⲁⲥ ⳽ⲱⲟⲡⲟⲓⲟⲩ ⲕⲁⲓ ⲟⲙⲟⲟⲩⲥⲓⲟⲩ ⲉⲛ ⲙⲟⲛⲁⲧⲓ[2] | ⲧⲉ]ⲥⲥⲁⲣⲉⲥ ⲕⲁⲓ
ⲁⲥⲕⲁⲧⲏⲥ ⲉⲛ ⲃⲁⲃⲩ[ⲗⲱⲏ] + [

Seal and ribbon still close a fold of the papyrus above line 1 (*cf* no 119)

Verso]ⲛ ⲙ ⲙⲡⲥⲟⲱⲛⲉ[3] ⲏ̅ ⳽.   Hand of 1

122 —Papyrus, complete, 21 × 6½ cm   Script irregular, ligatureless   *Recto* →
Receipt (ἀπόδειξις) by Moui, a deacon, to Apa Severus, for the contribution (διάγραφον[4]) to the δημόσιον of the 10th Indiction, paid by 'his men'   *Cf* the Severus in no 121

+ ⲁⲛⲟⲕ ⲙⲟⲩⲓ ⲡⲓⲉⲗⲁⲭⲓⲥⲧⲟⲥ | ⲉⲁⲓⲁⲕ/ ⲡⲣⲱⲙⲡⲙⲁ ⲛⲕⲁⲧⲟⲓ | ⲉⲓⲥϩⲁⲓ ⲕⲉⲣⲱⲙⲉ | ⲉⲩⲅⲁⲣⲧⲏⲕ
ⲧⲟⲕ | ⲁⲡⲁ ⲥⲉⲩⲏⲣⲟⲥ | ⲍⲉⲁⲓⲍⲓ ⲁⲡⲗⲏⲣⲟⲩ ⲧⲟⲟⲧⲕ | ϩⲁⲡⲉⲩⲧⲓⲁⲕⲣⲁⲫⲟⲛ ⲉⲕⲧⲓ ⲙⲟϥ | ⲛⲁⲕ ϩⲛⲧⲉ‐|
ⲙⲟⲥⲓⲟⲛ ⲉⲧⲉⲕⲁⲧⲉⲥ ⲛⲁ/ | ⲉⲩⲱⲣⲉ⳽ ⲛⲁⲕ | ⲁⲓⲥⲙⲛ ⲧⲓⲁⲡⲟ|ⲧ⳽ⲓⲥ ⲛⲁⲕ | ⲉⲓⲥⲧⲏⲭⲓ ⲉⲣⲟⲥ | ⲙⲟⲩⲓ
ⲡⲁⲓⲁⲕ/ | ⲥⲧⲏⲭⲓⲓ +

Verso + ? ? ⲁⲡⲁ ⲥⲉ | [ⲩⲏⲣⲟⲥ

123 —Papyrus, complete, 10½ × 16 cm   Script ligatureless, uneven   *Verso* →
Receipt by Severus, a priest, for tax-money of the current, 1st Indiction, from Apa Markos and Shenoute and for one (measure) of 'good' wine

Verso ϯ ⲥⲉⲩⲏⲣⲟⲥ ⲡⲓⲉⲗⲁᵡⲉⲛⲡ/ ⲡⲕϩⲉⲣⲁⲓ ϩⲁⲡⲁ ⲙⲁⲣⲕⲟⲩⲥ | ⲍⲉⲛⲁⲩ[5] ⲧⲣⲓⲙⲏⲥ ⲛⲛⲟⲩⲃ ⲩ᷍ ⲧ ϩⲉⲧ
ⲟⲩⲡⲁϣⲉ | ϩⲁⲡⲕⲧⲉⲙⲟⲥⲏ ⲁⲩⲱ ⲟⲩⲡⲁϣⲧⲣⲓⲙⲏⲥ ⲛⲛⲟⲩⲃ ϩⲁϣⲓⲛ[ⲟ]ⲩ[ⲧ]ⲉ ϩⲓⲧⲟⲟⲧⲃ ⲉϥⲓⲃⲁⲗⲟⲩⲏ ⲟⲩⲁ
ⲛⲏⲣⲡ | ⲧⲓⲁⲛⲟⲩⲃ ϩⲁⲧⲉⲣⲟⲙⲡⲉ ⲧⲁⲓ ⲡⲣⲱⲧⲉ ⲓⲁ/ | ⲙ̅ ⲡ̅ⲁ ⲩ, ⲁ ⲥⲉⲩⲏⲣⲟⲥ ⲡⲣ/ ⲧⲓⲥⲧⲟⲓⲭⲓ +

Recto remains of an earlier account, in red ink

---

[1] In 5 ⲛⲉⲉϥ is doubtless to be read 'Africa' in a similar connection in the Jkôw papyri (Brit Mus Or 6210, 6222, 1), in reference to the supply of sailors for the annual *cursus* against the Greeks   *V* BECKER in *Zeitschr f Assyr* xx 90

[2] Formula usual in the Jkôw texts, *v* Br. Mus. Cat, Pl 5, Or 6204
[3] *V* ro 119
[4] *V* CRUM, *Ostraca* no 410 &c., KRALL no ccxi
[5] For ⲍⲉⲉⲓⲥ ⲥⲛⲁⲩ.

124.—Papyrus, 2 fragments, $6\frac{1}{2} \times 16\frac{1}{2}$ and $9\frac{1}{2} \times 14\frac{1}{2}$ cm Script various Some in red ink

Receipts for taxes paid by the monastery, or the 'rock,' of Apa Thomas[1] They are issued by Apollo 'of the οὐσία'[2] and by Pachomo 'of (the monastery of) Ama Sophia,' and addressed to Apa George, the archimandrite or head (*lit* great man) of the former monastery

Recto ↑

I] ϩ ᎒ γ´ ιβ βικτ, απο δημοϲ ϩ ογτον τριϲϲδεκτ, ιδ, χρ ῦ ο ιε δεκ[| μ̄ γ ιδ, ιδ μελχισεδεκ στοι χ +

Below this, in red ink,]αϐικ, ογϲι[α]ϲ | +απλω πατογϲια πεϥϲϩαι μπαικεον ντπετρα | ϭεω]ργιοϲ παρχημιατριτηϲ [

II] ϩϲτικα . | α]πλω πεϥ . . πατ]ογϲια στηχ̄η +| ϲ]ϩαι μπαικε[ο]ν μπμονοϲτη]ριον ν]απα θωμαϲ ϩιτοττηγτη απα ϭεωργιοϲ |]ϲ ϫεϲ ογπεϣε (above ηϭολοκ, ῆ ϩ) αϲει ετοοτ ϩιτοττηγτη | α]κτι   . ογ ναι ϩιτιρομπε ϫαι τριϲκετηκ]α |]/ απλω πατογϲια στηχ [+] |

Verso →

I] απα ϭεωρϭε πνοϭ νρωμε ϫεϲ ϣομητ ι |] | πεκαημμοϲιον ϲч/ ῆ γ ομεοϲ νεομο[. . ν]-ϩολοκ, ϩαη |] αιρομπε ϫαι τριτηϲ ιδ, παϩωμμω ϲιοι̅ ϲϭραфε μ́ | μ̄ κα | ια ϫ |

Another hand   α]μα ϲογфια πεϥϲϩαι μπαικεον ναπα θωμαϲ |] ϭεορϭε πνοϭ νρωμε | ϲνοοϩϲ ηϭολοκ, ϲч/ ῆ ιβ αϭει εϫωωτ [

II   +[3] παϩωμμω ναμ[α ϲογфια πεϥ]ϲϩαι | ϩιτοοϥ ναπα ϭεωρϭε πνοϭ νρωμε ϫεεϲ [| εϫωωτ ϩαϫιρομπε ται τριϲ κεϫηκα[| ϲϭραф μ́ фαωф νϭ ια ϩ +παϩ[ωμμω | ϲ]ϩαι μπαηκεων ναπα θωμαϲ ϩιτοοτκ | ϫ]εεϲ ϣμογη ϩολοκ, αϭει εϫωωτη |]ιϲ κεϫεκατηϲ ιδ, +] παϩωμμω στοι̅ χ [

125.—Papyrus, a fragment, 18×12 cm (1) *Recto* ↑ Script sloping, irregular uncials

Receipt (ἀπόδειξις), issued by   of Teròt enapake[4], for a tax (?) paid by the δίκαιον of a monastery, through its administrator (προνοητής)

+ανοκ [5 | πανε ϲιϲϩαι μππαι[καιον | [.]ϣτερ[6] ϩιτοοτκ ντ[ον] απα θ[| ναιτηϲ ϫεαιϫι απληρογ τοο[τκ | εκτι μμοϥ ναι ϩααπα εϲιακ π[| ϩατιρομπε ται τριϲτηιϫε[κατηϲ ινα/ | ετεναιμε ϲο νιρατη εκ[.]νον ϭε[| αιϫιμ ττιαποϫιϫιϲ νακ απ[| +ϐικτωρ πρ/ αϐεπιτρεπε ναι [| +ανοκ ϐικτωρ πρ/ πϣϲ μπμ[| πρωμϲϭρωτ ναπακε ειϲ[ϩαι

---

[1] The archimandrite and the 'father' of this monastery occur in our papyri (*v* Index), but it is not mentioned elsewhere Πετρα presumably corresponds to τοογ The 'πέτρα of Siut occurs in ZOEGA 370, CLEDAT'S *Baouit* 1 43, in no 139 here 'the π of Apa Victor'

[2] To whose estate does this refer? *Cf* the use in Brit Mus nos 162, 629, and the obscure expressions in KENYON, *Catal* 11 30 235.

[3] Not line 1

[4] This recurs in a fragment in the series Brit Mus Or 6201 A &c *V* here no 196, note

[5] This line erased to give room for the address of the text on *verso*

[6] *Cf* KRALL no cxxx and here no 187, which make it probable that the monastery here is that of S Phoebammon Is it possible to connect this with Boh ϣοεϩ and so with фατιοϲ фοιϐαμμων νταϭορα, TURAIEF, *Materialie* no 7?

126.—Papyrus; a fragment, 15 × 18 cm   Script   small, ligatured   *Recto* ↑

Document, perhaps relating to taxation   Visible are the names μερκουρο͞υ ιουστο͞υ, παμβω ζοιτ, [τ]αχυμῑ ανουφο͞ο, γρηγ͞ υπο͞, each with a sum of money opposite it; below these, a total γι, ιϊ ιδγ, below which, in a different hand,] ⲣⲱⲣⲧⲉ ⲡϣⲉ ⲛⲡⲙⲁⲕ, ⲁⲑⲁⲕⲁⲥⲉ ⲡⲣⲱⲙⲉ ϣⲙⲟⲩⲛ ⲧⲓⲥⲧⲟ͞ⲓ .... | ⲉⲧ[ⲓ   .]ⲁ, ⲕⲑⲉ ⲉⲥⲥ⳨ⲏ⳨ⲅ ⲉⲙⲟⲥ + ⲁⲛⲟⲕ ⲍⲱⲣ[ⲟⲟ]ⲉ ⲡϣⲉ ⲛⲡⲙⲁⲕ, ⲗⲉⲟⲛⲧⲓⲟⲥ | ⲁⲓ]ⲥ⳨ⲣⲁⲓ [ⲥ⳨ⲁⲣ]ⲟϥ ⲭⲛϥⲛⲟⲓ +

Verso blank

127—Papyrus, almost complete, 21 (?) × 31½ cm   Script   small, rarely ligatured   *Recto* ↑

Agreement (ὁμολογία) between the community of Tlêtm [1] and a landowner, as to the rent to be required of him   Cf the phraseology of TURAIEF, *Materialie po Archeol Christ Egipta*, no 6, and KRALL no cxlv

+ [ⲧⲕⲟⲓⲛ,] ⲛⲡⲧⲙⲉ ⲧⲗⲏⲧⲙ ϩⲓⲧⲟⲟⲧⲛ ⲁⲛⲟⲕ ϩⲏⲗⲓⲁ[ⲥ] ⲙⲛⲓⲱⲥⲏⲫ ⲕⲁⲡⲏⲅⲉ ⲙⲛⲟⲩⲛⲉⲓϣ ⲙⲛⲡⲁⲙⲟⲩⲛ ⲙⲛⲉⲛⲱⲭ | ⲙⲛⲡⲥⲉⲉⲡⲉ ⲛⲉⲟⲩⲟⲟⲉⲓ ⲡⲉⲛⲧⲙⲉ ⲧⲗⲏⲧⲙ 'ⲉⲛⲥⲣ[ⲁⲓ ⲛ]ⲁⲡⲁ ⲁⲫⲟⲩ ⲡ[ⲗ]ⲁⲙ̄ⲡ̄ⲣ̄ⲟ̄ⲧⲁⲧⲟⲥ ⲡϣⲉ ⲛⲡⲙⲁⲕⲁⲣ, ⲗⲉ ..| ⲡⲣⲱⲙⲉ ϣⲙⲟⲩⲛ ⲭⲉⲉⲡⲓⲁⲏ ⲉⲣⲉⲧⲁⲕ [2] ⲟⲩ⳽ⲟⲓ ϩⲛⲟⲩⲁⲡⲉⲛ, [3] ⲛϣⲟⲩⲙⲟⲩⲧⲉ ⲉⲣⲟϥ ⲭⲉⲫⲟⲓ ⲛⲧⲙⲏⲧⲉ ⲁⲕⲉⲓ ⲉⲃⲟⲗ | .. ⲭⲉⲁⲭⲟϥ ⲛⲡⲕⲁⲣⲡⲟⲥ ⲛⲧⲉⲧⲁⲣⲧⲏⲥ ⲓⲛ[ᵈ] ⲁⲕϭⲛⲧϥ ⲁϥϣⲁⲁϫⲉ [4] ⲡⲉⲕϣⲭⲟ ϩⲓⲱⲱϥ ⲗⲉⲡⲟⲛ | ⲁⲛⲡⲓⲑⲉ ⲙⲛⲛⲉⲛⲉⲣⲏⲩ ⲧⲁⲣⲉⲕⲃⲓ ⲧⲉⲅⲁⲥⲟⲩ [. ..] ⲱⲡⲣϥ ⲛⲡⲓⲧⲙⲉ ⲟⲩⲱⲧ ⲧⲗⲏⲧⲙ ⲛⲥⲭⲟⲟⲩ ⲛⲡⲉⲓⲕⲁⲣⲡⲟⲥ | ⲛⲟⲩⲱⲧ ⲧⲉⲧⲁⲣⲧⲏⲥ ⲓⲛⲁ, ⲧⲉⲛⲟⲩ ⲟⲩⲛ ⲧⲉⲛⲣ̄ⲟⲙⲟⲗⲟⲅⲓ ⲭⲉⲛⲉⲛⲉ- [ϣ'ⲁ[ⲙⲁ]ϩⲉ [5] ⲙⲟⲛ ⲉⲗⲁⲁⲩ ⲛⲁⲅ[ⲙⲟ]ⲥⲓⲟⲛ ϩⲁⲣⲟⲟⲩ | ⲟⲩⲁⲉ ⲭⲉⲛⲉⲛⲉϣⲙⲙⲁϩⲉ ⲙⲟⲛ ⲉⲭⲟⲟⲩ ⲡⲁⲣⲉ ⲡ[ⲕⲁⲣⲡⲟⲥ ⲛⲧⲉⲓⲣⲟⲙⲉ ⲧⲁⲓ [6] ⲧⲉⲧⲁⲣⲧⲏⲥ ⲓⲛⲁ ϣⲁⲥⲛⲥϭ | ⲁⲗⲗⲁ ⲛⲥⲧⲓ ⲧⲙⲉⲧⲟⲩⲉ ⲛⲛⲉⲣⲁⲧⲛ ⲙⲛⲡ ... ⲥⲛϩ .. ⲉⲛⲃⲟⲩⲗⲏ ϩⲁⲡⲉⲕϩⲛⲁⲙ [ⲁⲛⲥⲣⲁ]ⲓ [ⲛ]|ⲧⲉⲓⲣⲟⲙⲟⲗⲟⲥⲓⲁ ⲛⲁⲕ ⲉⲛⲥⲧⲟ͞ⲓ ⲉⲣⲟⲥ ⲛⲧⲛ ... ⲗⲁⲁⲩ ⲛⲁⲙ[ⲫⲓⲃⲟⲗⲉ]ⲓⲁ ⲉⲛⲱ[ⲣⲕ ⲛⲡⲛⲟⲩⲧⲉ] | [ⲡⲁⲛⲧⲟ]ⲕⲣⲁⲧⲱⲣ ⲙⲛⲡ[ⲟⲩϫ]ⲁⲓ ⲛⲛ[ⲉⲧⲁⲣⲭⲉⲓ] ⲉⲭⲱⲛ ⲭⲉⲛⲉⲛ- ϣⲡⲁⲣⲁⲃⲁ ⲙⲟⲛ ⲡⲣⲟ[ⲥ .... | in middle ⲧⲣⲓⲧⲏⲥ | Remains of two more lines, giving signatures in different hands, the first being ⲓⲱⲥⲏⲫ

'The community (κοινότης) of the village of Tlêtm, (represented) by us, Helias and Joseph, the headmen, and Wêeish and Pamoun and Fnoch and the rest of the husbandmen of our village, Tlêtm, we write to Apa Aphou, the illustrious (λαμπρότατος), son of the late Le , of Shmoun   Seeing that (ἐπειδή) thou hast (?) a field in   , which is called the Middle Field, thou didst set about (?) to plant it for the crop (καρπός) of the 4th Indiction and didst find it to be hard (to till) and thou wast not able to plant it, and (λοιπόν) we did agree (πείθειν) together that thou shouldst take their price (?) (and shouldst)   it for this same village, Tlêtm, and shouldst plant them for this same crop (καρπός) of the 4th Indiction, so (οὖν) now we agree (ὁμολογεῖν) that we shall not be able to make a claim on (?) thee for any tax (δημόσιον) on their account, nor ever to make a claim on (?) thee beyond

---

[1] Τλῆθμις P AMHERST cxxii, VITELLI no 50, now Ethidem

[2] Equivalent to ⲟⲩⲛⲧⲕ-?

[3] ϩⲛⲙⲙⲁⲛⲉ might be read. ⲕ possibly cancelled

[4] Cf ⲭⲁⲭⲱ, applied in Num xiii 21 (PEYRON) to land

[5] ? Cf ⲙⲙⲁϩⲉ in no 148

[6] 'This (current) Indiction' seems impossible, owing to the 3rd, in the last line.

them, except for (παρά) the crop (κ) of this 4th Indiction, but (ἀλλά) that thou shalt pay the
11 carats and the . . corn-tax (ἐμβολή) for thy freight. We have drawn up this
agreement (ὁμολογία) for thee, concurring (στοιχεῖν) therein, any doubt (ἀμφιβολία),
and swearing by God Almighty (παντοκρ) and the health of those that rule (ἄρχειν) over us,
that we shall not be able to contravene (παραβαίνειν) thee, according to (πρός)' ... 'The
3rd Indiction' occurs doubtless in the date of writing

Verso blank

GUARANTEES

128.—Papyrus, a fragment, 13 × 22 cm.   Script ligatured   Ink red   *Recto* ↑
Deed of Surety (ὁμολογία) for certain persons who had been entrusted to the writers'
custody and whom they undertake to produce when required, at Tnouhe[1] 'The nome of
Touhô' is mentioned[2]

]ⲙⲙⲟⲟⲩ ϩⲙⲡⲧⲟⲡϥ ⲧⲟⲩϧⲱ ⲁⲕⲉⲛⲧⲟⲩ ⲁⲕⲡⲁⲣⲁⲇⲓⲇⲟⲩ ⲙⲙⲟⲟⲩ ⲉⲧⲟⲟⲧ[ⲛ │ ⲛⲁⲩ ⲛⲓⲙ ⲛϣⲁⲕϣⲓⲛⲉ
ⲛⲥⲱⲟⲩ ⲉⲧⲟⲟⲧⲛ ⲧⲛⲉⲛⲧⲟⲩ ⲧⲛⲡⲁⲣⲁⲇⲓⲇⲟⲩ ⲙⲙⲟⲟⲩ ⲛⲁⲕ ⲛⲧⲛⲟⲩϧⲣⲉ ⲉⲓ ⲁⲛ ⲙⲟ[ⲓ]ⲧⲉ ⲧⲛⲥⲱⲕ
ϩⲁⲣⲱϥ ⲛⲓⲙ[3] │ ⲛϣⲁⲃⲉⲓ ⲉⲃⲟⲗ ⲉⲣⲟⲟⲩ ⲉⲩⲱⲣϫ ⲛⲁⲕ ⲁⲛⲥⲱⲛ ⲧⲓⲣⲟⲙⲟⲗⲟⲅⲓⲁ │ ⲛⲁⲕ ⲉⲛⲥⲧⲟⲓ⁽ˣ⁾ ⲉⲣⲟⲥ
ⲉⲛⲱⲣⲕ ⲉⲛⲛⲟⲩⲧⲉ ⲛⲡⲁⲛⲧⲟⲕⲣⲁⲧⲱⲣ ⲙⲛⲡⲉⲩϫⲁⲓ ⲛⲛⲉⲛϫⲟⲉⲓⲥ ⲉⲧⲁⲣ⁽ˣ⁾ ⲉϫⲱⲛ ⲧⲁⲣⲛϥⲩⲗⲁⲥⲥⲉ ⲛⲏⲧⲛ │
ⲡⲣⲟⲥ ⲧⲉⲥⲥⲟⲙ + │ ⲙ . . . ⲉⲓ ⲛ ⲥⲟⲣⲟⲥⲁⲣⲟ . . ⲑⲏ⁽ˣ⁾ ⲁⲁⲟⲓⲁ ⲥⲉⲩⲏⲣ⁽ᵒᶾ⁾ ⲥ ⲕ . . . │
ⲫ[about 12 let] ⲁⲡⲟⲗⲗⲱ ⲫⲟⲓⲃ ⲥⲓ ⲃ . ..│ + ⲁⲛⲟⲕ ... ⲗⲙⲙ ⲡⲁⲧⲛⲟⲩϧⲣⲉ ⲧⲓⲟ ⲙⲙⲛⲧⲣⲉ + │
[+ ⲁⲛⲟⲕ ⲓⲱϩⲁⲛⲛⲏⲥ ⲡϣⲏⲛⲙⲙⲁⲕ ⲙⲛⲁ ⲡⲣⲱⲙⲉ ϣ'ⲙⲟⲩⲛ] │ ⲧⲓⲟ ⲙⲙⲛⲧⲣⲉ +

129.—Papyrus, a fragment, 10½ × 32½ cm   Script rarely ligatured   *Recto* →
Deed relating to a surety for the *sacho*[4] of Paul, and consisting of a letter addressed
by Theodoracius, a high official, to the sureties, and of their undertaking and signatures
The whole, including these signatures, seems to be by the hand of the notary, excepting
the four crosses themselves

+ ⲁⲛⲟⲕ ⲡⲕⲩⲣ/ ⲑⲉⲟⲇⲱⲣⲁⲕⲉ ⲡⲉⲛⲇⲟϾ/ ⲛⲓⲗⲗⲟⲩ[5] ⲡⲣⲱⲙⲉ ϣⲙⲟⲩⲛ ⲉⲓϩⲁⲓ ⲛⲓⲟⲣⲇⲁⲛⲏⲥ │
ⲙⲛⲙⲁⲣⲕⲟⲥ ⲙⲛⲃⲓⲕⲧⲱⲣ ⲙⲛⲃⲓⲕⲧⲱⲣ ⲟⲛ ⲙⲛⲁⲡⲁ ⲕⲟⲗⲗⲟⲅⲟⲥ ⲛⲉⲣⲱⲙⲉ ϣⲙⲟⲩⲛ │ ϫⲉⲉⲡⲉⲓⲇⲁ
ⲁⲧⲛⲉⲁⲛⲧⲓⲫⲱⲛⲏ[6] ⲛⲁⲓ ⲉⲡⲉⲡⲣⲟⲥⲱⲡⲟⲛ ⲉⲩϣⲁⲭⲟ ⲙⲡⲁⲩⲗⲉ │ ⲡⲣⲟⲥ ⲧⲉⲧⲛⲉⲁⲛⲧⲓⲫⲱⲛⲏⲥⲓⲥ ⲁⲩⲱ ⲁⲧⲛⲉⲛⲧϥ
ⲛⲁⲓ ϫⲛⲉⲓⲛⲉⲁⲙⲙⲫⲓⲃⲁⲗⲉ │ [

---

[1] 'The Sycomore' A place? *Cf.* ⲧⲛⲟⲩϧⲣⲉ in a
Theban (?) ostracon, TURAIEF in *Bull Ac. Imp* '99, 440
[2] *V* KRALL no cxvi
[3] For ⲥⲱⲕ *cf* REVILLOUT, *Actes* 57, 61, here no 199,
Br Mus Or 6205 (JꞭôw) ⲧⲁⲣⲛⲥⲱⲕ ϧⲁⲡⲣⲟⲥⲧⲓⲙⲱⲛ ⲛⲓⲙ
[4] A title, not yet adequately explained Sometimes
a clerical official (CRUM, *Ostraca* no 36), *cf* *Rev égypt*
x 164, where *sacho*-clothes are contrasted with 'secular',

κοσμικός, also here, in a list (*v.* Index) ϩⲱⲃⲉⲥ ⲛⲟⲩⲓ ⲥⲁⲭⲟ
and Berlin P 4977 ϩⲟⲓⲧⲉ ⲛⲥⲁⲭⲱ Appears as in the
employ of another, in present and another text here and
Brit Mus nos 627 1089 In Brit Mus no 571 apparently like ⲥⲁϧ, *cf* *PSBA* XXI. 249.
[5] Ἐνδοξότατος, ιλλούστριος *Cf* the κόμης in no 207
[6] *V* KRALL cxvi, Brit Mus no 457

Verso

ετιϩοⲙολοϲια [......] ⲉⲣⲉϩⲱϥ ⲛⲓⲙ ⲉ[ⲡⲱ]ⲏⲡⲉ ϭⲏⲡⲟⲕⲉⲓⲥ[ⲑⲁ]ⲓ [ⲛⲏⲧⲛ .]. ⲉⲡⲉⲧ[ⲛ]ⲟⲩⲣⲝ
ⲟⲩⲛ ⲁⲛϲⲙⲙ ϯϩⲟⲙⲟⲗⲟϲⲓⲁ ⲛⲏⲧⲛ ⲁⲩⲱ ⲁⲡⲟⲩⲁ ⲡⲟⲩⲁ ϩⲓⲱⲱⲛ ⲧⲓ ϣⲟⲙⲧ ⲛⲥⲧⲁⲩⲣⲟⲥ | ⲉⲣⲟⲥ ⲛⲧϥϭⲓⲝ

ⲉⲧⲉ ⲫⲁⲙ ⲑ ⲓⲛⲁ, ⲓ + $\underline{|\overset{\sigma\eta\mu\iota/}{||}|}_{\iota\text{o}\rho\delta\alpha\nu\eta\varsigma}$ $\underline{|\overset{\sigma\eta\mu\iota}{|}|}_{\mu\alpha\rho\kappa\text{o}\varsigma}$ $\underline{|\overset{\sigma\eta\mu\iota/}{|}|}_{\beta\iota\kappa\tau\text{o}\rho\text{o}\varsigma}$ $\underline{|\overset{\sigma\eta\mu\iota/}{|}|}_{\beta\iota\kappa\tau\text{o}\rho\text{o}\varsigma}$ | + ⲁⲛⲟⲕ ⲓⲟⲣⲇⲁⲛⲏⲥ ⲙⲛⲙⲁⲣⲕⲟⲥ

ⲙⲛⲃⲓⲕⲧⲱⲣ ⲙⲛⲃⲓⲕⲧⲱⲣ ⲟⲛ ⲙⲛ (blank[1]) ⲧⲓⲥⲧⲟⲓⲭ, | ⲉⲧⲓϩⲟⲙⲟⲗⲟϲⲓⲁ ⲛⲑⲉ ⲉⲥⲥⲏϩ ⲉⲙⲟⲥ + ⲁⲛⲟⲕ
ⲓⲱⲁⲛⲛⲏⲥ ⲙⲛⲟ ⲛⲧⲁⲓⲥϩⲁⲓ ϩⲁⲣⲟⲟⲩ ⲝⲉⲥⲟⲩⲛⲟⲓ ⲁⲛ ϥ

130.—Papyrus, a fragment, $17\frac{1}{2} \times 13$ cm   Script ligatureless   *Recto* ↑

Agreement (ὁμολογία) addressed by several sureties (ἐγγυητής) to Theodosius and Longinus, both of high rank, and relating to a single person, (whom they undertake to produce) at their own risk   The hand is apparently that of the first surety

+ ⲉⲛ ⲟⲛⲟⲙⲁⲧⲓ ⲧⲟⲩ ⲡⲁⲧⲣⲟⲥ ⲕⲁⲓ ⲧⲟⲩ ⲩⲓⲟⲩ [| ⲉⲅⲣⲁⲫⲏ ⲫⲁⲱⲫⲓ ⲉⲡⲛ̈ⲁ̇ⲕⲁⲓⲇⲉⲕⲁⲧⲏ ⲧⲏ[ⲥ |
+ ⲁⲛⲟⲕ ⲛⲉⲥⲅⲩⲏⲧⲏⲓ ⲉⲟⲩⲁ ϩⲩⲡⲟⲅⲣⲁⲫⲉ [[| ⲛⲓ ⲅ ⲛⲛⲉⲥⲅⲙⲓⲟⲛ ⲛⲛⲟⲩⲁ ⲡⲟⲩⲁ ⲉⲟⲩⲁ [[| ⲉⲃⲁⲗⲏ[ⲗⲟⲩ
ⲙⲙⲟϥ ϩⲓⲱⲱⲥ[2] ϩⲁⲡⲉϥⲡⲣ[| ⲛⲧⲱⲧⲛ ⲛⲕⲩⲣ̄, ⲑⲉⲟⲇⲟⲥⲉ ⲡⲉⲛⲇⲟⲝⲟⲧ[ⲗⲟⲛⲅⲓⲛⲉ ⲡⲙⲉⲅⲁⲗⲟⲡⲣⲉⲡⲉⲥ-
ⲧⲁⲧⲟⲥ ⲛ[|ⲙⲏⲧⲓ̈ⲥⲡⲉ ⲛⲡⲁⲟⲛⲉ ⲡⲉⲃⲟⲧ ⲛⲧⲓⲣⲟⲙⲡ[ⲉ | ⲟⲛⲟⲙⲁⲍⲉ[3] ⲙⲙⲟϥ ⲛⲡⲉϥⲡⲣⲟⲥⲱⲡⲟⲛ ⲙ[|
ⲛⲁⲧⲗⲟⲟⲩⲥ ⲛⲁⲧⲥⲧⲁⲩⲣⲟⲥ ⲛⲁⲧⲉⲭⲛⲙⲁ ⲛⲛⲟⲡⲁⲭⲟⲥ[4] | ⲉⲧⲛⲁϩⲩⲡⲟⲙⲛⲏⲥⲕⲉ ⲛⲙⲟⲛ ⲉⲧⲃⲏⲏ[ⲧ | ⲛⲁⲧⲗⲁⲁⲩ
ⲛⲡⲣⲟⲫⲁⲥⲓⲥ ⲛϭⲩⲡⲟⲕⲉⲓⲥ[ⲑⲁⲓ | ⲛⲧⲟⲟⲧϥ ⲛϣⲟⲣⲡ ⲛϩⲉ[5] ⲛⲓⲙ ⲛⲧⲁⲛⲟⲩ[| ϩⲟⲙⲟⲗⲟϲⲓⲁ ⲛⲏⲧⲛ ⲁⲛⲥⲧⲟⲓⲭⲉⲓ
ⲉⲣⲟⲥ [ⲛⲡⲁⲛⲧⲟⲕⲣⲁⲧⲱⲣ ⲙⲛⲛⲉⲩⲭⲁⲓ ⲛⲛ[| ⲛⲣⲁϩⲧ ⲛϣⲉ ⲛⲡⲙⲁⲕⲁⲣ, ⲥⲩⲥⲧⲁⲥⲉ ⲡ[| ⲡⲗⲉⲛⲧⲓⲁⲣⲏⲥ[6]

$\underline{|\overset{\sigma\eta\mu}{||}|}_{\phi[\iota\lambda\text{o}\theta]\overset{v}{\epsilon}\overset{u}{\text{o}}}$ + ⲁⲛⲟⲕ ⲫⲓⲗⲟ[ⲑⲉⲟⲥ |

Verso   remains of a Greek account, containing the amîr's name, ραζιδ[7] ειλ[δ] αμιρ̄

131.—Papyrus, a fragment, 9×14 cm   Script sloping, ligatureless   *Recto* ↑

Deed of Surety, in similar phraseology to that of no 129, with a fine of 6 *solidi*
The list on *verso* is presumably that of the sureties

]ⲛⲧⲓⲡⲟⲗⲓⲥ ⲛⲟⲩⲱⲧ ϣⲙⲟⲩⲛ ⲝⲉⲧ[|] ⲉⲡⲁϭⲟⲙⲉⲛⲏ ⲛⲧⲓⲣⲟⲙⲡⲉ ⲧⲁⲓ ⲉⲕⲧⲏ[ⲥ |] ⲛⲧⲁⲛϣⲏⲣⲡⲟⲛⲟ-
ⲙⲁⲍⲉ ⲙⲙⲟϥ [|] ⲛⲧⲟⲟⲧⲛ ⲙⲛⲧϥ ⲧⲛⲡⲁⲣⲁⲇⲓⲇⲟⲩ ⲙⲙⲟϥ [|]ⲛⲁⲧ[ⲥ]ⲭⲏⲙⲁ ⲛⲙⲟⲛⲁⲭⲟⲥ ⲫⲟⲅⲛ
ⲛⲙ[| ⲛ]ⲁϯ ⲥⲟⲟⲩ ⲛ[ϩⲟ]ⲗⲟⲕⲟ[ⲧ,] ⲛⲛⲟⲩ⳰ ⲛⲓⲧ[ⲛ]

Verso   legible are μαιο̄ͧ απο ερμ̄ͭ, απα νοκ̄, μην̄ͧ, κλλ̄ σιρ̄ͬ απο ωφελιο[8], κοιν̄ͧ αβ̄ σενου̇, κοιν̄ͧ νοταριο̇, μην̄ͧ απο πλο̇, απολλω νι[

---

[1] Apa Colluthus' name is wanting
[2] Sc this ὁμολογία
[3] ? [ⲛⲧⲁⲛϣⲏⲣⲡ]ⲟⲛⲟⲙⲁⲍⲉ, cf no 131
[4] Cf no 131 'Without word without cross, without monk's habit' Presumably there is a difference in meaning from the common ⲛⲁⲧϭⲁⲡ ⲛⲁⲧⲛⲟⲙⲟⲥ (cf ἄνευ δίκης καὶ κρίσεως, δίχα παντὸς νομου &c) In Krall no cxiii without word (?) or cross or Sunday (κυριακή) or festival-day , so in *ib* cxiv and here no 132. In deeds of surety from Jkôw (Brit. Mus Or 6212, 6226[14]), 'without word or cross or festival day   Cf perhaps Crum, *Ostraca* no 42 In Turaief, *Materialie* no 6 and Krall cxlv is an obscure phrase of similar purport

[5] Cannot be the same as in Krall cxxv
[6] Λεντιάριος *lintiarius* (Herwerden)
[7] شيد,
[8] A place? Cf the name Ωφέλιος, Brit Mus Catal p 450

132.—Papyrus, a fragment, $18\frac{1}{2} \times 14$ cm   Script clumsy, ligatureless   *Recto* ↑

Deed of Surety (ἐγγύα, ὁμολογία) relating to certain villagers who had been delivered to the amir   The writer (sing) now undertakes to produce them for the person addressed   On *verso* a similar text, possibly by the same hand, mentioning the amir Nagea[1] and the place Pma npeshoeij[a]

]ⲛⲁϭⲉ[a] ⲡⲉⲙϩⲓⲧ ⲛⲡⲙⲟⲩⲛ ⲉ̇ϭⲣⲁⲓ ⲛⲁⲡⲁ [|] ⲉⲛⲁⲡⲁⲧⲓⲙⲉⲛⲉ ⲁⲩⲏⲧⲟⲩ ⲙⲡⲉⲛ[δ] ⲛⲁⲙ[ⲓⲣⲁ |]ⲉ ⲛ[ⲙ]ⲟⲥ ⲉⲡⲓⲡⲧⲓⲙⲉ ⲁⲕϣⲓⲛⲉ ⲛⲥⲁⲧⲉⲩⲛⲥⲁ [| ϣ]ⲓⲛⲉ ⲛⲥⲱⲟⲩ ⲛⲧⲟⲧⲛ ⲧⲛⲛⲁⲡⲁⲣⲁⲧⲓⲧⲟⲩ ⲛⲙⲟⲩ [| ϩⲱϥ] ⲛⲙ ⲉⲡⲱⲡⲉ ϩⲁⲡⲓϩⲱϥ ⲟⲩⲱⲣⲝ ⲛⲁⲕ ⲁⲓⲥⲙ[ⲛ|ⲧ]ⲉⲓϩⲟⲙⲟⲗⲟⲅⲓⲁ ⲛⲑⲉ ⲉⲥⲛⲏ ⲛⲙ[ⲟⲓ] + [

Below this the names of guarantors and (?) guaranteed

]ψ̅ⲩ̅ᵡ	γ	πετρ ιακκ⁄		
]	?	βικ⁄	?	s a εσλα
]	a	πτολ⁰⁄ φοιβ⁻		s σοφια γαμ αυ⁻ [4]
]	β	οννοφρ μ⁻		s σοφια γαμ αυ⁻
]	β	(blank)		

Verso   (the upper part apparently blank)

]ⲧ ⲙⲛⲡⲉϩⲏⲧ [10 letters |] ⲛⲁⲡⲁ ⲃⲓⲕⲧⲱⲣ ⲡⲁⲛⲁⲓⲕⲉⲩⲭⲏⲥ[5] . . [|] illegible]ⲥⲧⲟⲥ[6] ⲛ[ⲁⲙ]ⲉⲣⲁ ⲛⲁⲥⲉⲁ ⲡϣⲥ ⲛⲟⲩⲛⲏ[|]ⲧⲓⲙⲉ ⲁⲧⲛⲉϣⲓⲛⲉ ⲧⲓⲥⲥⲛⲁ ⲛϩⲟⲙⲟ[ⲗⲟⲅⲓⲁ |]ⲛⲉⲙ ⲛⲁⲧⲗⲟⲥ[ⲟⲥ] ⲛⲁⲧⲅⲁⲩⲣⲟⲩ[7] . . [|]ⲧⲛ ⲙⲛⲡⲉⲧ ⲉⲡⲟⲩⲝⲓⲓϥ ⲉⲛⲁⲣϭ . ⲛ [|]ⲟⲥ ⲛⲁⲡⲁⲓ[8] ⲡⲣⲉⲙⲛⲙⲁ ⲛⲡϣⲟⲉⲓⲝ ⲧ[

133.—Papyrus, a fragment, $38\frac{1}{2} \times 9$ cm   Script various   *Recto* ↑

List of those who go surety for Elias, with the amounts guaranteed   Each line is in a different hand

] + ⲁⲛⲟⲕ ⲃⲓⲕⲧⲟⲣ ⲛⲡϣⲛⲡⲙⲁⲕⲁⲣⲓⲟⲥ ⲙⲛⲡⲁ ⲧⲓⲉⲥ[ⲥⲓⲁ ⲛϩⲏⲗ]ⲓⲁⲥ ⲛⲥ̄[9] ⲝⲟⲩⲱⲧ ϩⲟⲗⲟⲕ⁄ [ⲛ̄] ⲕ | + ⲁⲛⲟⲕ ⲓⲉⲣⲏⲙⲓ ⲡϣⲛⲡⲙⲁⲕ⁄ ⲁⲡⲁ ⲕⲩⲣⲓⲉ ⲡⲣⲙⲁⲓⲟⲥⲕⲟⲣⲓ[δ 10] ⲧⲓⲉⲥⲥⲩⲁ | ⲛϩⲏⲗⲓⲁⲥ ⲛⲥ̄ ϣⲟⲙⲛⲧ ⲛϩⲟⲗⲟⲕ⁄, ⲛ̄ γ | + ⲁⲛⲟⲕ ⲁⲡⲟⲗⲗⲱ ⲡϣⲥ ⲛⲡⲙⲁⲕⲁⲣⲓⲟⲥ ⲟⲩⲉⲛⲟⲃⲣ ⲧⲓⲉⲛⲥⲓⲁ ⲛⲏⲗⲓⲁⲥ ⲛⲧⲓ . ⲛ ϥⲧⲟⲟⲩ ⲛϩⲟⲗⲟⲕ⁄, ⲛ̄ δ | + ⲁⲛⲟⲕ ⲙⲏ   ⲧⲓⲉⲥⲥⲓⲁ ⲛϩⲏⲗⲓⲁⲥ ⲧⲓ . ⲟⲩ ⲛⲙⲛⲧ ⲛϩⲟⲗⲟⲕ⁄, γⲓ, ⲛ̄ ι | another line, ending γ⁄, ⲛ̊ ι

134.—Papyrus, a fragment, $19\frac{1}{2} \times 13$ cm   Script ligatureless   *Recto* ↑

Undertaking, with surety (ἐγγύη), by Theodore, a vine-dresser, addressed to   , regarding the cultivation of the latter's vineyard   On *verso*, in another hand, a payment (or ? receipt) of money by Theodore, here called an ἐντάγιον[11]

---

[1] *Cf* ⲛⲁⲕⲉⲁ, Brit Mus no 586   May be أغا, أباب or أغا   The father's name perhaps begins عبد
[a] Unknown   Possibly translates γυμνάσιον
[3] The place whence guarantors and guaranteed come   Perhaps read ⲛⲁϭⲉ (*cf* ⲛⲁⲕⲉ in no 123) or *cf* ⲧⲙⲟⲩⲛⲣⲁϭⲉ in a fragment, Brit Mus. Or 6201 A &c
[4] γαμετὴ αὐτοῦ.
[5] ἀντιγεοῦχος   Occurs in *Sphinx* x 2, KRALL clxvii,

and probably Brit Mus no 1114.
[6] Probably for εὐκλεέστατος
[7] *V* no 130
[8] *V* Brit Mus Catal, p 448
[9] ἐγγύη
[10] *Cf* Μερὶς Διοσκορίδου, MITTEIS, *Urk* no 90
[11] As in nos 196, 215, Brit Mus no 458, GRENFELL, *Gk. Papyri* ii, no xcvii.

+ ⲁⲛⲟⲕ ⲑⲉⲟⲇⲱⲣⲉ ⲡⲓⲥⲙⲉ ⲡϣⲉ ⲛⲡϭⲱ[ⲗ | ⲧⲓⲕⲟⲩ ⲇⲉ ⲉⲓϣⲟⲟⲡ ϩⲓⲯⲁϩ ⲓⲱϩⲁⲛⲛ[ⲏⲥ [1] | ⲡϣⲉ
ⲛⲡⲙⲁⲕⲁⲣⲓⲟⲥ ⲛϣⲟⲩⲣⲡⲉϥⲙⲉⲉ[ⲅⲉ | ⲡⲣⲱⲙⲉ ϣⲙⲟⲩⲛ ⲍⲉⲧⲓⲣⲁϣⲉ ⲧⲓϩⲟⲙ[ⲟⲗⲟⲅⲉⲓ [2] ⲛⲡⲉⲧⲣⲟⲥ ⲡⲉⲥⲙⲉ
ⲧⲁⲣⲉϥⲣⲏⲕϭⲟⲟⲙ [| ⲛⲡⲁ[.   ⲡⲉ]ⲃⲟⲧ ⲛⲧⲓⲣ[ⲟ]ⲙⲡⲉ ⲛϱ[| ⲕⲁⲛ ⲁⲃ . . .[ⲕ]ⲁⲛ ⲁⲃⲉ . ϩ . . . .[| ⲛϫⲓⲛⲥϥ .
ⲱⲃ . . ⲧⲁϥϫⲓ[| ⲛⲡⲉϥⲕⲁⲣⲡⲟⲥ ⲍⲛⲛⲉⲟⲩⲥⲙⲁϩ ⲕ[| ⲕⲙⲁⲩ ⲁⲩⲱ ⲍⲛⲛⲁⲕⲁ ⲟ . ⲗ . ⲱ . ⲫⲁ [| ⲡⲁⲙⲫⲓ-
ⲃⲟⲗⲉⲓⲁ (above ⲛⲁⲕ) ⲉⲡⲓ ⲧⲱ ⲧⲁⲧⲓ [| ⲡⲉⲕϭⲱⲙ ⲁⲩⲱ ⲛϣⲁⲓⲟⲩ[| ⲡⲉⲥⲙⲉ ⲛⲁⲕ ⲕⲁⲧⲗⲟⲅⲟⲥ |
ⲡ . . ⲡⲧⲱϣ ⲛϭⲱⲙ ⲛⲡ[| ⲡⲡⲁⲛⲧⲟⲕⲣⲁⲧⲱⲣ ⲙⲛⲡ[ⲟⲩ]ϫⲁⲓ | ⲛⲧⲓⲉⲥⲧⲅⲏ ⲥⲩⲱⲣⲍ ⲛⲁⲕ ⲟⲩⲛ | ϩⲓⲧⲛⲛⲁ-
ⲥⲧⲁⲩⲣⲟⲥ ⲁⲙⲡⲁⲣⲁ[ⲕⲁⲗⲉ |

Verso]ⲱⲣⲉ ⲡⲣⲱⲙⲡⲙⲁ ⲛⲁⲡⲁ ϣⲙⲟⲩⲧⲉ ^{sic}]] ⲡⲣⲱⲛⲟⲏⲧⲏⲥ ⲡϫⲥ ⲛⲡⲙⲁⲕⲁⲣ/ | ⲍ]ⲉⲉⲕ ⲕⲁⲓⲡⲁϣⲉ
ϩⲟⲗⲟⲕⲟⲧⲧⲓ |] ⲧⲣⲙⲏⲥⲓⲛ ϩⲛⲧⲁⲥⲫⲁⲗⲉⲓⲁ | ⲣⲟⲉ]ⲓⲥ ⲙⲡⲉⲓⲉⲛⲧⲁⲥⲓⲛ ⲛⲁⲕ |]ⲓⲛⲁ°/ α + $\frac{\sigma\eta\mu/}{\theta\epsilon o\delta\omega\rho}$ + ⲁⲛⲟⲕ |

]ⲥⲧⲟⲓⲭⲉⲓ ⲉⲡⲓⲉⲛⲧⲁⲥⲓⲛ ⲛⲑⲉ ⲉϥⲥⲏϩ ⲙⲙⲟⲥ + |] ⲡⲣⲱⲙⲉ ϣⲙⲟⲩⲛ ⲛⲧⲁⲓ ^{sic} ϩⲁⲣⲟϥ +

135.—Papyrus; a fragment, 46 × 20 cm   Script ligatured   *Recto*, top *selis* →, rest ↑
At the top, remains of a Greek and Arabic protocol in 3 or 4 ll of large, brown characters,
of which line 1 begins εν ονομ[ατι

Deed of Surety (ἐγγυητικὴ ὁμολογία[3]), addressed in the 1st pers plur to a high official
of Shmoun[4]   It probably guarantees the work of Apollo Elias for 5 months to come

[Entirely obliterated] | ⲏⲩ ⲙⲛⲛⲉⲩⲥⲙⲙⲟⲛ ⲛⲁⲟⲩⲱⲛⲁϩ ⲉⲃⲟⲗ ϩⲉ[ⲡ]ⲉⲛⲧ ⲛⲧⲓⲉⲥⲧⲅⲩⲧⲓⲕⲏ[|
ⲛⲧⲡ[ⲟⲗⲓⲥ] ⲧⲁⲓ ϣⲙⲟⲩⲛ ⲙⲡⲉⲥⲧⲟϣ ⲍⲉⲉⲡⲓⲁⲛ ⲁⲛⲡⲁⲣⲁⲕⲁⲗⲉⲓ ⲛⲙⲱⲧⲛ ⲧⲁⲣⲉⲧⲛ[ⲉ | ⲉ . . . . ⲧⲓ ⲉⲃⲉⲣϱⲱϭ
ⲡⲣⲟⲥⲩⲛⲏⲑⲓⲁ ⲛⲧⲓⲟⲩ ⲕⲉⲃⲟⲧ ⲛϩⲟⲟⲩ ⲁⲧⲛⲉϣⲓⲛⲉ[| ⲧⲓ ⲙⲉ . . . . . . ⲍⲟⲩⲣⲱⲙⲛⲡⲥⲙⲙⲟⲛⲁⲥⲧⲉ ^н [5] ⲁⲡⲟⲗⲗⲱ
ϩⲏⲗⲓⲁⲥ ⲛⲧⲁⲛ . [| ⲡϱⲱϥ ⲟⲩⲱⲛⲁϩ ⲛⲏⲧⲛ ⲉⲃⲟⲗ ⲍⲉϥϣ[ⲁ]ϣⲱⲡⲉ ⲡⲟⲗⲉ ⲕⲩⲣⲟ ⲕ . . . | . . . . ⲉⲍⲱⲛ ϩⲁⲣⲟϥ
ⲛⲧⲉⲧⲛϣⲱⲡⲉ ⲛⲧⲱⲧⲛ ⲛⲉⲍⲁⲕⲓⲛⲁⲩ[ⲛⲟⲥ . ^c]ⲱⲛ [|]ⲙⲛ ϩⲟⲙⲟⲗⲟⲅⲉⲓⲁ ⲛⲏⲧⲛ ϩⲁⲣⲟϥ ⲁⲩⲱ [ⲉ]ⲕϣⲁⲛ-
ϣⲱⲡⲉ . . . ⲛⲉⲓ ⲛⲥⲉⲡ[| [2 quite illegible lines] | + εγρ μ [rest illegible] | ⲡⲁⲧⲉⲣⲙ[ⲟ]ⲩ[ⲧⲉ] . .
ⲧⲓⲥⲧⲓⲭⲉ ⲕⲓⲣⲉ ⲁⲡⲟⲗⲗ[ⲱ] ⲓⲥⲁⲕ ⲉⲛⲱⲭ . ⲕⲟ [| ⲕⲩⲣⲁⲕ[ⲟⲥ] ⲉⲣⲏⲛ[

Verso traces of 1 line at top

136.—Papyrus, a fragment, 4 × 12½ cm   Script ligatureless   *Recto* ↑
End of a Deed of Surety, the author of which was a woman[7]

ⲉⲥⲥ]ⲅⲏ ⲛⲥⲧⲟ^xⲓ ⲉⲣⲟⲥ ⲛϣⲟⲣⲕ ⲛⲡⲛⲟⲩⲧⲉ ⲡⲡⲁⲛⲧⲟⲕⲣⲁⲧⲱⲣ |] ⲁ ⲧⲥⲧϣⲏⲣⲡⲉϫⲁⲓ ⲧⲓⲥⲧⲟ^xⲓ ⲉⲧⲓϩⲟⲙⲟⲗⲟ/
ⲉⲥⲟ ⲛⲉⲥⲥⲅⲏ | ⲧ]ⲏⲣⲉ ⲛⲧⲓϩⲟⲙⲟⲗⲟⲅⲓⲁ ⲉⲥⲟ ⲛⲉⲥⲥⲅⲏ $\frac{\sigma\eta\mu}{\pi\epsilon\tau o}$[8] + ⲁⲛⲟⲕ |]ϣⲙⲛ ⲛⲧⲁⲓⲥϩⲁⲓ ϩⲁⲣⲟⲟⲩ
ⲍⲛⲥⲟⲩⲛⲟⲉⲓ ⲁⲛ + |]

---

[1] Apparently a place, in Br Mus Or 6201 b &c
ⲡⲉⲣⲱⲙⲉ ⲛⲯⲁϩ ⲓⲱϩⲁⲛⲏⲥ Cf ⲡⲥⲁⲣⲕⲏⲥ (sic, not ⲛⲁⲣⲕⲟⲩ),
Vitelli, *Papiri* no 73, and Krall cxiii ⲛⲉϱⲣ[ ]ⲱⲣ
But possibly read ⲧⲁϱ-

[2] A phrase common in contracts, v Krall cxiii, cxxvii,
Brit Mus no 1073 Cf. ὁμολογῶ ἑκουσίως, οἱ ἑκουσία γνώμῃ

[3] Cf ll 2 and 8 and no 136 The phrase is frequent
in the Jkôw papyri, e g Brit Mus Or. 6205

[4] Perhaps the pagarch or amîr, from the phrase in line 3

[5] Enclitic -ⲡⲉ twice is suspicious, but 'the monastery
of Apollo' can scarcely be read

[6] ἐξακίνδυνος, with the meaning of ἀκίνδυνος In Jkôw
papyri, Br Mus Or 6201 &c, ⲧⲁⲉⲣⲧⲏⲅⲧⲛ ⲉⲛⲁϫⲓⲕⲉⲛⲧⲓⲛⲟⲥ
ϩⲁⲣⲟϥ

[7] To read ⲉⲧϣⲏⲣⲡⲛ would be quite unusual here

[8] Reading certain, name new.

137.—Papyrus, a fragment, 14 × 33 cm   Script sloping, almost ligatureless   *Recto* ↑
Deed of Surety (ἐγγύη), addressed by 3 guarantors[1], presumably from Thone[2], to a superior, on behalf of one person

]ⲙⲏⲧⲛ ϩⲁⲧⲉⳓⲡⲁⲣⲁⲥⲱⲧⲛ[3] ⲛⲁⲧⲗⲁⲁⲩ ⲛⲁⲙⲫⲓⲃⲟⲗⲥⲓⲁ ⲁ[ⲅⲱ] ϩ̇ⲱ]ⲕⲓ [ⲛⲙ[4]] | ⲥⲡⲱⲛⲉ ⲩ̇ⲛⲟⲕⲉⲓⲥⲑⲉ[5]
ⲛ̇ⲧⲥ̇ⲧⲏⲙⲛ̇ⲧⳓⲟⲉⲓⲥ ⲉⲅⲁⲥⲫⲁⲗⲥⲓ ⲛ̇ⲡⲉ̇ⲅⲅⲩⲏ ⳨ | ⲥⲅⲣⲁⲫ/ ⲧⲩⲃⲓ ⲓⲁ ⲓⲛ⸌ᵟ/ ⲡⲣⲱⲧⲏⲥ ⳨   ⳨ ⲁⲛⲟⲕ
ⲕⲩⲣⲁⲕⲟⲥ ⲡϣⲉ ⲛ̇ⲁⲡⲟⲗⲗⲱ ⲓⲥⲧⲟⲓⲭⲉⲓ ⲉⲧⲉⲉⲅⲅⲩⲏ ⳨ | ⲁⲛⲟⲕ ⲁⲡⲁ ⲙⲟⲛⲉ ⲡϣⲉ ⲛ̇ⲁⲡⲟⲗⲗⲱ ⲙⲛ̇ⲧⲁⲩⲣⲓⲛⲉ
ⲡⲉⲙⲣⲓⲥ[6] ⲡϣⲉ ⲛ̇ⲫⲏⲩ ⲧⲉⲛⲥⲧⲟⲓⲭⲉⲓ ⲉⲧⲓⲉⲅⲅⲩⲏ ⲁⲛⲟⲕ ⲧⲁⲩⲣⲓⲛⲉ ⲡⲓⲟⲙⲛⲓⲕⲟⲥ ⲛⲉⲱⲛⲉ ⲁⲓⲥϩⲁⲓ ϩⲁⲣⲟⲟⲩ
ⲛ̇ⲧⲁⲅⲉⲡⲓⲧⲣⲟⲡⲉ ⲛⲁⲓ | ⲉⲓⲥⲟⲩⲛⲟⲉⲓ ⲛⲉϩⲁⲓ ⲁⲛ ⳨ ⳨ ⲁⲛⲟⲕ ⲥⲁⲣⲁⲡⲱⲛ ⲡϣⲛ̇ ⲛⲁⲡⲁ ⲙⲟⲛⲉ ⲝⲉⲧⲉⲟ
ⲕⲁⲛ|ⲣⲉ ⲉⲧⲉⲁⲥⲡⲁⲗⲓⲛ ⳨ ⲁⲛⲟⲕ ⲡⲉⲣⲓⲧ ⲉϣⲉ ⲫⲓⲃ ⲝⲉⲧⲓⲟ ⲙⲡⲣⲉ ⲉⲧⲁⲥⲫⲁⲗⲓⲛ ⳨ | ⳨ ⲁⲛⲟⲕ ⲡϭⲱⲗ
ⲡϣⲉ ⲛ̇ⲓⲱⲁⲛⲛⲏⲥ ⲛ̄ ⲡⲣⲙⲛⲉⲱⲙⲉ ⲅⲓⲟ ⲛ̇ⲙⲉⲧⲣⲉ ⲉ|ⲁⲓⲁⲥⲫⲁⲗⲓⲁ ⳨⳨⳨ | ⳨ δι εμου ταυρινο εγραφ ⳨⳨⳨

138.—Papyrus, a fragment, 17 × 12 cm   Script ligatured   *Recto* ↑   12+ lines
Deed of Surety, ⲉⲛⳓⲁ (ἐγγύα *sic*)   Only the final phrases, ⲉⲅⲱⲣⳝ ⲟⲩⲛ, the oath by God and the health of the rulers, and the witnesses   The latter are ⲕⲩⲣⲓⲁ[ⲕⲟⲥ] son of with the title ⲡⲣⲁⲕⲛ/[7],   son of ⲓⲱⲁⲛⲛⲉ, ⲙⲁⲟⲁⲓⲟⲥ son of .   Two of them come from ⲡⲕⲟⲩⲓ ⲗⲩⲥⲓⲙ̄[8]   All are in the same hand

CONTRACTS

139.—Papyrus, 2 fragments, together 15 × 25½ cm   Script   unskilled, ligatureless   *Recto* ↑

Agreement (δόξον[9]) between David and Praxia[10], regarding a marriage[11]

+ ϩⲙ̇ⲡⲣⲁⲛ ⲙ̇ⲡⲕⲟⲩⲧⲉ ⲛ̇ϣⲟⲣⲡ ⲁⲛⲟⲕ ⲇⲁⲩⲉⲓⲇ ⲉⲓⲥϩⲁⲓ ⲙⲡⲣⲁⳝⲥⲓⲁ ⲝⲉⲛ̇ⲧⲁⲓⲡⲓⲑⲉ ⲛⲉⲙⲙ ⲁⲣⲅⲓⲛⲏ ⲧⲟⲩϣⲉⲉⲣⲉ ⲙ̇ⲡⲁ|ϣⲏⲣⲉ ⲁⲓⲥⲙⲛⲧⲥ ⲛⲏⲙⲙ ⲉϣⲟⲙⲧ ⲛ̇ϩⲁⲗⲁⲕⲟⲣⲧⲉ ⲙⲛ̇|ⲟⲩⲧⲣⲓⲙⲥⲛ ⲙ̇ⲛⲟⲩⲗⲏⲛⲓⲧⲥ ⲙ̇ⲛⲟⲩⲕⲁⲕⲗⲓⳓⲉ ⲙ̇ⲛⲟⲩ[ⲅ]ⲉⲗⲟ.ⲉ [ⲙⲛ]ⲟⲩϣⲛϩⲉⲣⲓⲁ ⲙⲛ̇ⲟⲩⲙⲛ̇ⲧⲱⲧⲉ ⲁⲅⲱ ⲧⲁⲣⲛ̇ⲣⲧϣⲉⲗⲉⲥⲧ [ⲙⲛ|ⲛⲏ]ⲛⲏⲣⲏⲩ ⲟⲡⲁϣⲉ ⲉⲣⲟⲓ [about 14 lett ⲛⲏ]ⲛⲏⲣⲏⲩ ϩⲉⲓⲡⳝⲓ ⲙⲛ̇ⲧⲓ ⲁⲩ[about 16 lett] | ⲧⲓⲧⲓ ⲡϭⲃⲉⲕⲉ ⲙ̇ⲛⲛⲉⲛⲛⲏⲣ[ⲏⲩ + ⲁⲛⲟⲕ ⲇⲁⲩⲉⲓⲇ ⲡⲉⲧϣ|ⲣⲡⲉϩⲁⲓ ⲧⲓⲥⲧⲏⲭⲉ | .]ⲉⲛⲁ ⲕ̄ ⲡϣⲟⲓ ⲛⲁⲧⲙⲉⲧⲣⲉ ⲛⲁⲡⲁ ⲃⲓⲕ|ⲧⲱⲣ

'I have consented (πείθειν) with thee and thou hast assigned[12] (?) thy daughter to my son, and I have agreed with thee upon 3½ *solidi* and a napkin (?)[13] and a   [14] and a

---

[1] Assuming that στοιχεῖν and ⲣⲙⲛⲧⲣⲉ have here the same meaning   [2] *V* no 119
[3] 'Presence,' 'delivery'?   *Cf* BGU 362, viii 9, price of bricks σὺν παραγωγῇ
[4] There is perhaps space for more than this
[5] ὑποκεῖσθαι
[6] Apparently a title   Perhaps for ⲡⲥⲁⲛⲉⲙⲣⲓⲥ, 'seller of *mustum*'   But Is lxiii 2 has ⲙ =πατητος, which the Boh takes for a person, ⲣⲉϥϩⲱⲙⲓ   Perhaps the same man in KRALL no lxii
[7] πράκτωρ

[8] *Cf* KRALL cclv.   Two villages named Lysimachis in KENYON, *Catal* ii 96, but the MS is from the Fayyûm
[9] This word, for a judicial decision, in Brit Mus Or 4678, 4884 (Jême papyri)   A Brit Mus fragment in Or 6201 A &c begins ⲛⲁⲓⲛⲉ ⲛ̇ⲁⲟϩⲟⲛ ⲛ̇ⲧⲁⲓ[
[10] Fem of Πραξίας
[11] The only Coptic document relating to marriage is the contract *Recueil* vi 70
[12] ? From ⲧⲛⲟ   ⳨ ⲕⲛ̇ⲓ cannot be read   [13] ? λέντιον
[14] Either for ⲕⲁⲗⲗⲓⳓⲉ καλίγιον (Brit Mus nos 1096, 1103 &c) or formed with ⲕⲁⲛ- (v CRUM, *Copt MSS* 32)

L

[1] and a . [2] and a comb[3], and that we should hold the wedding together, half[4] (the expenses being) mine (?) . together, in buying and selling . . . we should give his wage in common ' David and a witness (in a different hand), from 'the πέτρα[5] of Apa Victor,' sign

Verso   + птоϩ̣ои иалгеіа [space] аипрассіа +

140 —Papyrus, a fragment, 10½ × 17 cm Script uneven, ligatureless. *Recto* ↑.
Undertaking (ὁμολογία) as to work to be done, too fragmentary to be intelligible

] сω ϫωωτн[| а]ипалаиалı ииои [|]саерϩωб̣[6] иıе етаи[|]тпоλıс иатиатафрои ϩиλа[ау|]ωи[7] ииррωб ероı ϩωс . ш . λϯϩирωб |]иак аісии тıϩоиолоϲıа иак сıстоі-χеі̇ рос |ᵉр]исоре ише ипиакаріос ϩахаріас тıстоı |]с ише ипиакар/ [ϲе]ωрϲе пр[ω]ıе-
. . . .|]ᵉ (blank)

141 —Papyrus, a fragment, 9½ × 9 cm Script moderately ligatured. *Recto* ↑
Undertaking (ὁμολογία) by a workman to perform his work diligently, but saving (φυλάσσειν) his own freedom (ἐλευθερία)[8]

т]етиеϩупорсıа тнре иатоииеу[е |]оут ебоλ ϩиоуспоуаи аϫи |]е алλа тафуλ/ итаϯλϯϯоϯрıа | иı]ı етиеоуашıоу ϫе ϫниеиееи[| о]уи аісии тıϩоиолоϲıа ннт[и |]иеуϫаı инетар̇ͯ еϫωи тароеıс | аио|и иакаре тıстоı етıϩоиолоϲıа + | ишоурпесиıееуе ' иолλоусе пеитасшшпе иир̣е̣[10] |]е ише[11] ипиакар/ шеиоуте прωие | ши]оуи тıо̣ ииетре +

142 —Papyrus, a fragment, 7 × 8 cm Script moderately ligatured *Recto* (?) ↑
Undertaking (ὁμολογία) by Peter, a hired workman Line 1 probably relates to his wages, l 2 to the conditions by which he is bound

о]уϭос исıı иио̣уϩ̣олок̇т̇/ |]еиеϩ еı ϫе еıшаиоуωш |]еıте ϩапабеке аиои петрос |]тıϩоиолоϲıа ннтı |

Verso remains of a Greek account of expenses during a year, mentioning two churches and signed by Eustephius[12], an οἰκονόμος

+θεδωρ[α]κ̇ λκρωσ̄ δ/ ιω[| ﬡ πακτ, επαυλεως διαφᵉ τ ¯η αγῑ ε[| φαμ ¯θ ιδ/, ζ εω φαμ ¯θ ινδ⁰/, η θυμῑᵃ κερατ[| + ευστεφ[ι]ος ελͯ/ οικ⁰/ στοι̇ +

---

[1] Unknown
[2] ? Coptic and Greek combined The context suggests ἔριον, ἔρια
[3] *V* Brit Mus no 1096
[4] Quite uncertain Read ? апаше, but not оупаше
[5] *V* no 124
[6] таер- scarcely possible
[7] ϩω]ωк would imply a mutual undertaking
[8] *Cf* no. 144
[9] Different hand
[10] *Cf* nos 146,161 and VITELLI, *Papiri* p 119 γενάμενος γραμματεύς, *Rev egypt* iv 61 γενόμενος διάκονος, KRALL no cxxvii 27 'Late' or 'deceased'?, *v* PREISIGKE, *Gr Pap Strassburg*, no 20
[11] Different hand
[12] This name in VITELLI no 64, MITTEIS no 26

143.—Papyrus, a fragment, 16 × 14 cm   Script clumsy uncials   *Recto* ↑.
Undertaking (here merely χάρτης) addressed to a bishop, by Colluthus, an artizan[1]

] пепіскопос епіэн аіⲃⲱⲕ ⲉⲃⲟⲗ ⲉⲡⲧⲟⲡⲟⲥ ⲙ̅ⲡ|ⲅⲁⲙⲟⲥ ⲁⲡⲁ ⳉⲁⲣⲉ ⲁⲓⲣⳉⲱ[ⲃ] | ⲉⲣⲟϥ ⲧ̅ⲛⲟⲩ
ⲡ̅ⲛⲧⲁⲓⲁⲁⲃ ϯⲕⲱ ⲙ̅ⲙⲟϥ ⲉⲃⲟⲗ ⲉⲡⲧⲟⲥ | ⲁⲩⲱ ϯⲁⲡⲟⲧⲁⲥⲉ ⲧⲙ̅ⲣⳉⲱⲃ ⲉⲣⲟϥ |ᵃ ⲁ̅ⲱ ⲕⲟ ⲙ̅ⲡ̅ⲭⲟⲉⲓⲥ ⲉⲛⳉⲁⲙ
ⲛⲓⲙ | ⲁⲛⲟⲕ ⲕⲟⲗⲗⲟⲩⲑⲟⲥ ⲡⳉⲁⲙ ϯⲥⲧⲏⳉⲉⲓ ⲉⲡⲓⲭⲁⲣⲧⲏⲥ ⲛⲑⲉ ⲉϥⳉⲏⳉ | ⲙ̅ⲙⲟϥ ϯ ⲁⲩⲱ ⲛⲧⲁⲓⲕⳉⲁⲓ
ⲡⲓ|ⲭⲁⲣⲧⲏⲥ ⲛⲥⲟⲩⲙⲛⲧⲁⲥⲉ | ⲛ̅ⲭⲟⲓⲁⲕ ⲛ̅ⲧⲁⲉⲕⲁⲧⲉⲥ | ⲛⲁⲉⲕⲁⲓⲁⲛⲟⲥ ϯ

'Seeing that I went out to the τόπος of the holy Apa Hare[2] and worked there, now
I do resign (?) it (*sc* the work done ?) to the τόπος (?), and I renounce[3] (ἀποτάσσειν) working
there   And thou art master of every artizan'   Dated 16th Choiak, 10th Indiction.

Verso   part of a rough scroll ornament

144.—Papyrus, 30 × 33 cm   2 *selis*-joins visible, 13 cm apart   Script irregular, liga-
tured   *Recto* ↑.
Undertaking (ὁμολογία) by a sailor to work for a year on board a ship named 'The
Apa Severus'

+ ⲁⲛⲟⲕ ⲓⲱ[ⳉⲁ]ⲛⲛⲏⲥ ⲡ̅ⲛⲉⲉⲃ ⲡ̅ϣⲉ ⲛ̅ⲡⲙⲗⲁⲕ ⳅ[ⲉⲱⲣ]ⳅⲉ ⲡ[ⲣⲱⲙⲉ ϣⲙⲟⲩⲛ ⲉⲓⲥⳉⲁⲓ ⲛ̅ⲧⲉⲱⲣⳅⲉ |
ⲡ̅ⲛⲉⲉⲃ ⲡ̅ϣ[ⲉ ⲛⲁ]ⲉ̄ⲗⲁⲥ ⲛ̅ⲡ̅ⲣⲱⲙⲉ ϣⲙⲟⲩⲛ ⲟⲛ ⳉⲉⲉⲛⲉⲓⳉⲛ ⲛ̅ⲁⲓⲡⲉⲓⲑⲉ ⲛ̅ⲧⲁⲗⲉ ⲛⲉⲙⲁⲕ ⳉⲱⲕ | ⲛ̅ⲉⲃ
ⲉⲧⲕ[ⲟⲩ] ⲕⲁⲣⲁⲃⲓⲛ ⲛⲁ[ⲡⲁ ⲥⲉ]ⲅⲏⲣⲟⲥ [ⲧⲁⳉⲓ] ⲛ̅ⲧⲟⲟⲧⲕ ⲉⲙⲓⲥⲱⲥⲓⲥ ⳉⲙ̅ⲡⲉⲟⲟⲩ ⲉⲧⲉⲥⲟⲩⲙⲛ̅ⲧⲏⲛ̅ⲛⲉ | ⲛ̅ⲡⲁⲣ-
ⲙⲟⲩⲧⲉ ⲡⲉⲃⲟⲧ [ⲛ̅]ⲓⲣⲟⲙⲡⲉ ⲛⳉⲓⲱϣⲥ ⲁⲉⲕⲁⲧⲏⲥ ⲓⲛⲁⲁᵒ/ ⲥⲟⲡ ϣⲁⳉⲱⲕ ⲉⲧⲉⲥⲣⲟⲙⲡⲉ ⲉⲧⲉⲡⲁⲟⲡⲥ | ⲡⲉⲃⲟⲧ
ⲥ̅ⲩ̅ ⲉⲛⲁ[ⲉⲕ]ⲁⲧⲏⲥ ⲓⲛⲁⲁᵒ/ ⲧⲉ[ⲛⲟⲩ ⲁⲉ ϯⲣⲟⲙⲟⲗⲟ]ⳅⲉⲓ ⲧⲁⳉⲱ ⲉⲓⲟ ⲛ̅ⲡⲉⲃ ⲉⲧⲓⲕⲁⲣⲁⲃⲓ | ⳉⲓⲉⲗⲉⲩⲑⲉⲣⲓⲁ
ⲛⲓⲙ ⲛⲁⲧⲟⲕⲛⲉⲩⲉ ⲛⲁⲧⲕⲁⲧⲁⲫⲣⲟⲛⲉⲓ ⳉⲙ̅ⲡⲉⳉⲱⲡ ⲗⲁⲁⲩ ⲉⲛⲉⲛⲉⲣⲏⲩ | ⳉⲙ̅ⲡⲉⲧⲉⲣⲉⲡⲛⲟⲩⲧⲉ ⲛ̅[ⲁⲛ]ⲧϥ
[ⲉⳉ]ⲟⲩⲛ ⲉⳉⲱⲛ ⲁⲩⲱ ⲧⲓⲡⲓ ⲧⲁⲛⲁⲗⲟⲥⲓⲁ ⲛⲁⲡⲟⲧⲁⲕⲧⲟⲓ [ⳉ]ⲁⲁⲡⲁ[4] ⲥⲉⲅⲏⲣⲟⲥ | ⳉⲁⳉⲛ̅ⲡⲉⲟⲟⲩ ⲉⲑⲛ̅
ϣⲁⳉⲱⲕ ⲉⲧⲉⲥⲣⲟⲙⲡⲉ ⲁⲩ[ⲱ] ⲣϣⲁⲛⲧⲉⲥⲣⲟⲙⲡⲉ ⳉⲱⲕ [ⲉⲛ̅ⲧ]ⲛ̅ⲡⲉⲓⲑⲉ | ⲙ̅ⲙ̅ⲛⲉⲛⲉⲣⲏⲩ ⲧⲛ̅ⲟⲩⳉ̅ⲣ̅ⲛⲓⲥⲱⲕ
ⲙ̅ⲙⲛⲉ[ⲛ]ⲉⲣⲏ[ⲩ ⲁⲗⲗⲁ ⲉ]ⲓϣⲁⲛⲟⲩⲱϣ [ⲉⲡ]ⲱⲣ̅ⳉ ⲉⲃ[ⲟⲗ] | ⲉⲙⲟⲕ ⲥⲓⲟ ⲛ̅ⲛⲉⲉⲃ ⲛⲉⲙⲁⲕ ⲉⲧⲓⲕⲟⲩⳉⲓ ⲕⲁⲣⲁⲃ[ⲛ
ⲉⲡⲓ ⲧ]ⲱ ⲧⲁⳅ]ⳓ ⳉⲟⲗⲟⲕⲥⲛⲁⲩ ⲉⲛⲟⲩ ⲥⲡⲣⲟⲥⲧⲓ | . . . . ⲛ̅ⲡⲉⲧϣⲟⲟⲡ ⲛⲁⲓ [about 12 lett] ⲙⲟⲟⲩ
ⲉⲡⲉⲓⳉⲛ ⲧⲁⲓⲧⲉ ⲑⲉ ⲛ̅ⲧⲁⲥⳉⲟⳉⲛ̅ ⳉⲓⲧⲙ̅ⲓⲛⲧⲉ ⳉⲓⲟⲩⲥⲟⲡ ⲉⲥⲁⲑⲛ ⲉⳉⲣⲉⲓ ⲉⳉⲟⲩⲛ ⲙ̅ⲙⲓⲛⲉⲛⲉⲣⲏⲩ ⲧⲁⲧⲁⲗⲉ
ⲛⲉⲙⲁⲕ ⲉⲧⲓⲕⲟⲩⳉⲓ | ⲕⲁⲣⲁⲃⲓⲛ ⲉⲩⲱⲣ̅ⳉ ⲟⲩⲛ ⲁⲓⲙⲛ̅ ⲧⲓⳉⲟⲙⲟⲗⲟⳅⲓ[ⲁ ⲛ̅]ⲁⲕ ⲉⲓⲥⲧⲟⲓⲭⲉⲓ ⲉⲣⲟⲥ ⳉⲓⲧⲙ̅ⲙⲁⲥⳉ-
ⲙⲉⲓᵒ/ | ⲁⲓⲕⲱⲣϣ ⳉⲛ̅ⲕⲁⲓⲉⲗⲉⲩⲑⲉⲣⲟⲥ ⲁⲩⲣⲙⲉⲧⲣⲉ ⲉⲣⲟⲥ ⲉⲓⲱⳉⲛ ⲉⲡⲛⲟⲩⲧⲉ ⲛⲡⲁⲛⲧⲟⲕⲣⲁⲧⲱⲣ ⲡⲉⳅⲁⲓ | ⲉⲛⲉⲧ-
ⲁⲣ̅ⲭⲉⲓ ⲉⳉⲱⲛ ⲧⲁⲣⲓⲣⲟⲉⲓⲥ ⲛⲁⲕ ⲡⲣⲟⲥ ⲧⲉⳅⳓⲟⲙ ⲉⲩⲣ μ̅ φⲁⲣⲙ̅ ^θ ⲓⲉ ⲓ^δ, ⲇⲉⲕⲧ/ ⟦│├┤│⟧ ^σημον + ⲁⲛⲟⲕ ⲓⲱⲁⲛⲛⲏⲥ | ⲡ̅ⲛⲉⲉⲃ
ⲉⲧϣⲏⲣ̅ⲥⳉⲁⲓ ⲧⲓⲥⲧⲟⲓ ^Χ ⲉⲧⳉⲣⲟⲙⲟⲗᵒ/ ⲛⲟⲉ ⲉⲥⳉⲏⳉ ⲉⲙⲟⲥ + | + ⲁⲛⲟⲕ ⲁⲓⲟⲥⲕⲟⲣⲉ ⲡ̅ϣⲉ ⲛ̅ⲡⲙⲁⲕⲁⲣⲓⲟⲥ
ⲑⲉⲟⳉⲱⲣⲉ ⲡⲣⲱⲙⲉ ϣⲙⲟⲩⲛ ϯⲟ ⲙ̅ⲙⲛ̅ⲧⲣⲉ ⲉⲧⳉⲣⲟⲙⲟⲗⲟⳅⲓⲁ + | + [ⲁⲛⲟⲕ . .]ⲧⲟⲣⲉ ⲡ̅ϣⲉ ⲛ̅ⲡⲙⲁⲕⲁⲣⲓⲟⲥ
ⲑⲉⲟⳉⲟⲥⲉ ⲡⲣⲱⲙⲉ ϣⲙⲟⲩⲛ ϯⲟ ⲙ̅ⲙⲛⲧⲣⲉ ⲉⲧⳉⲣⲟⲙⲟⲗⲟⳅⲓⲁ | [

Verso + ⲑⲟⲙⲟⲗᵒ/ ⲛⲓⲱⲁⲛⲛⲏⲥ [ⲡ̅]ⲛⲉⲉⲃ [space] ⲡ[ⲣⲱ]ⲙⲥ ϣⲙⲟⲩ[ⲛ]

---

[1] Supposing this very rare word to be that in ⳉⲁⲙⳉⲉ,
ⳉⲁⲙⲕ̄ⲗⲉ   V Brit Mus no 459
[2] ? Hatre who had a monastery at Aswân (Eg Expl
Fund's *Report*, 1902–3, 62), or Ἄρειος, Ἄρη, Αri (Brit
Mus no 321, *cf* SPILGELBERG, *Eigennamen*, no 15)
[3] Or 'decide' not to work
[4] For ⳉⲁ- perhaps ⲉ- should be read

'I, John, the sailor, son of the late George, of Shmoun, write to George, the sailor, son of Melas, likewise of Shmoun   Seeing that (ἐπειδή) I have agreed (πείθειν) to embark with thee as sailor upon the little ship (καράβιον¹) "Apa Severus", and (to receive) hire (μίσθωσις) of thee² from to day, the 15th of Parmoute of the year in which we now are, the 10th Indiction, henceforth, until the fulfilment of its year, namely the month Paope, in God's will, of the 11th Indiction³, now therefore I undertake (ὁμολογεῖν) to remain as sailor on this ship, in all freedom⁴ (ἐλευθερία), without sloth (ὀκνεῖν) or neglect (καταφρονεῖν) (It is agreed) that we will conceal nothing, one from the other, of what God shall bring to us, and we will give (to each other) the proportion fixed (ἀναλογία, ἀπότακτος) from (? the takings of) the "Apa Severus", from to-day henceforth, until the fulfilment of its year   And if its year be fulfilled and we agree (πείθειν) together, we will set sail again together   But if I wish to part from thee, while I am a sailor with thee upon the little ship, thereupon (ἐπὶ τῷ) I will pay 2 gold solidi as fine (πρόστιμον), (all) that I have (being at thy disposal)   For (ἐπειδή) thus it hath seemed good (ἔδοξε⁵) between us together, from henceforth, that we should make common cause and that I should embark with thee upon the little ship   For thy assurance, therefore, I have drawn up this agreement (ὁμολογία) for thee and do consent (στοιχεῖν) thereto by my signs (σημεῖον)   And I have begged other freemen (ἐλεύθερος) and they have witnessed it, while I swear by God Almighty and by the health of them that rule (ἄρχειν) over us, that I will observe (it), according to its terms'   After the date and John's signature, those of 2 witnesses

145.—Papyrus, a fragment, 8½ × 20 cm   Script   sloping uncials   *Recto* ↑
Agreement (ὁμολογεῖν) between   (*plur*) and the δίκαιον of a monastery (τόπος) 'Our father the bishop' and 'the rest of the clergy'⁶ are mentioned

ϫΟΥ ΜΠΝΕΓΕΡΗΥ ΧΩΡΙϹ ΛΑΑΥ Π[| ϳΑ ϩΜΠΕΡΙϹΡΑΦΗ ϩΙϹΥΝΑΡΠΑϹΗ ΕΝϩΟΜΟΛΟϹΕΙ | ϳΤΟΥ
ΝΤΙϥΕ ΠΑΙΚΑΙΟΝ ΜΕΝ ΝΠΙΤΟΠΟϹ ΕΤΟΥΑΑΒ | ϳΠΕΝΕΙΩΤ ΕΤΟΥΑΑΒ ΠΕΠΙϹΚΟΠΟϹ [ΜΝ]ΒΙΚΤΩΡ | ΠϹΕΕΠΕ
ΝΝΕΚΛΗΡΙΚΟϹ ΝΤ..Μ.... ...| ΜΝΠ]ϹΩΟΥ ΚΑΤΑ ΚΑΙΡΟϹ ϫΙΝΕΤΕΝΟΥ ϢΑΕΝΕϩ ..Κ ΧΑΡ |

Verso   traces of accounts

146 -Papyrus, a fragment, 17 × 19 cm   Script   ligatured   *Recto* ↑
End of an Agreement (ὁμολογία), showing the date⁷ and witnesses' signatures

ϳΝΑΚ ΕΙϩΥΠΟϹΡΑ[ΦΕ | ϳΕ ΕΡΟϹ ΑΥΜΕΤΡΕ ΕΡΟϹ ΕΙΩΡΚ ΠΡΟ[| ΠΡΟϹ ΤΕϹϹΟΜ + ΕΠϥ ΙΕ
ΠΑΧΩΝ ϛ ΑΡ ΙΑ ΙΝᵟ + +⁸ ΑΝ[ΟΚ | ΤΙϩΟΜΟΛΟϹΙΑ ΘΕ ϹϩΠϩ ΜΟϹ + +⁹ ΑΝΟΚ [| .]
ΑΝΤΙΝΟΟΥ ϮΟ ΜΜΝΤΡΕ ΕΤΕΙϩΟΜΟΛΟϹΙΑ ΝΤ[| ϳΙϹΙΑΩΡΟϹ ΠϹΙϹΛᵡ/ ΝΑΙΑΝΟ/ ΠϢΕ ΝΠΜΑΚΑΡΙΟϹ |
.. ΑΙϹΩ]ΤΜ ϩΙΤΜΠΕΤϹΜΜΝΕ ΜΜΟϹ + +¹⁰ ΑΝΟΚ Ϲ[| ϢΩΠΕ ΝΠΡϵ/¹¹ ϮΟ ΜΜΕΤΡΕ ΕΤΙϩΟΜΟ-
ΛΟϹΙΑ ΝΤΑΙ[|

---

¹ The writer takes this as feminine
² This use of μίσθωσις should indicate that John hired the ship, but the rest of the deed scarcely bears this
³ Perhaps Paope is an error, for as it stands, the term is but for five or six months   ⁴ V no 141
⁵ For this form of δοκεῖν, v Br t Mus no 1175, REVIL-

LOUT, *Actes*, p 51, and here no 174
⁶ As probab y in KRAII clxiii
⁷ V KENYON, *Catal* 1 197, iii 280, and Brit Mus no 420
⁸ Different hand   ⁹ Original hand?
¹⁰ Different hand   ¹¹ V no 141

147.—Papyrus; a fragment, 8 × 9½ cm   Script · few ligatures   *Recto* ↑, excepting the lowest part

End of an Agreement (ὁμολογία) and witnesses' signatures, two being from Neuoi[1]

]τιϩοⲙⲟⲗⲟⲥⲓⲁ | ⲛ]ⲡϭⲧⲁⲁⲩ ⲧⲁⲧⲁⲁⲩ ϩⲁⲣⲟϥ ⲛϩⲟⲩⲛ |]ⲁⲓⲥⲙⲛ ⲧⲓⲁⲥⲫⲁⲗⲓⲁ ⲛⲁⲕ ⲉⲓⲥⲧⲟ^χ ⲉⲣⲟⲥ | ⲧⲁⲣ]ⲉϥⲩⲗⲁⲥⲉ^(sic) ⲛⲁⲕ ⲡⲣⲟⲥ ⲧⲉⲥϭⲟⲙ | ⲥ]ⲟⲗⲟⲙⲱⲛ ⲧⲓⲥⲧⲟ^χ ⲉⲧⲓⲁⲥⲫⲁⲗⲓⲁ |]ⲕⲟⲥ ⲡⲣⲱⲙⲛⲉⲩⲟⲓ ⲛⲧⲁⲩⲕⲟⲣϣⲧ ⲁⲓⲥϩⲁⲓ |]ⲙⲙⲁⲕⲁⲣⲓⲟⲥ[2] ⲓⲱ. ⲥⲏⲡ ⲡⲣⲱⲙⲛⲉⲩ[ⲟⲓ |]ⲭⲉ[3] ⲉⲧⲓⲁⲥⲫⲁ +

148.—Papyrus, a fragment, 15½ × 8 cm   Script ligatured   *Recto* ↑.

From an Undertaking (ὁμολογία) by Maria (or Marianus) perhaps relating to land cultivation, the salt mentioned[4] being possibly a manure.

]ⲡϣⲏⲣⲉ ⲙⲙⲁⲕⲁⲣ/ ⲁⲛ .... |]ⲭⲓⲛⲉⲡⲟⲟⲩ ⲉⲧⲉⲥⲟⲩⲥⲛⲁⲩⲡⲉ |]ⲩⲓ ⲉⲡⲱⲡⲉ ⲉϥⲧⲓ ϩⲙⲟⲩ ,] ⲧⲉⲕⲃⲁ ⲉⲡⲁⲧⲉⲧⲛⲥ[5] |]ⲭⲓⲛⲛⲉⲧⲛⲉⲁⲙⲁϩⲉ | ⲉⲡ]ⲓ ⲧⲱ ⲧⲁⲧⲓ ⲥⲟⲟⲩ ⲛϩⲟⲗⲟⲕ/ | ⲡⲡⲁⲛⲧⲟⲕ]ⲣⲁⲧⲱⲣ ⲙⲛⲛⲉⲩⲭⲁⲓ |]ϩⲙⲟⲩ ⲉⲩⲛⲧϥ ⲧⲁⲧⲁⲙⲟ[6] | ϩⲟⲙ]ⲟⲗⲟⲥⲓⲁ ⲛⲑⲉ ⲉⲥⲥⲏϩ ⲙⲙⲟⲥ |]ⲓⲟ[7] ⲙⲙⲛⲧⲣⲉ + |]⁸ .... ⲁⲙⲟⲩⲛ ⲧⲓⲟ ⲙⲙⲛⲧⲣⲉ +

Verso. +ⲑ[ⲟⲙⲟⲗ]ⲟⲥⲓⲁ ⲙⲁⲣⲓⲁ [

149.—Papyrus, a fragment, 15½ × 17 cm   Script · moderately ligatured   *Recto* ↑

The end of an Agreement (ἀσφάλεια) by Herwoj, a husbandman, with the signatures of witnesses

] ⲉⲭⲱⲛ ⲧⲁⲣⲓⲣ[ⲟⲓⲥ ⲡⲣⲟ]ⲥ ⲧϭⲟⲙ ⲉⲧⲓⲁⲥⲫⲁⲗ/ ⲉⲩⲣ μ [.] θ ιᵈ/ ⲁ[ⲛⲟⲕ] | ϩⲉⲣⲟ[ⲩ]ⲟϫ ⲡⲟ[ⲩ]ⲟⲓⲉ ⲧⲓⲥⲧ]ⲟⲓⲭⲉⲓ ⲉⲧⲓⲁⲥⲫⲁⲗ/ + ⲓⲱⲁⲛ[| ⲕⲁⲣⲓⲟⲥ ⲥⲉⲩⲏ[ⲣⲟⲥ] ⲡⲣⲱⲙⲉ ϣⲙⲟⲩⲛ +ⲟ ⲙⲙⲛⲧⲣⲉ + | ⲅⲉⲱⲣⲅⲉ ⲡⲣⲱⲙⲉ ϣⲙ[ⲟⲩⲛ] ⲧⲓⲟ ⲙⲙⲛⲧⲣⲉ ⲉⲧⲓⲁⲥⲫ[ⲁⲗ ⲛⲧⲏ ⲉⲧⲥⲙⲛⲉ ⲛ[ⲙⲟⲥ + | + ⲕⲟⲗⲗⲟⲩⲑⲉ ⲛϣⲉ ⲛⲡⲙⲁⲕⲁⲣ/ ⲓⲁ[ ]ⲉ ⲡⲛⲟⲙⲓⲕ°/ [| ϣⲱⲡⲉ ϩⲓⲧⲟⲟⲧ ⲁⲩⲱ ⲁⲓⲥϩⲁⲓ ϩⲁϩⲉⲣⲟⲩⲟϫ ⲡⲟⲩⲟⲓⲉ ⲡⲉⲓⲧ^(sic)

Verso, and on *Recto* at right angles to the above, a Greek account (earlier), headed + γ^ν ^τ μηχαν^ ρξβ   Each line begins with στο^χ ορ^γ (the first of these being throughout by another hand), which is followed apparently by a name   Among these are Αροης[9], Ψω[10], Τζαμουλ[11], Πετζρωτζ[12], the last two being of interest for their transcription of ϭ

150.—Papyrus, a fragment, 7½ × 10 cm   Script various   *Recto* ↑.

End of an Agreement (ὁμολογία) relating to land. The scribe (νομικός) Ammône is possibly the 'notary' of another text (v Index)

---

[1] *V* Brit Mus nos 1041 ('north of Shmoun'), 1059 ('west of Shmoun') KRALL, p 208, compares Nawâi, opposite Rodah, so too AMELINEAU, *Géogr.* 286 (the parallel Greek cited omits it)

[2] Different hand   [3] Different hand

[4] I can find no other such reference to salt in the papyri As manure (*sebach*) it was perhaps known in antiquity, *v*, *e g*, WILCKEN in *Archiv* ii 308

[5] For ⲙⲛⲁⲧⲉⲧⲛ-   [6] This word corrected

[7] and [8] Perhaps one hand

[9] *Cf* ⲁⲣⲥⲓⲥ, SPIEGELBERG no 26

[10] *Cf* ⲛⲉϥⲯⲱ, CRUM, *Ostr* no 445

[11] ϭⲁⲙⲟⲩⲗ

[12] ⲡⲉⲭⲣⲱϫ or ⲡⲉϭⲣⲱϭ.

ⲛⲉⲕⲁⲛⲱⲛ ⲉⲧⲟⲩⲁⲁⲃ ⲛⲧⲉⲕ[ⲕⲗⲏⲥⲓⲁ¹ |]ⲁⲕⲟⲥ² ⲡⲓⲥⲗⲁⲭⲓⲥⲧⲟⲥ ⲛ[|]ⲕⲟⲥ ⲡⲁⲓⲁⲕ°/ ⲛⲕⲱⲧⲉ ϩⲛⲡ[³
|] ⲓⲱϩⲉ⁴ ⲛⲫⲟⲩⲛ ⲛⲧⲏⲛⲉ°+ [|] ⲉⲧⲓϩⲟⲙⲟⲗⲟⲅⲓⲁ +   + ⲑⲉⲟⲁ[|]ⲉ +   +⁶ⲁⲙⲙⲱⲛⲉ ⲡⲛⲟⲙⲓⲕ/ ϩⲙ[

151.—Papyrus, a fragment, $17\frac{1}{2} \times 10$ cm   Script upright, ligatureless   *Recto* ↑.
Undertaking (ὁμολογία) by a lessee or tenant, referring to the annual rent, to his own payment of expenses (δαπάνη) and wages and to the fine in case of default   Written by a νομικός

ⲁⲥⲫⲁⲗⲉⲓⲁ ⲉⲣⲟϥ ⲉⲧⲃⲉ ϫⲉⲛⲧⲁⲩⲣⲙⲉⲗⲗⲟⲡⲧⲱ⁷ [| ⲧ]ⲉϥϣⲉ ⲁⲓⲟⲩⲱϣ ⲉⲛⲁ[ⲁ]ϥ ⲛⲏⲧⲛ ⲉⲃⲟⲗ⁸ [|]ⲣⲁⲓ
ⲛⲟⲩⲡⲁϣⲧⲣⲙⲛⲥⲓⲙ ⲧⲉⲣⲟⲙⲡ[ⲉ |]ⲟⲟⲧ ϩⲁⲡϩⲱⲃ ⲧⲥⲙⲟⲩ ⲧⲓϩⲟⲙⲟⲗⲟⲅⲉⲓ[|]ⲉⲣⲟϥ ϩⲓⲁⲁⲡⲁⲛⲏ ϩⲓⲃⲉⲕⲉ
ϩⲛⲡⲁϥⲓⲁ[ⲓⲕⲟⲛ |]ⲛⲡⲁϥⲓⲁⲓⲕⲟⲛ ⲟⲩⲁⲉ ϫⲛⲛⲓϣϫⲟⲟⲥ [| ⲥⲩⲛ]ⲧⲉⲗⲉⲓ ⲛⲙⲟⲥ ⲛⲏⲧⲛ ⲛⲡⲁⲣⲙⲟⲩⲧ[ⲉ |]ⲧⲏⲥ
ⲓⲛⲁⲓⲕⲧⲓⲟⲛⲟⲥ ⲁⲩⲱ ⲛⲧⲟⲥ ⲟⲛ ⲉⲑⲏ⁹ ϣ[|]ⲏϩ ⲁⲛ ⲉⲓ ⲁⲉ ⲛⲛⲓⲫⲩⲗⲁⲥⲥⲉ ⲛⲏⲧⲛ ⲡⲣ[ⲟⲥ |]ⲛⲟⲩⲃ ⲛⲡⲣⲟⲥⲧⲓ
ⲙⲟⲛ ⲉⲓⲅⲩⲡⲟⲛⲉⲓⲥⲟⲁⲓ ⲛ[| ϩ]ⲟⲙⲟⲗⲟⲅⲓⲁ ⲛⲏⲧⲛ ⲉⲓⲟⲣⲏ ⲛⲡⲛⲟⲩⲧⲉ ⲡⲡ[ⲁⲛⲧⲟⲕⲣⲁⲧⲱⲣ |] ⲉⲅⲣ/ ⲫⲁⲙ̅ β ιⲑ̅ ε
+¹⁰ⲓⲱⲁⲛⲛⲏⲥ ⲡⲉⲓⲉⲗ̅(ⲥⲓⲥ) ⲡϣⲉ[|]ⲁⲡⲟⲣⲉⲓ ⲙⲟⲥ +   +¹¹ⲁⲛⲟⲕ ⲕⲱⲛⲥⲧⲁⲛⲧⲓ[ⲛⲉ |]ⲙⲟⲥ ⲁⲓⲧⲉⲓ ⲛⲙⲟⲓ +
+ ⲁⲛⲟⲕ ⲃⲁⲥⲓⲗⲉ | ϩⲟⲙⲟⲗⲟ]ⲅⲓⲁ ⲛⲧⲁⲡⲉⲧⲥⲙⲛⲉ ⲙⲙⲟⲥ [| ⲡⲛ]ⲟⲙⲓⲕ/¹² ⲛⲧⲁⲧⲓϩⲟⲙⲟⲗⲟⲅⲓⲁ ϣⲱⲡⲉ
ϩ[ⲓⲧⲟⲟⲧ

152—Papyrus; a fragment, 18×13 cm   Script ligatured   *Recto* ↑
Agreement (ὁμολογία), with receipt for money paid

ϣ]ⲙⲟⲩⲛ ⲧⲡⲟⲗⲓⲥ ⲉⲓⲥϩⲁⲓ ⲛⲁⲡⲁ ⲓⲱϩⲁⲛⲛⲏⲥ ⲡⲉⲛⲁⲟϫ̅(ⲥⲓⲥ)ⲧ/ |]ⲓⲥ ϫⲉⲉⲡⲓ ⲁⲱ ⲧⲓϩⲟⲙⲟⲗⲟⲅⲉⲓ ϫⲉⲁⲓϫⲓ
ⲁⲩ¹³ |] ⲙⲙⲟⲟⲩ ⲛⲁⲓ ⲧⲓⲛⲟⲩ ⲟⲛ ⲧⲓϩⲟⲙⲟⲗⲟⲅⲉⲓ |]ⲧⲉⲓϩⲟⲙⲟⲗⲟⲅⲉⲓⲁ ⲛⲁⲕ ⲉⲓⲥⲧⲟⲓ̅ⲭ̅ ⲉⲣⲟⲥ |]ⲧⲁⲣⲉⲓϥⲅ̅λ
ⲡⲣⲟⲥ ⲧⲉⲥϭⲟⲙ + ⲉⲩⲣⲁⲫ/ μ̅ υ̅ τ̅ α ιⲇ̅/ θ̅]ⲙⲟⲥ ⲉⲥⲥⲏϩ ⲉⲙⲟⲥ + ⲁⲛⲟⲕ ϣⲉⲛⲟⲩⲧⲉ ⲡⲥⲩⲛ | ⲧⲉⲧⲛⲥⲓⲥ
ⲙⲡⲉⲧⲥⲙⲛⲉ ⲙⲙⲟⲥ | ϩ]ⲟⲙⲟⲗⲟⲅⲉⲓⲁ ϩⲓⲧⲛⲧⲉⲧⲛⲥⲓⲥ ⲙⲡⲉⲧⲥⲙⲛⲉ ⲙⲙⲟⲥ |]ⲁⲩⲱ ⲧⲓⲟ ⲛⲙⲛⲧⲣⲉ +

153.—Papyrus, a fragment, 12×33 cm   Script sloping semi-uncials   *Recto* ↑
Undertaking (ὁμολογία) by Theodosius, a priest, relating apparently to certain clerical functions

]ⲛⲕⲗⲏⲣⲓⲕⲟⲥ ⲉϣⲁⲩⲃⲱⲕ ⲉⲡⲧⲁϣⲉⲟⲉⲓϣ ϩⲙⲡⲟⲩⲱϣ ⲛⲡⲛⲟⲩⲧⲉ | ⲙⲓϫⲓ ⲗⲁⲁⲩ ⲛⲕⲁⲓⲥⲟⲡ ϩⲁⲡⲁⲣⲁ
ⲙⲉⲣ[. .] ϩⲁⲡⲁⲡⲁⲥ ⲟⲩⲁⲉ ⲟⲛ ⲙⲛ̅ϯ¹⁴ ⲗⲁⲁⲩ | ϩ]ⲱϥ ⲛⲓⲙ ⲉϣⲁϥⲉⲓ ϩⲟⲩⲛ ϩⲙⲡⲧⲁϣⲉⲟⲉⲓϣ ϫⲓⲛⲛⲟⲩⲕⲟⲩⲓ
ϣⲁⲟⲩⲛⲟϭ |]ⲓⲥ ⲛⲛⲉⲕⲗⲏⲣⲓⲕⲟⲥ ⲛⲛⲙⲁ ⲛⲫⲁⲥⲓⲟⲥ ⲕⲟⲗⲃⲉ ⲉⲓⲧⲉ ϩⲟⲙⲧ ⲛⲃⲁⲣⲱϩ (above ⲃⲁⲗⲟⲧ)
ⲟⲩⲁ[ⲉ |]ⲃⲱⲕ ϩⲁⲡⲓϣⲱϥ ⲛⲧⲉⲡⲙⲁ ⲧⲁⲁⲩ ϩⲓⲱⲧ ϩⲓⲛⲉⲧⲛ[ⲏ]ⲩ ⲙ[ⲛ]ⲉⲥⲱⲓ ⲛⲧⲉ |]ⲁⲥⲓⲟⲥ ⲑⲉⲟⲁⲱⲣⲉ
ϩⲛⲡⲁⲙⲟⲩ ⲁⲩⲱ ϩⲛⲡⲁⲱⲛⲁϩ ⲙⲉⲛⲧⲟⲓⲥⲉ ⲛⲧⲉⲛⲧⲟⲥ |]ϣ̅ϯ ⲗⲟⲅⲟⲥ ⲛⲡⲁⲡⲁⲥ ⲕⲁⲧⲁ ⲣⲟⲙⲡⲉ ϫⲛⲛⲉⲩϩⲱⲡ
ⲗⲁⲁⲩ ⲉⲣⲟϥ ⁻(ⲥⲓⲥ) |]ⲫⲱϥ ⲕⲁⲗⲱⲥ ϯ ⲁⲛⲟⲕ ⲑⲉⲟⲁⲟⲥⲓ ⲛⲉⲗⲁⲭ/ ⲡⲡⲣⲉⲥⲃⲩⲧ/ ϯⲥⲧⲟⲓⲭⲉⲓ ⲧⲓϩⲟⲙⲟⲗⲟⲅⲓⲁ +

---

¹ ? *Cf* Brit Mus no 1013   ² Different hand
³ 'We happening to be in'   *Cf* -ἀράγειν, Brit Mus
no 395
⁴ Not ⲥⲉⲧⲓⲱϩⲉ
⁵ 'The inner dyke' seems grammatically impossible
Perhaps read ⲛⲧⲕⲛⲉ
⁶ First hand   ⁷ ?? μολυβτουργός
⁸ Of land 'handed over' by outgoing tenant   *Cf*

no 159
⁹ Also in no 158 and Brit Mus no 1013   *Cf Archiv
f Pap* iii. 420, καὶ αὐτῆς ἐφεξῆς
¹⁰ Different hand   ¹¹ Different hand
¹² First hand
¹³ ⲁⲩⲱ ⲁⲓⲡⲗⲏⲣⲟⲩ.
¹⁴ The ϯ has two dots, here in the opposite, not parallel,
angles   *Cf* Brit Mus nos 472, 1121 &c

'] clergy (κληρικός) that go to the "preaching" ¹, by God's will,   [I will not] take aught again as   ² or as παπᾶς³, nor will I give aught,   ] everything that shall come in to the "preaching", from a small thing to a great,   ] the clergy (κλ.) of the place⁴ of St Colluthus, whether bronze   ⁵, or (? εἴτε)   ] go on account of this matter, and that the place entrust me therewith and them that come after me,   ]St Theodore, at my death or during my life   But (μέντοι γε),   ] be able to render account (λόγος) as παπᾶς annually, for they shall hide naught from him,   ] the matter well.'

Verso address erased

154—Papyrus, a fragment, 9½ × 10 cm   Script rarely ligatured   *Recto* ↑.

Deed of Security (λόγος), with the formula 'Lo, here is the word of God to thee⁶' The writer had sealed it with his ring

πλο]ϭοϲ ϲπϊογτε ϊτοοτ[ϊ | εϩ]ογϊ επεκηι ϫεϊϊαρϊϵθοογ ϊα[κ | ϫε ϫεϊϊαϲγϊχωρε ϊρωϫϵ[ε |]ακϊωτ ϫϊϊεϊαϫϕιϐαλϵ ϵρ[| ϐογλ]ιϛϲ ϊπειλοϭοϲ ϲπαϛογρ ϻ επαγ̄ ᵞ ιϊ[

155.—Papyrus, a fragment, 11 × 10½ cm   Script almost ligatureless   *Recto* →

Deed of Security (cf the preceding), issued by the community (κοινότης) of Tbaké npestratê⁷, addressed to a woman.

+ ϩϫϊπραϊ ϊϊϊϊογτε τϊ[οϊϊοτηϲ | ϯϐακε ϊπϲϲτρατϊ | ϩϫϊπϲ[| ϲτο αϊοϊ κγριαϊ, ϣεϊογτε [| ροϲ ϫϊαϊοϐϊοϊ ερϫϊαϲ[| ϫϊϊκοϲϫϊα ϕοιλϊϫϊω[ϊ | πϲϊπε τϊρϐ ϊερωϫϊ[| ϊα τϲϛϊϫϊε ϊαϐραϛαϫϊ [|..]ϊλοϭοϲ ϊϊϊϊογτε ϊτοο[τ

Verso] [space] ϛαϊαϊα ϩιτοοτϐ..| ᵃⁱᶜ ϫϊϯϐακε +

156.—Papyrus, complete, 18 × 19 cm.   Script irregular, seldom ligatured.   *Recto* ↑.
Text cancelled by lines drawn across it

An Acknowledgment (ἀσφάλεια) by Jamoul of Pamata, to Rashid (or Ar-Rashid), amir (of Shmoun⁸)

¹ This must have an unknown, technical meaning.
² A mistake for παραμονάριος unlikely
³ ? Head of the monastery   Cf Br Mus no 544, Crum, *Ostr* no 308, n   But here *t* not merely of clerical functions, *cf* Br Mus no 1156 and a letter here, where an ἄρχων is called ρεϫϊπαπα.
⁴ Translates τόπος, either 'church' or 'monastery'.
⁵ ϐαρωϩ occurs in Brit Mus no 1171, Crum, *Ostr* no 379   If ϐαλοτ is a correction=ϐαρωτ, then *v ib* no 459
⁶ This is used either, as here, in a promise that the recipient shall not be further troubled, that nothing further

shall be required of him, *i e* as a kind of receipt, or in an order to perform specified work   V Crum, *Ostr* no 107 ff, Brit Mus no 1024, *WZKM* 1902, 265, Hall, *Copt and Gk Texts*, pp 99, 100, 147, Guidi in *Rendic* 1906, 475
⁷ Tbake in Krall no clxxxii and apparently here no 205   Cf a fragment in Brit Mus Or 6201 b &c, ϥϫϊϯϐακε   The second word perhaps = στρατηγός οι στρατηλάτης, v Br Mus no 1051
⁸ The same amir in a document, Brit Mus Series Or 6201 a &c   Perhaps αϊα for αϊογ

+ ⲧϫⲁⲙⲟⲩⲗ ⲛϣⲉ ⲛⲡⲙⲁⲕⲁⲣⲓⲟⲥ ⲁⲡⲁ ⲉⲓⲥⲁⲁⲕ ⲡⲣⲉⲙⲡⲁⲙⲁⲧⲁ ⲙⲡⲉⲙϩⲓⲧ ⲛϣⲙⲟⲩⲛ ⲧⲡⲟⲗⲓⲥ
ⲉⲓⲥϩⲁⲓ ⲕⲁⲡⲁ [ⲁ]ⲣⲁϣⲓⲧ [... .]ⲁⲙⲓⲣⲁ | The remainder (15 ll) is mostly illegible It relates
to the repayment of money, ⲧⲓϣⲟⲟⲡ ⲛϩⲉⲧⲉⲙⲟⲥ ⲧⲁⲡⲗⲏⲣⲟⲩ ⲙⲟⲛ. The date of writing is
ⲥⲟⲩ... ⲙⲡⲉϩⲃⲟⲧ ⲧⲱⲃⲉ ⲛⲧⲉⲓⲣⲟⲙⲡⲉ ⲧⲁⲓ ϩⲉⲛⲧⲉⲕⲁⲧⲏⲥ ⲓⲛⲁ,. Among the witnesses is
ⲁⲓⲟⲥⲕ[ⲟⲣⲟⲥ] the deacon, son of the late ⲕⲟⲥⲙⲁ ⲡⲣⲙⲁⲛⲧⲓⲛⲟⲟϫ

157.—Papyrus, a fragment, 12 × 35½ cm Script much ligatured *Recto* ↑ Text
cancelled by cross-lines

End of an Agreement (ἀσφάλεια) by Theodore, son of Leontius, with signatures of
two witnesses and a scribe

]ⲉ ⲛⲧⲁⲓⲁⲓⲁⲥⲧⲓⲗⲉ ⲙⲙⲟϥ ϩⲛⲧⲓⲁⲥⲫⲁⲗⲉⲓⲁ |]ⲉϥ ϩⲛⲡⲉⲙ[..]ⲛⲧⲁⲓⲥⲙⲛⲧϥ ⲛⲏⲧⲛ ⲁⲩⲱ ⲧⲁⲁⲡⲟⲧⲁⲥⲥⲉ
ⲛⲧⲛⲟⲙⲏ[1] | ⲡⲉⲧϣ]ⲟ]ⲟⲡ ⲛⲁⲓ ⲧⲏⲣϥ [ϩⲩⲡⲟ]ⲣ̄ [ⲛ]ⲁⲕ ⲉⲩⲱⲣϫ ⲛⲁⲕ ⲁⲓⲥⲙⲛ ⲧⲓⲁⲥⲫⲁⲗⲉⲓ ⲛⲁⲕ | ⲉⲓϩⲩⲡⲟ-
ⲅⲣⲁⲫⲉ ⲉⲣⲟⲥ ⲛⲧⲁϭⲓϫ ⲉⲓⲥⲧⲟⲓ̈ ⲉⲓⲱⲣⲕ ⲉⲡⲛⲟⲩⲧⲉ ⲡⲡⲁⲛⲧⲟⲕⲣⲁⲧⲱⲣ ⲙⲡⲡⲟⲩϫⲁⲓ ⲛⲛⲉⲧⲁⲣ ⲉϫⲱⲛ
ϫⲓⲛⲛⲓϣⲡⲁⲣⲁⲃⲁ ⲙⲙⲟⲥ + | ⲉⲩⲣ μ̄ φαρμ ι ω δ, δ + + [2]ⲁⲛⲟⲕ ⲑⲉⲟⲇⲱⲣⲉ ⲡϣⲉ ⲛⲡⲙⲁⲕⲁⲣ ⲗⲉⲟⲛⲧⲓ
ⲡⲣⲱⲙⲉ ϣⲙⲟⲩⲛ ⲧⲓⲥⲧⲟⲓⲭⲉⲓ ⲉⲧⲓⲁⲥⲫⲁⲗⲉⲓⲁ | ⲕⲟⲉ ⲉⲥⲥⲏϩ ⲙⲙⲟⲥ + + [3]ⲫⲟⲓⲃⲁⲙⲙⲱⲛ ⲡⲉⲗ
ⲡⲣⲉ ⲛϣⲉ ⲛⲡⲙⲁⲕⲁⲣⲟⲥ ⲕⲟⲗⲗⲟⲩⲑⲉ ⲡⲣⲱⲙⲉ ϣⲙⲟⲩⲛ ϯⲟ ⲙⲧⲣⲉ + | + [4]ⲃⲉⲛⲓⲁⲙⲓⲛ ϩⲁⲡⲛⲁ
ⲛⲛⲟⲩⲧⲉ [ⲡⲣ]ⲉ ⲛϣⲉ ⲛⲡⲙⲁⲕⲁⲣ/ ⲓⲁⲕⲱⲃ ⲡⲣⲱⲙⲉ ϣⲙⲟⲩⲛ | ⲧⲓⲟ ⲙⲙⲛⲧⲣⲉ + [5]ⲁⲛⲟⲩϥ ⲡⲉⲓⲉⲗ̄ⲭ,
ⲛϩⲩⲡⲟⲇⲓⲁⲕ/ ⲡⲣⲱⲙⲉ ϣⲙⲟⲩⲛ ⲛⲧⲁⲧⲓⲁⲥⲫⲁⲗ, ϣⲱⲡⲉ ϩⲓⲧⲟⲟⲧ +

LEASES

158.—Papyrus, a fragment, 55½ × 35 cm 3 *selis*-joints visible, 14 cm. apart Script
sloping semi-uncials *Recto* ↑

Lease (μίσθωσις) of land by Sophia, daughter of Mercurius (ll 2, 34) of Shmoun,
to Macarius, son of George, of the ἐποίκιον of 'Pawan ⲉⲛⲓⲟⲧ[6].'

ⲡϣⲉ ⲛⲡⲙ]ⲁⲕⲁⲣⲓⲟⲥ ⲅⲉⲱⲣⲅⲉ ⲡⲣⲱⲙⲡⲁⲟⲩⲁⲛ [ⲛⲱⲧ ϩⲙⲡⲧⲟϣ ⲛϣⲙⲟⲩⲛ
ⲕⲩⲣⲁ ⲥⲟⲫⲓⲁ ⲧⲧⲓ]ⲙⲓⲱⲧⲁⲧⲏ ⲧϣⲉ ⲛⲡⲕⲩⲣ/ ⲙⲉⲣⲕⲟⲩⲣⲓⲟⲥ ⲧⲣⲱⲙⲉ ϣⲙⲟⲩⲛ ⲟⲛ
ⲡⲉⲧϣ]ⲣⲛⲥϩⲁⲓ] ⲙⲁⲕⲁⲣⲉ [ⲡ]ⲟⲩⲟⲟⲓⲉ [ϩⲛ|ⲟ[ⲩ]ⲱϣ ⲕⲁⲧⲣϩⲧⲏϥ[7]
ⲉⲣⲉⲡⲭ]ⲣⲟ[ⲛ]ⲟⲥ ⲛⲧⲙⲏⲧⲉ ⲛⲣⲟⲙⲡⲉ [ⲛⲡ| ϫⲓⲡⲉⲧⲛⲁⲥⲡⲟⲣⲁ
ⲓⲛⲁⲓⲕⲧⲓⲟ]ⲛⲟⲥ ⲡⲕⲁⲣⲡⲟⲥ ⲇⲉ ϩⲓⲛⲟⲩⲱϣ ⲛⲡⲛⲟⲩⲧⲉ
ⲓⲛⲁⲓⲕ[ⲧⲓ]ⲟⲛⲟⲥ ⲁⲩⲱ ⲛⲧ[ⲟ]ⲥ ⲟⲛ ⲉⲑⲏ[8] ⲛⲡⲉⲧⲁⲓⲁⲫⲉⲣⲉⲥⲑⲓ
]ϩ .. ⲧⲓⲧⲉ ⲙⲉⲛ ⲛⲕⲁϩ ⲛⲁⲓⲥⲧⲱⲧⲉ ⲇⲉ ⲛϣⲁϥ[9]

5

---

[1] *Cf* a phrase in no 167 and ἀποταττόμενος τῷ προ-
νομίῳ τῶν ἐγγυη-ῶν in *Pap Oxyrh* cxxxvi
[2] Different hand This signatured was specially cancelled
[3] Different hand [4] Different hand
[5] First hand, specially cancelled
[6] In series Br Mus Or 6201 A &c, a place ⲡⲁⲩⲁⲛⲓⲱⲧ
(reading rather doubtful) *Cf* perhaps ⲡⲟⲩⲁⲛ ⲡⲉϣⲟⲟⲥ

Brit Mus. no 1071, KRALL vi, and ⲡⲟⲩⲁⲛ in this Catal
(*i* Index), also Ποαμπινουφω *BGU* 860, Ποαμπιμηπις
VITELLI no 2 But ⲡⲁ- is a difficulty, *cf* ? ⲡⲁⲟⲩⲟⲛ
ⲛⲛⲟⲩⲃ ZOEGA 336
[7] *V* KRALL cxxvii 9, clxxix [8] *V* no 151
[9] Occurs *WZKM* 1902, 266 *Cf* ϣⲁϥⲉ 'desert', contrasted with cultivable land, ⲕⲁϩ as in Brit Mus no 1073
At beginning of line, should be ⲥⲧⲱⲧⲉ

]ⲡⲓⲟⲟⲣ ⲙⲛⲡⲉⲧⲁⲛϧⲏⲕⲉⲓⲥⲑⲁⲓ ⲉⲣⲟ ⲥⲧⲉⲡⲧⲉⲧⲁⲣⲧ[ⲟⲛ]

]ⲛⲙⲁ ⲛⲕⲱⲧⲉ[1] ⲙⲛⲧⲣⲥⲱ ⲙⲛⲧⲁϣⲉ ⲛ[ⲡⲧⲏ]ⲛⲉ[2]

10 ⲧϭⲓⲛ]ⲕⲱ ⲉϧⲟⲩⲛ[3] ⲙⲛⲧϭⲓⲛⲉⲓ ⲉⲃⲟⲗ ⲙⲛⲡⲥⲉⲉⲡⲉ ⲛⲛⲉⲇⲓⲕⲁⲓⲟⲛ

]ϫⲉ ⲛ[ⲥⲉ]ⲧⲱϭⲉ ⲛϣⲁϥ ϧⲓⲕⲁϧ ⲕⲁⲧⲁ ⲧⲛⲟⲙⲱⲛⲓⲁ[4] ⲛⲁⲡⲁ

ⲧⲁ ..[ⲙⲛⲧ]ⲕⲩⲣⲁ ⲉⲩⲗⲟⲅⲓⲁ ⲧ[ϣⲏ]ⲏⲣ[ⲉ] ⲛⲡⲟⲩⲙⲁⲕⲁⲣⲓⲟⲥ ⲛϧⲁⲓ ⲡ   [ⲕ]ⲁⲓⲛⲙⲓⲥⲩ

                                ]ⲙⲉⲣⲟⲥ ϧⲙⲡⲕⲣⲓⲛϧ[5] ⲛⲛⲓⲱϧⲉ

ⲛⲙⲓⲥⲩ ϧⲙⲡⲕⲁⲓⲣⲓⲛϧ ⲛⲛⲓⲱϧⲉ ⲛⲡⲉⲙⲛⲧ ⲛⲛⲉϭⲟⲟⲙ

15]ⲙⲛⲡⲟⲩⲛⲙⲓⲥⲩ ⲙⲉⲣⲟⲥ ϧⲙⲧϣⲟⲙⲧⲉⲣⲓⲛϧ ⲛⲛⲓⲥⲉⲧⲱϧⲉ ⲛⲡⲉⲙⲛⲧ ⲉϥϧⲟⲟⲩⲧⲛ[6]

.ⲥⲉⲧⲓⲁϧϧⲟⲩⲱⲣ[7] ⲙⲛⲡⲟⲩⲛⲙⲓⲥⲩ ⲙⲉ[ⲣⲟⲥ] ϧⲙⲧϣⲟⲙⲧⲉⲣⲓⲛϧ ⲛⲛⲓⲥⲉⲧⲓⲁϧϭⲱⲙ ⲉⲩⲟⲛⲁϧ[8] ⲉⲩⲧⲁϧⲏⲩ

ⲉⲣⲁⲧⲟⲩ ⲙⲛⲧⲡⲁϣⲉ ⲛϣⲉⲛ ⲛ[ⲓⲙ ⲉϥ]ϧⲣⲏ ϧⲓⲱⲟⲩ ⲕⲉⲧⲓ ⲕⲁⲣⲡⲟⲥ ⲙⲛⲕⲉⲧⲓ ⲁⲛ ⲙⲛⲡⲉⲃⲛⲛⲉ [ⲙⲛ]

ⲧⲣⲁϣ[9] ⲙⲛⲡⲧⲉⲧⲁⲣⲧⲟⲛ ⲙⲉⲣⲟ[ⲥ] ....ⲡϣⲏⲓ ⲥⲛⲁⲩ [ⲉⲓⲧⲉ] ⲛⲁⲡⲉⲙϧⲓⲧ ⲉⲣⲉⲙⲁ ⲛⲕⲱⲧⲉ ⲥⲛⲁⲩ

ϧⲓⲭⲟϥ ⲉⲓⲧⲉ ⲡⲁϧⲟⲩⲛ ⲙⲛⲡⲉⲡⲟⲓⲕⲉ[ⲓⲟⲛ] ⲙⲛⲛⲉⲩⲙⲁ ⲛⲕⲱⲧⲉ ⲛⲛⲉⲣⲥⲟⲟⲩⲉ ⲙⲛⲡⲧⲉⲧⲁⲣⲧⲟⲛ

20 ⲙⲉⲣⲟⲥ ϧⲙⲫⲟⲟ[ⲩⲧⲛ] ⲛ........ ⲉⲧⲉⲛⲉϧⲁⲣⲧⲏ[ⲥ]ⲓⲥ[10] ⲙⲛⲡⲧⲉⲧⲁⲣⲧⲟⲛ ⲙⲉⲣⲟⲥ ϧⲙⲛⲓⲥⲁ

.ⲏ ϧⲉ [ⲉ]ⲧⲉ[ⲡⲧⲁⲩ]ⲣⲏⲗⲁⲥⲧⲏⲣⲓⲛ[11] ⲙⲛⲡⲧⲉⲧⲁⲣⲧⲟⲛ ⲙⲉⲣⲟⲥ ϧⲙⲡⲉⲡⲟⲓⲕⲉⲓⲟⲛ ⲉⲩⲙⲟⲩⲧⲉ ⲉⲣⲟϥ

ϫⲉⲡⲁⲟⲩⲁⲛ ⲛⲓⲱⲧ ⲙⲛⲡⲧⲉⲧⲁⲣⲧⲟⲛ ⲙⲉⲣⲟⲥ ϧⲛⲧⲉⲕⲕⲗⲏⲥⲓⲁ ⲉⲩⲙⲟⲩⲧⲉ ⲉⲣⲟⲥ ϫⲉⲡⲁⲣⲭⲉⲁⲅⲅⲉⲗⲟⲥ

ⲙⲏⲭⲁⲏⲗ[12]

ⲙⲛⲡⲧⲉⲧⲁⲣⲧⲟⲛ ⲙⲉⲣⲟⲥ ϧⲛⲧⲓⲟⲩϧⲉ ⲙⲛⲧϭⲓⲛⲕⲱ ⲉϧⲟⲩⲛ ⲙⲛⲧϭⲓⲛⲉⲓ ⲉⲃⲟⲗ ⲙⲛⲇⲓⲕⲁⲓⲟⲛ [ⲛⲓⲙ]

ⲉⲧⲁⲛϧⲏⲕⲉⲓⲥⲑⲁⲓ ⲉⲛⲓⲥⲟⲟⲩ ⲙⲛⲛⲓⲱϧⲉ ⲉⲩϣⲟⲟⲡ ϧⲙⲡⲥⲛⲧⲓⲙⲁ ⲛⲡⲁⲟⲩⲁⲛ ⲛⲓⲱⲧ ϧⲛⲛⲉⲥⲁ ⲛ-

25 ⲣⲟⲉⲓⲥ ⲛⲙⲓⲥⲱⲗ[13] ⲛⲡⲉⲃⲧⲟⲟⲩ ⲛⲭⲟⲩⲱⲧ ϧⲛⲧⲟϣ ⲛⲧⲓⲡⲟⲗⲓⲥ ⲧⲁⲓ ϣⲙⲟⲩⲛ ⲛⲟⲩⲛⲙⲓⲥⲩ ⲙⲉⲣⲟⲥ ⲙⲉⲛ

ϧⲛⲛⲓⲱϧⲉ ⲧⲁϧⲟⲟⲩ ϧⲛⲛⲁⲥⲣⲱϧ ⲛⲕⲁⲣⲡⲟⲥ ⲛⲓⲙ ⲉⲓⲟⲩⲁϣⲃ[14] ⲧⲁⲧⲓ ⲛⲉ ϧⲁⲡⲉⲩⲫⲟⲣⲟⲥ ⲧⲉⲣⲟⲙⲡⲉ

ⲉⲧⲉⲛⲁⲓⲛⲉ ϣⲟⲙⲉⲧ ⲛϧⲟⲗⲟⲕⲟⲧⲧⲓⲛ ⲛⲛⲟⲩⲃ ⲙⲛⲟⲩⲧⲣⲓⲙⲏⲥⲓⲛ ⲛⲭⲟⲩⲧⲥⲛⲟⲟⲩⲥⲉ ⲟⲩϧⲟⲥ ⲛⲕⲉⲣⲁⲧⲓ

ⲉⲡⲟⲩⲁ ⲡⲟⲩⲁ ⲛⲡⲭⲓⲙⲟⲟⲩ[15] ⲛϣⲟ ⲇⲉ ⲧⲟ ⲙⲏ ⲅⲉⲛⲟⲓⲧⲟ ⲉϥϣⲁⲛϣⲱⲡⲉ[16] ⲛⲁⲛ ⲁⲓϫⲟ ⲛⲁⲛ ⲛⲡϫⲟ ⲕⲁⲛ

ⲁϧⲱⲃ ⲛⲓⲙ ⲉⲡⲁⲛⲛⲟⲩⲧⲉⲡⲉ[17] ϣⲱⲡⲉ ⲧⲁⲧⲓ ⲧⲛⲁϣⲉ ⲛⲛⲓⲫⲟⲣⲟⲥ[18] γι, χρ̄, ῑ γγ απο κτ, κβϛ τ̄ ν̄

ζῡγ αλε

---

[1] *Lit* 'turning-place', joined here and l 19 with 'cattle-fold' In l 18 wells have 'turning-places' attached to them *Cf* the ἰδρεύματα with ὄργανα belonging to them, VITELLI no 50. The verb l 32 (*v* note l 33) refers to irrigation by means of cattle, so in no 159, 10, and Brit. Mus no 1115 *Cf* probably κυκλευτήριον, KENYON, *Catal* iii 266 *V* CRÖNERT & WILCKEN on κυκλευειν, *Arch f Pap* iii 116, iv 201

[2] ZOEGA's examples and Habak 1 10 show this = χῶμα 'dyke'

[3] *Cf* Brit Mus no 1023, KRALL no 1 12

[4] *V* Brit. Mus no 1016, since which publication Greek instances have appeared VITELLI nos 13, 73, MITTEIS no 21, KENYON iii, pp 259, 268 It has been taken to indicate a community of property

[5] *V* KRALL xcii, xcv, whence the meaning 'part is conjectured

[6] ZOEGA 295, ϧⲟⲟⲩⲧⲛ = MIGNE *PL* 73, 952 *via* = ὁδός (Moscow, Synodal Libr, MSS 452, 163, communicated by O. von LEMM)

[7] Hwôi should be a place (KRALL cclv, Brit Mus 1159, here no 211), but the context and ⲓⲁꞝⲕⲁϧ Brit Mus 1073, ⲓⲁϧⲙⲁϧⲉ KRALL xcii, make this doubtful

[8] ⲉⲩⲟⲩⲟⲛⲁϧ

[9] Here and l 32, ⲕⲁϣ fem *Cf* VITELLI no 50, share in καλαμία

[10] *Cf* KENYON, *Catal* iii 259

[11] Hardly space for so much in gap Or read ἡλιαστήριον, VITELLI, *l c*

[12] *Cf* Brit Mus no 397, a share in a church

[13] *Cf* GRENFELL-HUNT, *Fay Towns*, 154, μαγδῶλον, πυργομάγδωλ

[14] *Cf* Corp Rain i, no xlii, εἰς σποράν ἣν ἐὰν βουλη θῶμεν

[15] *Cf* Brit Mus. no 1172, here no 166

[16] *Cf* P Amh lxxxv, ὕφαμμος (*v* GENTILLI, *Contr d'Affitto*, p 363), GRENFELL, *Gk Papyri* i, no lvii, τῷ δὲ ἀβμόχῳ, τὸ μὴ εἴη

[17] *V* Brit Mus no 1013

[18] *V* GENTILLI, *op cit*, 299

30 ⲡ[ⲓ]ϥⲟⲣⲟⲥ ⲟⲩⲛ ⲛ̄ⲭⲣⲏⲥⲓⲕⲟⲛ ⲧⲁ[ⲧ]ⲁⲁϥ ⲡⲉ ⲛ̄ⲙⲉⲥⲟⲣⲏ ⲡⲉⲃⲟⲧ ⲧⲉⲣⲟⲙⲡⲉ ⲁⲩⲱ ⲧⲁⲓ̄ⲟ̄ ⲛ̄ⲙⲉⲣⲁ ¹ ⲛ

. . . . . ⲡⲉⲡⲣ . . . ⲛⲧⲡⲉ ⲛ̄ⲡⲕⲁⲓⲣⲟⲥ ⲛ̄ⲧⲓ ⲭⲣⲩⲥⲓⲕⲟⲛ ⲉⲓⲧⲓ ⲛ̄ⲣⲡ ϩⲓⲁⲡⲁⲡⲏ ⲡⲟⲩⲛⲙⲓⲥⲩ

ⲍⲉ ⲛ̄ⲙⲉⲣⲟⲥ ϩⲛ̄ⲡⲉϩⲟⲟ[ⲙ ⲙⲛ̄]ⲧ̄ⲛⲁϣ ⲧⲁⲕⲱⲧⲉ ⲉⲣⲟⲟⲩ ϩⲛ̄ⲛⲁⲧ[ⲉ]ⲃⲛⲟⲟⲩⲉ ⲙⲛ̄ⲛⲁⲧⲣⲟⲫⲟⲟⲩ

ⲙⲛ̄[ⲛⲁⲃ̄ⲃⲥ̄ⲕⲉ] ⲁ[ⲙⲛ̄]ⲟⲩ ² ⲧⲉⲡⲣⲱ [ⲙ̄]ⲥⲛ .. .[ⲛ̄]ⲙⲟⲟⲩ ³ ⲥⲛ̄ⲧⲉ ⲉⲡⲉⲃⲟⲧ ⲡⲱϣⲙ ⲍⲉ ⲛ̄ⲙⲟⲩ ⲛ̄ⲙⲛ̄ⲧ

ⲉⲡⲓ ⲧⲱ ⲛ̄ⲧⲟ ⲛ̄ⲕⲩⲣⲁ ⲥⲟⲫⲓⲁ ⲛ̄ⲧⲉⲃⲓ ⲧⲓⲁϣ ⲛ̄ⲡⲥⲉⲛⲛⲙⲁ ⲛ̄ⲛⲓⲣⲡ ⲉⲩⲁϣⲱⲡⲉ ϩⲛ̄ⲡⲟⲩϩⲛⲙⲓⲥⲩ

35 ⲙⲉⲣⲟⲥ ϩⲛ̄ⲡⲉⲥ̄ϩⲟⲟⲙ ⲙⲛ̄ⲧⲡⲁϣⲉ ⲛ̄ⲡⲉ . . [ⲛ̄]ϣⲏⲕ ⲛⲓⲙ ⲥⲧⲣⲏⲧ ϩⲓⲟⲩ ⲧⲁⲃⲓ ⲧⲡⲁϣⲉ ϩⲱⲱⲧ

ⲙⲛ̄ . . . ϩ . . ⲉ ϩⲣⲓⲥⲉ ⲧⲁⲧⲓ ⲍⲉ ϩⲁⲡⲗⲟⲩⲥ ⲛ̄ⲧⲉⲅⲩⲛⲑⲉⲓⲁ ⲛ̄ⲡⲭⲱⲗⲉ ⲅⲉⲣⲟⲙⲡⲉ

ⲡⲟⲩⲕⲉⲣⲁⲧⲓⲛ ⲟⲩⲥⲟⲥ ϩⲁⲣⲁⲁⲣ ⁴ ⲙⲛ̄[ⲟⲩ]ⲗ̄[ⲁ]ⲥ̄ⲏ ⲛ̄ⲓⲣⲡ ⲁⲥ ⲙ̄ⲙⲟⲩⲉⲓ ⲙⲉⲙⲣⲓⲥ ⲙ̄ⲛⲟⲩⲇⲓⲥⲕⲁⲣⲓⲛ ⁵

ⲉϥⲥⲟⲣϩ ⲉⲃⲟⲗ ⲙⲛ̄ⲭⲟⲩⲱⲧ ⲛ̄ϩⲁⲗⲱⲙ ⲙ̄ⲛⲧⲉⲭⲣⲉⲓⲁ ⲛ̄ϩⲁⲁⲥϥ ⲛ̄ⲡⲭⲱⲗⲉ [ⲙ̄]ⲛⲧⲉⲭⲣⲉⲓⲁ ⲛ̄ⲛⲉϩ

ⲁⲛⲟⲕ ⲛ̄ⲛⲓϣ̄ϫ . . ⲛ̄ⲟⲩⲟ . . . . ⲧⲏ . . . . ⲡⲉⲭⲣⲟⲛⲟⲥ ⲛ̄ⲧⲙⲛ̄ⲧⲉ ⲛ̄ⲣⲟⲙⲡⲉ ⲉⲓⲁ

40 . . . . ⲥⲓⲁ . [ⲛ̄ⲛⲟⲙ]ⲟⲥ ⲧⲁⲓ ⲉⲧⲓ ⲛ̄ⲧⲉⲍⲟⲩⲥⲓⲁ ⲛⲟⲩⲟⲛ ⲛⲓⲙ ⲉⲧⲙ̄ⲓⲥⲟⲟⲩ ⲍⲉⲉϥ

ϣ[ⲁⲛⲧ̄ϣⲟ]ⲣⲡⲉ ⲛ̄ⲣⲟⲙⲡⲉ ⲛ̄ⲉⲓⲟⲩⲱϣ [ⲛ̄]ⲃⲱⲕ ⲛⲁϥ ⲛ̄[ⲓ]ⲃⲱⲕ ϫⲓⲛ̄ⲛⲓϣⲃⲱⲕ ⲡⲁⲓ ⲁⲛⲟⲕ ⲛ̄

ⲡⲓϫⲱⲕ ⲡⲉⲭⲣⲟⲛⲟⲥ ⲛ̄ⲧⲙⲛ̄ⲧⲉ ⲛ̄ⲣⲟⲙⲡⲉ ⲉⲓ ⲍⲉ ⲉⲓϣⲁⲛⲟⲩⲱϣ ⲛ̄ⲃⲱⲕ ⲡⲁⲓ ⲧⲁ . . ⲟⲛ̄ϫⲛⲉ

ϩⲁⲑⲏ ⲧⲁϫⲱⲕ ⲡⲉⲭⲣⲟⲛⲟⲥ ⲛ̄ⲧⲙⲛ̄ⲧⲉ ⲛ̄ⲣ[ⲟ]ⲙⲡⲉ . . . . ⲧⲁⲧ̣[ⲥ] ⲙⲛ̄ⲧ . . .]ⲏ ⲛ̄ϩⲟⲗⲟⲕⲟⲧⲧⲓⲛ

ⲛ̄ⲛⲟⲩⲃ ⲛ̄ⲡⲣⲟⲥⲧⲓ[ⲙⲟⲛ ⲛⲁⲧϭⲁⲡ] ⲛⲁⲧⲛⲟⲙⲟⲥ ⲛ̄ⲁⲧⲗⲁⲁⲩ ⲛ̄ⲁⲙ̄ⲫⲓⲃⲟⲗⲉⲓⲁ ⲉⲓⲅⲩⲡⲟⲕⲉⲓⲥⲑⲁⲓ ⲡⲉ

45 ⲙ̄ⲡⲣⲱⲃ ⲛⲓⲙ ⲉⲡⲱⲓⲡⲉ ⲉⲧⲃⲉⲡⲟⲩⲱⲣ[ϫ] ⲟⲩⲛ ⲁⲓⲥⲱⲛ ⲧⲓⲙⲥⲟⲱⲥⲉ ⲡⲉ ⲁⲓⲧⲓ ⲥⲧⲁⲩⲣⲟⲥ ⲉⲣⲟⲥ

ⲛ̄ⲧⲁϭⲓϫ ⲁⲩⲥϩⲁⲓ ϩⲁⲣⲟⲓ ϫⲓⲧⲓⲛⲟⲓ ⲁⲛ ⲁⲓⲡⲁⲣⲁⲕⲁⲗⲉⲓ ⲛ̄ϩⲛⲕⲁⲓⲉⲗⲉⲩⲑⲉⲣⲟⲥ ⲁⲩⲣ̄ⲙⲛ̄ⲧⲣⲉ

[ϩⲁⲣⲟⲓ ⲉⲓⲟⲣⲕ ⲉⲡⲛⲟⲩ]ⲧⲉ ⲡ[ⲁⲛⲧⲟ]ⲕⲣⲁⲧⲟⲣ ⲙ̄ⲡⲉⲩϫⲁⲓ ⲛ̄ⲛⲉⲛϫⲓⲥⲟⲟⲩⲉ ⲉⲧⲁⲙⲁⲣⲧⲉ

[ⲉϫⲱⲛ ⲧⲁⲣⲉⲓⲣⲟⲥ]ⲓⲥ ⲡⲉ ⲡⲣⲟⲥ ⲧⲉⲥϭⲟⲙ + ⲉⲅⲣ/ ⲫⲁⲱⲫⲓ ⲁ/ ⲓⲛⲇ°/ ⲓⲁ ¦̶ ¦̶ ¦̶ $\overset{\sigma\iota\mu\iota\text{o}\nu}{|\ |\ |}$ +

[+ ⲁⲛⲟⲕ ⲙⲁⲕⲁⲣⲉ ⲡⲟⲩ]ⲟⲟⲓⲉ ⲛ̄ϣⲉ ⲛ̄ⲧⲉⲱⲣⲡⲉ ⲧⲓⲥⲧⲟⲓⲭⲉⲓ ⲉⲓⲧⲓⲁⲥⲫⲁⲗⲉⲓⲁ ⲛ̄ⲑⲉ ⲉⲥⲛ̄ϩ ⲛ̄[ⲙⲟⲥ]

50 + ⁶ ⲁⲛⲟⲕ ⲁⲡⲁ ⲕⲩⲣⲓ ⲛ̄ϣⲉ ⲛ̄ⲁⲑⲁⲛⲁⲥⲓⲟⲥ . . . . . . ϫⲓⲛ̄ⲉⲓⲟⲓ] ⲁⲛ + ⲙⲛ̄ⲁ ⲡϣⲉ ⲛ̄

ⲡⲙⲁⲕⲁⲣ[ⲓⲟⲥ . . . . . . ⲧⲓⲟ ⲙ̄ⲙⲛ̄ⲧⲣⲉ + ⁷ [ⲁⲛⲟⲕ] ⲓⲱⲁⲕⲓⲛⲉ ⲡⲓⲥⲗⲁⲭ ⲙ̄ⲡⲣ/ ⲛ̄ϣⲉ ⲛ̄ⲡⲙⲁⲕⲁⲣⲓⲟⲥ

ⲫⲓⲗⲟⲑⲉⲟⲥ

ⲡⲣⲱⲙⲉ ϣⲙⲟⲩ̄ⲛ ⳿ⲧⲟ ⲙ̄ⲙⲛ̄ⲧⲣⲉ +   +ⲍⲁⲭⲁⲣⲓ[ⲁⲥ] ⲡⲓⲉⲗⲁⳃ/ [ⲛ̄ⲣ/] ⲡϣⲛ̄ⲙⲁⲕ . . ⲡⲁ

About 9 cm blank below this

Lines 1-15 show that the lease is for a period of 10 years[8], from the seed-time (κατασπορά) of the   year of the Indiction The property consists of the lessor's shares in various vineyards, fields &c, with the usual rights attaching (διαφέρεσθαι) thereto, according to the κοινωνία of Apa T   and Eulogia, step daughter (?) of Sophia Among the lands to be leased are some on the west of the vineyards and a share in the third-portion of fields on the west of the highroad (l 15) From here we may translate 'and (?) the   fields and thy half share (ἥμισυ μέρος) in the third-portion of the

---

¹ Cf ? Brit Mus no 1073

² This obscure phrase also in no 160 and GRENFELL, op cit, no lviii, ἑτοίμως ἔχω κυκλεῦσαι τὸ αὐτὸ γεωργιον ἐκ τῆς ἐμῆς ζωῆς, τῶν και τρεφομένων παρ' ἐμοῦ Cf also κυκλεύειν, KENYON, Catal i 171, and l 10 above

³ ⲧⲓ ⲙⲟⲟⲩ, KRALL no xci Cf ⲧⲓ ⲥⲕⲁⲓ, ib xcii In Br Mus no 434 ro, the debtor (lessee) shall give 3, in no 427 4 waterings to the field

⁴ Presumably = ⲧⲣⲁⲁⲣⲉ, Brit Mus no iiii Cf

KRALL no ccxlii, where it occurs in similar lists of contributions (farm and dairy produce &c) In no 159 one is valued at 2 carats

⁵ ⲅⲓⲥⲕⲁⲣⲏⲛ in KRALL ccxlii 44, as here in no 159 Presumably = δισκάριον

⁶ Different hand

⁷ Different hand

⁸ Cf WASZYNSKI, Bodenpacht i 91 Anm, and here no 163

gardens under cultivation (?) and in good condition (?), and the half of all the trees growing therein, those that bear fruit and those that do not, and the dates and the reeds and the 4th part [of the] 2 wells, but that on the north, wherein are 2 watering-places (?), and that within the farm (ἐποίκιον), with their watering-places for the rushes, and the 4th (l 20) part of the highroad   the outfit (ἐξάρτυσις) and the 4th part of the   the cattle shed (ταυρηλαστήριον) and the 4th part of the farm (ἐποίκ) called "Pawan eniôt" and the 4th part of the church (ἐκκλ) called the Archangel Michael('s), and the 4th part of the sycomore, and entrance and exit and all rights (δίκαιον) appertaining to (ἀνήκεσθαι) these vineyards and these fields, which are in the property (κτῆμα) of "Pawan eniôt" in the (l 25) migdôl watch-towers of the Eighty, in the nome of this town (πόλις) of Shmoun And (μέν) thy half share (ἥμ μέρ) in the fields I will sow with my seed, of whatsoever crop (καρπός) I wish, and will pay thee as their rent (φόρος) yearly, namely, 3 gold solidi and a tremis of 22½ carats (κεράτια), for each of the water-taking (fields)   But (δέ) the (desert-) sand, if it should happen (to come), which heaven forbid (τὸ μὴ γένοιτο), whether (κἄν) I have sown or (κἄν) have not sown, or if (κἄν) anything (sent) of God have befallen, I will pay half the tax (φόρος), namely, 3⅛ gold solidi less 22½ carats by the Alexandrian (?) standard   (l 30) And (οὖν) this rent in coin (χρυσικόν) I will pay thee in the month Mesore, yearly, and my 19 days (ἡμέρα) of   at the period (καιρός) of paying the money (rent), I paying wine and expenses (δαπάνη)   But (δέ) thy half-share (ἥμ μ) of the vineyards and the reeds I will water (?) them with (?) my beasts and my   and my herdsman's wage   And (μέν) in winter I will give (them) 2 waterings a month, but (δέ) in summer 10 waterings, whereupon (ἐπὶ τῷ) thou, the lady (κυρά) Sophia, shalt take the half of the produce (γένημα) of wine, and it shall be in thy (l 35) half-share (ἥμ. μ) of the vineyards, and the half of every tree that grows therein, while I likewise take the half and   the labour, but (δέ) pay according to (λόγος) the custom (συνήθεια) of the vintage, yearly, 1½ carats (κερ) for   and a measure of old wine and one of new (mustum) and a well filled (?) dish (δισκάριον) and 20 cheeses and the needful amount (χρεία) of loaves and the needful amount (χρ) of oil   I shall not be able to   the period (χρ) of these 10 years, while I (l 40)   , which gives power (ἐξουσία) to every one that lets (μισθοῦν), that if he fulfil the first year and wish to depart, he may depart.   I however shall not be able to depart ere I have completed the period (χρ) of these 10 years   But if (εἰ δέ) I shall wish to depart, and   before I shall have completed the period (χρ) of these 10 years   , I am ready (ἕτοιμος) to pay   gold solidi as fine (πρόστιμον), without judgement, without law (νόμος), without any doubt (ἀμφιβολία), while I am at thy disposal (ὑποκεῖσθαι) (l 45) with all that is mine   For thy security then (οὖν), I have drawn up for thee this deed of lease (μίσθωσις) and have set a cross (σταυρός) thereto with my hand, and they have written for me, because I know (νοεῖν) not how   And I have requested (παρακαλεῖν) other freemen (ἐλεύθερος) and they have witnessed it   And I swear by God Almighty (παντοκράτωρ) and the health of our lords that rule over us, that I will observe this deed of lease (μίσθ) for thee, in accordance with (πρός) its authority   I wrote it (ἔγραψα) on the 1st Phaophi, 11th Indiction'   Here follow the σημεῖον of the lessee and the signatures of 3 or 4 witnesses

M 2

159 —Papyrus, a fragment, 22 × 35 cm   Script seldom ligatured   *Recto* ↑.

Lines 1–5 and the letters ϩⲱ in 6 are supplied by a fragment, 6 × 9½ cm, in the British Museum (Or 6201 A &c)

Lease (μίσθωσις) of land by   to Iōnobr[1] (Onnophrius), a husbandman and vinedresser

]ϣⲉ ⲧⲁⲧⲁⲗⲟⲟⲩ ⲉ . [| ⲧⲏⲣⲥ ⲛⲁⲉⲛⲧⲟⲙⲉ ⲧⲁ[| ⲧⲓϩⲟⲙⲟⲗⲟⲅⲓ ⲁⲛⲟⲕ ⲓⲱⲛ[ⲟ]ⲃⲣ[| ϣⲏⲣⲡⲉϩⲁⲓⲥϥ
ⲛⲑⲉ ⲉⲃⲟ ⲙⲙ[ⲟⲥ | ⲟⲩⲁⲁⲧ ⲙⲛⲧⲕⲁϣ[2] ⲧⲏⲣⲥ ⲁⲩⲱ[| ⲓⲁ ⲓⲛ[δ]/ ⲧⲁⲡⲱ .. ⲛ]ⲃⲱ ⲛⲉ[ⲗⲟⲟⲗⲉ about 22 lett]
ⲧⲁⲉⲛⲧⲟⲩ ⲛⲁⲕ ⲉϩⲣⲁⲓ | ϣⲁⲧⲟⲩϫⲱⲱⲗⲉ[3] ⲙⲛⲧⲟⲓⲙⲉ [about 25 lett]ⲱⲱ[.]ⲁⲫⲟⲣⲟⲥ ⲥⲓ ⲁⲉ ⲉⲕϣⲁⲛ-
ⲁⲁϥ | ⲛϭⲱⲙ ⲧⲁϫⲓ ⲡⲁⲃⲉⲕⲉ ⲛⲑⲉ ⲛⲟ[ⲩⲟⲉⲓⲉ ⲛⲓⲙ about 12 more]ϣⲏⲛ ⲛⲓⲙ ⲉϥⲣⲏⲧ ⲉⲣⲟⲟⲩ
ⲙⲛⲛⲉⲩⲭⲣⲏⲥⲓⲥ[4] | ⲧⲏⲣⲟⲩ ⲉⲩⲟⲛϩ ⲉⲛⲓⲥⲉ ⲥⲡⲉ[. . . .]ⲡⲁⲅ[. . . . . .ⲗⲉⲓⲁ[5] ⲧⲏⲣⲥ ⲛⲧⲡⲁϣⲉ
ⲛⲧⲁⲙⲛⲧⲟⲩⲟⲉⲓⲟⲉⲓⲉ | 10 ⲧⲁⲧⲓ ⲛⲉⲩⲅⲁⲙⲟⲟⲩ[6] ⲛ[ⲁ]ⲩ ⲧⲉ[ⲡⲣ]ⲱ ⲙⲉⲛ ⲧⲁⲕⲱⲧⲉ[7] ⲉⲣⲟⲟⲩ ⲛⲙⲟⲩ ⲛⲁⲙⲛⲧⲏ
ⲁⲩⲱ ⲡϣⲱⲙ ⲧⲁⲕⲱⲧⲉ ⲉⲣⲟⲟⲩ ⲛⲙⲟⲩ ⲛⲙⲛⲧⲥⲛⲟⲟⲩⲥ ⲁⲩⲱ [. . . ⲧⲁ]ⲛⲁϫⲝ[8] ⲛⲙⲟⲩ ⲛⲥⲩⲙⲟⲩⲅⲏ ⲁⲩⲱ
ⲛⲉϣⲁϫⲟⲥϥ ⲉⲣⲟⲟⲩ ⲡⲱⲓⲡⲉ[9] ⲁⲩⲱ ⲉⲣϣⲁⲛⲁⲡⲟⲩⲅⲡ ⲟⲩⲱϣ | ⲉⲃⲱⲕ ⲛⲁϥ ⲛⲁⲧⲉⲣⲟⲩⲟⲉⲓⲉ [ⲛ]ⲁⲛ ⲧⲓⲟ
ⲛϥⲣⲉⲧⲟⲙⲙⲟⲥ ⲧⲁⲣⲁϣⲧ[10] ⲛⲙⲁ ⲧⲏⲣϥ ϭⲙⲉ ⲟⲩⲟⲉⲓⲉ ⲧⲁⲉⲣⲧⲉϥϩⲩⲡⲟⲩⲣⲅⲓⲁ ⲛⲙⲛⲧⲟⲩⲟⲉⲓⲉ ϩⲓⲙⲛⲧⲟⲙⲉ
ⲁⲩⲱ ⲧⲁϫⲓ (above ⲧⲁ) ⲧⲟ ⲟⲩⲟⲉⲓⲉ ⲙⲛⲧⲁⲧⲟ ϭⲙⲉ ⲛⲕⲁⲣⲡⲟⲥ ⲛⲓⲙ ⲉⲃⲁϣⲱⲡⲉ ⲉⲧⲉⲡⲟⲩⲟⲛ ⲉⲩⲧⲟⲟⲩ|ⲡⲉ
ϩⲁⲙⲛⲧⲟⲩⲟⲥⲓⲥ ⲁⲩⲱ ⲡⲟⲩⲟⲛ ⲉⲩⲧⲟⲟⲩ ϩⲁⲙⲛⲧⲟⲙⲉ ⲁⲩⲱ ⲁⲛϩⲁⲗⲱⲙⲁ ⲛⲓⲙ ⲉⲃⲁϣⲱⲡⲉ ϩⲓⲡⲙⲁ |
15 ⲧⲓⲧⲁⲁϥ ϩⲩⲡⲓⲟⲙ ⲉⲓⲁⲉ ⲁⲛϫⲓⲣ ⲉⲓⲁⲉ ⲁⲛϩⲁⲗⲱⲙⲁ ⲛⲓⲙ ⲁⲩⲱ ⲧⲁⲧⲓ ⲡⲁⲥⲩⲛⲏⲑⲉⲓⲁ ⲧⲉⲣⲟⲙⲡⲉ ⲉⲧⲉ-
ⲛⲁⲓⲛⲉ | ϩⲁⲙⲛ ⲅⲟⲩⲟⲉⲓⲉ ϩⲓⲙⲛⲧⲟⲙⲉ (ⲛⲡⲭⲱⲱⲗⲉ above) ⲗⲁⲩ ⲥⲩⲛⲧⲉ ⲛⲉⲣⲡ ⲁⲥ ⲧⲁⲓⲟⲩ ⲛϩⲁⲗⲱⲙ ⲧⲁⲓⲟⲩ
ⲛⲏⲓ[11] ⲛϭⲁⲗϭⲉ ⲁⲓⲥⲕⲁⲣⲓⲛ ⲥⲛⲁⲩ | ⲟⲩϩⲛⲥⲧⲉ ⲛⲛⲉϩ ⲟⲩⲅⲁⲁⲣ ϩⲁⲕⲉⲣⲁⲧⲓⲛ ⲥⲩⲛⲧⲉ[12] ⲁⲩⲱ ⲡⲉⲡⲁϫⲟϥ[13]
ⲉⲃⲟⲗ ⲛⲡⲭⲱⲱⲗⲥ ⲧⲓⲧⲁⲁϥ ϩⲓⲡⲓⲟⲙ ⲁⲩⲱ ϩⲁⲙⲡⲟⲩⲱϣ ⲙ̄ⲡ̄ⲛⲟⲩⲧⲉ ⲅⲁⲟⲩⲱϩ ϩⲁⲡⲉⲕⲧⲛⲙⲁ ⲁⲩⲱ
ⲙⲙⲛⲥⲁⲡⲉⲭⲣⲟⲛⲟⲥ ⲛⲧⲙⲓⲥⲑⲱⲥⲓⲥ ⲧⲁⲕⲁ ⲡⲉⲕⲙⲁ ⲛⲁⲕ ⲉⲃⲟⲗ ⲛⲑⲉ ⲉⲃⲟ ⲙⲙⲟⲥ | ⲁⲩⲱ ϫⲓⲛⲛⲉⲓⲉⲣⲧϣⲟⲣⲡ
ⲡⲣⲟⲙⲡⲉ ⲧⲁϫⲟⲟⲥ ϫⲉⲓⲟⲩⲱϣ ⲉⲃⲱⲕ ⲛⲁⲓ ⲉⲙⲛⲧⲓ ⲧⲁϫⲱⲕ ⲡⲉⲭⲣⲟⲛⲟⲥ ⲛⲧⲙⲓⲥⲑⲱⲥⲓⲥ ⲉⲓϣⲁⲛⲟⲩⲱϣ |
20 ⲉⲃⲱⲕ ⲛⲁⲓ ⲙⲡⲉⲥϫⲱⲕ ⲧⲓⲙⲓⲥⲑⲱⲥⲓⲥ ⲧⲓⲟ ⲛϥⲣⲉⲧⲟⲙⲙⲟⲥ ⲧⲁⲧⲓ ⲥⲟⲟⲩ ⲛϩⲟⲗⲟⲕⲟⲧⲛ ⲛⲉⲩⲥ̄ⲧ̄/[14] ⲛⲁⲧϩⲁⲡ
ⲛⲁⲧⲛⲟⲙⲟⲥ ⲛⲁⲧⲗⲁⲁⲩ ⲛϩⲱϥ | ⲛⲁⲙⲫⲓⲃⲟⲗⲉⲓⲁ ⲉⲓⲱⲣⲕ ⲙⲡⲛⲟⲩⲧⲉ ⲡⲁⲛⲧⲟⲕⲣⲁⲧⲱⲣ ⲙⲙⲡⲉⲩϫⲁⲓ
ⲛⲉⲛϫⲓⲥⲟⲟⲩⲧⲉ ⲛⲉⲛⲣⲱⲟⲩ ϫⲓⲛⲛⲉⲓⲉϣⲡⲁⲣⲁⲃⲁ ⲛⲗⲁⲁⲩ ⲛϣⲁϫⲉ | ⲉϥⲥⲛⲏ ϩⲛⲧⲙⲓⲥⲑⲱⲥⲓⲥ ⲉⲅⲱⲣϫ ⲛⲁⲕ
ⲁⲓⲥⲙⲛ ⲧⲓⲙⲓⲥⲑⲱⲥⲓⲥ ⲛⲁⲕ + ⲉⲅⲣ/ ⲉⲡⲉⲓⲫ ⲕⲉ ⲥⲩ̄ⲛ̄ ⲓⲁ ⲓⲛ[δ], + |——+——| συμιου / ανοκ ιωνοβρ πϣⲉ
                                                               οννουφριου
ⲛⲡⲁⲗⲁⲩ ⲛⲟⲩⲟⲉⲓⲉ ⲁⲩⲱ ⲡⲉϭⲙⲉ ⲧⲓⲥⲧⲟⲓⲭ/ ⲧⲓⲙⲓⲥⲑⲱⲥⲓⲥ ⲛⲑⲉ ⲉⲥⲥⲛⲏ ⲉⲙⲟⲥ + ⲕⲟⲗⲗⲟⲩⲑⲉ | ⲡⲓⲉⲗⲁⲭ/
ⲙⲡⲣ̄ⲉ̄, ⲡϣⲉ ⲛⲡⲙⲁⲕⲁⲣ/ ⲃⲓⲕⲧⲱⲣ ⲡⲣⲱⲙⲧⲉⲥⲥⲓⲱ[15] ⲛⲧⲁϥⲕⲟⲣϣⲧ ⲁⲓⲥϩⲁⲓ ϩⲁⲣⲟϥ ϫⲓⲛⲃⲏⲟⲓ ⲥϩⲁⲓ ⲁⲛ ⲁⲩⲱ
ⲧⲓⲟ ⲙⲙⲧⲣⲉ + | + ⲛⲟⲥⲙⲁ ⲡⲓⲗⲁⲭⲓⲥⲧⲟⲥ ⲡⲣ̄ⲉ̄, ⲧⲓⲟ ⲙⲉⲧⲣⲉ + + ⲁⲛⲟⲕ ⲁⲡⲁ ϩⲱⲣ ⲡϣⲉ ⲛⲕⲏⲛⲁ
ⲧⲓⲟ ⲛⲙⲛⲧⲣⲉ ⲉⲧⲓⲙⲓⲥⲑⲱⲥⲓⲥ ⲛⲉⲩ ⲥⲛⲏ ⲙⲟⲥ +

☥ ΔΙ ΕΜΟΥ ΚΟΥΛΛΟΥΘΟΥ ΒΙΚΤΟΡΟΣ ΣΥⲛ̄ ΕΓΡ/ ⲕ̄ⲉ̄ ΒΟⲏ̄ ☥

<hr/>

[1] So in Brit Mus no 1080
[2] Fem as in no 158
[3] For ? ϣⲁⲛⲧⲟⲩ- ϣⲁⲁⲧ ⲛⲟⲩ- is hardly possible
[4] Cf REVILLOUT, *Actes* ⲓ̄ⲃ̄
[5] ? ⲫⲓⲗⲟⲕⲁⲗⲉⲓⲁ Cf Brit Mus no 1064, note
[6] ⲅⲁⲙⲟⲟⲩ in a letter here, v Index Perhaps 'proportion', 'portion' of water
[7] V no 158
[8] Cf ⲛⲟϫϥ, ZOEGA 490, the only instance
[9] Altered from ⲡⲱⲕ
[10] Assuming this to be from ⲣⲱϣⲉ.
[11] Cf Boh ⲛⲓ ζεῦγος Lev v 11
[12] Wrong gender   [13] For ? ⲡⲉⲧⲛⲕⲁ-
[14] V KRALL v, lvi, Brit Mus no 1014 ⲉⲩⲥⲧⲁⲑⲉⲙⲱⲛ for εὐσταθμον
[15] KRALL lv   Cf VITELLI no 50, Σεσιν

Lines 1–5 show the lessee's name and a reference to 'all the reeds' From line 6
'] 14th Indiction, and I will . the vines (?) and deliver them to thee,
until (?) they be gathered But (μέντοι γε) .. rent (φόρος) But if (εἰ δέ) thou make
of it a vineyard, I shall receive my wage like every husbandman, of every tree
that grows thereon, with the full use (χρῆσις) of them appertaining (ἀνήκεσθαι) to
whole . of the hall of the husbandman's duty (l 10) And I will give them their
watering in winter (+μέν) I will irrigate (?) them with 15 waters and in summer I will
irrigate (?) them with 12 waters and . I will sprinkle (them with) 8 waters, and what
I sow thereon (shall be) mine And if Anoup shall wish to depart and not to be husbandman for thee, I am ready (ἕτοιμος) to suffice for the whole property (lit place), (both as)
vinedresser and husbandman And I will perform its husbandman's and vinedresser's
service (ὑπουργία) and receive my share as husbandman and my share as vinedresser,
in every crop (καρπός) that there shall be, namely, the 4th part for husbandry and the
4th part for vinedressing And all expenses (ἀνάλωμα) that shall occur upon the property,
(l 15) we will add it (?) to the vat, whether it be (εἴτε) ointment or (εἴτε) any expense (ἀν)
And I will give my customary presents (συνήθεια) annually, namely, for husbandry and
vinedressing at the vintage, 2 measures of old wine, 50 cheeses, 50 pairs of loaves,
2 dishes (δισκάριον), a sixth (ξέστης) of oil, a at 2 carats (κερ) And what we shall (?)
expend at the vintage, we will add to the vat And if God will, I will dwell on the estate
(κτῆμα), and after the period (χρόνος) of this lease (μίσθ), I will give over thy property
(lit place) to thee, even as it (now) is And (I undertake) that I will not pass the first year
and (then) say, I wish to depart, unless (εἰ μή τι) I have fulfilled the period (χρ) of this lease
(μίσθ) If I shall wish (l 20) to depart and have not fulfilled this lease (μίσθ), I am prepared (ἕτοιμος) to pay 6 solidi of proper weight (εὐστάθμος), without judgement, without law
(νόμος), without any matter of doubt (ἀμφιβολία) I swear, by God Almighty (παντοκρ) and
the health of our lords the kings, that I shall not be able to transgress (παραβαίνειν) any
word written in this lease (μίσθ) As an assurance for thee, I have drawn thee this lease
(μίσθ) I wrote it (ἔγραψα) on the 29th Epeiph, by God's will (σὺν θεῷ), 14th Indiction '
Here follow the σημεῖον of the lessee and signatures of 3 witnesses, one of whom, the
priest Victor, of Tsesiō, had acted as scribe

160.—Papyrus This is the *recto* of no 120 Script almost ligatureless Probably
by scribe of no 211 Fibres ↑

Lease of land The nature of the cultivation is uncertain, the lessee undertakes to
pluck[1], pound[2], and card[3] its product and to deliver its crop (καρπός) to the δημόσιος λόγος[4]

---

[1] Cf ϩⲱⲱⲗⲉ in a fragment Brit Mus Or 6201 A &c,
ⲛϫⲣⲉⲱⲥ ⲛⲁⲕ ⲙⲛⲧⲁⲥⲉ ⲙⲁⲣ ⲉⲗⲁⲥ ⲧⲁⲓ̈ϫⲓ ⲁⲥⲛⲗ[ⲏ|ⲣ[ⲟⲩ]
ⲛⲧⲉⲩ̈ϫⲓⲕⲁ ⲙ̈ⲙⲏⲛ ϫⲥⲛⲁⲩ ⲛⲓ̈ⲙ ⲉⲣⲉⲡⲉⲕⲙⲁϩⲉ ⲡⲁⲉⲓ ⲉ̈ⲃⲟⲗ
ⲧⲏⲉⲓ ⲧⲏϩⲟⲟⲗⲟⲩ ⲛⲁⲕ Hence and from Zoega 528 perhaps pluck', 'gather' But v Brit Mus no 171, ⲥⲕⲏ (1),
ⲡⲁⲧⲉⲫⲩⲥⲓⲥ ⲙ̈ⲡⲣⲱⲙⲉⲛⲥ ϩⲱⲱⲗⲉ ϩ̈ⲡⲟⲩϩⲱ̈ⲃ ⲟⲩϩⲱ̈ⲃ ⲁⲉ

ⲛⲧⲉ ⲛⲥⲁⲧⲁⲕⲁⲥⲡⲉ ⲙⲟⲩⲏ ⲉⲃⲟⲗ ϩ̈ⲙⲡϩⲱⲱⲗⲉ, which omitted
by the Greek (*PG* lxxxviii 1953 D), seems parallel to
πίπτειν
[2] V *PSBA* xxvii 170
[3] Cf ⲕⲱⲕ in Isa xix 9, 'carded,' σχιστος, of flax
[4] V no 116

]ⲉⲣⲟϥ ϩⲛⲛⲁⲧⲃⲛⲟⲟⲩⲉ ⲙⲛⲛⲁⲧⲣⲟⲫⲟⲟⲩⲉ ⲙⲛⲛⲁⲃⲉⲕⲉ ⲁⲙⲏⲩ¹ [| ⲛϩⲟⲟⲗⲉϥ ⲧⲁϩⲟⲟⲗⲉϥ ⲧⲁⲥⲟⲙⲉϥ ⲧⲁⲛⲟⲕⲕⲉϥ ⲧⲁⲁⲁϥ ⲛ | ⲧⲁⲡⲁⲣⲁⲍⲓⲁⲟⲩ ⲛⲡⲉϥⲕⲁⲣⲡⲟⲥ ⲉⲡⲁⲛⲙⲟⲥⲓⲟⲥ ⲗⲟⲅⲟⲥ ϩⲁⲣⲟ[| ⲉ ⲁⲁⲛ ⲡⲁⲣⲁ ⲡⲓⲧⲣⲓⲙⲏⲥⲓⲛ ⲥⲛⲁⲩ ⲛⲛⲟⲩⲃ ⲛⲧⲁⲕⲧⲁⲁⲩ ⲛⲁⲓ [| ⲓⲁⲡⲁⲣⲁⲍⲓⲁⲟⲩ ⲙⲙⲟϥ ⲟⲛ ⲉⲡⲁⲛⲙⲟⲥⲓⲟⲥ ⲗⲟⲅⲟⲥ ⲁⲍ[ⲛ | ⲫⲩⲗⲁⲥ]ⲥⲉ ⲛⲁⲕ ⲡⲣⲟⲥϭⲟ]ⲙ ⲛⲧⲓ[ⲙⲓⲥⲟⲱⲥⲓⲥ |

161.—Papyrus, a fragment, 10 × 10 cm Script ligatured *Recto* ↑

End of a Lease (μίσθωσις) by .   to Phoebammon, showing the witnesses' signatures

ⲣ]ϩⲱϥ ϩⲓⲱⲱϥ ⲧⲉⲛⲟ[ⲩ | ϩⲟⲟ]ⲩ ⲉⲧⲉⲥⲟⲩ ⲙⲛⲧⲍⲙⲛⲡⲉ ⁿⁱᶜ ⲛ[|]ⲍⲉⲩⲧⲉⲣⲁ ⁱⁿ ⲧⲁⲣϩ[ⲱϥ |]ϩ ⲉⲣⲉ[. . . .] ⲉⲧⲉⲩϩⲁ [|] ⲁⲓⲥⲙⲛ ⲧⲓⲙⲓⲥⲑⲟⲟⲩⲥⲓⲥ ⲛⲁⲕ ⲁ[ⲙ]ⲁϩϥ ⲛⲁⲕ ⲉⲛϥⲙⲁ ϩⲁⲡⲟⲩⲱϣ [ⲛⲡⲛⲟⲩⲧⲉ |]ⲉ ⲛⲉⲃⲟⲧ ⲛⲧⲉⲓⲣⲟⲙⲡⲉ ⲉⲧⲏⲏⲩ ⲧ [|] ┼┼┤ ᵒˢᵉᵐⁱᵒⁱ + ⲁⲛⲟⲕ ⲫⲟⲓⲃⲁⲙⲙⲱⲛ ⲡϣ[|] ϯⲥⲧⲟⲓⲭⲉ ⲉⲧⲉⲓⲙⲓⲥⲑⲟⲟⲩⲥⲓⲥ + ᵩₒᵢβ

+ ⲁⲛⲟⲕ [| ⲡⲉ]ⲁⲕ, ⲫⲟⲓⲃⲁⲙⲙⲱⲛ ⲡⲣ[ⲱⲙ]ⲉ ϣⲙⲟⲩⲛ[ ]ⲁⲓ]ⲉϩⲁⲓ ϩⲁⲣⲟϥ ⲍⲛⲉϥⲛⲟⲓⲉ ⲁⲛ ⲁⲩⲱ ϯ[| ⲑⲉⲟⲍⲱⲣⲉ ⲡϣⲉ ⲛⲡⲙⲁⲕⲁⲣ, ⲁ . .[

Verso address, illegible

162.—Papyrus, a fragment, 15½ × 7½ cm Script ligatured *Recto* ↑

Lease (μίσθωσις) of 3 arouras from   to Christopher

ⲡⲣ[ⲱⲙⲉ ϣⲙⲟⲩⲛ ⲟⲛ ⲧⲓⲣⲁϣ[ⲉ] |]ⲥⲩⲛ ⲑⲉⲱ ⲉⲕⲧⲏⲥ ιᵟ, ⲉⲑⲏ |]ⲛ ⲥⲉⲙⲉϩ ⲥⲉϣⲁⲁⲧ² ⲛⲑⲉ ⲉⲅⲟ [ⲛ]ⲙⲟⲥ|]ⲉⲓⲏⲃⲧ ϩⲓⲍⲛⲧⲏⲟ³ ⁿⁱᶜⁿᵒᵞⲱⲧ ⲛⲥⲁ ⲛ ⲛ]ⲡⲟⲩⲁϣϥ ϩⲁⲟⲗⲟⲩ ⲧⲁⲧⲓ ⲛⲁⲕ |]ⲧⲟⲙⲉ ⲛⲟⲩⲟⲟⲓⲉ ⲛⲁⲙⲁⲓⲟⲛ⁴ |ⲡⲣ]ⲟⲫⲁⲥⲓⲥ ⲧⲁⲧⲁⲗⲟ ⲛⲉⲥⲟⲩⲟ |ⲉ]ⲩⲱⲣⲍ ⲛⲁⲕ ⲁⲓⲥⲙⲛ ⲧⲙⲓⲥ͞ⲱ, | ⲭⲣⲓⲥⲧ]ⲟⲫⲟⲣⲉ⁵ ⲡⲧϣⲏⲣⲡ |]ⲧⲓⲟ ⲙⲛⲧⲣⲉ +

Verso +ⲙⲓⲥⲑ͞ⲱ, ⲁⲣⲟ̈ ⲟ[

163—Papyrus, a fragment, 12 × 29½ cm Script moderately ligatured *Recto* ↑

Lease (μίσθωσις) from a monastery to   , for 12 years⁶

ⲍ]ⲓⲛⲉⲧⲓⲣⲟⲙⲡⲉ ⲛⲟⲩⲱⲧ ⲉⲥⲏⲏⲩ ⲉⲩⲛ̅ ⲧⲣⲉⲓⲥ | ⲡⲉⲭ̅ⲣⲟⲛⲟⲥ ⲛⲧⲙⲛⲧⲥⲛⲟⲟⲩⲥⲉ ⲛⲣⲟⲙⲡⲉ ⲙ[ⲛ̅ϣ̅ϣⲟⲙ ⲍⲉ |]ⲉ ⲛⲥⲉⲧⲱϩⲉ ϣⲁⲛⲧⲓⲍⲱⲕ ⲡⲉⲭ̅ⲣⲟⲛⲟⲥ ⲛⲧⲙⲛⲧⲥⲛⲟⲟⲩⲥⲉ ⲛⲣⲟⲙⲡⲉ ⲉⲓ ⲍⲉ ⲉⲓϣⲁⲛⲟⲩⲱϣ |]ⲉⲡ . ⲟⲣⲟⲥ⁷ ⁿⁱᶜⲛⲧⲙⲛⲧⲥⲛⲟⲟⲩⲥⲉ ⲛⲣⲟⲙⲡⲉ ⲉϥⲡⲗⲏⲣⲟⲩ ⲉⲓⲕⲛⲁⲩⲛⲉⲩⲉ ⲛⲏⲧⲛ | ⲉⲩⲱⲣⲍ ⲟⲩⲛ ⲛⲡ[ⲉ]ⲓⲙⲟⲛⲁⲥⲧⲏⲣⲓⲟⲛ ⲉⲧⲟⲩⲁⲁⲃ ⲁⲛⲥⲙⲛ ⲧⲙⲓⲥⲟⲱ, ⲛⲏⲧⲛ |]ⲛⲕⲁⲓⲉⲗⲉⲩⲑⲉⲣⲟⲥ ⲁ[ⲩ]ⲣⲙⲛⲧⲣⲉ ⲉ[ⲣⲟⲥ [

---

¹ *V* no 158, l 32
² *V* KRALL exc, Brit Mus no 1021   Perhaps 'whether they be full or lacking' in weight
³ *Cf* KRALL i 12, ⲕⲱ ϩⲟⲩⲛ also fem

⁴ The identical phrase in a fragment Br Mus. Or 6201 B &c *V* no 166   ⁵ Different hand
⁶ An unusually long lease   *V* here no 158
⁷ ⲡⲉⲭ̅ⲣⲟⲛⲟⲥ or ⲡⲉⲫⲟⲣⲟⲥ ?

164.—Papyrus, a fragment; 17½ × 6½ cm.   Script   small, ligatured   *Recto* ↑

Lease of land for 4 years (?) from the δίκαιον of (the monastery of) St Severus, through its φροντιστής¹, to George (?), son of Philotheus   The yearly rent is to be paid in corn

ⲡⲙ]ⲁⲕ, ⲫⲓⲗⲟⲑⲉⲟⲥ ⲡⲣⲱⲙⲉ ⳃⲙⲟⲩⲛ | ⲟ]ⲓⲧⲟⲟⲧⲕ ⲁⲡⲁ ⲡⲉⲑⲏⲅ ⲡⲉⲫⲣⲟ[ⲛⲧⲓⲥⲧⲏⲥ |]ⲓ̅ ⲛⲁⲕ ⲛⲃ̅ⲅⲟ
ⲛⲣⲟⲙⲡⲉ ⲛⲥⲁⲛ| ⲥⲥ]ⲡⲏⲅ ⲥⲅⲏ̃ ⲡⲣⲱⲧⲏⲥ ⲓ̅δ̅, ⲛⲛⲉⲧⲁⲓⲁⲫ[ⲉⲣⲓⲥⲟⲉ |]ⲉ ⲛⲙⲁ ⲉⲅⲙⲟⲩⲧⲉ ⲉⲣⲟ[ⳃ ⲭⲉⲁⲛⲁ|]ⲡⲉⳃⲫⲟⲣⲟⲥ ⲧⲉⲣⲟⲙⲡⲉ ⲛⳃⳍ[ⲟ]ⲙⲉⲧ ⲛⲣⲓ | ⲑⲉⲧⲟ]ⲙⲟⲥ ⲧⲁⲡⲗⲏⲣⲟⲩ ⲛⲛⲟⲕ ⲉⲓ[| ⲃ]ⲣⲣⲉ ⲉⲡⲁⲛⲟⲩⲟⲩ ⲉⲅⳃⲗ-
ⳃⲱⲗ ⳇ |] ⲙⲛ ⲑⲱⳃ ⲛⲓⲙ ⲉⲓ̈ⲱⲡⲉ ⳃⲁⲛ[|]ⲉⲣⲟⲥ ⲉⲓⲱⲣⲕ ⲛⲛⲛⲟⲩⲧⲉ ⲛⲡ[| ⲥⲉⲱ]ⲡⲥⲉ ⲛⳃⲉ ⲛⲡⲙⲁⲕ, ⲫⲓⲗⲟ[ⲑⲉⲟⲥ | ⲛ]ⳃⲉ ⲛⲡⲙⲁⲕ, ⲛⳃⲟⲩⲣⲡⲉⳃⲙ[ⲉⲅⲉ |]ⲙⲛⲧⲣⲉ ✝ | ⲛⳃ]ⲉ ⲛⲡⲙⲁⲕ, ⲙⲛⲛⲁ
ⲛⲧⲁⲓⳍⲁⲓ ⳍⲁⲣ[

Verso]ⲉⳃⲙⲙⲉ ⲛⲙⲟⲥ ⲛⲡⲁⲓ[ⲕⲁⲓⲟⲛ | ⲫⲁⳃⲓⲟⲥⲉⲅ̈ⲏⲣⲓⲟⲥ

165.—Papyrus, almost complete, 8½ × 30½ cm   Script   clumsy semi uncials   *Recto* ↑

Agreement (ἀσφάλεια) between the heirs of Victor and the φροντιστής and ἀποκρισάριος of a monastery

✝ ⲁⲛⲟⲛ ⲛⲉⲕⲗⲏⲣⲟⲛⲟⲙⲟⲥ ⲛⲃⲓⲕ[ⲧⲱⲣ ⲡ]ⲉⳍⲣⲏⲣ² ⳍⲓⲧⲛⲉⲛⲱⲭ ⲡⲉⳃⳃⲏⲣⲉ ⲙⲛⲥⲁⲣⲁ ⲧⲉⳃⳃⲉⲉⲣⲉ
ⲙⲛⲧⲉⲅ|ⲅⲉⲛⲓⲁ ⲙⲛⳍⲉⲗⲁⲣⲓⲁ ⲙⲛⲡⲁⲧⲓ .ⳡⲩ ⲙⲛⲧⲁⲙⲁⲛⲉ ⲧⲉⲛⲙⲁⲅⲧⲉ ⲙⲁⲣⲓⲁ ⳍⲛⲟⲩⲁⳃⲙⲟⲩⲟⲩ³ ⲉⲛⲥⳍⲁⲓ | ⲛⲡⲙⲟⲩⲛⲁⲥⲧⲏⲣⲓⲟⲛ ⲉⲧⲟⲩⲁⲁⲃ ⲛⲁⲡⲁ ⲭⲉⲣⲏⲙⲱⲛ ⳍⲓⲧⲛⲁⲡⲁ ⳍⲱⲣ ⲡⲉⲫⲣⲟⲛⲧⲓⲥⲧⲏⲥ ⳍⲓⲧⲛⲫⲓⲃ-
ⲁⲙⲟⲩ | ⲡⲁⲡⲟⲕⲣⲏⲥⲁⲣⲏⲥ ⲭⲉⲉⲡⲓⲛ ⲙⲛⲧⲁⲓⲟⲩⲣⲏⳃ⁴ ⲛⲙⲁⲩ ⲛⲡⲉⲙⳍⲓⲧ ⲛⲧⳃⲟ ⲛⲡⲁⲏ ⲉⳍⲛ ⲁⲕⲥⲉⲡ-
ⲭⲱⲣⲓ | ⲛⲁⲕ ⲭⲓⲛⲛⲡⲕⲟⲟⳍ ⲛⲡⲁⲏ ⲉⲡⲁⲏ⁵ ⲉⲡⲉⲉⳃⳃ ⳃⲁⲅⲡⳍⲓⲣ ⲁⲓⲟⲩⲱⲛ ⲛⲡⲁⲣⲟ ⲉⲡⲉⲉⳃⳃ ⲉⲡⳍⲓⲣ
ⲧⲓⲛⲟⲩ | ⲧⲛⲱ ⲛⳍⲉⲭⲉⲙⲟⲥ ⲧⲓⳃ ⲟⲩⲡⳃⳃⲙⲉⲛⲧ ⲛⲥⲟⲩⲟ ⲛⲛⲧⲛ ⲛⳃⳃⲟⲣ ⲛⲙⲟⳃ ⲉⲧⲉⲣⲟⲁⲥⲡⲉ⁶ ⲭⲓⲛ|ⲡⲟⲟⲩ
ⲉⳍⲣⲁⲓ ⲉⲧⲉⲥⲟⲩⲟⲟⲩ ⲛⲛⲥⲟⲩⲣⲡⲛⲉ ⲛⲟⲉⲛⲛⲁⲧⲏⲥ ⲛⲁⲓⲕ, ⲁⲩⲱ ⲉⲕⳃⲁⲛⲟⲩⲱⳃ⁷ ⲉⲃⲛⳃ | ⲛⲧⲟⲟⲧ ⲧⲉⲧⲛⲱ
ⲛⲛⲡⲭⲟⲉⲓⲥ ⲉⲧⲁⳃⳃⲓ ⳃⲟⲣ ⲛⲧⲟⲟⲧⲛ ⲉⲛⳃⲁⲛⲟⲩⲱⳃ ⳍⲱⲱⲛ ⲉⲧⲁⳃ ⳃⲟⲣ | ⲧⲛⲟⲩⲛⲓ ⲛⲡⲉⳃⲣⲟ ⲉⳍⲛ
ⲛⲡⲉⲉⳃⳃ ⲙⲛⲕⲟⲟⳍ ⲙⲡⲉⲛⲏ ✝ ⲉⲧⳍⲁ ⲙⲛⲥⲟⲩⲣⲏ ⳅ̅ ⲑ̅ ⲓⲛⲁ, | ⲁⲩⲱ ⲁⲛⲟⲕ ⲁⲛⲭⲱⲛⲉ ⲡⲁⲡⲁⲥ, ⲛⲧⲁⲅ-
ⲁⲭⲓⲟⲩ ⲛⲙⲟⲓ ⲁⲓⲥⳍⲁⲓ ⳍⲁⲣⲟⲟⲩ ⲭⲉⲥⲉⲛⲟⲓ | ⲛⲥⳍⲁⲓ ⲁⲛ ⲁⲩⲱ ✝ⲱ ⲛⲙⲛⲧⲣⲉ ✝ ✝ ✝ ✝ ⲥⲉⲙⲟⲛ
ⲁⲅⲣⲁⳍⲙ ⲡⲗⲁⳃⲁⲛⲉ ✝ ⳃⲛⲁⲟⲩⲧ[. . .]ⲣⲉ

Verso, in semi Greek script   + ⲁⲥⲫⲁⲗ/ ⲥⲉⲛⲟⲙ̈ ⳇ ⲛ, ⲕⲩⲣ/ ⲃⲓⲕ, ⲫⲣⲏⲣ⁸ ⲁⲡ ⲟⲩⲟⲓ|ⲙⲟⲩ
ⲉⲧⲃⲉⲡⲟⲩⲣⲉⳍ +

'We, the heirs (κληρονόμος) of Victor, the . .   , represented by Enoch, his son, and Sara, his daughter, and Teugenia⁹ and Helaria and Pati u and Tamane, our mother being Maria, from Waiemow, we write to the holy monastery of Apa Chaeremôn, represented by Apa Hôr, the φρ, and by Phoebammon, the ἀπ   Seeing that (ἐπειδή) I have not a bare-space (?) on the north of the wall of my house, northward, thou didst give us leave (συγχωρεῖν) (of occupation), from the corner of my house, eastward, as far as the street, and

---

¹ As a monastic official, KRALL cxvii 8, clxiii, here no 165   In Brit Mus no 379 it appears to vary with διοικητής
² A quite unknown word
³ Unknown
⁴ V CRUM, *Ostr*, no 81, note.
⁵ Presumably superfluous

⁶ Possibly ⲣⲟ βγ, though γ can scarcely be read, nor have I found ⲣⲟ, 'part,' thus used
⁷ ⲉⲕ- altered from ⲥⲛ-, or *vice versâ*
⁸ Possibly ⲫⲣⲓⲁⲣ.
⁹ 'Then relatives' (for γενεά) is less likely, though Greek names with preformative Copt ⲧ- are rare

I have opened my door eastward, upon the street, so now we are prepared ($\check{\epsilon}\tau o\iota\mu os$) to give you (*pl*) half a third (?) of corn as rent therefor, that is,   . , from to-day onward, being the 6th of Mesore of the 9th Indiction   And[1] if thou shalt wish to take it from me, ye have the right not to receive rent of us   If we, on the other hand, shall wish not to pay rent, we will open our door on the north, eastward of the corner of our house'   Signature of the scribe and witness and $\sigma\eta\mu\epsilon\hat{\iota}o\nu$ of the magistrate

166—Papyrus, a fragment, 21 × 9 cm   Script small, few ligatures   *Recto* →

Lease ($\mu\acute{\iota}\sigma\theta\omega\sigma\iota s$), wherein a previous one is referred to, from the $\delta\acute{\iota}\kappa\alpha\iota o\nu$ of a monastery ($\tau\acute{o}\pi os$) to the $\kappa\hat{\nu}\rho\iota s$ Hamoi

+ ⲡⲁⲓⲕⲁⲓⲟⲛ ⲙⲡⲧⲟⲡⲟⲥ ⲉⲧⲟⲩⲁⲁ[ⲃ | ⲛⲉⲙ̣ⲯⲩⲭⲏ ⲙⲛ̄ⲓⲱⲙⲁ ⲁⲡⲁ ⲕⲩⲣ[| ⲛⲁⲓⲁⲕ° ⲙ̄ⲙⲡⲓⲥⲡⲉ
[ⲛ] . .   ⲟⲟⲩ [| ⲛⲉⲩⲣⲁⲛ ⲛⲉⲣⲁⲓ ⲛⲡⲕⲩⲣⲓⲥ ⲣⲁⲙⲟⲓ [[| ⲝⲉⲉⲡⲓⲁⲏ ⲛ̄ⲧⲁⲧⲛⲉⲥⲙ ⲟⲩⲙ̄ⲓⲥ̄ ⲛⲁ[ⲛ] ⲛⲉⲙⲉⲛ
ⲛ̄ⲧⲁⲩⲝⲓ ⲙⲟⲟⲩ ⲉⲛ.ⲅ.ⲁ [| ⲙ̄ⲙⲉⲛⲕⲟⲟⲩⲉ ⲛ...ⲝⲓ ⲡⲣⲉ ⲅ [| ⲡⲙⲉⲗⲧⲏ ⲛ̄ⲁⲓⲕⲧⲓⲟⲛⲟⲥ ⲉⲧⲉⲧⲛ̄
ⲥ̄[ⲧⲓⲁⲧⲉ[2] | ⲛ̄ⲧⲟⲡⲉ [ⲡⲟ]ⲩⲅⲟⲟⲓ̄[3] ⲧⲉⲛⲟⲩ ⲧⲏⲣ̄ⲟⲙⲟⲗⲟⲅⲉ | ⲏⲁⲡⲝⲱⲕ ⲛ̄ⲡⲭⲣⲟⲛⲟⲥ [ⲛ̄ⲧ]ⲙ | ⲡ̄ⲣⲟⲗⲟⲏ,
ⲛⲁⲛⲏ̇ⲟ ⲧⲓ ⲙⲟⲥ̄ ⲛ̄ⲧ̇ⲓ[| ⲧⲙⲙⲉ̇ ⲛⲏⲧⲛ̄ ⲁⲛⲥⲧⲟⲓ̄ⲭ ⲉⲣⲟⲥ ⲧ̄ | +[4]ⲓ.. ⲁⲏⲛⲥ ⲡⲉⲓⲉⲗⲁⲭͭ | ⲡⲣⲱⲙⲉ ⲏⲙⲟⲩⲛ
ⲧⲓⲥⲧⲟ[| +[5]ⲁⲡⲁ ⲕⲩⲣⲓ ⲡⲉⲓⲉⲗⲁⲭ ⲛ̄ⲡⲣ̄ ⲛⲏⲉ ⲛⲡⲙ[ⲁⲛ | +[6]ⲁⲙⲏⲏⲗ ⲡⲓⲉⲗⲁⲭͭ ⲛ̄ⲁⲓⲁ[ⲕ |

Verso   traces of an earlier text

167.—Papyrus a fragment, 12 × 18 cm   Script moderately ligatured   *Recto* ↑

End of a Lease ($\mu\acute{\iota}\sigma\theta\omega\sigma\iota s$) from   to Apostolus and George, with witnesses' signatures

]ⲛⲉⲃⲟⲧ ⲛ̄ⲧⲓⲣⲟⲙⲡⲉ ⲛⲟⲩⲱⲧ ⲉϥ̄ⲁⲟⲙⲏ ⲓⲇ̄, |]ⲧⲉⲫ ⲉⲥⲁⲣⲉⲥⲛⲁⲓ ⲛⲏⲧⲛ ⲉⲛ̄ⲕⲏⲧⲩⲛⲉⲩⲉ ⲙⲛ |]ⲉⲩⲱⲣⲝ
[ⲛⲁ]ⲕ ⲁ[ⲓ]ⲉⲣⲁⲓ [ⲧ̄]ⲙⲓⲥⲑⲟⲩⲥⲓⲥ ⲛⲁⲕ | ⲉⲗⲉⲩⲑⲉⲣⲟⲥ [ⲧⲣ]ⲉⲩⲣⲙ̄ⲛⲧⲣⲉ] ⲉⲣⲟⲥ ⲉⲛⲱⲣⲕ ⲛ̄ⲡⲛⲟⲩⲧⲉ |]ⲉⲝⲱⲛ
ⲧⲓⲫⲩⲗⲁⲥⲥⲉ ⲛⲏⲧ[ⲛ] ⲡⲣⲟⲥ ⲧⲉⲥⲟⲙ + | ⲁⲛⲟⲛ ⲁⲡⲟ]ⲥⲧⲟⲗⲟⲥ ⲙⲛ̄ⲅⲉⲱⲣⲅⲉ ⲡⲉ ⲏⲏⲏⲣⲓⲣⲁⲓ ⲧⲓⲥⲧⲟⲭⲉⲓ +|
ⲁⲓⲟⲥ]ⲕⲟⲣⲉ ⲡⲉⲛⲧⲁϥⲏⲱⲡⲉ ⲛ̄ⲡ̄ⲡⲣ̄ⲉ[7] ⲡⲣⲱⲙⲉ ⲏⲙⲟⲩ[ⲛ] |]ⲣⲟⲥ[8] ⲛⲏⲉ ⲛⲡⲙⲙⲁⲕⲁⲣ, ⲅⲉⲱⲣⲅⲉ ⲡⲣⲱⲙⲉ [

Verso   an account (*v* below)

168.—Papyrus, a fragment, 7 × 18 cm   Script semi uncials   *Recto* ↑

Lease to a husbandman, for 5 years

]ⲁⲗⲟ ⲉⲓⲟ ⲛⲟⲩⲅⲟⲟⲓⲉ |]ⲛ̄ ⲉⲓⲁⲡⲟⲧⲁⲥⲉ ⲛ̄ⲧⲃⲟⲏⲑⲉⲓⲁ ⲛⲛⲛⲟⲙⲟⲥ[9] |]ⲟⲩ ⲉϥ̄ⲏⲁⲛⲣ̄ⲧⲏⲟⲣⲡⲉ ⲡⲣⲟⲙⲡⲉ
ⲛ̄ϥⲟⲩⲱⲏ |]ⲝ[ⲱ]ⲕ ⲡⲉⲭⲣⲟⲛⲟⲥ ⲛ̄ⲧⲓⲧⲓ ⲛ̄|ⲭⲣⲟ]ⲛⲟⲥ ⲛ̄ⲧⲓⲧⲓ ⲛ̄ⲡⲣⲟⲙⲡⲉ | ⲡⲣ̄]ⲟⲥⲧⲓⲙⲟⲛ ⲕⲁⲧⲁⲗⲁⲁⲩ |

---

[1] The following conditions are obscure, there being several alternative readings ⲉⲛϣⲁⲛ-, ⲛⲓⲟⲟⲧⲉ ⲧⲛⲱ   [4,5] and [6] Different hands
[2] Νηστία, *v* Index   [7] *Cf* no 141   [8] Different hand
[3] Recurs in no 162 'The husbandman's *oipe*-measure'   [9] *Cf Archiv f Pap* iii 421, $\dot{\alpha}\pi o\tau\alpha\tau\acute{o}\mu\epsilon\nu os$ $\pi\acute{\alpha}\sigma\eta$ $\beta o\eta\theta\epsilon\acute{\iota}\alpha$ $\nu\acute{o}\mu\omega\nu$, also no. 157 here

169.—Papyrus, a fragment, 17 × 16½ cm   Script sloping, ligatureless   *Recto* ↑

Agreement (ἀσφάλεια), probably regarding a Lease   An amount of corn (? as rent) is to be delivered at (the lessor's) house, in Shmoun   House-property seems likewise to be dealt with

]ⲙⲛ̄ⲧⲛ ⲇⲉ ⲛ̄ⲧⲟⲓⲡⲉ ⲛ̄ⲧⲁⲡⲉ[1] ⲡⲉⲥ̄ⲱϣ ⲥⲓ/ ⲥⲓ/ ⲁⲣ̄ᵗ/ [|]ⲡⲟⲩⲱϣ ⲛ̄ⲡⲛⲟⲩⲧⲉ ⲛⲉⲡⲏⲡ ⲡⲉⲃ[ⲟⲧ |]ⲟⲩ ⲛⲁⲕ
ⲉⲡⲛⲕⲏⲛ ϩⲙϣⲙⲟⲩⲛ[| ϣⲣⲣ]ⲉ ⲛⲛⲁⲡⲟⲩⲟⲩ ⲉⲅⲁⲣⲉⲥⲕⲉ ⲛⲁⲕ[|]ⲥ̄ ⲧⲓⲡⲣⲟⲑⲉⲥⲓⲁ ⲉⲡⲓ ⲧⲱ ⲛ̄ⲕⲁⲙⲁ[ⲣ̄ⲧⲉ |
]ⲉⲡⲉⲥ̄ⲣⲟ ⲟⲩⲛ ⲉϩⲛ̄ⲧ ⲙⲛⲛⲉϥⲁⲓⲕ[ⲁⲓⲟⲛ[2] |] ⲙⲙⲟϥ ⲛⲛⲉⲙⲉⲥⲑⲁⲓ ⲉⲣⲟϥ ⲛ[| ⲛ]ⲓⲙⲉ ⲉⲛⲟⲩⲁϣϥ ⲛⲱϫⲓ ϣⲥⲟⲣ[|
ⲡⲛⲟⲩ]ⲧⲉ ⲡⲡⲁⲛⲧⲟⲕⲣⲁⲧⲱⲣ ⲭⲓⲛⲓϣⲡ[ⲁⲣⲁⲃⲁ |] ⲭ̄ⲟⲓⲁⲛ ⲓⲛ ⲓⲛⲁ/ . $\overset{\sigma\nu\mu\iota\sigma\nu}{\underset{?\ ?}{\vdash\!\!\vdash\!\!\vdash}}$ + ⲁⲛⲟⲕ [|] + ⲁⲛⲟⲕ
ⲡ . . . ⲁⲥ̄[3] ⲡϣⲉ ⲛ̄ⲗⲉⲟ[ⲛⲧⲓⲟⲥ | ⲁ]ⲛⲟⲕ[4] ⲁⲛⲑⲉⲙⲙⲓⲟⲥ ⲡⲛⲟⲧⲁⲣ/ ⲡ[| ⲁⲛ]ⲟⲕ⁵ ⲕⲟⲗⲑⲉ ⲡϣⲉ ⲛ̄ⲡⲙⲁⲕⲁⲣⲓ[|
] ⲉⲧⲓⲁⲥⲫⲁⲗⲓⲁ +

170—Papyrus, a fragment, 9 × 18½ cm   Script almost ligatureless   *Recto* ↑

Probably a Lease   A field named Teshnē   [6] is perhaps mentioned

ⲡϣ]ⲉ ⲛ̄ⲡⲙⲁⲕ/ ⲧⲣⲏⲥⲟⲣⲉ ⲛ̄ⲣⲱⲙⲉ ϣⲙⲟⲩⲛ ⲉⲓⲥϩⲁⲓ ⲛϥⲣⲁϩ ⲡⲓⲗ[|]ϥ ⲉϥⲥⲟⲣϭ ⲉ̄ⲃⲟⲗ[7] ⲉϩⲱϥ ⲛⲓⲙ
ⲡⲁⲓ ⲛ̄ⲧⲁⲓⲡⲟⲭϥ ⲉⲡϭⲟⲓ ⲉⲧⲉϣⲓⲛ [|]ⲉⲧⲓⲧⲟⲩ ⲛ̄ⲥⲟⲩⲟ ⲛ̄ⲧⲛⲟⲩⲓ ⲛⲟⲓⲡⲉ[3] ⲁⲩⲱ ⲧⲁⲧⲓ ⲛⲉⲕ[|]ⲭⲛⲛⲓⲁⲣⲙⲟⲩⲧⲉ
ⲛⲑⲉ ⲛ̄ⲧ[| ϩ]ⲟⲗⲟⲕⲧ ⲛⲟⲩⲃ̄ ⲛⲁⲧϩⲁ[ⲡ |] ⲡⲣⲟⲥ ⲧⲉⲥⲥⲟⲙ . . [

171—Papyrus, a fragment, 7½ × 35 cm   Script ligatured, *cf* Br Mus Catal, Pl 14, no 1024   *Recto* ↑

Lease (μίσθωσις) of a house, whereof the boundaries (γειτνία) are given   The annual rent is 2 carats   This deed is subsequent to a ὁμολογία previously drawn up by the lessor   The lessee (?) signs in Greek

ⲅⲉ]ⲱⲣⲅⲉ ⲡϣⲉ ⲛ̄ⲡⲁⲩⲗⲟⲥ ⲡⲉⲙϩⲣⲓⲧ ⲧⲕⲁⲙⲁϣⲉ ⲕⲓⲛ ⲧⲱⲓⲧⲉ ⲡⲉϥⲧ ⲡⲛⲓ ⲛⲁⲡⲁ ⲃⲓⲕⲧⲱⲣ ⲡϣ+
ⲛⲁⲡⲟⲩϥ ⲡⲁⲓⲛⲉ | ⲛⲉⲥⲉⲓⲧⲛⲓⲁ ⲧⲁⲧⲓ ⲛⲁⲕ ϩⲁⲡⲉϣϣⲟⲣ ⲧⲉⲣⲟⲙⲡⲉ ⲛ̄ⲕⲉⲣⲁⲧⲛ ⲥⲛⲧⲉ ⲅⲩ/ ⲕ/ β ⲡⲓϣϭⲟⲣ
ⲟⲩⲛ ⲧⲁⲧⲁⲁⲃ ⲧⲉⲣⲟⲙⲡⲉ | ⲡⲣⲟⲥ ⲧϭⲟⲙ ⲛ̄ⲧⲉⲕϩⲟⲙⲟⲗⲟⲅⲓⲁ ⲛ̄ⲧⲁⲛⲥⲙⲛ̄ⲧⲥ ⲛⲁⲓ ⲉⲡⲉⲕⲱⲣⲭ ⲟⲩⲛ ⲁⲓⲥⲙⲛ
ⲧⲓⲙⲓⲥⲑⲱⲥⲓⲥ ⲛⲁⲕ ⲉⲓⲅⲩⲡⲟ|ⲅⲣⲁⲫⲏ ⲉⲣⲟⲥ ⲛ̄ⲧⲁϭⲓⲝ ⲉⲅⲣ̄$\overset{\alpha}{}$ ⲡⲁⲩⲛⲓ δ [. . . . . . .] + [.]ⲟ̄ᵗ ⲅ︦ⲓⲟⲥ
ⲓⲁⲕⲕⲱⲃⲟⲩ ⲁⲡⲟ ⲉⲣⲙⲟⲩⲡⲟⲗ[ᵉ]/ | . ⲥⲧ ⲙⲟⲓ ⲛ ⲡⲁⲣⲟⲩⲥⲛ |ⲙⲓⲥⲑⲱⲥⲓⲥ about 10 lett + ⲁⲛⲟⲕ ⲧ]ⲁⲩⲣⲓⲛⲉ
ⲡⲣⲱⲙⲉ ϣⲙⲟⲩⲛ | ⲧⲓⲟ ⲙⲙⲛ̄ⲧⲣⲉ ⲉⲧⲓⲙⲓⲥⲑ[ⲱⲥⲓⲥ | [. . .]ⲙⲛ̄ⲧⲣⲉ ⲉⲧⲓⲙⲓⲥ[ⲑⲱⲥⲓⲥ

Verso part of an Account beginning + λογ/ χρυσιον   It consists of names, each preceded by δ/

---

[1] Name or title? *Cf* KRALL xxxiv, clxvii
[2] *Cf* phrases in KRALL cxxv
[3] Possibly ⲡⲉⲓⲣⲟⲥ.
[4] and [5] Different hands

[6] *V* KRALL cxxx and perhaps Br Mus no 1014   Or ? not a name, merely 'garden'
[7] *V* no 158, 38 for this verb.
[8] *V* Br Mus no 1043

172.—Papyrus, a fragment, 8 × 11½ cm   Script neat, ligatureless   *Recto* ↑

Lease (μίσθωσις) of part of a house, giving its boundaries   *Cf* phrases in Krall cxxv and Br Mus no 1015

] ⲡⲣⲱⲙⲉ ⲙⲙⲟⲩⲛ [|] ⲡⲉⲛⲧⲉⲛⲁⲓⲁⲉⲛᵀ/ ⲙⲁ°/ ⲉⲑⲏ ⲙⲡⲉⲧⲁ[ⲓⲁⲫⲉⲣⲉⲥⲟⲉ¹ |] ⲡⲉⲁⲛⲧ ⲉⲧⲉⲛⲁⲓⲛⲉ
ⲛ[|]ⲓⲥⲱⲣⲉⲝ ⲅⲛⲟⲁⲉⲓⲧ ⲉⲣⲉⲡⲉⲩⲣ[ⲟ |] ⲛⲧⲝⲓⲛⲉⲡⲱⲣ ⲛⲉⲙ[|] ⲉⲣⲱⲧⲛ ⲅⲏⲧⲏϣⲱⲧⲉ ⲙⲡ[|] ⲁⲓⲣⲁⲓⲟⲛ
ⲛⲓⲙ ⲉⲧⲁⲛⲅⲏⲕ/ ⲉⲡⲉⲧⲏ[² |]ⲧⲓ ⲛⲏⲧⲛ ⲅⲁⲡⲉⲩϣⲟⲣ ⲧⲉⲣⲟⲙⲡⲉ ⲛ[| ⲕⲁ]ⲧⲁ ⲣⲟⲙⲡⲉ ⲧⲉⲣⲟⲙⲡⲉ ⲁⲩⲱ
ⲛⲁⲩ ⲛⲓⲙ [| ⲟⲩ]ⲱϣ ⲙⲡⲟⲟⲛⲉⲥ ⲉⲃⲟⲗ ⲝⲛⲛⲉⲧⲛϣⲁⲛ[³

Verso ⳨ μισθ/ μερᵛ οικᵛ ευνο [space]

173.—Papyrus, a fragment, 24½ × 27 cm   A complete *selis* is 14 cm   Script sloping, often ligatured   *Recto* ↑

Lease (μίσθωσις) of 10 arouras from   to Paul, son of Agene⁴, of Pchental⁵, who employed Teleme⁶, headman of his village, to write for him

ⲉⲩϣⲏⲩ ⲉⲅⲟⲩⲟⲝ [|] ⲅⲁⲧⲙⲛⲧⲉ ⲛⲥⲉⲧ[ⲓⲱⲣⲉ | ⲕⲁⲧⲁ ⲣ[ⲟ]ⲙⲛ[ⲉ ⲛⲟ]ⲩⲟⲉⲓϣ ⲛⲓⲙ ⲉⲛϫⲟ ⲙⲙⲟⲟⲩ[|
ⲛⲡⲉⲛⲓⲱⲧ ⲁⲩⲉ[ⲛ]ⲉ ⲛⲧ.ϥ ⲙ .. ⲉⲥ ⲛⲁⲕ ⲛ ⲓⲟⲩ . ⲧⲏϣⲁ[| ⲧⲟⲙⲟⲥ ⲧⲓ ⲙⲁⲁⲃⲉ [ⲛ]ⲕⲉⲣⲁⲧⲛ ⲧⲓⲧⲁⲁⲩ
ⲛⲁⲕ ⲧⲉⲣⲟ[ⲙⲡ]ⲉ ⲧⲉⲣⲟ[ⲙⲡⲉ | ⲛ ⲕ. ⲉⲓⲉ ⲛ ... ⲡⲛ ⲧⲓⲁⲡⲟⲇⲓⲝⲓⲥ ⲛⲁⲕ ⲧⲛⲡⲗⲏⲣⲟⲩ ⲙⲙ[| ⲙⲟⲟⲩ
ⲛⲧⲱⲃⲉ ⲡⲉⲃⲟⲧ ⲧⲉⲣⲟⲙⲡⲉ ⲧⲉⲣⲟⲙⲡⲉ ϫⲓⲛⲉⲡⲕⲁ]ⲣⲡⲟⲥ | ⲛⲧⲡⲉⲁⲧⲏⲥ ⲙⲁ// ϣⲁⲟⲩⲟⲉⲓϣ ⲛⲓⲙ ⲉⲛⲁⲁⲩ
ⲉⲛϫⲟ ⲙⲙ[| ⲉⲅⲱⲣϫ ⲟⲩⲛ ⲛⲁⲕ ⲁⲛⲥⲙⲛ ⲧⲓⲙⲓⲥⲑⲱⲥⲓⲥ ⲛⲧϭⲓϫ [ⲛ]ⲡⲁ[ⲡⲉ] | ⲛⲡⲉⲛⲅⲓⲙⲉ ⲧⲉⲗⲉⲙⲉ ⲉⲛⲱⲣⲕ
ⲉⲡⲛⲟⲩⲧⲉ ⲡⲡⲁⲛⲧⲟⲕⲣ[ⲁ]ⲧⲱⲣ | ϫⲉⲡⲉ[ⲛ]ⲉϣⲡⲁⲣⲁⲃⲁ ⲙⲙⲟⲕ ⲡⲣⲟⲥ ⲧϭⲟⲙ ⲛⲧⲉⲙⲙⲓⲥⲑⲱⲥ[ⲓⲥ] | ⳨ ⲉⲅⲣⲁⲫⲉⲛ
ⲙ̄/ ⲫⲁⲱⲫ/ ⲓⲑ ⲓⲛⲇ/ ⲇ +   + ⲁⲛⲟⲕ ⲡⲁⲩⲗⲓ ⲡϣⲉ ⲙⲡⲓⲁⲕ/ | ⲁⲩⲉⲛⲉ ⲡⲣⲱⲙⲡⲉⲅⲛⲧⲁⲗ ⲧⲓⲥⲧⲟⲓⲭ/ ⲉⲧⲙⲓⲥ-
ⲑⲱⲥⲓⲥ ⲛⲟⲉ ⲉⲥ[ⲏ]ⲅ | ⲙⲙⲟⲥ ⲅⲁⲣⲟⲓ ⲙⲛⲡⲁⲥⲛⲏⲩ +   + ⲁⲛⲟⲕ ⲧⲉⲗⲉⲙⲉ ⲡⲁⲡⲉ ⲛⲡⲉ[ⲅⲛⲧⲁⲗ] | ⲁⲓⲥⲅⲁⲓ
ⲅⲁⲣⲟⲟⲩ ⲁⲩⲱ ⲧⲓⲟ ⲙⲙⲛⲧⲣⲉ +   +⁷ⲁⲛⲟⲕ ⲓⲉⲣⲏⲙⲓⲁⲥ ⲡϣⲉ ⲙ[ⲁⲡⲟⲗⲗⲱ ⲡⲣⲱⲙⲡⲉⲅⲛⲧⲁⲗ ⲟⲛ ϯⲟ
ⲙⲙⲛⲧⲣⲉ ⲉⲧⲉⲙⲙⲓⲥⲑⲱⲥⲓⲥ + | +⁸ⲁⲛⲟⲕ ⲁⲛⲁ ⲅⲱⲣ ⲡϣⲉ ⲛⲡⲣⲁⲉⲓⲥⲕⲉ⁹ ⲡⲣⲩⲙⲡⲉⲅⲛⲧⲁⲗ ⲧⲓⲟ ⲙⲙⲉⲧⲣⲉ
ⲉⲧⲉⲙⲙⲓⲥⲑⲱⲥⲓⲥ +

Verso blank

174.—Papyrus, a fragment, 39 × 9 cm   Script ligatured   *Recto* ↑   Above, remains of an Arabic (?) protocol

Agreement (ὁμολογία) addressed by   to the δίκαιον of a monastery, relating to a heritable Lease (ἐμφύτευμα) in certain land.

¹ *Cf* Krall cxxvii 12
² Was ⲉⲡⲉⲕ[
³ Was ⲛⲛⲉⲕ-
⁴ A name almost confined to Middle Egypt (except Grenfell, *Gk Pap* ii, xc, Edfu)   In Hall, *Copt and Gk Texts*, p 132, a martyr with Serenus, at Tehne, *ib* 145, a saint named with Apollo   Var ⲁⲅⲓⲛⲉ Krall cxiii, ⲁⲅⲉⲛⲁ *ib* xxix, ⲁⲕⲛⲛⲉ Clédat, *Baouit* ii 82, Αγενις Vitelli no 65, Αγανιος Kenyon, *Catal* iii 247. *Cf* Παγένης *BGU* 21, ⲅⲁⲅⲉⲛⲉ (? fem) Br Mus no 1086 (The Rev P Peeters S J suggests the Roman family-name Aggenus, Agennus, Agenus, Agenius, used here as a personal name)
⁵ Ⲡⲉⲉⲛⲧⲁⲗ Kenyon, *Catal* i 173, Ⲡⲉⲉⲛⲧⲁⲗⲓⲥ *BGU* 553 Perhaps Behdâl, near Miniah
⁶ ⲓ.ⲩⲏ, Karabacek   But *cf* Ⲡⲧⲟⲗⲉⲙⲁⲓⲟⲥ
⁷ Different hand   ⁸ Different hand
⁹ ? Πρίσκος

ⲥϩ]ⲁⲓ ⲛⲡⲇⲓⲕⲁⲓⲟⲛ ⲉⲧⲟⲩⲁⲁⲃ | ϩⲓ]ⲧⲟⲟⲧⲛ[1] ⲡⲉⲑⲉⲟⲫⲓⲗⲉⲥⲧⲁⲧⲟⲥ | ⲉⲓ]ⲱⲧ ⲙⲡⲁⲡⲁ ⲍⲁⲭⲁⲣⲓⲁⲥ |]ⲙⲟⲟⲩ ⲁⲧⲛⲉⲧⲓ ⲟⲩⲥⲉⲧⲓⲱϩⲉ |]ϥⲟⲛϩ ⲡⲉⲙⲫⲩⲧⲉⲩⲙⲁ |]ⲟⲉ̣ ⲇⲓⲁⲕⲟ/ ⲁⲥⲇⲟⲍⲏ[2] ⲧⲁⲣϥ |]ⲕ ϩⲱⲱⲧ ϩⲓⲧⲟⲟⲧϥ ⲉⲡⲇⲓⲁⲕⲟ/ |]ϫⲓⲛⲉⲡⲟⲟⲩ ⲉⲑⲏ ⲉⲧⲉⲥ | ⲉⲙ]ⲫⲩⲧⲉⲩⲙⲁ ⲉⲧⲉⲛⲁⲙⲉ ϣⲙⲟ[ⲩ] (ⲡ above) |] ⲉⲥⲉⲓⲭⲏ[3] ϣⲁⲉⲛϩ + ⲉⲩⲣ/ μ́ | ϩⲟ]ⲙⲟⲗⲟⲅⲓⲁ ⲛⲑⲉ ⲉⲥⲥⲏϩ ⲙⲙⲟⲥ | ⲓⲱ]ϩⲁⲛⲛⲏⲥ ⲡⲣⲙⲁⲛⲧⲓ/ |]ⲉ ⲙⲙⲟⲥ + |]ϯⲟ ⲙⲙⲛⲧⲣⲉ ⲥⲧⲓϩⲟⲙⲟⲗⲟⲅⲓⲁ |]ⲙⲛⲛⲁ ⲡⲣⲙⲁⲛⲧⲓⲛⲟⲟⲩ |

175.—Papyrus; a fragment, $5\frac{1}{2} \times 15$ cm Script *v* Pl I *Recto* ↑

Deed relating to a heritable Lease (ἐμφυτευτικὴ ὁμολογία) L I apparently shows the date, which would be A M 437 = A.D 721. L 2 has an obscure reference to the Thebaid

ⲧ]ⲉⲧⲣⲁⲕⲟⲥⲓⲟⲥⲧⲟⲩ ⲧⲣⲓⲁⲕⲟⲥⲧⲟⲩ ⲉⲃⲇⲟⲙⲟⲩ ⲉⲛ ⲥⲙⲟⲩⲡ[ⲟⲗⲉⲓ |] ⲓ[.].ⲣⲓⲥⲧⲟⲩ[4] ⲑⲏⲃⲁⲓⲇⲟⲥ + |] ⲉϫⲱⲟⲩ ⲡⲉⲙⲫⲩⲧⲉⲩⲧⲓⲕⲏ ϩⲟⲙⲟⲗⲟⲅⲓⲁ ⲥⲩⲟⲣϫ [|] ϣⲁⲉⲛⲉϩ ⲉⲩⲥⲙⲙⲛⲉ ⲛⲙⲟⲟⲩ ⲙⲛⲛⲉⲩⲉⲣⲏⲩ ϩⲛ[

176.—Papyrus; a fragment, 8×14 cm Script ligatureless *Recto* ↑

From a Deed relating to a heritable Lease (ἐμφύτευμα) One party appears to be the 'master'[5] George and Hatre On the *verso* a Greek tax receipt

]ⲉ̣ ϫⲉⲣϣⲁⲛⲁⲡⲁ ⲃⲁⲥⲓⲗⲉ ϩⲱⲱ[ϥ | ⲟⲩⲱ [ⲅ]ⲁⲣ ⲛ ⲃ̅ⲓ̅ ⲡⲓⲕ.ϥ.. ..[| ⲛⲧⲟⲟⲧⲟⲩ ⲛⲡⲥⲁϩ ⲅⲉⲱⲣⲅⲉ ⲙⲛϩⲁⲧⲣⲉ [| ⲧⲉⲣⲟⲙⲡⲉ ⲉⲡⲓ ⲧⲱ ⲛⲧⲟϥ .ⲛ .ⲛⲁⲣⲓ[| . .. ⲓ ⲉϣⲁⲣⲉϥⲁϩ ⲅⲉⲱⲣ[ⲅⲉ . | ⲉⲃ̣ⲁⲡⲁⲣⲁⲃⲁ ϩⲩⲡⲟⲕⲉⲓⲥⲑⲁⲓ ⲁⲩⲱ ⲙ ⲛⲉ.[| ⲉⲩⲕⲏⲃ[6] ⲛⲧⲉⲛⲓⲁⲛⲧⲓⲥⲩⲅⲅⲣⲁⲫⲟⲛ[7] ⲛⲉⲙⲫⲉ[ⲧⲉⲩⲙⲁ (?) | ϥϩⲟⲙⲟⲗⲟⲅⲉⲓ ⲇⲉ ⲛⲧⲟϥ ⲁⲡⲁ ⲃⲁⲥⲓⲗⲉ ϫⲉ̣ ϫ[| ⲉ ⲟⲩ (ⲟⲩ above) ⲛⲡⲉⲧⲣⲓⲙⲏⲥⲓ[ⲛ] ⲥⲛ[ⲁⲩ] ⲛ̣ⲛ̣ⲟⲩⲃ ⲛ[

Verso, in another hand

+ ⲑⲱⲑ ⲕ̅ⲑ̅ ⲉⲥⲭ ⲇ/ ⲕⲩⲣⲟⲩ ⲇⲓⲟⲥⲕⲟⲣⲉ̣ ..[| ⲁⲡⲟ ⲇⲏⲙⲟⲥⲓⲟⲩ ⲧⲉⲥⲥⲁⲣⲉⲥⲕⲁⲓⲇⲉⲕⲁⲧ[ⲏⲥ] | ⲓⲛⲇ/ $ⲁⲣ^{ⲟ}$[8] ⲉⲛ γι/ $\overset{θ}{ἀρ}$ α + ⲇⲱⲣⲟⲑⲉⲟⲥ ⲥⲧⲟⲓ. | blank

177.—Papyrus, a fragment, $15\frac{1}{2} \times 12$ cm Script ligatured *Recto* ↑

Deed of Authorization (ἐπιτροπή), addressed to a woman The writer undertakes certain duties as to the reeds and plants and as to 'enclosing their walls' Two places, Shbêk[9] and Pma nserge, are mentioned.

1 One would expect 2nd rather than 1st plur

2 *V* no. 144

3 Ἰσχύειν, *cf* Br Mus no 1013 and here no 183

4 Before ⲣ possibly ⲭ A local name?

5 ⲥⲁϩ 'teacher, master' (= διδάσκαλος in New Test), so, as here, apparently a title of respect (Br Mus nos 1172, 1183, KRALL xcv &c, an abbess ⲧⲥⲁϩ, *Bull Inst fr* v, fasc 1, pl xi), or joined with a designation of trade, occupation (Br Mus nos 1037, 1066 carpenters, here nos 215, 216 corn or fruit-dealers, CLÉDAT, *Baouit* ii 97 builder, *ib* 159 ἐξηγητής, Paris 131[3] 34 goldsmith &c) As a church official, = reader (Br Mus no 144, Leyden *MSS* p 153, *cf* CLEDAT *l c* 98, ⲣⲉϥⲱϣ) The ⲥ ⲛⲧⲙⲉ, a village official (= νομικός, KRALL cxxxviii), colleague of the headman (Br Mus no 1079), acts as scribe (*ib* 461, KRALL v), *cf* the ⲥⲁϫⲟ, *PSBA* xxi 249

6 Refers to the doubling of the rent (or price) in case of default

7 *V* Br Mus no 1013

8 *V* CRUM *Ostr*, no 409, note

9 Recurs in Br Mus Or 6201 B &c

ϥⲟ]ⲓⲃⲁⲙⲙⲱⲛ ⲡϩⲓⲉⲣ[ⲉⲩⲥ[1] | ⲡⲉ]ⲭⲟ[2] ϩⲛϣⲃⲏⲕ ⲉⲓ[ⲥϩⲁⲓ | ⲡ]ⲙⲁⲏ, ⲕⲟⲙⲓⲥ ⲧⲣⲙ[| ⲟⲩⲟⲉⲓ]ϣ
ⲁⲓⲡⲉⲡⲟⲟⲩ ⲉⲧ[ⲉⲥⲟⲩ |]ⲕⲁⲓⲁⲉⲕ[t], ⲓⲛ[8], ⲡⲉ[| [.]ⲕⲧⲙⲁⲁ ⲡⲙⲁ ⲕⲥⲉⲣⲅⲉ [| ⲕⲁⲙ ⲙⲛⲛⲉⲅⲉⲛⲧⲏⲅ
ⲧⲁⲁⲓⲧ[| ⲧⲁⲱⲣϥ ⲛⲉⲩⲝⲟ ⲉϩⲟⲩⲛ ⲧⲉ[| ⲗⲁⲁⲩ ⲛⲕⲁⲧⲁϥⲣⲟⲛⲏⲥⲓⲥ ⲛ[

Verso +ⲉⲡⲓⲧⲣⲟ̅π̅ ⲧ̅ω̅ ⲉⲙⲙ[| . .[|

178.—Papyrus, a fragment, $5\frac{1}{2} \times 28$ cm   Script ligatured   *Recto* ↑
Beginning of a Deed, from   .   the deacon, son of ⲁⲱⲣⲟⲑⲉ of Shmoun, to Apa
Taurinus, relating to a former lease, ⲝⲉⲡⲓⲁⲏ ⲁⲏⲥⲩⲙⲏ ⲟⲩⲙⲓⲥⲑⲱⲥⲓⲥ ⲕⲁⲓ. Taurinus is
apparently the ⲙⲉⲥⲟⲧⲉⲣⲟⲥ (μειζότερος[3])   The text was cancelled by cross-lines

RENT RECEIPTS

179.—Papyrus; complete; $22 \times 13\frac{1}{2}$ cm   Script ligatured. *Verso* →
Tax Receipt, in very short terms

+ ⲁⲛⲟⲕ ⲁⲓⲟⲥⲕ, ⲙⲛⲁⲡⲟⲗⲗⲱ | ⲝⲉⲁⲛⲝⲓ[4] ⲡⲉⲕⲏⲁⲕⲧⲱⲛ | ⲁⲃⲉⲓ ⲉⲧⲟⲟⲧⲛ ⲧⲛⲥⲧⲟⲓ̅ⲭ̅ + The rest
is blank

Recto   remnants of Greek accounts (earlier)

180.—Papyrus, a fragment, $7\frac{1}{2} \times 13$ cm   Script sloping uncials   *Verso* →
Tax Receipt from Eulogia to the 'master'[5] Phoebammon, for $1\frac{1}{2}$ carats, being the rent
(πάκτον) for her share (μέρος) in

+ ⲉⲅⲗⲟⲅⲓⲁ ⲧⲉⲥⲥϩⲁⲓ ⲛⲡⲥⲁϩ ϥⲟⲓⲃⲁⲙ[ⲙⲱⲛ | ⲏⲧⲟⲟⲧⲛ ϩⲁⲡⲡⲁⲕⲧⲟⲛ ϩⲁⲡⲁⲙⲉⲣⲟ[ⲥ | ⲉⲧⲉⲛⲁⲓⲡⲉ
ⲟⲩⲕⲩⲣⲁⲧⲓⲛ ⲟⲩⲥⲟⲥ ϩⲁ[| ⲱⲣⲝ ⲟⲩⲛ ⲁⲓⲥⲧⲟⲓⲭⲉⲓ + ⲉⲅⲗⲟⲅⲉ̅ⲓ̅ⲁ [| blank

Recto   remains of Greek text (earlier)

181.—Papyrus, complete, $9\frac{1}{2} \times 18\frac{1}{2}$ cm.   Script moderately ligatured   *Recto* ↑
Receipt (ἀπόδειξις) by the δίκαιον of the 'altar'[6] of St George, represented by the
priest Shenoute, to Apa Philotheus, for the rent (φόρος) of certain fields, *viz* **2 tremissia**
yearly

---

[1] Ἱερεύς, *cf* Br Mus no 1031   In a Br Mus fragment, Or 6201 B &c, ϥⲓⲉⲣⲉⲩⲥ ⲛⲡⲧⲟⲟⲩ.
[2] Σχολαστικός
[3] The Jkôw papyri make it clear that this is the Greek
equivalent to ⲗⲁϣⲁⲛⲉ.
[4] ⲝⲉ indicates the elliptic brevity to which the formulae

are reduced
[5] *V* no 176
[6] So in Krall lxxvi   *Cf* the similar use of τόπος,
e g here no 145, of εὐκτήριον, Krall clx, μοναστήριον,
ib lxxxvi, πέτρα, here no 124   In Br Mus no 1046
ⲙⲁ and φιλοπόνιον seem identical

+ ⲡⲁⲓⲏⲁⲓⲟⲛ ⲛⲡⲟⲩⲥⲓⲁⲥⲧⲏⲣⲓⲟⲛ ⲉⲧⲟⲩⲁⲁⲃ ⲫⲁⲙⲟⲥ ⲅⲉⲱⲣⲅⲉ | ϩⲓⲧⲟⲟⲧ ϣⲉⲛⲟⲩⲧⲉ ⲡⲣ̄ ⲉⲓⲥϩⲁⲓ
ⲁⲡⲁ ⲫⲓⲗⲟⲑⲉⲟⲥ ⲝⲉⲁⲓⲝⲓ | ⲁⲅⲱ ⲁⲓⲡⲗⲏⲣⲟⲩ ⲛⲧⲟⲟⲧⲕ ⲉⲛⲉⲫⲟⲣⲟⲥ ϩⲁⲛⲓⲱϩⲉ ⲉⲕϫⲟ ⲙ(above ⲉⲕ ⲛ
ⲙ[ ]ⲛⲟϥ ⲛⲉⲅⲙⲟⲟⲩ) | ⲉⲅϣⲟⲡ ϩⲁⲙⲡϣⲉⲛⲡⲟⲩⲥ[1] ⲉⲧⲉⲛⲁⲓⲛⲉ ⲥⲛⲁⲩ ⲉⲅⲣⲉⲙⲛⲥⲓⲛ | ⲉⲛⲟⲩⲃ ϩⲁⲧⲓⲣⲟⲙⲛⲉ
ⲧⲁⲓ ⲉⲕⲧⲏⲥ . . .[2] ⲛ̄ ⲙ̄ⲩ ⲉⲅⲱⲣⲝ ⲛⲁⲕ ⲁⲓ|ⲥⲙⲛ ⲧⲓⲁⲡⲟⲗⲉⲓϫⲓⲥ ⲛⲁⲕ ⲉⲓⲥⲧⲟⲓ̄ ϣⲉⲛⲟⲩⲧⲉ ⲡⲣ̄ ⲥⲧⲟⲓ̄ +

Verso   Greek accounts (earlier)

182.—Papyrus, a fragment, 10 × 9½ cm   Script moderately ligatured   *Recto* ↑

Receipt by Phoebammon, son of George, for rent (?) paid by   All written by
one hand

ⲅⲉⲱⲣ]ⲅⲉ ⲡⲣⲱⲙⲉ ϣⲙⲟⲩⲛ ⲉⲓⲥϩⲁⲓ [|] ⲝⲉⲁⲓⲝⲓ ⲁⲅⲱ ⲁⲓⲡⲗⲏⲣⲟⲩ ⲛⲧ[ⲟⲟⲧⲕ] ⲛⲡ[ ]ⲉ ⲡⲉϩⲟⲧ
ⲛⲁⲕⲁⲧⲏⲥ ⲓⲛᵈ/ ϣⲁⲥⲟⲩ[|] ϩⲟⲗⲟⲕⲟⲧⲧ]ⲛ ⲛⲓ[ⲟ]ⲩⲅ ⲉⲅⲟ ⲛϫⲟⲩⲧⲉ|ⲛⲟⲟⲩⲥ |]ⲕⲃ̵ ⲉⲕ̄/[3] ⲉⲧⲃⲉⲡⲉⲕⲱⲣϫ
ⲟⲩⲛ [|] ⲁⲣ]ⲭⲉⲓ ⲉϫⲱⲛ ⲧⲁⲣⲓϥⲅⲗⲁⲥⲥⲉ ⲛⲁⲕ ⲉ|] ✝ ⲁⲛⲟⲕ ⲫⲟⲓⲃⲁⲙ[ⲙⲱⲛ |] ⲡϣⲉ ⲛⲡⲙⲁⲕⲁⲣ/
ϣⲉⲛ[ⲟⲩⲧⲉ | ⲛ]ⲧⲁⲓⲥϩⲁⲓ ϩⲁⲫⲟⲓⲃⲁⲙⲙⲉ[ⲱⲛ

Verso   ⲫⲟⲓⲃⲁ]ⲙⲙⲱⲛ ⲡϣⲉ ⲛⲅⲉⲱⲣⲅⲉ [space] ⲡⲣⲱ[ⲙⲉ

PARTITIONS

183.—Papyrus, a fragment, 13 × 23 cm   Script ligatureless   *Recto* ↑.

Preliminary phrases to a Deed of Settlement (διάλυσις), addressed by   of
Shmoun, to .   , a woman, styled τιμιωτάτη[4]   It is to be deposited in the public
library[5]

]ⲟⲩⲁⲧⲣⲟ̄ⲧⲏϥ ⲉⲝ[| ⲧⲓⲁⲓ]ⲁⲗⲅⲥⲓⲥ ⲉⲥⲟⲣϫ ϩⲛⲁⲥⲫ[ⲁⲗⲉⲓⲁ ⲛⲓⲙ | ⲉⲥⲓⲥ]ϫⲩ ⲉⲥⲧⲁⲭⲣⲏⲩ ⲛⲁⲧⲡⲁⲣⲁⲃⲁ-
ⲥⲓⲥ ⲛⲁⲧⲕⲓⲙ ⲝⲓⲛ[|]ⲛⲉ[.]ⲉ ⲁⲅⲱ ⲉⲓⲕⲱ ⲛⲙⲟⲥ ⲉϩⲣⲁⲓ ϩⲛⲧⲁⲛⲉ[| ⲧⲁ]ⲡⲛⲱⲙⲛ ⲙⲛⲧⲁⲡⲣⲟⲁⲓⲣⲉⲥⲓⲥ
ⲛⲁⲧⲗⲁⲁⲩ ⲛⲕⲣⲟϥ [|] ⲁⲡⲁⲧⲏ ϩⲓⲁⲛⲁⲅⲕⲏ ϩⲓⲡⲉⲣⲓⲅⲣⲁⲫⲏ ϩⲓⲥⲩⲛⲁⲣⲡⲁⲅⲏ ⲁⲛⲟⲕ [|] ⲡϣⲉ] ⲛⲡⲙⲁⲕⲁⲣ/
ⲗⲉⲟⲛⲧⲓⲛ ⲡⲣⲱⲙⲉ ϣⲙⲟⲩⲛ ⲉⲓⲥϩⲁⲓ ⲛⲓ[ⲧ ⲧⲓ]ⲙⲓⲱⲧⲁⲧⲏ ⲧϣⲉ ⲛⲡⲙⲁⲕⲁⲣ/ ⲇⲁⲙⲓⲁⲛⲉ ⲡⲛ ⲅⲁϥϣⲱ[ⲡⲉ[6] |
ⲣⲱⲙⲉ]ⲉ ϣⲙⲟⲩⲛ ⲟⲛ ⲧⲓⲣⲁ[ϣⲉ] ⲧⲓϩⲟⲙⲟⲗⲟⲅⲉⲓ ⲁⲛ[ⲟ]ⲕ[

184.—Papyrus, a fragment, 17 × 15 cm   Script ligatured   *Recto* ↑

A Family Settlement (γενικὴ διάλυσις), addressed by   (*plur*) to Apa Prashe

]ⲙⲛⲛⲉⲓⲁⲛϩⲁⲗ[ⲱⲙⲁ about 11 lett] |]ⲓⲁ ⲛⲓⲙ ϩⲛⲙⲁ ⲛⲓⲙ ⲉⲅⲛⲁⲉⲙⲫⲁⲛⲓⲍⲉ |]ⲛ ⲁⲡⲁ ⲡⲣⲁϣⲓ
ⲙⲛⲛⲉⲕⲕⲗⲏⲣᵒ/ ϣⲁⲉⲛⲉϩ ⲁⲛⲥⲙⲛ | ϩ]ⲛⲓⲥⲧⲣⲛⲉⲛⲉⲕⲉ ⲛⲁⲕ ⲛⲡⲙⲉϩⲥⲟⲡ ⲥⲛⲁⲩ | ⲧ]ⲁⲩⲟⲥ ✝ⲣⲟⲛ ⲡⲉⲧⲛⲟⲓ

---

[1] ? A place *Cf* Br Mus no 1055, ⲛⲉϣⲉⲛⲡⲁⲕⲏⲛⲉ
[2] Signs perhaps stenographic, ⲓⲛⲁ/ ⲅⲓ/ can scarcely
be read
[3] ⲉⲕ̄ⲧ/ might be read, not ⲉⲩⲥⲧ/

[4] *Cf* no 158
[5] δημοσία βιβλιοθήκη   Deeds relating to monastic
affairs placed in the library of the monastery, REVILLOUT,
Actes 83, 97   [6] *V* no 141

ΝϹϩΑΙ ϩΙѠѠΝ | ϹΤΑϪΥΡΟϹ ΕΡΟϹ ΕΤϤϪΙϪ ΑΝΚѠΡϢ ϩΝΝΑΙΕΛΕΥΘΕΡ⁰, | ϩΟΜΟΟϳϒϹΙΟΝ ΜΠΕΥϪΑΙ ΕΝΕΤΑΡΧΕΙ ΕϪѠΝ |] ΤΗΡϹ ΝΤΙϹΕΝΙΚΗ ϪΙΑΛϒϹΙϹ ΕΡΕΤΝϩΥΠΟϹΤΑϹΙϹ |] ΤΕϹΒΕΒΑΙѠϹΙϹ ϪΝΝΕΝϢΧΡѠ ΝΛΑΑΥ | ϩΥΠ]ΕΝΑΝΤΙΟΥ ΕΤϪΟΜ ΕΤΙϹΕΝΙΚΗ ϪΙΑΛϒϹΙϹ |

SALES

185.—Papyrus, a fragment, 14 × 13½ cm Script small, moderately ligatured *Recto* ↑

Agreement (ὁμολογία) apparently relating to the Sale (? or lease) of land Perhaps a place, Hôtr, is mentioned

[text in Coptic]

Verso blank

186—Papyrus, a fragment, 5½ × 8½ cm Script ligatureless *Recto* ↑

Presumably from a Deed of Sale (? or of Gift)

[text in Coptic]

Verso parts of 2 lines in a Greek hand, giving a date, ινδ/

187.—Papyrus, a fragment, 13 × 6 cm Script ligatureless *Recto* ↑

Probably from a Deed of, or relating to, Sale A monastery or church of St Phoebammon is named[5]

[text in Coptic]

188.—Papyrus, a fragment, 44 × 37 cm Script even, ligatured, hand of nos 204 and perhaps 173 *Recto*, top *selis* →, rest ↑

---

[1] This rare verb appears to imply consent or agreement with An equally obscure instance in *WZKM* 1902 266 ΑΝΟΚ perhaps, not ΕΡΟΚ

[2] Note the peculiar form of negative
[3] *V* no 141
[4] This form in Br Mus no 1064
[5] *Cf* no 125

Above the text, a protocol,' in tall, brown characters like those in Br Mus nos 171, 1077

Undertaking (ὁμολογία) by John, a deacon, of Shmoun, to the κῦρις, Apa Mercurius[1], to whom he had formerly sold certain fields M had then agreed to pay 3 carats yearly as their tax (δημόσιον), representing both ἐμβολή and χρυσικόν, since they produced no corn For this John thanks him and now undertakes not to demand any additional tax payments Reference is further made to handing the deed of sale (πρᾶσις) to M and to the latter's inheritance in the said land

ⲁⲛⲟⲕ ⲓⲱⲁⲛⲛⲏⲥ ⲡⲉⲓⲉⲗⲁⲭ︦ ⲛⲁⲓⲁ︦ⲟ/ ⲡϣⲉ ⲛⲡⲙⲁⲕⲁⲣⲓⲟⲥ ⲃⲓⲕⲧⲱⲣ ⲡⲣⲱⲙⲉ ϣⲙⲟⲩⲛ ⲉⲓⲥϩⲁⲓ
ⲛⲡⲕⲩⲣ/

ⲁⲡⲁ ⲙⲉⲣⲕⲟⲩⲣⲓⲟⲥ ⲡϣⲉ ⲛ . . ⲁ ⲡⲣ︦ⲟ/[2] ⲁⲡⲁ ⲁⲥⲏ . ⲅ ⲡⲣⲱⲙⲉ ϣⲙⲟⲩⲛ ⲟⲛ ϫⲉⲉⲡⲉⲓⲁⲏ ⲁⲓⲧⲓ .
ⲥⲱ[ⲧ]ⲉ ⲛⲱϩⲉ ⲛⲁⲕ ⲉⲃⲟⲗ . ⲓ ⲉⲗⲁ ⲧⲁ̅ⲧⲉ ⲥⲉⲧⲓⲱϩⲉ ⲥⲅ ⲗⲓ ⲥⲟⲩ ⲉ̄ⲩⲛ ⲡⲙⲁ ⲉⲧⲙⲙ[ⲁ]ⲩ
. . . . . . ⲛⲉ ⲉⲛⲃⲉⲭ (rest illegible)

5 [ ]ⲁⲕ . . ⲉⲗⲟⲩⲉⲓⲧⲉ ⲡⲣⲟⲥ ⲧϭⲟⲙ ⲛⲧⲉⲡⲣⲁⲥⲓⲥ ⲛⲧⲁⲓⲙⲙⲛⲧ ⲛⲁⲕ ⲙ . ⲣⲟⲙ[ⲡⲉ]
. . . . . ⲉⲓ ⲁⲓⲡⲁⲣⲁⲕⲁⲗⲉⲓ ⲙⲟⲕ ⲙⲛϩⲛⲕⲁⲓⲉⲗⲉⲩⲑⲉ]ⲣⲟⲥ ⲓⲁⲣⲉⲕ ⲁ . .
[.ⲁ]ⲕϫⲓ ⲧⲓⲡⲁⲣⲁⲕⲗⲏⲥⲓⲥ ⲁⲕⲧⲓ ϣⲟⲙⲧⲉ ⲛⲕ[ⲉ]ⲣⲁ[ⲧⲏ ϩⲁⲡⲁⲛⲙⲟⲥⲓⲟⲛ ⲉⲣⲱⲟⲩ ⲕⲁ[ⲧⲁ]
ⲣⲟⲙⲡⲉ ϩⲁⲉⲙⲃⲟⲗⲏ ϩⲓⲭⲣⲩⲥⲓⲕⲟⲛ ⲉⲡⲉⲓⲁⲏ ⲙⲛⲧⲁⲩ[ⲥⲟ]ⲩⲟ ⲙⲙⲁⲩ + ⲅⲉⲛⲟⲩ ϩⲣⲁⲓ
[ϩⲛ] ⲉ . ⲧⲓ ⲁⲩⲱ ⲧⲓⲉⲩⲭⲁⲣⲓⲥⲧⲁ ⲛⲁⲕ ϫⲉⲛϫⲓ ⲧⲁⲡⲁⲣⲁⲕⲗⲏⲥⲓⲥ ⲉⲧⲟⲟⲧ ⲁⲛⲁⲛ[ⲁⲍⲓ-]

10 [ⲍⲟⲩ] . . . . . ⲛⲁⲕⲉⲣⲁ[ⲧ]ⲓⲁ ϩⲁⲣⲟⲟⲩ ⲕⲁⲧⲁ ⲣⲟⲙ[ⲡⲉ] ⲫ︦ ⲗⲟⲓⲡⲟⲩ
. . [ⲛⲡⲁⲛⲧⲟ]ⲕⲣⲁⲧⲱⲣ ⲙ[ⲛⲡⲟⲩ]ϫⲁⲓ ⲛⲛϫⲓⲥⲟⲟⲩⲉ
ⲟⲩⲧⲉ ⲙⲃⲟⲗⲏ ⲟⲩⲧⲉ ⲭⲣⲩⲥⲓⲕⲟⲛ ϣⲁⲉⲛⲉϩ ⲟⲩⲟⲉⲓϣ [rest illegible]
ⲛⲉⲧⲛⲏⲩ ⲙⲡⲉⲥⲱⲓ ϫⲓⲛⲛⲉⲓϣⲡⲟⲩϫ ϭⲉⲗⲁⲁⲩ ⲛⲁⲛⲙⲟⲥⲓⲟⲛ ϩⲁⲣⲟⲕ[3] ⲛⲥⲁ[rest illegible]
. . . . ⲡⲉⲩⲁⲛⲙⲟⲥⲓⲟⲛ ⲉⲛⲁⲣⲭⲁⲓⲟⲛ . . ⲟⲩⲁⲉ ⲛ[rest illegible]

15 . ⲕ ⲟⲩⲁⲉ ⲉⲙⲃⲟⲗⲏ ⲟⲩⲧⲉ ⲭⲉⲓⲣⲟⲅⲣⲁⲫⲉⲓⲁ ⲁⲗⲗⲁ ⲛⲧⲁⲕⲁⲁⲩ [ⲥⲉⲧ-]
ⲓⲱϩⲉ ⲛⲧⲁⲕⲁⲁⲩ ⲛⲁⲓ ϩⲛ[ⲡ]ⲙⲁ ⲉⲧⲙⲙⲁⲩ ϩ[ⲩⲡⲟ]ⲕⲉⲓⲥⲟ ⲛⲧⲛⲡⲁ[
ⲉ . [ⲁⲥ]ⲫ[ⲁⲗ]ⲉⲓⲁ ⲇⲉ ⲛⲁⲕ ⲁⲓⲁⲛⲁⲍⲓⲟⲩ ⲛⲁⲕ ⲛⲧⲉⲡⲣⲁⲥⲓⲥ ⲛⲧⲉ[
. . . ⲣⲱⲙⲙⲁ ⲛⲡⲁⲗⲗⲁⲁⲓ[4] ⲉⲡⲉⲓⲁⲏ ⲧⲟⲩⲉⲓ ⲛⲧⲁⲓⲧⲁⲁⲥ ⲛⲁⲕ ⲧⲁⲣ[ⲉ]ⲕⲕⲗⲏⲣⲟ/ ⲛⲧⲁ[
ϩⲁⲧⲉⲥⲙⲁⲁⲩ ⲁⲩⲱ ⲅⲟⲩⲉⲓ ⲧ ⲡⲣⲁⲥⲓⲥ ⲛⲧⲉⲥⲧⲱⲧⲉ[5] ⲉⲧⲃⲉⲡⲉⲓϩⲱϥ ⲟⲩⲛ ⲁⲓⲣϩⲟⲙⲟⲗⲟⲅ[

20 . . ⲁ . . ⲙⲉϩ ⲛⲧⲉⲡⲣⲁⲥⲓⲥ ϩⲁⲓⲙⲟⲧⲛⲉⲥ ⲛⲁⲕ[6] ϫⲉⲟⲩⲉⲓ ϩⲛⲡⲉⲛⲧⲁⲓ . . ⲁ . . . ⲁⲓⲉⲧ ⲟⲩⲉⲓ
. . . ⲁⲛ . ⲙ ⲗⲁⲁⲩ ⲛⲧⲁⲥϩⲓⲙⲉ[. . ⲉ]ⲩⲱⲣϫ ⲟⲩⲛⲁⲕ ⲁⲓⲥⲙⲛ ⲧ[
ⲛϩⲟⲙⲟⲗⲟ[ⲅⲓⲁ ⲛⲧⲁϭⲓϫ ⲧⲏⲣⲉⲥ ⲁⲩⲱ ⲁⲓⲕⲱⲣ[ϣ ⲛϩⲛⲕⲁⲓⲉⲗⲉⲩⲑⲉⲣⲟ]ⲥ ⲁⲩⲣ[
ⲑⲓ . . . . . ⲥ ϣⲁⲉⲛⲉϩ ⲟⲩⲧⲉ ⲁⲛⲟⲕ ⲟⲩⲧⲉ ⲛⲁⲕⲗⲏⲣⲟ/ ϩⲁⲛⲁ . . . . ⲁⲛⲉⲓ-
[ⲉⲙⲃⲟⲗⲏ ⲟ]ⲩⲧⲉ ⲭⲣⲩⲥⲓⲕⲟⲛ ⲛϣⲟⲣ[

25 . . . . ⲙⲛ[ⲡⲟⲩ]ϫⲁⲓ ⲉⲛⲉⲓϫⲓⲥⲟⲟⲩⲉ

Verso blank

[1] Perhaps the same person as in Br Mus no 1136 and here no 158
[2] Perhaps ⲛⲡⲙⲁⲕⲁⲣ︦/
[3] Perhaps ⲉϫⲱⲕ
[4] 'The place (´τόπος) of Palladius' Unknown
[5] V Br Mus nos 1013, 1061 and here no 158
[6] For this phrase v Krall no clvii

189.—Papyrus, a fragment, 10 × 16 cm   Script ligatureless   *Recto* ↑

Deed of Sale (πρᾶσις), in the form of a receipt for payment of 1 *solidus* (+?), 'by the city standard,' as the price of a large plank of wood (?)[1], described as in a rough, unworked state[2] and old   Its size is also given

]. ιϲ ⲛ̄ϣⲉ ⲛ̄ⲡⲙⲁⲕⲁⲣⲓⲟⲥ ⲓⲟⲩⲥⲧⲁ ⲡⲣⲱⲙⲡⲉ . ⲕⲗⲟ | ⲙ ⲙⲡϣⲏⲣⲉ ⲙ̄ⲡⲣⲏⲥ ⲛ̄ⲧⲡⲟⲗⲓⲥ ⲧⲁⲓ
ϣⲙⲟⲩⲛ ϫⲉⲧⲓϩⲟⲙⲟⲗⲟⲅⲉⲓ ϫⲉⲁⲓϫⲓ ⲁⲅⲱ ⲁⲓⲡⲗⲏⲣⲟⲩ ⲛ̄ⲧⲟⲟⲧⲛ̄   . | ⲙ̄ⲡⲟⲟⲩ ⲉⲧⲉⲥⲟⲩ ⲃ̄ⲧⲟⲟⲩⲡⲉ
ⲙ̄ⲡⲁϣⲟⲛⲉ ⲡⲉⲃⲟⲧ ⲛ̄ⲧⲓⲣⲟ[ⲙⲡⲉ] | ⲧⲁⲓ ⲅⲣⲓⲧⲏⲥ ⲓⲛⲁⲓⲕⲧⲓⲟⲛⲟⲥ ⲛ̄ⲧⲁⲓⲕⲁⲓⲁ ⲧⲓⲙⲏ ⲛ̄ⲧⲛⲟϭ | ⲙ̄ⲡⲟϭⲉ ⲛ̄ϩⲟⲓ
ⲛ̄ϣⲉ ⲛ̄ⲙⲁⲃⲥⲛⲟⲟ[ⲩⲥ] ⲛⲏ   ⲁ ⲗⲉ | ⲛⲁⲫⲓⲗⲟⲕⲁⲗⲏⲧⲟⲛ ⲛⲁⲡⲁⲥ ⲉⲥϣ[| ⲛ̄ⲧⲁⲓⲧⲁⲁⲥ ⲛⲁⲕ ⲉⲃⲟⲗ ⲡⲣⲟⲥ
ⲑⲉ ⲛ̄[| [ⲉ]ⲧⲉⲡⲁⲓⲡⲉ ⲟⲩϩⲟⲗⲟⲕⲟⲧⲧⲓ[ⲛ | [. .] ⲛ̄ⲡϣⲓ ⲛ̄ⲧⲡⲟⲗⲓⲥ ϭ, ⲭⲣ, ⲛ̄ ⲁ[

Verso +ⲧⲉⲡⲣⲁⲥⲓⲥ ⲛ̄ⲧⲡⲟϭⲉ ⌈space⌉ ⲛ̄ϩⲟⲓ ⲛⲁⲡⲁⲥ ⲁⲅⲱ ⲛ | ⲛⲁⲫⲓⲗⲟⲕⲁⲗⲏ ϩⲁ .. |

190.—Papyrus, a fragment, 12½ × 25 cm   Script rarely ligatured   *Recto* ↑

Deed of Sale (πρᾶσις) by   , son of Taurinus, son of Apostolus[3], of arable land, to Leontius, a subdeacon   The price is 4 *solidi*, already paid   The village Telbont is named[4]

]ϣⲉ ⲛ̄ⲧⲁⲩⲣⲓⲛⲉ ⲛ̄ϣⲉ ⲛ̄ⲁⲡⲟⲥⲧ[. ⲡⲣⲱⲙⲉ ϣⲙⲟⲩⲛ ⲟⲛ ⲉⲓⲥϩ[ⲁⲓ | [ⲛ̄ⲗⲉⲟⲛⲧ]ⲛ ⲫⲩⲡⲟⲇⲓⲁⲕⲱⲛ
ⲛ̄ϣⲉ ⲙ̄ⲡⲙⲁⲕⲁⲣⲓⲟⲥ ⲑⲉⲟⲇⲱⲣⲉ ⲡⲣⲙ[ⲧⲓ]ⲡⲟⲗⲓⲥ | [ϩⲟⲟⲩ ⲧ .ⲉ ⲛ̄ⲡⲣ[ ]ⲧⲓ]ⲛⲕ....ⲥ ⲉⲣⲟⲥ ⲕⲁⲧⲁ
ⲙ̄ⲛⲧϫⲟⲉⲓⲥ |]ⲧⲁⲁⲥ ⲉⲃⲟⲗ ⲛ̄ⲧⲁⲁⲥ ⲛ̄ⲟⲩ[about 8 lett]ⲛⲕⲱ̄ⲛ[5] ⲡⲛⲉⲛϣⲏⲣⲉ | ⲛⲥ̄ϫⲟⲥ ⲛⲥⲟⲗⲉⲥ[6] ⲛ̄ϭⲓ
ⲛ̄ⲕⲱ[ⲥⲓⲥ   . ⲉⲧⲉⲥⲟⲩϫⲟⲩⲧ | ⲙ̄ⲡⲁⲣϩⲟⲧⲡⲡⲉ ⲛⲉⲛⲧⲏⲥ ⲛ̄ⲁ, ⲉⲣⲉⲧ[.] ⲉ ⲁⲉ' ⲧⲉⲗ-
ⲃⲟⲛⲧ ⲉⲥⲙ | ⲉⲧⲟⲩⲙⲟ]ⲩⲧⲉ ⲉⲣⲟⲩ ϫⲉⲁⲣⲭⲁⲡ, ⲉⲡⲣⲟⲥ ⲛ̄[ⲉⲥⲧⲉ]ⲧⲙⲁ ⲛⲁⲣⲭⲁⲓⲟⲛ ⲉⲡⲩⲧⲉⲩϩⲟ |
ⲁⲓⲕⲁⲓⲱⲙⲁ ⲧⲏⲣⲟⲩ ⲕⲁⲧⲁ ⲧⲉⲕⲛ[ⲉⲗⲉⲩⲥⲓⲥ] ⲛ̄ⲧⲟ]ⲕ ⲡⲉⲧϣⲟⲡ ⲁⲡⲁ ⲗⲉⲟⲛⲧⲓ | ⲧⲧⲙⲛⲧⲉ ⲧⲁⲓ ⲃ̄ⲧⲟⲟⲩ
ⲛ̄ϩⲟⲗⲟⲕⲟⲧⲧ[ⲛ   .]ⲏⲛ ϭ, ⲭⲣ ⲛ̄ ϫⲉⲥⲥⲣ̄, | ⲧⲓϩⲟⲙⲟⲗⲟⲅⲉⲓ ϫⲉⲁⲓϫⲓⲧⲉ [..] ⲛ̄ⲛⲁϭⲓϫ
ⲙ̄ⲛⲛⲟⲩⲕ | ⲙⲁⲣⲧⲩⲣⲟⲥ ⲉⲩ ⲙ ⲉⲛ[.] ⲉⲧⲉ[..]ⲟⲥ ⲑⲩ]ⲡⲟⲅⲣⲁⲫⲏ ⲉⲡⲟⲩⲁ |]ⲩⲛ[

Verso + ⲡⲣⲁⲥⲓⲥ ⲙⲁⲣⲟⲥⲁⲟ ?

DEBTS

191.—Papyrus, complete, 24 × 8½ cm   Script ligatureless   *Recto* ↑

Undertaking (ἀσφάλεια) by Pebe to repay a debt to Leontius

ϯ ⲁⲛⲟⲕ ⲡⲉⲃⲉ ⲛ̄ϣⲉ ⲛ̄ⲓⲱⲁⲛⲛⲏⲥ ⲡⲉⲩⲙⲙⲁ̄ϫⲟⲥ[7] ⲡⲣⲱⲙⲉ ϣⲙⲟⲩⲛ ⲉⲓⲥϩⲁⲓ | ⲛ̄ⲗⲉⲟⲛⲧⲓ ⲛ̄ϣⲉ
ⲛ̄ⲅⲁⲧⲣⲉ ⲡⲣⲱⲙⲉ ϣⲙⲟⲩⲛ ⲟⲛ ϫⲉⲧⲓⲭⲣⲉⲱⲥⲧⲉⲓ ⲛⲁⲕ | ⲛⲕⲁⲑⲁⲣⲱⲥ ⲛⲁⲓ ⲁⲡⲟⲕⲣⲟⲧⲟⲥ[8] ⲛⲟⲩⲧⲣⲓⲙⲏⲥⲓⲛ
ⲛⲥⲁϣⲃⲉ ⲟⲩϭⲟⲥ ⲛ̄ⲕ[ⲉ]ⲣ[9] | ⲛ̄ⲡϣⲓ ⲛ̄ⲡⲣⲁⲕⲟⲧⲉ ⲅ/ ⲧⲣⲏ/ ⲍ/ ⲍⲩ̈ⲅ ⲁⲗ/, + ⲛⲁⲓ ⲟⲩⲛ ⲧⲓⲟ ⲛ̄ϩⲉⲓⲟⲙⲟⲥ |

---

[1] ⲡⲟϭⲉ ⲛ̄ϩⲟⲓ (*verso*) piece of meadow, but l 6 recalls the known phrase,=σανίς (Ezek xxvii 5, Rossi, *Papiri* I, iii 12), unless here ' wooded meadow ' *Cf* no 213

[2] The single instance of ἀφιλοκάλητος in Sophocles, *Lex*, relates to an 'unswept' cell But φιλοκαλεῖν is applied to land, KENYON *Catal* ii 326

[3] Grandparents named, no 204

[4] Θελβῶνθις *V* KRALL no ⲥⲭⲁⲓⲛ   [5] Foi ⲕⲱ on ?
[6] ωλ 'gather crops ' *V* ZOEGA 583, here no. 162
[7] *V* KRALL, p 28
[8] Of thirteen instances, all but two read thus (KRALL vi ἀποκρίτ, ib xlviii ἀποκρίτ) In Pap Amb ch 14 the editors read ἀποκρ[ί]τως
[9] *Tremission* of same value as in no 158

ⲧⲁⲧⲁⲁϥ ⲛⲁⲕ ⲙⲛⲧⲉϥⲙⲛⲥⲉ ⲛⲛⲁⲩ ⲛⲓⲙ ⲉⲕⲟⲩⲁϣϥ ⲉⲣⲉⲧⲙⲛⲥⲉ ⲏⲡ | [ϫ]ⲓⲛⲡⲟⲟⲩ ⲉⲧⲉⲥⲟⲩⲥⲛⲁⲩ
ⲛⲧⲱⲃⲉ ⲛⲉⲃⲟⲧ ⲛⲧⲓⲣⲟⲙ[ⲡⲉ . . . .] | ⲓⲛⲁ°, ⲉⲑⲛ ⲛⲁⲧϩⲁⲡ[1] ⲛⲁⲧⲛⲟⲙⲟⲥ ⲛⲁⲧⲗⲁⲁⲩ ⲛⲁⲙⲫⲓ-
ⲃⲟⲗ[ⲉⲓⲁ ⲧⲁⲧⲁⲁϥ] | ⲛⲁⲕ ⲛⲛⲁⲩ ⲛⲓⲙ ⲉⲕⲟⲩⲁϣϥ ⲉⲡⲓ ⲧⲱ ⲧⲁⲧⲓ ⲅⲣⲙⲛⲥⲓⲛ ⲥⲛ[ⲁⲩ . . ⲉⲡⲉⲕ]ⲱⲣⲉϫ ⲟⲩⲛ
ⲁⲓⲥⲙⲛ ⲧⲓⲁⲥⲫⲁⲗⲉⲓⲁ [ⲛ]ⲁⲕ ⲉⲓⲱⲣⲕ ⲉⲡⲛⲟⲩⲧⲉ ⲡⲡⲁⲛ[ⲧⲟ]ⲕⲣⲁⲧⲱⲣ ⲧⲁⲣⲓⲣⲟⲉⲓⲥ ⲛⲁⲕ ⲡⲣⲟⲥ ⲧⲉ[ⲥ]ϭⲟⲙ

$$\theta \;\overset{\sigma\iota\mu\iota\sigma\nu}{\underset{\pi\epsilon\beta\eta\sigma\varsigma}{\mid\!+\!\mid}}$$

ⲉⲓⲥⲩⲡⲟⲕⲉⲓⲥⲟⲁⲓ ⲛⲁⲕ ⲙⲛ|ϩⲱⲃ ⲛⲓⲙ ⲉⲡⲱⲡⲉ ⲉⲅⲣ, ⲧⲩⲃⲓ β ⲓⲛδ, θ ⊢⊣ + ⲁⲛⲟⲕ ⲡⲉⲃⲉ | ⲡϣⲉ
ⲛⲓⲱⲁⲛⲛⲏⲥ ⲧⲟⲓⲥⲧⲟⲓⲭⲉⲓ ⲉⲧⲓⲁⲥⲫⲁⲗⲉⲓⲁ ⲛⲑⲉ ⲥⲥⲛ̣ϩ ⲉⲙⲟⲥ + | + ⲁⲛⲟⲕ ⲅⲉⲱⲣⲅⲉ ⲡϣⲉ ⲛⲡⲙⲁⲕⲁⲣⲓ[ⲟ]ⲥ
ⲙⲛⲛⲁ ⲡⲣⲱⲙⲉ ϣⲙⲟⲩⲛ ⲛⲧⲁⲓⲥϩⲁⲓ | ϩⲁⲣⲟϥ ϫⲛⲃⲛⲟⲓ ⲁⲛ +[2] ⲁⲛⲟⲕ ⲅⲣⲏⲅⲟⲣⲉ ⲡϣⲉ ⲛⲭⲣⲓⲥⲧⲟⲇⲱⲣⲉ
ⲡⲣⲱⲙⲉ | ϣⲙⲟⲩⲛ ⲧⲓⲟ ⲙⲙⲛⲧⲣⲉ ⲉⲧⲓⲁⲥⲫⲁⲗⲉⲓⲁ ⲛⲧⲁⲓⲥⲱⲧⲙ ϩⲓⲧⲛⲡⲉⲧⲥⲙⲓⲛⲉ | ⲙⲙⲟⲥ +[3] ⲁⲛⲟⲕ
ⲓⲱⲁⲛⲛⲏⲥ ⲡⲉ[ⲓ]ⲉⲣⲁⲭⲓⲥⲧⲟⲥ ⲛⲁⲓⲁⲕ, ⲧⲓⲟ ⲙⲙⲛⲧⲣⲉ |ⲛⲧⲣⲉⲧⲓⲁⲥⲫⲁⲣⲓⲁ ⲛⲑⲉ ⲉⲓϩⲏϩ ⲉⲙⲟⲥ +
Verso +ⲧⲁⲥⲫⲁⲗⲉⲓⲁ ⲛⲡⲉⲃⲉ ⲡⲉⲩⲙⲙ ⲡϣⲉ ⲛⲓⲱϩⲁⲛⲛⲏⲥ

'I, Pebe, son of John, the σύμμαχος, of Shmoun, do write to Leontius, son of Hatre,
likewise of Shmoun, saying I owe (χρεωστεῖν) thee, clear and (ἀποκρότως), a
tremision of 7½ carats, by Alexandrian standard, that is (γίνεται), 7½ *trem* of Alexandrian
weight (ζυγῷ) This then (οὖν) I am ready (ἕτοιμος) to pay thee, with its interest, at any
time that thou wish, the interest being reckoned from to-day, the 2nd of Tôbe, of the
Indiction and onward, without judgment, without law (νόμος), without any doubt
(ἀμφιβολία), and to pay it thee at any time that thou wish, (otherwise,) then (ἐπὶ τῷ) to
pay 2 *tremisia* For thy assurance therefore (οὖν) I have drawn up this undertaking
(ἀσφάλεια), swearing by God Almighty (παντοκρ) that I will observe it for thee, according
to (πρός) its authority, I being at thy disposal (ὑποκεῖσθαι) with all that is mine' Then
the author's σημεῖον and assent (στοιχεῖν) and the signatures of the scribe and 2 witnesses

192.—Papyrus; a fragment; 12 × 15 cm   Script almost ligatureless except last line
Recto ↑

Acknowledgment of debt of 2 *solidi* less (παρά) 6 carats, by a woman to a nun,
Ama Ei   , the interest being at (πρός) ⅓ of   .

]ⲱⲛ ⲧⲣⲱⲙⲉ ϣⲙⲟⲩⲛ ⲉⲓⲥϩⲁⲓ ⲛⲁⲙⲁ ⲉⲓ[|] ⲛϩⲟⲗⲟⲕⲟⲧⲧⲓⲛ ⲥⲛⲁⲩ ⲡⲁⲣⲁ ⲥⲟ ⲉⲡⲟⲩⲁ ⲡⲉⲩ[ⲁ |]ⲉ
ⲙⲛⲧⲟⲩⲙⲛⲥⲉ ⲡⲣⲟⲥ ⲟⲩⲧⲉⲧⲁⲣⲧⲟⲛ ⲉ[|]ⲛ ⲛⲡⲁⲣⲙⲉϩⲟⲧⲡⲏⲛ ⲛⲧⲡⲉⲙⲛⲧⲏⲥ ⲓⲛ[|] ϥⲁⲙ ⲓⲉ ⲓⲛⲁ̣ ⲡⲉⲙⲛⲧⲏⲥ
ϯ ⲛ̄ ⲁⲥ ⲓβ' ⲍ, +[4] ⲙⲁ[

193.—Papyrus, a fragment, 7 × 31 cm   Script large, clumsy uncials. *Recto* ↑
Acknowledgment by two vinedressers of Sikeôs[5], of the loan of 1 *solidus* less (παρά)
6 carats[6], from the 'master' Callinicus   The term is for two months

---

[1] *V* no 130
[2] and [3] Different hands
[4] Different hand

[5] *Cf* ⲡⲙⲁ ⲛⲥⲓⲕⲉ, in a fragment in Br. Mus Or
6201 B &c
[6] *V* no 192

+[ⲃⲁⲛⲉ] ⲡ̣ϣⲉ ⲛⲁⲡⲁⲗⲟ ⲙⲛⲓⲱⲥⲏⲫ ⲛⲉϭⲙⲛⲟⲩ ⲛⲥⲓⲕⲉⲱⲥ ⲛⲉⲩ|ⲥϩⲁⲓ ⲛⲯⲁϩ ⲕⲁⲗⲗⲓⲛⲓⲕⲉ ϫⲛⲧⲛ-ⲭⲣⲉⲱⲥⲧⲏ ⲛⲁⲕ ⲛ̈ⲟⲗⲟⲕⲟ|ⲧⲧⲓⲛ [sic] ⲡⲁⲣⲁ ⲥⲟ ⲧⲛⲧⲁⲁϥ ⲛⲁⲕ ϣⲁϣ̈ⲟⲩⲙⲛⲧ [sic] ⲛⲫⲁⲣⲙⲟⲩ|ⲑⲓ ⲡⲉⲛⲧⲕⲁⲓⲇⲉ-ⲕⲁⲧⲏⲥ ⲓⲛⲇⲓⲕ/ ⲛⲧⲁⲛϫⲓⲧϥ ⲛⲧⲟⲟⲧⲕ | ⲉⲩⲡⲉⲩϣⲁⲛ ⲉⲅⲣⲁⲫ/ ⲙⲉⲭⲓⲣ ⲓ ⲉ ⲓⲛⲇ ⲃⲁⲛⲉ ⲥⲧⲟⲓⲭⲉⲓ ⲙⲟⲓ +[[1]

Verso (on right half only, owing to the manner of folding the leaf) 1 line, at end of which ⲫⲁⲣⲙⲟⲩⲑⲓ ⲓ ⲓ̣ⲉ ⲓⲛ[ⲇ/]

194.—Papyrus, a fragment, $6\frac{1}{2} \times 15\frac{1}{2}$ cm Script seldom ligatured *Recto* ↑ Above l 1 a cross

Acknowledgment of a debt by , son of Pehmot of [2] One witness is from Hage[3]

]ⲥ ⲡϣⲉ ⲙⲡⲉϩⲙⲟⲧ ⲡⲣⲱⲙ.ⲁⲁⲧ ϩⲙⲡⲧ[ⲟϣ | ⲭⲣⲉ]ⲱⲥⲧⲉ ⲛⲁⲕ ⲕⲁⲑⲁⲣⲟⲥ ⲕⲁⲓ ⲁⲡⲟⲕⲣⲟⲧⲱ[ⲥ |]ⲧⲁ-ⲧⲁⲁⲩ ⲛⲛⲁⲩ ⲛⲙ ⲉⲕⲟⲩⲁϣⲟⲩ ⲛⲛⲁ[| ⲡⲁ]ⲭⲱⲛ ⲓⲁ ⲁⲣⲭ/ ⲓⲛ ⲓ$^{\delta}$/ + ⲁⲛⲟⲕ ⲙⲁⲑⲉⲓⲁⲥ ⲡ[| ⲃⲓ]ⲕⲧⲱⲣ ⲡϣⲉ ⲙⲙⲏⲛⲁ ⲡⲣⲱⲙ ⲛϩⲁϭⲉ ⲁⲓⲉ[

Verso the address, illegible

195.—Papyrus, a fragment, $28 \times 25\frac{1}{2}$ cm Script regular, ligatureless *Recto* ↑.

Undertaking (ἀσφάλεια) as to the repayment of a debt of 20 *solidi*

]ⲧⲣⲓⲙⲏ ⲛⲉⲓ[. . . . ⲛⲉⲓϫⲟ]ⲩⲱⲧ ⲛ[ϩ]ⲟⲗⲟⲕ$^{\tau}$/ ⲟⲩⲛ ⲧ[|] ⲙⲙⲟⲛ ⲙⲙⲟⲟⲩ [ϩ]ⲙⲡⲟ[ⲩⲱϣ ⲙⲡⲛⲟⲩⲧⲉ . . . . ⲛ]ⲥⲛⲁⲩ ⲛⲉⲃⲟⲧ ⲛ[| ϫⲓ]ⲛⲉⲡⲟⲟⲩ ⲉⲧⲉⲥⲟⲩϫⲟⲩ[ⲧ . . . .] ? | ⲛⲁⲅⲗ]ⲁⲁⲩ ⲛⲡⲣⲟ-ⲫⲁⲥ[ⲓⲥ[4] about 15 let]ⲁ ⲛⲁⲕ ⲥⲓⲥⲧⲟⲓⲭⲉⲓ | [ⲉⲓⲱⲣⲕ ⲛ]ⲡⲛⲟⲩⲧⲉ ⲡⲡⲁⲛⲧⲱⲕⲣⲁⲧⲱⲣ ⲧⲁⲫⲩⲗⲁⲥⲥⲉ ⲛⲏⲧⲛ ⲡ[ⲣⲟ]ⲥ ⲧ[ϭⲟⲙ |] + ⲁⲛⲟⲕ ⲇⲁⲙⲓⲁⲛⲉ ⲡϣⲉ ⲙⲡⲙⲁⲕ/ ⲛϣⲟⲩⲣⲡϥⲙⲉⲥⲩ[ⲉ . . . . .]ⲉ ⲡⲣⲱⲙⲉ ϣⲙⲟⲩⲛ ϯⲥⲧⲟⲓⲭ | |+ⲁⲛⲟⲕ ⲓⲱⲁⲛⲛⲏ[ⲥ . . . . . ⲛϣⲟⲩⲣⲡⲉϥⲙ]ⲉⲩⲉ ⲗⲉⲟⲛⲧⲓⲟⲥ | [ⲧⲡⲟ ⲙⲙⲛ]ⲧⲣⲉ ⲉⲧⲓ[ⲁⲥ]-ⲫⲁⲗⲓⲉⲓⲁ ϩⲓⲧⲛ[ⲧⲁⲓⲧⲏⲥⲓⲥ ⲙⲡ]ⲉⲧⲥⲙⲓⲛⲉ ⲙⲙⲟⲥ + +[5] ⲁⲛⲟⲕ | ⲙⲉ]ⲥⲩⲉ ⲉⲧⲛⲁⲛⲟⲩϥ ⲡⲙⲁⲕ/ ⲁⲡⲁ ⲕⲩⲣⲓ ⲡⲣⲱⲙⲉ ϣⲙⲟⲩⲛ ϯⲟ ⲙⲙⲛⲧⲣⲉ ⲉⲧⲓⲁⲥⲫⲁⲗⲉⲓⲁ ϩⲓⲧⲛⲧⲁⲓⲧⲏⲥⲓⲥ |

196.—Papyrus, a fragment, $21\frac{1}{2} \times 36$ cm Script moderately ligatured *Recto* ↑

Agreement (ἀσφάλεια) as to debt The writer, Theodore, son of Leontius, owes to a monastery the price of certain grain supplied *Lacunae* make the exact meaning uncertain The text was cancelled by cross-lines

ϣⲙ]ⲟⲩⲛ ⲉⲓⲥ[ϩ]ⲁⲓ[ⲙⲡ]ⲇⲓⲕⲁⲓⲟⲛ ⲉⲧⲟⲩⲁⲁⲃ ⲙⲡⲁϫⲟⲉⲓⲥ |] ϫⲉⲧⲓⲭⲣⲉⲱⲥⲧⲉⲓ ⲛⲏⲧⲛ ⲕⲁⲑⲁⲣⲱⲥ |] ⲉⲣⲟⲓ ϩⲓⲡⲁⲗⲟⲅⲁⲣⲓⲛ ⲛⲧⲉⲥⲥⲁⲣⲉⲥⲕⲁⲓⲇⲉⲕ$^{\tau}$/ |] ⲙⲙⲛⲧⲥⲛⲟⲟⲩⲥ ⲛϩⲟⲗⲟⲕ$^{\tau}$/ | ⲛⲉⲩ[ⲥ]ⲧ^{o} ⲛ[ϫⲟⲩⲧⲥⲛⲟⲟ]ⲩⲥ ⲛⲕⲉⲣⲁⲧⲛ ⲡⲣⲟ[ⲥ about 16 let] ⲕⲁ ⲛⲁⲧⲛⲕⲣⲟϥ ϩⲁⲡⲉⲛⲧⲉⲕⲁⲓⲇⲉⲕ$^{\tau}$/ ⲓⲛⲇ^{o}/ | ⲛⲧⲟⲟⲧϥ ⲛⲧⲉⲧⲛⲉⲡⲗⲏⲣ[ⲟⲩ ⲙ]ⲙⲟϥ ϩⲱⲱⲧⲧⲏⲩⲧⲛ ⲛ[about 12 let]ⲁⲡⲟⲇⲉⲓⲝⲓⲥ ⲛⲧⲉⲧⲛⲉϫⲓ ⲧⲉⲧⲛⲉⲁⲡⲟ$^{\delta}$ | ϩⲁⲡⲉⲛⲧⲉⲕⲁⲓⲇⲉⲕ$^{\tau}$/ ⲓⲛⲇ/ γι/ σι/ αρ/ $\overset{\xi}{}$ $\overset{o}{\nu}$ ιβ/ η ⲡⲉⲓⲥⲉ ⲛ[ⲣ]ⲧⲟϥ ⲛ[ⲥⲟⲩⲟ] ⲟⲩⲛ ⲧⲓϩⲟⲙⲟⲗⲟⲅⲉⲓ ⲧⲁⲧⲁⲁⲩ ⲉⲡⲥⲁⲛⲕⲓⲛϩⲣ | ϩⲁⲣⲱⲧⲛ ⲛⲉⲡⲏⲡ ⲡⲉⲃⲟⲧ ⲛⲧⲓⲣⲟⲙⲡⲉ ⲛϩⲓⲱⲱⲥ ⲡⲣⲱⲧⲏⲥ ⲓ[ⲛⲇ/ ⲛⲁⲧⲗⲁⲁⲩ ⲛϩⲩⲡ]ⲉⲣⲑⲉⲥⲓⲥ ⲁⲩⲱ ⲡⲉⲓⲛ̊ ιβ/ η

[1] Perhaps nothing more here
[2] The first letter probably ⲡ or ⲛ
[3] *Cf* ⲧⲙⲟⲩⲛϩⲁϭⲉ in a Br Mus fragment (Or 6201 A &c), ⲧⲱϩⲱ ⲛϩⲁϭⲉ, Krall ccxlii.
[4] *V* no 130
[5] Different hand

ⲧⲓⲣⲟⲙⲟⲗⲟⲅⲉⲓ | ⲧⲁⲝⲓ ⲉⲛⲧⲁⲧⲟⲩ ⲛⲏⲧⲛ ⲉⲣⲟⲟⲩ ⲟⲛ ⲟⲁⲛⲟⲩⲟⲩϣ ⲙⲡⲛⲟⲩⲧⲉ ⲟⲁⲧⲓⲣⲟⲙⲡⲉ ⲛⲟⲩⲱⲟ̄ⲧ ⲡⲉⲛ-
ⲧⲉⲕⲁⲓⲆⲉⲕᵀ, ⲓⲛⲆ°, ⲛⲧⲉⲧⲛⲉⲧⲓ ⲡⲥⲉⲉⲡⲉ | ⲛⲧⲉⲛⲉⲭⲓ ⲧⲉⲧⲛⲉⲁⲡⲟᵈ ⲉⲣⲉⲡⲉⲧϣⲟⲟⲡ ⲛⲁⲓ ⲧⲏⲣϥ ⲟⲩⲡⲟⲕ°,
ⲛⲏⲧⲛ ϣⲁⲛⲧⲓⲡⲗⲏⲣⲟⲩ ⲙⲙⲱⲧⲛ ⲡⲣⲟⲥ ⲧϭⲟⲙ ⲛⲧⲓⲁⲥⲫⲁⲗⲉⲓⲁ ⲉⲓⲱⲣⲕ | ⲉⲡⲛⲟⲩⲧⲉ ⲡⲡⲁⲛⲧⲟⲕⲣⲁⲧⲱⲣ
ⲧⲁⲣⲉⲓⲣⲟⲥⲓⲥ ⲛⲏⲧⲛ ⲡⲣⲟⲥ ⲧϭⲟⲙ ⲛⲧⲓⲁⲥⲫⲁⲗⲉⲓⲁ ⲉⲩⲱⲣⲭ ⲛⲏⲧⲛ ⲁⲓⲥⲙⲛⲧⲓⲁⲥⲫⲁⲗⲉⲓⲁ ⲛⲏⲧⲛ | ⲛⲧⲁⲓⲟⲁⲓⲥ
ⲧⲏⲣⲥ ⲛⲧⲁϭⲓⲝ ⲁⲓⲕⲱⲣϣ ⲟⲛⲕⲁⲓⲉⲗⲉⲅⲟⲉⲣⲟⲥ ⲧ̄ⲁⲣⲉⲩⲣⲙⲛⲧⲣⲉ ⲉⲣⲟⲥ + ⲉⲅⲣ̄ ⲙ̄ ᴾ̄ ᴷ̄ ⲡ̄ ⲕⲉ ⲓⲛⲆ°, ⲁ + ⲁⲛⲟⲕ |
ⲑⲉⲟⲆⲱⲣⲉ ⲡϣⲉ ⲛⲙⲙⲁⲕⲁⲣ/ ⲗⲉⲟⲛⲧⲓⲛ ⲧⲓⲥⲧⲟ̄ᵡ ⲉⲧⲓⲁⲥⲫⲁⲗⲉⲓ[ⲁ] ⲛ̄ϭⲟⲉ ⲉⲥⲡ̄ϩ ⲙⲙⲟⲥ ⲛⲧⲁⲓⲥⲟⲁⲓⲉⲓⲥ ᵒᵘᵘ ⲧⲏⲣⲥ
ⲛⲧⲁϭⲓⲝ + |

Verso (cancelled)   + ⲁⲥⲫⲁⲗᵉ, ⲥⲓ, ρ̄ ξ ν̄° ⲓⲃ η [

'.   of Shmoun, I write to the holy δίκαιον of my lord[1] [,   ] I owe (χρεωστεῖν) you,
clear and   (καθαρῶς, ἀποκρότως) [,   ] me, with (?) my λογάριον[2] of the 14th Indiction
[,   ] 12 *solidi*, of full weight (εὐσταθμος) of 12 carats, according to (πρός) [,   ] without
fraud, for the 15th Indiction, from him (?), and that ye on your part receive them fully
(πληροῦν) [,   ] receipt (ἀπόδειξις) and that ye receive your receipt (ἀπ.) for the 15th Indiction, that is for (γίνεται) 60 *artabae* of corn at $12\frac{1}{6}$ (?) *solidi*[3]   These 60 *artabae* then (οὖν)
I undertake (ὁμολογεῖν) to deliver to the artichoke-seller[4] on your behalf, in the month Ἐπέπ,
of this year in which we are, the 1st Indiction, without any delay (ὑπέρθεσις[5])   And for
these $12\frac{1}{6}$ (?) *solidi* I agree (ὁμολ) also to hand you an acknowledgment (ἐντάγιον), if God will,
for this same 15th Indiction, and you shall pay the remainder and shall have your receipt
(ἀπόδ), all that I have being at your disposal (ὑποκεῖσθαι), until I shall fully pay (πληροῦν)
you, according to (πρός) the authority of this agreement (ἀσφάλεια)'   Then the usual oath
and date of writing, 25th Pachôn, 1st Indiction   'And I have requested other freemen
(ἐλεύθερος) that they would witness it'   There are however no signatures

Also, on *verso*, a list of names, with amounts of grain (σι, α̅ρ̅) or money (α̅ρ̅ⁱ) opposite
each, headed + συν ελ° τρι ινδ°, θωθ ι ινδ°, δ   Among them are Μαρκου στιπῑ̄, Πηρπ,
Θεοδωρου πρ̄ τ παπας.   Several names are followed by the place of residence or origin,
απο κᵉ,[6], απο θωτᵉ[7], απο τερτεμω̄[8], απ[ο]φεως   Much is illegible

197.—Papyrus, a fragment, $19\frac{1}{2} \times 18$ cm   Script ligatureless   *Recto* ↑
Undertaking (ἀσφάλεια) to repay a debt, addressed by Justa, a merchant, to   ,
a woman   The text was cancelled by cross-lines

] ⲟⲁⲗⲟⲕ[|] ⲡⲛⲟⲩⲃ ⲛ̄[|] ⲛⲁⲧⲗⲁⲁ[ⲩ] ⲛⲁⲙⲫⲓⲃⲟⲗⲉⲓⲁ ⲉⲣⲉⲡⲉⲧϣ[ⲟⲟⲡ |] ⲁⲓⲥⲙⲛ ⲧⲓⲁⲥⲫⲁⲗⲉⲓⲁ

ⲛⲉ ⲉⲓⲥⲧⲟⲓⲭⲉⲓ ⲉⲣⲟⲥ [| ⲙ]ⲛⲧⲣⲉ ⲉⲣⲟⲥ ⲉⲓⲱⲣⲕ ⲛⲛⲟⲩⲧⲉ ⲡⲡⲁⲛⲧⲟ[ⲕⲣⲁⲧⲱⲣ |]ⲟⲥ +╫ + ⲁⲛⲟⲕ

---

[1] Cf KRALL LXXVII
[2] Recurs KRALL CXI   Cf CRUM, *Ostr* no 415
[3] The η (or ? κ) should have the stroke above if a
fraction
[4] KRALI CCXLV compares κινάρα, while Paris MS 44,
81 *b* has ⲕⲓⲛⲁⲣⲏ 'lotus.'   Br Mus no. 1114 and a
letter here (v Index) mention bundles of it

[5] V Pap Amh cli
[6] Or ηᵉ,
[7] Cf Θοτέως (gen), MITTEIS, *Urk*, no 15
[8] Τερταμώθ, KENYON, *Catal* III 123 (? cf Τερτεμβῦθις)
From a fragment, Br Mus Or 6201 B &c, where ⲧⲉⲣⲱⲧ-
ⲟⲁⲗⲉ=ⲧⲉⲣⲧⲟ/ⲕ/ on *verso*, it appears that Τέρτον, Τερτ- in
Greek texts=ⲧⲉⲣⲱⲧ in Coptic

ιογϲτⲁ ⲡⲉϣⲱⲧ ⲡⲉ[ⲅ|] ⲁⲛⲟⲕ¹ ⲍⲁⲭⲁⲣⲓⲁⲥ ⲡϣⲉ ⲛⲡⲙⲁⲕⲁⲣ/ ⲅⲉⲱⲣⲅⲉ ⲡⲣⲱⲙ[| ²ⲛ]ϣⲟⲩⲣⲡⲉⲙⲉⲉⲩⲉ
ⲡⲉⲧⲣⲟⲥ ⲡⲣⲱⲙⲉ ϣⲙⲟⲩⲛ ⲧⲓⲟ ⲛ[| ⲣⲱ]ⲙⲉ ϣⲙⲟⲩⲛ ⲧⲓⲟ ⲛⲁⲙⲛⲧⲣⲉ ⲉⲧⲓⲁⲥⲫⲁⲗⲉⲓⲁ ⲛⲑⲉ ⲉⲥ̇ⲛ[ϩ ³]ⲛⲁⲡⲁ
ⲃⲓⲕⲧⲱⲣ ⲡⲛⲣ̅ ⲡⲣⲱⲙⲉ ϣⲙⲟⲩⲛ ⲛⲧⲁⲧⲓⲁ[ⲥⲫⲁⲗⲉⲓⲁ | ⲛ]ⲃⲛⲟⲓ ⲁⲛ + + +

198.—Papyrus, a fragment, $5\frac{1}{2} \times 19$ cm   Script small, ligatured   *Recto* ↑

Undertaking (εὐχρηστητικὴ[4] ἀσφάλεια) by Damianus, as to the payment (or repayment) of money   The price of a donkey is mentioned   The deed was written by a νομικός

ⲛⲧⲧⲓⲙⲉ ⲛⲡⲓⲱ ⲛⲧⲁϥϣ| ⲉϣⲁⲕⲉⲓ ⲉⲧⲡⲟⲗⲓⲥ ⲁⲛ ⲡⲛⲟⲟⲩ ⲛ ⲣ[ⲱ]ⲙⲉ ⲉⲡⲱⲕⲛⲉ . ⲕⲉⲣ . . . . . ⲡⲁⲛ ⲅⲟ[|
ⲧⲁⲡⲗⲏⲣⲟⲩ ⲛⲁⲟⲕ ⲉⲡⲉ[ⲓ . . . . . ⲛϩⲟⲗⲟ̅ⲕ̅/ ⲉⲓⲡ̅ⲟⲕ̅ⲑ, ⲙⲙⲡⲉⲧϣⲟⲟⲡ ⲛⲁⲓ ⲧⲏⲣϥ[| ⲉⲓⲱⲣⲕ ⲛⲡⲛⲟⲩⲧⲉ
ⲡⲡⲁⲛⲧⲟⲕⲣ[ⲁⲧⲱ]ⲣ ⲧⲁⲣⲟⲉⲓⲥ [ⲛⲁⲕ ⲡ]ⲣⲟⲥ ⲧⲥⲟ[ⲙ ⲛⲅ]ⲉⲩⲭⲣⲓⲥⲧⲉⲛⲧⲓⲕⲏ ⲁⲥⲫⲁⲗⲉⲓⲁ | $\overset{\sigma\eta\mu}{\underset{\delta\alpha\mu\iota-}{\hat\mu\;\overset{\nu}{\bar\tau}\;\beta\;\iota^\delta,\;\beta\;\text{†††}}}$

+ ⲁⲛⲟⲕ ⲇⲁⲙⲓⲁⲛⲉ ⲡⲉⲧϣⲏⲣⲡ[ⲉϩⲁⲓ ⲧ]ⲓⲥ ⲅⲟ̅ⲓ̅ $\overset{X}{}$ ⲉⲧⲓⲉⲩⲭⲣⲓⲥⲅⲉⲛⲧⲓⲕⲏ ⲁⲥⲫ̅ⲁ̅ⲗ̅ +   + [ⲁⲛⲟⲕ | ⲡⲛⲟⲙⲓⲕⲏ/
ⲛⲧⲡⲟⲗⲓⲥ ϣⲙⲟⲩⲛ ⲧⲓⲟ ⲛⲁⲙⲛⲧⲣⲉ ⲉⲧⲓⲁⲥⲫⲁⲗⲉⲓⲁ ⲛⲧⲁⲥϣⲱⲡⲉ ϩⲓⲧⲟⲟⲧ [ⲁ]ⲩⲱ ⲁⲓ[ⲥ]ϩⲁⲓ ϩⲁⲡⲉⲧⲓ
ⲥⲧⲁⲩⲣⲟⲥ +   +[5] ⲁⲛⲟⲕ ⲕⲟⲥⲙⲁ ⲡϣⲉ ⲛⲡⲙⲁⲕ/ ⲁⲛⲧⲱⲛⲉ [

199.—Papyrus, a fragment, $34\frac{1}{2} \times 21$ cm   Script thin, moderately ligatured, *cf* Brit Mus Catal, Pl 4, Or 6205, ll 1–3   *Recto* ↑   The text is cancelled by cross-lines, often obliterating the writing

Undertaking (ὁμολογία) as to payment (or repayment) of money   The amir (of Shmoun), Abû Saal[6], is mentioned, also Hamoi, the νοτάριος

,ⲍⲟⲉⲓⲥ ⲁⲃⲟⲩ ⲥⲁⲁⲗ ⲡⲉⲩⲕⲗⲉⲥ/ [ⲛⲁⲙⲓⲣⲁ | ⲡ]ϣⲉ ⲛⲡⲙⲁⲕ/ ϣⲥⲛⲟⲩⲧⲉ ⲡ[ⲣⲉ]ⲙⲧⲉⲛⲡⲟⲗⲓⲥ ⲉⲃⲟⲗ
[ⲍⲉ |]ⲥⲓⲁ ϩⲁⲡⲙⲁ [ⲥⲧⲙ]ⲙⲁⲩ ⲁⲩⲱ ⲛϭⲛ ϩⲁⲙⲟⲓ ⲡⲛⲟ̅ ⲥϭⲛⲏⲩ | ⲧⲓⲉⲩϩⲣ ϩⲓⲙⲡⲟⲩⲱϣ ⲙⲡⲛⲟⲩⲧⲉ
ⲡ[ϩ]ⲟⲩⲛ ⲛⲙⲛⲧⲛ |] ⲛⲉⲃⲟⲧ ⲛ]ⲡⲣⲟⲙⲉ ⲧⲁⲓ ⲡⲉⲛ ⲅⲉⲛ[ⲁⲓⲁ]ⲉⲕ[ⲁⲓⲏⲥ ⲓⲏ̅ⲑ, |]ⲉ ⲅ̅ⲛ̅ⲡⲣⲟⲑⲉⲥⲙⲓⲁ ⲧⲏϩⲟⲙⲟⲗⲟⲅⲉⲓ
ⲧⲛⲥⲱⲛ[7] ϩⲁϩⲱϥ |]ⲧⲛⲙⲛ ϩⲁⲟⲩ[. . . .]ⲉ[ ]ϩ ⲛⲉⲓϩⲱϥ | ⁸]ⲉⲩⲗⲟⲅⲛⲙⲉⲛⲟⲥ . . . . [ⲧⲓ-]
ϩⲟⲙⲟⲗⲟⲅⲓⲁ ⲛⲏⲧⲛ ⲛⲥⲧⲟⲓⲭ[ⲉⲓ ⲉⲣⲟ]ⲥ + [ⲛⲏ]ⲧⲛ ⲡⲣⲟⲥ ⲧⲉⲥⲥⲟⲙ ⲉⲅⲣ̅ $\hat\mu\;\alpha\theta^\nu,\;\kappa\epsilon\;\iota^\delta,\;\iota\epsilon$ | ϩⲟⲙⲟⲗ]ⲟ[ⲅⲓ]ⲁ
ⲛⲑⲉ ⲉⲥⲛ̇ϩ ⲥⲙⲟⲥ] +⁹ ⲁⲛⲟⲕ [| ϩⲟⲙⲟⲗⲟⲅⲓⲁ ⲛⲑⲉ ⲉⲥⲥⲛ̇ϩ ⲙⲙⲟⲥ + |] ⲧⲓⲥⲧ[ⲟⲓⲭ]ⲉⲓ ⲉ ⲧⲓϩⲟⲙⲟⲗⲟⲅⲓⲁ ⲛⲑⲉ
ⲉⲥⲥⲛ̇ϩ ⲙⲙⲟⲥ + |]¹⁰ ⲧⲓⲟ ⲙⲙⲛⲧⲣⲉ ⲉⲧⲓϩⲟⲙⲟⲗⲟⲅⲓⲁ [| ⲙⲉ]ⲉⲩⲉ¹¹ ⲕⲟⲗⲗⲟⲩⲑⲉ ⲡⲣⲱⲙⲉ [|]ⲡⲉⲧⲓ
ⲥⲧⲁⲩⲣⲟⲥ ⲍⲛⲃ[ⲛⲟⲓ ⲁⲛ

Verso   list of names (none remarkable) and money, in a Greek hand, mostly cancelled

200.—Papyrus, a fragment, $10\frac{1}{2} \times 19$ cm   Script ligatureless   *Verso* →

Agreement (ἀσφάλεια), whereby Anoute¹² undertakes to return a borrowed .   , when required, or to pay a fine of 1 *solidus*

¹ and ² Different hands   ³ Original hand   παραλ (*leg* ϲαραλ)   ⁷ V no 128
⁴ A new word   ⁶ Different hand   ⁸ This line added between the others
⁶ Recurs in Br Mus Or 6721 (10) (Jême)   Probably   ⁹ ¹⁰ and ¹¹ Different hands
= ج   V *Mitth Ram* ii 162   *Cf* Ciasca, *Papii* i, no. vi,   ¹² Ἀνουθις, Kenyon, *Catal* iii 255

ⲫ̄ ⲁⲛⲟⲕ ⲁⲡⲟⲩⲧⲉ ⲡⲟⲩⲟⲉⲓ ⲛⲉϥϩⲣⲁⲓ ⲛⲛⲁⲡⲁⲩⲗⲉ ⲡϣⲉ ⲏⲡ[| ⲁⲡⲁ ⲕⲟⲗⲑⲉ ϫⲉⲉⲡⲓⲁⲛ ⲁⲓⲕⲟⲣϣ ⲁⲛϯ
ⲧⲟⲣⲕⲁ¹ ⲛⲁⲓ ϩ.[| ⲙⲡⲛⲟⲩⲧⲉ ⲛⲁⲩ ⲛⲓⲙ ⲉⲕⲛⲁⲣⲭⲣⲓⲁ ⲙⲙ[ⲟⲥ. | ⲙⲟⲥ ⲧⲁⲁⲥ ⲛⲁⲕ ⲛ[ⲧⲉ]ⲥϭⲉ ⲁⲩⲱ
ⲉⲣϣⲁⲛⲧ [| ⲙⲟⲓ ⲧⲁϯ ⲟⲩⲅⲣⲁⲙⲛⲉⲥⲓⲛ ⲛⲁⲕ ϩⲁⲣⲟⲥ ⲛⲁⲧ[| ⲫ̄ ⲁⲛⲟⲕ ⲁⲡⲟⲩⲧⲉ ϯⲉⲭⲉⲓⲟⲛ ⲉⲧⲉⲓⲁⲥ-
ⲫⲁⲗⲉⲓⲁ + [| ⲡⲣⲉⲥⲃⲩⲧⲉⲣ, ⲧⲁϥⲕⲟⲣϣ ⲁⲓⲥϩⲁⲓ ϩⲁⲣⲟϥ ϫⲉ..[| ϯⲟ ⲙⲛⲧⲣⲉ +

Recto traces of an earlier text

201.—Papyrus, a fragment, 9½ × 8 cm   Script ligatureless, sloping; *cf* CRUM,
Ostraca, 'Hand A' *Recto* ↑   The text is cancelled by cross lines

Undertaking by the δίκαιον of a monastery (or church)² to repay a loan to a woman

ⲫ̄ ⲡⲁⲓⲕ[ⲁⲓⲟ]ⲛ ⲙⲡ[| ⲉⲧⲟⲩⲁⲁⲃ [ⲛ]ⲁⲡⲁ ⲑ[| ⲓⲟⲩⲥⲧⲉ ⲡⲉⲡⲣⲟⲉ[ⲥⲧⲱⲥ | ⲙⲙⲁⲣⲓⲁ ⲧⲙⲁⲁⲩ [|
ⲧⲛⲭⲣⲱⲱⲥⲧⲉ ⲛ[ⲉ | ⲡⲛⲟⲩϥ ⲧⲓⲧⲁⲁϥ ⲛⲉ [| ⲡⲣⲟⲥ ⲡϣⲁⲁⲣ ⲉϥϣⲱ[ⲡⲉ³ | ⲕⲁⲣ]ⲡⲟⲥ ⲛⲧⲉⲥⲥⲁⲣⲉⲥⲕⲁⲓⲁ[|
ⲓⲛⲁⲟ/, ⲉⲥⲧⲣⲁⲫ, ⲙⲡⲛ[| ⲧⲣⲓⲥⲛⲁⲉⲛⲁ[ⲧⲏⲥ | + + + ⲁⲛⲟⲕ ⲡⲛⲁⲡⲁ | ⲡⲉⲧⲣⲁⲫⲉⲩⲥ ⲛⲧⲁⲓⲛⲁ[ⲛⲁ |
ⲉ]ⲛⲓⲧⲣⲉⲡⲛ ⲛⲁⲓ ϩⲁⲙⲡⲣⲁⲛ[| ⲁⲓⲥϩⲁⲓ +

Verso [space] ⲓⲟⲩⲥⲧⲉ +

202.—Papyrus, a fragment, 9½ × 12½ cm   Script ligatureless *Recto* ↑.
Agreement (ἀσφάλεια) by Nahrow as to the payment (or repayment) of corn⁴

]ⲧⲉⲕⲁⲡⲟⲑⲏⲕⲏ ϩⲛⲑⲟⲟⲩⲧ [| ϩⲟⲙⲟⲗⲟⲅⲓ ⲁⲛⲟⲕ ⲛⲁϩⲣⲟⲟⲩ ϫⲉ |]ⲧ ⲛⲁⲓ ⲧⲁⲧⲁⲁⲩ ⲡⲣⲟⲥ ⲧⲉⲩⲁⲩ-
ⲛⲁⲙⲓⲥ | ⲉⲡ]ⲓ ⲧⲱ ⲧⲁⲣⲩⲡⲟⲕⲓⲥⲑⲁⲓ ⲙⲛϩⲱϥ ⲛⲓⲙ | ⲡⲛⲟⲩⲧⲉ ⲡⲡⲁⲛⲧⲟⲕⲣⲁⲧⲱⲣ ⲙⲛⲛⲉⲩⲭⲁⲓ |] ⲡϣⲉ
ⲛⲁⲡⲟⲗⲗⲱ ⲧⲓⲥⲧⲟⲓⲭⲉⲓ ⲉⲧⲓⲁⲥⲫⲁⲗⲉⲓⲁ | ⲉ]ⲛⲓⲧⲣⲱⲙⲛ ⲛⲁⲓ ⲁⲓⲥϩⲁⲓ + ⲁⲛⲟⲕ ⲃⲁⲛⲉ ⲡϣⲉ ⲛ |ϩⲓ]ⲁⲓⲕⲟⲛ⁵
+ + +⁶ ⲕⲩⲣⲟⲥ ⲡⲉⲗⲭ, ⲛⲁⲓⲁⲕⲟⲛ ⲧⲓⲟ ⲛⲙⲛⲧⲣⲉ + | ⲙ]ⲛⲧⲣⲉ + *sic*⁷ ⲧ]ⲓⲁⲥⲫⲁⲗⲉⲓⲁ ϣⲱⲡⲉ ϩⲓⲧⲟⲟⲧ +

203—Papyrus, a fragment, 17 × 17 cm   Script clumsy, ligatureless *Recto* ↑
Agreement (ἀσφάλεια) by George as to payment due for corn   The place Pekrot⁸
is named

]ⲛⲟ ⲙⲧⲣⲉ + |]ⲏⲛ..ⲥⲧⲓ⁹ ϩⲟⲗⲟⲕⲟⲧⲧⲛ ⲥⲛⲁⲩ ϩⲁⲅⲧⲉⲙⲙⲉ⁹ ⲡⲉⲓⲥⲟⲩⲟ | ⲛⲓⲙ ⲉⲛϣⲱⲡⲉ ϩⲉⲛⲟⲥⲱⲛ
ⲛⲁⲕ ϣⲁⲛⲧⲉⲕⲙⲟⲩϩ ⲙⲟⲟⲩ |¹⁰ ⲡⲛⲟⲩⲧⲉ] ⲡⲡⲁⲛⲧⲟⲕⲣⲁⲧⲱⲣ ⲧⲁⲣⲉⲓⲣⲟⲉⲓⲥ ⲛⲁⲕ ⲡⲣⲱⲥ | ⲁ]ⲥⲫⲁⲗⲓⲁ +
ⲉⲓⲥⲣⲁⲫⲏ ⲫⲁⲓ ⲕ ϛ ⲓⲛⲁ/, |++]+ [ⲧⲉ]ⲱⲣⲅⲉ +ⲁⲛⲟⲕ ⲅⲉⲱⲣⲅⲉ ⲡⲉⲧϣⲉⲣⲡ ⲥϩⲁⲓ |ⲧ]ⲓⲁⲥⲫⲁⲗⲓⲁ ⲑⲉ
ⲉⲥⲥⲛϩ ⲙⲟⲓ + ⲁⲛⲟⲕ ϩⲱⲣⲥⲓⲕⲓⲟⲥ | ⲙ]ⲁⲕⲁⲣⲓⲟⲥ ⲡⲁⲩⲗⲟⲥ ⲡⲣⲱⲙⲡⲉⲕⲣⲟⲧ ⲁⲓⲥϩⲁⲓ ϩⲁⲣⲟⲃ ϫⲉⲛ |] ⲧⲓⲟ
ⲛⲙⲥⲧⲣⲉ + ⲁⲛⲟⲕ ⲙⲏⲛⲁ ⲡϣⲉ ⲛϥⲣⲩⲃⲁⲙⲙⲱⲛ |]ⲛⲧⲁⲃⲏⲥ ⲧⲓⲟ ⲛⲙⲉⲧⲣⲉ ⲧⲓⲁⲥⲫⲁⲗⲓⲁ +

Verso a drawing of a cup or chalice

---

¹ The word has been altered
² Of St Theodore (*v* nos 153 and 238) or Thomas
(*v* no. 124)
³ *V* no 210, KRALL XXIX and xli   ϣⲁⲁⲣ apparently
' valuation ' here

⁴ Since ἀποθήκη is used
⁵]ⲁⲓⲕⲟⲛ cou'd be read
⁶ and ⁷ Different hands
⁸ Unknown   ⁹ Corrected
¹⁰ *V* KRALL XXIX for the verb

204—Papyrus, a fragment, 17 × 15 cm   Script *cf* Br Mus Catal, Pl 14, no. 1024 for the type   *Recto* ↑.

Agreement (ἀσφάλεια) by Trashe (Trasias) of Takala[1] (Takales), to deliver 9 *artabae* of corn, already paid for, to the brothers Andreas (?) and Herakleides, at their house in Shmoun, in Paône of the next year, free of carriage[2]   Two witnesses sign

+ ⲁⲛⲟⲕ ⲧⲣⲁϣⲉ ⲧϣⲉ ⲛⲙⲁⲣⲑⲁ ⲧϣⲉ[3] ⲛⲙⲉ[. .] | ⲧⲣⲱⲙⲉⲧⲁⲕⲁⲗⲁ ϩⲙⲡⲧⲟϣ ⲛϣⲙⲟⲩⲛ + ⲉⲓⲥϩⲁⲓ [ⲛ]- | ⲁⲛⲇⲣⲉⲁⲥ[4] ⲙⲛϩⲏⲣⲁⲕⲗⲉⲓⲇⲉ ⲛⲉⲥⲛⲏⲩ [| ⲛⲉⲩⲉⲣⲏⲩ ϫⲉⲧⲓⲭⲣⲉⲱⲥⲧⲓ ⲛⲏ[ⲧⲛ . . . .] | ⲯ[ⲓⲧ] ⲛⲉⲣⲧⲟⲩ ⲛⲥⲟⲩⲟ ⲛⲧⲁⲓⲡⲗⲏⲣⲟⲩ ⲛⲧ[ⲟⲟ]ⲧⲏⲩ[ⲧⲛ] | ⲛⲧⲉⲩⲅⲙⲉⲛ ⲥⲓ, ⲛ[5] ⲥⲓ, ⲑ ⲛⲁⲓ ⲧⲁⲧⲁⲁⲩ ⲛⲏⲧⲛ [| ⲛⲧⲥⲧⲛⲟⲓⲡⲉ[6] ⲙⲡⲁϣⲛⲓ ⲉ ⲓ̄ⲉ̄ ⲛⲁ̄, ⲛⲥⲟⲩⲟ ⲉⲛ[ⲁⲛⲟⲩⲟⲩ] | [ⲥⲩϣ]ⲗⲙ̄ϣⲱⲗ ⲉⲩⲧⲃⲏⲩ ⲁⲩⲱ ⲧⲁⲁⲗ .[7] [| ⲛⲡⲉⲧⲛⲏⲓ ϩⲛϣⲙⲟⲩⲛ ⲛⲛⲁⲧ- ϩⲙⲙⲉ [| ⲉⲓ ϫⲉ ⲙⲛⲧⲁⲁⲩ ⲛⲏⲧⲛ ⲧⲁⲧⲓ ⲯⲓⲧ [| . . . . ⲧⲓⲙⲏ + ⲉⲧⲣ, ⲭⲟⲓ[ⲁⲕ] | ⲍ ⲓ̄ⲛⲁ̄°, ⲁ̄[8] + ⲁⲛⲟⲕ ⲧⲣⲁϣⲉ ⲧⲉⲧ[| ⲉⲧⲓⲁⲥⲫⲁⲗⲉⲓⲁ + ⲁ[ⲛⲟ]ⲕ ⲓⲁ[| ⲛϣ[ⲉ ⲛⲡ]ⲙⲁⲕⲁⲣⲓⲟⲥ ⲁⲫⲟⲩ ⲡⲣⲱⲙⲉ ϣⲙⲟⲩ[ⲛ | ⲛⲧⲁⲓⲥϩⲁⲓ ϩⲁⲣⲟⲥ ϫⲉⲛⲥⲛⲟⲉⲓ ⲁⲛ | ⲁⲩⲱ ⲧⲓⲟ ⲙⲛⲧⲣⲉ + + ⲁⲛⲟⲕ ⲓⲱⲁⲛⲛ[ⲏⲥ] | ⲡϣⲉ ⲛⲕⲟⲗⲑⲉ ⲡⲣⲱⲙⲉ ϣⲙⲟⲩⲛ ϯⲟ ⲙⲛⲧⲣⲉ ⲉⲧⲓ|ⲁⲥⲫⲁⲗⲉⲓⲁ +

Verso + ασφαλ, σι, θ . . .[9] [space] τρασιας μ . . ωσαρεπικ | τακαλες

205—Papyrus, a fragment, 15 × 27 cm   Script ligatured   *Recto* ↑

Agreement (ἀσφάλεια) by Athanasius of Tbakeile[10], to repay to Apa Severus a loan of , oil and incense (?)

+ ⲁⲑⲁⲛⲁⲥⲉ ⲡⲣⲱⲙⲉⲧⲃⲁⲕⲉⲓⲗⲉ ϩⲙⲡⲧⲟϣ ϣⲙⲟⲩⲛ ⲧⲡⲟⲗⲓⲥ ⲉⲓⲥϩⲁⲓ ⲛⲁⲡⲁ ⲥⲉⲩⲏⲣ[ⲟⲥ | .] ⲡⲣⲱⲙⲉ ϣⲙⲟⲩⲛ ⲧⲡⲟⲗⲓⲥ ϫⲉⲉⲛⲉⲓⲁⲛ ⲧⲁⲡⲁⲣⲁⲅⲉⲗⲉ ⲙⲟⲛ ⲧⲁⲣ[ⲉⲕ . . . . . . | [. . . .] ⲛⲁ ⲛⲁⲓ ⲉϫⲱⲛ ⲉϩⲙⲡⲟⲟⲩ ⲛⲣⲟⲟⲩ ⲉⲧⲉⲥⲟⲩϫⲟⲩⲧⲁⲥⲉⲡⲉ ⲙ . . ⲫ . | [about 15 let]ⲃⲉ ⲙⲛⲥⲛⲁⲩ ⲛ[ⲍ]ⲛⲥⲧⲉ [ⲛ]ⲉϩ ⲛⲁ[about 10 let] | ⲙⲛϥⲧⲟⲟ̄ ⲛⲍ[ⲛⲥⲧ]ⲉ ⲛⲥⲧⲉ ϣ[.] ⲛ[.| ⲱ]ⲣⲏϫ ⲛⲁⲕ ⲟⲩⲛ ⲁⲓⲥⲙⲛ ⲧⲉⲓ[ⲁⲥⲫⲁⲗ]ⲉⲁ ⲛⲁⲕ ⲉⲓⲥⲧⲟⲓ ⲉⲣⲟⲥ ⲉⲓⲱⲣⲕ ⲉⲡⲛⲟⲩⲧⲉ | ⲉ]ⲧⲁⲣⲭⲉ ⲉϫⲱⲛ ⲕⲁⲧⲁ ⲕⲉⲣⲟⲥ ⲛⲓⲙ ⲧⲁⲣⲏⲣⲟⲉⲓⲥ ⲛⲁⲕ ⲡⲣⲟⲥ ⲧϭⲟⲙ ⲧⲉⲓⲁⲥⲫⲁⲗⲉⲁ + |]ⲣⲱⲙⲉⲧⲃⲁⲕⲉ ϯⲟ ⲙⲛⲧⲣⲉ + |ϯϯϯ| ⲁⲛⲟⲕ [about 10 let] ⲁⲑⲁⲛⲁⲥⲉ | . . . | ⲁⲛⲟⲕ ⲥⲁⲙⲟⲩⲏⲗ .   ⲉⲧⲟⲥ ⲡⲣⲱⲙⲉ[ϣⲙⲟⲩⲛ [|] ⲁⲩⲱ ⲧⲓⲟ ⲙⲛⲧⲣⲉ +   Most of the last two lines is illegible

206.—Papyrus, 2 disconnected fragments, each 8½ × 8 cm   Script ligatured   *Recto* ↑

Undertaking by Enoch, a husbandman, to repay 100 jars of wine, in Tôbe of (the current ?) year, with a fine for non-delivery   If any be spoilt, it shall be exchanged   The place Pma nleonti(us) is mentioned

---

[1] *Cf* ? KRALL clx 16
[2] *V* KRALL xxii, cxxxii
[3] Grandparents named, *cf* no 190
[4] 3rd letter rather ⲁ.
[5] Like an angular ħ, =? ἀρτάβαι
[6] *V* KRALL cxxviii
[7] Not ⲧⲁⲧⲁⲗ[ⲉ]

[8] ⲁ might be read Above, in place of ⲓⲉ, one expects ⲉ ⲓⲛⲁ,
[9] Mr KENYON suggests εν αλληλεγγυ(η) and possibly μαρθας   επι κ(ωμης) in the next gap
[10] One witness is from Tbake (*v.* no 155) Are they variants of the same ?

ⲉⲛⲱ]ϫ ⲡⲟⲩⲟⲟⲓⲉ ⲛϣⲉ ⲛⲡⲙⲁ[ⲁⲕⲁⲣ, ?].... ....ⲟⲩ ...[|]..ⲉ ⲛϣⲉ ⲛⲡⲙⲁⲕⲁⲣ,
....[?] ⲕⲁⲑⲁ'ⲣ[ⲱⲥ] ⲕⲁⲓ ⲁⲡⲟⲕⲣⲟⲧⲱⲥ [|]ⲛⲡⲗⲏⲣⲟⲩ ⲛⲧⲉⲩⲁⲓⲕⲁⲓⲁ ⲧⲙⲁ[ⲏ ?]ⲧⲟⲡⲟⲥ ⲧⲁⲡⲗⲏ-
ⲣⲟⲩ ⲕⲙⲟⲕ [ⲛ]ⲙⲟⲟⲩ[|] ⲡⲕⲁ]ⲣⲟⲥ ⲉⲛϫⲱⲱⲗⲉ ⲛⲡⲕⲩ[?]ⲛⲥ ⲙⲁ°, ϣⲉ ⲛⲕⲁⲗⲟⲅⲥ ⲛⲏⲣⲡ [|]ⲙ ⲉⲓⲟ
ⲛⲟⲩⲟⲟⲓⲉ ⲉⲣⲟⲥ ⲉⲩⲙⲟⲩⲧⲉ ⲉ[ⲣⲟⲥ ϫⲉ ?] ⲛ]ⲕⲁⲗⲟⲅⲥ ⲛⲏⲣⲡ ϩⲙⲡⲥⲉⲛⲙⲙⲁ ⲛⲏ [|ⲡ]ⲙⲁ ⲛⲗⲉⲟⲛⲅⲏ ⲛⲏⲣⲡ
ⲛⲃⲃⲣⲉ ⲉⲛⲁ[ⲛⲟⲩⲅ ?]] ⲛⲁⲕ ⲉⲣⲟⲟⲩ ϣⲁⲧⲱϭⲉ ⲡⲉⲃⲟⲧ ⲛⲧ[|]ⲗⲱⲙⲛⲥⲉ ϣⲁⲕϭⲛⲧⲅ[1] ϩⲓⲱⲟⲩ
ⲉϥⲧ[?]] ⲕⲙⲟⲟⲩ ⲧⲁⲧⲁⲁⲩ ⲛⲁⲕ ⲛⲏⲣⲡ ⲉⲛⲁⲛ[ⲟⲩⲅ |] ⲛⲛⲡⲗⲏⲣⲟⲩ ⲕⲙⲟⲕ ⲛⲛⲏⲣ[ⲡ ?]ⲉⲡⲓ ⲧⲱ
ⲧⲁⲧⲓ ⲃⲧⲟⲟⲩ ⲛϩⲟⲗⲟⲕ[

Verso ⲉⲛⲱ]ϫ ⲡⲟⲩⲟⲟⲓⲉ ⲛϣⲉ ⲛⲡⲙⲙⲁⲕ, [space] [?]] illegible

207—Papyrus, complete; $11\frac{1}{2} \times 18$ cm   Script rarely ligatured   *Recto* ↑

Undertaking (ἀσφάλεια) by John and Athanasius, vinedressers, to repay to the κύρα
Eudoxô, daughter of the κόμης Theodoracius [2], 141 new (?) wine jars, whereof the former
will supply 53, the latter 88

+ ⲁⲛⲟⲕ ⲓⲱϩⲁⲛⲏⲥ ⲙⲛⲁⲑⲁⲛⲁⲥⲉ ⲛⲉϭⲙⲏⲅ ⲛⲧⲉ ⲡⲙⲟⲩⲟⲩⲏ ⲉⲓⲥϩⲁⲓ ⲛⲧⲉⲡϫⲟⲉⲓⲥ ⲕⲩⲣⲁ | ⲉⲩⲇⲟϫⲟⲩ
ⲧϣⲉ ⲛⲡⲙⲁⲕⲁⲣⲓⲟⲥ ⲡⲕⲟⲙⲉⲥ ⲑⲏⲩⲧⲱⲣⲁⲕⲏ ϫⲉⲧⲉⲛⲭⲣⲉⲱ^{sic}ⲥ | ⲛⲏⲧⲛ ⲕⲁⲑⲁⲣⲟⲥ ⲕⲁⲓ ⲁⲡⲟⲕⲣⲟⲧⲱⲥ ⲛϣⲉ
ϩⲙⲉ ⲙⲛⲟⲩⲅⲥ ⲛⲗⲁⲅⲩ ⲛⲕⲟⲩϥⲟⲛ | ⲛⲃ̄ⲣⲉ ⲁⲛⲟⲕ ⲙⲉⲛ ⲓⲱ[ϩⲁ]ⲛⲏⲥ ⲧⲓⲭⲣⲉⲱⲥⲧⲉ ⲛⲧⲁⲓⲟⲩ ⲙⲛϣⲟⲙⲧ |
ⲁⲩⲱ ⲁⲛⲟⲕ ⲁⲑⲁⲛⲁⲥⲉ ⲧⲓⲭⲣⲉⲱⲥⲧⲁ ⲛⲃⲧⲟⲟⲩ ⲛⲭⲟⲩⲱⲧⲉ ⲙⲛϣⲟⲙⲟⲩⲏ | ⲥⲩ, ⲕⲟⲩϥ· ⲙ̄^c3̄ ⲣ̄ⲙⲁ ⲕⲁⲓ
ⲧⲉⲛϣⲟⲟⲡ ϩⲉⲧⲟⲓⲙⲱⲥ ⲧⲉⲛⲧⲁⲁⲩ ⲛⲏⲧⲛ | [ⲛⲛ]ⲁⲩ ⲛⲓⲙ ⲉⲧⲛⲉⲟⲩ[ⲁϣ]ⲥ ⲛⲛⲁⲧϭⲁⲛ ⲛⲛⲁⲧⲛⲟⲙⲟⲥ | [ⲛⲛⲁ]ⲧ-
ⲗⲁⲁⲩ ⲛϩⲣⲱϥ ⲛⲛⲁⲙⲫⲓⲃⲟⲗⲉⲓⲁ + ⲉⲩⲣ^a ⲑⲱ: ⲅ ⲓⲛⲁ// ⲏ | ✝ ⲁⲛⲟⲕ ⲧⲁⲙⲓⲁⲛⲟⲥ ⲡⲧⲓⲁⲕⲟⲛ ⲧⲓⲟ
ⲕⲙⲛⲧⲣⲉ + ⲁⲛⲟⲕ ⲉⲛⲱϫ | ⲛϣⲉ ⲙⲡⲛⲟⲩⲧⲉ ⲛⲧⲁⲓⲥϩⲁⲓ ϩⲁⲣⲟⲟⲩ ϫⲉⲛⲥⲟⲩⲛⲟⲓⲉ ⲁⲛ | ⲁⲩⲱ ⲧⲓⲟ
ⲙⲙⲛ/ⲣ̄^c +

Verso ⲁⲥⲫⲁⲗ^a ⲛ^a ⲝ^a ⲓⲱ^a [space] (the rest illegible)

208.—Papyrus, a fragment, $11 \times 8\frac{1}{2}$ cm   Script sloping uncials   *Recto* ↑

Undertaking (? ἀσφάλεια) as to the supply of 40 jars of wine, to be delivered in
Mesore   The addressee bears apparently a title[4]

✝ ⲁⲛⲟⲕ ⲕⲟⲗⲑⲉ ⲛϣ[ⲉ | ⲉⲓⲥϩⲁⲓ ⲛⲡⲣⲱⲙϩⲧⲟ ⲁ[| ⲡⲣⲱⲙⲉ ϣⲙⲟⲩⲏ ⲟⲛ ϫⲉⲧ[| ϩⲙⲉ ⲛⲛⲁⲧⲟⲩⲥ
ⲛⲏⲣⲡ [| ϩⲟⲓⲧⲉⲙⲟⲥ ⲧⲁⲧⲁⲩ ⲛ[ⲁⲕ | [ⲛ]ⲁⲧⲏⲥ ⲓⲛⲁ/ ⲙⲛⲥⲟⲣ[| [ⲛ]ⲁⲙⲫⲓⲃⲟⲗⲓⲁ .ⲛⲡⲓ[| ⲥⲩⲱⲣϫ ⲛⲁⲕ
ⲟⲩⲛ ⲁⲓ[| ⲛⲁⲕ ⲁⲛⲟⲕ ⲕⲟⲗⲑⲉ ⲛⲡ[|]ⲗⲓⲁ ⲛⲧⲁⲓⲥϩⲁⲓ ⲉⲓⲥ[

Verso traces of an earlier text

---

[1] *Cf* KRALL xxix and VITELLI no 65, 13
[2] *Cf* ? no 129   [3] ? μοῦσθου, *v* KRALL ccxxxiv
[4] *Cf* KRALL xlviii and a letter here (*v* Index) In both
the personal follows ⲡⲣⲱⲙϩⲧⲟ, also in a fragment B₁
Mus Or 6201 A &c, while in another, Or 6201 B &c.

ⲡⲉϩⲧⲟ alone seems to be a title Perhaps = ἱππεύς But
is the form ⲣⲱⲙ- allowable, except with place-names ? In
Alexandria there was a bath named ὁ Ἵππος (LUMBROSO
in Clugnet's Βίος τοῦ Ἀββᾶ Δανιήλ, 113) Might this be
imitated thence ?

209.—Papyrus, a fragment, 19½ × 17 cm   Script large, few ligatures   *Recto* ↑.

Undertaking (ἀσφάλεια) by Theodore, as to the delivery of 1800 jars of wine, due at the vintage (καρπός) of the ensuing year, to be supplied from his own estate (κτῆμα). Theodore was his own scribe   One witness signs

] пэіакшн . [|]ре пршме щмоүн | хеіхрешстеі на]к каѳаршс | каі апокротшс
мптхмни нще | ккалоүс сі, каѕ/ ,аш | наі татааү нак нтеіромпе таі | есннү ппкарпос
мносѕонс м̊ | татааү нак ѕппактмма ѕітасфші¹ | епапооү еікінаүноү нак ерооү |
[. . . . . . щ]атшбе певот | [натлааү намфі]ьолеіа еіоьк | [мпноүте пантократшр
таріфүласе | [нак прос тѕом н]тіасфалеіа | еграф/ м ѳ м̊ ⲍ + анок ѳеодшре |
тістоіхеі етіасфалеіа аүш анок | аісѕаіс тнрс птаѕіх +   + анок пща | пр̅ нще мпмакаріос
колѳе пршме щмоүн | тіо мнтре +

Verso blank

210—Papyrus, a fragment, 11 × 20 cm   Script   moderately ligatured   *Recto* ↑

Undertaking (ἀσφάλεια) to supply wine, in its jars, at a valuation (?)²

]анок щепоүте та[.] щмоүн е   . мпрп н[| ѕппеүкоүфон ппщаар е[ч]ащшпе
. . . .   [| таті петепоүч нптн (above нѕах[а]р) натѕап натном[ос натл]ааү н[ам-
фіьолеіа [| таріфүласе нптн прос тѕом нтіа[сфал]еіа + еүр [| ссрнне пршме щмоүн
тістоіхеі етіа[сфал]еіа нѳе ес[снѕ | нще мпмакаріос бінтшр пршме щмоүн [| пмакаріос
ісак пршме щмоүн тіо мнтре +

211.—Papyrus, a fragment, 12½ × 13 cm   Script   few ligatures   *Recto* ↑

Undertaking as to supplying a material the nature of which is uncertain   perhaps flax   'Thy balance' (καμπανός) is mentioned.   It is due partly in Thoout, partly in Paope   The village Hwôr³ is named

мна]ктіонос ен ерм[оүпол]еі |] .пр[ш]мнтмме ѕоүшр ѕмптощ щ[м]оүн | тполіс
хеіхрешсті нак каѳаршс к[аі | п]оліс таі щмоүн ппекнампанос еретаро птаѕт⁴
ѕ[|]тммн нтоотк прос ѳе нтансүмфшнеі ерос нем[а]к а[|]ч еѕме [нлі]тра нлас нѕшке⁵
оүн тіо нѕетоімос ан[ок |] . .тпаще мен ѕіооү нѳооүт ткапаще хе кпаоп[е |

212.—Papyrus, a fragment, 14½ × 8½ cm   Script various   *Recto* ↑

Undertaking by Pgôl (Pkulis⁶) to supply something to the 'master' Phoebammon, the καρπώνης⁷, who recurs in nos 215, 216   It is to be delivered in Paône

---

¹ Unintelligible   ѕі-, in this and preceding word, ? for ѕп-

² *V* no 201

³ *V* here no 158

⁴ *Cf* ? ароү (fem), Rossi, *Pap* i, v 51, perhaps an instrument of torture   Here it is of lead

⁵ Epithet of flax, 'combed'? Or a noun, beginning a new clause?

⁶ The equation has not occurred hitherto   *Cf* Pegôsh=Pekusis.

⁷ *Cf*. Br Mus no 1060, also Kenyon, *Catal* iii 115, a καρπ officially appointed for Hermopolis.

πε]αϩ ϕοιβαμμων πκαρπωνες | παω]ηε ητειρομπε ται ϩ̄ ιηᴧ, | ϩετοιμαι ταοπογ
εροκ μπηᴧγ | ϳε ηογρωμε ηπεη ογατ[. . | ,ος †††
^{сμιон} + анок |] †о мμнтре +анок |
^{инκλιογ πρ/}
ε]ϩᴧισογ αγω †о мμнтре |]ηταϥ ϣμογη ηϩολοκο^τ, |

Verso + ασϕᴧλεια πϲω[ᴧ

213.—Papyrus, a fragment, 10 × 7½ cm   Script ligatureless   *Recto* ↑
Acknowledgment of a loan of (or debt for the price of) certain shirts[1] (καμίσιον)

] ϩηταχρια μεηταᴧη[ασκη [2] ρειсо ηποϭε ηκαμις[η | ηπμε[. .]ενερапᴧ[| ϣομτε ηποϭε
κᴧ[| ηπαρμϩοτη πεβοτ[| τατι ογτριᴧηειη ηατ[ᴧ | καριος αηογϥ πρ[

RECEIPTS

214.—Papyrus, a fragment, 13 × 21½ cm   Script *v* Pl 9   *Recto* ↑
Undertaking (ὁμολογία) by Antony, a deacon, not to make further claims (ἐνάγειν)
regarding 40 *solidi*, already paid
The signature of each witness is in a different hand.   One of them is an 'interpreter'

]ηϩολ[| ϩο]λοκοττιη ϩιωωογ εγϣαατ ᴧ[η | μηсоог εнаногог теног огн τιϩομολοϭει
ϫεᴧпеϩμε ηϩολ[οκοττιη]|ει ετοοτ ητεγϩε· ηπειϩοог ηογωτ ϫηπειενеϲе ηακ ϩᴧρооγ ο[γτе |
огте ϭεᴧᴧγ ηρωμε επωηε εγωρϫ ηᴧκ ᴧιсᴧη τιϩомоλоϭιа ηᴧ[κ | αγω[4] ερϣαηᴧнееηеϲе[5]
ηᴧκ ϩᴧрооγ тᴧᴧᴧη ηᴧмериᴧ[ноϲ[6] | ероϲ + μ̄′ π̄ ι αρ̄^χ· ἰ^χ/, γ + анτωнε пιελ/ ηᴧιᴧκ/ пϣιп-
ᴧᴧκαρ/ ϩηρᴧκλειᴧη πρωμϩ[| ϲ анок ηιϲеϩ птнркогмᴧη[8] тιо мμнтре ϲ + анок
ᴧггсκριτε[9] пϣе | ϑεоϩωре πρωμε ϣμогη †о мμнтре على

وسهد مسلم بن سار الهدى على
اربعس دسر دعها الى ادوده صاحب هو كانت لادنته | عبد سودرس ن فانه وس دري سودرس ن
فانه من اربعس دسر الى الى ادوده   Prof C H BECKER translates the Arabic (from a facsimile)
'Muslim[10] b Bashsher (?), from H   [11], testifies as to the 40 dinars, that he has paid
them to Antonius, magistrate of How (Diospolis)[12]   They were[13] to be required by
Ant of Severus b Bane, and now S b B is free[14] as to the 40 dinais (due) to
Antonius'

---

[1] *Lit* 'pieces of shirts'   Recurs in a PETRIE fragment (Dêr
Balaiza).   The precise qualification is obscure   Cf PARIS
131[6], 37 (of effeminate monks) сенᴧкω ηсωог ηπηоϭе
ηλεϩιτωη ηеоог (? ειᴧᴧγ *v Hist Laus* λλχιι) ηπᴧпᴧ-
χωριτηс пϲеᴧᴧιο пᴧг прсηϣтηι ηκорᴧϭен (? κοράκι-
νος) ϩιᴧολοχε (μολόχη) ϩιεᴧριειη (? ερᴧιη KIRCHER)
[2] V KRALL XXIX   [3] Cf Br Mus no 1037
[4] This line was inserted later
[5] The 3rd є was cancelled

[6] A fragment in Br Mus Or 6201 A &c, ᴧιcᴧιιе
ηᴧκ ητειᴧпоᴧеιϭιс еειρε (*sic*) ᴧᴧoк ηᴧᴧериᴧιноϲ
ϩᴧпειϩолок/
[7] V no 146
[8] 1 є نحم الرحمان
[9] 'Ασυγκράτιος   [10] B's reading
[11] B's reading   I prefer المدى=пρωме ϣмогη   Cf
KRALL iii ηᴧτηολιϲ
[12] I think distance would make this unlikely
[13] B's reading   [14] B's reading

P

215.—Papyrus, complete; 19 × 11½ cm　Script irregular, ligatureless. *Recto →*.

Receipt (ἀπόδειξις, ἐντάγιον) by Apa (A)môn, cucumber seller, of Hanepioor[1], to the 'master' Phoebammon, the καρπώνης of Shmoun[2], for half (the price of) the cucumbers from the (monastery) of St Phoebammon

+ φοιβαμων δεδωκ/ απο τησυκιλ[3] εφ ημισ　｜ ἤ αρ/ ας τε　?　｜ illegible ｜ τιμο
τι αν̅ στοι + ｜　　　　　　+ ⲁⲛⲟⲕ ⲁⲡⲁⲙⲱⲛ ⲡⲥⲁⲣⲃⲟⲛⲧⲉ[4] ⲡⲣⲱⲙ|ⲅ̅ⲁⲛⲉⲡⲓⲟⲟⲣ ⲉⲓⲥϩⲁⲓ
ⲛ̅ⲯⲁϩ ϥⲟⲓⲃⲁⲙⲙⲱⲛ ｜ ⲡⲕⲁⲣⲡⲱⲛⲏⲥ ⲡⲣⲱⲙⲉ ϣⲙⲟⲩⲛ ϫⲉⲁⲓϫⲓ ｜ ⲁⲩⲱ ⲁⲓⲡⲗⲏⲣⲟⲩ ⲛⲧⲟⲟⲧⲕ ⲛⲧⲡⲁϣⲉ
ⲛ̅|ⲧⲃⲟⲛⲧⲉ ⲛϥⲁⲥⲓⲟⲥ ϥⲟⲓⲃⲁⲙⲙⲱⲛ ｜ ⲉⲧⲉⲛⲁⲓⲛⲉ ⲟⲩϩⲟⲗⲟⲕⲟⲧⲧⲛ ⲟⲩⲥ̄ⲟⲥ ｜ + ⲅⲓ� ⲭⲣ ⲛ̅ ⲁⲥ ⲉⲅⲱⲣϫ
ⲛⲁⲕ ⲟⲩⲛ ⲁⲓⲥⲁⲛ ｜ ⲡⲓⲉⲛⲧⲁⲙⲛ ⲛⲁⲕ ⲉⲓⲥⲧⲟⲓⲭⲉⲓ ⲉⲣⲟⲥ̅ + ⲉⲅⲣ ⲙ̅ᵃ | ϩⲱⲃⲓ ⲁ ⲓⲏ̄/, β ┼┼┼ + ⲁⲛⲟⲕ
ⲁⲡⲁⲙⲱⲛ ｜ ⲧⲓⲥⲧⲟⲓⲭⲉⲓ ⲉⲧⲓⲁⲡⲟⲇⲉⲓⲍⲓⲥ ⲛⲑⲉ ⲉⲥⲥⲏϩ ⲛⲁⲥⲟⲥ + ｜ + ⲁⲛⲟⲕ ϣⲉⲛⲟⲩⲧⲉ ⲛⲧⲁⲓⲥϩⲁⲓ ϩⲁⲣⲟϥ ｜
ϫⲉⲛϥⲛⲟⲓ ⲁⲛ +

Verso + ⲉⲛⲧⲁⲅⲓ/　　ⲓ/ ϥⲟⲓβ　?　　?

216.—Papyrus, a fragment, 7½ × 13 cm　Script uneven, some ligatures　*Verso →*
Receipt by Victor, a carpenter, to the καρπώνης (v last no.), for 2 *solidi* towards (?) the price of the crop (καρπός) from the orchard (πωμάριον) of the προάστειον[5]

+ ⲁⲛⲟⲕ ⲃⲓⲕⲧⲱⲣ ϥⲁⲙϣⲉ ⲉⲓⲥϩⲁⲓ ⲛ̅ⲯⲁϩ ϥⲟⲓⲃⲁⲙⲙⲱ[ⲛ] ｜ ⲡⲕⲁⲣⲡⲱⲛ/ ϫⲉⲉⲛ ϩⲟⲗⲟⲕ/ ⲥⲛⲁⲩ
ⲛⲛⲟⲩⲃ ⲁⲅⲥⲓ ⲧⲟⲟⲧ ｜ ⲉϩⲣⲁⲓ ⲉⲧⲧⲓⲙⲛ ⲛⲡⲕⲁⲣⲡⲟⲥ ⲛ̄ⲡⲡⲱⲙⲁⲣⲓ ⲉⲛⲡⲣⲟⲁⲥⲧⲓⲟⲛ[6] ⲛⲡⲟ[ⲇ] ｜ ⲉⲧⲉⲥⲟⲩ-
ⲙⲛⲧⲟⲩⲉⲉⲡⲉ ⲛⲡⲁϣⲛⲉ ⲡⲉⲃⲟⲧ ⲛⲧⲓⲣⲟⲙⲡⲉ ⲧⲁ[ⲓ] ｜ ⲉⲕⲧⲏⲥ ⲓⲛⲁϩᵒ ⲅⲓ ⲭⲣ ⲛ̄ β ⲉⲅⲣ ⲙ̅́ ⲡ̅ ᵛ ⲁ ⲓᵟ/ +[7] ┼┼┼
+ ⲁⲛⲟⲕ ｜ ⲃⲓⲕⲧⲱⲣ ϥ[ⲁⲙ]ϣⲉ ⲧⲓⲥⲧⲟⲓⲭⲉⲓ +

Recto remains of a letter, ⲕⲣⲡⲕⲟⲥ̄ ⲛϩⲱⲥϥ ⲧⲉⲕⲧⲓ legible

217—Papyrus, almost complete, 21 × 13 cm　Script clumsy, ligatureless　*Recto →*
Receipt by Benjamin for various articles

+ ⲁⲛ[ⲟⲕ ⲃⲥⲗⲓⲁ]ⲙⲓⲛ ⲉⲓⲥϩⲁⲓ ⲛⲧⲁⲥⲱⲛ ｜ (added above ⲃⲓⲕ[ )ⲑⲉ[. . ϩⲙ]ϥⲱⲃ ⲛⲧⲁⲥϥⲁⲗⲓⲁ ｜
ⲙⲡⲉⲛⲁⲩ ⲟⲩⲥ̄ⲟⲥ ⲛϩⲟⲗⲟⲕⲟⲧⲧⲛ ｜ ⲡⲉⲥⲛⲁⲩ ⲛ[.]ⲥ ⲁⲩⲱ ⲧⲡⲁϣⲉ ｜ ⲙⲙⲁⲧⲛⲥⲉ ⲉⲓⲥ ⲟⲩϩⲟⲓⲧⲉ ⲁⲥⲉⲓ ｜
ⲉⲧⲟⲟⲧ ϩⲁⲟⲩⲡⲁϣⲉ ⲛϩⲟⲗⲗⲟⲕⲧⲧ ｜ ϩⲙⲡⲱⲃ ⲛⲧⲁⲥϥⲁⲗⲓⲁ ｜ ⲁⲩⲱ ⲟⲩⲡⲁⲗⲗⲓⲛ ϩⲁϥϫⲥ ⲥⲛ|ⲕⲉⲣⲁⲧ̄ⲓ
ϩ[ⲟ]ⲙⲁⲓⲟⲥ ⲟⲛ ⲟⲩⲡⲉⲛ|ⲧⲉⲛⲧⲏⲥ ⲙ̄ⲙⲟⲛⲟⲭⲟⲥ ϩⲁⲟⲩⲧⲉⲣᶜ̄ ｜ ⲟⲙⲉⲓⲟⲥ ⲟⲩⲡⲁϣⲧⲉⲣ̄ⲙⲉⲥⲛ ⲛ̄ⲃⲏⲧ ｜
ⲟⲙⲉⲟⲩⲥ ⲕⲉⲛⲧⲉⲛⲁⲣⲓⲟⲛ ⲥⲛⲁⲩ ｜ ⲛϣⲉⲃⲛⲏⲉ [ⲁ]ⲛⲟⲕ ⲃⲥⲗⲓⲁⲙ̄[ⲛ] ｜ ⲉⲓⲥⲧⲏⲭⲉⲓ ϩⲣⲁⲓ ϩⲙ̄ϥⲱⲃ ⲙ̄|ⲡⲉⲥⲛⲁⲩ
ⲟⲩⲥ̄ⲟⲥ ⲛϩⲟⲗⲟⲕⲟ[ⲧⲧ]ⲛ ｜ ⲉⲓⲥ ⲛⲁⲓ ⲁⲅⲉⲓⲉⲓ ⲉⲧⲟⲟⲧ

---

[1] Recurs in a letter here (*v* Index)
[2] *V* nos 212, 216
[3] Σικνήλατον　But a fem is wanted here
[4] Recurs in no 235　Is it a variant of ⲥⲁ ⲛ̄-? *Cf.* ⲥⲁⲣⲏϩ CLÉDAT, *Baouît* ii 160, Pl cviii, apparently a

monastic official, also in Br Mus Or 6201 B &c
[5] A south and a north orchard occur in VITELLI no 50
[6] Corrected
[7] The two dates are hard to reconcile　Instead of the cross, perhaps ⲟ

'I, Beḥamın (Benjamın), wrıte to my sıster,   In regard to the matteı of the
agreement (ἀσφάλεια) as to the 2½ *solıdı*, the[1] 2   and the half   [2], lo, a garment
has reached me, worth a ⅓ *solıdus*, as regards the agreement (ἀσφ), and a cloak (παλλίον)
woıth 9 carats, *ıtem* (ὁμοίως) a monk's cloak (? ἐπενδύτης) worth a *tremısıon*, *ıtem* a ½ *tremısıon*-
worth of palm-branches, *ıtem* 2 *centenarıa* of palm-fibre[3] I, Beḥamın, assent (στοιχεῖν) ın
regard to the matter of the 2½ *solıdı*.   Lo, they have reached me'

DOUBTFUL

218.—Papyrus, a fragment, 8½ × 9½ cm. Scrıpt lıgatureless. *Recto* ↑
     Probably from the begınnıng of a legal document   Thε person mentıoned ıs from
Sbêht[4] (Lower Apollınopolıs)

]пще нпшакᷓ фоіβа[ллιωн | прωлесвнϩт тпο[λιс

219.—Papyrus, a fragment, 9½ × 7 cm   Scrıpt lıgatureless   *Recto* ↑
     Begınnıng of a document by the κοινόν of ɑ church or monastery

ϯ пкоιпωн є[| лениωснϕ [| пще нвιнт[ωр | лентапноүт[є | (space) ϯ сенпаλн п[|
фоіβаллιωн [

220.—Papyrus, a ɬragment, 2½ × 13 cm   Scrıpt moderately lıgatured   *Recto* ↑
     Document from the δίκαιον of St Phoebammon's monastery[5], represented by a deacon

+ паικαιοп етоүаав нϕασιос фо[ιβαλλιωн |. пι]еλаᵡ наιак, еісϧаι напост[

221—Papyrus, a fragment, 14 × 14 cm   Scrıpt of Greek type, lıgatuıed   *Recto* ↑
     The σημεῖα of Dıonysıus and Agenê, authors of a legal document

Besıde these, апа ϯ ᵃϯ паллоппнсιο and below thıs, ϧаро]үт хеллаүпоι аүω тιο
шлетре +

---

[1] Or ? ипеспаү, '(ın payment) for the 2'
[2] Greek?
[3] Used for monk's clothıng (шүнн нщ), Parıs 131[6],
37   Hence σεβένιον
[4] Dêr Balaιϻa, whence a group of documents came
(ʋ Crum ın Petrıe's *Gızeh and Rıfeh*), ıs there repeatedly
called 'the monastery of the ἄγιος Apa Apollo, ın the νομός
of the πόλις Sbêht,' a town otherwise ıdentıfied wıth the

Lower Apollınopolıs (Amélıneau, *Géogr* 463)   The sıte
oɬ the latter ıs thus fixed at the present Kôm Esfaht, 8 m.
further South   W Max Müller had proposed Sbêht=
Edfu (*Rec* xxı 199)
[5] *V* no 125
[6] *V* Br Mus no 1013 and p 521
[7] Unıntellıgıble, as Agenê ıs masculıne (ʋ no 173) Can
тa- here be that whıch follows the other names ?

LISTS AND ACCOUNTS

222.—Papyrus, complete, 30 × 17 cm   Script small, ligatureless   *Recto* ↑

A List (λόγος) in 30 lines, being the names of those who are to pay the poll tax[1] ⲉⲩⲧⲓ ⲁⲛⲧⲣⲓⲥⲙⲟⲥ, for the 8th Indiction   All names are double, the second being usually that of the father   Each is followed by ⲟⲩⲧⲣⲙⲏⲥⲓⲛ (or ⲧⲉⲣⲙⲏⲥⲓⲛ) and ⲛ̄ ⲅ̇,   Remarkable among the names are ⲅⲁⲣⲟⲟⲩ[2], ϭⲁⲛⲁⲅ[3], ⲡⲥⲓⲛⲗⲁⲣⲏⲥ, ⲡⲉⲧⲣⲁ, ⲓⲱⲅⲁⲏⲏⲥ ⲡⲉⲙⲡⲟ[4] ⲕⲟⲗⲟⲕⲟⲉⲩⲥ, ⲫⲱⲕⲁ, ⲡⲉⲣⲓⲉⲓⲃ, ⲥⲓⲕⲓⲁⲥ ϣⲏⲛⲟⲩⲧⲉ, ⲡⲁⲛⲅⲁⲗⲱⲙⲁ[5], ϣⲉⲧⲱⲣ, ⲡⲥⲁⲅⲁ, ⲁⲡⲁ ⲕⲓⲣⲉ ⲡⲥⲁⲭⲟ ⲁⲙ̇[6], ⲡⲉⲕⲡⲟ ⲧⲁⲕⲏⲗ, ⲕⲁⲗⲉⲫⲟⲣⲉ   The last 3 lines are ⲁⲩⲱ ⲧⲉⲣⲙⲏⲥⲓⲛ ⲥⲛⲁⲩ ⲃⲉⲅⲉ [about 15 let] | ⲁⲩⲧⲓ ⲁⲡⲟⲟⲩⲧⲉ[7] ⲉⲡⲟⲩⲁ ⲡⲟⲩⲁ ⲉⲥⲣⲁⲫ,   ? | ⲥⲓ, ⲭⲣ, ⲛ̄ ⲑ ⲕⲁⲓ ⲛ̄ ⲥ,, after which some words have been erased or are in a fainter ink

Verso   Remains of another List of names, in a different hand   Legible are ⲓⲱⲅⲁⲏⲏⲥ ⲡ̇ⲁⲛⲧⲏⲧϥ[8], ⲡⲉⲧⲣⲁ ⲡⲣⲱⲙⲉ ⲅⲟ., ⲡⲁⲛⲅⲁⲗⲱⲙⲁ

223—Papyrus, a fragment, 15 × 25 cm   Two texts   Script of (*a*) Greek, of (*b*) sloping semi-uncials   Fibres on (*a*) ↑

(*a*) Remains of an Account, wherein the following names &c occur   ]ⲁⲡⲁ ηλιας,]ⲁⲣⲧⲟⲕⲟⲡⲟⲩ, φιβ γναφεως εις τουω[9], πηλις[10] κ/ πετρο̅ απο νησου[11], κερμαεις στρατ/ ὑ ἐλυκας, παυλος οικονο/ απο νησου, ανουφ/ αλισου, του μαρτυρ/, των πεντη   Opposite each is a numeral, preceded by ϧ/[12]

(*b*) The Coptic consists of pen-trials   ⲁⲛⲟⲕ ⲫⲏⲃⲁⲙⲙⲱⲛ several times, Psalm l 1–3 (incorrectly) ⲛⲁ ⲕⲁⲓ ⲡⲕⲟⲩⲧⲉ ⲕⲁⲧⲁ ⲡⲕⲕⲟϭ ⲕⲡⲁ ⲕⲁⲧⲁ ⲡⲁϣⲁⲓ ⲕⲧⲉⲕⲙⲕⲧϣⲁⲛⲟⲧⲏϭ ϥ̄ⲱⲧⲉ ⲉⲃⲟⲗ ⲙⲡⲁⲕⲟⲃⲉ ⲓⲁⲁⲧ ⲉⲃⲟⲗ ⲅⲛ̄ⲧⲁⲁⲕⲟⲙⲓⲁ ϫⲉϯⲥⲟⲟⲩⲛ ⲁⲛⲟⲕ ⲙⲡⲁⲕⲟⲃⲉ ⲁⲩⲱ ⲧⲁⲁⲕⲟⲙⲓⲁ ⲙⲡⲁⲙⲧⲟ ⲉⲃⲟⲗ ⲕⲟⲩⲟⲉⲓϣ ⲕⲓⲙ, epistolary formulas [+ ⲅⲁⲑⲏ] ⲕϥⲱϥ ⲕⲓⲙ ϯϣⲓⲕⲉ ⲁⲥⲡⲁⲍⲉ ⲙⲡⲉⲅⲗⲟϭ ⲛⲧⲉⲕ &c

---

[1] *V* no 120   This view of ἀνδρισμος is proposed by H I BELL

[2] *Cf* Ⲁⲣⲟⲟⲩ, Br Mus no 1075

[3] *Cf* ⲕⲁⲛⲁⲅ, *l c*, 386

[4] 'The dumb man'   Its recurrence below shows it not to be a name

[5] Followed by 'his son', so must be a name   Recurs on *verso*

[6] ἀμπελουργος

[7] Plur of ⲁⲡⲟⲧ?

[8] Reading certain   Appears to be a trade-name

[9] Same form in KRALL cxvi   But there it is a nome-capital, here probably *cf* the village Ⲧⲟⲟⲩ, KENYON, *Catal* III 111, VITELLI no 50 &c

[10] *Cf* ⲡⲉⲗⲓⲥ, Br Mus no 438, ⲡⲉⲗⲉⲓⲥ *Recueil* xv 3

[11] Not known in the Hermopolite district

[12] ἀρταβη

224.—Papyrus, complete, $31\frac{1}{2} \times 8$ cm   Script ligatured   *Recto* →
'List of names, apparently of monastic officials   Each occupies a separate line

⳨ ⲙⲏⲛⲁⲥ ⲡⲣⲉⲥ⳰, ⲁⲡⲁ ⲅⲁⲟⲟⲣ[1] ⲡⲣⲉⲥ⳰, ⲁⲡⲁ ⲍⲁⲭⲉⲅⲧ ⲡⲣⲉⲥ⳰, ⲁⲡⲁ ⲡⲁⲩⲗⲟⲥ ⲡⲣⲉⲥ⳰, ⲁⲡⲁ
ⲓⲱⲁⲛⲛⲏⲥ ⲡⲣ/, ⲁⲡⲁ ⲑⲉⲟⲇⲱⲣⲟⲥ ⲡⲣⲉⲥ⳰, ⲑⲉⲟⲇⲱⲣⲟⲥ ⲇⲓⲁⲕ/, ⲁⲡⲟⲗⲗⲱⲛⲓⲟⲥ ⲇⲓⲁⲕ/, ⲁⲇⲣⲓⲁⲛⲟⲥ ⲇⲓⲁⲕ/,
ⲁⲛⲧⲓⲛⲟⲟⲥ ⲇⲓⲁⲕ/, ⲃⲓⲕⲧⲱⲣ ⲡⲣⲉⲥ⳰, ⲁⲑⲁⲛⲁⲥⲓⲟⲥ ⲇⲓⲁⲕ/, ⲯⲁⲧⲏⲥ ⲇⲉⲩⲧⲉⲣ/,[2] ⲉⲥⲛⲟⲩⲑⲏⲥ ⲇⲉⲩⲧⲉⲣ/,
ⲁⲡⲁ ⲡⲁⲗⲱⲥ[3], ⲁ[   ], ⲃⲓⲕⲧⲱⲣ ⲟ ⲧⲏⲥ ⲗⲉⲯⲟⲕ/,[4] ⲫⲟⲓⲃⲁⲙⲙⲱⲛ ⲑⲩⲣ/,[5] ⲓⲱⲁⲛⲛⲏⲥ ⲁⲡ
ⲛⲟⲥⲟⲕⲟⲙ,[6] ⲓⲱⲁⲛⲛⲏⲥ ⲟ ⲧⲏⲥ ⲗⲉⲯⲓ.], ⲁⲡⲁ ⲓⲁⲕⲱ⳰ [   ], ⲕⲁⲗⲗⲓⲛⲓⲕⲟⲥ ⲧⲉⲕⲧ/,[7] ⲡⲁⲛⲁⲭⲱⲣⲉ,
ⲁⲧⲁⲱⲛⲓⲛⲉ[8].

225.—Papyrus, complete, 25×14 cm   Script small, Greek type   *Recto* →
List of names, possibly relating to a tax on goldsmiths[9]

[χρ]υσοχοων απο[10] ιζ̅ⲥ̅ ⲛ̅ ι̅θ̅ⲋ̅   Then these names, in 10 lines, with two sums of money
opposite each   ⲓⲥⲁⲕⲓⲟ ⲕⲟⲥⲙ, ⲥⲧⲉⲫⲁⲛ ⲡⲣⲉⲥ⳰, ⲑⲉⲟⲇⲱⲣⲟ ⲡⲉⲧⲣⲟ, ⲫⲟⲓⲃ ⲡⲉⲧⲣⲟ, ⲁⲡⲁ ⲕⲧ ⲡⲉⲧⲣⲟ,
ⲁ . ⲥ ⲕⲟⲥⲙ, ⲅⲉⲱⲣⲅⲓ ⲁⲃⲁⲥⲧ,[11] ⲁⲙⲙⲱ ⲁⲓ, ⲥⲧⲉⲫ/ ⲛⲣ, ⲍⲁⲭⲁⲣⲓ ⲥⲉⲛⲟⲩ, ⲁⲡⲟⲗⲗⲱ ⲃⲓⲕⲧ, ⲁⲡ[12] ⲫⲓⲗⲛⲙⲱⲛ.
Below these, in a Coptic hand, ⳨ ⲁⲛⲟⲕ ⲥⲧⲉⲫⲁⲛⲉ ⲡⲣ̄ⲉ ⲙⲛⲑⲉⲟⲇⲱⲣⲉ ⲧⲓⲥⲧⲟⲓ̄ˣ ⳨

226.—Papyrus, complete, $17\frac{1}{2} \times 11$ cm   Script small, ligatured   *Recto* ↑
'List (γνῶσις) of the men that have not paid the κλάσμα[13], from among the ⁱ⁴,'
followed by the names of 5 men   Then, 'This is (the money) that has been extracted in
the year, for the registration (καταγραφη)[15], having been previously fixed as regards
Sarapamon'   The third section seems to relate to money paid[16]

⳨ ⲧⲉⲩⲛ ⲛⲛⲉⲣⲱⲙⲉ ⲛⲡⲟⲩⲧⲓ ⲕⲗⲁⲥⲙⲁ | ϩⲛⲛⲉⲓⲟⲟⲩⲛ | ⲥⲁⲣⲁⲡⲁⲙ ϩⲱⲣ | ⲓⲟⲩⲥⲧⲁ ⲥⲁⲣⲁⲡⲁⲙⲱⲛ |
ⲡⲟⲩⲥ ⲥⲁⲣⲁⲡⲁⲙⲱⲛ | ⲯⲉⲛⲟⲩⲧⲉ ⲥⲁⲣⲁⲡⲁⲙⲱⲛ | ⲓⲟⲩⲥⲧⲁ ⲙⲏⲛⲁ | ⲟⲓⲛ ⲉ |

⳨ ⲛⲁⲓ ⲕⲉⲛⲧⲁⲩⲧⲟⲩ ⲉⲃⲟⲗ ⲛⲧⲣⲟⲙⲡⲉ | ϩⲓⲧⲕⲁⲧⲁⲅⲣⲁⲫⲏ ⲛⲧⲁⲩⲟⲩⲱ ⲉⲩⲥⲙⲛⲧⲟⲩ | ϩⲁⲥⲁⲣⲁⲡⲁⲙⲱⲛ ⲁⲡⲟ ⲛⲁ̅ⲥ ⲛ̅ⲥ ⲕⲟⲩⲫ ⲛ̅ ⲁ |

⳨ ⲛⲁⲓ ⲕⲉⲛⲧⲁⲩⲧⲁⲗⲟ ⲉⲣⲟⲟⲩ | ϩⲁⲕⲩⲣⲓⲁ ⲛ̅ ⲅ̅ ϩⲁⲥϣⲟⲩ ⲛ̅ ⲅ̅ | ϩⲁⲙⲏⲛⲁ ⲛ̅ ⲅ̅ ⲅⲓ ⲛ̅ ⲁ

---

[1] Recurs here (v Index) and (? ⲁⲅⲟⲟⲣ) REVILLOUT, *Actes* 100   Cf Aⲅⲟⲣ, Br Mus no 1075, and Ἀκῶρις
[2] δευτεράριος
[3] Recurs KENYON *Catal* ii 326
[4] I cannot identify this
[5] θυρωρός   [6] νοσοκομεῖον, v Br Mus no 1077
[7] τέκτων   [8] Not ⲁⲡⲁ ⲙⲱⲛⲓⲛⲉ
[9] An instance from prechristian times, WILCKEN, *Gr Ostr* i 403
[10] Or α̅π̅ ⲛ̅
[11] Cf Br Mus no 1075, Αβα Στεκς

[12] Ἀγενις?
[13] In Br Mus no 605 this occurs in connection with the ἐμβολή (sic) tax   The Br Mus Aphroditô (Jkôw) papyri use κλάσματα as 'items' or 'details' of a καταγραφή, tax-register (H I BELL)
[14] Unknown word, found in KRALL lxxviii, xciv, and in a letter here (v Index)   Name of a trade or office Mr GRIFFITH suggests 'bath-man', cf ⲥⲓⲟⲟⲩ-ⲛ
[15] V KRALL iii
[16] The precise meanings of ⲧⲁⲗⲟ are yet to be distinguished

227.—The same MS as no 40

Verso An earlier text, in a small hand, was an Account containing the following names, several of which are uncommon ⲙⲓⲛⲁ ϩⲉⲣⲏⲥ, ⲓⲁϩⲁⲛⲏⲥ ⳨ ⲗⲉϣⲓ[1], ⲁⲡ[ⲁ ⲕ]ⲓⲣⲓ ⲡⲁⲙⲁⲣⲏⲥ ϩⲁⲧⲙⲟⲓⲥⲓⲣ[2], ⲁⲡⲟ ⲥⲓⲣⲓ ⳨ ⲙⲉⲣⲛⲟⲣⲉ ⳨ ⲱⲅⲗⲟϩⲏⲩ[3], ⲡⲁⲙⲓⲛ ⳨ ⲥⲱⲙⲟⲟⲛ, ⲥⲓⲱⲛ, ⲃⲓⲕⲧⲱⲣ ⲡⲁϩⲁⲙⲓⲟⲟⲣ[4], ⲡϣⲟⲙ ⲁⲡⲟ ⲧⲁϩⲣ· ⲡⲥⲁⲭⲟ[5] ϩⲙⲃⲁⲧⲙⲉⲛⲉ . . ⲣⲉ

228.—Papyrus; a fragment, $4\frac{1}{2} \times 4\frac{1}{2}$ cm   Script small, some ligatures   *Verso →*.
From a List of names

⸱ ⲅⲁⲓⲟⲥ ⲛ̅ⲣ̅ ⲁⲁⲣⲓⲁⲛ ⸱[| ⲁⲃⲓⲭⲉⲣ [| ⲁⲁⲣⲓⲁⲛⲟⲥ ⲧⲁⲙⲟⲧ[|

Recto   ]ⲉϥⲉ ⲓⲉⲍⲓⲁ[6] · ⲁⲁⲣⲓⲁⲛⲉ [and traces of an earlier text

229—Papyrus, a fragment, $6\frac{1}{2} \times 7\frac{1}{2}$ cm   Script small, ligatured   *Verso →*
A List of names, followed each by obscure words

]ⲕⲁ ⲁϩ[| ⲡⲉⲗⲟⲟ .   ⲁ ⲁϩⲥⲏⲧⲁⲛ [| ⲁⲛⲟⲩⲡ ϩⲟⲩⲙⲛⲟⲩ ⲁϩⲥⲏ (sic) [| . . . . . . ⲟⲙⲉⲛ ⲁϩⲥⲏⲧⲁⲛ[|
ⲕⲟⲩⲗⲟⲉ ⲅⲉⲟⲣ ⲁϩⲥⲏⲧⲁⲛ ⲟⲁⲙⲉ |

230—Papyrus, a fragment, 15×7 cm   Script ligatured, irregular   *Recto →*
From a List of names, in 2 (or more) columns   Among the few legible are ⲡⲕⲩⲗⲓⲥ[8], ⲡⲁⲙⲓⲛ, ⲓⲟⲩⲥⲧⲉ, ϩⲁⲧⲣⲉ.

231.—Cloth of pink colour[9], $7 \times 8\frac{1}{2}$ cm   Script large, clumsy uncials
Apparently three names   ⲙⲁⲛⲧⲓϩⲏ[10] | ⲁⲡⲁ ⲕⲟⲗⲟⲉ | ⲕⲁⲥⲃ[11] | Above ! 1 the cloth is folded once or twice and tacked down

232.—Papyrus, a fragment, $13\frac{1}{2} \times 12$ cm   Script ligatureless, except 1st line
Recto →. Not from the Ashmunaïn collection

An Account relating to taxation

---

[1] *Cf* ? ⲡⲁϣⲉ.
[2] ⲙⲁⲣⲏⲥ seems to be further south than Shmoun, *v* Br Mus nos 1153, 1154   With next *cf* ? Τεμσῖρις, WESSELY, *Studien* v, no 9
[3] *Cf* ? *Journ As*, 1888, 372, ⲡⲓⲗϩⲏⲩ, *Führ Rain* no 684, Pilheu, assuming a misreading in our text
[4] *Cf* حبور, Br Mus no. 865 n

[5] ابو طاهر ?
[6] *V* no 129
[7] يزيد
[8] *V* no 212
[9] *Cf* the RAINER *Führer*, 1894 p 12
[10] Or -ⲥⲓϩⲏ
[11] Or -ⲥⲱ or -ⲥⲙ (قاسم ?)

+ λογ ετπρ̄θ, απ̄ δημσι̇̈ ϩ ανδρισμου πεμτη[ϛ ῑν̣̇], followed by names with sums of money opposite each. Among them . ⲯⲏⲓ̇ϩⲱⲣ[1], ⲥⲁⲗⲱⲙ[2], ⲧⲉϭⲣⲟⲙⲡⲉ[3], ϥⲱⲕⲁ, ⲡⲉϭⲱϣ, ⲥⲁⲣⲉ[4], ⲡⲁϥⲟⲣⲉ.

233.—The *verso* of no 167

An Account (λόγος)

+ ⲡⲁⲙⲡⲉ ⲡⲗⲟⲩⲟⲥ ⲕⲡ[ⲏ]ⲧⲓⲥⲁⲧⲟ ⲉϩⲣⲁⲓ̇ ⲛ̇ⲥⲱⲩ[6] + | ⳗ[7] ϭⲉⲱⲣⲧⲉ | The following names and words have each a sum of money (ⲛ̄) and an amount of corn (ⲥ̄ⲧ ⲁ̄ⲣ) opposite them ⲙⲟⲛⲉ ⲙⲛ̄ⲍⲁⲭⲁⲣⲓⲁⲥ, ⲕⲟⲗⲑⲉ ⲑⲁⲡⲁⲥⲓⲁ, ⲥⲙ̄ⲡⲥⲟⲩϭⲉ, ϥⲓϥ, ⲉϩⲱⲧⲉ, ⲁⲡⲁⲕⲩⲣⲉ, ϩⲁⲩⲥⲁⲓ.

234.—Paper, a fragment, 14 × 11½ cm   Script of ZOEGA's 9th class

An Account, very obscure in detail   It shows Muslim names, and numerals (? money), with dates, and other words

ϩⲙ̄ⲡⲣⲁⲛ ⲉⲡⲛⲟⲩⲧⲉ ⲡϣⲟⲣⲡ ϩⲱⲃ[8] | ⲡϣⲟⲣⲡ ⲛϩⲟⲟⲩ: ⲉⲧⲁⲱϩ ⲡⲉ | ⲡⲟⲩⲱϣ ϩⲓⲡⲁⲃⲉ ⲙⲁⲥⲉ: | ⲡⲉⲡⲥⲓⲧⲉ ⲛⲁϭⲟⲧⲉ[9]: ⲥⲁⲧⲁⲕⲉ[10] | ⲁϭⲟⲧⲉ: ⲁ: ⲁⲡⲟⲩⲗⲟⲩϭⲉⲣ[11]: ⲁ: | ⲙⲉϩⲟⲙⲉⲧ[12]: ⲉⲓ: | ⸢ⲕⲁⲑⲉ ⲟⲩⲙⲛ̄ⲧⲉ ⲛⲁϭⲟⲧⲉ | ⲥⲁⲧⲁⲕⲉ —✝: ⲁⲡⲟⲩⲗⲟⲩ|ϭⲉⲣ: —✝ ⲡⲣⲁⲥⲧⲉ | [ⲓ̈ⲣⲁ: ⲏ: ⲥⲁⲧⲁⲕⲉ: ⲁϭⲟⲧⲉ | [ⲁ]ⲡⲟⲩⲗⲟⲩϭⲉⲣ: ⲁ: ⲙⲉϩⲟⲙⲉⲧ | [—]✝: ⲁⲡⲟⲩⲗⲟⲩϭⲉⲣ |]: ⲥⲁⲧⲁⲕⲉ | [

235—Papyrus, a fragment, 12½ × 15 cm   Script ligatured   *Recto* and *verso* uncertain

An Account, consisting of names with numerals opposite each   Among them ⲕⲟⲗⲗ̇ ⲁⲣⲭⲉⲗⲗⲓ̄, ⲱⲣ ⲛ̄ⲗⲓⲁⲥ, ⲥⲓⲱⲛ, ⲭⲁⲏⲗ, ⲙⲟ̄ⲡ ⲯⲁⲣⲃⲟⲏⲓ̄[13], ⲱⲙⲓⲥⲉ, ⲙⲉⲣⲕⲩ, ⲉⲓⲥⲁⲕ, ⲡⲓⲗⲉⲓⲑⲉⲟⲥ, ϩⲁϭⲉϭ[14], ⲡⲉϭⲱϣ.

236.—Papyrus, a fragment, 13½ × 12 cm   Script v Pl **7**   *Verso* →

An Account of 13 names with numerals opposite each   Among them are ⲧⲉⲗⲉⲙⲏ, ⲑⲉⲟⲇⲱⲣ (ⲱⲓⲟ), ⲓ̇ⲟⲩⲥⲉⲟ[15], then 'the total' ⲧⲁⲗϭⲟⲙⲗⲉ[16], and after this, ϫⲟⲣⲡⲉ ⲛ̄ⲕⲓⲣⲁⲕⲏ ⲣⲕ ⲧⲙⲉϩⲥⲛⲏⲧⲉ ⲛ̄ⲕⲓⲣⲁⲕⲏ, ⲡⲁⲡϩⲏⲩ[17], ⲁϫⲙⲏⲧ[18]. At bottom of the list, ⲡⲉⲛⲧⲁⲛ̄ⲥⲉⲡⲉ[19] ⲁⲣ̊ ⲁ

Recto remains of an Arabic text (earlier)

---

[1] ' Son of Horus '? Perhaps in a letter here (v Index, ϩⲱⲣ), v SPIEGELBERG, *Eigennamen*, p 33 (7)

[2] V CRUM, *Ostr* no 51

[3] Τεκρομπιας, Br Mus no 1077 and Or 6212

[4] V Br Mus no 580

[5] V p 56 n 6 above

[6] Cf ? Br Mus. no 580 for a similar name

[7] διά

[8] *Suppl* ? ⲛⲓⲙ

[9] Scarcely ⲁϭⲟⲗⲧⲉ, as it occurs often

[10] ؟ صدقة

[11] ؟ ابو الورر

[12] محمد

[13] 'The cucumber-seller'   V no 215

[14] حجاج

[15] يوسف

[16] الجملة

[17] ? ⲁⲡⲁ ⲡϩⲏⲩ

[18] احمد

[19] Not ⲁϥ- or ⲁⲃ-

237—Paper, a fragment, $5\frac{1}{2} \times 7\frac{1}{2}$ cm　Script　rough uncials
From a List of names with numeral opposite each

] ⲁⲓⲁ ⲑⲟⲩⲛⲁ[1]—β |]ⲛⲧⲥⲏⲣⲭⲏ[2]--β |]ⲣⲕⲉ—α | ⲁⲓⲁ ⲡⲁⲡⲟⲣⲉ[3]—γ | ⲫⲓⲗⲟⲑⲉ—α |
ⲟⲩⲉⲛⲟ]ⲃⲣⲓ—β |

Verso Arabic account

238.—Papyrus, complete, $45\frac{1}{2} \times 18\frac{1}{2}$ cm　3 *selis*-joints, 15 cm apart　Script small, regular (*cf* CRUM, *Coptic MSS*, pl 3, XIV)　*Recto* ↑

Inventory of the movable property of a church of St Theodore, presumably at Ashmunain[4]　Its author, Ignatius, perhaps recurs in TURAIEF, *Materialie*, no 7　Several of the objects are difficult to identify

```
+ ϩⲙⲡⲟⲩⲱϣ ⲙⲡⲛⲟⲩⲧⲉ ⲡⲁⲓⲡⲉ ⲡⲓⲙⲃⲉⲛⲧⲟⲛ ⲙⲫⲁⲅⲓ ⲑⲉⲟⲇⲱⲣ
  ⲙⲡⲕⲁⲕⲁⲣⲏ ϩⲓⲧⲟⲟⲧϥ ⲙⲡⲁⲓⲁⲕ, ⲓ[ⲥⲛⲁⲧ]ⲉ ⲙⲡⲟⲟⲩ ] ⲥⲟⲩ-[5]
  ⲙⲛⲧⲁⲥⲉⲡⲉ ⲙⲡⲁⲣⲙⲟⲩⲧⲉ ⲡⲥⲃⲟⲧ ⲛⲧⲉⲓⲣⲟ[ⲙⲡⲉ     ⲙⲡ]ⲁ
  ⲟⲩⲕⲟⲩⲓ ⲛ[ … ⲙⲙⲁⲥ]ⲏⲛⲥⲓⲛ           ⌈a⌉
5 ⲡⲟⲧⲏⲣⲓⲛ ⲥⲛⲁⲩ ⲛ̄ϩⲁⲧ                 |β]
  ϣⲟⲙⲧⲉ ⲛⲕⲟⲭⲗⲓⲁⲣⲓⲛ ⲛ̄ϩⲁⲧ            [γ]
  [ⲟ]ⲩⲉⲍⲁⲥⲕⲉⲗⲟⲛ ⲛⲧⲁϩ ⲅ              [a]
  [. . ]ϣ[. . ] ⲙⲙⲁⲡⲡⲁ               |ⲋ]
  ϣⲙⲟⲩⲛ [ⲛⲛⲟ]ϭ ⲛⲕⲁⲧⲁⲡⲉⲧⲁⲥⲙⲁ         η
10 ⲥⲟⲉⲓ ⲛⲕⲟⲩⲓ ⲛⲕⲁⲧⲁⲡⲉⲧⲁⲥⲙⲁ ⲛⲟⲩⲥⲓⲁⲥⲧ[ⲏ] [ⲋ]
  ⲭⲟⲩⲧⲥⲁϣϥⲉ ⲛⲟⲩⲏⲗⲟⲛ ⲛⲣⲟ          κζ
  ⲥⲟ ⲛⲥⲓⲛⲁⲓⲱⲛⲓⲛ ⲙⲡⲗⲟⲩⲙⲁⲣⲓⲕ,       ⲋ
  ⲟⲩⲥⲓⲛⲁⲓⲱⲛⲓⲛ ⲛⲁⲡⲧⲓⲥⲕⲓⲛ            α
  ⲧⲓⲟⲩ ⲛⲥⲧⲣⲱⲙⲁ ⲛⲕⲟⲣⲁⲓⲛⲁ           ε
15 ⲟⲩⲉⲙⲡⲣ[ⲟⲙ]ⲁⲗⲓⲛ ⲙⲡⲉⲣⲥⲓⲁⲧⲓⲕ,      α
  ⲟⲩⲥⲁⲕⲓⲛ ⲙⲯⲓⲙⲓⲑⲓⲟⲛ ⲙⲡⲟⲕϥ           α
  ⲥⲧⲁⲧⲁⲣⲉⲁ ⲥⲛ[ⲧⲉ]                   β
  ⲃⲧⲟ ⲙⲫⲓⲛ ⲁ ⲙⲙⲁⲥⲛⲏⲥⲓⲛ ⲙⲛⲟⲩϩⲣⲉⲛⲉ
    ⲛⲧⲁⲣⲥⲓ                          ε
  ⲃⲧⲟⲟⲩ ⲛⲥⲕⲉⲡⲁⲥⲙⲁ ⲛⲅⲃⲟⲓ           δ
20 ⲟⲩⲥⲕⲉⲡⲁⲥⲙⲁ ⲙⲙⲉⲧⲁⲝⲉ              α
  ⲟⲩⲥⲕⲉⲡⲁⲥⲙⲁ ⲛϩⲓⲥ[ⲁⲩ]ⲣⲓⲕ,         α
  ⲕⲟⲩⲓ ⲛⲥⲕⲉⲡⲛ ⲥⲛⲁⲩ ⲛⲗⲉⲩⲣⲕ,        β
```

ⲟⲩⲕⲟⲩⲓ ⲛⲥⲕⲉⲡⲛ ⲛⲁ[ϥ] ⲛⲛⲉⲃⲓⲱ ⲛⲁⲓⲧ　α
ⲟⲩⲫⲁⲥⲁⲣⲓⲛ ⲛⲅⲓⲥ　α

Bawit, *v* CLÉDAT II 82, 120
[4] The same church probably as in Br Mus no 1100 A similar inventory in GRENFELL & HUNT, *Gk Pap* II, p 161
[5] Not space for ⲙⲡⲟⲟⲩ ⲉⲧⲉⲥⲟⲩ.

[1] Or ⲑⲟⲩⲛⲁ
[2] *Cf* ⲧⲥⲉⲣⲭⲟⲩ, ⲧⲥⲉⲗⲭⲟⲩ, Br Mus no 414　Perhaps contains the name of the goddess Selket　ⲧⲥⲉⲣⲕⲁϩ, ⲧϣⲓⲣⲕⲁϩ, Br Mus Or 6721 (1) is probably different
[3] *V Aeg Zeitschr* xl 61　The name is common at

[ⲥ]ⲛⲧⲉ ⲛⲛⲟϭ ⲛⲗⲉⲕⲁⲛⲏ ⲛⲃⲁⲣⲱⲧ   β
ⲟⲩⲡⲟⲧⲏⲣⲟⲡⲗⲓⲧⲏⲥ ⲙⲛⲧⲉϥⲃⲁⲥⲓⲥ   α
25 ⲥⲛⲧⲉ ⲛⲥⲕⲁⲫⲛ ⲛϭⲟⲙⲛⲧ   β
ⲟⲩⲕⲟⲩⲓ ⲛⲕⲁⲃⲕⲁⲃⲛ   α
ϣⲟⲙⲛⲧ ⲛⲕⲟⲩⲓ ⲛⲧⲩⲥⲁⲓ   γ
ⲕⲟⲩⲓ ⲛⲥⲱⲙⲁⲣⲓⲥⲧ ⲥⲛⲧⲉ ⲟⲛ   β
ⲧⲓⲟⲩ ⲛⲕⲏⲣⲓⲁⲛ.   ε
30 ϣⲟⲙⲧⲉ ⲛⲥⲓⲧⲗⲁ ⲛⲃⲁⲣⲱⲧ ⲛⲡⲟⲗⲩϥⲁⲓ   γ
ⲕⲉⲗⲱⲗ ⲥⲛⲁⲩ ⲛϭⲟⲙⲛⲧ   β
ⲥⲁϣϥ ⲛⲟ.ⲟ. ⲛⲃⲁⲣⲱⲧ   ζ
ⲟⲩⲕⲟⲩⲓ ⲛⲟⲥⲥⲓⲛⲟⲥ   α
ⲟⲩⲭⲁⲣⲓⲥⲉⲧⲓⲟⲛ ⲛⲥϩⲓⲙⲉ   α
35 ⲟⲩϣⲙⲟⲩ ⲛⲟⲩⲱ[ϫ]ⲉ   α
ⲟⲩⲥⲓⲧⲗⲁ ⲛϫⲱⲕⲙ   α
ⲟⲩⲙⲁⲛϭⲁⲗⲏ   α
ⲉⲙⲡⲱⲧ ⲥⲛⲧⲉ ⲛⲧⲁⲗⲟ ⲕⲁⲙⲁⲥⲛ   β
ⲟⲩⲑⲩⲙⲓⲁⲧⲏⲣⲉⲓ   α
40 ⲟⲩϩⲣⲁⲃⲇⲟⲥ ⲙⲡⲉ[ⲛⲓⲡ]ⲉ   α
ⲟⲩⲡⲁϣϫⲉⲥⲧⲏⲥ ⲛⲛⲉϩ   ϛ
ϣⲃⲉ ⲛⲕⲟⲩⲓ ⲛⲕ[ⲁⲛ]ⲓⲥⲕⲉ ⲛⲥⲱⲣ ⲥⲟⲩⲟ ⲉⲃⲟⲗ   ο

45 ⲟⲩⲗⲉⲕⲁⲛⲏ ⲟⲛ ⲛⲃⲁⲣⲱⲧ ⲛⲁⲧⲙⲁⲁϫⲉ   α
ⲟⲩⲕⲟⲩⲓ ⲛⲗⲉⲕⲁⲛⲏ ⲟⲛ ⲛⲃⲁⲣⲱⲧ   α
ⲟⲩⲕⲟⲩⲓ ⲛⲥⲕⲁⲫⲛ ⲟⲛ ⲙⲛⲡⲉⲥⲟⲩⲃⲉ   α
ⲟⲩⲕⲟⲩⲓ ⲛϭⲁⲗⲁϩⲧ ⲛϭⲟⲙ[ⲛ]ⲧ   α
ⲟⲩⲥⲟⲩⲙⲁⲣⲓⲥⲧ ⲉⲥⲡⲟϫⲧ   α
50 ⲟⲩⲛⲟϭ ⲛⲟⲩⲁⲁⲩ ⲛⲃⲁⲣⲱⲧ   α
ⲧⲓⲟⲩ ⲛⲧⲣⲟ ⲛⲃⲁⲣⲱⲧ   ε
ⲟⲩϫⲟⲓ ⲛⲃⲁⲣⲱⲧ ⲛⲉϫⲁⲗⲩⲭⲛ   α
ⲟⲩⲕⲟⲩⲓ ⲛϭⲣⲟⲟⲙⲡⲉ ⲛⲃⲁⲣⲱⲧ   α
ⲟⲩⲕⲟⲩⲧⲟⲩⲗⲉ   α
55 ⲟⲩⲕⲁⲙⲡⲁⲛⲟⲥ ⲛⲁⲧⲉϣⲛⲧⲉ   α
ⲟⲩⲥⲛⲁⲗⲓⲥ ⲛϣⲱϥ   α
ⲟⲩⲡⲁϣⲉ ⲛϭⲁⲗⲁϩⲧ ⲛϭⲟⲙⲛⲧ   α
ⲧⲓ ⲛⲧⲛⲃⲉ   ε
ⲟⲩⲕⲣⲁⲃⲁⲧⲧⲛ   α
60 ⲃⲧⲟⲟⲩ ⲛⲥⲕⲁⲙⲙⲓⲛ   δ
ϣⲟⲙⲛⲧ ⲛϣⲏⲗⲕⲓⲗ ⲙⲛⲛⲉⲅⲁⲗⲏⲥⲓⲥ   γ
ⲟⲩⲗⲁϩⲛ ⲛⲏⲣⲡ   α
ⲙⲁϥⲟⲩⲉ ⲛϫⲱⲱⲙⲉ   λα

+ ⲓⲥⲛⲁⲧⲉ ⲡⲉⲓⲉⲗⲁ/ ⲛⲇⲓⲁⲕ/ ⲛϣⲉ ⲛⲛⲙⲁⲕⲁⲣⲓⲟⲥ ⲑⲉⲟⲇⲱⲣⲉ ⲡⲣⲱⲙⲉ
ϣⲙⲟⲩⲛ ⲧⲓⲥⲧⲟⲓⲭⲉⲓ ⲉⲡⲓⲙⲙⲉⲛⲧⲟⲛ ⲛⲟⲉ ⲉϥⲥⲏϩ ⲙⲙⲟⲥ +

Verso, near top   ]ⲁⲧⲓ ⲑⲉⲟ [

'By the will of God This is the Inventory (*inventum*) of the (church of) St (ἅγιος) Theodore, at the Caesareum, (made) by the deacon Ignatius, the 16th day of the month Parmoute, in this th year of the Indiction

A small . of magnesium (μαγνήσιον[1]), 2 silver cups (ποτήριον), 3 silver spoons (κοχλιάριον), a six-legged-vessel (ἑξασκελόν[2]) of lead, napkins (μάππα[3]), 8 large curtains (καταπέτασμα[4]), 6 small altar curtains, 27 door hangings (οὐῆλον), 6 linen cloths (σινδόνιον) embroidered (πλουμαρικός), a linen cloth for an awning (ἀντίσκιον), 5 curtain like coverings (στρῶμα, κορτίνα), a Persian embroidered garment (ἐμπλουμάριον[5], περσιατικός), a patchwork[6] bag (σάκκιον) of white-lead (colour, ψιμύθιον), 2 candlesticks (στατάρεα[7]), 4 of magnesium

[1] *V* BERTHELOT, *Introd à l'ét de la Chimie,* 221, on the difficulty of identifying various senses of μαγνήσια. *Ib* 255, it appears to sometimes=hematite Mr G F Hill refers me to Forcellini, *s v magnes,*=*lapis Heraclius* In a Jkôw text a *xestes* of magnesium occurs *V* also no 239 here

[2] *Cf* ἑξασκελής (SOPHOCLES)

[3] BUTLER, *Churches* ii 109 'dalmatic' *Cf* KIRCHER 118, 121.

[4] On this curtain *v* GELZER's *Leont von Neapolis,* p 132

[5] *Cf* ἔμπλουμος Perhaps 'peach-coloured' instead of 'Persian' *Cf* ⲡⲉⲣⲥⲁⲧⲓⲕⲟⲛ (*sic*) in a fragment, Berlin P 57¹⁷

[6] ⲡⲟⲕϥ=πέταλον, Exod xxix 6 (*cf* Lev viii 9)

[7] *Statarium* (*stantarium*), κονδολυχνιος, *Corp Glossar* iii 270

(φι   , μαγνήσιον) and a .... girdle (? ρέκος), 4 linen coverings (σκέπασμα), a silk (μετάξιον) covering (σκ), an Isaurian (ἰσαυρικός[1]) covering (σκ), 2 small white coverings (σκ, λευκός), 2 large brass dishes (λεκάνη), a vessel for cup-washing (ποτηροπλύτης) with its stand (βάσις), 2 bronze bowls (σκάφιον), a small water-vessel (καβκάβιον[2]), 3 small saucepans (τήγανον) and 2 small ladles (? ζωμάρυστρος[3]), 5 candle-lighters[4], 3   . brass buckets (σίτλα, πολύφανος[5]), 2 bronze pitchers, 7 brass   , a small hook (ὄγκινος), a woman's . . (χαρισήτιον[6]), a peg used in weaving[7] (?), a bucket (σίτλα) for washing, a hoe (μάκελλα[8]), 2   [9] for weaving (?) shirts (καμάσιον), a censer (θυμιατήριον), an iron[10] staff (ῥάβδος), half a *xestes* of oil[11], 70 small baskets (κανίσκιον) for distributing corn[12], (col 2) a small covering (σκέπη) of goatskin (αἴγειος) for bees, a cotton cap (? φακιόλιον[13]), a brass dish (λεκάνη) without handles and a small brass dish (λεκ) and a small bowl (σκάφιον) with its lid, a small iron caldron, a   [14] ladle (? ζωμάρυστρος), a large brass vessel, 5 brass wheels (τροχός), a brass boat[15] with six lights (ἐξάλυχνος), a small brass dove[16], a cup (? κοτύλη[17]), a measure (κάμπανος) without   , scissors (σπαλίς) for hair-cutting, an iron half(-measure) caldron, 5 bricks[18], a bier (κραββάτιον), 4 benches (σκάμνιον), 3 bells with their chains (ἅλυσις), a measure[19] of wine, 31 books[20]

Ignatius, the humble deacon, the son of the late Theodore, I assent (στοιχεῖν) to this inventory, as it is written'

239—Papyrus, complete, 12 × 15 cm   Script ligatureless   *Recto* ↑
List of articles stolen from the writer's house

+ⲡⲁⲓⲛⲉⲥⲕⲉⲉⲅⲉ ⲛⲧⲁⲅⲃⲓⲧⲟⲩ ϩⲓⲡⲁⲏⲓ ⲛⲭⲓⲟⲩⲥ | ⲟⲩϩⲁⲙⲉ[21] ⲟⲩⲛⲉⲗⲉⲃⲓⲛ ⲛⲉⲕⲱⲧ | ⲟⲩⲥⲟⲩⲙⲁⲣ-ⲣⲉⲥⲧⲏ[22] ⳤ ⲟⲩⲗⲁⲥⲓⲛ[23] ⲛⲉϩⲛⲱϩⲧ | ⲟⲩⲥⲡⲁⲗⲓⲥ[24] ⲛϩⲁⲟⲩⲉ ⲟⲩϣⲟⲧ ⲛϣⲁⲓ[25] | ⲟⲩⲙⲁϣⲉ ⲛϣⲓⲣⲏⲛⲉ | .ⲟⲩⲓ[26] ⲥⲛⲁⲩ ⲛⲃⲁⲣⲱⲧ ⲧⲓ ⲛⲟⲓⲡⲉ ⲛⲥⲟⲩⲟ | [ⲟⲩ]ⲫⲁϭⲁⲣⲉⲛ ⲛⲉϩⲙⲉ | ⲟ[ⲩ] . ⲕⲟⲥ ⲙⲁⲕⲛⲓϭⲉⲛ[27] ⲉϣⲁⲩⲃⲓ ⲛⲙⲟⲩⲛ ⲛⲍⲏⲥⲧⲏⲥ ⲛⲛⲏϩ ⲟⲩⲉⲓⲛⲉ ⲛϩⲁⲙⲙⲉ | ⲟⲩⲕⲁⲧⲏⲛⲉ ⲙⲛⲉⲛⲓⲛⲉ ⲟⲩⲭⲁⲣⲓⲥⲧⲓⲟⲩ[28] ⲛⲉϩⲙⲉ

---

[1] Or ἱστορικός ? 'painted,' *historiatus*

[2] ? καυκάλιον   [3] *V* no 239

[4] *Cf* κηριάπτης : But ⲕⲏⲣⲓⲁⲛⲉ could be read

[5] Perhaps *πολύφανος

[6] *Cf* no 239 ⲭⲁⲣⲓⲥⲧⲓⲟⲩ, also ? Crum, *Ostr* no 459 ⲭⲁⲣⲓⲥⲟⲛ

[7] ⲟⲩⲱϫⲉ Isa xxxviii 12 ἐκτέμειν (of weaving), Paris 131[6] 47 ⲉⲣⲉⲛⲉⲣϭⲟⲙⲉ ⲛ[ⲁ]ⲱⲟⲣ ⲛⲥⲉⲣⲉⲓⲟⲡⲉ ⲛⲥⲉⲧⲥⲁⲃⲟ ⲉⲧⲥⲟⲫⲓⲁ ⲙⲡⲥⲱⲣⲉ ⲛⲥⲉⲟⲩⲱϫⲉ ⲛⲧⲉⲓϣⲧⲏⲛ ⲛⲥⲁⲣⲧⲡⲉ, in Br Mus no 171 ⲉⲣⲉ=χειρουργεῖν, also in Zoega 592   *V* also Crum, *Ostr* nos 403, Ad 57

[8] Hence the Coptic and Arabic (مكلة) forms

[9] First word unknown : ⲧⲁⲗⲟ related to weaving, Lev xix 19, I⳽ iii 23, Zoega 375, *PSBA* xxix 305 *Cf* too the weaver's tax, ⲛⲧⲉⲙⲟⲥⲉ (δημόσιον) ⲛⲧⲁⲗⲉ ϣⲓⲕⲏ, in 2 receipts from Dêr Balaiza (Petrie, *Gizeh and Rifeh*)

[10] Scarcely space for ⲛⲉⲛⲓⲡⲉ   [11] Or 'for oil'

[12] Does this refer to seed-time ? ⲥⲟⲩⲟ would scarcely be used for the eucharistic elements : But *v* no 253 here *Cf Can Athanas*, p 125, note

[13] Or φάκελος : *Cf* ⲫⲁϭⲁⲣⲉ in nos 239, 243, 246, and *v* Butler, *op cit*, ii 148

[14] ? Γor ⲛⲟⲭϭ 'broad'

[15] *Cf* πλοιάρια in Grenfell's list, *Gk Pap* ii 161

[16] *V* Kraus, *RE* ii 822

[17] *Cf* ⲕⲟⲩⲧⲟⲩⲗⲏ no. 240, ⲕⲟⲩⲇⲟⲩⲗⲏ no 254

[18] *Cf* ⲕⲟⲩⲧⲟⲩⲗⲏ no. 240, ⲕⲟⲩⲇⲟⲩⲗⲏ no 254

[18] Scarcely bricks of clay, *cf* no 242

[19] Or 'for wine'

[20] Books entered last, as in Crum, *l c*

[21] *Cf* ϩⲁⲙⲉ ⲛⲧⲱⲡ (*sic*) in Br Mus no 420, and *ib* no 395 ⲟⲩϩⲁⲙⲉⲧⲱⲡ ⲉϥⲧⲟϩ ⲉⲭⲟⲉ, parallel with ϣⲙⲟⲩ. The meaning 'peg' would also suit the ϩⲁⲙⲉ which at Abydos marked the river's rise (*v* Crum in M A Murray's *Osireion*, p 42)

[22] ? ζωμάρυστρος, *v* no 238   [23] *V* no. 242

[24] *V* no 238 and Br Mus no 699

[25] Assuming this the word applied to cloth in Matt ix 16

[26] Not ⲕⲟⲩⲓ   [27] *V* no. 238

[28] *V* no. 238 *Cf* χαριστίων *campana*, *Corp Glossar* iii 197

'These are the things (σκευή) that have been stolen from my house   A peg (?)   A builder's ax   A ladle (?)   A steel for   fire   A (pair of) tailor's scissors (σπαλίς) A new cushion   A (pair of) scales for weighing incense   2 brazen .   5 *oipe* measures of[1] corn   A woman's head cloth (φάκελος, φακιόλιον)   A   of magnesium that holds 8 *xestai* of oil   A carpenter's knife   An iron chain (*catena*)   A woman's   .

Verso (earlier)   remnants of a Greek list of names, with sums of money opposite each Among them   αροου, τζωωρ[2], παλαυ.

240.—Papyrus, a fragment, 7½ × 13 cm   Script seldom ligatured   *Recto* ↑.
List of vessels in metal, apparently deposited at Shmoun

] προς θε ητληπιλτηλη[3] ιιοος ϩιτιτηωсιс + нiскеʏ[н[4] | оʏплнλлнн[5] нвλλωт ечϭoλϭ[6] нвнвɪ] | оʏсɪлɪл[7] нвλλωт нѥрɪιλ | оʏз[е]стнс нсω ιιооʏ нвλλωт | оʏноʏтоʏλн нсω ιιооʏ нв[л]λωт | оʏχωннн нιιλϩ сλрсɪн [8]

Verso   ]..тлɪϭλλωоʏ евoλ [space] + ϩɪωιιоʏ[н

241.—Papyrus, a fragment, 32 × 12 cm   Script rarely ligatured   *Recto* ↑
A List of various articles of property, including land

] оʏχωιιιιε н[н]ϣλλ[ιιос | .ϭ. н снлʏ ноʏω. [| оʏϩнвϲ нвλрωт [| оʏϩлʏ нвλрωт [| тн нслтω нлврлн . н[9 | оʏноʏɪ клт...ιιιλ [| ϣλλооʏ[10] сннтε нвλр[ωт | снлʏ ноʏнλн[11] нϩвɪос | снлʏ ноʏнλн нкл[| ϣоιιнт нλоʏтнр нвλрωт [| со[12] нсетɪωϩе нιιλϩ | с.теϩ нто.т.н[| лʏω оʏсетɪω[ϩε | ...не прос [| εγρ[α] µ̄ θ̄ω̄θ̄ α[| +ιωснφ πιελλχ̄ [| тιстнχε επιεн . .[13 [

242.—Papyrus, a fragment, 6 × 12½ cm   Script sloping semi-uncials. *Recto* →
A List of various articles.

] ϩнвϲ снлʏ нϩоιιнт нлɪ[| лιιιπεʏϩλλʏсɪс лιιπε[| н . рωн λлɪн[14] снлʏ нн[| нϩоιιнт · оʏкελωλ нϩ[оιιнт | нвλрωт · оʏтнве[15] нϩ[оιιнт | сооʏ ιιπλλλɪн ϣιιоʏн [|] нϭооʏ[нε

243.—Paper; complete, 21 × 18 cm   Script of ZOEGA's 9th class.   The leaf was many times folded

[1] Or 'for'   [2] Cf χωωρε
[3] διαδηλοῦν Or read τιλстнλн διαστέλλειν ?
[4] This word added in a different hand
[5] ? πανάριον   [6] For ? ϭорϭ
[7] I cannot identify this
[8] σαλσίκων. V KRALL in *Mitth Rain* v 35   In Paris 44, 85 a, σαρσικια شراشق, next to λουκανικον   In Vienna *Denkschr* xxxvii 229 σαρσικάριος

[9] I cannot identify this
[10] 'Wheel'? Cf GIUDI, *Framm Copti*, vi, p 378, and a letter here (v Index)
[11] *Velum* V no 238   [12] Different hand
[13] Apparently not ἐντάγιον or ἔγγραφον.
[14] V no 239
[15] Clearly not an ordinary 'brick' Cf ? Br Mus no. 1059 and CRUM, *Ostr* Ad 58

Q 2

A List of clothes and of articles in metal[1]   Many of the names are clearly tran-
scripts from the Arabic and their identification here is but tentative

>ⲭ< ⲡⲟ̄ⲥ ⲓ̄ⲥ ⲡⲉⲭ̄ⲥ̄ ⲁ ⲱ ※
    ⲟⲩⲉⲧⲧⲉ   ⲏ̄ η
    ⲟⲩⲙⲁⲭⲁⲛⲉ
    ⲟⲩϩⲁⲗⲏⲕ ⲛⲟⲩⲣⲏⲧⲉ
5 ⲥⲱ ⲙⲛⲁϭⲉ ⲛⲁⲛⲡⲁⲡⲁⲗⲉ
    ⲟⲩⲃⲃⲟⲥ ⲛⲁⲧϯⲡⲁϭ
    ⲁⲩ ⲟⲩⲁⲣⲣⲓⲧⲉ : ⲁⲩ ⲟⲩⲕⲁⲗⲗⲁⲥⲥ
    ⲛⲁⲧϯⲡⲁϭ ⲁⲩ ⲟⲩⲁⲗⲕⲁⲧ-
    ⲣⲁⲡⲟⲩⲗⲗⲓ ⲟⲩⲛⲱⲣⲡ ⲛⲁⲧϯⲡⲁϭ
10 ⲁⲩ ⲛⲉϥϣⲟⲧ ϣⲱⲙⲧⲉ
    ⲛⲁⲙⲙⲁⲗϩⲁⲃⲉ ⲁⲩ ⲟⲩⲥⲁⲃⲁⲛⲉ
    ⲥⲛⲏⲧⲉ ⲙⲙⲁⲧⲧⲏⲗⲉ ⲙⲛⲱⲣϣ
    ⲁⲩ ⲟⲩⲕⲁⲗⲗⲁⲥⲉ ⲛⲥⲱⲣⲧ ⲁⲩ ⲟⲩⲛⲁⲗ-
    ⲗⲓⲛ ⲁⲩ ⲁⲗⲛⲁⲛⲁ ⲛⲛⲱϩⲙⲉ
15 ⲁⲩ ϣⲟⲙⲉⲧ ⲛⲕⲁⲗⲗⲁⲥⲉ
    ⲟⲩϫⲓⲁϩϩⲁⲣⲏⲣⲉ ⲁⲩ ⲥⲟⲟⲩ ⲟⲩϫⲓ
    ϣⲱⲱ̅ⲛ̅ⲧ : ⲁⲩ ⲟⲩⲁⲗⲙⲓϭⲁⲣ
    ⲛⲁⲗⲕⲁⲧⲣⲁⲛⲟⲩⲗⲗⲓ : ϯⲟⲩ
    ⲙⲫⲁϭⲁⲣⲉ ⲛϩⲱⲃⲉⲥ
20 ⲕⲟⲩⲓ ⲥⲁⲭⲟ : ⲁⲩ ⲥⲛⲁⲩ ⲛⲁⲗ-
    ⲙⲓϭⲁⲣ : ⲁⲗⲙⲁⲗⲁϥⲃ̅ⲉ̅

ⲛϩⲱⲃⲉⲥ ⲁⲥⲥⲁⲓⲛϩ
    ⲁⲩ ϭⲧⲱ ⲛⲁⲗⲙⲁⲗⲁϥ
    ⲛⲁⲟⲩⲉⲛ ⲥⲥⲧⲛⲙ : ⲁⲩ ⲥⲛⲏ-
25 ⲧⲉ ⲙⲙⲁⲛⲧⲉⲗⲉ ⲙⲙⲱⲣⲁⲡⲉ
    ⲁⲩ ϣⲱⲙⲧⲥ ⲛϩⲁⲗⲥⲉⲥ
    ⲁⲩ ⲟⲩⲥⲟⲩⲣⲉ ⲛⲛⲟⲩϥ (later ink)
(col 2) ⲛⲗⲁⲩ ⲛϭⲁⲣⲱⲧ
    ⲟⲩⲁⲙⲁⲛⲁⲣⲓ : ⲁⲩ ⲟⲩⲁⲧⲓⲁⲥⲥ
30 ⲁⲩ ⲟⲩⲁⲗⲡⲣⲓⲕ ⲁⲩ ϣⲱⲙⲧⲉ
    ⲛⲁⲥⲥⲁⲓⲛⲓ ⲁⲩ ⲛⲗⲁⲭⲉⲣⲛⲏ
    ⲁⲩ ⲥⲛⲏⲧⲉ ⲛⲁⲗϩⲁⲥⲁⲭⲓ
    ⲁⲩ ⲟⲩⲉⲓ ⲛⲕⲟⲩⲓ ⲁⲩ ⲟⲩⲗⲁⲁⲩ
    ⲛϯ ⲥⲧⲟⲓ ⲉⲓϩⲣⲁⲓ ⲁⲩ ⲧⲣⲟϩⲧⲉ
35 ⲁⲩ ⲟⲩⲁⲗⲭⲛⲣⲛⲓⲛ ⲁⲩ ⲟⲩ-
    ⲁⲗⲁⲑⲛⲧⲓ ⲥⲛ̄ⲛ̄ ⲛϩⲣⲟϥ ⲙⲡⲉ-
    ⲛⲓⲛⲉ ⲁⲩ ⲥⲛⲏⲧⲉ ⲛⲭⲁϩⲗⲉ
    ⲁⲩ ϣⲟⲙⲉⲧ ⲛϩⲱⲃⲉⲥ ⲛϭⲁⲣⲟⲧ
    ⲁⲩ ⲥⲛⲏⲧⲉ ⲛⲕⲟⲩϫⲟⲩ ϩⲁⲛⲏϩ
40 ⲁⲩ ⲟⲩⲕⲟⲩⲓ ⲗⲱⲕ ⲉⲛϭⲁⲣⲟⲧ
    ⲁⲩ ⲟⲩⲛⲟϭ ⲉⲧⲟⲩⲕⲁⲛⲉⲥ
    ⲁⲩ ⲥⲛⲏⲧⲧⲉ ⲙⲙⲁⲉⲓⲥ ⲛϫⲉ

'The Lord Jesus Christ   A ⲱ — A set of towels[2], (worth) 8 *solidi*   A   [3]
An ankle (*lit* foot) ring   (5) Six   of cloaks[4]   A brocaded[5] garment and[6] a cloak[7] and
a brocaded cap[8] and a (garment of) Katrabbul make[9]   A brocaded coverlet[10] (10) and its
pillows[11]   3 bed covers[12] and a towel[13]   2 handkerchiefs for spreading[14] and a woollen
cap and a cloak[15] and a veil of . . .[16] (15) and 3 caps worked with silk[17] and 6 woven and

---

[1] If church property, *cf* the ‮امر كثير الدساح وثياب متاع‬
‮العابد الى حّدا‬, found in the Cairo churches in the 11th
century   MAKRIZI, *Ḥiṭaṭ* ii 495
[2] ‮عدد‬ LANE   Why a sum of money here only is not
clear
[3] Presumably Arabic
[4] ? *Anabalus cf* KIRCHER 120 ⲁⲛⲁⲛⲗⲓⲛ   But perhaps
Arabic   For ⲛⲁϭⲉ *v* no 213
[5] ‮الدساح‬ *V* KARABACEK, *Mittelalt Gewebe* (1882) 22 ff,
A. v KREMER, *Culturgesch* ii 290
[6] Note ⲁⲩ always for ⲁⲩⲱ.
[7] ‮اليرداء‬ In Paris 44, f 100=περιβόλαιον
[8] ‮قلنسوة, وثوبة‬
[9] ‮طرثولي‬, named after the district W of Baghdad
(⸀ LE STRANGE, *Baghdad* 113, M STRECK, *Alte Landsch
Babyloniens* 232)   This stuff appears not to be known

(Mr G LE STRANGE), though Baghdad was famous for
textiles   *V* KARABACEK, *l c*, 28, 29, *Fihr Rain* no 738,
KREMER ii 286   This should be the etymology of the
hitherto unexplained *quadrapolus, quadrapulus* (not *quadru-
plus*, BEISSEL, *Bilder* 268), used in the *Liber Pontif* (i 499,
ii 55, DUCHESNE) of costly altar-cloths, curtains   The
earliest instance relates to *ca* 790
[10] Said ⲛⲱⲣⲡ not elsewhere   Boh ⲫⲱⲣϣ also rare
Mus Guim xvii 57
[11] But in Rossi i, v 42 clearly 'bag'   [12] ‮الحلقة.‬
[13] σαβανον is transcribed ‮اشيه‬ (Dozi)
[14] ‮يمندل‬ Berlin Ostr P 4977 ⲙⲁⲛⲧⲏⲗⲓ   Same as in
l 25?   But why the *fem* ending?   Sense of ⲛⲱⲣϣ here
obscure
[15] ταλλιον, ‮بلس‬   [16] ? ‮الإعاع‬ or ‮كة‬
[17] ‮حرير‬ For ϫⲓ *v* no 244

a head-cloth[1] of Katrabbul make   5 turbans of linen (?)[2] (20) . . .   and 2 head-cloths (A) linen (?) mantle[3] (worked with) pearls[4] and 4 mantles of *stibium* colour[5] and (25) 2 square[6] handkerchiefs and 3 chains[7] and a gold pin

The articles of metal   a candlestick[8] and a cup[9] (30) and a jug[10] (?) and 3 dishes[11] and the   . [12] and 2 . .[13] and a small one and a thing for giving forth incense and the cauldron (35) and a hand basin[14] and a perfume-box[15] 2 iron stoves[16] and 2 ovens[17] and 3 brass lamps and 2 small vessels for oil[18] (40) and a small brass vessel and a large vessel[19] and 2 .   [20] of wood '

Verso, in a different hand   ⲛⲁⲛⲟⲩ ⲡⲛⲟⲩⲥ ⲡⲁⲣⲁ ⲛⲛⲟⲩϥ ⲧⲉⲥⲟⲫⲓⲁ ⲡⲁⲣⲁ ⲡⲱⲛⲉ ⲙⲙⲏ[21] In the other direction, part of an earlier Arabic text

244.—Papyrus, a fragment, 35 × 19 cm   Script clear, few ligatures   *Verso →*

A List of clothes or altar coverings, curtains &c[22]   Opposite each item is ⲉⲓ̅ⲇ̅ (= εἶδος) α   Many of the descriptive terms used are rare and difficult of appreciation[23] The identifications here are merely suggestions

] ⲉⲟ ⲛ [ⲛ]ⲁⲓⲥⲓⲟⲛ ⲛⲁⲅⲁⲛ ⲛⲛⲉⲃⲓⲱ
[ⲟⲩⲡ]ⲁⲗⲗⲓⲛ ⲛⲗⲉⲩⲕⲟⲛ ⲛⲁⲓⲥⲓⲟⲛ ⲛⲥⲙⲉⲣⲛⲉⲱⲛ
ⲟⲩⲥⲙⲉⲣⲛⲉⲟⲛ ⲛⲛⲉⲡⲣⲓⲥⲟⲛ ⲛⲁⲓⲥⲓⲟⲛ ⲉϥϫⲓⲛⲟⲩⲓ ϣⲱⲡⲧ ⲛⲯⲙⲙⲟⲩ
ⲟⲩϣⲧⲛ ⲛⲟⲛⲓⲭⲉⲟⲛ ⲉⲥϫⲓⲕⲟⲧ ϩⲓⲥⲡⲁⲑⲏ
5 ⲟⲩϣⲧⲛ ⲛϩⲱⲗ ⲉⲥϫⲓⲕⲟⲧ ϩⲓⲥⲡⲁⲑⲏ

[1] المعبر
[2] φακιόλιον, *v* no 238 I assume ϩⲱⲃⲥ to = ϩⲃⲟⲥ (*cf* l 22), but possibly a verb, 'covering,' with ⲥⲁϫⲟ as object, for which *v* no 129
[3] ملف, but should here be *fem* (*cf*. l 23).
[4] الصيني, or 'Chinese' الصيني
[5] *V* no. 244   [6] مربعة   [7] ἅλυσις
[8] منارة   [9] طاسة   [10] ادريق ?
[11] صينية , سيني, 'ABD AL-LAṬĪF 571
[12] Assuming ⲛ- the article ϫ might be read for ⲝ Possibly for ⲛⲁⲗϫⲉⲣⲡⲏⲛ, *cf* l 35
[13] Arabic, unidentified
[14] Altered from -ⲕⲉⲛ الكرنيب χέρνιψ, Dozy
[15] العنقل   [16] For ϩⲣⲱ
[17] *Cf* ? Boh ϫⲁϧⲙⲓ.
[18] Taking ⲕⲟⲩ- for ⲕⲟⲩⲓ *V* CRUM, *Ostr* no 465 ⲕⲟⲩⲝⲟⲩ ⲛⲧⲓ ⲛⲉϩ in a Br Mus Jkôw papyrus
[19] ?? δοκάνη
[20] مخشب 'a place where wood grows,' not possible here Perhaps for μαγίς ?
[21] Not a biblical quotation
[22] Other lists STERN in *Aeg Z* '85, 41, CRUM, *Copt MSS*, no xlvii Three words mean 'garment', 'covering' here ϣⲧⲏⲛ, ϩⲃⲟⲥ, ⲡⲁⲗⲗⲓⲟⲛ The 1st in the Bible varies with ϩⲟⲓⲧⲉ for ἱμάτιον (*v* Matt ix 20 and Mark v 27, Matt xxiv 18 and Mark xiii 16 and Acts ix 39 in WOIDE) or χιτών The 2nd, here, ZOEGA 316, Br Mus no 1114, KRALL ccxlv, *fem* (? distinct from ϩⲃⲱⲱⲥ, ϩⲃⲟⲟⲥ *masc*), in Lev xvi 4, 23 = λινοῦς, Boh ⲓⲁⲩ, *cf* ib 32, where λινῆν is Sa' ⲉⲓⲁⲁⲩ In NT ὀθόνη, ὀθόνιον is rendered by Sa' ϩⲃⲱⲱⲥ, Boh ϩⲃⲱⲥ ⲙⲁⲩ, ϣⲉⲛⲧⲱ ⲙⲁⲩ Instances of 'linen' are Berlin P 4977, contrasted with ⲥⲟⲣⲧ 'wool,' ZOEGA 628 ⲧⲟⲩⲓ ⲛϩ , CRUM, *Ostr* no 368 ϩⲟⲓⲧⲉ ⲛϩ ZOEGA 316 *ull* = MIGNE, *PG* 65 261 στιχάριον λινοῦν = *PL* 73 981 *tunica linea* But it also acquired, as here, a general meaning, *e g* Br Mus no 480, CRUM, *l c* Ad 62, *Eliasapok* 122 ϩ ⲛϣⲛⲥ, *Pistis* 375 ϩ ⲛⲥⲓⲁⲁⲩ. The ⲡⲁⲗⲗⲓⲟⲛ, besides being the monk's cloak, is a secular head-covering, *Can Eccles* 43 I AGARDE, also a bed-cover, *Vita Joh Eleemos* §§ xxi, xxvii, *Mirac S Menas* no 5, here perhaps an altar-cloth, as in the *Liber Pontif*, passim (*Cf* the use of *vestis*) On the *ballin* in Coptic church *v* BUTLER, *Churches* ii 118
[23] Comparable, if not identical, names of stuffs and garments, compounded of botanical terms, may be found in KARABACEK, *Mittelalterl Gewebe*, pp 4, 5, 33 &c., and the same in *Oesterr Monatsh f d Orient* xi 253/4, Latin names in the 'Charta Cornutiana' (*Liber Pontif* i, cxlvii) *Cf* also Br Mus. Or. 6211 ϣⲧⲏⲛ ⲛⲟⲩϩⲣⲧ

ογϣτη ηψελιθηη εcϫιϗοτ ϩιcπαθη

ογϣτη ηαγαη ϫωπεϩ εcϫιϗοτ ϩιcπαθη

ογϣτη ηλεγϗοη εcϣοητ ηαηαϩ

ογcлερηεοη ηπαλλεηηη εϥϫιϣωητ

10   ογλοογ ηπαλλεcηη ηαιcιοη

ογπαλλιη ηαγαη cϥαϭιηα

ογπαλλιη ηϫωλ

ογπαλλιη ηηαγαη ϫωπεϩ

ογϣτη ηπαλαεικ ηαγαη εϧιω

15   ογλιαλλωτ οη εϣοητ εcπαθη ϩιϗοτ

ογϩλιος εcτροφηη εcϫιηωλεα ϩιαποωλε

ογϩϧος οη εcϫιαποωλε

ογϩϧος ηαηαϩ ηcτηλι

ογϩϧος ηαηαϩ ηαγειαγαη

20   ογϩϧος οη ηαηαϩ

ογϩϧος ηοccια εcϫιϗοτ

ογϩϧος ηαηαϩ οη

ογϩϧος ηπγλη (altered from ? ηγλη)

ογϩϧος εcϫιαποωλε

25   ογϩϧος εcϫιηολεα ϩιαποωλες ηαιcι/

ογϩϧος ηcτροφηη εcϫιηολεα ηαιcι/

ογϩϧος οη εcϣοητ ηαηαϩ

ογϩϧος ηαποωλε

ϣολιτ[. .]ϗαλιϗη . . . η . .   πηογϥ

30   cηαγ ηλοτ[

ϣολιτε ηεπιχερη

λιτcηοογce ηϩαλαcιc ερεπηαθιλια ϩιογ

] of goat's hair (αἴγειος), honey-coloured   A white (λευκός) goat's hair covering (παλλίον) of Smyrna fashion[1] (σμυρνίος)   A cypress-coloured (κυπαρίσσινος) Smyrna (covering) of goat's hair, having a little white lead (ψιμύθιον)-coloured pattern woven therein[2]   An onyx-coloured[3] (ὀνύχιος) robe, having wheels[4] and stripes[5] (σπάθη)   (5) An onion(?)-coloured robe, having wheels and stripes (σπ)   A white-lead (ψιμ)-coloured robe, having wheels and stripes (σπ)   A robe of apple hue[6], having wheels and stripes (σπ)   A white (λευκός)

[1] Or 'myrrh-coloured,' though the next occurrence of the word makes this less likely

[2] ϫι as here and below recurs in CRUM, *Copt MSS* no xlvii ϫιcταγρος, Berlin P 4977 ϩοιτε εϥϫιχεριc (χειρίς).

[3] *Cf* ? the spice 'onycha,' Exod xxx 34, also ὀνύχινος, applied to a garment in *Pap. Oxyrh* cxiv

[4] *V Liber Pontif* i 432, 'ornavit in rotis' Perhaps *cf* the angel's στιχαριον whereon were 'great wheels τροχος,

Mus Guim xvii 131

[5] For σπάθη *cf* Br Mus Or 6201 A &c., fragment of letter,]ιωαηηηc περιχγτηc ϣπτω[ρ]s ηλιο ηπαλλιη ηπλεϗαηος[|]ηος ϫεεητοϥη(ε) πεcπαθη ηταπϗορογc (? κορεύς) ταϥ πε ογωϣ ογη τεγηογ | [τεηαϫι τιεπιc]-τολη πωλεϭ ηϫεϗαηος εϧολ ϗαη παλλιη ετϥρη (? πιεϩρε) ϗαη πεcπαθη[

[6] *Cf* Br Mus. no 476, ογλωτιϩ ηϫλιπεϩ εcϣο[ητ (*sic*)

robe woven with *anah*-signs[1]   A Smyrna (cloak), palm-embroidered (πάλμενος[2]), having a woven pattern   (10) A palm-embroidered (παλ) garment of goat's hair (αἴγ)   A covering (παλ.) of lentil (? φάκινος)[3] hue   An onion coloured (?) covering (παλ)   An apple hued covering (παλ)   A . . robe of honey-colour (15) and a woollen garment (μαλλωτός[4]), woven with stripes (σπ) and wheels   A dress of . (στρόφιον)[5], having skirts (ποδέα[6]) and shoulder-straps (ἐπωμίς[7]), and a dress with shoulder-straps (ἐπ)   A dress of *stibium* colour[8] with *anah*-signs   A dress of variegated colour with *anah*-signs, (20) and a dress with *anah*-signs   A dress of (ὀγγία[9]), having wheels, and a dress with *anah* signs   A dress of felt (? πῖλος[10])   A dress having shoulder straps (ἐπωμίς)   (25) A dress of goat's hair (αἴγ), having socks (ποδ) and shoulder-straps (ἐπ)   A goat's hair dress of . (στρόφιον), having socks (ποδ), and a dress woven with *anah*-signs   A dress with shoulder-straps (ἐπ).   3 . of shoes (? καλίγιον) of gold (? colour).   (30) 2 coverlets (? λῶδιξ) 3 . . . (? ἐπιχείριον[11]).   12 chains (ἄλυσις) with the collar (κάθημα) attached thereto

Recto   The earlier text, a Greek list of names and sums of money in several columns.   Among them ιωαννου κακινα, περσοῦ, μηνα κουι, περητ, μαρκου σανηρπ, μηνασιου, σενουθ κουκιρ.

245.—Papyrus, a fragment, $9\frac{1}{2} \times 17$ cm   Script. almost ligatureless   *Verso →*
List of clothes and the like

]ιϣωι ογναγνακες ⲙⲡογⲗⲱⲧⳅ . ⲁⳇᵀ. ⲛ̄ ⲇ |Ⳇⲁⲡⲱⲛ ογναγνακες ογⲗⲱⲧⳅ ⲙ . . ⲁⳇᵀ. ⲛ̄ ⲇ|]ⲥⲓⲛⲁ̇ προс ⲥⲟ ⲉⲫⲟⲗⲟⲛ/ ⲉⲛϣⲱⲡ ⲙⲙⲟⲟⲩ |]ⲧⲉ ⲉⲫⲟⲗⲟⲛ, ⲥⲁⲛⳅⲛⲙⲓ̄ⲟ̄[12] ⲛ̄ ⲃ |Ⳇⲧⲟⲟⲩ ⲡ̄ⲣⲟⲗⲟⲛ ⲛⲥⲓⲛⲁ̇ ⲉ̄ⲃ̄ϣⲱⲡ ⲙⲙⲟⲟⲩ . . ⲧⲥⲁⲃⲛ̄ⲙⲁ/ ⲛ̄ η |]ⲙ̄ⲛ̄ϣⲁⲟⲅⲡ ⳅⲟⲗⲟⲛ/ ⲛⲥⲓⲛⲁ̇ προс ⲥⲟ . . . . . . ⲛ̄ ⲓⲇ/ |]ⲟⲉϥ ⲛⲟⲩⲧⲣⲓⲙ ⲛ̄ⲡⲙⲟⳅ/[13] ⲛ̄ α γ/ |]   ⲛ̄ ⳅ |

Recto   remains of a Greek account

246.—Papyrus, complete, 13×6 cm   Script ligatureless   *Verso ↑*
List of clothes and the like   Above | 1 a cross.

+ⲟⲩϣⲧⲏⲛ ⲉⲙⲁⲗⲗⲱ̄' | ⲟⲩⲥⲱⲛⲁⳅ ⲛⲁⲓⲥⲩ[ⲡ]ⲧⲓⲟⲛ ⲛⲁⲅⲁⲛ | ⲟⲩⳅⲃⲟⲥ ⲛⲟⲡⲡⲓⲁ | ⲟⲩⲥⲩⲗⲗⲁ ⲛⳅⲧⲟ ⲙⲛⲛⲉⲥⲭⲁⲗⲙⲟⲥ | ⲟⲩⳅⲅⲧⲏ ⲛ̄ⲕⲫⲁⲥⲁⲣⲏ | ⲟⲩⳅⲅⲧⲏ ⲛⲥⲁⲃⲁⲛⲉⲛ | ⲟⲩⳅⲅⲧⲏ ⲛⲁⲗⲉⳅⲁⲙⲁⲣⲏ | blank

---

[1] Can this be the *crux ansata* ⳨ ? Phonetically it is possible (Sᴇᴛʜᴇ) (Cf Lᴇɪᴘᴏʟᴅᴛ, *Schenute* 29) Very rare on Coptic textiles, v Swᴏʙᴏᴅᴀ in *Arch Ehrengabe f De Rossi*, 103, 105, Taf vi, Fᴏʀʀᴇʀ, *Fruhchr Altert aus Achm*, Taff viii 4, xii 1, 2   As an ornament in books Turin, Sa'id *Eccl*, fly-leaf, and Pap Bruce, ed C Sᴄʜᴍɪᴅᴛ, p 38, on stelæ Cʀᴜᴍ, *Copt Monum* (Cairo), pll xxvi–xxxi The only Coptic word ⲁⲛⳅ, αὐλή, is unsuitable   But cf no 254

[2] Not in the dictionaries   Cf ? *palmatus*

[3] Recurs in a letter here (v Index)

[4] Cf no 246   In no. 247 ⲙⲉⲗⲗⲱⲧ.   But *Miss franç* i 408 ⲙⲉⲗⲱⲧ ⲛ̄ϣⲁⲣ, probably = μηλωτή

[5] στροφεῖον, a sort of headdress, Pap Oxyrh xxxiii, can scarcely be compared

[6] Recurs Kʀᴀʟʟ ccxl

[7] Kʀᴀʟʟ ccxlv ⲁⲡⲱⲱⲙⲓⲥ   Cf Cʀᴜᴍ, *Copt MSS* no xlvii ⲁⲡⲡⲟⲩⲙⲓⲥ, Kɪʀᴄʜᴇʀ 117 ⲁⲡⲟⲙⲓⲥ

[8] Recurs in no 243

[9] Recurs in no 246

[10] Or 'a door (τύλη) curtain'

[11] No such word in the dictionaries

[12] I can suggest nothing here   Apparently recurs in next line

[13] ? μόδιος   Very rare in the papyri (Vɪᴛᴇʟʟɪ no. 60) and scarcely appropriate in this list

'A woollen robe¹. A coloured Egyptian cloak² A dress of   ³. A horse's saddle (*sella*) with its bridle A pair (? ζεύγη) of head cloths⁴. A pair of towels A pair of napkins (?)⁵ '

247.—Papyrus, a fragment, 6½ × 9½ cm. Script rough uncials *Verso* →.
A List of clothes

]ογπαλλιν ΝογωΒϣ [| ογπαλλιν ΝογωΒϣ ο[ΙΙ | *ditto* [| ✝ Νϩβοος Νϣοιτ Ν[| ογΜελ-
λωτ⁶ οΝ ΝϣΟ[ΙΙτ | ϥ]τοογ Νκαλακιλλα .⁷ [|] Νφασ[⁸

248—Papyrus, 2 fragments, the larger, 9½ × 7 cm Script uncials, early type
Recto →
Account of wine supplied to various persons

Frag I ΝλοΓος ΝΝρΗΝ[Frag II]οΝΙ[] λαϩΝ ξ̄ [|]ω πρωΝπαπλοογ⁹ ογ-
λαϩ[Ν |]κος ογλαϩΝ .[|]Νιρος λαϩΝ ϲΝτε[| ϲαρ|απιωΝ παρϲγΝταρ/¹⁰ ογλαϩΝ
[|]ΝΗΙ Νταγ́Ντογ́Ν¹¹ εϩραι ΝΝ[|]Ναι Ντενοογϲ ΝΝο [| ϲ]ϩιΝε λεοΝτΗΝ ϣ[|] πεγϲοΝ
ιερ[ΝΝιαϲ |

249.—Papyrus, a fragment, 10 × 5½ cm Script very small, few ligatures. *Verso* →
Account (λόγος) of oil supplied to various persons, some of them oil or fruit dealers

ειϲ ΝλοΓος ΝεΝεϩ τ[| ϩαΝϣορπ Νϲοπ¹² [| ϩαροι αΝοκ Νται[| ϩαΝοΝε πϲαΝΝε[ϩ | ϩααπα
κγρε [Π]ϲαΝ[Νεϩ | ϩαΝΝερο Νταιτα[| ϩακαται¹³ πκαρπω[ΝΗϲ | ϩαπετρος πϲαΝΝεϩ [| ϩαιω-
ϩαΝ[ΝΗ]κ παΝτεχ¹⁴ [| ϩαϩγλοφγλαι ετ¹⁵ [| ϩαπκγογ [| ϩακα ι πκαρπω[ΝΗϲ |

Recto.]εΝαγ πετιρουπε ιε |] π̊ ε ϑ βϲ λ/π ⅄ μϲ¹⁶ |] π̊ ιϡ ϑ ηϲ λ/π ⅄ ιαϲ |] π̊ β (illegible).

250—Papyrus, a fragment, 17½ × 7 cm Script small, ligatured *Recto* →
List (γνῶσις) of oil bought of the persons named, for (?) the 9th and 10th Indictions

✝τϲΝΝωϲιϲ ΝΝεΝεϩ Ν[ΝΝΝα¹⁷ Ν[.]ϭογλε ϩα|ϩΝΝατΗϲ ΝΝϪεκαττΗϲ ιΝ⁸ / | ✝ ϩααΒραϩαΝ
ελαι/¹⁸ λε | ϩαπιλατος ελαι/ | ϩαϥαΝΝεϩ ελαι/ | ϩαιωϲΗφ ελαι/ [| ϩαιωϲΗφ [| Νϩολοκ/
[| (space) | ϩαροογ [

¹ *V no 244*
² καυνάκης *V no 245* In Paris 131⁶, 37 ϭογπαϭες Νλααγ ³ *V no 244* ⁴ *V no 238*
⁶ And in Br Mus Or 6211 (Jkôw) 'Αλλαξιμάριον Paris *scala* ʕ4, 86a has λαϩιΝαριΝ جلمة, equivalent to ϲαΒαΝοΝ
⁶ *V no 244* ⁷ καράκαλλον, a hood.
⁸ φαϭαρε, φακιόλιον *V no 238*
⁹ *V Br Mus no 1076*, also GOODSPEED's Papyri (*Chicago Dec Public*, vol v) p 20 and Cairo no 10270
¹⁰ *Argentarius* ¹¹ Read -Ντογ
¹² *Cf* this expression in Br Mus no 1086
¹³ Recurs below καΝαι can hardly be read
¹⁴ ?? ἀντιγεοῦχος *V no 132*
¹⁵ Or read ϩα ϩγλο (for ϩλλο) φγλακτ[.
¹⁶ The 2nd and 3rd abbreviations ? for πλεῖον λίτραι, though the latter word is not usually so represented
¹⁷ First Ν probably cancelled An unknown place-name
¹⁸ ἐλαιουργός, though] 6 might suggest merely ἐλαιον

251.—Papyrus, a fragment, 21 × 6 cm Script neat, ligatureless *Recto* and *verso* uncertain

Remains of Accounts, headed] . ⲡⲉⲗⲉ ⲓⲅ̄/ ϣⲁⲣⲟ[and relating in part to oil,]ⲛⲉϩ ⲛⲧⲁⲛⲧⲁⲁⲩ ⲉⲃⲟⲗ ϩⲓⲧ[ⲛ, *var* ⲛ[. The following are legible —

] ⲛⲣⲱⲙⲉ ⲗⲉⲡⲗⲟⲛ̄/ or ⲣⲱⲗⲡⲗⲟⲛ̄/ Another headed ⲁ]ⲡⲁⲣⲭⲏ ⲉⲡⲉⲓⲕⲁⲣⲡⲟⲥ, followed by ϩⲁⲫⲁⲛⲣⲟⲥ[1] ϩⲓⲧⲛⲗⲁⲕ[ⲁⲣⲉ, ϩⲁⲧⲁⲥⲙ̄ⲡⲟⲧⲉ[2] ϩ̄ⲧ̄ⲧⲏ, ϩⲁⲡⲁⲡϫⲟⲗ ϩⲓⲧⲛϫⲁⲭⲁⲣⲓⲁⲥ, ϩⲁⲡ-ϣⲉⲛⲟⲩⲧⲏⲗⲉ [, ϩⲁⲧⲁⲡⲧⲥⲓⲃⲗⲉ ϩⲓⲧⲛ[, ϩⲁⲧⲃⲉⲣⲥⲱⲧ[3] ϩⲓⲧⲛ[. On *verso* the names ⲡⲁⲥⲟⲛ ⲛⲟⲗⲗ[ⲟⲩⲑⲉ], ⲕⲩⲣⲟⲥ, ⲕⲩⲣⲓⲁⲕ/, ⲗⲏ(sic)

252.—Papyrus, a fragment, 22 × 18 cm Script rarely ligatured *Recto* ↑
Account of charges by a builder (?) The numerals presumably represent money[4]

]ⲉⲡⲏⲓ ⲛⲁⲡⲁ ⲣⲁϣⲉ ϫⲓⲧⲁⲓ | ⲛ̄ⲧⲓⲣⲟⲙ̄ⲡⲉ ⲧ[ⲁⲓ] | ⲓⲁ ⲛⲁϩ | above ⲟ——[5], ϩⲁⲧⲛⲓⲥⲉ[6] ⲛ̄ⲧⲁⲓⲕⲟⲧⲉ ⲁⲓⲣⲟⲩϩⲟⲟⲩ ϩⲓⲱⲱⲥ / ⲇ̄′ | ϩⲁⲛⲉⲓⲧⲏ ⲛ̄ⲧⲁⲓⲡⲟⲛⲕⲟⲩ ⲉⲃⲟⲗ ⲁⲓⲣϩⲟⲟⲩ ⲥⲛⲁⲩ ϩⲓⲱⲱⲟⲩ (ⲗⲉⲛⲡⲓⲱ above) / ⲅ̄ | ϩⲁⲛⲉⲥⲡⲏⲗⲁⲓⲟⲛ ⲛ̄ⲧⲁⲓϫⲡⲟϥ ⲛ̄ⲧⲁⲡⲉⲕⲱⲧ ⲥⲗ̄ⲛ̄ⲧϥ / ⲅ̄ⲇ̄′ | ϩⲁⲧⲉ[about 14 let] ⲉϥ | ϩⲁⲡⲣⲟ ⲛⲧⲁⲓⲥⲗⲛ̄ⲧϥ ⲛ̄ⲧⲁϥⲁⲙ̄ϣⲉ ⲣⲟⲩϩⲟⲟⲩ ϩⲓⲱⲱϥ ⲁ | ϩⲁⲛⲓⲉⲓϥⲧ ⲛ̄ⲧⲁⲓϣⲟⲡⲟⲩ ⲛⲧⲉ ⲁⲡⲁ ⲑⲉⲟⲇⲱⲣⲉ ⲡⲡⲣ⳽ / ⲇ̄′ | ϩⲁⲧϣⲉ[7] ⲛⲓⲁⲓⲧⲁⲁⲥ ⲉⲡⲉⲕⲗⲁⲃⲁⲕ[/ ⲁ | ϩⲁⲛⲧⲱⲃⲉ ⲛ̄ⲧⲁⲓⲡⲟⲛⲕⲟⲩ ϩⲙ̄ⲡⲉϥ-ⲥⲧⲁⲃⲗⲟⲛ ⲗⲉⲛⲡⲁⲓⲱ / ⲁ | ϩⲁⲧϫⲟ ⲛ̄ⲧⲁⲓⲟⲩⲁϩⲥ ⲉⲃⲟⲗ ϩⲓϫⲛ̄ⲛⲉⲡⲱⲣ[8] / ⲁ | ϩⲁⲧⲉⲡⲱ[9] ⲛⲛⲡⲣⲟ ⲛ̄ⲫⲓⲣ / ϥ̄

Verso [+] ⲡⲗⲟⲩⲟⲥ [. . . . .] ⲛⲁⲡⲁ ⲣⲁϣⲉ

' for the house of Apa Rashe, since I have this year of the 14th Indiction, as follows (οὕτως) For the   . which I built, taking a day thereto, ¾ For the earth that I removed, taking 2 days thereto, with the donkey, 3 For the cave (σπήλαιον) which I acquired and which the builder set in order, 3½ For the   , 5½ For the door which I made and which the carpenter worked a day upon, 1 For the nails I bought of Apa Theodore the priest, ¼ For the wood (?) that I put to the couch, 1 For the bricks which I took over to his stable (στάβλον) with my donkey, 1 For the wall which I added (?) to the roof, 1 For the bolt of the street door, ½ '

253.—Papyrus, complete, 20 × 17½ cm Script ligatured *Recto* ↑
Account of various expenses, apparently supplied by the persons named

---

[1] ? ἀγρός as a place-name
[2] Possibly ⲛ for ⲗ Hardly the place in AMÉLINEAU, *Geogr* 415
[3] Cf ⲃⲉⲣϭⲟⲟⲩⲧ, Fargût, Farshût (AMELINEAU, *op cit* 178), though this lies much further south
[4] The preceding stroke elsewhere = γίνεται
[5] = οὕτως *V* KENYON, *Catal* III 248 (BELL) *V* also Br Mus no 1076
[6] *V* Br Mus no 329 In a Jême pap Louvre E. 7986, ⲡⲏⲓ ⲉⲧⲉⲣⲉⲓⲡⲟϭ ⲛⲛⲓⲥⲉ ϩⲓⲱⲱϥ Meaning still

uncertain
[7] Perhaps for ⲧⲓⲟⲟⲥⲉ ⲛⲓϫⲉ The next word (reading certain) apparently in a letter here as ⲓ ⲣⲁⲃ̄ⲁⲕⲧⲏ, but feminine Cf GRENFELL & HUNT, *Gk Pap* II 161, κραβάκτιον
[8] This verb similarly in Br Mus no 1089 and *ib* no 112, also in a letter here (*v* Index), ERMAN, *Kopt Volksltl* 27, and *Rec égypt* IX 152, KRALL CIV The meaning is not certain
[9] *V* Br Mus no 259 and Lord AMHERST'S Pachomius papyrus a door ⲱⲓⲧⲏ ⲱⲟⲩⲧ ϩⲓⲕⲗⲗⲉ ϩⲓⲗⲟⲭⲗⲟⲥ ϩⲓⲉⲛⲱ

R

ϩⲁⲛⲧⲁϩ¹ ⲁⲣϣⲓⲛ ⲇ/ ⲡϣⲉ ⲡϣⲟⲛⲉ² ⲛ̅ ⲅ′ | ϩⲁⲛⲏϩ ϩⲓⲧⲛⲓⲉⲣⲉⲙⲓⲁⲥ ⲡⲣ/ ϩⲓⲑⲏⲛⲛⲏⲧⲉ ⲛ̅ ⲅ′ |

ϩⲁⲑⲏⲙ . ⲥⲛ ϣⲟⲛⲧⲉ ⲇ/ ⲓⲱⲁⲛ ⲁⲡⲟ · ⲟⲩⲡ̅³ ⲛ̅ ⲅ′ | ϩⲁⲛⲉⲥⲟⲩⲟ ⲛⲧⲉⲡⲣⲟⲥⲫⲟⲣⲁ ϩⲓⲧⲛⲙⲁⲣⲕⲟⲥ ⲛ̅ ⲅ′ |

ϩ′ⲁ] . ⲟϥ ϩⲓⲧⲛⲓⲁⲕⲱ ⲁⲛⲧⲱⲛ ϩ ⲁⲡⲁ ⲧⲏⲣ ⲛ̅ ⲇ′ | ϩⲁⲡ ⲧⲁⲃ ϩⲁⲧⲁⲗⲱⲧ ⲇ/ ⲁⲗⲗⲉⲓⲁ⁴ ⲛ̅ ⲋ′ |

[ϩⲁ] . ⲕⲏ ϩⲓⲧⲛⲥⲉⲛⲟ/ ⲛ̅ ⲁ | traces of 7 more lines

Verso remains of a Greek account

254—Papyrus, a fragment, 22 × 18½ cm. Script ligatured *Recto* ↑

An Account, in 17 lines, of various expenses, headed ⲡⲁⲛⲓ̇ ⲟⲩϣⲙⲟⲩⲛ, with a sum of money, preceded by ⲕ̅ ⁵, opposite each. Legible are ϩⲁⲡⲣⲓⲣ, ϩⲁⲁⲡⲉⲧ⁶, ϩⲁⲧⲉⲛϣⲱⲧ⁷, ϩⲁⲁⲡⲁ ⲓ̅ⲱ̅ ⲛⲡⲓⲉⲣⲟⲯⲁⲗⲧ⁸ ⲛ̅ ⲁ, ϩⲁⲧⲕⲟⲩⲁⲟⲩⲗⲏ⁹, ϩⲁⲧⲧⲙⲏ ⲛⲉⲛⲟⲩⲫ/, ϩⲁⲧⲉⲩϩⲙⲙⲉ, ϩⲁⲛⲧⲟⲃⲉ ⲛⲉⲥⲟⲓ, ϩⲁⲛⲉϩ, ϩⲁⲑⲩⲙⲓⲱⲙⲁ, ϩⲁⲛⲁⲛⲁϩ¹⁰ ⲉⲡⲉⲥⲧⲣⲱⲙⲁ ⲥⲛⲁⲩ ⲉⲡⲓ¹¹

255.—Papyrus, a fragment, 25½ × 11 cm. Script seldom ligatured *Recto* (?) ↑
Not from the Ashmunain collection

Account of various expenses

] ⲛⲉⲣⲱⲙⲡⲟϩⲉ ⲡⲓϣⲟⲧⲉ ⲡⲁⲑⲁⲕ[¹² | ⲁⲡⲟⲗⲗⲱ ⲡⲁⲃⲓⲗ ϩⲁⲛⲁϩⲟⲟⲩ ⲛⲧ[| ⲡⲁⲓⲁⲕ/ ⲙⲱⲩⲥⲏⲥ ⲡⲥⲁⲛⲏⲣⲡ [| ⲛⲉϩⲟⲟⲩ ⲉⲣⲉⲁⲡⲁ ⲑⲱⲙⲁⲥ ϩⲁⲧⲛ ϩⲙⲡⲱϩⲉ | ⲡⲓⲧⲁⲛϫⲟϥ ⲉⲃⲟⲗ ⲉⲛϫⲱⲱⲗⲉ [| ⲡⲉⲛⲧⲁⲛⲣⲱⲙⲉ ⲥⲟⲟϥ ⲛⲧⲁⲩⲉⲓ ⲉⲃⲟⲗ¹³

Below this and on *verso*, in different script and ink, a list of names, with sums of money opposite each. Among them βησαμων, σαθουλ¹⁴, απα ρασιος¹⁵, απα ωρ

256.—Papyrus, a fragment, 9½ × 7 cm. Script few ligatures *Recto* ↑
Account of various expenses.

] ϩⲁⲥⲛⲟⲩⲧⲉ ⲁⲡⲟ . ⲧⲁⲡⲱ[| ϩⲁⲛϩⲁⲓ ⲛⲧϣⲉ ⲛⲁⲡⲁ ⲛⲕⲩⲣ[| ϩⲁⲛⲥⲟ̇ ⲛⲉⲱⲣ ⲁⲡⲟ ⲑⲁⲗⲗ[¹⁶ | ϩⲁϩⲱⲣ ⲡⲁⲡⲙⲁ ⲛⲡϣ[| ϩⲁⲧⲉⲕⲕⲗⲏⲥⲓⲁ ⲙⲙⲁⲛⲡⲣⲟ[| ϩⲁⲧⲉϣⲙⲏ ⲛⲡⲙⲁ ⲛ.[| ϩⲁⲧⲧⲙⲏ ⲛⲧ.....[| .. ⲫⲁⲥⲓⲥ̇ ⲃⲓⲕ/ [

Verso remains of Accounts in the same (?) hand

---

¹ For ? ⲧⲱϩ   ² Or ϣⲟⲡⲉ
³ *V* no 119
⁴ الليت Cf ⲁⲗⲗⲉⲓⲁⲓ KRALL liv .ⲁⲗⲱⲧ presumably not a name
⁵ ⲕⲉⲣⲁⲧⲓⲁ   ⁶ Or ⲁⲡⲟⲧ.   ⁷ Unknown
⁸ ⲓⲉⲣⲟⲯⲁⲗⲧⲏⲥ Given among church officials, with ψάλτης and ψαλμωδός, in Paris 44, 60 *b*, so too, after the lector, in Br Mus no 514
⁹ *V* no 238
¹⁰ *V* no 244 Here too it seems to be an ornament on

a mat or shawl
¹¹ For ? ⲛⲧⲓ, an abbreviation ?
¹² The place might be ⲡⲓϣⲟⲧⲉ, KRALL cxviii (but *cf* *provenance* of this text), ⲛⲟϩⲉ being part of its name Or perhaps Shôtep, with 'Athanasius following
¹³ 'For what the men drank on departing'
¹⁴ Cf Boh ϣⲁⲑⲟⲩⲗ 'ichneumon' *V* probably KRALL lxi 8
¹⁵ *V* CRUM, *Ostr* no 116
¹⁶ KRALL cclxii 23 Cf Θαλλου, VITELLI no 50

257.—Papyrus, a fragment; 7 × 9 cm   Script ligatured   *Recto* ↑
Account of various expenses

+ αηϩαλωμⲁ̄ ⳝⲉⲣⲡⲓⲓ | ϩⲁⲡⲕⲁⲁⲗⲁⲕⲩ ⲛⲁⲧⲁⲡⲁ[| ϩⲁⲡⲏⲛⲧⲁⲓⲧⲁⲁⲩ ⲛⲟⲉⲟⲛ[1] ⲉⲃⲕⲏ[| ϩⲁⲡⲏⲛⲧⲁⲓ-
ⲧⲁⲁⳙ ⲛⲟⲥⲟⲛ ⲉⳙⲕⲏ [| ϩ[ⲁ

258—Papyrus, a fragment, 9 × 14 cm   Script moderately ligatured   *Verso* →
Account of various expenses, partly in Greek and often obscure

]ϩ[ⲁ] ⲁⲁⲃ ⲡⲁⲑⲁⳝ ⲙⲏⲕⲉⲛⲟ̄[2] ⲡⲣⲟⲥ ⲧⲕⲉⲅ̄ⲗⲉⲅⲥⲓ[ⲥ | ϩⲁⲡⲁⲣ[3] ⲧⲁⲗⲗ̄ ⲃⲁⲗ° ⳣ̄ ⲉⲣ̄ ⲥⲅ́ | ϩⲁⲡⲁⲣ
ⳝ ⲉⲣ̄ ⳣ̄ ⲟⲥⲕⲁⲣ̄ | ϩⲁⲧ . ⲉⲛ ⲉⲃⲓⲕ,̄ ⲡⲉⲡⲓⲥⲧⲓⲕⲩ̄ ⲡⲁⲃⲉⲗ°[4] | ϩⲁⲓⲙⲉ̄ ⲛⲁⲃⲣⲁϩⲁⲙ ⲡⲉⲅⲩⲙⲙ̄[5] ⲡⲁⲣⲉ̄ ⲧⲁ[

Recto remains of another Account

259.—Papyrus, a fragment, 13 × 11 cm   Script ligatureless   *Verso* →
The end of an Account of various expenses[6]

]ⲣⲉ ⲛⲉⲣⳡⲁⲧⲉⲓ — ⲛⲟⲃ ⲓ |]ⲉⲥⲟⲩⲁⲛ ⲁⲗϩⲁⲓ — ⲛⲟⲃ ⲓ |]ⲁⲛⲟⲩⲱⲙ ⲛⲁⲛ — ⲛⲟⲃ ⲓ | ⲧ]ⲁⲣⲓⲭⲉⲛ
— ⲛⲟⲃ ⲁ | ⲷ———— ⳙ

Recto remains of an Arabic account (earlier)

260.—Papyrus, a fragment, 8½ × 17½ cm   Script rarely ligatured   *Verso* →
List of Doves, supplied (?) at different dates

+ ⲡⲁⲓⲡⲉ ⲡⲗⲟⳡⲟⲥ ⲙⲛⲉⲥⳡⲣⲟⲟⲙⲡⲉ ⲓⳡ | + ϩⲁⲥⲟⲩⲙⲧⲟⲩⲉ (ⲟⲩⳡ erased) ⲡⲉⲣⲓⲥⲧⲉⲣ β | ϩⲁⲥⲟⲩ-
ⲙⲧⲥⲛⲟⲟⲩⲥ ⲡⲉⲣⲓⲥⲧⲉⲣ ? | ϩⲁⲥⲟⲩⲙⲛⲧⲁ ⳝⲧⲉ ⲡⲉⲣⲓⲥⲧⲉⲣ γ | ϩⲁ[ⲥⲟⲩⲙⲧ ? ⲡⲉⲣ (ⲓⲟ) δ | ϩⲁⲥⲟⲩⲙⲛⲧⲁ . ⲓⲓ
ⲡⲉⲣⲓⲥⲧⲉⲣ β | blank

Recto part of a letter

261.—Papyrus, a fragment, 13 × 7½ cm   Script cf ZOEGA's 4th class   1 (?) column
Verso →.

List of Books

ⳡ ⲁⲡⲁ ⲥⲓⲗⲁ[ⲥ | ⲡⲭⲱⲱⲙ⸗ⲉ | ⲡⲭⲱⲱⲙⲉ [| ⲡϣⲟⲙⳡⲧ [| ⲡⲕⲁⲧⲁ ⲙ[| ⲡⲉⲅⲁⲡ⳿ⲡⲉ[ⲗⲓⲟⲛ | ⲧⲙⲁⲣ-
ⲧⲩ[ⲣⲓⲁ | ⲁⲡⲁ ⲛⲁϩⲣ[ⲟⲟⲩ[7] | blank

Recto part of a list or account (earlier)

---

[1] ? Θέων
[2] νοτάριος
[3] ⲁⲣⳡⲁⲧⲏⲥ, ἐργάτης, ⲉⲣⳡ = ἔργον
[4] Victor πιστικὸς Βαβυλῶνος   For πιστ v Index
[5] Despite KRALL's quotation, *Rainer Mitth* ii 60, there are cases in which σύμμαχος seems something more than

'messenger   KRALL no ccxxiii (engaged in tax-collect-ing), Br Mus Gk Pap *Inv* 1515 (paid for work ὑπουργία on a mosque, H I Bᴠ11)
[6] ⲛⲟⲃ = ⲛⲟⲩⲃ, simply 'money'
[7] V *Synaxarium*, 7th Hathor

262.—Papyrus, 2 disconnected fragments, the larger, 8½ × 11½ cm   Script *recto*, moderately ligatured, of Greek type, *verso*, almost ligatureless, uneven

Recto ↑   An Account, showing the names of various garments

ⲟⲙ̄/[1] ⲡⲧⲓⲁⲕⲟⲛ ⲃ̄ⲓⲕⲧ[ⲱⲣ | ⲟⲙ̄/ ⲧⲓ ⲕⲟⲗⲗⲟⲉ [| lacuna | ⲟⲙ̄/ ⲓⲱⲁⲛⲛⲁ [ ] ⲟⲙ̄/ ⲧⲁⲗⲁⲩ[2] — — ⲛ̄[| ⲟⲙ̄/ ⲕⲁⲙⲓⲥⲓⲁ   ⲍ ⲁⲥ[3]   ιβ[| ⲟⲙ̄/ ⲧⲓ ⲕⲁⲙⲓⲥⲁ   ⲍ ⲁ [| ⲟⲙ̄/ ⲡⲗⲟⲩⲙⲁⲕⲓⲁ[4] . . ⲩ [| illegible   ⲩ ⲁ[| ⲟⲙ̄/ ⲡⲗⲟⲩⲙⲁⲕⲓⲁ ⲁⲩ ⲥⲓⲙ . ⲛⲁⲍⲓⲥ ⲛ̄ ⲉⲥ [| ⲟⲙ̄/ ⲙⲁⲣⲓϩⲁⲙ ⲛ̄ ⲁ[|

Verso →   A List (γνῶσις) of the articles (σκευή) belonging to the deceased (μακ)

ⲧⲁⲓⲧⲉⲥⲛⲱⲥⲓⲥ ⲛⲛⲉⲥⲕⲉⲩⲏ ⲛⲧⲁⲩ | ⲥⲟⲩ ⲛ̄ⲧⲟⲟⲧϥ ⲛ̄ⲡⲙⲁⲕⲁⲣ[| In the remaining lines can be read ⲟⲩⲃ..ⲛ ⲙⲛⲟⲩⲙ ⲉ , ⲟⲩⲧⲟⲟⲧⲥ ⲕⲙⲁⲧⲥ[5], ⲟⲩⲁϫⲉⲗⲉⲓ ⲛⲉⲱϩⲉ, ⲟⲩⲛⲟⲩ̈ϫⲟⲩ, ⲟⲩⲡⲁⲗⲗⲓⲛ ⲉϫⲱⲗ ⲉⲡⲁ[, ⲟⲩϩⲙⲛ ⲉϣⲧⲏⲛ ⲉⲥϩⲟ.[, ⲟⲩⲥⲉⲃⲗⲉⲓⲛ ⲉⲛⲛⲉ[ⲡⲉ

263.—Papyrus, complete (?), 12½ × 8 cm   Script ligatured, of late type   *Recto* ↑
An Account of expenses

ⲧⲓ[6] ⲩ β ⲛⲧ..ⲁⲕⲉ ⲛⲁⲣⲙ.| ⲩ β ⲓⲱⲁⲛⲛⲏⲥ | ⲁ ϩⲁⲧⲁⲣϩⲁⲙ[7] | ⲩ ⲁ ⲥⲁⲗⲙⲁ[8] ⲁ | ⲉ ϩⲁⲛ̄ ⲁ ϩⲟⲗⲟⲕ/ | ⲁ ⲧⲡⲁⲣⲑⲉⲛⲟⲥ ⲕⲟⲩⲓ ⲧⲓⲣⲟ | β ⲕⲱⲙⲛⲧⲉ | ⲁ ⲕⲱⲥⲧⲓⲛⲉ | blank

264.—Papyrus, a fragment, 5½ × 5 cm   Script   sloping uncials   *Recto* ↑
Account (λόγος) of sheep, wool &c

+ ⲡⲁⲓⲡⲉ ⲡⲗⲟⲅⲟⲥ [| ⲛⲉⲥⲟⲟⲩ ⲙⲛⲃ̄[ⲁⲁⲙⲡⲉ | ⲛⲥⲟⲣⲧ ⲕⲁⲓⲟ[| ⲡⲗⲱϫⲱⲛ.[| ⲟⲩⲁⲗⲡⲁⲥ[9] | ⲛⲕⲁⲩⲛⲁⲕ[10] |

265—This is the *verso* of no 108
List of months, with numerals opposite each   The forms are ⲑⲟⲟⲩⲧ, ⲡⲁⲟⲡⲉ, ϩⲁⲑⲱⲣ, ⲭⲓⲁⲭ, ⲧⲱⲃ̄, ⲙⲉⲭⲓⲣ, ⲡⲁⲣⲙⲉϩⲟⲧ, ⲡⲁⲣⲙⲟⲩϯ, ⲁ̈ⲡϣⲟⲟⲥ, ⲡⲁⲱⲛⲉ ⲉⲛⲡⲏⲡ

266.—This is the later text of the palimpsest no 88, *q v*
From a Word-list, in single column, showing Greek and Coptic words[11] beginning with ⲍ and ⲟ, but classed here merely on phonetic, not grammatical, principles[12]   They are

---

[1] ὁμοίως
[2] A name? *Cf* ⲧⲁⲗⲟⲩ, Ταλοῦς
[3] Presumably ζεύγη, *cf* Crum *Osti oco* Ad 36, Kᴇɴʏoɴ, *Catal* ii 314, Bi Mus no 1103
[4] πλουμάκιον, *plumatium*
[5] ⲧⲟⲟⲧⲥ obscure   Tha it should = δίφρος (Bꜱʜᴀɪ) seems due to confusion with ⲧⲟϭⲥ, v Job xxix 17, Prov ix 14, Rossi I iii 47   In Paris *Scala* 44, 122a is the phrase ⲁϥϩⲓⲧⲉ ⲁⲩⲥⲕⲟⲧⲉⲩⲉ ϣⲁⲛⲧⲉⲛⲉϥⲥⲱⲙⲁ ⲉⲣϩⲁⲭⲓϥ ϩⲓⲧⲉⲛⲡⲣⲁϥⲧ ⲙⲛ̄ⲧⲱⲧⲛⲉ الكل تعب وداح حتى ان حسده تمل بصرة
Kɪʀᴄʜᴇʀ 432 gives يربش, which might be suitable here.

[6] Possibly ⲁⲓⲧⲓ or +ⲧⲓ (imperat).   The sign following = κεράτια, *cf* pieceding no and Br Mus nos 1090, 1131
[7] If this is قرد, *cf* the use in Br Mus no 459, where the coin seems likewise unsuitab'e
[8] Or ⲡⲁⲗⲙⲁ
[9] Arabic is improbable with this script   [10] κανυάκης
[11] *V* Kʀᴀʟʟ in *Mitth Rainer* iv 132 and no 113 here, next to which the present text ought to have been placed
[12] Note that ⲍ, in the Coptic words = ⲕⲓ, while in the Greek it sometimes = ⲍξ-

separated into groups according to the vowel following the initial letter   A considerable space in the MS divides the first from the second syllables, and the incompleted words show that the latter were added after all the first syllables had been written down

ⲍⲁⲓⲧⲏⲥ, ⲍⲁⲧⲉ, ⲍⲁⲧⲟ, ⲍⲁⲡⲁ, ⲍⲁⲡⲉ, ⲍⲁⲡⲓ, ⲍⲁ (sic), ⲍⲁ

ⲍⲉⲛⲟⲥ, ⲍⲉⲥⲧⲏⲥ, ⲍⲉⲡⲁⲣ, ⲍⲉⲥϯ[1], ⲍⲉⲧⲟⲩ, ⲍⲥ, ⲍⲉ.

ⲍⲏⲣⲱⲛ, ⲍⲏⲛⲱⲛ, ⲍⲏⲧⲏⲣ, ⲍⲏⲣⲃⲉ, ⲍⲏ, ⲍⲏ.

ⲍⲓⲣⲓⲛ, ⲍⲓ (6 times)

ⲍⲟⲙⲉ, ⲍⲟⲙⲉⲥⲩ, ⲍⲟⲣⲉⲓⲥ, ⲍⲟⲣⲣⲓⲙ, ⲍⲟⲟⲩⲛ, (verso) ⲍⲟⲣⲓⲉⲧ, ⲍⲟⲩⲧⲛ.

ⲍⲩ (7 times)

ⲍⲱ (7 times)

ⲟⲁ (6 times)

ⲟⲏ, ⲟⲏ.

ⲟⲓⲡⲉ, ⲟⲓⲥⲓⲕ, ⲟⲓⲙⲉ, ⲟⲓ (4 times)

---

[1] ἔξεστι

LETTERS

267.—Paper, 2 fragments, the larger, 19 × 17 cm   Script of Zoega's 9th class
26 lines   The leaf was folded while the ink was wet, an impression therefore of other
lines often crosses and obscures the text   Parts of ll 1–4 are given from this impression
on the *verso*

Official Letter from the bishop of Shmoun to his flock, relating to a theft   One
exactly similar is published by Steindorff, in *Aeg Zeitschr* xxx 37, fragments of others are
among MSS in Mr De Ricci's hands[1] and, apparently, in *Mitth Rainer* v 33   Cf also
Br Mus no 633 and the Arabic letter, *ed* Reinhardt, in the Ebers *Festschrift*, p 89

ⲉⲅⲏ̄ [. . ⲟⲁⲙⲡ]ⲏⲁ ⲙ̄ⲡⲛⲟⲩⲧⲉ ⲡⲓⲉⲗⲁ̄ ⲉⲛⲉⲡⲓⲥⲕⲟⲡⲟⲥ] | ⲛ̄ⲧⲉ ⲧⲓⲡⲟⲗⲓⲥ ⲙⲙⲁⲓⲡⲉⲭ̄ⲥ̄ ϣⲙⲟⲩⲛ
ⲙ̄ⲡⲉⲥⲧⲟⲟ[ϣ²] | ⲧⲏⲣⲟⲩ ⲛⲁⲙⲉⲣⲁⲧⲉ ⲉϯⲙⲉ ⲙ̄ⲙⲟⲟⲩ ⲟⲙ̄ⲡⲟ̄ⲥ̄ ⲭⲉⲣⲉⲧⲉ] | ⲉⲣⲉ[ⲡⲟ̄ⲥ̄ ⲥⲙⲟⲩ ⲉⲣ]ⲱⲧⲛ
ⲟⲛⲥⲙⲟⲩ ⲛ[ⲙ ⲙ̄ⲡⲙⲁⲕ] |[ⲁⲩⲱ ⲛⲉⲛⲟⲩⲣⲁⲛ ⲙ̄ⲛⲛⲉⲧⲛ̄]ϣ[ⲏⲣⲉ ⲙ̄ⲛⲛⲉⲧⲛ̄ϣⲉ]ⲉⲣⲉ ⲙ̄ⲛⲛⲕⲁ ⲛⲓⲙ ⲉⲧϣⲟⲟⲡ
ⲛⲏⲧⲛ̄ [ⲟⲁⲙⲏⲛ] | ⲉⲡⲓⲧⲁ³ ⲇⲉ ⲁⲡϩⲱⲃ ⲡⲱⲟ ϣⲁⲣ ⲭⲉⲁⲩⲃⲱⲕ ⲉⲟⲟⲩⲛ | ⲉⲡⲏⲓ ⲉⲧⲙⲁⲁⲩ ⲛⲥⲁⲟⲩⲉⲡ⁴
ⲁⲩϥⲓ ⲟⲩⲉⲣⲧⲟⲩ | ⲉⲥⲟⲩⲟ ⲛⲁⲙⲉⲥⲟ⁵ ⲛⲁⲣⲣⲁⲡⲱ⁶ ⲛ̄ⲥⲓⲡⲉⲛ ⲛⲁⲙⲉⲥⲛ̄ⲏ⁷ ⲙ̄ⲡⲁⲡⲟⲓ ⲙⲉⲟⲩⲁⲗⲉⲕⲧⲱⲣ ⲗⲟⲓ̄
ⲉⲓⲧⲉ | ⲟⲟⲟⲩⲧ ⲉⲓⲧⲉ ⲉⲟⲓⲙⲉ ⲉⲓⲧⲉ ϣⲙ̄ⲙⲟ ⲉⲓⲧⲉ ⲣⲙ̄ⲛϯⲙⲉ ⲛ̄ⲧⲁϥϫⲟⲡⲟⲩ ⲛ̄ⲛⲉϥⲟⲩⲟⲛⲟⲟⲩ ⲉⲃⲟⲗ |
ⲉϥⲉϣⲱⲡⲉ ⲟⲁⲡⲥⲁⲟⲟⲩ ⲙ̄ⲡⲛ̄ⲟ̄ⲙ̄ⲟ̄ ⲙ̄ⲛⲛⲉⲡⲣⲟⲫⲏⲧⲏⲥ ⲁⲩⲱ ⲉⲃⲟⲗ ⲟⲓⲧⲧⲁⲡⲣⲟ ⲛ̄ⲧⲁⲙⲛ̄ⲧⲉⲗⲁ̄ⲭ̄ | ⲉϥⲉϣⲁⲣ⁸
ⲉⲣⲟⲟⲩ ⲛⲑⲉ ⲛ̄ⲧⲁϥϣⲁⲣ ⲉⲥⲟⲇⲟⲙⲁ ⲙ̄ⲛ̄ⲕⲟⲙⲟⲣⲣⲁ ⲉϥⲉⲉⲓ⁹ ⲟⲣⲁⲓ ⲉϫⲱⲟⲩ ⲛ̄ⲡⲉⲥⲁⲟⲟⲩ | ⲛ̄ⲧⲁ-
ⲡⲟⲩⲕⲁⲗⲛⲙ̄ⲯⲓⲥ ⲙ̄ⲛ̄ⲡⲉ[ⲡⲗⲏⲕⲏ ⲙ̄ⲡⲱⲱⲙⲉ ⲛⲓⲱⲃ ⲙ̄ⲛ̄ⲡⲉⲥⲁⲟⲟⲩ | ⲙ̄ⲡⲙⲉⲟⲣ̄ⲡ̄ ⲛⲯⲁⲗⲙ̄ ⲉⲣⲉⲛ̄ⲥⲁⲟⲟⲩ
ⲛⲁϣⲱⲡⲉ ⲛ̄ⲑⲉ ⲛ̄ⲟⲩⲛⲉⲟ ⲟⲓⲛⲉⲩⲕⲉⲉⲥ ⲁⲩⲙⲉⲣⲉⲛ̄ⲥⲁⲟⲟⲩ | ⲉϥⲉϣⲱⲡⲉ ⲛⲁⲩ ⲙ̄ⲡⲟⲩⲉϣ ⲡⲉⲥⲙⲟⲩ
ⲉϥⲉⲡⲱⲧ | ⲥⲁⲃⲟⲗ ⲙ̄ⲙ̄ ⲉⲓϣⲁϫⲉ ⲉⲟⲩⲟⲛ ⲛⲓⲙ ⲛ̄ⲧⲁϥϭⲟⲡ ⲛⲓⲥⲟⲟⲩ ⲙ̄ⲛ̄ⲛⲓⲥⲓ[ⲡⲉ]ⲛ ⲙ̄ⲛ̄ⲛⲓⲡⲁⲡⲟⲓ
ⲛⲓ[ⲉϥⲟⲩⲟⲛⲟⲟⲩ] | ⲉⲃⲟⲗ ⲛ̄ⲡⲉⲛⲧⲁϥⲙⲉ ⲉⲣⲟⲟⲩ ⲉϥϫⲓ ⲙ̄[. . .] | ⲁⲩⲱ ⲡⲗⲁ̄ⲥ̄ ⁿᵃᵗ ⲛⲁⲧⲁⲣⲓⲕⲉ ϥⲉϣⲱⲡⲉ
ⲛ̄ⲣⲙ̄ⲟⲉ | ⲉⲧⲃⲉⲟⲩⲡⲗⲏⲣⲟⲫⲟⲣⲓⲁ¹⁰

'With God('s help)¹   , by the mercy of God, the humble (ἐλάχιστος) bishop of
this Christ-loving city (πόλις) Shmoun and its whole nome   My beloved, whom I love
in the Lord, greeting (χαίρετε)   The Lord bless you, with every spiritual and heavenly
(πνευματικός, ἐπουράνιος) blessing, and your sons and your daughters and everything that
is yours   Amen   Thereafter (ἔπειτα) the matter hath reached us, that they have entered
the house of the mother of Sawep and have taken an *artaba* of corn and 6 *quarts* of
flax (σίππιον) and 2 (?) chickens and a cock (ἀλέκτωρ), now (λοιπόν) whether (εἴτε) it be man
or (εἴτε) woman or stranger or native that hath taken them and doth not make them
known, he shall be under the curse of the law (νόμος) and the prophets   And by the
mouth of my humility (·ἐλάχ) He shall be wroth with them, even as He was wroth with

---

[1] Mr De Ricci generously allowed me the use of his
copies

[2] As in the parallel texts ⲧⲏⲣⲟⲩ presumably for ⲧⲏⲣϥ

[3] لما الما   Cf Br Mus nos 549, 633   May not the
frequent ἐπειδή be sometimes for ἔπειτα?

[4] ? شعب   V Br Mus no 658   Gk Pap *Inv* 1514
has Σζωειπ   Or ?ضوب   What is ' Du'eib, *Führer Rainer*,
no 551 ?

[5] ⲛⲁⲙⲥ =? ⲛⲉⲙ, *cf* no 368   Yet here we have ⲙ̄ⲛ̄
frequently

[6] *V* p 56 above

[7] ⲥⲛⲏⲧⲉ, as ⲛⲁⲡⲟⲓ is fem, v *Mitth Rain* iv 128

[8] *V* Spiegelberg in *Sphinx* v 200

[9] ⲉⲓⲛⲉ

[10] Seems displaced here   *cf* Steindorff

Sodom and Gomorrah, and He shall bring upon them the curses of the Apocalypse and the plagues (πληγή) of the book of Job and the curses of the 108th Psalm And these curses shall be as it were oil in their bones "They have loved cursing it shall be theirs They desired not blessing it shall depart far from them" I mean any one that shall have taken the corn and the flax and the chickens and shall not display them unto such as have known them, he . And the blameless tongue shall go free For an assurance (πληροφορία)'

268.—Papyrus, almost complete, 19 × 14 cm Script heavy, uncials of early type[1]
V Plate 2 *Recto* ↑
Letter from Apa Shoi to 'his dear brother, Apa John'
This, the following 6 numbers, and no 276 are addressed to John, whom, judging by the relative antiquity of script in all of them and by certain incidental names and phrases, I take to be the same person He was presumably a monastic dignitary Several more of our papyri, apparently of a like age, may also belong here, although no John is named in them And *cf* perhaps Br Mus Greek Catal iii, Pap 981 ('4th cent', *provenance* unknown)[2]

апа щoеι пепресбүте|рос мптооу мпномт[3] петιоаι мпечмерιт | нсон апа ιωаннне
оаθн | ∆е ноωб нιм †щιне ерок | аүω несннү тнроү ката | пеүран непетещще | гарпе
етреneι щарон алλа | ерщанпхоеιс ронач тιнаeι | теноүσе †сдι нак етбепен|коүeι
нщнре папноүте | етрекртексом нммач | ката пноүте ксооүн мпоιсе epeι[4] eхωч аүω
тнр|мнтре оароч епιсте пен|еιωт апа пансе перадатехаι мпωб[5] ачeισe[6] | ебоλ оι
[. м]пнщнрер|на мпωб τ+н]оүσе н|токпе пен[. . . .][7] мннса|мпноүιе [о]үхаι оαмпхоеιс |
нсон [ммерιт

Verso blank

'Apa Shoi, the priest (πρεσβ) of the mount of Pnomt, writeth to his dear brother, Apa John Before all things I greet thee and all the brethren by (κατά) their names For (γάρ) we ought to have come to thee, yet (ἀλλά) if it please God, we will come So now I write to thee concerning our young son, Papnoute, that thou mayst exert thyself with him according to (κατά) God('s grace) Thou knowest the trouble that is upon him, and we do testify thereto Seeing that (ἐπειδή) our father Apa Paêse ' The rest is obscure

269.—Papyrus, 3 disconnected fragments, the largest 13 × 9½ cm Script uneven, tolerably early uncials V Plate 3 *Recto* →
Letter from Apa Shoi to 'his dear father, Apa John'[8], greeting others also and 'all the brethren that are with thee'. St Paul is quoted[9]

---

[1] Possibly written more carefully by the scribe of no. 269 But *cf* the difference in terms of salutation

[2] WILCKEN would make this John a bishop, *Arch f Pap* iv 558

[3] An unknown place 'Mount here presumably = monastery

[4] Above eι a letter, perhaps τ'

[5] Alternatives are нерадтехλιнтоωб All very uncertain

[6] Oι cισe

[7] Does not look like хоeιc

[8] Shoi perhaps the writer of no 268 V also no 301

[9] †онү suggests 1 Cor xiii 3, but it hardly seems suitable

ⲁⲡⲁ ϣⲟⲓ ⲡⲉⲧⲉϩⲁⲓ ⲛⲡⲉⲕⲙⲉⲣⲓⲧ ⲛⲓⲱⲧ ⲁⲡⲁ ⲓⲱϩⲁ|ⲛⲛⲉ ϩⲙⲡϫⲟⲓⲥ ⲭⲁⲓⲣⲉⲧ⳽ ϩⲁⲧⲉϩⲏ [ⲙ]ⲉⲛ
ⲛⲣⲱⲃ | ⲛⲙ ϯϣⲓⲛⲉ ⲉⲣⲟⲕ ⲡⲁⲙⲉⲣⲓⲧ ⲛⲓⲱⲧ ⲁⲩⲱ ⲁⲡⲁ ⲑⲉ|ⲟⲧⲣⲉ ⲙⲛⲁⲡⲁ ⲱ[ⲛⲟⲫⲣ]ⲉ[1] ⲙⲛⲁⲡⲁ
ⲑⲉⲟⲫⲓⲗⲉ | ⲙⲛⲛⲉⲥⲛⲏⲩ ⲧⲏⲣⲟⲩ ⲉϫⲛⲙⲙⲉⲕ⳽ ϯⲣⲁϣⲉϭⲉ | ⲉⲙⲁ[ⲧ]ⲉ ϫⲉⲧⲙⲛⲧⲙⲁⲓⲛⲟⲩⲧⲉ ⲉⲧⲛϩⲏⲧⲕ |
[. . . . .]ⲛϩⲁϩ ⲛⲥⲟⲡ ⲉⲧⲣⲉⲛⲙⲉⲧⲉ|[ⲭⲥ　　　　　　　　]ⲛⲁ ⲧⲁⲓ ⲉⲧⲉⲣⲉ|[. . . . . . 　　. . .]ⲧⲉ⳽
ⲟⲩ ⲙⲟⲛⲟⲛ ⲁⲛⲟⲛ [. . . . . ⲧ]ⲏⲣⲟⲩ ⲕⲁⲧⲁ ⲛⲉⲩ[　　　　　　　　ⲙ]ⲏⲛ[ϩ]ⲏⲕⲉ ⲙⲛ[
. . . 　　.]ⲡⲉ ϯⲙⲉⲉⲩⲉ | [. . . . .]ⲡⲉⲛⲧⲁⲡⲁⲩⲗⲟⲥ | [. . . . .]ϩⲱⲕ
ⲛ . . ⲁⲓⲁⲁⲧ | [. . . . 　. 　　　]ⲛⲁ[ϯ]ϩⲏⲩ ⲙⲡⲉ| ? |[. . . . . .] ⲉⲣⲟⲥ ϫⲉ[. .ⲧⲟⲛ[　　　] | |
[. . .]ⲡⲁⲙⲉⲣⲓⲧ ⲛⲉⲓⲱⲧ ϯⲣⲁϣⲉ ⲉⲙⲁ[ⲧⲉ] ⲙⲛⲓ. . .ⲁⲓ ⲉⲛⲧⲁⲧⲉⲕ[ⲙⲛⲧ]ϣⲁⲛⲉϩⲧⲏϥ ⲛⲁϩ[2] | ⲉⲃⲟⲗ
ϩⲙⲡⲉⲩⲟⲓⲥⲉ ⲧⲏⲣ[ⲟ]ⲩ ⲛⲥⲉⲛϩⲧⲟ ⲟⲛ |[ ] ⲛⲧⲉⲡⲉⲕϩⲏⲧ ⲟ ⲛⲙⲧⲟⲛ ⲉⲧⲃⲉⲡⲉⲉⲓ | [. . .] ⲉⲛⲅⲁⲧⲛⲛⲁⲩ ⲛⲁⲕ
ⲉⲧⲃⲏⲧⲟⲩ ⲉⲧⲣⲉⲕ|[. .] ⲕⲁⲧⲁ ⲡⲉⲧⲉϩⲛⲁⲕ blank

270—Papyrus, a fragment, 29 × 11 cm　Script　*v* Plate 4　*Cf* that of nos 313, 399,
and of the Psalter, *Fuhrer Rainer*, Taf vii　Recto →

Letter from Porphyra[3] to Apa John, whom he addresses as 'thou man of God', and
whose help he entreats once again　He then narrates his interrogation at the βῆμα of the
prefect (ἡγεμών), and ends with salutations to Theodore, Petosiris[4] and ' all those with thee '

The idiom is remarkable, showing several Aḥmimic forms[5]

ⲡⲟⲣⲫⲩⲣⲁ ⲡⲉⲧⲉϩⲁⲓ ⲛⲁⲡⲁ | ⲓⲱϩⲁⲛⲉⲥ ϯⲣⲡⲁⲣⲁⲕⲁⲗⲓ ⲙⲙⲟⲛ | ϯⲥⲁⲡⲓ ⲙⲙⲟⲛ ϯⲥⲟ[ⲟ]ⲩⲛⲉ |
ϫⲉⲁⲕⲛⲁⲉ ⲛⲁⲓ ⲛϩⲉⲛ[.] | ⲛⲁⲉ ⲛⲁⲓ ⲟⲛ ⲙⲡⲓⲕⲉⲥⲟⲡ [ⲙ]ⲡ̣ⲣ̣ⲧ ⲱⲡ ⲛⲥⲙⲁⲓ ⲕⲁ[ⲧ]ⲁ ⲛ . . . . | ϫⲉⲛⲧⲁⲡⲣⲱⲙⲉ
ⲧⲁ . . . | ⲥⲟⲟⲕ ⲙⲡⲉϯ ⲱⲡ ⲛⲉⲙⲁⲓ ϩⲛ|ⲃⲟⲗ ⲛⲡⲁⲣⲙⲁⲧⲁⲩ　ⲟⲛⲁ ⲉⲣⲟⲕ | ϯⲥⲁⲡⲉ ⲙⲙⲟⲛ ⲡⲣ[ⲱ]ⲙⲉ
ⲙⲡⲛⲟⲩⲧⲉ ϯⲟⲩⲱϣ ⲉⲟⲉϥⲣⲉⲕ[6] ⲙⲙⲉ ϫⲉⲛⲧⲁⲓϫⲟ[ⲥ] ϫⲉⲟⲩ | ϩⲛⲃⲏⲙⲁ ⲉⲓ |ⲧⲁϥⲏⲕⲉ|ⲙⲱⲛ ϫⲛⲟⲩⲓ
ϫⲉ[ⲛⲧ]ⲕⲟⲩⲉⲟⲩ | ⲡⲉϫⲁⲓ ϫⲉⲁⲛⲕⲟ[ⲩ . .ⲅⲟ ⲁⲛ | ⲡⲉϫⲉϥ ϫⲉ . 　ⲥⲟⲟⲩⲛⲉ | ⲡⲉϫⲁⲓ ϫⲉⲁ[. . . . . .]ⲡⲉ
ⲁⲓ|ϫⲟϥ ϩⲉⲛϩ[.]ⲡⲁⲣⲁⲕ|ⲁⲗⲓ ⲙ'ⲙⲟⲛ ϯⲥⲁⲡⲉ ⲙ[ⲙⲟⲛ]ϩⲁⲣϩ |ⲃⲉⲗⲉ ⲡⲁⲡⲁⲓⲕ [. .ⲙⲟ]ϥ |ⲛⲁⲓ ϫⲉⲃⲟⲏⲑⲉⲓ
ⲛⲁ[. . . .]|ⲛⲟⲥ ⲉϩⲁⲓ ⲟⲩⲉⲡϥ ⲧⲟ[ⲗⲏ　　　] | ϫⲉⲅⲁⲓⲁⲛⲕⲱⲡⲓⲉ[7] ϯⲧⲣ| | ϯϣⲓⲛⲉⲥ ϩⲁⲣⲟⲧⲛⲛ[| ⲉⲁⲡⲁ
ⲑⲉⲟⲥⲱⲣⲉ ϯⲩ⳽ⲛ|ⲉ ⲉⲁⲡⲁ| ⲡⲉⲧⲟⲥⲓⲣⲓⲥ ⲡⲉⲛⲓⲱⲧ] ϯϣⲓⲛⲉ | ⲉⲛⲉⲧⲛⲉⲙⲉⲛ ⲧⲏⲣⲟⲩ] | blank

271—Papyrus, a fragment, 11 × 17½ cm　Script　early, upright uncials, of a type
unusual in private documents　*V* Plate 4　Recto →

Letter from　　　　　to 'his brother' John, greeting several persons, requesting the
recipients' prayers, and asking that the πραιπόσιτος should send Palô[8], (to remain) till he
recover from his illness

]ⲉϩⲁⲓ ⲙⲡⲉϥⲥⲟⲛ ⲁⲩⲱ ⲡⲉϥ |]ⲓⲱⲁⲛⲛ[ⲉ] ϯϣⲓⲛⲉ ⲉⲣⲟⲕ ⲧⲟⲛⲉ | [ϩⲛⲧⲁϥⲯⲩ]ⲭⲏ ⲧⲏⲣⲥ [ⲙ]ⲛⲡⲛⲁ̄
ⲁⲩⲱ ϯϣⲗⲏⲗ | ⲉⲡⲛ[ⲟⲩⲧ]ⲉ ⲉⲧⲣⲉ[ⲕ]ⲟⲩϫⲁⲓ ⲛⲁⲓ ⲁⲩⲱ ⲛ'ⲛϣⲗⲏⲗ ⲉϫⲱⲉⲓ ⲁⲩⲱ ϯϣⲓⲛⲉ ⲉⲑⲉⲟⲥⲱⲣⲟⲥ |

---

[1] Not space for ⲱⲣⲟⲛⲛⲟⲩⲧⲉ, which no 271 suggests
Perhaps ⲱⲣⲛⲛⲟⲩⲧⲉ　Onnophrius is rarely if ever found
with ⲱ

[2] Possibly ⲛⲁ ϩⲙⲛ, *v* end of preceding line

[3] Porphyra masc apparently unknown　Only Πορφύριος
is found　Forms Jus a, Petra therefore not analogous

[4] Πετοσῖρις, a name practically extinct after the 3rd or
4th century

[5] *Cf* the usage of the *Acta Pauli*, and here nos 292,
35², 396

[6] Altered　One expects a verb, 'relate to thee '

[7] ϫⲉⲩ added later

[8] Recurs in a Jkôw (Aphroditô) fragment　*Cf* ? ⲡⲁⲗⲟⲩ,
ⲡⲁⲗⲁⲩ

ллпаропноүте¹ ллмерıт ҙллхоеıс | †ноүѕе еεıсҙаı [ллан ллкра . . оүл л|лепрепосıтос
лчхооү ѕапалω пшн|ре лсатрωнⳡле² лечıтч³ епⳑла шан|[т]ечⳑо ечшωпе ллон пехаү
лаεı | [

272.—Papyrus, 2 fragments, the larger, 10 × 9 cm   Script   early type, v Pl 4   Recto →

Letter to 'the beloved in the Lord' Apa John (v no 268)   It contains a request as to
an old man who had been put in custody⁴   Reference is made to his daughter, long
deceased, to his son in law and to the magistrate

a |cҙаı лапа ıωаллнс | лл]ерıт ҙллхоеıс хаıре |] лıлл †ѕıле епекоүхаı |

b | сүлтакч хетаı | пı]ноүте тоше лпечсωлт | ет]в̅епаı †аѕıоүѕе ллмок | ıе оүѕⲗⲗⲟ
ечнⳑ еҙоүл | лıⳑалллωн пархωл л |] ехıфаı лтечшеере | ҙⲗⲗⲟ ѕе еıс оүлоѕ л | течⳑ-
шеере лоү ел | л]капн етречıωт | т]аѕоч лсхооү л|

273 —Papyrus, almost complete, 25½ × 15½ cm   Script   of early type   V Pl 10
Recto →

Letter from Kelbaule⁵, his 'servant', to Apa John

|.   .] пеıтсҙаı лпечллерıт | [лεıωт ıωа]лнс лееллпе лıı шарок | [. . .   . . .]
пеоү . сωв аүω †шωпе | ллпıшεı . .] шарок ката тсүлнⳑн|сıс⁶ ллпе[.]тн т+лоү
шⳑнⳑ ехωεı | лтелı[оүте †ѕѡⲙ паı †лноү шарок | тепоүѕе ıс пелсол ⲯелтсапıс⁷
аεı|тлⲙⲟⲟⲩч шарок (хеаⲙархωл хоос ⲛⲁⲓ above) хеⲅⲣⲏⲓ етвеоү|пракⳑа оүаⲛⲁⲡⲧⲉⲥⲛ
лрⲱⲙⲉⲡⲉ | ката тсүлтесıс аⲗⲗⲁ оүⲱⲃ ката ⲯⲱⲙⲁ тепоүѕе лепратⲙⲁ лѕеⳑ | (above
хеаⲣⲓ оүспоⲩⲁⲛ лтсҙаı ⲛⲁ[л]а ıωалнс ⲡⲡⲣⲉⲥ⁹) | еıωⲣⲉⲡⲉ еаⲡⲙⲟⲟⲩ чıточ еⲛⲁⲓⳃⲁ⁹ |
лекⲥⲁⲕⲧⲱⲣⲏⲥ аүлаү ҙⲱⲟⲩ епⳃⲱⲃ | хечⲥⲱⲙⲉ аүхⲟⲟⲥ ⲛⲁⲥ хеⲥⲙⲙⲉ | лⲫⲛⲥⲙⲙⲟⲛ етвеⲅⲥⲛ-
кооүе ⲙⲁⲣⲉ|чⲕⲁⲁⲩ ⲛⲁⲕ еⲃⲟⲗ еⲱⲁⲣⲉⲡⲁⲣⲭⲱⲛ | ⲱⲡⲅⲧⲛⲟⲩ ҙⲁⲣⲟⳃ еⳃⲛⲗ еҙⲟⲩⲛ ⲛⲥⲉ†
оⲩⲕⲟⲩⲉⲓ еⲡⲟⲩⲁ ҙⲁⲣⲟⳃ т+ⲛⲟⲩⲅⲉ аⲡⲉ|хе лⲙⲟⳃ ⲛⳃⲓⲁⲅⲉ ⲑⲉ ерⲟⲕ хеⳃⲅⲣⲏⲓ ауⲁⲑⲟⲛ ⲛⲓⲙ
етеⲛⲛⲁⲱⲁⲁⲩ ⲛⲉⲙⲁⳃ аⲣⲓⲥⲟⲩ хетеⲛ ⲟⲟⲩⲛⲉ¹⁰ лпечⲅⲱⲱ †ѕⲓⲙⲉ еⲡⲉⲥⲛⲟⲩ тнⲣⲟⲩ ⲉⲧⲣⲁ|ⲧⲛ
ката ⲛⲉⲩⲣⲁⲛ оүхаı ҙⲙⲡⲭⲟⲉⲓⲥ | ⲡⲁⲉⲓⲱⲧ ⲙ̅ⲉⲣⲓⲧ †ѕⲓⲙⲉ ерⲟⲕ ⲡⲁⲉⲓⲱⲧ | [ⲙⲉ]ⲣⲓⲧ [. .]ⲡⲉⲕҙⲙⲅⲁⲗ
ⲕⲉⲗⲃⲁⲩⲗⲥ | [about 10 let] ⲡⲁⲉⲓⲱⲧ ⲙⲉⲣⲓⲧ

'   writeth to his dear father, John.   I had decided to go to thee   , and
I was sick and unable [to go ?] to thee, according to the information (? συνείδησις) of
So now pray for me, that God may give me strength to come to thee   And now here is

---

¹ Does this form one name?   Cf ? Pap Tebtunis 81,
'Αρπνοῦτις. If not, пноүте is difficult   With аро cf арооү
² Σατορνεῖλος   ⁸ Possibly a letter before ллч-
⁴ Cf nos 273, 311 and ωⳑ еҙоүл in Rossi I, v 26
⁵ Recurs in a Jkôw pap   Cf Καλαβελις, Καλάβαιλις,
BGU, ? Κελλαβαεύς, Kenyon, Catal 1 193, also каⳑа-
ⲙⲁⲅⲗⲉ, Crum, Ostr no 345.
⁶ It is difficult to give this the same meaning here and

below   Cf the use in Pap Oxyrh cxxiii
⁷ An unknown name   For теаⲙⲥ Sir H Thompson
suggests an abbreviated form of *dd ḥp ef ʿnḫ* (comparing
Tεῶs = *dd ḥr*)
⁸ This insertion inevitably disturbs the construction
⁹ For ʿcaҙ   Or cf no 320
¹⁰ Supposing an old-Saïdic form, as e g in the *Elias
Apokalypse*

S

our brother Psenteapis, I have sent him to thee, because the magistrates (ἄρχων) told me, saying that he is troubled regarding a matter of business (πρᾶγμα) He is a man valuable (ἀναγκαῖος) as to judgment (συνείδησις? reliability), yet weak in body (σῶμα) So now the business (πρ)—'be diligent (σπουδή),' they said, ' and write to Apa John the presbyter'—is one of fields which the (river's) water hath carried away, and they are those of the 'master' (?) tax-collector (ἐξάκτωρ). And they saw how the affair was becoming difficult, and they said to him, 'Appeal unto the prefect (ἡγεμών) for other (fields), that he would concede them unto thee,' and the magistrates (ἄρχ) will have pity on him, while he is imprisoned, each of them giving a little on his behalf Now, therefore, suffer (ἀνέχεσθαι) him to relate to thee the manner in which he is troubled Any benefit (ἀγαθόν) that thou canst do unto him, that do, for I am acquainted with his trouble I greet all the brethren that are with thee by their names Farewell in the Lord, my dear father I greet thee, my dear father, [I,] thy servant Kelbaule   , my dear father'

Verso ⲧⲁⲁⲥ ⲛⲁⲡⲁ ⲓⲱⲁⲛⲛⲏⲥ

274—Papyrus, a fragment, 7½ × 7 cm Script relatively early, v Pl 2 *Recto* →.
Letter from   to (his) 'lord and master', John

ⲕⲩⲣⲓⲱ ⲧⲱ ⲧⲉⲥⲡⲟ[ⲧⲏ | ⲉⲓⲁ]ⲛ]ⲛⲏⲥ ⲟⲁⲑⲏ ⲙ[| ⲛⲧ[.]ⲣⲁⲍⲓⲟⲩ ⲡⲉⲛ[| ⲡⲉ[.]ⲧ︤ⲭ︥ ⲉⲧⲙⲧⲁⲧⲉ[| ⲁⲥ︤ϥ︥ .]ⲓⲱⲱⲧ ⲛⲧⲙ[| ⲧⲁⲥⲱⲛⲉ ⲟⲛϣⲏⲣ [| ϯ ⲛⲉⲩⲁⲉⲓ ⲉⲃⲟⲗ ⲉⲙⲡⲁ | ⲛⲁⲉⲧⲉⲥ ⲁ︤ϥ︥ⲧⲁⲛⲟ ⲧ[| ⲡⲉ[.]ⲗⲁⲁⲩ ⲉⲓ ⲉⲃⲟ[ⲗ|

Verso traces of an account

275.—Papyrus, a fragment, 4 × 11 cm Script of no 396, but here *Recto* ↑
Letter from (?) Theodore (*or* Theodosius) to (?) John, whose charity he appears to be praising, while making a request

]ϣⲉ ⲁ︤ⲭ︥ⲛⲛ︤ⲭ︥ⲏⲣⲁ[1] ⲙ[ⲛ]ⲛⲟⲣ[ⲫⲁⲛⲟⲥ |]ⲛⲉⲓⲱⲧ ⲭⲉⲕⲁⲥ ⲧⲉⲭ︤ⲣ︥ⲓⲟⲩ[2] ⲉ︤ϥ︥[|]ⲛⲱⲣⲁ ⲣ︤ⲛ︥ⲡⲁⲣⲟⲣⲁ[3] ⲙ̄ⲙⲁⲓ |
blank

Verso](4) ⲓⲱⲛⲛⲉ ⲑⲉⲟⲇⲱ[

276.—Papyrus, a fragment, 26 × 6 cm Script early type, v Pl 3 *Recto* →.
Letter from Germanus ⲅⲉⲣⲙⲁⲛⲟⲥ, ⲡⲧⲁⲗⲁⲓⲡ[ⲱⲣⲟⲥ], to ⲁⲡⲁ ⲓⲱⲟⲁⲛⲛⲏⲥ, greeting also those with him ⲙⲛⲛ[ⲉⲥⲛⲏⲩ ⲉⲧ]ⲛⲙⲙⲁ︤ϥ︥ ⲟⲙⲡⲭⲟⲉⲓⲥ ⲭⲁⲓⲣⲉ] The writer is evidently making an appeal on behalf of ⲡⲉⲓⲣⲱⲙⲉ ⲉⲛⲧⲁ︤ϥ︥ⲉⲓ ⲛ[ⲁ︤ⲛ︥   ] ⲭⲉⲙⲁⲕⲁⲣⲓ A woman and her son, something given in pledge]ⲧⲁⲁ︤ϥ︥ ⲛⲉⲩⲱ, and poverty [ⲙ]ⲛⲧⲟⲙⲛⲕⲉ are referred to

Verso some words, apparently not the address

---

1 ⲭ altered from ⲭ
2 For ? ⲧⲁⲁⲭⲓⲟⲩ
3 ? πάρωρος
4 Half of a cross ✕

277.—Papyrus, a fragment, $37\frac{1}{2} \times 18$ cm (height and width complete)   Script
v Pl 11   *Recto* ↑

Letter from a high official to the person (2nd sing) responsible for the 'strangers'
resident in or passing through the pagarchy.   The affairs of such strangers ($\phi\upsilon\gamma\acute{\alpha}\delta\epsilon\varsigma$)
are a conspicuous element in the Jkôw (Aphroditô) documents[1], whence it is indeed
probable that the present letter is from the governor himself   The opening words, 'the
men of Peiom (Fayyûm) and those of [Hnes?] and those of Shmoun and those of Kôs[2],'
presumably indicate the districts whence the 'strangers' had come

³неρ]ωµπειοµ µннα| п]ашµоγп µµпакωс | ше]µιο еµпаαγθе¹ |н пеγραн нотнооγ |
5 |αιϥ сγтωш нак |ϳι ансеϩαιнε акµнооγε наι | п]ωт⁵ жеλααγ ερωµε ϩιωоγ |]тнроµпе
н жµпеµооγ епе |]наι λοιпоν тιτиш тепρωϥ | 10 |є нак акεµ тсιнатаграфн наι |
]нооγ оγа ϩµпентансϩαισоγ наι] оптос тнιοι | ан [жн]аоγ коλеι µµок етµтноγсоγ
шатенογ | [. .]к . ϩ . α нтак[с]ϩαинсϥ н[а]ι ϩιω[о]ϥ αγω τι |[. . . .]µпіθε ненп ше µιο
еϐоλ⁶ ϩιтекпаϲаρ | 15. [. . ше µιο нтеµµıне шатепрофιсµια н[. . .] |αγω т]ιωρк нак
µппоγте жε[а]µε савнλ етϐε[ппо[γ]те µоη µεκα оγшµιο поγωτ енапеıпаϲаρ |
[н]таı[оγ]ωнϩ пеγρ[ан н]ак еϐоλ⁷ еıжε пıтаϲρ[п]ехρоное ϩιωоγ еıжε пıпϥααϐ еıµнтсι
тапаρϩιста | 20 [п]µоγ λοιпоν екажι насϩαι αηαγ еλααγ ншµειο нтеıµıне еϐоγнϩ
ϩιтекпаϲаρ нтаıсϩαι пеγραν нак | ϩµннтаγпωϩ ϩιωоγ жιпεµптн проµпе епекнт |
нтеркнтоγсоγ⁸ наι несоγтн ϩιтооτϥ µпаρωµε | еϐατι насϩαι нак еıс ϩннте он аµпаρас-
теλε⁹ µпаρωµε | 25 жннϲααтн еϐоλ шαнтϥжι неµµειо нтеıµıне | нтотн нктноγсоγ
наı нµµαϥ αγω оптос ешωпе | нпаткеıµε ерооγ шапооγ ωш ϩιπαϩоγ + (verso) + αγω
акеıµε спµα еγϩιωоϥ αγω аксевтωоτϥ |стεıнтноγсоγ еεı нкоγρωµε еϲϳρнш¹⁰ пρϥката-|
30.-фρонеı еϐшооп ϩαоγσорнϲε нϐωп етϥϥγхн | ан ϩоλωс λοιпоν е[к]ажι нтаεпιстоλн |
тнооγ неµµειо етıµµαγ наı несоγтн | [about 10 let шактнооγϥ наι µннраν |[ппеγеı]оτε
µµпραν ппеγτιµε µµпраν ппеγ | 35]ωн епτι[µε нтакентоγ еϐоλ | ϩιωоγ ϩιтекпаϲаρ
αγω тнооγ пеγшнρε |ϩіпеϩіоµε нµααγ µµпноγϐ нιαнжιтγ | blank

[1] *V* Becker in *Z f Assyr* xx 96 and H I Bell's
article in *Journ Hell St*, 1908
[2] The context makes it very improbable that this is the
Kôs (Kûs) between Keft and Luksor   The alternative is
that which the legend of Christ's sojourn in Egypt identi-
fies with Koskam (Paris 131⁵, 102, Sermon of Timothy of
Alex, птооγ ккωс=Br Mus, Or 604 32 a col 1 *fenôta
dabra Quesquám*, and again later), placed by the Arabic
versions of this legend (Br Mus *Arab Cat*, *Suppl* p 820),
by Abû Sâlih 78 a and the *Synaxarium* (6th Haṭûr) at or
close to Al-Muḥarraḳ, i e a little S W of Al-Kûssîyah, some
texts indeed identifying Koskam and Ḳûṣṣîyah (Budge,
Mirac of Virgin, Meux MS, 1900, pp 67 and 125,
Amélineau, *Géogr* 555)   This Kôs-Koskam-Ḳûṣṣîyah then
=*Cusæ*, other forms of which name (as H I Bell points
out) closely resemble it   Geo. Cypr. Κοῦσος, Hierocl
Ἀκούασα, *Byz Zeitschr* ii 25 Κούσις   Amélineau has
seen (*Géogr* 494) that this is the Kôs S of Terôt, reached

by the travellers from Bawît (Zoega 366)   The Kûs, named
with Shmoun and 'the low land' (اسفل الارض) as Dr Wessely
informs me) as an administrative district in *Führer Rainer*
no 725, is presumably the same   Hence the form Al-
Kûssîyah, originally applied to such a district, subsequently
(like Al-Ahnassîyah) restricted to its chief town
[3] About 12 letters are missing from ll 1 to 5
[4] Altered.   Perhaps only one a   The word should be
αὐθεντικόν, presumably not the present document   *Cf* Br
Mus no 1211
[5] Or ογωτ
[6] Or in some technical sense? *Cf* no 323
[7] еϐоλ may belong to ка
[8] *Cf* ? нтарк-, Br Mus no 1102
[9] *Cf* Br Mus Pap *Inv* 1341 (Aphroditô), ἐπετρέ-
ψαμε[ν] γὰρ τῷ ἀποστόλῳ ἡμῶν μὴ ἀποκινηθῆναι ἐκ σοῦ ἄχρις
ἂν κτλ (Bell's copy)
[10] 'In danger' of punishment? The precise meaning of
these phrases is obscure

In the other direction, the address $+\epsilon\pi\iota\sigma\tau\grave{o}\ \overset{\lambda}{\tau}\ \overset{\nu}{\iota}$ [

(l 6) '] which thou hast written and sent me,   ] no man among them,   ] this year, or (ἤ) since the water[1],   ] to me   But (λοιπόν) I am decided that the matter,   ] thee (and) thou hast drawn me up this list (καταγραφή),   ] send one of those (of whom) thou hast written to me   Indeed (ὄντως) I know (νοεῖν) not what hath hindered (κωλύειν) thee from sending them hitherto   which thou didst write me concerning them   And I (desire that ?) thou consent (πείθειν) to remove the strangers from thy pagarchy (παγαρχία) these strangers until a   's delay (προθεσμία)   And (?) I swear to thee by God that of a truth, excepting for the sake of God, I will surely excuse not one stranger of those from these pagarchies whose names[2] I have shown thee, whether (εἴτε) he have spent time (χρόνος) there, or whether (εἴτε) he have not, but (εἰ μή τι) I will produce (παριστάναι) him[3]   And (λοι) when thou shalt receive my letters, see to each such stranger, dwelling in thy pagarchy, whose names I have written unto thee, of such of them as have fled away, from 15 years and under[4], that thou send them to me carefully, by my man, who will give thee my letters   Lo, too, I have charged (παραγγέλειν) my man that he quit thee not ere he shall have received the aforesaid strangers of thee and thou send me them with him   And verily (ὄντως) if thou hast not taken knowledge of them till to-day—Read on the back—(verso) and know the place where they are, and prepared them for sending, then art thou a man in danger and neglectful (-καταφρονεῖν), liable to be ensnared, that valueth his own life (ψυχή) not at all (ὅλως)   But (λοι) when thou shalt receive my epistle (ἐπιστ), send me these strangers carefully   send it me, with the names of their fathers and the names of their villages   the village whence thou hast taken them in thy pagarchy   And send (the names of) their children and their wives with them and the money that thou hast taken '

278 —Papyrus, 2 unconnected fragments, the larger, 9 × 8½ cm   Script small, ligatured   Recto →

Letter from Flavius Mercurius, a pagarch, through Severus[5], to the headmen of the villages and the priests (ἱερεύς)[6] of the homesteads (ἐποίκιον), that are (?) rated in his σιγίλλιον   It relates to certain workmen (ἐργάτης) to be supplied   Details are not clear It is to be noted that for the smaller local subdivisions, the clergy are the responsible officials

$+$ φλ μερ[κουρε[7] συ] παγα$\overset{χ}{ρ}$ δι εμο$\overset{υ}{}$ σευηρο | ⲡⲉϥⲥϩⲁⲓ [ⲛⲛⲁⲡ]ⲏⲅⲉ ⲛⲛⲥⲧⲓⲙⲉ ⲙⲛⲛⲉϩⲓⲉⲣⲉⲩⲥ | ⲛⲛⲉⲡⲟⲓⲕⲉⲓⲟⲛ [ⲉⲧ ⲅ]ⲁⲥⲥⲉ ⲉⲡⲁⲥⲓⲅⲉⲗⲗⲓⲛ ⲥⲭⲉⲇⲟⲛ[8] | ⲥⲛⲣⲁϩⲉ ⲛⲱ[ϣ ⲛⲛ]ⲁⲥϩⲁⲓ ⲛⲛⲉⲧⲛⲉⲧⲛⲟⲟⲩ[9] ⲛⲉⲣ-

---

[1] I e the inundation   [2] I e of the strangers

[3] 'Except I have him produced' would seem more logical

[4] Cf Br Mus no 1079, where the returnable age is 14 and upwards, ⲉϩⲣⲁⲓ   The reference here to the wives and children of the strangers would rather require ' upwards ' But Matt 11 16 shows that ⲉⲛⲉⲥⲏⲧ must have its usual meaning   [5] Cf no 319

[6] V ro 177   It should be read in Br Mus no 1180, 1 1   Cl Ganneau, Reu d'Arch v 389, gives an instance from mediaeval Palestine

[7] Probably not space for the full name

[8] Σχεδόν would seem merely to add emphasis

[9] ' Do not stay (spend time) reading my letter and not sending '

ϲⲁⲧⲏⲥ | ⲉⲧⲧⲁⲥⲥⲉ ⲏ[　　] ⲛⲁⲙⲙⲱⲛⲉ ⲡⲁⲣⲥⲩⲙⲙ̄ ⲛ̄ⲧⲕⲟⲩ⳿ | ⲛⲁⲗⲗⲁϲⲛ[1] ⲁ[. . .]ⲙⲡⲣⲕⲟⲧ ⲉⲡⲓⲛⲁⲩ
ⲥⲭⲉⲇⲟⲛ | ⲉⲓⲙⲏⲧⲓ ⲛⲧ[ⲉⲧⲛ]ⲉⲧⲛⲟⲟⲩϲⲟⲩ ⲛⲁⲩ ⲁⲩⲱ | ⲙⲡⲉⲣⲓⲧ[. .]ⲉ ⲛⲟⲩ.ⲉ ⲙⲡⲉ[

279.—Papyrus, complete, 9 × 6½ cm   Script v Pl 1   Recto →

Letter requesting Apa Cyrus, son of Colluthus, to supply 3 camels (2 on the 7th, 1 on the 8th), for water-drawing at the amir's house   Dated 7th Phamenoth, 5th Indiction[2].   Cf Br. Mus nos 1167–1169

ⲟⲩⲱϣ ⲛ̄ⲧⲟⲕ ⲁⲡⲁ ⲕⲩⲣⲓ | ⲕⲟⲗⲗⲟⲩⲑⲉ ⲛ̄ⲧⲛ ϣⲟⲙⲉⲧ | ⲉϫⲁⲙⲟⲩⲗ ⲉⲡⲙⲁ ⲛ̄ⲙⲁϩ|ⲙⲟⲟⲩ ⲉⲡⲏⲓ ⲉⲡⲉⲛ^ⲁ ⲛⲁⲙⲓⲣⲁ | ⲥⲛⲁⲩ ⲛ̄ⲥⲟⲩⲥⲁϣϥ ⲟⲩⲁ | ⲛ̄ⲥⲟⲩϣⲙⲟⲩⲛ ⲙ̄′ ⲫⲁⲙ^ⲑ ⲍ ⲉ ⲓ^ⲇ/ | Below the text, a clay seal without engraving, which, when the papyrus was folded, lay inside

280.—Papyrus, complete, 9½ × 18 cm   Script seldom ligatured   Recto ↑

Letter from Zacharias, 'his servant', to his lord, the *comes*

+ ⲛϣⲟⲣⲡ ⲙⲉⲛ ⲛ̄ϩⲱϥ ⲛⲓⲙ ⲧⲓⲡⲣⲟⲥⲕⲩⲛⲉⲓ ⲙ̄ⲡⲉⲓⲙⲉⲙⲧⲭⲟⲉⲓⲥ | ⲁⲓϫⲓ ⲛ̄ⲛⲉⲥϩⲁⲓ ⲛ̄ⲧⲉⲧⲛⲙⲉⲙⲧⲭⲟⲉⲓⲥ
ⲁⲓⲛ̄ ⲛⲉⲧⲛⲥ̄ϩⲁϩⲟⲛ ⲁⲓⲡⲟⲗϩⲟⲩ ⲙⲛⲡⲥⲁϩ ⲃⲓⲕⲧⲱⲣ ⲡⲓⲟⲟⲩⲛ[3] ⲁⲓϣⲓⲛⲉ ⲟⲩⲛ ϫⲉⲛⲧⲁⲡⲉⲥⲕⲁⲛⲧⲁⲗⲟⲛ |
ϣⲱⲡⲉ ϩⲓⲛⲙ ⲁⲓⲣⲉ [ⲉⲣⲟ]ϫ ϫⲉⲛ̄ⲧⲁϥϣⲱⲡⲉ ϩⲓⲟⲙ̄ ⲙⲁⲕⲁⲣⲉ | ⲁⲓⲛ̄ⲧⲥ ⲁⲓⲡⲉⲣⲙⲁⲧⲓⲥⲉ[4] [ⲙ̄]ⲙⲟⲥ ⲁⲓϫ[ⲓ]
ⲧⲉⲥⲉⲅⲅⲩⲏ ϫⲉⲛ̄ⲛⲉⲥⲙⲁϫⲉ ⲛ̄ⲉϩ | ⲁⲩⲱ ⲉⲓⲥ ϣⲙⲟⲩⲛ ⲛ̄ⲕⲟⲙⲙⲁ[5] ⲛ̄ϣⲉ ⲁⲓ[ⲧⲛ̄ⲟ]ⲟⲩⲥⲟⲩ ⲛ̄ⲧⲉⲧⲛⲙⲛⲧⲭⲟⲉⲓⲥ |
ⲛ̄ⲧⲁⲓϩⲉ ⲛⲉⲓⲕⲟⲁϩ ⲉⲧⲣⲉⲩ[6] ⲛⲉⲩⲭⲣⲏⲥⲙⲟⲩ ⲁⲓⲥⲟⲣⲡⲟⲩ ⲁⲓⲧⲛ̄ⲟⲟⲩⲥⲟⲩ ⲛⲏⲧⲛ | ⲁⲩⲱ ⲛ̄ⲕⲱⲣϣ̄
ⲙ̄ⲡⲁϫⲟⲉⲓⲥ ⲙ̄ⲡⲉⲧⲛⲛⲁ ⲧⲁϩⲟⲓ ⲛⲧ̄ⲧⲛⲉⲧⲓ ⲫⲟⲓⲃⲁⲙⲙⲱⲛ | ⲫⲱⲣⲓⲧ (above ⲙ̄ⲙⲧⲥⲱ) ⲛⲧⲉⲧⲛ̄ⲥ̄ϩⲁⲩⲟⲛ
ⲛ̄ϥⲟⲩⲁϩ ⲧⲁⲕⲉ ⲛⲁⲓ[7] ⲛ̄ⲥⲟⲩⲧⲱϥ ⲡϣⲛⲙ ⲛ̄ϫⲁϭⲉ ⲛⲁⲓ | ⲁⲩⲱ ⲉⲓⲥ ⲡⲓⲟⲛ̄ⲭⲟⲣⲟⲥ ⲁⲓⲛⲟⲟⲩϥ ⲛ̄ⲧⲉⲧⲛⲙⲉⲙⲧ-
ⲭⲟⲉⲓⲥ ⲙ̄ⲡⲉϥϩⲟⲩⲣ[8] + ϫⲉⲥⲛ̄/

Verso + ⲧⲁⲁⲥ ⲛ̄ⲡⲁϫⲟⲉⲓⲥ ⲡⲕⲟⲙⲟⲥ [space] ϩⲓⲧⲛ̄ϫⲁⲭⲁⲣⲓⲁⲥ ⲡⲉϥϩⲁⲩⲟⲛ +

'Before everything, I salute (προσκυνεῖν) your lordship   I have received your lordship's letters and have brought your servants and caused them to agree with the 'master' Victor, the   I enquired, therefore (οὖν), on whose account the disturbance (σκάνδαλον) had happened, and I found that it had happened on account of the wife of Macarius   Her I brought and bastinadoed (πελματίζειν), and I took her surety (ἐγγύη) that she would not again (lit ever) quarrel (μάχεσθαι)   And here are eight pieces (κόμμα) of wood which I have sent unto thy lordship   I found these bits remaining over (? λείπειν) they will not (?) be of use (χρησιμεύειν), and I cut them (up? off?) and have sent them unto you   And I beseech my lord, that your kindness reach me, and that you give Phoebammon, the guardian, and

---

[1] *V* no 342

[2] I had hesitated to read ε ι^δ/, but Messrs KENYON & GRENFELL both read so   [3] *V* no 226

[4] Of πελματίζω I find only one instance (*Etymol. Magn*).   Cf ϣⲛ ⲛ̄ⲡⲉⲗⲙⲁ as a punishment, CRUM, *Copt. MSS*, no xi

⁻ In KRALI ccxiii, ROSSI, *Nuov Cod* 64, Br Mus no 1202

of wood, as here   In Leont Neapol xix, GELZER, of marble

[6] Altered   The ⲛ following is superlined and so, the scribe being elsewhere consequent, should not end a word   But with ⲛⲁⲩ- cf ⲛⲛⲉⲥ- above

[7] Oι ⲧⲁⲕ ⲉⲛⲁⲓ? ⲧⲁⲕⲉ for ⲧⲱϭⲉ seems improbable

[8] Cf CRUM, *Ostr*, Ad 48 n   For the ring-key, v GAYET, *l'Art Copte* 58, STRZYGOWSKI's Cairo Catal, p 337

the ass unto thy servant (? ι e me), so that he continue to bake (?) for me, and that I may have a few loaves baked　And here is the bolt (μοχλός), I have sent it to your lordship, with its key　(I salute) thee, master (δεσπότα) '

281—Papyrus, almost complete, 10 × 32 cm　Script　clear, seldom ligatured.　*Recto* ↑
Note that ϩ has the form of ϫ

　　Letter from the headmen of Pouan[1], his 'servants', who 'venture (τολμᾶν) to write to their lord, Apa Victor'　He had written to them, but his messenger could not be found, and they now request him to represent them before the *comes* and arrange the despatch of certain business

　　+ ⲛⲉⲧⲛϩⲙϩⲁⲗ ⲛⲁⲡⲛⲏⲅⲉ ⲙⲡⲟⲩⲁⲛⲡⲉ ⲉⲩⲧⲟⲗⲙⲁ ⲉⲩⲥϩⲁⲓ ⲙⲡⲉⲩϫⲟⲉⲓⲥ ⲁⲡⲁ ⲃⲓⲕⲧⲱⲣ ϩⲁⲑⲏ
ⲛϭⲱⲃ] | ⲛⲓⲙ ⲧⲓⲡⲣⲟⲥⲕⲩⲛⲉⲓ ⲛⲧⲉⲕⲙⲛⲧϫⲟⲉⲓⲥ ϩⲙⲡϫⲟⲉⲓⲥ ⲭ̅ⲥ̅/ ⲉⲡⲉⲓⲁⲏ ⲁⲧⲉⲕⲙⲛⲧϫⲟⲉⲓⲥ ⲥϩⲁⲓ ⲛⲁⲛ
ϩⲓⲧⲛ[　] ⲕⲟⲥⲧⲁⲛⲧⲓⲛⲉ ⲡⲁⲛⲃⲁⲗⲛⲁⲓ[2] ⲡⲣⲟⲩⲣⲓⲧ ⲁⲛϣⲓⲛⲉ ⲛⲥⲱϥ ⲙⲡⲉⲛϩⲉ ⲣⲟϥ ϩⲙⲡⲧⲙⲉ ⲙⲁⲣⲉ-
ⲧⲉⲕ[ⲙⲛⲧϫⲟⲉⲓⲥ] | ⲉⲣⲛⲉⲛⲡⲣⲟⲥⲱⲡⲟⲛ[3] ⲙⲙⲁ ⲙⲡⲕⲟⲙⲉⲥ ⲛⲃⲧⲛⲟⲟⲩ ⲛⲣⲱⲙⲉ ⲛⲁⲛ ⲉⲃⲥⲙⲉ[4] ⲉⲣⲟϥ ⲁⲛⲟⲛ
ⲡⲁⲡⲟⲗ[ⲥⲟⲩ[5] ⲙⲛⲛⲉⲩ]ⲉⲣⲛⲟⲩ ⲧⲉⲛⲧⲉⲡⲣⲱⲙⲉ[6] ⲧⲛⲟⲟⲩ ⲧⲉⲩⲭⲁⲣⲓⲥⲧⲓⲁ ⲛⲏⲧⲛ ϫⲉⲁⲓⲡⲱⲗϭ ⲛⲁⲓ ⲅⲁⲣ
ⲧⲉⲛⲑⲁⲣϭ̅ⲉ̅[7] ⲙⲙ[.　　　] | ⲙⲡⲕⲟⲙⲉⲥ ⲁⲩⲱ ⲉⲧⲃⲉϥⲟⲗⲟⲕⲟⲧⲧⲓ ⲙⲙⲁⲕⲁⲣ ⲉⲧⲛⲉⲥϩⲁⲓ ⲛⲁⲛ ⲉⲧⲛⲃⲧ̄
ⲉⲛϣⲁⲛⲉⲓ ⲉϩⲣⲁⲓ ⲧⲉ[ⲛ . . . .] | ⲡⲙⲉⲣⲓⲥⲙⲟⲥ[8] ⲉⲩϣⲁⲛⲧⲁⲗⲟϥ ⲛⲁϥ ⲉⲡⲙⲉⲣⲓⲙⲟⲥ ϣⲁⲕϩⲉ ⲣⲟϥ
ⲉⲙⲡⲟⲩⲧⲁⲗⲟϥ ⲛⲧⲟϥ ⲛϣⲁⲃⲧⲁ[. . . . .] | +ⲟⲩϫⲁⲓ ϩⲙⲡϫⲟⲉⲓⲥ +

Verso　ⲧⲁⲁⲥ ⲙⲡⲉⲛϫⲟⲉⲓⲥ ⲡⲉⲛⲡⲣ[ⲟⲥⲧ]ⲁⲧⲏⲥ [space] ⲡⲕⲩⲣⲓⲥ ⲁⲛⲁ ⲃⲓⲕⲧⲱⲣ + ϩⲓⲧⲛⲛⲉϥϩⲙϩⲁⲗ |
ⲛⲁⲡⲛⲏⲅⲉ ⲙ[ⲡⲟⲩ]ⲁⲛ +

282.—Papyrus, a fragment, 9 × 31 cm　Script　ligatureless　*Recto* ↑
　　Letter from　　　　to his 'God guarded master and brother, the lord Theodore, the great *comes*'[9]　It treats of various matters, giving instructions as to payment for certain clothes and the purchase of provisions　The bishop and *dux* are mentioned, also Antinoe

　　]ϣⲁⲣⲥⲛⲁⲓⲁⲕⲱⲛ ⲉⲓⲱⲛ ⲉⲓ ⲉⲧⲡⲟⲗⲓⲥ ⲧⲁϫⲙ ⲡⲕⲩⲣ/ ⲁⲡⲁ ⲕⲩⲣⲓ ⲡⲁⲧⲉⲡⲗⲁⲧⲉⲁ[10] ⲙⲛⲁⲡⲁ ⲁⲑⲁⲛⲁⲥⲉ
ⲙⲛⲡⲕⲩⲣⲓ ⲁⲡⲁ ⲕⲩⲣⲓ ⲡϣⲉ ⲛⲗⲁⲕⲟⲛ[11] |]ⲡⲉⲡⲓⲥⲕⲟⲡⲟⲥ ⲇⲉ ⲛϩⲟⲩⲟ ϣⲁⲩⲡⲁⲣⲁⲕⲁⲗⲉⲓ ⲙⲙⲟϥ[12] ⲛⲉϥϫⲓⲛⲟⲩ
ⲡⲁⲟⲩϩ ϩⲁⲣⲟⲓ ⲁⲩⲱ ⲙⲡⲣⲧⲓ ⲗⲁⲁⲩ ⲙⲡⲇⲓⲁⲕⲟ/ ⲁⲑⲁⲛⲁⲥⲉ ϣⲁⲛⲧⲉϥ |]ϩⲟⲧⲉ ⲉⲡⲉⲓ ⲉϥⲃⲏⲕ . ⲙⲡⲉⲡⲓⲥ-
ⲕⲟⲡⲟⲥ[13] ⲁⲩⲱ ⲉϣⲱⲡⲉ ⲙⲡⲉⲁⲡⲁ ⲁⲑⲁⲛⲁⲥⲉ ⲃⲓ ⲛⲁⲥⲧⲣⲟⲙⲓⲛ ⲉⲡⲉϥⲏⲓ ⲃⲓⲧⲟⲩ ⲉⲡⲱⲛ ⲉⲧⲟⲕ ⲙⲛϩⲱϥ |]ⲟⲓⲙⲉ
ϣⲁⲛⲧⲉⲡϫⲟⲉⲓⲥ ϫⲓ ⲙⲟⲉⲓⲧ ϩⲏⲧⲛ ϥⲛⲏⲧ ⲉⲡⲁⲏⲓ ⲁⲩⲱ ⲕⲱ ⲡⲉⲓⲛϭⲓ ⲙⲡⲏⲓ ⲧⲓⲧⲟⲟⲃⲉϥ ⲉϫⲱⲡⲣⲟ ⲁⲩⲱ ⲕⲱ
ⲁⲛⲧⲓⲛⲟⲟⲩ | ⲧ]ⲣⲓⲙⲛⲉⲓⲛ ⲛⲏ[.　　　]ⲉⲓⲱⲛⲉ ⲧⲣⲟⲥⲓⲥ ⲧⲁϥ ⲛⲁⲓ ϩⲁⲟⲩϩⲃⲟⲥ ⲁⲩⲱ ⲙⲛⲡⲟⲧⲉ[14] ⲛⲏϫⲟⲟⲥ
ϫⲉⲗⲓⲧⲓ ⲟⲩⲕⲉⲣⲁⲧⲓⲛ ⲛⲁϥ ϩⲓⲱⲱϥ[15] | ⲉ]ⲉϣⲁⲛϫⲟⲟⲥ ⲟⲛ ϫⲉⲁⲓⲟⲩⲱϫⲉ[16] ⲛⲥⲁⲃⲁⲛⲛⲏ[17] ⲛⲁϥ ϫⲓⲧⲟⲩ ⲉⲓ

---

[1] *V* no 158
[2] ?? *Balneæ*　No such place-name is found
[3] *V* no 321　　　　'ⲥⲙⲙⲉ
[5] Read ⲡⲉⲧⲛⲁ- or ⲧⲉⲛⲛⲁ-　[6] Read ⲧⲉⲛⲧⲣⲉ-
[7] θαρρεῖν　For the inserted ϭ, *cf* Br Mus no 1123
[8] Should refer to partition of property　But *cf* phrases in Krall lxiv, lxv

[9] So the Greek address　But the Coptic line accompanying it has simply 'My brother, Apa Th'
[10] πλατεῖα as a place-name is unknown
[11] *Cf* ? Λάκων, *Pap Amh* cxxviii
[12] Altered　　　　[13] First letters not ⲙⲛ nor ⲛϭⲓ
[14] Altered from ⲙⲛⲛⲟⲧⲉ　　　　[15] Altered
[16] *V* no 238
[17] *V* no 246

ⲇⲉ ⲙⲛⲉ ⲍⲓ ⲡⲧⲣⲓⲙⲏⲥⲓⲛ |]ⲉ ⲍⲓ ⲟⲩⲕⲉⲣⲁⲧⲓⲛ ⲛⲥⲁⲣⲥⲓⲕⲛ ϩⲓⲧⲁⲡⲧ [1] ϩⲓⲫⲁϭⲓⲛⲁ ⲧⲛⲟⲟⲩⲥⲟⲩ ⲛⲁⲓ ⲟⲩⲕⲉ ⲣⲁⲧⲓⲛ ⲥⲁⲣ |] ⲁⲩⲱ ⲉϣⲱⲡⲉ ⲁ.... ⲟⲩⲉ ⲧⲛⲟⲟⲩ ⲟⲩⲱⲙ ⲛⲗⲁⲁⲩ ⲟⲩⲱⲙ ⲛⲁⲓ ⲁⲩⲱ ⲉϩⲁⲓ ϩⲱϥ ⲛⲓⲙ |]ⲕⲟⲟⲩⲛ ⲁⲛ ⲍⲛⲧⲁⲧⲛ   ⲟⲩⲟⲩ ⲁⲩⲱ ⲧⲣⲟⲃⲟⲩ +

Verso + τω θεοφυλ[a], μ̄ δεσπ̄/ αδελφω κυρω [space] θεοδωρος τω μεγαλ° κομ⟩, π[| ο αδελφ[|
+ⲡⲁⲥⲟⲛ ⲁⲡⲁ ⲑⲉⲟⲇⲱⲣⲉ [space] ⲧⲓⲡⲓⲥⲧⲟⲗⲏ ⲙⲡⲕⲩⲣ[| ⲡⲁ[ⲧ]ⲡⲗⲁⲧⲉⲁ +

283.—Papyrus, 2 fragments, the larger, 12 × 23 cm   Script irregular, *cf.* Br Mus
Catal, Pl 14, no 1024   *Recto* ↑
Letter to a *comes*, to whom, the writer says, he has sent the fishermen

ⲉ]ϩⲁⲓ ⲛⲡⲉϥϫⲟⲉⲓⲥ ⲡⲕⲟⲙⲓⲥ ϫⲉϩⲁⲑⲛ ⲛ[|]ⲧⲓⲧⲁⲙⲟ ⲛⲧⲉⲧⲛⲙⲉⲉⲧ[|]ⲁⲙⲉ[| ? lines lost |]ⲁⲧⲛⲙⲙⲉ [|]ⲁⲣ ⲉⲡⲓϩⲟⲟⲩ ⲉⲩⲧⲓ ⲙⲟⲟⲩ ⲉⲃⲟⲗ [|]ⲉⲙⲁ ⲛⲛⲉⲛⲧⲁⲩⲧⲁⲁⲩ ⲛⲁⲓ ⲟⲉ ⲉⲧⲕⲕⲉⲗⲉⲩⲉ ⲙⲟⲥ |]ⲛⲧⲱϣ ⲁⲓⲧⲛⲟⲟⲩϥ ⲛⲏⲧⲛ ⲉⲧⲃⲉⲡⲉⲟⲩⲱϣⲉ ⲇⲉ ⲉⲓⲥ ϩⲏⲏⲧⲉ ⲁⲓⲡⲛⲟⲟⲩⲥⲟⲩ ⲛⲧⲉ |]ϩⲉⲓⲧ ⲉⲧⲃⲉⲁⲡⲁⲛⲓⲁⲥ ⲇⲉ ⲙⲛⲃⲓⲕ ⲧⲱⲣ ⲉⲓⲥ ϩⲏⲧⲉ ⲁⲩⲗⲟ ⲉⲩϩⲏⲡⲟⲩⲣⲛ ⲉϣⲱⲡⲉ ⲧⲉⲧ |]ⲕⲉⲗⲉⲩⲉ ⲧⲱϣ ⲟⲩⲁ ⲛⲁⲓ ⲙⲟⲛ ⲙⲓϣⲡⲱⲗϭ [2] ⲙⲛⲛⲁⲡⲟⲕⲣⲓⲥⲓⲥ ⲉⲧⲉϩⲱⲥⲓⲁ ⲙⲡⲛⲟⲩⲧⲛ |]ⲁⲧ⳨ ⲟⲩϫⲁⲓ ϩⲙⲡϫⲟⲉⲓⲥ +

Verso blank

284.—Papyrus, a fragment, 11½ × 21 cm   Script ligatureless   *Recto* ↑
Letter from   to 'his lord, the *comes*'   The dyke (χῶμα) is often mentioned, and
the cattle to be pastured (?) there.

]ⲛⲡⲉϥϫⲟⲉⲓⲥ ⲡⲕⲟⲙⲓⲥ ϫⲁⲓϣⲱⲡ ⲛⲁϩⲓⲥⲉ ⲧⲏⲣⲟⲩ ϩⲓⲡⲉϥ |]ⲱⲣⲟϥ ⲁⲩϭⲟⲗⲡϥ ⲁⲓϫⲟⲟⲩ ⲉϩⲣⲁⲓ ⲁⲓϣⲁϫⲉ ⲛⲉⲙⲁⲟⲩ |]ⲧⲛⲏⲣϥ ϭⲟⲙ ⲉⲣⲟⲛ ϩⲛⲛⲛⲧⲉϥⲛⲟⲟⲩⲥ ⲉⲛⲛⲧⲟⲩ ⲉⲡⲉⲭⲱⲙⲁ |ⲛ]ⲉⲥⲥⲣⲱⲥ[3] ⲁⲩⲱ ⲁⲓⲱϩⲁⲛⲛⲏⲥ ⲛⲁⲡⲉ ⲛⲉⲩⲛⲧⲣⲱϥⲓ[4] ⲛⲁⲓ |]ⲣⲱⲙⲙⲉ ᵗⁱᶜⲅⲙⲉ ⲧⲏⲣⲟⲩ ϫⲉⲁⲛⲧⲓ ⲗⲟⲅⲟⲥ ⲛⲁⲛ ⲁⲕϭⲱⲛ ⲛⲉⲛ | ⲛ]ϫⲁⲕⲁ ⲛⲏⲣⲱⲙⲉ ⲛⲁⲛ ⲉⲃⲟⲗ ⲁⲛ ⲡⲕⲩⲥⲉⲡⲉ ⲛⲁⲡⲱⲣⲕ ⲉⲃⲟⲗ [|] ϫⲉⲛⲛⲉⲡⲉⲛⲅⲓ ⲗⲟⲅⲟⲥ ⲛⲁⲩ ⲡⲉϫⲁⲩ ⲛⲁⲓ ϫⲉⲁϩ̄ⲣⲁ[5] ⲁⲕⲧⲓ |]ϣⲟⲛⲧⲉ ⲉⲓⲥ ϩⲏⲧⲉ ⲉⲓⲥ ⲡⲗⲟⲥ ⲁⲓϫⲟⲟⲩϥ ⲛⲏⲧⲛ |]ⲛϥⲱⲃ ⲁⲩⲱ ⲃⲱⲓⲱⲛ' ϫⲟⲟⲩ ⲛⲛⲏⲟⲩϥ ⲛⲁⲓ ⲛⲡⲉⲭⲱⲙⲁ |]ⲉⲙ ⲛⲁⲓ ⲁⲛ ⲉⲃⲟⲗ ⲉⲣⲱϥ ⲁⲩⲱ ⲡⲉⲧⲛⲛϫⲟⲟⲩ ⲁⲡⲟ |]ⲁⲩⲡⲱⲧ

Verso]ϭⲟⲡⲟⲩ ⲉⲩⲣⲱϥⲧ ⲛϩⲛϩⲣⲟⲧⲉ ⲛⲁⲓ ⲛⲉⲩ |]ⲛⲕⲁⲓⲗⲉⲅⲟⲩⲉ[7] ϫⲉ....... ⲑⲉ ⲛⲁⲩ ϩⲓⲟⲛⲟⲩϥ ⲁⲓϩⲥ |]ϩⲁⲕⲱ ⲛⲓⲁ ⲛⲁⲡ ⲁⲡⲟⲗⲗⲱ ⲇⲓⲁϩ̄ⲏⲧ[8] ⲁⲣⲏⲥ ⲡⲕⲩⲟⲩⲁ |]ⲟⲩ ⲧⲁϫⲟⲟⲩⲥⲟⲩ ⲛⲏⲧⲛ ⲁⲩⲱ ⲉϣⲱⲡⲉ ⲧⲉⲧⲛⲛⲏⲣⲁⲓ |]ⲙⲛⲛⲁⲟⲩⲛⲏⲣⲓϫⲉ ⲛⲁⲓ ⲉⲃⲟⲗ ⲧⲁϫⲟⲟⲩ ⲡⲁⲓ ⲛⲏⲧⲛ ⲉϩⲣⲁⲓ |]ⲧⲕⲣⲓⲥⲓⲥ ⲛⲡⲉⲭⲱⲙⲁ

In other direction ⳨ ⳨ ⊕ᵗⁱᶜ ⳨ [⳨, the round mark having been crossed by the ribbon

285.—Papyrus; almost complete, 34 × 13 cm   Script moderately ligatured   *Recto* ↑.
Letter from Zacharias to 'his sincere friend (γνήσιος φίλος) Rashid, the most glorious
(ἐνδ) amir'[9], referring to the taxes of certain villagers

---

[1] An unknown noun
[2] This verb, with ⲙⲛ-, refers usually to a person
V no. 280
[3] Here and in] 1 perhaps for ⲡⲉⲕ-
[4] Or -ⲧⲣⲱϥⲛ   Apparently the village in KENYON,
Catal iii 225

[5] *Cf* ? the interjection ⲁϩⲉ
[6] *V* no. 320 &c
[7] κελεύειν
[8] Or ϣⲓⲁϩ̄ⲏⲧ
[9] *V* nos 280, 319

[+] ϩⲙⲡⲣⲁⲛ ⲉⲡ[ⲛⲟⲩⲧⲉ] ⲍⲁⲭⲁⲣⲓⲁⲥ ⲡϥϭⲁⲓ ⲙⲡϥⲅⲛⲏⲥⲓⲟⲥ ⲛⲫⲓⲗⲟⲥ[1] ⲣⲁϣⲓⲁ ⲡⲥⲛ ⲧⲓⲣ[ⲏⲛ]ⲏ
ⲛⲁⲕ ⲙⲉⲛⲉⲛⲥⲁⲛⲁⲓ | [ϩ]ⲉⲛⲣⲱⲙ[ⲡ]ⲧⲓ[ⲙⲉ] ⲛⲡⲓⲁϩⲡⲉ . ⲙⲟⲙ[2] ⲉⲅⲉⲛⲧⲁⲩϩⲛⲣⲱⲙⲉ ϩⲛⲡⲉⲙϩⲓⲧ ⲛϣⲙⲟ[ⲩⲛ]
ⲗⲟⲓⲡⲟⲛ ⲕⲉⲗⲉⲩⲉ | [. .]ⲏⲛ . ⲛⲥⲟⲩⲡⲟⲗⲅⲟⲩ ⲉⲃⲟⲗ ⲥⲡ[ⲉ]ⲅⲁⲓⲁⲥⲣⲁⲫⲟⲛ ⲁⲩⲱ ⲉ[ϣⲱⲡ]ⲉ ⲁⲩϣⲁⲧⲟⲩ
ⲛⲟⲩⲗⲁⲁⲩ (nothing ?) | [.... .]ⲁⲩ ... ⲁⲩⲱ ⲧⲉⲓⲣⲏⲛⲏ ⲛⲧⲕⲉⲛ[ⲁⲟ]ϫ [ⲛⲭⲟⲉ]ⲓⲥ + ⲉⲩⲣ/ $\bar{\mu}$
ⲫ[ⲁⲙ]$^\theta$ ⲕⲉ ι^δ, ⲏ +

Verso ⲣⲁⲥⲍⲓⲇ ⲉⲛ$^\delta$ ⲁⲙⲓⲣ̄ ⲧⲁ ⲣ ⲍ[ⲁ]ⲭ[ⲁ]ⲣ.. + $\overset{v}{\rho}$ ⲁⲡⲟ ?

286.—Papyrus, a fragment, $7\frac{1}{2} \times 12$ cm   Script ligatured   *Recto* ↑

Letter to an amír, named Abou Pilal[3], [ⲡⲉⲛⲭⲟ]ⲉⲓⲥ ⲡⲉⲓ[ⲱⲧ] ⲁⲃⲟⲩ ⲡⲓⲗⲁⲗ ⲡⲉⲩⲕⲗ/ ⲛⲁⲙ[ⲓⲣⲁ].
Beyond the mention of ⲛⲣⲱⲙⲉ ⲕⲁⲱⲣⲟⲉ[ⲉ], there is nothing to note

287.—Papyrus, a fragment, 17×16 cm   Script *v* Pl 6   *Recto* ↑

Letter to a high official[4], addressed as 'dear brother', regarding the affairs of 'the young deacon Mone'   Above the text, a cross

ⲑⲉⲟⲫ$^\delta$ⲩⲗⲁⲕ$^\top$/ ⲛⲉⲛ$^\lambda$ ⲙⲙⲉⲣⲓⲧ ⲛⲥⲟⲛ ϫⲉⲁⲩⲧⲁⲙⲟⲛ |]ⲁϭⲓⲛ ⲉⲧⲡⲟⲗⲓⲥ ⲁⲛⲟⲩⲱϣ ⲉⲥϩⲁⲓ ⲉⲡⲧⲓ | ⲉⲧ]-
ⲃⲉⲡⲕⲟⲩⲓ ⲇⲓⲁⲕ^o, ⲙⲟⲛⲉ ⲉⲧⲛⲉⲥⲟⲟⲩⲛ ϫⲉⲁⲛⲧⲓ |] ⲛⲁϥ ⲛϥ[ⲧⲁⲁϥ ⲉⲃⲟⲗ above) ⲗⲟⲓⲡⲟⲛ ⲕⲉⲗⲉⲩⲉ[5]
ⲧⲉⲧⲛⲥⲥⲣⲟⲩⲡⲥⲧⲛⲁⲛ$^{\overline{ⲟⲧ}}$ |] ⲁⲩⲱ ⲕⲉⲗⲉ[ⲩⲉ] ⲛⲡⲉⲣϣⲱⲡ ϩⲣⲉ[6] ⲛⲁⲛ |]ⲡⲉⲛ ⲅⲁⲧⲛⲉϣⲟⲡϥ ⲥⲙⲛⲡⲉⲧⲛⲉⲗⲟⲥⲟⲥ |
ⲥ]ⲉⲉⲡⲉ ⲛⲧⲁⲅⲛⲉⲝⲓⲧϥ ⲉⲛⲟⲩϥ ⲉⲧⲛⲉϭⲱⲡⲉ |]ⲟⲧϥ ⲉϥϣⲁⲛϭⲱⲡⲉ ⲉⲣⲱⲧⲛ[7] ⲧⲉⲧⲛⲉⲧⲓ ⲛⲁϥ | ⲑ]ⲉⲟⲫⲩⲗ/
ⲛⲉⲛ$^\lambda$ ⲙⲉⲣⲓⲧ ⲛⲥⲟⲛ ϩⲓⲧⲛⲉⲓⲥϩⲁⲓ +

Verso   remnants of the address

288 —Papyrus, a fragment, $14\frac{1}{2} \times 11$ cm   Script curved uncials   Not from the Ashmunaín collection

Letter from   to Taurínus, a bishop   Besides complimentary phrases, 'the monastery' and 'wool' are referred to[8]

]ⲧⲏⲣϥ ⲙⲡⲁϩⲏⲧ ⲙⲛⲧⲁⲯⲩⲭⲏ | ⲡϩⲩⲡⲟⲡ]ⲟⲁⲓⲟⲛ ⲛⲛⲉⲩⲟⲉⲣⲏⲧⲉ ⲙⲡⲁ |] ⲁⲩⲱ ϯⲥⲟⲡⲛ ⲟⲛ ⲧⲉⲧⲛ |
ⲓ]ⲡⲉⲩⲟⲩⲟⲓⲱ ⲛⲛⲉⲧⲛⲡⲣⲟⲥⲉⲩⲭⲏ |]ⲉⲧⲏϫⲟⲟⲛ ⲛⲥⲙⲁⲓ ⲛⲧⲉⲡⲛⲟⲩ |] ϩⲙⲡϫⲟⲉⲓⲥ ⲭⲉⲣⲉⲧⲉ |]ⲓⲧⲏⲛⲩⲧⲛ
ⲉⲑⲉⲛⲉⲉⲅⲉ |]ϥⲁϫⲉⲟⲩⲥⲟⲙ ⲛⲧⲉⲧⲛ |]ⲁϫⲓ ⲛⲥⲟⲣⲧ ⲛⲏⲧⲛ |]ⲁⲙⲟⲧⲛⲟⲩ ⲛⲁⲕ ⲁⲩⲱ |]ⲧⲁⲅⲁⲡⲏ ⲛⲉⲙⲁⲛ |
]ⲡ ⲛⲥⲟⲣⲧ ⲛⲉϥⲧⲁⲁⲩ |]ⲥⲥⲙⲟⲧⲛⲟⲩ ⲛⲁⲛ[9] |]ⲱⲕ ⲃⲓⲣⲟⲟⲩϣ ϩⲁⲛⲉⲛ | ⲉⲃⲟ]ⲗ ϩⲓⲧⲟⲧⲏⲩⲛ ⲥ̄ⲩⲛⲏⲩ |

---

[1] *Cf Pap Amh* clv, Kᴇɴʏoɴ, *Cat* iii 244 Misunderstanding γνήσιος in Br Mus no 1011, I added a needless *sic*

[2] *Cf* such names as ⲡⲓⲁϩⲟⲉ, *Pap Amh, l c*, and several with initial Πⲁ-

[3] ابو بلال   ⲉⲓⲱⲧ seems unlikely referring to an amír

[4] Θεοφυλακτος, ενδοξοτατος apply to a *comes* (here no 282, Br Mus no 1114), or pagarch (Br Mus no 1156) or 'headman (here no 339)

[5] *V* no 308   [6] *V* no 346

[7] *Cf* Br Mus. nos 1031, 1103, where this verb is equally obscure

[8] The unusual forms ⲥⲟⲡⲉⲛ and ⲙⲟⲧⲛ- (transit) may be noted   [9] *Cf* nos 343 387

(verso, in other direction)]ει ϫεαπϫαϫε |] ϫεογηϫοιι ηηετη |] ηιιι ετωογη εϫωη |]ϯ ηηογϫρο ιιπιε |]ωη ηαι ητε πηογτε | τ]ετηϩαιβηс αγω |]ε ογαι ηαη

In the original direction   + ταας ιιπετφορι ιιπεχ̅с̅ ϩ[ηογιιε¹ | ταγριηε πεπιсκο[ποс

289.—Papyrus, 2 disconnected fragments, the larger, $11\frac{1}{2} \times 21\frac{1}{2}$ cm   Script sloping uncials, cf CRUM, *Ostraca*, Pl I, no 71   *Recto* ↑

Letter from Sarapamon, head (?) of the community of the 'rock' of Apa Thomas[2], to   , archimandrite[3] of another monastery   Gaps and many illegible letters make details obscure   His humility (-ἐλάχιστος) does obeisance (προσκυνεῖν) and (greets   by this letter), till such time as God shall make him worthy to do so in person (κατὰ πρόσωπον), and so fulfil his joy   He relates that certain youths have fled from the monastery (μοναστ) and gone south, to the τόπος of   There they had induced (πείθειν) certain sailors (?) trading in grain, to take them north   The writer has therefore sent his son, the deacon Germanus, to seek the fugitives, and begs his 'most saintly (ὁσιώτατος) father' to authorize (προτρέπειν) that undertaking (λόγος) be given them in his name (that they shall suffer) nothing beyond (παρά) their strength and that no man shall   (παρέρχεσθαι) them in any wise (and that they shall be readmitted) as before, in peace (εἰρήνη)   'For thy most saintly (ὁσ) fatherhood knoweth (νοεῖν) the storms of youth (and how such) as these are not of experience for going abroad, neither know they what it is seduceth (?) them'   He begs therefore that the archimandrite will persuade (πείθειν) and despatch them, that he may continue (to be grateful) also in this respect (μέρος)   He asks that he may be worthy to have news of his correspondent's health by letter (ἐπ), that his joy may be full

✝ ηϣορπ ιιεη ιιπϣαϫε ηταιιητελαχ̅, τηπροсκγηει αγω τ]ιαсπαϫε   ?   ]| ϣαητε-
πηογτε αατ ιιπϣα ηρπι κατα προсωποη ητεπαρα[ϣε ϫωκ εβολ   ?   ]| κογι ηϣηρε
πωτ ϩιιιιοηαсτηριοη αγει ερηс επτοποс ηαπ[α   ?   ]επαс[. . .]| ηεεγ βηκ επсαη сογο⁴
αγπιθε ιιιιοογ ετρεϥϫιτογ⁵ εϩητ ηιιιιαγ [?   παρα]καλει ητετη϶ϩοсιωτατοс ηειωτ
ειс πεηϣηρε ηϫιακωη ϩεριιαηε αιτηιιοογϥ   ?   ]ηϣιηε η|сωογ ητετηπροτρεπε . . .
ϣϭ . τετητι λοϭοс⁶ ηαϥ ϩιιπαρ[αη   ?   λα]λαγ ηϩωβ παρα | τεγϭοιι ογϫε ϫεηπε-
ρωιιε παρελθε⁷ ιιιιοογ κατα λααγ ηсηοτ [?   ϫ]οη ητεγϩε ϩη̄ϯ|ρηηη ϫετετη-
ϩοсιωτατοс ηειωτ ηοι ηηϩοειιι ητηητϣηρε .[?   ]ϫ ηειιιιε ϫεηсε|ϫοητ αη εβωκ
επϣιιιιο ογϫε ηсεсοογη α[η] ιιπετϥι ιιιιοογ ϫε   ?   παρακα]λει ητετηιιητ|ειωτ
ταρετηπιθε ιιιιοογ ητετητηποογсογ ηαη ταρηιιογη εβο]λ εη   ?   τετιιι|ητειωτ

¹ The same style of address in *Rev égypt* ix 137, 139, 142 &c and CRUM, *Ostr* no 50   Contrast Br Mus no 1121   All these are to bishops

² V nos 124, 294

³ ὁσιώτατος usually a bishop's epithet   *Rev égypt* ix 143, 145 &c, Br Mus nos 449, 514   Here οσιότης (as in a frag. Br Mus Or 6201 B) was intended, or a form with ιιητ-, v the gender.   Cf θεοφιλία in no 339

⁴ Or ? ηε сγβηκ, or εγβηκε (βεκε)   The sense of

сακ is uncertain   'Corn-grinding' (ωκε) seems unlikely   Cf in a Balaiza (PETRIE) fragm сακβητ an obscure noun, and Br Mus no 487, тсакιιοογ

⁵ All but illegible, ϫ above quite uncertain

⁶ Cf the formula, 'Here is God's word to thee,' CRUM, *Ostr* nos 107 &c, and especially GUIDI in *Rendic* 1906, 15

⁷ Exact meaning doubtful, as in CRUM, *l c*, no 111   Cf ? the obscure use in *Pap Amh* clv

T

ϩⲙⲡⲉⲓⲕⲉⲙⲉⲣⲟⲥ [1] ⲡⲉⲧⲛⲟⲩϫⲁⲓ ⲇⲉ ⲉⲧⲛⲁⲕⲟⲩϥ ⲙⲁⲣⲛⲙⲡϣⲁ ⲛⲉⲙⲉ ⲉⲣⲟϥ ϩⲓ[ⲧⲛ   ? ⲉⲡⲓ]ⲥⲧⲟⲗⲏ
ⲛⲧⲉⲡⲉⲛ|ⲣⲁⲛ, ϫⲱⲕ ⲉⲃⲟⲗ ϯ ⲟⲩϫⲁⲓ ϩⲛⲧϭⲟⲙ ⲛⲧⲉⲧⲣⲓⲁⲥ ⲉⲧⲟⲩⲁⲁⲃ ⲛϩⲟⲙⲟⲟⲩⲥ[ⲓⲟⲥ   ? |

Verso]   ? ⲁⲣⲭⲓⲙⲁⲛⲇ, [space] ⲥⲁⲣⲁⲡⲁⲙⲙⲱⲛ ⲛⲧⲡⲉⲧ|ⲣⲁ ⲛⲁⲡⲁ ⲑⲱⲙⲁⲥ

290.—Paper, complete, 19 × 14 cm   Script upright, of Zoega's 9th class   28 lines
The leaf was folded six times in width, once in height   Phrases and words are often
separated by a colon

Letter addressed in adulatory terms to a superior, whom the writer begs to accompany
him to 'Apa Antonius', presumably the famous monastery in the eastern desert, mentioned
also in a Cairo papyrus (8025)

ϯ ⲥϯ ⲁⲛⲟⲕ ⲡⲓⲣⲉϥⲉⲣⲛⲟⲃⲉ ⲙⲓⲭⲁⲏⲗ ⲡⲓⲙⲡⲱ ϯϣⲓⲛⲉ ⲁⲩⲱ ϯⲉⲣϩⲟⲩⲟ ⲡⲣⲟⲥⲕⲓⲛⲉ ⲁⲩⲱ ϯⲛⲁϩⲧ
ϩⲓϫⲙⲡⲁϩⲟ ⲉⲓⲟⲩⲱϣⲧ ⲛⲛⲉⲟⲩⲉⲣⲏⲧⲉ ⲙⲡⲁϫⲟⲉⲓⲥ ⲛⲉⲓⲱⲧ ⲡⲁⲡⲁ (5) ⲑⲉⲱⲇⲟⲣ ⲡϣⲟⲩⲧⲁⲓⲟϥ ϩⲓⲧⲙⲡⲛⲟⲩⲧⲉ
ⲙⲛⲛⲣⲱⲙⲉ ⲡⲉⲧⲥⲙⲁⲙⲁⲁⲧ ϩⲙⲡⲉϥⲃⲓⲟⲥ ⲁⲩⲱ ⲉⲧⲟⲩⲁⲃ ϩⲙⲡⲉϥϩⲏⲧ ⲡϣⲟⲩϣⲟⲩ ⲛⲧⲁⲯⲩⲭⲏ ⲁⲩⲱ
ⲡⲥⲟⲗⲥⲗ ⲙⲡⲁϩⲏⲧ ⲉⲣⲉⲡⲟⲥ ⲓ̅ⲥ̅ ⲡⲉⲭ̅ⲥ̅ ⲧⲁⲙⲟⲓ ⲉⲡⲉⲕϩⲟ ϩⲛⲟⲩⲣⲁ(10)ϣⲉ ⲉⲡⲉⲓⲇⲏ ⲉⲓⲥ ϩⲁϩ ⲛϩⲟⲟⲩ
ⲉϫⲓⲛⲧⲁⲉⲓ ⲉⲧⲁⲓⲁⲕ[ⲟⲛ]ⲓⲁ [2] ⲉⲓϣⲓⲛⲉ ⲛⲥⲁⲃⲱⲕ ⲉϩⲟⲩⲛ ⲁⲡⲁ ⲁⲛⲧⲱⲛⲓ ⲙⲡⲉⲛⲁⲗⲇⲁⲓ [3] ⲉⲓϣⲓⲧ ⲉϩⲟⲩⲛ
ⲉⲧⲃⲉⲛⲁⲗⲇⲉϭⲟⲥ [4] ⲉⲩϩⲓⲡⲧⲟⲟⲩ [5] ⲟⲩⲇⲉ ⲙⲡⲉⲧϩⲟⲧⲉ ⲕⲁⲁⲧ ⲧⲁⲉⲓ ⲧⲁ(15)ϭⲉⲛ ⲡⲉⲕϣⲓⲛⲉ ⲗⲟⲓⲡⲟⲛ ⲉⲓⲥ
ⲧⲓⲙⲉⲧⲁⲛⲓⲁ [6] ⲥⲧⲃⲉⲡⲛⲟⲩⲧⲉ ⲧⲉⲕⲉⲓ ⲧⲉⲛⲃⲱⲕ ⲉϩⲟⲩⲛ ⲉⲁⲡⲁ ⲁⲛⲧⲱⲛⲓ ⲧⲉⲛⲟⲩⲉϩ ⲡⲉⲛϩⲟ ϩⲓⲭⲛⲛⲉⲛⲉⲣⲏⲩ [7]
ⲁⲣⲏⲩ ϣⲁⲛⲉⲣⲡⲥⲙⲡϣⲁ [8] ⲧⲉⲛⲟⲩⲉϩ ⲛⲉⲛⲕⲉⲉⲥ ϩⲙⲡⲙⲁ ⲉⲧⲙⲙⲁⲩ (20) ϯⲙⲉⲉⲩⲉ ϫⲉϣⲁⲩⲉⲣϩⲱⲃ
ⲥⲧⲁⲣⲣⲉϭⲛⲓ [9] ϩⲙⲙⲉϩⲥⲟ ⲛⲕⲩⲣⲓⲁⲕⲏ ⲧⲉⲛⲃⲱⲕ ⲉϩⲟⲩⲛ ϩⲙⲡⲥⲟⲩϣ ⲙⲡⲛⲟⲩⲧⲉ ϩⲛⲧⲙⲉϩⲥⲁϣϥⲉ
ϣⲁⲛϫⲟⲡ ⲡⲁⲗⲙⲁⲣⲙⲉⲗ [10] ⲧⲉⲛⲁⲗⲛ ⲉⲣⲟϥ ⲁⲛⲟⲛ ⲡⲉⲥⲛⲁⲩ ϯϣⲓⲛⲉ ⲉⲣⲟⲕ ⲕⲁⲗⲟⲥ (25) ⲁⲩⲱ ϯ ⲡⲁϣⲓⲛⲉ
ⲙⲡⲁϫⲟⲉⲓⲥ ⲛⲉⲓⲱⲧ ⲛϭⲩⲅⲕⲙⲛⲟⲥ ⲡⲡ ⲥⲧⲉⲫⲉⲛ ⲙⲙⲡⲙⲉⲓⲱⲧ ⲁⲡⲟⲩⲗⲓⲟⲩⲙⲏⲛ [11] ⲙⲛⲛⲓⲥⲛⲏⲩ ⲧⲏⲣⲟⲩ
ⲟⲩϫⲁⲓ ϩⲙⲡⲟ̅ⲥ̅ ⲁⲙⲏⲛ ⲡⲡ ⲥⲁⲅⲟⲗ ϣⲓⲛⲉ ⲉⲣⲟⲕ ⲕⲁⲗⲟⲥ

'With God('s help)'   I, the sinner Michael, the dumb man, greet and greatly reverence
(προσκυνεῖν) and cast myself upon my face, worshipping the feet of my lord father, Papa
Theodore, honorable before God and man, who is blessed in his life and holy in his heart,
the pride of my soul (ψυ) and solace of my heart   The Lord Jesus Christ show me thy
face in gladness!   Now (ἐπειδή) it is many days since I came to the service (διακονία) and
sought means to go to Apa Antonius, and the   have not been able to bring me
(thither), because of the   that are on the desert, nor (οὐδέ) did fear suffer me to go
and visit thee   But (λοιπόν) I humbly beg (-μετάνοια), for God's sake, that thou come and that
we go to Apa Antonius and lay our faces one to another   perhaps we shall be held worthy
to lay our bones there   I think that they will be preparing the caravan (?) on the 6th Sunday
(κυριακή) and we (will) go thither, if it be God's will, on the 7th   we will take the litter (?)

---

[1] Cf ἐν τῷ μέρει τούτῳ, 2 Cor ix 3 &c

[2] Some 'service' connected with monastic life   V Br
Mus no 463   [3] Arabic ⲁⲗϭⲁⲉⲓϣⲓ less likely

[4] Arabic   [5] 'Desert' rather than 'monastery'

[6] V Br Mus no 547, note

[7] A locution unknown to me   Scarcely = 'embrace' here

[8] ⲁⲣⲏⲩ ϣⲁⲣⲉ- in Krall ccxviii 19, 22, Erman, Kopt
Volkslitt 6

[9] ? الرعية

[10] محمل   The sacred litter sent since 1272 (Lane, *Mod
Eg*, ch xi) to Mekka, cannot be here in question

[11] Doubtless ابو اليمن a name common among Christians, several are mentioned by Abû Sâlih in Fatimite
and Aiyubite times   Cf Cairo 8025, ⲁⲡⲟⲩⲗⲓⲟⲩⲙⲉⲗ and
here no 309 *verso*

and mount thereon, both together   I greet thee much (καλῶς)   And give my greeting to my lord father the *hegumenus*, Papa Stephen, and my father Apouhoumên and all the brethren   Farewell in the Lord   Amen.   Papa Saul greets thee much (καλῶς)'

Verso blank

291—Papyrus, complete, 6½ × 36 cm   Script even, sloping uncials, *cf* CRUM, *Ostraca*, Pl 1, no 71   *Recto* ↑   Not from the Ashmunain collection

Letter to an ecclesiastical superior

ϯ ⲉⲓⲥ ⲡⲉⲓⲙⲏⲓ ⲛϣⲱⲗϩ ⲛⲕⲟⲩⲓ ⲛⲕⲛϩⲏⲣ¹ ⲁⲓⲧⲛⲛⲟⲟⲩⲥⲟⲩ ⲙⲛϣⲙⲟⲩⲛⲉ ⲙⲙⲁⲓⲣⲉ ⲛϩⲙⲉ ⲁⲩⲱ ⲟⲩⲙⲁⲓⲣⲉ | ⲛⲉⲣⲃⲛⲛⲉ² ⲙⲛϣⲟⲗ ⲥⲛⲁⲩ ⲛⲱϥ ⲉⲣⲉⲙⲛⲧⲁⲥⲉ ⲛⲃⲱ³ ϩⲓⲱⲟⲩ ⲁⲩⲱ ⲥⲁϣϥ ⲟⲩⲥⲟⲥ ⲛⲗⲓⲧⲣ, ⲛⲥⲧⲏⲙⲟⲩ⁴ ⲉⲡⲁ|ⲡⲣ, ⲙⲁⲣⲕⲟⲥⲛ ⲡⲉⲓⲥⲟⲧⲡ ⲇⲉ ⲉϩⲱⲃ ⲛⲓⲙ ⲧⲛⲁⲥⲡⲁⲍⲉ ⲙⲡⲉⲣϩⲗⲟϭ ⲛⲧⲉⲕⲙⲛⲧⲙⲁⲓⲛⲟⲩⲧⲉ ⲉⲓⲙⲡϣⲁ ⲛⲧⲁⲓⲟ ⲛⲓⲙ | ⲙⲛⲛⲉⲕⲙⲉⲣⲁⲧⲉ ⲉⲧⲙⲙⲁⲕ ⲕⲁⲧⲁ ⲣⲁⲛ ⲉⲛⲁⲟⲩϫⲁⲓ ϩⲓⲛⲛⲉⲧⲛϣⲗⲏⲗ ⲉⲧⲟⲩⲁⲁⲃ ⲏ ⲁⲅⲓⲁ ⲧⲣⲓⲁⲥ ϯ

'Here have I sent these 10 sprigs of small artichokes and 8 bundles of straw and a bundle of papyrus and 2 bunches of lettuce, having 16 leaves on each (?), and 7½ liters of *stibium* (?), belonging to the priest Mark   Yet (δέ) what is above all valuable   we greet (ἀσπάζειν) the sweetness of thy piety, that is worthy of all honour, and our beloved that are with thee, by name   May we keep health through thy saintly prayers   The Holy Trinity'

292.—Papyrus, 2 disconnected fragments, the larger, 10 × 19½ cm   Script early uncials   *V* Pl 5   *Recto* →

Letter to a superior, whom the writer entreats to remember him and no longer to regard him as a stranger, citing Matt ix 12   He professes his devotion and asks for a letter, while referring to one previously written to 'my brother Comodus'   The idiom is peculiar, *e g* ⲉⲓ = ⲓ, ϣϣⲉⲉ, ⲉⲛⲛ- = ⲙⲛⲧ-, ⲙⲉⲉⲩ, ⲕⲁⲁⲥ, ⲛⲥⲁⲣ, ⲛⲁⲉ⁶.

ⲕⲓ ⲧⲁⲁϥ ϩⲱⲟⲩ ⲙⲙⲛⲗⲁ | ⲕⲣⲟ ⲉⲑⲉ ⲧⲓⲟⲩⲁϣⲕ ⲙⲙⲟⲥ ⲉⲓⲧⲉⲥⲉ ⲉⲧⲃⲉⲡⲟⲩⲱϣ ⲉϯⲟ ⲙ | ⲡⲟⲃⲉ ⲉⲩⲟϣ ⲉⲙⲁⲧⲉ ⲡⲉⲧⲉϣϣⲉⲉⲛⲉ ⲉⲓⲣⲉⲕⲣⲡⲁⲙⲉⲉⲩ ⲛⲣⲉϥ | ⲓⲁⲧⲉⲕⲙⲓⲛⲉ ⲁⲩⲱ ⲉⲧⲓⲁⲉⲓⲏⲩ ϩⲓⲙⲡⲛⲟⲩⲧⲉ ⲛⲧⲉⲕϩⲉ ⲛⲡ ⲉⲛⲁ ⲛⲁⲩ |] ⲡⲉⲟⲩⲟⲝ ⲛⲥⲁⲣ ⲉϣⲱⲡⲉ ⲙⲙⲉϥϫⲓ ⲡⲁⲥⲛ ⲉⲣⲟϥ ⲕⲁⲧⲁ ⲑⲉ | ⲅⲉⲕⲟⲩⲥⲉ ⲡⲁⲓⲱⲧ ⲉⲧⲧⲁⲉⲓⲏⲩ ϯⲡⲁⲣⲁⲕⲁⲗⲉⲓ ⲙⲙⲟⲕ ⲕⲁⲁⲥ ⲉⲕⲉⲣ |] ⲥⲣⲟⲉⲓ ⲛⲑⲉ ⲛⲛⲓϣⲙⲙⲟ ϯⲧⲏⲥ ⲅⲁⲣ ⲉⲣⲟⲕ ϩⲙⲡⲁϩⲏⲧ ⲡⲁⲣⲁ ⲛⲉⲧ | ⲕⲣ ⲙⲙⲟⲕ ϩⲙⲡⲥⲱⲙⲁ ⲡⲁϩⲏⲧ ⲛⲁⲉ ⲙⲟⲕϩ ⲉⲙⲁⲧⲉ ϫⲉⲛⲛⲱⲡ ⲙ | ⲕ ⲟⲩⲧⲉ ϩⲓⲛⲛⲉⲧⲟⲩⲏⲩ ⲙⲙⲟⲕ ⲛⲕⲧⲁⲉⲓⲟ ⲅⲁⲣ ⲁⲛ ⲙⲟⲉⲓ ⲉⲣⲡⲁⲙⲉⲉⲩ | ⲕⲧ ⲉϣⲱⲡⲉ ⲉⲣⲛⲁⲕ ⲡⲁⲓⲱⲧ ⲉⲧⲧⲁⲉⲓⲏⲩ ⲥⲣⲁⲉⲓ ⲛⲟⲩ- ⲉⲡⲓⲥⲧⲟⲗⲏ ⲙ | ϯ ⲙⲙⲟⲉⲓ ⲉⲧⲟⲟⲧϥ ⲛⲑⲉ ⲛⲧⲁⲕⲥϩⲁⲉⲓ ⲙⲡⲁⲥⲟⲛ ⲕⲟⲙⲟⲍⲉ ⲉⲕⲅⲩⲏ | ϫⲉ ⲡⲁⲉⲓ ϫⲉⲁⲕⲥϩⲁⲉⲓ ⲛⲁϥ ⲉⲧⲃⲏⲧϥ ⲛⲕⲧⲙⲥⲱϣⲧ ⲉⲧⲁⲙⲛⲗⲁⲁⲩ | ϫⲟ ⲛⲁ . ⲕⲁⲧⲁ [ⲛ]ⲉϩⲃⲛⲟⲩⲉ | a line lost here | ϫⲟⲥ

¹ *V* Bi Mus no 1114
² *Cf* ⲉⲣⲃⲁⲓⲛ ﺭﺏ KIRCHER 198 (PEYRON's reference, p 41, is incomplete), LABIB, *Dict*, ﺭﻳﺱ
³ Possibly 'stalk' rather than 'leaf'

⁴ ? Variant of ⲥⲧⲙ
⁵ Perhaps recurs in VITELLI no 64   Κόμμοδος seems improbable
⁶ For the last *v* nos 6 and 314

T 2

ⲛⲕⲧⲉⲟⲩⲟ.ⲟⲛ.ⲓⲧⲉ ⲛⲁϥ ϧⲛⲟⲩ[|]ⲕ ⲉⲥⲥⲡⲥⲱⲛⲕ ⲁⲛⲟⲕ ⲛⲅⲁⲣ ⲙⲡⲓϣⲕⲛ | ⲡ]ⲁⲉⲓⲱⲧ ⲉⲧⲧⲁⲉⲓⲏⲩ ⲁⲩⲱ ⳁϣⲗⲏⲗ |]ⲭ̅ⲥ̅ ⲛⲧⲉⲩⲣⲏⲏ ⲙⲡⲉϧⲟⲟⲩ ⲛϥ |] ⲛⲟⲩⲛⲟϭ ⲛⲟⲩⲟ]ⲉⲓϣ ⲁⲩⲱ ⲛϥⲕⲧⲟ ⲙⲡⲉⲕ |] ⲛϥⲧⲣⲉⲕⲗⲟ ⲛⲛϭⲱϣⲧ ⲉⲣⲟⲉⲓ ⲛⲑⲉ ⲛⲛⲓϣⲙⲙⲟ |]ⲱ ⲛⲑⲉ ⲛⲟ[ⲩⲁ] ⲛⲛⲥⲕⲙ[ⲉ]ⲣⲁⲧⲉ [

Verso blank

293—Papyrus, a fragment, $6\frac{1}{2} \times 25$ cm　　Script　*v* Pl 5.　*Cf* no 352 and Brit Mus *Catal*, Pl 1, no 395　*Recto* ↑

Letter from　　　　　to his 'dear father, Apa Hagor[1]'

]ⲧⲁⲕϫⲟⲟⲩ [ⲛ]ⲁⲓ [ⲙⲡⲁⲉⲓ]ⲱⲧ ⲡϫⲓⲁⲕⲱⲛ ϫⲉⲕⲁⲧⲁ ⲡⲁⲛⲁϣ ⲉⲧⲟⲩⲧⲛ̅ ⲙⲛⲛⲉⲡⲉⲣⲏⲩ |]ⲛⲉ ϧⲓⲧⲛⲙⲛⲧⲉ ⲙⲡⲛⲕⲩⲣⲓⲥ ⲁⲡⲁ ⲃⲓⲕⲧⲱⲣ ⲫⲁⲣⲁⲛⲧⲏⲥ[2]　ⳁⲛⲟⲩ ⲁⲛⲟⲕ ⲙⲉⲛ ϣⲁⳁⲛⲟⲩ ⲡⲁⲗⲟⲅⲟⲥ |]ⲁⲃⲟⲗⲉⲓ ⲙⲉⲛ ⲉϣⲱⲡⲉ ⲛⲧⲟⲕ ⲕⲟⲩⲱϣ ⲉⲃⲟⲗ ⲡⲗⲟⲅⲟⲥ ⲉⲃⲟⲗ ⲕⲟ ⲙⲡⲉⲕϫⲟⲉⲓⲥ[3] ⲡⲛⲟⲩⲧⲉ ⲡⲁ |] ⲙⲡⲁⲛⲁϣ ⲁⲩⲱ ⲉⲧⲃⲉⲡⲙⲁ ⲛⲡⲁⲛⲟⲩⲡ ⲉⲕϣⲁⲛⲉⲓ ⲉⲣⲛⲉ ⲛⲟⲩⲱϣ ⲕⲱ |] ϣⲁⲛⲛⲁⲧⲛⲁϥ ⲛⲁⲙⲙⲁ ⲡⲗⲓⲛ ⲙⲡⲣⲧⲉⲧⲉⲛⲯⲩⲭⲏ[4] ⲟⲗⲓⲧⲱⲣⲓ ⲉⲣⲟⲓ ϧⲛⲗⲁⲁⲩ ⲉ | ⲛⲉ]ⲛⲉⲣⲏⲩ ⳁ ⲟⲩϫⲁⲓ ϧⲙⲡϫⲟⲉⲓⲥ +

Verso　ⳁ ⲧⲁⲁⲥ ⲙⲡⲁⲙⲉⲣⲓⲧ ⲛⲓⲱⲧ ⲁⲡⲁ ϧⲁ [space] ϭⲟⲣ ϧⲓⲧⲛ[

294.—Papyrus, a fragment, $6\frac{1}{2} \times 30$ cm　　Script sloping, ligatureless　*Recto* ↑

Letter from　　　　　to 'the pious and reverend Apa Amoun, father of the 'rock'[5] of Apa Thomas', referring to a deed of gift (δωρεά) of a garden, and ending, 'And believe me, that nothing that I can do for you will I conceal from you'

[+] ⲁⲓϫⲓ ⲧⲉⲡⲓⲥⲧⲟⲗⲏ ⲛⲧⲉⲕⲙⲛⲧⲙⲁⲓⲛⲟⲩⲧⲉ ⲁⲩⲱ ⲉⲓⲥ ϧⲏⲏⲧⲉ ⲁⲓⲥϧⲁⲓ ⲥⲧϫⲁⲥⲣ[6] ⲥⲁⲓϧⲱⲛ ⲥⲧⲟⲟⲧⲟⲩ | ⲭⲁⲃⲟⲩⲧ 16 ⲗⲉⲧ]ⲥⲧⲟⲥ ϫⲉⲛⲟⲩⲉⲓ ⲉⲃⲟⲗ ϧⲙⲡⲉⲓϧⲱⲃ ⲉⲡⲉⲓϫⲏ ⲁⲓⲱϣ ⲧϫⲱⲣⲉⲁ ⲛⲧⲉϣⲛⲏ | ⲭⲁⲃⲟⲩⲧ 12 ⲗⲉⲧ] ⲧⲁⲁⲥ ⲛⲏⲧⲛ ⲉϧⲟⲩⲛ ⲉⲡⲉⲧⲣⲁ ⲁⲩ[ⲱ] ⲡⲓⲥⲧⲉⲩⲉ ⲛ]ⲁⲓ ϫⲉϧⲱⲃ ⲛⲓⲙ ⲉⳁⲛⲁϣⲙϭⲟⲙ | [ⲉⲁ]ⲁϥ ⲛⲏⲧⲛ ⳁⲛⲁϧⲟⲡϥ ⲉⲣⲱⲧⲛ ⲁⲛ ⲟⲩϫⲁⲓ ϧⲙⲡϫⲟⲉⲓⲥ ⳁ

Verso　[+ ⲧⲁ]ⲁⲥ ⲙⲡⲙⲁⲓⲛⲟⲩⲧⲉ ⲁⲩⲱ ⲉⲧⲧⲁⲓⲏⲩ [space] ⲁⲡⲁ ⲁⲙⲟⲩⲛ ⲡⲉⲓⲱⲧ ⲛⲧⲡⲉⲧⲣⲁ ⲛⲁⲡⲁ ⲑⲱⲙⲁⲥ [　　ⳁ　　 |

295—Papyrus, a fragment, 14×22 cm　　Script ligatureless, *cf* Crum, *Ostraca*, Pl 1, no 71, though the type is different　*Recto* ↑　Note the breathing here on ⲏ (ἤ), as in Smuthian and other parchment MSS.

Letter to an ecclesiastical (?) superior, regarding a dispute as to the management (διοίκησις) of certain commemorative offerings (προσφορά)[7]

]ⲁⲓϫⲟⲟⲥ ⲉⲣⲟⲟ[ⲩ ϫ]ⲉ[.. ⲡⲟ]ϣϥ ⲡⲉϫⲁⲩ ⲛⲁⲓ ϫⲉⲙⲡⲟ[ⲩ.·] |] ⳁⲡⲁⲣⲁⲕⲁⲗⲉⲓ ⲛⲧⲉⲕⲙⲛⲧⲉⲓⲱⲧ ⲉⲧⲣⲥⲕⲣⲧⲁⲅⲁ |]ⲛ̅ ⲛⲥⲉϥⲓⲧϥ ⲛⲁⲩ ⲧⲏⲣϥ ⲉⲡⲉⲓ ⲉⲛϣⲁⲛⲕⲁⲁϥ ⲛⲧⲉⲓϧⲉ | ,ⲗⲁⲁⲩ ⲇⲓⲟⲓⲕⲛⲥⲓⲥ ⲛϧⲏⲧϥ

---

[1] *V* no 224

[2] *I e* 'of Pharan' in Sinai　(The ref Tattam, *Lex* 872, appears to be wrong, Zoega clix does not show the word)

[3] A similar locution, *Mission franç* iv 824

[4] Read ⲙⲡⲣⲧⲣⲉ-

[5] *V* nos. 124, 289

[6] A line over ⲥⲣ supports this reading　Person or place?

[7] *V* Crum, *Ostr* no 135, Br Mus nos 398, 399, 445

ⲁⲩⲱ ⲁⲛⲉⲥⲏⲏⲩ ⲃⲱⲕ ⲉⲃⲟⲗ | ⲙⲡⲡⲁⲣⲁⲅⲉ ⲙⲙⲟϥ ϫⲓⲛⲙⲡⲭⲱⲱⲗⲉ ⲟⲩⲇⲉ ⲡⲕⲉ(ⲣⲱⲙⲉ cancelled) |
ⲇⲓⲟⲓ]ⲕⲏⲧⲏⲥ [1] ⲙⲡⲓⲛⲁⲩ ⲉⲣⲟϥ ϫⲓⲛⲙⲡⲭⲱⲱⲗⲉ ⲟⲩⲇⲉ | ⲗⲁⲩ ⲛϭⲱⲃ ⲉⲓⲥ ϭⲏⲏⲧⲉ ⲁⲓⲧⲁⲙⲉ ⲧⲉⲕⲙⲛⲧⲉⲓⲱⲧ *(sic)* |
]ⲕⲟ ⲉϥϣⲁⲛⲡⲟϣϥ ⲅⲁⲣ ⲡⲟⲩⲁ ⲡⲟⲩⲁ ⲛⲁϥⲓ ⲣⲟⲟⲩϣ ϩⲁ |]ⲡⲣⲟⲥⲫⲟⲣⲁ ⲛⲧⲉⲕⲙⲁⲕⲁⲣⲓⲁ ⲛⲙⲁⲁⲩ ϭⲱ |
ⲥⲉⲙⲏⲛ ⲉ |]ⲧⲉⲙⲙⲛⲧⲉⲓⲱⲧ ϫⲉⲛϥⲛⲁⲕⲁⲁⲩ ⲁⲛ ⲉϫⲓ ⲗⲁ]ⲁⲩ ⲙ | ⲁⲛⲟ]ⲕ ϩⲱⲱⲧ ⲛϥⲛⲁϥⲓ ⲁⲛ ⲏ̄ ⲛⲥⲉϥⲓⲧϥ
ⲧⲏⲣϥ ⲛⲧⲉ | ⲡⲣⲟⲥⲫⲟⲣⲁ ⲗⲟ ϩⲓϫⲱⲓ ⲛ̄ ⲛⲥⲉⲡⲟϣϥ ⲛⲧⲁⲣϫⲟⲉⲓⲥ ⲉⲡⲁ |]ⲁⲣⲓ ⲧⲁⲅⲁⲡⲏ ⲛⲥⲱⲗⲏⲗ ⲉϫⲱⲛ
ⲛⲧⲉⲡϫⲟⲉⲓⲥ ⲛⲁϩ [2]] | ⲛⲁⲛ ⲡⲉⲛⲙⲉⲣⲓⲧ ⲛⲉⲓⲱⲧ + ⲛ ⲁⲅⲓⲁ ⲧⲣ[ⲓ]ⲁⲥ + + +

296.—Papyrus, a fragment, 11 × 21½ cm   Script ligatureless   *Recto* ↑

Letter from 'the humble'   , 'who ventures to write to his lady mother,' whose feet he kisses   He, from the mention of his 'son, Apa Mena', is perhaps an abbot, she an abbess   He has a request to her   'I know (that everything that thou dost ask) of the Lord befalleth'   'If I should do all, yet could not I repay (thee for all) thou hast done for me'

]ⲉⲗⲁⲭⲓⲥⲧⲟⲥ ⲡϥⲧⲟⲗⲙⲁ ϥϭϩⲁⲓ ⲉⲣⲁⲧϥ *(sic)* ⲛⲧϥϫⲟⲉⲓⲥ ⲙⲙⲁⲁⲩ |] ⲛϭⲱϥ ⲛⲓⲙ ⲧⲓⲁⲥⲡⲁⲍⲉ ⲉⲡⲛⲥⲏⲧ
ⲉⲛⲟⲩⲟⲩⲣⲏⲧⲉ ⲁⲩⲱ ⲧⲓϣⲓⲛⲉ | ⲕ]ⲁⲧⲁ ⲛⲉⲩⲣⲁⲛ ⲁⲩⲱ ⲉⲡⲉⲓⲇⲏ ⲁⲡⲁⲥⲟⲛ ⲇⲓⲟⲥⲕⲟⲣⲟⲥ ⲉⲓ ⲉϩⲣⲏ ⲁϥϫⲟⲟⲥ |
ⲥ]ⲏⲛⲙⲙⲁ[.]ϣ ⲉⲩⲟ ⲛⲓⲅⲛⲓ[ⲛⲉ]ⲙⲏⲛⲉ ⲉⲣⲭⲱⲗⲏ [3] ⲙⲡⲣⲱⲙⲉ |]ⲉϥϣⲏⲣⲉ [ⲧⲓⲡⲁ]ⲣⲁⲕⲁⲗⲉⲓ ⲟ[ⲩⲛ] ⲙⲙⲟ
ⲧⲁⲣⲉⲧⲁⲩⲟ ⲡⲁⲣⲁⲛ |]ⲛⲁϩ[.ⲛ.ⲉ..ⲉⲓⲣ[ⲉ ⲛ]ⲙⲟⲥ ⲛⲧⲁⲩϣⲱⲡⲉ ⲧⲓⲥⲟ[ⲟⲩⲛ] |]ⲟϥ ⲛⲧⲟⲟⲧϥ ⲙⲡϫⲟⲉⲓⲥ
[ⲉ]ϣⲁϣⲱⲡⲉ ⲁⲩⲱ ϩⲱϥ ⲛⲓⲙ |]ⲛ ⲯⲁⲙⲁⲣⲉⲩ [4] ϭϩⲁⲓ ⲛⲁⲓ ⲧⲁϫⲉⲓⲧϥ ⲡⲉ ⲙⲡⲣ[. .] |]ⲉ ⲁⲩⲱ ⲉⲓϣⲁⲛⲉⲣ
ϩⲱϥ ⲛⲓⲙ ⲇⲓⲁⲥⲙⲁϩⲥ [5] ⲁⲛ [..]].ⲁⲣⲁⲁⲩ ⲛⲁⲓ ⲁⲩⲱ ϣⲓⲛⲉ ⲉⲅⲁⲥⲱⲛⲉ ⲧⲁⲅⲁⲡⲏ ⲧⲟⲛⲟⲩ |]ϣⲓⲛⲉ
ⲉⲧⲁⲭⲟⲉⲓⲥ ⲙⲙⲁⲁⲩ ⲧⲟⲛⲟⲩ ⲁⲩⲱ ⲧⲁϣⲟⲙⲧⲉ |ⲡ]ⲁϣⲏⲣⲉ ⲁⲡⲁ ⲙ[ⲏ]ⲛⲁ ϣⲓⲛⲉ ⲉⲣⲟ ⲧⲟⲛⲟⲩ ⲁⲩⲱ ⲡⲣⲟ[. .] |
ϣ]ⲓⲛⲉ ⲉⲣⲟ ⲧⲟⲛⲟⲩ ⲁⲩⲱ ⲧⲓϣⲓⲛⲉ ⲉⲅⲁⲅⲁⲡⲏ ⲧⲁⲥⲱⲛ[ⲉ] | ⲟ]ⲩϫⲁⲓ ϩⲙⲡϫⲟⲉⲓⲥ ⲛ ⲁⲅⲓⲁ ⲧⲣⲓⲁⲥ ⳨ ⳨

Verso ⳨ ⲧⲁⲁⲥ ⲛⲧⲁϫⲟⲉⲓⲥ ⲙ [space] ⲙⲁ]ⲁⲩ

297.—Papyrus, a fragment, 8½ × 22 cm   Script   sloping, ligatureless   *Recto* ↑

Letter to a superior, wherein reference is made to 'the father of orphans and judge of widows'

Above l 1 a cross

⳨ ⲡⲣⲟⲥ ⲧⲉⲧⲛⲕⲉⲗⲉⲩⲥⲓⲥ ⲁⲓϫⲟⲟⲩ ⲉⲃⲟⲗ ⲙⲡⲉϥ | ⲁⲓϫⲟⲟⲩϥ ⲛⲏⲧⲛ ⲉⲡⲉⲓⲇⲏ ⲟⲩⲛ ⲁⲛⲕⲟⲩⲓ [ ] ⲙⲡⲉⲓⲱⲧ
ⲛⲛⲟⲣⲫⲁⲛⲟⲥ ⲙⲡⲛⲉⲕⲣⲓⲧⲏⲥ ⲛ[ⲛⲉ]ⲭ[ⲏ]ⲣ[ⲁ | ⲛⲉϥ⳨ⲉⲩⲥⲛⲱⲙⲛ ⲛⲁⲓ ⲧⲁϭⲛⲧⲟⲩ ⲧⲁⲛⲁⲁⲩ ⲉⲃⲟⲗ ⳨

Verso] [central space] ⲭ̅ⲙ̅ⲅ̅

298.—Papyrus, complete, 15 × 12 cm   Script ligatured   *Verso* →

Letter to a superior regarding the measurement of certain land and money transactions

---

[1] Here presumably the administrator of private property, not a magistrate   *Cf* nos 354, 369.

[2] ⲡⲁⲣⲙⲉⲛ

[3] χολή   *Cf* CRUM, *Ostr*, no. 325, here no. 305

[4] Apparently Σαμαρεύς as a name   *Cf* perhaps CLÉDAT *Baouit*, pl xxix, ⲁⲡⲁ ⲯⲁⲙⲁⲣⲓⲧⲏⲥ, and CRUM, *l c*, p xviii, not 3

[5] For ⲧⲓⲛⲁϣⲙⲁϩⲉ (*fem*)

ⲥⲛ ⲧⲡⲣⲟⲥⲏ, ⲛⲧ[ⲥ]ⲕ[ⲙ]ⲉⲧ[ⲭⲟ]ⲉⲓⲥ ⲉⲥ ⲛⲁⲕⲁϩ ⲁⲓϣⲓⲧⲟⲩ | ⲉⲥ ⲡⲉⲩⲡⲟⲡⲉ[1] ⲁⲓⲭⲟϥ ⲛⲁⲕ ⲉϩⲣⲁⲓ | ⲁⲩⲱ ⲉⲥ ⲛⲥⲣⲟⲙⲉ ⲧⲁⲗⲃⲁⲗⲉ[2] ⲁⲓⲁⲡⲁⲛⲧ[3] ⲉⲣⲟⲩ ϩⲁⲡϣⲁϥ[4] ⲁⲩⲙⲁϩⲉ[5] ⲙⲟⲓ · ϥ | ⲁⲓⲉⲛⲧϥ ⲉⲭⲟⲧⲓ ⲛⲧⲉⲣⲟⲁⲙ | ⲗⲟⲓⲡⲟⲛ ⲥϭⲁⲓ ⲛⲉⲕⲛⲟⲓⲉⲙ[6] | ⲛⲁⲓ ⲧⲁⲱⲡ ⲉⲭⲟϥ ⲧⲓⲡⲣⲟⲥⲕ, ⲡⲉ | blank

Recto remains of an earlier Arabic text and of a still earlier account in Greek numerals

299 —Papyrus, a fragment, 16½ × 15 cm   Script ligatureless   *Verso* →

Letter to a superior, of obscure purport

ⲧⲡⲣⲟⲥⲕⲩⲛ ⲁⲩⲱ ⲡⲁⲥⲡⲁⲍⲉ ⲙⲡⲁ |]ⲁⲡⲁⲭⲟⲉⲓⲥ ⲭⲓ ⲛⲉⲡⲓⲥⲧⲟⲗⲟⲟⲩⲉ |]ⲉⲣⲏⲥ ϩⲓⲧⲟⲟⲧⲃ ⲉⲡⲁⲩⲗⲟⲥ ⲡⲛⲉⲉⲃ |]ⲉ ⲉⲛⲛⲉⲩⲟⲩⲁⲉⲓⲉ ⲉⲩⲭⲉⲣⲟⲩ |]ⲅⲉ ⲭⲉⲙⲁⲛⲭⲓⲛⲥ ⲧⲛⲛⲁϩⲟⲩ |]ⲉⲙⲁⲛ ϩⲁⲡⲭⲱⲱⲕ · · · |]ⲟⲩⲉ ⲧⲁⲕⲱ ϩⲟⲩⲛ ⲉⲛⲉⲩⲉϣⲟⲓ |]ⲛⲛⲕ ⲉⲓⲉ ⲥϭⲁⲓ ⲉⲛⲁⲡⲛⲩⲉ |]ⲙⲡⲁⲭⲟⲉⲓⲥ ϣⲱⲡⲉ ⲉⲧⲃⲉ] ⲧⲱϩ ⲉⲙⲁ ⲁⲗⲗⲁ ⲥⲁⲓⲧⲁⲁⲩ |]ⲕⲁⲕ ϣⲁ ⲓ ⲕ ⲉⲛⲟⲩⲏⲣ · |]ⲥⲁⲧⲉⲧⲁⲥⲉ ⲙⲙⲟⲕ ⲛⲁⲓⲉ |]ⲕ ⲭⲉⲓ ⲁⲙⲟⲩ ⲉϩⲣⲉϩ ⲉⲧⲃⲉ |]ⲁⲕ ⲁⲭⲓⲛⲡⲁⲧⲱⲭⲟⲥ + ⲧⲓⲡⲣⲟⲥ |]

Recto   + [ⲡⲁ]ⲭⲟⲉⲓⲥ ⲛⲛⲁ[space] ⲓ

Also traces of an earlier text, the address of which is visible

+ [ⲧⲁⲁⲥ] ⲛϥⲟⲓⲃⲁⲙⲙⲱⲛ [space] ⲡⲛⲁⲣⲡⲱⲛⲛⲉ][7] ϩⲓⲧⲛ[ⲍⲁ]ⲭⲁⲣⲓⲁⲥ |

300. —Papyrus, a fragment, 10 × 10 cm   Script ligatureless   *Recto* ↑

Letter to a superior, apparently from an absent member of his household ('our honorable house')   Antinoe is mentioned

ⲛ]ϩⲱϥ ⲛⲙⲙ · · · ⲣⲕ   ⲥⲃ[| ⲟⲩ]ⲉⲣⲏⲧⲉ ⲛⲙⲧⲕⲙⲛⲧⲏ |]ⲛⲡⲉⲛⲛⲓ ⲧⲏⲣϥ ⲛⲉⲩⲗⲟⲥ[ⲓⲙⲉⲛⲟⲥ |]ⲏⲥ ⲙⲛⲥⲟⲛϣⲙⲙ[8] ⲡⲛⲉⲉ[ϥ |] ⲕ.ⲟ]ⲗⲗⲁⲑⲟⲛ ⲉⲩϩⲛⲁⲛⲧⲓⲛⲟⲟ[ⲩ |]ⲃⲧⲟⲟⲩ ⲛϣⲟⲡ ⲁ[|]ⲧⲁⲡⲟⲟⲛ[ⲕⲏ |]ϩ ⲛⲛⲉ[|

Verso   ⲧ]ⲁⲁⲥ ⲛⲡⲁⲙⲉⲣⲓⲧ ⲛⲭⲟⲉⲓⲥ ⲛⲉⲓⲱⲧ [

301 —Papyrus, a fragment, 13 × 10½ cm   Script   moderately ligatured, early type   *Recto* →

Letter to a superior, containing a request   The script and the mention of Apa Shoi suggest a connection with nos 268, 269

] ⲙⲡⲁⲟⲩⲱϣ ⲁⲗⲗⲁ] ⲛⲁⲥ ⲭⲉⲁⲙ[ ] ⲛⲥⲭⲓⲭⲉⲓ |] ⲉⲁⲡⲁ ϣⲟⲉⲓ ⲁⲓⲧⲛⲛⲟⲟⲩϥ |] ⲭⲟⲉⲓⲥ [ⲡ]ⲁⲉⲓⲱⲧ ⲉⲉⲓⲁⲍⲓⲟⲩ |]ⲙⲁⲣⲉⲥⲱ ⲉⲣⲟⲉⲓ ⲉ |] ⲭⲉⲙⲛⲗⲁⲁⲩ ⲛⲁⲁⲛⲧⲓ[9]] ⲟⲩⲉϩⲥⲁϩ[ⲛ]ⲉ ⲛⲁⲓ ⲙⲡⲓⲧⲥⲉ[10] |]ⲉϩⲁⲓ ⲛⲁⲥⲓ ⲉⲧⲃⲉ ϣⲟⲓ ⲁⲩⲁⲑⲟ | ⲁ]ⲓⲁⲛⲁⲅⲕⲁⲍⲉ ⲉⲙⲟϥ ⲉⲧⲃⲛⲧⲕ | ⲙ]ⲡⲣⲧⲥⲟ ⲧⲁⲁⲍⲓⲱⲥⲉ ⲉⲃⲟⲗ |]ⲣⲱⲃ [ ] ⲙⲡⲁϩⲉⲗ ⲅⲁⲣ ⲁⲛ |]ⲉϩⲁⲧⲱⲧⲛ [.ⲉ |

---

[1] From ? ⲡⲱⲱⲛⲉ 'transfer'

[2] ?? لبلة   Cf no 374

[3] ἀπαντᾷ   [4] V ro 158

[5] 'They took of me'   This seems to be the meaning in no 324 &c

[6] Recurs in Br Mus no 1116   Perhaps نعمك 'thy

pleasure'   But a fragment in Br Mus Or 6201 b has ⲁⲩⲱ ⲡⲉⲕⲛⲟⲉⲙⲁ ⲟⲩⲛⲟϭⲛⲉ

[7] V no 212

[8] This name ⲓⲥ ⲥⲟⲛⲭⲙⲙ, ⲥⲁⲛⲣⲙⲙ in Br Mus no 386

[9] ? ἀντιλέγειν

[10] Sic   Read here ⲧⲥⲧⲉ and below ⲧⲥⲧⲟ

302—Papyrus, a fragment, 13 × 13½ cm   Script almost ligatureless   *Recto* ↑
Letter from Paul of Simou[1], a servant, giving news and saying that he is sending certain things

ϯ ⲡⲉⲕϭⲁⲟⲩⲟⲛ ⲡⲁⲩⲗⲉ ⲡⲣⲱⲙⲉⲓⲙⲟⲩ [| ϩⲁⲑⲛ ⲙⲙ ⲛϧⲱϥ ⲛⲓⲙ ϯⲡⲣⲟⲥⲕ[ⲩⲛⲉⲓ | ⲁⲓⲧⲛⲟⲟⲩϥ ⲛⲁⲕ ⲉϩⲣⲁⲓ ⲉϥⲧⲓ ⲕⲁ[| ⲁⲅⲉⲛⲉⲕⲉ ⲛⲉⲙⲁϥ ⲛⲧⲣⲟⲙ.ⲋ.[2][| .. ⲉⲥ ⲧⲁⲁⲡⲟⲗⲟⲩⲅⲓⲍⲉ ⲛⲁⲕ[| ⲁⲩⲱ ⲉⲓⲥ ⲥⲟⲁϣⲓ[3] ⲥⲛⲁⲩ ⲛ [| ⲁⲩⲱ ϣⲉⲡⲛⲟⲩⲧⲉ ϩⲉⲡⲁϩⲉ.[| blank

Verso   ϩⲓ|ⲧⲛⲡⲉⲕϭⲁⲟⲩⲟⲛ ⲡⲁⲩⲗⲉ ⲡⲣ.   .[4]

303—Papyrus, a fragment, 8 × 9½ cm   Script moderately ligatured.   Possibly the same as no 302   *Recto* ↑
Letter from Paul the βοηθός, of Parow', his servant, to Theodoracius the χαρτουλάριος[6], mentioning Easter (ἀνάστασις)[7]

+ ⲡⲉⲧⲛⲉϭⲁⲟⲩⲟⲛ [ⲡ]ⲁⲩⲗⲉ ⲡⲃⲱⲏⲑⲟⲥ | ⲑⲉⲩⲇⲱⲣⲁⲕⲉ [ⲡ]ⲉⲭⲁⲣⲧⲟⲗⲁⲣⲏ[ⲥ | ϩⲁⲧⲁⲛⲁⲥⲧⲁ[ⲥⲓ]ⲥ ⲙⲡⲉⲭ̄ⲥ̄ ⲉⲓⲥ.[| ⲛⲕⲗⲉⲅⲉ ⲛⲛⲉⲧ[ⲛ]ⲉϭⲁⲟⲩⲟⲛ ⲛⲥⲟ[ⲩ | ⲛⲉⲙⲁⲛ ⲧⲁⲓⲙ [| ⲛⲛⲏ ⲉⲣⲏⲥ ⲁⲩ[| ⲛⲁⲓ ⲝⲉⲩⲛⲉⲧ[| ⲛϩⲱⲃ ⲁⲭⲛⲧⲉⲧⲛ[ⲉ |

Verso   ϩⲓ|ⲧⲛⲡⲉⲕϭⲁⲟⲩⲟⲛ ⲡⲁⲩⲗⲉ ⲡⲃⲱⲛⲑ/ ⲛⲡⲁⲣⲟⲟⲩ

304—Papyrus, a fragment, 8 × 10½ cm   Script almost ligatureless   *Recto* ↑
Letter to (?) Phoebammon   It contains the phrase [ⲡ]ϣⲁ ⲛⲧⲁⲛⲁⲥⲧⲁⲥⲓⲥ ⲙⲡⲉⲭ̄ⲥ̄.

305—Papyrus, a fragment, 10½ × 14 cm   Script ligatured   *Recto* ↑
Letter, probably from a servant (ϭⲁⲟⲩⲛ) to his master   Shmoun is mentioned

ⲡⲉ]ⲥⲧⲟⲗⲙⲁ ⲉϥⲥϩⲁⲓ ⲙⲡⲉϥϫⲟⲉⲓⲥ | ϯⲡⲣⲟⲥⲕⲩⲛⲏ ⲛⲧⲉⲛⲉⲙⲛⲧϫⲟⲉⲓⲥ |]ⲉⲓⲣⲭⲟⲗⲛ ⲛⲥⲁϥ ⲉⲧⲃⲉ |]ⲉⲛ ϩⲩϣⲙⲟⲩⲛ ⲁⲑⲓⲛ ⲛϩⲉⲣⲟⲩⲟⲝ [|]ⲝⲉⲓⲱϩⲁⲛⲛⲏⲥ ⲡⲓⲁϩ ⲛ̇ⲅⲓⲙⲉ[8] |]ⲓⲁⲥ ⲡⲉϥⲥⲱⲙⲁ ⲁϥϫⲓ ⲡⲉϥⲉⲛ-ⲅⲁⲧⲓⲛ [|]ϣⲁⲛⲧⲉⲛⲉϩⲉ ⲉϭⲟⲗ ⲛⲥⲱⲛ [|]ⲛⲛⲙⲉⲓϩⲟⲧⲉⲣⲟⲥ[9] ⲧⲁⲣϥϩ̇ⲱ ⲉⲣⲟⲛ [|]ⲛ̇ϫⲟⲉⲓⲥ ϫⲉⲥⲛ +

Verso   ]ⲉⲧⲓ [space] ⲭ̄ⲙ̄ⲅ̄ ⲯⲑ̄ [

306.—Paper, a fragment, 8½ × 10 cm   Script sloping, ligatureless   ⲛ is ν
Letter from a servant (ν address), referring to financial transactions with flax and barley, and mentioning Apourrōshet (Abû 'l Rashîd)

] ϯϣⲙⲉ ⲧⲉⲕⲙⲛⲧϣⲁⲗ.[|].ⲡ̄ⲟ̄ⲥ̄ ϩⲁⲣⲉϩ ⲉⲡⲉⲕⲱⲛϩ[10] ϥϯ[ⲭ]ⲁ[ⲣⲓⲥ ⲛⲁⲕ ϩⲓⲡⲁⲣϩⲏⲥⲓⲁ ϥⲛⲁ ⲡⲉⲕⲣⲁϣⲉ.[|] ⲛⲁⲓ ⲉⲣⲉⲡⲟ̄ⲥ̄ ⲛⲁⲁⲛ ⲁⲡⲟⲩⲣⲣⲱϣⲉⲧ |]ϫⲓ ⲡⲉⲉⲛⲉ ⲛⲉϥⲥⲛⲛⲉⲛ ⲁⲩⲱ ⲁϥⲧⲁ [ⲓ]ⲟⲩⲥⲧⲉ

---

[1] *V* no 401   [2] Not ⲣⲟⲙⲡⲉ
[3] *V* Br Mus no 1102   [4] I cannot read ⲓⲙⲟⲩ here
[5] *Cf* in Br Mus Or 6201 ⲁ, ϥⲟⲓ ⲛⲧⲁⲡⲁⲣⲟⲟⲩ
Another ⲡⲁⲣⲟⲃ is an ἐποίκιον in a Jkôw fragment
[6] Scarcely the high official in nos 129, 207
[7] Not generally so designated   *V* next no and Crum, Ostr no 60 n   [8] He recurs in no 329
[9] *V* no 178   [10] *V* nos 309, 317, 337

ⲁϥⲟⲩⲁϩⲛⲉϥ¹ ⲉⲙⲟϥ ⲧⲉⲃⲓ ⲥⲱ |]ⲧⲕⲓⲣⲁⲕⲏ ⲧⲉϥϯ ϥⲧⲟⲟⲩ ⲇ ⲉϩⲟⲗⲟ | ⲁⲩ]ⲱ ⲧⲉϥϯ ϥⲧⲟⲟⲩ ⲇ ⲛⲁⲕ
ϩⲓⲧⲁⲣⲁ . |]ⲡⲉⲛϣⲓⲛⲉ ⲛⲁⲓ ⲙⲛⲛⲉⲕⲁⲡⲟⲕⲣⲁⲥⲓⲥ ϯ |]ⲟⲩⲁⲕⲛⲉϥ ⲉⲙⲟⲕ ⲥⲩⲙⲟⲩⲛ ⲉϩⲟⲗⲟⲕ ⲛⲟⲉ |]ⲓⲥ
ⲁⲓⲧⲁⲁⲩ ⲉⲁⲡⲱⲣⲣⲱϣⲉⲧ | (verso) ⲡ]ⲉⲛⲛⲟⲩⲥ ⲉϩⲟⲩⲛ ⲉⲡⲉⲕⲉⲣⲡϣⲃⲉϣ . |]ⲅ ⲇ ⲛϥⲧⲟⲟⲩ ⲉⲛⲉⲣⲧⲟϥ
ⲉⲓⲱⲧ ⲙⲉⲥⲛⲧⲉ | ⲉⲓ]ⲱⲧ ϩⲁⲑⲏⲕ ⲉⲧⲁⲓⲧⲁⲁⲩ ⲛⲕⲁϩ ⲁⲩⲱ ⲛⲉϩⲟⲙⲧ |]ϩ.ⲁ.ⲭⲛ ⲉⲃⲟⲗ ⲭⲟⲟⲩ ⲡⲉⲛϣⲓⲛⲉ
ⲛⲁⲓ .. |

In the other direction, the address   ⲡⲉⲕϭⲁⲟⲩ[ⲟⲛ |] ⲁⲡⲗⲱ [

307—Papyrus   The *recto* of no 260   Script   semi uncials
Letter from his 'servant', Philip², to 'his lord', beginning ⲡⲉⲕ]ϭⲁⲟⲩⲟⲛ ⲫⲓⲗⲓⲡⲡⲟⲥ
ⲡⲉⲧⲡⲣⲟⲥⲕⲏⲙ ᵐᵉᵐⲙⲡⲉϥ̇ⲭⲟⲉⲓⲥ ⲕⲁⲧⲁ ⲧ [|] 6 more lines containing the words] ⲡⲁⲛϫⲓⲣ ⲁⲓⲥⲁⲕⲧϥ³
ⲙⲉⲓⲗⲟ ϩⲓⲭⲱϥ ϣ[ⲁⲛ ϭ, and ending [ⲟⲩ]ⲭⲁⲓ ϩⲙⲡⲭⲟⲉⲓⲥ ⲧⲉⲥⲡⲟⲧⲁ /

308—Papyrus, a fragment, 9 × 18½ cm   Script   large, rarely ligatured   *Recto* ↑
Letter from his 'servant', John, to a superior   He is venturing (τολμᾶν) to send
some fish and other things

+ ⲡⲉⲧⲛⲉϩⲙϩⲁⲗ ⲓⲱϩⲁⲛⲛⲉ ⲡⲣⲱ[ⲙ | ⲉϥϩⲁⲓ ⲙⲡⲉϥⲭⲟⲉⲓⲥ ⲡⲕⲟⲙ[ⲉⲥ] ϩⲁⲑⲏ | ⲉⲓⲥ ⲡⲉⲓϣⲏⲙ
ⲛⲧⲏⲃⲧ ⲁⲉⲓⲧⲟⲗⲙⲁ ⲁ[ⲓ | ⲙⲛⲛⲟⲩⲗⲁⲃⲛⲉ⁴ ⲕⲉⲗⲉⲩⲉ⁵ ⲙⲁⲣⲉⲩϫⲓⲧⲟⲩ ⲁⲩⲱ [] ⲙⲛⲧⲟⲟⲩ ⲧⲉⲧⲛⲙⲛⲧⲭⲟⲉⲓⲥ
ⲛⲁⲛ ⲁⲣ[ⲓ | ⲧⲁⲕⲁⲡⲏ ⲛⲉⲙⲁⲛ ⲣⲱⲱⲡⲉ + ⲇⲉⲥⲡⲟⲧ[ⲁ |

Verso (different hand?) χμγ ηθ

309.—Paper, a fragment, 10½ × 7 cm
Script   *cf* CRUM, *Coptic MSS*, Pl 3, xv
Letter from a servant to his master
ϥ... ⲡⲉⲕϩⲙϩⲁⲗ [| ϯⲡⲣⲟⲥⲕⲏⲛⲁⲓ̇ ᵐᵉᵐ ⲙ[|
ⲙⲉⲧⲭⲟⲉⲓⲥ ⲙ[| ⲉⲣⲉⲡⲟⲥ ϩⲁⲣⲉϩ | ⲛⲡⲉⲕⲱⲛⲁϩ
ⲁ[| ϫⲉⲛⲧⲁⲓϩⲁⲓ [| ⲁⲓⲥϭⲛ ⲟⲩⲉⲣⲧⲟϥ [

Verso An Arabic Receipt (later) 'Abd
al-Masih⁶, brother of Abu 'l-Yumin, has paid
اﻟﺞ, for A H 388 = A D 998, ⅓+⅛ *dinar* and
½+⅓ *kirât*, towards the taxes حرج of Ashmu
nain   Scribe   ? Bishai بشاى, son of Shanu-
dah⁷

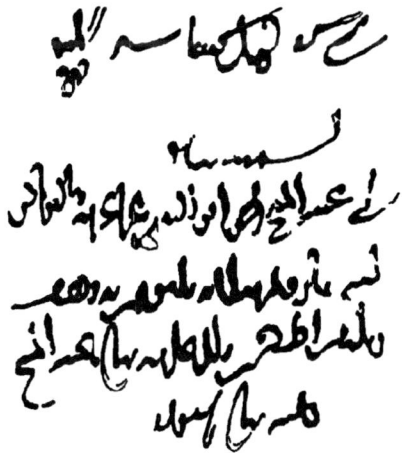

310—Papyrus, a fragment, 17 × 12 cm   Script   fine, of ZOEGA's 1st class, but for ⲙ,
which is rounded   *V* Pl 1   *Recto* →
Letter from a widow   The script, the very high figures involved and the reckoning
in 'talents'⁸ point to the 4th century

¹ Unknown verb
² *V* Br Mus no 1107 &c
³ ⲥⲓⲕⲉ varies with ⲟⲛⲟ in the alchimistic texts
⁴ ? λαβις   *V* Br Mus no 1114
⁵ Same use of this in no. 287   *Cf* κελευσον (*v* Br
Mus no 613)

⁶ Does Χριστόδουλος occur so early? For the next
name, *v* no 290
⁷ For this tentative reading I depend wholly on KARA-
BACEK, *Mitth Rain* ii, Taf III (esp no 5) and pp 160 ff
The Berlin *Arab Urkunden* no 7 is a similar receipt.
⁸ *V* KENYON, *Catal* iii 237

 acoγ aq[. . . . . . .] · ʍʍ|cwc ap[. . . ¹] etʍʍaγ | ϫeγ teqʍaaγ ac̄ пкe|ϣwϫп
eптaqceeпe epнc | 5 aγw ʍʍпcwc aпeϣwт | oп etʍʍaγ ɓw[к] eʒнт | aqaпacкaʒe ʍʍoq |
aqтaaq нтноγapχwп ² | прʍпaпa ³ aqʒoγ[.]a epoq | 10. ϫeoγптaı ʍʍıaϣϥe | нтɓa
нɓıнϣwр ⁴ · epoq | aqoтпq eʒoγн · aqϫı|тq нɓoнc ϣaптqcɓaı | пaq eпeqϣнpe eпʒнaq
aп | 15 aqтaaт нтпʒγпapнc ⁵ | нaптıноoγ a[⁰. . .]ı п̄aı|тı epoe[ı] aqкaaт [eɓoʌ] | [т]eпoγce
eq[. . . .]a | . e ʍʍ[o]ı eϫп . e | 20. ʍʍпaнce · oγдe ʍʍпıoγwʍ н|ʒн]тoγ ʍʍпcw н|ʒн-
тoγ [eı]o нχнpa eıc | ʍʍпcп[тo]oγc нpoʍпe | ϫıптa[. . . . н]тaq|25 -ʌo ʒa | н̄ |

'   price and he   Thereafter that   sent his mother and she brought
southward the rest of what remained   And thereafter that merchant too went north
and constrained (ἀναγκάζειν) him and delivered him to a magistrate (ἄρχων), a *papa*, and
he   him, saying, 'He is my debtor for 170,000 talents'   And he shut him up and
maltreated him, till, against his will, he wrote (making over) to him his children   He
delivered me to the   . of Antinoe, and he   to enquire of (αἰτεῖν) me and he
let me go   Now therefore   . . . . me to (?)   and Taêse.   Neither (οὐδέ) have I
eaten thereof (?) nor have I drunk; and I am a widow (χήρα) now 12 years, since I
ceased to

Verso   remains of a Greek (?) list or account.

311.—Papyrus, a fragment, **22 × 16** cm   Script   early uncials   *V* Pl 3   *Recto* →

Letter, citing Jeremiah's weeping over Jerusalem and Christ's pity for the blind,
and begging the recipient's good offices with the prefect (ἡγεμών), 'I know [that whatsoever]
thou shalt say, God will grant it thee.'   The writer, describing his miserable state, says
that he has sold his clothes   The recipient perhaps a monastic superior (*v* the last line)

L 4 ıcp]нʍıac pıʍe ʒaθıнʌ ⁷ aı[.] |] īc ϣнʒтнq ʒaнɓʌʌeeγ aq | teıʒe ϣнʒтнк
oп ноγwʒʍ ʒa |]aпaнpıпe ʍʍoı ʍʍптpa |]r̄ eγϣaпoγwʒ oп cтooтoγ |]a нʒнг ʒıппıeк-
ϣʌнʌ |]poı aγoγw ɣap eγ† ʒoı ⁸ eıc caʍϣe |]eıнʌ eʒoγн eтɓe[oγ] ⁹ †пapaкaʌı | ʒʍoт
нтoorq ʍʍφнceʍwн †ceoγнc |] eкнaϫooγ пноγтe нaтaaq нaк apı | ʍʍптaʌeпwpoc aı†
нaʒoıтe eɓoʌ eı |]ʍwt aqтaʌe pwq eʒpaı ϫeaγeıc oγтa |]пaɓpcɓıc ¹⁰ нaʍe eıoнʒ
eгaнa[п]н ʍʍпноγтe |]pнc нтoγoнʒт e[п]ʒнceʍwн |] aп aпoχн ¹¹ пaϫ[oeı]c †ceoпc
ʍʍ] к ʒппϣopп ¹² ʒa[ʒт]нк eкϣaннa | eϣwпe eкϣaннa c[ϫнo]γaceɓнc | cwтʍ ϫeʍʍп-
ϣaϫe [. . .]oк aннa |]oγт[.]тʒwн eʍa[ ] нaн eтɓe |]aʌa ʒwc ʍʍпoʌıт[. . . .] eт |]ϣıпe epoн
пaʍ[. . . . .] | eтнʍʍaн тнpoγ кaтa нeγ[paн . . .]ϫwı

¹ Not space for eϣwт
² Note the use of this preposition, and in l 15
³ *Cf* Br Mus no 1156, KENYON, *Cat* ıı 160, 299, where
пaпa, πάπας, need not be an ecclesiastical title (but *v* DEISS-
MANN, *Licht v Ost* 150)   But the force of pʍ- is not clear.
⁴ I know of no other instance of this in Coptic documents
⁵ *V* HALL, *Copt and Gk Texts*, p 69 (5) ʒıпapıc,
possibly a title   If ʒγ were explicable, пapнc might be
'on the south of A'

⁶ Perhaps ʍ, not a
⁷ Unusual in Sa'idic, perhaps archaic   *V* RAHLFS's
Sah Psalter, p 18 n
⁸ *Cf* Pishs 279, 26, where pʒoı is obscure ('be ready,
desirous'?)
⁹ Not space for more   For нʌ eʒoγн *v* no 272
¹⁰ Βρέβις, *brevis*
¹¹ *V* no 352
¹² ʔ те]кɟн пϣopп

U

312.—Papyrus; 2 disconnected fragments, the larger, 11 × 6 cm   It is not possible to ascertain their exact distance apart   Script small uncials of early type, *v* Pl 5
Recto →

Letter to a revered personage, asking for an application on the writer's behalf to the *primicerius*[1]   In l 4 наɪͅкар might be read, but the emperors Trajan and Maurice, thus combined, would be hard to explain   Presumably neither is intended[2]   In l 5 perhaps a title *ἀπὸ ὑπομνημάτων*, thus accounting for the genitive plural[3]

```
]ιραϫι[ο]ү[ | ] ммελн[. .]ετρεηϣн[ϩтнк      αϫιογ мпριмикнрос ετβнт |      ] ͼαρ
τραιαнος αγω маγρισις | ϩ]γпомннммιатωн ϛτρεγ |] τεнογσε пαιωτ ϯπι |] ϩωβ[  ?  ]нα
ϩιτοотн εροογ κατα | ]нτεκμнτατͼαθος [   ?   | ] пнογτε ϯ тоотн нͅϩнтογ |]ͼαρ нακ пαιωτ
[   ?   н]ογτε ϫετεϣϫн ετϩιωωτ | ].н κατα ογμ[   ?   огϣ]нϩτηϥ мнογαͼαпн |
]γ нαι ϩнογαн[   ?   ]γ нταнεннͼαн тнρογ | ]мαγ ϩωστε ετ[   ?   ] нϩεннοογε
εγϣαατ εϐολ нϫн | τεнογσε пαιωτ [   ?   пλαϫοϛιϲ ϩлмпнογτε | о]βϣн εροι αλ[λα
   ?   ма]ρεнκнα ταϫοι ϩнογϛεпн· | ι]εκμнτн[   ?   α]γω τεκμнτατͼαθος · |
τεϛρω[   ?   ]пεμτο εϐολ [μп]нογτε  (blank)
```

313.—Papyrus, a fragment, 14 × 13½ cm   Script *v* Pl 5   *Recto* →

Letter from   . to his 'dear brother', whose prayers and help are asked   'But we are confident (*θαρρεῖν*) that all things whereunto thou dost set thy hand, God it is doth work (*ἐνεργεῖν*) with thee therein and bringeth them to pass'   The writer is further sending herewith, fastened up[4], the letter which he had received from the bishop   He speaks also of a woman, apparently suffering from an internal malady

```
]ϛϛτ огϣψγχн αϛϫοος ͼαρ | ϫεε|ρ|επαϣнρε [ϩ]ατнγ κατα огαпαͼ|κн .αγτρɪτα[α]ϥ
εογρα[ ]. ероι εειϩнϣ αλλα τнθαρρισε ϫεϩω[ϥ] нιμ ετн|ναϩ|ι τ]оотн εροογ пнογτε
ετεпεргϛι ннͼ|μαн нͅϩнтογ εϛ|ϲοογτн мμοογ пεικϛγα | он тнпιͼτεγε ϫεпϛ|пαρατͼοг
н[ακ] ан | ειϲ τͼ|ειϲτолн он ϛнταпεпιͼκопоϲ τн[н]о|огϛ нα[ι] αιτннογ нακ εͼмнр ται
ϫϛ|εκϛϛι[με] εнϩ[ .]ϛρια нτεκμнτχρнͼτοͼ[5] [ . . . ͼ]αρ αϛϛι ϛϐολ ϊнα ϫεϛκϛ|ϛιμε
ϫ[ϛ      ]οͼпε αγω ногκογι αнпε | пεϛн[      ]γϛϭιμε ϫωϐε ннϛιτοογ[н      ]ϫε пετпϛϛογн
ρωκϩ | ϛϫн[      ] ϩнτϛ ετεпεϛϣнρε ϯϣιпε ϛ[ρон мннͼτιμμα]н τнρ[ογ] нα|τα п]εγραн |
[6] ογϫ[αι ϩлп]ϫ|ϛοϛ|ιϛ пμϛ|ριτ [нϛо]н εнϣλнλ | εϫω[ι +]
```

314—Papyrus, a fragment, 28 × 7 cm   Script large, ligatureless, of early type
Recto →

Letter to a superior or some revered personage[7], begging his benevolence for 'the

---

[1] Or possibly plural

[2] KENYON's suggestion   The script seems too early for M 's reign   Trajan, Valens' general (*ob* 378), is not known to have been in Egypt   Br Mus Gk Catal iii 228 names Trajan, an eparch at Hermopolis, in 357

[3] *Cf* *ab actis*, *a memoria* and 2 Sam. viii 16 *ἐπὶ τῶν ὑπομνημάτων*, *a commentariis*   Genitives thus are rare in Coptic   ZOEGA 282 απο λογκωη, Cairo 8462 αнотрιϐογпон (*sic*)

Usually not declined   Cairo 8432 анотριϐοτнос, Br Mus no 255 αпокомιτος, 355 αпотраμοϲιτος, Paris 44 121 *b* αпотраμματικος, Rossi, *Nuov Cod* 16 αпоϥρнтωρ

[4] *I e* closed with the usual ribbon and seal (though I know of no other instance of моγρ with this meaning)

[5] *V* no 314

[6] These are short lines, as in *Pap Amh* cxlv

[7] *Cf* perhaps phrases in no 313

brothers Joseph the deacon and Ammoniôn the reader', concerning whom Isaac had gone to law[1] The idiom is archaic[2]

Remnants of 5 lines, beginning ⲡⲁ[.

L 5 ends ϩⲁⲑⲏ ⲛϩ[ⲱ]ϥ [ⲙ]ⲛ[sic] | ϯϣⲓⲛⲉ ⲥⲣⲟⲕ | ⲧⲟⲛⲟⲩ ⲕⲁⲧⲁ | ⲑⲉ ⲛⲧⲁⲓⲁⲁⲛ [ⲉ]ⲓ[3] | ⲉⲃⲟⲗ ⲉⲧⲃⲉⲛⲉⲥⲛⲏⲟⲩ ⲓⲱⲥⲏϥ | ⲛⲧⲓⲁⲕⲟⲛⲟⲥ | ⲙⲛⲁⲙⲙⲱⲛⲓⲱⲛ | ⲡⲁⲛⲁⲅⲛⲱⲥⲧⲏⲥ [ⲛ]ⲑⲉ ⲛⲧⲁⲧⲉⲕⲙⲛ[ⲧ]ⲭⲣⲓⲥ ⲧⲟⲥ ⲡⲱϩ ⲛϣⲁⲟⲩⲟⲛ ⲛ[ⲓ]ⲙ ⲙⲁ|ⲣⲉⲡⲱϩ ⲛϣⲁ[ⲛ]ⲉⲥⲛⲏⲟⲩ ϩⲱⲟⲩ ⲉⲓⲱⲥⲏϥ ⲙⲉⲛⲁⲙⲙⲱ|ⲛⲓⲱⲛ ϥⲱ[ϥ] ⲛⲅⲁⲣ | ⲛⲧⲁⲓⲣⲁ[ⲍ]ⲟⲩ ⲙⲟⲕ | ⲉⲧⲃⲉⲛⲉⲥ[ⲛⲏⲟⲩ] ⲍⲉ|ⲕⲁⲁⲥ ⲉⲛ[ⲉ..]ⲁⲣⲟ|ⲛ[4] ⲅⲁϩⲉ.[. .]ⲕ | Traces of 5 more lines

315—Papyrus, a fragment, 8 × 18 cm Script rarely ligatured *Recto* ↑
Letter to a superior, asking charity and mentioning the 'place of Apa Macarius' and the 'lord bishop'

ⲁⲡⲁϩⲏⲧ] ⲙⲧⲟⲛ ⲧⲟⲛⲟⲩ ⲍⲉⲧⲉⲧⲛⲥⲓⲣⲉ ⲛⲡⲁⲙⲉⲩⲉ | ϯⲉⲧⲛⲣⲧⲁⲅⲁⲡⲏ ⲙⲛ̅ϥⲛⲥⲉ ⲛⲣⲱⲙⲉ ⲕⲁⲓ | ⲍ]ⲁⲩϥ ⲛⲁⲓϭⲓⲧⲛ ϩⲣⲁⲓ ⲛⲡⲙⲁ ⲛⲁⲡⲁ ⲙⲁⲕⲁⲣⲉ |]ⲍⲱⲛ ⲁⲩⲱ ⲉⲓⲥ ⲧⲉⲡⲓⲥⲧⲟⲗⲏ ⲁⲓⲍⲓⲧⲉ ⲁⲓⲍⲁⲩⲉ |]ⲙⲟⲥ ϯⲡⲣⲟⲥⲕⲩⲛⲉⲓ ⲛⲏⲧⲛ ⲧⲟⲛⲟⲩ ⲁⲩⲱ ⲁⲛⲟⲕ | ⲍⲟⲉⲓⲥ ⲡⲉⲡⲓⲥⲕⲟⲡⲟⲥ ϣⲁⲛϯⲙⲛϣⲁ ⲛⲁⲩ ⲉⲣⲱⲧⲛ

Verso + ⲧⲁⲁⲥ ⲛⲡⲁⲍⲟⲉⲓⲥ ⲛⲓⲱⲧ ⲁⲡⲁ ⲱ[

316—Papyrus, a fragment, 7 × 18½ cm Script ligatureless *Recto* ↑ Not from the Ashmunain collection
Letter from 'his son' John to Apa Daniel, asking for help

ⲛⲟⲍⲧ ⲁⲍⲟⲩⲛ ⲁ[| ⲛϩⲱϥ ⲧⲁⲓⲙⲉ ⲣⲟϥ ⲙⲁⲗⲗⲟⲛ ⲍⲉ ⲟⲛ ⲍⲉⲡⲉⲛⲥⲕⲟ|ⲡⲟⲥ ⲍⲉϥⲟ ⲛⲁϣ ⲙⲙⲓⲛⲉ ⲛⲡⲁⲣⲁⲕⲁⲗⲓ ⲙⲡⲁⲍⲟⲉⲓⲥ | ⲡⲉⲓⲱⲧ ⲧⲁⲣⲉϥⲕⲁⲧⲁⲣⲁⲛⲉ ⲛⲙⲙⲉⲩⲉ ⲧⲏⲣⲟⲩ ⲛ|ⲛⲉⲧϣⲁⲍⲉ ⲛⲉⲙⲁϥ ⲉϥϣⲓⲛⲉ ϩⲙⲡⲁϩⲱϥ ⲍⲉⲙⲛⲧⲁⲓ|ⲣⲱⲙⲉ ⲉϥⲛⲁϣⲓⲛⲉ ϩⲙⲡⲁϩⲱ[ϥ][sic] ⲥⲁⲣⲟⲧⲛ[5] ⲁⲩⲱ ⲉⲓⲧⲁ|ⲭⲣⲏⲟⲩ ⲉϩⲣⲁⲓ ⲉⲍⲙⲡⲛⲟⲩⲧⲉ ⲛⲙⲙⲏⲧⲛ ⲉⲡⲓ ⲉⲕϣⲁⲛⲛⲁⲩ | ⲥⲣⲟⲓ ϩⲙⲡⲉⲧϣⲟⲟⲡ ⲙⲙⲟⲓ ⲡⲁⲛⲧⲱⲥ ⲕⲛⲁϣⲓⲛⲉ | (*verso*) ϩⲙⲡⲁϩⲱϥ | ⲗⲏⲡⲟⲛ ⲙⲁⲣⲉⲡⲉⲕⲛⲟϭ ⲛⲁ | ⲙⲛⲧⲉⲕⲛⲟϭ ⲛⲁⲛⲁⲡⲉ ⲉⲧⲟϣ ⲉϩⲟⲩⲛ ⲉⲣⲟⲓ ⲛⲉⲩ | ⲡⲉⲥⲛⲏⲗⲗⲟⲥ[6] ⲛⲛⲓ ⲉⲣⲏⲥ ⲙⲛⲡⲁⲥⲟⲛ ⲛⲁⲗⲓ|ⲛⲉⲭⲉ ⲧⲛϣⲁⲍⲉ ⲛⲉⲙⲁⲩ ⲧⲓⲧⲓ ⲡϩⲟⲗⲟⲕ[o] | ⲥⲛⲁⲩ ⲛⲁⲩ ⲧⲟⲩⲧⲓ[7] ⲉⲛⲧⲁⲕⲉⲟⲛ [

Above l 1 of *verso* the address + ⲧⲁⲁⲥ ⲙⲡⲁⲍⲟⲉⲓⲥ ⲛⲥⲓⲱⲧ ⲁⲡⲁ ⲧⲁⲛⲓⲏⲗ ⲓⲱϩⲁⲛⲛⲥ ⲡⲉϥϣⲏⲣⲉ

'cast me in to   matter, that I may know it, but more still (μᾶλλον δέ) what thy intention (σκοπός) is I beg (παρακαλεῖν) my lord father that he bring to nought (? καταργεῖν) all the thoughts of them that talk with him, while he enquireth into my affair[8] For I have none that will enquire into my affair save you, and I confide in God and you For (ἐπεί) if thou shouldst see me in the state wherein I am, thou wouldest certainly (πάντως) enquire into my affair But (λοιπόν) let thy great pity and thy great

---

[1] Taking ⲉⲓ ⲉⲃⲟⲗ in the sense (= ἐνάγειν) frequent in the Jême deeds

[2] Cf the forms ⲛϣⲁ-, ⲛⲅⲁⲣ (*v* no. 292)

[3] Above the line Perhaps ⲓ only

[4] Perhaps o belongs to the next line

[5] The normal form should be ⲛⲥⲁⲃⲗⲗⲱⲧⲛ

[6] ? ⲛⲉⲍ ⲡⲉⲥⲕ Cf CRUM, *Ostr* no 61 and ⲃⲱⲕ ⲡⲉⲥⲕ

in Leyden *MSS* p 486 (*sic*) and TURAIEF in *Bull Ac Imp* 1899, 440

[7] One expects ⲥⲟⲩⲧⲓ, though ⲛⲧⲟⲩ-, ⲧⲟⲩ- is to be met with in Saïdic

[8] Or ? 'prying into my affair', in spite of the false concord.

love (ἀγάπη) that are so great toward me, make endeavour (σκυλμός) to come southward with my brother Callinicus, that we may talk with them and give them the 2 *solidi* and that they give a receipt (ἐντάγιον)   .

317—Paper, complete; $17\frac{1}{2} \times 5$ cm   Script   much faded, *cf* ZOEGA's 9th class
   Letter to a superior, whom the writer, *inter alia*, asks for some vinegar

+ cṗ̄ аι.... ..| ϯπροϲⲛ̄, ⲁⲩⲱ | ⲧιⲁⲥⲡⲁ̄ⲍⲉ ⲙ̄|ⲟⲩⲝⲁι ⲛ̄ⲧⲥⲕⲙ̄|ⲛ̄ⲧⲙⲉⲣιⲧ ⲛ̄|ⲥⲟⲛ ⲉⲧⲧⲁⲏⲩ |
ⲉⲣⲉⲡⲭⲟⲉιⲥ ϩⲁ|ⲣⲉϩ ⲉⲡⲉⲕⲱⲛϩ¹ | ϩⲛ̄ ϯⲧⲁⲙⲟⲛ | ⲝⲉⲁⲡⲉⲛ. | 7 lines, almost wholly illegible |
ⲙ̄ⲛ̄ⲧⲥⲟⲛ ⲝⲟ|ⲟⲩ ⲟⲩⲗⲁⲕⲟⲛ | ⲉϩⲛⲙⲝ ⲉϥⲝⲏϥ² ⲛⲁⲓ ⲧⲁ|ⲉⲩⲭⲁⲣιⲥⲧⲟⲩ | ⲛⲁⲕ .. ·|

Verso   remains of an Arabic text (earlier)

318—Papyrus; a fragment, $8 \times 9\frac{1}{2}$ cm   Script   moderately ligatured   *Recto* ↑
   Letter to an ecclesiastical (?) superior, mentioning an application to the amir on behalf of an old man   Bousiris is named

]ⲕ, ⲛⲙⲉⲣιⲧ ⲛ̄ⲭⲟ[ⲉι]ⲥ   ? | ⲡⲣⲟⲥ]ⲉⲗⲑⲉ ⲡⲉⲛⲁ ⲛⲁⲙⲓⲣⲁ ⲉⲧⲃⲉⲡϩⲗ̄ⲗⲟ |ϯⲧⲱϣ ⲟⲩⲥⲩⲙⲙⲁⲭ
ⲛⲁⲩ ⲧⲁⲣⲉⲩⲛ ϩ [|] ⲧⲁⲙⲟⲓ ⲝⲉⲛⲣⲱⲙⲛⲟⲩϭⲓⲣⲉ [|]ⲃ̄ⲱⲕ ⲁιⲥⲛⲧⲟⲩ [|]ⲁⲩ ⲉιⲟⲩⲱϣ ϭⲱ. [

Verso   +ⲧⲱ [ⲑ]ⲉⲟⲫⲩⲗ/   ?   [

319.—Papyrus, complete, $34\frac{1}{2} \times 16$ cm   Script   *v* Pl 11   *Verso* →.
   Letter (called ⲥιⲅⲓⲗⲗιⲟⲛ) from a pagarch, through his son³, to certain villages and⁴ to the inhabitants of Psoi-Ptolemais   It relates to the collection of taxes.   KRALL's nos iii and iv are documents of the same class

[   ]ⲫⲗ/ ⲥⲉⲛⲟⲩᶿ ⲥⲩⲛᶿ ⲡⲁⲅⲁⲣ ⲭⲇι, ⲉⲙⲟ ⲍⲁⲭⲁⲣιⲁ ⲩⲓᵒ ⲁⲩ̄ ⲡϥ̄ϭⲣⲁι ⲛⲛⲁⲡⲛⲏⲅⲉ | ⲡⲛⲉⲙⲙⲁ ⲉⲧⲧⲁⲥⲥⲉ⁵
ⲥⲧⲥⲛ̄ⲱⲥⲓⲥ ⲛ̄ⲧⲁιⲧⲁⲁⲥ ⲛ̄ⲡⲁⲥⲟⲛ | ⲁⲡⲁ ⲁⲫⲟⲩ ⲝⲉⲧⲉⲧⲛⲉⲥⲟⲟⲩⲛ ⲝⲉⲁⲡⲉⲓⲱⲧ ⲝⲏⲣ̄ⲡⲁⲣⲁⲅⲅⲉⲓⲗⲉ | ⲛⲏⲧⲛ
ⲉⲧⲃⲉⲛⲉⲥⲟⲩⲟ ⲛ̄ⲧⲉⲙⲃⲟⲗⲏ ⲙ̄ⲡⲧⲁⲅⲟⲣⲁⲥιⲁ· ⲙⲛ̄|ⲧⲉⲥⲡ[ⲉⲣ]ⲙⲟⲩⲃⲟⲗιⲁ ⲛ̄ⲧⲥⲛⲥⲟⲟⲩⲝⲟⲩ ⲉιⲥ ϩⲏⲏⲧⲉ ⲟⲩⲛ !
ⲁιⲧⲛ[ⲟⲟ]ⲩ̄ϥ ⲁιⲡⲁⲣⲁⲅⲅⲉⲓⲗⲉ ⲛⲁϥ ⲧⲁⲣⲉϥϣⲓⲛⲉ ⲛ̄ⲥⲁⲧⲥⲛⲥⲉⲙ̄|ⲃⲟⲗⲏ ⲙ̄ⲛ̄ⲧⲉⲧⲛⲉⲥⲡⲉⲣⲙⲟⲩⲃⲟⲗιⲁ ⲙ̄ⲛ̄ⲧⲉⲧ-
ⲛⲁⲅⲟⲣⲁⲥιⲁ | ⲉⲥⲡⲗⲏⲣⲟⲩ ⲁⲩⲱ ⲁιⲡⲁⲣⲁⲅⲅⲉⲓⲗⲉ ⲛⲁϥ ⲧⲁⲣϥ̄ϭⲱⲧⲛ̄ | ϩⲛ̄ⲧⲣⲁ̅ ⲛⲉⲩⲡⲟⲣⲟⲥ ϩⲛ̄ⲛⲉⲧ-
ⲛⲉⲧιⲙⲉ ⲛ̄ⲥⲟⲩⲅ̄ⲩⲡⲟ̄ⲙ[ⲉⲭⲉ] | 10 ⲛⲙⲟⲟⲩ ⲁⲩⲱ ⲁιⲡⲁⲣⲁⲅⲅⲉⲓⲗⲉ ⲛⲁⲩ ⲧⲁⲣⲟⲩⲛⲟⲩϩ ⲩ̄ⲡⲟⲩⲅⲣ̄ⲟⲥ | ⲉⲃⲟⲗ⁷
ⲕⲁⲧⲁ ⲧιⲙⲉ ⲛ̄ⲥⲟⲩⲧⲟϣϥ̄ ⲉⲕⲁιⲙⲁ ⲁⲩⲱ | ⲁιⲡⲁⲣⲁⲅⲅⲉⲓⲗⲉ ⲛⲁϥ ⲟⲛ ⲝⲉⲛⲛⲟⲩⲧι ⲟⲩⲉⲣⲧⲟϥ ⲛ̄ⲥⲟⲩⲟ ⲛ̄ |
ⲙⲟⲓⲁϩ⁸ ⲛ̄ⲧⲱⲁϩ ⲡⲣⲱⲙⲉ ⲉⲩⲟιⲝⲛ̄ⲛⲕⲁϩ ϣⲁⲛⲧⲟⲩ|ⲡⲗ[ⲏⲣⲟⲩ ⲛ̄]ⲧⲉⲙⲃⲟⲗⲏ ⲙ̄ⲛ̄ⲧⲉⲥⲡⲉⲣⲙⲟⲩⲃⲟⲗιⲁ

---

¹ *V* nos 306, 337   ² *V* no 348
³ The *waly* represented by his son, *Führ Rain* nos 554, 558
⁴ Assuming that δέ in l 22 implies contrast, these villages should be near Psoi, 150 miles south of Shmoun   Can the writer then be pagarch of Shmoun?   Yet in no 215 Hanepioor and in KRALL ccxlii Pbôah seem near the latter, so too Φβύ, *Arch f Pap* iv 452 and (? same) Βῶυ, *ib* 429

⁵ Or merely 'are entered, reported'   *V* Br Mus nos 1079, 1131, KRALL iii, here no 278
⁶ Apparently a tax in WILCKEN, *Ostr* i 132
⁷ The difference between ϭⲱⲧⲛ̄ and ⲛⲟⲩϩ ⲉⲃⲟⲗ is not clear
⁸ *Cf* Br Mus no 1055   Greek perhaps μώιον, *Pap. Hibeh* 49, 8 n, Eg Expl. Fund, *Arch Rep* 1905-6, 14.

ⲙⲏ|ⲧⲁⲅⲟⲣⲁⲥⲓⲁ ⲙⲙⲏⲅⲅⲁⲏⲙⲟⲥ ⲟⲁⲡⲗⲱⲥ ⲕⲡⲉⲣⲧⲣⲉⲅ|ⲟⲛ ⲟⲓⲱⲟⲧⲧⲏⲅⲧⲏ ⲧⲓ ⲡⲣⲟⲫⲁⲥⲓⲥ ⲕⲁⲧⲁ
ⲧⲓⲯⲩⲭⲏ[1] | ⲁⲓⲡⲁⲣⲁⲅⲅⲉⲓⲗⲉ ⲛⲁⲅ ⲍⲉⲉⲣ̄ⲱⲁⲛⲟⲅⲟⲟⲓⲉ ⲉⲛⲁⲟⲅ|ⲧⲓⲙⲉⲛⲉ ⲧⲓ ⲟⲩ̄ⲟ[.] [2] ⲕⲥⲟⲅⲟ ⲏ ⲟⲩⲃⲓⲣ
ⲕⲧⲱⲁⲟ | ⲉⲛⲟⲅⲣⲱⲙⲉ ⲭⲱⲣⲓⲥ ⲉⲟⲁⲓ ⲉⲛⲱⲡⲉ ⲏ ⲟⲩⲟⲛ ⲉⲛⲁⲡⲁⲉⲓⲱⲧ 20 -ⲛⲉ ⲕⲥⲟⲛⲁⲣ̄ⲟ ⲛⲉⲧⲛⲟⲟⲅⲅ ⲛⲁⲓ
ⲧⲁⲣⲉⲧⲓ ⲥⲃⲱ ⲛⲣⲱⲙⲉ ⲥⲱⲁⲅⲣⲁⲧⲥⲱⲧⲙ ⲟⲙⲡⲉⲓⲧⲟⲱ ⲕⲧⲱⲧⲏ | ⲍⲉ ⲛⲉⲣⲉⲛⲓⲯⲟⲓ ⲟⲩⲱⲱ ⲧⲉⲧⲛⲉⲧⲱⲱ
ⲥⲣⲁⲙⲙ̄ ⲥⲛⲁⲅ | ⲉⲅⲧⲏⲱ ⲉⲛⲉⲅⲡⲟⲣⲟⲥ ⲕⲥⲟⲅⲅ̄ⲩⲡⲟⲍⲉⲭⲉ ⲛⲡⲉⲥⲟⲅⲟ | ⲕⲡⲃⲱⲁⲟ ⲁ̄ⲛⲟⲁⲛⲉⲡⲓⲟⲟⲣ
ⲙⲙⲛⲉϥⲉⲡⲟⲓⲕⲓⲛ ⲍⲛⲛⲉⲧⲛⲉ [3]ⲁⲙⲫⲓⲃⲁⲗⲉ ⲁⲓⲃⲟⲅⲗⲗⲓⲍⲉ ⲛⲡⲉⲓⲥⲓⲅⲉⲗⲗⲓⲛ[4] ⲛ̄ⲛⲁⲍⲟⲩⲣ + |

+ ⲉⲅⲣⲓ ⲙ̄ $\overset{\chi}{\pi}$ ⲕⲏ ⲓ$^{\delta}$ⲓ ⲁ$\overset{\chi}{\rho}$ ⲁ +   ⓛ ⲛ̄

' Flavius Senouthius, by God's will pagarch, through me, Zacharia his son, writeth unto the headmen of the places that are indicated (τάσσειν) on the list (γνῶσις) which I have given to my brother Apa Aphou Ye know that my father hath already charged (παραγγέλειν) you concerning the corn of the corn-tax (ἐμβολή) and the purchase money (ἀγορασία) and the seed-corn (σπερμοβολία), that ye should gather them in Here, then (οὖν), I have sent him and have charged (παρ) him that he require your corn-tax (ἐμβ) and your seed-corn and your purchase-money (ἀγ) in full (πληροῦν) And I have charged (παρ) him to choose well to-do scribes (γραμματεύς, εὔπορος) from your villages, that they may receive (ὑποδέχεσθαι) them, and I have charged (παρ) them that they appoint a representative (ὑπουργός) for each (κατά) village and set him over another place. And I have further charged (παρ) them that they give (or sell) not an *artaba* of corn nor a bundle (?) of straw to any man upon earth, ere he have fulfilled the corn-tax (ἐμβ) and the seed-corn (σπερ) and the purchase-money (ἀγορ) and their general tax (δημόσιον), in short (ἁπλῶς), let none among you give occasion against himself (πρόφασις, κατά, ψυχή) I have charged (παρ) him that, should an husbandman belonging unto a village sell (?) unto any man a   of corn or (ἤ) a basket of straw, without (χωρίς) a writing of mine or (ἤ) one of my father's, he shall bind him and send him unto me, that he may teach the men, if they be disobedient in this nome But (δέ) ye, men of Psoi, I desire that ye set up two scribes (γρ), being of authority and well-to do (εὔπ), that they may receive (ὑποδέχ) the corn of Pbôah and Hanepioor and its homesteads (ἐποίκιον), so that ye fail (ἀμφίβαλλειν) not I have sealed (βουλλίζειν) this order (σιγίλλιον) with my ring ' Then the date and the clay seal, the design (not inscription) on which is no longer recognizable

Recto Protocol (fibres →) in 4 lines of tall, brown characters, 1 and 3 of which begin with a sign or letter resembling φ The end of an Arabic line can perhaps be discerned

320.—Papyrus, complete, 30½ × 13 cm Script *v* Pl 10 *Recto* →
Letter relating to the assessment and collection of taxes from certain localities Though complete, the text is unusually difficult of exact interpretation.

---

[1] Or 'to the detriment of his soul'

[2] > ⲥⲓⲝ (*v* Br Mus no 1066) or ⲥⲗⲱ, though neither have been found used of grain, or ⲥⲟⲛ ὀλίγα, Revel iii 4

[3] Altered from (*sic*) ⲍⲉⲛ-

[4] KRALL iii and iv are thus named

Above 1 1, ⲭⲙⲅ

ⲫ︦ ⲕⲩⲣⲁⲕⲟⲥ ⲡⲉⲧⲥϩⲁⲓ ⲛⲡⲥⲁϩ ⲇⲓⲟⲛⲩⲥⲓ | ϫⲉϩⲁⲑⲏ ⲙⲉⲛ ⲛϩⲱⲃ ⲛⲓⲙ ϯϣⲓⲛⲉ | ⲉⲣⲱⲧⲛ ⲁⲩⲱ
ⲉⲡⲓⲇⲏ ⲁⲓⲃⲱⲕ ⲇⲓⲁⲛⲁⲕⲁⲍⲉ ⲙⲟⲉⲛⲉⲥⲧⲉ ⲛⲡⲙⲁ ⲛⲁⲡⲁ ⲃⲁⲛⲉ | 5 ⲉⲧⲃⲉⲡⲕⲱⲙⲏⲕⲁⲑⲏⲕⲏⲥ¹ ⲁⲩ² ⲉϩⲣⲁⲓ |
ⲛⲡⲥⲁϩ ⲡⲉⲧⲣⲁ ⲁϥϫⲟⲟⲩ ⲧⲉⲡⲓⲥⲧⲟⲗⲏ | ⲛⲁⲓ ⲉⲃⲟⲗ ϫⲉⲡⲣϫⲁϫⲉ³ ⲙⲛⲡⲣⲱⲙⲉ | ⲛⲡⲙⲁ ⲁⲇⲉⲗⲫⲏ⁴ ⲡⲉϫⲁⲩⲟⲩ
ϫⲉϣⲁⲣⲉⲡⲙⲁ ⲁⲇⲉⲗⲫⲏ ϯ ϣⲉ ϫⲟⲩⲧⲏ ⲃⲱⲓⲟⲉ | ⲧⲟ ⲃⲱⲕ ⲛⲡⲙⲁ ⲡⲥⲁϩ ⲡⲉⲧⲣⲁ ⲛⲁⲩ ϫⲉϣⲁⲣⲉⲡⲕⲱⲙⲏ-
ⲕⲁⲑⲏⲕⲏⲥ ⲉⲓ ⲧⲱⲛ ⲉⲙⲙⲟⲛ ⲡⲣⲱⲥ⁵ ⲡⲙⲁ ⲁⲇⲉⲗⲫⲏ ⲡⲣⲱⲥ ⲡⲙⲁ | ⲛⲁⲡⲁ ⲃⲁⲛⲉ ϣⲁⲣⲉϣ ⲥⲉ ⲙⲛⲟⲩⲁ |
ⲉⲓ ⲛⲙⲁⲩⲟⲩ⁶ ⲉⲣⲉⲡⲁⲩⲟ ⲛⲙⲥⲩ ⲧⲱⲛ | 15 ⲉⲕⲁⲧⲟⲛ⁷ ⲧⲁⲗⲩⲟⲩ ⲉϫⲱⲟⲩ⁸ ⲉⲕⲧⲟⲥ | ⲟⲩⲙⲉ ϯⲛⲟⲩ
ⲉϣⲱⲡⲉ ⲛⲟⲩⲱϣ ⲗⲁⲭⲁ | ⲉⲣⲟⲟⲩ ⲉⲓ ϫⲁϫⲉ ⲙⲛⲡⲥⲁϩ ⲡⲉⲧⲣⲁ (ϫⲉ above)ⲉϥⲟⲩⲱϣ | ⲕⲟⲩⲫⲏⲥⲛ
ⲛⲡϣⲉ ϫⲟⲩⲧⲏ ⲙⲛⲧⲉⲩϥⲩⲙⲉ | ⲁⲩⲱ ⲡⲉⲩⲁⲩⲟ ⲛⲙⲥⲩ ⲧⲱⲛ ⲉⲕⲁⲧⲟⲛ | 20 ⲉϣⲱⲡⲉ ϥⲟⲩⲱϣ ⲕⲟⲩⲫⲏⲥⲛ
ⲛⲁⲓ ϩⲁⲡⲙⲁ | ⲡⲁⲇⲉⲗⲫⲏ ⲧⲏⲛϣⲓⲛⲉ ⲥⲁⲛⲁⲩ ⲉⲡⲙⲁ | ⲛⲁⲡⲁ ᵇᵉ︦ⲛⲉ (ϫⲉⲛⲁⲩ above) ⲉⲓⲉ⁹ ⲧⲱⲛ ⲉⲓⲁⲧ
ⲉⲃⲟⲗ | ⲙⲟⲛ ⲧⲁϥⲥϩⲁⲓ ⲛⲁⲓ ϫⲉⲡⲣϫⲁϫⲉ | ⲙⲛⲡⲙⲁ ⲁⲇⲉⲗⲫⲏ ⲡϥⲥϩⲁⲓ ⲉⲧⲃⲉⲡⲙⲁ | 25 ⲛⲁⲡⲁ ⲃⲁⲛⲉ
ϯⲛⲟⲩ ⲉⲓⲙⲉ ϫⲉϣⲁϥⲕⲁ | ⲕ︦ⲁ ⲡⲓⲉⲕⲁⲧⲟⲛ ⲉϩⲛⲕⲟ︦ⲡ ⲙⲁ¹⁰ ϩⲓⲡⲙⲁ | ⲡⲁⲇⲉⲗⲫⲏ ⲙⲛⲧⲉⲩϩⲛⲙⲉ ϫⲉ |
(verso) ϫⲉⲛⲙⲙⲥⲛ ⲉϣⲱⲡⲉ ϣⲁϥⲕⲁ ⲫⲏⲕⲁⲧⲟⲛ ⲉⲓⲕⲟⲥⲙⲉⲛⲧⲉ ⲙⲛⲧⲉⲩϩⲛ|30-ⲙⲉ ⲉⲓ ⲥϩⲁⲓ ⲛⲁⲓ ⲉⲃⲟⲗ
ϫⲉⲙϣⲓⲛⲉ | ⲥⲁⲓⲥⲉⲉⲡⲉ ⲛⲡⲙⲁ ⲛⲁⲡⲁ ⲃⲁⲛⲉ | ⲉϣⲱⲡⲉ ⲟⲛ ⲉϥⲟⲩⲱϣ ϣⲁϫⲉ | ⲙⲛⲟⲩⲟⲛ ⲛⲙⲟⲟⲩ ⲁⲛ¹¹
ⲉⲓⲉ ⲥϩⲁⲓ ⲛⲁⲓ | ϫⲉⲁϥⲏⲕⲁⲧⲟⲛ ⲉϩⲛⲕⲟⲛⲧⲁ ⲙⲁ | 35 ⲙⲛⲧⲉⲩϩⲛⲙⲉ ⲉⲓ ⲉⲧⲟⲟⲧ ⲧⲁⲧⲙⲓϫⲁϫⲉ ⲛⲙⲙⲁⲩⲟⲩ
ϩⲁⲯⲁ¹² ⲛⲓⲕⲱⲙⲏⲕⲁⲑⲏⲕⲏⲥ ⲟⲩϫⲁⲓ ϩⲙⲡϫⲟⲉⲓⲥ | ⲉⲡⲉϫⲉ ⲡⲉϫⲁⲩⲟⲩ ϫⲉϣⲁⲣⲉⲡⲙⲁ ⲁⲇⲉⲗ|ⲫⲏ ϯ ϣⲉ
ϫⲟⲩⲓⲏⲧⲏ ⲡⲙⲁ ⲁⲡⲁ ⲃⲁⲛⲉ | 40 . . ⲛⲁϯ¹³ ⲯⲉⲉⲡⲉ ⲁⲩⲱ ⲑⲏⲙⲉ ⲛⲡⲟⲩⲁ | ⲡⲟⲩⲁ ⲫ︦ⲫ︦ⲫ︦

'Cyriacus (Kyrakos) writeth unto the 'master' Dionysius, saying Before all things
I greet you And because that (ἐπειδή) I went and constrained (ἀναγκάζειν) the monastery
of the place of Apa Bane regarding the village   (κωμηκαθηκης), they have gone
to the 'master' Petra and he hath despatched the letter (ἐπιστολή) to me, saying, 'Be
not at enmity with the men of the place of Adelphius' They said, the place of Ad payeth
125 Give us thy help (βοηθεῖν) and go to the place of the 'master' Petra, see whither
the village   (κωμ) belongeth, whether (?) to (πρός) the place of Ad (or ἤ?) to (πρός)
that of Apa B The 161 will be their part, the 2½ of the hundred (δύο ἥμισυ τῶν ἑκατόν)
being imposed on them, besides (ἐκτός) the freight-charge If now thou desire to share
(? λαχεῖν) therein, so contend with the 'master' Petra, for he would remit (κουφίζειν) the
125 with their freight-charge and the 2½ of the hundred If he desire to remit (κου) these
for the place of Ad and that we should seek to impose them on the place of Apa B ,
then see thou and inform me For he hath written to me, saying, 'Be not at enmity with
the place of Ad ', he wrote not concerning the place of Apa B So now, learn whether
he will excuse (?) the 161 upon the place of Ad with their freight-charge, or no If he
should excuse (?) the 125 with their freight-charge, so write to me to require the remainder
from the place of Apa B Further, if he desire not to speak with one among them, so write
to me, saying, 'I have received the 161,' that I may not contend with them as to the share (?)

---

¹ Perhaps an official, so not the κωμηκάτοικος 'villager'
of MITTEIS, Urk 99 Neither κωμηκαθηγητης nor οικητής is
known Such a word as *κωμηκαθηγησις is excluded by the
gender A compound of χῶμα is scarcely possible

² Altered from ⲁⲩⲉⲓ

³ Unknown as a verb, that in Br Mus. no 169 being
presumably different Possibly = ⲣϫⲁϫⲉ

⁴ ? 'Αδέλφιος Cf ⲇⲓⲟⲛⲩⲥⲓ above

⁵ A clause crucial for the sense, but obscure ⲉⲓ
? 'appertain to', 'regard', if ⲕⲱⲙⲏⲕ were an impost or the

like, and if ⲧⲱⲛ = ⲉⲧⲱⲛ πρός as merely directive is unlikely
The use of ⲉⲙ ⲙ︦ⲟⲛ too is doubtful

⁶ Lit go with them', possibly in some technical sense,
'is their assessment' ?

⁷ Presumably the name of a tax

⁸ V no 323

⁹ ⲉⲓⲉ is difficult here, but 3rd fut would be more so.

¹⁰ Why are the same numbers now expressed in Greek ?

¹¹ ⲁⲛ for ⲟⲛ would be improbable here

¹² Has been altered Cf no 273   ¹³ Half effaced

of the village. (κωμ). Farewell in the Lord. For (ἐπειδή) they said, 'The place of Ad. doth pay 125, the place of Apa B. shall (?) pay the rest and the freight-charge of each.''

321.—Papyrus, complete, 19 × 40 cm. Script ligatured, uneven. *Recto* ↑
Letter from Prashe, probably at Babylon, to the amir, regarding tax-collection

1 ☩ ϩⲙⲡⲣⲁⲛ ⲕⲡⲛⲟⲩⲧⲉ ⲡⲣⲁϣⲉ ⲡⲉⲧⲛⲉⲥⲁⲟⲅⲟⲛ ⲉϥⲥϩⲁⲓ ⲛ[ⲡⲉⲩ]ⲕⲗⲉⲓ ⲛⲁⲙⲓⲣⲁ ϯⲣⲏⲛⲏ ⲛⲁⲕ ⲉⲃⲟⲗ
ϩⲙⲡⲛⲟⲩⲧⲉ ⲙⲙⲛⲥⲁⲛⲁⲓ ⲧⲁⲣⲉⲧⲉⲕⲙⲛⲧϫⲟⲉⲓⲥ

2 ⲉⲓⲙⲉ² ⲉⲧⲃⲉⲛⲉⲓⲣⲱⲙⲉ ⲉⲩϩⲁⲣⲧⲏ ⲏ ⲛⲧⲉⲡⲁϫⲟⲉⲓⲥ ϫⲓ ⲡⲉⲩⲉϫⲁⲅⲓ³ ⲛⲧⲉⲧⲛⲉⲧⲛⲟⲟⲩϥ ⲛⲁⲓ ⲉϩⲣⲏⲧ ⲉⲡⲉⲓ
ⲥⲟⲩⲧⲓ ⲁⲛⲁⲥⲕⲉ ⲉⲣ[ⲟⲓ] ⲉⲧⲃⲏⲏⲧⲟⲩ ⲁⲩⲱ ⲥⲟⲩⲧⲓ ϩⲃⲁ⁴ ⲛ-

3 ⲛⲁⲙⲙⲉⲁ⁶ ⲡ . . ⲁⲣⲓ⁶ ⲉⲩⲧⲓ ⲁⲛⲁⲥⲕⲉ ⲉⲣⲟⲓ ⲉⲧⲃⲉⲡⲉϫⲁⲅⲓ ϣⲁϩⲣⲁⲓ ⲉⲡⲙⲟⲩ ⲁⲩⲱ
ⲁⲩϩⲓⲧⲛ ⲉϩⲟ[ⲩ]ⲛⲡⲉ ⲁϯ ⲡⲉⲛⲡⲉ⁷ ⲉⲣⲟⲛ ϩⲁⲡⲉⲓϩⲱϭ

4 ⲁⲩⲱ [ⲧ]ⲁⲣ[ⲓ]ⲧⲁⲙⲟ ⲧⲉⲕⲙⲛⲧϫⲟⲉⲓⲥ ⲉⲧⲃⲉⲡⲣⲱⲙⲉ ⲛⲧⲁⲧⲛⲉⲥϩⲁⲓ ⲛⲁⲓ ⲉϩⲣⲏⲧ ϫⲥⲧⲁⲗⲟⲟⲩ ⲛⲁⲓ ⲉⲣⲏⲥ
ⲁⲡⲉⲛⲁⲟϩⲟⲧⲁⲧⲟⲥ ϫⲟⲉⲓⲥ ⲡⲥⲩⲛⲃⲟⲩⲗⲟⲥ⁸ ⲕⲉⲗⲉⲩⲉ

5 ⲧⲁⲣⲟⲩⲥϩⲁⲓ ⲛⲉⲣⲱⲙⲉⲃⲁⲃⲩⲗ⁽ⲱ⁾, ⲧⲏⲣⲟⲩ ϫⲓⲛⲡⲉⲕⲟⲩⲓ ϣⲁⲡ[ⲛ]ⲟϭ ⲉⲡⲉⲓ ⲉⲧⲃⲉⲡⲉⲓϩⲱϭ ⲡⲁⲓ ⲛⲡⲉⲛϣⲧⲁ-
ⲗⲟⲟⲩ ⲉⲣⲏⲥ ⲛⲏⲧⲛ ⲁⲩⲱ ⲉϣⲱⲡⲉ ⲡⲁϫⲟⲉⲓⲥ

6 ⲕⲉⲗⲉⲩⲉ ⲃⲟⲩⲱϣ [ⲛⲡ]ⲉϫⲁⲅⲓⲛ⁹ ⲧⲁⲧⲛⲟⲟⲩϥ ⲛⲏⲧⲛ ⲉⲣⲏⲥ ⲁⲩ[ⲱ] . ⲉⲓ . . . . ⲥⲟ . ⲛϥⲥϩⲁⲓ ⲉϩⲣⲏⲧ
ⲉⲡⲉⲛ ⲡⲥⲩⲙⲃⲟⲩⲗⲟⲥ ϣⲁⲓⲁⲥⲫⲁⲗⲓⲍⲉ

7 ⲙⲙⲟⲟⲩ ⲧⲁⲧⲛⲟⲟⲩⲥⲟⲩ ⲛⲏⲧⲛ ⲉⲣⲏⲥ ⲉⲡⲉⲓ ⲉⲣⲉⲡⲟⲩⲥⲙ . ⲟⲩ ⲉⲡⲁϫⲟⲉⲓⲥ ⲉⲡⲉⲓϩⲱϭ ⲡⲁⲓ ⲁⲛⲡⲉ ϫⲓⲛⲉⲑⲉ
ⲛⲧⲁⲡⲁϫⲟⲉⲓⲥ ⲥϩⲁⲓ ⲛⲁⲕ ⲉϩⲣⲏⲧ

8 ϣⲁⲓⲁⲥⲫⲁⲗⲓⲍⲉ ⲙⲙⲟⲟⲩ ⲧⲁⲧⲛⲟⲟⲩⲥⲟⲩ ⲛⲏⲧⲛ [rest illegible]

9 [all illegible till end,] ϩⲓⲧⲟⲟⲧϥ

10 ϯⲡⲣⲟⲥⲕ̄ ⲛⲡⲁϫⲟⲉⲓⲥ ϩⲓⲧⲛⲡⲉⲓⲥϩⲁⲓ μ̄ φαρμοῦ ⁱⁿ ⲓⲏ ⲓⲱ^δ δ

'In the name of God! Prashe, your servant, writeth to the most renowned (εὐκλεέστατος) amir. Peace unto thee from God. Thereafter (I write) that thy lordship may know concerning those men that are with thee, or else (? ἤ) that my lord take their ἐξάγιον and send it northward to me. For (ἐπεί) I am in difficulty (ἀνάγκη) because of them and Mohammed, thy representative (πρόσωπον), is perturbed , I being in the utmost difficulty[10] as to the ἐξάγιον, and we were brought in and put in irons on this account. And (I would) inform thy lordship as to the men of whom thou didst write northward to me, saying, Send them south to me. The most glorious (ἐνδοξότατος) governor (σύμβουλος) hath commanded to inscribe all the men of Babylon, from small to great, so (ἐπεί) for this cause have we not been able to send them south unto you. And if my lord bid and desire the ἐξάγιον, that I should bring it southward to you and and he write northward to

---

¹ The gap might hold more than this
² For this form v no 322
³ From Br Mus no 444 and *Pap Rhind* ii (Edinburgh), where 1st, 2nd and 3rd ἐξάγιω of the year occur, it should be a sort of tax
⁴ ⲡⲉϥϯ ϩⲃⲁ 'excitable', GIRON, *Légendes* 63.
⁵ *Cf* Br Mus Or 6721 (3) (Jême), where 'the πρ of the most glorious amir is mentioned, and Or. 6218 (Jkôw) the πρ of the pagarch, also no 281 here.

⁶ The last letters might be ⲉⲣⲟⲓ (? ⲛⲁⲣⲁⲣⲟⲓ)
⁷ Σιδηροῦν. The Aphroditô letter, Br Mus no 1358, tells how the pagarch's agent (at Babylon) had been imprisoned for failure to pay certain taxes (H I BELL)
⁸ Title of the Muslim governor. *V* C H BECKER, *Papyri Schott-Reinhardt* i 35. Occurs too in ROSSI *Papiri* I i, Tav 4 a, and in VOLLERS-LEIPOLDT, *Katal d islam. Hss zu Leipzig*, p. 410
⁹ Or [ⲡⲉⲩ]
¹⁰ *Lit.* 'constrained unto death'.

the most glorious (ἐνδ) governor (σύμβ), I will put them under guard (ἀσφαλίζειν) and send them south to you   For (ἐπεί) not   .. my lord for this very matter from the beginning when my lord wrote northward to us, I will put them under guard (ἀσφ) and will send them to you   I make obeisance to (προσκυνεῖν) my lord by this letter 18th Pharmouthi, 4th Indiction'

Verso the address in one line, illegible

322—Papyrus, complete, 15×11 cm   Script moderately ligatured   *Recto* ↑
Letter relating to the collection of village taxes   It is difficult to translate intelligibly

+ ταρεκε␣␣¹ ␣εεπε[ι␣]␣ [a]␣[␣]␣a τι ␣εϩιο␣␣² ␣␣ρερнc³ | ␣aϥ aнϩοτογ εϩολ ετϭι␣-
aπαιτει | ␣␣οο[γ] ϭн cρϩε нει нak ειнaϭн cρϩε | ␣ϣαττaϩλa⁴ ␣περογaϩ нacϩaι ϩннeкϭιϫ⁵ |
␣ϣaнтнπλнρογ ннeктi␣␣e επι πετε|ϣaнϣϣωτ ␣␣оϥ ϩнттaϩλa ␣ειλο | ειτι ␣␣aнλaϩιн
eπcкϩaλ cнaγ ϣaн|тнπλнρογ н␣␣oн⁶ aγω ϭωπ ογρeϥ|ρоειc нak ϩaϩτнk⁷ тоϣϥ eнϭγριaноc |
ϣaнтнπλнρογ н␣␣oϥ ϫннekc␣␣ | τι␣␣н ноγa ϣaнтcкϫι [π]eϥϫ␣кaιoн⁸ нтооτϥ | aγω eιc
τιeπιc[τολн a]ιтнооγc нak | τ␣.....]aн[...].ˣ н .e. ϩιωωϥ | ϫнн.ι. .cт..e... + |
eπει тaнaϭннтe⁹

Verso the address, apparently erased, excepting the initial +

('I write) that thou mayest know that, seeing (ἐπειδή) Mena hath made the women his heirs (?? κλῆρος), we have erased them in regard to demanding (taxes ἀπαιτεῖν) of them
find leisure to go to thee, I shall have leisure until the (? making up of the) register (τάβλα)   Lay not down my letters from thy hands, ere thou hast paid (πληροῦν) (? on behalf of) thy villages   For (ἐπεί) as to that which thou lackest in the register, I will not cease to lay a bandage (*lit* strap μαγκλάβιον) upon thy two eyes, until I shall have paid (πλ) thee (it)   And take thee a watchman and assign him unto Cyriacus, until thou shalt have paid it, for thou shalt not fix a price (τιμή) for any one till thou shalt have received of him his   (δίκαιον)   And see, I have sent thee this letter (ἐπιστολή) .   For (ἐπεί) it is (a matter of) importance (ἀνάγκη)'

323—Papyrus, complete, 20×20½ cm   Script moderately ligatured   *Recto* ↑   A clay seal and ribbon were attached.

Letter from Jeremias, notary, to his 'altogether God-beloved, most honorable brother' Elissaius, deacon and notary

+ ␣␣нncaтрac␣␣н тϣорπ нcπιcτολн нak ϩιтооτϥ нλογнac παπ␣␣a ␣περογορ¹⁰ | aϥει

---

¹ I find only two letters commencing thus elliptically, here no 321, Br Mus no 1156, both address superiors *Cf* also ϩωcтe таρeк-, Br Mus nos 1064, 1065
² After ␣e all quite uncertain
³ An instance of κλῆρος for κληρονόμος, REVILLOUT, *Actes* 99   But the parallel text, Br Mus Pap civ, shows this as probably an error   In Br Mus no 1051 кρнρcc is equally obscure, and there κλῆρος seems still less suitable
⁴ *V* no 401   ⁵ *Cf* KRALL ccxxviii 9

⁶ I have no idea what this phrase means
⁷ ϩaϩτнk might be ' into thy house or merely pleonastic with нak
⁸ 'Just rights seems unsuitable   *V* perhaps KRALL clxxxiii, here no 358
⁹ This in another ink and ? hand, added perhaps by the author, not his scribe
¹⁰ *V* no 211 and perhaps KRALL cxiii. 3   But here it should include a personal name

ⲉⲃⲟⲗ ϩⲓⲧⲟⲟⲧⲛ ϩⲛⲡⲧⲣⲉϥⲉⲣⲡⲁϣⲉ ⲙ̄ⲡⲣⲟⲟⲩⲧⲛ ⲉⲅⲩⲏⲏ ⲉⲣⲏⲥ ⲁϥⲥⲙⲛ | ⲟⲩⲉⲡⲓⲥⲧⲟⲗⲏ ⲛⲁⲓ ⲉϥⲟ ⲛ̄ⲕⲟⲩⲓ
ⲛ̄ⲯⲩⲭⲏ[1] ϫⲉϣϣⲱⲡⲉ ⲙ̄ⲁⲛⲁϩⲉⲣⲁⲧⲛ ⲛⲙ̄ⲙⲁϥ[2] | ⲧⲏⲛ ⲛⲥⲉⲓⲱϩⲉ ⲉⲃⲟⲗ ϩⲓϫⲱϥ ⲙⲁϥⲃⲱⲕ ⲉϩⲟⲩⲛ
ⲉⲡϥⲧⲙⲉ ⲛϥϫⲟ ⲟⲩϫⲓⲥⲉ[3] | ⲛⲉⲓⲱϩⲉ ⲗⲟⲓⲡⲟⲛ ⲉϥϣⲁⲛⲉⲓ ⲛⲁⲕ ⲉⲣⲏⲥ ⲁϩⲉⲣⲁⲧⲕ ⲛⲙ̄ⲙⲁϥ ⲛⲥⲛ ⲟⲩⲛⲟϭ |
ⲙ̄ⲙⲉⲣⲟⲥ ⲛⲉⲓⲱϩⲉ ⲉⲃⲟⲗ ϩⲓϫⲱϥ ⲛ̄ⲧⲁⲗⲟϥ[4] ⲉϫⲛ̄ⲛⲉⲣⲱⲙⲉ ⲙ̄ⲡⲉϩⲟⲩⲟⲣ | ⲛⲥⲁⲛⲁⲥⲭⲁⲍⲉ ⲙ̄ⲙⲟⲟⲩ
ⲛⲥⲟⲩϫⲟⲟⲩ ⲡⲉⲥⲉⲡⲉ ⲉⲙⲁⲛⲉⲛ ⲑⲉ ⲛ̄ⲁⲓⲟⲓⲕⲉⲓ ⲙ̄ⲙⲟϥ | ⲁϩⲉⲣⲁⲧⲛ ⲛⲙ̄ⲙⲁϥ ⲟⲛ ϣⲁⲛⲧⲁⲉⲓ ⲉⲣⲏⲥ ⲉⲣϣⲁⲛ-
ⲧⲉⲭⲣⲉⲓⲁ ϣⲱⲡⲉ | ⲧⲛ̄ⲕⲟⲩⲫⲓⲍⲉ ⲛⲟⲩϣⲏⲙ ⲛ̄ⲁⲏⲙⲟⲥⲓⲟⲛ ⲛⲁϥ ϩⲁⲣⲟⲟⲩ ϣⲁⲛⲁⲁⲥ ⲁⲗⲗⲁ ⲡⲁⲛⲧⲱⲥ |
ϭⲱ ϩⲓⲧⲛⲡϥϩⲱⲃ ⲛ̄ⲁⲓⲟⲓⲕⲉⲓ ⲙ̄ⲙⲟϥ ⲛ̄ⲧⲓ ⲡⲁⲣⲁⲯⲩⲭⲏ ⲛⲁϥ | ϣⲁⲛⲧⲁⲉⲓ ⲉⲣⲏⲥ ϯⲁⲥⲡⲁⲍⲉ ⲛ̄ⲧⲉⲕ-
ⲑⲉⲟⲫⲓⲗⲉⲓⲁ ϩⲓⲧⲛ̄ⲛⲉⲓⲥϩⲁⲓ +

'After that I had drawn up the first letter (ἐπ) unto thee, (sent) by the hand of Lukas of Pma npehwor, and he had left us, when he had done half the journey, going southward, he drew up a letter (ἐπ) to me, being disheartened, (and saying) that if we stay not by him and relieve him of (the burden of) these fields, he will not enter his village and (will not) sow a   of land   But (λοιπόν) when he cometh south to thee, stay by him and relieve him of a large portion (μέρος) of fields and impose it on the men of Pma npehwor and compel (ἀναγκάζειν) them to send the remainder which thou canst not find means to manage (διοικεῖν)   And stay by him till I come south   If need (χρεία) arise that we remit (κουφί- ζειν) for him a little of the tax (δημόσιον) on their account, we will do so   But by all means (ἀλλὰ πάντως) continue (to attend) to his affair and manage (διοικ) it, and give him heart (παραψυχή), till I come south   I greet (ἀσπ) thy piety (θεοφίλεια) by these letters'

Verso ⲧⲱ ⲧⲁ ⲡ̄ ⲑⲉⲟⲫⲓⲗ/ ⲧⲙⲁⲓ/ ⲁⲇⲉⲗⲫⲱ [space] ⲉⲗⲓⲥⲥⲁⲓⲱ ⲇⲓⲁⲕ°, ϩ ⲛⲟ + ⲓⲉⲣⲉⲙⲓⲁⲥ ⲛⲟ +

324.—Papyrus, complete, 13 × 21 cm   Script · moderately ligatured   *Recto* ↑
Letter from Mohammed, son of   , perhaps to Victor

⸱ ⲃⲓⲕ/[5] | ⲁⲕⲟⲗⲗⲟⲅⲟⲥ ⲧⲁⲙⲟⲓ ⲡⲁⲡⲙⲁ ⲛⲉⲩⲣⲁϣⲉⲓ[6] ϫⲉⲛⲧⲁⲛϣⲁⲡⲉ ⲟⲩⲱⲙ | ⲟⲩⲱⲙ ⲛⲉⲁⲏ-
ⲙⲟⲥⲓⲱⲛ ⲙ̄ⲡϥⲧⲙⲉ ⲉⲕϣⲱⲡ ⲡⲉⲧⲛⲁⲓ ⲛⲁⲥϩⲁⲓ ⲛⲁⲕ | ⲉⲕⲟⲩⲱϣ ⲁⲁϥ ⲛⲁⲡⲉ ⲛⲓϣⲁⲧϥ ⲉⲡⲉ[ⲛ]ⲧⲁϥ-
ⲟ[ⲩ]ⲱϣⲡ ϩⲁϫⲓⲛⲉⲡⲉⲓⲙⲁ[7] | ⲉⲡⲁϩⲟⲩ ⲉϣⲱⲡⲉ ⲁⲛⲧⲟϣϥ[8] ⲉⲓⲉ ⲛⲡⲣⲙⲁⲅⲉ[9] ⲙⲙⲟϥ ⲉⲗⲁⲁⲩ | ϩⲁⲡⲁϩⲟⲩ
ϯ ⲉⲓⲁⲧⲛ ⲉⲡⲉⲧⲉϣⲁⲕϣⲁⲧϥ ⲉⲙⲟϥ ⲉϩⲟⲩⲛ ⲉⲡⲉⲕⲏⲓ | ⲁⲗⲗⲁ ⲉⲕϣⲁⲛⲧⲟϣϥ ϫⲓⲛⲉⲡⲉⲓⲙⲁ ⲉⲑⲏ ϣⲁⲛϣⲓⲛⲉ |
ⲛⲥⲁⲛⲁⲏⲙⲟⲥⲓⲱⲛ ⲉⲧⲟⲟⲧϥ ⸱ μ̄ θ ⲕⲃ /

Verso ⸱ ⲥⲅⲛ̄ ⲙ[ⲁ]ⲙⲉ ϯ ....ⲁ̄ [space] ⲃⲓ[ⲛ̄/] · ⲟⲁⲣ ⲛ[ⲟ]ⲗⲗⲟⲩ ⸱ | ⲁⲙⲁⲉ..

'Colluthus (he of Pma neurashei) hath informed me that its headman hath devoured the tax-money (δημόσιον) of his village   When thou receivest him that shall give thee my

[1] Cf μικροψυχεῖν
[2] Or 'support him'   An instance with ⲙⲛ- ?, CRUM, *Ostr* no 314   Neither this nor the next verb is clear in meaning
[3] V Br Mus no.1013 &c
[4] V no 320
[5] Preceding the name is a sign somewhat resembling δ   If Victor is the addressee, διά would be out of place
[6] ⲩ altered from ⲥϥ   The name has neither a Coptic,

Greek nor Arabic appearance   Rashîd (v KRALL LXVI 19) is, on all grounds, unlikely
[7] V Br Mus no 1054 and no 144 here for the preposition
[8] For ⲧⲱϣ thus v no 136   But perhaps 'If thou so decide', and similarly below (v ZOEGA 342)
[9] V Br Mus nos 1107, 1158, KRALL CIV, TURAIEF, *Materialy* no 6, here nos 148, 298, 370, assuming this = ⲁⲙⲁⲅⲉ   Cf ⲙⲉϭⲓ in KRALL CXL, CXLVII, Br Mus no 582

Λ

letter, if thou wilt, make him headman and require of him what he¹ hath squandered, from this time (*lit.* place) backward. If thou appoint him, then take not aught of him for the past Keep an eye upon that which thou dost require of him, in thy house. But (ἀλλά) if thou wilt appoint him, so shalt thou, from this time onward, demand of him the tax-money

The 22nd of Thoth '

325.—Papyrus, a fragment, 13 × 26 cm   Script sloping, rarely ligatured   *Recto* ↑

Letter from Mark of Plêtm², his 'servant', to 'the most glorious amîr' It relates to the taxes (διάγραφον) payable by the districts north and south of Shmoun The amîr (?) is begged to provide a pass (σιγίλλιον³) for some one.

+ ϩⲙⲡⲣⲁⲛ ⲙⲡⲛⲟⲩⲧⲉ ⲙⲁⲣⲕⲟⲥ ⲡⲉⲧⲛⲉⲥⲁⲟⲩⲟⲛ ⲡⲁⲡⲗⲏⲧⲙ ⲡⲉϥϫⲉⲁⲓ ⲉϥⲡⲣⲟ[ⲥⲕⲩⲛⲉⲓ |]ⲭⲉⲧⲓⲣⲏⲙⲛ
ⲙⲡⲛⲟⲩⲧⲉ ⲉⲥⲉϣⲱⲡⲉ ⲛⲁⲕ ⲙⲛⲛⲥⲁⲛⲁⲓ ⲉⲓⲥ ⲕⲟⲙⲥ ⲡⲙⲁⲧⲟ[ⲓ | [............]ⲕ ⲙⲡⲁϫⲟⲉⲓⲥ
ⲉⲧⲧⲁⲓⲏⲟⲩ ⲧⲁⲣⲉⲡⲥⲧⲓⲁ ϣⲱⲡⲉ ⲛⲧⲉⲡ[| [.]ⲛⲁⲓⲁⲕⲣⲁⲫⲟⲛ ⲛⲉⲛⲣⲱⲙⲉ ⲡⲉⲙϩⲓⲧ ⲛϣⲙⲟⲩⲛ ⲙⲛⲡⲣⲏⲥ
ⲛϣⲙⲟⲩⲛ [| ⲛϥⲥⲙⲛ ⲟⲩⲥⲓⲕⲉⲗⲉⲛ ⲛⲡⲓⲣⲱⲙⲉ ⲉⲡⲱϩⲛⲉ ⲉϥϩⲛⲧⲁϩⲣⲟⲩϫ⁴ [ϫ]ⲉϥⲫⲓⲗⲟⲑ[ⲉⲟⲥ | ⲫⲟⲛ ⲛⲁⲛ
ⲁⲩ[ⲱ ⲧⲓ]ⲡⲁⲣⲁⲕⲁⲗⲉⲓ ⲛ[ⲡ]ⲁϫⲟⲉⲓⲥ ⲛⲁⲅⲁⲑⲟⲥ ⲉⲓ |

Verso]ⲛⲡⲉⲩⲕⲗ/ [space] ⲛⲁⲙⲓⲣⲁ ⲡⲉⲧⲛⲉⲥⲁⲟⲩⲟⲛ ⲙⲁⲣⲕⲟⲥ ⲡⲁⲡⲗⲏⲧⲙ +

326.—Papyrus, a fragment, 7½ × 7½ cm   Script moderately ligatured   *Recto* ↑

Letter from Isaac to the κῦρις Christodorus ° (*or* Christophorus), beginning, 'I desire that, so soon as ye receive this letter ' It relates to a payment (καταβολή) of taxes⁶ Antinoe is mentioned

[+ ⲟⲩ]ⲱϣ ⲧⲉⲩⲛⲟⲩ ⲉⲓⲛⲁϫⲓ⁷ ᵗⁱᶜ ⲧⲓⲉⲡⲓⲥⲧⲟ[ⲗⲏ |]ⲟⲓ ⲉϩⲣⲁⲓ ⲉⲥⲟⲟⲩⲧⲛ ⲙⲛⲧⲕⲁⲧⲁⲃ[ⲟⲗⲏ | ⲁ]ⲛⲧⲓⲛⲟⲟⲩ
ⲉⲛϣⲁⲁⲧ ⲉⲩⲫⲟⲗⲗⲓⲥ⁸ |]ⲡⲉⲧⲛⲣϩⲱⲟϥ ϣⲁⲩⲥⲓⲁⲛ[ⲉ⁹ |]ⲁⲧⲉ ⲛⲧⲁⲓⲧⲛⲟⲟⲩ ⲡⲉⲓϩⲱ[| ⲧⲛ]ⲟⲟⲩϥ ⲛⲏⲧⲛ
ⲧⲁⲣⲉⲩⲧⲓ ⲛⲏ ⲋ ⲛ[|]ⲛ ϫⲓⲛⲉⲉϣⲁⲓⲛⲁⲩ ⲉⲛⲕ[|]ⲕⲁⲣⲁⲃⲏⲛ¹⁰ + ⲕⲁⲓ ⲅⲁⲣ ϣⲁⲣⲉ | [ⲱϣ] ϩⲓⲙⲁϩⲟⲩ |
(*verso*) ⲡ]ⲛⲟⲩⲧⲉ ⲇⲉ ⲡⲉⲧⲥⲟⲟⲩⲛ ⲕⲩⲣⲓ ⲭⲣⲓ[|]ⲩⲙⲁϩ ⲧⲉⲕⲛⲁⲧⲁⲃⲟⲗⲏ ⲛⲗ[ⲏⲛ| (in other direction)
]. ⲉⲥⲛⲏⲩ¹¹ + ϩⲓⲧⲛⲥⲁⲕ[

327.—Papyrus, a fragment, 8½ × 21 cm   Script seldom ligatured   *Recto* ↑.

Letter from Bane, a village scribe¹², to Apa Victor¹³, his superior, referring to certain payments

¹ Presumably the peculating headman
² Πλῆθμις, WESSELY, *Studien* v 73
³ V KRALL cxx and KENYON, *Catal* i 231
⁴ *Cf* بجس 'Abd al-Latîf 689, Abû Sâlih 55 b, or possibly بجلس, though ب = ϫ would be abnormal
⁵ A κῦρις Christodorus in KRALL xxix, Br Mus no 1145.
⁶ V CRUM, *Ostr* no 409   ⁷ For ⲉⲧⲉⲧⲛⲛⲁ-.

⁸ *Cf.* Leont Neap (GELZER) 77, δεκα (φόλλεις), ἐστιν δὲ ὅτε καὶ κεράτιν, misunderstood by me, *Ostr* Ad 15, note CLUGNET's Ἀββᾶ Δανιήλ, pp. 12, 32, show φόλλις = κεράτιον as a labourer's day-wage The Coptic version (*ib* 84) gives φ. = ἄρκιον (ἀργύριον)
⁹ Σιαίνω, 'disturb, trouble' *Cf* Br Mus nos 1131, 1209.
° Καράβιον   ¹¹ Apparently not ⲛⲉⲥⲛⲏⲩ.
¹² V Br Mus. no 1079 &c   ¹³ V ? nos 281, 293.

✝ ⲡⲉⲧⲛⲉϭⲁⲩⲟⲛ ⲃⲁⲛⲉ ⲡⲥⲁϩ ⲛⲧⲓⲙⲉ ⲡⲉϥⲥ[ϩⲁⲓ | ⲁⲡⲁ ⲙⲏⲛⲁ ϫⲉϩⲁⲑⲛ ⲙⲛ ⲛϧⲱϥ ⲛⲓⲙ ⲧⲓⲡⲣⲟⲥⲕ[ⲩⲛⲉⲓ | ⲧⲁⲓⲥⲩⲛ ⲧⲉⲕⲙⲛⲧϫⲟⲉⲓⲥ ⲉⲃⲟⲗ ⲁⲩⲱ ⲅⲓ ⲗⲟⲅⲟⲥ [| ⲉⲓⲁⲧⲛⲟⲟⲩ ⲡⲛ̄ ⲁ ⲕ,[1] ⲓⲃ ⲛⲁⲕ ⲉϩⲣⲁⲓ ⲁⲩⲱ ⲉⲓⲥ ϫⲟⲥⲓⲥ ⲁⲓⲧ[| ✝ⲟⲩϫⲁⲓ[2] ϩⲙⲡϫⲟⲉⲓⲥ ⲙⲟⲛ ⲛⲡⲁⲧⲛϫⲓⲧ ⲉⲡⲣⲱⲙⲉ ⲛⲧⲱ[| ⲛⲁϫⲟⲟⲩⲥⲟⲩ ⲛⲏⲧⲛ ⲉϩⲣⲁⲓ ⲛⲡⲉϩⲟⲟⲩ ⲉⲧⲉⲙⲙⲁⲩ ⲙⲛⲡⲓϣ[| ⲫϫⲓⲧⲟⲩ ϣⲁⲧⲛⲟⲩ ✝

Verso] [space] ⲁⲡⲁ ⲃⲓⲕⲧⲱⲣ ✝ ϩⲓⲧⲛⲃⲁⲛⲉ ⲡⲥⲁϩ ⲛⲧⲓⲙⲉ

328.—Papyrus, a fragment, 9½ × 7 cm. Script small, ligatured *Verso* →.

Letter giving instructions as to the taxes required of the villages under the recipient's charge. The phrases 'a *tremis* of each (κατά) village,' 'I will require of thee 10 *solidi*,' occur

]ᵲ.ⲭ̄ ⲡⲉⲧⲛⲁⲧⲓ ⲛⲁⲥϩⲁⲓ ⲛⲁⲕ | ⲛ]ⲣⲱⲙⲡⲉⲛⲧⲓⲙⲉ ⲁⲕⲁⲁⲩ | ⲟ]ⲩⲧⲣⲓⲙⲏⲥⲓⲛ ⲕⲁⲧⲁ ⲧⲓⲙⲉ ϩⲛ | ϩⲩⲡ]ⲟⲩⲣⲅⲉⲓ ⲉⲣⲟⲕ ⲁⲩⲱ ⲑⲁⲣⲣⲉⲓ | ϫⲉ ϣⲁⲓϣⲁⲧⲕ ⲙⲙⲛⲧ ⲛϩⲟⲗⲟⲕ̄ | ⲁⲃⲁ]ⲉⲗⲗⲁ ⲉⲡⲉⲓ ⲛⲡⲁⲧⲉⲕⲥⲟⲩⲱ |]ⲁϩⲉ ⲛⲡⲁⲓ ⲉⲛⲉⲩϫⲓⲁⲥⲧⲣ̄ |]ⲧⲉϩⲓⲏ ⲉⲥⲱϣ ⲛⲡⲣⲕⲇ |]ⲅ ⸱

Recto the address, ⸱ σὺν ⷿ ομαρ υⷷ αβδερ̄[3] [space], and, in the other direction, remains of an Arabic letter in semi-Cufic script (earlier), relating likewise to taxation[4]

329.—Papyrus, a fragment, 8¼ × 11½ cm. Script almost ligatureless *Recto* ↑.

Letter relating to taxation and mentioning a village scribe found also in no. 305

].ⲥϣⲏⲣⲉ ⲓⲱϩⲁⲛⲛⲉ ⲯⲁϩ ⲛⲧⲓⲙⲉ ⲛ[| ϩⲁⲑ]ⲛ ⲙⲛ ⲛϧⲱϥ ⲛⲓⲙ ⲧⲓⲡⲣ[ⲟⲥ]ⲕⲩ[ⲛⲉⲓ | ⲡ]ⲛⲟⲩⲧⲉ ⲉⲃⲁⲣⲟⲉⲓⲥ ⲉⲣⲱⲧⲛ ⲉⲡⲉ[|]ⲉϥ ⸱ ⲁⲁⲧ[5] ⲉⲡⲉⲓ ⲉϩⲣⲁⲓ ⲛⲏⲧⲛ [| ⲕⲁ]ⲧⲁⲃⲟⲗⲏ ϩⲓⲡⲟⲩⲱϣ [ⲙⲛ]ⲡⲛⲟ[ⲩ]ⲧⲉ [|]ⲡⲁⲉⲓⲱⲧ ⲙⲛⲁⲡⲁ ⲥⲟⲗⲟⲙⲱⲛ ⲡ[|]ⲁⲁⲥ ⲉⲧⲃⲉϥⲱϥ ⲉⲡⲧⲓⲙⲉ ⲁⲩⲱ [|] ⲃⲗⲟⲓⲑⲉ[6] ⲧⲛⲟⲟⲩ ⲛⲁⲛ ⲙⲟⲛ ϣ[ⲗ]ⲏⲗ [|

Verso] μγ ⸍θⲓ,[7] [

330.—Papyrus, 3 fragments, the distances between which cannot be determined, the largest, 8 × 11 cm. Script moderately ligatured *Recto* →.

Letter (since the 2nd person is used), difficult of interpretation. It is divided into paragraphs, each beginning elliptically with ωσδε (ὥστε)[8]. The writer seems to complain that, when sent south, the pagarch had not assisted him, but had paid greater respect to (him who bore) 'the false name, archimandrite'. The sum of 1263 *solidi* is in question, also a tax-instalment (διάγραφον), further 'the house of the nuns' and something stolen and given to 'another monastery'

---

[1] κεράτια. [2] Perhaps ✝ instead of ✝.
[3] Presumably the author, though standing first
[4] The words من طول (v. no. 401) and رسول occur
[5] I cannot read ⲕⲁⲁⲧ [6] V nos 284, 320 &c
[7] No trace of χ. Presumably it stood on the left of the space

[8] A fragment of a letter in Br Mus Or 6201 A is similarly divided thrice by ϩⲱⲥⲧⲉ, introducing in each case a request, while another letter, *ib*, begins ✝ϩⲱⲥⲧⲉ ⲧⲁⲣⲉⲕⲕⲱ ⲛⲙⲁ⸱⸱ Here however it does not appear to serve that purpose

]ꙙππαθαποκρηⲥⲓⲥ [1] | [ⲱⲥ]ⲁⲉ ϩⲛⲡⲧⲣⲉⲕϭⲁⲓ ⲧⲁⲃⲱⲕ | ⲉⲣⲏⲥ ꙙⲡⲉⲡⲡⲁⲧⲁⲣ̄ ⲧⲓ ⲧⲟⲟⲧ | ⲁⲗⲗⲁ
ⲁϥⲧⲓ ⲧⲉⲡⲣⲟⲧⲓⲙ̄[2] ꙙⲡⲣⲁⲛ [3] ⲛⲛⲟⲩⲝ ⲝⲉⲁⲣꙙⲁⲛ̄ | [ⲱⲥⲁⲉ . . .]ⲉ[. .] ⲥⲛⲟⲩⲁⲁⲍⲉ ⲛϣⲟⲣϣⲣ | [. . . . . .]ⲁⲣ
[ʼ ?]]|

ⲥⲁⲭ[ⲟ . .]ⲕⲟⲩⲓ | ϣⲏꙙ ⲛⲛⲟⲩⲃ ⲟⲛ ⲉⲛꙙⲁ | ꙙⲡⲛ̄ ﹐ⲁⲥⲅⲝ | [ⲱ]ⲥⲁⲉ (ⲟⲛ above) ⲝⲛⲛⲉⲩⲧⲓ
ⲗⲁⲁⲩ ϩⲁ[.] |

[. .]ⲉ ⲉⲩⲟⲩⲱꙙ ⲉⲩⲥⲱ ⲉⲩⲫⲟⲣⲉⲓ |ⲛⲧⲁⲕ﹒[5] ⲁⲩⲱ ⲛⲁⲇⲓⲁⲅⲣⲁⲫⲟⲛ | ⲱⲥⲁⲉ ⲧⲁⲣⲉⲧⲉⲧⲛⲉⲛⲧⲟⲩ ⲛⲁⲓ
ⲉϩⲟⲩⲛ | ⲟⲩⲁ ⲟⲩⲁ ϩⲓⲧⲟⲟⲧ ⲥⲉⲝⲓ ⲧⲉⲩ|ⲁⲛⲁⲅⲱⲥⲛ ⲝⲉϩⲛⲁϣ ꙙꙙⲛⲉ|ⲛⲉ| ⲱⲥⲁⲉ ⲝⲉⲡⲉⲩⲇⲓⲁⲅⲣⲁⲫⲟⲛ
ⲛⲁⲣⲭ|ⲁⲓⲟⲛⲡⲉ ⲛ̄ ⲭ |

(*verso*)] ⲱⲥⲁⲉ ⲉⲧⲃⲉⲡⲏⲓ ⲛⲛⲓ|ⲙⲟⲛⲁⲭⲏ | ⲱⲥⲁⲉ ⲉⲧⲃⲉⲡⲉⲕⲥⲟⲛ ⲁ[ⲩⲱ] | ⲱⲥⲁⲉ ⲉⲧⲃⲉⲡⲉϥⲉⲓⲱⲧ
[ⲁⲩⲱ] | ⲛⲉϥⲥⲛⲏⲩ ⲛⲧⲁⲩⲃⲱ[ⲕ . .] | ⲉⲛⲝⲱ[. . . . . .]] |

ⲉϥϩⲱⲃⲅ ꙙⲙⲟⲟⲩ ⲉϥ[.]|ⲗⲉ ꙙⲙⲟⲟⲩ ⲉⲕⲉⲙⲟⲛⲁⲥⲧⲏⲣ̄ | blank

331.—Papyrus, almost complete, 10×21 cm Script irregular, some ligatures
Recto ↑

Letter wherein the writer tells his 'dear lord brother' that he has sent Apa Zacharias's man, 'that thy pity may attain us to (the extent of) 5 *solidi* For I have been taken to the place of payment (-καταβάλλειν) and they have [6] '

+ ⲁⲓⲣⲁϣⲉ ⲛⲧⲁⲓϭⲛ ⲧ ⲉⲡⲡⲣⲟⲫⲩⲥⲓⲥ ⲁⲓⲥϩⲁⲓ ⲉⲓϣ[ⲓⲛⲉ] ⲉⲅⲉⲕ|ꙙⲛⲧꙙⲉⲣⲓⲧ ⲛⲝⲟⲉⲓⲥ ⲛⲥⲟⲛ ⲧⲉⲡⲣⲟ|
ⲫⲩⲥⲓⲥ ⲧⲉ [ⲧ]ⲁⲓ[7] ⲉⲓⲥ | ⲡⲣⲱⲙⲉ ⲡⲕⲩⲣ/ ⲍⲁⲭⲁⲣⲓⲁⲥ ⲁⲓⲝⲟⲟⲩϥ ⲛⲁⲛ ⲧⲉⲛ|ⲉⲕⲛⲁ ⲧⲁϩⲟⲛ ⲉⲡⲧⲓⲟⲩ
ⲛϩⲟⲗⲟⲕ̄/ ⲉⲡⲓ ⲥⲁⲩⲃⲓⲧ ⲉⲛꙙⲁ ⲛ|ⲕⲁⲧⲁⲃⲁⲗⲗⲓ ⲥⲟⲩⲧⲓ ⲧⲓϣⲓⲛⲉ ⲧⲉⲕꙙⲛⲧꙙⲉⲣⲓⲧ | ⲛⲝⲟⲉⲓⲥ ⲛⲥⲟⲛ
ϩⲓⲧⲛⲛⲉⲓⲥϩⲁⲓ +

Below the text, a clay seal bearing a figure difficult to recognize
Verso the address, illegible

332.—Papyrus, a fragment, 10½×31 cm. Script ligatureless *Recto* ↑

Letter from Colluthus to his 'saintly lord father', begging the loan of 2 *solidi*, to be repaid as in the preceding year, so as not to anger him[8] He has had no opportunity to buy[9] the wine (? as instructed)

Above l 1, ⲭꙙⲥ

ϯ ϩⲁⲑⲏ ꙙⲡϣⲁⲝⲉ ⲛⲧⲕꙙⲉⲧⲉⲗⲁⲭⲓⲥⲧⲟⲥ ⲧⲛⲡⲣⲟⲥⲕⲩⲛⲉⲓ ꙙⲡ[ϩⲩⲡⲟⲡⲟⲇⲓⲟⲛ] | ⲛⲧⲉⲧⲛꙙⲉⲧⲝⲟⲉⲓⲥ
ⲓⲱⲧ ⲉⲧⲟⲩⲁⲁⲃ ⲛⲉⲛⲝⲟⲉⲓⲥ ⲓⲟⲧⲉ ⲉⲧⲟⲩ[ⲁⲁⲃ ⲧⲓ]ⲡⲁⲣⲁⲕⲁⲗⲉⲓ | ⲛⲧⲉⲧⲛꙙⲉⲧⲝⲟⲉⲓⲥ ⲓⲱⲧ ⲉⲧⲟⲩⲁⲁⲃ ⲛⲁⲓⲱⲧⲉ
ⲝⲉⲕⲁⲁⲥ ⲉⲣⲉⲅ[ⲉⲧⲕꙙⲉⲧⲝⲟⲉⲓⲥ] | ⲓⲱⲧ ⲉⲧⲟⲩⲁⲁⲃ ⲛⲁⲃⲟⲏⲑⲓ ⲉⲣⲟⲓ ⲉϩⲟⲗⲟⲕⲟⲧⲓⲥ ⲥⲛⲁⲩ ⲧⲁⲧⲁⲁⲩ [ⲛ]ⲧⲉⲧⲛ-

---

[1] Is ⲑ for ⲧ ?
[2] ? πρότιμη as substantive
[3] Possibly a letter before ⲛ
[4] Uncertain whether there was more in this line Possibly it precedes immediately the second fragment
[5] ⲛ perhaps erased Perhaps nothing after ⲕ

[6] The phrase is apparently incomplete, ⲧⲓ being without an object
[7] *V* Br Mus no 1137
[8] λυπεῖν, as in Rossi, *Nuov Cod* 37, 38 ⲧⲓⲁ- apparently for ⲛϯⲛⲁ-
[9] The rare verb ⲧⲟⲟⲩ

ⲙⲉⲧϫⲟⲉⲓⲥ ⲓⲱⲧ | ⲉⲧⲟⲩⲁⲁⲃ ⲛⲥⲟⲩⲟ ⲛⲑⲉ ⲥⲛⲟⲩϥ ⲁⲩⲱ ⲉⲣϣⲁⲛⲡϫⲟⲉⲓⲥ ⲧⲱϣ ⲧⲛ . ⲉ[1] ⲛⲉⲧⲛϣⲗⲏⲗ |
ⲉⲧⲟⲩⲁⲁⲃ ⲛⲟⲉ ⲙⲡⲓⲗⲩⲡⲓ ⲙⲙⲱⲧⲛ ⲛⲉⲛⲟⲩϥ ⲧⲓⲁⲗⲩⲡⲓ ⲁⲛ ⲛⲧⲣⲟⲙⲡⲉ ⲁⲩⲱ ⲧⲛⲡⲁⲣⲁⲕⲁⲗⲉⲓ | ⲛⲧⲉⲧⲛ-
ⲙⲉⲧⲓⲱⲧ ⲉⲧⲟⲩⲁⲁⲃ ⲉⲧⲃⲉⲟⲩϩⲟⲗⲟⲥⲟⲧⲥⲉ ⲛⲏⲣⲡ ϫⲉⲧⲉⲧⲛⲙⲉⲧϫⲟⲉⲓⲥ ⲓⲱⲧ | ⲉⲧⲟⲩⲁⲁⲃ ⲥⲟⲟⲩⲛ ϫⲉⲙⲡⲛⲥⲛ
ⲑⲉ ⲛⲧⲟⲟⲩ ⲉⲡⲁⲣⲁⲕⲁⲗⲉⲓ ⲛⲧ[ⲉⲧⲛⲙⲉⲧϫⲟⲉⲓⲥ ⲓⲱⲧ] | ⲉⲧⲟⲩⲁⲁⲃ ϫⲉⲕⲁⲁⲥ ⲉⲧⲉⲧⲛⲙⲉⲧϫⲟⲉⲓⲥ ⲓⲱⲧ ⲛⲁⲃⲟⲏⲑⲓ
ⲉⲣⲟⲓ + ⲟⲩϫⲁⲓ ϩⲙⲡϫⲟⲉⲓⲥ ⲡⲁ|ϫⲟⲉⲓⲥ ⲓⲱⲧⲉ ⲉⲧⲟⲩⲁⲁⲃ + ⲏ ⲁⲅⲓⲁ ⲧⲣⲓⲁⲥ +

Verso [+ ⲧⲁⲁⲥ ⲙⲡⲁϫⲟ]ⲉⲓⲥ ⲓⲱⲧ ⲉⲧⲟⲩ[space]ⲁⲁⲃ + ϩⲓⲧⲛⲕⲟⲗⲗⲟⲩⲑⲟⲥ ⲡⲉⲗⲁⲭ/

333.—Papyrus, a fragment, $4\frac{1}{2} \times 34\frac{1}{2}$ cm Script few ligatures *Recto* ↑
Letter to a 'brother', with a request for clothes

ⲡⲁⲣⲁ]ⲕⲁⲗⲉ ⲛⲉⲕⲙⲛⲧⲥⲟⲛ ⲧⲁⲣⲉⲕⲧⲓ ϣⲟⲙⲧⲉ | [ⲛⲏⲧⲛ about 28 letters] ⲁⲓⲧⲁⲁⲩ ϩⲓⲱⲟⲩ ⲙⲟⲛ
ⲡⲛⲟⲩⲧⲉ ⲥⲟⲟⲩⲛ ⲙⲙⲗⲁⲁⲩ | ⲛϩⲏⲧⲛ ⲛⲡⲙⲁ ⲉⲩϣⲁⲛⲉⲓ ⲧⲁϯ ⲟⲩⲉⲓ ⲟⲩⲁ[2] ϩⲓⲱⲟⲩ ⲙⲁⲣⲉⲡⲉⲕⲛⲁ ⲧⲁϩⲟⲓ
ⲛⲧⲓ ⲧϣⲟⲙⲧⲉ ⲛⲏⲧⲛ ⲛⲁⲩ | ⲉⲩⲛⲏⲩ ⲉϩⲏⲧ ⲁⲩⲱ ⲧⲛⲟⲟⲩ ⲡⲉⲕⲟⲩⲱ ⲉⲧⲛⲁⲛⲟⲩϥ ⲛ[ⲁⲓ] ⲧⲁⲣⲓⲉⲓⲙⲉ
ⲉⲡⲉⲕⲟⲩϫⲁⲓ ⲛⲧⲉⲡⲁϩⲏⲧ ⲉⲙⲧⲟⲛ | + ⲟⲩϫⲁⲓ ϩⲙⲡϫⲟⲉⲓⲥ ⲡⲁⲙⲁⲓⲛⲟ[ⲩⲧ]ⲉ ⲛⲥⲟⲛ +

'I entreat thy brothership that thou wouldest give [me] three robes   God
knoweth, there are here no robes, that, when they come, I might give one to each of
them   Let thy kindness reach me and give them the three robes, when they come
northward   And send thy good news to me, that I may know of thy health and my heart
be at rest   Farewell in the Lord, my pious brother'

334.—Papyrus, a fragment, 16×19 cm Script uneven, seldom ligatured *Recto* ↑
Above l 1 a cross
Letter, the writer of which begs for (the loan of?) an ox for (use as far as?) the ferry
He offers to make and deliver various articles of clothing, perhaps in payment of a debt

+ ⲧⲛⲡⲁⲣⲁⲕⲁⲗⲉⲓ ⲛⲧⲉⲧⲛⲙⲉⲙⲛⲧϫⲟⲉⲓⲥ [.]ⲉ[. .]ⲓⲉ[. . . . .] | ⲟⲩⲧⲃⲛⲏ ⲛⲁⲓ ϣⲁⲡⲉϫⲓⲟⲟⲣ ⲙ[.] ϣ
. . ⲭⲣⲉⲓⲟⲥⲧⲉⲓ ⲛ|ⲟⲩϩⲟⲗⲟⲛ/ ⲧⲉⲧⲛⲉⲉⲣⲧⲁⲥ[ⲁⲡ]ⲏ ⲛⲧⲉⲧⲛⲉⲧⲁⲁϥ ⲛⲁⲓ ⲉⲧ|ⲛⲡⲉⲟ]ⲩⲱϣ ⲟⲩϫⲩ[ⲅⲏ][3] |
ⲛⲥⲁⲃⲁⲛⲏⲛ ⲉⲛⲁⲛⲟⲩⲥ ⲉⲛⲧⲁⲓⲥⲙⲛⲧⲉ ⲧⲁⲧⲛ[ⲟ]ⲟⲩⲥ ⲛⲏ[ⲧⲛ] ⲉ[ⲧ]ⲉⲧ[ⲛ]|ⲟⲩⲱϣ ϣⲟⲙⲛⲧ ⲛⲉⲡⲓⲕⲓⲫⲁⲣⲛ[4]
ϣⲁⲓⲧⲛⲟⲟⲩⲥ[ⲟⲩ] . . . . ⲛ | ⲥⲛⲁⲩ ϩⲁⲟⲩϩⲟⲗⲟⲛ[5] ⲉⲧⲛⲉⲟ[ⲩ]ⲉϣ ⲃⲧ[ⲟⲟⲩ] . . . . . ϩⲉ . . . . | . . . ⲉⲧⲛⲁⲛⲱ
ⲁ̄ⲛⲧⲛⲟⲟⲩ ϣⲁⲓⲧⲛⲟⲟⲩϥ ⲛⲛ[ⲧⲛ . . . .]| ⲧⲓ ⲉⲙⲛⲟⲗⲓⲟⲛ ⲉ ⲱⲩ [| ⲁⲧⲛⲉⲉⲣⲧⲁⲅⲁⲡⲏ ⲛ[| ϩ]ⲓⲃⲟⲗ ⲇⲉⲥⲡ[6] +

335.—Papyrus, complete, 10×14 cm Script ligatured *Recto* ↑
Letter from[6] Titoue to the presbyter Peter, referring to certain sailors who had been
sent to the latter, claiming of him 2 *solidi*

---

[1] Altered   [2] For ? ⲉⲟⲩⲁ   [4] ? *ἐπικεφάλαιον* Not found in the sense of headdress
[3] Cf Br Mus no 1103 Frag in Br Mus Or 6201ʙ,   [5] 'Two for a *solidus*'
ⲧⲥⲟ ⲛϫⲩⲧⲛ ⲛⲥⲓⲛϫⲱⲛⲛ   [6] Assuming the abbreviations to = [π]ϥ[ός] and π[α]ϥ[ά]

ρ̄ πετρ/ πρ/ τιτογε |⸱ απετρος ταμοι ϫⲛⲧⲁϥⲧⲁⲗⲉ ⲛⲛⲉⲉϥ ϩⲁⲣⲟⲛ | ⲉⲩⲧⲁϩⲟ ⲛⲉⲛⲁⲩ
ⲛϩⲟⲗⲟⲕᵀ, ⲉⲣⲟⲕ ⲉϣⲱⲡⲉ ⲧⲁⲉⲉⲧⲉ | [ⲡⲣ]ⲟⲥ ⲑⲉ ⲛⲧⲁϥⲧⲁⲙⲟⲓ ⲉⲧⲟ [.]ⲉⲩ ⲟⲛ ⲁⲩⲱ | ⲕⲉ[. . . . .]ⲉⲣ[. . . .
.]ⲉⲕ[. . . . .]ⲓⲧⲁⲧⲛ[.] | ⲛϥⲣⲱⲙⲉ ⲕⲡ[. .]ⲉϣⲁϥⲧⲁⲕⲟⲛ ϩⲁⲡⲉⲓϩⲱⲉ . | χ̄/ μ̄ ι ϝ ῑδ̄/

At the lower edge of the leaf, a clay seal with traces of a Cufic inscription

336 —Papyrus, a fragment, 8 × 17½ cm   Script rarely ligatured   *Recto* ↑.

Letter containing various requests and referring to a loan on security

]ⲉϩ ⲏ ⲟⲩⲛⲗⲁⲁⲩ ⲛⲁⲅⲁⲡⲏ ⲉⲡⲁⲡⲛⲟⲩⲧⲉ ⲛⲉϥ ⲛⲧⲏⲙⲛⲧⲉ[1] ⲟⲉ ⲉⲧⲉⲕ |]ⲉⲓ ⲉⲛⲉϣⲁⲛⲟⲩⲁϩ ⲗⲁⲁⲩ
ⲛⲉⲟⲩⲱ ⲛⲉϫⲓ ϣⲏⲧ ⲛϩⲟⲗⲟⲕᵀ, ⲛⲉⲧⲛⲟⲟⲩⲥⲟⲩ |]ⲧⲁⲁⲩ ⲛⲁⲛ ϣⲁⲛⲁⲡⲟⲗⲟⲩⲧⲍⲉ ⲙⲙⲟⲟⲩ ⲉⲛⲉⲩⲭⲁⲣⲓⲥⲧⲉⲓ
ⲛⲁϥ |]ⲙⲉⲟⲩⲱϣ ⲟⲛ ϩⲙⲡⲟⲩⲱϣ ⲛⲡⲛⲟⲩⲧⲉ ⲛⲁⲕⲧⲟⲩⲃⲗⲗⲉ ⲁⲛ |]ϩⲏⲧ ⲉϥϩⲟⲟⲩ ⲉⲛⲉⲃⲗⲗⲉ ⲗⲟⲓⲡⲟⲛ
ⲁⲣⲓ ⲁⲡⲁⲧⲟⲟⲧⲛ ⲛⲧⲉⲛⲉ. |

337.—Paper, a fragment, 8 × 13 cm   Script irregular, almost ligatureless   ⲛ is ν and ⲩ ʃ

Letter to a woman, perhaps asking for money

+ ⲥⲏ̄ ϯⲡⲣⲟⲥⲕ/ ⲙⲡⲟⲩϫⲁⲓ ⲛⲧⲟⲩⲙ|ⲉⲧⲙⲉⲣⲓᵀ ⲛⲥⲱⲛⲉ ⲉⲥⲧ[ⲁⲓ]ⲏⲩ ⲉⲣⲉⲡⲟⲥ̄ ϩⲁⲣⲉϩ ⲉⲡ|ⲟⲩⲱⲛϩ[2]
ⲙⲉⲡⲟⲩϣⲏⲣⲉ ⲙⲉⲡⲉϥⲓⲱ ⲉⲣⲉ|ⲡⲟⲥ̄ ⲛⲁⲁⲩ ⲛⲏ ⲁⲩⲱ ⲉⲥ ⲧⲉⲣⲛⲟⲉⲓⲛ[3] ⲉϩⲱⲱⲃ ⲛⲓⲙ ϫⲉⲙⲉⲓϩⲟⲙⲉⲧ ⲉⲧⲟⲟⲧⲛ
ⲉⲥ|[12 letters]ⲡⲉⲧⲥϩⲛⲁⲓ ⲡⲉ|ᶫ

338.—Papyrus, complete, 20½ × 32½ cm   Script small, ligatured   *Recto* ↑.

Letter to a high official, regarding 2 shiploads of acacia wood[4]   *Lacunae* make details obscure

[+] ⲉⲓⲥ ⲡⲉⲓϫⲟⲓ [ⲥⲛ]ⲁⲩ [ⲁ]ⲓⲟⲧⲡⲟⲩ ⲛϣⲟⲛⲧⲉ ⲁⲓⲕ[ⲁ]ⲁⲩ ⲉⲃ[ⲟⲗ ⲛ]ⲉⲟⲩⲡⲁⲓ ⲁⲑ/ β̄ ϩⲓⲧⲟⲟⲧⲉϥ ⲛⲛⲉⲩ-
ⲡⲓⲥⲧⲓⲕⲟⲥ[5] ⲉⲩⲧⲁⲗⲏⲩ | ⲉϫⲱⲟⲩ ⲁⲩⲱ ⲉⲓⲥ ⲡⲣⲁⲛ ⲛⲛⲉⲭⲏⲩ ⲙⲛⲡⲣⲁⲛ ⲛⲛⲉⲡⲓⲥⲧⲓⲕⲟⲥ ⲉⲩⲧⲁⲗⲏⲩ ⲉϫⲱⲟⲩ
ⲙⲛⲡⲕⲁⲧⲁⲧⲓⲙⲉ ⲛⲧⲁⲩⲧⲁⲗⲟⲟⲩ | ϩⲓⲱⲟⲩ ⲁⲓⲥⲙⲛⲧϥ ⲛⲧⲉⲛⲥⲉⲩⲕⲗ̄/ ⲛϫⲟⲉⲓ[ⲥ . . .]ᵀ ⲉⲧⲧⲁⲓ|ⲏ̄ⲩ ⲥⲁⲡⲉⲥ[ⲏⲧ]
ⲛⲧⲓⲉⲡⲓⲥⲧⲟⲗⲏ [ⲁⲩ]ⲱ ⲉⲓⲥ ᶠ [.]ⲁ. ⲁⲛⲟ[. .]ⲅⲉ | [. . . .]ⲃⲓⲧⲟⲩ (ⲉϩⲏⲧ above[6]) ⲛ̄ⲏⲩ ϩⲓⲡⲁϩⲟⲩ ⲛ̄ⲛⲉⲓⲥϩⲁⲓ
ⲛⲡ[. .] ⲁⲓⲟⲧⲡ ⲕⲁⲧⲟⲥⲛⲅⲉ ⲅⲁⲣ ⲛⲁⲓⲁⲛⲟⲙⲏ[7] ⲁⲓⲥϩⲁⲓ ⲛⲏⲩ[. .] | ϩⲓⲧⲟⲟⲧϥ ⲛⲛⲉⲩⲡⲓⲥⲧⲓⲕⲟⲥ ⲉⲩⲧⲁⲗⲏⲩ
ⲉϫⲱⲟⲩ ⲥⲟⲩ[. . ⲛ]ⲡⲟⲟⲩ ⲧⲁⲣⲉⲡⲁϫⲟⲉⲓⲥ ⲉⲓⲙⲉ ⲁⲓⲥϩⲁⲓ ⲧⲓⲡⲣⲟⲥⲕ̄ⲩ | ⲁⲩⲱ ⲧⲓⲁⲥⲡⲁⲍⲉ ⲉⲛⲏϥⲩⲡⲟⲡⲟⲁⲓⲟⲛ
ⲛⲧⲉⲛⲥⲉⲩⲕⲗ̄/ ⲛϫⲟ[ⲥⲓ]ⲕ ⲉⲧⲧⲁⲓⲏ̄ⲩ . . . ⲁⲑ/ β̄

---

[1] Or ⲉⲡⲁⲡⲛⲟⲩⲧⲉⲡⲉ ϩⲛⲧⲛ-   [2] *V* nos 306, 317
[3] *V* no 344   For ⲧⲉⲣ- *cf* ⲓⲉⲣⲁ- of the future, also the Boh forms in *Bessarione* vii 19 (Guidi)
[4] *Cf* Kenyon, *Catal* iii 186, where it is used in making agricultural implements   On acacias as taxable church property, *v* Krall iii (read ⲛⲁⲛⲥⲉⲕⲕⲗⲏⲥⲓⲁ)

[5] So used in Justinian (Sophocles) and Leont Neap (Gelzer 55, 60)   In Krall lxiv, lxv (*cf* Br Mus. no 675) the meaning is obscure   *Cf* Becker, *Pap Schott-R* i 47, 49, where the ship's نیس, and امس are clearly distinct
[6] The insertion stands almost above ϩⲓⲡⲁϩⲟⲩ
[7] *V* Kenyon, *Catal* i 223, *Pap Amh* cliv

In a different hand (?) and ink.

εἰτ/ λιβ‹ ¹ παχουι ² ναῦ απο παγ λυκωᶜ³ δ/ πιλατο̊ πιᵗ⁴ απο ρου[β]εες . . αμηρ̊   ακθ̦ γ |
χωριο̊ θμουμηρᶜ°   ακθ̦ ν   χωριο̊ πνομφ.ᶜ   ακθ̦ λβ   χωριο̊ ψ ᶜ   ακθ̦ η |
εἰτ/ λιβᶜ μηνα ναῦ απο παγ ερμουπολᶜ   εἰτ/ χ̈ μουναει ⁶ δ/ πιλατο̊ πιᵗ απο ρουβεες εν χωριο̊
αραβων   ακθ̦ μ[ ] |

Verso. ϥ εγρ/ [   ] blank | +[ι]διᵂ αγθ̦ θεοφυλο̊ δεσπ̊ μων ευεργ [space] τω . . . . . . τ̊ατ̊
. ψας υμας

Also (fibres ↑), in a different hand.

+ πλοϲ/ ҥ̅ογ̅υποϲταϲιϲ [ℳ̅πℳακαρ, ͛[α]ne | ϩαππαⱦ⃛ ⁸ ετλακ [. . .]ⲅн | ϩαππ아͛
εἰϧοι ⁹ ϲι αρ[ᵀ .]ℳ | ϩαⲡ[ℳ]a ҥ̅ϩραϲ[ιοϲ κο]λλ⃛ | ϩατεϲτιⲱϩε ҥ̅[ка]ϩ . . κοℳιϲ | ϩαππⲁⱦ⃛,
επεϩⲣⲓπⲁρ . ¹⁰ | ϩαⲡⲣⲟ⃛ β ҥ̅πϩⲟⲓ . . . . | ϩⲁⲁⲡⲁ ͛ⲓκⲧ/ [. . .] | ϩⲁⲡⲉⲫⲟⲣⲟⲥ ҥ . . ⲁⲛ ⲫⲁⲁⲕ . ⲣ̊ⲟ̊
γενα   Each item has a figure opposite it, preceded by / ¹¹. Their total concludes the
column γϥ ⱱ̊ γ / γϲ

Then a second account, headed ⲁϥⲱ̊ ¹² ϩⲁⲡⲁнⲓⲓ̊ ⲉⲡⲉ ⲗⲁϲⲅн ⲁϥ   .ⲁ ⲓ̅ⲅ | ϩⲁⲡⲁнⲓⲓ̊
εἰϧⲟⲓ | ϩⲁⲡⲉϫⲉⲥⲧнⲥ ҥϩ | ϩⲁⲡⲟⲓ, кнᵈ ⲓⲍ, with the total below γϥ ⱱ̊ γ / ϲ

'Lo, I have loaded the 2 ships with acacia (wood) and have despatched them this
day, the 2nd of Hathor, in charge of their supercargos (πιστικός) that are aboard them
And here are the names of the ships and the names of the supercargos that are aboard
them and the list of (κατά) villages where they were loaded ¹³, I have drawn it up for your
renowned (εὔκλεια)   . , honored lordship, at the bottom of this epistle (ἐπ)   And see,
the   that have been brought north come on the back of this letter   for
I have loaded 2 jars (κάδος) for distribution (διανομή)   I have written the   at the
hand of their supercargos (πισ) that are aboard them, that my lord may know   I have
written and do worship (προσκυνεῖν) and kiss the footstool (ἀσπάζειν, ὑποπόδιον) of your
renowned (εὐκλ), honored lordship   (Written ?) on the 2nd of Hathor'

The accounts on the *verso*—'The list of the property (λόγος, ὑπόστασις) of the late
Bane'—have no connection with the foregoing

339.—Papyrus, almost complete, 12 × 21 cm   Script moderately ligatured   *Recto* ↑.
Letter from Apa Cyrus to the headman, Phib

+ ϩⲁⲑн ℳⲉн ⲛϩⲱϥ ⲛⲓⲙ ⲧⲓⲩⲓⲛⲉ ⲛ̅ⲓⲣⲕ̅ⲑⲉⲟⲫⲩⲗ⃛ / ¹⁴ нⲁ̅ⲙⲉⲣⲓⲧ ⲛ̅ϫⲟⲉⲓⲥ ⲛⲓⲱⲧ | ϯⲡⲁⲣⲁⲕⲁⲗⲉⲓ
нⲁⲙⲟⲕ ⲛⲥ̅ϣⲓⲛⲉ ⲛ̅[ⲥⲁ]ⲫⲱϥ ⲛⲛⲉⲓⲱϩⲉ ⲉⲅⲛ̅ⲧⲟⲟⲧ̅ϥ | ⲛ̅[ⲡⲛ]ⲟϭ ⲛ̅ⲣⲱⲙⲉ ¹⁵ ⲛ̅ϣⲓⲛⲉ ⲛⲥⲁⲫⲱϥ . . .¹⁶

¹ H I Bell suggests Εἰς τὸ λίβερνον (λίβυρνον), a kind
of large ship (Suidas)   The expected names of the ships
appear wanting
   ² Cf ⲡⲁⲕⲟⲅⲓ, in Jkôw texts, e g Br Mus Or 6205
   ³ The pagarchy of Lycopolis   Below, that of Hermopolis   Παγαρχία and νόμος seem identical
   ⁴ Πιστικός.
   ⁵ Cf ⲧⲙⲟⲩⲙнⲣ in the Antinoite nome, Petrie, *Gizeh
and Rifeh* 41
   ⁶ Cf ? Br Mus no 1171, ⲧⲙⲟⲩнⲁⲣⲓ
   ⁷ Cf addresses of Br Mus nos 1115, 1156

⁸ *Pactum*
   ⁹ It will be noticed that Psoi-Ptolemais, far south of
Shmoun, occurs here twice   Cf no 319
   ¹⁰ *Riparius*   V *Pap Amh* cxlvi
   ¹¹ κεράτιον   V Kenyon, *Catal* iii 276
   ¹² V Bi Mus. no 1076
   ¹³ For ⲧⲁⲗⲟ ϩⲓ- v Br Mus no 1119
   ¹⁴ θεοφιλία (v Br Mus nos. 481, 1151) or θεοφιλέστα-
τος?   For the gender cf ὁσιώτατος in no 289
   ¹⁵ V Crum, *Ostr* no 119
   ¹⁶ Not ϩⲱⲥⲧⲉ, possibly ⲁⲩⲱ

ⲧⲁⲣⲉⲕⲙⲉ ⲭⲥⲁⲡⲟⲕ ⲟⲩ|ⲃⲁⲓⲁⲛⲙⲟⲥⲓⲟⲛ¹ ⲧⲉⲣⲭⲣⲉⲓⲁ ⲛϣⲉ ⲛⲛⲁ⁴ ⲉⲣⲟⲓ ⲉⲡⲟⲟⲩ ⲁⲩⲱ ⲛⲧⲛⲟⲉⲓ³
ⲛⲡⲁⲧⲉⲡⲟⲟⲩ ϣⲱⲡⲉ ⲭⲉⲣⲉⲛⲁⲓⲱϩⲉ ϩⲓ⁴ ⲧⲱⲛⲉ ⲁⲗⲗⲁ ⲉϥϭⲱⲛ ⲗⲟⲉⲓϭⲉ ⲭⲉⲓⲟⲩⲱϣ | ⲭⲁⲣᵀ ⲉⲣⲟⲟⲩ
ⲉⲡⲓ ⲉⲥ ⲡⲁⲭⲁⲣᵀ ⲛⲓⲧⲟⲟⲧ ⲉϥϣⲁⲛⲟⲩⲱϣ ⲛⲉⲓ ⲉϥⲟⲟⲩⲧⲛ . ⲉ . | ϫ . . ⲙ]ⲥⲧⲁ ⲕⲁⲗⲟⲩ⁵ ⲥⲛⲡⲉ ⲙⲉⲓ⁶
ϣⲁⲣⲟϥ ϣⲁⲛⲧⲉⲡⲉⲛϫⲟⲉⲓⲥ ⲡⲉⲩⲕⲗ⁷⁷ ||[. .]ⲓ ⲡⲁⲭⲁⲣᵀ ⲧⲁⲡⲣⲟⲥⲁⲣⲑⲉ⁸ ⲉⲣⲟϥ ϩⲁϩ . ⲙ . ⲉ ϣⲁϥⲛⲕⲁⲁⲧ
ⲉⲃⲟⲗ | [.]ⲟϥ ⲕⲓ ⲛⲁⲓ ⲁⲁⲥ ⲗⲟⲓⲡⲟⲛ ⲧⲓⲡⲁⲣⲁⲕⲁⲗⲉⲓ ⲙⲙⲟⲕ ⲛⲧⲟϣⲁⲭⲉ ⲛⲥⲙⲁϥ | [ϫⲉⲓ]ⲥ ϥⲧⲟ ⲛⲣⲟⲙⲡⲉ
ⲛⲡⲉϥⲧⲓ ⲗⲁⲁⲩ ⲛⲁⲓ ⲁⲩⲱ ⲧⲣⲟⲙⲡⲉ ⲧⲁϥⲃⲱⲕ] | ⲛⲁϥ ⲁϥⲧⲓ ⲛⲁⲛⲣⲱⲙⲉ ⲛⲁⲩ ⲧⲏⲣⲟⲩ ⲛⲡⲉϥⲧⲓ ⲛⲁⲓ
ⲁⲛⲟⲕ ⲡⲗⲏⲛ | ϩⲉ ⲛⲓⲙ ⲉϥⲟⲩⲱϣ ⲧⲓ ⲛⲁⲓ ⲡⲣⲟⲥ ⲧⲣⲟⲙⲡⲉ ⲙⲁⲣⲉϥⲧⲓ ⲁⲩⲱ ⲉϣⲱⲡⲉ | ϫⲓ ϥⲟⲩⲱϣ ⲭⲟ
ⲛⲁⲓⲱϩⲉ ⲉⲑⲛ ⲙⲁⲣⲉϥⲥⲙⲛ ⲭⲁⲣᵀ ⲛⲁⲓ ⲉⲣⲟⲟⲩ⁹ ⲉϣⲱⲡⲉ ⲙⲙⲟⲛ | [ⲙⲁ]ⲣⲉϥⲛⲁ ⲛⲁⲓⲱϩⲉ ⲛⲁⲓ ⲉⲃⲟⲗ
ϩⲓⲛⲁⲁϩ ⲛⲓⲙ ⲉϥⲟⲩⲱϣ ϩⲓⲧⲛⲛⲥⲓⲥ[ϩⲁⲓ] ϯϣⲓⲛⲉ | ⲉⲣⲟⲕ +

'Before all things, I greet thy God favoured ($\theta\epsilon o\phi\iota\lambda\iota\alpha$?), beloved lord and fatherhood
I beg ($\pi\alpha\rho\alpha\kappa\alpha\lambda\epsilon\hat{\iota}\nu$) thee to enquire into the matter of the fields that the 'great man' holds,
and to enquire into the matter   , that thou mayest know that I am a ⲧⲁⲗ ($\delta\eta\mu\acute{o}\sigma\iota o\nu$)-
payer (lit bearer) I have need ($\chi\rho\epsilon\iota\alpha$) of pity for myself, this day, and that thou
mayest be aware ($\nu o\epsilon\hat{\iota}\nu$), ere to-day pass, that my fields are very But ($\dot{\alpha}\lambda\lambda\acute{\alpha}$) he maketh
pretence, saying, 'I wish for a deed ($\chi\acute{\alpha}\rho\tau\eta\varsigma$) regarding them' For ($\dot{\epsilon}\pi\epsilon\iota$) see, I hold my
deed ($\chi\acute{\alpha}\rho$) If he wish to come to the road, rightly ($\mu\epsilon\tau\grave{\alpha}\ \kappa\alpha\lambda o\hat{\nu}$), nay, I will
not go to him, till our lord, the renowned ($\epsilon\dot{\nu}\kappa\lambda\epsilon\acute{\epsilon}\sigma\tau\alpha\tau o\varsigma$) my deed ($\chi\acute{\alpha}\rho$) and
I approach ($\pi\rho o\sigma\epsilon\lambda\theta\epsilon\hat{\iota}\nu$) him on account of (?) and he let me go free
And ($\lambda o\iota\pi\acute{o}\nu$) I beg ($\pi\alpha\rho\alpha\kappa$) thee to speak with him, for it is 4 years that he hath paid
me nothing, and the year that he departed, he paid all the men their (money), but me
he paid not But ($\pi\lambda\acute{\eta}\nu$) let him pay me yearly, in what soever way he will And if
he wish to sow my fields henceforth, let him draw up for me a deed ($\chi\acute{\alpha}\rho$) regarding
them, if not, so let him deliver unto me my fields, with any land he will I greet thee
by these letters'

Verso [+ ⲧ]ⲁⲁⲥ ⲛⲡⲁⲡⲉ + [space] ⲫⲓⲃ + ϩⲓⲧⲛⲁⲡⲁ ⲕⲩⲣⲉ +

340.—Papyrus, complete, 19 × 17 cm Script clumsy, ligatureless, resembles that
of no 393 *Verso* → The *recto* is palimpsest, but both texts were perhaps by the same
scribe The earlier was insufficiently erased, and it is difficult to say to which text
ll 1-3 *recto* belong

  Letter from his servant, Agathonicus, to Apa Phoebammon He recounts his
dealings with the husbandmen of Pathethnoube and Pepôgm [10], whom he has employed
in certain agricultural processes [11] He tells of his difficulties (or experiments) with a
water-wheel (?), as to which he requests instructions There is also a question as to
reed gathering, but little of the whole can be confidently interpreted

---

¹ ϭⲓ perhaps implying oppression
² 'A hundred mercies' seems improbable
³ Altered   ⁴ 'A qualitative? or ϩⲓⲧ ⲱⲡⲉ?
⁵ V Cʀᴜᴍ, *Ostr* no 107 ⁶ For ⲙⲉⲓⲉⲓ
⁷ Possibly 2 or 3 letters at end One expects 'amir',
dux or *comes*

⁸ *Cf* no 318
⁹ Was ⲉⲣⲟϥ
¹⁰ For the 1st, *cf* ? Πⲉⲧⲟⲭⲛⲟῦⲃⲓⲥ (Ⲧⲟⲭⲛⲟῦⲃⲓⲥ), *BGU* 55²,
P Amh lxxı, the 2nd occurs perhaps in Kʀᴀʟʟ cxlv
¹¹ The verb *ⲛⲟⲩϭϩ* is difficult neither 'yoke' nor *coire
facere* (Lev xix 19) seems suitable to a meadow

✝ ϯτⲁⲗⲟ ⲛ̄ⲧⲉⲧⲛⲉⲙⲛ̄ⲧϫⲟⲉⲓⲥ ϫⲉ[ⲉⲓⲥ] ⲡⲉⲟⲩⲟⲓⲉ | ⲙⲡⲁⲧⲉⲑⲛⲟⲩⲃⲉ ⲁⲓⲣⲉⲩⲛⲁϩⲃ̄ ⲫⲟⲓ ⲙⲡⲟⲟⲩ
ⲉⲧⲉⲧ|ⲕⲟⲩⲓ ⲛⲉⲥⲧⲓⲁⲧⲉ[1] ⲛ̄ⲧⲁⲓⲕⲁ ⲡⲙⲟⲟⲩ ⲉϩⲟⲩⲛ ⲉⲡ|ⲥⲟⲟⲙ ⲙⲟⲛ ⲁⲛⲁⲡⲓⲡⲱϫⲙ ϩⲱⲟⲩ ⲧⲥⲟ ⲧⲉⲩⲭⲟ |
5 ⲉ︦ⲏ ⲛ̄ⲧⲁⲓⲯⲡⲱⲗⲥ̄ ⲟⲩⲛ ⲙⲛⲟⲩⲥⲛⲁ ϫⲟⲥ[2] | ⲁⲓⲧⲣⲉⲛ[. .].ⲁⲧⲉⲑⲛⲟⲩⲃⲉ ⲛⲁϩⲃ̄ ⲫⲟ[ⲓ] | ⲙⲟⲛ
ⲡⲉ[about 15 let] | ⲁⲩⲱ ⲁⲓⲭ[ⲟⲟⲩ ⲛ̄ⲧⲓⲉⲡⲓⲥⲧⲟⲗⲏ ⲙⲛⲧⲛ ⲛ]. ⲉϩⲁⲓ . . . ⲛⲁⲓ ⲡⲟⲟⲩ ⲥ . . ⲛ̄ⲧⲉⲫⲓⲗⲟⲩⲉ |
10 ⲥⲧϣⲁⲛⲟⲩϫⲉ ϣⲁⲧⲉⲓⲙⲉ ⲉⲧⲉⲥⲥⲟⲙ ⲁⲩⲱ | ⲧⲓⲟⲩⲁⲉ ⲧⲉⲡⲓⲥⲧⲟⲗⲏ ⲉⲧⲙⲙⲁⲩ ⲁⲛ ⲁⲩⲱ | ⲉⲓⲥ ϣⲟⲙⲛⲧ
ⲛ̄ϩⲟⲟⲩ ϫⲛ̄ⲧⲁⲓⲛⲁϩⲃ̄ ⲫⲟⲓ ⲛ̄ⲧ|ⲙⲟⲩ ⲁⲩⲱ ⲕⲁⲧⲁ ⲧⲉⲏ ⲛ̄ⲧⲁⲓϫⲟⲟⲥ ⲉⲣⲱⲧⲛ | ϫⲉⲁⲓϫⲓ ϣⲁⲗⲟⲟⲩ[3] ⲉⲡⲉ ϣ ⲟ ⲣ
ⲙⲡⲓϫⲓⲧⲉ | 15 ⲁⲓⲉⲛ ϣⲁⲗⲟⲟⲩ ⲉϩⲣⲁⲓ ⲁⲓⲙⲁⲣⲥ̄ ⲛⲃⲛ̄ | ⲁⲓⲧⲁⲁⲥ ⲉⲡⲉⲥⲛ̄ⲧ ⲧⲁⲛⲁⲩ ϫⲉϣⲁⲥϯ ⲧⲉⲓ|ϩⲁⲗⲟⲟⲩ[4]
ⲧⲁⲓ ⲉϣⲱⲡⲉ ϣⲁⲧⲉⲣⲉ ⲟⲩⲉⲓ ϩⲁ|ⲧⲏⲧ[ⲛ] ϫⲓⲧⲉ ⲉϣⲱⲡⲉ ⲙⲟⲛ ⲉϩⲣⲁⲓ ⲛ̄ⲧⲱϣ | ⲛⲁⲓ ⲧⲁ̄ⲧⲏ ⲛⲟⲩⲉⲓ[5] ϩⲁⲧⲏⲓ
ⲙⲟⲛ ⲛⲥⲁⲧⲉⲓ|20-ϩⲁⲗⲟⲟⲩ ⲧⲁⲓ ⲙⲉⲥϯ ⲁⲩⲱ ⲙⲛ ⲓ ⲛⲁⲓ | ϫⲉⲛⲟⲩⲱϣ ⲕⲱⲟⲣⲉ ⲛⲁϣ ϫ . ⲛⲉⲡⲫⲁ
ⲉϣⲱⲡⲉ | ⲙ̄ⲡⲓϣⲕⲱⲟⲣⲉ ⲛⲁⲧⲉⲅⲱ ⲛ̄ⲧⲁⲓⲉ ⲱϣ ϩⲓⲡⲁϩⲟⲩ | (recto) ⲙⲁⲗⲗⲟⲛ ⲧ(rest illegible) |
(illegible) ⲁⲩϫⲟⲟⲥ ϫⲉ [about 12 let] ⲛⲉⲥⲧⲁⲃⲗⲟⲛ ⲉⲓⲥ | ⲡⲉⲥⲣⲱⲙⲉ ⲁⲥⲉⲓ ⲧⲁⲁⲃ ⲛⲁⲥ ⲉϣⲱⲡⲉ
ⲉⲥϫⲓ ⲥⲟⲗ | 5 ϣⲓⲛⲉ ⲛⲥⲁⲡⲉⲥⲉⲣⲱⲥ ⲥⲟⲩⲧⲁⲁⲃ ⲛⲁⲃ ⲙⲟⲛ | ⲉⲓⲥ ⲥⲟⲟⲩ ⲛ̄ϩⲟⲟⲩ ϩⲛ̄ⲧⲟⲟⲧⲩ ⲃⲟⲏⲑⲓⲁ[6] ⲟⲩⲛ |
ⲧⲉⲧⲛⲉⲥϩⲁⲓ ⲛⲁⲓ ⲉⲧⲃⲉⲫⲱⲃ ⲛ̄ⲧϣⲁⲗⲟⲟⲩ | ⲙⲟⲛ ⲡⲛⲟⲩⲧⲉ ⲥⲟⲟⲩⲛ ϫⲉⲁⲓϣϫ ⲛⲛⲏⲩ ⲉⲣⲟⲥ ⲙ̄ⲙⲏⲛⲉ[7]
ⲉϣⲱⲡⲉ ⲁⲛⲟⲕⲛⲉ ⲉ ϣⲁⲓⲧⲛⲛⲉ ⲙⲟⲥ|10 ⲛ̄ⲃⲟⲗ ⲧⲁⲧⲓ[.].ⲉ ⲙⲟⲥ ⲟⲩϫⲁⲓ ϩⲓⲧⲛ̄|ϫⲟⲉⲓⲥ ϫⲉ[ⲥⲡⲟ]ⲧⲁ ✝

In the other direction ✝ ⲧⲁⲁⲥ ⲙ̄ⲡⲁϫⲟⲉⲓⲥ ⲁⲡⲁ [space] ⲫⲟⲓⲃⲁⲙⲙⲱⲛ ϩⲓⲧⲛⲡⲉⲧⲛⲉⲥⲁⲩⲟⲛ
ⲁⲃⲁⲑⲟⲛⲓⲕⲉ ✝. Beyond this, traces of 2 lines, in the hand of the earlier text, with witnesses' signatures

341.—Papyrus, almost complete, 11 × 18 cm   Script almost ligatureless   *Recto* ↑

Letter giving instructions regarding the treatment of certain vineyards   Above the text, a cross

ⲉⲡⲉⲓⲁⲏ
✝ ⲛ̄ⲧⲁⲡⲉⲓⲟⲩⲟⲓⲉ ⲉⲡⲟⲓⲛⲉ ⲉⲓ ⲉⲃⲧⲁⲗⲟ ⲙⲙ[ⲟ]ⲓ | ϫⲉⲉⲕⲁⲛⲁⲅⲕⲁⲍⲉ ⲙⲙ[ⲟ]ⲥ ⲧⲁⲣⲉϥⲕⲱⲧⲉ[8] ⲉ ⲛⲉⲥ ⲱⲙ |
ⲉⲡⲙⲁ ⲙⲡⲛ̄ⲓⲗⲗⲏⲥ[9] ⲁ[ⲓ]ⲑⲁⲩⲙⲁⲍⲉ ⲟⲩⲱϣ ⲟⲩ[ⲛ] |ⲙ̄ⲡⲉⲣ[ⲡⲁ]ⲣⲁⲅⲉ[10] ⲙⲙⲟϥ ⲁⲛⲓ ⲛⲉⲛⲟⲩϥ ⲧⲉⲙ-
ⲡⲁ ⲣⲙⲟ[11] | ⲡⲉⲛⲧⲁϩⲟⲓ ⲉϩⲣⲁⲓ ⲛⲥⲟⲟⲩⲧⲛ ✝

'Seeing (ἐπειδή) this husbandman of mine hath come and told me that thou dost compel (ἀναγκάζειν) him to water (?) the vineyards at Pma mpnilles, I was surprised (θαυμάζειν)   (My) desire therefore (οὖν) is   pass him not by (παράγειν) and bring the money, so that   .   properly'

Verso   the address .ⲉⲩ]ⲁⲟⲕⲓⲙⲱ̅ⲧ [space] (illegible)

342.—Papyrus, a fragment, 17 × 33 cm   Script ligatureless   *Recto* ↑   Above l 1, a cross

[1] Cf no 342 'The Little Fast' appears to commence the Pascha   assuming νηστία and ⲙⲟⲩⲣ ⲉϩⲟⲩⲛ identical, v Oxford MS Hunt 3, ⲣⲙⲑ, where the 3rd Sat in Mechir is headed ⲉⲭⲙⲡⲕⲩⲣⲓⲕⲙⲁ (v Crum, *Ostr*, no 18 n) ⲉⲧⲉⲛ-ⲕⲟⲩⲓ ⲙⲙⲟⲩⲣ ⲉϩⲟⲩⲛⲉ, while ⲣϫⲁ, the next Sat, is headed ⲡⲛⲟϭ ⲙⲙ ⲉϩⲟⲩⲛ=الصوم من السبت الثاني   V also Crum, l c, no. 60 n and Leipoldt in K Vollers's Leipzig Catalogue (1906), 421

[2] σύμμαχος   [3] V no 241

[4] V no 159
[5] Presumably διοικεῖ, as in ro 9
[6] V no 320
[7] ? 'The carpenter is expected daily'
[8] V no 158, 16, and Krall cxii
[9] A place?
[10] V Crum, *Ostr* no 61 n, Bi Mus no 462, but the meanings suggested scarcely suit here
[11] Quite uncertain   Perhaps ϫⲉⲙⲡⲉⲫⲙⲟ

Y

Letter from the headmen of Tóhe[1] to a superior, regarding 20 workmen engaged upon his dyke (χῶμα)

[+] ⲛϣ[ⲟ]ⲣⲡ [ⲙ]ⲉ[ⲛ] ⲛⲛϣⲁϫⲉ ⲧ[ⲉⲛ]ⲡⲣⲟⲥⲕⲩⲛⲉⲓ ⲛⲧⲉⲕⲙⲛⲧⲙⲉⲣⲓⲧ ⲛϫⲟⲉⲓⲥ ⲛⲥⲟⲛ ⲁⲛϫⲓ ⲛⲉⲥϧⲁⲓ
[ⲛ]ⲧⲉⲕ . . | ⲁⲩⲱ [ⲉ]ⲛⲃⲉⲡ[ⲉⲓ]ϫⲟⲩⲱⲧ ⲛⲣⲙ̄ . .[2] ⲉⲛ ⲡⲉⲕⲭⲱⲙⲁ ⲉⲛⲡⲁⲣⲁⲕⲁⲗⲉⲓ ⲛⲧⲉⲕⲙⲛⲧⲙⲉⲣⲓⲧ ⲛⲥⲟⲛ
ⲛ.ⲱ..ϩ... | ⲛⲣⲁⲥⲧⲉ ⲉⲧⲉⲧⲕⲟⲩⲓ ⲛⲉⲥⲧⲓⲁⲧⲉ[3] ⲛⲧⲙⲉⲛ ⲁⲡⲟⲕⲣⲓⲥⲓⲥ ⲛⲁⲛ ϣⲁⲛⲧⲱϣ ⲛⲛϧⲱϣ ⲧⲛⲧⲛⲛⲟⲟⲩ
ⲛⲉⲣ[ⲅⲁⲧⲏⲥ ⲛⲁ]ⲕ | ⲁⲩⲱ ⲡⲛⲟⲩⲧⲉ ⲡⲉⲧⲥⲟⲟⲩⲛ ⲙ̄ⲡⲉⲛⲛⲁ ⲛⲉⲛϫⲟⲉⲓⲥ ⲡ̄ⲭ̄ⲁⲣ̄[4] ⲧⲁϩⲟⲛ ⲧⲁⲗⲗⲁⲩⲏ[5] ⲛⲧⲁⲥⲉⲓ
ⲉϩⲣⲁⲓ ⲛⲧⲟⲥ ⲛⲛϣⲁⲛⲧⲛⲛⲟⲟⲩⲥ ⲉⲡⲉⲥⲏⲧ + ⲟⲩϫⲁⲓ ϩⲙⲡϫⲟⲉⲓⲥ +

Verso ⲧⲁ[ⲁⲥ   ?   ] ϩⲓⲧⲛⲛⲁⲡ[ⲛⲅⲉ] | ⲉⲛⲧⲱϩⲉ +

343.—Papyrus, 2 disconnected fragments, 10 × 11½, 13½ × 14 cm   Script sloping uncials   *Recto* ↑

Letter to a superior (perhaps an advocate), regarding dykes and canals, and the work to be done on them

ϩⲣ]ⲛⲧⲱⲣ[6] ⲧⲏⲣⲟⲩ ⲁⲩⲱ[| ⲉⲓⲱ]ⲧ ⲓⲱⲥⲏⲫ[7] ⲡⲁⲣⲭ[|]ⲟⲩ ⲙⲙⲟⲟⲩ ⲥⲟⲩ[| ⲃⲟⲏⲑⲉ ⲉⲣⲟⲛ ⲁⲛⲕⲁⲣ[|
[ⲡ]ⲁⲣⲭⲏ[?   ]. ⲧϥⲙⲟⲧⲛⲟⲩ ⲕ[ⲁⲗ]ⲱⲥ ⲧⲁϫⲣⲟⲟⲩ | ⲁⲣⲓ ⲁⲅⲁ[ⲡⲏ... .]ⲉⲛϣ[?   ϫ]ⲁⲧⲉ
ⲛⲡⲉⲛⲧ[8] ⲧⲓⲧⲁⲥⲧⲁⲛⲟ ⲡⲉⲛⲭⲱⲙⲁ ⲙⲟⲛ ⲃ̄ⲧⲁϫⲣⲏⲩ ⲕⲁⲧ[ⲁ   ?   ]ϩⲓⲧ ϫⲉϩⲱⲥ ⲁ ⲡⲛⲟⲩⲧⲉ ⲧⲓ
ⲧⲛⲛⲟϭ | ⲛⲥⲟⲫⲓⲁ ⲛⲏⲧⲛ ⲁⲧⲉⲧⲛⲉⲙ[9]   ?   ]ⲛⲕⲟⲩⲓ ⲉⲓⲙⲉ ⲁⲣⲓ ⲧⲁⲅⲁⲡⲏ ⲙⲁⲣⲉⲩ ⲙⲟⲩⲧⲛ ϥⲟⲗⲧ[10]
ⲛⲧⲁϥⲡⲱ[?   ]ⲡⲛⲟⲩⲧⲉ ⲉⲩⲕⲁⲁⲥ ⲉⲃⲟⲗ ⲛⲧⲕⲁⲓⲣⲟⲙⲡⲉ | ⲛⲁⲩⲧⲏⲣⲟⲩ ⲙⲟⲩⲧⲛ ϥⲟⲗⲧ [?   ]ⲁ
ⲉⲧⲛⲉϣⲁⲛⲣⲧⲁⲅⲁⲡⲏ ⲧⲉⲧⲛⲉϣⲓⲛⲉ | ⲥⲁⲫⲟϫ ⲡⲉϣⲁϥⲛ ⲙⲙⲟⲧⲛ[?   ]ϫ̄ ⲛⲧⲉⲛϣⲏⲣⲉ ⲛⲛⲉⲣⲱⲙⲉ
ⲥⲙⲙⲉ | ⲁⲩⲱ ⲉⲡⲉⲓⲇⲏ ⲁⲧⲛⲕⲉⲗⲉⲩ[ⲥ   ?   ]ⲅ̄ ⲟⲩⲏⲣ ⲛⲣⲱⲙⲉ ⲣϩⲱϥ ⲉⲧϫⲁⲧⲉ[11] | ⲛⲙⲁⲃ̄ⲧⲁⲥⲉ
ⲛⲣⲱⲙⲉ ⲣϩⲱ[ϥ   ? |] ⲡⲁϫⲟⲉⲓⲥ +

344.—Paper, a fragment, 8 × 11 cm   Script sloping, ligatureless

Letter relating to the building of a wall   Much is obscure. The writer complains that, of the 5 workmen (ἐργάτης) sent him, '3 are sick and not one hath done me proper[12] work'   Later he says 'I was at pains to write unto thee and thou hast not sent me any reply' (ἀπόκρισις)

]ⲉⲙⲙⲟⲓ ϩⲁⲛϩⲱϥ ⲛϫⲟ | ⲁⲩⲱ ⲡⲉⲛⲧⲁⲕⲟⲩⲟϭⲣⲉϥ[13] | ⲛⲁⲓ ⲡⲉϯⲟⲩ ⲛⲁⲣⲕⲁⲧⲉⲥ | ⲁϣⲟⲙⲉⲧ ϣⲱⲛⲉ
ϩⲓⲱⲱϥ | ⲁⲩⲱ ⲡⲉⲟⲩ ⲉⲣⲟϩⲣⲱϥ ⲉϥϣⲏϣ | ⲛⲁⲓ ⲁⲩⲱ ⲉⲣⲉⲡϥⲓⲗⲟ[14] ⲉⲧⲟⲉⲛϫⲟ ⲡⲛⲟⲩⲧⲉ ⲙⲉⲛⲁⲕ
ϩⲓⲡⲕⲟⲧ | ⲛϫⲟ ⲁⲩⲱ ⲉⲥ ⲧⲉⲕⲛⲟⲉⲛ[15] ϫⲉⲁⲡⲁⲗⲟⲩⲁⲕ ⲧⲁⲕⲟ ⲁⲩⲱ ⲙⲓⲕⲓ | ⲗⲟϭ ⲉⲙⲙⲁⲩ ϣⲟⲡ ⲧⲉⲕⲛⲟⲉⲛ |
(*verso*) ⲟⲩ ϩⲉⲣⲏϭ ⲛⲉϭⲟⲙⲉⲧ ⲛⲁⲓ | ⲙⲟⲛ ⲁⲓϩⲟⲥⲉ ⲉⲥϧⲁⲓ ⲛⲁⲕ | ⲡⲉⲕⲉⲣ ⲟⲩⲁⲡⲟⲕⲣⲟⲥ ⲛⲁⲓ | ⲁⲩⲱ

---

[1] *V* no 92, note, adding from Br Mus Or 6201 A &c , ⲧⲱϩⲉ ⲙⲡⲁⲗⲟⲩⲗⲟⲩ

[2] Assuming this an abbreviation for ἐργάτης   There is not space for the full word.

[3] *V* no 340   [4] χαρτουλάριος

[5] 'Discount' *V Pap Amh* xxxi, note, also here no 278

[6] A ῥήτωρ in *Pap Oxyrh* cli, perhaps in Br Mus no 1023 (reading there correct)

[7] ⲫ corrected from ⲡ

[8] First ⲓ perhaps erased   It has 2 dots, 2nd ⲓ has not

[9] ? διοικεῖν

[10] *V* nos 288, 387, where ⲙⲟⲧⲛ- seems to mean 'pay', 'deliver to'   In ZOEGA 299 ⲉⲙⲟⲧⲛⲉϥ simply = ποιῆσαι, *PG* 65, 372 D   [11] ⲉⲧϣⲁⲧⲉ

[12] I do not know whether ϣⲛϣ can be interpreted thus

[13] *V* no 368, Br Mus no 1143 and probably KRALL ccxxviii. 11

[14] Did the text show a Mid Eg tendency, one might read ⲉⲣⲉⲡϥⲓⲗ (ϩⲓⲡ) ⲗⲟ.

[15] νοεῖν   *V* no 337

ⲁⲓⲡϩⲱϥ ⲧⲁϥϩ|ⲣⲱϣϣ ⲉⲍⲟⲕ ⲁⲩⲱ ϣⲟⲡ | ⲙⲉⲕⲟⲩⲟϩ ⲛ̄ⲡⲟⲩⲙⲉ ⲡⲁⲓ | ⲙⲉⲡⲁⲣⲣⲁ. ⲅⲁ¹ ϣⲟⲡ ⲙ[ⲉ]ⲕⲓϩ̣ⲉⲩ
ⲟⲩⲣⲱⲙⲉ ⲟⲩⲟϩ ⲛ̄ⲉϩⲟⲙ|[ⲉⲧ   Along margin of *recto* ⲙⲉ ⲛⲁϥ ⲁϣⲟⲡ ⲙⲟⲛ, and of *verso*
ⲡϣⲓⲛⲉ ⲛⲁⲓ ⲧ̄ϣⲓⲛ[ⲉ

345.—Papyrus, a fragment, 10×8 cm   Script seldom ligatured   *Recto* ↑.
Letter containing nothing noteworthy except ⲁⲩⲱ ⲡϣⲁⲁⲣ ⲉⲛⲉϥⲓⲱ[ⲧ] and [ⲁⲩ]ⲱ ⲡϣⲁⲁⲣ
ⲉⲡⲓⲱⲧⲡⲉ ⲁⲣ ⲕ[, referring to the value² of barley
Verso part of a legal document

346.—Papyrus, complete, 18½×23½ cm   Script moderately ligatured   *Recto* ↑
Folded about 11 times in height and width
Letter from Iszem (هشم), son of Belal (بلال)³, to Severus, son of Bane⁴ It relates
to the fodder to be supplied by a certain village The letters ϥ and ⲩ (sing and plur) are
indistinguishable

+ ⲁⲩⲕⲟⲩⲓ ϩⲙⲡⲉⲕϩⲱϥ ⲉⲓ ϣⲁⲣⲟⲓ ⲙⲡⲉⲛⲧⲁⲕⲁⲁϥ ⲁⲩⲱ ⲁⲓⲛⲁⲩ ⲙⲡⲉⲓϩⲱϥ ⲡⲁⲓ | ⲁⲓⲣϩⲟⲧⲉ
ϫⲛⲧⲉⲕϩⲣⲟϣ⁶ ⲉϫⲛ̄ⲡⲣⲱⲙⲉ ⲉⲧϣⲟⲡ ϩⲣⲉ⁶ ⲉⲓⲥ ⲁⲙⲙⲱⲛⲉ ⲡⲛⲟⲧⲁⲣ⁷ | ⲁⲓⲧⲛⲟⲟⲩϥ ⲛⲁⲕ ⲗⲟⲓⲡⲟⲛ
ⲁⲛ[ⲁ]ⲩ ⲉⲡϩⲱϥ ⲛⲧ[ⲁⲓ]ϫⲛⲟⲩⲕ ⲉⲣⲟϥ ⲉⲛⲧⲁⲩϣⲟⲡ | ϩ[ⲣ]ⲉ ⲉϥⲏⲣⲧ ⲛϭⲓⲝ ⲙⲉϭⲓⲝ⁸ ϩⲣⲁⲓⲥϥ [..]ϫ ⲁⲩⲱ
ⲥϩⲁⲓ ϩ[..]ⲁⲓ⁹ ⲉϫⲛⲡⲉⲣⲱⲙ|ⲡⲧⲙ̄ⲉ ϩⲁⲡⲉϩⲣⲉ ⲉⲃⲟⲗ ⲛⲡⲣⲱⲙⲉ ⲛⲧⲁϥϣⲟⲡ ⲛϭⲓⲝ ⲙⲛϭⲓⲝ ⲁⲩⲱ | ⲡⲉⲧⲉϣⲁⲕϩⲣ
ⲧⲣⲟϥ ⲛⲧⲁϥϫⲟ ⲟⲩⲕⲁϩ ⲧⲛⲟⲟⲩϥ ⲛⲁⲓ ⲁⲩⲱ ⲟⲩⲱⲛⲁϩ ⲡϩⲱϥ ⲛⲁⲓ | ⲉⲃⲟⲗ ϫⲛⲧⲁϥϫⲟ ⲟⲩⲟⲩⲏⲣ ⲛⲥⲟⲩⲟ
ⲟⲩⲏⲣ ⲛⲓⲱⲧ ⲟⲩⲏⲣ ⲛϩⲣⲉ ⲏ ϫⲛⲧⲁϥϫⲟ | ⲉⲧⲁϣⲉ ⲏ ϫ[ⲏ]ⲧⲁϥϣⲟⲡ ⲡⲕⲁϩ ⲁϥϫⲟϥ ⲥϩⲁⲓ ⲡⲁⲓ ⲧⲏⲣϥ
ϩⲁⲣⲧⲕ ⲛⲡⲁⲧⲥⲕⲉϩⲁⲓⲥϥ | ⲛⲁⲓ ⲁⲩⲱ ⲛⲡⲣⲕⲱⲗⲩ ⲛⲣⲱⲙⲉ |ⲛ̄ⲧⲁⲩϣⲟⲡ ⲛϭⲓⲝ ⲙⲛϭⲓⲝ ⲉⲧⲉⲛⲛⲕⲁ¹⁰
ⲡⲉⲩϩⲣⲉ|ⲛⲁⲩ ⲉⲃⲟⲗ ⲧ̄ ⲑ ⲧⲩ/ ⲁ

'Somewhat of thy matter hath reached me, of what thou hast done, and I have seen this thing and have been afraid lest thou art hard upon the men that are buying fodder See here, I have sent unto thee **Ammonius, the notary** (νοτάριος) Now (λοιπόν) see to the matter as to which I enquired of thee, (namely,) that fodder hath been bought (while still) standing, and directly Write it   and write   against the villages for fodder, on account of (?) that man who bought directly And him thou shalt find to have sown land, send me, and set forth for me the matter, as to how much corn, how much barley, how much fodder he hath sown, or (ἤ) whether he hath sown up to the half, or (ἤ) whether he hath bought the land and hath sown it Write down all this for thyself, ere thou write it to me And hinder (κωλύειν) not such men as have bought directly, whose fodder we (?) do excuse them 9th Tubi, 4th Indiction'

Verso ⲋ συν ισζεμ υἱ βηλαλ [space] σευηρω βανου ⲋ

---

¹ After ⲁ a ligature or abbreviation Arabic?
² *V* no 201, also KRALL in *WZKM* xiv 234
³ *Cf* no 286
⁴ Severus (dat) is apparently the recipient, though he, as a rule, is named first S perhaps recurs elsewhere, *v* nos 117, 214
⁵ An elliptical subjunctive?   ⁶ *V* no 287

⁷ These 2 words inserted in a blank, in different ink. *V* perhaps no 150
⁸ *Lit* 'hand and *or* with hand' The phrase is unknown to me, it may refer to private dealing, regardless of the due contribution or of official inspection
⁹ Perhaps 3 letters missing, ϩⲁⲣⲟⲓ or ϩⲣⲁⲓ?
¹⁰ ⲉⲓⲉⲧⲛⲕ- might be read

Y 2

347.—Papyrus, complete, 6×21 cm. Script clumsy, ligatureless *Verso* → Not from the Ashmunaın collection

Letter from George to his 'father', Apa Kolthê (Colluthus), to whom he is sending beans Heracleopolis Magna is mentioned

+ ⲧⲁⲁⲥ ⲉⲡⲁⲓⲱⲧ ⲡⲁ ⲕⲟⲗⲑⲏ ϩⲓⲧⲉⲛⲅⲉⲱⲣⲅⲉ | ⲉⲓⲥ ⲝⲟⲩⲟⲧ ⲛⲉⲣⲧⲟϥ ⲛⲟⲩⲣⲱ ⲁⲗⲁⲩ ¹ ⲁⲓⲧⲉⲛⲟⲟⲩ-
ⲥⲟⲩ | ⲛⲁⲕ ⲛⲧⲁⲡⲁⲥⲟⲛ ⲙⲱⲩⲥⲏⲥ ⲡⲣⲙⲉϩⲛⲓⲥ ⲧⲁⲁⲩ ⲛⲁⲓ | ⲁⲩⲱ ⲟⲩⲟⲓⲡⲉ ⲧⲁⲣⲉⲕϥⲓⲧⲉ ⲛⲁⲕ ϣⲓⲛⲉ ⲛⲥⲟⲟⲩ
ϩⲓⲧⲉⲛⲡⲁˢⁱᶜ ⲓⲥⲁⲁⲕ ⲁⲩⲱ ⲉⲓⲥ ⲧⲟⲓⲡⲉ ⲁⲓⲧⲉⲛⲟⲟⲩⲅ ⲛⲁⲕ | ⲛⲧⲁⲓϣⲓⲧⲟⲩ ⲙⲟⲥ ⲁⲩⲱ + ⲟⲩϩⲟⲧⲉ ² ⲛⲏⲣⲡ
ⲛⲛⲉⲉϥ | ϩⲁⲣⲟⲟⲩ ⲟⲩⲝⲁⲓ ϩⲙⲡⲝⲟⲉⲓⲥ

Recto. + ⲧⲁⲁⲥ ⲉⲡⲁⲓ[space]ⲱⲧ ⲡⲁ ⲕⲟⲗⲑⲏ | ϩⲓⲧⲉⲛⲅⲉⲱⲣⲅⲉ

Parts of an earlier protocol, in large, brown characters, are visible on *recto*

'Here are 20 *artabae* of white beans which I have sent thee, of what my brother Moses from Hnıs gave to me And an *oıpe* (thereof I wish) that thou take for thyself Ask for them from the *papa* (?) Isaak And lo, I have sent thee the *oıpe*, having measured them therewith³ And give a *hots* worth of wine to the sailors as their wage Farewell in the Lord'

348.—Papyrus, a fragment, 13½×21 cm Script of the same type as nos 341, 360
V Pl 8 *Recto* ↑ Through the first lines, part of the Arabic protocol,]ﻋﻤﻞ

Letter from Simeon, his son, to Silôn⁴ He informs him that, thanks to God, who had guided him, Amrous⁵ had reached them safely Among the subjects of the letter are certain transactions in flax, but the script is difficult and details remain obscure

+ ⲥⲩⲛ ⲧⲓⲣⲏⲛⲏ ⲛⲛⲟⲩ ⲛⲁⲕ ⲙⲡⲉⲕⲥⲱⲟⲩϩ ⲉϩⲟⲩⲛ ⲧⲏⲣϥ ⲧⲓⲧⲁⲙⲱ ⲍⲉ ⲛⲙⲱⲛ ⲝⲉⲡⲟ| ⲡⲓⲥϩⲁⲓ
ⲛⲁⲕ ⲁⲡⲛⲟⲩⲧⲉ ⲝⲓ ⲙⲟⲉⲓⲧ ⲉⲁⲙⲣⲟⲩⲥ ⲁϥⲓ ⲛⲁⲛ ⲉϥⲛⲁϩⲙ ⲉⲗⲁⲁⲩ ⲉⲡⲉ⁶ ⲛⲉⲣⲙⲉ[ⲟ]ⲧ [ⲉⲡⲛⲟⲩⲧⲉ] | ϣⲏⲡ⁷
ⲁⲩⲱ ⲁⲓⲝⲓ ⲛⲧⲉⲕⲥϩⲁⲓ ⲁⲓⲱϣⲥ⁸ S ⲁⲓⲉⲓⲙⲉ ⲉⲡⲉⲧⲉⲛϩⲏⲧⲉ ⲉⲣⲉⲧⲁⲥⲟⲩⲣⲁ ⎾ | ⲑⲏⲛ ⲁⲡⲥⲙⲡⲟ⁹ ⲧⲁⲗⲱ ϩⲁⲟⲏⲛⲕ
ⲁⲕⲟⲩⲱⲣⲡ ⲛⲁⲡⲁ ⲗⲟⲅⲁ¹⁰ ⲛⲁⲓ ⲉϣⲟⲣⲡ ⲉⲙ[| ⲁⲕⲟⲩⲱⲣⲡ ⲛⲁⲓ ϩⲓⲡⲁⲥⲁⲅⲉ ϩⲁⲛ ⲁⲇ/ ⲁⲛⲥⲛⲧⲟⲩ ⲉⲩⲝⲏϥ¹¹
ⲁⲕⲝⲟⲟⲩ ⲛⲁⲓ [| ϩⲁⲛ ⲁⲇ/ ⲕⲇ ⲛⲧⲁⲥⲟⲩⲣⲁ ⲧⲁⲗⲱ ⲛⲛⲓϣⲁⲁⲣ ⲛⲁⲓ ⲁⲛ ⲟⲩⲇⲉ ⲛⲧⲛⲛⲁⲩ ⲉϩⲱⲃ ⲁ . ⲧ[|
ⲟ̄ⲣⲱ ⲛⲁⲕ ϩⲁⲛⲉⲥⲕⲉⲩⲉ ⲉⲧⲕⲏ ⲫⲓⲣ ⲉⲧⲟⲟⲧⲛ ⲝⲉϣⲱⲛ ⲁⲕⲕⲟⲃⲟⲩ ϩⲓⲝⲱ[| ⲁⲗⲗ ⲙⲉⲃⲓⲕⲛ ϩⲓⲟⲟⲩ ⲉⲩⲓ ⲛⲧⲁⲩⲉⲣ-
ⲟⲩⲟⲩⲙⲉⲧ ⲛⲁⲓ ⲛⲟⲛⲏϣ ⲁⲛ ⲁⲛϣⲱⲛ ⲛⲕⲟ̄ⲏ[| ϥⲟⲗ ⲁⲕⲥϩⲁⲓ ⲛⲁⲓ ⲝⲉⲉϥⲟⲗ ⲛⲉ ϩⲓ ⲛⲉⲥⲓⲙⲡ ⲛⲥ̄ⲓⲗⲗ¹² ⲛ̄ⲉⲛⲟⲛ
ⲙⲉⲩⲕⲛ̄ [| ⲣⲟⲙⲡⲉ ⲉϥⲓⲙⲉ ⲛⲛⲁⲥ̄ⲓⲗⲗ ⲛⲕⲟ̄ⲩϩⲃⲟⲥ¹³ ⲁⲩⲱ ⲁⲕⲥϩⲁⲓ ⲛⲁⲓ ⲝⲉⲛⲉⲥⲓⲙⲡ (above ⲛⲙⲱⲛⲥⲛⲥ)
ⲁⲕⲙ[| ⲧⲉϥⲉⲣϣⲉⲗⲉⲉⲧ ϩⲁⲛ ⲁⲇ/ ⲁⲩⲱ . ⲏ ⲝⲏⲕ ⲝⲉⲉϥⲟⲗ ⲛⲉ ϩⲓⲛⲁⲥ̄ⲓⲗⲗ [| ⲝⲉⲧⲙ[

---

¹ V Krall vııı ⲁⲗⲁⲩ often in the alchimistic texts (Stern, *Aeg Z* 1885, the Bodleian papyrı &c)

² V Crum, *Ostr* no 348

³ As in Matt vıı 2 &c Cf Krall lx

⁴ An unknown name

⁵ ﺱﺭﻣﻋ, elsewhere ⲁⲙⲃⲣⲟⲩ, ⲁⲙⲃⲣⲟⲥ

⁶ ⲛⲡⲉⲟⲟⲩ Cf the phrase in Krall ccxxvııı 3

⁷ V 2 Cor ıx 15

⁸ Fem ? because confused with ἐπιστολή

⁹ The letter above is for ⲟⲩ, in ll 9, 10 apparently

different

¹⁰ Recurs *Ann du Service* vııı 84

¹¹ Cf Br Mus no 1103, γεννημα ⲉϥⲝⲏϥ The word is also applied to vinegar, *ıb* 161, Bodl Pap Copt *a* 1, here no 317, Berl *Kopt Urk* 21 (2), 7, to nıtre In these instances 'acid, sour' (cf Peyron, ⲝⲏⲃ) is more fitting than 'hot'

¹² ⲥ̄ⲓⲗⲗⲉ or ⲥ̄ⲓⲗⲗⲁ Cf ? ﺩﺟﻞ 'corn-stalks', Lane

¹³ Altered

Verso ⲓⲛⲕⲉⲱⲟⲩϩ ⲗⲁⲁⲩ ⲁⲩ· ⲉϩⲟⲩⲛ ⲛⲏⲓ ⲉϩⲣⲏⲧ ϧⲙⲡⲟⲩⲱϣ ⲙⲡⲛⲟⲩⲧⲉ ⲁⲩⲱ ⲙ[| ⲡⲉ ⲥⲟⲩ-
ⲗⲁⲙⲁⲛ ⲙⲟⲛ ⲛⲉϥⲥⲡⲛ ⲥⲙⲟⲛⲧ ⲁⲛ ⲟⲩⲭⲁⲓ ϧⲙⲡⲭⲥ *sic*

The address is + ⲧⲁⲁⲥ ⲥⲡⲁⲙⲉⲣⲓ ⲙⲓⲱ ⲥⲓⲗⲱⲛ [space] ϧⲓⲧⲛⲥⲩⲙⲉⲱⲛ ⲡⲉϥϣⲏⲣ

349.—Papyrus, 16 × 23½ cm. Script ligatured and difficult, perhaps that of no 372
V Pl 8   *Recto* ↑

Letter from Apa Kire (Cyrus) to his 'dear father', Mena   So little has been read
with certainty, that the sense remains obscure   It relates to business transactions, sums
of money[1] and *litræ* of flax (σιππον = στίππιον) being mentioned   Arabic words occur

+ ϧⲙⲡⲣⲁⲛ ⲉⲡⲛⲟⲩⲧⲉ ⲛϣⲟⲣⲡ ϩⲱⲃ ⲛⲓⲙ [. . ⲉⲓⲥϧⲁⲓ ⲉⲓϣⲓⲛⲉ ⲡⲁⲙ[ⲉⲣⲓⲧ] | ⲛⲓⲱⲧ ⲙⲙⲛⲁ
ⲙⲙⲡⲁⲙⲉⲣⲓⲧ ⲛⲥⲟⲛ ⳁⲁⲭⲁⲣⲓⲁⲥ [about 14 let]ⲁⲩ ⲙⲛⲫ·ⲉ ⲙⲛⲁⲓⲉ [|] ⲙⲛⲟⲩⲛⲟⲃⲉⲣ ⲙⲡⲟⲩⲭⲁⲓ
ⲡⲁⲡⲉⲕⲏⲓ ⲧⲏⲣϥ ⳅⲓⲡⲉⲕⲟⲩⳝ ϣⲁⲡⲛⲟϭ ⲧⲓⲧⲁⲙⲟ ⲕⲙⲟⲕ ⲡⲁⲓⲱⲧ ⲭⲉⲣϣⲁⲛⲡⲛⲟⲩⲧⲉ ⳅⲓ ⲙⲟⲉⲓⲧ[2] ⲉⲭⲁⲏⲗ
ⲡϣⲱⲧ ⲉⲥⲟⲩϣⲓⲛⲉ[3] ⲧⲟⲟⲧϥ ⲛⲥⲁⲟⲩ. . | 5 ⲉⲣⳅ·η ϧⲓⲱⲱⲥ ⲛϣⲁⲣⲉⲡⲛⲟⲩⲧⲉ ⳅⲓ ⲙⲟⲉⲓⳅ [ⲛ]ⲁϥ
ⲧⲏⲉⲓ ⲧⲟⲟⲧⲕ ⲥϧⲁⲓ ⲡⲉϥ . . | ⲛⲁⲓ ⲛⲉⲩⲗⲓⲥⲓⲁ[4] ⲁⲩⲱ ⲡⲁⲓⲱⲧ ϣⲉⲡⲛⲟⲩⲧⲉ ⲁ[.]ϣⲁⲁⲣⲁⲧ ϣⲁⲧ . . . ⳅⲉⲛ
. . | ⲛⲧⲁⲩⲛⲧⲟⲩ ⲁⲩⲱ ⲛⲁⲧⲡⲉⲩϧⲟⲕϧⲏ[5] ⲙⲟⲛ ϣⲉⲡⲛⲟⲩⲧⲉ ⲛⲏⲓ . . ⲕⲥ ϧⲓⲁⲓ ⲟⲩⲁ | ⲁⲡⲓⲥⲛⲉ ⲃⲟⲗ
ϧⲓⲟϥ ϧⲁⲥⲕⲁⲩ . .ⲑⲉ ⲛⲓⲧⲁⲩⲉ ⲉϧⲟⲩⲛ ⲉⳅⲱⲓ ⲁⲩⲱ ⲡⲁⲓⲱⲧ ϣⲱⲡⲉ ⲁⲡⲛⲟⲩⲧⲉ ⳅⲓ ⲙⲟⲉⲓⲧ ⲉⲡⲓϧⲏⲩ
ⲡⲁⲧⲗⲟⲕⲉ ⲁⲛⲏⲓ : η ⲉⲓ ⲧⲟⲟⲧⲕ . ⲕ ⲥϧⲁⲓ | 10 ⲛⲁⲓ ⲁⲩⲱ ⲡⲁⲓⲱⲧ ⲛⲧⲁ λ̄ κθⳝ ⲥⲓⲡⲡⲟⲛ ⲥⲉⲉⲛⲉ ϧⲁⲧⲛⲓ
ⲙⲟⲛ ⲁⲓ . . . . . | ⲛⲁⲕ ⲟⲩⲁⲓ ⲥⲟⲡ ⲁⲗⲗⲁ ⲉⲣⲉⲡⲛⲟⲩⲧⲉ † ⲭⲁⲣⲓⲥ ⲉⲣⲟϥ ϣⲁⲓⲭⲟⲩⲥⲟⲩ ⲛⲁⲕ ⲁⲩⲱ
ⲡⲁⲓⲱ|ⲧ ⲁⲓⲧⲡⲧⲱⲛⲟⲩ ⲭⲉⲣϣⲁⲛⲡⲛⲟⲩⲧⲉ ⲡⲓⲱⲉ[6] ⲧⲟⲩⲕⲱ ⲃⲟⲗ ⲛⲟⲉ [ⲛ]ⲧⲁⲗⲁⲩ | ⲕⲁⲧⲁ λ̄ ιβⳝ ϧⲁ : α
ϧⲛⲁⲗⲟⲩⲥⲁⲧ . . ⲉⲣϣⲁⲛⲡⲛⲟⲩⲧⲉ ⲡⲓⲱⲉ ⲧ[ⲟⲩ]ⲕⲱ ⲃⲟⲗ | ⲛⲟⲉ ⲛⲧⲛⲁⲩ ⲛⲛⲉⲗⲁⲁⲩ ⲕⲱⳅⲟⲩ ϣⲁⲣⲉ-
ⲡⲛⲟⲩⲧⲉ ⲕⲏ : α ⲉϧⲣⲁⲓ ϧⲓⲱⲱϥ | 15 ⲡⲁⲗⲭⲁⲗⲏⲥ ⲛⲏⲧⲛ ⲉⲩⲕⲱ ⲃⲟⲗ . ⲁⲗⲗⲁ ⲧⲓⲟⲩⲱϣ ⲡⲁⲃⲏⲕⲉ
ϧⲓⲱⲃ | ⲧⲉⲕⲟⲩⲱϣ η ⲓⲕⲇ′ ϧⲁⲧⲛⲓ ϧⲁⲛⲥⲓⲡⲡⲟⲛ ⲛⲧⲁⲓⲕⲁⲁⲩ ⲉⲃⲟⲗ ϧⲁⲧⲛⲙⲉⲣⲟⲩⲁⲛ[8] | ⲁⲩⲱ ⲡⲛⲟⲩⲧⲉ
ⲡⲉⲧⲥⲟⲟⲩⲛ ⲭⲙⲡⳅⲛ : ⲕⲇ′ ⲟⲩⲁⲗⲁ ⲧⲉⲩ : μή ⲁⲓ ⲭⲛⲟⲥ ⲉⲃⲟⲗ | . . . ⲧϣⲓⲛⲉ ⲉⲣⲟⲕ ⲟⲩⳅⲁⲓ ϧⲙⲡⳅⲟⲉⲓⲥ[9] |
(*verso*) ⲟⲩⲁⲗⲁ ⲁⳅⲓⲧⲉ ⲥⳅⲁⲕⲉ ⲁⲓⲟϭⲙⲉ ⲁⲩⲱ ⲁⲓⲥϧⲁⲓ ⲛⲁⲕ ϧⲁ ϧⲁⲧⲭ|20 ⲛϧⲁⲗⲃⲉⲉⲥ[10] ⲗⲟⲓⲡⲟⲛ ⲡⲁⲓⲱⲧ
ⲛⲡⲉⲡϧⲱϥ ⲧⲓ ⲥⲙⲟⲛ ⲛⲁⲕ ⲁⲕⲥϧⲁⲓ ⲛⲁⲓ ⲁⲗⲗⲁ | ⲡⲁⲓⲱⲧ ⲧⲓⲥⲟⲟⲩⲛ ⲁⲛ ⲉⲡⲁⲥⲏⲩ ⲁⲛⲟⲕ ϧⲁⲧⲏⲕ ⲁⲗⲗⲁ
ϣⲱⲡⲉ ⲡϧⲱϥ ⲧⲓ ⲉⲙⲧⲟⲛⲁⲕ ⲧⲉⲕⲭⲟⲩϥ ⲛⲁⲓ ⲛⲟⲥ ⲉϥϧⲟⲩϩ ϧⲁⲧⲏⲕ ϣⲱⲓ ϣⲁⲕⲡⲓⲟⲉ ϧⲁⲧ : ⲥ ⲉⲓ[11]
ϣⲁⲓ|ⲧⲁⲁⲥ ⲛⲁⲕ ϣⲱⲡⲉ ⲧⲉⲕⲡⲓⲟⲥ ⲧⲓⲣⲏⲛⲏ ⲛⲁⲕ[12] ⲁⲩⲱ ⲡⲁⲓⲱⲧ . η   ϣⲓⲛⲉ ⲛⲣⲱⲙⲉ ⲧⲏⲣⲟⲩ ϧⲁⲧⲛⲓ
ⲕⲁⲗⲱⲥ ⲁⲩⲱ ⲡⲁⲓⲱⲧ ⲉⲓⲁⲕⲱⲛ ⳅⲓⲛⲟⲩⲓ ⳅⲡ[. . .] ⲭⲉⲣ|25ϣⲁⲛⲡⲛⲟⲩⲧⲉ ⳅⲓ ⲙⲟⲉⲓⲧ ⲉⲣⲙⲛⲁ ϣⲓⲛⲉ
ⲧⲟⲟⲧϥ ⲛⲥⲁ : ⲕⲉ ⲛϧⲟⲗⲟⲕ ⲉⲧⲟⲟⲧϥ | ⲁⲩⲱ ⲁϥⳅⲟⲟⲥ ⲭⲉϣⲓⲛⲉ ⲧⲓⲭⲁⲏⲗ ⲟⲛ ⲛⲥⲁⲕⲓ λ̄ ⲓⲉ ⲁⲩⲱ ⲡⲁⲓⲱⲧ
[. . .] | ⲉⲣⲟⲕ ⲁⲩⲱ ⲙⲉⳅⲏⲩ[13] ⳅⲉϣⲱⲡ ⲡⲉⲥⲛⲁⲩ ⲕⲁⲗⲓⲕⲉⲛ[14] ⲛⲁⲓ ⲁⲩⲱ ⲡⲁⲓⲱⲧ ϣⲉⲡⲛⲟⲩⲧⲉ

---

[1] The : preceding the figures should stand for ϧ̄
[2] V *Mitth. Ram* v 46
[3] Alternative readings, ⲡϣⲱ ⲧⲉⲛⲟⲩ
[4] εὐλογία 'safety' V Bi Mus no 1155
[5] Reading certain   A new verb, unless = ϧⲟⳅϧⳝ
[6] This locution in KRALL cxxviii 19
[7] Cf ⲉⲓⲣⲉ ⲡⲁⲗⳝⲁⲁⲗⲏⲥ الحلال (STERN), *Aeg Z* 1885,
104, 118

[8] مروان
[9] *Verso* continues the text, notwithstanding this final
salutation
[10] Perhaps -ⲃⲉⲉ only
[11] For ⲉⲓⲉ. V no 353
[12] Presumably = 'it is well'
[13] V no 352   [14] καλίγιον

пικ, ⳾ αϥ[1] ⲛⲧⲁⲡⲉϩⲁⲓ ⲛⲁⲓ ⲍⲉⲛⲁⲧⲕⲱⲣⲁⲛⲉ ⳽ⲡⲉⲡⲛⲟⲩⲧⲉ ⲛⲡⲓ⳽ⲛⲏ ⲗⲁⲁⲩ | ϧⲓⲟϥ ⲛⲡⲉⲓ · β ⲉⲩ⳽ⲱⲙⲉ
ⲁⲓⲧⲁⲁⲩ ⲕⲁⲧⲁ λ̅ ⲓⲁ ϧⲁ : α ⲧⲓⳝⲓⲛⲉ ⲉⲣⲟⲛ ⲕⲁⲗⲱⲥ

In other direction

+ ⲧⲁⲁⲥ ⲡⲁⲙⲉⲣⲓⲧ ⲛⲓⲱⲧ ⲙⲏⲛⲁ (ϧⲗⲟ below) + [space] ϧⲓⲧⲛⲁⲡⲁ ⲕⲓⲣ̀ ⲡⳝⲏⲣ̀

350—Papyrus, a fragment, 17×12 cm　Script thin, ligatured　*Recto* ↑
Letter of instructions as to transactions relating to wine (?), flax, ropes, corn and money

]ⲕⲟⲟⲩ ⲛⳝⲉ ⲛⲕⲟⲗⲁⲑⲛ ⲛⲁⲛ ⲧ[| ⲧⲁⲧⲁⲭⲏ[2] ⲧⲁⲧⲁⲁⲩ ⲉⲃⲟⲗ ϧⲁⲧⲛⲟ[ⲟⲩ |]ⲣⲟϥ ⲁⲩⲱ ⳽ⲓ ⲛⲉⲓⲁⲥ-
ⲫⲁⲗⲓⲁ ⲛⲧⲟⲟⲧϥ ⲛⲙ[|] ⲉⲣⲟϥ ⲧⲉϥⲧⲁⲗⲟ ⳝⲏⲧ ⲙⲉ[ⲥ]ⲛⲧⲉ ⲛⲕⲟⲗⲁⲑ[ⲛ[3] |] ⲛⲡⲙⲏⲛⲧ ⲛϧⲟⲗ°, ⲛⲡⲓⲙⲁ
ⲁϥⳝⲛⲟⲩⲓ[|]ⲧⲁⲧⲓ ⲡⲁⲅⲉⲛⲛⲙⲁ ⲛⲁⲕ ⲗⲟⲓⲡⲟⲛ ⳽̅ | ⲧⲏ]ⲟⲟⲩ ⲛⲁⲓ ⲉϧⲏⲧ ⲁⲩⲱ ⲅⲉⲛ⳽ⲁⲧϥ ⲛⲕⲟⲗⲗ[|]ⲉ-
ⲥⲓⲡⲡⲱⲛ ⲛⲁⲓ ⲙⲛⲛⲉⲥⲡⲁⲣⲧⲱⲛ ⲙⲛ[ⲁⲩ]ⲱ ⳽ⲛⲟⲩ ⲫⲟⲓⲃⲁⲙⲱⲛ ⲛⲡⲉⲣⲕⲁⲍ[|]ⲉⲧⲁⲉⲓ ⲉⲣⲏⲥ ⲁⲩⲱ ⲛⲡⲉⲣⲧⲓ
ⲧⲟⲡⲉ ⲛⲣⲱⲙⲉ[|] ⲛⲙⲟϥ ⲉϧⲁⲓ ⲛⲁⲓ ⲁⲩⲱ ⲁϧⲉⲣⲁⲧⲕ ⳽ⲁⲛⲧⲟⲩⲁ[|] ⲁⲩⲱ ⳽ⲁⲧ ⲡ⳽ⲛⲕⲟⲩⲙⲉⲧⲁ[4]
ⲛⲡ⳽ⲟⲙⲉⲓ ⲛϧⲟⲗ[ϥ |]ⲧⲱⲛ ⲏ ⲛⲟⲩϥ ⲁⲩⲱ ⲁⲣⲓ ⲡⲣⲟⲟⲩ⳽ ⲛⲡⲱ ⲕⲁⲗ[ⲱⲥ |]ⲟ⳽ ϧⲓⲡⲁϧⲟⲩ | (*verso*)
] ⲕⲁⲗⲱⲥ ⳽ⲁⲛⲧⲟⲩⲧⲁⲗⲟ ⲧⲉⲩⲙⲟⲩⲛⲉ [|]ϧⲏⲓ ⲉⲛⲁⲛⲟⲟⲩ ⲁⲩⲱ ⳽ⲛⲟⲩ ⲁⲛⲁⲥⲧⲁ[ⲥⲥ |] ⲛⲧⲉϥⲃⲓ ⲧϥ⳽ⲏⲧ
ⲛⲕⲟⲩⲗⲁⲑⲛ ⲉⲩⲧⲁⲕⲏ[ⲩ |]ⳝⲓ ⲥⲛⲁⲩ ⲛϧⲟⲗⲟⲕ[ⲧ ⲛⲓⲥⲟⲩ ⲛⲡ⳽ⲁ[|]ⲡⲉⳝⲱⳝ ϥ⳽ⲁⲛⲏⲣⲡ ⲉⲡⲓ ⲁⲓⲧⲁⲁⲩ
ⲛⲁϥ [|]ⲉ ⲛⲛⲉⲛⲉⳝ ⳽ⲁⲛⲧⲉⲩ[⳽]ⲟⲟⲩ ⲛⲁ[|]ⲟⲟⲩ ⲡⲉⲩⲣⲱⲙⲉ ⲉϧⲏⲧ ⲛⲉⲙⲁ[|] . . ϧⲙⲡⳝⲟⲉⲓⲥ +

351.—Paper, a fragment, 8½×8 cm　Script moderately ligatured, but difficult
Letter greeting Abū Geber[6] and relating to wine, corn &c.

]ⲛⲁⲓ ⲁⲩⲱ ⲡ⳽ⲏⲛ̄ ⲛ⳾̄ ϭⲉⲡⲉⲣ[6] |] ⲁⲩⲱ ϧⲛ ⲡⲉϥ⳽ⲏⲛ̄ ϧⲁⲣⲟⲓ |]⳽ⲁⲣⲟϥ ϭⲟⲡ ⲕⲱⲗⲗⲟⲅⲑ ⳽ⲱ |
]ⲙ ⳽̄ ⲥⲛⲁⲩ ⲉⲛⲁⲗϭⲱⲣⲱⲡ[7] |]ⲛϧ . ⲉⲓ ⲁⲩⲱ ⲧⲛⲟⲟⲩ ⳗ̄ δ |]ⳝⲓ ⲡⲉⲥⲟⲩⲟ |]ϧⲟⲟϥ ⲁⲩⲱ |

Verso　Arabic (earlier).

352—Papyrus, a fragment, 18½×19 cm　Script of relatively early type; *v* Pl **5**
Recto ↑

Letter from　　　　to his 'dear lord', Apa Colluthus　It relates to corn which the
writer had been bidden to send, to orders received from the *comes* and to various other
matters

The idiom shows several semi Achmīmic forms[8]

ⲡ]ⲣⲙⲣⲟⲧⲟ[9] ⲁⲡⲁ ⲕⲟⲗⲗⲟⲅⲑⲉ ϧⲁⲑⲛ ⲙⲛ ⲛⲣⲱ⳽ | ⲧ]ⲉⲕⲙⲉⲧⳝⲟⲉⲓⲥ ⲕⲉⲗⲉⲅⲉ ⳽ⲉⲧⲁⲗⲟ ⲛⲉⲥⲟⲩⲟ |
]ⲙⲡⲟⲩⲉⲉⲓ ⲛⲣⲱⲙⲉ ⲉⲛⲏϧⲉ ⲛⲁⲓ ⲅⲁⲣ ⲛⲓ |]ⲉⲉⲥ ⲛⲁⲓ ⳽ⲉⲉ⳽ⲁⲓ ⲛⲉ⳽ⲓ ⳨ⲟⲩ ⲛⳝⲉ ⲛⲣⲧⲟⲃ |] ⲡⲉⲭⲉⲃ ⳽[ⲉⲁ-
ⲡ]ⲕⲟⲙⲉⲥ ⲕⲉⲗⲉⲅⲉ ⲛⲁⲓ ⲛ⳨ϧⲉ ⲁⲓ⳽ⲓⲥⲉ ⲙⲡⲓⳝⲉⲛ | ⲡⲕⲟ]ⲙⲉⲥ ⲙⲁⲣⲉⲃⲥϧⲁⲓ ⲉⲣⲏⲥ ⲛⲉⲃ ⲉⲡⲓ ⲡⲣⲟⲥ ⲑⲉ
ⲉⲓⲙⲉ[10] ⲉⲣⲟⲃ ⲉⲃⲙⲉⲉⲩⲉ |]ⲛⲥⲉⲡⲉ ϧⲁⲉⲃⲣⲉ ⲥⲱ⳽ⲉ ⲛⲧⲉⲣⲓⲉⲙⲉ ⳽ⲉⲁⲃⲕⲱⲧⲉ ⲥⲛⲁⲧⲉ | ⲉⲡ]ⲓⲥⲧⲟⲗⲙⲁ[11] ⳽ⲁⲧⲉ-

---

[1] Or ⲡⲓⲕⲓ　The oblique stroke may = κεράτια
[2] V Br Mus no 1141
[3] Κόλλαθον, κολλάθιον is treated as fem in KRALL
cccxxiv *Mitth Rain* v 32, Br Mus nos 334, 657, 1097,
1041 (ⲥⲛⲧⲉ ⲛⲕ, but ⲥⲛⲁⲩ⳽ⲟ ⲛⲕ)
[4] This compound name recurs in CRUM, *Copt MSS*
no lii, cf ? *Mission franç* iv 702　ⲕⲟⲩⲙⲏⲛⲧⲉ alone n

REVILLOUT, *Actes* 74, ⲕⲱⲙⲏⲛⲧⲓ in ? Jköw frag
[6] Cf Br Mus nos 586, 707, Rainer *Führer*, Taf viii,
ⲁⲃⲟⲩ ϭⲁⲃⲁⲣ
[6] Or ϭⲉⲡⲓⲣ　حراب, pl of حَرْب[7]
[8] ⲛⲉⲉⲓ, ⲛⲉⲃ, ⲉⲛⲏϧⲉ, ⲛⲉⲭⲉⲃ, ⲁⲧⲛ, ⲁⲛ-, ⲥⲟⲟⲩⲛⲉ　Cf
nos 270 &c
[9] V no 208
[10] Altered　Perhaps ⲉⲓⲣⲉ　[11] ἐπίσταλμα　V below

παχοεις ει αιχοοβ εροв χεκαατ τααπ |]ηρ εвϣογειτ ииεχεв χεειογωϣ ηααπογχοογε¹ |
α]τπς τα λοιπον εϣωπε ηαερταταπη ηcει ερηc τι |]κογλητη² αη εει ϙιχι επιстολη ητε
πκοιιεc τεπιρωιιε |]ογτε ηταιερвολ εcηϣε ηικογι cοογηε τηρογ ηπραιιῖῖ³ |]οвε εροογ
επι ηαвωη ϙιηεει αη χιταιαπε πχοι ϙιι |] εηαχι ϣητ ταιογ ηρтов ηαρϣιη ηcαπογ εροη
ηcογο |] ιιε ειc πεπιстολιια ητοοτ αγω αιταλο ηεει επχοι ιιπωρ εв | χ]ειλιαc τετρακοcιαc
ογκтοηκοηта ⁱⁱᶜεπια⁴ тηοογ πογω ηαι ηϙωв ηιιε |] οε тαϙοι ιιηηεχηγ εcгραφ/ αποcοιι/
α χ η ιηα/ + + +

Verso. +тααc ιιπαιιεριт ηχοε[ιc [

In the other direction]χεαιικογι χοοв χεηαχι ηρηπ αη εϣ⁵ (blank)

353 —Papyrus This is the *verso* of no 125 Script ligatureless. Fibres →
Letter relating to transactions regarding dates and corn

ϯ ϙаογ ιιεη ηϙωϥ ηιιε τιϣιηε εροκ η[| ιιητεκϙιιιε ιιηηεκϣηρε ιιη[| ηηα⁶ επιтη
αιπωρχ ηειιακ та[| вγηε ιιιηογтριιιηcιη ϙαπιιητ [| εηρтογ ηвγηε αγει ετοοт ката
п[| ιιηcιη ιιωη πηογτε πεταπληρογ [| ει⁷ χι ιαχι πετριιηcιη εχωcογο⁸ η[| ιιακ
ϣαπεχγηοογ αγ[α]ιιαϙε ιιοι [| ηρтογ ηcογο ϙαροϥ татааγ ηта[| τι ϙιιιε ϙαροογ εϣωπε
ϯⁱⁱᶜтcοογ[ι]η | αγω ηcτι ϙγιιε ϙαροογ ει ταιιοει т[| ϣαρεπεϥϙωϥ cωп ϣιιογιη ηρтογ
ηc[ογο | πεταχιτϥ ετεπετωπ⁹ cωп ϣιιο[γη | [.]ϙ εροη ειιπεκτι η[| ιιωη ϣεπηογтε
ωκο[| εχωει ϙαητειιοcιωη ιι[| ιιηι[| τι παϣη[| ϙατηκ ιι[

On *recto*: ϯ тααc ηη[

354. —Papyrus; a fragment, 9 × 11 cm Script rarely ligatured *Verso* →

Verso Letter from the priest (ἱερεύς) Enoch of Tesh   ¹⁰, his 'servant', to Apa
Shenoute, a διοικητής¹¹ Corn is the subject dealt with But the text is palimpsest and
often hard to read

ϯ πετηcαγοη εηωχ φιερεγc¹² ητεϣ[| απα ϣεηογтε παικαιτηc ϙαθη ιιεη [| ηογοcιϣ
ηιιε cc χε τιταιιο ιιιιοη χε[| ετιιαπαcογ. λη¹³ ακχοοc χεια[| ιιπεκι ηcαcογο ειc παιωτ
ϯ[| ϣε πηογϯ ηcαογοιπε ηογ[| ηαв εвχω ιιιιοc ερεπεϥ [| ϣοοπ ηαη αη[| таιιιαγ χ+η[

Recto The address·]παικαιτηc ϙιτηπεϥcαγοη εηωχ and traces of an earlier text
(perhaps not that visible on *verso*)

---

¹ Plur of ἀποχή *V* no 311
² ? Contains the verb κωλυειν *Cf* no 277
³ ? γράμμα
⁴ These high figures recall no 310
⁵ This presumably relates to the preceding text, but is
suddenly broken off
⁶ ? For ηηαπεκηι

⁷ For ειε? *Cf* Br Mus no 1116, here no 349
⁸ ω altered
⁹ The т in ιωη and in l 6 та is almost identical with ϭ
¹⁰ *Cf* τεϣηκ, perhaps a place, KRALL cxxx
¹¹ *V* no 369
¹² Priest as 'servant' in no 355·
¹³ Or ϫ for λ Perhaps contains αἴτημα.

355 —Papyrus, a fragment, $7\frac{1}{2} \times 21\frac{1}{2}$ cm   Script almost ligatureless   *Recto* ↑

Letter from 'your servant Apollo' the ἱερεύς[1], to a superior, mentioning 40,000 reeds, 4 workmen and a measure[2] of honey

[+ ⲡⲉ]ⲧ[ⲡⲉ]ⲥⲁⲟⲩⲟⲛ ⲁⲡⲟⲗⲗ[ⲱ ⲡ]ⲣ]ⲉⲣⲉⲟⲥ ⲡⲉϥⲧⲟⲗⲙⲁ ⲉϥⲥϩⲁⲓ ⲁⲉ| [ϩ]ⲁⲑⲏ ⲙⲉⲛ ϩⲱⲃ ⲛⲓⲙ
ⲧⲓⲡⲣⲟⲥⲕⲏⲛⲉ ⲙⲡⲉⲟⲟⲩ ⲛⲧⲉⲧⲛⲉⲙⲉ[ⲧⲭⲟⲉⲓⲥ | ⲭⲟⲉⲓⲥ ⲭⲉⲉⲓⲥ ⲡⲉϥⲧⲟⲟⲩ ⲛⲧⲃⲁ ⲛⲕⲁϣ ⲁⲡⲉϥⲧⲟⲟⲩ
ⲛⲣⲕⲁⲧⲏⲥ [| ⲉⲃⲁⲣⲟⲉⲓⲥ ⲉⲣⲱⲧⲛ ⲙⲉⲡⲕⲁⲡ ⲉⲛⲉϥⲓⲱ ϣⲟⲟⲛ ϩⲁⲧⲏ[

Verso]ϧⲟ [space] ⲭⲙ̅ⲙ̅ ϥⲟ ⳨⳨⳨

356 —Papyrus, a fragment, $6\frac{1}{2} \times 7\frac{1}{2}$ cm   Script very small, ligatured   *Recto* ↑

Letter to a superior, mentioning the places Delke and   ndôg[3], and speaking of gathering fodder in the meadow

]ⲓ ⲉⲓⲡⲣⲟⲥⲕⲏⲛⲉ ⲡⲁⲙⲉⲣⲓⲧ ⲛⲭⲟⲉⲓⲥ ⲓⲱⲧ[|] ⲉⲣⲟⲟⲩ ⲉϩⲟⲩⲛ ⲉⲁⲏⲗⲕⲉ ⲉⲥⲁⲃ ⲁⲩⲱ ⲡⲉ[|]ⲛⲁⲱϭ
ⲉⲣⲁⲥⲧⲉ ⲁⲩⲱ ⲡⲉⲣⲕⲁ ⲛⲁⲃ[| ⲉⲃⲟⲗ ⲁⲛ ϩⲟⲗⲟⲥ ⲁⲩⲱ ⲧⲛⲟⲩ ⲛⲉϭⲁⲙⲟⲩⲗ̅[|]ⲁⲃ ⲁⲥⲱⲗ ϩⲣⲉⲥⲟⲩ ⲛⲫⲟⲓ
ⲁⲩⲱ[|]ⲧ ⲫⲟⲓⲃⲁⲙⲙⲱⲛ ⲙⲉⲛⲡⲁⲓⲁⲛ, ⲧⲁⲩⲣⲓⲛⲉ[|] 1 blank

Verso]ⲧ ⲉ̇ⲧ̇ⲁ̇ⲓ̇ⲏ̇ⲩ̇ (sic)

357. —Papyrus, a fragment, $15\frac{1}{2} \times 16$ cm   Script ligatured   *Recto* ↑

Letter from John to (Apa) Severus, a merchant (πραγματευτής)   It seems to contain a request or instructions as to certain buildings or land

[+ⲛ]ϣⲟⲣⲡ ⲙⲛ ⲛϩⲱϥ ⲛⲓⲙ ⲧⲓⲡⲣⲟⲥⲕⲩⲛⲉⲓ ⲁⲩⲱ [|] ⲧ]ⲏⲣϥ ⲙⲉⲛⲧⲉⲙⲙⲁⲁⲩ ⲙⲉⲛϣⲉⲛⲟⲩⲧⲉ ⲡⲉⲧⲛ-
ϣⲏⲣⲉ[|]ⲓⲥ ⲛⲧⲁⲓϫⲛⲟⲩⲧⲏⲩⲧⲛ ⲉⲣⲟⲥ ⲛⲉⲥϩⲁⲓ ⲡϣ ⲛ[|]ϥ ϩⲟⲗⲟⲥ ϫⲓⲛⲉⲟⲥ ⲛⲧⲁⲓⲥⲁⲧⲛ ⲉⲃⲟⲗ ⲗⲟⲓⲡ[ⲟⲛ |
]ⲅⲉ ϩⲓⲧⲟⲟⲧϥ ⲛⲡⲣⲱⲙⲉ ⲉⲃⲁⲧⲓ ⲛⲁⲥϩⲁⲓ ⲛⲁⲕ ⲭⲉⲟⲩ [|] ⲉⲥⲛⲁⲩ ⲛⲕⲟⲟϩ ⲙⲙⲁ ⲙⲁⲣⲥⲩⲡⲟⲟⲛⲟⲩ ⲉⲃⲟⲗ
ϩⲓⲍⲛ[|] ⲁⲩⲱ ⲧⲓ ϭⲓϫ ⲛⲁϥ ϩⲁⲣⲟⲓ ⲡⲉⲧⲉⲛⲧⲁⲓϫⲛⲟⲩⲕ ⲉⲣⲟϥ ϣ[|]ⲛⲕⲱⲣϣ ⲙⲙⲟϥ ⲉⲧⲃⲉⲛⲉⲣⲟ ⲙⲡⲏⲓ
ⲡⲁⲛⲧⲟⲥ ⲛⲥⲟⲩ[|] ⲛⲧⲉⲕⲙⲛⲧϫⲟⲉⲓⲥ ⲛⲥⲟⲛ ⲙⲉⲛⲡⲟⲩϫⲁⲓ ⲙⲡⲉⲛⲏⲓ ⲧⲏⲣϥ[

Verso.]ⲓⲁ ⲥⲥⲩⲏⲣⲟ̅ ⲡⲣⲁⲅ⳽ + ⲓⲱϩⲁⲛⲛⲏⲥ ⲡⲉⲕ .   ⲡⲉⲓⲏⲛ[

358. —Papyrus; a fragment; 13×22 cm   Script small, ligatured   *Recto* ↑
13 + lines

Letter, mostly illegible   It relates to money matters and wine (?) ⲧⲓ ϥⲧⲟ ⲛⲕⲟⲗⲗⲁⲑⲉ.

The last 6 lines are   ϩⲁϩⲧⲏⲩ ⲥⲩϭⲱⲡ | ⲗⲟⲓⲥⲉ ⲁⲛⲟⲛ ⲣⲱ . ⲉ ⲛⲕⲁⲩⲗⲉϩ ⲛⲁⲕ ϩⲟⲗⲱⲥ
ⲣⲱ [ⲛ]ⲉⲧⲛⲁⲛⲟⲩϥ ⲉⲓⲥ ϩⲏⲏⲧⲉ ⲁⲓⲥϩⲁⲓ ⲛ|ϩⲉⲣⲟⲩϫ ⲉⲧⲃⲏⲏⲧⲟⲩ ⲡⲟⲛⲕⲟⲩ ⲉⲃⲟⲗ ϩⲁϩⲧⲏⲩ ⲛⲁⲕ ⲁⲕⲧⲁⲁⲩ

---

[1] *V* no 354

[2] ⲕⲁⲓ a corn measure, *Aeg Z* xx 39   *Cf* Bi Mus nos 1135, 1205   In the alchimistic pap Bodl Copt (P) *a* 1, a mixture is to be put into a cloth ⲉⲩⲧⲟⲉⲓⲥ ⲉⲥⲕⲁⲣⲉϩ and tied to (*or* in) a ⲕⲁⲡ

[3] The first is ⲧⲣⲁⲗⲕⲉ in KRALL lviii   *Cf* in Br Mus O1

6201 B, a fragment, ⲡⲉⲡⲟⲓⲕⲓⲟⲛ ⲛⲡⲟϣ ⲛⲧⲏⲗⲕⲉ ϩⲙⲡⲧⲟϣ [ⲛϣⲙⲟⲩⲛ ⲉⲣⲉ ⲡⲧⲟⲡ]ⲟⲥ ⲛⲫⲁⲧⲓⲟⲥ ⲁⲡⲁ ⲁⲡⲟⲗⲗⲱ ϩⲙⲡⲉⲓ-ⲧⲟϣ [ⲛⲟⲩⲱⲧ]. Now ـلبـ, AMÉLINEAU, *Géogr* 175   The τόπος referred to would therefore be that at Bawit, some 7 miles further south   For the second name, *cf* formations like ⲙⲁ ⲛⲧⲱϭ

ⲕⲁⲛ ⲉⲡⲉⲕⲧⲁⲁⲩ ⲧⲁ⳽ⲛ | ⲑⲉ ⲧ[ⲁ.]ⲝ. ⲡⲁⲇⲓⲕⲁⲓⲟⲛ ⲉⲅⲟⲟⲧⲟⲩ ⲉⲡⲉⲓ ⲙⲡⲟⲟⲩ ⲉϣⲁⲛⲥϩⲁⲓ ⲛⲁⲓ ϩⲁⲟⲩϩⲱⲃ
ⲡⲉⲛⲗⲉϩ¹ ϩⲓⲭⲱⲓ | ϩⲛⲟⲉⲓⲙⲉ ⲕϩⲁϩⲧⲏⲓ ⲁⲩⲱ ⲁⲓⲧⲓ ⲡⲕⲁⲓⲛ η ⲙⲡϣⲉ ⲛϩⲱⲣ ⲁⲩⲱ ⲡⲛ γ ⲙⲡϣⲉ ⲙⲡⲣⲁϣⲉ
ⲉⲡⲭⲱⲕ | ⲉⲡⲛ ⲕ ⲛⲧⲁⲕⲧⲛⲛⲟⲟⲩⲥⲟⲩ ⲛⲁⲓ ϩⲓⲧⲟⲟⲧⲩ ⲉⲁⲡⲁ ⲧⲏⲣ ⲡⲉⲛⲟⲩϫⲁⲓ ⲇⲉ ⲉⲧⲛⲁⲛⲟⲩⲥ ⲥⲱ ⲉⲕⲥϩⲁⲓ |
ⲉⲙ[ⲟ]ⲕ ⲛⲁⲓ ⲙⲙⲡⲉⲧⲉⲕⲟⲩⲁϣⲩ ⲧⲁⲁⲩ ⲉⲡⲉⲓ ⲕⲁⲗⲱ² ⲧⲓϣⲓⲛⲉ ⲉⲧⲉⲕⲙⲛⲧⲥⲟⲛ ϩⲓⲧⲙⲛⲉⲓⲥϩⲁⲓ +

359.—Papyrus, a fragment, 11 × 10 cm. Script seldom ligatured Recto ↑
Letter from Theodore to Apa Enoch, an ἀρχισυμμαχός Wine in the cellar (κελλάριον), the tower (πύργος²) and a cell are mentioned

+ ⲟⲩⲱϣ ⲧⲉⲩⲛⲟⲩ ⲉⲕⲁϫⲓ [| ⲡⲉⲛⲏⲣⲡ ⲉⲧϩⲛⲡⲕⲉⲗⲗⲁⲣ[ⲓⲛ | ⲉⲡⲡⲩⲣⲅⲟⲥ ⲙⲛⲛⲁⲧⲣⲓ ⲙ[| ⲟⲩⲱⲛ
ⲉⲙⲟⲟ[ⲩ | ⲧⲉⲩⲧⲁⲁⲩ [| ⲙⲙⲣⲕⲁⲁ | ⲛⲥⲁⲡⲉⲩ | ⲁⲓ[

Verso ⲁ]ⲡⲁ (space) ⲉⲛⲱⲭ ⲡⲁⲣⲭⲓⲥⲩⲙⲙ | +ϩⲓⲧⲛⲑⲉ[ⲟⲇⲱ]ⲣⲉ..

360.—Papyrus, a fragment, 5½ × 18 cm Script rarely ligatured Recto ↑.
Letter asking that 2 σκεύη of wine may be sent, 'because of this soldier (that is come?) to us'

] ⲙⲁⲣⲉⲧⲉⲕⲙⲛⲧⲙⲁⲓⲛⲟⲩⲧⲉ ⲛⲥⲟⲛ ⲉⲣⲡϩⲱⲩ⁴ ⲛⲥⲧⲛⲟⲟⲩ |]ⲥⲛⲁⲩ ⲛⲥⲕⲉⲩⲉ ⲛⲛⲏⲣⲡ ⲛⲁⲛ ⲛⲥⲟⲟⲩⲧⲛ
ⲉⲧⲃⲉⲡⲉⲓⲙⲁⲧⲟⲓ |]ⲉ ϩⲓⲭⲱⲛ +

Verso +ⲡⲙⲁⲓⲛⲟⲩⲧⲉ ⲛ[|] ⲁⲕ^ω/.[

361.—Papyrus, a fragment, 37 × 31 cm. 2 selis-joints visible. Script irregular, often ligatured Recto ↑
Letter from . to a superior ('thy fathership') The writer relates first that he ('we') had caused the son of Anastasius to swear regarding a money matter and had disputed with him to the uttermost ('unto death'⁵), with the result, apparently, that payment was promised by the 3rd day of the Feast⁶ The affairs of 2 βοηθοί, Papô⁷ and Phoebammon, are then dealt with, and it is suggested that letters should be written them, for 'thy word is different from⁸ that of other men' A guarantee, cancelled in compliance with the addressee's instructions, is referred to

The writer's idiom is faulty and peculiar (somewhat Middle Egyptian), and frequent corrections make the reading uncertain

ϯ ⲁⲛϫⲓ ⲛⲛⲉⲡⲉⲥⲧⲟⲗⲏ ⲛⲧⲉⲕⲙⲛⲧⲉⲓⲱⲧ ⲁⲛⲁϣⲟⲩ ⲁⲛⲁⲥⲡⲁⲥⲉ ⲙⲙⲟⲟⲩ ⲧⲛⲧⲁⲗⲟ ⲛⲧⲉⲕⲙⲛⲧⲉⲓⲱⲧ |
ϫⲉⲁⲛⲱⲣⲕ ⲉⲡϣⲉ⁹ ⲛⲁⲛⲁⲥⲧⲁⲥⲉ ⲉⲧⲃⲉϥⲟⲗⲟⲕⲧⲥⲉ ⲁⲛⲥⲱϫⲉ¹⁰ ⲛⲉⲙⲁϥ ϣⲁⲁⲥϩⲣⲁⲓ ⲉⲡⲙⲟⲩ ⲡⲉϫⲉϥ

---

¹ Can this be the ἅπαξ λεγομενον in Job xi 18, μέριμνα?
² ? ἐπὶ καλῷ
³ V Crum, Ostr no 310 n , also Zoega, p 95 infra, 'the village tower'
⁴ Cf ⲣⲏⲛⲟϭ ⲛϩⲱϥ, Br Mus nos 1131, 1207
⁵ Recurs in no 321 Cf biblical ἕως θανάτου
⁶ Berlin Ostr, P 1076, ⲛϣⲟⲙⲧ ⲙⲙϣⲁ Cf here

no 385 Presumably the Paschal festival
⁷ Cf ⲡⲁⲡⲟ, Br Mus no 1086
⁸ Assuming ⲟⲩⲱⲧ=ⲟⲩⲉⲧ Otherwise one must translate 'the same as', which gives less sense
⁹ 'Adjure' (Mitth Rain v 120, Br Mus nos 1007, 1008)
¹⁰ For ? ϣⲱϫⲉ

Z

ⲭⲉⲉⲧⲛⲁⲧⲙⲁⲧ ⲛϭⲓⲛⲉ ⲛⲥⲟⲓ ⲙⲡⲁⲓϩⲟⲟⲩ ⲥⲛⲁⲩ ⲛⲧⲉⲣⲉϥϫⲟⲟⲥ ⲛⲧⲥⲓϩⲉ ⲁⲓⲃⲉⲓ ⲛⲉⲩϩⲟⲟⲓ ⲧⲏⲣⲟⲩ ⲁⲓⲃⲟⲕ
ⲉⲣⲟϥ ⲁⲓϭⲛ ⲡϣⲟⲓ ⲡⲟⲩⲁⲥ ⲛⲁⲛ ⲁϥⲛⲟ[..] ⲉⲧⲟⲟⲧⲛ ⲉⲧⲣⲉϥⲧⲁⲁϥ ⲛⲁⲛ ϣⲁ|5-ⲁⲡϣⲁⲙⲛⲧ ⲛⲡϣⲁⲁ
ⲁⲩⲱ ⲉⲧⲃⲉⲡⲁⲡⲱ ⲡⲃⲟⲛⲑⲟⲥ ⲭⲉⲉⲡ[ⲉⲓ]ⲇⲏ ⲁⲕⲉⲓⲛ ⲡⲗⲟⲅⲟⲥ ⲉⲧⲁ.[.] ⲡϣⲙⲟⲩⲛ ⲛ[about 21 let]ⲙ
ⲁⲛⲭⲟⲟⲥ ⲭⲉⲉⲩⲁϥⲁⲛϥⲉⲓⲃⲟⲗⲛ ⲭⲉⲉⲓ|ⲁϣϣⲉⲅⲅⲛⲩⲧⲉ ⲙⲡⲕⲥⲉⲉⲛⲉ ⲁⲛⲭⲟⲟⲥ ⲭⲉϣⲁⲛϯ ⲥⲟⲟⲩ ⲛⲣⲧⲟϥ
ⲛⲥⲟⲩⲱ ϥⲧⲟⲟⲉⲓ ⲉⲣⲟⲛ ⲛ|ⲛⲉⲥⲟϣϥ[1] ⲁⲩⲱ ⲉⲧⲃⲉⲫⲱϭ ⲛⲛⲓⲕⲁⲛⲉ[2] ⲁⲛⲁⲗⲉϥ ⲁⲛⲛⲧϥ ⲉϩⲟⲩⲛ
ⲙⲡⲁⲧϥϣⲁϫⲉ[3] ⲉϥϣⲁⲛϣⲁⲩ[4] | ⲉⲡⲉⲙⲟⲩ ⲉⲣⲉⲡⲛⲟⲩⲧⲉ ⲛⲁⲧⲁⲁϥ ⲛⲁⲭⲁⲩ[5] ⲧⲛⲧⲁⲙⲟⲕ ⲁⲩⲱ
ⲉⲧⲃⲉⲫⲱϭ ⲙⲡⲁⲡⲱ ⲡⲃⲟⲛ|ⲧⲟ-ⲑⲟⲥ ⲁⲓϫⲁ... ⲭ[ⲱ] ⲙⲙⲟⲥ ⲛϭⲉⲓⲛⲉ ⲥⲁⲡⲉⲧⲉⲡⲟⲛ ⲉⲓⲟⲩⲱϣ ⲡⲁϩⲟ-
ⲗⲟⲕⲟⲧⲥⲉ ⲥⲛⲁⲩ ⲧⲁϩⲁⲩ|ⲟⲩ ⲛⲁϥ ⲉϩⲣⲁⲓ ϥⲧⲁⲁⲩ ⲉⲛⲙⲁ ⲉⲧⲉⲣⲟⲓ ⲧⲁⲗⲟ ⲉⲓⲧⲉⲓ ⲙⲛⲥⲉ ⲙⲛⲥⲧϭⲣⲉ
ⲭⲉⲉⲣⲉⲡⲁ ϣⲙⲟⲩⲧⲉ | ⲛⲙⲁⲛ ⲉⲓⲧⲛⲉⲥ ⲙⲡⲉⲓϭⲉⲓⲛⲉ ⲛⲛⲁⲩ ⲛⲧⲁϥϫⲟⲟⲥ ⲛϯϩⲉ ⲁϥⲟⲓⲃⲁⲙⲙⲓⲟⲛ
ⲡⲃⲟⲛⲑⲟⲥ ⲉⲓ ⲉⲣⲟϥ ⲁⲓⲥⲱϫⲉ ⲛⲉⲙⲁϥ ⲭⲉⲁⲃⲟⲕ [... ...] ⲛⲉⲥⲛⲏⲩ ⲛⲧⲥⲉⲓⲙⲉ[6] ⲛⲁⲥ ⲁⲩⲱ ⲉϣⲱⲡⲉ
ⲉⲕⲁⲙϥⲉⲓⲃⲟⲗ[ⲛ] | [ⲉ]ⲧⲃⲉⲛⲉⲥⲟⲩⲟ ⲁⲛⲟⲕ ⲉⲧⲁⲧⲁⲁⲩ ⲛϩⲟⲩⲛ ⲉⲡⲁⲛ ⲛⲟⲩⲱϣ ⲟⲩⲛ ⲙⲁⲣⲉⲧⲥⲕⲙⲛⲧⲉⲓⲱⲧ
ⲉϩⲣⲁⲓ ⲟ[ⲩ]|15-ⲉⲡⲉⲥⲧⲟⲗⲏ ⲉⲃⲟⲗ ⲛⲁⲩ ⲟⲩⲓⲁ ⲙⲫⲟⲓⲃⲁⲙⲙⲓⲟⲛ ⲟⲩⲉⲓⲁ ⲙⲡⲁⲡⲱ ⲟⲩⲱϣ ⲡⲉⲛϣⲁϫⲉ ⲟⲩⲱⲧ
ⲡⲁⲣⲱ|ⲙⲉ ⲛⲓⲙ ⲁⲩⲱ ⲭⲓⲙⲡⲛⲁⲩ ⲛⲧⲁⲡⲉⲕϩⲣⲣⲁⲩ[7] ⲧⲁϩⲟⲛ ⲉⲧⲃⲉϥⲫⲟⲓⲃⲁⲙⲙⲓⲟⲛ ⲡⲁ.. ⲉⲛ..| [..]ⲭⲁϥ
ⲁⲛⲃⲁⲗ ⲡϣⲧⲟⲣⲉ ⲉⲃⲟⲗ ⲁⲩⲱ ⲕⲁⲧⲁ ⲑⲉ ⲛⲧⲁⲛⲭⲟⲟⲥ ⲭⲉ[about 15 let] | [.ⲃⲟ]ⲛⲑⲟⲥ ⲙⲡⲥⲛϭ[8] ⲛⲁⲉⲓⲛ
ⲉⲃⲟⲗ ϣⲁⲁⲃ[

Parts of 8 more lines are visible, but nothing consecutive can be read beyond the phrase (l 24)] ⲉⲕⲟⲩⲱϣⲧⲁⲣⲕⲟⲓ ⲙⲙⲁⲩ [

362.—Papyrus, almost complete, 17 × 16 cm   Script ligatured, v Pl 7   Recto ↑

Letter the contents of which, but for a reference to 2 *solidi*, are obscure   The name Aioob (ابوٯ) occurs

+ ⲥⲧⲏ̊ ⲧⲓⲣⲏⲛⲏ ⲛⲁⲕ ⲁⲓⲥϩⲁⲓ ⲛⲉⲓⲥϩⲁⲓ | ⲛⲁⲕ ⲛⲧⲁⲉⲓ ϩⲓⲧⲓⲁⲡⲟⲛⲣⲓⲥⲓⲥ ⲉⲧⲁⲡϣ..ʼ|ⲧⲉ ⲁⲩⲱ
ⲁⲩⲧⲁⲙⲟⲓ ⲭⲛⲧⲁⲅⲉⲓ ⲉ[.]ⲣⲱⲙ[.] | ⲕⲱ ⲕⲁⲗⲁⲛⲧⲓⲣⲅⲛ[10] ⲁⲅⲓ ⲥⲛⲁⲩ ⲉϩⲟⲗ[ⲟⲕⲧ/] | ⲁⲩⲱ ⲡⲡⲉⲧⲥⲙⲟⲛⲧ
ⲁⲛⲡⲉ ⲡⲗⲏⲛ ϩⲉ | ⲧⲓ ⲥⲛⲁⲩ ⲉϩⲟⲗⲟⲕⲧ ⲡⲁⲓϣⲟⲃ ⲙⲛ ϣⲁϣⲱⲡⲉ | ⲧⲟⲩⲁⲗⲟⲟⲩ ⲛⲁⲕ ⲛⲛⲁϩ ⲁⲩⲱ
ⲙⲡⲉⲣϣⲓⲛⲉ | ⲭⲛⲧⲁⲕⲕⲁⲗⲉ ⲛⲙⲟⲕ ϩⲱⲱⲕ ⲙⲟⲛ | ⲧⲟⲟⲩ ⲛⲉⲩⲭⲣⲓⲁ[11] ⲛⲙⲟⲕ ⲧⲓⲣⲏⲛⲏ ⲛⲁⲕ +

Verso blank

363 —Papyrus, a fragment, 3½ × 14 cm   Script sloping semi-uncials   Cf CRUM, *Ostraca*, Pl I, no 71   Recto ↑

Letter referring to certain money, which is to be received and weighed

+ ⲁⲣⲓ ⲧⲁⲅⲁⲡⲏ ⲛⲅϫⲓ ⲡⲉⲓⲧⲣⲓⲙⲛⲉⲛ ⲛⲧⲟ[ⲟⲧϥ ⲛⲡⲡⲣⲉⲥⲃⲩⲧⲉⲣⲟⲥ ⲛϭϣⲓⲧϥ (ⲛⲁϥ erased) ⲁⲩⲱ
ⲧ[ⲓ ⲧ]ⲡⲁϣⲉ ⲛϩⲟⲗⲟⲕⲟⲧⲧⲛ ⲛⲁϥ ⲟⲛ ⲛⲛ[.ⲁⲁⲛ ⲧⲓϫⲉϩ . ⲛⲧⲁⲧⲁⲁⲥ ⲛⲁⲛ [

---

[1] For ʼ ϣⲱⲭⲛ (cf ⲥⲱⲭⲉ above) assuming the rest of the phrase omitted   Or ʼ The rest may be neglected ʼ (ⲕⲉ abso lutelv, LAGARDE, *Aeg* 240, Rossi ii, ii 28)

[2] For ʼ ⲛⲁⲡⲁⲥⲕⲛ, ʼthe matter of importanceʼ

[3] Or ϣⲁⲩ ⲉⲉϥ-

[4] ϣⲁⲩ[ⲉ] possible

[5] ⲁⲧϣⲁⲩ

[6] ⲥⲕⲉⲩⲛ ⲛⲧⲉⲥϩⲓⲙⲉ

[7] Reading certam , ? ϩⲣⲟⲟⲩ ʼvoiceʼ, command

[8] For ? ⲛⲉⲭ-   [9] ? For ϩⲛⲧⲓ   [10] Or read ⲧⲓⲟⲩⲛ

[11] For ⲙⲙⲟⲛ ⲛⲧⲟⲟⲩ ⲛⲉⲩⲭⲣⲓⲁ. Χρεία thus in *Aeg* Z ʼ85, 30, Bˡ Mus nos 591, 592 (note the Mid. Eg tendency here, shown by ϩⲉ)

364.—Paper; a fragment; 10×6½ cm. Script *cf* Zoega, Tab vi, n. xxxviii and Br Mus *Catal*, Pl 7, no 190 for the type

Letter referring to money ϩογλογκοττη and showing the word ниаллаивапи, *i e* an Arabic form of μαγκλάβιον[1] One line is напроллпϩωбεн.[, a place-name found elsewhere[2] The form пос̄ occurs.

365.—Papyrus; a fragment; 14×22 cm Script rounded, clumsy uncials. *Recto* ↑ Note the peculiar superlineation Not from the Ashmunain collection[3].

Letter from Pahōm to the *papa* Victor Apparently there is inconsistency in the pronominal suffixes

✝ ϩαθη λεн ῑἼπϣαχε (sic) εροτῑ επιχε αιε[ι]| εϩητ ακϯ ῑ̄λαῑῑ ῑπϣε παι ακχοος παι [χε]|ῑρωλε ογωϣ πιχнιλ ῑппипε αγω τ[| λπαϩρε ϩασορετ ϯнογ εις πρωλ[ε]| εϣωπε κογωϣ εταατ нас ειс τα[ατ] | ταϣαχε ῑιαк εις ῑ̄λτρα⁴ αιςιλντογ [| ετбеῑϲλοιῑ⁵ ῑпсαϥ ῑλωϋсне χεῑ[πκ]|сλντογ наι ϣα·ϯнογ· рτακαιн πιсκελα λο[κ]⁶ πικχιτι πας χεαπϥοιλε⁶ еι пak ϩρнт αϥχοος [χε]|αιсῑλντογ αιр̄ηοτ⁷ снαγ⁷ εроϥ⁷ αιϩε ερ[⁸ | πεϥϲῑλντογ ϯнογ λαρϲпсαϥ λωϋсне · εϩαι[| ῑпϩαλ ϭ̄ϲῑлтог ταϩατроогϣ·ταεı пак εϩн[т| огχαι ϩ̄λпχοεıс

'Before speaking, I (greet) you Seeing that (ἐπειδή) I went north and thou didst give me the piece of wood and didst say to me that the men wish for the small iron (tool ?) and the . colour for wool, here then is the man If thou wouldest give them him, do so (?), and I will speak with thee (on the matter) See, I have made the caps (μίτρα) As for the of the 'master' Moses, in as much as thou (?) hast not yet made them for me, be so kind (-ἀγάπη) as to bestir thyself (σκύλλειν) and take them (?) to him For the workman went north to thee and said that he had made them and had set two 'wheels' thereon (But) I found that he had not made them So now let the 'master' Moses write to the workman, that he may (?) make them and that I be freed from care and come north to thee Farewell in the Lord.'

Verso. ✝ ταας ῑ̄ппапα бικτ [space] ωр ϩιῑ̄πϩαϩω[λ

366.—Papyrus, a fragment, 8×15 cm Script almost ligatureless *Recto* ↑.

Letter, probably from a superior, since no salutations are used and instructions are given The 'place' of Petei is mentioned

✝ λογρωλε ει εϥπροсελθε наı [| ϩιϣρп пταγриnε паплα ῑпετрος [пτεγ-]|ног ετϊϊαχι (sic) птιεπιсτολн тиоог .... | ϣαптϥнαϩϥ⁹ ππсте ? | пιερκααϥ εκτοϥ ? | т]ετнελλϥιбολ[ε] (sic) αιϯпоϲраϕε εрос + | +¹⁰ βασιλιος υπεγρ¹¹ × ×

Verso. address, illegible

<hr/>

[1] *V* no 322

[2] A fragment in Br Mus Or 6201 A, πρωλ[пτγλн] прοбн ϩλпτοϣ неλϩıτ (*cf* Vitelli no 75, βορρινη μερίс) птιπολıс таι ϣλογп and пεıрос папε птпγλн пϩобн.

[3] On the frame is the name 'A Pettersen'

[4] *V* Kircher 119.   [5] ? Gloves

[6] *Cf* пϩαλ below, though the name Paham (never found in Shmoun texts) might be intended

[7] A kind of ornament, *v* no 244

[8] To judge by the other lines, there should not be space for [ос λ]   [9] *Cf* ногϩ εбολ in no 319

[10] Different hand and ink   [11] *Cf* Krall cxlv 19

367.—Paper, a fragment, $5\frac{1}{2} \times 12$ cm. Script Brit Mus *Catal*, Pl 6, no 465
Letter with instructions   Unusually obscure

] ⲁⲩ̅ ⲉϣⲟⲡ ⲁ|ⲃⲣⲁϩⲁⲙ ⲥϧⲁⲓ ϧⲓⲭⲟⲩ ⲡⲉⲗⲙⲟϩⲁⲁⲗ[1] | ⲙⲉⲕⲏϣ ⲧⲉⲕϭⲟⲡ ⲟ̅ⲗⲁⲁⲩ̅[2]: ⲗⲓⲡⲟⲛ |
ⲁϧⲧⲟⲣ ⲙⲟⲩ ϣⲓⲛⲉ ⲧⲉⲩⲃⲱϣ ⲡⲉⲩ|ϧⲟⲩ[3] ⲁⲩ̅ ⲁⲙⲟ̈ ⲛⲁⲓ ⲉⲡⲥⲁⲙ ⲛⲉⲧϣⲱⲗ | ⲟ̈ⲭⲁⲓ ϧⲙⲡⲟ̅ⲥ̅ +

368—Parchment, complete, 20×14 cm   Script slightly sloping, of ZOEGA's 9th class   29 lines

Letter from Joseph to his 'dear and honoured brother', Phoebammon   Such is the irregularity of the idiom, that little is intelligible   The urgent affairs of Joseph's daughter are in question and Peter is bearer of this letter relating thereto, George having previously been sent, but in vain   Two witnesses, provided apparently by the recipient at the writer's instance, sign below

ⲥϥ̅ⲏⲓ ϧⲙⲡⲣⲁⲛ ⲉⲡⲛⲟⲩⲧⲉ ⲛϣⲟⲣⲡ ⲉϩⲱϥ ⲛⲓⲙ ⲁⲛⲟⲕ ⲥⲓⲥⲏϥ ⲉⲓⲥϧⲁⲓ ⲉⲓϣⲓⲛⲉ ⲣⲟⲕ ⲡⲁⲙⲉⲣⲓⲧ
ⲛⲥⲟⲛ ⲉⲓⲧⲁⲓⲏⲩ ⲫⲓⲃⲁⲙⲉ ⲉⲣⲉⲡⲟ̅ⲥ̅ ⲕⲁⲁⲕ[4] ϥϯ ⲭⲁⲣⲓⲥ ⲛⲁⲕ ϧⲙⲡⲁⲣϧⲟⲩⲥⲓⲁ· (5) ϥⲛⲁ ⲡⲉⲕⲣⲁϣⲉ ⲛⲁⲓ
ϣⲁⲡⲁⲛⲓⲃⲉ ⲛϧⲁⲓⲉ ⲙⲉⲛⲉⲛⲥⲁⲛⲁⲓ ⲉⲣⲉⲡⲟ̅ⲥ̅ ⲕⲁⲛ ⲉⲓⲥ ⲡⲁⲥⲟⲛ ⲡⲉⲧⲣⲟⲥ ⲁⲓⲟⲩϧⲟⲣⲣⲉⲩ[6] ⲛⲁⲕ ⲛⲁⲙⲉⲡⲁⲥϧⲁⲓ[7]
ⲗⲓⲡⲟⲛ ⲉⲧⲃⲉⲡⲟ̅ⲥ̅ ⲉⲧⲃⲉⲣⲱⲙⲉ ⲁⲛ ⲡⲉϣⲁⲡⲟ̅ⲥ̅[8] ⲉⲣⲁⲕⲁⲡⲏ ⲙⲙⲟⲩ ϧⲓⲡⲁⲧⲁ(10)ϣⲉⲣ ⲧⲁⲁⲩ ⲉⲡⲉⲧⲣⲟⲥ
ⲡⲉϣⲁⲕⲧⲁⲩ ⲛⲁⲩ ⲁⲩⲉⲓ ⲧⲟⲟⲧ ⲉⲙⲟⲛ ⲁⲓⲟⲩϧⲉⲣ ⲉⲥⲓⲱⲣϭⲉ ⲡⲱϣ ⲁⲡⲁⲥⲏ ⲡϣⲛ ⲛⲡⲁⲗϧⲁⲙⲓⲟⲟⲣⲓ[9]
ⲙⲡⲉⲕⲅⲁⲁⲩ ⲛⲁⲩ ⲗⲓⲡⲟⲛ ⲉⲧⲃⲉⲡⲟ̅ⲥ̅ ⲛⲛⲉⲕϧⲁⲩⲉϭ[10] ⲉⲙⲟⲓ ⲁⲛ ⲧⲁⲉⲓ ⲣⲏⲥ ⲁⲩ ⲁⲛⲟⲕ ⲟⲩⲣⲱ(15)ⲙⲉ
ⲙⲉⲩⲓⲱ ⲛⲥⲱⲓ ⲁⲩⲱ ⲉⲓⲁϧⲉ ⲛⲁⲩ ⲉⲥⲁⲓⲉ ⲥⲁⲓⲉ ⲙⲟⲛ ⲉⲓⲙⲡⲉ[11] ⲉⲓⲥ ϯⲁϧⲉ ⲙⲡⲓⲧⲁϣⲉⲣ ⲁⲩⲱ ⲡϧⲟⲟⲩ ⲉⲧⲁⲓϯ
ⲛⲓϧⲟⲙⲉⲧ ⲛⲁⲕ ⲙⲉⲗⲁⲁⲩ ⲭⲟⲟⲩ ⲉⲣⲟⲕ ⲁⲩ ⲁⲛⲟⲕ ⲉⲡⲁⲣ[12] ⲡⲟ̅ⲥ̅ ⲁⲩⲱ ϣⲟⲡⲉ ⲉⲕⲉⲣϧⲟⲧⲉ ϧⲁⲣⲟⲓ ⲙⲉϣϭⲟⲙ
(20) ⲧⲁⲑⲁⲗⲗⲉⲗⲉ ⲭⲱⲕ ϧⲁⲣⲟⲟⲩ ϭⲟⲡ ⲡⲁⲥϧⲁⲓ ⲧⲉⲕⲟⲩⲁϧⲩ ϧⲁⲧⲏⲕ ⲁⲩⲱ ⲧⲉⲛϯ ϥⲧⲟⲟⲩ ⲉⲣⲱⲙⲉ
ⲙⲡⲓⲥⲧⲟⲥ ⲉⲭⲱϥ ⲁⲩⲱ ϣⲟⲡⲉ ⲟⲩⲣⲱⲙⲉ ⲡⲁⲧⲉϣⲗⲱⲧⲡⲉ[13] ϧⲁⲧⲏⲕ ⲧⲁⲁⲩ ⲉⲙⲛⲧⲣⲉ ⲉⲭⲱϥ ⲧⲉⲕⲧⲁⲁⲩ ⲛⲁⲩ
ⲓⲉϥⲉⲛⲧⲟⲩ ⲛⲁⲓ (25) ⲉⲓⲥ ⲡⲣⲁⲛ ⲉⲡⲛⲟⲩⲧⲉ ⲣⲟⲕ[14] ϣⲁⲕϯ ⲡⲕⲟⲧ ⲛⲁⲓ ⲉⲣⲏⲥ ϧⲁⲛⲓϧⲟⲙⲉⲧ ⲁⲛⲟⲕ[15] ⲡⲁⲡⲁ
ⲕⲗⲁⲩⲧⲉ ⲉⲓⲟ ⲙⲙⲛⲧⲣⲉ ⲁⲛⲟⲕ[16] ⲡⲁⲓⲁⲕ ⲥⲁⲭⲉⲟⲥ ⲛⲩ ⲛⲁⲁⲏⲏⲗ ⲉⲓⲟ ⲙⲙⲛⲧ ⲉⲡⲓⲥϧⲁⲓⲉⲓⲁⲉⲓⲥⲏϥ ⲥϧⲁⲓⲉⲥϥ.

Verso blank

369—Papyrus, complete, 8×17 cm   Script moderately ligatured   *Recto* ↑
Letter from Taurinus to Stephanacius, a διοικητής[17]   Very obscure

Above the text, a cross   + ⲧⲓ ⲟⲩⲡⲁϣⲉ ⲛϧⲟⲗⲟⲕ[1], ⲛⲯⲁⲛⲁⲡⲟⲧ ⲛϥⲥⲙⲛⲧⲉ ⲛⲁ[ ][18] | ⲡⲓⲁⲗ[19]
ⲙⲟⲛⲟⲛ ⲙⲁⲣⲉϥⲥⲙⲛⲧⲟⲩ ⲛⲁⲛⲟⲩϧⲟ[ⲩ] | ⲁⲩⲱ ⲕⲁⲛ ⲛⲡⲉⲕⲉⲓ ⲛⲁⲓ ⲟⲛ ⲙⲁⲣⲓϭⲛ ⲛⲉⲕϧⲏⲩⲅⲉ | ⲁⲕⲁⲁⲩ

[1] Arabic
[2] 'Thou canst not take some'   But ordinary grammar forbids this   Or ⲙⲉⲕⲏϣ for ⲙⲉϣⲁⲕ?
[3] 'But urge him (and) enquire if (?) he is desirous of their matter'
[4] *Cf* Br Mus no. 582 &c
[5] *V Milth Rain* v 28 for this and following phrase
[6] For ? ⲟⲩⲟⲣϧⲉⲩ   *V* no 344
[7] ? ⲛⲉⲙ=ⲙⲡⲛⲁⲥϧⲁⲓ, *v* no 267
[8] This form of relative below and KRALL ccxxviii 23, ccxxxvi, ERMAN, *Kopt Volkslitt* 27
[9] ? A *nisbeh* from the place Hamiûr, *v* no 227
[10] 'Hinder, prevent perhaps suitable, but what is the verb?
[11] ? ⲙⲡⲉ, 'Indeed no'
[12] ⲙⲡⲁⲣⲁ   *v* Br Mus no 1132
[13] ? بشتل, W of Deirout
[14] ? *Cf* the frequent +ⲓⲕ ⲡⲗⲟⲧⲟⲥ, no 154 above
[15] Different hand
[16] Original hand
[17] Either the writer is a person of very exalted position (note the tone employed, the absence of all salutations), or διοικητής is not here the local magistrate, but a private servant, *cf* no 295
[18] ⲧⲉⲕⲧ[ⲉ] cannot be read
[19] *V.* Job xli 22,=ἐξάλειπτρον, μυρηψήτριον

ε[π]ει πνογτε πεθο ιιεπτρε ει . ϯ.] | ιιεκιητωογη ϩαροι¹ παντωс ϲαρ χεειιιαι|εχολαϲε
ιιπειιιιιι ιιιαιει επειηϲϯ+ | αγω αιιαγ αιιαϲηαϲε ιιιεϲϲθογι ϲι τεγεϲϲγη | ϲογηρϩωϲ ιιαϲι
εϲϲαιρϲτωϲ πεϲϩριτογϩω² +

'Give half a *solidus* to the jar-seller, that he may therewith make for me (?) perfume-
pots Only (μόνον) let him make them good And even if (κἄν) thou come not to me
again, let me find that thou hast done thy work For (ἐπεί) God is witness   thou
shalt not be able to bear with me For indeed (πάντως γάρ) if I spend (more) time (σχολάζειν)
here, I shall go eastwards —And see and compel (ἀναγκάζειν) his apprentices, take sureties
(ἐγγύη) of them that they will work for him, especially (ἐξαιρέτως) while he is at Touhô'

Verso. [+] ταϩϲ ιι ϲτεφαιιαιε [space] ιιαιοιη¹, + ϩιτιιταγριιε +

370.—Paper, a fragment, 22 × 9 cm Script 2 hands, both of ZOEGA's 9th class
Letter of obscure purport The writer mentions his children who are hungry, money
and loaves which the recipient has *Verso* over 21 lines

] ρειιοι | [. . . . . . . ιιι]οιιετ ιιϲω|[λωιιοττειι ϩαροι τογ | [. .]ιϲι ϩαϲτιιιι |[. . . .]ϩ
τιιιϲιϲ εϲω | [. . | ετειιιια ιιαιιιηρε | [.]ιι εγϩοιιερ³ ογαλ|[. . .]α ϩειε ιιτακϲοπ⁴ ιιεϲαϲε |
ϩαϲτιιιι ακογϲορε ιιαγ εογ|οτεϲι εθολ ογαλααπαπ|πε⁵ αγ ιιπειιαιιαϲε ιιιιοογ⁵ αιι ιιεϲαϲε
εγϩιιιε|ογοι⁷ ιιειιεγϲιτιιο ιιαγ | εθολ ϲεγϲοπογ ιιαιι | ιιιαιιταϲωϲι εροιι ια|θωιιιι εθολ⁸
ελααγ ιιιιιι | ιιειιτακ ιιεγρωιιε ιιπαθ|ροει⁹ ιιιι εϲωλωιιοτ|τειι ϩιτϩωϲι ιιιαιθωιιιι | εθολ
ϯιιιιηιε ροιι ιια|λοϲ ιϲ ογϲαι ϩιιπ̄ϲ̄

Recto the earlier text Only small parts of the lines remain The name
[α]θογϲϲωρωρ, [α]θωϲϲωρωρ¹⁰ occurs

371.—Papyrus, a fragment, 16½ × 10½ cm Script small, ligatureless *Recto* ↑
Letter, perhaps mentioning Fustât

L 3] αιταAϲι ιιιιταϲτε ιι | εϲιθωϲτε εθολ . . πειιϲιριτ | ϯε αϲιρϩιιαϲι αγ[ϲ]οοϲ ϲα |
]ϲογϲογταϲτε ιιτ[ω]θ[ε] |]ι ερατϲι ιιιιογϲιϲραϲι εροι |]πεϲιφωϲατοιι¹¹ τηρϲι ιιιιιιιιηε |
ϩλο]ιιλειι παρα πιιιι αιϲωτιι |] τιιιιιηιε ιιαιιερι̇τ ιιιιιιηρε |]ιιηρε ογϲαι ϩιιπχωεις |] αγω
τιϲϩαι ιιαιοϲιι/ ϲεπαιιειιϲρω¹² |]ϲ ιιιιιιειιϲιιηγ

¹ In MS CURZON 110, ϲλϩ, ϲλιι, τωογιι ϩα- appears
to mean 'depart from'
² Note Yâkût's variants, in 516, الدخوّ الطخوّ, 'in the
northern Saîd, on west bank' Apparently the form طحا
has since replaced this The dialect of KRALL'S cxvi
implies for his τογϲω proximity to the Fayyûm If this be
Tahâ al-'Amudain, then Tahâ al-Madinah (the nome-capital)
must be different For the latter was in the prov of Ashmunain (Abû Sâlih 74 a) and was probably the Tahâ SE of
Tûh al-Hail (AMELINEAU, *Géogr* 524), i e τωϲε ταπεϲτωωρ
(*v* no 92 above) 'Pergoush (read درحوش Abû Sâlih 86 a,
cf Paris 302 f 27 درحاش) in the nome of Touhô' (ZOEGA 367)
hardly helps to locate it, for the speaker is residing S of Kôs

(Kûssiyah) Nor can we draw conclusions from Cairo stele
8329 τογϲω ιιεϲογ on a stele from S of Siût (F PETRIE,
1907) and ? in KRALL xcviii may be different again
³ [θω]ιι or [εθο]λ Note Boh ϲοιιερ
⁴ Or ειιτακ- or ιι (ῆ) ται-
⁵ Read ? αλλαπαιιε الينا 'bread crumbs', ALMKVIST
in 8th Or Congr ii 394
⁶ *V.* no 324   ⁷ Perhaps the town, *v* no 147
⁸ This verb in Br Mus. no 1152
⁹ θ added above   ¹⁰ ابو السرور
¹¹ Φοσσᾶτον The preceding πε perhaps the article
Cf A J BUTLER *Arab Conquest* 340
¹² ιια altered from ιια

372.—Papyrus, a fragment, 32 × 10 cm   Script much ligatured, *v* Pl 7   *Verso* ↑

Letter from   to his 'dear and honoured brother Phoebammon, son of Basil'
Beyond the fact that previous letters and money are in question, I can, owing to the
difficulty of reading, say little as to the contents

+ ϩⲁⲙⲡⲣⲁⲛ ⲉⲛⲛⲟⲩⲧⲉ ⲛϣⲟⲣⲡ[| ϣⲓⲛⲉ ⲉⲡⲟⲩⲭⲁⲓ ⲉⲡⲁⲙⲉⲣⲓⲧ ⲛⲥⲟⲛ ⲉⲧⲧⲁⲓ̅ ⲛ.[| ⲁⲓⲥϩⲁⲓ ⲡⲉⲓⲥϩⲁⲓ
ⲛⲁⲕ ⲙⲡⲟⲟⲩ ⲡⲁⲓ ⲥⲱ ⲓⲍ [| ⲙⲥⲁⲛⲁⲓ ⲁⲓⲥϩⲁⲓ ⲕⲓⲥⲛⲏⲧⲉ[1] ⲛⲥϩⲁⲓ ⲛⲁⲕ [| 5 ⲛⲉⲧϩⲓϫⲱⲟⲩ ⲁⲩⲱ ⲟⲩϩⲁⲓ
ⲡⲁⲡⲉⲕ[| ⲡⲉ ⲅⲁⲃⲣⲓⲏⲗ ⲧⲁⲕⲥϩⲁⲓⲉⲃ ⲁⲓⲛ[| ⲁⲕⲁⲁⲥ ⲓⲉⲧⲉϩⲣⲁⲧⲏⲕ ⲁⲓⲧⲏⲡⲟⲟⲩ [| ⲣⲱⲙⲉ ⲥⲛϩ ⲥⲟⲟⲩ
ⲛⲛⲉϣϣⲟⲡⲧ ⲡⲛ[| β ⲉϩⲟⲗⲉⲛ ⲛⲁⲥ ⲉⲧⲉϩⲣⲁⲧⲁⲡⲯⲩⲭⲏ ⲛ[| 10 ⲁⲓⲥϩⲁⲓ ⲛ̄ ⲕ ⲉϩⲟⲗⲉⲛ ϣⲉⲛⲟⲩⲧⲉ ⲁⲩⲱ
[| ⲁⲓⲉⲣⲛⲟⲩⲃ ⲛ̄ ⲕβ ⲉϩⲟⲗⲉⲛ ϩⲓⲟⲩ 5 ⲁⲓⲛⲛ ⲡ[| ϣⲁⲛ ⲥϥ̄ ⲡⲁⲥⲛⲧⲓ ⲛⲁⲕ ⲧⲓⲁⲥ [| ⲙⲟⲛ ⲁⲛϩⲓⲥⲉ ⲉⲛⲧⲓ
ⲟⲥⲉ ϣⲁⲡⲉⲛ[| ϩⲁⲣⲟϥ ⲛⲛⲉⲙⲁⲓ ⲁⲩⲱ ⲁⲓⲥϩⲁⲓ ⲛⲁⲕ ⲛⲉⲓ [| 15 ⲛⲁⲃ ϩⲁⲧⲏ ⲧⲁⲧⲁⲓⲟⲩⲃ ⲁⲩⲱ ⲁⲩⲥ[|
ⲛⲁⲕ ⲁⲩⲱ ⲉⲧⲃⲉⲟⲩ ⲣⲱⲙⲉ ⲉⲓⲥ ⲕⲓϩⲛ[| ⲥⲩⲟⲛⲅ ⲉⲃⲟⲗ ⲁⲗⲗⲁ ⲡⲓϧⲏⲩ ⲡⲁⲓ[| ⲡⲉⲣⲧⲓ ⲟⲥⲉ ⲉⲥⲟⲟⲩ 5
ⲁⲓϫⲟⲩⲓⲥⲟⲩ ⲛⲁⲕ [| ⲛⲉⲧⲁⲓⲥⲟⲡⲟⲩ ⲁⲕⲧⲁⲁⲩ ϩⲁⲡⲉⲕϣⲏⲣⲉ [| 20 ϭⲓ ⲧⲕⲥϩⲁⲓ ⲛⲁⲓ ⲥϥ̄ ⲧⲓϭⲓϣ ⲁⲛ
ϣⲁ[| ⲧⲉⲕⲥⲟⲡⲟⲩ ⲧⲉⲕⲧⲁⲁⲩ ϩⲓⲟⲓⲕ ⲡϩ[| ϩⲱⲃ ⲉⲣⲟⲓ ⲁⲩⲱ ⲁⲓⲥϩⲁⲓ ⲛⲕⲓⲣⲓ ⲟⲩⲏⲣ[| ⲱⲙ ⲛ̄ ⲓⲥ ⲡϩⲛⲧ
ⲡⲁϫⲟⲛ ⲁⲩⲱ ⲛⲟⲩ̣[| ⲟⲩⲡⲉ ⲁⲩⲛϣⲙⲟⲉⲓⲛⲉ ϩⲁ.. ⲧⲏⲣⲟⲩ [| 25 ⲁⲣϣⲡⲉ ⲙⲟϥ ⲥϥ̄ ϣⲱⲡⲉ ⲁⲕⲉⲣ.ⲡ[|
ⲡⲉⲕⲛⲓϣ ϣⲱⲡ.ⲡⲉ[| ⲧⲏⲙⲟⲥ ⳨

Above the text, the address   + ⲧⲁⲁⲥ ⲉⲡⲁⲙⲉⲣⲓⲧ ⲛⲥⲟⲛ ⲉⲧⲧⲁⲓ̅ [space] [| ⲫⲟⲓⲃ̅ ⳿ⲅ̄ ⲃⲁⲥⲓⲗⲉ
ⲉⲣⲉⲡϫⲟⲓⲥ [space] [ⲕⲁⲁϥ

Recto   part of an Arabic text (earlier); *v.* Pl 9   This Prof C H BECKER reads
tentatively   والحكم السك والخمل علمه إن ساء اللّه | أطال اللّه دعاك وأعزّك واكرمك بالمسد (1)ؤ
فى المحرم سنة تسع عشرة وثلثمائة   He does not venture to read the difficult words, in
another hand, beyond l 1   Of the date, Muharram, A H 319 = Jan –Feb A D 931, he says
there is no doubt   This gives a *terminus a quo* for dating the Coptic text

373—Paper, a fragment, 16½ × 12 cm   Script sloping, ligatureless, but often
ambiguous

Letter dealing with various matters

The opening lines, mostly illegible, contain greetings, ⲙⲛⲁⲡⲁ ? , ⲡⲓⲱⲧ ⲉⲡⲁⲣⲙ[,
ⲙⲛⲛⲁ̅ⲓ̅ ? , ⲙⲛϭⲓⲛⲓⲗ[3] ⲙⲛⲡ̅ⲡ̅ ϩⲛ[| ⲙⲛⲡⲓⲱⲧ ⲉⲡⲁⲅⲣⲓⲏⲗ ⲙⲛⲡⲥⲉⲡⲉ ⲛⲥⲛⲗ[| ⲉⲣⲉⲡⲟ̅ⲥ̅ ϩⲁⲣⲥϥ
ⲉⲡⲉⲩⲥⲱⲟⲩϩ ⲉϩⲟⲩⲛ [| ⲁ]ϫⲛⲭⲣⲟⲛ꞉ ⲁⲩⲱ ⲙⲡⲥⲁⲛⲁⲓ ⲛⲉϩⲓⲟⲙⲉ [| ⲙⲛⲧⲁⲭⲁⲛⲗ ⲧⲁⲥⲱⲛⲉ · ⲙⲛⲁⲛ[|
. ⲁⲩ · ⲙⲛⲧⲁⲙⲓⲛⲁ ⲁⲙⲉ[| ⲛϥⲏ . . ⲩϥⲏⲓⲏ[4] ⲙⲉⲛⲧⲉϣⲉⲣⲉ [| ⲉⲣⲉⲡⲟ̅ⲥ̅ ⲥⲙⲟⲩ ⲉⲣⲟⲟⲩ · ⲛⲉⲙⲟⲩ ⲛⲓⲙ [|
ⲛⲁⲧⲁ ⲑⲉ ⲧⲁϥⲥⲙⲟⲩ · ⲛⲁⲥ]ⲣⲁϩⲁⲙ [| ⲁⲩⲱ ⲙⲛⲥⲁⲛⲁⲓ ϫⲁⲉⲓ ⲉⲃⲟⲗ ϩⲓ[| ⲉⲥϩⲁⲓ · ⲁⲓϫⲟⲟⲩⲥⲟⲩ ⲛⲛⲧⲛ
ⲛ[| ⲁⲡⲁϩⲣⲛⲧ ⲃⲱⲗ ⲉⲃⲟⲗ · ⲙⲓ[| ⲁⲩⲱ ⲉⲧⲃⲉⲧⲁⲡⲟⲗⲟⲥ · ⲉⲧⲥϭⲟ[| (*verso*) ⲁⲩⲱ ⲉϣⲱⲡⲉ ⲁⲁⲣⲕⲁⲧⲏⲥ ·
ϥ[| ⲙⲉⲟⲩⲛⲁⲧⲉⲛⲁⲧⲟⲓⲛⲓⲥⲓ · ⲧⲉ[| ⲁⲩⲱ ⲛⲓⲥⲁⲡⲁⲃⲟⲧ · ⲉⲓ ⲧⲓϣⲓⲛⲉ ϩ[| ⲁⲗⲁ ⲉⲣⲁⲡⲁⲧⲟⲟⲧ ᵗ ⲧⲏⲩⲧⲛ ⲧ[|
ⲛⲁⲓ · ⲉⲓ ⲧⲁⲧⲓ ⲟⲩⲧⲉⲣϩⲁⲙ ϩⲁ[| ⲟⲩ · ⲉⲣⲉⲛⲥⲁⲕⲓ ⲟⲛ ϩⲓⲱⲱⲥ꞉ ⲙⲉ[| ⲡϩⲁⲓ ⲉⲧⲭⲉⲛⲥⲁⲩϩⲁⲣⲉ[5] ⲕⲁⲛ
[| ⲛⲡⲉϭⲱ ⲛⲁⲧⲟⲩⲟⲣϩⲥ · ⲡⲉⲧϣⲓⲩ [| ⲉⲩⲥⲛ · ⲡⲉⲛϣⲁϫⲛⲏ ⲡⲉⲥϩⲁⲓ ⲉⲣⲏ[ⲥ | ϩⲓⲙⲁ ⲛϭⲁⲟⲩⲟⲛ ·

---

[1] Perhaps ⲕⲉⲓ- and in l 16   A similar ligature in l 11,
here read as S

'Vielleicht ein Kaufmannzeichen ذلك,' BECKER

[3] Or ϭⲓϭⲓⲗ

[4] Or ⲙⲛⲫⲏⲓⲏ

[5] حوذم   One would expect the article ⲁⲗ-

ϣⲁϥⲉⲥⲛⲗ[1] ⲉⲣⲟⲓ [| ⲟⲩⲉⲡ · ⲉⲡⲁⲙⲁⲣⲁ[2] · ⲛⲥⲓⲟⲩⲟⲩⲉⲧ ⲉⲥ[| ⲉⲅⲁⲩϩⲁⲣⲉ ϣⲁϥⲉⲥⲛⲗ ⲉⲣⲟⲓ[| | ⲧⲉⲧⲃⲱⲕ · ⲧⲉⲧⲛ ⲡϣⲓⲛⲉ · ⲙⲡⲁ| ⲙⲙⲉⲕⲓⲣⲁ · ⲉⲣⲉⲡⲟⲥ[| | ⲡⲓⲱⲧⲉ ⲙⲟⲧ[

Along margin of *recto*, a line containing ⲑⲟⲧⲉⲣ ⲡⲟⲩϣⲏⲣⲉ

374.—Papyrus, a fragment, 28 × 25 cm Script ligatured, cf Pl 7, no 362 *Recto →*

Letter dealing with various matters 'The amîrs' are often mentioned Its interest however lies in the reference to Hnês (Heracleopolis) as being further south[3] It was therefore written presumably at Babylon. ⲧ and ϥ are generally indistinguishable.

�]ⲁⲓ ⲙⲙⲡ . . . ⲓ ⲗⲟⲩⲗⲉⲓ ⲁⲩⲱ ϩⲁⲡ | �] . . ⲗⲟⲓⲡⲟⲛ ⲉⲣϩⲱⲃ ⲛⲟⲉ ⲉⲕⲟⲩⲱϣ | ⲕⲛⲁⲕ ⲧⲓⲟⲟⲩⲥⲟⲩ ⲉⲣⲏⲥ ⲙⲁⲛ | ⲧⲁⲉⲓ ⲛⲁⲕ ⲙⲙⲡϣⲁⲗⲟⲩ[4] ϩⲛⲁⲉ | ⲧⲉ ⲥⲟⲟⲩⲛ ⲧ ⲛⲓⲧⲟⲩ ⲛⲁⲕ ⲧⲁⲁⲩ | . . ⲉⲃⲟⲗ ⲉⲣϩⲱⲥ ϩⲓⲧⲉϥⲧⲙⲏ ⲛⲟⲉ ⲉ[ⲕⲟⲩ]ⲟⲱϣ [. . . . . .] ⲉⲡⲣⲱϥ | ⲛϣⲁϥⲛⲡϣⲁ ⲛⲁⲁⲩ ⲉⲓⲥⲙⲛⲧⲩ ϩⲓⲡⲁⲛⲓ ⲙⲙⲡⲃⲟⲗ ⲉⲡⲁⲛⲓ ⲉⲡⲉⲓ | ϣⲉⲡⲛⲟⲩⲧⲉ ⳉⲉⲡⲁϩⲛⲧ ⲧⲁϩⲣⲏⲩ . . . . . . ⲧⲉ ⲛ ⲁⲩⲱ ⲛⲥϩⲛⲁⲓ ⲛⲛⲉⲕ|ⲥⲁⲁⲧ ϣⲁⲛⲧⲉⲡ-ⲙⲟⲟⲩ ⲥⲟⲗⲡ[5] ⲁⲛ ⲁⲩⲱ ⲁⲓⲣⲁϣⲓ ⲉⳉⲱⲡⲙⲁ ⲛⲧⲁⲛ|ⲥⲙⲛⲧⲩ ⲕⲁⲗⲱⲥ ⲁⲩⲱ ⲛϣⲁⲡⲛⲟⲩⲧⲉ| ⲛⲛ ⲉⲡⲓⲥⲟⲟⲩ ⲉⲧⲓ|ⲣⲟⲙⲡⲉ ⲧⲁⲓ ϣⲁⲛⲥⲙⲛ ϩⲱⲥ ⲛⲓⲙ ϩⲓ . . ⲛ]ⲉⲕϭⲓⳉ ⲁⲩⲱ | ⲁⲩⲥⲱⲱ ⲛⲥⲣⲁⳉⲁⲙ ⲉⲡⲁⲙⲉⲣⲁ ⲁⲩⲧⲱϣ ⲥⲛ[. . ⲁ]ⲙⲉⲣⲁ ⲉⲣⲟⲛ ⲉϣ[ ] ⲧⲁⲗⲛⲁⲗⲗⲁ[7] | ⲁⲩⲱ ⲡⲁⲧⲉⲡⲣⲱϥ ⲉⲡⲁⲙⲉⲣⲁ[. .] ⲛⲉϣⲉⲛⲑⲙⲙ[8] | ⲙⲙⲡⲉϥⲉⲣⲏⲩ ϣⲱ ⲉⲃⲟⲗ ϣⲁⲛⲧⲟⲩϭⲗⲟ ⲡⲛⲟϥⲥ | ⲉⲡⲁⲙⲁϩⲉ ⲙⲙⲟⲟⲩ ⲉⲣⲟϥ ⲁⲩⲱ ⲁⲩⲥⲱⲣ . . . . . ⲡⲱⲛⲉ | ⲛⲉⲣⲱⲙⲉ ⲉⲩϩⲓⳉⲱⲧⲁⳉⲓⲉ ⲁⲩⲱ . . . ⲛⲛⲩ ⲉϩⲣⲏⲧ |]ⲁⲙⲉⲣⲁ ⲉⲩⲓⲛ ⲉⲣⲏⲥ ⲉⲣⲏⲥ [ ] ⲛⲁϥ ⲉϥⲁϣⲓ ⲛⲣⲱⲙⲉ ⲡϥⲥⲧⲟⲩ ⲉϩⲣⲧ |] ⳉⲉϣⲁⲛⲁⲩ ⲧ[

Verso Scarcely two consecutive words are legible, but the closing words are] ⲡⲉⲧⲣⲟⲥ ϣⲓⲛⲉ ⲉⲣⲟⲕ ⲕⲁⲗⲱⲥ | ⲁⲩⲱ ⲣⲁⲙⲁⳉⲁⲛ[9] ϣⲓⲛⲉ ⲉⲣⲟⲕ.

375.—Papyrus; a fragment, 9 × 24 cm Script small, almost ligatureless *Recto ↑*

Letter to a superior, consisting, so far as preserved, of declarations of the writer's devotion and desire—like that of the blind for light—to see the recipient, whose wife, Cyra[10], and her children he also salutes.

+ ⲛϣⲟⲣⲡ ⲙⲛ ⲛϩⲱϥ ⲛⲓⲙ ⲧⲓⲡⲣⲟⲥⲕⲩⲛⲉⲓ ⲉⳉⲓⲫⲩⲡⲟⲡⲟⲇⲓⲟⲛ ⲛⲟⲩⲉⲣⲏⲧⲉ ⲙⲡⲁⲙⲉⲣⲓⲧ ⲛⳉⲟ[ⲉⲓⲥ] | ⲛⲥⲟⲛ ⲛⲡⲣⲟⲥⲧ/[11] ⲙⲛⲧⲁⲙⲉⲣⲓⲧ ⲛⳉⲟⲉⲓⲥ ⲛⲥⲱⲛⲉ ⲕⲩⲣⲁ ⲙⲛⲡⲉⲥϣⲏⲣⲉ ⲙⲙⲡⲉⲧⲛⲉⲛⲓ ⲧⲏⲣϥ ⲡⲛⲟⲩⲧⲉ] | ⲡⲉⲧⲥⲟⲟⲩⲛ ⳉⲉⲡⲁϩⲛⲧ ⲙⲧⲟⲛ ⲧⲟⲛⲟⲩ ⲉⲧⲁⲓⲥⲱⲧⲙ ⲡⲉⲧⲛⲉⲟⲩⳉⲁⲓ ⲉⲧⲛⲁⲛⲟⲩϥ ⳉⲉⲁⲧ[ⲛ]ⲉϥⲣⲡ[. . .] | [. .] ⲡⲛⲟ[ⲩ]ⲧⲉ ⲡⳉⲛⲁⲡⲗ[ⲏⲣ]ⲟⲫⲟⲣⲉⲓ ⲙⲙⲱⲧⲛ ⳉ[ⲉⲧ]ϣⲓⲛⲉ ⲛⲥⲁⲡⲉⲧⲛⲉⲟⲩⳉⲁⲓ ϩⲓⲧⲛⲟⲩⲟⲛ ⲛⲓ[ⲙ] | ϥⲛ . | ⲉⲧⲁϩⲉ ⲙⲙⲓⲛ ⲉⲙⲟⲓ ⲉⲑⲉ ⲙⲡⲃⲗⲗⲉ ϥⲟⲩⲱϣ ⲉⲛⲁⲩ ⲉⲡⲟⲩⲟⲉⲓⲛ ⲧⲁϭⲉⲧⲉ ⲧⲁⲓ ⲉⲓⲟⲩⲱϣ | ⲉⲛⲁⲩ ⲉⲡⲁⲙⲉⲣⲓⲧ ⲛⳉⲟⲉ[ⲓⲥ ⲛⲡ]ⲣⲟⲥⲧ/ ⲡⲛⲟⲩⲧⲉ ⲛⲉⳉⲛⲁ[ ] ⲛⲛⲉϥϣⲉ ⲧⲁⲁⲡⲁⲛⲧⲁ ⲉⲡⲁⲙⲉⲣⲓⲧ | | [

Verso + ⲧ[ⲁⲁ]ⲥ ⲛⲡⲁⲙⲉⲣⲓⲧ ⲛⳉⲟ[ⲉⲓⲥ

---

[1] Can this be a Coptic verb? It recurs below

[2] The amîr

[3] 'To the south of Hnês' would require ⲉⲡⲣⲏⲥ or ⲡⲣⲏⲥ

[4] ϣⲁⲗⲟⲩ cannot be read An uncatalogued fragment in a similar script in this collection has the phrase ⲉⳉⲱ ⲙⲙⲟⲥ ⳉⲛⲧⲁⲛϣⲁⲗⲓⲟⲩ ⲉⲣⲟⲓ (perhaps ⲉⲣⲁⲓ), while a letter in Br Mus Or 6201 A has ⲧⲓ ⲁⲣⲧ ⲕⲩ ⲛⲁⲣϣⲓⲛ ⲕⲱⲁⲡⲗⲟⲩⲥ ⲧⲙⲱⲡⲁⳉⲏ ϩⲁⲛ ⲁ ⲛⲧⲁⲛϣⲁⲗⲓⲟⲩ ⲉⲣⲁⲓ ⲛⲁⲓ ⳉⲉⲧⲁⲁⲩ ⲛⲁⲥ. And the word occurs in 2 Balaiza fragments, but without instructive context

[5] 'Not with my consent shalt thou depart ere the (inundation) water hath been apportioned' Cf ⲥⲱⲗⲡ in Br Mus nos 1116, 1146 Yet one might here read ⲥⲟⲗⲥ

[6] Perhaps a derivate of حكر

[7] Cf ⲓ ⲕⲁⲗⲉ in no 298

[8] نعمة is a common name, نعّام less so

[9] رمضان

[10] Cf ? the lady in Br Mus nos 1105, 1106 In ḤRALL no cxlix 6 read ⲕⲩⲣⲁⲥⲉⲓ, cf Br Mus no 530 note

[11] προστάτης

376—Papyrus, a fragment, 14½ × 11 cm. Script ligatured, *cf.* Pl 7, no 236 for the type *Recto* ↑

Letter of obscure purport, from 'his brother', Severus, son of Agênah (?)

ⲧⲉⲧⲛⲉⲉⲩⲕⲁ ⲙⲉⲣⲓ ⲛϫⲟⲉⲓⲥ ⲛⲥⲟⲛ | ⲙⲉⲣⲓ ⲛϫⲟⲉⲓⲥ ⲛⲥⲟⲛ ⲉⲛⲛⲁϧⲙ ⲡⲉϧⲙⲟⲧ | [ⲉⲡⲛⲟⲩⲧⲉ
ϣⲏⲡ¹   ⲧⲉⲧⲙⲉⲧⲙⲉⲣⲓ ⲛⲥⲟⲛ ϫⲉⲛⲧⲁⲩⲧⲁⲙⲟⲓ | ⲡⲣⲉϫⲟϥ ⲉⲃⲟⲗ ϧⲁⲡⲣⲱⲙⲉ ⲛⲉⲧⲙⲉ | ⲗϭⲉⲙⲉ²
ⲉϧⲣⲁⲓ ⲧⲁϥⲧⲁⲁϥ ⲗⲟⲓ ⲡⲁⲥⲟⲛ | ϫⲟⲟⲩϥ ⲧⲉϥϫⲓ ⲟⲩⲉϧⲣⲁⲓ ⲛⲁⲓ ⲛⲛⲉϭⲡⲁ | ϫⲉⲛⲡⲉⲛⲧⲓ ⲗⲁⲁⲩ ⲡⲁⲣⲉ ⲛ°ⲗⲁ
ⲡ+ϣ | ϫⲓ ⲉⲡⲣⲱϥ ⲟⲛ ⲛⲥⲁⲧⲉⲛ ⲗϥ ⲉϧⲣⲁⲓ |] ϧⲟⲗⲟⲥ ϫⲓ ⲟⲩⲉϧⲣⲁⲓ ⲛⲁⲓ ⲉⲛⲉϥⲣⲱⲙⲉ | ϫⲉⲛ ⲡⲣⲁⲛ ⲉⲃⲟⲗ
ⲉⲕⲉⲥⲟⲛ + ⲉϥ ... |

Verso the address in Arabic, ⁴ من أحمد سورس بن اعانه [

377.—Papyrus, a fragment, 14 × 13 cm Script ligatured, *cf* Pl 7, nos 236, 362 for the type *Verso* →

Letter of obscure purport

ⲡⲉϧⲙⲟⲧ ⲉⲡⲛⲟⲩⲧⲉ ϣⲏⲡ⁵ ⲛⲡⲓⲛⲁⲩ ⲉϥϧⲣⲁⲓ ⲉⲡⲱⲧⲡⲉ | ϫⲓⲥ ⲉⲓⲙⲏⲧⲓ ⲟⲩⲁ ⲛⲧⲁϧⲱⲣⲟⲃⲉ |] . ⲁϣ⁶
ⲉⲛⲧⲁⲓⲉⲓⲙⲉ ⲥⲡⲉⲧⲓⲛⲉⲥϫⲁⲓ ⲉⲧⲛⲁⲛ|ⲟⲩϥ   ⲉⲧ]ᵉ ⲧⲓ ⲧⲟⲟⲧⲧⲏⲩⲧⲛ ⲧⲓⲧⲁⲙⲟ ⲛⲧⲉⲧ |]ⲛⲧⲁⲁⲡⲟⲗⲗⲱ
ⲡⲁⲧⲉⲗⲓⲗⲥ⁷ ⲧⲓ ⲛⲁ̄ⲓ ⲉⲧⲣⲁⲥϧⲁⲓ |] ϧ ⲁϧϫⲱ ⲙⲙⲟⲥ ϫⲉϥϫⲓϫⲱⲡⲉϧⲣⲁⲛ | ⲗⲱ ⲙⲛⲁⲡⲟⲗⲗⲱ ⲧⲉⲧⲛⲉ-
ⲕⲉⲗⲉⲩⲉ ⲧⲉⲧⲛⲉⲧⲛⲟⲩ ⲥⲱϥ |]ⲕ ϧⲛⲧⲉⲥ ⲉⲡⲡⲗⲓⲧⲱⲣⲛ ⲛⲥⲱϥ ⲙⲁϧ ⲡⲉⲃⲣⲁⲛ |]ⲟⲩ ϫⲓⲧⲁⲗⲡⲁⲣⲁ ⲛⲁϧ
ⲁⲩⲱ ⲡⲉϥϧⲁⲓ ⲉⲡⲁⲙⲱϧ | blank

Recto End of an unpointed Arabic text (earlier)   Legible هذا كاتاس اسعل وى [
كلك علك نعبد وتم اللّٰه السا اى له لى معصوٍ(؟) كرمك امر

378.— Papyrus, a fragment, 6½ × 15½ cm Script ligatured *Recto* ↑

Letter from Yezid, son of 'Abd er-Rahman, to Athanasius George, son of Colluthus⁸, from Great Mjêw⁹, on the north of Shmoun The subject is obscure

ⲉⲓϥ ⲓⲉ̄ϫⲉⲓⲁ ⲅ ⲁϥⲙⲉⲣⲁⲙⲁⲛ ⲡⲓϧⲉϧⲣⲁⲓ ⲛⲁⲑⲁⲛ ⲅⲉⲱⲣⲅⲉ ⲕⲟⲗⲟ̄ | ⲡⲣⲱⲙⲧ[ⲛ]ⲟϭ ⲛⲁϫⲏⲩ ⲛⲡⲛⲟⲓⲧ
ϣⲙⲟⲩⲛ ϫⲉⲛⲁⲓⲛⲉ ⲧ|ⲁⲧⲛ ϧⲛⲛⲙⲟ ... ⲁⲩ ϧⲛⲡⲉⲁⲓⲁⲥⲧⲟⲗ ϧⲛⲡⲃⲟⲗ |]ⲟⲩⲡⲁϣⲉ | Parts of 2 more
lines show figures.

379.—Papyrus, a dilapidated fragment, about 21 × 16 cm Script ligatured, *cf*
Pl 7, no 362 for the type *Recto* (?) ↑

Letter noticed here on account of the following phrase on *verso* ϫⲉⲥϧⲁⲓ ⲛϣⲓⲛⲉ ⲛⲁⲓ
ⲙⲡⲛ+ⲕ ⲓⲉⲓⲥⲃ ⲡⲗⲏⲛ ϧⲉ ⲡⲟⲩⲱ¹⁰ ⲙⲡⲉϥⲣⲱⲙⲉ ϧⲁⲣⲟⲓ ⲕⲁⲗⲱⲥ ⲁⲩⲱ ϫⲓⲛⲟⲩⲃ ϫⲁⲓϫⲓ | ⲧⲁⲡⲁ.. .
ⲛⲁϧ ⲕⲟⲡⲟⲗⲭⲫ≡ⲓⲓⲓⲏ | ⲁⲩⲱ ϧⲟⲗ[The Coptic appears to be a direct continuation (its first

---

¹ *Cf* no 348   ² Altered   ⁷ Not ⲓⲉⲗⲟⲗⲉ Apparently a place
³ Perhaps ϫ for ⲧ A coin or measure which I do not   ⁸ Or Colluthus perhaps the grandfather But the reading
recognize   is uncertain
⁴ Perhaps اعانه ⲁⲣⲉⲛⲉ *v* no 173   ⁹ A place ⲧⲙϫⲏⲩ in a fragment, Br Mus Or 6201 ʙ
⁵ *V* nos 348, 376   ⁶ Not ⲡⲁϣⲉ   ¹⁰ *V* Br Mus no 1150

word is ⲁⲩⲱ) of 3 Arabic lines immediately preceding it and beginning, after the *basmala*,
اكرمك اللّٰ   Above them is the writer's name من داود بن ادرهم

The cryptogram in the 4th line does not yield to the usual keys[1].

380.—Papyrus, a fragment, 18½×9 cm   Script   ligatured, *cf* Pl 8, no 348 for
the type   *Recto* ↑.

Letter, wherein the following phrases are legible ⲡⲁϫⲟⲉⲓⲥ ⲧⲓⲧⲁⲙ[ⲟ],   ⲉⲓⲟϩⲉ ⲣ[ⲁ]ⲧⲕ
ⲉⲡⲁⲃⲉⲗⲱⲛ 'while I await thee at Babylon',   [ⲙⲉϩ]ⲟⲙⲉⲧ ⲡⲁⲗϩⲟⲩϣϣⲁⲣ[2] ⲛⲏⲩ ⲛⲁⲓ,
ⲁϩⲙⲏⲧ[3] ⲡⲁⲗ[,   ⲁⲩⲱ ⲟⲛ ⲕⲍ̅[4] ⲫⲓⲃ̅ ⲙⲛⲏⲅ̄ ϫⲁⲏⲗ,   (*verso*) ϣⲁⲓⲕⲱ ⲃⲁⲃⲉⲗⲱⲛ 'I will stay
at B',   ⲁϩⲙⲏⲧ ⲁⲩⲱ ⲁⲡⲣⲁϩⲙⲉ[5]. Further, ⲡⲛⲟⲩⲧⲉ shows the ligature noticed in no 390

381.—Papyrus; a fragment; 14×10 cm   Script   sloping, ligatureless   *Verso* →
Letter referring to the *dux* and the amir and their journeys   Shmoun is mentioned

+ ⲁⲓϫⲓ ⲛⲉⲥϩⲁⲓ ⲛⲧⲉⲕⲙ̣ⲛⲧ | ⲟⲩⲭ[ⲁ]ⲓ [ⲁ]ⲑⲁⲩⲙⲁϩⲉ .[| ⲛⲏⲩ ⲉϩⲣⲏ ⲙⲡⲉⲕⲁⲛⲉ[| ϣⲙⲟⲩⲛ
ⲙ̄ⲛⲛⲣⲁⲙ[| ϫⲟⲉⲓⲥ ⲙⲡⲁⲟⲩϫ ⲛⲕⲱⲣϣ ⲉ [| ⲁⲩⲱ ⲛⲉⲡⲧⲁϥⲁⲩ ⲁⲑⲁⲛⲁⲥⲉ ⲡⲣⲟ[| ⲛⲧⲁϥϩⲉ ⲟⲩϣⲏⲙ
ⲛ̄ⲱϣⲉ ⲉⲩⲕⲏ[6] | ⲁϥⲃⲁⲕ ⲗⲉⲥⲥ[6] ⲙⲟϥ ⲁϥⲙⲟⲩⲣ ⲛⲧ[| ϩⲏⲧⲕ ϣⲁⲛⲧⲉⲕⲛ̄ϫⲟ ⲛ̄ⲱϣⲉ ⲥⲓⲥ[| ⲡⲁⲙⲉⲣⲁⲥ
ⲛⲏⲩ ⲉⲣⲏⲥ ϩⲓⲫⲟⲟⲩⲧ[ⲛ | ⲉϩⲣⲏ ⲉⲓⲥ ⲛⲉϩⲓⲛⲏⲩ ⲛ̄ⲧⲓⲭⲁⲗⲁ[| ⲛϩⲟⲟⲩ ϣⲁⲛⲧⲟⲩⲡⲁⲣⲁⲧⲉ ⲉⲣⲏⲥ [| ⲛϣⲁⲩ-
ⲧⲁⲁⲩ ⲉϩⲟⲩⲛ ⲛⲥⲟⲩⲙⲟⲧⲛ ϩⲓ | ϩⲓⲛ̄ϣⲱ ϩⲓϫⲱⲟⲩ ϣⲁⲛⲧⲉⲛⲛⲁⲩ [| ⲁⲩⲱ ϣⲉⲡⲛⲟⲩⲧⲉ ⲛⲧⲉⲓⲉⲣϩⲟⲧⲉ
ⲁⲛ[| ⲙⲉ̣ϣϭⲟⲙ ⲙ̄ⲙⲟⲓ ⲟⲩⲱⲙ ⲛⲉⲓⲃⲁ[| ⲉϥⲕⲏ ⲛ̄ϣⲱ ⲉ̣ϥⲧⲟⲩⲙⲟⲩⲧⲛ ⲛⲥⲉ[| ⲁⲩⲱ ⲡⲉϩⲟⲟⲩ ⲛⲧⲁⲡⲁⲟⲩϫ
ⲙ̄ⲛⲛⲁⲙⲉ[ⲣⲁⲥ | ⲃⲁⲡⲉ ⲉⲧⲃⲉⲛⲓⲱϣⲉ ⲁⲙⲛⲟⲩⲧⲉ ⲁⲥ ⲙ̄ⲡⲟⲩ[

Recto (same hand) + ⲙⲟⲛⲉ ⲛ̄ⲧⲁϩⲉ ⲉⲣⲟϥ ⲡⲣⲟⲩϩⲉ ⲉⲧⲙ̣[.

(A Greek hand, earlier)]ⲁⲡⲟ χειρος σου,   ] δοκιμησει.

382.—Papyrus; a fragment, 13½×12 cm   Script   much ligatured and ambiguous
Cf Pl 7, no 362   *Recto* ↑
Letter treating of various matters   The writer's 'dear mother' is several times
mentioned

]. ⲕⲱ ⲃⲟⲗ ⲉⲡϩⲟⲓ ϣⲁⲛⲧⲕⲛ ⲙ̣[| ⲡ]ⲟⲩⲱϣ ⲙ̄ⲡⲛⲟⲩⲧⲉ ⲁⲩⲱ ⲡⲁⲙⲉⲣⲓ̄ ⲛⲥⲟⲛ [|]ⲛ ⲡϣⲓ ⲛⲛ̄ ⲣ
ϩⲓⲡⲇⲁⲙⲟⲥⲓⲟⲛ ⲁ[| ϫ̣ⲉⲙⲏⲥ[7] ⲉⲡⲁⲧⲟⲩⲧⲁⲛⲉⲕ ⲧⲉϥⲉⲓ ⲥϩⲟⲩⲛ[|]ⲛⲡⲁⲙⲉⲣⲓ̄ ⲛϫⲟⲉⲓⲥ ⲛⲥⲟⲛ ⲉϩⲁⲓ ⲛⲁϥ
ⲧϥ[|] ⲡⲉⲧⲛⲉⲣⲭⲣⲓⲁ ⲁⲩⲱ ⲉⲓⲟⲩⲏϩ ⲉⲃⲟⲗ ϩⲓⲡⲏ |]ⲉⲡⲛⲟⲩⲧⲉ ⲧⲓ ⲡⲓⲧⲱϣ ⲉⲛⲁⲧⲁ[8] ⲁⲛⲟⲕ ⲇⲉ ⲡⲉ |
]ⲉϣⲡⲱⲗⲉϭ ⲡⲣⲱ ⲟⲉ ⲛⲧⲁⲕⲥϩⲁⲓ ⲛⲁⲓ |]ⲛϣⲓⲛⲉ ⲛⲧⲁⲙⲉⲣⲓ̄ ⲛⲙⲁⲁⲩ ϫⲉⲥϣⲟⲟⲛ |] ϩⲓϫⲟⲓ ⲙ̄ⲡⲟⲉ ⲉⲓⲕⲱ
ϩⲉⲛϩⲟⲟⲩ ⲡϩⲟⲟⲩ |]ⲉⲣⲟⲥ ⲕⲁⲗⲱⲥ ⲛⲛⲉⲥⲕⲁ ⲟⲩⲁ ⲛⲧⲁⲗⲓ ⲉⲣⲟⲥ |]ⲧ ⲉⲓⲕⲱ ⲣⲏⲥ ⲧⲓⲟ ⲙ̄ⲡⲑⲁⲣ̄[9] ϫⲉⲛⲧⲟⲕ |
ⲉ]ⲧⲉⲃⲉⲛⲁⲗϭⲟⲩⲡⲉ[10] ⲛⲧⲁϫⲟⲟⲩⲥⲟⲩ ⲛ[| ϩ]ⲁⲣⲟⲓ ⲕⲁⲗⲱⲥ ⲙⲛⲏⲅ̄ ⲥⲓⲁ[11] ⲙⲛⲏⲗ[

---

[1] Its last letter possibly ⲃ   *V* Crum, *Ostraca*, no 488
[2] Mohammed rarely thus, *v* no 234   The next word
perhaps جلّاب, a kind of tax-collector (Dozy)
[3] احمد   [4] κῦρις   [5] ادرهم
[6] *Cf* ⲗⲉⲥⲓ, Crum, *Copt MSS* p 78   In Br Mus

no 580, 17 read? ϩⲓⲗⲉⲥ (=ⲗⲁⲥ) ⲉⲛϣⲉⲉⲓ
[7] Possibly ⲉ after 2nd ⲥ   [8] ⲛⲁⲛⲟⲩϥ cannot be read
[9] ? θάρρος   *Cf* the frequent use of θαρρεῖν
[10] *Cf Miltt Rain* v 55 ⲧⲁⲗϭⲟⲩⲡⲛⲉ جلّة
[11] *V* Br Mus no 1142

Verso (in other direction)]ⲁⲓϣⲓⲛⲉ ϩⲁⲣⲟⲓ ⲕⲁⲗⲱⲥ ⲁⲩⲱ ⲧⲁⲙ[ⲁⲁⲩ |] ⲁⲩⲱ ⲙⲁⲣⲉⲧⲁⲙⲁⲁⲩ
ⲝⲟⲟⲩ ⲡⲉϭϣⲓⲛⲉ ⲛⲁⲓ |] ϣⲉⲛⲉⲧⲉⲣⲓ ⲙⲟⲛ ϣⲱⲡ ⲡⲟⲟⲩ ⲧⲕⲝⲓⲧⲟⲩ |]ⲟⲩ ⲉⲡⲁⲓ ⲉⲣⲟⲛ ⲁⲛ ⲉϩⲣⲁⲓ ϩⲛⲧⲓⲣⲟⲙ̈
ⲧⲁⲓ |] ⲁⲓⲥϩⲁⲓ ⲛϥϣⲭⲁⲧ ⲛⲁⲓ ⲉ̇ⲝⲱⲛ̈ ⲓⲁ |] ϣⲁⲛⲧⲓⲥⲱⲕ ⲉⲑⲏ ⲟⲛ |] +

383 —Papyrus, a fragment, $11\frac{1}{2} \times 17$ cm   Script   rarely ligatured, irregular   *Recto* ↑
Letter from Papostolus, son of Bane, of Bousiris in the nome of Shmoun, to his
brother, Abba Severus   It relates to an agreement (ἀσφάλεια) belonging to Bane, son of
John (?), at present in S's hands   On the back was the copy (ἴσον) of Bane's account
(λόγος)

+ ⲁⲛⲟⲕ ⲡⲁⲡⲟⲥ⳿ⲓ ⲡϣ[ⲉ ⲛ]ⲡⲙⲁⲛ, ⲃⲁⲛ[ⲉ | ⲡⲟⲩⲥⲓⲣⲉ ϩⲛⲡⲧⲟϣ ⲛϣⲙⲟⲩⲛ ⲧⲡⲟⲗⲓⲥ [| ⲡϣⲥ ⲛⲡⲙⲁⲕ,
[. . . . ⲡ]ⲣⲱⲙⲉ ϣⲙⲟⲩⲛ [ⲧⲟ]ⲩ ⲛⲟⲩⲱⲧ ⲝⲉⲟⲩⲉⲛⲧⲕⲃⲁⲛⲉ ⲡϣⲥ ⲛⲓⲱ | ⲕ ⲉⲣⲉⲟⲩⲁⲥⲫⲁ̄ ⲛⲧⲟⲟⲧⲕ
ⲥⲧⲱⲃⲧⲉ . ⲉⲝⲱ ⲙⲟ . . [| ⲡⲛⲉⲃⲓⲗⲏⲣⲟⲩ ⲙⲟⲓ ⲙⲟⲥ ⲧⲏⲣⲉ ⲁⲓⲉⲓ ⲁ[ⲥ]ⲡⲁⲣⲁⲕⲁⲗⲉⲓ ⲙⲙⲟⲛ | ⲁⲩⲱ
ⲁⲕⲧⲁⲛϩⲟⲩⲧ[. .]ⲏ ⲉⲛⲁⲕⲛⲉ ϣⲁⲕⲥⲙⲛ ⲗⲟ[ϭ]ⲟⲥ | ⲉⲙⲁⲃ ⲛⲕⲟⲣ ⲥⲣⲟⲃ[. . . ⲁ]ⲥⲫⲁⲗⲉⲓⲁ ⲁⲗⲗⲁ ⲛⲓ,ⲧⲓ
ⲧⲉ[|] (inserted above following ⲛⲁⲥⲫⲁⲗ[ ) | ⲧⲓ . ⲉⲱ ⲛⲁⲃ ⲝⲉⲛ[

Verso ҇ⲗ︦ⲟ︦ⲩ ⲥⲟⲛ [space] ⲁⲩⲱ ⲉⲛⲛⲉⲓⲟⲥ ⲁⲃⲃⲁ ⲥⲥⲩⲏⲣ︦ⲟ︦ⲥ̄ + | ϩⲓⲧⲛⲡⲁⲡⲟⲥ⳿ⲧ ⲡⲁⲡⲟⲩⲥⲓⲣ+ + Below
this, in another (?) hand, [ⲛⲁⲓⲛ]ϯ ⲫⲓⲥⲟⲛ ⲛⲛⲗⲟⲩ̈ ⲛⲃⲁⲛⲉ ⲡⲛⲟ̇ (rest illegible) | . . . . ⲁϥⲝⲟⲟⲥ
ⲝⲉϥⲥⲙⲟⲟⲛⲧ ⲉⲣⲉⲡⲁ [   ] ⲡⲁⲣⲁⲣⲟϥ ⲉ̅ϥ̅ | ⲛⲉⲛⲧⲁϥⲝⲟⲟⲥ ⲝⲉⲛⲧⲁⲓⲝⲓⲧϥ ⲛⲛ[   ] ⲅ̄

384 —Papyrus, a fragment, 7×17 cm   Script   moderately ligatured   *Recto* ↑
Above l 1 a cross   ϩ has the form ꙅ
Letter to a woman, beginning ⲛⲓ]ⲙ ⲧⲓϣⲓⲛⲉ ⲉⲧⲟⲩⲙⲙⲉⲣⲓⲧ | and containing greetings
from ⲓⲁⲛⲛⲉ ⲛⲛⲟⲩ, [ⲁⲡ]ⲟⲗⲗⲱ, ⲉⲩⲫⲙⲓⲁ, ϣⲉⲛⲟⲩⲧⲉ, ⲥⲓⲃⲟⲩⲧ[1] (masc)   It continues, giving instruc-
tions as to various articles of property belonging to the writer, ⲁⲩⲱ ⲃⲱⲓⲟⲥ[2] ⲉⲧⲃⲉ|ⲙⲟⲩⲅⲉ
ⲧ[ⲛⲟⲟ]ⲩϥ ⲛⲁⲓ ⲙⲛⲛⲁϩⲟⲓⲧⲉ ϩⲓⲧⲛⲡⲉⲧⲣⲁ | ⲏ ⲙⲙⲟⲛ . ⲗⲁⲕⲧⲉ ⲁⲩⲱ ⲥϩⲁⲓ ⲡⲣⲁⲛ ⲉⲡⲣⲱⲙⲉ ⲛⲁⲓ |
ⲧⲁⲉⲓⲙⲉ [ⲉⲣ]ⲟϥ ⲉⲧⲃⲉⲫⲱ̈ⲃ ⲉⲧⲉⲕⲣⲁⲃⲁⲕⲧⲏ[3] ⲧⲁⲝⲓ ⲧϥⲉⲛⲟⲩⲏ | ⲧⲁ† ⲛⲉⲛⲟ]ⲩⲧϥ ⲛⲏⲧⲛ | (*verso*) ⲁⲩⲱ ⲝⲓ
ⲛⲉⲥⲟⲩⲟ ⲛⲧⲉ[4] ϣⲉⲛⲟⲩⲧⲉ ⲧⲟϭⲟⲩ ϩⲙⲡⲟⲩⲱϣ | ⲉⲡⲛⲟⲩⲧⲉ ⲁⲩⲱ ⲉⲡⲙⲁⲝⲉ ⲡⲣⲟⲥⲕⲩⲛⲉⲓ ⲙⲙⲱⲧⲛ |
ⲟⲩⲝⲁⲓ ϩⲙⲡⲝⲟⲉⲓⲥ +

385. —Papyrus, 15×19 cm   Script   *recto*, ligatureless, *verso*, almost so   *Recto* ↑
Recto   Letter to a superior, wherein 'the 7th day of the feast'[5] and a rent (φόρος) of
80 *artabae* of corn are mentioned

ⲡⲣⲟⲥ]ⲕⲩⲛⲓ ⲛⲧⲉⲛ[| ⲝⲉⲧⲁⲁⲃ ⲛⲁϥ [about 12 letters]ⲛⲟⲩ ϣⲏⲙ ⲙⲉ | [ⲁⲓⲟⲩⲟϭⲡϥ ⲁⲓⲧⲓ [ⲡⲧⲣⲓ-]
ⲙⲏⲥⲓⲟⲛ ⲛⲁⲩ ⲁⲓϩⲓⲥⲉ ⲉⲓ[| ⲛⲛⲉ ⲛⲝⲟⲉⲓⲥ ⲙⲟⲛ ⲧⲉⲭⲣⲓⲁ ⲛⲁϥⲧⲉ ⲡⲉⲭⲁⲩ ⲝⲉⲙ | ϣⲁⲛⲥⲁⲙϥ ⲙⲡⲛϣⲁ
ϩⲙⲡⲟⲩⲱϣ ⲛⲛⲛⲟⲩⲧⲉ ϣⲁⲓⲛⲉϩ ⲟⲩϩ[| ⲛⲧⲉⲕⲙⲛⲧⲝⲟⲉⲓⲥ + ⲁⲩⲱ ⲉⲧⲃⲉ ⲁⲛⲟⲩⲡ ⲛⲧⲁⲧⲁ[| ⲉⲛⲧⲏⲧⲛ
ϥⲧⲟⲟⲩ ⲛⲭⲟⲩⲱⲧ ⲛⲡⲉⲣⲧⲟⲩ ⲛⲥⲟⲩⲟ ⲛⲫⲟⲣⲟⲥ ⲉ[| ⲉⲥⲕⲏ ⲉⲃⲟⲗ ⲛϩⲏⲧϥ ⲧⲉⲧⲛⲟⲓ ⲅⲁⲣ ⲝⲉϥⲁⲓϭⲱϣⲧ
ⲛⲥⲁ[| ⲙⲛⲝⲟⲉⲓⲥ ⲕⲉⲗⲉⲩⲉ ⲝⲓ ⲉϩⲣⲁⲓ ⲛⲁⲓ ⲛⲧⲉⲡⲉⲧⲛⲥⲟⲛ ⲡⲉⲗⲗ[6]

---

[1] Hardly a Coptic name
[2] *V* nos 284, 320 &c   [3] *V* no 252
[4] For ⲛⲓⲙ-?   [5] *V* no 361

[6] *Cf* ⲡⲉⲗⲟⲩⲥⲧⲣⲉ, ⲛⲓⲗⲟⲩⲥⲧⲣⲓⲟⲥ as a name , but in
Jême only (Br Mus nos 376, 385, 418).   Here perhaps
ⲗ̇.ⲗⲟⲩⲥⲧⲣⲓⲟⲥ as a title

Verso Letter from Shenoute to . . and Silas, relating to vine-cultivation. The condition of the fields is dealt with and ploughing referred to The vine-dressers, he learns, have fled he will neither pursue them nor make them promises (λόγος) The recipients are instructed to seek out others to replace them, taking a due of half a *solidus* of each This is apparently to go towards the expense of reeds (?) and of ploughing Isaac had sued the writer for a *tremis* (as rent ? tax ?) for the vineyards this is apparently to be settled, but the phrases are obscure, as indeed are many details, though the reading is usually certain

[+ ai]ϫι ⲛⲉⲛⲥϧⲁⲓ ⲉⲛⲥϧⲁⲓ ⲛⲁⲓ ⲉⲧ[ⲃⲉ]ⲡⲓϣϧⲉ ϫⲉⲁⲩ[. . .]ⲟ ⲡⲛⲟⲩⲧⲉ ⲥⲟⲟⲩⲛ ⲧⲓⲟ ⲛ̄ⲉϣⲡⲏⲣⲉ[1]
ⲛ[ⲙⲟⲛ . . .] | [.] ϧⲁⲧⲏⲕ ⲧⲁⲕ ⲙ . . ⲥϧⲁⲓ ϫⲉ[. .]ⲏⲣ ϣ ⲉ[ ] | [. .] ⲛⲉⲕⲁⲉⲓ ⲡⲁ[. . .
. . . . . ⲡ]ⲗⲏⲛ ⲧⲓⲥⲟⲟⲩⲛ | [ϫⲉ]ⲛⲏⲣ ⲡⲉⲛϧ[ⲱⲃ . . . . . .]ⲑⲉ ⲛ̄ⲧⲁⲕⲥϧⲁⲓ ⲛⲁⲓ | [ⲉ]ⲧⲃⲉⲛⲉϭⲙⲏⲩⲟⲩ ϫⲉⲁ[ⲩⲡ]ⲱⲧ
ⲡⲣⲱⲧⲟⲛ ⲙⲉⲛ | ⲙ̄ⲡⲱⲧ ⲉⲥⲱⲟⲩ ⲟⲩⲇⲉ ⲟⲛ ⲙ̄ⲧⲓ ⲗⲟⲅⲟⲥ ⲛⲁⲩ ⲁⲩⲱ ⲧⲓⲙⲉⲩ | ϫⲙ̄ⲡⲁⲧⲉⲙⲙⲁⲓⲟⲩⲙⲁ[2]
ⲛ̄ⲣⲁⲧⲟⲙⲉ ⲁⲛⲁⲩ ⲟⲩⲛ ⲉϧⲛⲥ|ⲙⲏⲩⲟⲩ ⲉⲛⲁⲡⲟⲩⲟⲩ ⲧⲁⲁⲩ ⲉⲣⲟⲟⲩ ⲁⲩⲱ ⲁⲛⲁⲩ ϫⲉⲕⲁϣ|ϫⲓ ⲟⲩⲡⲁϣⲉ
ⲛ̄ϧⲟⲗⲟⲕⲟⲧⲧⲓ ⲉⲧⲟⲟⲧⲏ ⲉⲡⲟⲩⲁ ⲡⲟⲩⲁ ϧⲙ̄ⲛⲉϭ|ⲙⲏⲩⲟⲩ ⲉⲛⲁⲧⲁⲁⲩ ⲉϧⲟⲩⲛ ⲉⲟⲩⲱϧ ⲧⲁⲁⲩ° ⲛ̄ⲛⲉϭⲁⲙ[4] |
ⲥⲟ[ⲩⲥ]ⲕⲁⲉⲓ ⲛⲓϣϧⲉ ⲁⲩⲱ ⲉⲡⲓⲇⲏ ⲁⲓⲥⲁⲕ ⲉⲓ ⲃⲟⲗ ⲛⲉⲙⲁⲓ | ⲉⲩⲧⲣⲓⲙⲏⲥⲓ ϧⲁⲛϭⲟⲟⲙ ⲉⲛⲁⲭⲣ[5] ϧⲓⲧⲃ
ϣⲟⲡⲃ | ⲉϧⲣⲉ ⲁⲩⲱ ⲛ̄ⲛⲉⲛⲧⲁⲁⲩ ϧⲓⲧⲃ ⲉⲧⲉϣⲟⲓ[6] ⲧⲁⲁⲃ ⲉⲡⲉⲃ|ⲙⲁ ϧⲁⲡⲗⲱⲥ ⲑⲉ ⲉⲕⲟⲩⲱϣ ⲙⲁⲣⲉⲛⲕⲁⲙ
ⲙⲟⲩⲣ | ⲡⲕⲁⲙ ⲙⲟⲛ ϧⲟⲟⲩⲛ ϫⲉ[. .] ⲁⲩⲱ ⲡⲛⲟⲩⲧⲉ | ⲥⲟⲟⲩⲛ ϫⲉⲛ . ⲩⲙⲉ ⲛ̄ϭⲣⲟⲙ ⲣ ⲣ.ⲁⲩ
ϧⲏⲩ | ⲣⲟⲙⲡⲓ[. .]ⲕⲁϧϥ ⲙ̄ⲡ ⲉϧⲉⲛⲁⲕ ⲉⲥⲟ[.] . .

The address is on the other side, above the text [. . . .]ⲱⲧⲛ ⲙ̄ⲛⲥⲓⲗⲁⲥ + ϧⲓⲧ|ϣⲉⲛⲟⲩⲧ[ⲉ

386.—Papyrus, a fragment, 4 × 30½ cm Script ligatureless *Recto* ↑

Letter from Cosma to Victor, 'his brother,' giving various information and instructions

[+] ⲛ̄ϣⲟⲣⲡ ⲙⲉⲛ ⲛ̄ϧⲱⲃ ⲛⲓⲙ ⲧⲓϣⲓⲛⲉ ⲛ̄ⲧⲉⲕⲙⲛ̄ⲧⲥⲟⲛ ϧⲙ̄ⲡϫⲟⲉⲓⲥ ⲭⲥ̄, ⲧⲓⲧⲁⲙⲟ ⲛ̄ⲧⲉⲕⲙⲛ̄ⲧⲥⲟⲛ |
]ϫⲉⲕⲁⲧⲁ ⲑⲉ ⲛ̄ⲧⲁⲓⲉⲓ ⲉⲃⲟⲗ ϧⲓⲧⲟⲟⲧⲕ ⲁⲕϫⲟⲟⲥ ϫⲉϣⲁⲓⲃⲱⲕ ⲧⲁϫⲓ ⲧⲡⲁϣⲉ ⲛ̄ϧⲟⲗⲟⲕⲟⲧⲧⲓ ⲛ̄ⲥⲟⲩ[ⲟ |
]ⲉϧⲛ̄ϣ[. . .]ⲃⲱⲕ ⲅⲁⲣ ⲧⲁⲕⲁⲡⲉ ϫⲏⲩ ⲡⲉϣⲛⲉⲣ[7] ⲥⲛⲁⲩ ⲛⲁⲓ ⲁⲩⲱ ⲁⲣⲓ ⲧⲁⲕⲁⲡⲉ ⲧⲓ ϧⲧⲏⲕ [|] ⲁⲩⲱ
ⲧⲓϣⲓⲛⲉ ⲉⲛⲉⲓⲕⲉⲧⲓ ϣⲏⲣⲉ ⲁⲩⲱ ϫⲏⲩ ⲡⲉⲛ[|] ϧⲙ̄ⲡϫⲟⲉⲓⲥ [

Verso + ⲧⲁⲁⲥ ⲙ̄ⲡⲁⲥⲟⲛ ⲃⲓⲕⲧⲱⲣ [space] ϧⲓⲧⲛ̄ⲕⲟⲥⲙⲁ ⲡⲉⲕⲥ[ⲟⲛ

387.—Papyrus, a fragment, 10 × 8½ cm Script. moderately ligatured *Recto* ↑.

Letter, giving various instructions.

ⲧⲓ]ⲟ ⲛ̄ϣⲡⲏⲣⲉ ⲙ̄ⲙⲟⲛ ⲉⲡⲓⲛⲟϭ ⲉⲛ[|]ⲁⲩⲉⲓ ⲥⲓⲙⲁⲩ ⲧⲣⲉⲡⲛⲟⲩⲧⲉ ⲛⲟⲓ [|]ⲁⲛⲁ ϧⲁⲧⲣⲉ ⲉⲃⲟⲗ ⲁⲛⲗⲟ
ⲉ[ⲛ |]ⲧⲓⲙⲏ ⲛ̄ⲧⲁⲓⲙⲟⲧⲛⲟⲩ ⲛⲁⲕ[8] [|] ⲟⲉⲓⲕ ⲉⲧϧⲛ̄ⲧⲉⲙⲙⲛ̄ⲧⲉ ⲛ[ⲙ |]ⲛ ⲁⲛⲛⲁ ϥⲟⲓ ⲉⲃⲟⲗ[9] ⲉⲣⲉ[|]ϫⲓ

---

[1] *V* no 398
[2] Corrupt? Sense could be made by omitting ⲙⲁⲓ
[3] 'That they may be again (*or* in addition) paid (*or* may continue to pay)'
[4] ? = ⲕⲁⲙ below Scarcely for ϭⲱⲙ, as its plural occurs below

[5] A new word? ⲭⲣ[ⲟ]ϫ for ϭⲣⲟϭ would be abnormal in this idiom
[6] One is tempted to take ⲓ for a disjunctive particle
[7] ? 'Send 2 half-measures of oil'
[8] *Cf* no 343   [9] *Cf* no 382, l 1

ⲛⲁⲡⲗⲱ[1] ϫⲉⲁϩⲉⲣⲁⲧⲕ ⲉϥⲱ[ⲃ2] |]ⲣⲁⲓ ⲙⲉⲛⲡⲁⲥⲟⲛ ⲁⲩⲱ ⲁⲛⲟⲕ ⲁ[ ]]ⲁⲡⲉⲓϩⲱⲃ ⲁⲓϫⲟⲟⲥ ϫⲉⲙⲉⲥⲉⲣ[ ] ⲡ]ⲉⲓϩⲱⲃ ⲁⲩⲱ ⲧⲓϣⲓⲛⲉ ⲡⲁⲥⲟⲛ ⲁ[ ]

Verso   ]ⲛϫⲟⲉⲓⲥ ⲛⲓⲱⲧ ⲁⲡⲁ [

388 —Papyrus, a fragment, 14 × 8 cm   Script uneven, rarely ligatured   *Verso* →
Letter, giving instructions as to the purchase of various articles

⸎ ⲥⲩⲛ ⲁ[ ]ⲉ[3] ⲥⲓⲱⲣⲙⲉ [| ⸎ ⲥⲩⲛ ⲉⲕϣⲁⲛϫⲓ ⲛⲛⲁⲥϩⲟ[ⲓ | ⲧⲓ ⲥⲏⲓⲧⲉ ⲕⲟⲓⲡⲉ ⲛⲓⲱⲧ | ⲉⲁⲃⲣⲁ-
ϩⲁⲙ ⲁⲩⲱ [| ϣⲡ ϣⲥⲙⲛⲧ ⲉϣⲗⲁⲉⲓ[ⲛ4 | ⲁⲩⲱ ⲟⲩⲡⲁϣ ⲛϣⲛⲉ ⲙⲛ[| ⲉⲥⲓⲙ ⲁⲩⲱ ⲁⲙⲟⲩ ⲣⲏ[ⲥ | ⲡⲉ
ⲡⲉⲛⲁⲣⲏⲧ[5] ⲧⲁⲭⲏ ⸎   [| ⲁⲩⲱ ϫⲓ ⲛⲟⲩⲁⲡⲓⲟⲛ ⲧⲉⲩⲕⲁ[| ⲉⲕⲁⲥ ⲉϩⲟⲩⲛ ⲛⲁⲓ   blank

Recto   remains of an Arabic text (earlier), naming Derût, الى درن طور   .

389 —Papyrus, a fragment, 13½ × 11½ cm   Script late, ligatured   *Recto* ↑
Apparently two texts, since the *recto*, mostly illegible, ends with ⲧⲓⲡⲣⲟⲥⲕ⸍ ⲁⲩⲱ ⲧⲓ[

Verso   probably same hand   Its writer gives certain instructions and threatens his displeasure

]ⲣⲱⲙⲉ ⲧⲛⲟⲟⲩ ⲉⲛ[.]| ϣⲓⲛⲉ ⲛⲥⲱϥ ⲉⲓⲥ ⲥⲟⲡ[. . .6] | ⲛⲡⲉⲛⲉⲓⲙⲉ ϫⲉⲧⲃⲉⲟⲩ ⲗⲟⲓ[ⲛ] | ⲧⲁⲙⲟⲓ
ⲉⲛⲧⲱϣ ⲉⲡⲣⲱϥ | ⲁⲩⲱ ⲥⲉⲣϣⲓⲡⲉ ⲉⲣⲟⲥ ⲉⲡⲉⲃϩⲱϥ | ⲉⲡⲉⲓ ⲕⲥⲟⲟⲩⲛ ⲛⲟⲥ ⲛⲧⲁⲓⲥⲁⲁⲧⲕ | ⲉⲃⲟⲗ ϩⲓⲭⲱⲥ
ⲁⲩⲱ ⲉⲕϣⲁⲛ|ⲕⲁ ⲟⲩϣⲁϫⲉ ⲛϣⲱⲡⲉ ϩⲓⲡⲉⲃ|ϩⲱϥ ⲙⲉⲕⲉϣⲧⲱⲟⲩⲛ ϩⲁⲧⲁ|ⲁⲣⲓⲕⲉ ⲗⲟⲓ ⲥϩⲁⲓ ⲛⲁⲓ ϫⲉⲃ|ϣⲓⲛⲉ
ⲛⲥⲱϥ ⲉⲧⲃⲉⲟⲩ ⲛⲉⲁⲓⲁ[7] | ⲧⲓⲡⲣⲟⲥⲕ⸍ +

390.—Papyrus, a fragment, 11 × 11 cm   Script ligatured, *v* Pl 6   The ligature
in ⲛⲟⲩⲧⲉ, l 2, recurs in a papyrus dated A D 827[8]   *Verso* →
Letter of invitation

⸎ ⲧⲏⲣⲏⲛⲏ ⲛⲁⲕ ⲉⲃⲟⲗ | ϩⲓⲧⲙⲡⲛⲟⲩⲧⲉ ⲧⲓⲧⲁⲙⲟ | ⲙⲙⲟⲕ ϫⲉⲡϣⲁ | ⲡⲟⲟⲩ ⲗⲟⲓⲡⲟⲛ | ⲁⲙⲟⲩ ⲉϩⲣⲁⲓ
ϣⲁⲕ|ⲥⲱ ϩⲁⲣⲟⲓ ⲙⲡⲟⲟⲩ |[.] ⲙⲡⲣⲥⲱ ⲛⲁⲧ .|

'Peace unto thee from God   I (would) inform thee that to day is the festival   Come up then (λοιπόν) and stay to day with me   Be not .. '

Recto   an Arabic text (earlier), showing the name Nasr, كتاب الى نصر   .

391 —Papyrus, a fragment, 7½ × 9½ cm   Script some ligatures   *Recto* ↑
From a letter   ]ⲛ. . .ⲉ ⲛⲙⲓⲧⲁⲱ[ⲗ9 | ϩⲁⲑⲏ ⲙⲛ ⲡϩⲱϥ ⲛⲓⲙ ⲧⲓ[|] ⲧⲉⲧⲛⲉϫⲓ ⲡⲉⲓⲕⲟⲩ[ⲓ |
ⲓⲱ]ϩⲁⲛⲛⲏⲥ ⲫⲓⲉⲣⲉⲩ[ⲥ10 | ϩⲁⲗⲱⲙ ⲟⲩⲣⲁⲁⲣ[11] ⲟ[ⲩ

---

[1] ? Apollo   [2] V KRALL ccxxviii 6, ccxl   [8] The Rainer *Führer*, 1894, Taf. viii   V also nos 380,
[3] Not ⲁⲛⲟⲕ   [4] 'Nasturtium'   [5] ? ⲁⲣⲏⲃ   405
[6] Space for ⲥⲛⲁⲩ, but could this be thus used?   [9] V. no 158.
[7] ⲁⲓⲧⲓⲁ   [10] Ἱερεύς   V nos 177, 278   [11] V no 158

392.—Paper, a fragment, 9 × 12 cm.   Script . ligatured

Letter treating of various matters

ϯ ⳉ ϯϣⲓⲛⲉ ⲉⲣⲟⲕ ⲕⲁⲗⲱ̄ ⲉⲣⲉⲡⲟⲥ̅ ⲕⲁⲁⲕ ⲁⲓϫⲱ|ⲱⲃ ⲉⲣⲟⲕ ϩⲓⲧⲡⲁⲣ[1] ⲉⲕⲧⲁⲙⲟⲓ ϫⲉⲧⲛⲟⲩ ⲡⲉⲕⲥⲁϫⲟ[2] |
ⲛⲁⲓ ⲧⲁⲉⲣⲧⲉⲛⲁⲡⲟⲕⲣⲁⲥⲓⲥ ⲗⲟⲓ ϩⲓⲧⲁⲃⲓ |

Recto part of an Arabic account (earlier), mentioning Fustât, الفسطاط   .

393.—Papyrus, a fragment, 14 × 15 cm   Script clumsy uncials.   Resembles that of
no 340 and, in a less degree, that of no 165   *Recto* →

Letter from   . to his 'brother'

ϯ ϩⲁⲑⲏ ⲙⲛ ϩⲱⲃ ⲛⲓⲙ ϯϣⲓⲛⲉ ⲉⲡⲁⲥⲟ[ⲛ | ⲥⲡⲓϫⲏ ⲁⲕⲉⲓ ⲙⲡϩⲟⲟⲩ ⲙⲡⲓϭⲛ ⲑⲉ ⲛ[| ⲙⲁⲕ ⲙⲡⲣϭⲱ
ⲉⲛⲧⲁⲗⲉ ⲙⲟⲧⲉ ⲉ[ϩⲣⲁⲓ[3] | ⲉⲧⲃⲏⲧ ⲉⲙⲟⲛ ⲉⲕⲛⲏⲩ ⲁⲛ ⲉⲧⲃⲏⲧ ϩⲁ[| ⲕⲟⲩⲱⲛⲉ ⲛⲉⲛⲏⲩ [. ⲛ]ⲗⲏⲛ ⲙⲡⲣ |
ϫⲥⲕⲏⲛⲧ ⲁⲗⲗⲁ ⲉⲣⲉⲡⲁϩⲏⲧ ϩⲟⲥⲉ ⲛ[| ϫⲱⲣⲡ ⲉⲩⲧⲁϩⲟ ⲙⲟⲓ ⲁⲩⲱ ⲡⲣϭⲱ ⲉⲕ[| ⲙⲁⲓ ⲙⲟⲛ ⲛⲥⲛϩⲉ
ⲁⲛ ⲉⲓ[4] ⲙⲡⲉⲉⲛⲣⲣⲟⲩⲱ [| ⲡⲙⲁ ⲙⲡⲣⲟ ⲙⲡϩⲟⲟⲩ ⲉⲛⲉϩ ⲁⲩⲱ [|[ⲉ]ⲣⲟⲕ ⲥⲧⲃⲉⲛⲩϫⲁϫⲉ ⲛϫⲱ[.] ⲡϫⲱⲕ.. ⲁ[|
ⲙⲁⲩⲧⲁ ⲟⲥ ϫⲉⲡⲁⲛⲟⲩ ⲧⲓ ⲉ[| ⲥⲟⲩ ⲉⲕϣⲁⲉⲓⲙⲉ ⲡⲁⲥⲟⲛ ⲛ[| ⲙⲉⲓⲛⲁⲩ ⲉⲣⲟⲕ ⲉⲓⲉ ⲙⲡⲉⲕⲩⲱ[| ⲙⲉ ⲉⲓ
ⲧⲁⲛⲁⲩ ⲉⲣⲟⲕ ⲁⲩⲱ ⲉⲩⲱⲡ[ⲉ | ⲛⲁⲓ ϩⲁⲣⲟⲥ ⲉⲓⲥ ⲙⲡⲣⲣⲟⲩⲱ ⲛⲁⲓ ϣⲁ[| ⲁⲛⲟⲕ ϩⲱⲧ ⲟⲛ ⲓⲁⲣⲣⲟⲩⲱ
ⲛⲁⲕ [|] ϯϣⲓⲛⲉ [

394.—Papyrus, a fragment, 11 × 12 cm   Script almost ligatureless *Recto* ↑.

Apparently a letter, though beginning with the words, 'This is the judgement that
God hath given   '[5] It then proceeds to relate certain events

ϯ ⲡⲁⲡⲉ ⲫⲁⲡ ⲛⲧⲁⲡⲛⲟⲩⲧⲉ ⲧⲁⲁ[ϥ | ⲁⲧⲁϩⲱⲣ[6] ⲧⲥⲁⲃⲟⲓ ⲉϩⲛⲭⲁⲣⲧⲏⲥ ⲉⲓ[| ⲁⲩⲱ ⲁϥϫⲟⲟⲥ
ϫⲉⲁⲓϣⲗⲏⲗ [| ⲛⲉⲥⲕⲉⲩⲉ ⲛⲧⲁⲥⲱⲛⲉ ⲛⲁⲓ ⲉⲃ[| ⲛⲧⲓϩⲉ ⲉⲓⲉ ϣⲁⲥⲁⲁⲥ ⲛⲡⲉ[| ⲧⲉⲥϩⲓⲙⲉ ⲛⲧ[| ϣⲁⲩⲉⲓⲣⲉ
ⲡⲣ[ⲟⲥ | blank

395.—Papyrus, complete, 8 × 27 cm   Script sloping uncials, *cf* Hyvernat ix 2,
col 2 *Recto* ↑.

A writing exercise, in form of a letter

ϯ [ⲥ]ⲏⲛ̄ ϯⲡⲣⲟⲥⲕⲩⲛⲏ ⲉ[ⲡ]ⲟⲩϫⲁⲓ ⲛⲡⲁⲙⲉⲣⲓ[ⲧ] ⲛϫⲟⲉⲓⲥ ⲛⲓⲱⲧ ⲛ[ⲅⲣ]ⲓ ⲉⲡⲙⲁ ⲭⲟⲥ | ϩⲙⲡⲁϩⲏⲧ
ⲙⲛⲧⲁⲯⲩⲭⲏ ⲙⲛⲛⲥⲁⲛⲁⲓ ⲧⲓ(*sic*)

Lower down + [ⲥ]ⲏⲛ̊ ϯⲡⲣⲟ̊ⲕⲩⲛⲉ ⲛ(*sic*)   *Verso*. Arabic pen-trials

---

[1] ? The Virgin's church
[2] *V* no 129
[3] 'Do not continue to raise (thy) shoulders'   Can this
have the meaning of the modern idiom ?

[4] ? ⲉⲓⲉ.
[5] Is this comparable with the formula, ' Lo, here is God s
word' &c (*v* Crum, *Ostr* no 107, Br Mus no 1024)?
[6] *V* Krall clxvn, Cairo 8409 (clearly fem)

396—Papyrus, a fragment, 16×11½ cm.　Script of early type, v Pl 4　By the scribe of no 275　Note the careful superlineation　*Recto →*

Letter, whereof a woman is the subject, a conversation with her being reported　The dialect is fully Achmimic, but as differing in degree only from other of our texts, in which Saïdic preponderates, it is placed among them

ογ]ωμ εαεϥ ϯπαεϥ αγω αη θε |]αταϩ[.] πεμεϲ ϊ . . p̄¹ ϩαϱοpϊ² |]ϲε μμαϲ ϫεαpιϲμα ϫειϫε |]τπαϲε ντπϯϲτωτε πεϲ ωϊ |]εοϱε ετβεογ ατετμα ϫετε |]ϲωπε ϫε³ ϯπαϯ εη εηωωϫτ |]τϱεγ πεϲ αηαη αp̄ϲϱιμε⁴ |]εϭαμεγτε μα⁵ ϫεταϲωπε |] ϯπακωτ⁶ εη ογτε ϯπαϯ |]αιογ εϲϩαγπε ϩωκ ϫε |]ογϲϱιμε ογμ ϭπαλ |]ϲαϫϥε⁷ μμαι μμπα |]ϥ ϩωτ μπp̄(above κο)τε⁸ ντε⁹ |]μμαγ πμμαpϲ̄ αραι |]ϟ πηι πογμαϭ |]πογαιϫ

397—Papyrus, a fragment, 12½×13½ cm　Script uneven, moderately ligatured *Verso →*

Letter from John and his mother to his 'dear lord brother .　'

]πϩωβ πιμ αηοκ επϣ̄ μπτεϥμααγ | πϲε]επε πεπρωμ ϊπρογ τεπϣιπε εροκ |] τιταμο πμοκ παϲοπ ϫεοπϲ |].ϭ πϭα ταας τρομπε ετπτεκ | ϊϲ εϊ πτκϫι ογϭαπε¹⁰ ειειpε | ε]ϱαιϲογ πμοογ ηακ ϫεογϭαπε |]μ ϫεαπεκϲϱαι εϊ |]πατα π .μ |

Recto　✝ ταας πηαμεpϊ¹ πϫοειϲ πϲοη [, also remains of an earlier Arabic text

398—Papyrus, a fragment, 16×10 cm　Script v Pl 6　*Recto ↑*
Letter of uncertain purport

✠ ϩμπραη επηογτε τιϣιπε | τιο πτεκϣπιρε¹¹ πηαγ πϣα[| ϣιπε ϲωι ογϫε μεπτποϲογ | θεβηρε αη ερϣαππρωμε | αγω ειϲ ϩωριοπ αιτπο[ογ]ϥ | παι ϣαπτεκει παι εϱραι [| ποηριϲιϲ ϩαϱτηι αγω ε[| πετροϲ μππεικογι ϣ[ηρε | αγεπτογ ϫεερεπϣε ππα[| ε ϣαπει εϱραι περϭω | π[| πογωϣ επηογτε ϥ . [

399—Papyrus, a fragment, complete in height and width, 30×8½ cm　Script early type, almost ligatureless, *cf* that of no 270　*Recto →*

Letter to a woman¹², referring to legal affairs

✝ επειϫη [| πϲαπαγλος αϥ [| αγϲγπταϲη¹³ ε[| επϩαπ αποκ ϫε μπογϫι λααγ πϣ[α]ϫε ερ[|] πεπιϲι[..] αη κα . | επϩαπ [] τα . οϲ ϫ.[| αγω . πα] | αp̄ϫοος ϫ..[| μηρη . p

---

¹ After ι was ϲ or ω　　² 1st p was altered
³ ϫ was ϯ　　⁴ α was p
⁵ ? μμα fem　But μεγτε, if=μογτε, should have apa
⁶ ϛ was π
⁷ ϫϥ altered, former perhaps erased
⁸ p was ω　　⁹ π was τ.　　¹⁰ ? ἀγάπη

¹¹ Usually ϯο πϣπ μμοκ οι ϯpϣπ μμοκ
¹² Assuming l 6 to be a quotation
¹³ In literary texts συντάσσεσθαι usually=ϩωπ, but v Crum, *Ostr* nos 356, Ad 49　Sometimes it is 'bid fare well', ϲγπταϲε, Rossi, *Nuov Cod* 30, Giron, *Légendes* 64　Bodleian MS copt g 3 (a fragment apparently from Br Mus no 359)

[. . . . . . .] | ⲛϣⲁϫⲉ ⲥⲩ . . ⲛϫⲏ[. .] | ⲉⲣⲟⲥⲉ ⲧⲁⲕⲱ ⲥϩⲉ[. . . .] | ⲟⲩⲁⲁⲧ ϩⲁⲡⲁⲧⲟⲩ . . | ⲙⲟⲛⲟⲛ
ⲧⲁϧⲙⲟ[ⲟ]ⲥ   . | ϣⲁⲛⲧⲉⲓⲙⲏ ϫ . . .] | ϧⲏⲧⲧⲟⲩ ⲕⲁⲓ ⲥⲁⲣ[. . . .] | ⲙⲛⲧⲣⲉ ϫⲏⲙⲛⲣⲏ ⲁⲣ[. . .] |
ϩⲱⲣⲏ ⲛⲛⲟⲗ .]ϩⲁ[. .] | ϩⲁⲛ ⲡⲁⲓ[| ⲉⲓ [| ⲉⲩ[| ⲕⲱ[| ⲛ[| blank

400.—Papyrus, a fragment, 13 × 26½ cm   Script clumsy, ligatureless   *Recto* ↑

Letter from   . to 'our dear son' John, the purport of which is obscure   It opens
with greetings to several persons

]ⲙⲁⲕⲁⲣⲉ ⲉⲓⲥϩⲁⲓ |]ⲧⲛⲉ ⲛⲙⲙⲁⲏⲣⲉ ᶜⳑⲧⲁⲩⲣⲱⲩ ⲙⲛⲡⲉⲩϫⲁⲓ | [. . . ..]ⲟⲩ ⲉⲃⲟ[ⲗ] .
ⲉⲡⲛⲟⲩⲧⲉ ϫⲛⲧⲁⲙⲁⲛⲁ|ⲣ[ⲉ] . . . . . ⲉⲕⲟⲩ . . . ⲥⲟⲩⲛⲉ ϫⲟⲟⲩ ϩⲁⲗⲟ|ⲛⲟ[ⲧ] . . . . . . .ⲏⲥ
ⲁⲩ . . . . . ⲉϣⲏⲣⲉ ⲧⲁⲓⲥⲁⲛ ⲛⲓⲱ[1] | ϫⲉⲡ . . ⲛⲁⲛⲓⲭⲉ . . ⲉⲣⲡⲉ ⲉⲥⲟ [ⲛⲧⲓϧⲏ ⲁⲩⲉⲓ ⲉⲓⲣⲏⲥ ⲉⲧⲃⲉ
ⲡⲏ[ⲟⲩ]ⲧⲉ ⲥⲡⲓ ⲉⲓ ⲥⲛⲏⲕⲟⲩⲓ ϣ[ⲏⲣⲉ ⲁⲛⲛⲉ ϣⲁⲓⲧⲉⲧⲙⲥ | ⲱⲟ . . ϩⲛⲧⲉⲛ[ⲙⲛⲧⲉ ⲛϩⲟⲛⲛⲓⲕ . ⲧⲛⲏⲓ[2]
ⲁⲩⲱ ⲥⲧϣⲁⲛϣⲓⲛⲉ | [. . . . .] ϣⲏⲣⲉ ⲧⲓ ⲛϩ . .ⲥⲟⲥ ⲛⲁⲩ ⲁⲩⲱ ⲙⲁⲛⲟⲩⲣⲡⲉ |

Verso [ⲡⲉⲛⲙⲉⲣ]ⲓⲧ ⲛϣⲏⲣⲉ ⲓⲱ [space] ⲁ[ⲛⲛⲏⲥ   ?

401—Papyrus, a fragment, 13½ × 12 cm.   Script   small, ligatured.   *Verso* →

Letter, mentioning the place Tsesio[3] and concluding, 'But go if thou wilt or stay
if thou wilt'

]ϫⲛⲧⲁⲕⲉⲓ ⲉϩⲟⲩⲛ ⲉⲕⲛⲏⲧ ϣⲁⲡⲟⲟⲩ |.]ⲉⲓ ⲉϩⲟⲩⲛ ⲉⲧⲥⲉⲥⲓⲱ ⲗⲟⲓⲡⲟⲛ ⲧⲓⲱⲣⲕ | . . . .]
ⲉⲓ ⲉϩⲟⲩⲛ ⲉⲣⲟⲥ | .] ⲛⲓⲙⲙⲟⲟⲩ ⲉⲥⲱⲕ ⲉⲧⲧⲁⲃⲗⲁ[4] | ⲗⲟⲓⲡⲟⲛ ⲉⲕⲟⲩⲱϣ ⲉⲓ ⲉⲕⲟⲩⲱϣ | ⲥⲱ
+ [ⲙ́] ᶦᵟⳑ ⲓⲁ +

Recto   Remains of an earlier Arabic text, in unpointed semi-Cufic character[5]   It
is a list, probably relating to taxation, and consisting of names of Copts, followed by those
of their domiciles, several of which remain to be identified   The two last lines show
Muslim witnesses

⳽ ⲥⲩ̄ⲛ ⲛⲓⲩⲟⲡ[6] ϯ̄ ⲗⲁⲣ . [

[ⲥⲙ] [ ] ادى عمر بن افلو[7] من اهل سموا الصعرى°
[اد] [ ] د[طرو دن مبوس° من اهل سواڡ
[ⲓⲙⲁ دطرد من اهل دمو[10] قلمبى
[ ] نطر بن دصا[11] من أهل دلطس[12]
سهد على دلك عمر بن ادى دعم العد[]
? عبد اللّه بن سهاب° الحصر[]°[14]

---

[1] Difficult to read otherwise   Dots above ⲓ
[2] Not ⲡⲉⲧⲛⲏⲓ   [3] V no 159
[4] V no 322, whence it appears to relate to taxation
Cf ⲧⲁⲃⲗⲓⲛ *Aeg Z* 1885, 34, and طبل in *Mitth Rain* ii.
163   In Lagarde, *Aeg* 223 ⲧⲁⲃⲃⲁ (ⲧⲁⲃⲗⲁ) = κυβοις
[5] Cf B Moritz, *Ar Palæogr* pl. 106 (A D 731) or
C. H Becker, *P Schott-Reinh* i, no 1 (A D 710)
[6] ابو   Presumably the writer of the Arabic text   Cf
no 328

[7] Neither *f* nor *w* are elsewhere formed as here , but
the reading 'Apollo' is irresistible
[8] Cf ⲥⲓⲙⲟⲩ in no 302 and Br Mus no 1130
[9] For مساوس   But *m* is uncertain
[10] Cf De Sacy, *Abd al-Latif* 693 ادمر
[11] Possibly لكا.   Bisa is usually وصا and is a very rare
name
[12] May end with *n*
[13] I cannot read شهاب   1st letter ? *m*   [14] الحاصر ?

402—Papyrus, a fragment; 8 × 6½ cm   Script rarely ligatured   *Verso* →.

Letter containing the description of a man's features, referring to 'heavy eyebrows[1]', 'the hair of his beard' and a 'strap (μαγκλάβιον[2]) on his back'

] ϛ ογρωμε εϥтнϣпϲ | ν]εϥεμхнϩ рнт |]нвω ϩιтϲϥмор+т | м]анλавιν ϩнпεϥϲοι |

Recto · traces of an Arabic text in semi-Cufic script (earlier)

403—Papyrus, a fragment, 4½ × 14 cm   Script early type, v Pl 4   *Recto* ↑

Letter of uncertain purport

+ ϩαθн мεν мпϣахε +ϣιнε ε[| епειαн амογϲнϲ + хоутаϥтε ι | αϥвнтоу наι ειϲ ϩнп[3] ϲουϩ[| αγω ахιϲ мпαιωт нϥϣλнλ εϩ[раι | ϩιхοн ϩннογειрннι αγω αι | нϲϩαι επεнхοειϲ нιωт ετουααϥ [

Verso   traces of the address

404.—Papyrus, a fragment, 7½ × 13 cm   Script moderately ligatured   *Recto* ↑

Letter, the language of which is particularly obscure   In l 3 the Nile seems to be mentioned[4]

]нατω мλογ миикωмιϲ тнϲι επεн[ ]|ϭнтϥ αγω αικω енεμα тнроу [.] | раｊϲтε нтнγрιαнι λοιпον αмιι нпϥ [ ] |]εμαγ αγω ωрх енрок αмα ιϲι | пαнтοк]рατωр ετεннγ επι ετεμпιει |]тι επι ειнατεхε ετвнтнγтн |]λγп . таιтнοογ пαϣнрε αнογтε |

405.—Papyrus, a fragment, 4 × 13½ cm   Script late, ligatured   *Verso* →

Letter (?) containing the words, 'for a remembrance of the beginning of our holy fasts of Our Lord Jesus Christ, Our God'

]нι ει ϩιωωϥ [|] εγεрпмεγε нтαрхн ннεнннϲтια | е͡уογααв ннεнхοειϲ ι͡ϲ пε͡х͡ϲ пεннογτε[5] ι | н]ммнтн |

Recto   traces of an account

406.—Papyrus, a fragment, 6½ × 12½ cm   Script clumsy, ligatureless   *Recto* ↑

Letter mentioning—possibly addressed to—a tribune

ϲ]ϩαι ερατϥ мпετрιвογноϲ |]хοοϲ ероι ϩраι мпεннι |]ϥнι αιвωк мнтε   μαϲ |

---

[1] Cf Mus Guimet xxv 62 εрехωϥ рнт
[2] Occurs in Mitth Rain v 48 Possibly here refers to marks of punishment In Br Mus no 1113 read манλавιϲε 'μαγκλαβίζειν Cf Rev Egypol ix 170 ('200 strokes)

[3] Note this early form
[4] Νεῖλου? Nilopolis is unlikely   κατω is difficult 'the lower part of the river'?
[5] Ligature as in no 390.

407.—Papyrus; a fragment, $27\frac{1}{2} \times 10$ cm   Script *v* Pl 6   *Recto* ↑

Letter beginning ⲋ ⲧⲓⲡⲣⲟⲥⲕ/ ⲛⲧⲉⲕⲙⲛⲧⲙ[ⲉⲣⲓⲧ, and containing the phrases ⲣⲱⲙⲉ] ⲛⲅⲁ-
ⲗⲁⲓⲡⲱⲣⲟⲥ ⲡⲥⲁϩ ⲅⳇⲱⲣⳤⲉ,   ⲛⲥⲧⲱⲗⲙⲡⲣⲁⲧⲕ ⲉϣⲟⲉⲓϣ,   ⲁϣⲧⲉ ⲧⲁⲕⲟⲗⲁⲥⲓⲥ ⲉⲓϩⲓⲱⲱⲥ,   ⲛⲧⲉⲓ
ϣⲁⲣⲟⲓ ⲉⲥⲟⲟⲩⲧⲛ

408.—Papyrus, a fragment, 9×12 cm   Script · sloping uncials resembling Zoega's
9th class   *Verso* →

Letter of uncertain purport

ϯ ϩⲙⲡⲣⲁⲛ ⲙⲡⲛⲟⲩⲧⲉ ⲛϣⲟ[ⲣⲡ | ⲣⲁⲙⲁ ᴵˢⁱᶜ ⲉϭϩⲁⲓ ⲉⲓϣⲓⲛⲉ ⲁⲩⲱ ⲙ | ⲅⲏ ⲁⲩⲱ ⲭⲁⲕⲃⲱⲕ ⲛⲁⲕ
ϣⲁ[| ⲥⲁⲩⲧⲉ ⲉϥϩⲓⲧⲁⲯⲛ̅ⲭⲛ ⲭⲉⲛ[| ϩⲟ ⲙⲡⲉⲥⲕⲁⲁⲧ ⲁⲓⲅⲓ ⲙⲙⲟϥ ⲙⲟⲛ [| ⲧⲉⲗⲟⲥ ⲧⲓ ⲥⲱϣ ⲛⲁⲓ ϩⲓⲛⲁⲓⲙⲉ
ⲧⲏ[ⲣϥ | ⲧⲁⲉⲓ ⲁⲩⲱ ⲉⲥϩⲓⲉ ⲉⲛⲉⲥϣⲏⲣⲉ ⲛⲧ. | ⲁⲗⲁ¹ ϩⲁⲡⲉⲥϣⲓ ⲁⲗⲁ ϩⲁⲡⲛ̅ϣⲓ ⲛⲧⲉ[| ⲛⲧⲁⲛⲉⲣⲁⲧϣⲁⲭⲉ ⲛⲉⲙ
[. . .]ⲁϥ[

On the *recto*, the beginning of a Greek legal text, mentioning the χωρίον Pouanp
digeos²

]κου και ζωοπαιου σ̅ο̅υ π̅ν̅α̅μ̅α̅, |] ινδ θ ⫽   της παρουσης ινδικτιωνος |] π/   ωˢⁱᶜ ᵛ
απ χωριο
τουανπδιγεος |] λαμπροτ̅, + εβαιωδης + |

409—Papyrus, a fragment, 15×17 cm   Script clumsy uncials   *Recto* ↑.

Letter from Claudius 'his servant' to the κῦρις Apa Cyrus³, presumably an official
superior.

+ ϩⲁⲑⲏ ⲙⲛ ⲛⲉϩⲱϥ ⲛⲓⲙ ϯⲡⲣⲟⲥⲕⲏⲛⲉ | ['ⲛ]ⲧⲉⲕⲙⲛⲧϫⲟⲉⲓⲥ ⲉⲡⲓⲧⲉ ⲁⲡⲉⲓ ⲉⲣⲁⲓ ⲁⲛⲡⲁ[ⲣ]ⲁⲕⲁⲗⲉ
ⲙⲟⲕ ⲉⲉⲧⲃⲉⲧⲉⲥϩⲓⲙⲉ ⲧⲁⲣⲉⲛ[ⲁ]ⲁⲥ ⲛⲁⲛ ⲉⲃⲟⲗ ⲁⲕⲱⲣⲕ ⲭⲉⲙⲕⲁⲁⲥ | [ⲉⲃⲟⲗ ⲙⲡⲉⲅⲧⲛⲭⲱⲗⲁϩ⁴ ⲙⲙⲟⲟⲩ
ⲉⲃⲟⲗ | [ⲗ]ⲉⲡⲱⲛ⁶ ⲁⲓⲥⲡⲟⲩⲧⲁⲥⲥⲉ ⲁⲓϯⲛⲣⲉⲃⲛⲓⲕⲧⲟⲣ ; [ⲉ]ⲓⲛⲉ⁶ ⲉⲣⲱⲙⲉ ⲉⲁϥ̅ˢⁱᶜϫⲟⲗⲁϥ⁷ ⲉⲃⲟⲗ ⲉⲗⲉⲡⲱⲛ ⲁⲓ[ⲥ]ϩⲁⲓ
ⲉⲓⲡⲁⲣⲁⲕⲁⲗⲉ ⲙⲙⲟⲕ ⲧⲁⲣⲉⲕⲁⲁⲥ ⲛⲁϥ | [+ⲃⲟⲗ ϫⲉϩⲱϥ ⲛⲓⲙ ⲉⲧⲉⲣⲧⲉⲕⲙⲛⲧϫⲟⲉⲓⲥ | ⲛⲁⲧⲛⲟⲩⲥⲟⲩ ⲛⲁⲓ
ϩⲓⲧⲛⲡⲉⲕϩⲁⲟⲛ ⲧⲓⲛⲁ[ⲁ]ⲁⲩ ⲧⲁⲭⲏ (different hand) ⲁⲛⲟⲛ ⲧⲓⲡⲁⲣⲁⲕⲁⲗⲓ ⲛⲙⲱⲧⲛ | [about 14 let]
ⲛⲉⲕⲕⲁⲁⲥ ⲛⲁⲛ ⲉ[ⲃⲟⲗ

Verso (by the 2nd hand)   [+ⲧⲁⲁⲥ] ⲛⲛⲁⲭⲉⲓⲥ ⲛⲕⲓⲣⲉⲥ ⲁⲡⲁ ᵗ | ⲕⲓⲣⲉ ⲡⲉϥϩⲁⲟⲩⲟⲛ ⲕⲗⲁⲩⲧⲉ +

'Before all things I do obeisance (προσκυνεῖν) to thy lordship   Since (ἐπειδή) we came
up and requested (παρακαλεῖν) thee concerning the woman, that thou wouldst release her
unto us and thou didst swear, saying, 'I will not release her ere ye have drawn the
water,' then (λοιπόν) I was diligent (σπουδάζειν) and had Victor bring (?) the man that
had drawn it   And (λοιπ) I have written begging (παρακ) thee that thou wouldst release
her unto him   For everything which thy lordship shall send me by thy servant, I will

---

¹ ἀλλά   ἀλλά, expressing alternatives?   Guimet xvii 264, elsewhere = ϥⲱⲛⲕ
² Cf the forms in nos 158 note, 281   ⁵ Not space for ⲉⲗⲉⲡⲱⲛ as below
³ V no. 282   ⁶ Or ϣⲓⲛⲉ or ϭⲓⲛⲉ or possibly ⲭⲓ
⁴ Cf Br Mus nos 1036, 1130 Boh ϭⲱⲗϩ in *Mus*   ⁷ Or ϫⲟⲗϥϥ.

speedily (ταχύ) perform   And (λοιπ) I[1] beg (παρακ) you   would release her
unto us   . .'

410.—Papyrus, a fragment; $7\frac{1}{2} \times 16$ cm   *V* Pl 9   *Recto* (?) ↑

Text written in some system of cryptogram or stenography, representing probably a
Greek text   Some signs resemble those in the Rainer *Führer*, Taf xiii 444   Letters of
the ordinary alphabet are frequently used   Above this is a line of tall characters similar
to those in Crum, *Ostraca*, p 85 (facsim), Ad 6

Verso (?) the text continued

---

[1] This is a different person

MIDDLE EGYPTIAN MANUSCRIPTS

411.—Papyrus, a fragment, 8 × 11 cm   Text in one column   Script   heavy uncials, differing much on *recto* and *verso*   *V.* Pl 1 for *recto*[1]   On the *verso* there is an undeniable resemblance to the 10th century type of Bohairic hand from Nitria

Dioscorus of Alexandria, narrative relating to   The text corresponds to pp 59, 60, 275, 276 of NAU's Syriac version[2]

→ [ⲇⲓⲟⲥⲕⲟ]ⲣⲟⲥ ⲛⲛⲁϥ   ⌐ ⲡⲱⲧ ⲉⲃⲁⲗ ϩ[ⲛⲡⲏⲓ ⲙⲡⲉⲃ-]
     ] ⲛϫⲉ ⲟⲩⲉⲓ   ⲓⲱⲧ ⲛⲥⲁⲃⲏ[ⲗ ϫⲉⲁϥϫⲁⲓ]
[ϩⲙⲡⲁⲗⲗⲁ]ⲛⲧⲓⲟⲛ[3] ⲧⲁ   ⲛϫⲉ ⲉⲥⲁⲩ[4] ϫ[ⲉⲙⲁⲗⲟⲩϩⲱⲛ]
     ]ⲛⲟⲩ ⲉⲃⲁⲗ   ⲉϩⲟⲩⲛ ⲛϫⲉ ⲛ[ⲉϩⲁⲟⲩ ⲙ-]
[ⲛϫⲉ ⲡⲟⲗⲭ]ⲏ̣ⲣⲓⲁ · ⲁϥ   ⲡⲙⲟⲩ ⲙⲡⲁ[ⲓⲱⲧ ⲛⲧⲁϭⲱ-]
    ⲉϩ[ⲗⲏⲓ ⲡⲉϫⲉϥ   ⲧⲉⲃ ⲙⲛⲁⲥ[ⲁⲛ ⲓⲁⲕⲱϥ]
[ϫⲉ   ] ⲇⲓⲟⲥⲕⲟⲣⲟⲥ   ⲙⲡⲉⲓⲱⲥⲛϥ [ⲉⲗϩⲉⲙϩⲉⲗ]
    ⲙ̣ⲟⲟ]ⲛ ⲛϫⲗⲁⲛ ·   ⲛⲥⲁⲃⲏⲗ ϫⲉ[ⲛⲧⲁⲛⲉϥⲥⲏⲛ-]
                     ⲟⲩ ⲧⲉⲓϥ ⲉⲃⲁ[ⲗ ⲙⲡⲉ

412.—Paper; a fragment, 7½ × 10 cm   Script   uneven, of ZOEGA's 9th class, = Br Mus *Catal*, no 527, to which MS this appears to belong[5]

From a medical work, showing portions of 3 recipes   The second mentions 'raven's gall', 'camphor' and refers to a wine shop   It may be a preventive of intoxication

             ]ⲧⲟⲩⲃ̣[
ⲛⲁⲗⲙⲛϥⲗⲟⲩⲟⲩϭ[6] · ⲙⲉ[
ⲙⲟⲩⲣ[. . .]ⲁⲡⲁⲛ ⲙ[
———[   ]———[
ϭⲁⲡ ⲛⲥⲓϣⲓ ⲙⲡⲁⲃⲱⲛ[7] ⲉⲕⲁⲙⲡ[
ⲉⲓ ⲥⲉⲕ ⲛⲁⲗⲭⲁⲃⲱⲟⲣ[8] ⲟⲩⲟ[
ⲱⲙⲉ ⲉⲗϥⲉⲗ . . ⲣⲓⲗ ⲉⲡⲣⲓ ⲛⲟⲉ[

---

[1] *Cf* also the Leyden papyrus book (*MSS*, p 471)
[2] *Journ As*, 1903
[3] A not impossible form   The first visible letter is not ⲁ   The text here appears to differ from the Syriac
[4] *Cf* Gen xxvii. 41
[5] A difference in dialect alone prevents me connecting it also with Berlin, *Kopt Urk*, No 26 (P 8116, 8117), which is identical in script and measurements (Dr SCHUBART

kindly sent a photograph)   There may be a difficulty too in reconciling the *provenance* of the Br Mus and Berlin MSS with ours.
[6] ? المفلوج 'paralytic'
[7] Bile of various animals was used (*v* indices to BERTHELOT's *Chimie au Moyen Age*), but I do not find the raven's
[8] الكافور   So in the above Berlin MS   8116 a, 8

ⲙⲁ ⲛⲥⲟ ⲉⲣⲡ ϭⲁⲛ ϣⲁⲙϯ ⲉⲗⲉⲛⲣ[
ⲗⲁⲥ ⲙⲁⲕⲥⲱ ⲙⲉⲗϯϩⲓ[1] [

[ⲡ]ⲉⲛⲁϥ ⲉⲛⲁ . . . . . [

Verso Arabic

413.—Papyrus, a fragment, 11½ × 15 cm Script early, *v* Pl 3 *Recto* ↑

Letter from Phoebammon to Justus, giving certain information relating to agriculture, and making requests

ⲁ]ⲛⲁⲕ ⲫⲟⲓⲃⲁⲙⲙⲱⲛ ⲡⲉⲧⲥϩⲉⲓ [|]ⲥⲁⲛ : ϩⲙⲡⲁϩⲏⲧ ⲧⲏⲗϥ : ⲙⲛ[|]ϣⲱⲡ : ⲙⲡⲉⲭϩⲙⲁⲧ (sic) : ⲙⲏⲛ[|]ⲫϯ ⲛⲉⲧⲓ ⲡⲉⲕⲃⲉⲕⲏ ⲛⲉⲕ : ⲁⲩⲱ [| ⲧ]ⲁϩⲁⲕ ⲙⲡⲉⲗⲕⲉⲟⲩ ⲥⲩⲱⲥϥ ⲛ[| ϣ]ⲁⲧⲉⲡⲙⲁⲟⲩ : ⲕⲱⲧⲓ : ϩⲛϩⲱ[| ⲧ]ⲉⲃⲛⲁⲟⲩⲓ · ⲉⲧⲃⲁⲗⲧⲉⲓ : ⲁⲩⲱ [|]ⲓ · ⲙⲡⲉⲛϣⲧⲁⲟⲩⲁⲁⲥ : ⲛⲉ[|]ϣⲓ : ⲛⲙⲉⲩ : ⲁⲩⲱ ⲁⲗⲓ ⲧⲁⲕⲁⲡ[ⲏ | ⲁⲩ]ⲱ ⲁⲗⲓ ⲧⲁⲕⲁⲡⲏ : ϩⲉⲓ ⲛⲛϭⲁⲙⲟⲩ[ⲗ |]ⲛⲧⲁϥ ⲫϯ : ⲁⲩⲱ ⲧⲁⲁⲕ : ⲙⲡⲉⲧⲉⲗ[ⲉ |]ϩⲓⲟⲩⲓ ⲉⲗⲁⲟⲩ : ⲁⲩⲱ ⲉⲛⲁⲁϫⲟⲩ ⲉⲃⲁ[ⲗ

Verso ⲧ]ⲉⲓⲥ ⲓⲟⲩⲥⲧⲉ [space] ϩⲓⲧⲥⲫⲟⲓⲃⲁⲙⲙⲱⲛ

414.—Papyrus, a fragment, 11½ × 9 cm Script sloping, ligatureless *Recto* ↑

Letter addressing the recipient as 'my brother' and referring to transactions in corn[2]

: ιθ ⲁϩⲁ ⲡⲁⲥⲁⲛ ⲫⲁ[| ⲧⲓ ⲉⲃⲁⲗ ⲧⲉⲓϩⲛ[| ⲛⲉⲧⲉⲥⲛⲓ ⲛⲉϥ ⲁϩⲁ ϩⲙⲁ[| ⲡⲓⲁⲓ ⲁϩⲁ ⲡⲁⲥⲁⲛ ⲉϣⲱⲡⲉ [| ϣⲁⲛ ⲥⲟⲩⲁ ϩⲁⲗⲁⲓ ⲙⲡ[| ⲛⲁⲃⲧⲛⲁⲩⲥⲉⲧ ⲉϣⲱ| | ⲧⲓ : α ⲥⲟⲩⲁ ⲛⲉⲥⲁϣⲛ[| ϭⲱⲙ[. .]ⲧ ⲛⲁϥ ⲥⲓⲙ [| ⲧⲓ[. . .]ⲟϥ ⲛⲉϥ ϣ[| small parts of 5 more lines

Verso (↑) Arabic

415—Papyrus, a fragment, 4½ × 25 cm Script rarely ligatured *Recto* (?) →

Letter of obscure purport 'Thy soul,' the writer says, 'will contend with mine'

]ⲛⲡⲉⲕⲉⲓ ⲛⲁⲕ ⲟⲛ ϩⲁⲓⲧⲓ[3] ⲛⲟⲩ[|]ⲟⲩ ⲗⲁⲓ ϣⲁⲗⲉⲧⲉⲕⲯⲩⲭⲏ ϫⲓ ϩⲉⲡ ⲙⲉⲧⲱⲓ ⲁⲩⲱ ⲗⲁ ϩⲁⲓⲧⲓ[|] ⲧⲉⲧⲉⲑⲁⲧⲓ ⲛⲛⲟⲩϯ ⲡⲁϣⲏⲗⲓ ⲗⲉⲗⲃⲁϣⲧⲁⲕ ⲙⲁⲓ ⲧⲁⲙⲟⲩ[|]ⲙⲁ ⲡⲁⲧⲛⲁⲕ ⲟⲛ ϩⲁⲓⲧⲓ ⲁⲩⲱ ⲛϣⲟⲡⲓ ⲕϭⲓⲛ ⲕⲁⲣⲁⲕ [

The fragment has been used in a binding (?), and the other side is covered with brown glue

[1] Perhaps ⲙⲉⲕϯϩⲓ

[2] The preceding the numerals presumably = ϋ̊

[3] This seems to recur in l 4 Can ⲛⲁⲕ=ⲁⲛⲁⲕ and ϩⲁⲓ- be the perfect prefix (*cf* the *Acta Pauli* and *Aeg Z*, 1898, 139)? Otherwise the dialect appears Fayyûmic

BOHAIRIC MANUSCRIPTS

BIBLICAL

416 [9]—Paper, a volume in modern binding, 110 foll, 28×20 cm 1 col of about 20 lines, with Arabic opposite it as far as p. 41 b Script 2 modern hands, the second starting at p 42 a and showing a good example of contemporary calligraphy On the fly-leaf, the usual elaborately-coloured (red, yellow, green) cross

Job, complete Of this MS, TATTAM, to whom it belonged (fly-leaf 'Tatt 373'), says[1] that it was copied, while he was in Egypt, 'from an ancient one in the patriarch's library,' and then collated[2] with a MS 'belonging to the Rev Mr SCHLEINITZ'

417 [8]—Paper, a volume in modern binding, 206 foll , the page 17½×13 cm Script a heavy 14th century hand Initials and stops, up to fol 60, in red 1 col , 15 lines Paged incompletely In each quire, of 5 double leaves (qu 7, renovated, is of 3 leaves), omitting qu 1, the paging is upon the *rectos* of its first half only, thus in qu 2, only pp ⲓⲁ̄ to ⲓⲉ̄ are paged This shows that the paging (which seems to be in the original scribe's hand) was done before the leaves had been folded or written upon Foll 61-65 are renewed by a somewhat later, foll 126, 133-135 by a quite modern scribe

I Foll 1 a—60 b, Proverbs i 1—xiv 26 (the end of a quire) The other MSS of this book likewise end here (v Br Mus no 724) and, being all of younger date than ours, may be but copies of it The text is divided into paragraphs, but not into larger sections Once or twice there is an orthographic correction بلس in the margin For editions of the book, v Br Mus *Catal*, l c

II Foll 61 b—206 b, Job, complete This text was used by TATTAM for his edition (1846), as is evident from the final computation 'found in only one of the three copies' he used (v his p 181) and to be read on fol 206 b of the present MS[3] The main divisions of the text are at chh iv 1, vi 1, ix 1, xi 1, xii 1, xv 1, xvi 1, xviii 1, xix 1, xx 1, xxi 1, xxii 1, xxiii 1, xxv 1, xxvi 1, xxvii 1, xxix 1, xxxii 1, *ib* 17, xxxiv 1, xxxv. 1, xxxvi 1, xxxviii 1, xxxix 33, xl 1, xlii 1, *ib* 7 Orthographic corrections are indicated by بلس, doubtful (? faulty) places as بحرّر 'collated' (or 'to be collated'), a blank on fol 65 b as سهو, preferable readings as صح or, on the authority of the oldest copy, فى الاصل[4]

---

[1] *Job* preface The fly-leaf shows too the price he paid for it 200 peasters'

[2] In 1839, says a note on p 109 a V the companion volume, Br Mus no 725

[3] This computation however is also in Br Mus no 724,

fol 49 b, and there too breaks off with ⲧⲏⲣⲟⲩ

[4] On fol 204 b, this refers to the numeral ⲥ (200), which the older MS wrote ⲟⲣ على هذا المثال, thus indicating a considerable age

The final note (fol 206 b) states that the book was the property (ملك) of 'the poor servant of (الله) Almighty God', Michael, deacon of the church of Atrib, who hopes for His pardon, mercy and grace

Fol 61 a, an Arabic note (probably not much later than the Coptic script), detailing the 36 times that the various limbs and features of a newly baptized boy are to be signed with the holy oil[1]   عنه الرسم بالدهن المقدس بعد صعود الطفل من المعمودية المعمودين

وللنون رسمًا نفصله الماوج والجبهه ة العم ة الإذنان ة معاصل اليدين داحلاً وحارجاً ة المرفعان ة المكبان داحلاً وخارجاً ة الإبطان داحلاً وحارجاً ة الركبتان ة معاصل الرحلى (sic)ة العلى داحلاً وحارجاً ة ومن الابط الايمن الى الحصر ة ومن الابط الشمال الى الحصر ة نم ذلك وكمل

The MS belonged to TATTAM[2], v first fly-leaf, bearing the note 'Tatt 372'   Chapters too and verses are throughout marked in his hand

418 [12].—Paper, 258 foll, in modern native binding, paged on *versos*, 30½ × 22 cm Script   (1) foll 5 a-93 a, a regular, if somewhat sprawling 18th century hand, (2) foll 93 b to end, a stiffer, more compact hand   Initials, stops, the letters Ⲫ, Ⳉ, Ϧ in red   1 col of (1) 20-24 and (2) 25 lines, with Arabic opposite it

Foll 5 a-214 b   Jeremiah

Foll 215 a-232 b   Lamentations, with the Prayer of Jeremiah

Foll 232 b-249 b   Baruch, beginning (as a sequel to Jeremiah) with ch liij

Foll 249 b-258 b   The Epistle of Jeremiah

An Arabic colophon by the scribe, on fol 258 b, states that the work was ended on the 29th Abib, A M 1512 = A.D 1796

The MS belonged to TATTAM, as a note of contents at the beginning and the marking of chapters and verses in his hand throughout indicate[3]

419 [10]—Paper, 147 foll (first 2 and last 6 blank), in modern native binding, paged on *versos*, 31 × 22½ cm   Script a regular, 18th century hand   Head lines, initials, stops, the letters Ⲫ, Ⳉ, Ϧ in red   1 col of 18-22 lines, with Arabic opposite it

Daniel, opening with the History of Susanna   The apocryphal 14th vision is on p p̄ⲕⲏ̄ b

The text is preceded by 4 pp of Arabic, giving a sketch of contemporary biblical history, a summary of the prophecies and 6 ethical reasons for their revelation (the

---

[1] V VANSLEB, *Histoire* 203, TUKI, *Rituale* 32
[2] Presumably that given him by Lord Prudhoe, v *Job*, preface

[3] Presumably it is that given him by the Duke of Northumberland, v *Proph Maj* I, Præfatio

display of divine might, confounding of idolatry, humiliation of Babylon &c)   It is

headed معده مل كتاب دانيال السى فيها شرح اموره واحتصار عرض دوته فارض دانل

It begins سعى ان نعلم ان ندمال سعف ورودا الى دانل من حرقمال(sic) باحدى عشره سه

and ends والسادس ان نكون ذلك دادسه وممالا لما نكون من ادساط دس اللّه فى جميع الملدان

عد طهور مسدد دالحسن واشتمال مواهب روح فدسه على المومس به امس

A note by the scribe, on p 141 a, states that the work was finished on the 29th Misrâ,
'the end of the year' عام سنه A M 1511 = A D 1795   The scribe was Claudius, *hegumenus,*
'serving حادم [1] the great martyr Apa Tir' اپا تير, in Siût [2]

The MS belonged to TATTAM, as numerous marginal variants (in ink) and the chapter
and verse notation (in pencil) in his hand show [3]

420 [11].—Paper, 119 foll, paged on *versos*, European binding, 23 × 15 3 cm   Script
quite modern   Initials, stops &c in red, cross on fly-leaf, head-piece and largest initials in
red, green and yellow   1 col of 20 lines, with Arabic opposite it

Daniel, beginning with the History of Susanna and terminating with that of Bel
(13th vision)

The MS belonged to TATTAM, as the chapter and verse notation and an occasional
variant in his hand show [4]

421.—Papyrus, 6 fragments, the largest, 8 × 6 cm   Script   a heavy, Bohairic hand of
the 10th century, similar to those of the Vatican MSS or the CURZON *Catena*, v Brit
Mus *Catal*, Pl 11, no 739

A Gospel MS, unique hitherto in being in the Bohairic dialect though upon
papyrus   Other fragments of the volume are Brit Mus no 739

The largest fragment here shows St Matthew xxi 14-16, 23-25, as follows

14	]nⲅⲁⲗ[		*Verso* 23	]ⲙⲛⲙⲡⲓ
	]ⲣⲫⲁϣ[			]ⲕⲓⲣⲓ ⲛ[
	] [			]ⲟⲅ ⲛⲓⲙ ⲛ[
15	]ⲓⲉⲡⲉⲩⲉ ⲛ[		24	]ⲣⲟⲩⲱ ⲛ[
	]ⲁϥⲁⲓⲟⲩ ·[			] ϯⲛⲁϣⲉⲛⲟ[
	] ⲉⲃⲟⲗ ϩⲉⲛⲛ[			]ϣⲱⲛ ⲁⲣⲉⲧ[
16	] ⲭⲉⲱⲓⲁⲛⲛⲁ [			]ⲛⲟⲕ ϩⲱ ϯⲛ[
	]ⲭⲣⲉⲙⲣⲉⲙ [			]ⲁⲓ ϩⲉⲛⲁϣ [
	]ⲕⲉⲱⲓⲉ [		25	]ⲱⲙⲓ ⲛⲧⲉ[

[1] V Br Mus no 729, note
[2] Not in Abû Sâlih or Makrizi, but now one of the two
churches in Siût, v list appended to اللولوه الدهية فى الراتيل
الروحة, Cairo, 1896

[3] V *Proph Maj*, Præfatio viii, 'Copto-Arabicus in folio'
[4] V *Proph Maj*, Præfatio viii, 'Copto-Arabicus in
quarto et recenter transcriptus'

422 [15].—Paper , 287 (*sic*) foll , in oriental binding (wooden boards with coarse leather back), paged on *versos*, 35 × 26 cm , 1 col of 25 lines   Script a regular, 14th century hand, excepting foll 1–39, 269–285 (286, 287 blank), which are by a much later scribe, foll 74, 126, 215 being also in a later, though again different, hand   These last 3 foll replace coloured and gilded[1] initial pages, which have been cut out   Most initials, head-lines, stops &c, the letters Ϧ, Ϩ are in red , larger initials with marginal scrolls in red, green and yellow

The MS is described at length as M, in HORNER's Bohairic New Testament 1, p cxii

The Four Gospels   St Mark begins on fol 74 *a*, St Luke on 126 *a*, St John on 215 *a*

The words, fol 74 *a*, ⲁⲛⲉⲣϧⲏⲧⲥ ϩⲉⲛⲧϫⲟⲙ ⲛⲧⲉ ⲫϯ ⲛⲥⲉⲛⲡⲓⲉⲑⲛⲁⲛⲉϥ ⲛⲧⲉ ⲡⲉϥⲉⲛϫⲟⲗⲏ ⲁⲛⲥⲃⲉ &c are intended to translate the familiar ﺍﺑﺘﺪﻯ ﺑﻌﻮﻥ ﺍﻟﻠﻪ ﻭﺣﺴﻦ ﺗﻮﻓﻴﻘﻪ ﻧﻜﺘﺐ ﺍﻟﺦ

The scribe's name is on fol 214 *a* ⲁⲣⲓ ⲡⲁⲙⲉⲩⲓ ⲥⲟⲃⲉⲫϯ ⲁⲛⲟⲕ ⲡⲓⲉⲗⲁⲭⲓⲥⲧⲟⲥ ⲥⲓⲙⲱⲛ ⲡⲓⲣⲉⲙⲧⲁⲙⲡⲉϯ[2] ⲡⲓⲁⲧⲙⲡϣⲁ ⲙⲙⲟⲩϯ ⲉⲣⲟϥ ϫⲉϫⲓⲁⲕⲟ, ⲕⲉ ⲕⲁⲗⲓⲅⲣⲁⲫⲟⲥ.

Fol 214 *b*, this Arabic note of dedication[3] by Ibrahim of Shubra, dated A M 1230 = A D 1514

ﺑﺸﺎﺩﺭ ﺍﻷﺭﺑﻌﻪ ﺍﻟﻜﺘﺎﺏ ﺍﻟﻤﻘﺪﺱ ﻫﺬﺍ   ﺍﻟﺨﻼﺹ ﺍﻟﻠﻪ ﻳﺎ ﻟﻠﺮﺏ ﺍﻟﺨﻼﺹ ﺍﺑﺪﺍً ﺩﺍﺋﻤﺎً ﻟﻠﻪ ﺍﻟﻤﺤﺪ
ﺍﺩﺭﺍﻫﻢ ﺍﻻﺳﻌﺪ ﺍﻟﺸﻤﺲ ﺍﻟﺸﺘﺎﺱ ﺍﻟﻤﻜﺮﻡ ﺍﻻﺭﺩﻛﺴﻰ ﺍﻟﺪﺗﻦ ﺍﻟﻤﺒﺎﺭﻙ ﺍﻟﻮﻟﺪ ﺍﺑﻨﻪ ﻭﺣﺘﻤﺴﻪ ﻭﻗﻌﺪ ﺍﻟﺤﺒﺎﻩ ﺍﺩﻫﺎﺭ
ﻧﻮﺍﺩﻯ ﺍﻻﺩﻣﺾ ﺩﺍﻟﺪﻳﺮ ﺍﻟﻤﻌﺮﻭﻑ ﺑﺴﺎﻯ ﺍﻣﺎ ﺍﻟﻌﻈﻴﻢ ﺍﻟﻘﺪﺱ ﺩﻳﺮ ﻋﻠﻰ ﻋﻠﻤﻪ ﺍﻟﻠﻪ ﺩﺍﺭﻙ ٠ ﺍﻟﺴﺮﺍﻭﻯ
ﻣﻦ ﻗﺒﻞ ﺳﻠﻄﺎﻧﺎً ﺍﻟﻌﻠﻤﺎﻧﻴﺲ ﻣﻦ ﻭﻻ ﺍﻟﺮﻫﺒﺎﻥ ﻣﻦ ﻻﺣﺪٍ ﻭﻟﻴﺲ ﻭﺩﻛﺮﻭﻩ ﺍﻟﺮﻫﺒﺎﻥ ﻓﻴﻪ ﻟﻴﻌﺮﻭﺍ ﺍﻻﻃﺮﻭﻥ
ﺩﺍﻟﺮﻫﺒﺎﻥ ﻋﺎﻣﺮﺍً ﺩﺍﻡ ﻣﺎ ٠ ﺍﻟﺒﻼﻑ ﻭﺟﻮﻩ ﻣﻦ ﻟﻮﺣﺪٍ ﺍﻟﻤﺬﻛﻮﺭ ﺍﻟﺪﻳﺮ ﻭﻣﻌﺘﻪ ﻋﻦ ﺗﺨﺮﺟﻪ ﺳﺨﺎﻧﻪ ﺍﻟﺮﺏ
ﻭﺍﻟﺤﺪﺍﻡ ﻭﺍﻟﻜﻬﺪ ﺍﻟﺮﻫﺒﺎﻥ ﻣﻦ ﺗﺨﻮﺩﻩ ﻓﻤﻦ ﻭﺍﻟﻤﺎ ﺍﻟﻜﺒﺮﻩ ﻭﺣﻌﻞ ٠ ﺍﻟﺪﻭﺍﻡ ﻋﻠﻰ ﺩﻛﺮﻩ ﺍﻟﻠﻪ ﻋﻘﺮﻩ
ﺍﺑﺪﺍً ﺩﺍﺋﻤﺎً ﻟﻠﻪ ﻭﺍﻟﺴﻜﺮ ﺍﻣﻦ ﺍﻟﻤﻌﻤﺲ ﺍﻟﻤﻮﺍﺻﻌﻴﻦ ﺍﻟﻄﺎﺑﻌﻴﻦ ﺍﻟﺴﺎﻣﻌﻴﻦ ﺍﻻﺩﻣﺎ ﻋﻠﻰ ﻳﺤﻞ ﺍﻟﺮﺏ ﻭﺳﻼﻡ
ﺷﺎﻛﺮﺍ[6] ﺍﻟﻤﺮﺳﻤﻪ[7] ﺍﻟﺮﺏ (؟) ﻣﻦ ﺍﻟﻠﻪ ﺳﻌﺪﻩ ﺍﻟﺨﺎﺩﻡ ﻳﻮﺣﻨﺎ ﺍﻟﺤﻘﻴﺮ ﻛﺒﻪ ٨٥٠ ﺍﻟﻤﺒﺎﺭﻙ ﻃﻮﺑﻪ ﺷﻬﺮ ﻟﺢ٬
ﺑﻌﺪﻩ ﻋﻠﻰ ﻟﻠﺮﺏ

The MS belonged to TATTAM[8], as a pencil note, 'Tattam 400,' on the inside of the binding (beginning) and the chapter and verse notation in his hand testify

423 [14].—Paper, 150 foll (last blank) in a fine native binding, partly renewed , paged on *versos*, 17 7 × 26½ cm , 1 col, 19 lines, with Arabic opposite it   Script a regular, 14th century hand   Initials, stops, the letters Ϧ, Ϩ in red , head lines, quire-

---

[1] Fol 214 *b* retains plain traces of this

[2] *V* Br Mus no 1132   *Mission* iv 607 shows it to be in the nome of Oxyrhnchus ﻃﺒﺪﻯ is almost opposite Maghâgha

[3] Translated by HORNER   Pointed here as in MS

[4] There were several Shubras, v AMÉLINEAU, *Geogr* ,

[5] I cannot find the monastery thus named elsewhere   In the later note, fol 285 *a*, the name is spelt ﺑﺸﻮﻯ

[6] HORNER takes this apparently for ﻟﺘﺎﺭﻳﺦ

[7] HORNER takes the writer of this note for John, 93rd (94th) Patriarch, doubtless he who also wrote the note, HORNER, *l c*, lxiv *infra*

[8] Presumably no 3 in the list, *ZDMG* vii 94

ornaments, larger initials, and marginal scrolls, as well as the elaborate cross on fol 1 *b*, red, green, blue and yellow   Gilding also is used in this cross and in all the head-lines The MS is described by HORNER, in his Bohairic New Testament III, p lxi

Foll 2 *a*—99 *b* The Revelation of St John   The margins are full of Arabic glosses, in a contemporary (?) hand and red ink, giving closer versions of the Coptic (sometimes headed ق) or, in black, a divergent Arabic (headed غ)   Rarely the reading of another copy (نسخة or نسخة الاصل) is given, or the Coptic emended

The liturgical rubrics, indicating the hymns and antiphons proper to the lessons from the Apocalypse, whereof HORNER (III, p lxvi) has given a translation, are, in this MS, as follows[1]. Certain of them are found in the liturgical books

Ch 1 10—ⲏ̄ ⲅ̄ ⲟⲃⲁⲃ̅ⲗ̅ ⲥϭⲁⲓ ⲛⲏⲛ ⲉⲧⲁⲕⲛⲁⲩ ⲉⲣⲱⲟⲩ
ⲉⲧⲁⲓⲉⲛⲕⲟⲧ.

II 1—ⲏ̄ ⲧ̄ ϩⲱⲃ ⲛⲁⲓⲡⲉ ⲛⲏ ⲉⲧⲉϥϫⲱ ⲙⲙⲱⲟⲩ ⲕⲓⲣⲓ ⲡⲁⲟ̄ⲥ.

II 18—ⲏ̄ ⲓⲱⲥⲏⲫ ϯⲥϧⲓⲙⲓ ϫⲉⲓⲉⲍⲁⲃⲉⲗ
ⲏ̄ ϯⲕⲓⲃⲱⲧⲟⲥ.

III 7—ⲏ̄ ϭⲱϣⲧ ⲫⲏ ⲉⲑⲛⲁϭⲣⲟ ϯⲛⲁⲁⲓϥ
ⲃⲱϩⲉⲙ ⲁⲙⲟⲩ ⲧⲉⲕⲛⲁⲩ

III 14—ⲅ̄ ⲏ̄ ⲡⲓⲙⲅ̄ⲥ ϭⲓ ⲛⲁⲕ ⲛⲟⲩⲫⲁϧⲣⲓ
ⲃⲱϩⲉⲙ ⲁⲛⲓⲙⲁⲧⲟⲓ ϭⲓⲥⲓ.

IV 1—ⲅ̄ ⲓⲱⲃ ⲁⲓⲛⲁⲩ ⲁⲛⲟⲕ ⲓⲱⲁⲛⲛⲏⲥ
ⲃⲱϩⲉⲙ ⲉⲧⲁⲩⲉⲛ ⲛⲓϭⲓⲥⲓ.

V 1—ⲅ̄ ⲡⲓⲡⲣⲟⲫⲏ ϩⲏⲡⲡⲉ ⲁϥϭⲣⲟ ⲛϫⲉ ⲡⲓⲙⲟⲩⲓ
ⲃⲱϩⲉⲙ ⲡⲓⲛⲉⲙⲕⲉⲙ.

VI 1—ⲅ̄ ⲟⲩⲫⲁⲣⲓⲥⲉ ⲁⲓⲛⲁⲩ ⲉⲟⲩϩⲑⲟ ⲛⲭⲁⲙⲉ
ⲃⲱϩⲉⲙ ⲛⲓⲣⲱⲙⲓ ⲉⲧⲧⲁⲗⲏⲟⲩⲧ.

VII 9—ⲅ̄ ϯⲣⲁϣⲓ ⲁⲓⲛⲁⲩ ⲉⲟⲩⲛⲓϣ ⲫⲏⲣⲓ
ⲃⲱϩⲉⲙ ⲁⲓⲛⲁⲩ ⲥ̄ⲧ̄ ⲛⲭⲗⲟⲙ[6].

VIII 1—ⲅ̄ ⲛ̅ⲉϣⲟϣⲧ ⲁⲩⲭⲁϥ ϣⲱⲡⲓ ϧⲉⲛⲧⲫⲉ
ⲃⲱϩⲉⲙ ⲁϫⲁⲙ ⲁⲃⲉⲗ.

IX 6—ⲅ̄ ⲛⲁⲓⲟ̄ⲧ̄ ⲡⲓϩⲟⲩⲓⲧ ⲛⲟⲩⲟⲓ ⲁϥⲓⲛⲓ
ⲅ̄ ⲁⲛⲁⲩ ⲉⲛⲁϫⲓϫ.

---

[1] Words underlined are in red   It will be observed how irregularly this has been carried out   Abbreviations are for ⲏ̄ⲭⲟⲥ and ⲟⲩⲱϩⲉⲙ (presumably identical here with ϩⲱⲣⲉⲙ)   It is difficult to distinguish between the two, both seem to correspond to رد (cf HORNER, Conseer Serv 320 with TUKI, *Euh* 1 ⲣϫ, ⲣⲏⲛ &c and Br Mus no 894) Referred, as here, to a biblical text, ⲟⲩⲱϩⲉⲙ must be the response sung in conjunction with a lection (ⲥⲟⲛ ⲛⲱϣ), *v* Br Mus nos 144 n, 147, 326 and many instances in margins of homiletic or narrative texts (e g Eg Expl Fund, *Report* 1901-02, p 52 *supra*)

[2] Recurs *Aeg Z* xxxix 109

[3] Recurs *l c* 109   Note the Sa'idic form retained.

[4] TUKI, *Miss* ⲥⲛⲅ̄

[5] *Aeg Z, l c*

[6] Br Mus no 894

[7] Cf *Aeg Z* ⲉⲓⲥ ⲛⲉϣⲟϣⲧ

[8] *Aeg Z, l c*

X I—ⲱ̄ⲅ ⲧⲉⲡⲣⲱ ⲁⲓⲛⲁⲩ ⲉⲅⲁⲅⲅⲉⲗⲟⲥ
ⲭ̄ⲏ ⲁⲓϫⲉⲙ ⲡⲓⲥⲛⲟⲩ.

XI I—ⲱ̄ⲅ ⲡⲓⲍ̄ ⲛⲁⲍⲓⲱⲙⲁ ⲛⲁⲓⲛⲉ ⲛⲃⲱ ⲛϫⲱⲓⲧ
ⲃⲱϧⲉⲙ ⲕⲁⲧⲁ ⲛⲓⲭⲱⲣⲟⲥ.

XII I—ⲱ̄ⲅ ϧⲁⲙⲟⲓ ⲟⲩⲥⲟⲙⲁ ⲉⲥϫⲟⲗϧ ⲙⲫⲣⲏ
ⲃⲟ ⲛⲟⲩϭⲣⲟⲙⲡϣⲁⲗ

XIII I—ⲱ̄ⲅ ⲡⲁⲓⲱⲧ[1] ⲡⲁⲣⲭ̄ ⲁⲓⲛⲁⲩ ⲉⲟⲩⲛⲓϣϯ ⲙⲡⲟⲗⲓⲥ
ⲃⲱϧⲉⲙ ⲡⲁⲥⲁϩ.

XIII II—ⲱ̄ⲅ ⲁⲓⲛⲉϫ ⲡⲓⲱ̄ⲙ ⲫⲁⲓⲡⲉ ⲫⲙⲁ ⲛⲧⲟⲩⲡⲟⲙⲟ
ⲃⲱϧⲉⲙ ⲫⲁⲛⲓⲧⲉⲛϧ[2]

XIV I—ⲱ̄ⲅ ⲁⲓⲛⲁⲩ ⲉⲟⲩϧⲓⲛⲃ ⲁⲓⲛⲁⲩ ⲉⲟⲩϧⲓⲛⲃ
ⲃⲱϧⲉⲙ ⲟⲩⲕⲉⲙⲕⲉⲙ.

XIV 12—ⲱ̄ⲅ ϯⲭⲱⲣⲁ ⲱ ⲟⲩⲛⲓⲁⲅⲟⲩ
ⲃⲱϧⲉⲙ ⲛⲑⲱⲧⲉⲛ ⲇⲉ[3].

XIV 17—ⲱ̄ⲅ ⲁⲛⲓⲛⲉ ⲛⲁⲓ ⲁⲓⲛⲁⲩ ⲉⲟⲩⲛⲓϣϯ ⲛϣⲫⲏⲣⲓ
ⲭ̄ⲏ ⲡⲓⲛⲟⲩⲃ

XV 5—ⲱ̄ⲅ ⲁⲩⲣⲉⲙⲙⲁⲟ ⲛⲏ ⲉⲧⲁⲡⲑⲉⲟⲗⲟⲅⲟⲥ
ⲃⲱϧⲉⲙ ⲧⲉⲛⲟⲩⲱϣⲧ

XVI 12—ⲱ̄ⲅ ⲉⲩⲫⲣⲁⲛⲉ ⲁⲩⲉⲣⲫⲉⲅⲓ[4]
ⲃⲱϧⲉⲙ ⲁⲇⲁⲙ ⲁⲃⲉⲗ.

XVII I—ⲱ̄ⲅ ⲁⲓⲃⲱⲕ ⲉⲃⲟⲗ ⲁⲓⲛⲁⲩ ⲉⲟⲩⲥⲟⲙⲓ
ⲭ̄ⲏ ⲡⲣⲟⲗⲟⲅⲟⲛ[5].

XVIII I—ⲱ̄ⲅ ⲉⲑⲃⲉⲟⲩⲥⲟⲙⲓ[6] ϯϧⲓⲙⲓ ⲉⲧⲁⲕⲛⲁⲩ ⲉⲣⲟⲥ
ⲃⲱϧⲉⲙ ⲡⲁⲥⲁϩ.

XIX II—ⲭ̄ⲏ ⲧⲥϧⲣⲱⲙⲙⲁⲛⲓⲁ ⲁⲓⲛⲁⲩ ⲉⲟⲩϧⲟⲟ ⲛⲟⲩⲱⲃϣ
ⲭ̄ⲏ ⲃ̄[7].

XX 6—ⲱ̄ⲅ ⲙⲉⲛⲧⲁⲓⲇⲱⲣⲟⲛ ⲟⲩⲙⲁⲕⲁⲣⲓⲟⲥ
ⲭ̄ⲏ ⲧⲥϭⲟⲥⲓ ⲭ̄ⲉⲛⲓ̄.

XXI I—ⲱ̄ⲅ ⲁⲓⲛⲁⲩ ⲉⲧ̄ ⲁⲓⲛⲁⲩ ⲉⲟⲩⲃⲁⲕⲓ ⲉⲑⲛⲉⲥⲱⲥ
ⲭ̄ⲏ ⲁⲓⲛⲁⲩ ⲉⲧ̄ ⲛⲭⲗⲟⲙ.

XXI 21—ⲭ̄ⲏ ⲉϣⲱⲡ ⲛⲑⲟⲕ ⲑⲃⲁⲕⲓ ⲙⲡⲓⲛⲓϣϯ ⲛⲟⲩⲣⲟ
ⲭ̄ⲏ ⲥϣⲱⲡ ⲛⲑⲟⲕⲡⲉ ⲡⲁⲥⲱⲧⲏⲣ.

---

[1] *Aeg Z , l c*   [2] Br Mus no 893   [6] *Aeg Z l c*, Br Mus no 972

[3] *L c*   [4] ? ⲫⲙⲉⲅⲓ   [7] The 2nd 'authentic' mode

[5] A liturgical term ?

On fol 93 a a passage is introduced into ch xxi 19 (after κεκοσμημένοι), indicated as a hymn to be sung by the bishop[1] After it, ver 19 is continued, ΙΩΑ ΛΕΓΙ. Ver 21 is headed ερεπενϲωτηρ ϫενιωα λεϲι.

On fol 99 b, after the end of ch xxii, is the following, by the original scribe

ελα S ϩαλιοϲραφο̅ πετρο̅ ✗ ⲁⲅⲁ   كل مصحف حلمان دوحما بسلام من الرب
هو برحمتك نصع رحمة مع المهتم والعادى والعارى والمسكس الخاطى ناقله وله المجد الى
الابد لدهور وعلمنا رحمته

On fol 100 a, the following Blessing (with Arabic), to be recited before the Apocalypse[2], πιϲⲙⲟⲩ (البركة) ετοⲩωϣ ⲙⲙⲟⲥ (sic) ϫⲁϫⲉⲛϯⲁⲡⲟⲕⲁⲗⲩⲯⲓⲥ εⲑⲟⲩⲁⲃ

ϲⲙⲟⲩ εⲣⲟⲓ ⲓⲥ ϯⲙⲉⲧⲁⲛⲟⲓⲁ ⲭⲱ ⲛⲏⲓ εⲃⲟⲗ ⲡⲁⲥⲏⲛⲟⲩ ⲛⲉⲙⲛⲁϣⲏⲣⲓ ⲧⲱⲃϩ εϫⲱⲓ ϩⲓⲛⲁ
ⲛⲧⲉⲡⲁϭ̅ ⲓⲏ̅ⲥ̅ ϯ ⲡⲓⲕⲁϯ ⲛⲏⲓ ⲛⲧⲁⲱϣ ϫⲉⲛⲡⲉϥⲛⲟⲙⲟⲥ ⲛⲅⲁⲣⲉϩ ⲉⲛⲉϥⲉⲛⲧⲟⲗⲏ ⲛⲧⲁϯ ⲱⲟⲩ
ⲙⲡⲉϥⲣⲁⲛ ⲉⲑ̅ ⲟⲩⲟϩ ⲛⲧⲁϫⲱ ⲛⲱⲧⲉⲛ ⲛϯⲁⲡⲟⲕⲁⲗⲩⲯⲓⲥ ⲛⲧⲉ ⲡⲓⲁⲅⲓⲟⲥ ⲓⲱⲁⲛⲛⲏⲥ ⲡⲓⲉⲩⲁⲅⲅⲉⲗⲓⲥⲧⲏⲥ
ⲟⲩⲟϩ (100 b) ⲡⲓⲡⲁⲣⲑⲉⲛⲟⲥ ⲡⲓⲙⲉⲛⲣⲓⲧ ⲛⲧⲉ ⲫϯ ϫⲉⲛⲟⲩⲙⲉⲑⲙⲏⲓ ⲉⲣⲉⲡⲉϥϲⲙⲟⲩ ⲉⲑⲟⲩⲁⲃ ϣⲱⲡⲓ
ⲛⲉⲙⲁⲛ ⲡⲉⲛⲛⲓϲⲙⲟⲩ ⲛⲧⲉ ⲛⲏ ⲉⲑⲟⲩⲁⲃ ⲧⲏⲣⲟⲩ ⲉⲧϫⲉⲛⲧⲫⲉ ⲛϩⲟⲩⲟ ⲇⲉ ⲛϩⲟⲩⲟ ⲡⲓⲥⲙⲟⲩ ⲛⲧⲉ
ⲅⲉⲛⲟⲥ ⲧⲏⲣⲉⲛ ϯⲑⲉⲟⲧⲟⲕⲟⲥ ⲉⲑⲟⲩⲁⲃ ϯⲁⲅⲓⲁ ⲙⲁⲣⲓⲁ ϯⲣⲉϥϫⲫⲉϥϯ ϫⲉⲛⲟⲩⲙⲉⲑⲙⲏⲓ. The blessings are then asked of ⲛⲓⲣⲉϥⲉⲣⲟⲩⲱⲓⲛⲓ (الديوان) Michael, Gabriel, (101 a) Raphael and Souriel, of the 4 bodiless (العم متشسد) Beasts and 24 Elders, of John, πρόδρομος, βαπτιστής (السائف والصائع), the priest, son of the priest, kinsman (دو حسب) of Emmanuel[3], of the 144 virgin children (اطفال), of the Apostles, (101 b) of the 3 holy children (صبى), of the archdeacon and protomartyr Stephen, of the victorious martyr, the morning star, my lord king George, of SS Theodore Stratelates and Theodore the Eastern and his (Ar their) 2 companions, (102 a) of St Mercurius φιλοπάτηρ and St Apa Mena, of St Apa Victor and κῦρι Claudius, his fellow, and of all the martyrs, and of our righteous father the great Abba Antonius and the just Abba Paul, (102 b) of the 3 SS Macarius and Abba John and Abba Pishoi (دمشاى), of the Romans Maximus and Dometius, of Abba Moses and Abba John the Black, of Abba Pachom and Theodore, his disciple, of Abba Shenouti the archimandrite (103 a) and his cross bearing children, of Benipi (حنى) and his disciple, the presbyter John, of the great Abba Parsoma the Naked, of the whole choir of the cross-bearers &c, (103 b) of St Mark, evangelist and apostle, light of the land of Egypt, of our father archbishop NN and of our fathers the orthodox bishops, and above all ⲛϩⲟⲩⲟ ⲇⲉ ⲛϩⲟⲩⲟ, of the all-holy Trinity (104 a) ⲛⲥⲉϣⲱⲡⲓ ⲛⲭⲗⲟⲙ ⲛⲱⲟⲩ ⲟⲩⲭⲗⲟⲙ ⲛⲭⲁ ⲛⲟⲃⲓ ⲉⲃⲟⲗ ⲛⲥⲉⲓ ⲉϩⲣⲏⲓ ⲉϫⲉⲛⲧⲁϥⲉ
ⲙⲡⲓⲗⲁⲟⲥ ⲧⲏⲣⲉϥ ⲉⲧⲟⲩⲟⲩϯ ϫⲉⲛⲧⲁⲓⲁⲅⲓⲁ ⲛⲉⲕⲕⲗⲏⲥⲓⲁ ⲛⲓⲛⲓϣϯ ⲛⲉⲙⲛⲓⲕⲟⲩϫⲓ ⲛⲓϧⲉⲗⲗⲟⲓ ⲛⲉⲙ-
ⲛⲓⲁⲗⲱⲟⲩⲓ ⲛⲓϩⲱⲟⲩⲧ ⲛⲉⲙⲛⲓϩⲓⲟⲙⲓ ⲛⲉⲙⲛⲓⲁⲣⲭⲱⲛ ⲉⲧⲑⲟⲩⲏⲧ ϫⲉⲛⲡⲁⲓⲙⲁ ϯⲛⲟⲩ ⲛⲏ ⲉⲧⲁⲩⲓ ⲛⲉⲙⲛⲏ
ⲉⲧⲉⲙⲡⲟⲩⲓ ⲛⲉⲙⲛⲏ ⲉⲧⲁⲩϫⲟⲥ ⲛⲁⲛ ⲉⲑⲃⲏⲧⲟⲩ ϫⲉⲁⲣⲓ ⲡⲉⲛⲙⲉⲩⲓ (104 b) ϫⲉⲛⲡⲏⲓ ⲙⲡⲟϭ̅ ⲟⲩⲟϩ ϯϯϩⲟ
ⲉⲣⲱⲧⲉⲛ ⲱ ⲛⲁϣⲏⲣⲓ ⲛⲉⲙⲛⲁϣⲉⲣⲓ ⲉⲧⲑⲟⲩⲏⲧ ⲉⲡⲓⲙⲁ ϯⲛⲟⲩ ϩⲓⲛⲁ ⲛⲧⲉⲧⲉⲛϥⲁⲓ ϫⲁⲣⲟⲓ ϫⲉⲛⲡⲁϣⲟϥⲧ ⲟⲩⲟϩ
ⲛⲧⲉⲧⲉⲛϣⲱⲡ ⲉⲣⲱⲧⲉⲛ ⲛⲧⲁϫⲓⲛⲥⲁϫⲓ ⲉⲃⲟⲗ ϫⲉⲫⲏ ⲉϯϫⲱ ⲙⲙⲟϥ ⲛⲱⲧⲉⲛ ⲫⲱⲓ ⲁⲛⲡⲉ ⲁⲗⲗⲁ ⲫⲁⲫϯ
ⲉⲧⲟⲛϭⲛⲉ. The writer goes on to ask indulgence for his shortcomings, to exhort to

[1] V HORNER iii, p lxviii
[2] Cf ? MAI, Scr Vet Nov Coll V, Codd Copt, no xvi

[3] So in the Sinuthian liturgy, Paris MS 68 ⲡ̅ⲍ̅, and Luki's Theotokia cie

watchfulness ϣⲣⲱⲓⲥ and, God being prone to mercy, to repentance   He speaks thus
from love toward his hearers, silence would be blameworthy ⲛ̅ⲧⲁϣⲱⲡⲓ ⲉⲓⲭⲏⲃ
ϧⲁⲡⲉⲧⲉⲛⲛⲟⲃⲓ.   He desires that they may be all (106 a) saved together and his sadness
turned to joy   Finally he addresses Christ on behalf of those whose names he had
already given, that they and he be remembered in the heavenly Jerusalem, ⲉⲛⲟⲩⲟⲝ
ⲝⲉⲛϯⲯⲩⲭⲏ ⲛⲉⲙⲡⲓⲥⲱⲙⲁ, that the peace of God may encompass them on all sides
'Say with me, my children and my brethren together, Amen'

Fol 106 b has the scribe's colophon, referring to the preceding ذكر, and dated
A M 1091 = A H 777 (= A D 1375)   After the date, it continues الشيخ اهتمام من وذلك
صع اهتمامه الله ادام مجاهد مساجدل الارحن الشيخ ابن ووابل الامجد المكرم الشماس المحترم الاجل
والعمل العلم سلعه برحمته هو المسيح يسوع سبدنا مبر امام رحمه ده لبعد الحسن الذكار هذا
والعمل الطويل العمر الله وبسعد الاجل طول التملا بعد السما ملكوب الى بعده بما وبوصله
الابدا والى والى الان من المعزدين ملائكته وبحرسه المسيح يسوع تربما الصحيح والاىمان السكل
حطاياه معثره وبذكره حلله وبسن عطله عن بصعح ان بطالعه من كل بسال داقله والمسكين • امىن
الابدى حماه الاخرة وفى وماىه وستس ثلثس الواحد عوص محاربه والله وزلله

Along the margin, ⲡⲓϧⲏⲕⲓ ⲡⲓⲕⲉⲣⲙⲓ ⲡⲓⲉⲗⲁⲭⲓⲥⲧⲟⲥ ⲙⲟⲛⲁ̅ⲭ̅ ⲥ̅ ⲡⲣⲉⲥⲃ̅ⲧ̅ ⲡⲉⲧⲣⲟⲥ ⲡⲁ-
ⲧⲣⲟⲡⲭⲏ ⳿ ⲛⲁⲓ ⲛⲁϥ ⲁⲙⲏⲛ.   The scribe came therefore from Dronkah, S of Siût[1]

Also, in a later hand, a note of dedication to the church of the Virgin in Hârat
Zuwailah (Cairo), 'زوىله بحاره السنه الست دعه على وقف المقدس الكتاب هذا

The latter portion of the volume, foll 109–149, is in Arabic

Foll 149–142   An Introduction to the Revelation, in rhymed prose, addressing
readers or hearers as 'beloved brethren', 'O my masters (السادة) present here'   In the
MS CURZON 15 of the Revelation[3], p ⲡⲉ, this is attributed to the AWLÂD AL 'ASSÂL
العسال اولاد وصعها نعدمه and is to be read 'before the reading of the Revelation in
Arabic'   The piece does not appear to be noticed in lists of their works[4]   It begins
نعوسا اشبرى الذى الرحوم والادس الارمان وحون وحوده السابغ الازلى العدوس الاب بسم
الذى الادهان المصلى الصعات • والصفات الاقادم المثلث • الذاب الواحد الاله الاىمان نادس
الجحدمه الادواب وكسر دنه عدونه من ما كل نغس وعتغ • بصلله وحلاصا دىمه فداىا
• وعرده (؟) اندهاده بعد الشك اغناف وقطع • حسه وطغات فامامه بصواىم   The writer quotes
Ps cxx(cxxi) 4 and (147 a) refers to the day for which he writes as 'the day which
the Lord hath made, the time that He hath prepared for mercy and made ready
This is the day the greatest of the week, whereon appeared the living Light,
the day whereon He opened the broad road to paradise, whereon types were made
clear in a plain tongue (العصى باللسان الرموز واعلنت)'   Gabriel dons a white robe
(حلاب), the token of joy (146 b), Michael arrays him in a garment (حله) of gladness,

---

[1] Cf Journ Theol Stud v, 558, 563   The scribe of
MS Hunt 256 (A D 1388) was Senouthius ⲛ̅ⲧⲉ ⲙⲟϣⲗⲟⲥ
(ملص) ⲁⲡⲁ (ἀπό) ⲭⲣⲓⲟⲛ (χωρίον) ⲁⲧⲣⲁⲡⲭ ⲥⲁϥⲣⲏⲥ
ⲛ̅ϯⲡⲟⲗ ⲗⲉⲩⲟⲩ (Λύκου) (pp ⲣϥⲍ, ⲥⲅ̅ⲋ)

[2] This explains the fragment let in to the fly-leaf, v
HORNER III, p lxii
[3] V HORNER'S Boh NT. III, p lxiv
[4] V MALLON in Journ As 1906 (II), 521

brightly glittering (بارقه النور) Further quotations are from Ps xcix(c) 4, Jer ix 23, James (cited, 146 a, as 'Peter, chief of the apostles') i 9, 10, Matt v 3, xxiii 27, 26 Finally the intercession of the Virgin, 4 Beasts, 24 Elders, saints, apostles, is recommended On 143 a is a rubric, introducing John, the Apostle and Evangelist, and sketching his history. On 142 b, a the writer concludes with a wordy profession of his inadequacy and a prayer for indulgence

It is evident therefore that the book was intended for use in the Easter service[1] The following rubric, from the above CURZON MS, gives the ritual of procession and hymn to follow the reading of the Revelation

دم بعد ذلك تعرى الرويا عربما على المنحلمه؛ لما حيث الشرف وبعد دمام الرويا العربى نعال لحن ⲙⲏⲛ ⲁⲅⲩⲱⲡⲓ ⲛⲉⲙⲉⲛ نقال امس كمربالنصوں ثلاث مرات بالكبر والمواقبس؛ وبطوقوا الهمكل ثلاثه صورات وهم حاملس كتاب السعر وللّه الاعاده وبعد ذلك حمعه بتبدوا بالسوءاى؛ حكم دربيب بطام بس العرج المدوں بكتاب الترنبب وبكمله العباس كعادة ست العرج وبصروقوا بسلام الرب امس

On 140 b begins an Arabic version of the Revelation It appears to be that whence the variants in red ink in the first part of this MS are drawn (v above) A later hand has added the Coptic sections in the margin

---

[1] A rubric in no 16, fol 311, refers to its being read on Easter Eve V also the *Gauharah an-nafisah* of Ibn Sabbâ' (Cairo, 1902), p 170

[2] In the Cairo *Euchologion* 105, written الاحلية. Mr EVETTS suggests ἀναλόγιον The etymology given (? by the editor) in Ibn Sabbâ', p 96, is fantastic

[3] MARCUS BEY SIMAIKA informs me that بالكبر is 'at length', the notes being each long sustained by many repetitions of the syllables sung to them It is contrasted with دمح (TUKI, *Missale* 151), which implies reading, instead of singing The باقوس is (now) a metal cymbal

[4] Presumably for سواعة *Horologion*

LECTIONARIES

424 [16].—European paper, 344 foll, paged on *versos*, in a restored native binding, 51 × 34½ cm , 27 lines with Arabic opposite   Script a large, regular hand   Head-lines, stops and the usual letters in red , large initials, sectional divisions in red, green and yellow   On the fly leaf an elaborately ornamented cross   Dated, fol 343 *a*, A M 1477 = A D 1761

Lectionary for the Paschal season (Palm Sunday ϯⲕⲩⲣⲓⲁⲕⲏ ⲛⲧⲉ ⲡⲉⲩⲗⲟⲥⲓⲙⲉⲛⲟⲥ till Easter Day ϯⲕⲩⲣⲓⲁⲕⲏ ⲛⲛⲓϣϯ ⲉⲧⲉϯⲁⲛⲁⲥⲧⲁⲥⲓⲥ ⲛⲧⲉ ⲡⲉⲛⲟ̅ⲥ̅)[1]   In the final subscriptions it is entitled رسم الصعايني الكبير   Lessons (from the Old and New Testaments) are given for the 5 canonical hours of each day, interspersed with 12 Homilies   The lessons for each day are preceded by those for the foregoing night, the 1st hour of the former being ' First hour of the night ⲉϫⲱⲣϩ باللی of —— ', the 1st of the latter being ' Early morn, ϣⲱⲣⲡ باكر, of —— '   The opening lessons, for Palm Sunday morning, are Ps cxxi 1, John xii 1, Ps lxvii, Luke xix 1[2]   Those for the night of Monday (i e Sunday night) begin on fol 21 *a*, those for Monday on 32 *a*, for the night of Tuesday on 57 *b*, for Tuesday on 69 *a*, for the night of Wednesday on 105 *b*, for Wednesday on 117 *a*, for the night of Thursday on 139 *a*, for Thursday on 150 *b* (here ritual, lessons and prayers for the service of the Basin اللقان λακάνη, 168 *a*), for the night of Friday παρασκευή on 201 *b*, for Friday on 242 *a* (with ritual for the Exaltation of the Cross, 258 *a*³), special lessons of the 11th and 12th hours of Friday on 291 *a*, for the Saturday of Joy (*sic*) on 301 *b*, for the σύναξις on 314 *a*, for Easter Sunday on 332 *b* and evening, ⲣⲟⲩϩⲓ ⲙⲙⲉ, on 342 *b*

Among the lessons are the passages from Ecclesiasticus, Wisdom, and Joshua, printed by Bouriant from a similar book⁴, and practically identical in extent with ours   He has also printed the incidental Homilies[5] by Shenoute (foll 38 *b*, 55 *b*, 74 *a*, 120 *a*, 182 *b*), Severus[6] (137 *a*), Athanasius (289 *b*, 303 *a*)   Those of Chrysostom on 152 *b*, ⲟⲩⲟⲛ ϩⲁⲛϩⲃⲏⲟⲩⲓ ⲉⲛⲙⲉⲩⲓ ⲉⲣⲱⲟⲩ and 194 *b*, ϯⲛⲁⲩ ⲅⲁⲣ ⲉⲟⲩⲙⲏϣ ⲙⲡⲓⲥⲧⲟⲥ, are not printed , only those on 80 *b*, ϯⲟⲩⲱϣ ⲇⲉ ⲟⲩⲛ and 251 *a*, ⲟⲩ ⲡⲉⲧⲉⲛⲛⲁϣϫⲟⲟϥ

Two hymns occur among the lessons fol 306 *a*, on Saturday morning, ⲁⲩⲁϣ ⲡⲉⲛⲥⲱⲣ ⲉⲛϣⲉ ⲛⲧⲉ ⲡⲓⲥⲧⲁⲩⲣⲟⲥ, containing a narrative of the Crucifixion , and fol 341 *a*, on Sunday morning, ϭⲓⲟⲩⲱⲓⲛⲓ ϭⲓⲟⲩⲱⲓⲛⲓ ⲱ ⲡⲓⲧⲱⲟⲩ ⲛⲧⲉ ⲛⲓϫⲱⲓⲧ, ' Be thou illumined, O Mount of Olives '   The lesson from 1 Corinthians for Saturday's σύναξις is also to be sung يطلب السلام عليكم

---

[1] *Cf* Br Mus no 1247
[2] As in Lagarde, *Orientalia* p 7
  Cf Br Mus no 774
[4] *Recueil de Trav* vii 82

[5] *V* Br Mus no 774, Codd Vatic Copt xxxi and xxxiv
[6] 'Severian' in Bouriant and in Ethiopic (Wright's *Cat* ccvii)   But the passage is not in Migne , it might recall the homily in Zoega p 120

On foll 68 *b*, 116 *b* the sections end with the verses

اطلب العلم ما متى •   اىما العلم ﻻالطلب

رحم اللّه الدى قرى •   ودعا الدى كىب

A reader's or owner's note on fol 116 *b* and subscriptions by the scribe, on 343 *a*, *b*, state that the MS. was dedicated to the church of St George, above the great church of the Virgin of Hârat Zuwailah[1] (الح السى ىعه ﻻاعلا روىله or داعلا حارى كسسه ﻻعلوا), in Dair al-Habash, by حاد اللّه اىو ناﻻرس   The scribe was Colluthus ڡلمہ, priest of the church of the Virgin at the Steps[2] in Babylon الدرح ساىلوں in Old Cairo, and the date A M 1477 = A D 1761   Above this subscription is the name (in Coptic) and seal of Mark, the 106th patriarch

The MS belonged to TATTAM, as a note on the fly-leaf in his hand shows

Fol 344 does not belong to this MS   It is an episcopal letter   *V* no 461

425 [6, 7].—Paper, 4 foll in a modern binding, now 25 × 17½ cm   Foll 1, 3 are from the same MS, in one col of 21 lines, fol 2, from another MS, has 20 lines, fol 4, from a third, has 21   Scripts all may be of the 14th century, fol 4 being probably the earliest   Red initials, stops &c are used in all

I Foll 1, 3 (the last and first leaves of quire ⲕⲉ)   The Psalter   Fol 3 has Pss cxliii 13–15, cxliv 1–8, fol 1 has the Ode of Moses (Exod xv 1–10), with an ornamental heading, indicating a new section of the volume

II Fol 2, p ⲧⲍ̄ⲩ̄   A Lectionary, showing 1 Cor ix 7 (end of a lesson), 1 John v 14–19   *Incipits* and *explicits* in Arabic (later) in the margins

III Fol 4   A Lectionary, showing Mark ix 43–50, and, for Morning Prayer of the 3rd day of the Forty Days' (fast, Ar المعىس الصوم من الاولہ الحمعه من الثلتا الىوم), Ps xxiv 11, 12, and Matt ix 9 (beginning of a lesson), *incipit* in Arabic

[1] *V* BUTLER, *Churches* 1 271   [2] This church in MAI iv 194   *V* Abû Sâlih, foll 41 *b*, 43 *b*

LITURGICAL

426 [59]—Paper, 284 foll [1], paged on *versos*; 14.4 × 12 cm, with modern blank leaves at beginning and end, foll 1–3 being also relatively modern additions, in European binding   16 lines with Arabic opposite.   Script   heavy, regular, ⲅ rests upon a horizontal stroke   Subordinate parts (the deacon's) are in a neat, sloping hand (*e g* foll 79–85)   Initials, stops, head-lines, the letters ⲫ, ⲋ in red, quire-ornaments, larger initials and scrolls in red, green and yellow, so too occasional birds and animals in the margins (foll 159, 223, 251 &c)   But the first lines of the principal prayers &c are gilt [2], while facing the beginning of each Anaphora (foll 115 *b*, 182 *b*) is a beautifully illuminated page, in red, blue and gold arabesques, ornaments in similar style and colours heading the subsequent texts

The Anaphoras of SS Basil, Gregory and Cyril, mainly for the priest's use, though giving the deacon's part with tolerable fullness   The initial text=ⲡ ⲣϥⲏ of the Cairo *Euchologion*.   The Anaphora proper of Basil begins on fol 57 *b*, the diptychs on fol 76 containing only the names of Mark, Severus, Cyril, Gregory, Basil, Anthony, Paul and Macarius   This is followed by the list of patriarchs, which ends with Cyril b Laklak (*ob* A D 1243), so dating the MS, or its original [3]   The Anaphora of Gregory begins on fol 116 *a*, that of Cyril on 183 *a*, with the prayer of John ⲃⲟⲥⲧⲣⲓⲕⲟⲥ on 186 *a* [4], and, after it, one attributed elsewhere to Severus [5]   One or two prayers found here appear to be lacking from the printed editions (on foll 258 ⲉⲁⲕϯ ⲛⲁⲛ ⲙ̄ⲡⲓϧⲙⲟⲧ, 261 ⲛⲑⲟⲕ ⲡⲟ̄ⲥ̄ ⲫⲏ ⲉⲧⲁϥϥⲓⲣⲓ)   The Anaphoras are followed by 6 prayers   before and after food (=*op cit*, pp ⲯⲅⲁ, ⲯⲅⲁ), at private offerings ⲟⲩⲥⲓⲁ ⲛⲟⲩⲁⲓ (beg ⲧⲉⲛϯϩⲟ ⲉⲣⲟⲕ ⲡⲭ̄ⲥ̄ ⲡⲉⲛⲛⲟⲩϯ ϭⲓ ⲛⲛⲁⲓⲟⲩⲥⲓⲁ), after the diptychs (*op cit*, ⲧⲟⲏ), then, added in a later hand (perhaps belonging to another MS) at the ἀσπασμός [6] (*op cit*, ⲅⲅⲁ) and, in yet another hand, one at Morning Incense (*op cit*, ⲗⲏ)   On fol 278 *b* is a note, possibly by the original scribe, ending thus ⲕⲁⲗⲓⲟⲕⲣⲁⲫⲟⲥ ⲥⲓⲙⲱⲛ | ⲫϯ ⲛⲉⲙ ⲧⲁⲅⲁⲡⲏ |] ⲁ̄ⲥ̄, and therefore written in A D 1288

The MS has been studied, constantly annotated (with cross and biblical references and with translations of words) and paged throughout by a 17th or 18th century hand [7] In 1835 it was the property of J Enschede of Haarlem, for whom C Leemans examined it   Subsequently (as his writing on foll 269, 270 shows) it became Tattam's

---

[1] Foll 70, 101 are bound upside down

[2] Fol 175 *b* has such letters simply painted yellow showing inadvertently the stage preliminary to gilding

[3] After Cyril, Severus of Antioch is added, in the Cairo edit and Br Mus no 817 he stands after Benjamin (*ob* 1331)   May this indicate that the types of those texts are of this later date ?

[4] In the Arabic يوحنا العامل, in the Cairo ed, ⲣⲁ, ϥⲅ̄ⲟ

[5] يوحنا المثلث الطوبى 'the thrice blessed'   Presumably both refer to Chrysostom, who sometimes replaces John of Bostra, *v* Renaudot (1847) 1 203, 282   (Bostra and Basora are clearly confused, for Paris 129 [20], f 122 has the prayer Ren ii 421 *infra* as by J bishop ⲛⲃⲁⲥⲧⲣⲓⲕⲟⲩ)

[6] *V* Cairo ed ϥⲥ̄ⲣ, *cf* Renaudot 296

[6] صلاة الصلح

[7] Much like Petraeus's hand in MS Bodleian Or 325

427 [19].—European paper, 192+22 blank foll, paged on *versos*, 15 8 × 10 5 cm , in native binding, 13 lines, with Arabic opposite Script a regular, 18th century hand Initials, stops &c red , larger initials, quire and some sectional ornaments and the cross on the 1st fly-leaf, red, yellow and black. Dated, fol 190 b, A M. 1465 = A.D 1749

The Euchologion, حولاحى χολοϭιοη, containing (1) foll 1–3, the ceremonial تردبس as to the 36 'crossings' رشومات, occurring in the liturgy 18 made upon the sacramental elements, 18 upon the clergy and people, also 6 مو والدٮ, i e upon the bread after touching the wine and conversely, and instructions علم as to the 'indications' or 'pointings' (i e with the finger) الشارٮ, occurring in the anaphoral service[1], (2) foll 4–127, the Anaphora of St Basil, giving mainly the priest's part and corresponding pretty closely with the Cairo edition[2], (3) the priest's part in the Prayer of Morning Incense[3], (4) 8 of the prayers سمة appended in the printed text to the Anaphoras[4]

The long Arabic subscription, foll 190–192, shows that the MS was written by Saʻd, the scribe of no 431, who sold it in A M 1480 to Fadl Allah Abû ʻAbd al-Masîh, for 367 *ryáls*[5] (about £8 10s.), the binding ٮحلٮد having cost 25 (? *ryáls*, 11s 6d) Salib, deacon حادم of the Virgin's Church at العدووٮ[6], is likewise prayed for On fol 192 b a note gives the climax ووٮ of the Inundation[7] and the proclamation thereof خبرو as having occurred on the 3rd of Misra in A H 1178 = A D 1764, and is followed by a short prayer

This MS was in TATTAM's collection.

428 [51], foll. 111–122.—Paper, 12 foll, paged on *versos*, 18 × 13 cm , 1 col, 15 lines, with Arabic opposite Script characterized by ﻣ of the form u and γ resting on a horizontal stroke. A few initials, head-lines and stops (not the letters ⲫ, ⲋ) in red

The Anaphora of Cyril The sequence of the leaves is 111–116 121, 117, 118, 119, 120, 122, the first corresponding to p ⳁⲟⲉ of the Cairo *Euchologion*

429 [52]—Paper, 205 foll, from various MSS, in a restored native binding , the leaves here described, 15 7 × 10 cm , not paged Script an uneven, modern hand (but the text is principally Arabic) Title and rubrics in red

Foll (counting from end) 2–17 The Service of the Holy Lamp[8], كٮاٮ صلاٮ ٮردبٮ (؟) العدٮل المعٮس 'First let him gather 7 priests كهٮ, and let them fill a lamp with olive oil and put therein 7 wicks ٯٮائل, then set it aside ووٮدرون, then let him say the Thanksgiving شهٮٮ (ϣⲉⲛⳉⲙⲟⲧ)' The liturgy following corresponds to some extent with TUKI's print (*Rituale*, pp ⲣⲗⲟ ff) The 1st prayer is that on T p ⲣⲙⲉ. The

---

[1] All this is on pp ⲅⲁⳁ ff of the Cairo *Euchologion* (1902)

[2] *Op cit*, p ⲣ⳽ⲏ.   [3] *Op. cit*, pp ⲕ and ⲗⲁ

[4] *Op cit*, pp ⳃⲏ ff The first is a Greek piece = RENAUDOT (ed 1847) i 73

[5] *V* LANE, *Mod Eg* (1837) ii 380

[6] A former suburb of Cairo *V* Abû Ṣâlih, fol 44 a, Makrizi, *Churches*, no 18   [7] *V* LANE ii 259

[8] I e Extreme Unction. *V* VANSLEB, *Hist* 213 and cf LEGRAIN in *Ann du Serv des Ant* viii 253

D d

Arabic lessons (fol 6) are James v 10-20, Ps vi 2, 1 (*sic*), John v 1-7 (this is not complete), Eph vi 12-18 (not in TUKI). Coptic lessons (fol 8 *b*) Ps xxiv 17, 18, Matthew vi 14-18 (with Arabic) The Arabic prayers which follow these (fol 10 *a*) are apparently neither in TUKI nor in Br Mus no 438 The 1st begins 'We pray Thee, O Lord, God of might (=sabbaoth), Merciful, mighty in all things, to look upon Thy servant, NN ' The 2nd 'O Lord, pitiful and of great mercy, who desirest not the death of the sinner ' The 3rd 'O Lord of peace سلم, physician of bodies and spirits ' The 4th · 'O ye Saints, unto whom belongeth healing . ' This last is by far the longest

This MS was TATTAM'S it bears his name on the fly leaf

For the final portion of the volume *v* no 458

For the Arabic portions *v* Addenda

430 [17].—European paper, 420 foll, paged on *versos*, in European binding, $28\frac{1}{2} \times 22$ cm 17 lines, with Arabic opposite it Script a good 19th century hand Smaller initials, head lines, stops &c in red, larger initials in red and yellow Dated, on p ⲧⲏⲃ *b*, ⲁ ⲙ 1549 – ⲁ ⲇ 1833

The Psalmodia (الصلوودية, elsewhere Theotokia), for the service (تكريم) of the month of Kihak, containing the 7 Theotokias, 4 Odes and Hymns (تسبيح) for that month [1]

The arrangement of this copy differs widely from that of TUKI's print it contains many more pieces [2] and much resembles Br Mus no 863 The preliminary sections however, up to p ⲗⲉ, correspond generally to the first 23 pp of TUKI The following table shows the disposition of the successive groups of hymns and their corresponding places in TUKI's edition, the pages of the latter being given in figures Where these are absent, the piece is not found in TUKI

P ⲁ = TUKI p ⲓ, ⲥⲉⲛⲫⲣⲁⲛ
 ⲓ = 7, ⲧⲱⲟⲩⲕⲟⲩ
 ⲓⲁ = 5, Ps ⲓ
 ⲓⲍ = 20, *Madih* [3] on the Resurrection, to be said only between Easter (القيامة) and
       the end of Hatûr
 ⲕⲃ = ⲓⲟ (the Psalter extracts are in a different sequence)
ⲗⲃ = 264 *b* [4], *Absâliyah* on 1st Ode
 ⲗⲋ = 23, 1st Ode (Moses)
 ⲙ = 27, ⲗⲱⲃⲱ, *Madih*

---

[1] An analysis and description of the Theotokia by MALLON in *Rev Or Chret* 1904, 17

[2] But these often much resemble the hymns printed for the corresponding occasion, they may indeed open with identical phrases.

[3] Written indifferently مديح or مديحة throughout

[4] 261-270 are numbers erroneously given twice over in TUKI

ⲙⲃ = 268 *b*, *Absâlıyah* on Theot. for 2nd Day

ⲙⲅ, another, ⲁⲍⲁⲙ ⲉⲧⲓ ⲉϥⲟⲓ... ⲁϥⲛⲁϩⲙⲉϥ.

ⲙⲍ = 81, Theotokıa for 2nd Day

ⲛⲉ = 87, ⲗⲱⲃϣ

ⲛⲁ, *Tarh*[1] on preceding Theot, ⲁⲍⲁⲙ ⲡⲓϣⲟⲣⲡ.

ⲛⲉ = 271, *Absâlıyah* on Theot for 3rd Day

ⲛⲍ, another, ⲁϥϯ ⲥⲱⲧⲡ.

ⲝ = 90, Theotokıa for 3rd Day.

ⲝⲉ = 95, ⲗⲱⲃϣ

ⲝⲋ, *Tarh* on preceding Theot., ⲡⲓⲭⲗⲟⲙ.

ⲝⲍ = 274, *Absâlıyah* on 2nd Ode

ⲟ, another, ⲁⲙⲱⲓⲛⲓ ⲙⲁⲣⲉⲛϩⲱⲥ.

ⲟⲅ = 28, 2nd Ode (Davıd)

ⲟⲋ = 32, *Madîh,* ⲙⲁⲣⲉⲛⲟⲩⲱⲛϩ.

ⲟⲏ, *Tarh* on preceding Ode, ⲙⲁⲣⲉⲛⲉⲣⲯⲁⲗⲓⲛ

ⲟⲏ = 277, *Absâlıyah* on Theot for 4th Day

ⲡⲃ, another, ⲁⲙⲱⲓⲛⲓ ⲧⲏⲣⲟⲩ ⲛⲛⲓⲥⲧⲟⲥ.

ⲡⲋ, another, ⲁⲣⲉϭⲓⲥⲓ ⲛⲝⲉ(*leg* ⲉⲝⲉⲛ)ⲛⲓⲙⲉⲅⲓ.

ϥⲁ = 99, Theotokıa for 4th Day

ϥⲋ = 105, ⲗⲱⲃϣ, ⲓⲉⲍⲉⲕⲓⲏⲗ.

ϥⲏ, *Tarh* on preceding Theot, ⲛⲓⲧⲁⲅⲙⲁ

ϥⲑ = 280, *Absâlıyah* on Theot for 5th Day

ⲣⲃ, another, ⲁⲡⲟⲥ ⲫϯ.

ⲣⲍ = 108, Theotokıa for 5th Day

ⲣⲓⲋ, *Madîh* before ⲫϯ ⲫⲏ ⲁⲧϣⲙⲁⲩ

ⲣⲓⲏ = 118, ⲗⲱⲃϣ, ⲫϯ ⲫⲏ ⲁⲧϣⲙⲁⲩ ⲉⲣⲟϥ.

ⲣⲓⲑ, *Tarh* on preceding Theot, ⲙⲱⲩⲥⲏⲥ ⲅⲁⲣ.

ⲣⲕ = 284, *Absâlıyah* on 3rd Ode

ⲣⲕⲅ, another, ⲁⲣⲓ ϩⲙⲟⲧ

ⲣⲕⲋ[2], an alternative (مصر[3]), ⲁⲡⲁϩⲏⲧ.

ⲣⲕⲍ *b* = 33, 3rd Ode (Three Chıldıen)

ⲣⲗ = 286, *Absâlıyah* on precedıng Ode

ⲣⲗⲁ = 189, on same

ⲣⲗⲉ = 38, Doxology on same

ⲣⲗⲋ, *Tarh* on preceding Ode, ⲁϥⲧⲁϩⲟ.

ⲣⲗⲍ, *Absâlıyah* on the Vırgın, Angels, Apostles &c, ⲁⲙⲱⲓⲛⲓ ⲙⲁⲣⲉⲛⲟⲩⲱϣⲧ.

ⲣⲙⲋ, another, ⲁⲙⲱⲓⲛⲓ ⲧⲏⲣⲟⲩ ⲋⲉⲛⲟⲩⲑⲉⲗⲏⲗ.

ⲣⲙⲑ = 38 *b*, Lıtany (الطلبات[4]).

ⲣⲛⲍ = 266, Doxology to be saıd here and at the Incense (رفع البخور)

ⲣⲛⲑ = 269, Doxology to Gabrıel

---

[1] The طرح ıs gıven ın Arabıc, except for the openıng phrases

[2] Pp ⲣⲕⲋ, ⲣⲕⲍ are by error repeated, but ın the first pair the figures are erased

[3] MS مصر

[4] = ⲛⲓⲧⲱⲃϩ

ⲣⲙⲑ *Rubric* after ϣⲱⲡⲓ ⲛⲑⲟ (46) and *tarh* to the proper saint[1] (صاحب النهار),
sing the *tarh* ⲭⲉⲣⲉ ⲛⲉ ⲱ ϯⲡⲁⲣⲑⲉⲛⲟⲥ

ⲣϙⲁ, *Absâlîyah* on ⲛⲉⲕⲛⲁⲓ, ⲁⲓⲛⲁⲉⲣϧⲏⲧⲥ.

  ⲣϙⲋ, Doxology on the Great Fast, for the nights of Sundays (حدون) in Kihak,
ⲛⲉⲕⲛⲁⲓ ⲱ ⲡⲁⲟ̅ⲥ̅.

  ⲣϙⲑ, *Tarh* on preceding, ⲧⲉⲛϯϩⲟ ⲉⲣⲟⲕ

ⲣⲟ, *Absâlîyah* for Friday, ⲁⲓⲉⲣⲉⲧⲓⲛ.

  ⲣⲟⲁ = 290, another, ⲁⲛⲟⲕ ⳝⲁⲡⲓϫⲱⲃ.

  ⲣⲟⲋ, another, ⲁⲡⲟ̅ⲥ̅ ⲫϯ.

  ⲣⲡ, *Madîh* for the same, ادى ناسم اللّه العدوس

  ⲣⲡⲃ = 121, Theotokia for Friday

  ⲣⲡⲉ, *Madîh* on preceding Theot., before the لش, in rhymed Arabic, ادى ناسم
الرب سوع • واطلب من فصله بحشوع

  ⲣⲡⲍ = 125, ⲁⲓⲛⲁⲙⲟⲩϯ.

  ⲣⲡⲏ[2], *Tarh* on preceding Theot., ⲧⲥⲙⲁⲣⲱⲟⲩⲧ ⲛⲑⲟ.

ⲣⲡⲑ = 293, *Absâlîyah* on Theot. for Saturday

  ⲣϥⲅ, another, ⲁⲡⲟ̅ⲥ̅ ⲫϯ ⲥⲱⲧⲡ

  ⲣϥⲅ = 130, Theotokia for Saturday

  ⲥⲃ, *Tarh* on preceding Theot., ϯⲁⲧⲟⲩⲗⲉⲃ

ⲥⲃ, *Absâlîyah* to Gabriel before the 1st شارب[3], ⲁⲓⲛⲁⲉⲣϧⲏⲧⲥ.

  ⲥⲋ = 135, 1st شارب

  ⲥⲏ, *Tarh* after the foregoing, ⲭⲉⲣⲉ ⲛⲉ ⲱ ϯⲡⲁⲣⲑⲉⲛⲟⲥ.

ⲥⲏ, *Absâlîyah* to Gabriel at the 2nd شارب, ⲙⲱⲓⲛⲓ ⲧⲏⲣⲟⲩ ⳝⲉⲛⲟⲩⲣⲁϣⲓ.

  ⲥⲓⲃ, 2nd سارب, ⲭⲉⲣⲉ . . . . ϯⲉⲕⲩⲛⲏ.

  ⲥⲓⲅ, *Tarh* on foregoing, to Gabriel, ⲭⲉⲣⲉ ⲡⲛⲓϣϯ ⲛⲅⲁⲃⲣⲓⲏⲗ

ⲥⲓⲉ = 296, *Absâlîyah* on next following, ⲁⲛⲟⲕ ⳝⲁⲡⲓϫⲱⲃ.

  ⲥⲓⲏ, Doxology on Theot. (*sic*), ⲱ ⲡⲉⲛⲟ̅ⲥ̅ ⲓ̅ⲏ̅ⲥ̅

  ⲥⲕ, *Tarh* after preceding, ⲛ̅ⲭ̅ⲥ̅ ⲡⲓⲗⲟⲅⲟⲥ.

ⲥⲕⲁ = 299, *Absâlîyah* on 4th Ode

  ⲥⲕⲁ, another, a mixture (موشع) of Greek and Coptic[4], ⲁⲕϣⲏⲡⳝⲓⲥⲓ ⲛⲉⲙⲏⲓ

  ⲥⲕⲍ, another, ⲙⲱⲓⲛⲓ ⲙⲁⲣⲉⲛⲟⲩⲱϣⲧ.

  ⲥⲗ = 46, 4th Ode (David)

  ⲥⲗⲁ, *Tarh* on preceding, ⲁϭⲓ ⳝⲉⲛⲛⲉⲧⲛϫⲓϫ

ⲥⲗⲉ = 303, *Absâlîyah* on Theot. for Sunday

  ⲥⲗⲏ, *Madîh* by Abû 's-Sa'd of Abûtîg (الابونسيى), to precede ⲁⲓⲕⲱϯ, اىرى عىرى امىح
وسول[5]

  ⲥⲗⲑ, *Absâlîyah* on same Theot., ⲁⲓⲕⲱϯ ⲛⲥⲱⲕ.

  ⲥⲙⲅ = 51, another to Our Lord and throughout the year

  ⲥⲙⲉ = 54, ⲗⲱⲃϣ, ⲗⲟⲓⲡⲟⲛ

---

[1] Presumably this refers to the Antiphonary
[2] Practically = 122
[3] Plur of (ⲅ) شارى ⲭⲉⲣⲉ (misread in Br Mus no 864)
[4] A number of Greek words are introduced into the
Coptic sentences

[5] Hymns by this author are printed on pp 24-29, 94,
183 of اللولو الهية of Yuhannâ Girgis and Gubrân Efendi
Ni'mat Allah (Cairo, 1892), but not the present piece
V below

ⲥⲙⲋ, *Absâlyah* on same Theot., ⲁⲓⲥⲱⲧⲉⲙ ⲛϫⲉ ⲥⲓⲱⲛ.

ⲥⲙⲍ, another, on ساموكﻭي (ⲥⲉⲙⲟⲩϯ), ⲁⲙⲱⲓⲛⲓ ⲛⲓⲗⲁⲟⲥ.

ⲥⲙⲏ = 54 ff and 305 ff, Theotokia for Sunday including lections from St Luke, interspersed with passages from this Theotokia and their 7 paraphrases نفاسمر (*cf* p ⲧⲗⲉ)

ⲥⲙⲑ = 63, *Tarh* on foregoing, at the 1st ⲥⲉⲙⲟⲩϯ.

ⲥⲛⲁ, *Absâlyah* at 2nd ⲥⲉⲙⲟⲩϯ, ⲁϥϯ ⲛⲁⲗⲏⲟⲓⲛⲟⲥ.

ⲥⲛⲏ, another, ⲁⲙⲱⲓⲛⲓ ⲛⲓⲗⲁⲟⲥ ⲋⲉⲛⲟⲩⲥⲏⲛ.

ⲥⲛⲁ, from Theotokia, ⲥⲉⲙⲟⲩϯ.

—, *Tarh* to Virgin, on 2nd ⲥⲉⲙⲟⲩϯ, ⲱ ⲟⲩⲙⲁϯ.

ⲥⲛⲃ, *Absâlyah* on 7th سمير, ⲁⲓⲛⲁⲉⲣϧⲏⲧⲉ.

ⲥⲛⲋ, *Madih* on the Seven (*sc* Theotokias[1]), Arabic couplets, each with a Coptic refrain beginning ⲙⲁⲣⲓⲁ.

ⲥⲛⲏ, 7th سمير, ⲥⲟⲗⲥⲉⲗ ⲛⲛⲓⲉⲛⲕⲗⲏⲥⲓⲁ.

ⲥϥ, ⲍ ⲛⲥⲟⲡ ⲙⲙⲏⲓ

ⲥϥⲁ, Greek *Troparion* (قطبـ) to Virgin, ⲭⲉⲣⲉ ⲛⲉ ⲙⲁⲣⲓⲁ (Coptic throughout).

ⲥϥⲋ, *Tarh* after ⲍ ⲛⲥⲟⲡ, ⲁⲙⲱⲓⲛⲓ ⲛⲓⲡⲓⲥⲧⲟⲥ.

ⲥϥⲍ, *Absâlyah* على الاوﻧﺎﺭ to a stringed instrument, ⲁⲩⲥⲁϫⲓ.

ⲧ, ⲥⲱⲧⲉⲙ ⲱ ⲛⲁⲙⲉⲛⲣⲁϯ

ⲧⲋ, *Madâih* to Virgin for the كنيسـة in Kihak, ﺳﺖ ﻧﺎ مريـمكى.

ⲧⲉ, *Madih* before ⲁⲩⲙⲟⲩϯ (begins as last).

ⲓⲍ = 68, ⲁⲩⲙⲟⲩϯ.

— = 307, *Tarh* after foregoing

ⲧⲏ, *Absâlyah* on following.

ⲧⲓⲁ = 68, final ﻧﻔﺴﻴﺮ on ⲥⲉⲙⲟⲩϯ, ⲧⲉⲟⲓ ⲛϧⲩⲕⲁⲛⲟⲥ.

ⲧⲓⲏ = 75, between Easter and end of Hatûr

ⲧⲓⲑ, *Tarh* on the spiritual labourers[2] العيد الروحانيين, to the melody (بطربـ) of ϭⲓ ⲟⲩⲱⲓⲛⲓ, ⲁϥⲙⲟⲩϯ ⲛϫⲉ ⲡϭⲥ.

ⲧⲕⲃ = 315, *Absâlyah* on ⲛⲉⲛⲛⲁⲓ.

ⲧⲕⲉ, *Tarh*, ⲛⲉⲛⲛⲁⲓ ⲱ ⲡⲁⲙⲟⲩϯ, by priest only, to same طربـة as before

ⲧⲕⲏ = 152, Angelic Hymn, followed by a *Tarh*

ⲧⲗ, *Subscription*. The end of what must be read in the Seven and the Four, on the Sundays (حدود) in Kihak

ⲧⲗ, What must be read at Evening Prayer in Kihak, on Sunday nights

— = 235, *Absâlyah* on Theot of Saturday

ⲧⲗⲁ, *Madih* to Virgin, Arabic and acrostical, امدح فى عدرى وبتول[3]

ⲧⲗⲉ = 130, Theotokia for Saturday (as above) This section consists of the 9 successive 3-strophe divisions of this Theotokia (*v* Tuki), after each of which come 6 paraphrases[4] (نفاسمر) In the 1st of these, the 'Greek' (رومى), the 4 lines of the strophe rhyme alternately, in the 2nd, 'the Replacer' (مبدل), the lines (all but the last) generally rhyme in pairs, while the last

---

[1] ⲍ ع, or on the 7th ﻧﻔﺴﻴﺮ, as before   *V* the next
[2] Refers to Matt xx 8
[3] Printed on p 20 of the above hymn-book.
[4] Given by Tuki, 240 ff, without any headings.

of one strophe serves again as the first of the next ; in the 3rd, 'the Bohairic' (بحيرى), the 4 lines again rhyme alternately   The 4th series is the composition of the above Abû 's-Sa'd[1], the 5th, that of the *mo'allim* Gabriel of Kâu[2] (القاى), this series is regularly followed by a blank, as if for the insertion of another, the 6th is that of the patriarch Mark[3]   The 4th, 5th and 6th series are in Arabic only[4].   The 8 remaining divisions of the Theotokia are upon pp ⲧⲁⲍ, ⲧⲁⲗⲉ, ⲧⲏ, ⲧⲏⲁ, ⲧⲏⲟ, ⲧⳓⲅ, ⲧⳓⲏ, ⲧⲟⲃ

ⲧⲟⲍ, *Tarûhat* for Sundays in Kîhak

—, 1st Sunday, ⲁⲥϣⲱⲡⲓ ⲥⲉⲛⲛⲓⲉϩⲟⲟⲩ (= Luke 1 5-23, but with constant divergence from the biblical text), followed by another (ولد اصا), a paraphrase, in Arabic, of the same story (to 1 25)

ⲧⲟⲏ, 2nd Sunday, ⲥⲉⲛⲓⲁⲃⲟⲧ ⲙⲙⲁϩϩⲍ (= *ib* 1 26-38), with a highly apocryphal paraphrase, in Arabic

ⲧⲟⲑ, 3rd Sunday, ⲁⲥⲧⲱⲛⲥ ⲇⲉ (= *ib* 39-56), with an Arabic paraphrase as before

ⲧⲏⲁ, 4th Sunday, ⲁⲛⲓⲥⲛⲟⲩ ⲇⲉ ⲙⲟϩ (= *ib* 57-80), with paraphrase as before.

ⲧⲏⲅ = 141, What must be read at Morning Prayer, after the Psalms

ⲧϥⲃ = 152, Angelic Hymn (تسبحة)

ⲧϥⲛ = 160, Doxologies to the Saints   Not so numerous nor in the same sequence as Tuki's   Severus of Antioch is included (ⲩⲓⲅ)   The last is to the reigning (الحاطر *sic*) patriarch

ⲩⲓⲉ, *Madih* on the Doxology ⲕⲉ ⲅⲁⲣ (above p ⲣⲛⳓ), composed by Al Bardanûhy[5], Arabic, acrostical

ⲩⲓⳓ = 205, final Doxology

ⲩⲓⳓ, Preface (ٯدمة) to Creed, ⲧⲉⲛϭⲓⲥⲓ ⲙⲙⲟ ⲑⲙⲁⲩ.

ⲩⲓⲏ, The Creed (امانة المجمع), (قانون الامانة التى رتبها ربنها المجامع), ⲥⲉⲛⲟⲩⲙⲉⲑⲙⲏⲓ ⲧⲉⲛⲛⲁϩϯ.

The MS is adorned with full-page paintings, in *gouache* and gold, overlaid with varnish   They are either by a European hand, or imitated from western modals   On the fly-leaf is a Crucifixion, on p ⲕⲁ a picture of David, on ⲙⲍ, ⲙⲏ Adam and Eve in Paradise, on ϥ the 7 Archangels (?), on ⲣⲍ the burning bush (Moses wearing a modern bishop's mitre), on ⲣⲕⲍ the 3 Children, on ⲥⲕⲟ the Cross &c, on ⲥⲛⲃ the Virgin and Child   On ⲣⲛⲃ are marginal ornaments in the same style, including a double eagle

This volume was in TATTAM's collection, as various notes in his hand testify

431 [20] —European paper, 370 foll[6], paged on *versos*, 21 5 × 30 5 cm, in a European binding, wherein the outer sides of a previous native binding are preserved   19 lines,

[1] Printed *op cit*, p 24

[2] This, I presume, is the meaning of the *nisbah*

[3] I cannot ascertain which of the 7 Marks is intended

[4] These hymns and their sequence are different in no 431   In Cambridge Univ Libr, Add 3064, their titles and sequence are 'Greek', Abû 's-Sa'd, the Patriarch,

Al-Bardanûhy (*v* below), 'Arabic'

[5] From the village دردهة, between Al-Kais and Qolosna. Some of his hymns are printed in the above book, pp 51, 140, but there this is ascribed (p 58) to Gâdd Allah, an author represented on pp 156, 202

[6] Fol 322 is misplaced, it should follow 189

with (usually) Arabic opposite, in a regular 18th century script, probably all by one hand   Initials, stops, head-lines &c are in red.   Dated, fol 369 a, A M 1478 = A D 1762.

The Psalmodia or Theotokia, here simply ما دصمه وى شهر كدهك المبارك The arrangement, in the first portion of the volume, is practically identical with that of no 430, but later on the sequence of the pieces differs considerably from that   The 1st Ode is on fol 25, the 2nd Theotokia on 33, 3rd Theot. on 41, 2nd Ode 50, 4th Theot 57, 5th Theot 67, 3rd Ode 81, 6th Theot 116, 7th Theot 125, 4th Ode 151, 1st Theot (Sunday) 160   Fol 224 b = no 430, p ⲧⲏⲅ, fol 243 = Tuki 160[1].   On fol 268 are the Doxologies for the chief festivals, to precede those on 'The Seven and the Four'   On 287 b is the Deacon's Office, ⲓⲥ ⲡⲁⲧⲏⲣ.   Fol 319 b gives the series of paraphrases on Sunday's Theotokia, = no 430, p ⲧⲗⲉ   But though these same texts are, so far as they go, found there too, they are here designated (and in this sequence) 'Greek', 'Little' (الصغير)[2], 'the Replacer' (المعبر), 'Arabic,' the last being the compositions of Abû 's-Sa'd   On fol 343 b begin other hymns (لحن), each with its ذرلكس[3], among them, on fol 345, one relating to Thomas (John xx)   On 359 b is the Creed   On 366 a part of the Deacon's Office again, ⲁⲙⲏⲛ ⲁⲙⲏⲛ ⲁⲙⲏⲛ ⲓⲥ ⲡⲁⲧⲏⲣ..... ⲉ[ⲥ]ϣⲟⲡ ⲛⲉⲙⲁⲕ...   The last piece is a وطعه رومى, to follow the Pauline lesson

Fol 369 a, b has a wordy colophon, giving the scribe's name as Sa'd سعد[4], deacon of the church of كوم احسن[5], near Kalyûb[5], who wrote it for the 'archon' and deacon, Lutf Allah, called b as-Sabbâg, of Al-Kais, but resident in Misr

The MS was in Tattam's collection

432 [18].—European paper, 201 foll, paged on *versos*, in native binding, 15 7 × 10 6 cm   Some 15 lines, without parallel Arabic   Script an uneven 18th century hand   Stops, head-lines, initials &c red, sectional ornaments red, yellow and green   On the 1st fly-leaf an elaborately coloured cross by a later hand   Dated, on fol 201, A M. 1467 = A D 1751

The Psalmodia or Theotokia   The quires, as far as fol 157, and perhaps after 183, are in confusion   A native hand has, subsequently to their present disordering, frequently adapted the guiding catch-words to this erroneous arrangement, so increasing the confusion   The proper order of the leaves is as follows   14-28, 2-13, 29-87[6], 148-157, 138-147, 128-137, 118-127, 108-117, 98-107, 88-97, 158-183, [gap of ? foll], 184-201.

The text, like that of no 430, shows the two series of Odes and Theotokias combined   On p ⲕⲍ is the hymn preceding the 1st Ode, on p ⲗⲋ that preceding the 3rd Theotokia, on p ⲙⲁ that preceding the 4th, and so on   These hymns, 'due to be read in the month Kihak,' and on p ⲣⲉ.   Next follow Doxologies for use between New Year

---

[1] On 262 b is a hymn to العمر ابو شنودة, not the same as that printed by Leipoldt, *Aeg Z* xliii *152*

[2] Can this and the title of the same series in no 430, 'Bohairic,' be the same word, misread in one case?

[3] *Cf* Br. Mus no. 906   But v the explanation

(παραλλάξ) of P Peeiers, *Byz Z* 1907, 302, which is indeed supported by Br Mus no 894

[4] *V* no 427   On fol 57 a, his father was 'Attiyah عطية

[5] Now written Ishfîn.

[5] One fol , between 74 and 75, has been cut out

(عبد السرور) and the Festival of the Cross, on p ρζ others for that festival, p ρι for Christmas (ⲧⲟⲧⲉ ⲣⲱⲕ); then those for Baptism (Epiphany), Lent, the Saturday of Lazarus, several for Palm Sunday, for Easter (ⲧⲟⲧⲉ ⲣⲱⲕ again), Ascension, then *Absâliyât* for Lent, Pentecost, the Apostles, one for general use (سنوى) ⲁⲓⲥⲱⲧⲉⲙ ⲉⲛⲓⲥⲁϣ (Tuki 228), a *troparion* for alternate chanting (فى التوزيع) in Lent. On p ⲣⲡⲅ are the 9 Arabic paraphrases (نعاسير) for Kihak by Abû 's-Sa'd (*v* no 430, p ⲧⲗⲉ ff), here without author's name. Then follow two *Madâih*, after which begins (fol 182) the Deacon's Office from the Anaphora[1] ⲁⲙⲏⲛ ⲁⲙⲏⲛ, ⲓⲥ ⲡⲁⲧⲏⲣ ⲁⲅⲓⲟⲥ. On fol 185 is the list of Patriarchs, ending with John the 105th (1727). The 12 virtues of the Holy Spirit, *troparia* for the Dominical festivals, for Christmas and for the سعادة of the (newly) married[2], and a *Madih* for Kihak, to the melody of (بطرخ) ⲕⲁⲓ ⲅⲁⲣ (Tuki 266), end the volume.

On the last leaf is the scribe's note　he was the قمص Colluthus كاتب, schoolmaster (حاتم الاطفال)[3] at Siût, and wrote this مجموع at the behest of the deacon George, son of the *mo'allim* Gabriel, resident in (العاطف) the neighbourhood (ناحية) of the same town.

This volume is from TATTAM's collection.

433 [69]—Paper; 217 foll, paged on *versos*, in a restored native binding; 21 × 14·7 cm. 15 lines. Script an even, 18th century hand. Initials, stops, Arabic headings &c in red. Hymns ابصاليات. All are acrostical, a few only are found in TUKI's *Theotokia*.

(1) To the melodies *Watos* (βάτος) and *Adam* alternately, for certain festivals of the calendar, beginning with New Year's Day يوم السرور, ⲁⲙⲱⲓⲛⲓ ⲧⲏⲣⲟⲩ ⲛⲧⲉⲛϯ ⲱⲟⲩ ⲙⲡⲟⲩⲣⲟ. Those following are to John the Baptist (2nd Thoth), ⲁⲓⲛⲁⲉⲣϩⲏⲧⲥ and ⲁⲕϭⲓⲥⲓ ⲁⲗⲏⲟⲩⲥ, the Cross (7th Thoth[4]), ⲁⲣⲓⲯⲁⲗⲓⲛ ⲱ ⲛⲓⲡⲓⲥⲧⲟⲥ and ⲁⲗⲏⲟⲩⲥ ⲧⲉⲛⲛⲁϩϯ, the Virgin (21st Thoth), ⲁⲙⲱⲓⲛⲓ ⲧⲏⲣⲟⲩ ϧⲉⲛⲟⲩⲑⲉⲗⲏⲗ and ⲁⲓⲛⲁϩϯ=Tuki ⲥⲗⲁ, the latter being also for the 21st of each month and for the eve of all Sundays, the Virgin again, ⲁⲓⲥⲱⲧⲉⲙ=ⲧ ⲥⲕⲏ, George (7th Hatûr), ⲁⲗⲏⲟⲩⲥ ⲁϥϣⲁⲓ ⲛⲁⲛ and ⲁⲗⲏⲟⲩⲥ ⲧⲉⲛⲛⲁϩϯ ⲉⲣⲟⲕ, the Four Beasts (8th), ⲁⲙⲱⲓⲛⲓ ⲧⲏⲣⲟⲩ ⲱ ⲛⲓⲗⲁⲟⲥ and ⲁⲙⲟⲩ ϣⲁⲣⲟⲓ ⲙⲫⲟⲟⲩ, Michael (12th), ⲁⲣⲉϩ ⲉⲣⲟⲛ ⲱ ⲉⲙⲙⲁⲛⲟⲩⲏⲗ and ⲁⲓⲧⲱⲃϩ ⲙⲙⲟⲕ, Menas (15th), ⲁⲩⲣⲁϣⲓ ϣⲱⲡⲓ and ⲁⲓⲛⲁϩϯ ⲉⲣⲟⲕ ⲡⲁⲛⲟⲩϯ, the Twenty four Elders (24th), ⲁⲓⲉⲣϩⲉⲗⲡⲓⲥ ⲉⲣⲟⲕ and ⲁⲣⲉϩ ⲉⲣⲟⲓ, Mercurius (25th), ⲁⲙⲱⲓⲛⲓ ⲙⲁⲣⲉⲛϯ ⲱⲟⲩ and ⲁⲙⲱⲓⲛⲓ ⲧⲏⲣⲟⲩ ⲙⲫⲟⲟⲩ, Sergius and Bacchus (10th Babeh), ⲁⲙⲱⲓⲛⲓ ⲧⲏⲣⲟⲩ ⲱ ⲛⲓⲡⲓⲥⲧⲟⲥ and ⲁⲙⲱⲓⲛⲓ ⲛⲧⲉⲛϯ ⲱⲟⲩ, Theophanius, called also ⲧⲉⲝⲓ, فرج and روس[5] (21st Babeh), ⲁⲓⲉⲣϩⲉⲗⲡⲓⲥ ⲉⲣⲟⲕ and ⲁⲓⲧⲱⲃϩ ⲙⲙⲟⲕ.

(2) Fol 101 *a* ابصاليات for the month Kihak　to Shenoute, رئيس الموحدين (1st Kihak, sic[6]), ⲁⲣⲉϩ ⲉⲣⲟⲛ ⲱ ⲛⲭ̅ⲥ̅ and ⲁⲓⲧⲱⲃϩ ⲙⲙⲟⲕ ⲡⲁⲟ̅ⲥ̅, Entry of the Virgin into the Temple and Martyrdom of 'the new martyr' Pistauros ⲛⲓ⳨ صلب[7] (3rd), ⲁⲙⲱⲓⲛⲓ

---

[1] *V* no 431 and Br Mus no 890
[2] *V* Br Mus no 889
[3] His name 's found also on p ⲍ̅ⲍ *a*
[4] This should be the 17th

[5] *V PSBA* xxix 135 n　These 2 hymns tell nothing of him　He lived, according to Makrizi (*Churches*, no 1), after A D 1398
[6] Not thus in the calendars
[7] *V* no 435

ⲛⲧⲉⲛⲟⲩⲱϣⲧ and ⲁⲙⲱⲓⲛⲓ ⲡⲓⲣⲉϥϫⲁⲉⲓ, Isi (Paèsi) and Thecla (8th), ⲁⲙⲁⲉⲣϧⲏⲧⲥ and ⲁⲗⲏⲑⲱⲥ ⲧⲉⲛⲓⲁϧϯ, Barbara[1] (do), ⲁⲙⲁⲉⲣϧⲏⲧⲥ ⲱ ⲛⲓⲡⲓⲥⲧⲟⲥ and ⲁⲓⲧⲱⲃϩ ⲙⲙⲟⲕ ⲡⲁⲛⲟⲩϯ

(3) Fol 130 b ‎الابصالات‎, *Watos* and *Adam*, for the Sundays in Kihak, on the Theotokias, preceded by one at Evening Prayer ‎صلاة السلام‎ = ⲦⲨⲔⲒ ⲥⲗⲉ   The suc ceeding hymns are given by Tuki on pp ⲥϥⲏ b, ⲥⲟⲁ, ⲥⲟⲍ, ⲥⲡ (here one not in Τ, ⲁⲓⲉⲣⲉⲧⲓⲛ ⲁⲛⲟⲕ ⲡⲓⲕⲉⲣⲙⲓ), ⲥϥⲩ, ⲧⲅ, ⲧⲓⲉ, ⲥϥⳉ (here 2 to Gabriel, for 22nd Kihak), ⲥⲡⳉ

(4) Fol 176 a ‎الابصالات‎ for the Vigil παραμονή ‎برمون‎ of Christmas, i e the 28th Kihak, on the successive Theotokias, according to the week-day upon which that date falls   That for Monday is ⲁⲟⲩⲣⲁϣⲓ ϣⲱⲡⲓ ⲙⲫⲟⲟⲩ, the others are respectively ⲁⲙⲁⲅ- ⲙⲟⲣⲧⲟⲥ ϣⲁⲛϧⲏⲧ ⳪ⲁⲉⲗⲁⲁⲙ, ⲁⲣⲓϥ ⲁⲗⲓⲛ ⲱ ⲛⲓⲡⲓⲥⲧⲟⲥ, ⲁϥϯ ⲥⲁϫⲓ ⲙⲙⲱⲩⲥⲏⲥ, ⲁⲙⲁⲉⲣϧⲏⲧⲥ ⲱ ⲛⲓⲡⲓⲥⲧⲟⲥ, ⲁⲙⲱⲓⲛⲓ ⲱ ⲛⲓⲭⲣⲏⲥⲧⲓⲁⲛⲟⲥ, ⲁⲣⲓϥ ⲁⲗⲓⲛ ⲕⲁⲗⲟⲥ   Similarly on Christmas (29th Kihak) the 7 appropriate hymns are ⲁⲣⲓⲉⲧⲓⲛ ⲛⲧⲟⲧ, ⲁⲩⲙⲓⲥⲓ ⲛⲁⲛ ⲙⲫⲟⲟⲩ, ⲁⲙⲱⲓⲛⲓ ⲧⲏⲣⲟⲩ ⲛⲧⲉⲛϩⲱⲥ, ⲁϥϯ (as at the Vigil), ⲁⲙⲱⲓⲛⲓ (as at the Vigil)   In the middle of this last the volume ends   It is impossible to say how much is lost

A large number of the hymns have, as a last strophe, a petition on behalf of 'Nicodemus', ⲁⲛⲟⲕ ⲡⲓⲕⲉⲣⲙⲓ ⲛ, possibly their composer[2], others end with a similar but anonymous prayer

A note on fol 179 a states that the MS was dedicated perpetually to the church of SS Cyrus and John in Old Cairo[3] ‎مصر العدينة‎, while one on fol 208 b tells that the cost was borne by the deacon ‎سنار‎, son of Michael, overseer ‎ناطر‎ of that church

This MS belonged to Prof H MIDDLETON, who acquired it at Dair Mari Tadrus

434 [62]—Paper, 97 foll, several being blank, in native binding of plain red velvet Paging, beginning at the end[4], on *versos* ⲣⲟⲁ‾-ⲥ‾ⲓ‾ⳉ 21–25 lines, 20½ × 15 cm.   Script regular but cramped   Head-lines, stops, initials &c and the usual letters in red   Dated (fol 94 b) A M 1325 = A D 1609

A Collection of Hymns to the tone *Adam*, for various festivals throughout the year, entitled (fol 9 a) ‎دنرى   ست بعض ابصالات ادام لن دكر منه من الملايكه الح‎ (v. also the colophon)   The collection is similar to that of no 69, cf also Br Mus Catal, no 890

Foll 3, 4, a hymn to the Virgin for general use, ‎سوى‎, followed by 4 blank leaves and perhaps not properly belonging to the rest of the book

The saints honored (besides various festivals of Christ, the Virgin and Archangels) are Abraham, Isaac and Jacob, Anthony, Barsauma the Naked, Bifâm (Phoebammon)

---

[1] The text mentions her festival in the church of ⲅⲁⲣⲁⲃⲓⲁ ⲛⲓⲡⲣⲟⲙⲉⲟⲥ ‎حارة الروم‎, presumably that destroyed in A D 1318 (Makrizi, *Churches*, no 3)   Yet the proximity here of hymns to Paèsi and Thecla may indicate the other ch of B (v BUTLER, *Churches* i 235, Makrizi, l c, no 9)

[2] The name Nicodemus is not in use among the Copts
[3] V AMÉLINEAU, *Geogr* 577
[4] Presumably with a view to an Arabic text and, perhaps, since 171 is the lowest figure, as a second volume

E e

of Wasîm, Claudius, George the Great, George of Alexandria (7th Hatûr), John Baptist, Marina[1], Mercurius, Mena, Peter and Paul, Shenoute, Theodore the Eastern, Theodore Stratelates, Victor   The dates of their commemoration are those usual in the calendar   The hymns to the Virgin on the 2nd, 3rd and 1st Theotokias (fol 18 ff) are in Tuki, pp 268 *b*, 271, 303

Fol 85 *b* has a hymn for a martyr 'who has no *psali*', his name is to be inserted at the end of each strophe رجع   On 87 *a* is one for 2 saints falling upon the same day, on 88 *a*, one for all saints

All hymns (excepting one to Christ at New Year, fol 82 *b*) are acrostical, hence perhaps the poverty of invention which they display

The colophon, fol 94 *b*, names Girgis[2], son of the deceased *mo'allim* Barsûm, as provider of the book, in the following terms   دم وكمل هذا المجموع المبارك الذى هو

على الابصالهاب الادام حاصه وبعض معرده من الواطس[3] على اسم من ذكر وسه من الاعماد

هور ما وحن وكان العراع الح   وكان المهم تلك من ماله وكنه وتعبد الاح الحبس المحد

المحبوب المولا الرئيس الدين الاردكسى السمح المكس سمدى حرحس نحل المسح فى الاحصان

الابراهيمه المعلم درسوم على دلك وكسد لعسد[4] لستعع دركنه وبعرى سه الرب الاله صاحد كمور

النحس والرحمه   والباسح المسكس دصرب المطاهده الح

435 [22 and 21] — European paper, 142 and 155 foll respectively, paged on *versos*, several being blank at each end, in modern native binding of red leather, 30 × 21 3 cm ; 1 col of some 25 lines, with Arabic opposite   Script a coarse but regular 18th century hand   Initials, head lines, stops &c in red, quire and other ornaments in red, green, yellow and black, so too an elaborate cross on the fly-leaf of each volume   The subscription to each volume bears its date the first, 19th Kîhak, A M 1515 = A D 1799, the second, 4th Amshîr of the same year

The Antiphonary, *Difnâr*[5], for the months of Tût and Bâbeh, Hatûr and Kîhak.
Title (22) دفنار دوى سهر دوت وبابه . سنى (21), دفنار   سنى   شرح كتاب دفنار دومى تحدم[6] سهر هور وكهيك

The work consists of Hymns appropriate to the saints and festivals of the calendar[7]. For each day there are 2 hymns, but if more than one commemoration is inscribed for the same day, each has usually but a single hymn   The praise of more saints than one may be combined in a single hymn   The hymns are called ⲯⲁⲗⲓ ⲙⲟⲥ, rarely

---

[1] Date (23rd Hatûr) omitted

[2] Assuming the preceding *al malîn* to be but a title (as ? in Abû Salih, f 39 *a* &c)   In Horner's Boh N Test i, p xcix, it is apparently a name

[3] I notice but one to this tone the last (fol 92), on the Ascension

[4] May we hence assume, the scribe being given no name, that in reality Girgis himself wrote the book ?

[5] The Göttingen MS (Lagarde, *Orient* 43) has in full اددمارى Abû 1-Barakât, Paris 203, f 108 *b*, cf Br Mus no 920, ⲧϥⲱⲛⲁⲣⲓ. Elsewhere دفنار

[6] Cf this verb in MS Curzon 134, ⲕⲁⲧⲁⲙⲉⲣⲟⲥ ⲉϥⲉⲣ-ϧⲱⲃ تحدم ⲛ̇ⲉⲛⲛⲓⲕⲓⲡⲓⲁⲕⲏ &c

[7] Perhaps a reference to its use on p ⲣⲛⲉ of no 430   Its place is at Evening Prayer, after the Psalms and Theotokia, before the Incense (Cairo *Euchologion*, pp ⲍ, ⲕ)

(towards the beginning of the month) طرح¹   They are in the usual 4-verse strophe and
of varying length, some have but 6 strophes, others 16 or 20   The first of the two hymns
is to the tone (ἦχος لَحن) *Adam*, the second to that of *Watos*, rarely (towards the
beginning of the month) this order is inverted   Each of the *Adam* hymns closes with
the words ϩⲓⲧⲉⲛⲛⲓ⳨ϩⲟ ⲛⲉⲙⲛⲓⲡⲣⲟⲥⲉⲩⲭⲏ ⲛⲧⲉ NN, the *Watos* hymns with ⲧⲱⲃϩ ⲙⲡⲟ̅ⲥ̅
ⲉϩⲣⲏⲓ ⲉϫⲱⲛ ⲛⲧⲉϥⲭⲁ ⲛⲉⲛⲛⲟⲃⲓ ⲛⲁⲛ ⲉⲃⲟⲗ, or where these are inapplicable, with others,
e g (17th Hatur) the Cross ϩⲓⲧⲉⲛⲧϫⲟⲙ ⲉⲧϭⲟⲥⲓ ⲛⲧⲉ ⲡⲓⲥ̅⳨̅ⲥ̅ ⲡⲟ̅ⲥ̅ ⲁⲣⲓ ϩⲙⲟⲧ ⲛⲁⲛ ⲙⲡⲭⲱ ⲉⲃⲟⲗ
ⲛⲧⲉ ⲛⲉⲛⲛⲟⲃⲓ and ϫⲉϥⲙⲁⲣⲱⲟⲩⲧ ⲛϫⲉ ⲡⲟ̅ⲥ̅ ⲓⲏ̅ⲥ̅ ⲛⲉⲙⲡⲉϥⲥ̅⳨̅ ⲛⲣⲉϥⲧⲁⲛϧⲟ &c   Few hymns
are throughout acrostical, i e with initials of successive strophes following the letters of the
alphabet (7th, 9th, 12th Hatûr), sometimes this system is maintained through part of the
hymn (22nd Hatûr) or in alternate strophes only (3rd Kihak), often the same letter or
word is used as initial for every strophe (7th Tût, 21st Babeh, 21 Kihak)   The first
hymn is now and then interrupted midway by the rubric من هاهنا يقال قدام عيد فلان,
indicating that the remainder is to be sung before the picture (εἰκών) of the saint²
Sometimes the hymns apostrophize the saint to whom they refer, at other times his
story is told in narrative form

The basis of the work, so far as the narrative hymns are concerned, is clearly the
Synaxarium   This would not apply to the many pieces which consist merely of pious
meditations upon the subject under commemoration³   But the stories in the Synax
are of course never fully narrated   only selected incidents and features are alluded to
Where the Synax gives no story, the Antiphonary alludes to none   Not infrequently
however materials appear to have been used beyond what the Synax —at any rate in its
usual recensions forms—offers, the following are instances   At the festival of Chrysostom
(16th Tût and 17th Hatûr) Theophilus and Epiphanius are mentioned, 'Jezebel' is alluded
to and 'Theognostus' is the deceased owner of the coveted vineyard, the people of
the isle 'Atrakis'⁴ are converted by his preaching   The notice of Severus of Antioch
(2nd Babeh) makes reference to his exile in Egypt, how, on attending a church there
and finding none to whom he might give the ἀσπασμός, he kisses the picture of the
Virgin and Child, whereupon his lips cleave thereto and he is thus recognized by the
congregation⁵   Of Paul of Tamma (7th Babeh) we are told how he brought to life,
baptized and again sent to rest certain dead pagans, and we learn there that the name
ⲡϣⲟⲓ (ⲛⲧⲉ) ⲓⲉⲣⲏⲙⲓⲁⲥ was commemorative of the prophet's visit to Pshoi⁶   On the 11th
Hatûr the martyrdom of Michael of Damietta is added   Once a monk in Shihet, he had
removed to Cairo⁷, married a Muslim⁸ wife and become apostate, yet only to repent 8
days later, make public profession of his faith and, despite the 'king of Misr's' efforts

---

¹ In Bâbeh and Hatûr   But in the Borgian copy
(*Copto* 60) this word regularly replaces مديح   The verb
مدح is in these texts rendered by ⲉⲩⲫⲟⲙⲓⲛ (εὐφημεῖν)
Cf ⲉⲩⲫⲩⲙⲓⲁ, *Theotokia* ⲣ̅ⲕ̅ⲉ̅

² Pictures are mentioned in these volumes of the
following   the Baptist, Stephen, the Virgin, Sergius and
Bacchus, Matthew, the Apostles, George, the 4 Beasts,
Michael, Gabriel, Mena, Onnofrius, Cosmas and Damianus,
the 24 Elders, Mercurius, Paese and Thecla, Behnam,

Christmas   Cf the lists in BUTLER, *Churches* 1 50 ff,
101 ff &c
³ There is no question of direct translation, especially
impossible in hymns acrostical and the like.
⁴ V Bi Mus nos 308, 983
⁵ The little said in the Lives of Severus as to his sojourn
in Egypt does not refer to this (GOODSPEED's Ethiop *Conflict*,
p 713, but the 2nd hymn appears to refer to that work)
⁶ V BASSET's *Synax*, 25th Kihak, and *Aeg Z* xl 61.
⁷ ⲧⲙⲟⲗⲓⲥ ⲧⲣⲉϥϫⲣⲟ المدينة القاهرة   ⁸ Ἀγαρηνός

to persuade him, suffer death by fire   The 'new' martyr Salib ⲡⲓⲥⲧⲁⲩⲣⲟⲥ too (3rd Kihak), 'who came at the eleventh hour, yet received the whole day's wage,' is unknown to the Synax   Evidence of the later introduction of this piece may be seen in the absence of the usual Arabic parallel to the short Coptic text, the version مسير being added, and at greater length, subsequently[1]   As a consequence of his public profession, he was sent in chains to Cairo   There he was tortured and paraded through the city, bound to a crosslike frame and mounted on a tall camel, while a herald cried his accusation before him   After execution, his body was to be burnt, but the flames refused to devour it and, having been secured by the faithful, it was deposited by the patriarch in a church[2]   Again the martyrs Behnâm and Sarah (14th Kihak) have, we are told, no place in the Synax, but are found in the Antiphonary[3]   This must apply however to the particular recension used, for others show even two versions of their story[4]   Various lesser divergencies from the available texts of the Synax are observable   the hymns to Macaiius of Tkôw (27th Bâbeh) are evidently compiled with the help of the narrative of Dioscorus, the name of the priest is given who baptized Eustathius Placidus (27th Tût), Cleophas (1st Hatûr) was one of the disciples who journeyed to Emmaus, the number of the Nicene fathers (9th Hatûr) was foreshadowed by that of Abraham's servants[5], the number of pieces into which James the Persian (27th Hatûr) was cut is 32, the place of martyrdom of Cosmas and Damianus (22nd Hatûr) is Aegae (ⲉⲅⲉⲁⲥ ⲧⲛⲟⲗⲓⲥ[6], Sarapamon (or Saiapion) foretells the conversion and martyrdom of Arian (28th Hatûr)   'The Book of Testimonies' (i e the ⲡⲗⲏⲣⲟⲫⲟⲣⲓⲁⲓ) of Peter the Iberian (1st Kihak) is cited with the works of Timothy and Severus

Confusions are not infrequent   e g 24th Tût, Gregoiy the monk and Gregory Theologus, 21st Hatûr, the last named and Gregory Thaumaturgus   On the 23rd Hatûr we read that, in place of Dionysius of Corinth, 'The Book of Hymns' كتاب الطارح has D the Areopagite[7]

That the author, though a poor Coptic scholar, was familiar with the literature is evident from the quantity of Greek words employed, many of them of but rare occurrence in ordinary texts[8]   It might even seem, here and there, that he had drawn upon Gieek texts, cf the phrases   archbishop of ⲧⲣⲱⲙⲁⲓⲓⲁ ⲧⲱ ⲟⲛⲟⲅⲁⲉⲁ ⲁⲩⲧⲏⲥ وما اما امرو روم (9th Bâbeh), ⲁⲉⲡⲁϥⲟⲩⲱⲉ ⲏⲟⲩⲱⲓⲕ .. ⲁⲗⲗⲁ ⲟⲩϥⲁⲃⲁ ⲕⲁⲧⲁ ⲣⲟⲩⲅⲓ (30th Bâbeh), ⲇⲉⲏⲛⲓ-

---

[1] As in the fragment Br Mus no 888
[2] It appears from the expressions used (اولاد هذه الكنيسة, حسا اتيب السا البوم اها لحسد, فرحون البوم) that this is the church to which the present MS belonged   From the history of Salib in Paris MS arabe 152, f 92 we learn that he came from اشاد (ⲡϣⲟⲧⲉ, Kiall Rechtsurk cxviii) near Ashmunain, that he was brought in custody to Cairo tortured and executed (as above), in موضع ان صربوا مع الارقاب (f 100 b), on the 3rd Kihak, A M 1129 = A D 1413   Not to be confused with his namesake of 28th Miyazya also martyred by the Muslims   He was from the town Maksur (? مقصور) and was buried beside the blessed John of Harkâl (or Herkalt), i e Heraclea in Pontus (cf Br Mus no 865 n, Synax 4th Sane)

[3] فانه لم يوحد فى السكارلكن فى كتاب الديار
[4] V Forget's Synai, pp 158 and 288   Our hymn seems to resemble the 2nd of these texts   V also Wüstenfeld 181   Cf G Hoffmann, Auszüge 17
[5] Gen xiv 14
[6] V PSBA xxx 132
[7] V PSBA xxix 293
[8] E gg ἀντίχριστος, ἀπανθρωπος, αικινον (Paris 44, 81a ⲁⲩⲕⲉⲛⲟⲛ, ⲁⲩⲕⲏ 'ebony', cf Kircher 175 ⲉⲩⲕⲏⲛⲱⲛ السمكار 'pium', Almkvist), βοινευρον, γενεαλογεῖ, διαβάλλειν, ἐξουσιαστής, ζωγράφος, θεραπευτής, ἱστορεῖν, κατόρθωμα, μιτάτωρ (رسور), νυμφαγωγός, ὀπτασία, σκάφος, σπεῖρα, φάβα, χηροτρο ̣ια (احسار, احمار), χειραγωγία)

ϩⲟⲟⲩ ⲙⲡⲓⲡⲁⲡⲁⲥ ⲃⲓⲕⲧⲟⲣⲟⲥ (11th Hatûr) Possibly however these mean no more here than the frequent Greek locutions to be found throughout the Theotokia and other liturgical books

It is abundantly clear, from the strange forms of many proper names, that the Coptic text of the narrative hymns is mainly a version from the Arabic, witness the following examples ⲁⲃⲗⲁⲣⲓⲟⲛ ادلاريوس, ⲁⲡⲁ ⲧⲟⲗⲟⲥ اناطلس for اناطلس[1], ⲁⲡⲣⲁⲕⲟⲥ ادراكس for ? ⲓⲉⲣⲁⲝ[2], ⲁⲩⲏⲁⲙⲟⲥ for اودانوس, ⲁⲉⲣⲟⲩⲅⲓ دروى for ? حاروحى (George[4]), ⲑⲁⲣⲁⲉⲁ طرداك Τιριδάτης, ⲙⲁⲗⲁⲧⲓⲏⲏ ملاينسى for Μελιτηνή[5], ⲡⲁⲗⲁⲣⲓⲁⲛⲟⲥ and ⲟⲓⲡⲟⲣⲓⲛⲟⲥ دسوردينوس for نالاردانوس وديسورديدوس, ⲥⲃⲱⲛ اصعون, ⲥⲱⲣ صور instead of ⲧⲩⲣⲟⲥ, ⲭⲟⲩⳅⲁ حورى for حورى ⲭⲱⲣⲓ. Cf also the locution (vol 2, ⲗⲇ a) ⲉⲧⲁϥⲧⲁⲥⲟⲟϥ ⲉⲧⲉϥⳙⲩⲭⲏ ثم رجع الى نفسه[6] On the other hand, ⲁⲧⲁⲑⲟⲩ, ⲁⲙⲁⲛⲟⲩ, ⲕⲁⲣⲡⲟⲩ &c may be reminiscent of the genitives in the diptych lists[7]

As to the authorship and date of the Antiphonary, VANSLEB states[8] that it was the work of the patriarch Gabriel b Turaik (1131–1146) But the words in Abû 'l-Barakât's list, on which he presumably relies, are[9] كتاب السجد المصرية ونستر الى الطردرك انا عبردال من درنك وكتاب الدمارى ومعناه (space[10]) وهو نسمل على دماحمد الاعمان وايانئس العدسس والاسهاك, whence it appears that for the *Difnâry* no author is named Further, on the 9th Tut the eclipse is commemorated which occurred in A D 1242, showing that the source here drawn upon (a recension of the Synax) was compiled after the time of Gabriel[11] Seeing that it is unknown at what period the earliest recension of the Synax arose—the reputed authors, Peter al Jamil of Malig and Michael of Atrib, lived respectively before 1363 and *ca* 1425[12]—we cannot rely upon the relationship of the two works as a guide in dating

A book bearing the name Ἀντιφωνάριον was in use about the 8th century That is roughly the date of the Fayyûm papyrus in which, among other books, the name occurs[13] None of the known copies of the present work is older than the 18th century[14] Their texts appear to correspond with ours

The present copy belonged to TATTAM, as his handwriting (with date 1840) on the fly-leaf of each volume and often in the margins, shows He paid '210 piastres' for it

The following may serve as specimens of the hymns The line division within the strophes here follows the metre, not the fortuitous divisions by the scribe

---

[1] Abû 'l-Barakât's calendar (Paris 203, f 257 b) has اطلماوس Ptolemaus
[2] V Br Mus no 986, though no Hierax appears in the Synaxarium
[3] Cf Hypatius and Andreas, (Synax 20th Sept)
[4] Perhaps George, the friend of Abraham (v 9th Tûbah, 18th Bashans, PSBA xxix 289) FORGET 202, BASSET 266 give this variant Ethiop (Or 658 171 a) too Dârûdî, but that is inconclusive Or cf the name ⲧⲟⲩⲣⲟⳅⲁ, BALESTRI-HYVERNAT, Acta i 202
[5] Abû 'l-Barakât المدلا
[6] As in Acts xii 11, where cf the Coptic
[7] PSBA xxx 259

[8] Histoire 62
[9] Paris 203, f 108 b
[10] Showing that the meaning of the name was no longer known
[11] RENAUDOT, Hist. 513, even supposes that a later Gabriel is intended
[12] Works of Peter described by Abû 'l-Barakât, v RIEDEL in Gotting Nachr 1902, 688 ; Michael's date (on what authority ?) by ASSEMANI in Mai iv 93
[13] CRUM, Copt MSS p 61
[14] The Gottingen MS 1788 (LAGARDE, Orient 43), the Vatican (Borgian) MS 1738 I have procured specimens of both by the kindness of Prof PIETSCHMANN and Mgr EHRLE

Vol 1, p ⲕ̅ⲁ̅ b   Moses   اليوم الثامن من شهر دوب موسى النبي وركردا الكاهن

مديح بلحن اظام ⳡⲁⲗⲓ ⲛ̄ⲭⲟⲥ ⲁⲇⲁⲙ

1   Ⲁⲙⲟⲩ ϣⲁⲣⲟⲛ ⲫⲟⲟ ⲩ
ⲱ ⲡⲓⲭⲣⲏⲥⲟⲥⲧⲟⲙⲟⲥ
ⲱϣ ⲉⲃⲟⲗ ⲉⲣⲟⲛ
ⲥ̄ⲛⲟⲙⲛ̄ϯ ⲛ̄ⲧⲑⲱⲟⲩⲧⲉ

2   Ⲉⲓⲛⲁ ⲛ̄ⲧⲉⲕⲧⲁⲙⲟⲛ
ⲉⲡⲧⲁⲓⲟ ⲙ̄ⲡⲁⲓⲣⲱⲙⲓ
ⲉⲧⲁϥⲥⲁϫⲓ ⲛⲉⲙⲫ̄ϯ
ϧⲓϫⲉⲛⲡⲧⲱⲟⲩ ⲛ̄ⲥⲓⲛⲁ

3   Ⲁϥϯ ⲫⲓⲱⲧ
ⲥⲁϫⲓ ⲛⲉⲙⲙⲱⲩⲥⲏⲥ
ϫⲉⲁⲛϫⲉⲙ ⲭⲁⲣⲓⲥⲙⲁ
ⲙ̄ⲡⲁⲙⲑⲟ ⲉⲃⲟⲗ

4   Ⲁ̄ϥⲛⲁⲩ ⲉⲡⲓⲃⲁⲧⲟⲥ
ⲉϥⲙⲟϩ ϧⲉⲛⲡⲓⲭⲣⲱⲙ
ⲉⲃⲟⲗ ϩⲓⲧⲛϣⲁϥⲉ
ⲟⲩⲟϩ ⲣⲱⲕϩ ⲁⲛ

5   Ⳳ ⲟⲩⲙⲁⲧⲏ ⲛ̄ⲑⲟⲕ
ⲱ ⲙⲱⲩⲥⲏⲥ ⲡⲓⲡⲓⲡⲣⲟⲫⲏⲧⲏⲥ
ϫⲉⲁⲙⲙⲡϣⲁ ⲙ̄ⲡⲁⲓⲛⲓϣϯ
ⲙ̄ⲙⲩⲥⲧⲏⲣⲓⲟⲛ

6   Ⲭⲉⲁⲛⲉⲣⲙ̄ⲙ̄ ⲛⲉϩⲟⲟⲩ
ⲛⲉⲙ ⲙ̄ ⲛⲉⲭⲱⲣϩ
ⲉⲛⲭⲏ ϩⲉⲛⲡⲓⲅ̄ⲛⲟⲫⲟⲥ
ⲉⲕⲥⲁϫⲓ ⲛⲉⲙⲫ̄ϯ

7   Ⲟⲩϣⲃⲱⲧ ⲅⲁⲣ ⲛϣⲉ
ⲁϥϭⲓⲧϥ ⲛ̄ϫⲉ ⲙⲱⲩⲥⲏⲥ

ⲉϩⲣⲏⲓ ⲉϥⲓⲟⲙ ⲛ̄ϣⲁⲣⲓ
ⲁⲩⲫⲱⲣϫ ⲛ̄ϫⲉ ⲛⲓⲙⲱⲟⲩ

8   Ⲉϥⲉⲣⲅⲩⲙⲛⲏⲛ ⲛⲁⲛ
ⲙ̄ⲡⲓϣⲉ ⲙ̄ⲡⲉⲥ̄ⲧ̄
ⲉⲧⲁⲅⲁϣ ⲡⲟ̄ⲥ̄ ⲉϫⲱϥ
ⲛ̄ⲙⲁⲣ̄ⲃ̄ ⲛ̄ⲁⲇⲁⲙ

9   Ⲟⲩϣⲫⲏⲣⲓ ⲁⲗⲏⲑⲱⲥ
ⲡⲉ ⲡϫⲓⲛ ⲉⲙⲏⲣ
ⲛ̄ⲛⲉⲛϣⲏⲣⲓ ⲙ̄ⲡⲓⲥ̄ⲗ̄
ϧⲉⲛⲫⲓⲟⲙ ⲛ̄ϣⲁⲣⲓ

10   Ⲙⲱⲩⲥⲏⲥ ⲡⲓⲡⲣⲟⲫⲏⲧⲏⲥ
ⲛⲁϥϯⲛⲟⲙϯ ⲡⲱⲟⲩ
ⲧϫⲟⲙ ⲙ̄ⲡⲓⲥⲉ̄ⲧ̄
ⲉⲥⲉⲣⲟⲩⲱⲓⲛⲓ ⲉⲣⲱⲟⲩ

11   Ⲉⲧⲥⲡⲓϣⲃⲱⲧ ⲉ̄ⲟ̄ⲩ̄
ⲛ̄ⲣⲉϥⲓⲣⲓ ⲛ̄ⲛⲓϣⲫⲏⲣⲓ
ⲉⲧⲁϥⲫⲱⲣϫ ⲙ̄ⲫⲓⲟⲙ
ϧⲉⲛⲧϫⲟⲙ ⲛ̄ⲧⲉ ⲫ̄ϯ

12   Ⲙⲱⲩⲥⲏⲥ ⲡⲓⲡⲣⲟⲫⲏⲧⲏⲥ
ⲛⲉⲙⲡⲓⲗⲁⲟⲥ ⲧⲏⲣϥ
ⲛⲁⲩϯ ⲱⲟⲩ ⲙ̄ⲡⲟ̄ⲥ̄
ϫⲉϧⲉⲛⲟⲩⲱⲟⲩ ⲅⲁⲣ ⲁϥϭⲓ ⲱⲟⲩ

13   Ⲉⲓⲧⲉⲛⲛⲓⲉⲩⲭⲏ

Vol 2, p ⲣ̅ⲉ̅ b   Onnophrius (2nd hymn)

ⲛⲑⲟϥ ⲟⲛ ⲛ̄ⲭⲟⲥ ⲃⲁⲧⲟⲥ   له ادضا بلحن واطس

1   Ⲡⲓⲥⲛⲟⲩ ⲅⲁⲣ ⲙ̄ⲡⲡⲁⲧⲓⲕⲟⲛ
ⲉⲧⲱϣⲉⲙ ⲛ̄ⲛⲉⲛⲯⲩⲭⲏ
ⲁⲛϣⲁⲛⲭⲱ ⲛⲁϩⲣⲉⲛⲓⲥⲛⲟⲩ ⲛⲓⲃⲉⲛ
ⲙ̄ⲡⲁⲓⲱⲛⲓϩ ⲛ̄ⲛⲉⲛⲓⲟⲧ ⲉ̄ⲟ̄ⲩ̄

2   Ⲛⲁⲓ ⲉⲧⲁⲩϭⲓⲥⲓ ⲛ̄ϩⲟⲩⲟ
ⲡⲁⲣⲁ ⲧⲫⲩⲥⲓⲥ ⲛ̄ϯⲙⲉⲧⲣⲱⲙⲓ
ⲉⲟⲃⲉϯⲥⲡⲟⲩⲇⲁ ⲉⲧⲥⲟⲩⲧⲱⲛ
ⲛ̄ⲧⲉ ⲧⲟⲩⲡⲣⲟϩⲉⲣⲉⲥⲓⲥ

3   Ⲉⲧⲓ ⲅⲁⲣ ⲛ̄ⲧⲁⲩⲫⲱⲛϩ ⲁⲛ
ⲥⲁⲃⲟⲗ ⲛ̄ⲛⲉⲛⲟⲱⲙ ⲛ̄ⲧⲫⲩⲥⲓⲥ
ⲁⲗⲗⲁ ⲁⲥϣⲓⲃϯ ⲛ̄ϫⲉ ⲧⲟⲩⲅⲛⲱⲙⲏ
ϧⲉⲛⲟⲩⲇⲓⲁⲕⲣⲓⲥⲓⲥ ⲙⲙⲏⲓ

4   Ⲟⲩϩⲱⲃ ⲛϣⲟⲩⲉⲣϣⲫⲏⲣⲓ ⲙ̄ⲙⲟϥ
ⲡⲉ ⲫⲃⲓⲟⲥ ⲙ̄ⲡⲁⲓⲣⲱⲙⲓ ⲛ̄ⲟⲩⲏⲓ
ⲡⲓⲛⲓϣϯ ⲛ̄ⲥⲱⲧⲛ ⲛ̄ⲧⲉ ⲡⲭ̄ⲥ̄
ⲡⲓⲑⲉⲟⲫⲟⲣⲟⲥ ⲁⲃⲃⲁ ⲟⲩⲛⲟⲫⲣ

5 Ⲫⲁⲓ ⲉⲧⲁϥⲃⲁϣϥ ϧⲉⲛⲟⲩϫⲱⲕ
ⲙ̄ⲡⲱⲟⲩ ⲅⲏⲣϥ ⲓⲧⲉ ⲡⲁⲓⲕⲟⲥⲙⲟⲥ
ⲉⲑⲃⲉⲧϩⲗⲏϫⲓ ⲛⲧⲉ ⲫ̄ϯ
ⲑⲁⲓ ⲉⲧϣⲟⲡ ⲥⲁⲃⲟⲩⲛ ⲙ̄ⲙⲟϥ

6 Ⲁϥⲥⲟⲧⲡ ⲛⲁϥ ⲉⲉⲣϣⲫⲏⲣ
ⲛ̄ⲛⲓⲑⲏⲣⲓⲟⲛ ϧⲓⲡϣⲁϥⲉ
ⲉϩⲟⲧⲉ ⲛ̄ⲧⲉϥϭ̄ⲙⲉ
ϧⲉⲛⲡⲓⲣⲱⲟⲩϣ ⲙ̄ⲃⲓⲱⲧⲓⲕⲟⲛ

7 Ⲛⲁⲓ ⲉⲧⲱⲙⲥ ⲙ̄ⲡⲓⲣⲱⲙⲓ ⲉϧⲣⲏ
ⲉⲡϣⲱϯ ⲉⲃⲟⲗ ⲙⲉⲙⲡⲧⲁⲕⲟ
ⲉⲩⲓⲣⲓ ⲙ̄ⲡⲓⲕⲁϯ ⲙ̄ⲃⲉⲗⲗⲉ
ⲉⲃⲟⲗ ϧⲁⲡⲓⲙⲙⲓ ⲙ̄ⲙⲏⲓ

8 Ⲉⲑⲃⲉⲫⲁⲓ ⲉϥϭⲓⲥⲓ ⲛ̄ⲧⲉϥⲥⲙⲏ
ⲙ̄ⲡⲣⲟⲫⲏⲧⲓⲕⲟⲛ ⲉϥϫⲱ ⲙ̄ⲙⲟⲥ
ϫⲉⲉⲑⲃⲉⲫⲁⲓ ⲁⲓⲟⲩⲉⲓ ᵉⁱᶜⲫⲏⲧ
ⲟⲩⲟϩ ⲁⲓϣⲱⲡⲓ ϧⲓⲡϣⲁϥⲉ

9 Ⲉⲓϫⲟⲩϣⲧ ⲉⲃⲟⲗ ϧⲁⲧϩⲏ ⲙ̄ⲫⲏ
ⲉⲧⲁϥⲛⲁϩⲙⲉⲧ ϧⲁⲟⲩⲥⲁⲑⲛⲟⲩ
ⲉⲓϣⲑⲉⲣⲑⲱⲣ ⲛⲧⲉ ⲫⲓⲟⲙ
ⲛ̄ⲧⲉ ⲡⲁⲓⲃⲓⲟⲥ ⲉⲧϣⲟⲡ ϯⲛⲟⲩ

10. Ⲡⲁⲓⲣⲏϯ ϧⲉⲛⲟⲩⲛⲟⲩ ⲥϥⲣⲏⲥ
ⲛⲉⲙⲟⲩⲕⲁϯ ⲙ̄ⲡⲛ̄ⲁⲧⲓⲕⲟⲛ

11 Ⲉϥⲑⲣⲟ ⲙ̄ⲙⲟϥ ⲥⲁⲡϣⲱⲓ ⲛⲛⲓϧⲱⲙⲓ
ⲛⲧⲉ ϯⲕⲁⲕⲓⲁ ⲙ̄ⲡⲟⲛⲏⲣⲟⲥ
ⲛⲁⲓ ⲉⲧⲱⲙⲥ ⲙ̄ⲙⲟⲛ ⲉⲡⲉⲥⲏⲧ
ⲉⲡⲕⲁⲧⲁⲕⲗⲓⲥⲙⲟⲥ ⲉⲛⲓⲡⲁⲑⲟⲥ

12 Ⲡⲁⲓⲣⲏϯ ⲉϥϣⲱⲡⲓ ⲛⲁⲓⲣⲱⲟⲩϣ
ⲉⲃⲟⲗ ϩⲁϯⲕⲣⲓⲥⲓⲥ ⲛ̄ϯⲛⲉϫⲓ
ⲁϥϣⲁⲛϣ ⲙ̄ⲙⲟϥ ϧⲉⲛⲡⲓⲉⲛⲧⲏϫ
ⲛⲉⲙϧⲁⲛⲃⲟⲧⲁⲛⲏ ⲛⲁⲧⲣⲓⲟⲛ

13 Ⲛⲟⲩⲓⲥ ⲛ̄ⲧⲉϥⲥⲁⲣϩ
ⲉⲛⲁⲡⲁⲛⲑⲣⲟⲡⲟⲛ ⲉϥϩⲱⲧⲡ ⲙ̄ⲙⲟⲥ
ⲉⲑⲣⲉⲥ̄ⲡⲉϫⲱ ⲙ̄ⲡⲓⲡⲛ̄ⲁ
ⲉⲑⲩ̄ ϧⲉⲛⲟⲩϩⲓⲣⲏⲛⲏ

14 Ⲭⲉⲁϥⲉⲣϩⲉⲗⲡⲓⲥ ϧⲉⲛⲡⲓⲡⲛ̄ⲁ
ⲟⲩⲟϩ ⲛⲁϥⲙⲉⲩⲓ ⲙ̄ⲡⲓⲡⲉϩϩⲏ
ϫⲉϥⲛⲁⲱⲛϧ ϧⲉⲛⲟⲩⲱⲛϧ
ⲛⲧⲉ ⲫⲣⲁϣⲓ ⲛⲁⲧⲥⲁϫⲓ ⲙ̄ⲙⲟϥ

15 Ⲧⲱⲃϩ ⲙ̄ⲡⲟ̄ⲥ ⲉϧⲣⲏⲓ ⲉϫⲱⲛ

HOMILIES

436 [41].—Parchment, a complete leaf, $33\frac{1}{2} \times 22\frac{1}{2}$ cm , pp —, $\overline{\text{ra}}$, the last of quire $\overline{\text{ī}}$ I col , 37 lines, in paragraphs   Script *of* HYVERNAT, *Album* xxii or xl 2

Homily treating here of Christ's burial and the visit of the women to the tomb The *quotations* are from St Mark   Salome is here called a rich woman who brought ointments to the tomb[1], and the angel is said to have taken the form of a youth in order that the women, and especially Salome, who was not used to the sight of angels, might not be terrified

P [ⲧⲉ]ⲟⲩ ⲁⲩϣⲱⲡ ⲛ̄ϩⲁⲛⲥⲟⲩⲛⲟⲩϥⲓ ϩⲓⲛⲁ ⲛ̄ⲧⲟⲩⲑⲁϩⲥⲉϥ ⲟⲩⲟϩ ϩⲁⲛⲁⲧⲟⲟⲩⲓ ⲙ̄ⲙⲁϣⲱ
ⲙ̄ⲫⲟⲩⲁⲓ ⲙ̄ⲛⲓⲥⲁⲃⲃⲁⲧⲟⲛ ⲁⲩⲓ ⲉⲡⲓⲙϩⲁⲩ ⲉⲧⲁⲫⲣⲏ ϣⲁⲓ ⲉⲧⲁⲙⲁⲣⲕⲟⲥ ϫⲉⲟⲩⲛ ⲉⲣⲫⲙⲉⲩⲓ ⲉⲑⲃⲉⲡⲓⲙⲁϩⲝ̄
ⲛ̄ⲥⲟⲡ ⲉⲧⲁⲛⲓϩⲓⲟⲙⲓ ϣⲉ ⲛ̄ⲱⲟⲩ ⲉⲡⲓⲙϩⲁⲩ ⲁϥϫⲉⲛⲁⲓ ⲙ̄ⲡⲁⲓⲣⲏϯ ϩⲟⲧⲉ ⲉⲧⲁⲫⲣⲏ ϣⲁⲓ ⲉⲧⲁⲥⲓ ⲛ̄ϫⲉ
ⲙⲁⲣⲓⲁ ϯⲙⲁⲅⲇⲁⲗⲓⲛⲏ ⲛⲉⲙⲙⲁⲣⲓⲁ ⲛ̄ⲧⲉ ⲓⲁⲕⲱⲃⲟⲥ ⲛⲉⲙⲥⲁⲗⲟⲙⲏ ⲙⲁⲣⲓⲁ ϫⲉⲟⲩⲛ ⲛ̄ⲧⲉ ⲓⲁⲕⲱⲃⲟⲥ
ⲛⲉⲙⲙⲁⲣⲓⲁ ⲛ̄ⲧⲉ ⲓⲱⲥⲏⲧⲟⲥ ⲛⲑⲟⲥ ⲣⲱ ⲟⲛⲧⲉ ⲑⲙⲁⲩ ⲙ̄ⲡ̄ⲟ̄ⲥ̄ ⲓⲁⲕⲱⲃⲟⲥ ⲅⲁⲣ ⲛⲉⲙⲓⲱⲥⲏⲧⲟⲥ ⲛⲉⲙⲥⲓⲙⲱⲛ
ⲛⲉⲙⲓⲟⲩⲇⲁⲥⲛⲉ ⲛⲓⲥⲛⲏⲟⲩ ⲕⲁⲧⲁⲥⲁⲣⲝ ⲛ̄ⲧⲉ ⲡ̄ⲟ̄ⲥ̄ ⲥⲁⲗⲟⲙⲏ ⲇⲉ ⲛⲉⲟⲩⲣⲁⲙⲁⲟⲧⲉ ⲛ̄ⲥϩⲓⲙⲓ ⲙ̄ⲡⲓⲥⲧⲏ ⲛⲑⲟⲥ
ⲅⲁⲣ ϩⲱⲥ ⲁⲥⲉⲣⲉⲧⲓⲛ ⲙ̄ⲡⲟⲩⲛⲁϥϯ ⲉⲑⲣⲉⲥⲓⲛⲓ ⲛ̄ϩⲁⲛⲥⲟϫⲉⲛ ⲉⲡⲓⲙϩⲁⲩ ⲟⲩⲟϩ ⲉⲑⲱϩⲥ ⲙ̄ⲡⲉϥⲥⲱⲙⲁ
ⲉⲧⲟⲩⲁⲃ ⲟⲩⲟϩ ⲥⲉⲛⲓϫⲓⲛⲑⲟⲣⲟⲩϣ ⲛⲱⲟⲩ ⲉⲡⲓⲙϩⲁⲩ ⲟⲩⲟϩ ⲉⲧⲁⲩϫⲁⲓ ⲛ̄ⲟⲩⲃⲁⲗ ⲉⲡϣⲱⲓ ⲁⲩⲛⲁⲩ
ⲉⲡⲓⲱⲛⲓ ⲉⲁⲩⲥⲕⲉⲣⲕⲱⲣϥ ⲓⲧⲁ ⲇⲉ ⲉⲧⲁⲩϣⲉ ⲥⲃⲟⲩⲛ ⲉⲡⲓⲙϩⲁⲩ ⲁⲩⲛⲁⲩ ⲉⲟⲩⲥⲉⲗϣⲓⲣⲓ ⲉϥϩⲉⲙⲥⲓ ⲥⲁⲟⲩⲓ-
ⲛⲁⲙ ⲉϥϫⲏⲗ ⲛ̄ⲟⲩⲥⲧⲟⲗⲏ ⲉⲥⲟⲩⲟⲃϣⲓ ⲡⲁⲓⲥⲉⲗϣⲓⲣⲓ ⲇⲉ ⲟⲛ ⲉⲧⲁϥⲥⲁϫⲓ ⲉⲣⲟϥ ⲛ̄ϫⲉ ⲡⲓⲉⲩⲁⲅⲅⲉⲗⲓⲥⲧⲏⲥ
ⲉⲟⲩⲁⲅⲅⲉⲗⲟⲥⲡⲉ ⲉⲑⲃⲉⲛⲓϩⲓⲟⲙⲓ ϫⲉⲟⲩⲛ ϩⲓⲛⲁ ⲛ̄ⲧⲟⲩϣⲧⲉⲙⲉⲣϩⲟϯ ⲁϥⲉⲣⲡⲉⲙⲟⲧ ⲛ̄ⲟⲩⲥⲉⲗϣⲓⲣⲓ ⲛ̄ϫⲉ
ⲡⲓⲁⲅⲅⲉⲗⲟⲥ ⲛ̄ϩⲟⲩⲟ ⲇⲉ ⲉⲑⲃⲉⲥⲁⲗⲟⲙⲏ ϫⲉⲟⲩⲛⲓ ⲧⲉⲥⲥⲩⲛⲏⲑⲓⲁ ⲁⲛ ⲧⲉ ⲉⲛⲁⲩ ⲉⲁⲛⲅⲉⲗⲟⲥ ⲉⲑⲃⲉⲫⲁⲓ
ⲁϥⲉⲣⲡⲉⲙⲟⲧ ⲛ̄ⲟⲩⲥⲉⲗϣⲓⲣⲓ ⲛ̄ϫⲉ ⲡⲓⲁⲅⲅⲉⲗⲟⲥ ⲟⲩⲟϩ ⲙⲁⲗⲓⲥⲧⲁ ⲉⲧⲁⲥⲛⲁⲩ ⲉⲣⲱⲟⲩ ⲥⲩⲉⲣϩⲟϯ (ⲡ ⲣ̄ⲃ̄)
ⲥⲁⲧⲟⲧϥ ⲁϥⲱⲗⲓ ⲛ̄ⲧϩⲟϯ ⲉⲃⲟⲗ ϩⲁⲣⲱⲟⲩ ⲓⲧⲁ ⲇⲉ ⲟⲛ ⲡⲉϫⲁϥ ⲛⲱⲟⲩ ⲛ̄ϫⲉ ⲡⲓⲁⲅⲅⲉⲗⲟⲥ ϫⲉⲙⲁϣⲉ
ⲛⲱⲧⲉⲛ ⲁϫⲟⲥ ⲛ̄ⲛⲉϥⲙⲁⲑⲏⲧⲏⲥ ⲛⲉⲙⲡⲉⲧⲣⲟⲥ ϫⲉϥⲛⲁⲉⲣϣⲟⲣⲡ ⲉⲣⲱⲧⲉⲛ ⲉϯⲅⲁⲗⲓⲗⲉⲁ ⲁⲣⲉⲧⲉⲛⲛⲁⲛⲁⲩ
ⲉⲣⲟϥ ⲙ̄ⲙⲁⲩ ϩⲏⲡⲡⲉ ⲁⲓϫⲟⲥ ⲛⲱⲧⲉⲛ ⲉⲑⲃⲉⲟⲩ ⲇⲉ ⲁϥⲉⲣⲫⲙⲉⲩⲓ ⲙ̄ⲡⲉⲧⲣⲟⲥ ⲙ̄ⲡⲁⲓⲙⲁ ϫⲉϩⲓⲛⲁ
ⲛ̄ⲧⲉϥⲉⲙⲓ ϫⲉⲁⲡ̄ⲟ̄ⲥ̄ ϣⲉⲡⲧⲉϥⲙⲉⲧⲁⲛⲓⲁ ⲉⲣⲟϥ ⲉⲑⲃⲉϯⲁⲣⲛⲏⲥⲓⲥ ⲛ̄ⲧⲉ ⲡⲓϫⲱⲗ ⲉⲃⲟⲗ ⲉⲁϥϯ ⲡⲣⲟⲑⲩⲙⲓⲁ ⲛⲁϥ
ⲉϧⲟⲩⲛ ⲉⲡⲁϣⲱⲛ ⲛ̄ϯⲙⲉⲧⲁⲡⲟⲥⲧⲟⲗⲟⲥ ϩⲓⲧⲉⲛⲛⲉϣⲟⲙϯ ⲛ̄ϫⲓⲛⲉⲣⲟⲛⲟⲙⲁϫⲓⲛ ⲙ̄ⲡⲉϥⲣⲁⲛ ϩⲓⲛⲁ ⲛ̄ⲧⲉϥ-
ϣⲧⲉⲙⲉⲣⲙⲕⲁϩ ⲛ̄ϩⲏⲧ ⲉⲡⲓϩⲟⲩⲟ ⲉⲑⲃⲉⲧⲁⲣⲛⲏⲥⲓⲥ ⲙ̄ⲛⲓϫⲱⲗ ⲉⲃⲟⲗ ⲑⲁⲓ ⲉⲧⲁⲥϣⲱⲡⲓ ⲛⲁϥ ⲕⲁⲧⲁ
ⲟⲩⲥⲩⲛⲗⲱⲛⲥⲓⲥ ϩⲓⲛⲁ ⲛ̄ⲧⲉ[about 15 let]ⲁⲥⲑⲉⲛⲏⲥ ⲙ̄ⲙⲓⲛ ⲉⲙⲙⲟϥ ⲟⲩⲟϩ ⲛ̄ⲧⲉϥϣⲧⲉⲙⲭⲁϩⲑⲏϥ
ⲉ[ⲣⲟⲕ] ϫⲉⲙⲙⲁⲅⲁⲧϥ ⲟⲩⲇⲉ ⲉϣⲧⲉⲙⲉⲣⲁⲛϯⲗⲉⲅⲓⲛ ⲟⲩⲇⲉ ⲛⲏ ⲉⲧⲉⲣⲉⲡ̄ⲟ̄ⲥ̄ ⲛⲁⲭⲟⲧⲟⲩ ⲡⲉⲧⲣⲟⲥ ϫⲉⲟⲩⲛ
ⲥⲉⲛⲓϫⲓⲛⲑⲣⲉϥⲥⲱⲧⲙ ⲉⲡⲉϥⲣⲁⲛ ⲉⲧⲁⲩⲉⲣⲟⲛⲟⲙⲁϫⲓⲛ ⲙ̄ⲙⲟϥ ϧⲉⲛⲡⲣⲱϥ ⲛ̄ⲛⲓϩⲓⲟⲙⲓ ϩⲓⲧⲉⲛⲙ̄ⲡⲓⲁⲅⲅⲉⲗⲟⲥ
ⲁϥϣⲱⲡⲓ ⲗⲟⲓⲡⲟⲛ ϧⲉⲛⲟⲩⲛⲓϣϯ ⲛ̄ⲡⲣⲟⲑⲩⲙⲓⲁ ⲛⲉⲙⲟⲩⲣⲱⲟⲩⲧϥ ⲛ̄ϩⲏⲧ ⲉⲛⲁϣⲱϥ ⲉⲁϥϣⲉⲡϩⲙⲟⲧ ⲛ̄ⲓⲟⲧϥ
ⲙ̄ⲡⲭ̄ⲥ̄ ϫⲉⲁϥⲁϣ ⲛⲁϥ ⲉⲃⲟⲗ ⲟⲩⲟϩ ⲁϥⲉⲣⲟⲛⲟⲙⲁϫⲓⲛ ⲙ̄ⲙⲟϥ ⲟⲛ ⲛⲉⲙⲛⲉϥⲙⲁⲑⲏⲧⲏⲥ ⲓⲧⲁ ⲇⲉ ⲟⲛ
ⲡⲉϫⲉ ⲡⲉⲩⲁⲅⲅⲉⲗⲓⲥⲧⲏⲥ ϫⲉⲉⲧⲁϥⲧⲱⲛϥ ⲛ̄ϣⲟⲣⲡ ⲙ̄ⲡⲓⲉϩⲟⲟⲩ ⲛ̄ϩⲟⲩⲓⲧ ⲛ̄ⲧⲉ ⲛⲓⲥⲁⲃⲃⲁⲧⲟⲛ ⲁϥⲟⲩⲟⲛϩϥ
ⲛ̄ϣⲟⲣⲡ ⲉⲙⲁⲣⲓⲁ ϯⲙⲁⲅⲇⲁⲗⲓⲛⲏ ⲑⲏ ⲉ[ⲧ

---

[1] Note this confusion of Salome μυροφορος with the rich harlot converted by Simeon   *V* Acad des Inscr *CR* 1903, 249, *Journ Theol St* vi 582

437 [42].—Parchment, a complete leaf, 33½ × 26 cm   Pp —, $\overline{\text{ҁⲁ}}$, the last of quire $\overline{\text{ⲁ}}$
1 col, 34 lines, in paragraphs   Script *of* HYVERNAT, *Album* xxxvii   No colours   The
verso is often illegible

Homily, apparently treating of charity and love to one's neighbour and *quoting*
Malachi ii 10, Amos vi 4, 5   The following are specimens of the text   ⲁⲛⲉⲣⲁⲥⲣⲓⲟⲥ ⲉϧⲟⲩⲛ
ⲉⲛⲏ ⲥⲧⲏⲡ ⲉⲧⲁⲓⲫⲩⲥⲓⲥ ⲛⲟⲩⲱⲧ ⲛⲉⲙⲁⲛ ⲟⲩⲟϩ ⲕⲁⲧⲁ ⲫⲣⲏϯ ⲛⲛⲓⲅⲉⲛⲉⲁ ⲛⲧⲉ ⲛⲁⲫⲱϯ ⲛⲁⲣⲭⲉⲟⲥ
ⲛⲏ ⲉⲧⲁⲡⲓⲕⲁⲧⲁⲕⲗⲏⲥⲙⲟⲥ ϣⲱⲡⲓ ⲉⲑⲃⲏⲧⲟⲩ ⲉⲡⲓⲁⲛ ⲉⲩⲓⲣⲓ ⲛϩⲁⲛⲥⲓⲛϫⲟⲛⲥ ⲟⲩⲟϩ ⲉⲩϭⲱⲧⲉⲃ
ⲛϧⲁⲛⲣⲱⲙⲓ

ⲙⲫⲱⲣ ⲟⲩⲛ ⲱ ⲡⲁⲙⲉⲛⲣⲁϯ ⲙⲡⲉⲛⲑⲣⲉⲛϣⲱⲡⲓ ⲛϩⲁⲛⲟⲓⲕⲟⲛⲟⲙⲟⲥ ⲉⲛϩⲱⲟⲩ ϧⲉⲛⲛⲏ ⲉⲧⲁⲩⲧⲏⲓ
(ⲡ $\overline{\text{ҁⲁ}}$)-ⲧ[ⲟⲩ

ⲑⲁⲓⲧⲉ ϯⲕⲁⲧⲏⲅⲟⲣⲓⲁ ⲉⲧϭⲓ ⲉϧⲟⲩⲛ ⲉⲛⲏ ⲉⲧϣⲟⲡ ϧⲉⲛϧⲁⲛⲧⲣⲩⲫ[ⲏ] ⲉⲩⲱϣϣ ⲙⲙⲱⲟⲩ ⲉⲛⲟⲩⲥⲛⲛⲟⲩ
ⲉⲧϣⲱⲡⲓ ⲟⲩⲟϩ ⲉⲑⲙⲟⲕϩ.

NARRATIVES, ACTS, MARTYRDOMS

438 [2 b].—Parchment, complete but for the outer edge, 31 × 19½ cm , 1 col , 30 lines
Script a heavy, square hand, of the Nitrian type

Elijah the Prophet   The text is merely a paraphrase of 1 Kings xix—xx 4   Elijah
is however spoken of almost as a Christian saint (ὁ ἅγιος Η), to whom, before his
translation, God promises powers similar to those granted to dying martyrs and saints
His help shall be especially efficacious to travellers by sea and land[1] and in times of
famine   The text may be from an Encomium.

]ϣⲟⲩ ⲛⲁⲕ ⲍⲉⲛⲡⲁⲓⲕⲟⲥⲙⲟⲥ ϯⲛⲟⲩ] ϫⲉ ⲙⲁϣⲉ ⲛⲁⲕ ⲑⲱϧⲥ ⲛⲉⲗⲓⲥⲉ[ⲟⲥ] ⲡϣⲏⲣⲓ ⲛⲓⲱⲥⲁⲫⲉⲧ
ⲙⲡⲣⲟⲫ[ⲏⲧⲏⲥ ⲛⲧⲉⲕϣⲉⲃⲓⲱ ⲁⲛⲟⲕ ⲅⲁⲣ ϯⲛⲁⲟⲩⲟⲑⲃⲉⲕ ⲉⲃⲟⲗ ⲉ[ⲃ].ⲉⲙⲛⲁⲩ ⲉϥⲙⲟⲩ ϣⲁⲧⲉⲩⲛ[ⲧⲉ]ⲗⲓⲁ
ⲛⲧⲉ ⲡⲁⲓⲉⲱⲛ ⲁⲗⲗⲁ ϯⲛⲁⲟⲩⲱⲣⲡ ⲛϧⲁⲛϧⲁⲣⲙⲁ ⲛⲭⲣⲱⲙ ⲛⲧ[ⲟⲩ]ⲟⲗⲛ ⲉⲡϭⲓⲥⲓ ⲉⲡⲙⲁ ⲛⲉⲙⲧⲟⲛ
[ⲉ]ⲧⲁⲓⲥⲥⲃⲧⲱⲧϥ ⲛⲁⲕ ϯⲛⲁⲧⲣⲉⲡⲉⲕⲣⲁⲛ ϭⲓ ⲱⲟⲩ ϧⲓϫⲉⲛ[ⲡⲕⲁ]ϧⲓ ⲙⲫⲣⲏϯ ⲉⲧⲁⲓϯ ⲱⲟⲩ ⲙⲡⲁⲃ[ⲱⲕ]
ⲙⲱⲩⲥⲏⲥ ⲟⲩⲟⲛ ⲛⲓⲃⲉⲛ ⲉⲧϧⲉⲛϧⲟϫϧⲉϫ [ⲛⲓ]ⲃⲉⲛ ⲁⲩϣⲁⲛⲧⲱⲃϩ ⲙⲙⲟⲓ ⲉⲩ[ϫⲱ] ⲙⲙⲟⲥ ϫⲉ ⲫϯ ⲙⲡⲓⲁ-
ⲅⲓⲟⲥ ⲛ[ⲗⲓⲁⲥ] ⲛⲁⲓ ⲛⲏⲓ ϯⲛⲁⲥⲱⲧⲉⲙ ⲉⲣⲱⲟⲩ ⲉⲩϧⲏϣ ϧⲉⲛⲫⲓⲟⲙ ⲓⲉ ⲛⲛⲓⲁⲣⲱ[ⲟⲩ] ⲓⲉ ⲛⲓⲙⲱⲓⲧ ⲙⲙⲟϣⲓ
ⲓⲉ ϧⲉⲛ[ⲟⲩϧⲉ]ⲃⲱⲛ ϯⲛⲁⲓ ⲛⲱⲟⲩ ⲛⲭⲱⲗϭⲙ ⲫⲏ ⲉⲧⲁϥ ⲫⲣⲱⲟⲩϣ ⲙⲡⲉⲕⲃⲓⲟⲥ] ⲛⲉⲙⲧⲉⲕⲡⲟⲗⲏⲧⲓⲁ
ⲛⲧⲉϥⲥⲃⲏ[ⲧϥ] ⲉⲟⲩⲱⲙ ϯⲛⲁⲥⲱⲗϫ ⲡⲛⲉϥ[ⲛ]ⲟⲃⲓ ⲛⲧⲁⲑⲣⲉϥϣⲱⲡⲓ ⲛⲉⲙⲁⲕ ϧⲉⲛ[ⲧⲭⲱ]ⲣⲁ ⲛⲧⲉ ⲛⲏ
[ⲉ]ⲧⲟⲛ]ϧ ⲁϥⲧⲱⲛϥ ⲛϫⲉ ⲡⲓⲁⲅⲓⲟⲥ ⲛⲗⲓⲁⲥ ⲙⲉ[ⲛⲉⲛ]ⲥⲁⲛⲁⲓ ⲁϥⲓⲣⲓ ⲕⲁⲧⲁ ⲡⲥⲁϫⲓ ⲙⲡⲟ̄ⲥ̄ ⲁϥϫⲓⲙⲓ
ⲛⲉⲗⲓⲥⲉⲟⲥ ⲡϣⲏⲣⲓ ⲛⲓⲱⲥⲁⲫ[ⲉⲧ] ⲉϥⲥⲭⲁⲓ ⲛⲓ̄ⲃ̄ ⲛϧⲉⲃⲓ ⲛⲉϧⲉ ⲁϥⲭⲱ[ⲗⲉⲙ] ⲁϥⲱⲗⲓ ⲛⲧⲉϥⲙⲉⲗⲱⲧⲏ
ⲁϥⲥⲁⲧ[ⲥ (verso) ⲉϧⲣⲏⲓ ⲉϫⲱϥ ϧⲉⲛⲟⲩⲛⲟⲩ ⲁϥⲕⲁ ⲛⲓϧⲉⲃⲓ ⲛⲥⲱϥ ⲁϥϭⲟϫⲓ [ⲛ]ⲥⲁⲡⲓⲁⲅⲓⲟⲥ ⲛⲗⲓⲁⲥ
ⲉϥϫⲱ ⲙⲙⲟⲥ [ⲛ]ⲁϥ ϫⲉ ϯⲛⲁⲙⲟϣⲓ ⲛⲥⲱⲕ ⲡⲁ[ⲓ]ⲱⲧ [ⲡ]ⲉϫⲉ ⲡⲓⲁⲅⲓⲟⲥ ⲛⲗⲓⲁⲥ ⲛⲁϥ ϫⲉϫⲉⲙⲡⲟⲛϯ ⲱ
ⲡⲁϣⲏⲣⲓ ϫⲉⲁⲡⲟ̄ⲥ̄ ⲓⲣⲓ ⲛⲟⲩⲛⲁⲓ ⲛⲉⲙⲁⲕ ⲁϥⲧⲁⲥⲑⲟ ⲛϫⲉ [ⲉ]ⲗⲓⲥⲥⲟⲥ ⲁϥϣⲱⲧ ⲙⲡⲓ̄ⲃ̄ ⲛϧⲉ[ⲃⲓ] ⲛⲉϧⲉ
ⲁϥⲫⲁⲥⲟⲩ ⲁϥⲧⲏⲓⲧⲟⲩ [ⲛ]ⲛⲓⲙⲏϣ ⲁⲩⲟⲩⲟⲙⲟⲩ ⲁϥⲙⲟϣⲓ [ⲛ]ⲥⲁⲡⲓⲁⲅⲓⲟⲩ ⲛⲗⲓⲁⲥ ⲁϥϣⲱⲡⲓ ⲛⲁϥ
[ⲙ]ⲙⲁⲑⲏⲧⲏⲥ [.]ⲧⲟⲛⲡⲉ ⲉⲧⲁϥϣⲱⲡⲓ ⲙⲉⲛⲉⲛⲥⲁⲛⲁⲓ ⲛⲉⲟⲩⲟⲛ ⲟⲩⲓⲟϧⲁⲗⲟⲗⲓ ⲛⲧⲉ ⲛⲁⲃⲟⲩ[ⲟ]ⲩⲑⲉ ⲡⲓⲥⲣⲁ-
ⲏⲗⲓⲧⲏⲥ ⲉϥϧⲉⲛⲧ ⲉⲫⲓⲟϧⲉ ⲛⲁⲭⲁⲁⲃ ⲡⲟⲩⲣⲟ ⲡⲉϫⲉ [ⲁ]ⲭⲁⲁⲃ ⲛⲛⲁⲃⲟⲩⲟⲩⲑⲉ ϫⲉⲙⲟⲓ ⲛⲏⲓ [ⲙ]ⲡⲉⲕⲓⲟϧ-
ⲁⲗⲟⲗⲓ ϫⲉϥϧⲉⲛⲧ ⲉⲫⲱⲓ [ⲁ]ⲛⲟⲕ ϯⲛⲁϯ ⲛⲁⲕ ⲛⲧⲉϥϣⲉⲃⲓⲱ [ϧ]ⲉⲛⲕⲉⲙⲁ ⲉϥⲥⲟⲧⲡ ⲉϧⲟⲧ ⲉⲣⲟϥ [ⲡ]ⲉϫⲉ
ⲛⲁⲃⲟⲩⲟⲩⲑⲉ ⲛⲁϥ ϫⲉⲛⲛⲉⲥϣⲱⲡⲓ ⲛⲏⲓ ⲉⲟⲣϯ ⲛⲧⲕⲗⲏⲣⲟⲛⲟⲙ[ⲓ]ⲁ ⲛⲛⲁⲓⲟϯ ⲛⲁⲕ ⲟⲩⲟⲛ ⲛⲧⲁⲕ
ⲛ[ⲟ]ⲩⲙⲏϣ ⲛⲁⲅⲁⲑⲟⲛ ⲙⲁⲣⲟⲩⲣⲱϣⲓ [ⲉ]ⲣⲟⲕ [ⲁ]ϭϣⲉ ⲛⲁϥ ⲛϫⲉ ⲁⲭⲁⲁⲃ ⲉϧⲟⲩⲛ ⲉⲡⲉϥⲏⲓ ⲁϥⲉⲛⲕⲟⲧ
ⲉϫⲉⲛⲡⲉϥϭⲗⲟϫ ⲁϥϧⲱⲃⲉ ⲙⲡⲉϥϧⲟ ⲙⲡⲉϥⲟⲩⲱⲙ ⲟⲩϫⲉ ⲙⲡⲉϥⲥⲱ ⲉϥⲟⲓ ⲛⲭⲟⲗⲓ ⲉⲑⲃⲉ[

439 [47 b].—Parchment, a complete leaf, 26 × 18 cm   Pp —, ⲗ̄   Script cf
HYVERNAT, *Album* xxxviii or xli 2   1 column, in paragraphs, 29 or 30 lines   No colours

Michael the Archangel, Miracles of   We have here the beginning of a story of
Elias, a rich citizen of Pemje (Oxyrhynchus), who gave alms at the monthly festivals[2]

---

[1] So in Mohammedan legend, v LANE, *Arab Nights*,
Introd , note 2

[2] On the 12th of each month, that in Hathor being
specially important

of the archangel, and of John, a thief Possibly from the Homily by Peter of Alexandria, *Cod Vatic Copt* lxi, which treats of Michael[1]

Ⲣ —. ⲉϩⲣⲏⲓ ⲉϥⲛⲟⲩⲛ ⲛⲧⲉ ⲁⲙⲉⲛϯ ⲁϥⲥⲟⲛϩϥ ⲉⲙⲁⲩ ⲁϥϯ ϯ ⲉⲣϣⲓϣⲓ ⲛⲛⲓⲁⲅⲓⲟⲥ ⲉⲑⲣⲟⲩⲥⲣⲟ ⲉⲣⲟϥ ⲛⲟⲩϣⲟ ⲛⲣⲟⲙⲡⲓ ⲱ ⲙⲓⲭⲁⲏⲗ ⲡⲓⲁⲣⲭⲏⲁⲅⲅⲉⲗⲟⲥ ⲉⲑⲟⲩⲁⲃ ⲛⲑⲟⲕ ⲟⲩϣⲟⲩⲙⲉⲛⲣⲓⲧ ⲧⲏⲣϥ ⲟⲩⲟϩ ⲟⲩⲭⲓⲛⲓ ⲙⲙⲟⲕ ϫⲉⲛⲁⲅⲁⲑⲟⲛ ⲛⲓⲃⲉⲛ· ⲛⲑⲟⲕⲡⲉ ⲉⲧⲁϥϯ ⲉⲛ ⲡⲓⲗⲁⲟⲥ ⲛⲧⲉ ⲛⲉⲛϣⲏⲣⲓ ⲙⲡⲓⲥⲗ ⲉϩⲣⲏⲓ ⲉⲛⲉⲕϫⲓϫ ⲉϥϫⲱ [ⲙⲙⲟⲥ] ⲙⲙⲱⲩⲥⲏⲥ ϫⲉϩⲏⲡⲡⲉ ⲓⲥ ϯⲛⲁⲟⲩⲱⲣⲡ ⲙⲡⲁⲁⲅⲅⲉⲗⲟⲥ [ϧⲁϫ]ⲱⲕ ⲥⲱⲧⲉⲙ ⲛⲥⲱϥ ϫⲉⲟⲩⲛ[ⲓ] ⲡⲁⲣⲁⲛⲡⲉ ⲉⲧⲭⲏ ϩⲓϫⲱϣⲡⲉ[2]· ϭⲉⲣⲙⲉⲟⲣⲉ ϩⲁⲣⲟⲕ ⲟⲛ ⲛϫⲉ ⲅⲁⲃⲣⲓⲏⲗ ⲡⲓⲁⲣⲭⲏⲁⲅⲅⲉⲗⲟⲥ ⲉϥⲥⲁϫⲓ ⲛⲉⲙⲁⲛⲓⲏⲗ ⲡⲓⲑⲉⲟⲫⲟⲣⲟⲥ ⲉϥϫⲱ ⲙⲙⲟⲥ ϫⲉⲁⲛⲟⲕ ⲉⲓⲭⲏ ϧⲉⲛⲡⲓⲡⲟⲗⲉⲙⲟⲥ ⲛⲧⲉ ⲡⲁⲣⲭⲱⲛ ⲛⲛⲓⲡⲉⲣⲥⲓⲥ[3]· ⲁϥⲓ ⲛϫⲉ ⲙⲓⲭⲁⲏⲗ ⲡⲁⲣⲭⲱⲛ ⲛⲧ .. ⲧⲱⲛ ⲟⲩⲟϩ ⲡⲁⲣⲭⲱⲛ ⲧⲉ ϣⲟⲣⲡ ⲁϥⲉⲣⲃⲟⲏⲑⲓⲛ ⲉⲣⲟⲓ ⲁⲓⲥⲟϫⲡϥ ⲙⲙⲁⲩ· ϫⲉⲛⲧⲁⲧⲁ[ⲙⲟ ⲙ]ⲙⲟⲛ ⲉⲛⲉⲕϩⲟⲣ[ⲁⲥ]ⲓⲥ (ⲣ ⲗ) ⲁⲧⲉⲧⲉⲛⲛⲁⲩ ⲱ ⲛⲁⲙⲉⲣⲁϯ ⲉⲡⲧⲁⲓⲟ ⲙⲡⲓⲁⲣⲭⲏⲁⲅⲅⲉⲗⲟⲥ ⲉⲑⲟⲩⲁⲃ ⲙⲓⲭⲁⲏⲗ ϫⲉⲟⲩⲛⲓϣϯ ⲡⲉ ϥϣⲟⲣⲉⲙ ⲛⲟⲩⲟⲛ ⲛⲓⲃⲉⲛ ⲉⲣⲉⲉϩⲛⲟⲩϥ[4] ϫⲏ ⲉⲣⲟϥ ϯⲛⲁⲁⲙⲱⲧⲉⲛ ⲇⲉ ⲟⲛ ⲉⲟⲩϩⲱⲃ ⲉⲁϥϣⲱⲡⲓ ϧⲉⲛⲡⲁⲓⲉϩⲟⲟⲩ· ⲛⲥⲟⲩⲟⲛ ⲟⲩⲣⲱⲙⲓ ⲇⲉ ϧⲉⲛϯⲡⲟⲗⲓⲥ ⲡⲉⲭⲉ ⲉⲡⲉϥⲣⲁⲛⲡⲉ ⲏⲗⲓⲁⲥ ⲉⲟⲩⲣⲁⲙⲁⲟⲡⲉ ⲉⲙⲁϣⲱ ⲉϥϯ ⲙⲡⲓϣⲁⲓ ⲙⲡⲓⲁⲣⲭⲏⲁⲅⲅⲉⲗⲟⲥ ⲙⲓⲭⲁⲏⲗ ⲕⲁⲧⲁ ⲁⲃⲟⲧ· ⲛⲁϥϯ ⲛⲗ ⲛϫⲉⲥⲧⲉⲥ ⲥⲛⲏⲣⲡ ⲛⲉⲙ ⲛϫⲉⲥⲧⲉⲥ ⲛⲛⲉϩ ⲕⲁⲧⲁ ⲁⲃⲟⲧ ⲛⲉⲙ ⲛⲕ ⲛⲕⲩⲡⲛⲁⲓⲁⲣⲓⲟⲛ[5] ⲉⲛⲱⲕ ⲛⲉⲟⲩⲟⲛ ⲟⲩⲣⲱⲙⲓ ⲇⲉ ϩⲱⲥ ⲡⲉϥⲣⲁⲛⲡⲉ ⲓⲱⲁⲛⲛⲏⲥ ⲉϥϣⲟⲡ ⲥⲁⲃⲟⲗ ⲙⲡⲥⲣⲟ ⲉϥⲟⲓ ⲛⲥⲟⲛⲓ· ⲉϣⲱⲡ ⲛⲧⲉⲛⲗⲓⲁⲥ ϯ ⲙⲡⲓϣⲁⲓ ⲙⲡⲁϭⲙⲟⲩϯ ⲉⲓⲱⲁⲛⲛⲏⲥ ⲉϧⲟⲩⲛ ⲉⲛⲉϩ ϫⲉⲉϥⲙⲟⲥϯ ⲙⲙⲟϥ ⲉⲑⲃⲉⲛⲉϥϩⲃⲛⲟⲩⲓ ⲁⲥϣⲱⲡⲓ ⲇⲉ ⲉⲧⲁⲛⲗⲓⲁⲥ ⲉⲛ ⲡⲓϭⲱⲗ ⲉⲛϣⲱ ϧⲉⲛⲡⲉϥⲁⲗⲟⲗⲓ ⲁϥϣⲓ ⲡⲓⲗ ⲛϫⲉⲥⲧⲉⲥ ⲛⲏⲣⲡ ⲛⲃⲉⲣⲓ ⲁϥⲧⲏⲓⲧⲟⲩ ⲉ[

440 [39].—Parchment, 2 leaves, 32½ × 24½ cm Script *v* HYVERNAT, *Album* XXXIII, which may be by the same scribe Described by FORBES ROBINSON, *Apocr Gosp* p XXVIII

Joseph the Carpenter, Death of The text corresponds (fol 1 bound in wrong order) to LAGARDE, *Aegyptiaca* p 3, ⲟⲩⲟϩ ⲁⲥϫⲱ — 4, ⲉϧⲟⲩⲛ ⲉⲡⲉϥⲛⲓ, (fol 2) to *ib* 7, [ϫⲉⲛⲟⲩ-ⲙⲉⲧ]ϧⲉⲗⲗⲟ ⲉⲛⲁⲛⲉⲥ — 8, ⲥⲧⲉⲟⲩⲟⲛ[ϣⲧⲩⲭⲏ]. F ROBINSON, *l c*, 221 ff gives the variants from LAGARDE and on pp 131, 134 translates the text

441 [46].—Parchment, 2 complete leaves, 28 × 19 cm Pp. — ⲛⲃ, — ⲓⲏ 1 column, 28 lines Script *cf.* HYVERNAT, *Album* XXXII and xlii 4 No colours

Mary the Virgin, Falling asleep of The MS is described by FORBES ROBINSON, *Apocryphal Gospels*, p XXVI The text is that of *Cod Vatic* lxi (ZOEGA p 94) = ROBINSON p 110, l 13—116, l 6, who on p 219 gives the variants

The Leipzig University, Vol XXVI, fol 1 (pp — ϧⲃ) is a leaf of the same MS and relates the attempt of the Jews to carry off and burn the Virgin's body so as to secure its miraculous benefits

---

[1] The mention of Oxyrhynchus recalls the Pseudo-petrine text, *ed* C SCHMIDT, pp 7, 31 (*Texte u Unt*, N F v)

[2] *Cf* Exod xxiii 20, 21 [3] *Cf* Dan x. 20

[4] This prosthetic ⲉ also in ⲉϩⲛⲟⲩⲓ below Other texts with this feature, *e g* AMELINEAU, *Rec de Trav* vi 166, ROSSI, *Cinque MSS*, p 83 ff

[5] Κεντηναριον

442 [47 a].—Parchment, the lower part of a leaf, 18 × 16 cm. 1 column, in paragraphs Script *cf* HYVERNAT, *Album* xviii, though the resemblance is but partial

Basilides, Martyrdom of   The passage corresponds to p 23, cap vii of the Ethiopic version *ed* PEREIRA (*Corp Scr Chr Or*, Acta Mart i, *Versio*)   *Cf* also AMÉLINEAU, *Les Actes* 163 ff, HYVERNAT, *Les Actes* i ff, *Synaxarium*, 11th Thoth   Leipzig University, Vols xxiv 14, 15 and xxvi 23 [1] are perhaps from the same MS

Fol *a*   ] ⲋⲉⲛⲟⲩϧⲟ ⲉϥⲙⲉϧ ⲛⲣⲁϣⲓ ⲡⲉϫⲁϥ ⲛⲁϥ ϫⲉⲭⲉⲣⲉ ⲃⲁⲥⲓⲗⲓⲧⲏⲥ ⲡⲓⲥⲧⲣⲁⲧⲩⲗⲁⲧⲏⲥ ⲛⲧⲉ ⲡⲭ̅ⲥ̅ ⲭⲉⲣⲉ ⲫⲏ ⲉⲧⲁⲡⲭ̅ⲥ̅ ⲥϧⲁⲓ ⲙⲡⲉϥⲣⲁⲛ ⲛϧⲣⲏⲓ ⲋⲉⲛⲥⲓⲱⲛ ⲛⲥⲙⲓⲗⲓⲙ ⲙⲃⲉⲣⲓ ⲭⲉⲣⲉ ⲫⲏ ⲥⲧⲁⲛⲥϥⲙⲉⲧⲛⲁⲏⲧ ϥⲟϧ ϣⲁⲡⲓⲟⲣⲟⲛⲟⲥ ⲛⲧⲉ ⲫ̅ϯ̅ ⲭⲉⲣⲉ ⲫⲏ ⲉⲧⲛⲁϣⲱⲡⲓ ⲛⲁⲣⲭⲩⲥⲧⲣⲁⲧⲩⲥⲟⲥ ⲋⲉⲛⲛⲓⲫⲏⲟⲩⲓ ⲙⲫⲣⲏϯ [

Fol *b*   ] ⲙⲡⲓϧⲏⲃ ⲓⲥ[8 or 9 let]ⲛⲓ ⲭⲉⲣⲉ ⲫⲏ ⲉⲧⲁⲩϭⲁⲥ ⲡⲉϥⲡⲁⲗⲗⲁⲧⲓⲟⲛ ⲛⲉⲙ ⲫⲁⲓⲟⲩⲥⲧⲟⲥ ⲛⲉⲙⲫⲁⲉⲩⲥⲓⲃⲓⲟⲥ ⲙⲫⲣⲏϯ ⲙⲫⲁⲗⲁⲅⲓⲁ ⲭⲉⲣⲉ ⲫⲏ ⲉⲧⲁⲩϣⲟⲛⲧ ⲙⲡⲉϥϫⲗⲟⲙ ⲋⲉⲛⲛⲓⲱⲛⲓ ⲙⲙⲁⲣⲅⲁⲣⲓⲧⲏⲥ ⲛⲧⲉ ⲧⲡⲟⲗⲓⲥ ⲙⲡⲓϧⲏⲃ ϫⲉⲛⲟⲩⲙϯ ⲙⲡⲉⲣⲉⲣϧⲟϯ ⲁⲛⲟⲕ ϯϣⲟⲡ ⲛⲉⲙⲁⲕ ⲁⲛⲟⲕⲡⲉ ⲙⲓⲭⲁⲏⲗ ⲡⲓⲁⲣⲭⲏⲁⲅⲅⲉⲗⲟⲥ ⲫⲏ ⲉⲧϣⲟⲡ [

443 [61]—Paper, 148 foll, paged on *versos* [2], in modern binding, 21 3 × 14 5 cm, 1 col, 15 lines   Script   a regular hand, slightly resembling HYVERNAT i or liii 2   Initials, head lines, stops, the letters ⲫ, ⲋ in red   Described by BUDGE, *Martyrdom and Miracles of St G*, 1888, p xii

St George, texts relating to

I Fol 1 (p ⲗⲃ), his Martyrdom   *Beg* ⲡⲓⲁ]ⲅⲓⲟⲥ ⲅⲉⲱⲣⲅⲓⲟⲥ ⲉϫⲛⲡⲓⲃⲏⲙⲁ, = BUDGE, *l c*, p 13, l 14

II Fol 59 *a*, Encomium by Theodosius, bishop of Jerusalem, on his Miracles, the building of his τόπος at Diospolis and the deposition there of his body, on the 7th of Hathor, = BUDGE, p. 38 ff

The 1st Miracle begins on fol 73 *a*, the 2nd on fol 82 *b*, the 3rd on 91 *b*, the 4th on 101 *b*, the 5th on 105 *b*, the 6th on 112 *a*, the 7th on 120 *a*, the 8th on 126 *b*   The concluding leaves of the book are, as now bound, in disorder   After fol 138 should follow foll 145, 146, after them, foll 139–144 (ⲣⲟⲏ)   Here a *lacuna* of 6 foll is followed by foll 147, 148 (ⲣⲛⲉ, ⲣⲛ5)   The last words are ⲛⲏ ⲉⲣⲉⲛⲁⲓⲛⲟⲩϯ ⲛⲧⲱⲟⲩ

Dr BUDGE gives the variants from this MS on p 214 ff of his work

The MS belonged to TATTAM

444 [51], fol 126 —Paper, 15½ × 10½ cm   P ⲣ̅ⲗ̅ⲃ̅   1 col of some 15 lines   Script relatively modern

St George, probably from an Encomium on   His name does not occur, but the

---

[1] *V* LEIPOLDT in K VOLLERS's *Katal*, p 391 &c
[2] From fol 39 onwards the paging, originally erroneous, was subsequently corrected

mention of the widow's crippled son, the queen's conversion and martyrdom, and the servants who secured the saint's body [1], make the ascription certain.

ϩⲓⲱⲓϣ ⲇⲉⲙⲡⲓⲣⲁⲛ ⲉⲧⲉⲙⲁⲣⲱⲟⲩⲧ · ⲛⲓϣⲫⲏⲣⲓ ⲛⲉⲙⲛⲓⲙⲏⲓⲛⲓ ⲉⲧⲁϥⲁⲓⲧⲟⲩ ⲛϫⲉ ⲫⲏ ⲉⲑⲟⲩⲁⲃ
ⲛϩⲟⲩⲟ ⲇⲉ ϯⲭⲏⲣⲁ ⲛⲉϧⲙⲓ · ⲑⲏ ⲉⲧⲁϥⲓⲣⲓ ⲙⲡⲉⲥϭⲁⲡ · ϩⲁⲡⲓⲛⲁ ⲁϥⲧⲁⲗϭⲟ ⲡⲉⲥϣⲏⲣⲓ · ⲙⲃⲉⲗⲗⲉ
ⲟⲩⲟϩ ⲛϭⲁⲗⲉ · ⲁϥⲧⲟⲩⲛⲟⲥ ⲉⲃⲟⲗ ⲇⲉⲙⲛⲛ ⲥⲧϣⲱⲛⲓ ⲛⲏ ⲉⲧⲁⲩⲛⲁⲩ ⲉⲩⲉⲣⲙⲉⲑⲣⲉ (verso) ⲟⲩⲟϩ
ⲁϥⲧⲁⲥⲑⲟ ⲛϥⲟⲩⲣⲟ ⲉⲡⲓⲛⲁϩϯ ⲛⲟⲣⲑⲟⲇⲟⲝⲟⲥ · ⲁⲥϣⲱⲡⲓ ⲉϯⲙⲉⲟⲩⲣⲟ · ⲁⲥⲟⲩⲛⲟϥ ⲛⲉⲙⲛⲓ⳥ · ⲡⲁⲗⲓⲛ
ⲉϥⲭⲏⲛ ⲡⲉϥⲁⲣⲟⲙⲟⲥ ⲇⲉⲛⲟⲩⲙⲉⲧⲥⲉⲛⲛⲉⲟⲥ · ⲛⲉⲙⲙⲉⲧϫⲱⲣⲓ · ⲟⲩⲟϩ ⲁϥⲉⲣϣⲁⲓ ⲛⲉⲙⲡⲭ̄ⲥ̄ · ⲇⲉⲛⲟⲙⲉⲧ-
ⲟⲩⲣⲟ ⲛⲛⲓⲫⲏⲟⲩⲓ ⲣⲟⲩϩⲓ ⲇⲉ ⲙⲡⲓⲉϩⲟⲟⲩ ⲁⲩⲓ ⲛϫⲉ ⲛⲉϥⲁⲗⲱⲟⲩⲓ ⲁⲩⲱⲗⲓ ⲙⲡⲉϥⲥⲱⲙⲁ

445 [38].—Parchment, a single leaf, $32\frac{1}{2} \times 21\frac{1}{2}$ cm , 1 column, 30 lines   Script identical with HYVERNAT, *Album* xxxiii   No colours

Pijimi, Life of[2]   *Published* by AMÉLINEAU, *Méms de la Miss* iv 247, and again by LEIPOLDT, *Sinuthii Vita* &c , i 77 (*Corp. Scr Chr Or*)   Leipzig University, Vols xxiv 9 and xxv 1 are probably from the same MS [3]

446 [49].—Parchment, a complete leaf, 32×24 cm   Pp —. ⲝ̄ⲍ̄, the last of quire ⲝ̄ , 1 column, 32 lines, divided into paragraphs   Script *v* HYVERNAT, *Album* xli 3, probably by the same scribe   Stops in red

Gregory of Nyssa, from the Oration on Gregory Thaumaturgus   The text corresponds to MIGNE, *Patr. Gr* 46, 925 B from ἡ δὲ συγκινηθεῖσα to *ib* C, καὶ ὅσα εἰκὸς ἦν

Other leaves from the same MS. are Leipzig University, Vol xxiv, foll 6, 28, 29, 34, 41, Vol xxv, foll 14, 17, 24 [4].   Six foll of a Saïdic version are MS Clarendon Press (WOIDE), fragm 54

447 [40, 43 a].—Parchment, 2 leaves and a fragment, $30\frac{1}{2} \times 19\frac{1}{2}$ cm , 1 col, 35 or 36 lines   Script *cf* HYVERNAT, *Album* xli. 1 and 2   No 40, fol 1 *b* is paged ⲡ̄ [5]

Sergius of Athribis, Martyrdom of.   *Cf* Synaxarium, 19th Mechir, and ZOEGA, p 30   The proper order of the leaves seems to be no 43, f 1 *b*, *a*, no 40, f 1 *a*, *b*, f 2 *b*, *a*   Leipzig University, Vol xxiv 13 is from the same MS [6] and probably precedes (though not immediately) no 43   The Leipzig leaf relates first the prayer of Sergius and

---

[1] These incidents are narrated on pp 305, 313, 324 of BUDGE's *St. George* and on pp 197, 202 of AMÉLINEAU's *Contes* ii

[2] Rather than of Shenoute, who only appears incidentally in the story.   The recurrence of this incident in the Synaxarium (*v* WUSTENFELD, p 172) merely shows

that that work drew upon the Life   The Leipzig leaves do not refer to Shenoute

[3] *V* LEIPOLDT, *l c*, pp. 390, 400

[4] *V l c*, p 389 &c

[5] Possibly a letter precedes ⲕ

[6] *V* LEIPOLDT, *l c*, p 391

Theodore his father[1] for all who commemorate or honour them, then the appearance of Christ promising to entrust their bodies and memorial chapel to Julius of ⲭⲃⲉⲅⲥ

No 43 tells how Julius undertook to write [Sergius's] history and to preserve his and his companions' bodies It also relates a miraculous cure worked by Sergius in prison and the summons, on the 13th Mechir, to trial before the magistrates, sitting on the πρόβλημα on the river bank, east of the town

No 40 The people cry out that they are Christians Thereat Cyprian the magistrate[2] is wroth and questions Sergius, who, confessing Christ, is reminded of the many who have suffered death for that name Euius[3], the general, bribes and threatens in vain, and Sergius is placed upon the ἑρμητάριον Here Christ again appears to comfort and encourage him, promising him fame like that of Victor, son of Romanus, and hailing him father of many martyrs Then Menesôn ⲁⲡⲁ ⲙⲉⲛⲉⲥⲱⲛ[4] the priest, hearing of Sergius's trial, goes with two deacons to the βῆμα There being invited to sacrifice, he sends to the church for baptismal water and oil, wherewith he anoints the crowd, who again confess their faith The heathen ἄνομος, further enraged, accuse him of enchanting their city Menesôn replies (sic expl).

448 [43 b].—Parchment, the bottom of a leaf, 15 × 19½ cm , 1 col, 33 lines Script appears identical with HYVERNAT, *Album* xxxvi Stops &c in red

Thomas (of Shentelet), Martyrdom of (v Synaxarium, 27th Payni and AMÉLINEAU, *Les Actes* 105)[5] Other fragments of the same MS are Leipzig University, Vol xxiv, foll 43, 45-48 The present leaf would come between foll 46 and 47 They relate how Thomas caused a statue of Apollo first to fall and crush those of other gods, then to pursue and almost strangle Culcian[6], the ἡγεμών, whereat the people declare for Thomas's god The saint is then imprisoned, and there twice refuses to do sacrifice . When in the boiling calderon χαλκίον he throws some of its contents and blinds the ἡγεμών, yet takes pity on him at Arian's entreaty and heals him Thereafter he is brought forth from prison and, as he leaves, is asked to heal one possessed He is placed upon the ἑρμητάριον and stretched till his bones separate Michael appears and cuts his chains Our present dilapidated leaf tells how, when brought out of prison and thrown to wild beasts, a she lion licks[7] his feet and in a human voice sings his praises

449 [48].—Parchment , a single leaf, 28 × 19 cm , 1 column, 27-29 lines, in para graphs Script cf HYVERNAT, *Album* xlii 1, also xli 1, though that of our leaf is less even than either, its ⲅ and ⲝ being especially clumsy, while ⲙ has the form ⲩ

---

[1] Theodore is called the σχολαστικός in ZOEGA, l c

[2] Cyprian is Theodore's brother and ἡγεμών of Athribis, v ZOEGA

[3] [ⲉ]ⲩⲓⲟⲥ V VON LEMM, Kl Kopt St, no viii

[4] Mentioned in ZOEGA, l c The name is presumably Μνάσων (Acts xxi 16, which the Boh appears persistently to misread)

[5] The Ethiopic Synaxarium gives the story, the Coptic generally appears to omit it Thomas of Tanphôt (HYVERNAT, Actes 100) is presumably a different person

[6] AMÉLINEAU has here Armenius, the governor of Alexandria, in the Ethiopic he is nameless Arian is in both Thomas's final executioner

[7] ⲗⲱⲭ̅ⲣ, not Boh in PEYRON V BALESTRI-HYVERNAT, Acta 1 30, 106

From a Discussion between an Archbishop and a Jew Mr F C CONYBEARE has kindly sought for this passage, but in vain, among the early apologies and dialogues of a similar nature He observes that the Christian claim to be the true keepers of the Law is a common feature of such compositions

Fol *a.* ϫⲉⲓⲥ ⲛⲉⲕⲛⲟⲩϯ ⲡⲓⲥ̄ⲗ̄ ⲛ[ⲏ ⲉ]ⲧⲁⲩⲥ[ⲛⲉⲛ ⲉⲃⲟⲗ ϫⲉⲛⲡ[ⲕⲁϩⲓ ⲛ̄ⲭⲏⲙⲓ[. . . . .]ⲟⲩ ⲛ[ⲓⲥⲧⲉⲕ]ⲓⲟⲩ ⲛⲡⲟⲩⲁⲣⲉϩ ⲉⲡⲉϥ[ⲛⲟ]ⲙⲟⲥ ⲁⲡⲟ̄ⲥ̄ ⲱ ⲛⲛⲓⲭⲣⲏ[ⲥ]ⲧⲓⲁⲛⲟⲥ ϩⲱⲟⲩ ⲁϥϯ ⲛⲱⲟⲩ ⲛⲡⲉϥⲥⲱⲙⲁ ⲛⲉⲙⲡⲉϥⲥⲛⲟ[ϥ] ⲡⲓⲙⲁⲛⲛⲁ ⲉⲧϩⲏⲡ ϯⲟⲓ . .[¹] ⲛⲟⲩϣⲟ ⲛⲣⲟⲙⲡⲓ ⲕⲉ ⲅⲁⲣ ⲛⲉⲛⲓⲟⲧ ⲉⲛⲁⲡⲟⲥⲧⲟⲗⲟⲥ ⲁⲩⲧⲥⲁⲃⲟⲛ ⲉⲡⲁⲓⲙⲁⲛⲛⲁ ⲉⲑⲟⲩⲁⲃ ⲫⲁⲓ ϩⲏⲡⲡⲉ ⲁⲛⲟⲛ ⲁⲛϣⲱⲡ ⲛⲁⲣⲉϩ ⲉⲡⲟⲩⲛⲟⲙⲟⲥ ϣⲁⲉⲃⲟⲩⲛ ⲉⲫⲟⲟⲩ ⲟⲩⲟϩ [. . . .]ⲗ ⲛⲛⲁⲣ[.]ⲡϥ ϣ[ⲁⲉ]ⲛⲉϩ ⲁⲛⲉⲕⲓⲟⲧ ⲟⲩⲱⲙ ⲛⲡⲓⲙⲁⲛⲛⲁ ⲁⲩⲙⲟⲩ ⲁⲛⲥⲓⲟⲧ ϩⲱⲟⲩ ⲟⲩⲱⲙ ⲛⲡⲓⲙⲁⲛⲛⲁ ⲁⲩⲱⲛϧ ϣⲁⲉⲛⲉϩ ⲡⲉϫⲉ ⲡⲓⲟⲩⲇⲁⲓ ϫⲉⲡⲱⲥ ⲕⲱ ⲛⲫⲁⲓ ⲛⲏⲓ ⲙⲏ ⲛⲓⲭⲣⲏⲥⲧⲓⲁⲛⲟⲥ ⲙⲱⲟⲩⲧ ⲛⲱⲟⲩ ⲁⲛ ⲡⲉϫⲉ ⲡⲓⲁⲣⲭⲏⲉⲡⲓⲥⲕⲟⲡⲟⲥ ϫⲉⲫⲙⲟⲩ ⲙⲏⲛ ⲛ̄ⲧⲉ ⲡⲁⲓⲕⲟⲥⲙⲟⲥ ⲟⲩⲱⲧⲉⲃ ⲉⲃⲟⲗⲡⲉ ⲫⲏ ⲛⲑⲟϥ ⲉⲑⲛⲁϩⲉⲓ ⲛⲛⲉⲛϫⲓϫ ⲛⲁⲙⲉⲛϯ ⲫⲁⲓⲡⲉ ⲡⲙⲟⲩ ⲛⲉⲛⲉϩ (fol *b*) [ⲡⲉϫⲉ ⲡ]ⲓⲟⲩⲇⲁⲓ ϫ[ⲉϥⲥϧ]ⲏⲟⲩⲧ [. . . .] ϫⲉ . . . . . .] ⲉⲛⲁ[. . . .]ⲁⲙⲉⲛϯ [ⲡⲉϫ]ⲉ ⲡⲓⲁⲣⲭⲏⲉⲡⲓⲥⲕⲟⲡⲟⲥ ϫⲉⲛϯ[ⲟⲩⲛⲟ]ⲩ ⲉⲧⲁⲩ[ⲥⲛ] ϯϣⲑⲏⲛ [ⲛ̄]ⲧⲉ ⲓⲱⲥⲏⲫ ⲛⲓⲁⲕⲱⲃ ⲡⲉϥⲓⲱⲧ ⲁϥ[ⲣⲓ]ⲙ[ⲓ] ⲉⲡⲉⲥⲏⲧ ϩⲓϫⲱϥ ⲟⲩⲟϩ ⲁⲛⲉϥϣⲏⲣⲓ ϯ ⲛⲟⲙϯ ⲛⲁϥ ⲉⲩⲟⲩⲱϣ ⲉⲥⲉⲗⲥⲱⲗϥ ⲛⲑⲟϥ ⲇⲉ ⲙⲡⲉϥⲟⲩⲱϣ ⲉⲥⲟⲗⲥⲉⲗ ⲁⲗⲗⲁ ⲛⲁϥϫⲱ ⲙⲙⲟⲥ ϫⲉϯⲛⲁϣⲉ ⲛⲏⲓ ⲉⲡⲉⲥⲏⲧ ⲉ[ⲁⲙⲉⲛϯ about 12 let]ⲥ ⲡⲁϣⲏⲣⲓ ⲡⲁⲗⲓⲛ ⲟⲛ ⲉⲧⲁϥⲟⲩⲟⲣⲡ ⲛⲛⲉϥϣⲏⲣⲓ ⲉⲭⲏⲙⲓ ⲉϣⲉⲡ ⲥⲟⲩⲟ ⲉⲧⲁϥⲛⲁⲩ ⲉⲣⲱⲟⲩ ⲛϫⲉ ⲓⲱⲥⲏⲫ ⲁϥⲥⲟⲩⲱⲛⲟⲩ ⲟⲩⲟϩ [ⲁϥ] .ⲓ ⲅ̄ⲉⲗ[²] ⲉⲣⲱⲟⲩ ⲉϥϫⲱ ⲙⲙⲟⲥ ϫⲉⲛⲑⲱⲧⲉⲛ ϩⲁⲛⲙⲏⲣ ⲉⲧⲁⲣⲥⲧⲉⲙ ⲉⲙⲟϣⲧ ⲙⲡⲓⲕⲁϩⲓ ⲛⲑⲱⲟⲩ ⲇⲉ ⲁⲩⲟⲩⲱϣⲧ ⲙⲙⲟϥ ⲉⲩϫⲱ ⲙⲙⲟⲥ ϫⲉⲱ ⲡ⳰ⲛ⳰ⲟ⳰⳽ ⲛⲉⲕⲉⲃⲓⲁⲓⲕ ϩⲁⲛⲣⲱⲙⲓ ⲁⲛⲛⲉ ⲛⲛⲁⲓⲣⲏϯ

'saying, Behold thy Gods, Israel, they that brought thee forth from the land of Egypt[³] [After that He had] called your fathers, they kept not His law (νόμος), and the Lord called the Christians instead and gave unto them His body and His blood, the hidden manna[⁴], to [reign?] for a thousand years For (καὶ γάρ) our fathers the Apostles taught us concerning this holy manna lo, we it is have kept their law (νόμος) unto this day and   for ever Thy fathers did eat this manna and are dead , but our fathers did eat of this manna and lived unto everlasting[⁵]'

The Jew said, 'How (πῶς) sayest thou this to me? Do Christians then not die?'

The Archbishop (ἀρχιεπ) said, 'The death indeed (μήν) of this world (κόσμος) passeth But he that shall fall into the hands of Hell (*Amenti*), this is death everlasting' (fol *b*)

The Jew said, 'It is written   .   Hell (*Amenti*)'

The Archbishop said, '[When?] they brought Joseph's coat unto Jacob, his father, he wept over it   And his sons encouraged him, wishing to comfort him , but (δέ) he would not be comforted, but rather (ἀλλά) said, I will go down to [Hell]   my son[⁶]. And again (πάλιν), when he sent his sons to Egypt, to buy corn, when Joseph beheld them, he knew them and [he]   them, saying, Ye are spies and are come to spy out the land But (δέ) they worshipped him, saying, O, our lord, thy servants are not men of this sort[⁷]'

---

¹ Not space for ⲛⲟⲩⲣⲟ, Rev xx 4   ⁴ Rev ii 17   ⁵ *Cf* John vi 58
² Possibly ⲅⲓϧⲉⲗ   ³ *Cf* Exod xxxii 4   ⁶ *Cf* Gen xxxvii 33-35   ⁷ *Cf* Gen xlii 8

450 [50].—Paper, 257 foll, paged on *versos*, in native binding Script tolerably regular Dated on last fol , A M. 1487 = A D 1771 The MS is incomplete and the quires in confusion their proper sequence is 141(ⲙⲙⲁ)-149, 1-9, 91-110, 40-49, 20-29, 60-69, 30-39, 10-19, 50-59, 70-89, 111-140, (*lacuna*), 90, 250-257 (ⲧ︤ⲟ︦).

Grammars and Vocabularies

I P ⲙⲁ *b* Ibn Kâtib Kaisar, التصريف. *Beg.* ⲉϥⲉⲥⲁϫⲓ من بول (= KIRCHER[1] 28 *a*, *v* MALLON[2] 125)

II P ⲛ︤ⲃ *a* Abû 'l-Faraj b al-ʿAssâl, المقدمة (*v* MALLON 122)

III P ⲟ︤ⲃ *a* Al Wajih al Kalyûbî, الكافد (*l c* 126).

IV P. ϙⲅ *a* At-Tikah (*sic*) b ad-Duhairî, المقدمة (*l c* 129)

V P ⲣⲛ︤ⲃ *b* Index to the Vocabulary following (but the index begins on ⲣⲛⲁ *b*), which is divided into 32 فصول The *Scala* (= KIRCHER 42) begins on ⲣⲛⲅ *b*; its 2nd chapter باب is on ⲣⲟⲉ *a*, its 3rd on ⲥⲗ︥ⲍ *a*, 4th on ⲥⲙⲁ *b*, 5th on ⲥϙ︤ⲃ *a*, 6th on ⲥϧ︤ⲉ *b*, 7th on ⲥⲟ︤ⲃ *b* (= K 215), 8th on ⲥⲟⲅ *a* (= K 221), 9th on ⲥⲛⲉ *b* (= K 238) After p ⲥϥ *b* (= K 245) is a *lacuna* P. ⲧ︤ⲃ = K 261

P ⲣⲛⲅ *a* has the scribe's name ⲓⲱ︦ⲁ ⲡϣⲏⲣⲓ ⲛ︦ⲓⲱ︦ⲁ ϣⲟⲩⲱⲟⲩ.

From TATTAM's collection

451 [58].—Paper, 163 foll and 8 blank, in Europeon binding, 30 × 22 cm Script a modern hand Dated, fol 9 *b*, A M 1555 = A D 1839

Grammars and Vocabularies The corresponding pages of 'The Baramous MS' are noted in the margins, fol 1 being p ⲕⲁ of that copy (which the sequel shows to have been in confusion)

I Fol 1 *b* As-Samannûdî, المقدمة (= KIRCHER 2 *a*, *v* MALLON 117)

II Fol 9 *b* Ibn Kâtib Kaisar (fol 12 = Baramous ⲥ)

III Fol 16 *a* Abû 'l-Faraj b al-ʿAssâl (= B p ⲕⲁ)

IV Fol 21 *b* Al Wajih al-Kalyûbî (= B ⲓⲁ)

V Fol 29 *a* Al Tikâ b ad-Duhairî (= B ⲕⲉ)

VI Fol 46 *a* The *Scala Magna* كتاب السلم (= B ⲍ︤ⲏ) KIRCHER's chap xxiv (p 225) is on fol 81 *a* After ⲡⲓⲡⲣⲟⲕⲩⲙⲉⲛⲟⲛ (K 236) follows ϯⲃⲁϣⲟⲣ &c (K 253), then ⲡⲓϧⲁⲧ &c (K 250) The sequence often differs subsequently from KIRCHER's Fol. 86 *b* = K 239, fol 87 *b* = K 243

---

[1] *Lingua Ægyptiaca Restituta*

[2] In *Mélanges de la Faculté Orientale*, Beyrout, vols i, ii, 1906, 1907

VII Fol 89 *b*   The Vocabulary of Ibn al-'Assâl (= K 275)
VIII Fol 136 *b*   That of As-Samannûdî [1], comprising words from the Psalter, N Test
and Liturgical books

This MS was in TATTAM's collection

452 [57].—Paper, 218 foll, in a modern binding like that of no 451, 28 × 20 cm
Script a modern hand   Dated, p ⲥⲏ *b*, A M 1556 = A D 1840

Grammars and Vocabularies.

I   Fol 4 *a*   Ibn Kâtib Kaisar
II   Fol 11 *a*   Al Wajih
III Fol 21 *a*   Al-Mu'taman b al 'Assâl, المعلم [2]
IV   Fol 29 *a*   Ibn ad-Duhairî
V   Fol 51 *b*   As Samannûdî, المعلم, beginning with the text MALLON 120 *infra*
VI   Fol 66 *b*   Paradigms, headed فلثو الاسم وهى and beginning ⲡⲁⲟⲥ, ⲡⲉⲛⲟⲥ, ⲛⲉϥⲟⲥ
VII Fol 69 *a*   *Scala Magna* السلم الكبر, = KIRCHER 42 (*v* MALLON 260)   The 10
chapters ابواب begin successively on foll 69 *a*, 77 *b*, 101 *b*, 104 *b*, 111 *b*, 113 *a*,
115 *b*, 117 *a*, 121 *a*, 125 *a*
VIII Fol 131 *a* Abû Ishak b al-'Assâl, Rhymed Vocabulary (= K 275)   There is an
omission at the end corresponding with K 476, ⲡⲟⲩⲛⲟϥ to 479, ϯ ϩⲓⲱⲧϥ

On the last fol is the scribe's colophon, which states that the MS was copied
from an old one كتاب قديم at Dair al-Baramûs [3] and corrected وانصاها by another at
Dair Abû 's-Sailain, in Cairo   The scribe was Takla Haimânôt [4], one of the clergy خادم
of the 'Maician Church' in the Azbakiyah   TATTAM has noted the correspondence of pages
with the original (which appears to have been in confusion), *viz* that p 6 of this copy
= 11 cf that, p 21 = 51, p 29 = 29, p 52 = 1, p 69 = 46   Thence it appears to follow
its model regularly to p 218 = 132

From p 69 TATTAM has likewise noted the correspondence with the 'Sahidic
Lexicon' p 69 = Sah ⲡⲙⲋ, and so consecutively till p 125, which = Sah ⲣⳃⲏ   This
Sa'idic vocabulary is sometimes termed 'No 3'

453 [53].—Paper, 337 foll, in European binding, 22 × 16 cm   Script a modern
hand   Dated, fol 297 *a*, A M 1559 = A D 1843

Grammars and Vocabularies

I   Fol 4 *a*   An introductory dissertation   Beg هذه الاحرف العطمه وهى انان وبلثوں
حرفا   On 4 *b*, a chapter entitled حروف نحتاج الى معرف نصرىفها   This ends
with the words ⲕⲁⲧⲁⲭⲟⲟⲛⲓⲟⲛ, ⲡⲓⲋⲱⲣ, ϯⲁⲧⲕⲓⲗⲉ, ⲡⲓϣⲉⲛⳃⲓ.

[1] *Cf* MALLON, *l c* 119 *infra*
[2] For this variant of his name *v* MALLON, *Journ As*
1905 (ii), 516
[3] On the present binding is *Turiani MS*, presumably
intended for As-Suryânî
[4] Who also wrote no 453 and Br Mus no 922
(MALLON)

G g

II   Fol 8 *a*   Abû 'l-Faraj b al-'Assâl, حـنـاوم.
III   Fol 13 *b*   Ibn Kâtib Kaisar
IV   Fol 19 *b*   Al-Wajîh
V   Fol 27 *a*   As-Samannûdî
VI   Fol 36 *b*   Ibn ad Duhairî
VII   Fol 55 *a*   Abû Shâkir b ar-Râhib, حـنـاوم, printed by MALLON, p 232   It
      enumerates the books whence it was drawn[1] and ends with the date of
      completion of the original = A D 1270[2], and of the present copy (as above),
      by the scribe Taklâ Haimânôt نكلا هـمـابوب[3]   Then follows the author's
      Grammar, the sources of all quotations being given in the margin up to
      fol 59 *a*   On fol 80 *a*, a section (? of the same) beginning[4] اعلم ابها الـناظر فى
      فى اقسام الكلام الـعـطى الح   On 83 *b*, a chapter[5] هـده الـحـروف الح
VIII Fol 90 *a*   A grammar entitled[6] كتاب مـحـتصر فى وواعـد اللغـه المصريه ونـظامـها والعرب
      فـمـا بـن البـحـرى والـصـعـدى   It opens with the alphabet and with lists of words,
      e g ϩⲉⲛⲓⲁⲙⲓⲛ, ϩⲁⲉⲙⲧⲓ, ϩⲏⲟⲗⲉⲉⲙ, ϩⲓⲟⲥ.   The Sa'idic consists in frequent equiva-
      lents (in red ink) for the Bohairic examples   A comparison with TUKI's
      Rudimenta shows that our MS is either a mere copy of that publication
      (issued in 1778) or that both are drawn from a common source   The former
      appears the most probable inference, TUKI's work having been done at Rome,
      presumably from a MS already there[7]
           It will be seen that the MS bears a close resemblance to Br Mus no 920,
      though the latter omits this final section   MS Paris no 53 is also of this type[8]
IX   Fol 183 *a*   The *Scala Magna*
X   Fol 230 *b*   The *Scala* of Abû Ishâk b al-'Assâl
XI   Fol 276 *b*   The *Scala* of As Samannûdî (*cf* Br Mus no 920, f 196 ff)
XII   Fol 323 *a*   List of Bishoprics, *published* by AMÉLINEAU, *La Géogr* 574[9].
XIII. Fol 325 *b*   List of Churches in Egypt, *published l c* 579
XIV   Fol 328 *b*   Lists of words from the Pentateuch, Antiphonarium, and Encomiums
      on St Michael   Final words ⲛⲓϩⲉⲣϫⲱⲟⲩ, ⲙⲉⲟⲉⲙⲱⲛ, ⲁⲁⲱⲛⲁⲓ, ⲛ̅ⲗ̅.

454 [54]—Paper, 192 foll in native binding, 21 × 17 cm   Script a modern hand
Dated, fol 178 *b*, A M 1514 = A D 1798

     Grammars and Vocabularies

I   Fol 4 *a*   Abû 'l-Faraj b al-'Assâl, حـنـاوم
II   Fol 9 *a*   Ibn Kâtib Kaisar
III Fol 15 *a*. Al Wajîh

[1] Among them the puzzling احينـل, for which MALLON
(236) suggests the plausible etymology, ⲁϫⲡ in the plural
[2] *Cf* no 454   [3] Scribe also of no 452
[4] *V* MALLON 259   [5] *L c* 260
[6] The title likewise of LORD AMHERST'S grammar, *v*
MALLON 263.

[1] According to HYVERNAT, *Etude sur le Versions* (*Rev
Bibl* 1896–97), p 18, TUKI's MS was recently in the
Borgian Museum
[2] This I owe to Father MALLON
[3] The foliation there given is incorrect.

IV Fol 25 *a* Ibn ad-Duhairî, and, fol 41 *a*, an introduction to his work, partly printed by MALLON 130

V Fol 41 *b* Abû Shâkır (= no 453, fol. 55 *a*) The date at which the original of this was completed was A M 980 = A D. 1264[1], its (?) scribe was Hannâ Abû Sulaımân, attached to the northern church of St. Michael, ın the lower Handak[2], السعلى

VI Fol. 42 *b* His grammar The sources of the examples are given in the margins (*cf* no 453)

VII Fol 66 *a* *Scala* of Abû Ishâk b al-'Assâl, with references for all the examples (a list of the abbreviations علائم نعسمر, indicating these sources, is given on fol 65 *a*)

VIII Fol 102 *b* As-Samannûdî, ܐܘܥܦܤ

IX Fol 108 *b*. His *Scala*

X Fol 136 *a* The short Preface = no 453, fol 80 *a*

XI Fol 139 *a* The *Scala Magna*, ending on fol 171 *b*

XII Fol 172 *a* The *Scala* on fol 307 *a* of no 453

XIII Fol 176 *a* List of Bishoprics (unfinished)

XIV Fol 178 *a* Certain *formulæ* used in the Ordination of a bishop (ⲉⲗⲁⲭⲓⲥⲧⲟⲥ ⲟ ⲧⲁⲡⲓⲛⲟⲥ ⲉⲡⲓⲥⲕⲟⲡⲟⲥ .).

XV Fol 178 *b* ⲉⲟⲃⲉⲛⲟⲱϣ ⲛϯⲕⲁⲍⲟⲫⲩⲗⲁⲕⲓⲟⲛ ..., ending with the scribe's (?) date, as above

XVI Fol 179 *a* Index to *Scala Magna*.

XVII Fol 180 *a*. Words from the Consecration of Lector, Sub-deacon &c

XVIII Fol 189 *a* List of Churches, as in AMÉLINEAU, *Geogr* 577

XIX. Fol 190 *b* List of Bishoprics, *beg* ⲁⲗⲉⲍⲁⲛⲁⲣⲓⲁ, ⲣⲁⲕⲟϯ, ⲟⲃⲁϣⲟⲩ, ϯⲣⲁϣⲓⲧ, ⲙⲉⲗⲉϫ, ⲁⲣⲃⲁⲟ Not identical with any of those printed by AMÉLINEAU, *op cit* 558 ff

XX Fol 191 *b* Greek proper names, used التكرير وى, = no 453, fol 327 *a* and Br Mus no 920, 261 *a*

This MS belonged to TATTAM

455 [68] —Paper, 268 foll , 22½ × 16 cm Script a modern hand

Grammars and Vocabularies On the fly leaf is a note 'Copy of the Coptic-Arabic dictionary in the possession of the Coptic patriarch at Cairo, of which he has allowed the transcription, I believe for the first time—John Bournely[3].'

I Fol 2 *a* Ibn ad-Duhairî

II Fol 29 *b* Abû Shâkır; *beg* قصدبا لما فانا وبعد, published by MALLON 233

---

[1] MALLON points out that in no 453 the year is A D 1270, while in Br Mus no 922 it is, as here, 1264 Does this indicate a difference in the works copied?

[2] *V* AMÉLINEAU, *Géogr.* 577 (*cf* 220)

[3] I cannot be certain of the reading of this name Perhaps Bowring

III   Fol 32 *b*   His مقعد, = *l c* 238 (though here somewhat longer), preceded by a list of abbreviations for the references in السلم المقعى of Abū Ishâk b al-'Assâl

IV   Fol 68 *a*   The *Scala* of Abû Ishâk

V   Fol 155 *b*   The *Scala Magna*

VI   Fol 256 *b*   The short Preface = no 453, fol 80 *a*

VII   Fol 263 *a*   Abū Ishâk's Introduction to his *Scala*, entitled مسر من قول واضع كتاب السلم المعلمس   Printed and translated by MALLON, 216, from Paris MS 51

456 [55] — Paper, 57 foll, in native binding, $22\frac{1}{2} \times 16$ cm   Script the Coptic is in TATTAM's hand, the Arabic by a native

Grammars

I   Fol 1 *a*   As-Samannûdi

II   Fol 20 *b*.   Ibn Kâtib Kaisar

III   Fol 33 *a*   Abû 'l-Faraj b al-'Assâl

IV   Fol 44 *b*   Al-Wajih

457 [56] — Paper, 139 foll, $20 \times 13\frac{1}{2}$ cm   Script as in no 456

The *Scala Magna* of Shams ar-Riâsah, followed, fol 133 *b*, by a list of words from the Consecrations of *hegoumenos*, priest and deacon   *Beg.* ⲁⲛⲁⲃⲁϯ ⲥⲉⲛⲡⲓⲗⲓⲡⲉⲗⲉⲟⲛ ⲥⲉⲛⲃⲁⲃⲩⲗⲟⲛ ⲛ̅ⲭⲏⲙⲓ ⲛⲉⲩⲥⲉⲃⲓⲟⲥ[1].   The last 5 foll of the volume are copied, by TATTAM, from a vocabulary

458 [52]   Foll 204–172 — Paper, 16×11 cm   Script a regular 18th or 19th century hand   The leaves are in confusion

The *Scala Magna*   The leaves correspond as follows to KIRCHER's print

Fol 204	=	K p 193 *infra*		Fol 183, 182	=	K 254–257
203		198 *supra*		181		251
202		264		180		253
201–192 (?)		57–70		179		257
191		114		178		258 *infra*
190–188		116–120		177		207
187–184		124–131		176–172		208–214

459 [51] — Paper, 126 foll   The volume is made up of parts of 11 MSS, the largest, $18\frac{1}{2} \times 13$ cm   Script all the hands are tolerably early (13th or 14th cent)

---

[1] *Cf* terms in the list of Cairo churches, AMÉLINEAU, *Géogr* 577

The Vocabulary of As-Samannūdī   With the exception of foll 35 &c (v no 114 above), 111 &c (v no 428), the volume appears to consist of this *Scala*   The following is the proper sequence of the leaves of the different MSS, so far as indicated by visible pagination   An asterisk = sequence not ascertained

MS. α, Foll 89, 1, 105, 106, 2*

MS β, Foll 9, 92, 26, 40, 3*, 7*, 8*, 123*.

MS. γ, Foll 41, 48, 4*

MS. δ, Foll 52, 67, 95-98, 5*, 24*, 46*, 68*, 99-101*

MS. ε, Foll 14, 10-13, 15, 90, 16-18*

MS ζ, Foll 29, 30, 28, 27, 26, 22, 23, 21, 20, 31-34, 39, 42, 43, 47, 91, 102-104, 108, 107, 110

MS η, Foll. 57-66, 71-88

MS θ, Foll 69, 70

MS ι, Foll 124, 125

LETTERS

460.—Papyrus, complete but dilapidated, $26\frac{1}{2} \times 21$ cm   Script   much ligatured
Verso ↑

Letter from Apa Mena, Theodore, Co . (?) and Bounophêr (Onnophrius) It
relates to Zôleman, son of Saeit (ﺳﻌﯿﺪ) and to the purchase of certain 'large vessels'
(σκευή) More than this it is difficult to ascertain, owing to the peculiarity both of
idiom and script The former, although the MS belongs to the Ashmunain collection,
is an almost pure Bohairic, but written with the help of Greek letters to express certain
of the Coptic sounds[1] The tail of the ϣ projects far to the left and then is looped
back to the right The initial of the name Zôleman can hardly be ϭ (which elsewhere
has the normal form) it is a mere curve, ſ, presumably derived from ζ and scarcely
distinguishable from ϩ 'and' Very puzzling is the sign in ll 2, 7, 12 Since ϧ does
not occur, this might be taken to represent it, yet it is difficult to account for an ϧ in
these 3 places It might be taken for ligatured ⲁⲗ, indeed in ll 12, 13 the doubtful
letters ⲁⲓ might well be read thus But in the former 3 cases, ⲁ cannot be so precisely
disconnected from the rest of the ligature Boh ϫ appears to be represented by ⲭ
Final ⲩ (in internal syllables as well as words) is merely a curve above the preceding
letter

+ ⲭⲧⲱⲓⲣⲁⲛ ⲫ̄ϯ ⲁⲛⲟⲕ ⲝⲁⲁⲡⲁ ⲙ̄ⲏ ϩ ⲑⲉⲟⲇⲱⲣⲟⲥ ϩ ⲕⲟ̄ [2]| ϩ ⲃⲟⲩⲛⲟⲫⲏⲣ ⲥⲛⲉⲭⲁⲉⲓ ⲉⲛⲱϣⲓⲛ]ⲓ
ⲥ . . . ⲉⲱ̄ⲣ ⲧⲓⲛⲟ̄ ⲝ [ⲍⲱ]|ⲗⲉⲙⲁⲛ ⲡϣⲏⲣⲓ ⲥⲛⲉⲓⲧ ⲡⲕ . . ϣ . ⲫⲛⲉ[ⲛⲓ]ϣⲧ | ⲉⲥⲕⲛⲃⲓ ⲧⲁⲫϣⲟⲡϥ
ϣⲁⲟ ⲭⲁⲥ ⲝⲉ ⲛⲁϣⲟⲛϥ ⲙⲏⲛ |ϩ-ⲝⲙⲏⲛ ϩ ⲙ . . . . ⲉⲣⲟⲕ ϣⲉⲙⲥⲫⲧⲁⲙⲟⲕ ⲛⲛⲓϣⲧ ⲉⲥⲕⲛⲃ[ⲓ]| ⲧⲉⲫⲧⲓ ⲛⲁⲕ
ⲭⲉⲙⲏⲛ ⲉⲣⲉⲙⲏϣ.ⲉ. ⲥⲁⲛⲙⲱ̄ ⲉⲭⲟ ϭ | ⲡⲟⲟⲩ ⲍⲱⲗⲉⲙⲁⲛ ⲓⲣ̄ⲉⲃⲓⲥⲁⲫ . ⲡⲛⲕⲁⲝⲉⲉⲓ̄ϯ ⲉⲛⲓϣⲧ |
ⲧⲟⲧⲟ̄ ϣⲟⲛϥ   ⲧⲫϣⲟⲡ ⲥⲕ[ⲛⲃⲓ] ⲛⲁⲣⲕⲟⲛ ⲁⲛ ⲟⲩⲧⲏⲛ . | ⲝⲓⲃⲱⲛⲉⲓ ϣⲁⲕⲝⲉⲥⲓ   ⲛⲉⲁⲣⲙⲟⲧⲓ[. . .]
ⲉϣⲟⲙⲧⲓ   ⲓⲟ ⲛ̄ⲝⲓϣⲟⲛ ⲛⲛ ϣⲉⲛⲟⲝⲓ ϣⲁⲕⲝⲙⲙ ⲛⲁⲛⲏϥ ϣⲁⲥ | ⲝⲥⲁⲧⲓⲁⲕⲟⲩ ⲣⲁⲟⲉⲓⲣⲁⲧⲁⲙⲉⲣ ϣⲟⲡⲁⲕ-
ⲥⲱ ⲥⲕⲛⲃⲓ | ⲛⲁⲛⲏϥ ϩ ⲭⲓⲭⲛⲙⲭⲁⲓ ⲭⲁⲃⲉⲙⲟⲉⲓⲧⲉⲕ . ⲥⲱⲧ̄ⲙ | ⲝⲉⲃⲟⲛ ⲥⲕⲛⲃⲓ ⲛⲁⲛⲏϥ ⲉⲥⲙⲙⲁⲧ . ⲧⲁⲓ .
ⲛⲁⲗⲁⲛⲁⲛ̃ | ⲉⲣⲱ̄ ϣⲁⲕⲝⲙⲙⲟ̄ ⲛⲁⲛⲏⲟ̄ ϣⲁⲡⲟ̄ ϩ ⲡⲟ̄ⲛⲁⲫⲏⲣ | 15 ⲧⲁⲉⲓ ⲉⲣⲏⲥ ϣⲟⲩ ϯ̄ϯ ⲟⲩϣ
ⲃⲟⲩⲛⲟⲫⲏⲣ ⲧⲁⲉⲓ ⲉⲣⲏⲥ ⲉⲓⲁⲉ . | ⲧⲓⲕⲁⲧⲟ ⲍⲱⲗⲉⲙⲁⲛ ⲡϣⲏⲣⲓ ⲥⲛⲉⲓⲧ ⲧⲁⲭⲏ ⲝⲉⲁⲕⲟⲥⲙⲁ | ⲥⲉⲡⲓⲕⲟⲝⲓ
ⲉⲓ ⲉⲣⲏⲥ ⲧⲉⲫⲟⲗⲟⲝⲓⲛ ⲟ̄ⲝⲁⲉⲓ ⲭⲉⲛⲛⲟ̄ⲥ̄ ⲁⲙⲏⲛ +

Recto . ⲁⲉⲓⲥⲭⲏⲧ ⲧⲁⲉⲓⲉⲡⲓⲥⲧⲟⲗⲟⲓ ⲛⲁⲕ ⲥⲱ ⲙⲛⲛⲝⲙⲏⲛ ⲛⲉⲛⲏ[ⲡ] and, at the other end of the
leaf, the address, whereof only ⲭⲉⲓⲧⲉⲛⲁⲡⲁ ⲙ̄ⲏ ϩ ⲡⲟⲩⲛⲟⲫⲏⲣ is legible Also remains of
an earlier text, apparently in the same idiom, since ⲧⲟⲟⲧϥ can be discerned

---

[1] *Cf Mitth Rainer* ii 57, v 41, Crum, *Copt MSS* xlii   [2] 1st letter ? ⲃ̇, instead of ⲁ ? a stroke

461 [16].—Papei , a sheet inserted at the end of the volume (v no. 424), 45 × 30½ cm
Script a tolerably even, 18th or 19th century hand *Verso* blank

Letter from 'the poor Athanasius, the bishop of Tapotheke (Abûtig)', named thus
above the text Above it too are ⲫ⳨ⲡⲉ ⲧⲁⲅⲉⲗⲡⲓⲥ ⲛⲛⲁⲉⲣϧⲟ⳨ and ⲥⲉⲛⲫⲣⲁⲛ ⲙⲫ⳨ ⲡⲓⲣⲉϥ-
ⲣⲉⲛϧⲏⲧ ⲡⲓⲛⲁⲛⲧ, also in form of an interlaced monogram, ⲟⲩⲟⲩ ⲥⲉⲙⲏⲛ ⲥⲧⲟⲥⲓ ⲙⲫ⳨[1]
Athanasius was, in A D 1789, resident in the monastery of Antonius in العرب[2], though
entitled 'bishop in the see of Abûtig'. Elsewhere he is 'bishop from the mon of
Ant , in the see of Abûtig'[3] But in Br Mus no 920 he is also ⲉⲡⲓⲥⲕⲟⲡⲟⲥ ⲓ̅ⲗ̅ⲏ̅ⲙ̅[4]
Does this mean that in 1806 he held the titular see of Jerusalem[5]? In 1811 he again
appears as bishop of Abûtig[6] He had been consecrated by the 107th patriarch, John
(1770–1797)[7]

The present letter was written from Upper Egypt to a friend in Fustât The clumsi-
ness of the language, besides several phrases obviously translated from Arabic, are
evidence that Coptic was but an artificial acquirement at the time

Ⲡⲓϧⲟⲩⲓⲧ ⲛⲧⲉ ⲥⲙⲟⲩ ⲛⲓⲃⲉⲛ ⲥⲧⲍⲏⲛ ⲉⲃⲟⲗ ⲛⲉⲙⲡⲓϧⲙⲟⲧ | ⲧⲏⲣⲟⲩ ⲉⲧϧⲱⲃⲥ ⲉⲃⲟⲗ ⲉϧⲣⲏⲓ ⲉϫⲉⲛ-
ⲡⲓϣⲏⲣⲓ ⲉⲓⲥⲙⲁⲣⲱⲟⲩⲧ | ⲫⲏ ⲉⲧⲉⲣⲥⲉⲃⲉⲥⲑⲉ ⲡⲓⲟⲣⲑⲟⲇⲟⲝⲟⲥ ⲡⲓⲇⲓⲁⲕⲱⲛ ⲉⲧⲧⲁⲓⲏⲟⲩⲧ | ⲡⲓⲁⲣⲭⲱⲛ ⲉⲧⲟⲓ
ⲛⲛⲓϣϯ ⲡⲓⲙⲉⲓ ⲡⲓⲙⲉⲛⲣⲓⲧ ⲥⲉⲛⲡⲓⲙⲁϧ |5-ϯ ⲉⲧⲥⲟⲩⲧⲱⲛ ⲛⲧⲉ ⲡⲉⲛⲟ̅ⲥ̅ ⲓ̅ⲏ̅ⲥ̅ ⲡⲭ̅ⲥ̅ ⲡⲓⲥⲁϧ ⲃⲁⲥⲟⲫ ⲫⲁ|ⲏⲗⲓⲁⲥ
ⲉϥⲉⲥⲙⲟⲩ ⲛϫⲉ ⲫ⳨ ⲉϧⲣⲏⲓ ⲉϫⲱϥ ⲥⲉⲛⲡⲓⲥⲙⲟⲩ ⲙ|ⲡⲛ̅ⲁ̅ⲧⲓⲕⲟⲛ ⲉⲧⲁⲩⲓ ⲉϧⲣⲏⲓ ⲉϫⲉⲛⲛⲉϥⲁⲡⲟⲥⲧⲟⲗⲟⲥ
ⲛⲉⲙⲛⲉϥ|ⲡⲣⲟⲫⲏⲧⲏⲥ ⲛⲉⲙⲉⲭⲉⲛⲓⲛ ⲉⲧⲓⲣⲓ ⲙⲡⲉϥⲟⲩⲱϣ ⲛⲥⲙⲛⲉϥ|ⲧⲟⲗⲏ ⲥⲉⲛⲥⲉⲛⲉⲁ ⲛⲓⲃⲉⲛ ϧⲓⲧⲉⲛ-
ⲛⲓⲡⲣⲉⲥⲃⲓⲁ ⲛⲧⲉ ϯⲡⲁⲣⲑ | 10 ⲛⲥⲛⲟⲩ ⲛⲓⲃⲉⲛ ⲁⲙⲏⲛ ⲙⲉⲛⲉⲛⲥⲁⲡⲓⲁⲓ ⲛⲧⲉ ⲛⲓⲥⲙⲟⲩ ⲥϧⲣⲏⲓ |
ⲉϫⲱϥ ⲛⲉⲙⲡⲓⲁⲥⲡⲁⲥⲙⲟⲥ ⲙⲡⲛ̅ⲁ̅ⲧⲓⲕⲟⲛ ϣⲁⲣⲟϥ ⲧⲉⲛⲛⲁ|ⲧⲁⲙⲟⲕ ⲡⲉⲛϣⲏⲣⲓ ϫⲉⲥⲭⲉⲛⲡⲓϩⲟⲟⲩ ⲉⲧⲁⲛ-
ⲉⲃⲟⲗ ⲛ|ϧⲏⲧϥ ⲉⲃⲟⲗ ⲥⲉⲛⲭⲏⲙⲓ ⲙⲡⲁϭⲓ ⲉⲣⲟⲛ ⲉⲃⲟⲗ ⲥⲉⲛⲟⲛⲛⲟⲩ | ⲛⲟⲩⲉⲡⲓⲥⲧⲟⲗⲏ ⲉⲧϣⲟⲡ ⲛϧⲏⲧⲥ
ⲛⲭⲉ ⲧⲉⲧⲉⲛϧⲓⲣⲏⲛⲓ | 15 ⲟⲩⲟϧ ⲡⲉⲛϧⲏⲧ ⲉϥϣⲟⲟⲣⲧⲉⲣ ⲉⲃⲟⲗ ϧⲓⲧⲉⲛⲟⲛⲛⲟⲩ ⲙⲁⲗⲓⲥⲧⲁ | ϫⲉⲁⲩⲧⲁ-
ⲙⲟⲛ ϫⲉⲥⲉⲛⲭⲏⲙⲓ ⲙⲡⲓⲙⲟⲩ ⲛⲟⲩϧⲟϯ ⲥⲉⲛⲟⲩϧⲟϯ | ⲟⲩⲟϧ ⲧⲉⲛⲯⲩⲭⲏ ⲁⲥⲉⲣⲙⲕⲁϧ ⲉⲙⲁϣⲱ
ⲉⲙⲁϣⲱ ⲉⲡⲁϣⲱϥ | ⲉϧⲣⲏⲓ ⲉϫⲱⲕ ⲱ ⲡⲁϣⲏⲣⲓ ⲙⲙⲉⲛⲣⲓⲧ ⲛⲉⲙⲉⲭⲉⲛⲡⲉⲛϣⲏⲣⲓ | ⲧⲏⲣⲟⲩ ⲉⲧϣⲟⲡ
ⲥⲉⲛⲭⲏⲙⲓ ⲁⲛⲟⲛ ⲇⲉ ϧⲱⲛ ⲧⲉⲛϯϩⲟ | 20 ⲉⲡⲭ̅ⲥ̅ ⲡⲉⲛⲛⲟⲩϯ ϩⲓⲛⲁ ⲛⲧⲉϥϭⲱⲗⲓ ⲉⲃⲟⲗ ϧⲁⲣⲟⲛ ⲛⲉⲙ-
ⲉⲃⲟⲗ | ϧⲁⲣⲱⲧⲉⲛ ⲛⲟⲩⲙⲟⲩ ⲛⲉⲙϩⲱⲃ ⲛⲓⲃⲉⲛ ⲉⲧϩⲱⲟⲩ ⲟⲩⲟϩ | ⲉϥϭⲟⲣⲉⲛⲛⲁⲩ ⲉⲡⲉⲧⲉⲛϩⲟ ⲥⲉⲛϧⲁⲛ-
ⲁⲅⲁⲑⲟⲛ ⲛⲓⲃⲉⲛ | Ϣⲓⲛⲓ ⲉⲣⲟⲛ ⲉϫⲉⲛⲡⲉⲛⲓⲱⲧ ⲛⲉⲙⲡⲉⲛⲛⲓ ⲧⲏⲣϥ ⲛⲉⲙⲛⲏ ⲉⲧ|ϧⲱⲛⲧ ⲉⲣⲟⲕ ⲧⲏⲣⲟⲩ
ϣⲓⲛⲓ ⲉⲣⲟⲛ ⲉϫⲉⲛⲛⲓⲟⲩⲏⲃ ⲛⲧⲉ ϯⲉⲕⲕⲗ|25-ⲏⲥⲓⲁ ⳼ⲉⲃⲓⲗⲉ ⲛⲉⲙⲛⲓⲇⲓⲁⲕⲟⲛⲟⲥ ϣⲓⲛⲓ ⲉϫⲉⲛⲡⲉⲛ|ϣⲏⲣⲓ
ⲥⲟⲗⲟⲙⲱⲛ ⲛⲉⲙⲙⲁⲣⲕⲟⲥ ⲡⲓⲣⲉⲙⲣϣⲓⲧⲧⲉ ⲛⲉⲙⲙⲁⲣ|ⲕⲟⲥ ⲟⲩⲟϩ ⲛⲉⲙⲡⲉϥⲛⲓ ⲧⲏⲣϥ ⲛⲉⲙⲡⲉⲣⲥⲱⲙⲁ
ⲛⲉⲙⲓⲥⲁⲁⲕ | ⲛⲉⲙⲛⲏ ⲧⲏⲣⲟⲩ ⲛⲣⲉⲙⲭⲱⲛⲟⲡ ϣⲓⲛⲓ ⲉϫⲉⲛⲁⲛⲧⲱⲛⲓ ⲛⲉⲙⲁⲃⲁ | ⲛⲟⲩⲃ ⲛⲉⲙⲥⲉⲛⲟⲩⲑⲓⲟⲥ
ⲡⲓⲣⲉⲙⲓⲱϯ ϣⲓⲛⲓ ⲉϫⲉⲛⲫⲃⲱⲕ ⲙⲡⲓ,30-ⲁⲥⲅⲉⲗⲟⲥ ⲫⲁⲓⲱⲥⲏⲫ ⲛⲉⲙⲡⲉϥⲥⲛⲟⲩ ⲛⲉⲙⲉϫⲉⲛⲫⲃⲱⲕ
ⲙ|ⲡⲓⲁⲅⲓⲟⲥ ⲡⲣⲉϥϭⲃⲁⲓ ⲛⲛⲓⲥⲛⲕⲉⲩ ⲛⲉⲙⲡⲉϥⲥⲛⲟⲩ ⲛⲉⲙⲡⲓϣⲏⲣⲓ ⲙ|ⲡⲥⲟⲛ ⲙⲡⲉϥⲓⲱⲧ ⲅⲉⲱⲣⲅⲓⲟⲥ ϣⲓⲛⲓ
ⲉϫⲉⲛⲡⲥⲁϩ ⲅⲉⲱⲣⲅⲓⲟⲥ ⲡⲓ|ⲥⲁⲛϭⲙⲓ ⲛⲥⲙⲛⲉϥϣⲏⲣⲓ ⲛⲉⲙⲡϣⲏⲣⲓ ⲛⲧⲉ ⲡⲉϥϣⲏⲣⲓ ⲅⲉⲱⲣⲅⲓⲟⲥ | ⲡⲓⲕⲟⲩϫⲓ

---

[1] *Cf* the Arabic corresponding to these 2 phrases in
another of Athanasius's books, HORNER, Boh NT 1, p lvii
infra and in Br Mus no 920, 267 *b*

[2] MS CURZON 147, last fol , whereof A was himself the
scribe, كاتبه

[3] MS CURZON 118 (A D 1795), last fol , من دير القديس
نكرى ابوته .

[4] Inadvertently omitted in my Catalogue

[5] At one time a metropolitan under Alexandria , *v*
VANSLEB, *Hist* 32

[6] HORNER 1, p cxxii

[7] *L c* lxxxii Elsewhere Peter Their names and
dates are uncertain , *cf* lists in STERN (Ersch and Gruber)
and Mrs BUTCHER s *Story of the Church*.

ⲛⲉⲙⲙⲏⲛ ⲥⲧⳓⲱⲛⲧ ⲉⲣⲱⲟⲩ ϣⲓⲛⲓ ⲉϫⲉⲛⲡⲁϣⲏⲣⲓ ⲭⲣⲓⲥ|35-ⲧⲟⲩⳉⲟⲗⲟⲅ ⲫⲁⲡⲓⲉⲡⲓⲥⲕⲟⲡⲟⲥ ⲛⲉⲙⲓⲱⲥⲏⲫ ⲫⲁⲡⲓⲡⲣⲉⲥⲃⲩⲧⲉⲣⲟⲥ | ⲛⲉⲙⲡⲉϥⲥⲟⲛ ⲛⲉⲙⲙⲓⲭⲁⲏⲗ ⲡⲓⲣⲉϥϩⲁⲩ ⲛⲉⲙⲑⲉⲟⲇⲟⲣⲟⲥ ⲡⲓⲣⲉϥ|ϣⲓ ⲛⲉⲙ ⲙⲓⲭⲁⲏⲗ ⲡⲓⲁⲣⲭⲏⲧⲥⲏⲧⲟⲛ ⲛⲉⲙⲙⲓⲭⲁⲏⲗ ⲡⲓⲕⲟⲧϫⲓ (*along margin*) ϣⲓⲛⲓ ⲉϫⲉⲛⲑⲉⲟⲇⲟⲣⲟⲥ ⲛⲉⲙ ⲥⲟⲗⲟⲙⲱⲛ ⲡⲓⲣⲉⲙⲫⲱⲧ ⲟⲩⲟϩ ⲁϫⲟⲥ ⲛⲱⲟⲩ ϫⲉⲡⲓⲙⲟⲩⳉ ⲁϥⲫⲟϩ ϣⲁⲣⲟⲛ | ϣⲓⲛⲓ ⲉϫⲉⲛⲙⲁⲣⲕⲟⲥ ⲡⲓⲣⲉϥⲥϧⲁⲓ ⲛϯⲕⲓϯ ⲛⲉⲙⲡⲉϥϣⲏⲣⲓ ϣⲓⲛⲓ ⲉϫⲉⲛⲡⲓⲥⲁϩ ⲓⲱⲥⲏⲫ ⲫⲁⲓⲁⲛⲟⲃⲟⲥ | 40 ⲛⲉϥ̇ⲛⲉϥϣⲏⲣⲓ ^sic ϣⲓⲛⲓ ⲉϫⲉⲛⲡⲉⲛϣⲏⲣⲓ ⲥⲉⲛⲟⲩⲑⲓⲟⲥ ⲫⲁⳉⲱⲣⲉⲁ ⲛⲉⲙⲉⲭⲉⲛⲫⲃⲱⲛ ⲫⲁⲡⲓⲫⲁⲙⲱⲛ ϣⲓⲛⲓ ⲉⲣⲟⲛ ⲉϫⲉⲛ ⲡⲉⲛϣⲏⲣⲓ ⲛⲓⲟⲩⲏⲃ ⲧⲏⲣⲟⲩ ⲛⲗⲁⲓⲕⲟⲥ ⲛⲉⲙⲛⲓⲟⲩⲏⲃ ⲧⲏⲣⲟⲩ ⲙⲙⲟⲛⲁⲭⲟⲥ ⲛⲉⲙⲙⲏⲛ ⲧⲏⲣⲟⲩ | ⲉⲧϣⲓⲛⲓ ⲉϧⲣⲏⲓ ⲉϫⲱⲛ ⲡⲁⲗⲓⲛ ⲛⲏ ⲧⲏⲣⲟⲩ ⲉⲧⳓⲁⲧⲟⲧⲉⲛ ⲛⲁⲓϣⲓⲛⲓ ⲉϫⲉⲛⲑⲏⲛⲟⲩ   ⲟⲩⲟϩ ⲡⲉϥ|ⲣⲉϥⲥϧⲁⲓ ⲡⲓⲣⲏⲕⲓ ⲡⲓⲕⲉⲣⲙⲁⲓ ⲡⲉⲧⲉⲛⲥⲟⲛ ⲅⲉⲱⲣⲅⲓⲟⲥ ⲫⲁⲕⲟⲥⲙⲁ ⲉϥϣⲓⲛⲓ ⲉϫⲉⲛⲑⲏⲛⲟⲩ ⲛⲉⲙⲥ|ϫⲉⲛⲟⲩⲟⲛ ⲛⲓⲃⲉⲛ ⲉⲧⲟⲩ ⲉⲣⲫⲙⲉⲩⲓ ⳉⲉⲛⲧⲁⲓⲉⲡⲓⲥⲧⲟⲗⲏ   ⲉϣⲱⲡ ⲇⲉ ⲁⲕϣⲁⲛϣⲓⲛⲓ ⲥϫⲉⲛⲫⲙⲟⲩ ⳉⲉⲛ|45-ⲫⲓⲁⲣⲓⲥ ϫⲉⲥϧⲏ ⳉⲉⲛⲡⲟⲣⲟⲛⲟⲥ ⲛⲧⲉ ϣⲗⲟⲗ ⲃ̄ ⲛⲉⲙⲕⲟⲥⲙⲁⲙ ^sic ⲙⲙⲁⲅⲁⲧⲟⲩ   ϯⲣⲏⲛⲏ ⲇⲉ ⲛ|ⲧⲉ ⲡⲟ̄ⲥ̄ ⲉⲥⲉϣⲱⲡⲓ ⲉϫⲉⲛⲑⲏⲛⲟⲩ ⲡⲓϣⲉⲡϩⲙⲟⲧ ⲇⲉ ⲫⲁϥϯ ϣⲁⲛⲓⲉⲛⲉϩ ⲧⲏⲣⲟⲩ ⲁⲙⲏⲛ

'(May) the first of every blessing (be) that fulfilled on and all grace (be) that over-shadowing the blessed, worshipful (-σέβεσθαι) son, the orthodox (ὀρθόδ), reverend deacon, the great ruler (ἄρχων), the loving and beloved, (who is) in the right (5) faith of Our Lord, Jesus Christ[1], 'master' Basoph[2], the son of Elias   May God bless him with the spiritual (πνευματικός) blessings that did descend upon His apostles and His prophets and upon such as do His will and His commandments (ἐντολή), in all generations (γενεά), through the intercession (πρεσβεία) of the Virgin (παρθ) (10) at all times   Amen

After the ascription of blessings unto him and the spiritual salutation (πνευμ, ἀσπασμός) to him, we shall inform thee (*sic*), our son, that, since the day whereon we came forth from Fustât, there hath not reached us from you a letter (ἐπ), wherein is (news of) your health[3], (15) and our mind is troubled regarding you, especially (μάλιστα) seeing we have been informed of the terrible plague[4] (that is) in Fustat, and our soul (ψυ) was very greatly grieved on thy account, O my beloved son, and that of all our children that are in Fustât But we, for our part, do beseech (20) Christ, our God, that (ἵνα) He will take from off us and you both plague and every evil thing, and that He will suffer us to see your face in all prosperity (ἀγαθόν)

Greet on our behalf thy father and all thy house and all them that are related unto thee   Greet on our behalf the priests of the church (25) (of) Zebile[5] and the deacons Greet our son Solomon and Mark of Rosetta[6] and Mark   [7] and all his house and Persôma[8] and Isaac and all those in Chônon[9]   Greet Antonius and Apa Noub and Senouthius, the men of Siôti[10]   Greet the Servant of the (30) angel (ἄγγελος), son of

---

[1] *Cf* phrases in the Arabic colophon of no 434

[2] واصف Very probably the person wrongly called 'Yûsuf' in Br Mus no 724, where the name is بواصف (Ⲓⲱⲁⲥⲁⲫ) He was scribe of MS Curzon 118 and dwelt in the Darb Adam, on the bank (رصيف) of the Azbakiyah pond (*l c*, f 165 *b*) ⲥⲁϩ in such a text would translate معلم

[3] *Lit* 'peace' *Cf* سلام

[4] *Lit* 'death' So below *Cf* ⲙⲟⲩ in Turaef, *Materialy*, no 12

[5] Hârah Zuwailah V Butler, *Churches* 1 271 Spelt

ⲍⲁⲃⲏⲗⲏ in Horner's Boh NT, 1, p cv, ⲍⲉϩⲟⲩⲗⲟⲛ else-where (*Bull Inst fi anç* 1 170)

[6] Thus spelt in the *Scala*, v Amélineau, *Géogr* 558 &c

[7] Apparently a name or epithet Pronounce ? *Ôshaj*

[8] Barsaumâ

[9] *Cf* ⲙⲟⲭⲟⲛⲟⲛ, Amélineau, *op cit* 578

[10] Perhaps for ⲧⲉⲙⲥⲓⲱⲧ Damsîs, or ϯⲡⲉⲣⲥⲓⲱϯ Gizah (*op cit* 580), possibly even for ⲥⲓⲱⲟⲩϯ Siût (*cf* ⲣⲉⲙϣⲧⲧⲉ above)

Joseph, and his brethren, and the Servant of the Holy One (ἅγιος)[1], the(ir) lordships' scribe, and his brethren and the son of his father's brother, George   Greet 'master' George the dyer, and his sons and his son's son, little George, and those related unto them   Greet my son (35) Christodulus of (the household of?)[2] the bishop, and Joseph of (the household of?) the presbyter, and his brother and Michael the overseer[3], and Theodore the weighing officer[4], and Michael the architect (ἀρχιτέκτων) and little Michael   Greet Theodore and Solomon the   [5], and tell them that the wax hath reached us   Greet Mark the scribe of the treasury[6] and his son   Greet 'master' Joseph, son of Jacob, (40) and his sons   Greet our son Senouthius, son of Dōrea[7], and the servant, son of Piphamōn   Greet on our behalf all our sons the lay (λαικός) priests[8] and all the monastic (μοναχός) priests and all such as do greet us   Further (πάλιν) all they that are with us will greet you

And his scribe, the poor cinder, your brother George, son of Cosma[9], would greet you and all them that are mentioned in this epistle (ἐπ)

And (δέ) if thou shouldest ask concerning the plague in (45) the southern country, (we would inform you) that it is in the diocese (θρόνος) of the Two Shmouns[10] and Koskam alone

And (δέ) may the peace (εἰρήνη) of the Lord be upon you   And (δέ) thanks are (due) to God unto all ages   Amen '

---

[1] This should be the translation of عبد القدوس , the preceding of عبد الملاك   Marcus Bey Simaika informs me that both are common among the Copts of to-day   The fashion thus to translate seems not unusual, v Lagarde, Aeg 238, PSBA xxix 201, 202   Of names now in use a large number are given on p 355 ff of the work cited on p 204, note

[2] I know not if φα- can have this meaning

[3] ? باطر

[4] ? وزان

[5] ρεμ- should imply a place-name   So here scarcely 'masons', 'sculptors' (the verb has a variety of meanings)

[6] Lu ' of money ' (drachmas)

[7] Probably intended for an Arabic name, perhaps درى though Simaika tells me that this is rare

[8] Presumably the secular clergy   Cf Cairo Euchol ⲭⲩ, ⲛⲉⲛⲓⲟϯ ⲙⲙⲟⲛⲁⲭⲟⲥ ⲕⲉ ⲛⲉⲛⲓⲟϯ ⲛⲗⲁⲓⲕⲟⲥ

[9] This is the translator of the Bohairic Apostolical Canons in A D 1804 (Lagarde, Aeg. 238, cf p iv infra)

[10] Ashmunain

ADDENDA

462.—Papyrus, a fragment, 17×38 cm (width complete). Script unusually large, sloping uncials, characterized (like several hands among the Ashmunain documents) by the absence of the middle tooth in ω and ⲱ   *Cf* Pl 10, no 159   *Recto* ↑

Will of Pouroush[1] and Archôntia, relating to land to be inherited by their son, Justa (Justus)   The only will hitherto found among Ashmunain papyri

ⲁ̀ⲛⲟⲕ ⲡⲟⲩⲣⲟⲩ[ϣ ⲙ̄ⲛⲁⲣⲭⲱⲛⲧⲓⲁ] |]ⲕⲁϩ ⲙ̄ⲡⲉⲛϣⲏⲣⲉ ⲓⲟⲩⲥⲧⲁ ⲉⲧⲁⲁ[ϥ ⲉⲃⲟⲗ] |] ⲙⲉⲛⲧⲟⲓⲅⲉ ⲇⲉ
ⲙ̄ⲛⲥⲁⲙⲙⲟ[ⲩ] ⲇⲉ ⲛⲁⲣⲭⲱⲛ[ⲧⲓⲁ   ]ⲧ̄ . . ⲛ̄ⲃ̄ϫⲉⲓ ⲡⲉⲓⲫⲟⲣⲟⲥ |] ⲛⲁⲥ ⲛ̄ϩⲟⲩⲛ ϣⲁⲓ[. . . .]ⲕ |] ⲁⲣ-
ⲭⲱ]ⲛⲧⲓⲁ . ⲙⲣⲉⲛⲧⲓ ⲧⲉϥⲟⲓⲕⲟⲥⲕⲉⲩⲏ [ⲛ]ⲁϥ ⲛ̄[. .] | ⲧ . ⲙ . . . ⲛ . . . ⲉⲧⲁⲛⲥⲙⲏⲛⲧⲉ ⲁ[ⲡⲟ]ⲛ ⲡⲟⲩⲣⲟⲩϣ
ⲙ̄ⲛⲁⲣⲭⲱⲛⲧⲓⲁ ⲙ̄[.] | ϫⲓⲛⲉϥϩⲟⲓⲧⲉ ⲛ̄ⲧⲓ ϩⲓⲱⲱϥ ⲙ̄ⲛⲛ̄ⲥⲁⲙⲙⲟⲩ ⲇⲉ ⲛⲉϥⲣϫⲟⲉⲓⲥ ⲛ̄ⲧⲓⲥⲓⲧⲓⲱϩⲉ |
ⲛ̄ⲧⲁⲛϣⲏⲣⲡⲉϩⲁⲓⲥ ⲛⲥⲉⲓ ⲉ̅ⲣⲁⲓ ⲉⲣⲟϥ ⲙ̄ⲛⲉ . [| ⲧⲉⲛⲉϣ . ⲧⲏⲛⲟⲩ ⲙⲟⲩϩ ⲉⲡⲉⲛⲧⲁⲛⲧⲁⲁϥ [

Verso blank

463.—Papyrus, a fragment, 10×7 cm   Script ligatureless   Fibres →.

Guarantee (ἐγγύη) by Theodore to the κῦρις Taurinus, regarding a working tenant, for whom he goes surety and whom he will himself replace in case of failure, provided Taurinus retain him (the tenant) until the covenanted term   *Cf* no 134

]ⲉⲛⲟ[|]ⲣⲁⲥ ⲛ̄ⲡⲉϥⲣ̄ⲟⲉ ⲉⲣⲉⲛⲕⲉ[. | . .]ⲓ . . ⲉⲡⲓ ⲧⲱ ⲛⲟ ⲛ̄ϩⲉ[ⲧⲟⲓⲙⲱⲥ ⲛ̄ⲡⲉϥϫⲉ ⲛϥⲣⲡ̄ⲧⲓ | ⲛ̄ⲣⲟⲙ̄ⲡⲉ
ⲛⲁⲕ ⲧⲁⲕⲱⲧⲉ[2] | ⲛⲁⲕ ⲁⲛⲟⲕ ⲁⲩⲱ ⲛ̄ⲡⲣⲣⲱⲙⲉ | ⲕⲱⲧⲉ ϩⲁⲣⲟⲓ ⲉⲡⲓ ⲧⲱ ⲧⲁⲧⲓ | ⲙⲁⲁϥ ⲛ̄ϩⲟⲗⲟⲕⲟⲧⲧⲓⲛ
ⲛⲁⲕ ϩⲁⲡⲉⲕⲥⲱⲙ ⲙ̄ⲛⲡⲉⲕ|ⲫⲟⲣⲟⲥ ⲛⲁⲧϩⲁⲛ ⲛⲁⲧⲛⲟ͞ⲙⲉ | ⲛⲁⲧⲗⲁⲁⲩ ⲛⲁⲙ̄ⲫⲓⲃⲟⲗⲉⲓⲁ | ⲁⲩⲱ ⲛ̄ⲧⲟⲕ ϩⲱⲱⲕ
ⲡⲕⲩⲣ/ | ⲧⲁⲩⲣⲓⲛⲉ ⲛⲁ . ⲧⲥⲕ[ϥⲟ]ⲛϥ | ⲃⲟⲗ ϣⲁⲛⲧⲉϥϫⲱⲕ ⲛⲉϥⲣⲟⲙ̄ⲡⲉ | . ⲉ . ⲛ̄ϣⲁⲛⲟⲩⲱϣ ⲉϥⲟⲛϥ |
[ⲉ]ⲃⲟⲗ |

Verso ⳨[3] ⲥⲏ ⲙⲛⲧⲛ ⲛ̄ϩⲟⲗⲟⲕⲟⲧⲧⲓⲛ | ⲛⲟⲩϥ ⲛⲁⲧⲗⲁⲁⲩ ⲛⲁⲙ̄ⲫⲓⲃⲟⲗ⳿ | ⲉⲓⲱⲣⲕ ⲁⲛⲟⲕ ⲑⲉⲟⲇⲱⲣⲉ |
ⲛ̄ⲡⲛⲟⲩⲧⲉ ⲛ̄ⲡⲁⲛⲧⲟⲕⲣⲁⲧⲱⲣ | ϫⲛ̄ⲛⲓϣ̄ⲡⲁⲣⲁϥⲁ ⲡⲣⲟⲥ | ϭⲟⲙ ⲉⲧⲓⲥⲅⲅⲩⲏ ⲉⲣⲉϩⲱϥ ⲛⲓⲙ | ⲉⲡⲱⲙⲉ ϩⲩⲡⲟ-
ⲕⲓⲥⲑⲁⲓ ⲛⲁⲕ | ⳨[4] ⲁⲛⲟⲕ ⲑⲉⲟⲇⲱⲣⲉ ⲡϣⲉ ⲛ̄ⲡⲁⲡⲛⲟⲩⲧⲉ ⲧⲓⲥⲧⲟⲓⲭ/ | ⲉⲧⲓⲥⲅⲅⲩⲏ ⲛ̄ⲑⲉ ⲉⲥⲥⲏϩ | ⲙⲙⲟⲥ
⳨[5] ⲁⲛⲟⲕ ⲙⲁⲕ|ⲁⲣⲉ ⲡⲓⲁ ⲡⲛⲟⲩⲧ[ⲉ

464.—Paper, complete, 9×6½ cm   Script *v* Pl 2

A Tax-receipt[6], obscure but interesting, as being dated, 'in this year 397'   The

---

[1] *V* Br Mus, p 449
[2] *V* nos 158, 159, KRALL cxi
[3] The text here is in the reverse direction and, there being traces of a line above that first preserved, the ⳨ is difficult to account for

[4] Different hand   [5] Different hand
[6] Before I had recognized the nature of this text, the Plates had been arranged   I was however still able to withdraw the description from its erroneous context and relegate it to this place

corresponding Arabic (*verso*, end of l 3) has 398. This is doubtless the Muslim era, in which 397=A D 1006-7

$$\overset{o}{\text{ñ}}_{/} \text{ s } \varrho\text{ı}\dagger\text{p}\text{o}\lambda\pi\text{e}\text{ τaı } \overline{\text{τ}\bar{\varsigma}} \mid \text{κπоо̄ } \overline{\text{аı}}^{1} \text{ εоγ } \overline{\text{κ}\bar{\varsigma}} \text{ ετω}\dot{\text{ß}}\text{·} \mid \varrho\text{ı}\text{αωηбıα}^{2} \text{ ελλωηсωρ } \mid \text{ ς ηαсαρ:}$$
$$\lambda\lambda\text{η } \text{ s } \overline{\text{ıı}}_{/} \text{ λεη } \mid \text{ ηεπεı απογλκαсελ } \mid$$

Mansur and Naser have paid a sum which, according to l 1 of the Arabic, should be 7 νομίσματα   Yet the sign following ñ/ is more like 'half', that for 7, in the dates, being differently formed   The meaning of ll 4, 5 is obscure possibly a transcript of Arabic words   Is Abu 'l-Kâsım another payer?   His name appears to terminate the last line of Arabic, which begins دع على بن مصور ونسر[3]

465.—Papyrus, complete , $6 \times 8\frac{1}{2}$ cm   Script seldom ligatured   *Verso →*. Not from the Ashmunain collection

Account (λόγος) for half a ξέστης[4] (?) of oil, paid to the boys who guard the vineyard-meadow

$$\dagger\varrho\text{аθωρ } \text{ı} \bar{\text{θ}} \text{ επλοκος ηεκογı } \mid \text{ ψηρε ετρε}\overset{sic}{\text{ıλ}} \text{ λλφоı λλ}\overline{\text{б}}\mid\text{ωλλ огηаψ }\overline{\text{ζ}}\text{ε[ε]τρ}^{\text{е}} \text{ ηηη}\varrho$$
$$\text{γεωργε ετηχε } +$$

Recto. A Greek Account

466 —Another fragment having been subsequently joined to that given on p 107 as no 219, the text now reads

$$\dagger \text{ ηκοıηωη επτıλλε [} \mid \text{ λλπιωсηφ ηалнгı[ε } \mid \text{ πψε ηÁ̄ıητωρ λλη[} \mid \text{ λλππαπιογτε πψε}$$
$$\text{ıı [} \mid \text{ space } \mid \dagger \text{ γεıιηалн λλππсεεπε [} \mid \text{ фоıÁалλλωη о Áоηθос [} \mid \text{]χοιιτη η[} \mid \text{]τоıı}$$
$$\text{ετс[}\mid\text{η]ψε [ıı}$$

The authors are the κοινόν and headmen of a village

---

[1] The second o was corrected to ıı, for ηaı
[2] The form of ϙıχη- usual *e g* in the alchemistic texts
[3] مس can scarcely be read in the Arabic
[4] Rather ξέστμξ or another diminutive form

467 [52].—The Arabic Texts bound together in no 429 fill foll 2–171 (counting from the end) The 3 hands in which they are written all appear tolerably modern

A. Foll 2–17. The Service of the Holy Lamp, described as no 429 above

B Foll 18–48, in a different hand   Four Prayers طلباب 1 'Prayer for general use' دعرى كل الإوقات Beg دا سمى نسوع المسبح ارجمى با سمى نسوع المسبح اسالك با سمى (each petition ends thus) 2 'Prayer to be said each day and may God accept the sayer' Beg سمحدانك لا الإه الا الا انك با رب كل سى 3 'Prayer for absolution, from the Gospel of Luke' Beg اعفر لى با مں ارسل الملاك لزكرىا والمصابات (each petition begins thus) با نعسى سمى 4 'Prayer composed from the Scriptures,' by بعض المحادسں الحطاه Beg سمى (each phrase, for half the prayer, begins with الذى احرجك مں العدم الى الوحود .(سمى).

C Foll 49–145   Prayers طلباب, 50 in number, by 'the virtuous and pious priest مس, Anbâ Peter of Sedment' السدمتى or السدمنى The 1st begins اللهم انا دعوىك اسمحبى Several are modelled closely upon the phraseology of the لى وفى النسىه فرح عى Psalter

D Foll 147–162 'The Ritual of the Service of Abû Tarabô, for him whom a mad dog hath bitten' الكلب الكلب (sic) لمں عطه درسب عمل ابو دربوا This curious magical service has been edited, in a rather more condensed form, by E GALTIER[2] Other copies of it are in the Vatican[3] and one, incomplete, in the Aberdeen University Library[4]

The sequence of the ritual differs in the MSS, those of GALTIER (G) and Aberdeen (A) resembling each other as against ours (R) The rubric, with which all open, is in R

واحد الكاهں سبع حراب مں دفسى بعمل فطر حمر دومه وفں بعبحں دلا ملح وسبع حساب طرده دلا ملح وقليل زيت طمس[5] وبسبر مں حمر وبوقں سراج حديدں درسب طمس ودبجمع سبع صعار موبسبں دكور وحاصه وهم صدام وبحلس المرىص الذى عصه الكلں الكلب فى الوسط وبعلف على كعبه حرج او محلاه وبسرك فبها الحمر والحبس واباء الحمر كلبں مبهم دعرده ثم دلا اداء فحار حديدں ماء حلوا ويكشف الكاهں راسه ويصلى معه السماس هكذى بقول الشبهبوب ودفوع البحور وهم درسلوا فى χ̄ς̄ ̄ ̄ epc̄ π̄, aλ, neλ neλ neλ π̄ بقولوا ثم τenoγώϣτ[6] fanterωon am̄n ten(oγ)ώϣτ m̄mok e π̄χ̄c̄[7] ̄ ̄ ̄ epc̄ π̄, aλ, neλ neλ neλ π̄ البحور وهم درسلوا فى الى احره دعال اوسمه المرىص باللحں السوى Here follow the Lessons in Coptic and Arabic[8] Eph iii 13–15 (Ar –17), Ps vi 1, 2, Matt xv 21–28, followed by the 'Response' مرں of the Gospel[9], the 3 Prayers (for fathers, peace and congregation) and this Blessing, ϧenoγmeϧmhi epepismoγ nte

---

[1] In the Fayyûm V Makrizi, Monasteries no 32, As-Safadî, Târîh p 22₁₉ Other works of Peter 'the Armenian RIEDEL, Katâl Abû 'l-Barakât p 698, MAI iv pp 248, 250, ZOTENBERG's Ethiop Cat p 73 His date, according to MAI's MS, should be A D 1200, not 1062

[2] Bulletin de l'Inst franç iv 105 The identification with Θεράπων has been questioned (P PEETERS in Anal Boll xxv 341) CL GANNEAU proposes Θεράπειων (Rec d Arch Or vii 369) Were it not that a different transcription (prosthetic l and ط for ت) seems needed, I would suggest درىوا = Τρυφω(ν), a saint of many transformations (z H GÜNTER, Legenden-Studien 66), to whom the demon appears in form of a fiery-eyed dog (MIGNE, P G 114, 1316 C)

[3] MAI iv 187, v 146 I have not consulted these MSS

[4] The MS belonged to DR GRANT BEY and is dated A D 1795   [5] Olive-oil V p 58 n

[6] Presumably the melody proper to the hymn in Theotokia p 141, cf Cairo Euchologion p 30 The following κυριε &c are doubtless from the Service of Morning Incense, but I cannot precisely identify each

[7] V Eucholog pp 19, 46 &c

[8] The lessons, and their sequence in the service, differ in the other MSS in G, Rom xv 1–4, Ps vi 3, 2, Joh v 1–18, in A, Rom vi 12, 13, Ps lxiv 4, 2, Joh v 1–18

[9] ? The Doxology, oγoϩ nooκπe etecepπpeπi nak, Cairo Eucholog 103

ⲡⲓⲁⲥⲕⲩⲧⲏⲥ ⲁⲃⲃⲁ ⲑⲁⲣⲡⲟⲩ ⲡⲓⲙⲟⲗⲟⲅⲓⲧⲏⲥ ⲁϥⲉⲓ ⲝⲟⲥ(sic) ⲧⲏⲣⲟⲩ ⲝⲉⲁⲙⲏⲛ ⲁⲥⲉϣⲱⲡⲓ Then comes the History سيرة of Abba Tarabō *Beg* كان فى زمان الاصطهاد۱ فى ايام الملك الكافر دعلادياۇس It relates how this pious and charitable person, zealous for martyrdom, suffered at the hands of the pagans and lay in prison until released by the edict of Constantine, and how thereafter he chanced to encounter at midday a mad dog, 'the water dripping from his mouth, والماء سائل fierce and walking awry, as one lame, turning this way and that, his eyes being as yellow gold and he like unto one drunken with wine,' من فاه٢ مستجمعًا يمشى على حسه منل الاعرج۲ يميل على هذه الناحمه وهذه الناحمه وعساه كالذهب الاصفر وهو كالسكران من الخمر Seeing him thus possessed, Abba T prays and Michael, forthwith coming to his aid, slays the dog with his wand عصا The evil spirit promises never more to enter where the names of God and Abba T may be, while the angel announces that God has given the saint power over 'this foul spirit', both in life and after death, so that when either man or beast be bitten and the victim cry on the God of Abba T, 'straightway, by the will of God, I (*sc* Michael) will take forth from him its poison and he shall not be shaken يزعزع, nor upset, nor terrified, neither shall aught of ill befall him, nor the mad dog's poison harm him   Make their sign in God's name and thine' A widow's only son, being bitten, is sent by his mother to Abba T, bearing a present of 7 unsalted loaves, 7 fresh, unsalted cheeses طرمس ملح بلا حساب, 7 bunches of grapes سمراب and a little olive-oil and wine, all wrapped in a white cloth الازار On learning his need, Abba T summons 7 pure boys سبعة غلمان حطبة and, bidding them follow him and respond to each word he shall say, he sets the widow's son with his gifts before him, placing in front of him the oil and wine and a jar وعاء of fresh water Then he turns 7 times round the bitten boy, followed by the 7 children, to whom he says, 'Welcome children مرحبا نكم ادها الاطفال, peace unto you,' while they reply, 'And unto thee peace, O master' He 'What seek ye?' They 'Healing we seek, for this unhappy one, that the mad dog hath bitten' He 'Depart in peace The Lord shall cure and heal him, for His trusty promise unto me, His servant, that do confess His name' Here follows a long prayer by Abba T, including Ps xc The ceremony concludes with further ritual The first of the 7 boys approaches the priest, the whole congregation meanwhile joining hands, and says, 'Peace unto thee, O teacher of teachers⁴' The priest replies, questioning him as before, but here healing is sought for all such as may have been bitten Then, as each time they repeat their circuits round the supplicant, 7 to right and 7 to left, they say, ⲛⲓⲥⲟⲉⲛⲥ ⲡⲓⲥⲟⲛⲉ⁵. Then the priest takes the first boy's hand and all bark يعوى like dogs and bite at the unleavened bread سهس من العطمر, until it is consumed, the victim standing in their midst the while and saying, 'By the prayers of the saintly Abba T, may the Lord accept your prayers and grant me healing speedily,' after which the priest dismisses them with his blessing⁶ To this ritual is appended the following charm, 'useful

---

¹ G الاطهار   ² G عرح من سوا, A *om*
³ G A المقطوع
⁴ Reading معلم المعلمين for معلم المعلم
⁵ MS A, ⲛⲓⲥⲟⲉ 'Perhaps meant for some form of πιστεύειν
⁶ MS A has lost some leaves here, but its last words show that the results of the ritual were to be ensured by

more material means 'and he (*sc* the victim) shall eat the piece of unleavened cake that has been placed in the oil and taken from the boys' (*plur*) mouths and shall be anointed with the oil and shall drink of the water and wash therewith, so shall he be made whole by the blessing of the saintly Abba T Thereafter the priest shall say the blessing &c'

against trembling[1]' فادة للحلم 'Let him write (this) upon two leaves of paper ورقتين and he shall be healed by God Almighty's leave And this is what he shall write In the name of God, the Compassionate, the Merciful Let the trembling حلم die out from the body of NN , the son of NN ' Here 3 magical signs[2], ⊏⎯⎯⎯⎯⎯⎯⊐, ⊏⎯⎯⎯⎯⎯⎯⊐, ⊏⎯⎯⎯⎯⎯⊐, the 1st 6, the 2nd 3, the 3rd 6 times 'O plant, sprouting in the body ! he that dieth, doth die, die, die, by the power of Him that liveth and dieth not' ايها النبات المنبوت فى جسم من يموت موت موت موت بعون الحى الذى لا يموت

E Fol 163 *a, b* A Charm against the Evil Eye This text, similar in several features to Syriac[3] and Greek charms[4], is found in identical form in Ethiopic[5]

بسم اللّه الخالق الحى الباطف رقوات العين والنظره لما كان سيدنا يسوع المسيح له المحن
دمشى على سحره طرده وهو وتلاميده[١] الاطهار وانا هو امراه عجور ولها مساهل نار تخرج من
فاها الى ذرا طولها سبون ذراعا ولها انماب ومخالب كمخالس الاسد وعيناها[١] نشغل كالذهب
وهى معرعه حنا[ً] احاب سيدنا يسوع المسيح له المحن وقال لتلاميده ما هاى[ا] وليس امرها كان
عنه محفى لكى حنى صارت دامره دما فعلوا ادها فعالوا له سيدنا هذه هى العد[ين] الشريره
الرديه الذى اذا نطرة[ً] سايره فى المح[ار] افلتنها دم دمها وانا نطره الى ورا[سه] فى
مسوارها ومطرنها دراكبها وانا نطره د[عره] بحلبي فطع لبها وانا نطره الى امراه واولا[د]دها[ا] (163ـ)
حياها ناذرب فى هلاكهم فاحاب سيدنا يسوع المسيح وقال لتلاميده ان كان هذه فعال هذه
العين الملعونه الرديه فخدوها واحرقوها بالنار ونزروها على الاربعه ارداج السرفى والغربى والعلى
والبحرى وسخرج هذه العين الملعونه الرديه من عندك حامل هذه الصلاه بعون اهباشر اهما
ادوداى الرب الصادووت الشناى (sic) وبشساعه الست السمه مريم العذرى وبعوه مارى مرقس
الابحملى وحميع الشهداء والعدسسى والابا والانمداء والرسل الاطهار والادرار الاى وكل اوان والى
دهر الدهرس امس   تم وكمل صلات العس النطره بعون اللّه تعالى امس

'In the name of God, the Creator, the Living ! Pronouncing of the charms of the Eye and the Glance[6] —When Our Master Jesus Christ (unto whom glory) was walking by the Lake of Tiberias He and His pure disciples, lo, an old woman, foith from whose mouth went flames of fire[7] to a length of 60 ells, and she had tusks and claws, like to the claws of a lion, and her eyes gleamed like gold, and she was very frightful to behold Our Master Jesus Christ (unto whom glory) answered and said unto His disciples, 'Who is this[8]?' And her being was not hid from Him, but in order that   what they would do unto her[9] And they said unto Him, 'O Our Master, this is the wicked Evil Eye,

---

[1] A symptom of hydrophobia

[2] Of a type not unlike those common in Muslim magic, e g Z f Assyr xx 409, line 14

[3] Cf those published by H Gollancz, *11th Or Congr* , Pt iv, esp pp 92 93

[4] Cf Reitzenstein, *Poimandres* 297, 298

[5] Two versions exist among the charms collected by Prof Littmann Dr W H Worrell (Michigan University), who is editing these (*Stud z abessin Zauberwesen*), has kindly supplied me with versions

[6] Ethiop , 'Prayer concerning Nadarâ ' Worrell hesitates, on phonetic grounds, to identify this with Arab نظر

[7] The Ethiop confirms this, though the form appears unknown

[8] The question in the Eth is the disciples', the reply Christ's But the following explanatory words are there wanting

[9] Reading لكن I do not understand the following words Perhaps يامر Eth has no parallel

which, when[1] she looketh upon a ship sailing in the sea, overturneth it with those therein, and when she looketh upon a horse in its course, upsetteth it with its rider; and when she looketh upon a cow about to be milked, cutteth off its milk, and when she looketh upon a woman and her children (163 *b*) before her[2], they go speedily to destruction' And Our Master Jesus Christ answered and said to His disciples, 'If these be the deeds of this accursed, wicked Eye, take ye her and burn her with fire and scatter her unto the 4 winds, the east and west and south and north' And the accursed, wicked Eye shall go forth from Thy servant that beareth this prayer, by the might of 'I am that I am'[3], Adonai, the Lord of Hosts, El Shaddai, and by the mediation of the Lady and Mistress Mary, the Virgin, and by the might of Mâri Marcus the Evangelist, and all the martyrs and saints and the fathers and the prophets and the pure and holy apostles, now and evermore and for ever and ever Amen Finished and completed is the prayer of the Eye and the Glance, by the help of God Almighty Amen'

F Foll 164-166 The Letter of Abgar to Christ, رسالة العبس ارعاندوس' الذى هو, and Christ's reply, الجواب من سيدنا المح The text is the same as that edited by HYVERNAT in TIXERONT's *Origines de l'Église d'Édesse*, pp 98, 200, ending with the names of the 7 seals affixed to the second Letter

G. Foll 167-171, in a different hand Extracts فصول from the Gospels Luke i 26-38, *ib* x. 38-42, Matthew xii 35-50, Luke i 39-56 Each ends with والمحد لله

---

[1] The same enumeration in Eth as here

[2] ? حداء

[3] *V* Exod iii 14 For this name, thus transcribed, and the following, *v* GOLDZIHER in *ZDMG*. xlviii 359 and

Z f Assyr xx 244, also the above Syriac charms, pp 79, 90, and L BLAU, *Altjud Zauberwesen* 103

[4] *Sic* for اوعاربوس

ADDITIONS AND CORRECTIONS

n = note.

Page 3, line 10   Read p̄λc̄

„   7, l 15   Read ϥⲡⲉⲕⲁⲩⲗⲏ

„   11, penul'   Read ⲛⲡⲉⲣⲓⲙⲛⲟⲩⲥⲓⲏ (ὑπερυμνοῦσιν)

„   14, no e 5   Cf Cod Vatic Arab clxxii, 99 b صاحب
الموت العظم فى الاسماء اشعيا

„   15, l 14   JUNKER (in Oriens Christ vi 332) points
out that this is identical with part of Brit Mus
no 161

,   16, l 4 from below, ⲛⲁⲧⲥ̄   The devil loq

„   17, n 2   Cf BALESTRI-HYVERNAT, Acta (CSCO)
I 194, ϥⲓⲱⲧ ⲙⲡⲁⲓⲙⲟⲛⲁⲥⲧⲏⲣⲓⲟⲛ, Mission franç
IV 175, ϥⲓⲱⲧ ⲙⲡⲁⲓⲧⲟⲡⲟⲥ, Hist Patr (EVETTS)
510, هذا الحبل ابل (of Macarius in Scete)

„   19, n 4   Read ⲁⲣⲭⲁⲅⲅⲉⲗⲟⲥ

„   24, l 21   Read ἀσκεῖν

„   29, l 19   I may here mention a fragment in the
collection of the Patriarch, at Cairo, which shows
the following colophon ⲁⲩⲱ ⲝ[. . . .]ⲙⲉ
ⲉⲃⲟⲗ ⲙⲡⲉϥⲃⲓⲟⲥ ⲛϭⲓ ⲡⲙⲁⲕⲁⲣⲓⲟⲥ ⲁⲡⲁ ⲓⲱⲣⲁⲛ-
ⲏⲏⲥ ⲡⲁⲡⲁⲭⲱⲣⲓⲧⲏⲥ ⲛⲥⲟⲩⲭⲟⲟⲧⲟⲧⲉ ⲙⲡⲉⲃⲟⲓ
ⲉⲁϣⲱⲣ ⲡⲉⲧⲉϣⲁⲩⲙⲟⲩⲧⲉ ⲉⲣⲟϥ ⲉⲱⲱϥ [ⲉⲛⲟⲩ]-
ⲉⲩⲛⲓⲁⲥⲓⲙⲁ ϫ[ⲉⲛ]ⲁⲣ[ⲁ]ϫ[ⲉⲓ]ⲕⲟⲥ ⲉⲛⲟⲩⲉⲓⲣⲏⲛ[ⲏ
&c   This fragment is from the MS of ZOEGA
no clxv, Brit Mus no 333   Another, from the
same MS and in the same collection, shows a
decided relationship with the chapter on John
of Lycopolis in the Hist Monach   The title
'Paradise', applied thus to a Life of John, is
noteworthy   (Cancel reference in note 6 to Brit
Mus 333)

,   38, l 5   For]ⲏⲡⲧⲉ[, read]ⲓⲣ ⲉⲛ ⲧⲱ [ⲡ]ⲡⲓ]ⲏⲁ |
This is perhaps, like no 81 ff, a Festal Letter
The Greek text was upon one side only

„   39, n 1   Add   the long 8th century Letter, lately
acquired for Berlin.

,   46, l 9   For Tôhe, v p 173, n 2

„   „ l 15   The full text in BASSET'S Synaxarium
(Patrol Or), 11th Kîhak

„   penult   On the Greek texts relating to these martyrs
v now KRUMBACHER in Munich Academy, Abh
xxiv Bd (iii), 78

„   47, l 25   Read about 13 letters

„   „ n 3   In BALESTRI-HYVERNAT, op cit, 13, a
wooden wheel, ⲭⲁⲗⲓⲁ, is used to saw the martyr's
body in two, cf ib 72 ἀστήριον, 113 τροχός

,   54, n 5   cik occurs in HYVERNAT, Actes 313, infra

,   59, n 3   ⲁⲛⲕⲉⲫⲟⲗⲟⲥ is merely ἐγκέφαλος The form
ⲁⲛⲕⲉⲫⲟⲗⲟⲥ also in BALESTRI-HYVERNAT, II,
144 &c

„   61, l 18   The formula should be ⲧⲉⲕⲕⲗⲏⲥⲓⲁ ⲛⲧⲡⲟⲗⲓⲥ
ⲙⲙⲁⲓⲛⲉⲭⲥ̄, though there is hardly space for
all that

„   63   A photograph of no 115 appears in CAETANI'S
Annali, ii (I), 696

„   68 l 20   For ⲣⲟⲙⲉ, read ⲣⲟⲙⲡⲉ

„.   69, l 15   For ⲥⲱⲛ, read ⲥⲁⲓⲛ

„   „ penult   ⲯⲁⲭⲟ is here rather a name, as such
it is frequently found in the Jkôw (Aphroditô)
papyri

Page 70, l 13   Read ⲉⲁⲡⲉϥⲓⲡⲣ[ⲟⲥⲱⲡⲟⲏ

„   „ n 4   PREISIGKE's publication (Griech Pap
zu Strassburg, 1 (II), 1908, nos 46 ff) of a series
of 6th century deeds of surety suggests an explanation of these formulae   Λόγος would be
'excuse', σταυρός and σχῆμα μοναχοῦ (?) would
refer to exemption or asylum, claimed on the
ground of proximity to sacred objects (cf P 's
θείων χαρακτήρων) or of monastic vows, while
'Sunday' and 'festival' would correspond to
P 's ἁγίας κυριακῆς   νε ἀπράκτου ἡμέρας (KENYON
suggests ἐν ἐμπράκτω ἡμέρα)   Cf also Pap
Oxyrh, cxxxv, cited by WENGER, Rechtshist
Papyrusstud 59

„   71, l 15   Traces of the protocol are visible, above
the text, on the verso

„   78, l 5 from below   Read ⲙⲉⲣ[ⲟⲥ]   Cf REVILLOUT,
Actes ⲕⲉ̄

,   82, l 3   For ⲉⲣⲟⲟⲩ, read ⲉⲣⲟⲟⲩ.

„   „ l 16   For ⲥⲱⲛ, read ⲥⲁⲓⲛ

„   „ n 5   A Balaiza fragment (now in the Bodleian),
with a list of utensils, has ⲛⲡⲓⲁⲝ ⲛϭⲱⲡⲉ̄

,   86, n 1   For 32, read 33

„   87, l 24   The occurrence of ⲗⲁⲩⲁⲛⲉ is to be noted
(cf Brit Mus Catal, p 522, infra)   But there
is no evidence whence the present MS came

„   88, no 166   For recto, read verso, and conversely

„   90, l 3   The following small piece has since been
added above l 1] ⲧⲓⲙⲉⲣⲓ ⲡⲣⲱⲙⲉ ϣⲙⲓ[

„   „ n 4   This name in Arabic ⲀⲘϥⲒⲚⲈⲀⲨ, Geogr
399, 403, the Synaxarium having ابلا Ib.,
123, one might read اعاني (cf HALL, l c), did
not Ethiopic 'Agâbiyos' confirm 'Agapit'

„   92, nos 179, 180   These are not tax, but rent
receipts

„   96, n 1   The picture kissed by Severus (v p 211,
l 28) is painted upon a ϥⲱϫⲓ ⲛϣⲉ لوح

„   98, n 1   Cancel reference to KRALL   ⲡⲁⲅⲱⲣⲱ there
is a man's name

„   107, no 219   V no 466

„   111, n 11   Or ? ابو الوصل

„   116, n 9   Discussed at length in ZDMG lxii 552

„   124, n 9   This needs modification   The script may
well be of the 8th century

„   165, ult ⲙⲉⲭⲏⲩ   Cf Brit Mus no. 1118, ⲙⲉⲭⲁϥ

,   193, n 1   On ⲟⲩⲱⲣⲉⲙ and related questions, v
JUNKER in Oriens Christianus vi (1906), 343

„   209, l 15   I have since noticed that this 'Nicodemus' occurs similarly in no 431, foll 67a
(=TUKI 284 supra, though the name is omitted)
and 115 b (Absdliyah for Friday), which correspond respectively to foll 43 a, 59 a of no 432
Further, no 431, fol 86 b similarly names
'Sergius' ⲥⲁⲣⲕⲓⲥ=nos 432, fol 52 a and 433,
177 b=TUKI 289 supra (omitting name)   These
hymns are all acrostical, so too are those
naming 'Nicodemus' (24 in all) in no 433

APPROXIMATE DATES OF THE MANUSCRIPTS

a = first half of century, b = second half

Number	Century or year	Number	Century or year	Number	Century or year	Number	Century or year
1	? 6–7	42	10–11	82	10–11	123	8 a
2	11–12	43	,	83	? ,,	124	8
3	? 6–7	44	,,	84	? 6–7	125	8–10
4	9–11	45	,,	85	10–11	126	8 a
5	? 6–7	46	,	86	7–8	127	8
6	4–5	47	,,	87	11	128	8, 8–9
7	? 6–7	48	,,	88 (a)	,	129	7–8
8	10–11	49	,,	— (b)	11–12	130	8 a
9 (b)	ca A D 1050	50	,,	89	10–11	131	,
10	6, 6–7	51	? 7	90	,	132	7, 7–8
11	11 a	52	?	91	11	133	7–8
12	? 7–8	53	10–11	92	10–11	134	,,
13	11 a	54	,,	93	11 a	135	,
14	10–11	55	,	94	10–11	136	7–8, 8
15	? 6–8	56	,,	95	,,	137	ca A D 600
16	4–5	57	,,	96	9–11	138	9
17	10–11	58	,,	97	A D 1006	139	6–7
18	? 6–8	59	,,	98	9–11	140	7–8
19	? 11	60	,,	99	11	141	8
20 (b)	,	61	,,	100	8, 8–9	142	,,
21	,,	62 (a)	10–12	101	6	143	6–7
22 (a)	6–7	— (b)	10–11	102	11	144	7 a
— (b)	10–11	63	,,	103	? 9	145	7
23	5–6, 6	64	,,	104	11	146	8
24	10–11	65	,	105	? 7–8	147	7–8
25	,,	66	19 a	106	11–12	148	,
26	,,	67	10–11	107 (b)	11	149	8 a
27	,,	68	,	108 (b)	10–11	150	8
28	,	69	,,	109	? 6–7	151	8 a
29	,	70	,,	110	11	152	8
30	,,	71		111	? 6–7	153	6–7
31	,,	72	,,	112 (b)	11–12	154	8
32		73	? 11–12	113	11	155	8, 8–9
33	,,	74	7	114	13–14	156	8 a
34	,	75	10–11	115	7–8	157	8
35	,,	76	,	116	8 a	158	? 7
36	,,	77	,,	117	8	159	6–7, 7
37	,,	78 (a)	6	118	8 a	160	7–8
38	,	— (b)	7–8	119	,,	161	8
39	,,	79	10–11	120	7–8	162	,,
40	,,	80	8–9, 9	121	8	163	,,
41	,,	81	? 10	122	6–7	164	6–7

I 1

Number	Century or year	Number	Century or year	Number	Century or year	Number	Century or year
165	6-7	217	? 6-7	270	4	323	8
166	8 a	218	7-8	271	4-5	324	8-9, 9
167	9, 8-9	219	6-7	272	,,	325	7-8
168	8 a	220	8	273	,,	326	7, 7-8
169	7-8	221	8 a	274	,,	327	7 a
170	,,	222	? 7-8	275	4, 4-5	328	8 a
171	,,	223	7	276	4-5	329	6-7
172	,,	224	6, 6-7	277	8 a	330	8 a
173	7	225	8, 8-9	278	8	331	8-9
174	8, 8-9	226	8-9, 9	279	,,	332	(a A D 600
175	A D 721	227	10-11	280	7-8	333	7
176	8 a	228	8-9	281	6, 6-7	334	8
177	,,	229	9-10	282	8 a	335	,,
178	7-8	230	6-7	283	7-9	336	,,
179	8-9	231	? 7-8	284	6-8	337	10-11
180	8 a	232	? 8	285	8 a	338	7-8
181	8, 8-9	233	8-9	286	,,	339	8
182	7-8	234	11	287	8-9	340	6
183	,	235	9	288	? 6-7	341	8
184	8	236	9-10	289	7, 7-8	342	7, 7-8
185	7-8	237	,,	290	11-12	343	6-7, 7
186	8	238	8	291	7-8	344	11
187	7-8	239	8 a	292	4-5	345	8
188	7 a	240	8	293	6 b	346	8-9
189	8	241	7-8	294	7-8	347	7, 7-8
190	7, 7-8	242	10-11	295	6-7	348	10
191	7-8	243	11-12	296	6, 6-7	349	,,
192	7	244	7-8	297	6-7, 7	350	8-9
193	6-8	245	7 a	298	9	351	9-10
194	7, 7-8	246	8 a	299	? 8	352	6 a
195	8	247	? 8	300	7-8	353	9-10
196 (a)	8 a	248	5-6	301	4-6	354	7-8
— (b)	8-9	249	8	302	6-7, 7	355	7
197	7	250	8 a	303	,,	356	8 a
198	7-8	251	,,	304	7, 7-8	357	8
199	8 a	252	,,	305	6-7, 7	358	8, 8-9
200	8	253	? 8	306	11	359	8
201	7, 7-8	254	8	307	8	360	7-8
202	7 a	255	7-8	308	6-7	361	? 6-7
203	? 7 a	256	8	309	10	362	9-10, 10
204	6-7	257	,,	310	5, 5-6	363	7
205	9, 9-10	258	8 a	311	4	364	11
206	8	259	7-8	312	5-6	365	? 6-7
207	7	260	8	313	4-5	366	7 a
208	6-8	261	? 7	314	5-6	367	11
209	7-8	262	ro 8 a, vo 8	315	6, 6-7	368	10-11
210	7	263	9	316	7-8	369	7-8
211	7-8	264	8	317	9-10	370	? 9-11
212	8	265	10-11	318	8	371	6-8
213	8 a	266	11-12	319	7-8, 8	372	after A D 931
214	,,	267	10-11	320	7 a	373	10-11
215	,,	268	4-5	321	8	374	9-10
216	,	269	,,	322	,,	375	8 a

Number	Century or year	Number	Century or year	Number	Century or year	Number	Century or year
376	9–10	401	8 a	421	9–10	446	9–10
377	„	402	8	422	14	447	„
378	8	403	6	423	A D 1375	448	„
379	10	404	7–8	424	A D 1761	449	„
380	9	405	9	425	? 14	450	A D 1771
381	7	406	6	426	? 14–15	451	A D 1839
382	9–10	407	9	427	A D 1749	452	A D 1840
383	8–9	408	8	428	13–14	453	A D 1843
384	8	409	? 6–7	429	18–19	454	A D 1798
385	10 8 a or 8 b	410	?	430	A D 1833	455	19
386	6			431	A D 1762	456	„
387	8, 8–9	**MIDDLE EGYPTIAN**		432	A D 1751	457	„
388	9	411	? 7–9	433	18	458	18–19
389	9–10	412	10–11	434	A D 1609	459	? 13–14
390	9	413	6, 6–7	435	A D 1799	460	8
391	7–8	414	? 8	436	9–10	461	18–19
392	10	415	? 9–10	437	„		
393	5–6			438	„	**ADDENDA**	
394	7–8, 8	**BOHAIRIC**		439	„	462	? 6–7
395	10–11	416	19	440	,	463	8
396	4, 4–5	417	14	441	„	464	A D 1006–7
397	9	418	18	442	„	465	7–8
398	„	419	A D 1795	443	„	466	6–7
399	6	420	19	444	? 17–18	467	18–19
400	6, 6–7			445	9–10		

CONCORDANCE BETWEEN OLD AND NEW NUMBERS

Crawford numbers	New numbers	Crawford numbers	New numbers	Crawford numbers	New numbers	Crawford numbers	New numbers
1	13	19	427	33	94	49	446
2	2	20	431	34	69	50	450
2 b	438	20 a	53	35	96	51	114, 428, 444, 459
3	11	21	435	36	72	52	429, 458, 467
4	14	22	435	37	97	53	453
5	12	23	68	38	445	54	454
6	425	23 a	69	39	440	55	456
7	,,	24 a	70	40	447	56	457
8	417	24 b	67	41	436	57	452
9	416	24 c	63	42	437	58	451
10	419	25	62, 85, 89, 90	43 a	447	59	426
11	420	26	91	43 b	448	60	66
12	418	27	92	44	92	61	443
14	423	28	69	45	94	62	434
15	422	29	87	46	441	66	63
16	424, 461	30	71	47 a	442	68	455
17	430	31	8	47 b	439	69	433
18	432	32	65	48	449		

INDEX

I NAMES OF PERSONS

numbers=pages   n = note   * = more than once on this page

II. NAMES OF PLACES

III   GREEK AND OTHER FOREIGN WORDS

ⲭⲣⲟⲛⲟⲥ, 80, 82, 84, 86, 88, 131
ⲭⲣⲩⲥⲓⲕⲟⲛ, 82, 95
ⲭ̅ⲣ̅ (*χρυσου*), 67, 81, 96, 106
χρυσοχοος, 109
ⲭⲣⲏⲥⲧⲁⲗⲗⲟⲥ, 48
ⲭⲣⲱ, 94
ⲭⲱⲙⲁ, 81 n, 135, 150 n, *162
ⲭⲱⲛⲏⲛ, 115
ⲭⲱⲣⲁ, 42
χωριον, 159, 185
ⲭⲱⲣⲓⲥ, 149

ⲯⲁⲗⲓ, 210, 214
ⲯⲁⲗⲙⲟⲥ, 115
ⲯⲉⲩⲧⲟⲡⲣⲟⲫⲏⲧⲏⲥ, 45
ⲯⲓⲙⲓⲑⲓⲟⲛ and vais, 112, 117, 118
ⲯⲩⲭⲏ, 71, 88, 149, 174, 181, 185, 188, 196, 213
—, ⲕⲟⲩⲓ ⲛ-, 153

ⲱⲣⲱⲕⲉⲓⲟⲩⲥ (?) 56
ϩⲱⲥⲧⲉ, 155 n, 156
ⲱⲫⲉⲗⲓⲥ (*ωφελειν*), 57

IV. COPTIC WORDS

(In consonantal sequence)

ⲁ-, with numerals ⲁϫⲟⲩⲱⲧ, 32, ⲁⲟⲩⲏⲣ, 34
ⲁⲉ- = ⲁⲁ- (ⲉⲓⲣⲉ), 182
ⲁⲓⲁⲓ, 46
ⲁⲃⲟⲕⲓ, fem, 27
ⲁⲃⲱⲕ, 187
ⲁⲑⲱⲣ, ⲁⲑⲩⲣ, month, 11, 15, 18, 20, 22, 45, 100, 158 *V* ϩⲁⲑⲱⲣ
ⲁⲉⲓⲱ, ⲁⲓⲱ, 7, 53 55 n
ⲁⲉⲓⲕ, 170
ⲁⲓⲕ, 231
ⲁⲉⲓⲏⲥ, 32
ⲁⲕⲏⲧ, vb, 58 n
ⲁⲗⲉ-, vb, 102 (?), 138, 170
ⲁⲗⲟ, *v* ⲗⲟ
ⲁⲗⲃⲓⲗ (?), ⲡ-, 122
ⲁⲗⲕⲉ, 18
ⲁⲗⲧⲕⲁⲥ, 48
ⲁⲗⲁⲩ, 56 59, 164 n *V* ⲗⲁⲁⲩ
ⲁⲙⲏⲟⲩ, ⲃⲉⲕⲉ 82, 86
ⲁⲙⲁϩⲉ, 65, 68, 77, 153 n, 167, 173, 175
ⲁⲙⲁϩⲧⲉ, 82, 89
ⲁⲛⲓ (ⲉⲓⲛⲉ), 161
ⲁⲛⲥⲙⲙⲉ, 48
ⲁⲛⲧⲟⲟⲩ, ⲡ-, 59
ⲁⲛⲟⲩⲏⲣϣⲉ, 135
ⲁⲛⲁϣ, 140
ⲁⲛⲁϩ ? *crux ansata*, 118, 119 n, 122
ⲁⲛϫⲓⲣ, 84, 141
ⲁⲡⲁ, 15, 18, *66–9, *71, 72, 73, *75, 78, 80, 81, 82, 84, *87–96, 98, *101, 102, 107–11, 120–3, 127–30, 133, 134, 135, 138, *140, 141, 142, *147, 148, 150, 155, 159, 160, 164, *166, 167, 168 n, *169, 170, 180, 185, 213, 222, 230, 231
ⲁⲡⲉ, ⲡ-, title, 89, 90, 135, 153, 160, 171 n *V* ⲁⲡⲏⲩⲉ
ⲁⲡⲟⲩ ? = ⲁⲡⲁ, 79 n
ⲁⲡⲏⲩⲉ, 68, 132, 134, 142, 148, 162, 235
ⲁⲡⲁⲥ, 96
ⲁⲡⲥⲓ, 122
ⲁⲡⲟⲟⲩⲧⲥ, 108
—, ⲥⲁⲛ-, 172
ⲁⲡⲟⲧ, 108 n
ⲁⲡⲁⲧⲟⲟⲧ-, ⲣ-, 158, 174
ⲁⲡϣⲟⲟⲓ, month, 124 *V* ⲡⲁⲭⲱⲛ
ⲁⲣⲟ (?), ⲧ-, 104
ⲁⲣⲟⲩ, 104 n
ⲁⲣⲓⲕⲉ, 180
—, ⲁⲧ-, 126
ⲁⲣⲏⲩ (? ⲁⲣⲏⲃ) 180
ⲁⲣⲏⲩ, 41
ⲁⲣⲟϣ, 55
ⲁⲣϣⲓⲛ, 9, 122, 167, 175 n
ⲁⲣⲉϩ, 2
ⲁⲥ, ⲏⲣⲡ, 82, 84
ⲁⲥⲓⲕ, 54 55
ⲁⲥⲟⲩ, 68 (?), 145
ⲁⲧⲉ- ? = ⲁⲧ-, 113
ⲁⲧⲃⲉⲥ, 49 n
ⲁⲩ = ⲁⲩⲱ, 57, 116, 172, 173
ⲁⲩⲁⲛ, 116–19
ⲁⲩⲉⲓⲁⲩⲁⲛ, 118
ⲁⲩⲉⲓⲥ, 145
ⲁⲫⲱⲫ, 217
ⲁϣⲉ, 47
ⲁϣⲏ, 41
ⲁϥ ⲛⲛⲉⲃⲓⲱ, 112
ⲁϩⲁ, 188
ⲁϩⲉ, vb, 132
— ⲣⲁⲧ-, 153, 166, 177, 180
ⲁϩⲣⲟ-, 33
ⲁϩⲣⲁ (?), 135
ⲁϫⲡ, 226 n
ϫⲉⲡ, 15
ⲁϭⲃⲉⲓ, 49
ⲁϭⲣⲏⲛ, 36
ⲁϭⲟⲧⲥ, 111

ⲃⲓ, *v* ϥⲓ
ⲃⲱ, 139
ⲃⲱ (ϥⲱ), 184
— ⲛⲉⲗⲟⲟⲗⲉ 84
ⲃⲏⲃ (?), 115
ⲃⲁⲕ, vb, 177
ⲃⲱⲕ ⲉⲃⲟⲗ, 75
ⲃⲏⲕ, 137
ⲃⲉⲕⲉ, ⲃⲓⲕⲉ 73, 74, 78, 84, 164, 165, 188
— ⲁⲙⲏⲟⲩ, 82, 86
—, ϫⲁⲓ- 2
ⲃⲁⲗ, 52, 59
ⲃⲟⲗ, ⲡ-, 175, 176
—, ⲛ-, 161
ⲃⲱⲗ, translation, 18, 19, 20
ⲃⲱⲗ ⲉⲃⲟⲗ, 16, 28, 51, 57, 140, 170, 174
ⲃⲉⲗⲉ, *v* ⲃⲗⲗⲉ
ⲃⲉⲗⲃⲓⲗⲉ, 47
ⲃⲗⲗⲉ, 158, 175
ⲃⲗⲗⲉⲉⲩ, pl, 145
ⲃⲁⲗⲟⲩ, 78, 79 n *Cf* ⲃⲁⲣⲱϩ
ⲃⲁⲗⲱⲧ, 115 *V* ⲃⲁⲣⲱⲧ
ⲃⲗϫⲉ, 94
ⲃⲁⲁⲙⲡⲉ, 124
ⲃⲏⲛⲉ (ⲃⲛⲛⲉ), 81
ⲃⲩⲛⲉ (ⲃⲛⲛⲉ), 167
ⲃⲉⲛⲓⲡⲉ, *v* ⲡⲉⲛⲓⲡⲉ

154, 157, 158, 160, 165, *170, 171, 175 *178, 234

cιιι 56, 57, 58 n, 60, 74 180

coм-, vb, 86

ιιιε, v cιιιε

cιιιε, 129, 134, 162.

cιιογ, 14, 45, 126, 170 195, 231

cιιαιιααι, 32 138

cιιογτ (cιιοτ), 9

cιιαϯ, 59

cιιαϩ 72

cааτ- (cιιιε), 175

— εϩολ, 131, 155, 168, 180

cωιιτ, noun 36, 129

cιιτε foundation, 45

cааιιϣ, 35

cιιαϥ (cιιοϥ) 188

cιιογϥ 157

cωιιϩ 35, 149

coιι 120

— nωϣ, 193 n

ceεnε, 68, 76, 79, 88, 150

— vb, 145, 165

conc, 15, 145

canc (conc), 128

concn, 136, 140

ιnoιoγ 56

cαp- (cа ϯ-), 106 n

ιαpϩonтε 111

cωp, vb, 175

— εϩολ, 45, 47, 113

cαpω-, prep, т' ncа-

cpϩ̄ε, 152

copn (coλn), 133

copϯ 44, 59, 116, 124, 136, 171

cαt- (cιтε), 55

— εϩpаι, 56 n, 111

cат- (cιϯ) 218

cετιωϩε, 81 86, 90, 91, 95, 115 159 234 V ειωϩε

cετιαϩϩογωp, 81

cεт- (cωтε), 146

cатε, 57

ιωτε, 8

cтo 175

cатω, 115

cтoι, 7, 116

cϯnογϩε 7

cтнιι, 116, 118, 139 n

cтнιιογ (?) 139

cωтn, 139, 148

cатεεpε, 48

ιpιp, 48

cтωт, 47

cтωιε nιωϩε, 95, 182 (?)

cтωтε nιϣαϥ, 80

cωтϥ, 37

cоγo, 65, 86, 87, 89, 95, 98, 101, 102, 113, *114 122 126, 137, 148, 149, 163, *166, *167, 170, *178, 179

coγа (coγo), 188

cнγ, 37

cooγnε (cooγn), 128, 129, 145

cаγnε (cooγn), 182

coγpε, 116

cooγтn, n-, 131, 154, 161, 169, 185

—, ϩnογ-, 48

cωoγϩ, 148

— εϩoγn, 16, 26, 164, 174

cooγϩε, 18, 19 *20

cooγϩε, egg, 56, 59

—, crown of head, 35

cаϫo, cаϫω, 69 n, 91 n 108, 110, 116 156, 181 V p 240

cωϣ, 185

cнϣ (cιιϣ), 94

cнϣε, 167

cιιϣε, cаϣε 9, 35, 48, 187

cιωϣε, 63

—, εϩpε-, 166

cωϣϥ, 2 26

cаϥ, 143, 168

cаϥ (?), 59

cιιωϯ, 31, 32

cоϥт (?), 55

cаϩ, 231, 232 n

cϩаι, peϥ-, 231, 232

cϩ vb, 114

cаϩ, 9, 44, 45, 69 n, 72, 89, 91 n, 92 98, 105, *106, 129 n, 133, 150, 171, 185

— nιιιε, 143, *155

cωϩp, 114 n, 124

cϩаι, make over in writing, 145

cειιιε (cϩιιιε), 170

cаϩт (cωϩε), 114 n

cаϩтε, *56, *57

cаϩoγ 126

cϩoγεp, 34 n

cϩoγopт, 31, 32, *33

ιιωϫε (? ϣωϫε), 169, 170

та-, daughter or wife of 174

ϯ with 2 dots, 78 n

гι εϩoλ, 95, 96

ϯ ιιn-, 16

тo, 56, 84.

тω εтω, 34

ιнϩε, 113, 115

тωϩε, mo th, 80, 90, 97, 103, 104, 106 124, 173, 235

тγϭι, month, 21 *22, 78, 97, 100, 163

тωϩε brick 121, 122.

тωωϩε vb, 134 135

тϩϩo 32 102

тϩιιn, тϩnooγε, 82, 86, 135, 157, 188

ϯϩι, 47

тнϩт (тϩт) 56, 57, 144

тωϩαϩ, 8

таке (·), vb, 133

тако, 162, 166

ϯкаc (гкаc), 52

ϯкаc (ϯ ткаc) 59

тoϩ (тωкc), 114 n

таλo, 37, 50, 55, 60, 75, 84, 86, 109, 134, 145, 150, 151, 153 *158, 159 n, 164, *106, 167, 170, 177, 181

— weave, 113, 114 n

— εϩpаι, 5, 28

тωλιι, 8, 185

гωιι, 31

тωλc, 48

тιιιε, 63, 68, 71, 90, 131, 132 134, 135, 136, 143, 148, 152, *153, *155, 176, 185, 235

—, pιιn-, 126

—, nата-, noun, 158

тooιιε, 35

таιιo, 13, 16, 26

тωn, whence?, 33, 150

—, ε-, 48 n

тнnε, 78 (?), 81

ιнιι (? тнo), 73

тonoγ, 141 *147, 175

тonε (тωnε), adv, 128

тωnε (?), 160

тnаγ (тnnooγ), 188

тnтωn, 165

таnϩo, 28

танpoγт, 178

ιon, n-, 31

тωn, 114 n

тιnкаc, n- (not ткаc), 55

таnεn, 54, 60

таnιт (?), 135

таpε-, elliptical, 151, 152.

таpкo 53 170

гppε, 32

тco, 54, 161

ιco = тcιo εϩoλ, 142

тcаϩo, 114 n

тcnкo, 36

ιωт nϩнт, 8

M m

ϭ = ϫ (ⲱⲣⲉϭ), 66 , (ϭⲛⲟ), 9
ϭⲱ, 141, 153, 180–3
ϭⲱⲃ, 129
ϭⲱⲃⲉ, 59
ϭⲃ̄ϣⲁ, 37
ϭⲟⲉⲓⲗⲉ, 32
ⲟ̄ⲥ, in Saʾidic texts, 7, 8, 9, 13, 15, 17, 22, *23, 54, 116, 126, 138, 143, 144, 158, 172–5, 181
ϭⲓⲕⲓⲧ, 231
ϭⲟⲗ 32, 143, 161
ϭⲱⲗ, ϭⲗ, gather, 47, 168
ϭⲱⲗ, ⲡⲓ-, 219
ϭⲱⲱⲗⲉ, ϭⲟⲟⲗⲉ, 26, 45
ϭⲁⲗⲟ ⲉⲃⲟⲗ, 115
ϭⲓⲗⲗⲉ (?), 164 ⲛ
ϭⲁⲗⲓⲗ, 47 ⲛ
ϭⲱⲗϩ, 185 ⲛ
ϭⲁⲗⲁϩⲧ, 56, 113
ϭⲱⲗϫ, 47
ϭⲟⲗϭ, ⲉϥ-, 115
ϭⲗⲓϭ, 47 ⲛ
ϭⲗⲟϭ ⲛⲉⲓⲙ. 57

ϭⲉⲗϭⲓⲗ, 47 ⲛ
ϭⲗϭⲓϫ, 171
ϭⲁⲙ (? ⲕⲁⲙ), 179
ϭⲟⲙ, miracle, 46 ⲛ
ϭⲱⲙ, 72, 84, 161, 234, 235
—, ⲥⲥⲧⲓⲁⲣ-, 81
ϭⲟⲟⲙ, plur, 72, 81, 161, 179
ϭⲟⲟⲙⲉ, ϭⲱⲙⲉ, 33, 129
ϭⲙⲉ, 72, *84, 179
ϭⲙⲏⲩ and vars, 98, 103, 179
ϭⲁⲙⲟⲩⲗ, 35, 133, 168, 188
ϭⲟⲙϭⲙ, 36
ϭⲟⲛⲥ, ϫⲓ ⲛ-, 145
ϭⲟⲩⲡⲁϭⲉⲥ, ϭⲱⲡⲁϭ, ⲟ ⲕⲁⲩⲛⲁⲕⲏⲥ
ϭⲁⲡ (ϭⲱⲡ), 187 188
ϭⲟⲡ, ⲟⲗⲓⲅⲁ, 149 ⲛ
ϭⲱⲡ, ϭⲟⲡ, 35, 54 7, 60, 126, 135, 138, 152, 153, 160, 166, 167, 168, *172, 173, 174
ϭⲱⲡⲉ, 136
ϭⲣⲟⲟⲙⲡⲉ, 113, 123
ϭⲁⲣⲧⲉ, 48
ϭⲱⲣⲉϫ, 90.

ϭⲱⲣϭ, 31
ϭⲟⲣϭ ⲉⲃⲟⲗ, 82, 89   V p 240
ϭⲣⲟϭ, 179 ⲛ
ϭⲣⲱⲱϭ, plui , 81
ϭⲣⲱϭ (?), 135
ϭⲟⲣⲏϭⲥ, 131
ϭⲟⲩⲙ, 21 ⲛ
ϭⲱⲧⲛ, 16
ϭⲉⲉⲣ (ϭⲱ), 27
ϭⲁⲩⲟⲛ and vars., 133, 134, *143, *144, 151, 154, 155, 167, 168, 174, *185
ϭⲟⲟⲩⲛⲉ, 115
ϭⲱϣⲧ, 178
ϭⲉϣϭⲱϣ, 60
ϭⲓϫ, ⲧⲓ, 168
— ⲙⲛ-, 163
—, a measure, 149 ⲛ
ϭⲟϫⲉ, 47.
ϭⲓϫⲓ, ⲥⲁⲡ-, 231
ϭⲁⲁϭⲉ, ϭⲁϭⲉ, 82, 133, 164, 173

V. ARABIC WORDS

(According to the Arabic alphabet)

اصلمودية, 202
اصالية, 208, 209, 210.
ⲁϫⲡ, احية, 226 ⲛ
حدود — احد, Sundays, 205
ادام, name of a melody, 209, 210
اطام, 214
اتّى, 144
ⲁⲣⲭⲱⲛ ارحس, 196
ازار, 237
اصل, 189, 193
ام الصلاة, 55 ⲛ
معلية , العلية, 197
دعارى , اديعارى, ⲁⲛⲧⲓⲫⲱⲛⲁⲣⲓⲟⲛ, 210 ⲛ
اهياشر اهيا (Hebrew), 238
اوشة, ⲉⲩⲭⲏ, 236.
ⲁⲁⲡⲁⲡⲉ (? ⲗⲁⲡⲁⲡⲉ, اللابة), 173
ⲁⲡⲟⲩ, ابو, 110
ⲁⲡⲟⲩⲥⲓⲣ (?), 56
ⲁⲣⲥⲛⲧⲁⲡ, ⲁⲣⲥⲛ (?), 110
ⲁⲛⲁⲣⲕⲁⲣϭⲁⲣ, 57.

ⲁⲗϩⲱⲣ (?), 57
ⲁⲙⲁⲣⲁ, 175
ⲁⲙⲉⲣⲁ, 71, 175
ⲁⲙⲉⲣⲁⲥ, 177
ⲁⲙⲓⲣⲁ, 63 ⲛ, *64, 71, 80, 100, 133, 136, 148, 151, 154
ⲁⲙⲏⲣ(ⲁ), 159
ⲁⲙⲓⲣ̄, 70, 136.

شور, 56 ⲛ
درلكس, 207
رمون, ⲡⲁⲣⲁⲙⲟⲛⲏ, 209 }
درّى, vb, 105
كتاب السبعة, 213   V صعة
سور, 56 ⲛ
صعة, 198
تنصرة — نصر, 224
ⲡⲁⲗⲗⲓⲱⲛ, ڤليس, 116 ⲛ
ديان, 189
ⲡⲁⲣⲁ (?), 176

ⲡⲣⲓⲕ أدريق), 116
ⲛⲁⲣⲡⲓⲉ درية, 56 ⲛ
تكل, ⲟ ⲙⲁⲧⲕⲁⲗ
ⲧⲏⲣⲕⲟⲩⲙⲁⲛ, ترجمان, 105 ⲛ
ⲑⲁⲁⲗⲗⲉⲗⲉ (?), 172

حس, 236
حمرة), 59 ⲛ
معار — حزى, 196
حزية — , 144
حلّ, 164 ⲛ
حلباب, 196
تحليد — جلد, 201
حلا — حلان, Revelation, 195
جموع — جمع, 208, 210
تحسير — حسر, 198
ϭⲟⲩⲡⲉ, حمة, 177
ϭⲱⲣⲱⲡ ? حزب, 166
ϭⲟⲙⲗⲉ, حملة, 111
ϭⲁⲩϩⲁⲣⲉ ? جوهر), 174, 175

ⲕⲁⲗⲗⲁⲥⲉ, قلوسة قلاسوة, 116.

ⲕⲁⲗⲉ ?, طلعة, 142

ⲕⲁⲗⲗⲁ ?, طلعة, 175

ⲕⲁⲛⲁ, كنة or صاع, 116

بالكسر — كر, 197 n

كتاب السحة, 213

تكرير — كرر, 227

كفاية, 224

كلب الكلب, 236

كولان, 139 n

ⲭⲓⲟⲓⲣⲉ, كثيراء, 55, 57 n

ⲭⲁⲃⲱⲣ, كابور, 187

لبانة, 173 n

ⲗⲱⲃϣ, لتس, 204

لحى, 193 n, 197, 198, 207, 211, 236

لساريح = ليح, 192 n

لقان, λακανη, 198

لوح, 240

بماجيد — مجد, 213

بمعانيس — معن, 236

مح, 59 n

مدلحة مدلح, 202 n, 210, 211 n

مرمة, 62 n

مطانية, μετανοια, 210

مقل, 57 n

مكس, 210

ملح, 236

محل, 114 n

أحلمة محلمة, 197

ميمر, 228

ⲙⲁⲧⲕⲁⲗ, متكل, 57

ⲙⲁⲗⲕⲁⲗ ?, متكل, 57

ⲙⲟⲩϭⲟⲁⲗ, ⲉⲗ- (?), 172

ⲙⲁϥⲙⲉⲗ, محمل, 138

ⲙⲱⲣⲁⲛⲉ, مربعة, 116

ⲙⲓϭⲁⲣ, معجر, 116

ⲙⲁⲕⲣⲁⲛⲓ, ⲁⲗ- (μαγκλαβιον), 171

ⲙⲁⲗϭⲁⲃⲉ, محلمة, 116

ⲙⲁⲗⲁϥ, ⲙⲁⲗϥⲃⲉ ?, ملف, 116

ⲙⲁⲧⲧⲏⲗⲉ, منديل, 116, 120 n

ⲙⲁⲛⲁⲣⲓ, ة مارا, 116

س, 238

مسر — سر, 196

أناشيد — شد, 213

بطى, 238

باطر, of church, 209, 233 n

بطرؤ, 238

نعيم, 142 n

نفس, ψυχη, 213

بواقس — ناوس, 197 n

بهش, 237

سرور, 208

واطس, βατος, a melody, 210, 214

اوتار — ور, 205

وَرد, 58 n

ورقة, 238

بوريع — ورع, 208

وزان (?), 233 n

موشع — وشع, 204

انصا — وصأ, 225

وعاء, 237

وما, 201

مولا — ولى, 210

ⲟⲩⲁⲣⲉ, ورس, 57, 58 n

VI   SUBJECT INDEX

No. 86

No. 411

No. 302

No. 175 (A.D. 721)

No. 7

PLATE I

No. 28

No. 36

No. 268

V. Addenda

No. 49

No. 55

No. 274

No. 311

N. 276

No. 413

No. 269

No. 271

No. 270

No. 272

No. 396

No. 403

PLATE 5

No. 352

No. 312

No. 292

No. 313

No. 293

PLATE 6

No. 407

No. 287

No. 390

No. 398

PLATE 7

No. 236

No. 352

PLATE 8

No. 348

PLATE 9

No. 410

No. 514

No. 372 verso

No. 272

No. 320

No. 139

PLATE II

No. 277

No. 319

No. 171

CPSIA information can be obtained at www.ICGtesting.com
Printed in the USA
LVOW111946130113

315520LV00023B/1734/P

9 781171 515654